Food Science Sourcebook

Second Edition

Part 2

Food Composition, Properties, and General Data

HERBERT W. OCKERMAN, Ph.D.

Professor of Animal Science
The Ohio State University
and
The Ohio Agricultural Research
and Development Center
Columbus, Ohio

An **avi** Book
Published by Van Nostrand Reinhold
New York

Dedicated to Frances

An AVI Book
(AVI is an imprint of Van Nostrand Reinhold)

Copyright © 1991 by Van Nostrand Reinhold
Library of Congress Catalog Card Number 90-21740
ISBN 0-442-23388-4

Manufactured in the United States of America

Published by Van Nostrand Reinhold
115 Fifth Avenue
New York, New York 10003

Chapman and Hall
2-6 Boundary Row
London, SE1 8HN

Thomas Nelson Australia
102 Dodds Street
South Melbourne 3205
Victoria, Australia

Nelson Canada
1120 Birchmount Road
Scarborough, Ontario M1K 5G4, Canada

16   15   14   13   12   11   10   9   8   7   6   5   4   3   2   1

Library of Congress Cataloging-in-Publication Data
Ockerman, Herbert W.
  Food science sourcebook/Herbert W. Ockerman.—2nd ed.
    p. cm.
  Rev. ed. of: Source book for food scientists. ©1978.
  "An AVI book."
    ISBN 0-442-23388-4
    1. Food—Dictionaries.   2. Food—Composition—Tables.
  I. Ockerman, Herbert W. Sourcebook for food scientists.
  II. Title.
  TX349.03 1991   90-21740
  664'.003—dc20   CIP

Preface to second edition, titled *Food Science Sourcebook*

It was realized, even prior to the printing of the first edition, that a book of this magnitude would never be complete and that at some point a line must be drawn and data currently available must be organized. This was done to get the first edition into print. However, prior to its printing, revisions and new data were becoming available for inclusion in the second edition (now titled *Food Science Sourcebook*), which includes most of the information in the first edition plus twelve additional years of collecting data.

The author wants to thank the many readers, colleagues, and students who have made suggestions on how the manuscript could become more useful. Most of the suggestions have been incorporated into this edition. Like the first edition, the second edition is certainly also not complete, and the author would certainly appreciate communications from readers and colleagues for suggestions and recommendations on how additional editions might be improved.

HERBERT W. OCKERMAN
Columbus, Ohio

Preface to first edition, titled *Source Book for Food Scientists*

The *Source Book for Food Scientists* materialized as the result of accumulating current data and relevant facts in the field of food science and technology. Since reference sources are often scattered, there has been a need for a one-volume data book of this type. A number of my colleagues have urged me to make my data bank available to others, hence this volume.

Such a book could be organized as follows: a dictionary interpretation of terms used in food science and technology; tabular material giving detailed information on food composition and properties; chemical formulas and structures; uses of foodstuffs; harvesting; slaughtering and related information concerning the meat industry . . . , in fact, almost any and every type of subject one might encounter dealing with food.

I have organized the material in two parts. Part 1 covers what I call my "personal dictionary" of pertinent information. Part 2 contains the tabular and general information that broadens the base of Part 1 with factual data.

I have found it invaluable. My earnest desire, now that the material is to be published, is that it will equally serve other food scientists and technologists working in various capacities in industry, government, and the academic community.

I wish to acknowledge the encouragement given me by Dr. Donald K. Tressler, President, AVI Publishing Company, and to express my appreciation for his belief and support in this project.

It is also a special pleasure for me to acknowledge the editorial assistance provided by Mrs. Lucy Long, Senior Editor at AVI, and to Mr. Gessner Hawley, Editor of the *Condensed Chemical Dictionary* and Co-editor of the *Encyclopedia of Chemistry*. It was their collaboration and assistance that transformed a very rough draft into a publishable manuscript. However, errors of omission or commission are mine alone to bear.

I would also like to thank the scores of publishers and authors who have granted me permission to reprint their copyrighted materials. Thanks are also extended to the many authors and contributors to government publications for information obtained from those sources. Specific acknowledgement is noted for each source as it appears in this book.

I also wish to extend grateful thanks to my wife, Frances, for her assistance in typing and proofreading. Her patience and help contributed much to the completion of this book.

This is the First Edition of the *Source Book* and I would greatly appreciate communications from readers for suggestions or recommendations on how to improve it and also to call to my attention errors that may be corrected in the next printing.

HERBERT W. OCKERMAN
Columbus, Ohio

Jan. 1, 1978

How to Use The *Food Science Sourcebook*
(important to obtain maximum utilization of this book!)

For ease of retrieval, this book has been organized into two parts. *Start your search in Part 1* and this, if necessary, will lead you to Part 2 by extensive cross-references. Part 1 consists of dictionary terms and descriptions wherein the definition usually contains detailed information on the subject and, where feasible, some data concerning its use or properties. With the majority of these *Sourcebook* terms and description in Part 1, there is a reference to Part 2, giving a list of subjects for further information. (See the breakdown of the **artichoke** entry below.)

Part 2 is composed of alphabetical sections containing food composition, properties, and general data designed as the basis for the initiation of a broader search for further information relevant to the dictionary term given in Part 1. Part 2 is, in truth, a "data book" of tables, figures, charts, formulas, etc.

Part 1 will lead the reader to a pertinent, appropriate section in Part 2, or one can refer to Part 2 independently of the Part 1 dictionary description because it is organized alphabetically; however, some information will be missed if the second approach is used.

Term

Generic name

Growth preferences

Description

artichoke (French; globe; true; *Cynara scolymus* **)**
A deep-rooted, 3- to 5-ft perennial, thistle-like plant, belonging to the daisy or thistle family; grows well in a cold, moist climate; the flower heads (green to purplish; small to 5-in. diam.) and "chokes," or unopened, tightly clinging fleshy petals, have scales with fleshy bases. 650 seed/oz; thin to 2–3 ft apart in rows 3–4 ft apart. In season Nov.–May; harvest when buds are compact and refrigerate as soon as picked.

Growing information

Size information

Size	Use
Small	Pickling, stews, casseroles
Medium	Salads
Large	Stuffing

Type information

Type	Where grown	Varieties
Conical bud	Europe	French or green French Thistle or prickly Violet
Globular head	U.S. and Europe	Giant bud Green or white globe Red Dutch Violet bud

Varieties

Other varieties	Commercial growth area	Cooking
Creole	Southern Louisiana	
Grande Beurre		Boiled and served with melted butter
Green Globe	California Gulf Coast	Most popular
Gros Vert de Laon		
Purple Globe		

Portion eaten —— The fleshy base of the scales is eaten raw, baked, —— Preparation methods
fried, stuffed, served with sauces, or preserved in oil;
the base of the flower head and the central leaf stalk

Canned information —— are also eaten.
Canned and frozen styles:
    Whole (one per can)
    Topped
    Hearts (packed in brine, vinegar, sauces, or olive oil)

Cooking information —— Bottoms
Cooking: trim ("choke," or scaly part discarded), boil 30–50 min or until tender in acidulated water

Weights —— 1 large artichoke cooked and drained = 15 oz
1 artichoke heart = 15 g
1 serving = $\frac{1}{2}$ lb
       = 1 med. artichoke

Composition —— Composition: moisture 86%; protein 3%; fiber 11%; ash 0.8%; pH 5.6
Store at 31–32°F, at 60–95% relative humidity; use —— Storage information
in 1–2 weeks.

For more information —— *See* **Chinese artichoke; Jerusalem artichoke**; —— Reference to Part 1 sections C, J, and A
other artichoke entries
See Part 2: Iron; Minerals, Food; Niacin; Phosphorus;
Potassium; Potassium-Rich Foods; Vegetable Compo- —— Reference to Part 2 sections I, M, N, P, and V
sition; Vegetable Plants; Vegetables, Canning Dates

Other ready-reference material that is to be found in the book:

Inside the front cover is a table for temperature conversion from Fahrenheit to Celsius or vice versa.

Inside the back cover will be found conversion factors for units of weight, units of liquid measure, oven temperatures, and units of volume.

And following is a list of the most-often-used abbreviations for quick reference.

Common Abbreviations

NOTE: Where the abbreviation denotes either the singular or plural, the spelled-out version of the abbreviation carries an asterisk (*).

A	ampere*
AAAS	American Association for the Advancement of Science
AOAC	Association of Official Analytical Chemists
apoth.	apothecary
approx.	approximately
atm	atmosphere
at. no.	atomic number
at. wt.	atomic weight
avg.	average
avdp.	avoirdupois
bp	boiling point
Brit.	British
Btu	British thermal units
bu	bushel*
cal	calorie*
°C	Centigrade or Celsius
ca.	circa or about
cc	cubic centimeter* (also cm^2)
CAMP	computer assisted menu planning
CFN	Council on Food and Nutrition of the American Medical Association
cg	centigram*
chem.	chemical or chemistry
cl	centiliter*
cm	centimeter*
CP	chemically pure
cps	cycles per second
cu.	cubic
cwt	hundredweight
d	density
dc	direct current
deg	degree*
df	degrees of freedom
dg	decigram*
diam.	diameter
dag	dekagram*
dal	dekaliter*
dl	deciliter*
dm	decimeter*

dwt	pennyweight
doz	dozen*
dr	dram*
e.g.	for example
EMF	electromotive force
equiv. wt.	equivalent weight
°F	Fahrenheit
FAO	Food and Agricultural Organization, United Nations
FDA	Food and Drug Administration
ffa	free fatty acid*
fl	fluid
FNS	Food and Nutrition Service, US Department of Agriculture
FNB	Food and Nutrition Board of the National Academy of Science–National Research Council
fp	freezing point
fpm	feet per minute
fps	feet per second
ft	foot*
g	gram*
gal	gallon*
gpm	gallon* per minute
gr	grain*
h	hectare*
hg	hectogram*
Hg	mercury
hhd	hogshead*
hp	horsepower
h	hour*
i.d.	inside dimension
i.e.	that is
imp	imperial
in.	inch*
IU	International Units

J	joule*		PER	protein efficiency ratio
			pk	peck*
			ppm	parts per million
K	kelvin		ppt	precipitate; parts per trillion
kcal	kilocalorie*		prob.	probable
K_{eq}	equilibrium constant		psf	pounds per square foot*
kg	kilogram*		psi	pounds per square inch*
km	kilometer*		psia	pounds per square inch atmosphere*
kW	kilowatt*		pt	pint*
l	liter* (more often spelled out to avoid misinterpretation with numeral one)		qt	quart*
lat	latitude			
lb	pound*			
			r	correlation
			R	Réaumur
m	meter*		rd	rod*
M	Molal		RDA	recommended daily allowance
max.	maximum		RH	relative humidity
MDR	minimum daily requirement (no longer used; see RDA)		rpm	revolutions per minute
med.	medium			
mg	milligram*		s	second*
MHz	megahertz		sig.	significant
mi	mile*		sp.	specific
MID	Meat Inspection Division, US Department of Agriculture		sp. gr.	specific gravity
			sq.	square
min.	minimum			
ml	milliliter*			
mm	millimeter*			
mo.	month*		tbsp	tablespoon*
mol. wt.	molecular weight		temp.	temperature
mp	melting point		tsp	teaspoon*
mps	meters per second			
mV	millivolt*			
			USDA	United States Department of Agriculture
No.	number (when followed by numeral)		USP	*US Pharmocopeia*
NFE	nitrogen free extract			
NIH	National Institutes of Health			
NMR	nuclear magnetic resonance			
NPU	net protein utilization		vit.	vitamin (rarely used)
NPV	net protein value		vol.	volume
NRC	National Research Council			
NSF	National Science Foundation			
			wt.	weight
o.d.	outside dimension			
opt.	optimum, optional		yd	yard*
oz	ounce*		yr	year*

Contents

Part 2

Food Composition, Properties, and General Data

Part 2

Food Composition,
Properties and
General Data

Acidulants

TABLE 2.A.1
Properties of some common food acidulants

Property	POMALUS® Malic Acid $HOCHCOOH$ $|$ CH_2COOH	Fumaric Acid $HOOCCH$ $||$ $HCCOOH$	Adipic Acid CH_2CH_2COOH $|$ CH_2CH_2COOH	Succinic Acid CH_2COOH $|$ CH_2COOH	Succinic Anhydride $CH_2C\,O$ $>O$ $CH_2C\,O$	Citric Acid CH_2COOH $|$ $HOCCOOH$ $|$ CH_2COOH	Tartaric Acid $HOCHCOOH$ $|$ $HOCHCOOH$
Appearance	White crystal. powder	White crystal. powder	White crystal. powder	White crystal. powder	White crystals	White crystals	White crystals
Crystal system	Triclinic crystal	Monoclinic prisms	Monoclinic prisms	Monoclinic prisms	Ortho-rhombic prisms	Monoclinic holohedra	Monoclinic sphenoidal prisms
Taste	Smooth tart	Tart	Tart	Tart	Burning tart	Tart	Bitter tart
Empirical formula	$C_4H_6O_5$	$C_4H_4O_4$	$C_6H_{10}O_4$	$C_4H_6O_4$	$C_4H_4O_3$	$C_6H_8O_7$	$C_4H_6O_6$
Melting point, °C	130°–132°	286°–287°	153°	188°	118.3°–119°[1]	153°	168°–170°
Specific gravity	1.601 (20°/4°)	1.635 (20°/4°)	1.380 (25°/4°)	1.564 (15°/4°)	1.503 (20°/4°)	1.542 (18°/4°)	1.7598 (20°/4°)
Bulk density, lb/ft³	57.3	32.6	40.5	55.0	47.2	56.2	50.2
Solubility in ethanol gm/100 ml @ 25°C	39.16	4.3	16.10	9.0	2.56	58.9	19.6
Solubility in ether gm/100 ml @ 25°C	1.41	0.56	0.92	0.66	0.64	1.84	0.59
Solubility in chloroform gm/100 ml @ 25°C	0.04	0.02	<0.01	0.02	0.87	<0.01	0.04
Ionization constant K_1	4×10^{-4}	1×10^{-3}	3.7×10^{-5}	6.5×10^{-5}	(See succinic acid)	8.2×10^{-4}	1.04×10^{-3}
K_2	9×10^{-6}	3×10^{-5}	2.4×10^{-6}	2.3×10^{-6}		1.8×10^{-5}	4.55×10^{-5}
K_3	..	—	—	—		3.9×10^{-6}	—
Heat of combustion, kcal/mole, 20°C	320.1	320.0	669.0	357.1	369.6	474.5	257.1
Heat of solution, kcal/mole solute	4.9	—	—	—	—	3.9	3.3
Viscosity 50% aqueous solutions, cps, @ 25°C	6.5	2	2	2	2	6.5	6.5
Standard free energy of anion formation, $\Delta F°_f$, kcal, @ 25°C, aqueous solutions	201.98	144.41	—	164.97	— (See succinic acid)	278.8	—
Sp gr saturated aqueous solutions, @ 5°	1.210	1.000	1.002	1.012		1.24	1.26
25°	1.250	1.000	1.005	1.024	"	1.28	1.27
75°	1.310	0.989	1.032	1.076	"	1.31	1.31

[1] Solidification point.
[2] Solubility too limited.

Source: Sausville, T. J. (1975). Acidulants. In *Encyclopedia of Food Technology*. A. H. Johnson and M. S. Peterson (editors). AVI Publishing Co., Westport, Connecticut.

Acre, Plants

TABLE 2.A.2
Number of plants per acre at given spacings

Inches	No. of Plants	Inches	No. of Plants	Inches	No. of Plants
12 × 1	522,720	24 × 6	43,560	40 × 30	5,227
12 × 3	174,240	24 × 9	29,040	40 × 36	4,356
12 × 4	130,680	24 × 12	21,780		
12 × 6	87,120	24 × 15	17,424	42 × 3	49,782
12 × 9	58,080	24 × 18	14,520	42 × 6	24,891
12 × 12	43,560	24 × 24	10,890	42 × 12	12,445
				42 × 18	8,297
15 × 1	418,176	30 × 3	69,696	42 × 24	6,223
15 × 3	139,382	30 × 4	52,272	42 × 30	4,978
15 × 4	104,544	30 × 6	34,848	42 × 36	4,148
15 × 6	69,696	30 × 9	23,232		
15 × 9	48,484	30 × 12	17,424		
15 × 12	34,848	30 × 15	13,939	48 × 3	43,560
		30 × 18	11,616	48 × 6	21,780
18 × 1	348,390	30 × 24	8,712	48 × 12	10,890
18 × 3	116,160	30 × 30	6,969	48 × 18	7,260
18 × 4	87,120			48 × 24	5,445
18 × 6	58,080	36 × 3	58,080	48 × 30	4,356
18 × 9	38,720	36 × 4	43,560	48 × 36	3,630
18 × 12	29,040	36 × 6	29,040	48 × 42	3,111
18 × 15	23,232	36 × 9	19,360	48 × 48	2,722
18 × 18	19,360	36 × 12	14,520		
		36 × 15	11,616	60 × 3	34,848
20 × 3	104,544	36 × 18	9,680	60 × 6	17,424
20 × 4	78,408	36 × 24	7,260	60 × 12	8,712
20 × 6	52,272	36 × 30	5,808	60 × 18	5,808
20 × 9	34,848	36 × 36	4,840	60 × 24	4,356
20 × 12	26,136			60 × 30	3,484
20 × 15	20,909	40 × 3	52,272	60 × 36	2,904
20 × 18	17,426	40 × 6	26,136	60 × 42	2,489
		40 × 12	13,068	60 × 48	2,178
24 × 3	87,120	40 × 18	8,709	60 × 54	1,936
24 × 4	65,340	40 × 24	6,534	60 × 60	1,742

Source: Mortensen, E., and Bullard, E. T. (1969). *Handbook of Tropical and Sub-Tropical Horticulture.* Agency for International Development, U.S. Department of State.

Acre, Trees

TABLE 2.A.3
Number of trees per acre at given spacings

Feet	No. of Plants	Feet	No. of Plants	Feet	No. of Plants
6 × 1	7,260	10 × 1	4,356	16 × 14	194
6 × 2	3,630	10 × 2	2,178	16 × 16	170
6 × 3	2,420	10 × 3	1,452		
6 × 4	1,815	10 × 4	1,089	18 × 4	605
6 × 5	1,452	10 × 5	871	18 × 6	404
6 × 6	1,210	10 × 6	726	18 × 8	303
		10 × 7	622	18 × 10	242
7 × 1	6,223	10 × 8	544	18 × 12	202
7 × 2	3,111	10 × 9	484	18 × 14	173
7 × 3	2,074	10 × 10	435	18 × 16	152
7 × 4	1,556			18 × 18	132
7 × 5	1,244				
7 × 6	1,037	12 × 2	1,815		
7 × 7	889	12 × 4	907		
		12 × 6	605	20 × 8	272
8 × 1	5,445	12 × 7	454	20 × 10	218
8 × 2	2,722	12 × 10	363	20 × 12	184
8 × 3	1,815	12 × 12	302	20 × 14	156
8 × 4	1,361			20 × 16	136
8 × 5	1,089			20 × 18	121
8 × 6	907	14 × 2	1,556	20 × 20	109
8 × 7	778	14 × 4	778		
8 × 8	680	14 × 6	518		
		14 × 8	389	24 × 12	151
9 × 1	4,840	14 × 10	311	24 × 16	114
9 × 2	2,420	14 × 12	259	24 × 20	92
9 × 3	1,613	14 × 14	222	24 × 24	76
9 × 4	1,210				
9 × 5	968	16 × 2	1,361	30 × 20	72
9 × 6	807	16 × 4	680	30 × 30	48
9 × 7	691	16 × 6	454	30 × 40	36
9 × 8	605	16 × 8	340		
9 × 9	528	16 × 10	272		
		16 × 12	227	40 × 40	27

Source: Mortensen, E., and Bullard, E. T. (1969). *Handbook of Tropical and Sub-Tropical Horticulture.* Agency for International Development, U.S. Department of State.

Alcoholic Solutions

TABLE 2.A.4
Various strengths of alcoholic solutions

Alcohol, Strength Desired Ml per Liter	Alcohol Required Grams	Ml
50	42.63	52.6
100	85.26	105.3
150	127.89	157.9
200	170.52	210.5
250	213.16	263.2
300	255.78	315.9
400	341.04	421.1
500	426.32 (proof)	526.3
700	596.84	736.8

NOTE: Alcoholic solutions: Specification requires 95% C_2H_5OH by vol. Sp gr = 0.810 at 25°. Mix and dil. to 1 liter.

Alcohol of any desired strength may be obtained by taking number of ml 95% alcohol equiv. to desired strength and dil. soln. to 95 ml. For example, to obtain soln. of 70% alcohol, take 70 ml 95% alcohol and dil. to 95 ml.

Source: Editorial Board, AOAC (1975). *Official Methods of Analysis of the Association of Official Analytical Chemists,* 12th Edition. Association of Official Analytical Chemists, Washington, D.C.

Altitude Adjustments For Baking

TABLE 2.A.5
Adjustments for high-altitude baking

	3000 ft	5000 ft	7000 ft
Reduce Baking Powder For each teaspoon, decrease	1/8 tsp	1/8–1/4 tsp	1/4–1/2 tsp
Reduce Sugar For each cup, decrease	no change	usually no change	1–2 tbsp
Reduce Lard For each cup, decrease	1–2 tbsp	2 tbsp	2–3 tbsp
Increase Liquid For each cup, add	1–2 tbsp	2–3 tbsp	3–4 tbsp
Increase Baking Temperature	6–10°F	10–15°F	15–25°F
Decrease Baking Time 5 to 10 minutes when recipes have been tested at sea level.			

NOTE: When two amounts are given, try the smaller adjustment first; then if cake still needs improvement, use the larger adjustment the next time you make the cake.

Source: Kitchen Classics. National Live Stock and Meat Board, Chicago.

Altitude Corrections For Boiling Water

TABLE 2.A.6

Altitude (feet)	Increase processing time if the time recommended is:	
	20 minutes or less	More than 20 minutes
1,000	1 minute	2 minutes
2,000	2 minutes	4 minutes
3,000	3 minutes	6 minutes
4,000	4 minutes	8 minutes
5,000	5 minutes	10 minutes
6,000	6 minutes	12 minutes
7,000	7 minutes	14 minutes
8,000	8 minutes	16 minutes
9,000	9 minutes	18 minutes
10,000	10 minutes	20 minutes

Source: USDA (1977). Canning, freezing, storing garden produce. USDA Agricultural Information Bull. *410*.

Amino Acids I

TABLE 2.A.7
Physical properties

Amino Acid	Chemical Formula	Molecular Weight	Melting Point	Specific Rotation				Iso-electric Point	Solubility g/100 ml solvent
				Solvent	g/100 ml	Temp °C	Value		
1 L-Alanine	$C_3H_7NO_2$	89.09	297	1.0 N HCl	5.79	15	+14.7	6.11 [1]	sl.sol.alc.; insol.acet., eth.; 16.51, w.
2 β-Alanine	$C_3H_7NO_2$	89.09	196	....	....	.....	0	6.90	v.sol.w.; v.sl.sol.alc.; insol. eth.
3 L-α-Aminobutyric acid	$C_4H_9NO_2$	103.12	285	20% HCl	....	20	+14.1	5.98	insol.eth.; 0.18, alc.; 28, w.
4 L-Anserine	$C_{10}H_{16}N_4O_3$	240.26	238-239	H_2O	5.0	20	+12.2	8.27	sol.me.alc., w.; sl.sol. alc.
5 L-Arginine	$C_6H_{14}N_4O_2$	174.20	238	6.0 N HCl	1.65	23	+26.9	10.76	v.sol.w.; insol.alc., eth.
6 L-Asparagine	$C_4H_8N_2O_3$	132.12	236	3.4 N HCl	2.24	20	+34.3	5.41	sol.dil.NH_4OH; v.sl.sol. alc.; insol.eth.; 2.46, w.
7 L-Aspartic acid	$C_4H_7NO_4$	133.10	269-271	6.0 N HCl	2.0	24	+24.6	2.98	sol.dil.HCl; v.sl.sol.alc.; insol.eth.; 0.50, w.
8 L-Canaline	$C_4H_{10}N_2O_3$	134.14	214	H_2O	1.6	21	−8.1	......	sol.w.
9 L-Canavanine	$C_5H_{12}N_4O_3$	176.18	184	H_2O	3.2	20	+8.1	8.2	sol.w.
10 L-Carnosine	$C_9H_{14}N_4O_3$	226.23	246-250	H_2O	2.0	20	+20.5	8.17	sol.w.
11 L-Citrulline	$C_6H_{13}N_3O_3$	175.19	222	1.0 N HCl	2.0	27	+24.3	5.92	v.sl.sol.w.; insol.alc.
12 L-Cystathionine	$C_7H_{14}N_2O_4S$	222.26	270-312	1.0 N HCl	1.0	22	+23.7	......	sol.HCl
13 L-Cysteic acid	$C_3H_7NO_5S$	169.17	289	H_2O	....	.....	+8.7	1.6	sol.a., alk., w.; insol.alc.
14 L-Cysteine	$C_3H_7NO_2S$	121.16	175-178	H_2O	2.0	21	−10.1	5.07	v.sol.w.; sol.a., alk.
15 L-Cystine	$C_6H_{12}N_2O_4S_2$	240.30	258-261	1.0 N HCl	1.0	24	−214.4	5.02	sol.a. [2], NH_4OH; insol. alc., eth.; 0.011 w.
16 L-3,5-Dibromotyrosine	$C_9H_9NO_3Br_2$	338.99	245 [3]	0.3 N HCl	....	20	−2.4	4.30	....
17 L-3,4-Dihydroxyphenylalanine	$C_9H_{11}NO_4$	197.19	280	4% HCl	1.0	25	−12.0	......	sol.a., alk.; insol.alc., eth.; 0.50, w.

(Continued)

Amino Acids I (Continued)

TABLE 2.A.7 (Continued)

Amino Acid	Chemical Formula	Molecular Weight	Melting Point	Specific Rotation				Iso-electric Point	Solubility g/100 ml solvent
				Solvent	g/100 ml	Temp °C	Value		
18 L-3,5-Diiodo-tyrosine	$C_9H_9NO_3I_2$	432.99	194	1.1 N HCl	5.1	20	+2.9	4.29 [L]	0.62, w.
19 L-Djenkolic acid	$C_7H_{14}N_2O_4S_2$	254.33	300-350	1% HCl	2.0	26	−44.5	....	0.10, w.
20 L-Ergothio-neine	$C_9H_{15}N_3O_2S$	229.30	290	H_2O	5.0	21	+116.0	....	....
21 L-Ethionine	$C_6H_{13}NO_2S$	163.24	272-284	0.2 N HCl	0.8	25	+23.5	....	sol.w.
22 L-Glutamic acid	$C_5H_9NO_4$	147.13	247	6.0 N HCl	1.0	22	+31.2	3.22 [L]	0.86, w.
23 L-Glutamine	$C_5H_{10}N_2O_3$	146.15	185-186	H_2O	....	19	+8.0	5.65	v.sl.sol.alc.; insol.eth.; 4.25, w.
24 Glycine	$C_2H_5NO_2$	75.07	290	....	....	......	0	6.20	0.43, 90% alc.; 24.99, w.
25 L-Histidine	$C_6H_9N_3O_2$	155.16	277	H_2O	1.1	25	−39.0	7.64	v.sl.sol.alc.; insol.eth.; 4.19, w.
26 L-Homocys-teine	$C_4H_9NO_2S$	135.19	232-233 [L]	....	....	......	....		sol.w.
27 L-Homocystine	$C_8H_{16}N_2O_4S_2$	268.36	282	1.0 N HCl	1.0	26	+77	5.53	v.sl.sol.w.
28 L-δ-Hydroxyly-sine	$C_6H_{14}N_2O_3$	162.20	220	6.0 N HCl	....	25	+17.8	9.15	sol.a., w.; insol.alc.
29 L-4-Hydroxy-proline	$C_5H_9NO_3$	131.13	273-274	H_2O	1.0	22	−75.2	5.82	v.sl.sol.alc.; insol.eth.; 36.11, w.
30 L-Isoleucine	$C_6H_{13}NO_2$	131.18	283-284	6.1 N HCl	5.1	20	+40.6 [L]	6.04 [L]	sol.h.ac.a.; insol.eth.; 0.09, alc.; 3.45 [4], w.; 4.12, w.
31 L-Lanthionine	$C_6H_{12}N_2O_4S$	208.24	270-295	2.4 N NaOH	5.0	22	+8.6	....	sol.NH_4OH, aq.HCl; insol.w.
32 L-Leucine	$C_6H_{13}NO_2$	131.18	337	6.0 N HCl	2.0	26	+15.1	6.04 [L]	sol.ac.a.; insol.eth.; 0.022, alc.; 2.17 [4], w.; 2.19, w.
33 L-Lysine	$C_6H_{14}N_2O_2$	146.19	224	6.0 N HCl	2.0	23	+25.9	9.47	v.sol.w.; v.sl.sol.alc.; insol.eth.
34 L-Methionine	$C_5H_{11}NO_2S$	149.21	283	0.2 N HCl	0.8	25	+21.2	5.74 [L]	insol.eth.; 5.75, w.; 5.62 [4], w.
35 L-Norleucine	$C_6H_{13}NO_2$	131.18	301	6.0 N HCl	4.3	20	+21.3	6.08 [L]	0.017 [L], alc.; 1.149 [L], w.
36 L-Norvaline	$C_5H_{11}NO_2$	117.15	291-292	20% HCl	5	20	+22.8	6.04	sl.sol.alc.; insol.eth.; 10.7 [5], w.
37 D-Octapine	$C_9H_{18}N_4O_4$	246.27	229-230	H_2O	....	17	+20.9	5.51	sol.w.
38 L-Ornithine	$C_5H_{12}N_2O_2$	132.16	225	H_2O	4.0	27	+16.5 [3]	9.70	v.sol.alc.; sl.sol.eth.; v. deliq.w.
39 L-Phenylalanine	$C_9H_{11}NO_2$	165.19	283	H_2O	1.9	20	−35.1	5.91 [L]	sl.sol.alc.; insol.eth.; 2.76 [4], w.; 2.96, w.
40 L-Proline	$C_5H_9NO_2$	115.13	220-222	0.5 N HCl	0.6	20	−52.6	6.3	insol.eth.; 1.55, alc.; 162.3, w.
41 Sarcosine	$C_3H_7NO_2$	89.1	210	....	....	......	0	6.12	v.sol.w.; sl.sol.alc.; in-sol.eth.
42 L-Serine	$C_3H_7NO_3$	105.09	228	1.0 N HCl	9.3	25	+14.5	5.68 [L]	insol.alc., eth.; 4.22 [4], w.; 5.023 [L], w.
43 L-Thiolhistidine	$C_6H_9N_3O_2S$	187.2	310 [6]	1.0 N HCl	1.0	25	−9.5	5.16	sol.a., w.; insol.alc., organic solvents
44 L-Threonine	$C_4H_9NO_3$	119.12	253	H_2O	1.0	26	−28.4	5.59	insol.alc., eth.; 20.1 [L], w.

(Continued)

Amino Acids I (Continued)

TABLE 2.A.7 (Continued)

Amino Acid	Chemical Formula	Molecular Weight	Melting Point	Specific Rotation				Iso-electric Point	Solubility g/100 ml solvent
				Solvent	g/100 ml	Temp °C	Value		
45 L-Thyroxine	$C_{15}H_{11}NO_4I_4$	776.88	235-236	0.13 N NaOH in 70% ethanol	3	......	−4.4	......	insol.alc., eth.; 0.001, w.
46 L-Tryptophan	$C_{11}H_{12}N_2O_2$	204.23	282	H_2O	1.0	20	−31.5	5.88	sl.sol.alc.; insol.eth.; 1.14, w.; 1.36[1/], w.
47 L-Tyrosine	$C_9H_{11}NO_3$	181.19	344	6.3 N HCl	4.4	20	−8.6	5.63	sol.alk.; insol.acet., eth.; 0.01, alc.; 0.0454, w.
48 L-Valine	$C_5H_{11}NO_2$	117.15	293	6.0 N HCl	3.4	20	+28.8	6.00[1/]	0.019[1/], alc.; 5.81[4/], w.; 8.85, w.

[1/] Value for the racemic (DL) mixture. [2/] Mixture of acetonitrile and perchloric acid. [3/] Value for the dihydrate. [4/] Value from reference 1. [5/] Value at 50°C. [6/] Decomposes without melting.

Contributors: Evans, Robert John; Ward, Wilfred H.; Sauberlich, H. E.

Specific Reference

[1] Sober, H. A., ed. 1970. Handbook of Biochemistry. Ed. 2. Chemical Rubber, Cleveland.

General References

[2] Andrews, S., and C. L. A. Schmidt. 1927. J. Biol. Chem. 73:651.

[3] Ashley, J. N., and C. B. Harington. 1930. J. Chem. Soc. London, p. 2586.

[4] Bergel, F. 1948. Biochem. Soc. Symp. 1:78.

[5] Block, R. J., et al. 1958. A Manual of Paper Chromatography and Paper Electrophoresis. Ed. 2. Academic Press, New York.

[6] California Foundation for Biochemical Research. 1958. Properties of the L- (Natural) Amino Acids. Rev. ed. Los Angeles.

[7] Cohn, E. J., and J. T. Edsall. 1943. Proteins, Amino Acids and Peptides. Reinhold, New York.

[8] Du Vigneaud, V., et al. 1942. J. Biol. Chem. 143:59.

[9] Dyer, H. M. 1938. Ibid. 124:519.

[10] Greenstein, J. P., and M. Winitz. 1961. Chemistry of the Amino Acids. J. Wiley, New York. v. 1-3.

[11] Howe, E. E. 1951. Amino Acids and Proteins. C. C. Thomas, Springfield, Ill. p. 3.

[12] Pollock, J. R. A., and R. Stevens, ed. 1965. Dictionary of Organic Compounds. Ed. 4. Oxford Univ. Press, New York.

[13] Riegel, B., and V. du Vigneaud. 1935. J. Biol. Chem. 112:149.

[14] Schmidt, C. L. A. 1945. The Chemistry of the Amino Acids and Proteins. C. C. Thomas, Springfield, Ill.

[15] Weast, R. C., ed. 1971-72. Handbook of Chemistry and Physics. Ed. 52. Chemical Rubber, Cleveland.

[16] West, E. S., et al. 1966. Textbook of Biochemistry. Ed. 4. Macmillan, New York.

[17] Wichers, E. 1952. J. Amer. Chem. Soc. 74:2447.

Source: Altman, P. L., and Dittmer, D. S. (editors) (1972). *Biology Data Book*, Vol. 1. Federation of American Societies for Experimental Biology, Bethesda, Maryland.

Amino Acids II

TABLE 2.A.8
Structure of amino acids

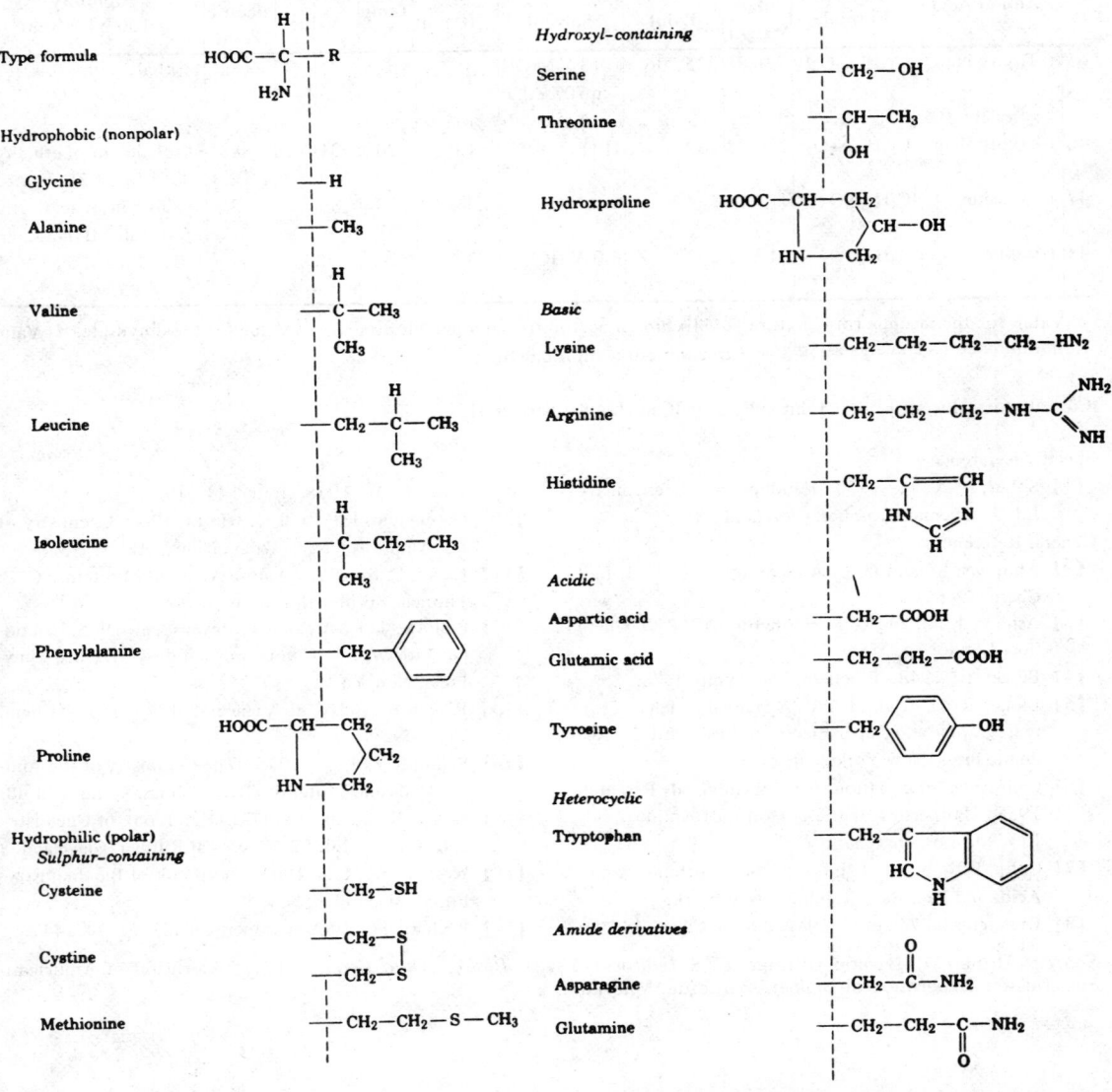

Source: Paul, P. C., and Palmer, H. H. (1972). *Food Theory and Applications*. John Wiley & Sons, New York.

Amino Acids, Solubilities

TABLE 2.A.9
Solubilities of the amino acids in grams per 100 grams of water

Amino Acid	Temperature, °C					Ref. No.
	0°	25°	50°	75°	100°	
DL-Alanine	12.11	16.72	23.09	31.89	44.04	1
L-Alanine	12.73	16.65	21.79	28.51	37.30	1
DL-Aspartic acid	0.262	0.778	2.000	4.456	8.594	1
L-Aspartic acid	0.209	0.500	1.199	2.875	6.893	1
L-Cystine‡ × 10^2	0.502	1.096	2.394	5.229	11.42	2
Diiodo-DL-tyrosine × 10	0.149	0.340	0.773	—	—	3
Diiodo-L-tyrosine × 10	0.204	0.617	1.862	5.62	17.00	1
DL-Glutamic acid	0.855	2.054	4.934	11.86	28.49	1
L-Glutamic acid	0.341	0.864	2.186	5.532	14.00	1
Glycine	14.18	24.99	39.10	54.39	67.17	1
L-Histidine	—	4.19	—	—	—	4
Hydroxy-L-Proline	28.86	36.11	45.18	51.67*	—	5
DL-Isoleucine	1.826	2.229	3.034	4.607	7.802	1
L-Isoleucine	3.791	4.117	4.818	6.076	8.255	2
DL-Leucine	0.797	0.991	1.406	2.276	4.206	1
L-Leucine	2.270	2.426†	2.887†	3.823	5.638	1
DL-Methionine	1.818	3.381	6.070	10.52	17.60	2
DL-Phenylalanine	0.997	1.411	2.187	3.708	6.886	1
L-Phenylalanine	1.983	2.965	4.431	6.624	9.900	2
L-Proline × 10^{-1}	12.74	16.23	20.67	23.90*	—	3
DL-Serine	2.204	5.023	10.34	19.21	32.24	2
L-Tryptophan	0.823	1.136	1.706	2.795	4.987	2
DL-Tyrosine × 10	0.147	0.351	0.836	—	—	3
L-Tyrosine × 10	0.196	0.453	1.052	2.438	5.650	1
D-Tyrosine × 10	0.196	0.453	1.052	—	—	3
DL-Valine	5.98	7.09	9.11	12.61	18.81	1
L-Valine	8.34	8.85	9.62	10.24*	—	6

*Value at 65°.

†Dunn and Stoddard (7) report 2.19 g at 25° for L-leucine rendered methionine-free by repeated recrystallization from 6 N HCl. Hlynka (8) found 2.20 g at 25° and 2.66 g at 50° for L-leucine rendered methionine-free [by S. W. Fox (9)] by fractional crystallization of the formyl derivative and identical values for D-leucine obtained by resolution of the DL form.

‡The following values were found by Loring and Du Vigneaud (10): DL-cystine (0.0049 g), D-cystine (0.0108 g), and meso-cystine (0.0056 g) at 25°.

References

1. Dalton, J. B., and Schmidt, C. L. A., J. Biol. Chem., 103, 549 (1933).
2. Dalton, J. B., and Schmidt, C. L. A., J. Biol. Chem., 109, 241 (1935).
3. Winnek, P. S., and Schmidt, C. L. A., J. Gen. Physiol., 18, 889 (1934-35).
4. Dunn, M. S., Frieden, E. H., and Brown, H. V., unpublished data.
5. Tomiyama, T., and Schmidt, C. L. A., J. Gen. Physiol., 19, 379 (1935-36).
6. Dalton, J. B., and Schmidt, C. L. A., J. Gen. Physiol., 19, 767 (1935-36).
7. Dunn, M. S., and Stoddard, M. P., unpublished data.
8. Hlynka, I., Thesis (1939), California Institute of Technology, Pasadena, California.
9. Fox, S. W., Science, 84, 163 (1936).
10. Loring, H. S., and du Vigneaud, V., J. Biol. Chem., 107, 270 (1934).

Source: Weast, R. C. (editor) (1974–1975). Handbook of Chemistry and Physics, 55th Edition. CRC Press, Cleveland. Used by permission of CRC Press.

Ammonia Solutions

TABLE 2.A.10
Various strengths of ammonia solutions

NH_3 Strength Desired Grams per Liter	Reagent Ammonia Required	
	Grams	Ml
5	18.52	20.6
10	37.04	41.1
15	55.55	61.7
20	74.07	82.3
25	92.59	102.9
50	185.18	205.8
75	277.77	308.6
100	370.37	411.5
150	555.55	617.3
200	740.74	823.0

NOTE: Ammonia solutions: Specification requires not <27% NH_3 by wt. Sp gr = 0.9. Mix and dil. to 1 liter.

Source: Editorial Board, AOAC (1975). *Official Methods of Analysis of the Association of Official Analytical Chemists*, 12th Edition. Association of Official Analytical Chemists, Washington, D.C.

Amylopectin I

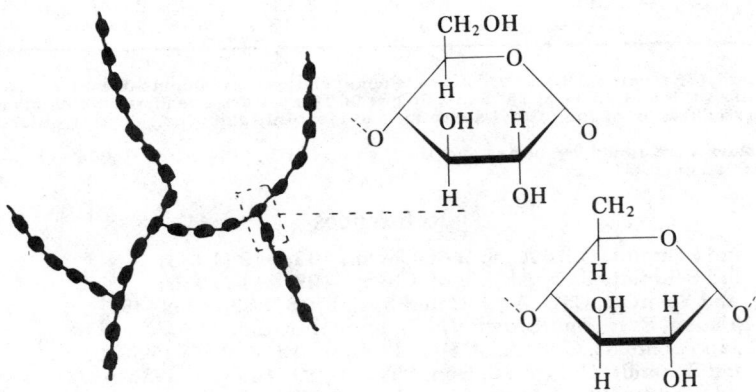

FIGURE 2.A.1
Conformation and structure of amylopectin

Source: Sone, T. (1972). *Consistency of Foodstuffs*. D. Reidel Publishing Co., Boston.

Amylopectin II

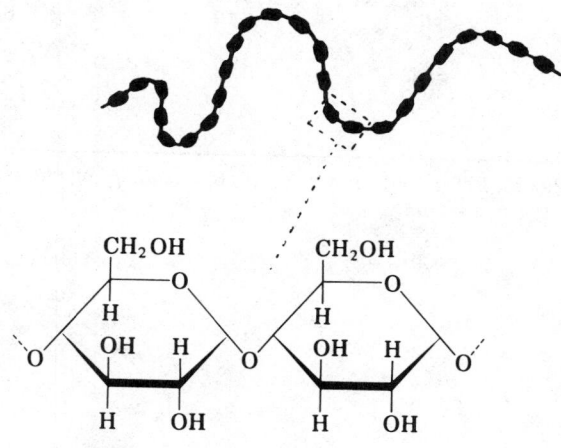

FIGURE 2.A.2
Point of branching of amylopectin molecule

Source: Pomeranz, Y. (editor) (1971). *Wheat Chemistry and Technology*, 2d Edition. American Association of Cereal Chemists, St. Paul, Minnesota.

Amylose I

FIGURE 2.A.3
Conformation and structure of amylose

Source: Sone, T. (1972). *Consistency of Foodstuffs*. D. Reidel Publishing Co., Boston.

Amylose II

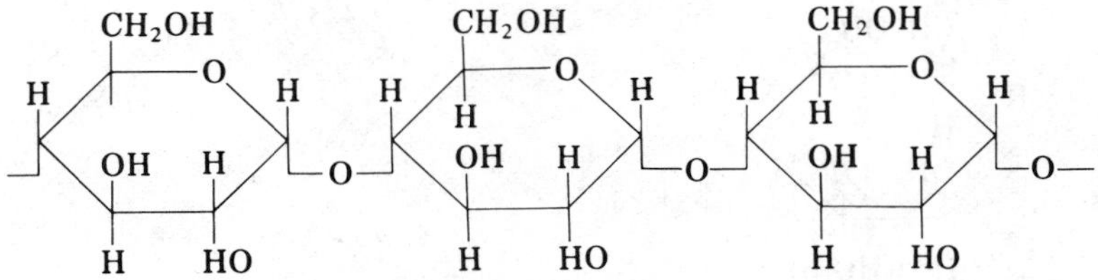

FIGURE 2.A.4
Section of amylose molecule

Source: Pomeranz, Y. (editor) (1971). *Wheat Chemistry and Technology*, 2d Edition. American Association of Cereal Chemists, St. Paul, Minnesota.

Amylose and Amylopectin

TABLE 2.A.11
Size and proportion of amylose and amylopectin in some starches

Plant Species	Amylose (%)	Glucose Residues per Molecule	Amylopectin (%)	Glucose Residues per Molecule
Tubers, roots or rhizome				
Tapioca	17	980	83	18,600
Potato	22	980	78	—
Lily	34	640	66	18,600
Seeds				
Corn, hybrid	22	490	78	30,850
Corn, waxy	0	—	100	—
Wheat	24	540	76	24,700
Rice	17	—	83	—

Source: Mallette, M. F., Althouse, P. M., and Clagett, C. O. *Biochemistry of Plants and Animals.* John Wiley & Sons, New York.

Animal, Foods, Composition

TABLE 2.A.12

Foods of animal origin: composition

(Values are per 100 g of edible portion of fresh, uncooked food, unless otherwise specified; values based on inadequate evidence are enclosed in parentheses)

Food	Water g	Food Energy Cal	Protein g	Fat g	Carbohydrate Total g	Carbohydrate Fiber g	Ash g	Ca mg	Fe mg	P mg	Vitamin A I.U.	Ascorbic acid mg	Niacin mg	Riboflavin mg	Thiamine mg
							Dairy Products								
1 Butter	15.5	716	0.6	81	0.4	0	2.5	20	0	16	3300[1]	0	0.1	0.01	Trace
2 Buttermilk	90.5	36	3.5	0.1	5.1	0	0.8	(118)	0.1	93	Trace	1	0.1	0.18	0.04
3 Cheese: Cheddar	37	398	25.0	32.2	2.1	0	3.7	725	1.0	495	1400	(0)	Trace	0.42	0.02
4 Cottage	76.5	95	19.5	0.5	2.0	0	1.5	96	0.3	189	(20)	(0)	(0.1)	0.31	0.02
5 Cream	51	371	9.0	37.0	2.0	0	1.0	68	0.2	97	(1450)	(0)	0.1	0.22	(0.01)
6 Swiss	39	370	27.5	28.0	1.7	0	3.8	925	0.9	563	1450	(0)	(0.1)	0.40	0.01
7 Cream, light	72.5	204	2.9	20.0	4.0	0	0.6	97	0.1	77	830	1	0.1	0.14	0.03
8 Milk, cow: whole	87	68	3.5	3.9	4.9	0	0.7	118	0.1	93	(160)	1	0.1	0.17	0.04
9 Skimmed	90.5	36	3.5	0.1	5.1	0	0.8	123	0.1	97	Trace	1	0.1	0.18	0.04
10 Milk, goat	87.4	67	3.3	4.0	4.6	0	0.7	129	0.1	106	(160)	1	0.3	0.11	0.04
							Meats								
11 Beef: chuck	65	224	18.6	16	0	0	0.9	11	2.8	167	(0)	0	4.5	0.17	0.08
12 Flank	61	247	19.9	18	0	0	0.9	12	3.0	186	(0)	0	4.8	0.18	0.09
13 Hamburger	55	321	16.0	28	0	0	0.8	9	2.4	128	(0)	0	3.8	0.14	0.07
14 Heart	77.6	108	16.9	3.7	0.7	0	1.1	9	4.6	203	30	4	7.8	0.89	0.58
15 Kidney	74.9	141	15.0	8.1	0.9	0	1.1	9	7.9	221	1150	13	6.4	2.55	0.37
16 Liver	69.7	136	19.7	3.2	6.0	0	1.4	7	6.6	358	43,900	31	13.7	3.33	0.26
17 Porterhouse	58	296	16.4	25	0	0	0.8	10	2.5	134	(0)	0	3.9	0.15	0.07
18 Rib roast	59	282	17.4	23	0	0	0.8	10	2.6	149	(0)	0	4.2	0.15	0.07
19 Round	69	182	19.5	11	0	0	1.0	11	2.9	180	(0)	0	4.7	0.17	0.08
20 Rump	55	322	16.2	28	0	0	0.8	9	2.4	131	(0)	0	3.9	0.14	0.07
21 Sirloin	62	254	17.3	20	0	0	0.9	10	2.6	147	(0)	0	4.2	0.15	0.07
22 Tongue	68	207	16.4	15.0	0.4	(0)	0.9	9	2.8	187	(0)	(0)	5.0	0.29	0.12
23 Brains	78.9	125	10.4	8.6	0.8	0	1.4	16	3.6	330	0	18	4.4	0.26	0.23
24 Lamb: leg roast	63.7	235	18.0	17.5	0	0	0.9	10	2.7	213	(0)	0	5.2	0.22	0.16
25 Liver	70.8	136	21.0	3.9	2.9	0	1.4	8	12.6	364	50,500	33	16.9	3.28	0.40
26 Kidney	77.8	105	16.6	3.3	1.0	0	1.3	13	9.2	237	(1150)	13	7.4	2.42	0.51
27 Shoulder roast	58.3	295	15.6	25.3	0	0	0.8	9	2.3	155	(0)	0	4.5	0.19	0.14
28 Pork: bacon	20	630	9.1	65	1.1	0	4.3	13	0.8	108	(0)	0	1.9	0.12	0.38
29 Ham, fresh	53	344	15.2	31.0	0	0	0.8	9	2.3	168	(0)	0	4.0	0.18	0.74
30 Ham, smoked	42	389	16.9	35.0	(0.3)	0	5.4	10	2.5	136	(0)	0	4.0	0.19	0.70
31 Heart	76.8	117	16.9	4.8	0.4	0	1.1	35	2.7	132	30	6	6.0	1.24	0.43
32 Kidney	77.1	114	16.3	4.6	0.8	0	1.2	11	8.0	246	130	13	9.8	1.74	0.58
33 Liver	72.3	134	19.7	4.8	1.7	0	1.5	10	18.0	362	14,200	23	16.7	2.98	0.40
34 Loin or chops	58	296	16.4	25	0	0	0.9	10	2.5	186	(0)	0	4.3	0.19	0.80
35 Salt pork, fat	8	783	3.9	85	0	(0)	3.5	Trace	0.6	Trace	(0)	0	(0.9)	(0.04)	(0.18)
36 Sausage	41.9	450	10.8	44.8	0	0	2.1	6	1.6	100	(0)	0	2.3	0.17	0.43
37 Spare rib, medium	53	351	14.6	32	0	0	0.8	8	2.2	158	(0)		3.8	0.17	0.71
38 Rabbit, domesticated	54	122	16	6	0	0	0.8	15	1.0	271			9.9	0.04	0.06
39 Seal, canned	66	183	19.1	10.6	1.4				11.4				4.9	0.09	0.04
40 Veal: cutlet	70	164	19.5	9.0	0	0	1.0	11	2.9	200	(0)	0	6.5	0.26	0.14
41 Leg roast	68	186	19.1	12.2	0	0	1.0	11	2.9	206	0	0	6.3	0.27	0.17
42 Liver	71	141	19.0	4.9	4	0	1.3	6	10.6	343	22,500	36	16.1	3.12	0.21
43 Shoulder roast	70	173	19.4	10.0	0	0	1.0	11	2.9	199	(0)	0	6.5	0.26	0.14
44 Stew meat	64	231	18.3	17.0	0	0	0.9	11	2.7	182	(0)	0	6.1	0.24	0.13
45 Venison	73	140	20	6.0	0	0	1.0	11	3.0	216					0.14
							Poultry and Eggs								
46 Chicken: broiler	71.2	151	20.2	7.2	0	0	1.1	14	1.5	200	(0)	(0)	10.2	0.16	0.08
47 Heart	69.6	157	20.5	7.0	1.6	0	1.3	23	1.7	142	30	6	5.2	0.91	0.12
48 Liver	69.6	141	22.1	4.0	2.6	0	1.7	16	7.4	240	32,200	20	11.8	2.46	0.20
49 Roaster	66.0	200	20.2	12.6	0	0	1.0	14	1.5	200	(0)	(0)	8.0	0.16	0.08
50 Egg, whole	74.0	162	12.8	11.5	0.7	0	1.0	54	2.7	210	1140	0	0.1	0.29	0.10
51 Egg white	87.8	50	10.8	0	0.8	0	0.6	6	0.2	17	(0)	0	0.1	0.26	0
52 Egg yolk	49.4	361	16.3	31.9	0.7	0	1.7	147	7.2	586	3210	0	Trace	0.35	0.27
53 Duck	54	326	16.1	29	0	0	1.3	9	2.4	172	0		6.0	0.23	0.16
54 Goose	50	354	16.4	32	0	0	0.9	9	2.4	176		9	5.6		0.15
55 Squab	58	279	18.6	22.1	0	0	1.5	12	3.0	217					
56 Turkey	58.3	268	20.1	20.2	0	0	3.8	23	3.8	320	Trace	(0)	8.0	0.14	0.09
							Fish and Shellfish								
57 Bluefish	74.6	124	20.5	4.0	0	0	1.2	23	0.6	243			1.9	(0.09)	(0.12)
58 Clam	80.3	81	12.8	1.4	3.4		2.1	(96)	(7.0)	(139)	110		(1.6)	0.18	0.10
59 Cod	82.6	74	16.5	0.4	0	0	1.2	10	0.4	194	0	2	2.2	0.09	0.06
60 Crab	80.0	86	16.1	1.6	0.6	0	1.7	(39)	(0.8)	(160)			2.7	0.06	0.14
61 Eel	71.6	162	18.6	9.1	0	0	1.0	18	0.7	202	1800		1.4	0.37	0.28
62 Flounder	82.7	68	14.9	0.5	0	0	1.3	61	0.8	195			1.7	0.05	0.06
63 Haddock	80.7	79	18.2	0.1	0	0	1.4	23	0.7	197			2.4	0.08	0.05
64 Halibut	75.4	126	18.6	5.2	0	0	1.0	13	0.7	211	440		9.2	0.06	0.07
65 Herring, Atlantic	67.2	191	18.3	12.5	0	0	2.7		1.1	256	110		3.4	0.15	0.02
66 Herring, Pacific	79.6	94	16.6	2.6	0	0	1.3			100			(2.2)	0.22	0.02
67 Lobster	79.2	88	16.2	1.9	0.5	0	2.2	61	0.6	184			(1.9)	0.06	(0.13)
68 Mackerel	68.1	188	18.7	12.0	0	0	1.2	5	1.0	239	(450)		8.4	0.35	0.15
69 Oyster	80.5	84	9.8	2.1	5.6		2.0	94	5.6	143	320		1.2	0.20	0.15
70 Perch, yellow	80	88	18.7	0.9	0	0	1.2	20	1.2	215			1.7	0.07	0.09
71 Salmon	63.4	223	17.4	16.5	0	0	1.0			(289)	310	9	7.2	0.23	0.10
72 Sardine, canned	57.4	214	25.7	11.0	1.2		(4.7)	386	2.7	586	220	(0)	4.8	0.17	0.02
73 Scallop	80.3	78	14.8	0.1	3.4	0	1.4	26	1.8	208	0		1.4	0.10	(0.04)
74 Shad	70.2	168	18.7	9.8	0	0	1.4		0.5	260			(8.4)	0.24	(0.15)
75 Shrimp, canned	66.2	127	26.8	1.4	0	0	5.8	115	3.1	263	60	(0)	2.2	0.03	0.01
76 Swordfish	75.8	118	19.2	4.0	0	0	1.3	19	0.9	195	1580		9.1	0.05	0.05
77 Tuna, canned	60.0	198	29.0	8.2	0	0	2.7	(8)	1.4	(351)	80	(0)	12.8	0.12	0.05
78 Whitefish	70	156	22.9	6.5	0	0	1.6	25	1.3	263			(4.2)	(0.09)	(0.09)

/1/ Year-round average.

Source: Spector, W. S. (editor). *Handbook of Biological Data.* Federation of American Societies for Experimental Biology, Bethesda, Maryland.

Antibiotic Standards

TABLE 2.A.13
International standards for antibiotics

Substance	Defined Potency, IU/mg	Equivalence of 1 IU to American μg	Calculated Purity of Standard on Basis of American μg%
Penicillin (sodium salt)	1670	Not used	99[1]
Phenoxymethylpenicillin (free acid)	1695	Not used	99[1]
Streptomycin (sulfate)	780	1 μg of base	97.5
Dihydrostreptomycin (sulfate)	760	1 μg of base	95.1
Bacitracin	55	Not used	Not known
Tetracycline (hydrochloride)	990	1 μg hydrochloride	99.0
Chlortetracycline (hydrochloride)	1000	1 μg hydrochloride	100
Oxytetracycline (base dehydrate)	900	1 μg anhydrous base	97.1
Erythromycin (base)	950	1 μg anhydrous base	95
Polymixin B	7874	Not used	Not known

[1] Independent estimate (Lightbown 1961).

Source: Grant, J. (editor) (1969). Hackh's Chemical Dictionary, 4th Edition. McGraw-Hill Book Co., New York.

Antioxidant Activity

TABLE 2.A.14
Comparative antioxidant activity

Additive	(%)	Schaal Oven, Thin Layer, 45°C Chicken Fat (Days to Reach 20 Meq Peroxides)	Pork Fat (Days to Reach 20 Meq Peroxides)
None		8	3
BHA	0.01	14	14
BHA	0.02	20	28
BHT	0.02	15	18
Tenox 2	0.05	28	32
α-Tocopherol	0.02	13	15
α-Tocopherol	0.05	13	15
α-Tocopherol	0.2	10	15
α-Tocopherol } Ascorbyl Palmitate	0.02 0.02	28	28
γ-Tocopherol	0.02	29	37
γ-Tocopherol	0.05	40	58
γ-Tocopherol	0.2	46	61
γ-Tocopherol } Ascorbyl Palmitate	0.02 0.02	53	67
Ascorbyl Palmitate	0.02	10	9

Source: Bauernfeind, J. C. (1975). Tocopherols. In Encyclopedia of Food Technology. A. H. Johnson and M. S. Peterson (editors). AVI Publishing Co., Westport, Connecticut.

Antioxidant Mixtures

TABLE 2.A.15
Some typical commercial antioxidant preparations

	BHA[1] (%)	BHT[2] (%)	Propyl Gallate (%)	TBHQ[3] (%)	Propylene Glycol (%)	Citric Acid (%)	Vegetable Oil (%)	Glyceryl Mono-oleate (%)	Sorbitan Mono-stearate (%)	Water (%)	Ethyl Alcohol (%)	Citrate Mono-glyceride (%)
Eastman Tenox BHT		X										
Eastman Tenox BHA	X											
Eastman Tenox 2	20				70							
Eastman Tenox 4	20	20	6			4	60	20				
Eastman Tenox 6	10	10	6		12	6	28	20	8			
Eastman Tenox 7	28		12		34	6						
Eastman Tenox 20				20	70	10						
Eastman Tenox 22	20			6	70	4						
Eastman Tenox 26	10			6	12	6						
Eastman Tenox R	20	10			60	20	28	28				
Eastman Tenox S-1			20		70	10						
UOP-BHA	X	X										
UOP Sustane												
UOP-Sustane 3F	66.7		20			13.3	60					
UOP-Sustane 6	18	22					40					
UOP-Sustane E	10											
UOP-Sustane W	10	10	6		8	6	28	30	2.5	47.5		
UOP-Sustane P	20	20										
Shell Ionol	6	X			X	2					60	
Griffiths G-16	6	13.5	5.5									X

[1] Butylated Hydroxy Anisole.
[2] Butylated Hydroxy Toluene.
[3] Tertiary Butylated Hydroquinone.

NOTE: Monotertiary butylhydroquinone has recently been introduced as a food grade antioxidant. Its advantages are claimed to be low odor, good fat solubility, and no discoloration in the presence of iron.

Source: Morse, R. E. (1975). Antioxidants. In *Encyclopedia of Food Technology.* A. H. Johnson and M. S. Peterson (editors). AVI Publishing Co., Westport, Connecticut.

Antioxidants, Formulas

TABLE 2.A.16
Composition and structure of several antioxidants

Compound	Common Designa- tion	Structure Formula
Propyl gallate	PG	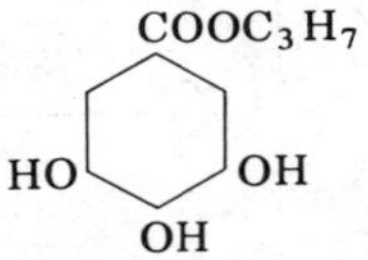$COOC_3H_7$ HO OH OH
		Commercial BHA is a mixture of two isomers: 2-*tert*-butyl-4-hydroxyanisole 3-*tert*-butyl-4-hydroxyanisole
Butylated hydroxyanisole (3-isomer)	BHA	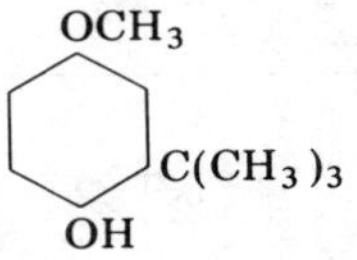OCH_3 $C(CH_3)_3$ OH
Butylated hydroxytoluene 2-6-*tert*-butyl-p-cresol	BHT	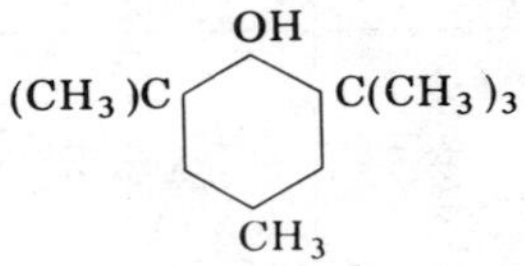OH $(CH_3)C$ $C(CH_3)_3$ CH_3
Citric acid	—	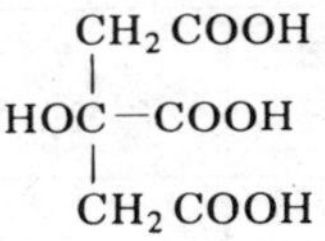CH_2COOH HOC—COOH CH_2COOH
Nordihydro- guaiaretic acid	NDGA	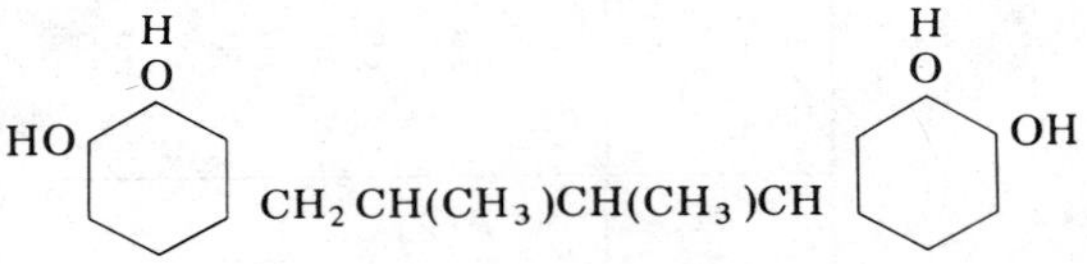H O HO $CH_2CH(CH_3)CH(CH_3)CH$ H O OH

Source: Mahlenbacher, C. V. (1960). *The Analysis of Fats and Oils*. Garrard Publishing Co., Champaign, Illinois.

Antioxidant Structure

TABLE 2.A.17
Lipid antioxidants acceptable for use in human food in the United States

Name	Use Limit	Structure
Butylated hydroxyanisole	0.02% of fat content	
Butylated hydroxytoluene	0.02% of fat content	
Dilauryl thiodipropionate	0.02% of fat content	$CH_2-CH_2-COO-CH_2-(CH_2)_{10}-CH_3$ S $CH_2-CH_2-COO-CH_2-(CH_2)_{10}-CH_3$
Thiodipropionic acid	0.02% of fat content	CH_2-CH_2-COOH S CH_2-CH_2-COOH
Propyl gallate	0.02% of fat content	

(Continued)

Antioxidant Structure (Continued)

TABLE 2.A.17 (Continued)

Name	Use Limit	Structure
Gum guaiacol	0.1% in fat	(phenol ring with OH and OCH$_3$)
Tocopherols	GMP[1]	(chroman structure with CH$_3$, HO, O, CH$_3$, and (CH$_2$CH$_2$CH$_2$CH$_3$)$_3$—CH$_3$ side chain)
Ethoxyquin	100 ppm in paprika and chili	(dihydroquinoline structure: H–N, CH$_3$ CH$_3$, CH$_3$, C$_2$H$_5$O)
2,4,5 Trihydroxy butyrophenone	0.02% of fat content	CH$_3$—CH$_2$—CH$_2$—C=O (attached to benzene ring with OH, HO, OH)
4 hydroxy methyl-2, 6-di tert-butylphenone	0.02% of fat content	(benzene ring with OH, C(CH$_3$)$_3$, C(CH$_3$)$_3$, OCH$_3$)

[1] In accordance with good manufacturing practices.

Source: Morse, R. E. (1975). Antioxidants. In *Encyclopedia of Food Technology*. A. H. Johnson and M. S. Peterson (editors). AVI Publishing Co., Westport, Connecticut.

Ascorbic Acid (*Requirements and Sources*)

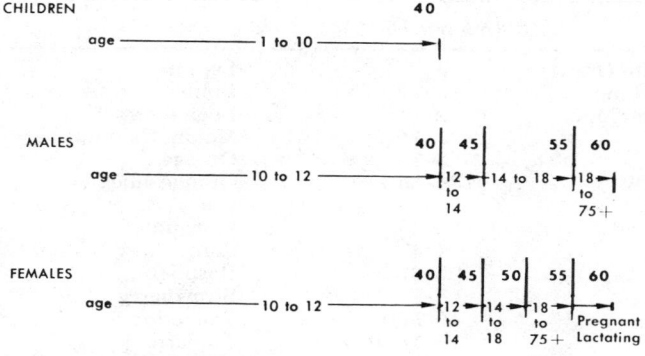

MILLIGRAMS

CHILDREN		40
age	1 to 10	

MALES — age — 10 to 12 — 40 | 45 | 55 | 60; 12 to 14 — 14 to 18 — 18 to 75+

FEMALES — age — 10 to 12 — 40 | 45 | 50 | 55 | 60; 12 to 14 — 14 to 18 — 18 to 75+ — Pregnant Lactating

GOOD SOURCES†

MILLIGRAMS

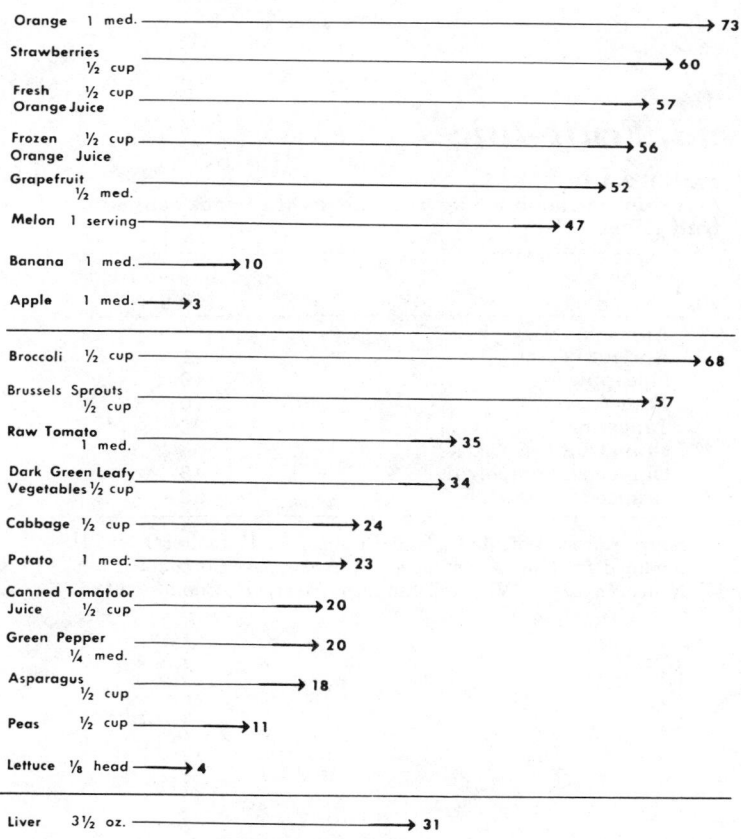

Food	mg
Orange 1 med.	73
Strawberries ½ cup	60
Fresh ½ cup Orange Juice	57
Frozen ½ cup Orange Juice	56
Grapefruit ½ med.	52
Melon 1 serving	47
Banana 1 med.	10
Apple 1 med.	3
Broccoli ½ cup	68
Brussels Sprouts ½ cup	57
Raw Tomato 1 med.	35
Dark Green Leafy Vegetables ½ cup	34
Cabbage ½ cup	24
Potato 1 med.	23
Canned Tomato or Juice ½ cup	20
Green Pepper ¼ med.	20
Asparagus ½ cup	18
Peas ½ cup	11
Lettuce ⅛ head	4
Liver 3½ oz.	31

†Average nutrient content as food is served. (Note 3½ oz equals approximately 100 g.)

FIGURE 2.A.5

Source: Lessons on Meat. (1974). National Live Stock and Meat Board, Chicago.

Ascorbic Acid, Food

TABLE 2.A.18
Ascorbic acid in fruits

	(mg per 100 g)		(mg per 100 g)
Apple, Blenheim Orange	3	Lemon	14–66
Bramley Seedling	16–22	Lime	32–58
Cox's Orange Pippin	2–14	Loganberry	20–48
Banana	1–15	Melon, Cantaloupe	15–53
Cherry	3–17	Orange	16–99
Currant (black)	136–353	Orange Juice	28–89
(red)	50	Pear	1–10
Gooseberry	28–47	Pineapple	10–63
Grape	1–4	Plum	0.5–5
Grapefruit	26–65	Raspberry	30
Greengage	0.5–7	Strawberry	46–77
Haw	49–500	Tangerine	10–36
Hip	10–1870	Tomato	13–39

Source: Sinclair, H. M., and Hollingsworth, D. F. (1969). *Hutchison's Food and the Principles of Nutrition.* Edward Arnold (Publishers), London, England.

Ascorbic Acid, Fruit Juices

TABLE 2.A.19
Ascorbic acid supplied by four ounces of various canned fruit juices

Fruit	Ascorbic Acid Mg
Apple	1.5
Apricot nectar	1.5
Pineapple	10
Tomato	20
Tangerine	32
Grapefruit	34
Orange and grapefruit	48
Orange	53

Source: Woodroof, J. G., and Phillips, G. F. (editors) (1974). Modified fruit juice beverages. In *Beverages: Carbonated and Noncarbonated.* AVI Publishing Co., Westport, Connecticut.

Asparagus Terms

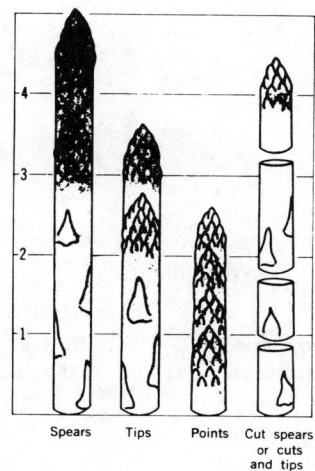

FIGURE 2.A.6
Identification of cuts of asparagus used for processing canned and frozen products

Source: USDA (1977). How to buy canned and frozen vegetables. USDA Home and Garden Bull. *167*.

B

Bacon Dressing

TABLE 2.B.1

Ingredients

2 slices of bacon, fried	2 tbsp sugar (optional)
Bacon fat from bacon	½ tsp salt
¼ cup vinegar	

Procedure

Fry the bacon until crisp, and crumble. Into the same pan (with the fat) add the vinegar, sugar and salt. Stir and pour hot over greens or salad. Finely chopped onions often are added to this type of salad dressing.

Source: Kintner, T. C., and Mangel, M. Vinegars and salad dressings. Univ. Missouri. Agric. Exp. Sta. Bull. *631*.

Bacterial Food-Borne Illnesses

TABLE 2.B.2

Name of illness	What causes it	Symptoms
Salmonellosis. Examples of foods involved: Poultry, red meats, eggs, dried foods, dairy products.	Salmonellae. Bacteria widespread in nature, live and grow in intestinal tracts of human beings and animals.	Severe headache, followed by vomiting, diarrhea, abdominal cramps, and fever. Infants, elderly, and persons with low resistance are most susceptible. Severe infections cause high fever and may even cause death.
Perfringens poisoning. Examples of foods involved: Stews, soups, or gravies made from poultry or red meat.	*Clostridium perfringens.* Spore-forming bacteria that grow in the absence of oxygen. Temperatures reached in thorough cooking of most foods are sufficient to destroy vegetative cells, but heat-resistant spores can survive.	Nausea without vomiting, diarrhea, acute inflammation of stomach and intestines.
Staphylococcal poisoning (frequently called staph). Examples of foods involved: Custards, egg salad, potato salad, chicken salad, macaroni salad, ham, salami, cheese.	*Staphylococcus aureus.* Bacteria fairly resistant to heat. Bacteria growing in food produce a toxin that is extremely resistant to heat.	Vomiting, diarrhea, prostration, abdominal cramps. Generally mild and often attributed to other causes.
Botulism. Examples of foods involved: Canned low-acid foods, smoked fish.	*Clostridium botulinum.* Spore-forming organisms that grow and produce toxin in the absence of oxygen, such as in a sealed container.	Double vision, inability to swallow, speech difficulty, progressive respiratory paralysis. Fatality rate is high, in the United States about 65 percent.

(Continued)

Table 2.B.2 (*Continued*)

Characteristics of illness	Preventive measures
Transmitted by eating contaminated food, or by contact with infected persons or carriers of the infection. Also transmitted by insects, rodents, and pets. Onset: Usually within 12 to 36 hours. Duration: 2 to 7 days.	Salmonellae in food are destroyed by heating the food to 140° F. and holding for 10 minutes or to higher temperatures for less time; for instance, 155° F. for a few seconds. Refrigeration at 40° F. inhibits the increase of Salmonellae, but they remain alive in foods in the refrigerator or freezer, and even in dried foods.
Transmitted by eating food contaminated with abnormally large numbers of the bacteria. Onset: Usually within 8 to 20 hours. Duration: May persist for 24 hours.	To prevent growth of surviving bacteria in cooked meats, gravies, and meat casseroles that are to be eaten later, cool foods rapidly and refrigerate promptly at 40° F. or below, or hold them above 140° F.
Transmitted by food handlers who carry the bacteria and by eating food containing the toxin. Onset: Usually within 3 to 8 hours. Duration: 1 to 2 days.	Growth of bacteria that produce toxin is inhibited by keeping hot foods above 140° F. and cold foods at or below 40° F. Toxin is destroyed by boiling for several hours or heating the food in a pressure cooker at 240° F. for 30 minutes.
Transmitted by eating food containing the toxin. Onset: Usually within 12 to 36 hours or longer. Duration: 3 to 6 days.	Bacterial spores in food are destroyed by high temperatures obtained only in the pressure canner.[1] More than 6 hours is needed to kill the spores at boiling temperature (212° F.). The toxin is destroyed by boiling for 10 to 20 minutes; time required depends on kind of food.

[1] For processing times in home canning, see Home and Garden Bulletin 8, "Home Canning of Fruits and Vegetables," and 106, "Home Canning of Meat and Poultry."

Source: USDA (1975). Keeping food safe to eat. USDA Home and Garden Bull. *162.*

Bacteria, Molds, and Yeasts

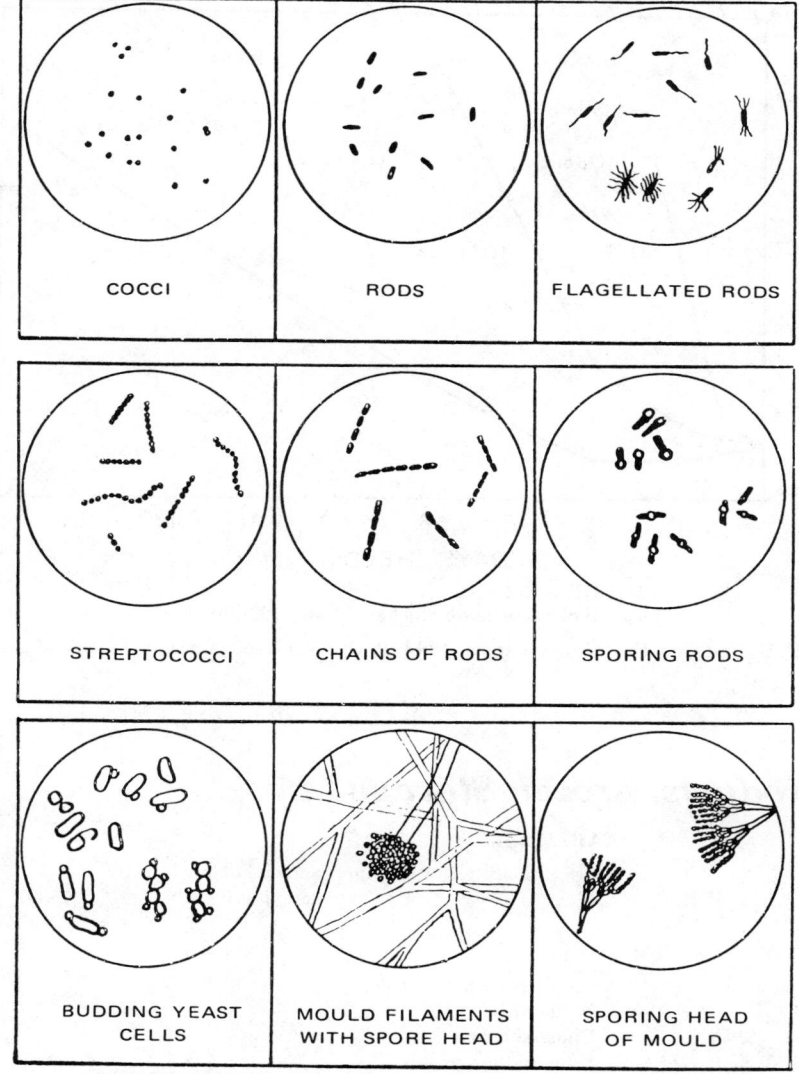

FIGURE 2.B.1
Microscopic appearance and identification of molds and yeasts

Source: Graham-Rack, B., and Binsted, R. *Hygiene in Food Manufacturing and Handling.* Food Trade press, London, England.

Bacteria on Chickens at Various Holding Temperatures

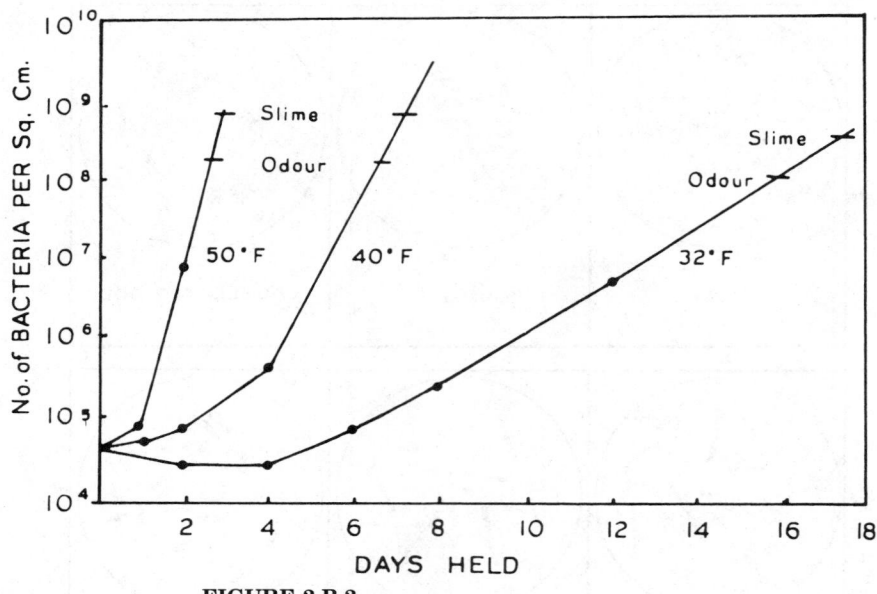

FIGURE 2.B.2
Growth of bacteria on chickens at 32, 40, and 50°F

Source: Snyder, E. S., and Orr, H. L. Poultry meat. Publ. *9*, Ontario Dept. Agriculture, Canada.

Baked Products, Frozen Storage Life

TABLE 2.B.3

Food	Approximate holding period at 0° F.
	(months)
Bread and yeast rolls (baked):	
White bread	6
Cinnamon rolls	3
Fruit and nut breads	3
Plain rolls	6
Cakes (baked):	
Angel	2
Chiffon	2
Chocolate layer	4
Fruit	12
Pound	6
Yellow	6
Pies (unbaked):	
Apple	8
Berry	8
Cherry	8
Peach	8

Source: USDA (1979). Breads, cakes, and pies in family meals: A guide for consumers. USDA Home and Garden Bull. *186*.

Banana, Areas of Production

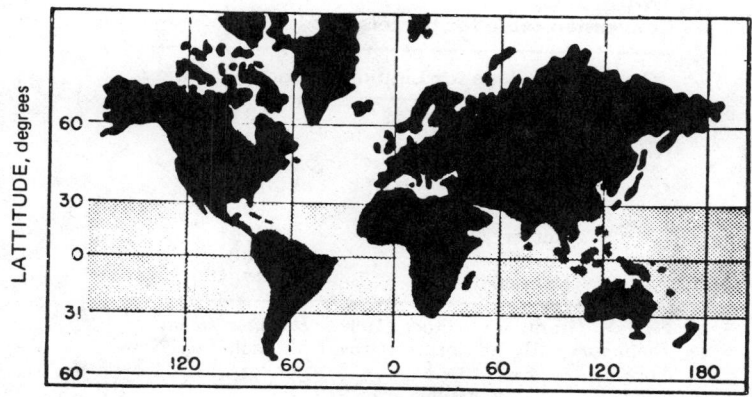

FIGURE 2.B.3
Zone of banana production

Source: Von Loesecke, H. W. Bananas. In *Economic Crops*, Vol. 1. Z. I. Kertesz (editor). John Wiley & Sons, New York.

Bananas, Composition

TABLE 2.B.4
Chemical composition of different varieties of ripe bananas[1] expressed as percentage of fresh pulp

Constituent	Gros Michel	Lady Finger	Lacatan	Plantain	Red[3] Banana
Moisture	75.9	70.6	71.6	63.8	73.3
Reducing sugars	10.73	6.19	8.15	18.89	4.10
Nonreducing sugars	6.12	13.38	10.01	0.00	16.08
Starch	2.93	4.13	6.54	11.69	4.12
Total carbohydrates	19.78	23.70	24.70	30.58	24.30
Protein	0.81	1.49	1.04	1.16	0.48
Crude fat	0.47	0.30	0.40	0.30	0.24
Pectin	0.34	0.57	0.41	0.43	0.62
Protopectin	0.34	0.29	0.35	0.37	0.43
Ash	0.76	0.70	0.77	0.85	0.84
Acidity, cc.[2]	4.46	4.27	4.06	9.00	4.05

[1] These analyses are for fruit the peel of which had developed a full yellow color.
[2] Cubic centimeters of N NaOH required to neutralize 100 g of pulp.
[3] Unpublished data, J. T. Manion, United Fruit Co., Research Dept., 1933.

Source: Von Loesecke, H. W. Bananas. In *Economic Crops*. Vol. 1. Z. I. Kertesz (editor). John Wiley & Sons, New York.

Barrel Size

TABLE 2.B.5
Conversion table for barrels

Compute Gallons for Liquids, Pounds for Solids	
Wine	31
Ale	36
Petroleum	42
Rosin	180
Flour	196
Butter	224
Pork, beef	200
Cement	376

Source: Grant, J. (editor) (1969). *Hackh's Chemical Dictionary*, 4th Edition. McGraw-Hill Book Co., New York.

Beans, Dry, Cooking

TABLE 2.B.6
Boiling guide for dry beans, peas, and lentils[1]

Vegetable (1 cup)	Amount of water	Approximate boiling time	Yield
	Cups	*Hours*	*Cups*
Black beans	3	2	2
Blackeye beans (blackeye peas, cowpeas)	2½	½	2½
Cranberry beans	3	2	2
Great Northern beans	2½	1 to 1½	2½
Kidney beans	3	2	2¾
Lentils	2	½	2½
Lima beans, large	2½	1	2½
Lima beans, small	2½	1	2
Navy (pea) beans	3	1½ to 2	2½
Peas, whole	2½	1	2½
Pinto beans	3	2	2½
Soybeans	4	2½	2½
Split peas	2	⅓	2½

[1] **Soak before cooking.**

Source: USDA (1980). Vegetables in family meals. USDA Home and Garden Bull. *105*.

Beans or Peas Planting Guide

TABLE 2.B.7

Type	Pounds of seed per 50-ft row	Depth of planting, inches	Spacing between rows, inches	Spacing in rows, inches		Days to harvest
				Seeds	Plants	
Snap beans, bush	¼–½	1–1½	18–30	1–2	2–4	50–60
Snap beans, pole	¼–½	1–1½	24–48	3–6	4–8	60–70
Lima beans, bush	¼–½	1–1½	18–30	2–4	4–8	65–75
Lima beans, pole	¼–½	1–1½	36	3–6	6–8	70–90
Peas, garden	¼	1–2	6 (double rows) 36–48	1–1½	1–1½	55–70
Peas, southern	¼–½	1–1½	30–54	2–4	2–4	55–80

Source: USDA (1977). Growing your own vegetables. USDA Agricultural Information Bull. *409.*

Beans, Peas, and Lentils Label

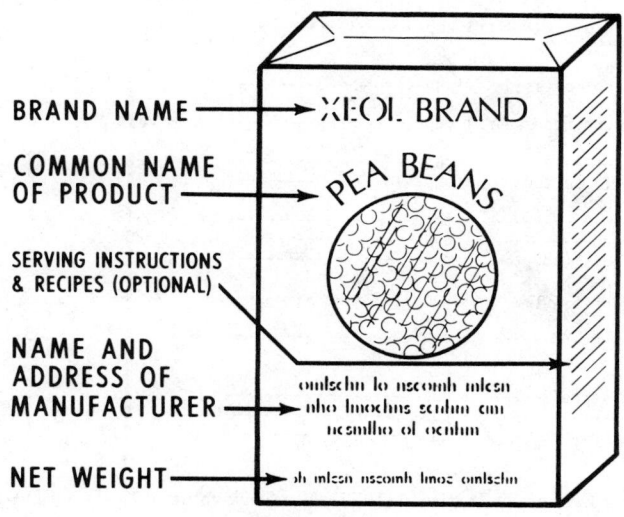

BRAND NAME → XEOL BRAND

COMMON NAME OF PRODUCT → PEA BEANS

SERVING INSTRUCTIONS & RECIPES (OPTIONAL)

NAME AND ADDRESS OF MANUFACTURER → omlschn lo nscomh mlcsn nho lmochns scnlnn cnn ncsmlho ol ocnlnn

NET WEIGHT → oh mlcsn nscomh lmoz onnlschn

FIGURE 2.B.4

Source: USDA (1970). How to buy dry beans, peas, and lentils. USDA Home and Garden Bull. *177.*

Beans, Peas, and Nuts

TABLE 2.B.8
Composition of beans, peas, and nuts [Dashes (—) denote lack of reliable data for a constituent believed to be present in measurable amount]

Item No. (A)	Foods, approximate measures, units, and weight (edible part unless footnotes indicate otherwise) (B)	Water (C)	Food energy (D)	Pro- tein (E)	Fat (F)
		Grams	Per- cent	Cal- ories	Grams	Grams
	Almonds, shelled:					
507	Chopped (about 130 almonds)----- 1 cup--------------------	130	5	775	24	70
508	Slivered, not pressed down (about 115 almonds). 1 cup--------------------	115	5	690	21	62
	Beans, dry:					
	Common varieties as Great North- ern, navy, and others:					
	Cooked, drained:					
509	Great Northern-------------- 1 cup--------------------	180	69	210	14	1
510	Pea (navy)------------------ 1 cup--------------------	190	69	225	15	1
	Canned, solids and liquid:					
	White with—					
511	Frankfurters (sliced)----- 1 cup--------------------	255	71	365	19	18
512	Pork and tomato sauce----- 1 cup--------------------	255	71	310	16	7
513	Pork and sweet sauce------ 1 cup--------------------	255	66	385	16	12
514	Red kidney---------------- 1 cup--------------------	255	76	230	15	1
515	Lima, cooked, drained---------- 1 cup--------------------	190	64	260	16	1
516	Blackeye peas, dry, cooked (with residual cooking liquid). 1 cup--------------------	250	80	190	13	1
517	Brazil nuts, shelled (6-8 large kernels). 1 oz--------------------	28	5	185	4	19
518	Cashew nuts, roasted in oil------- 1 cup--------------------	140	5	785	24	64
	Coconut meat, fresh:					
519	Piece, about 2 by 2 by 1/2 in--- 1 piece------------------	45	51	155	2	16
520	Shredded or grated, not pressed down. 1 cup--------------------	80	51	275	3	28
521	Filberts (hazelnuts), chopped (about 80 kernels). 1 cup--------------------	115	6	730	14	72
522	Lentils, whole, cooked----------- 1 cup--------------------	200	72	210	16	Trace
523	Peanuts, roasted in oil, salted (whole, halves, chopped). 1 cup--------------------	144	2	840	37	72
524	Peanut butter-------------------- 1 tbsp-------------------	16	2	95	4	8
525	Peas, split, dry, cooked---------- 1 cup--------------------	200	70	230	16	1
526	Pecans, chopped or pieces (about 120 large halves). 1 cup--------------------	118	3	810	11	84
527	Pumpkin and squash kernels, dry, hulled. 1 cup--------------------	140	4	775	41	65
528	Sunflower seeds, dry, hulled------ 1 cup--------------------	145	5	810	35	69
	Walnuts:					
	Black:					
529	Chopped or broken kernels----- 1 cup--------------------	125	3	785	26	74
530	Ground (finely)--------------- 1 cup--------------------	80	3	500	16	47
531	Persian or English, chopped (about 60 halves). 1 cup--------------------	120	4	780	18	77

Source: Consumer and Food Economics Institute (1977). Nutritive value of foods. USDA Home and Garden Bull. 72.

							NUTRIENTS IN INDICATED QUANTITY					
Fatty Acids												
Satu-rated (total)	Unsaturated		Carbo-hydrate	Calcium	Phos-phorus	Iron	Potas-sium	Vitamin A value	Thiamin	Ribo-flavin	Niacin	Ascorbic acid
	Oleic	Lino-leic										
(G)	(H)	(I)	(J)	(K)	(L)	(M)	(N)	(O)	(P)	(Q)	(R)	(S)
Grams	Grams	Grams	Grams	Milli-grams	Milli-grams	Milli-grams	Milli-grams	Inter-national units	Milli-grams	Milli-grams	Milli-grams	Milli-grams
5.6	47.7	12.8	25	304	655	6.1	1,005	0	.31	1.20	4.6	Trace
5.0	42.2	11.3	22	269	580	5.4	889	0	.28	1.06	4.0	Trace
——	——	——	38	90	266	4.9	749	0	.25	.13	1.3	0
——	——	——	40	95	281	5.1	790	0	.27	.13	1.3	0
			32	94	303	4.8	668	330	.19	.15	3.3	Trace
2.4	2.8	.6	48	138	235	4.6	536	330	.20	.08	1.5	5
4.3	5.0	1.1	54	161	291	5.9	——	——	.15	.10	1.3	——
——	——	——	42	74	278	4.6	673	10	.13	.10	1.5	——
——	——	——	49	55	293	5.9	1,163	——	.25	.11	1.3	——
——	——	——	35	43	238	3.3	573	30	.40	.10	1.0	——
4.8	6.2	7.1	3	53	196	1.0	203	Trace	.27	.03	.5	——
12.9	36.8	10.2	41	53	522	5.3	650	140	.60	.35	2.5	——
14.0	.9	.3	4	6	43	.8	115	0	.02	.01	.2	1
24.8	1.6	.5	8	10	76	1.4	205	0	.04	.02	.4	2
5.1	55.2	7.3	19	240	388	3.9	810	——	.53	——	1.0	Trace
——	——	——	39	50	238	4.2	498	40	.14	.12	1.2	0
13.7	33.0	20.7	27	107	577	3.0	971	——	.46	.19	24.8	0
1.5	3.7	2.3	3	9	61	.3	100	——	.02	.02	2.4	0
——	——	——	42	22	178	3.4	592	80	.30	.18	1.8	——
7.2	50.5	20.0	17	86	341	2.8	712	150	1.01	.15	1.1	2
11.8	23.5	27.5	21	71	1,602	15.7	1,386	100	.34	.27	3.4	——
8.2	13.7	43.2	29	174	1,214	10.3	1,334	70	2.84	.33	7.8	——
6.3	13.3	45.7	19	Trace	713	7.5	575	380	.28	.14	.9	——
4.0	8.5	29.2	12	Trace	456	4.8	368	240	.18	.09	.6	——
8.4	11.8	42.2	19	119	456	3.7	540	40	.40	.16	1.1	2

Beef and Dual-Purpose Cattle

TABLE 2.B.9
Breeds and their characteristics

Breed	Place of Origin	Color	Distinctive Head Characteristics	Other Distinguishing Characteristics	Disqualifications; Comments
Beef Breeds: **Angus**	Scotland; in the northeastern counties of Aberdeen, Angus, Kincardine, and Forfar.	Black	Polled	Comparatively smooth coat of hair. Somewhat cylindrical body.	Horns, scurs, or buttons. Red color. A noticeable amount of white above the underline, or in front of the navel, or on one or more legs. Calves from females less than 18 mo. of age when calf was dropped, or from bulls less than 6 mo. of age at the time of service.
Beefmasters (approx. ½ Brahman, and ¼ each Shorthorn and Hereford)	United States; on the Lasater Ranch, Falfurrias, Texas.	Red is the dominant color, but color is variable and is disregarded in selection.	The majority are horned, although a few are naturally polled.	Good milk producers under range conditions; heavy weaning and mature weights.	In order that each Beefmaster may be permanently identified with the breeder thereof, the breeds must use a prefix name such as ''Jones Beefmaster,'' ''Smith Beefmaster,'' etc., to designate his cattle. Thus, in a unique way, the responsibility for the continued improvement of the breed is placed squarely upon the individual breeder.
Belted Galloway	Scotland; in the southwestern district of Galloway.	Black with a brownish tinge, or dun; with a white belt completely encircling the body between the shoulders and the hooks.	Polled	Heavy coat of hair.	Red color, incomplete belt, other white marks, or scurs.

(Continued)

Beef and Dual-Purpose Cattle (Continued)

TABLE 2.B.9 (Continued)

Breed	Origin	Color	Head	Characteristics	Disqualifications / Remarks
Brahman	India (but a distinct American breed has been created through the amalgamation of several Indian types, probably with a small infusion of European breeding).	Gray or red preferred; either solid color, or a gradual blending of the two. However, there are brown, black, white, and spotted Brahmans.	Drooping ears. A long face.	Prominent hump over the shoulders. An abundance of loose, pendulous skin under the throat and along the dewlap. A voice that resembles a grunt rather than a low.	Brindle, gruella (a smutty or blackish red), or albino color. Cryptorchid bull. Freemartin heifer. Inherited lameness. Dwarf or midget characteristics.
Brangus (3/8 Brahman 5/8 Angus)	United States; on Clear Creek Ranch, Welch, Okla., owned by Frank Buttram, beginning in 1942.	Black	Polled	Slight crest over the neck. Smooth, sleek coat.	Horns. Off-color. White on underline or legs.
Charbray (3/4 Charolais, 1/4 Brahman to 7/8 Charolais, 1/8 Brahman, solid color, golden to white are registered)	United States; in the Rio Grande Valley of Texas.	Light tan at birth, but usually change to a cream white in a few weeks.	Horned	A slight hint of the Brahman dewlap remains.	To qualify for registration, Charbray cattle must have at least 1/4 Brahman. Charolais-Brahman of lesser percentages are recorded but not considered registered.
Charolais (usually spelled Charollais in France)	France; in the province of Charolles in Central France.	White or cream	Horned	Pink skin and mucus membranes.	The association disqualifies any animal that (1) has a black nose, (2) is spotted, or (3) has excessive dark skin pigmentation.
Devon	England; in the county of Devon.	Red; rich dark red is preferred.	Creamy white horns with black tips.	Yellow skin.	White other than in the switch or on small areas on the udder and belly.
Dexter	Ireland, in the southern and southwestern parts. They were named after their founder, a Mr. Dexter.	Black or red.	Head is rather long.	Small size and short legs. Mature bulls should not exceed 900 lbs. and mature cows 800 lbs. Some mature animals are less than 40 inches high.	Animals having white other than on the belly, switch, udder, or scrotum are disqualified for registry.

(Continued)

Beef and Dual-Purpose Cattle *(Continued)*

TABLE 2.B.9 *(Continued)*

Breed	Place of Origin	Color	Distinctive Head Characteristics	Other Distinguishing Characteristics	Disqualifications; Comments
Galloway	Scotland; in the southwestern province of Galloway.	Black; sometimes with a brownish or reddish tint; or dun.	Polled	Long curly hair.	White markings on feet or legs or above the underline.
Hereford	England; in the county of Hereford.	Red with white markings; white face and white on the underline, flank, crest, switch, breast, and below the knees and hocks. White back of the crops, high on the flanks, or too high on the legs is objectionable. Likewise, dark or smutty noses and red necks are frowned upon.			Calves from females less than 24 mo. of age when calf was dropped, or from bulls less than 12 mo. of age when service producing the calf occurred, cannot be registered.
Indu Brazil (Zebu)	Brazil	Light grey to silver grey; dun to red.	Prominent forehead and long drooping ears. Symmetrical horns drawing upward and to the rear.	Prominent hump over the shoulders. An abundance of loose, pendulous skin under the throat and along the dewlap. A voice that resembles a grunt rather than a low.	Brindle color combinations. White markings on the nose or switch. Absence of loose, thick, mellow skin. Weak and improperly formed hump.

(Continued)

Beef and Dual-Purpose Cattle (Continued)

(Continued)

TABLE 2.B.9 (Continued)

Polled Hereford	United States; in Iowa.	Red with white markings, white face and white on underline, flank, crest, switch, breast, and below the knees and hocks. White back of the crops, high on the flanks, or too high on the legs is objectionable. Likewise, dark or smutty noses are frowned upon.	Polled		No calf is eligible for registration unless its sire was at least 12 mo. of age at the time of conception, and its dam at least 24 mo. of age at the time of calving. Horned animals.
Polled Shorthorn	United States; in the north central states, chiefly Ohio and Indiana.	Red, white or any combination of red and white. A "smutty nose" or dark nose is objectionable.	Polled		Horned animals.
Red Angus	British Isles[1]	Red	Polled	Similar to black Angus, except for recessive red color.	Any color other than red.
Red Brangus	United States; from Brahman Angus cross, made in 1946. Registry chartered in 1956.	Red	Broad head with slightly curved forehead and straight profile; with medium sized, moderately drooping ears.	Males have crest immediately forward of the shoulders. Smooth, sleek coat.	White spotting other than on the underline, brindling or roan on the body, or black skin or mucus membrane. Long hair, or tight hide. Undersized; too rangy or too compact. Mature females with underdeveloped teats or udders. Mature males with an excessive or pendulous sheath, or the absence of a sheath.

Beef and Dual-Purpose Cattle (Continued)

TABLE 2.B.9 (Continued)

Breed	Place of Origin	Color	Distinctive Head Characteristics	Other Distinguishing Characteristics	Disqualifications; Comments
Santa Gertrudis (5/8 Shorthorn and 3/8 Brahman)	United States; on the King Ranch in Texas.	Red or cherry red.		Hair should be short, straight, and slick. Hide should be loose, with surface area increased by neck folds and sheath or navel flap.	White or other spotting; fawn, cream, or brindle color; black skin; long wavy hair; absence of neck folds.
Scotch Highland (or Highland)	Scotland	Silver, golden, light red, brindle, black, or dun.	Long, widespread horns and heavy foretop.	Long, shaggy hair, short head and short legs.	Mottled or spotted with white (white permissible on tip of tail or on udder), or polled.
Shorthorn	England; in the northeastern counties of Durham, Northumberland, York, and Lincoln.	Red, white or any combination of red and white. A "smutty nose", or dark nose is objectionable.	Rather short, refined, incurving horns.		No calf is eligible for registration unless its sire and dam were each at least 18 mo. of age at the birth date of the calf.
Dual-Purpose Breeds: **Milking Shorthorn**	England	Red, white, or any combination of red and white.	Fine horns that are rather short.		No calf is eligible for registration unless its sire and dam were each at least 18 mo. of age at the birth date of the calf.
Red Poll	England; in the eastern middle coastal counties of Norfolk and Suffolk.	Red, varying from light to dark red. Any white except in the switch is discriminated against. Also a smoky nose or dark spots on the nose are objectionable.	Polled		White above underline, above switch of tail, or on legs. Bulls with white on underline forward of the navel region; or with only one testicle. Solid black or blue nose. Scurs or any horny growth. Total blindness.

[1]In England and Scotland, both reds and blacks are registered in same association, without distinction. In the U.S., however, red colored animals have been barred from registry in the American Angus Association since 1917. Red Angus Association of America was organized in 1954.

Source: Ensminger, M. E. (1969). *Animal Science.* Interstate Printers & Publishers, Danville, Illinois. Reproduced with permission of the publisher.

Beef, Boneless Cuts

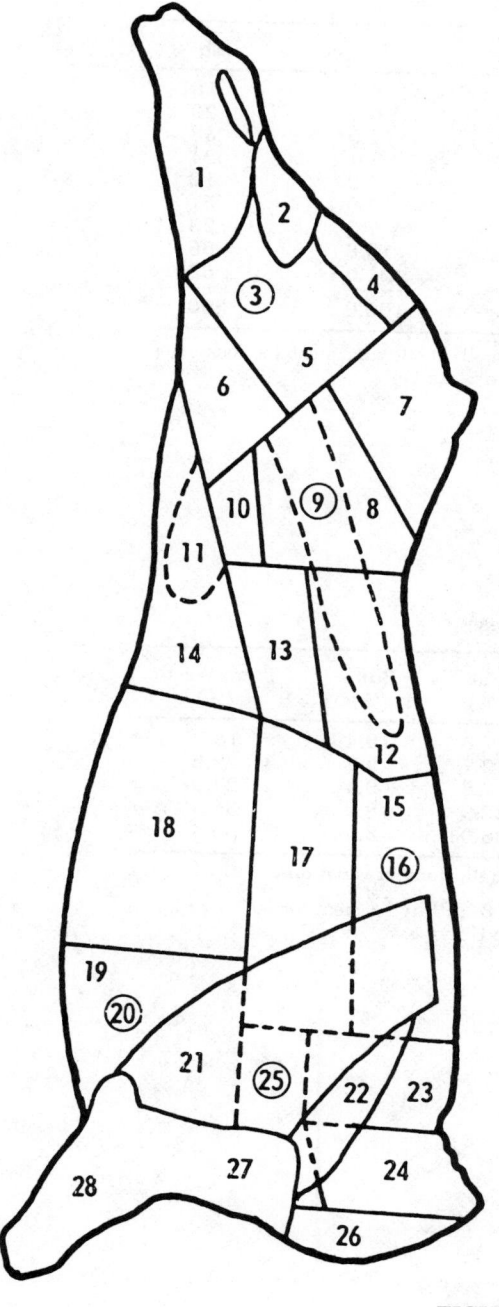

1. HINDSHANK MEAT
2. HEEL
3. TOP ROUND (INSIDE)
4. EYE OF ROUND
5. BOTTOM ROUND (OUTSIDE)
6. KNUCKLE
7. SIRLOIN RUMP
8. TOP SIRLOIN BUTT
9. TENDERLOIN
10. BOTTOM SIRLOIN BUTT
11. FLANK STEAK
12. LOIN STRIP
13. LOIN WING
14. FLANK MEAT
15. RIBEYE COVER
16. RIBEYE
17. RIB WING
18. SHORT PLATE
19. BRISKET
20. DECKLE
21. SHOULDER CLOD
22. CHUCK TENDER
23. CHUCK ROLL (BLADE END)
24. CHUCK ROLL (NECK END)
25. INSIDE CHUCK
26. NECK MEAT
27. ARMBONE MUSCLE
28. FORESHANK MEAT

RIB FINGERS
SKIRT
HANGING TENDER
TRIMMINGS

NOTE: Circled Numbers Lie Deeply

FIGURE 2.B.5

Source: Food inspection specialist. Department of the Army, TM 8-451 (1969).

Beef Carcass, Cutting Yield

TABLE 2.B.10
Beef carcass half (300 lb)

Retail Cut	% of Carcass	Lb
Porterhouse, T-bone & club steak	6.0	18
Sirloin steak	6.7	20
Round steak	11.0	33
Rib roast	8.0	24
Boneless rump	4.2	12
Chuck roast	17.0	51
Ground beef	7.5	23
Stew meat and miscellaneous	18.6	56
Bone, trimming and cutting loss	21.0	63
	100.0	300

Source: Simonds, L. A., and Vanstavern, B. D. Buying meat for locker or home freezer. Coop. Ext. Serv., The Ohio State Univ.

Beef Carcasses, Yield Grade

TABLE 2.B.11
Relative composition of beef carcasses[1]

Yield Grade	Retail Cuts (%)	Fat (%)	Bone (%)	Total Waste (%)
1	82.0	7.6	10.4	18.0
2	77.4	12.7	9.9	22.6
3	72.8	17.8	9.4	27.2
4	68.2	22.9	8.9	31.8
5	63.6	28.0	8.4	36.4

[1] Examples only—individual carcasses will show minor variations.

Source: Simonds, L. A., and Vanstavern, B. D. Buying meat for locker or home freezer. Coop. Ext. Serv., The Ohio State Univ.

Beef Chart

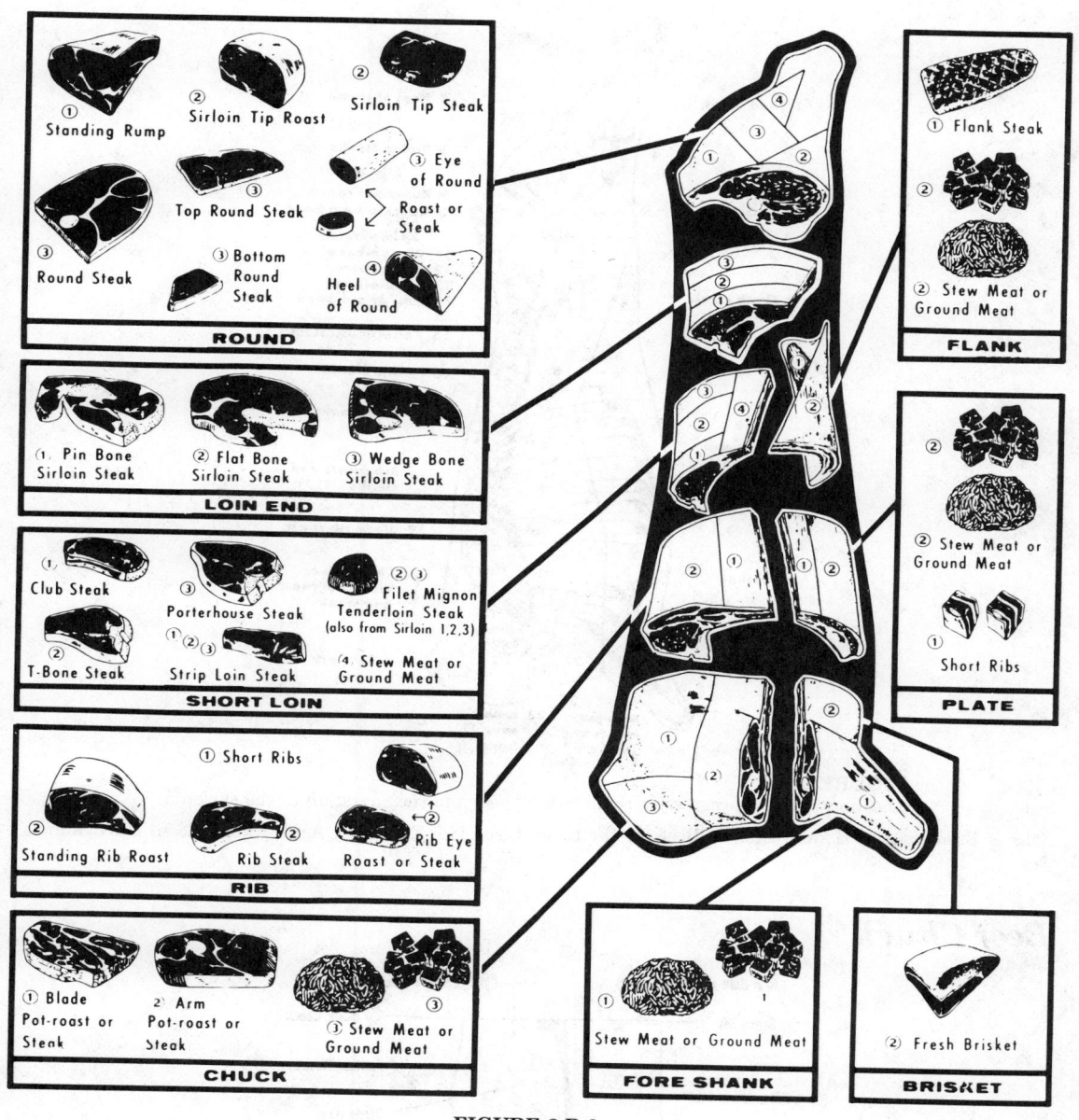

FIGURE 2.B.6

Source: How to buy meat for your freezer. USDA (1969) Home and Garden Bull. *166*; How to buy beef roast. USDA (1977) Home and Garden Bull. *146*.

Beef, Chicago-Style Cutting

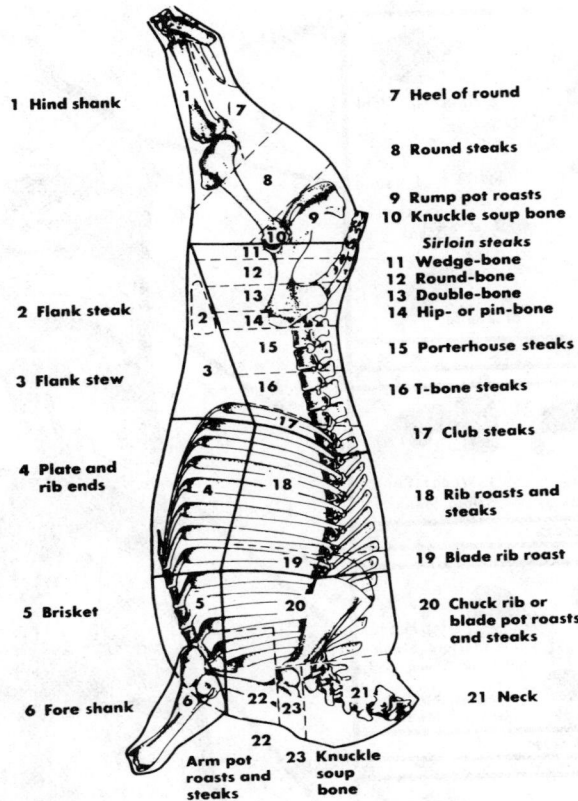

1 Hind shank

2 Flank steak

3 Flank stew

4 Plate and rib ends

5 Brisket

6 Fore shank

7 Heel of round

8 Round steaks

9 Rump pot roasts
10 Knuckle soup bone

Sirloin steaks
11 Wedge-bone
12 Round-bone
13 Double-bone
14 Hip- or pin-bone

15 Porterhouse steaks

16 T-bone steaks

17 Club steaks

18 Rib roasts and steaks

19 Blade rib roast

20 Chuck rib or blade pot roasts and steaks

21 Neck

22 Arm pot roasts and steaks

23 Knuckle soup bone

FIGURE 2.B.7
Location of the Chicago-style retail cuts of beef and their relation to the skeleton

Source: Breidenstein, B., and Bull, S. Beef for the table. Circ. *585*, Ext. Serv. Agric. Home Econ, Univ. Illinois.

Beef Chuck

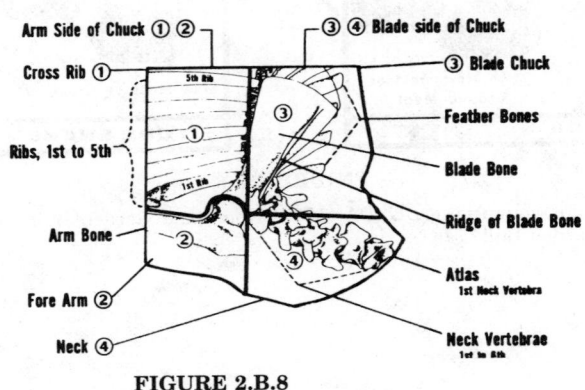

Arm Side of Chuck ① ②

Cross Rib ①

Ribs, 1st to 5th

Arm Bone

Fore Arm ②

Neck ④

③ ④ Blade side of Chuck

③ Blade Chuck

Feather Bones

Blade Bone

Ridge of Blade Bone

Atlas
1st Neck Vertebra

Neck Vertebrae
1st to 5th

FIGURE 2.B.8
Bone structure of a beef chuck

Source: Muscle Boning of the Chuck. National Live Stock and Meat Board, Chicago.

Beef, Cooking

TABLE 2.B.12
Timetable for cooking beef

| Cut | Roasted at 300°F Oven Temp | | Broiled[1] | | Braised | Cooked in Liquid |
	Meat Thermometer Reading (°F)	Time (min per lb)	Meat Thermometer Reading (°F)	Total Time (min)	Total Time (hr)	Total Time (hr)
Standing ribs	140 (rare)	18–20				
Standing ribs	160 (med)	22–25				
Standing ribs	170 (well)	27–30				
Rolled ribs	Same as above	Add 10–15				
Blade, 3rd to 5th rib (high quality only)	150–170	25–30				
Rump (high quality only)	150–170	25–30				
Tenderloin	140–170	20–25				
Beef loaf	160–170	25–30				
Steaks (1 in.)			140 (rare)	15–20		
			160 (med)	20–30		
Steaks (1½ in.)			140 (rare)	25–35		
			160 (med)	35–50		
Steaks (2 in.)			140 (rare)	30–40		
			160 (med)	50–70		
Beef patties (1 in.)			140 (rare)	12–15		
			160 (med)	18–20		
Pot roasts						
Arm or blade					3–4	
Rump					3–4	
Swiss steak					2–3	
Corned beef						3½–5
Fresh beef					3–4	3–4
Stew						2–3

[1] Panbroiling or griddle-broiling requires approximately one-half the time for broiling.

Source: Potts, B., Simonds, L., and Vanstavern, B. D. Meat specials really are special. The Ohio State Univ. Coop. Ext. Serv. Bull. *574.*

Beef Cuts

TABLE 2.B.13
Characteristics and cooking methods of beef cuts

WHOLESALE CUTS	RETAIL CUTS	CHARACTERISTICS	COOKING METHODS
Round (and Rump)	Round Steak (full cut)	Round or oval in shape with small round bone. One large muscle, three smaller ones.	Braise
	Top Round Steak or Pot-Roast	Most tender portion of round. Is one large muscle.	Braise; roast; panfry
	Bottom Round Steak or Pot-Roast	Not so tender as top round. Distinguished from top round by having two muscles.	Braise
	Tip Roast or Steak	Triangular cut; roast may contain kneecap. Steaks are boneless.	Braise; roast; broil; panbroil; panfry
	Standing Rump	Triangular in shape; contains portions of aitch (rump) bone and tail bone. Knuckle end of leg (round) bone usually removed.	Braise; roast (high quality)
	Rolled Rump	Boneless roll.	Braise, roast (high quality)
	Heel of Round	Boneless wedge-shaped cut from lower part of round. Weighs 4 to 8 pounds. Has very little fat and is least tender cut of round.	Braise; cook in liquid
	Hind Shank	Bony, considerable connective tissue, rich in extractives.	Cook in liquid (soup)
Sirloin	Sirloin Steak	Contains portions of back bone and hip bone. Wide variation in bone and muscle structure of the various steaks.	Broil; panbroil; panfry
	Pinbone Sirloin Steak	Lies next to the porterhouse. Contains pin bone which is the forward end of hip bone.	Broil; panbroil; panfry
	Boneless Sirloin Steak	Any boneless steak from the sirloin.	Broil; panbroil; panfry
Short Loin	Porterhouse Steak	Largest steak in short loin. Loin strip and tenderloin muscles. T-shaped bone. Tenderloin larger in porterhouse than in other short loin steaks.	Broil; panbroil; panfry
	T-Bone Steak	Same as porterhouse except tenderloin is smaller (porterhouse and T-bone used more or less interchangeably).	Broil; panbroil; panfry
	Club (Delmonico) Steak	Triangular-shaped; smallest steak in short loin. Tenderloin has practically disappeared.	Broil; panbroil; panfry
	Tenderloin Roast or Steak	Boneless tapering muscle. Most tender cut beef.	Roast; broil; panbroil; panfry

(Continued)

Beef Cuts   (Continued)

TABLE 2.B.13   (Continued)

Flank	Flank Steak	Oval-shaped boneless steak weighing ¾ to 1½ pounds. Muscles run lengthwise; usually scored to shorten muscle fibers. Less tender cut.	*Braise*
	Flank Steak Fillets	Sections of flank steak rolled and fastened with skewers.	*Braise*
	Flank Meat	Boneless. Coarse fibers. May be rolled, cut into stew or ground.	*Braise; cook in liquid*
Rib	Standing Rib Roast (Short Cut)	Contains two or more ribs from which short ribs and chine bone have been removed. Comparable to rib roast served in restaurants.	*Roast*
	Rolled Rib Roast	Boneless roll. Outer cover of roll consists largely of thin plate meat wrapped around rib eye.	*Roast*
	Rib Steak	Contains rib eye and may contain rib bone.	*Broil; panbroil; panfry*
	Short Ribs	Cut from ends of ribs; layers of lean and fat.	*Braise; cook in liquid*
Short Plate	Plate "Boiling" Beef	Cut across plate parallel with ribs.	*Braise; cook in liquid*
	Rolled Plate	When rolled the absence of the rib eye distinguishes this cut from the rolled rib.	*Braise; cook in liquid*
	Short Ribs	Cut from ends of ribs; layers of lean and fat.	*Braise; cook in liquid*
Square-Cut Chuck	Arm Pot-roast or Steak	Has a round bone and cross sections of 3–5 ribs. A small round muscle near the round bone is surrounded by connective tissue.	*Braise*
	Blade Pot-roast or Steak	Pot-roast contains portions of rib and blade bones. Steaks cut between ribs will not contain rib bone.	*Braise*
	Boneless Chuck	Any part of the square-cut chuck (except the neck) from which the bones have been removed.	*Braise*
	Boneless Neck	Any part of the neck without the neck bone.	*Braise; cook in liquid*
	English (Boston) Cut	A rectangular piece cut across 2 or 3 chuck ribs.	*Braise*
Brisket	Brisket	Layers of lean and fat. Presence of breast bone sure indication that cut is from the brisket.	*Braise; cook in liquid*
	Boneless Brisket	Same as above with ribs and breast bone removed.	*Braise; cook in liquid*
Fore Shank	Shank Knuckle	Knuckle or upper end of fore shank.	*Cook in liquid, braise*
	Shank Cross-Cuts	Small pieces cut across shank bone.	*Braise; cook in liquid*
Ground Beef	Loaf and Patties	Usually made from flank, shank, plate and chuck.	*Roast (bake); broil; panbroil; panfry; braise*

Source: Meat Manual, 6th Edition. National Live Stock and Meat Board, Chicago.

Beef Cuts and Uses

TABLE 2.B.14
Beef cuts and their uses

WHOLESALE CUT	DESCRIPTION	RETAIL CUTS	BEEF SPECIALTIES
ROUND	Well-flavored, with rump and hind shank off, has very little bone	Steaks, pot-roasts	Brains— Cream, scramble with eggs, cutlets
RUMP	Well-flavored, contains aitch bone, knuckle joint and tail bone. To facilitate carving some or all of bones are removed	Corn beef, pot-roasts, steaks	Heart— Braise, cook in water
LOIN END	Tender, juicy, varying amounts of bone	Sirloin steaks	Liver— Fry, roast whole or as loaf, braise
SHORT LOIN	Tender, juicy, contains portion of tenderloin	Porterhouse, T-bone, club steaks	Tongue (fresh, pickled or corned)— Cook in water
FLANK	Thin, practically boneless, coarse grained, well-flavored	Flank steak, stew meat	
RIB	Tender, juicy; contains rib bones and "eye" muscle	Roasts, rib steaks	Tripe— Cook in water, cream
CHUCK	Juicy, well-flavored, muscles run in different directions	Pot-roasts, steaks, stew meat	Oxtail— Soup, braise
BRISKET	Layer of fat and lean; contains rib ends and breast bone	Fresh brisket, corned brisket	
PLATE	Rib ends, layers of fat and lean	Short ribs, "boiling" beef, boneless roll	
SHANKS	Considerable bone, connective tissue, varying amounts of lean	Soup bones, cross-cut shanks	

Source: *Meat Buying Manual*. National Live Stock and Meat Board, Chicago.

Beef, Degrees of Doneness

TABLE 2.B.15
Internal temperatures of large beef roasts for the different degrees of doneness

Degree of Doneness	Color of Inside of Roast	Meat Thermometer Reading When Roast Comes from Oven*
Rare	Bright pink	120° to 125° F.
Medium	Pinkish brown	135° to 145° F.
Well done	Greyish or light brown	150° to 160° F.

* The temperatures at which color changes take place in beef as it cooks are considerably higher than the temperatures above indicate; however, large roasts continue cooking for some time after they are removed from the oven. Therefore, to prevent overcooking, roasts should be removed from the oven when the meat thermometer shows several degrees lower than the temperature at which the actual color change takes place.

Source: *Cooking Meat in Quantity*. National Live Stock and Meat Board, Chicago.

Beef, New York-Style Cutting

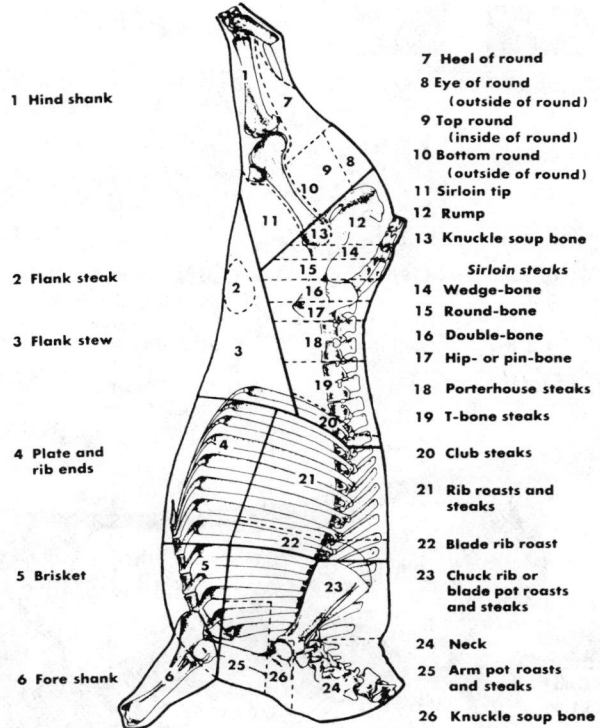

FIGURE 2.B.9
Location of the New York-style retail cuts of beef and their relation to the skeleton

Source: Breidenstein, B., and Bull, S. Beef for the table. Circ. *585*, Ext. Serv. Agric. and Home Econ., Univ. Illinois.

Beef, Percentages of Daily Recommended Allowances

TABLE 2.B.16
Percentages of daily recommended allowances[1] (based on $3\frac{1}{2}$ oz cooked lean beef)

	Age	Protein	Calories	Iron	Phosphorus	Magnesium	Thiamin	Riboflavin	Niacin	Vit. B-6	Vit. B-12
Children	1–3	129	20	25	24	14	14	49	50	61	206
	4–6	99	15	37	24	11	11	35	38	41	137
	7–10	82	11	37	24	9	8	33	28	31	103
Males	11–14	67	9	21	16	6	7	26	25	23	69
	15–18	55	9	21	16	5	7	22	23	18	69
	19–22	55	9	37	24	6	7	22	23	18	69
	23–50	53	10	37	24	6	7	24	25	18	69
	51+	53	11	37	24	6	8	7	28	18	69
Females	11–14	67	11	21	16	7	8	30	28	23	69
	15–18	62	13	21	16	7	9	28	32	18	69
	19–22	64	13	21	24	7	9	28	32	18	69
	23–50	64	13	21	24	7	10	33	35	18	69
	51+	64	15	37	24	7	10	35	38	18	69

[1]Figures based on 1974 National Research Council Recommended Dietary Allowances.

Source: Facts About Beef. (1974). National Live Stock and Meat Board, Chicago.

Beef Retail Yield

	Saleable Beef—lbs	Other lbs

• **CHUCK** *164.8 lbs (26.8% of total carcass)*

	Saleable Beef—lbs	Other lbs
Blade pot-roast	59.3	
Stew or ground beef	32.1	
Arm pot-roast	22.3	
Cross rib pot-roast	10.7	
Boston cut	9.9	
Fat and bone		30.5
TOTAL	134.3 lbs	30.5 lbs

• **BRISKET** *23.4 lbs (3.8% of total carcass)*

	Saleable Beef—lbs	Other lbs
Boneless	9.4	
Fat and bone		14.0
TOTAL	9.4 lbs	14.0 lbs

• **SHANK** *19.1 lbs (3.1% of total carcass)*

• **RIB** *59.0 lbs (9.6% of total carcass)*

	Saleable Beef—lbs	Other lbs
Standing rib roast	24.2	
Rib steak	12.4	
Short ribs	4.7	
Braising beef	2.7	
Ground beef	3.5	
Fat and bone		11.5
TOTAL	47.5 lbs	11.5 lbs

• **LOIN** *105.8 lbs (17.2% of total carcass)*

	Saleable Beef—lbs	Other lbs
Porterhouse steak	18.7	
T-bone steak	9.5	
Club steak	5.2	
Sirloin steak	41.4	
Ground beef	2.9	
Fat and bone		28.1
TOTAL	77.7 lbs	28.1 lbs

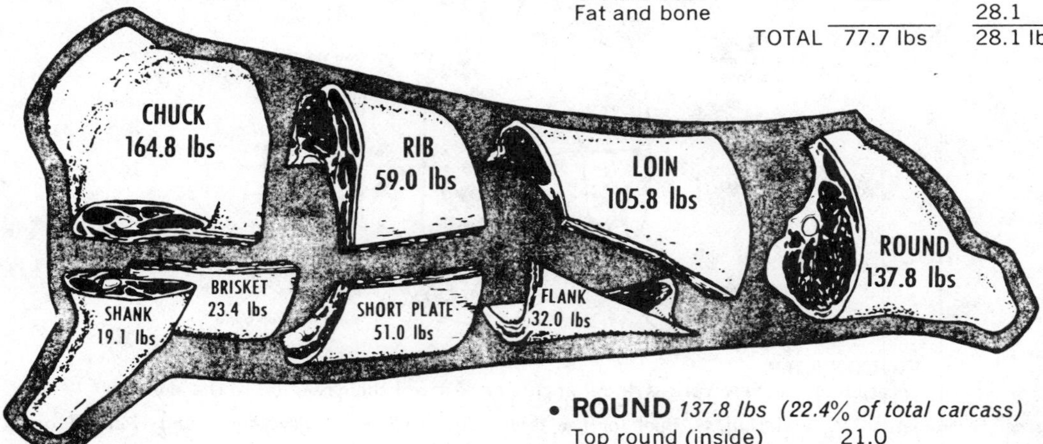

CHUCK 164.8 lbs · RIB 59.0 lbs · LOIN 105.8 lbs · ROUND 137.8 lbs · SHANK 19.1 lbs · BRISKET 23.4 lbs · SHORT PLATE 51.0 lbs · FLANK 32.0 lbs

• **ROUND** *137.8 lbs (22.4% of total carcass)*

	Saleable Beef—lbs	Other lbs
Top round (inside)	21.0	
Bottom round (outside)	20.3	
Tip	13.1	
Stew	8.3	
Rump	4.8	
Kabobs or cubes	2.1	
Ground beef	14.2	
Fat and bone		54.0
TOTAL	83.8 lbs	54.0 lbs

• **SHORT PLATE** *51.0 lbs (8.3% of total carcass)*

	Saleable Beef—lbs	Other lbs
Plate, stew, short ribs	40.8	
Fat and bone		10.2
TOTAL	40.8 lbs	10.2 lbs

• **FLANK** *32.0 lbs (5.2% of total carcass)*

	Saleable Beef—lbs	Other lbs
Flank	3.2	
Ground beef	12.6	
Fat		16.2
TOTAL	15.8 lbs	16.2 lbs

MISC. *22.1 lbs (3.6% of total carcass)*

	Saleable Beef—lbs	Other lbs
Kidney, hanging tender	3.6	
Fat, suet, cutting losses		18.5
TOTAL	3.6 lbs	18.5 lbs

SUMMARY	
(1000 lb choice steer)	
Dresses out 61.5%	**615 lbs**
Less fat, bone and loss	**183 lbs**
Saleable beef	**432 lbs**

FIGURE 2.B.10

Source: A Steer's Not All Steak. National Live Stock and Meat Board, Chicago.

Beef Rib Carving (Standing Roast)

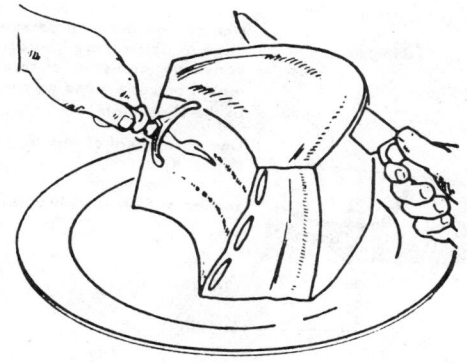

Place the roast on the platter with the largest end down to form a solid base. Insert the fork between the two top ribs. Starting on the fat side, carve across the grain to the rib bone.

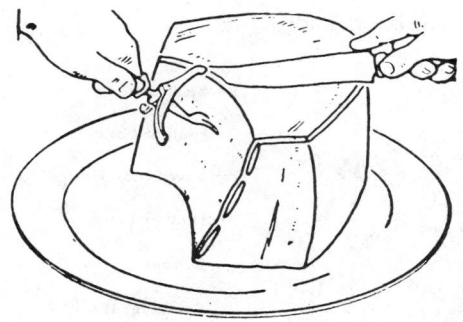

Use the tip of the knife to cut along the rib bone to loosen the slice. Be sure to keep close to the bone, to make the largest servings possible.

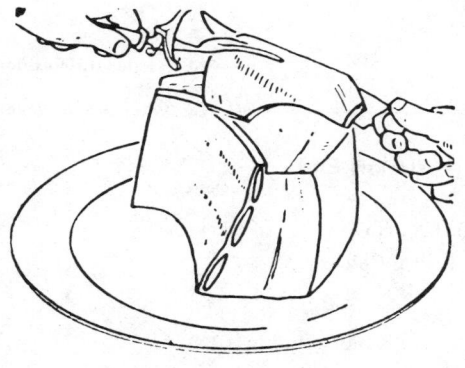

Slide the knife back under the slice and, steadying it with the fork, lift the slice to the side of the platter. If the platter is not large enough, place the slices on a heated platter close by.

FIGURE 2.B.11

Source: Carving Meat. National Live Stock and Meat Board, Chicago.

Beef Rib Nomenclature

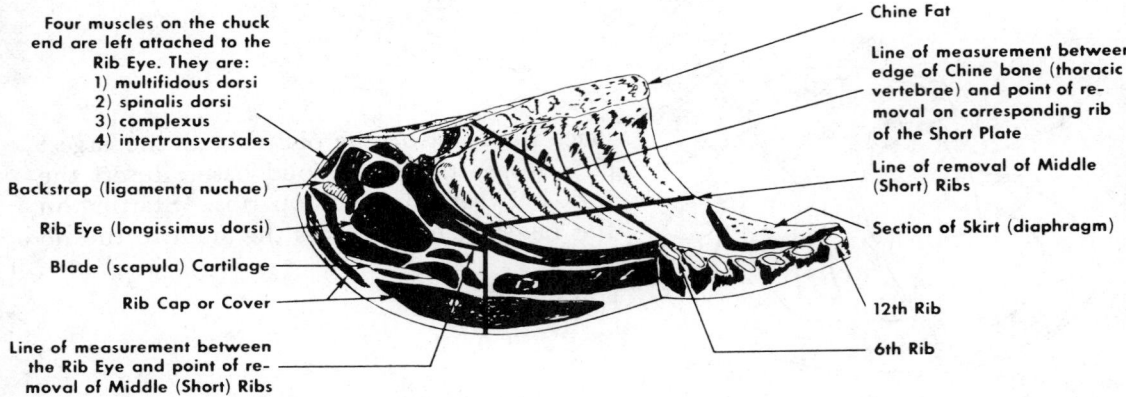

Four muscles on the chuck end are left attached to the Rib Eye. They are:
1) multifidous dorsi
2) spinalis dorsi
3) complexus
4) intertransversales

Backstrap (ligamenta nuchae)

Rib Eye (longissimus dorsi)

Blade (scapula) Cartilage

Rib Cap or Cover

Line of measurement between the Rib Eye and point of removal of Middle (Short) Ribs

Chine Fat

Line of measurement between edge of Chine bone (thoracic vertebrae) and point of removal on corresponding rib of the Short Plate

Line of removal of Middle (Short) Ribs

Section of Skirt (diaphragm)

12th Rib

6th Rib

View of Beef Rib from Chuck (Anterior) End

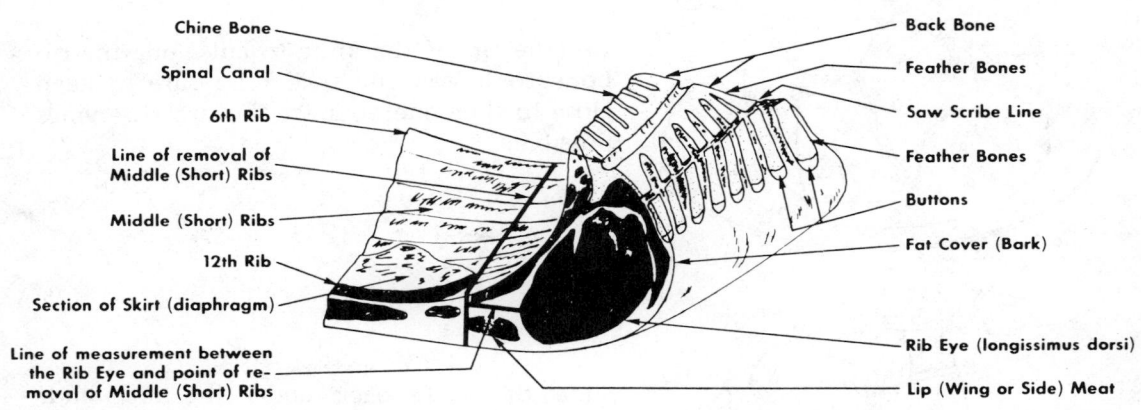

Chine Bone

Spinal Canal

6th Rib

Line of removal of Middle (Short) Ribs

Middle (Short) Ribs

12th Rib

Section of Skirt (diaphragm)

Line of measurement between the Rib Eye and point of removal of Middle (Short) Ribs

Back Bone

Feather Bones

Saw Scribe Line

Feather Bones

Buttons

Fat Cover (Bark)

Rib Eye (longissimus dorsi)

Lip (Wing or Side) Meat

View of Beef Rib from Loin (Posterior) End

FIGURE 2.B.12
Commonly used names for beef rib

Source: Merchandising Beef Ribs. National Live Stock and Meat Board, Chicago.

Beef Roasting

TABLE 2.B.17
Timetable for roasting beef

Cut	Approx. Wt. of Single Roast	No. of Roasts in Oven	Approx. Total Wt. of Roasts in Oven	Oven Temperature	Interior Temperature of Roast When Removed from Oven	Minutes per Pound Based on One Roast	Minutes per Pound Based on Total Wt. of Roasts in Oven	Approximate Total Time
	pounds		*pounds*					
Standing rib (3-rib)	6 to 8	1		300° F.	140° F. (rare) 160° F. (medium) 170° F. (well)	18 to 20 22 to 25 27 to 30		2 to 3 hours 2½ to 3 hours 3 to 4 hours
Standing rib (7-rib)	20 to 25	1		250° F.	125° F. (rare) 140° F. (medium) 150° F. (well)	13 15 17		4½ hours 5 hours 6 hours
Standing rib (7-rib)	23	1		300° F.	125° F. (rare) 140° F. (medium) 150° F. (well)	11 12 13		4 hours 4½ hours 5 hours
Rolled rib (7-rib)	16 to 18	1		250° F.	150° F. (well)	26		7 to 8 hours
Rolled rib (7-rib)	17	1		300° F.	150° F. (well)	24		6 hours
Standing rib (7-rib)		2	56	300° F.	140° F. (medium) 160° F. (well)		6 7 to 8	6 hours 7 hours
Chuck rib	5 to 8	1		300° F.	150° to 170° F.	25 to 30		2½ to 4 hours
Rump	5 to 7	1		300° F.	150° to 170° F.	25 to 30		2½ to 3½ hours
Round (rump and shank off)	50	1		250° F.	140° F. (medium) 154° F. (well)	12 14		10 hours 11 to 12 hours

Source: Cooking Meat in Quantity. National Live Stock and Meat Board, Chicago.

Beef Round, Bone Structure

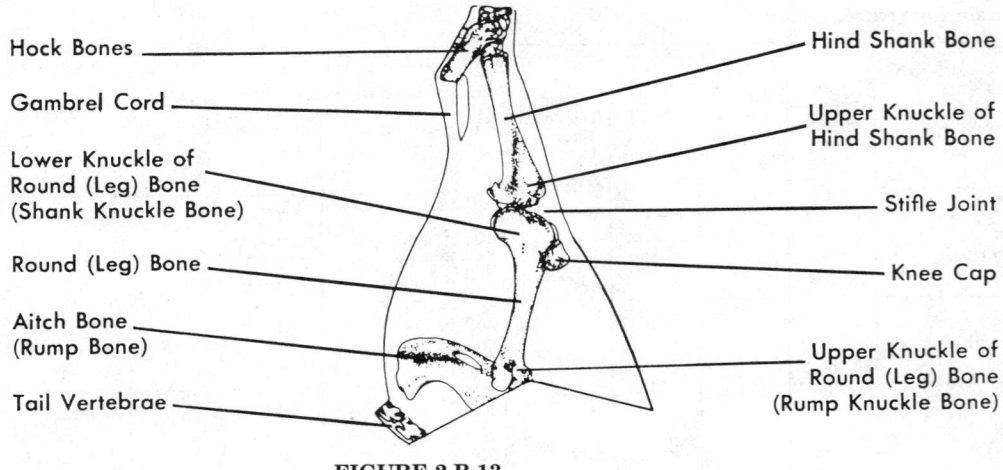

Hock Bones

Gambrel Cord

Lower Knuckle of
Round (Leg) Bone
(Shank Knuckle Bone)

Round (Leg) Bone

Aitch Bone
(Rump Bone)

Tail Vertebrae

Hind Shank Bone

Upper Knuckle of
Hind Shank Bone

Stifle Joint

Knee Cap

Upper Knuckle of
Round (Leg) Bone
(Rump Knuckle Bone)

FIGURE 2.B.13
Bone structure of a diamond round

Source: Merchandising Beef Rounds. National Live Stock and Meat Board, Chicago.

Beef Round Cuts

Cut through natural seam to split
boneless round into two pieces . . . Top
Round and Outside Round.

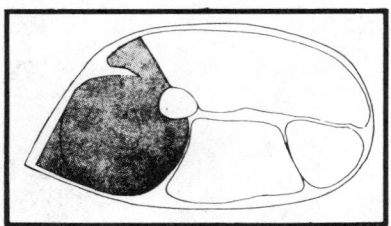

Shaded area indicates
location of tip (knuckle)

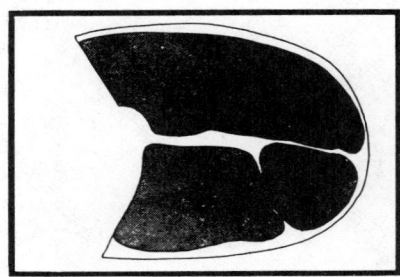

A Top (Inside) Round
B & C Outside (Bottom) Round
B Outside Round
C Eye of Round

FIGURE 2.B.14

Source: Merchandising Beef Rounds. National Live Stock and Meat Board, Chicago.

Beef Rounds

THREE POPULAR BEEF ROUNDS

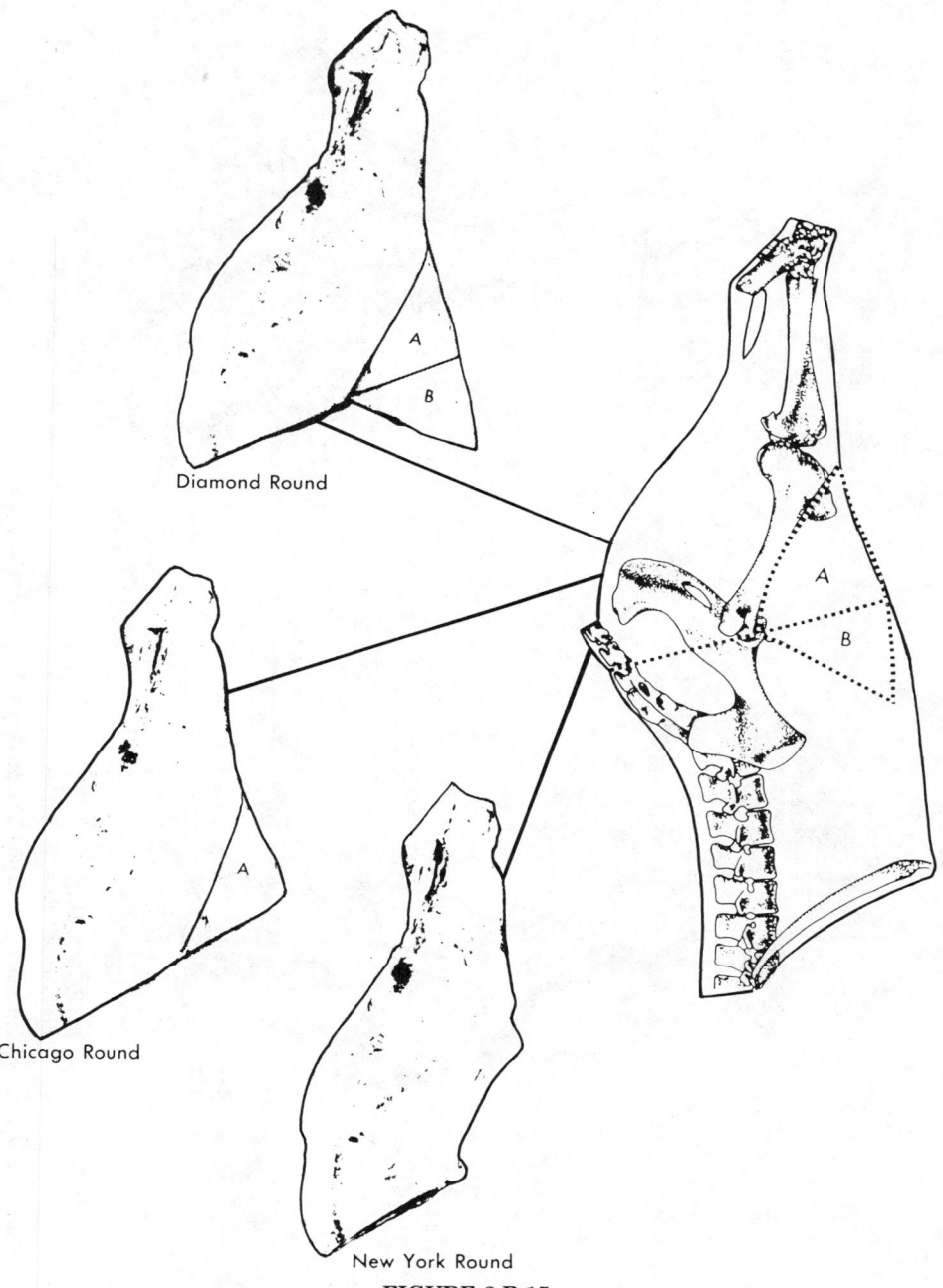

Diamond Round

Chicago Round

New York Round

FIGURE 2.B.15

Source: Merchandising Beef Rounds. National Live Stock and Meat Board, Chicago.

Beef Wholesale Cuts

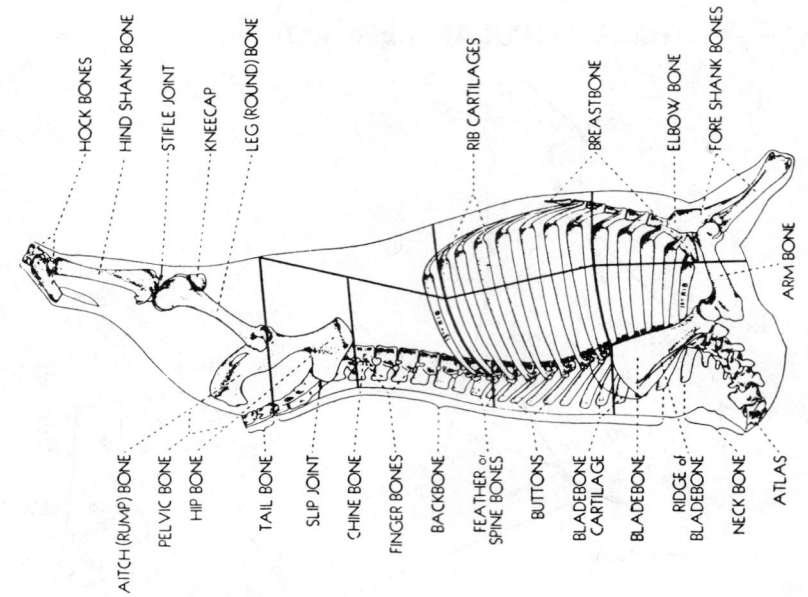

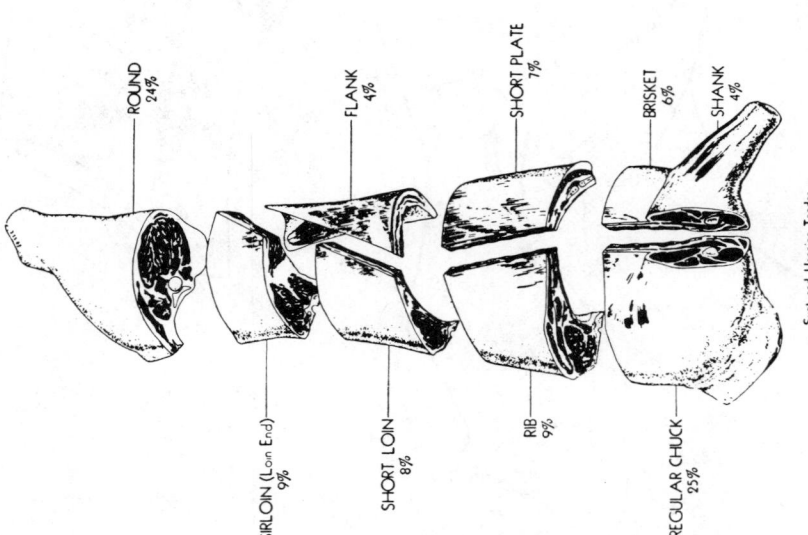

FIGURE 2.B.16

Beef carcass showing wholesale cuts (left) and location, structure, and names of bones (right)

Source: Cooking Meat in Quantity. National Live Stock and Meat Board, Chicago.

Beef Yields

TABLE 2.B.18
Approximate yields from wholesale cuts of beef (300-lb side, yield grade 3)

	% of Wholesale Cut	Pounds		% of Wholesale Cut	Pounds
Round (68 lbs.)			**Rib (27 lbs.)**		
Round Steak	39.7	27.0	Rib Roast (7″ cut)	67.8	18.3
Rump Roast (Boneless)	14.6	9.9	Lean Trim	12.6	3.4
Lean Trim	17.9	12.2	Waste (fat, bone, and shrinkage)	19.6	5.3
Waste (fat, bone, and shrinkage)	27.8	18.9	Total Rib	100.0	27.0
Total Round	100.0	68.0			
Trimmed Loin (50 lbs.)*			**Square-Cut Chuck (81 lbs.)**		
Porterhouse, T-Bone, Club Steaks	30.6	15.3	Blade Chuck Roast	33.0	26.7
Sirloin Steak	49.8	24.9	Arm Chuck Roast (Boneless)	21.5	17.4
Lean Trim	6.4	3.2	Lean Trim	25.9	21.0
Waste (fat, bone, and shrinkage)	13.2	6.6	Waste (fat, bone, and shrinkage)	19.6	15.9
Total Loin	100.0	50.0	Total Chuck	100.0	81.0

* Does not include Kidney knob and flank.

Source: USDA (1969). How to buy meat for your freezer. USDA Home and Garden Bull. *166.*

Beverage, Carbonated, Ingredients

TABLE 2.B.19
Primary ingredients commonly detected in carbonated beverages

Ingredients	Cola	Orange	Grape	Lemon-Lime	Root Beer
Water	x	x	x	x	x
Sugar	x	x	x	x	x
Phosphoric acid	x				
Citric acid		x	x	x	x
Caffeine	x				
Sodium benzoate		x	x		x
Carbon dioxide	x	x	x	x	x
Gum acacia	x	x			x
Caramel color	x				x
FDC colors		x	x		
Nutmeg oil	x				x
Methyl anthranilate			x		
Orange oil	x	x			
Lemon oil	x			x	x
Vanilla/vanillin	x				x
Lime oil	x			x	
Cinnamon oil	x				x
Ethyl acetate			x		
Ethyl alcohol			x	x	
Citral		x		x	
Kola nut extract	x				
Ascorbic acid		x			
Cassia oil	x				x
Clove oil	x				x
Ethyl butyrate			x		
Methyl salicylate					x

Source: Woodroof, J. G., and Phillips, G. F. (editors) (1974). Beverage acids, flavors, colors, and emulsifiers. In *Beverages: Carbonated and Noncarbonated.* AVI Publishing Co., Westport, Connecticut.

Biotin Content

TABLE 2.B.20
Biotin content of some selected foods

	γ/g
Royal jelly	1.70
Liver	0.96
Chocolate	0.32
Roasted peanuts	0.34
Peas	0.21
Cauliflower	0.17
Lima beans	0.098
Whole wheat	0.052
Sea foods	0.080

Source: Braverman, J. B. S. Introduction to the Biochemistry of Foods. ASP Biological and Medical Press (Elsevier Division), New York.

Bitter Flavors

TABLE 2.B.21
Classification of bitter flavors

Bitter Flavors		Complementary Flavors		
Aromatic-bitter	Bitter	Aromatic	Pungent	Sweet
Angelica	Aloe	Ambrette	Cardamom	Anise
Balm	Angostura	Clary sage	Cinnamon, Ceylon	Licorice
Calamus	Artichoke	Coriander	Clove buds	Star anise
Camomile, Hungarian	Blessed thistle	Imperatoria	Ginger	Vanilla
Camomile, Roman	Calumba	Lemon	Grains of paradise	
Cascarilla	Centaury	Liatris	Juniper	
Catmint	Chicory	(wild vanilla)	Mace	
Chinotti	Chirata	Melilotus	Nutmeg	
Condurango	Cinchona	Myrrh	Peppermint	
Dittany of Crete	Dandelion	Orange, sweet	Thyme	
Elder	Gentian	Orris		
Elecampane	Gentian, stemless	Saffron		
Galanga	Larch agaric	St. Johnswort		
Genepi	Quassia	Savory, summer		
Germander	Rhubarb	Tonka bean		
Hyssop	Southernwood	Valerian		
Marjoram, sweet	Walnut	Woodruff, sweet		
Mugwort				
Orange, bitter				
Rue				
Wormwood				
Wormwood, mountain				
Yarrow				
Yarrow, musk				
Zedoary				

Source: Furia, T. E., and Bellanca, N. (editors) (1971). Fenaroli's Handbook of Flavor Ingredients. CRC Press, Cleveland. Used by permission of CRC Press.

Bitters, Herbs

TABLE 2.B.22
Herbs and derivatives used to formulate bitters

Common name	Botanical name	Parts of plant used
Aloe	*Aloe* species	Concentrated leaf juice
Ambrette	*Hibiscus abelmoschus* L.	Seeds
Angelica	*Angelica archangelica* L.	Roots
Angostura	*Galipea cusparia* DC.	Bark
Anise	*Pimpinella anisum* L.	Fruits
Artichoke	*Cynara scolymus* L.	Leaves
Balm (lemon balm)	*Melissa officinalis* L.	Leaves and flowering tops
Blessed thistle	*Cnicus benedictus* L.	Leaves and flowers
Calamus	*Acorus calamus* L.	Rhizomes
Calumba	*Jatrorrhiza palmata* (Lam.) Miers	Roots
Camomile, Hungarian or German	*Matricaria chamomilla* L.	Flowers
Camomile, Roman or English	*Anthemis nobilis* L.	Flowers
Cardamom	*Elettaria cardamomum* Maton	Fruits
Cascarilla	*Croton eluteria* Benn.	Bark
Catmint	*Nepeta cataria* L.	Flowering tops
Centaury	*Erythraea centaurium* Pers.	Whole plant
Chicory	*Cichorium intybus* L.	Roots
Chinotti	*Citrus myrtifolia* Risso	Peels or the whole fruit
Chirata	*Swertia chirata* (Roxb.) Buch.-Ham.	Whole plant
Cinchona	*Cinchona* species	Bark
Cinnamon, Ceylon	*Cinnamomum zeylanicum* Nees	Bark
Clary sage	*Salvia sclarea* L.	Flowering tops
Clove	*Eugenia caryophyllata* Thunb.	Buds
Condurango	*Marsdenia condurango* Reichenb. f.	Bark
Coriander	*Coriandrum sativum* L.	Fruits
Dandelion	*Taraxacum officinale* Weber	Leaves and roots
Dittany of Crete	*Origanum dictamnus* L.	Leaves and flowering tops
Elder	*Sambucus nigra* L.	Flowers
Elecampane	*Inula helenium* L.	Rhizomes
Galanga	*Alpinia officinarum* Hance	Rhizomes
Genepi	*Artemisia glacialis* L.	Whole plant
Gentian	*Gentiana lutea* L.	Rhizomes and roots
Gentian, stemless	*Gentiana acaulis* L.	Whole plant
Germander	*Teucrium chamaedrys* L.	Flowering tops
Ginger	*Zingiber officinale* Rosc.	Rhizomes
Grains of paradise	*Aframomum melegueta* Rosc.	Seeds
Hyssop	*Hyssopus officinalis* L.	Leaves and flowers
Imperatoria	*Peucedanum osthruthium* (L.) Koch.	Rhizomes
Juniper	*Juniperus communis* L.	Berries
Larch agaric	*Polyporus laricis* Jacq.	Inner portion of the thallus
Lemon	*Citrus limonum* (L.) Risso	Peels
Liatris (wild vanilla)	*Trilisa odoratissima* (Walt.) Cass.	Leaves
Licorice	*Glycyrrhiza glabra* L.	Roots
Mace	*Myristica fragrans* Houtt.	Arillodes
Marjoram, sweet	*Marjorana hortensis* Moench.	Flowering tops
Melilotus	*Melilotus officinalis* (L.) Lam.	Flowers
Mugwort	*Artemisia pontica* L.	Leaves and flowering tops
Myrrh	*Commiphora* species	Gum resin

(Continued)

Bitters, Herbs (*Continued*)

TABLE 2.B.22 (*Continued*)

Common name	Botanical name	Parts of plant used
Nutmeg	*Myristica fragrans* Houtt.	Fruits
Orange, bitter	*Citrus aurantium* L. subspecies *amara* L.	Peels
Orange, sweet	*Citrus sinensis* L. Osbeck	Peels
Orris	*Iris pallida* L. and *I. germanica* L.	Roots
Peppermint	*Mentha piperita* L.	Flowering tops
Quassia	*Picrasma excelsa* (Sw.) Planch.	Wood
Rhubarb	*Rheum* species	Rhizomes
Rue	*Ruta graveolens* L.	Leaves
Saffron	*Crocus sativus* L.	Stems
St. Johnswort	*Hypericum perforatum* L.	Flowering tops
Savory, summer	*Satureja hortensis* L.	Flowering tops
Southernwood	*Artemisia abrotanum* L.	Leaves and flowering tops
Star anise	*Illicium verum* Hook. f.	Fruits
Thyme	*Thymus vulgaris* L.	Whole flowering plant
Tonka bean	*Dipteryx oppositia folia*	Seeds
Valerian	*Valeriana officinalis* L.	Rhizomes and roots
Vanilla	*Vanilla* species	Pods
Walnut	*Juglans regia* L.	Leaves and green nuts
Woodruff. sweet	*Asperula odorata* L.	Whole plant
Wormwood	*Artemisia absinthium* L.	Leaves and flowering tops
Wormwood, mountain	*Artemisia valesiaca* L.	Leaves and flowering tops
Yarrow	*Achillea millefolium* L.	Whole flowering plant excluding the root
Yarrow, musk	*Achillea moschata* Jacq.	Leaves and flowering tops
Zedoary	*Curcuma zedoaria* Rosc.	Bark

Source: Furia, T. E., and Bellanca, N. (editors). (1971). *Fenaroli's Handbook of Flavor Ingredients*. CRC Press, Cleveland. Used by permission of CRC Press.

Blood

TABLE 2.B.23
Analysis of the blood of animals and poultry

Animal	PCV %	Hgb g/100 ml	RBC X 10^6/cu mm	MCV ml X 10^{-12}	MCHC %	PPC g/100 ml
Horse Light breeds	30–50	11–19	7–12	34–58	31–37	6–8
Horse Heavy breeds	25–45	8–14	6–9	37–52	32–38	6–8
Ox	25–45	8–15	5–10	40–60	26–36	6–8
Sheep	25–50	9–16	8–16	25–50	30–38	6–7.5
Goat	20–37	8–14	8–18	18–34	30–40	6–7.5
Pig	32–50	10–16	5–8	50–68	30–35	6–8.5
Dog	37–55	12–18	5–9	60–77	30–35	6–7.5
Cat	27–45	8–15	5–10	40–55	30–35	6–7.5
Rabbit	35–45	9–15	5–7	60–68	31–35	5–7
Chicken	30–40	9–13	3	127	29	3–5
Turkey	39	11	2	203	29	3–5

Source: The Merck Veterinary Manual, 4th Edition (1973). Merck & Co., Rahway, New Jersey.

Blueberry Production

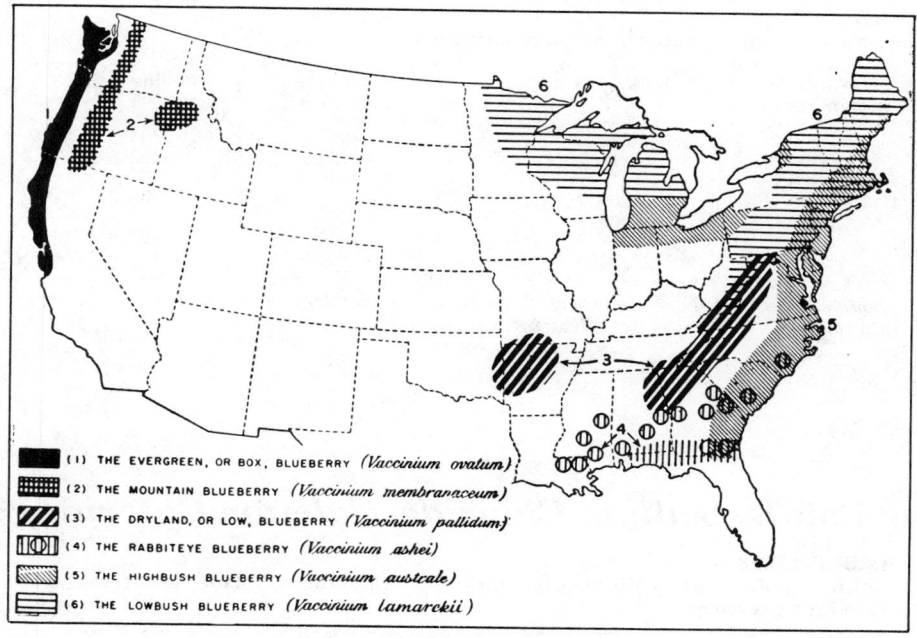

(1) THE EVERGREEN, OR BOX, BLUEBERRY *(Vaccinium ovatum)*
(2) THE MOUNTAIN BLUEBERRY *(Vaccinium membranaceum)*
(3) THE DRYLAND, OR LOW, BLUEBERRY *(Vaccinium pallidum)*
(4) THE RABBITEYE BLUEBERRY *(Vaccinium ashei)*
(5) THE HIGHBUSH BLUEBERRY *(Vaccinium australe)*
(6) THE LOWBUSH BLUEBERRY *(Vaccinium lamarckii)*

FIGURE 2.B.17

Source: USDA (1978). Commercial blueberry growing. USDA Farmers' Bull. *2254.*

Body Weight

TABLE 2.B.24
Suggested body weights

Height (in feet and inches)	Range of acceptable weight	
	Men (in pounds)	Women (in pounds)
4'10"		92–119
4'11"		94–122
5'0"		96–125
5'1"		99–128
5'2"	112–141	102–131
5'3"	115–144	105–134
5'4"	118–148	108–138
5'5"	121–152	111–142
5'6"	124–156	114–146
5'7"	128–161	118–150
5'8"	132–166	122–154
5'9"	136–170	126–158
5'10"	140–174	130–163
5'11"	144–179	134–168
6'0"	148–184	138–173
6'1"	152–189	
6'2"	156–194	
6'3"	160–199	
6'4"	164–204	

Note: Heights without shoes; weight, without clothes.
Source: USDA (1980). Nutrition and your health. USDA Home and Garden Bull. *232.*

Boiling Point, Altitude

TABLE 2.B.25
Boiling point of water at various altitudes

Altitude in Feet	Boiling Point °F.	Altitude in Feet	Boiling Point °F
0	212.0	4500	203.6
500	211.2	5000	202.6
1000	210.2	5500	201.7
1500	209.2	6000	200.7
2000	208.3	6500	199.8
2500	207.4	7000	198.8
3000	206.4	7500	197.9

Source: Desrosier, N. W. (editor) (1977). In *The Technology of Food Preservation*, 4th Edition. AVI Publishing Co., Westport, Connecticut.

Boiling Points, Sodium Chloride, Calcium Chloride

TABLE 2.B.26
Boiling points of sodium chloride and calcium chloride solutions at standard pressure

Temperature °F.	Per cent Sodium Chloride	Per cent Calcium Chloride
212	0	0
215	9.5	8.5
220	19.0	18.5
225	25.5	24.5
230	..	29.3
240	..	36.3
250	..	42.0
257	..	45.8

Source: Desrosier, N. W. (editor) (1977). In *The Technology of Food Preservation*, 4th Edition. AVI Publishing Co., Westport, Connecticut.

Bone

TABLE 2.B.27
Common and technical nomenclature of bones

Common name	Technical name
Neck bone	Cervical vertebrae (7 in beef and veal, lamb, pork, horse, & rabbit; 13–14 in chicken)
Atlas	First cervical vertebra
Backbone	Spine (vertebrae)
Button	Cartilage of spinous process (on all thoracic vertebrae)
Feather bone	Spinous process (on all thoracic vertebrae)
Finger bone	Transverse process (on all lumbar vertebrae)
Chine bone	Body of each vertebra

Backbone	Vertebrae	beef & veal	lamb	pork	chicken	horse	rabbit
	Thoracic	13	12–14	14–15	7	18	12
	Lumbar	6	6–7	6–7	} 14 fused	6	7–8
Slip joint	Sacral	5	4	4	}	5	3–4
Slip joint	Sacro-iliac diathrosis						
Tail bone	Caudal (coccygeal) vertebrae						

	Coccygeal	beef & veal	lamb	pork	chicken	horse	rabbit
	Total	18–20	16–18	20–23	5–6	15–21	14–20
	Carcass	2–3	2–4	20–23	5–6	2–3	0–2

Common name	Technical name
Blade bone	Scapula
Arm bone	Humerus
Foreshank bones	Ulna (7U) and radius (7R)
Forefoot bones	Pork: carpal, metacarpal, and phalangeal bones, dew claws and toes (digits)
	Lamb: carpal and metacarpal bones
	Chicken: 1st, 2nd, and 3rd digit and 2nd and 3rd metacarpal
Elbow bone	Olecranon process
Breast bone	Sternum, sternebrae (7; 6 in pork; 1 in chicken: keel of sternum)
Rib cartilages	Costal cartilages

Ribs	Ribs	beef & veal	lamb	pork	chicken	horse	rabbit
	No. of pairs	13	13–14	14–15	7	18	12

Common name	Technical name
Pelvic bone	Pelvis (os coxae)
Hip bone	Ilium
Rump (aitch) bone	Ischium
Leg (round) bone	Femur
Knee cap	Patella
Stifle joint	Femorotibial articulation
Hindshank bones	Tibia (includes fibula in pork, beef, and poultry)
Hock bones	Parts of tibia, fibula, and tarsal bones; removed in beef, veal, and poultry
Hindfoot bones	Pork: tarsal, metatarsal, and phalangeal bones, dew claws and toes (digits)
	Lamb: metatarsal and proximal phalangeal bones
Wishbone	Clavicle (in chicken)
Raven's beak	Coracoid (in chicken)

Source: Ockerman, H. W. (1975). Comparative anatomy of meat animals. In *Meat Hygiene*. Libby, J. A. (editor). Lea and Febiger, Philadelphia.

Bone Age

TABLE 2.B.28
Relationship between age and development of bones

Beef

Age	Ischiopubic Symphysis (Aitch Bone)	Cartilage Extension on the Dorsal Spine of the First 5 Thoracic Vertebrae
1 year old	May be cut with a knife	Cartilaginous extensions are soft and pearly white, no ossification; sharply delineated from soft red bone
2 years old	May be cut with a knife	Some evidence of ossification; red islets of bone appearing in cartilage
3 years old	May be cut with a knife with extreme difficulty	Cartilage partly ossified, grayish in color; red areas are more numerous in cartilage
4–5 years old	Must be cut with a saw	Less cartilage than bone; considerable ossification, outline of tip still visible
6 years old	Must be cut with a saw	Cartilage ossified into compact bony tissue but still definable from bone

Sheep

Age	Foreleg Ossification
Lamb	Red break joint
Yearling	White break joint
Mutton	White spool joint

Poultry

Age	Amount of flexibility (amount of cartilage remaining) in posterior end of keel of sternum
Broiler	Anterior half or less is ossified

Source: Ockerman, H. W. (1975). Comparative anatomy of meat animals. In *Meat Hygiene.* J. A. Libby (editor). Lea and Febiger, Philadelphia.

Bone and Body Weight

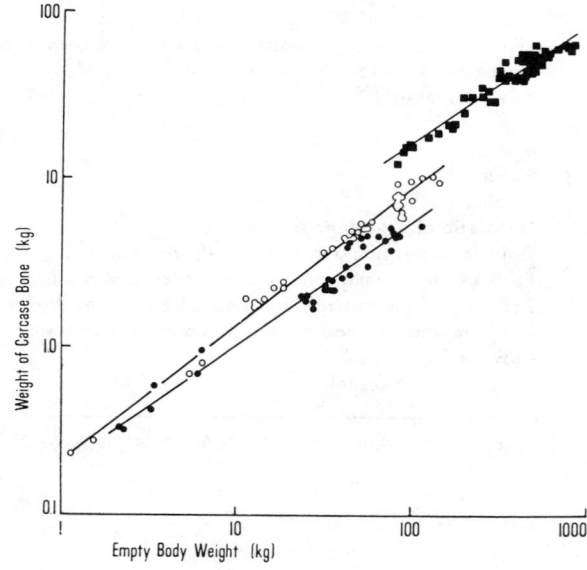

FIGURE 2.B.18
Weight of dissected bone in a carcass compared with empty body weight for sheep (●), cattle (■), and pigs (○)
Source: Tribe, D. E. (editor). *Carcass Compositions and Appraisal of Meat Animals.* CSIRO, Australia.

Bone in Retail Cuts

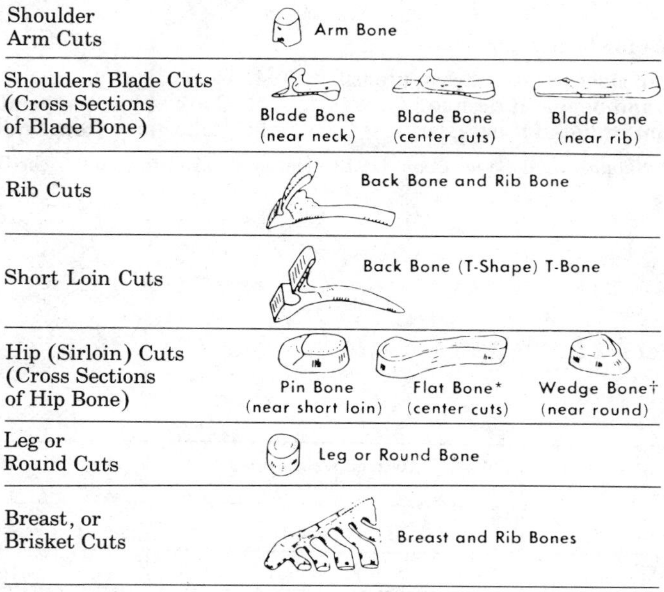

Shoulder Arm Cuts		Arm Bone
Shoulders Blade Cuts (Cross Sections of Blade Bone)	Blade Bone (near neck)	Blade Bone (center cuts)	Blade Bone (near rib)
Rib Cuts		Back Bone and Rib Bone
Short Loin Cuts		Back Bone (T-Shape) T-Bone
Hip (Sirloin) Cuts (Cross Sections of Hip Bone)	Pin Bone (near short loin)	Flat Bone* (center cuts)	Wedge Bone† (near round)
Leg or Round Cuts		Leg or Round Bone
Breast, or Brisket Cuts		Breast and Rib Bones

*Formerly part of "double bone" but today the back bone is usually removed leaving only the "flat bone" (sometimes called "pin bone") in the sirloin steak.

†On one side of sirloin steak, this bone may be wedge shaped while on the other side the same bone may be round.

FIGURE 2.B.19
Bones that identify groups of retail cuts of meat

Source: Lessons on Meat. (1974). National Live Stock and Meat Board, Chicago.

Bones, Composition

TABLE 2.B.29
Percentage composition of entire skeleton and certain bones of cattle

Age	Water	Fat	Protein	Ash
At birth	65.31	2.30	16.19	13.76
3 months	49.29	13.30	20.00	16.20
11 months	38.47	18.49	19.25	21.61
2 years	36.08	15.39	20.94	25.78
3 years	32.83	18.05	21.25	25.90
4 years	32.09	17.72	21.00	26.34
Rib bones	28.67	18.02	20.63	28.74
Round bones	26.09	29.96	19.63	23.20

Braising Meat I

TABLE 2.B.30
Recommended steps for braising meat

1. Brown meat on all sides in fat in heavy utensil.
2. Season with salt and pepper if desired.
3. Add small amount of liquid if necessary.
4. Cover tightly.
5. Cook at low temperature until tender.
6. Make gravy from liquid in pan if desired.

Source: Be a Smarter Shopper . . . a Better Cook. (1973). National Live Stock and Meat Board, Chicago.

Braising Meat II

TABLE 2.B.31
Timetable for braising

Cut	Average Weight or Thickness	Approximate Cooking Time
Pot-roast	3 to 5 pounds	3 to 4 hours
Pot-roast	5 to 15 pounds	3 to 5 hours
Swiss steak	1 to 2½ inches	2 to 3 hours
Round steak or flank steak	½ inch (pounded)	45 minutes to 1 hour
Stuffed steak	½ to ¾ inch	1½ hours
Short ribs	Pieces 2 x 2 x 2 inches	1½ to 2 hours
Fricassee	1 to 2 inch pieces	2 to 3 hours
Beef birds	½ x 2 x 4 inches	1½ to 2 hours
Stuffed lamb breast	2 to 3 pounds	1½ to 2 hours
Rolled lamb breast	1½ to 2 pounds	1½ to 2 hours
Lamb shanks	½ pound each	1 to 1½ hours
Lamb neck slices	½ to ¾ inch	1 to 1½ hours
Lamb riblets	¾ x 2½ x 3 inches	2 to 2½ hours
Pork chops or steaks	¾ to 1 inch	45 minutes to 1 hour
Spareribs	2 to 3 pounds	1½ hours
Stuffed veal breast	3 to 4 pounds	1½ to 2 hours
Rolled veal breast	2 to 3 pounds	2 to 3 hours
Veal cutlets	½ x 3 x 5½ inches	45 minutes to 1 hour
Veal steaks or chops	½ to ¾ inch	45 minutes to 1 hour
Veal birds	½ x 2 x 4 inches	45 minutes to 1 hour

Source: Cooking Meat in Quantity. National Live Stock and Meat Board, Chicago.

Braising Time

TABLE 2.B.32
Timetable for braising meat

Cut	Average Weight or Thickness	Approximate Total Cooking Time
BEEF		
Pot-Roast		
Arm or blade	3 to 4 pounds	2½-3½ hours
Boneless	3 to 5 pounds	3-4 hours
Cubes	1 to 1½ inches	1½-2½ hours
Short ribs	Pieces (2 in. x 2 in. x 4 in.)	1½-2½ hours
Round steak	¾ to 1 inch	1-1¾ hours
Stuffed steak	½ to ¾ inch	1½ hours
PORK		
Chops	¾ to 1½ inches	45-60 minutes
Spareribs	2 to 3 pounds	1½ hours
Tenderloin		
Whole	¾ to 1 pound	45-60 minutes
Filets	½ inch	30 minutes
Shoulder steaks	¾ inch	45-60 minutes
LAMB		
Breast, stuffed	2 to 3 pounds	1½-2 hours
Breast, boneless	1½ to 2 pounds	1½-2 hours
Riblets		1½-2½ hours
Neck slices	¾ inch	1 hour
Shanks	¾ to 1 pound each	1-1½ hours
Shoulder chops	¾ to 1 inch	45-60 minutes
VEAL		
Breast, stuffed	3 to 4 pounds	1½-2½ hours
Breast, boneless	2 to 3 pounds	1½-2½ hours
Riblets		2-3 hours
Chops	½ to ¾ inch	45-60 minutes
Steaks or cutlets	½ to ¾ inch	45-60 minutes
Cubes	1 to 2 inches	45-60 minutes

Source: Lessons on Meat. (1974). National Live Stock and
Meat Board, Chicago.

Bread and Flour Enrichment

TABLE 2.B.33
Federal standards for flour[1] and bread[2] enrichment

	Flour		Bread	
	Minimum Mg/Lb	Maximum Mg/Lb	Minimum Mg/Lb	Maximum Mg/Lb
Thiamine	2.0	2.5	1.1	1.8
Riboflavin	1.2	1.5	0.7	1.6
Niacin	16.0	20.0	10.0	15.0
Iron	13.0	16.5	8.0	12.5
Calcium[3]	500	625	300	800
Vitamin D[3] (USP units)	250	1,000	150	750

[1] Anon. (1941).
[2] Anon. (1952).
[3] Optional ingredients.

Source: Potter, N. N. (editor) (1973). Nutritive aspects of food constituents.
In Food Science, 2d Edition. AVI Publishing Co, Westport, Connecticut.

Brine, Meat Curing

TABLE 2.B.34
Brine, meat curing

Degrees Salinometer	Degrees Baumé	Specific Gravity	Salt (%)	Weight (Lb)	Salt (Lb/Gal.)
20	—	—	5.305	—	0.427
21	—	—	5.570	—	0.453
22	—	—	5.835	—	0.479
23	—	—	6.100	—	0.505
24	—	—	6.365	—	0.531
25	—	—	6.630	—	0.557
26	—	—	6.895	—	0.583
27	—	—	7.160	—	0.609
28	—	—	7.425	—	0.635
29	—	—	7.690	—	0.661
30	—	—	7.955	—	0.687
31	—	—	8.220	—	0.713
32	—	—	8.485	—	0.739
33	—	—	8.745	—	0.765
34	—	—	9.010	—	0.791
35	—	—	9.275	—	0.817
36	—	—	9.540	—	0.843
37	—	—	9.805	—	0.869
38	—	—	10.070	—	0.895
39	—	—	10.335	—	0.921
40	10.40	1.073	10.600	8.939	0.947
41	10.66	1.075	10.865	8.955	0.973
42	10.92	1.077	11.130	8.972	0.998
43	11.18	1.079	11.395	8.989	1.024
44	11.44	1.081	11.660	9.005	1.050
45	11.70	1.083	11.925	9.022	1.075
46	11.96	1.085	12.190	9.039	1.101
47	12.22	1.087	12.455	9.055	1.127
48	12.48	1.089	12.720	9.072	1.154
49	12.74	1.091	12.985	9.089	1.180
50	13.00	1.093	13.250	9.105	1.206
51	13.26	1.095	13.515	9.122	1.232
52	13.52	1.097	13.780	9.139	1.259
53	13.78	1.100	14.045	9.164	1.287
54	14.04	1.102	14.310	9.180	1.313
55	14.30	1.104	14.575	9.197	1.340
56	14.56	1.106	14.840	9.214	1.367
57	14.82	1.108	15.105	9.230	1.394
58	15.08	1.110	15.370	9.247	1.421
59	15.34	1.112	15.635	9.264	1.448
60	15.60	1.114	15.900	9.280	1.475
61	15.86	1.116	16.165	9.297	1.502
62	16.12	1.118	16.430	9.314	1.530
63	16.38	1.121	16.695	9.339	1.559
64	16.64	1.123	16.960	9.355	1.586
65	16.90	1.125	17.225	9.372	1.614
66	17.16	1.127	17.490	9.389	1.642
67	17.42	1.129	17.755	9.405	1.670
68	17.68	1.131	18.020	9.422	1.697
69	17.94	1.133	18.285	9.439	1.725
70	18.20	1.136	18.550	9.464	1.755
71	18.46	1.138	18.815	9.480	1.783
72	18.72	1.140	19.080	9.497	1.812
73	18.98	1.142	19.345	9.514	1.840
74	19.24	1.144	19.610	9.530	1.868
75	19.50	1.147	19.875	9.555	1.899
76	19.76	1.149	20.140	9.572	1.927
77	20.02	1.151	20.405	9.580	1.956
78	20.28	1.154	20.670	9.614	1.987
79	20.54	1.156	20.935	9.630	2.016
80	20.80	1.158	21.200	9.647	2.045
81	21.06	1.160	21.465	9.664	2.074
82	21.32	1.163	21.730	9.689	2.105
83	21.58	1.165	21.995	9.705	2.134
84	21.84	1.167	22.260	9.722	2.164
85	22.10	1.170	22.525	9.747	2.195
86	22.36	1.172	22.790	9.764	2.225
87	22.62	1.175	23.055	9.780	2.256
88	22.88	1.177	23.320	9.805	2.286
89	23.14	1.179	23.585	9.822	2.316
90	23.40	1.182	23.850	9.847	2.348
91	23.66	1.184	24.115	9.864	2.378
92	23.92	1.186	24.380	9.880	2.408
93	24.18	1.189	24.645	9.905	2.441
94	24.44	1.191	24.910	9.922	2.477
95	24.70	1.194	25.175	9.947	2.504
96	24.96	1.196	25.440	9.964	2.534
97	25.22	1.198	25.705	9.980	2.565
98	25.48	1.201	25.970	9.980	2.598
99	25.74	1.203	26.235	10.022	2.629
100	26.00	1.205	26.500	10.039	2.660

Source: Komarik, S. L., Tressler, D. K., and Long, L. (editors) (1974). Cured meats. In *Food Products Formulary*, Vol. 1, AVI Publishing Co., Westport, Connecticut.

Brix Table

TABLE 2.B.35

Relationship between degrees Brix, pounds of sugar to be added to 1 gal water, volume of syrup prepared from 1 gal water, and weight of sugar in 1 gal syrup

Degrees Brix 68°F	Pounds of Sugar to Be Added to Each Gallon of Water (lb)	Volume of Syrup from 1 Gallon of Water (Gal.)	Weight of Sugar Contained in 1 Gallon of Syrup (lb)	Degrees Brix 68°F	Pounds of Sugar to Be Added to Each Gallon of Water (lb)	Volume of Syrup from 1 Gallon of Water (Gal.)	Weight of Sugar Contained in 1 Gallon of Syrup (lb)
10	1.11	1.067	1.04	41	6.97	1.437	4.85
11	1.23	1.076	1.14	42	7.26	1.454	4.99
12	1.36	1.085	1.25	43	7.56	1.474	5.13
13	1.49	1.093	1.36	44	7.88	1.494	5.27
14	1.62	1.101	1.47	45	8.20	1.514	5.42
15	1.76	1.111	1.58	46	8.55	1.536	5.57
16	1.90	1.119	1.70	47	8.90	1.558	5.71
17	2.04	1.127	1.81	48	9.26	1.580	5.86
18	2.19	1.137	1.93	49	9.64	1.604	6.01
19	2.34	1.146	2.04	50	10.03	1.628	6.16
20	2.50	1.157	2.16	51	10.44	1.654	6.31
21	2.66	1.167	2.28	52	10.86	1.681	6.45
22	2.82	1.176	2.40	53	11.31	1.710	6.61
23	3.00	1.187	2.52	54	11.77	1.739	6.77
24	3.17	1.198	2.64	55	12.26	1.770	6.93
25	3.34	1.208	2.76	56	12.77	1.803	7.08
26	3.52	1.220	2.89	57	13.29	1.837	7.23
27	3.70	1.231	3.01	58	13.85	1.871	7.40
28	3.89	1.243	3.13	59	14.43	1.907	7.57
29	4.09	1.256	3.26	60	15.05	1.948	7.73
30	4.30	1.269	3.38	61	15.69	1.988	7.89
31	4.50	1.281	3.51	62	16.37	2.032	8.05
32	4.72	1.294	3.64	63	17.08	2.077	8.21
33	4.94	1.309	3.77	64	17.84	2.124	8.39
34	5.17	1.323	3.90	65	18.62	2.174	8.57
35	5.40	1.338	4.03	66	19.47	2.229	8.75
36	5.64	1.353	4.17	67	20.39	2.287	8.92
37	5.89	1.369	4.30	68	21.32	2.344	9.10
38	6.14	1.384	4.44	69	22.33	2.411	9.27
39	6.41	1.401	4.58	70	23.40	2.480	9.44
40	6.69	1.419	4.71				

Example: Sugar required to add to 50 gal. of water for 45° Brix

    Sugar = 50 × 8.2 = 410 lb

Volume of syrup

    Volume = 50 × 1.514 = 75.5 gal.

Sugar in 80 gal. of syrup of 40° Brix

    Sugar = 80 × 4.71 lb = 376.8 lb

Sugar for 100 gal. of syrup at 45° Brix

Water for 100 gal. of syrup at 45° Brix

    Water = 100/1.514 = 66.1 gal.

    Sugar = 66 × 8.2 = 542 lb

Source: Lock, A. (1969). *Practical Canning.* 3d Edition. Food Trade Press, London, England.

Brix, Temperature Correction

TABLE 2.B.36
Correction of Brix readings for temperatures above and below 68°F

	Temperature °F	Degrees Brix, and correction:									
		10	20	25	30	35	40	45	50	55	60
Subtract correction	40	0.5	0.6	0.7	0.8	0.8	0.9	0.9	0.9	0.9	1.0
	50	0.5	0.5	0.5	0.5	0.6	0.6	0.6	0.6	0.6	0.6
	60	0.2	0.2	0.2	0.2	0.2	0.2	0.2	0.2	0.2	0.2
Add correction	70	0.1	0.2	0.2	0.2	0.2	0.2	0.2	0.2	0.2	0.2
	80	0.5	0.6	0.6	0.6	0.6	0.6	0.6	0.6	0.6	0.6
	90	0.9	1.0	1.0	1.0	1.1	1.1	1.1	1.1	1.1	1.0
	100	1.3	1.4	1.5	1.5	1.5	1.5	1.5	1.5	1.5	1.5
	120	2.5	2.6	2.6	2.6	2.6	2.6	2.6	2.6	2.5	2.5
	140	3.8	3.8	3.8	3.8	3.8	3.8	3.7	3.7	3.6	3.6
	160	4.1	5.1	5.1	5.1	5.1	5.0	5.0	4.9	4.8	4.8
	180	6.7	6.5	6.4	6.3	6.3	6.3	6.2	6.1	6.0	5.9
	212	10.0	9.6	9.4	9.1	9.1	8.9	8.7	8.4	8.2	8.1

Example: Hydrometer reading, 44.4 at 140°F

Corrected reading: 44.4 + 3.7 = 48.1° Brix

Source: Lock, A. (1969). Practical Canning, 3d Edition. Food Trade Press, London, England.

Broiling Griddle, Meat

TABLE 2.B.37
Timetable for griddle-broiling meats

Cut	Approx Thickness	Approx Cooking Time		
		Rare (min)	Medium (min)	Well-done (min)
Individual servings of beef steaks	¾ in.	4	8	12
	1 in.	6	10	15
	1½ in.	10–12	15–18	20
Ground beef patties	¾ in.	4–5	8–10	12
	1 in. (4 oz)	6–8	10–12	15
Lamb chops	1 in.		10	15
	1½ in.		15	20–25
Ground lamb patties	¾ in.		10	12–15
	1 in. (4 oz)		10–15	15–20
Smoked ham slice	½ in.			6–10
Bacon				2–3

Source: Cooking Meats in Quantity. National Live Stock and Meat Board, Chicago.

Broiling Meat I

TABLE 2.B.38
Recommended procedure for broiling meats

1. Broil in oven or on outdoor grill.
2. If oven is used, set regulator for broiling. Preheat if desired.
3. Place 1-inch steaks, chops or patties 2 to 3 inches from heat . . . 3 to 5 inches for thicker cuts.
4. Whether broiling in oven or on outdoor grill, cook until meat is brown on one side.
5. Season browned side if desired.
6. Broil second side until done. Serve at once.

Source: Be a Smarter Shopper . . . a Better Cook. (1973). National Live Stock and Meat Board, Chicago.

Broiling Meat II

TABLE 2.B.39
Timetable for broiling (for type of broiler that cooks one side of meat at a time)*

Cut	Approximate Thickness	Approximate Cooking Time		
		Rare	Medium	Well-done
		minutes	*minutes*	*minutes*
Rib, club, T-bone, porterhouse, tenderloin or individual servings of sirloin beef steak	1 inch	15	20	30
	1½ inches	25	35	
	2 inches	35	50	
Sirloin beef steak (whole steak)	1 inch	20 to 30	30 to 40	
	1½ inches	30 to 40	40 to 50	
	2 inches	40 to 55	50 to 65	
Ground beef patties	1 inch (4 oz.)	15	20	
Shoulder, rib, loin and sirloin lamb chops or steaks	1 inch		12 to 15	
	1½ inches		17 to 20	
	2 inches		20 to 25	
Ground lamb patties	1 inch (4 oz.)		20	
Smoked ham slice	½ inch			10 to 12
	1 inch			16 to 20
Bacon				4 to 5

* There are automatic speed broilers which cook both sides of the meat at once and may, therefore, decrease the time to half or even a third of that given above.

Source: Cooking Meat in Quantity. National Live Stock and Meat Board, Chicago.

Broiling Time and Temperature

TABLE 2.B.40
Timetable for broiling *

Cut	Weight or Thickness	Approximate Total Cooking Time	
		Rare	Medium
BEEF	Pounds	Minutes	Minutes
Blade steak (high quality)—1 in.	1½ to 2½	24	30
1½ in.	2 to 4	40	45
Rib steak—1 in.	1 to 1½	15	20
1½ in.	1½ to 2	25	30
2 in.	2 to 2½	35	45
Rib eye steak—1 in.	8 to 10 ozs.	15	20
1½ in.	12 to 14 ozs.	25	30
2 in.	16 to 20 ozs.	35	45
Top loin steak—1 in.	1 to 1½	15	20
1½ in.	1½ to 2	25	30
2 in.	2 to 2½	35	45
Sirloin steak—1 in.	1½ to 3	20	25
1½ in.	2¼ to 4	30	35
2 in.	3 to 5	40	45
Porterhouse steak—			
1 in.	1¼ to 2	20	25
1½ in.	2 to 3	30	35
2 in.	2½ to 3½	40	45
Filet Mignon—			
1 in.	4 to 6 ozs.	15	20
1½ in.	6 to 8 ozs.	18	22
Ground beef patties 1 in. thick by 3 in.	4 ozs.	15	25
PORK — SMOKED			
Ham slice—			
½ in.	¾ to 1	Always cooked well done	10-12
1 in.	1½ to 2		16-20
Loin Chops—			
¾ to 1 in.			15-20
Canadian-style bacon			
¼ in. slices			6-8
½ in. slices			8-10
Bacon			4-5
PORK — FRESH			
Rib or loin chops	¾ to 1 inch	Always cooked well done	20-25
Shoulder steaks	½ to ¾ inch		25-30
LAMB			
Shoulder chops—			
1 in.	5 to 8 ozs.	Lamb chops are not usually served rare	12
1½ in.	8 to 10 ozs.		18
2 in.	10 to 16 ozs.		22
Rib chops—1 in.	3 to 5 ozs.		12
1½ in.	4 to 7 ozs.		18
2 in.	6 to 10 ozs.		22
Loin chops—1 in.	4 to 7 ozs.		12
1½ in.	6 to 10 ozs.		18
2 in.	8 to 14 ozs.		22
Ground lamb patties 1 in. by 3 in.	4 ozs.		18

*This time-table is based on broiling at a moderate temperature (350° F.). Rare steaks are broiled to an internal temperature of 140°F.; medium to 160°F.; well done to 170°F. Lamb chops are broiled from 170°F. to 175°F. Ham is cooked to 160°F. The time for broiling bacon is influenced by personal preference as to crispness.

Source: *Lessons on Meat*. (1974). National Live Stock and Meat Board, Chicago.

Buffer Solutions

TABLE 2.B.41
Composition of standard buffer solutions

Hydrochloric Acid Buffer		Acid Phthalate Buffer		Neutralized Phthalate Buffer	
To 50.0 ml of 0.2 M KCl add the ml of HCl specified		To 50.0 ml of 0.2 M $KHC_6H_4(COO)_2$ add the ml of HCl specified		To 50.0 ml of 0.2 M $KHC_6H_4(COO)_2$ add the ml of NaOH specified	
pH	0.2 M HCl, ml	pH	0.2 M HCl, ml	pH	0.2 M NaOH, ml
1.2	85.0	2.2	49.5	4.2	3.0
1.3	67.2	2.4	42.2	4.4	6.6
1.4	53.2	2.6	35.4	4.6	11.1
1.5	41.4	2.8	28.9	4.8	16.5
1.6	32.4	3.0	22.3	5.0	22.6
1.7	26.0	3.2	15.7	5.2	28.8
1.8	20.4	3.4	10.4	5.4	34.1
1.9	16.2	3.6	6.3	5.6	38.8
2.0	13.0	3.8	2.9	5.8	42.3
2.1	10.2	4.0	0.1	—	—
2.2	7.8	—	—	—	—

Phosphate Buffer		Alkaline Borate Buffer	
To 50.0 ml of 0.2 M KH_2PO_4 add the ml of NaOH specified		To 50.0 ml of 0.2 M H_3BO_3-KCl add the ml of NaOH specified	
pH	0.2 M NaOH, ml	pH	0.2 M NaOH, ml
5.8	3.6	8.0	3.9
6.0	5.6	8.2	6.0
6.2	8.1	8.4	8.6
6.4	11.6	8.6	11.8
6.6	16.4	8.8	15.8
6.8	22.4	9.0	20.8
7.0	29.1	9.2	26.4
7.2	34.7	9.4	32.1
7.4	39.1	9.6	36.9
7.6	42.4	9.8	40.6
7.8	44.5	10.0	43.7
8.0	46.1	—	—

Note: Dilute all final solutions to 200.0 ml. The standard pH values given in this table are considered to be reproducible to within ±0.02 of the pH unit specified at 25°.

Source: Food Chemicals Codex. Committee on Food Protection, National Academy of Sciences–National Research Council.

Butter and Butter Products, Composition

TABLE 2.B.42
Approximate composition of butter and butter products

Product	Fat (%)	Moisture (%)	Salt (%)	Curd (%)
Salted butter	80.5	15.8	2.4	0.9
Unsalted butter	81.0	18.05	—	0.95
Butter oil	99.0	1.0	—	—
Dry milkfat	99.9	0.1	—	—
Butterfat-vegetable fat blend	82.5	15.0	1.5	1.0
Butterfat-water emulsion	40.0	56.0	2.0	2.0 Emulsifier
Margarine	80.5	15.4	2.4	1.65

Source: Arbuckle, W. S. (1973). Dairy products. In *Quality Control For The Food Industry*, Vol. 2, 3d Edition. A. Kramer and B. A. Twigg (editors). AVI Publishing Co., Westport, Connecticut.

Butter Grade

U.S. Grade AA butter
  • has a delicate sweet flavor, with a fine, highly pleasing aroma.
  • is made from fresh sweet cream.
  • has a smooth, creamy texture with good spreadability.
  • has salt completely dissolved and blended in just the right amount.

U.S. Grade A butter
  • has a pleasing flavor
  • is made from fresh cream
  • is fairly smooth in texture.

FIGURE 2.B.20

Source: USDA (1979). How to buy dairy products. USDA Home and Garden Bull. *201.*

Cabbage Looper

FIGURE 2.C.1

Source: USDA (1978). Growing cauliflower and broccoli. USDA Farmers' Bull. *2239.*

Calcium

TABLE 2.C.1
Calcium content of some fresh vegetables and fruits

	mg/100 g		mg/100 g
Broccoli	103	Carrots	37
Spinach	93	Brussels sprouts	36
Snap beans	56	Onions	27
Lima beans	52	Lettuce	20
Artichokes	51	Grapefruit	16
Cabbage	49	Tomatoes	13
Tangerines	40	Oranges	11
Celery	39	Potatoes	7

Source: White, P. L., and Selvey, N. (editors) (1974). *Nutritional Qualities of Fresh Fruits and Vegetables.* Futura Publishing Co., Mt. Kisco, New York.

Calcium, Daily Recommendations (Requirements and Sources)

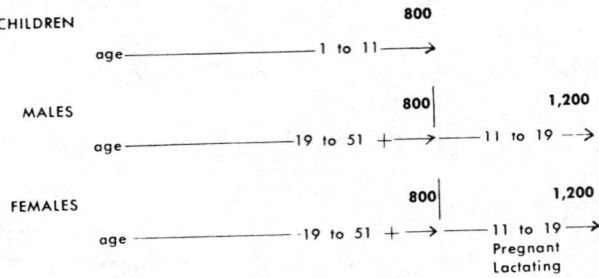

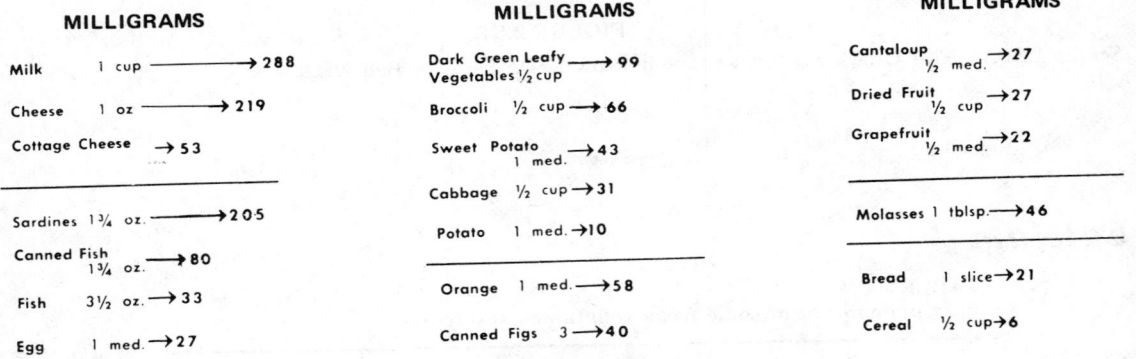

FIGURE 2.C.2

Source: Lessons on Meat. (1974). National Live Stock and Meat Board, Chicago.

Calcium Equivalents for Milk

TABLE 2.C.2

On the basis of the calcium they provide, the following are alternatives for 8 ounces of fresh whole milk:

1-1/3 ounces Cheddar cheese

1-1/2 ounces process American cheese

1-1/3 cups cottage cheese

1 cup cocoa made with milk

1 cup custard

1-1/3 cups ice cream

1 cup ice milk, soft serve

3/4 cup homemade macaroni and cheese

1 milkshake (made with 2/3 cup milk and
    1/2 cup ice cream)

1 cup oyster stew

1-1/2 to 1-2/3 cup canned cream soup,
    prepared with equal volume of milk

1 cup unflavored yogurt

Source: USDA (1979). How to buy dairy products. USDA Home and Garden Bull. *201.*

Calories, Basal, per 24 Hours

BOOTHBY AND SANDIFORD'S NOMOGRAPH

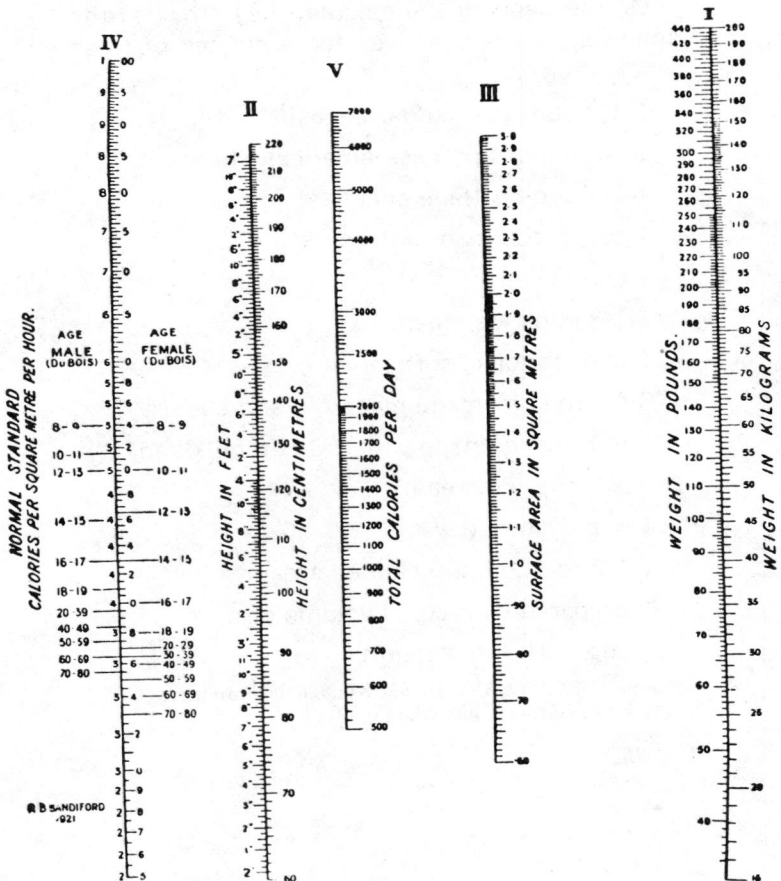

FIGURE 2.C.3

The weight (in pounds or kilograms) is shown on Scale I. The height (in inches and centimeters) is shown on Scale II. The surface area (in square meters) is shown on Scale III. The normal standard calories per square meter of body surface per hour are shown on Scale IV. The total calories per diem are shown on Scale V.

Directions—Keep the chart flat. Use a flexible ruler with a straight edge, or a strip of stiff paper such as a postcard. A) Locate the position of the weight and height on Scales I and II, respectively. Apply the straight edge of the ruler and note where it cuts Scale III. Read the figure on Scale III, which will give the surface area of the body in square meters. B) Locate the surface area on Scale III and the normal standard Calories per square meter per hour for the age and sex of the subject on Scale IV. Apply the straight edge of the ruler, and see where it cuts Scale V. Read this figure, which gives the total basal calories per 24 hours.

Source: Sinclair, H. M., and Hollingsworth, D. F. (1969). *Hutchison's Food and the Principles of Nutrition.* Edward Arnold (Publishers), London, England.

Calories, Daily Recommendations (Requirements and Sources)

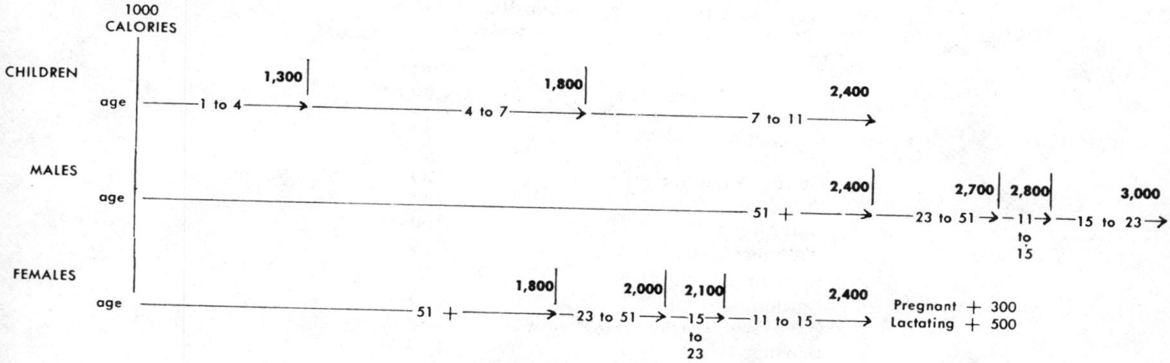

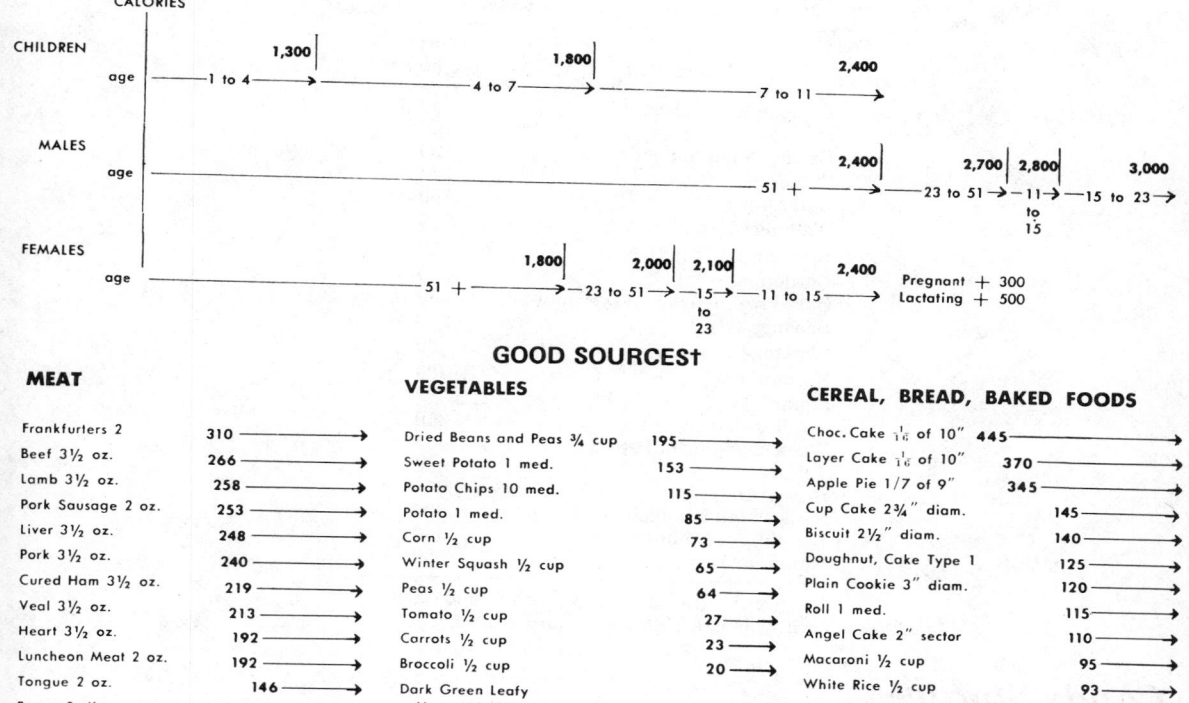

GOOD SOURCES†

MEAT

Frankfurters 2	310
Beef 3½ oz.	266
Lamb 3½ oz.	258
Pork Sausage 2 oz.	253
Liver 3½ oz.	248
Pork 3½ oz.	240
Cured Ham 3½ oz.	219
Veal 3½ oz.	213
Heart 3½ oz.	192
Luncheon Meat 2 oz.	192
Tongue 2 oz.	146
Bacon 2 slices	68

POULTRY, FISH, EGGS

Turkey 3½ oz.	190
Chicken 3½ oz.	183
Fish 3½ oz.	181
Oysters 6-9	80
Egg 1	80
Canned Fish 1¾ oz.	76

DAIRY PRODUCTS

Ice Cream ⅙ qt.	193
Custard ⅔ cup	190
Hot Chocolate ¾ cup	176
Whole Milk 1 cup	160
Ice Milk ½ cup	143
Cheese 1 oz.	105
Skim Milk 1 cup	90
Cottage Cheese ¼ cup	59
Butter 1 pat	50
Coffee Cream 1 tblsp.	30

VEGETABLES

Dried Beans and Peas ¾ cup	195
Sweet Potato 1 med.	153
Potato Chips 10 med.	115
Potato 1 med.	85
Corn ½ cup	73
Winter Squash ½ cup	65
Peas ½ cup	64
Tomato ½ cup	27
Carrots ½ cup	23
Broccoli ½ cup	20
Dark Green Leafy Vegetables ½ cup	19
Asparagus ½ cup	18
Summer Squash ½ cup	15
Green Beans ½ cup	15
Cabbage ½ cup	14
Cauliflower ½ cup	13
Lettuce ⅛ head	8
Green Pepper ¼ med.	4

FRUIT

Dried Fruit ½ cup	126
Fruit Cocktail ½ cup	98
Avocado ¼ med.	93
Canned Pineapple 2 sm. slices	90
Berries ½ cup	89
Melon 1 serving	88
Banana 1 med.	85
Apple 1 med.	70
Orange 1 med.	68
Grapefruit ½ med.	55
Orange Juice ½ cup	55
Cherries ½ cup	40
Peach 1 med.	35

CEREAL, BREAD, BAKED FOODS

Choc. Cake 1/16 of 10"	445
Layer Cake 1/16 of 10"	370
Apple Pie 1/7 of 9"	345
Cup Cake 2¾" diam.	145
Biscuit 2½" diam.	140
Doughnut, Cake Type 1	125
Plain Cookie 3" diam.	120
Roll 1 med.	115
Angel Cake 2" sector	110
Macaroni ½ cup	95
White Rice ½ cup	93
Cereal, prepared ¾ cup	71
Cereal, cooked ½ cup	65
Enriched White Bread 1 slice	60
Griddlecake 4"	60
Whole Wheat Bread 1 slice	55
Soda Cracker 2½" sq.	50

MISCELLANEOUS

Nuts ¼ cup	209
Peanut Butter 2 tblsp.	190
Sherbet ½ cup	130
Lard 1 tblsp.	125
Fudge 1 oz.	115
Mayonnaise 1 tblsp.	110
Soup 1 cup	103
Cola Beverage 8 oz.	95
Plain Gelatin Dessert ½ cup	70
French Dressing 1 tblsp.	60
Syrups 1 tblsp.	60
Jams, Jellies 1 tblsp.	55
Margarine 1 pat	50
Molasses 1 tblsp.	48
Sweet Pickles 2 sm.	22
Sugar 1 tsp.	15
Green Olives 2 "Mammoth"/4 med.	15

†Average nutrient content as food is served. (Note: 3½ oz equals approximately 100 g.)

FIGURE 2.C.4

Source: Lessons on Meat. (1974). National Live Stock and Meat Board, Chicago.

Calorie Utilization

TABLE 2.C.3
Approximate energy expenditure by a
150-lb person in various activities

Activity	Calories per hour
Lying down or sleeping	80
Sitting	100
Driving an automobile	120
Standing	140
Domestic work	180
Walking ($2\frac{1}{2}$ mph)	210
Bicycling ($5\frac{1}{2}$ mph)	210
Gardening	220
Golf; lawn mowing, power mower	250
Bowling	270
Walking ($3\frac{3}{4}$ mph)	300
Swimming ($\frac{1}{4}$ mph)	300
Square dancing, volleyball; roller skating	350
Wood chopping or sawing	400
Tennis	420
Skiing, 10 mph	600
Squash and handball	600
Bicycling (13 mph)	660
Running (10 mph)	900

Source: USDA (1980). Nutrition and your health. USDA Home and Garden Bull. *232*.

Candy Storage

TABLE 2.C.4
Expected storage life

Candy			Storage			
				Temperatures, °F. (°C.)		
Name	Moisture Content (%)	Relative Humidity (%)	68 (20)	48 (9)	32 (0)	0 (−18)
			Months	Months	Months	Months
Sweet chocolate	0.36	40	3	6	9	12
Milk chocolate	0.52	40	2	4	6	8
Lemon drops	0.76	40	2	4	9	12
Chocolate covered peanuts	0.91	40–45	2	4	6	8
Peanut brittle	1.58	40	1	$1\frac{1}{2}$	3	6
Coated nut roll	5.16	45–50	$1\frac{1}{2}$	3	6	9
Uncoated peanut roll	5.89	45–50	1	2	3	6
Nougat bar	6.14	50	$1\frac{1}{2}$	3	6	9
Hard creams	6.56	50	3	6	12	12
Sugar bonbons	7.53	50	3	6	12	12
Coconut squares	7.70	50	2	3	6	9
Peanut butter taffy kisses	8.00	40	2	3	5	10
Chocolate covered creams	8.09	50	1	3	6	9
Chocolate covered soft creams	8.22	50	$1\frac{1}{2}$	3	5	9
Plain caramels	9.04	50	3	6	9	12
Fudge	10.21	65	$2\frac{1}{2}$	5	12	12
Gum drops	15.11	65	3	6	12	12
Marshmallows	16.00	65	2	3	6	9

Source: Woodroof, J. G. (1968). Freezing candies. In *The Freezing Preservation of Foods*, Vol. 4, 4th Edition. D. K. Tressler, W. B. Van Arsdel, and M. J. Copley (editors). AVI Publishing Co., Westport, Connecticut.

Canned Food, Processing

TABLE 2.C.5
Classification of canned foods on the basis of processing requirements

Acidity Classification	pH Value	Food Item	Food Groups	Spoilage Agents	Heat and Processing Requirements
	7.0	Lye hominy	Meat	Mesophilic spore-forming anaerobic bacteria	High temperature processing 240°–250°F.
Low acid		Ripe olives, crabmeat, eggs, oysters, milk, corn, duck, chicken, codfish, beef, sardines	Fish Milk Poultry		
	6.0	Corned beef, lima beans, peas, carrots, beets, asparagus, potatoes	Vegetables	Thermophiles Naturally occurring enzymes in certain processes	
Medium acid	5.0 4.5	Figs, tomato soup Ravioli, pimientos	Soup Manufactured foods	Lower limit for growth of *Cl. botulinum*	
Acid		Potato salad Tomatoes, pears, apricots, peaches, oranges	Fruits	Non-spore forming aciduric bacteria	Boiling water processing (212°F.)
	3.7	Sauerkraut, pineapple, apple, strawberry, grapefruit		Acidic spore-forming bacteria	
High acid	3.0	Pickles Relish Cranberry juice Lemon juice	Berries High acid foods (pickles) High acid-high solids foods (jam-jelly)	Natural occurring enzymes Yeasts Molds	
	2.0	Lime juice	Very acid foods		

Source: Desrosier, N. W. (editor) (1977). Principles of Food Preservation by Canning. In *The Technology of Food Preservation*, 4th Edition. AVI Publishing Co., Westport, Connecticut.

Canned Spoilage Manifestations

TABLE 2.C.6

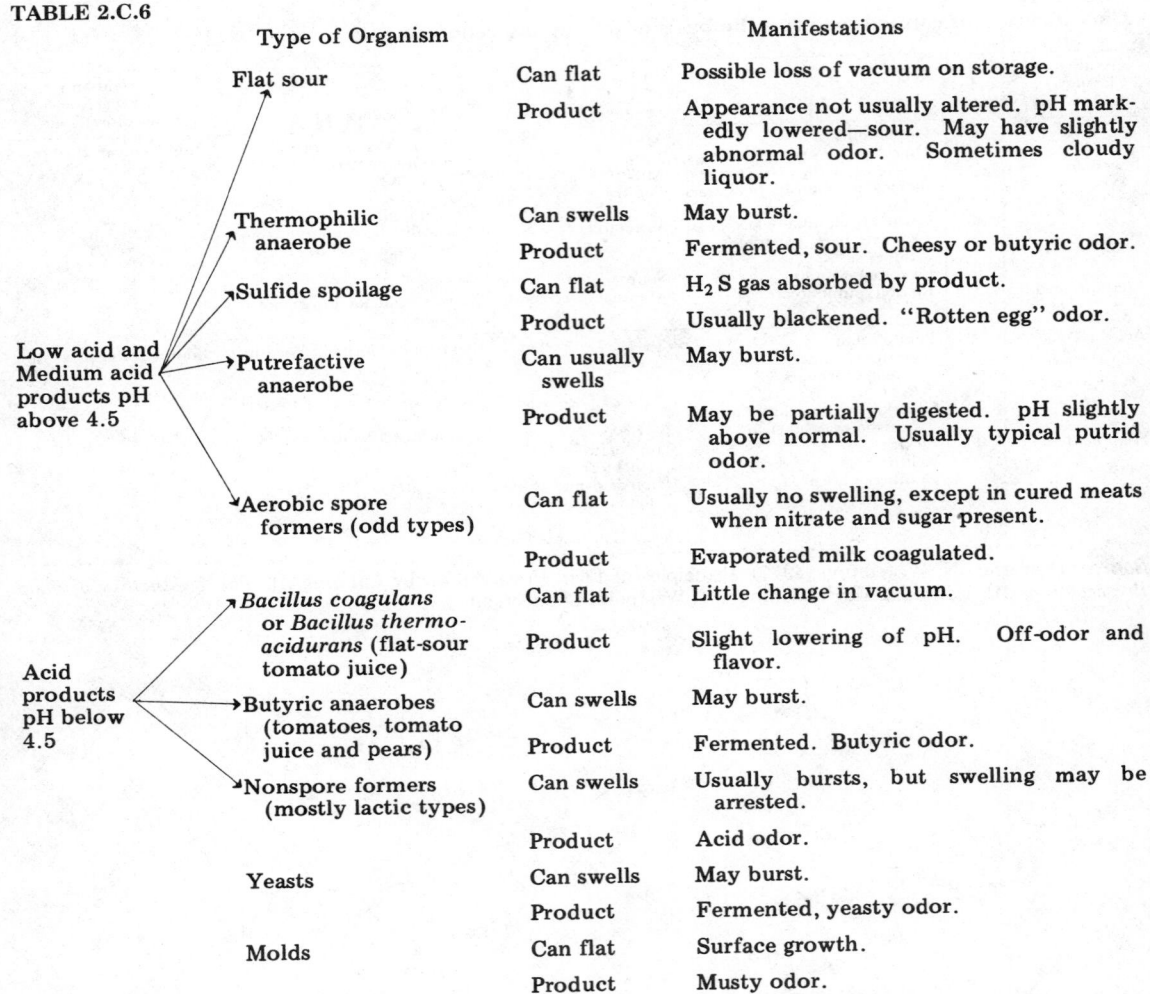

Type of Organism		Manifestations
Flat sour	Can flat	Possible loss of vacuum on storage.
	Product	Appearance not usually altered. pH markedly lowered—sour. May have slightly abnormal odor. Sometimes cloudy liquor.
Thermophilic anaerobe	Can swells	May burst.
	Product	Fermented, sour. Cheesy or butyric odor.
Sulfide spoilage	Can flat	H_2S gas absorbed by product.
	Product	Usually blackened. "Rotten egg" odor.
Putrefactive anaerobe	Can usually swells	May burst.
	Product	May be partially digested. pH slightly above normal. Usually typical putrid odor.
Aerobic spore formers (odd types)	Can flat	Usually no swelling, except in cured meats when nitrate and sugar present.
	Product	Evaporated milk coagulated.
Bacillus coagulans or Bacillus thermoacidurans (flat-sour tomato juice)	Can flat	Little change in vacuum.
	Product	Slight lowering of pH. Off-odor and flavor.
Butyric anaerobes (tomatoes, tomato juice and pears)	Can swells	May burst.
	Product	Fermented. Butyric odor.
Nonspore formers (mostly lactic types)	Can swells	Usually bursts, but swelling may be arrested.
	Product	Acid odor.
Yeasts	Can swells	May burst.
	Product	Fermented, yeasty odor.
Molds	Can flat	Surface growth.
	Product	Musty odor.

Low acid and Medium acid products pH above 4.5 — Flat sour, Thermophilic anaerobe, Sulfide spoilage, Putrefactive anaerobe, Aerobic spore formers (odd types)

Acid products pH below 4.5 — Bacillus coagulans or Bacillus thermoacidurans (flat-sour tomato juice), Butyric anaerobes (tomatoes, tomato juice and pears), Nonspore formers (mostly lactic types)

Source: American Public Health Association. *Recommended Methods for the Microbiological Examination of Foods.*

Canned Spoilage Related to pH

TABLE 2.C.7
Relation of pH to canned-food spoilage

Acidity Classification	Typical Foods	Spoilage Organisms
Low acid pH 5.3 and higher	Peas Corn Lima beans Evaporated milk White potatoes	Thermophilic group: Flat-sour types Thermophilic anaerobes, gas producers Sulfide spoilage organism, H_2S gas producers Mesophilic group: Putrefactive anaerobes, gas producers Aerobic formers
Medium acid pH 4.5–5.3	Spinach Green beans Asparagus Sweet potatoes Beets	Same as for low acid products but thermophilic anaerobes assume importance over flat-sour types. Abnormal growth of putrefactive anaerobes.
	(A recent study has indicated that a pH of 4.6 may be used as the dividing line between medium acid and acid products.)	
Acid pH 4.5 and lower	Tomato juice Pears Bananas Applesauce Fruit preserves	Spore formers: Aciduric flat-sour types—*Bacillus thermoacidurans* Butyric anaerobes, gas producers Nonspore formers—Lactobacilli Yeasts Molds

Source: American Public Health Association. *Recommended Methods for the Microbiological Examination of Foods.*

Canned Yield

TABLE 2.C.8
Approximate ratio of uncooked to canned products

Product	Amount Fresh Product Needed to Can 1 Qt	No. Quarts Canned Food to 1 Bushel	Approx No. of Pounds of Fresh Food in 1 Bushel
Apples	2–3 lb	20–25 qt	40–45 lb
Cherries	1–1½ qt	12 qt[1] (not pitted)	1 crate or 16 qt = 44 lb
Peaches	2–3 lb	18–20 qt	40–50 lb
Pears	2–3 lb	16–20 qt	50–55 lb
Plums	1½–2 lb	30 qt	50–55 lb
Raspberries	1¼–1½ qt	8–10 qt[1]	1 crate or 24 pt = 16 lb
Strawberries	2–2½ qt	7–8 qt	1 crate or 16 qt = 22 lb
Tomatoes	2½–3½ lb	16 qt	50–60 lb
Beans, green	1½–2 lb	18–22 qt	28 lb
Beets or carrots	2½–3 lb	16–20 qt	50–60 lb
Corn	8–12 ears	7–8 qt	70 lb
Greens	2–3 lb	5–6 qt	12 lb
Peas in pod	3¼–4 lb	7–8 qt	28 lb

[1]Quantities given are for a crate.

Source: Justin, M. M., Rust, L. O., and Vail, G. E. *Foods*, Revised Edition. Houghton Mifflin Co., Boston.

Cans, Construction

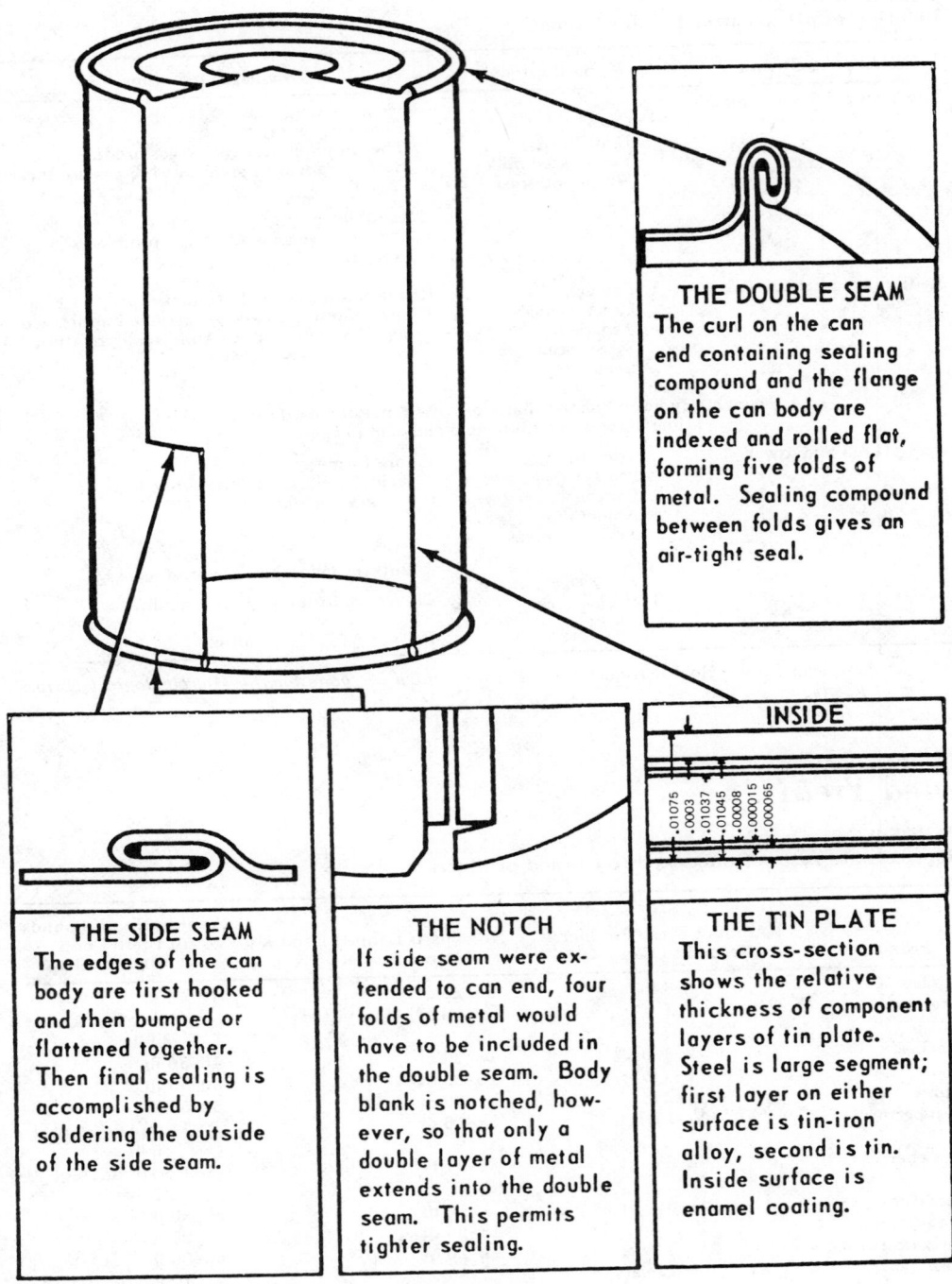

THE DOUBLE SEAM
The curl on the can end containing sealing compound and the flange on the can body are indexed and rolled flat, forming five folds of metal. Sealing compound between folds gives an air-tight seal.

THE SIDE SEAM
The edges of the can body are first hooked and then bumped or flattened together. Then final sealing is accomplished by soldering the outside of the side seam.

THE NOTCH
If side seam were extended to can end, four folds of metal would have to be included in the double seam. Body blank is notched, however, so that only a double layer of metal extends into the double seam. This permits tighter sealing.

THE TIN PLATE
This cross-section shows the relative thickness of component layers of tin plate. Steel is large segment; first layer on either surface is tin-iron alloy, second is tin. Inside surface is enamel coating.

FIGURE 2.C.5

Source: Food inspection specialist. Department of the Army, *TM 8-451* (1969).

Cans, Conversion Table

TABLE 2.C.9
Container size conversion—tin and glass

Name of Container 1	Diameter X Height 2	Min. Vol. Fil (Cu. In.) 3	Total Capac. Avoir ozs. Water at 68°F 4	No. 303 Can Equiv. 5	No. 2 Can Equiv. 6	No. 2½ Can Equiv. 7	No. 3 Cyl Can Equiv. 8	No. 10 Can Equiv. 9
2z Mushroom	202 X 204	5.45	3.60	0.207	0.170	0.117	0.068	0.032
5z Baby Food	202 X 214	7.63	4.80	.290	.238	.164	.095	.045
6z Jitney	202 X 308	9.42	6.00	.358	.294	.203	.117	.055
6½z	202 X 314	10.62	—	.404	.332	.229	.132	.062
Baby	208 X 211	9.32	6.00	.354	.291	.201	.116	.055
4z Pimento	211 X 200	7.18	4.90	.273	.224	.155	.089	.042
211 Baby Food	211 X 200	10.38	4.90	.395	.324	.223	.129	.061
4z Mushroom	211 X 212	11.19	7.15	.423	.348	.239	.138	.065
8z Short	211 X 300	12.34	7.90	.469	.386	.266	.153	.072
8z Tall	211 X 304	13.48	8.65	.512	.421	.291	.167	.079
No. 1 Picnic	211 X 400	17.06	10.90	.648	.533	.367	.212	.100
211 Cylinder (12r)	211 X 414	21.28	13.55	.809	.665	.455	.264	.125
Pint Olive	211 X 600	26.47	16.95	1.006	.827	.570	.329	.155
4z Flat Pimento	300 X 108	5.59	4.20	.212	.175	.120	.069	.033
7z Pimento	300 X 206	11.37	7.50	.432	.355	.245	.141	.067
	300 X 308	18.03	11.70	.685	.563	.383	.224	.106
No. 1 Square	300 X 308 X 308	26.96	—	1.025	.843	.580	.335	.158
No. 2½ Square	300 X 308 X 604	50.68	—	1.926	1.584	1.091	.629	.297
8z Mushroom	300 X 400	21.11	13.55	.802	.660	.545	.262	.124
No. 300	300 X 407	23.71	15.20	.901	.741	.511	.294	.139
No. 300 Cylinder	300 X 509	30.17	19.40	1.147	.943	.651	.375	.177
No. 1 Tall	301 X 411	25.99	16.60	.988	.812	.561	.323	.152
No. 303	303 X 406	26.31	16.85	1.000	.822	.566	.327	.154
No. 303 Cylinder	303 X 509	34.11	21.85	1.296	1.066	.734	.424	.200
No. 1 Flat	307 X 203	13.21	8.90	.502	.413	.298	.164	.077
No. 2 Flat	307 X 204	14.40	9.20	.547	.450	.310	.179	.084
Kitchenette	307 X 214	19.17	12.25	.729	.599	.413	.238	.112
No. 2 Squat	307 X 302	21.06	13.45	.800	.658	.453	.261	.123
No. 2 Vac. (12z Vac.)	307 X 306	22.90	14.70	.870	.716	.493	.284	.134
No. 95	307 X 400	27.63	17.75	1.050	.863	.595	.343	.162
No. 2	307 X 409	32.00	20.50	1.216	1.000	.689	.397	.187
No. 2 XT	307 X 506	38.30	—	1.456	1.197	.825	.476	.224
Jumbo	307 X 510	40.28	25.70	1.531	1.259	.867	.500	.286
No. 2 Cylinder	307 X 512	40.95	26.35	1.556	1.280	.886	.508	.240
No. 2 Tall	307 X 604	44.99	28.80	1.710	1.406	.969	.559	.264
29z	307 X 700	50.65	32.48	1.925	1.583	1.090	.629	.297
Quart Olive	307 X 704	52.62	33.70	2.000	1.644	1.133	.653	.308
32z (Quart)	307 X 710	55.43	35.54	2.107	1.732	1.193	.688	.325
	312 X 508	47.52	30.45	1.806	1.485	1.023	.590	.278
No. 1¼ (Veg.)	401 X 206	21.51	13.80	.818	.672	.463	.267	.126
No. 1¼ (Pineapple)	401 X 207.5	22.07	—	.839	.690	.475	.274	.129
No. 2½	401 X 411	46.45	29.75	1.765	1.452	1.000	.577	.272
No. 3 Vac	404 X 307	37.19	23.85	1.414	1.162	.801	.462	.218
No. 3	404 X 414	54.09	35.05	2.056	1.690	1.165	.672	.317
	404 X 506	60.80	38.95	2.311	1.900	1.309	.755	.356
No. 3 Cyl. (46z)	404 X 700	80.54	51.70	3.061	2.517	1.735	1.000	.472
No. 5	502 X 510	92.20	59.10	3.504	2.881	1.985	1.145	.540
No. 5 Squat	603 X 408	106.30	68.15	4.040	3.322	2.288	1.320	.623
No. 10	603 X 700	170.71	109.45	6.488	5.335	3.673	2.120	1.000
No. 12 (Gal.)	603 X 812	215.82	138.35	8.203	6.744	4.646	2.680	1.264
GLASS CONTAINERS								
8z		12.12	—	.461	0.379	0.261	.150	0.071
12z		18.18	—	.691	.568	.391	.226	.106
14z		21.21	—	.906	.663	.457	.263	.124
16z (No. 303 or 1 lb. jar)		27.97	—	1.063	.874	.602	.347	.164
30z No. 2½		48.06	—	1.827	1.502	1.035	.597	.282
32z		53.02	—	2.015	1.657	1.143	.658	.312
64z		115.20	—	4.390	3.069	2.487	1.434	.677
128z (1 gal. jug)		231.00	—	8.780	7.219	4.973	2.868	1.353

Instructions: To convert a given quantity of cans, glass jars or bottles of the size listed in column 1 to No. 303's, 2's, 2½'s or 10's *multiply* by corresponding factor in columns 5, 6, 7 and 8. To convert *from* 303's, 2's, 2½'s or 10's to a particular size in column 1, *divide* by corresponding factor. The equivalents are based on a comparison of minimum volume fill in cubic inches.

Source: National Canners Association and Agricultural Marketing Service.

Cans, Equivalent Sizes

TABLE 2.C.10
Case equivalents of various sizes of cans: The following table gives the equivalent in cases of 24 No. 303, 24 No. 2, 24 No. 2½, and 6 No. 10 cans of the more commonly used cans.

Case of		No. 303 equiv. cases	No. 2 equiv. cases	No. 2½ equiv. cases	No. 10 equiv. cases	Case of:		No. 303 equiv. cases	No. 2 equiv. cases	No. 2½ equiv. cases	No. 10 equiv. cases
48 6Z	=		.72	.59	.41	.441	24 #303	=	.....	.82	.57	.616
48 8Z Tall	=		1.03	.84	.58	.632	36 #303	=	1.50	1.23	.85	.924
24 8Z Tall	=		.512	.421	.290	.316	24 12Z Vac.	=	.87	.72	.49	.536
24 8Z Short	=		.469	.386	.266	.289	24 #2 Vac.	=	.87	.72	.49	.536
48 8Z Short	=		.94	.77	.53	.576	24 #2	=	1.22	.....	.69	.748
48 #1 Flat	=		1.05	.87	.60	.619	24 #2 Cyl.	=	1.56	1.284	.89	.960
48 #1 Pic.	=		1.30	1.06	.73	.800	24 #2½	=	1.77	1.45	....	1.088
24 #1 Tall	=		.99	.81	.56	.609	24 #3	=	2.08	1.71	1.16	1.268
48 #1 Tall	=		1.97	1.63	1.12	1.216	24 #3 Vac.	=	1.42	1.16	.80	.871
24 #1 Sqr.	=		1.02	.84	.58	.732	12 #29Z	=	.96	.79	.55	.593
24 #211 Cyl.	=		.80	.66	.46	.499	12 #32Z	=	1.05	.86	.60	.649
48 #211 Cyl.	=		1.61	1.32	.91	1.000	12 #3 Cyl.	=	1.53	1.26	.87	.944
24 #300	=		.90	.74	.51	.556	6 #10	=	1.62	1.33	.92	.....
24 #300 Cyl.	=		1.15	.94	.65	.707	6 #5 Squat	=	1.01	.83	.57	.623

The capacity of a 16 oz. and No. 2½ glass jar is approximately the same as the No. 303 and No. 2½ can respectively.

Source: The Almanac of the Canning, Freezing, Preserving Industries, 58th Edition. (1973). E. E. Judge & Son, Baltimore.

Cans, Sizes

TABLE 2.C.11
Dimensions and capacities of can sizes

Name	Dimensions	Total Capacity, avoir. oz. of Water at 68° F	No. 2 Can Equivalent
6Z	202 x 308	6.08	0.295
8Z Short	211 x 300	7.93	0.386
8Z Tall	211 x 304	8.68	0.422
No. 1 (Picnic)	211 x 400	10.94	0.532
No. 211 Cylinder	211 x 414	13.56	0.660
No. 300	300 x 407	15.22	0.741
No. 300 Cylinder	300 x 509	19.4	0.945
No. 1 Tall	301 x 411	16.70	0.813
No. 303	303 x 406	16.88	0.821
No. 303 Cylinder	303 x 509	21.86	1.060
No. 2 Vacuum	307 x 306	14.71	0.716
No. 2	307 x 409	20.55	1.000
Jumbo	307 x 510	25.8	1.2537
No. 2 Cylinder	307 x 512	26.4	1.284
No. 1¼	401 x 206	13.81	0.672
No. 2½	401 x 411	29.79	1.450
No. 3 Vacuum	404 x 307	23.9	1.162
No. 3 Cylinder	404 x 700	51.7	2.515
No. 5	502 x 510	59.1	2.8744
No. 10	603 x 700	109.43	5.325

Source: F. W. Green Co. (editor) (1967). *Glossary of Packaging Terms*, 4th Edition. Packaging Institute, New York.

Carbon Dioxide Dissolved in Water

TABLE 2.C.12
Gas volume test chart (showing volumes of carbon dioxide dissolved by 1 volume of water)

Gage pressures in bottle, lbs. per sq. in.

Temp °F in bottle	16[a]	18	20	22	24	26	28	30	32	34	36	38	40	42	44	46	48	50	52	54	56	58	60	62	64
45	2.7	2.9	3.1	3.3	3.4	3.6	3.8	4.0	4.1	4.3	4.5	4.7	4.8	5.0	5.2	5.4	5.6	5.7	5.9	6.1	6.2	6.4	6.6	6.8	6.9
46	2.7	2.8	3.0	3.2	3.4	3.5	3.7	3.9	4.0	4.3	4.4	4.6	4.7	4.9	5.1	5.3	5.4	5.6	5.8	6.0	6.1	6.3	6.4	6.6	6.8
47	2.6	2.8	2.9	3.1	3.3	3.5	3.6	3.8	4.0	4.1	4.4	4.5	4.6	4.8	5.0	5.3	5.4	5.6	5.8	5.9	6.1	6.3	6.3	6.5	6.7
48	2.6	2.7	2.9	3.1	3.2	3.4	3.6	3.7	3.9	4.1	4.2	4.5	4.6	4.8	5.0	5.2	5.3	5.5	5.7	5.9	6.0	6.2	6.3	6.5	6.6
49	2.5	2.7	2.8	3.0	3.2	3.3	3.5	3.6	3.8	4.0	4.2	4.4	4.6	4.7	4.9	5.1	5.2	5.4	5.6	5.7	5.9	6.1	6.2	6.4	6.6
50	2.5	2.6	2.8	3.0	3.1	3.3	3.5	3.6	3.8	3.9	4.1	4.3	4.5	4.6	4.8	5.0	5.1	5.3	5.5	5.6	5.8	6.0	6.1	6.3	6.4
51	2.4	2.6	2.7	2.9	3.1	3.3	3.4	3.6	3.7	3.9	4.1	4.2	4.4	4.5	4.7	4.9	5.0	5.2	5.4	5.5	5.7	5.9	6.0	6.2	6.3
52	2.4	2.5	2.7	2.8	3.0	3.2	3.3	3.5	3.6	3.8	4.0	4.2	4.4	4.5	4.7	4.8	5.0	5.2	5.3	5.5	5.6	5.7	5.9	6.1	6.2
53	2.3	2.5	2.6	2.8	3.0	3.1	3.3	3.5	3.6	3.7	3.9	4.1	4.3	4.4	4.6	4.7	4.9	5.0	5.2	5.3	5.5	5.6	5.8	5.9	6.1
54	2.3	2.4	2.6	2.7	2.9	3.1	3.3	3.4	3.5	3.6	3.8	4.0	4.2	4.3	4.5	4.6	4.8	4.9	5.1	5.2	5.4	5.5	5.7	5.9	6.0
55	2.3	2.4	2.6	2.7	2.8	3.0	3.1	3.3	3.4	3.6	3.7	3.9	4.1	4.2	4.4	4.5	4.7	4.8	5.0	5.1	5.3	5.4	5.6	5.7	5.9
56	2.2	2.4	2.5	2.6	2.8	2.9	3.2	3.2	3.3	3.5	3.7	3.8	3.9	4.1	4.3	4.4	4.5	4.7	4.9	5.0	5.2	5.3	5.5	5.6	5.8
57	2.2	2.3	2.5	2.6	2.8	2.9	3.1	3.2	3.3	3.4	3.6	3.7	3.9	4.0	4.2	4.4	4.5	4.6	4.8	5.0	5.1	5.2	5.4	5.5	5.7
58	2.1	2.3	2.4	2.6	2.7	2.8	3.0	3.1	3.3	3.4	3.5	3.7	3.8	3.9	4.1	4.3	4.4	4.5	4.7	4.9	5.0	5.2	5.3	5.4	5.6
59	2.1	2.2	2.4	2.5	2.6	2.8	2.9	3.1	3.2	3.3	3.5	3.6	3.8	3.9	4.1	4.2	4.3	4.5	4.6	4.8	5.0	5.1	5.2	5.3	5.5
60	2.1	2.2	2.3	2.4	2.6	2.7	2.9	3.0	3.1	3.2	3.4	3.6	3.7	3.8	4.0	4.1	4.3	4.4	4.6	4.7	4.9	5.0	5.2	5.3	5.4
61	2.0	2.1	2.3	2.4	2.5	2.7	2.8	2.9	3.1	3.2	3.3	3.5	3.6	3.7	3.9	4.0	4.2	4.3	4.4	4.6	4.8	4.9	5.0	5.2	5.3
62	2.0	2.1	2.2	2.4	2.5	2.6	2.8	2.9	3.0	3.2	3.3	3.4	3.6	3.7	3.8	4.0	4.1	4.2	4.4	4.5	4.7	4.8	4.9	5.1	5.2
63	2.0	2.1	2.2	2.3	2.4	2.6	2.7	2.9	3.0	3.1	3.2	3.4	3.5	3.6	3.8	3.9	4.0	4.2	4.3	4.4	4.6	4.7	4.8	5.0	5.1
64	1.9	2.0	2.2	2.3	2.4	2.5	2.7	2.8	2.9	3.1	3.2	3.3	3.5	3.6	3.8	3.9	4.0	4.1	4.2	4.4	4.5	4.7	4.8	4.9	5.0
65	1.9	2.0	2.1	2.2	2.4	2.5	2.6	2.8	2.9	3.0	3.1	3.3	3.4	3.5	3.6	3.8	3.9	4.1	4.2	4.3	4.4	4.6	4.8	4.7	4.9
66	1.9	2.0	2.1	2.2	2.3	2.5	2.6	2.7	2.8	3.0	3.1	3.2	3.3	3.5	3.6	3.7	3.8	4.0	4.1	4.2	4.3	4.5	4.6	4.7	4.8
67	1.8	2.0	2.1	2.2	2.3	2.4	2.6	2.7	2.8	2.9	3.0	3.2	3.3	3.4	3.5	3.7	3.8	3.9	4.0	4.2	4.3	4.4	4.5	4.7	4.8
68	1.8	1.9	2.0	2.1	2.3	2.4	2.5	2.6	2.7	2.9	3.0	3.1	3.3	3.3	3.5	3.6	3.7	3.8	3.9	4.1	4.2	4.3	4.4	4.6	4.7
69	1.8	1.9	2.0	2.1	2.2	2.4	2.5	2.6	2.7	2.8	3.0	3.1	3.2	3.3	3.4	3.6	3.7	3.8	3.9	4.0	4.2	4.3	4.4	4.5	4.6
70	1.7	1.8	2.0	2.1	2.2	2.3	2.4	2.5	2.7	2.8	2.9	3.0	3.1	3.3	3.4	3.5	3.6	3.8	3.9	4.0	4.1	4.2	4.3	4.4	4.5
71	1.7	1.8	1.9	2.1	2.2	2.3	2.4	2.5	2.6	2.7	2.9	3.0	3.1	3.2	3.3	3.4	3.6	3.7	3.8	3.9	4.0	4.1	4.2	4.3	4.5
72	1.7	1.8	2.0	2.0	2.2	2.2	2.4	2.5	2.6	2.7	2.8	2.9	3.0	3.2	3.3	3.4	3.5	3.6	3.7	3.8	4.0	4.1	4.2	4.3	4.4
73	1.7	1.8	1.9	2.0	2.1	2.2	2.3	2.4	2.5	2.6	2.8	2.9	3.0	3.1	3.2	3.3	3.4	3.5	3.7	3.8	3.9	4.0	4.1	4.2	4.3
74	1.6	1.7	1.8	2.0	2.1	2.2	2.3	2.4	2.5	2.6	2.7	2.8	2.9	3.0	3.2	3.3	3.4	3.5	3.6	3.7	3.8	3.9	4.0	4.1	4.2
75	1.6	1.7	1.8	1.9	2.0	2.1	2.3	2.4	2.4	2.5	2.6	2.7	2.9	3.0	3.1	3.2	3.3	3.4	3.5	3.6	3.7	3.8	3.9	4.0	4.1
76	1.6	1.7	1.8	1.9	2.0	2.1	2.2	2.3	2.4	2.5	2.6	2.7	2.8	2.9	3.0	3.1	3.3	3.4	3.5	3.6	3.7	3.8	3.9	4.0	4.1
77	1.6	1.7	1.8	1.9	2.0	2.1	2.2	2.3	2.4	2.5	2.5	2.7	2.8	2.9	3.0	3.1	3.2	3.3	3.4	3.5	3.6	3.7	3.8	3.9	4.0
78	1.5	1.6	1.7	1.8	2.0	2.0	2.1	2.3	2.3	2.4	2.6	2.6	2.7	2.8	2.9	3.0	3.1	3.3	3.3	3.4	3.5	3.7	3.8	3.9	4.0
79	1.5	1.6	1.7	1.8	1.9	2.0	2.1	2.2	2.3	2.4	2.5	2.6	2.7	2.7	2.9	3.0	3.1	3.2	3.3	3.4	3.5	3.6	3.7	3.3	3.9

[a]Figures in this column represent the volume of carbon dioxide gas (reduced to 0° and 760 mm.) dissolved by 1 volume of water at the temperatures indicated, if the partial pressure of the carbon dioxide gas is 760 mm. Hg. Solubility data correspond to Bohr and Bock published in Landolt-Börnstein, *Physikalische-Chemische Tabellen*. Figures in the body of the table were calculated for various temperatures and pressures based on the Boyle-Mariotte law for isothermal compression.

Source: Jacobs, M. B. (editor). *The Chemistry and Technology of Food and Food Products*, 2d Edition, Vol. 3. John Wiley & Sons, New York.

Carbon Dioxide, Weight and Volume

TABLE 2.C.13
Carbon dioxide, weight and volume

At Standard Temp and Pressure

One Cubic Foot Equals	0.1227 lb
One Cubic Foot Equals	957.5 oz
One Gram Equals	506 ml
One Liter Equals	1.976 gm
One Liter Equals	0.3532 cu ft
One Milliliter Equals	0.00198 gm
One Ounce Equals	0.0584 gm
One Pound Equals	8.1499 cu ft
One Pound Equals	7803.85 oz

Percent CO_2 by volume x 0.19428 Equals approximate percent by weight.
Percent CO_2 by weight x 5.1470 Equals approximate percent by volume

Source: Woodroof, J. G., and Phillips, G. F. (editors) (1974). In *Beverages: Carbonated and Noncarbonated*. AVI Publishing Co., Westport, Connecticut.

Casings, Animal

TABLE 2.C.14
Animal casings

Casing	Source
Rounds	Small intestine of cattle, sheep, goats, and pigs
Runners	Small intestines of cattle
Middles	Large intestines of cattle and pigs
Beef bungs	Caecum (blind gut)
Hog bungs	End of the intestinal tract, usually 5 to 6 ft of intestines, starting from the anus
Caps	Caecum or blind gut of the hog
Weasands	Esophagus of cattle
Bladders	Urinary bladder of cattle or hogs
Stomachs	Hog stomach, often called maws
Small casings	Small intestines of hogs, sheep, or goats

Source: Kramlich, W. E., Pearson, A. M., and Tauber, F. W. (editors) (1973). Sausages. In *Processed Meats*. AVI Publishing Co., Westport, Connecticut.

Casings, Hog

TABLE 2.C.15
Hog casings—sizes

Grades	Millimeters
Extra narrow	Under 28
Narrow medium	28 to 32
Selected medium	32 to 35
English medium	35 to 38
Wides	38 to 42
Extra wides	42 and over

Source: MacKenzie, D. S. *Prepared Meat Product Manufacturing.* American Meat Institute, Arlington, Virginia.

Casings, Hog and Beef

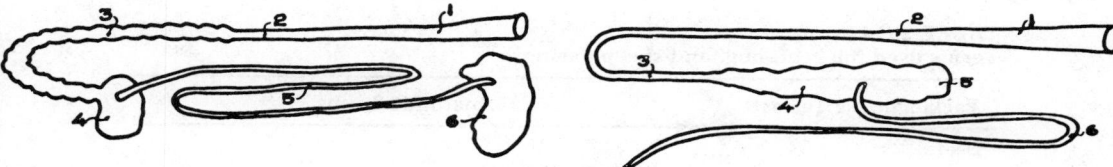

FIGURE 2.C.6
Hog casings (left): 1) bung; 2) second end; 3) middle; 4) cap; 5) small casing; 6) stomach. Beef casings (right): 1) fat end; 2) wide middle; 3) narrow middle; 4) bung; 5) blind end; 6) round

Source: Moulton, C. R., and Lewis, W. L. *Meat Through The Microscope,* Revised Edition. Institute of Meat Packing, The University of Chicago, Chicago.

Casings, Hog Bungs

TABLE 2.C.16
Hog bung casings—sizes

Grade	Width, Inches	No. of Pieces to a Tierce
Exports	2⅛ and over	400
Large primes	1¹⁵⁄₁₆ to 2⅛	500
Medium primes	1¹²⁄₁₆ to 1¹⁵⁄₁₆	550
Special primes	1⁹⁄₁₆ to 1¹²⁄₁₆	580
Small primes	1⁷⁄₁₆ to 1⁹⁄₁₆	600
Skips	1⁴⁄₁₆ to 1⁷⁄₁₆	700
No. 1 broken shorts—large and export primes		800
No. 2 broken shorts—all others except broken skips which are thrown away		1,050

Source: MacKenzie, D. S. *Prepared Meat Product Manufacturing.* American Meat Institute, Arlington, Virginia.

Casings, Sheep

TABLE 2.C.17
Sheep casings—sizes

Classification	Diameter (mm)	Length of Hank (yards)
Narrow	16–18	100
Narrow mediums	18–20	100
Special mediums	20–22	100
Wide	22–24	100
Extra wide	24–26	100

Source: MacKenzie, D. S. *Prepared Meat Product Manufacturing.* American Meat Institute, Arlington, Virginia.

Casings, Terms

TABLE 2.C.18
Terms used for beef, hog, and sheep casings

Packinghouse Terms	Anatomic Terms
Beef:	
Fat end	Rectum, anal end
Wide middle	Rectum, colonic end
Narrow middle } Middle	Colon
Bung Bung gut	Cecum
Blind end of bung } Cap	Cecum, blind end of, below ileoceal valve
Round	Small intestine, including duodenum, jejunum, and ileum
Weasand	Esophagus
Rennet	Omasum, or true stomach
Bladder	Urinary bladder
Hog:	
Bung	Rectum, anal end
Second end	Rectum, colonic end
Cap	Cecum
Casing Small casing }	Small intestine: duodenum, jejunum, and ileum
Middle Black gut Chitterling }	Colon
Bladder	Urinary bladder
Rennet	Stomach
Sheep	
Casing	Small intestine: duodenum, jejunum, and ileum

Source: Moulton, C. R., and Lewis, W. L. *Meat Through the Microscope*, Revised Edition. Institute of Meat Packing, University of Chicago, Chicago.

Cattle

TABLE 2.C.19
Market classes and grades

Cattle or Calves	Use Selection	Sex Classes	Age Wt. (Group)	Weight Divisions (lbs.)	(kg)	Commonly Used Grades
Cattle	Slaughter Cattle	Steers — Yearlings	Light / Medium / Heavy	800 down / 800–1000 / 1000 up	362.9 down / 362.9–453.6 / 453.6 up	Prime, Choice, Good, Standard, Commercial, Utility, Cutter, Canner
		Steers — 2-year-old and over	Light / Medium / Heavy	1100 down / 1100–1300 / 1300 up	499.4 down / 499.4–590.2 / 590.2 up	Prime, Choice, Good, Standard, Commercial, Utility, Cutter, Canner
		Heifers — Yearlings	Light / Medium / Heavy	750 down / 750–900 / 900 up	340.5 down / 340.5–408.6 / 408.6 up	Prime, Choice, Good, Standard, Utility, Cutter, Canner
		Heifers — 2-year-old and over	Light / Medium / Heavy	900 down / 900–1050 / 1050 up	408.6 down / 408.6–476.7 / 476.6 up	Prime, Choice, Good, Standard, Commercial, Cutter, Canner
		Cows	All ages	All weights		Choice, Good, Standard, Commercial, Utility, Cutter, Canner
		Bullocks (often called "beef" or "butcher" bulls & lower grades bologna bulls) — Yearlings	All weights			Prime, Choice, Good, Standard, Utility
		Bullocks — 2-year-old and over	Light / Medium / Heavy	1300 down / 1300–1500 / 1500 up	590.2 down / 590.2–681.0 / 681.0 up	Not quality graded but may be yield graded
		Stags	All ages	All weights		Choice, Good, Commercial, Utility, Cutter, Canner
	Feeder Cattle[1]	Steers — Yearlings	Light / Medium / Heavy / Mixed			Prime, Choice, Good, Standard, Commercial, Utility, Inferior
		Steers — 2-year-old and over	Light / Medium / Heavy / Mixed			Prime, Choice, Good, Standard, Commercial, Utility, Inferior
		Heifers — Yearlings	Light / Medium / Heavy / Mixed			Prime, Choice, Good, Standard, Commercial, Utility, Inferior
		Heifers — 2-year-old and over	Light / Medium / Heavy / Mixed			Prime, Choice, Good, Standard, Commercial, Utility, Inferior
		Cows	All ages	All weights		Prime, Choice, Good, Commercial, Utility, Inferior
		Bullocks	All ages	All weights		Ungraded
		Stags	All ages	All weights		Ungraded
	Milkers & Springers	Cows (milkers or springers)	All ages	All weights		Ungraded
Calves	Vealers	No Sex Class (Sex characteristics of no importance at this age)	Under 3 months	Light / Medium / Heavy	110 down / 110–180 / 180 up	49.9 down / 49.9–81.7 / 81.7 up	Prime, Choice, Good, Standard, Utility, Cull
	Slaughter Calves	Steers / Heifers / Bullocks	3 months to 1 year	Light / Medium / Heavy	200 down / 200–300 / 300 up	90.8 down / 90.8–136.2 / 136.2 up	Prime, Choice, Good Standard, Utility, Cull
	Feeder Calves	Steers / Heifers / Bullocks	Usually 6 mo. to 1 year	Light / Medium / Heavy / Mixed			Prime, Choice, Good, Standard, Utility, Inferior

NOTE: In addition to the above quality grades, there are the following yield grades: Yield Grade 1, Yield Grade 2, Yield Grade 3, Yield Grade 4, and Yield Grade 5. Thus, slaughter cattle may be graded for (1) quality alone, (2) yield grade alone, or (3) both quality and yield grades.
[1] Tentative standards proposed by USDA. Not official but widely used for many years and updated by 1977 USDA Grade Standards.

Source: Ensminger, M. E. (1969). *Animal Science*. Interstate Printers & Publishers, Danville, Illinois.

Cellulose Formula

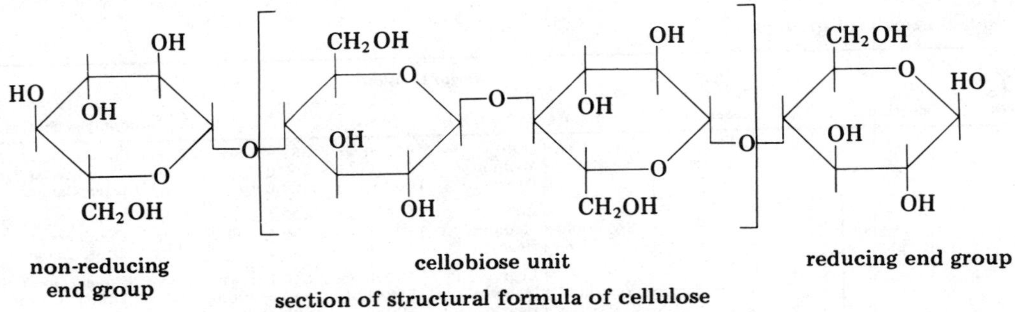
OH
HO
OH
CH₂OH
CH₂OH
OH
OH
OH
CH₂OH
CH₂OH
HO
OH
OH
O
non-reducing end group
cellobiose unit
reducing end group

section of structural formula of cellulose

FIGURE 2.C.7

Source: Braverman, J. B. S. *Introduction to the Biochemistry of Foods*. ASP Biological and Medical Press (Elsevier Division), London, England.

Cereal By-Products Composition

TABLE 2.C.20
Percentage composition of some cereal by-products

Feeding Stuff	Dry Matter	Ash	Crude Protein	Crude Fiber	Crude Lipide	N-free Extract
Brewer's grains	92.9	3.6	27.6	14.3	6.5	40.9
Corn gluten feed	90.9	6.3	25.5	7.6	2.7	48.8
Distiller's corn grains	92.9	2.5	28.3	11.4	8.8	41.9
Distiller's corn solubles	93.0	7.4	26.7	2.6	7.9	48.4
Winter wheat bran	89.9	6.2	15.5	8.9	4.2	55.1
Wheat middlings	89.7	4.5	18.0	7.4	4.7	55.1

Source: Mallette, M. F., Althouse, P. M., and Clagett, C. O. (1960). *Biochemistry of Plants and Animals*. John Wiley & Sons, New York.

Cereal Composition

TABLE 2.C.21
Composition of the edible portion (E.P.) and refuse in the material as purchased (A.P.)

Commodity and Description	Water	Protein	Fat	Carbohydrate Total (by Dif.)	Fiber	Ash	Calories (No. per 100 g)	Extraction Rate	Notes: Can Apply to Other Extraction Rates:	Refuse in A.P. (Percent)
	Percent of Edible Portion							Percent		
CEREALS										
Wheat, Medium[1] (or unspecified)										
Whole meal or flour	12	12.2	2.3	71.8	2.1	1.7	334	100	94 to 100	0
Flour, medium extraction	12	11.7	1.5	74.3	0.5	0.5	350	85	80 to 93	0
Flour, white, low extraction	12	10.9	1.1	75.5	0.3	0.5	370	72	Less than 80	0
Wheat, Hard[1]										
Whole meal or flour	12	13.8	2.0	70.2	2.4	2.0	332	100	94 to 100	0
Flour, medium extraction	12	13.4	1.4	72.7	0.4	0.5	350	85	80 to 93	0
Flour, white, low extraction	12	12.7	1.1	73.7	0.3	0.5	364	72	Less than 80	0
Wheat, Soft[1]										
Whole meal or flour	12	10.5	1.9	73.9	2.1	1.7	333	100	94 to 100	0
Flour, medium extraction	12	9.8	1.3	76.2	0.4	0.7	349	85	80 to 93	0
Flour, white, low extraction	12	8.6	1.1	77.9	0.2	0.4	365	72	Less than 80	0
Rice										
Husked or brown (only hulls removed)	13	7.5	1.8	76.7	0.8	1.0	357	80	75 to 82	0
Home-pounded, undermilled, parboiled	13	7.1	1.1	78.0	0.7	0.8	359	70	68 to 74	0
Milled, white	13	6.7	0.7	78.9	0.4	0.7	360	65	Less than 68	0
Rye										
Whole meal, dark flour	12	11	1.9	73.1	2.0	2.0	319	100	94 to 100	0
Flour, medium extraction	12	9	1.8	76.2	1.5	1.0	341	85	80 to 93	0
Flour, light, low extraction	12	7	1.2	79.1	0.9	0.7	349	70	Less than 80	0
Barley										
Whole seed, except hulls and groats	12	11	1.8	73.4	3.4	1.8	332	[2]65	60 to 70	0
Pearled, light or dark	12	9	1.4	76.5	0.8	1.1	346	[3]55	Less than 60	0
Oats										
Oatmeal, rolled oats	10	13	7.5	67.8	1.9	1.7	385	50	40 to 55	0
Maize (Corn)										
Grain or whole meal	12	9.5	4.3	72.9	2.1	1.3	356	100	97 to 100	0
Meal, coarse, bolted	12	9.3	4.0	73.5	1.4	1.2	360	93	90 to 96	0
Meal, fine, bolted and degerminated	12	8.4	1.2	77.8	0.5	0.6	363	85	Less than 90	0

(Continued)

Cereal Composition   (Continued)

TABLE 2.C.21 (Continued)

Commodity and Description	Water	Protein	Fat	Carbohydrate Total (by Dif.)	Fiber	Ash	Calories (No. per 100 g)	Extraction Rate	Notes: Can Apply to Other Extraction Rates:	Refuse in A.P. (Percent)
	Percent of Edible Portion							Percent		
CEREALS										
Buckwheat										
Hulled, groats, dark flour	13	11	2	72.4	1	1.6	330	(90)	85 to 100	0
Light flour	13	6.4	1.2	78.5	0.4	0.9	344	(60)	Less than 85	0
*Quinoa (*Chenopodium quinoa*)										
Whole seeds	12	12	5	68	6	3	342	100	90 to 100	0
Flour	12	11	4	71	3	2	341	(85)	Less than 90	0
Sorghum (*Sorghum vulgare*)	11	10.1	3.3	73.8	1.7	1.8	343	90	All rates	0
Millet										
Ragi (*Eleusine coracana*)	11	6.5	1.7	78.0	2.6	2.8	332	90	All rates	0
Foxtail (*Setaria italica*)	11	9.8	3.0	74.7	2.0	1.5	343	90	All rates	0
Proso (*Panicum miliaceum*)	11	11.8	2.4	72.8	2.2	2.0	338	90	All rates	0
Pearl or bajra (*Pennisetum glaucum*)	11	11.7	4.7	70.5	1.9	2.1	348	90	All rates	0
Unspecified millets	11	9.7	3.0	74.1	2.7	2.2	340	90	All rates	0
Hominy, Samp, Maize Grits	12	8.4	0.7	78.5	0.4	0.4	361	52	All rates	0
Macaroni, Spaghetti, Wheat Pastes	11	11	1.1	76.3	0.5	0.6	367	(69)	All rates	0
Farina, Semolina	Calculate composition from wheat flour, Item No. 3, 6, or 9.									
Mixed Grains, Meslin	Calculate from specific components, each country.									
Spelt	Calculate from wheat, according to extraction used.									

*More information needed.

[1]Medium wheat in this table is considered to have between 13.4% and 15.0% protein (as N X 5.83) on the water-free basis; soft wheat is considered to have less than 13.4% and hard wheat, more than 15.0% on the same basis.

[2]That is, 65% of common varieties. Of the naked or hull-less varieties, the corresponding extraction is 100% and the figures can apply to any extraction over 90%.

[3]That is, 55% of common varieties. Of the naked or hull-less varieties, the corresponding extraction is 85% and the figures can apply to any extraction under 90%.

Source: Chatfield, C. *Food Composition Tables for International Use.* Food and Agriculture Organization, United Nations, Rome.

Cereal Enrichment

TABLE 2.C.22
Review of cereal enrichment in the United States[1]

Product	B-1 Thiamin Min (mg/lb)	B-1 Thiamin Max (mg/lb)	B-2 Riboflavin Min (mg/lb)	B-2 Riboflavin Max (mg/lb)	Niacin Min (mg/lb)	Niacin Max (mg/lb)	Iron Min (mg/lb)	Iron Max (mg/lb)	Code No. Fed. Reg.
Enriched bread, or other baked products	1.1	1.8	0.7	1.6	10.0	15.0	8.0	12.5	17.2
Enriched flour[2]	2.0	2.5	1.2	1.5	16.0	20.0	13.0	16.5	15.1
Enriched farina	2.0	2.5	1.2	1.5	16.0	20.0	13.0	—	15.140
Enriched maca-roni products	4.0	5.0	1.7	2.2	27.0	34.0	13.0	16.5	16.9
Enriched noodle products	4.0	5.0	1.7	2.2	27.0	34.0	13.0	16.5	16.10
Enriched corn meals	2.0	3.0	1.2	1.8	16.0	24.0	13.0	26.0	15.513
Enriched corn grits[3]	2.0	3.0	1.2	1.8	16.0	24.0	13.0	26.0	15.514
Enriched milled white rice[3]	2.0	4.0	1.2	2.4	16.0	32.0	13.0	26.0	15.525

[1] Further information, including levels of optional ingredients, are given in Code of Federal Regulations, Title 21, Chapter 1 (1968), Superintendent of Documents, U.S. Government Printing Office, Washington, D.C. 20402.
[2] In enriched self-rising flour, calcium is also required between limits of 500 and 1500 mg per lb.
[3] Levels must not fall below 85% of levels shown after washing and rinsing.

Source: Milner, M. (editor) (1969). *Protein-Enriched Cereal Foods for World Needs.* American Association of Cereal Chemists, St. Paul, Minnesota.

Cereal Fortification

TABLE 2.C.23
Recommended[1] fortification per pound of cereal grain[2]

	Wheat	Flour	Rice	Corn	Millet	Sorghum	Barley	Universal Premix Cereals[3]
Vitamin A (IU)	5,000	5,000	7,600	3,500	5,000	5,000	5,000	5,000
Vitamin E (mg)	26	29	25	18	23	23	23	28
Thiamin (mg)	0	1.0	1.8	—	—	—	0.8	1.0
Riboflavin (mg)	0.8	1.0	2.0	1.0	—	0.7	1.0	1.0
Nicotinamide (mg)	0	10.5	18.0	7.0	6.0	—	3	10.0
Vitamin B-6 (mg)	0.6	1.8	1.4	0.3	1.0	1.1	0.9	1.0
Vitamin B-12 (mcg)	4	4	7.0	4	4	4	4	4.0
Folic acid (mcg)	218	364	400	364	—	—	0	200
Ascorbic acid (mg)	90	90	90	90	90	90	90	90
Calcium (g)	0.8	0.9	1.0	0.9	0.9	0.9	0.9	0.9
Iron (mg)	0	8	16	3	0	0	4	8.0
Iodine (mcg)	75	75	68	75	74	74	60	75
Phosphorus (mg)	0	400	760	0	0	0	200	400
Magnesium (mg)	0	160	270	0	0	0	0	50

[1] For grain-eating nations.
[2] Assume 300 g maximum consumed per day by children and 1 lb maximum by adults for all cereals except rice; assume child eats 200 g and adult 300 g of rice daily.
[3] Excluding rice.

Source: Milner, M. (editor) (1969). *Protein-Enriched Cereal Foods for World Needs.* American Association of Cereal Chemists, St. Paul, Minnesota.

Cereal, Nutrient Content

TABLE 2.C.24
Calorie and nutrient content of wheat and other cereals[1]

Cereal	Water	Calories	Protein[2]	Fat	Total carbo-hydrate (incl. fibre)	Calcium	Iron	Thiamin	Riboflavin	Nicotinic acid
	Grammes		.... *Grammes*			.... *Milligrammes*				
Wheat (hard)	12	332	13.8	2.0	70	37	4.1	0.45	0.13	5.4
Wheat (soft)	12	333	10.5	1.9	74	35	3.9	0.38	0.08	4.3
Rice	13	357	7.5	1.8	77	15	1.4	0.33	0.05	4.6
Maize	12	356	9.5	4.3	73	10	2.3	0.45	0.11	2.0
Barley	12	332	11.0	1.8	73	33	3.6	0.46	0.12	5.5
Rye	12	319	11.0	1.9	73	38	3.7	0.41	0.16	1.3
Oats	9	388	11.2	7.5	70	60	5.0	0.50	0.15	1.0
Sorghum	12	355	9.7	3.4	73	32	4.5	0.50	0.12	3.5
Millet, finger (*Eleusine corocana*)	12	336	5.6	1.5	78	350	5:0	0.30	0.10	1.4
Millet, bulrush (*Pen“nisetum americana*)	12	363	10.3	5.0	71	25	3.0	0.30	0.15	2.0

[1] Per 100 grammes. — [2] Protein content has been calculated by nitrogen × 5.83.

Source: Aykroyd, W. R., and Doughty, J. (1970). *Wheat in Human Nutrition*. FAO, United Nations, Rome.

Cereals, Vitamin and Mineral Content

TABLE 2.C.25
Vitamin and mineral content of various cereals[1]

	Nutrients per 350 g of Cereal Grains[2]							Recommended[3] Dietary Allowances	
	Whole Wheat	Wheat Flour	Rice	Corn	Millet	Sorghum	Barley	(1–3 yr of age)	Adults
Vitamin A (IU)	0	0	0	1,800	0	0	0	2,000	5,000
Vitamin D (IU)	—	—	—	—	—	—	—	400	—
Vitamin E (IU)	3.9	1.2	4.7	12	7.3	—	4.2	10	20–30
Thiamin (mg)	1.8	0.3	0.2	1.3	2.6	1.3	0.4	0.6	1.4
Riboflavin (mg)	0.4	0.2	0.1	0.4	1.3	0.5	0.2	0.7	1.4
Nicotinamide (mg)	15	3.5	6	7	8	14	11	8	17
Vitamin B-6 (mg)	1.4	0.2	1.4	1.7	—	—	0.9	0.6	2.0
Vitamin B-12 (mcg)	0.3	—	—	—	—	—	—	2.5	5.0
Folic acid (mcg)	140	28	—	25	—	—	50	100	400
Ascorbic acid (mg)	0	0	0	0	0	0	0	35	60
Calcium (mg)	160	55	85	70	70	100	55	800	800
Phosphorus (mg)	1,240	330	330	900	1,100	1,000	660	800	800
Magnesium (mg)	560	90	180	420	476	500[4]	600	150	350
Iron (mg)	12	3	3	8	24	15	7	10	14
Iodine (mcg)	15	14	14	15	16[4]	16[4]	32	60	100

[1] Data from report of President's Advisory Committee.
[2] Except for B-6 and E values.
[3] RDA reference.
[4] Estimated values.

Source: Milner, M. (editor) (1969). *Protein-Enriched Cereal Foods for World Needs*. American Association of Cereal Chemists, St. Paul, Minnesota.

Cheese Characteristics

TABLE 2.C.26
Characteristics of some popular varieties of natural cheeses

Kind or Name Place of Origin	Kind of Milk Used in Manufacture	Ripening or Curing Time	Flavor	Body and Texture	Color	Retail Packaging	Uses
Soft, Unripened Varieties							
Cottage, plain or creamed (Unknown)	Cow's milk skimmed; plain curd or plain curd with cream added.	Unripened	Mild, acid.	Soft, curd particles of varying size.	White to creamy white.	Cup-shaped containers, tumblers, dishes.	Salads, with fruits, vegetables, sandwiches, dips, cheese cake.
Cream, plain (U.S.A.)	Cream from cow's milk.	Unripened	Mild, acid.	Soft and smooth.	White.	3- to 8-oz. packages.	Salads, dips, sandwiches, snacks, cheese cake, desserts.
Neufchatel (Nû-shä-tel') (France)	Cow's milk.	Unripened	Mild, acid.	Soft, smooth similar to cream cheese but lower in milkfat.	White.	4- to 8-oz. packages.	Salads, dips, sandwiches, snacks, cheese cake, desserts.
Ricotta (Ri-cō'-ta) (Italy)	Cow's milk, whole or partly skimmed, or whey from cow's milk with whole or skim milk added. In Italy, whey from sheep's milk.	Unripened	Sweet, nutlike.	Soft, moist or dry.	White.	Pint and quart paper and plastic containers, 3-lb metal cans.	Appetizers, salads, snacks, lasagne, ravioli, noodles and other cooked dishes, grating, desserts.
Firm, Unripened Varieties							
Gjetost[1] (Yēt'ōst) (Norway)	Whey from goat's milk or a mixture of whey from goat's and cow's milk.	Unripened	Sweetish, caramel.	Firm, buttery consistency.	Golden brown.	Cubical and rectangular.	Snacks, desserts, served with dark breads, crackers, biscuits or muffins.
Mysost (Müs-ôst) also called Primost (Prēm'-ôst) (Norway)	Whey from cow's milk.	Unripened	Sweetish, caramel.	Firm, buttery consistency.	Light brown.	Cubical, cylindrical, pie-shaped wedges.	Snacks, desserts, served with dark breads.

(Continued)

Cheese Characteristics (Continued)

TABLE 2.C.26 (Continued)

Kind or Name Place of Origin	Kind of Milk Used in Manufacture	Ripening or Curing Time	Flavor	Body and Texture	Color	Retail Packaging	Uses
Mozzarella (Mō-tsa-rel'la) also called Scamorza (Italy)	Whole or partly skimmed cow's milk. In Italy, originally made from buffalo's milk.	Unripened	Delicate, mild.	Slightly firm, plastic.	Creamy white.	Small round or braided form, shredded, sliced.	Snacks, toasted sandwiches, cheeseburgers, cooking, as in meat loaf, or topping for lasagne, pizza, and casseroles.
Soft, Ripened Varieties							
Brie (Brē) (France)	Cow's milk.	4 to 8 weeks.	Mild to pungent.	Soft, smooth when ripened.	Creamy yellow interior; edible thin brown and white crust.	Circular, pie-shaped wedges.	Appetizers, sandwiches, snacks, good with crackers and fruit, dessert.
Camembert (Kăm'ĕm-bâr) (France)	Cow's milk.	4 to 8 weeks.	Mild to pungent.	Soft, smooth; very soft when fully ripened.	Creamy yellow interior; edible thin white, or gray-white crust.	Small circular cakes and pie-shaped portions.	Appetizers, sandwiches, snacks, good with crackers, and fruit such as pears, apples, dessert.
Limburger (Belgium)	Cow's milk.	4 to 8 weeks.	Highly pungent, very strong.	Soft, smooth when ripened; usually contains small irregular openings.	Creamy white interior; reddish yellow surface.	Cubical, rectangular.	Appetizers, snacks, good with crackers, rye or other dark breads, dessert.
Semisoft, Ripened Varieties							
Bel Paese[2] (Bĕl Pä-ā'-zĕ) (Italy)	Cow's milk.	6 to 8 weeks.	Mild to moderately robust.	Soft to medium firm, creamy.	Creamy yellow interior; slightly gray or brownish surface sometimes covered with yellow wax coating.	Small wheels, wedges, segments.	Appetizers, good with crackers, snacks, sandwiches, dessert.
Brick (U.S.A.)	Cow's milk.	2 to 4 months.	Mild to moderately sharp.	Semisoft to medium firm, elastic, numerous small mechanical openings.	Creamy yellow.[*]	Loaf, brick, slices, cut portions.	Appetizers, sandwiches, snacks, dessert.

(Continued)

Cheese Characteristics (Continued)

TABLE 2.C.26 (Continued)

Kind or Name Place of Origin	Kind of Milk Used in Manufacture	Ripening or Curing Time	Flavor	Body and Texture	Color	Retail Packaging	Uses
Muenster (Mün'stĕr) (Germany)	Cow's milk.	1 to 8 weeks.	Mild to mellow.	Semisoft, numerous small mechanical openings. Contains more moisture than brick.	Creamy white interior; yellow tan surface.	Circular cake, blocks, wedges, segments, slices.	Appetizers, sandwiches, snacks, dessert.
Port du Salut (Por dü Sá-lü´) (France)	Cow's milk.	6 to 8 weeks.	Mellow to robust.	Semisoft, smooth, buttery, small openings.	Creamy yellow.	Wheels and wedges.	Appetizers, snacks, served with raw fruit, dessert.
Firm Ripened Varieties							
Cheddar (England)	Cow's milk.	1 to 12 months or more.	Mild to very sharp.	Firm, smooth, some mechanical openings.	White to medium-yellow-orange.	Circular, cylindrical loaf, pie-shaped wedges, oblongs, slices, cubes, shredded, grated.	Appetizers, sandwiches, sauces, on vegetables, in hot dishes, toasted sandwiches, grating, cheeseburgers, dessert.
Colby (U.S.A.)	Cow's milk.	1 to 3 months.	Mild to mellow.	Softer and more open than Cheddar.	White to medium-yellow-orange.	Cylindrical, pie-shaped wedges.	Sandwiches, snacks cheeseburgers.
Caciocavallo (Kä´chō-kä-val´lō) (Italy)	Cow's milk. In Italy, cow's milk or mixtures of sheep's, goat's, and cow's milk.	3 to 12 months.	Piquant, similar to Provolone but not smoked.	Firm, lower in milkfat and moisture than Provolone.	Light or white interior; clay or tan colored surface.	Spindle or ten-pin shaped, bound with cord, cut pieces.	Snacks, sandwiches, cooking, dessert; suitable for grating after prolonged curing.
Edam (Ē´dăm) (Netherlands.)	Cow's milk, partly skimmed.	2 to 3 months.	Mellow, nutlike.	Semisoft to firm, smooth; small irregularly shaped or round holes; lower milkfat than Gouda.	Creamy yellow or medium yellow-orange interior; surface coated with red wax.	Cannon ball shaped loaf, cut pieces, oblongs.	Appetizers, snacks, salads, sandwiches, seafood sauces, dessert.

(Continued)

Cheese Characteristics   (Continued)

TABLE 2.C.26 (Continued)

Kind or Name Place of Origin	Kind of Milk Used in Manufacture	Ripening or Curing Time	Flavor	Body and Texture	Color	Retail Packaging	Uses
Gouda (Gou'-dá) (Netherlands)	Cow's milk, whole or partly skimmed.	2 to 6 months.	Mellow, nutlike.	Semisoft to firm, smooth; small irregularly shaped or round holes; higher milkfat than Edam.	Creamy yellow or medium yellow-orange interior; may or may not have red wax coating.	Ball shaped with flattened top and bottom.	Appetizers, snacks, salads, sandwiches, seafood sauces, dessert.
Provolone (Prō-vō-lō'-ně) also called smaller sizes and shapes called Provolette, Provoloncini (Italy)	Cow's milk.	2 to 12 months or more	Mellow to sharp, smoky, salty.	Firm, smooth.	Light creamy interior; light brown or golden yellow surface.	Pear shaped, sausage and salami shaped, wedges, slices.	Appetizers, sandwiches, snacks, souffle, macaroni and spaghetti dishes, pizza, suitable for grating when fully cured and dried.
Swiss, also called Emmentaler (Switzerland)	Cow's milk.	3 to 9 months.	Sweet, nutlike.	Firm, smooth with large round eyes.	Light yellow.	Segments, pieces, slices.	Sandwiches, snacks, sauces, fondue, cheeseburgers.
Very Hard Ripened Varieties							
Parmesan (Pàr'mě-zăn') also called Reggiano (Italy)	Partly skimmed cow's milk.	14 months to 2 years.	Sharp, piquant.	Very hard, granular, lower moisture and milkfat than Romano.	Creamy white.	Cylindrical, wedges, shredded, grated.	Grated for seasoning in soups, or vegetables, spaghetti, ravioli, breads, popcorn, used extensively in pizza and lasagne.
Romano (Rŏ-mä'-nō) also called Sardo Romano Pecorino Romano (Italy)	Cow's milk. In Italy, sheep's milk (Italian law).	5 to 12 months.	Sharp, piquant.	Very hard granular.	Yellowish-white interior, greenish-black surface.	Round with flat ends, wedges, shredded, grated.	Seasoning in soups, casserole dishes, ravioli, sauces, breads, suitable for grating when cured for about one year.

(Continued)

Cheese Characteristics (Continued)

TABLE 2.C.26 (Continued)

Kind or Name Place of Origin	Kind of Milk Used in Manufacture	Ripening or Curing Time	Flavor	Body and Texture	Color	Retail Packaging	Uses
Sap Sago[1] (Săp′-sä-gō) (Switzerland)	Skimmed cow's milk.	5 months or more.	Sharp, pungent cloverlike.	Very hard.	Light green by addition of dried, powdered clover leaves.	Conical, shakers.	Grated to flavor soups, meats, macaroni, spaghetti, hot vegetables; mixed with butter makes a good spread on crackers or bread.
Blue vein Mold-ripened Varieties							
Blue, spelled Bleu on imported cheese (France)	Cow's milk.	2 to 6 months.	Tangy, peppery.	Semisoft, pasty, sometimes crumbly.	White interior, marbled or streaked with blue veins of mold.	Cylindrical, wedges, oblongs, squares, cut portions.	Appetizers, salads, dips, salad dressing, sandwich spreads, good with crackers, dessert.
Gorgonzola (Gôr-gŏn-zō′-lä) (Italy)	Cow's milk. In Italy, cow's milk or goat's milk or mixtures of these.	3 to 12 months.	Tangy, peppery.	Semisoft, pasty, sometimes crumbly, lower moisture than Blue.	Creamy white interior, mottled or streaked with blue-green veins of mold. Clay colored surface.	Cylindrical, wedges, oblongs.	Appetizers, snacks, salads, dips, sandwich spread, good with crackers, dessert.
Roquefort[1] (Rŏk′-fĕrt) or (Rôk-fôr′) (France)	Sheep's milk.	2 to 5 months or more.	Sharp, slightly peppery.	Semisoft, pasty, sometimes crumbly.	White or creamy white interior, marbled or streaked with blue veins of mold.	Cylindrical, wedges.	Appetizers, snacks, salads, dips, sandwich spreads, good with crackers, dessert.
Stilton[1] (England)	Cow's milk.	2 to 6 months.	Piquant, milder than Gorgonzola or Roquefort.	Semisoft, flaky; slightly more crumbly than Blue.	Creamy white interior, marbled or streaked with blue-green veins of mold.	Circular, wedges, oblongs.	Appetizers, snacks, salads, dessert.

[1] Imported only.
[2] Italian trademark—licensed for manufacture in U.S.A.; also imported.

Source: USDA (1977). How to buy cheese. USDA Home and Garden Bull. 193.

Cheese Composition

TABLE 2.C.27
Composition of six cheeses representing different types

Cheese	Water (%)	Fat (%)	Protein (%)	Calcium (mg)	Vitamin A (Retinol) (μg)	Thiamin (mg)	Riboflavin (mg)	Nicotinic Acid (mg)
					per 100 g			
On the wet basis								
Cheddar	35.1	33.1	25.8	826	410	0.03	0.42	0.09
Emmental	34.9	30.5	27.4	1180	370	0.05	0.33	0.10
Edam	43.4	23.6	26.1	765	180	0.06	0.35	0.07
Camembert	51.3	22.8	18.7	382	420	0.05	0.45	1.45
Cottage cheese	78.3	4.2	13.6	94	51	0.03	0.25	0.10
Roquefort	40.0	30.5	21.5	315	372	0.03	0.70	1.20
On the dry basis								
Cheddar		51.0	39.7	1272	632	0.04	1.00	0.13
Emmental		47.0	42.2	1817	570	0.10	0.50	0.20
Edam		41.8	46.2	1354	319	0.11	0.60	0.12
Camembert		46.7	38.3	783	861	0.10	1.00	2.97
Cottage cheese		19.4	62.7	433	235	0.14	1.15	0.50
Roquefort		50.9	35.9	526	621	0.05	1.16	2.00

Source: Kon, S. K. (1972). Milk and milk products. In *Human Nutrition*. FAO, United Nations, Rome.

Cheese Grade Stamps

FIGURE 2.C.8

Source: USDA (1971). How to buy cheese. USDA Home and Garden Bull. *193*.

Cheese Label

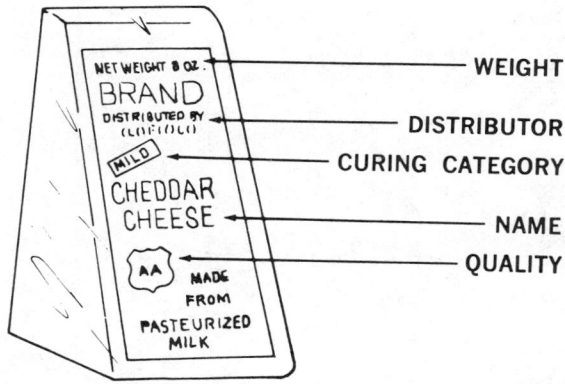

FIGURE 2.C.9

Source: USDA (1977). How to buy cheese. USDA Home and Garden Bull. *193.*

Cheese Shield

U.S. Grade AA cheese has
- fine, highly pleasing Cheddar flavor
- smooth, compact texture
- uniform color and attractive appearance.

FIGURE 2.C.10

Source: USDA (1979). How to buy dairy products. USDA Home and Garden Bull. *201.*

Cheese Skipper (*Enlarged*)

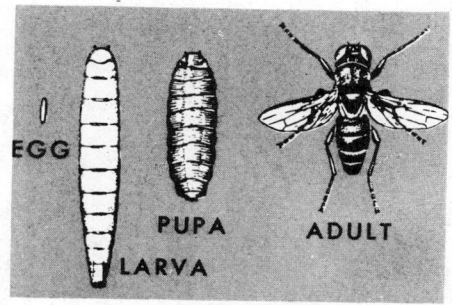

FIGURE 2.C.11

Source: USDA (1974). Protecting home cured meat from insects. USDA Home and Garden Bull. *109.*

Cheese, Vitamin Content

TABLE 2.C.28
Content of thiamin, riboflavin, nicotinic acid, and pantothenic acid in various cheeses[a]

Cheese variety[b]	Thiamin Average	Thiamin Range	Riboflavin Average	Riboflavin Range	Nicotinic Acid Average	Nicotinic Acid Range	Pantothenic Acid Average	Pantothenic Acid Range
					—(mg/kg)—			
Very hard								
Parmesan	0.23	0.20–0.26 (2)[c]	4.8	2.4–7.1 (2)	3.4	1.1–7.4 (4)	5.3	(1)
Romano[d]					0.77	(1)		
Hard								
Ripened by bacteria, without eyes								
Cantal	0.30	0.12–0.55 (7)	3.6	2.0–5.2 (2)	0.7	(1)	2.6	(1)
Cheddar	0.38	0.33–0.44 (2)	5.0	3.0–8.0 (11)	0.49	0.2–0.9 (4)	2.7	1.8–4.0 (5)
Cheshire			3.2	(1)	0.7	(1)	2.0	(1)
Colby			5.1	(1)	0.38	0.38–0.38 (2)	2.8	(1)
Edam	0.83	(1)	4.1	3.9–4.4 (2)	0.63	(1)	3.4	(1)
Gouda			4.3	(1)			4.8	(1)
Provolone	0.24	(1)	3.2	(1)	3.8	1.9–5.8 (2)		
Ripened by bacteria, with eyes								
Fontina[d]	0.21	(1)	2.0	(1)	1.5	(1)		
Gruyère	0.46	0.06–0.86 (2)	3.0	2.4–3.5 (2)	1.4	1.0–1.8 (2)	5.2	4.3–6.1 (2)
Swiss	0.43	0.22–0.72 (3)	3.2	1.9–6.0 (4)	1.7	0.7–3.1 (3)	3.0	2.0–4.4 (3)
Semisoft								
Ripened principally by bacteria								
Brick			4.6	4.2–5.1 (2)	1.0	0.9–1.1 (2)	2.9	2.8–2.9 (2)
Cornhusker			4.7	(1)	1.0	(1)	2.4	(1)
Münster					0.67	(1)		
Ripened by bacteria and surface microorganisms								
Liederkranz	0.80	(1)	6.1	6.0–6.2 (2)	2.4	0.5–4.3 (2)	14.4	9.0–19.9 (2)
Limburger	0.80	0.80–0.80 (2)	4.6	3.6–5.6 (3)	1.3	0.4–2.0 (3)	7.9	3.0–12.8 (2)
Port Salut[d]			2.8	(1)	0.64	0.59–0.7 (2)	2.1	(1)
Tilsiter	0.87	(1)	4.2	(1)				
Trappist[d]	1.18	(1)	6.6	(1)				

(Continued)

Cheese, Vitamin Content (Continued)

TABLE 2.C.28 (Continued)

Cheese variety[b]	Thiamin Average	Thiamin Range	Riboflavin Average	Riboflavin Range	Nicotinic Acid Average	Nicotinic Acid Range	Pantothenic Acid Average	Pantothenic Acid Range
Ripened principally by blue mold in the interior								
Blue[d]	0.27	0.18–0.36 (2)	6.0	4.5–7.2 (4)	7.8	2.8–12.5 (4)	12.6	7.8–20.5 (3)
Gorgonzola	0.40	0.12–0.68 (2)	4.3	4.3–4.4 (2)	3.2	—— (1)		
Roquefort[e]	0.30	—— (1)	6.0	4.1–7.8 (3)	5.9	4.7– 6.6 (3)	12.9	6.2–19.5 (2)
Stilton	0.50	0.24–0.75 (2)	3.0	—— (1)				
Soft								
Ripened								
Bel Paese	0.29	—— (1)	2.2	2.0–2.5 (2)	2.6	—— (1)		
Brie	0.60	—— (1)	5.9	2.8–9.0 (2)	3.8	0.5 – 7.0 (2)	7.4	0.9–14.0 (2)
Camembert	0.45	0.40–0.50 (2)	6.7	5.0–8.3 (4)	8.2	2.8 –11.6 (5)	7.1	0.4–14.0 (5)
Cresceenza	0.39	—— (1)	2.7	2.0–3.5 (2)	1.8	—— (1)		
Reblochon			4.1	—— (1)	1.1	—— (1)		
Robbiole	0.49	—— (1)	3.5	2.4–4.5 (2)	7.8	—— (1)	2.6	—— (1)
Unripened								
Cottage	0.26	0.18–0.34 (3)	3.3	2.8–4.3 (6)	0.92	0.7 – 1.15 (3)	2.2	1.8– 2.8 (3)
Cream	0.24	—— (1)	2.6	1.4–5.4 (6)	0.81	0.6 – 1.0 (3)	2.1	1.4– 2.7 (2)
Demisel			4.5	—— (1)	2.5	—— (1)	3.9	—— (1)
Mascarpone	0.17	—— (1)	1.3	—— (1)				
Mozzarella[d]	0.32	—— (1)	2.7	—— (1)	1.4	0.6 – 2.8 (2)		
Neufchâtel					0.86	—— (1)		
Petit Suisse			2.6	—— (1)	3.0	—— (1)	2.0	—— (1)
Pimento Cream			1.2	—— (1)				
Processed								
Brick			4.3	—— (1)				
Cheddar	0.20	—— (1)	5.1	4.3–5.6 (4)	0.88	0.8 – 1.0 (3)	5.7	4.3– 7.9 (2)
Limburger			3.5	—— (1)	1.4	—— (1)	5.8	—— (1)
Swiss	0.10	—— (1)	3.5	3.0–4.0 (2)	0.85	0.7 – 1.0 (2)	2.6	—— (1)

[a] Mean and range of average values obtained from publications of various groups of workers.

[b] Classified primarily according to Sanders (935).

[c] Figures in parentheses indicate number of references consulted.

[d] May be made from milk of species other than the cow.

[e] Made from ewe's milk.

Source: Hartman, A. M., and Dryden, L. P. Vitamins in milk and milk products. J. Dairy Sci., American Dairy Science Association.

Cheese, Vitamin Content (Continued)

TABLE 2.C.29
Content of vitamin B_6, biotin, folic acid, and vitamin B_{12} in various cheeses[a]

Cheese variety[b]	Vitamin B_6 Average	Vitamin B_6 Range	Biotin Average	Biotin Range	Folic Acid Average	Folic Acid Range	Vitamin B_{12}[c] Average	Vitamin B_{12}[c] Range
					(mg/kg)			
Very hard								
Parmesan	0.96	(1)[d]	0.030	0.017–0.043 (2)	0.073	(1)		
Romano[e]			0.013	(1)	0.068	(1)		
Hard								
Ripened by bacteria, without eyes								
Cantal					0.31	(1)	0.020	(1)
Cheddar	0.75	0.66–0.84 (2)	0.022	0.017–0.033 (3)	0.095	0.05–0.17 (4)	0.013	0.006–0.028 (6)
Colby	0.79	0.74–0.84 (2)	0.016	(1)	0.34	0.16–0.53 (2)	0.014	(1)
Edam	0.80	(1)	0.015	(1)	0.21	(1)	0.021	(1)
Gouda			0.017	(1)				
Kachkaval[f]	0.83	(1)	0.018	(1)	0.104	(1)	0.011	(1)
Provolone								
Svecia								
Ripened by bacteria, with eyes								
Gruyère	0.78	0.76–0.81 (2)	0.013	0.0084–0.017 (2)	0.101	0.098–0.104 (2)	0.016	(1)
Swiss	2.33	0.48–5.6 (3)	0.0051	0.0004–0.0094 (3)	0.072	0.064–0.08 (2)	0.018	0.009–0.028 (4)
Semisoft								
Ripened principally by bacteria								
Brick	0.73	(1)	0.022	0.016–0.028 (2)	0.20	(1)		
Cornhusker	0.79	(1)	0.012	(1)	0.104	(1)		
Münster	0.84	0.76–0.93 (2)	0.012	0.011–0.014 (2)	0.33	0.12–0.53 (2)	0.016	(1)
Ripened by bacteria and surface microorganisms								
Liederkranz	1.24	0.60–1.89 (2)	0.030	0.020–0.041 (2)	1.21	(1)	0.010	(1)
Limburger	0.54	0.2–0.89 (2)	0.086	0.020–0.200 (3)	0.58	(1)	0.015	(1)
Port Salut	0.50	0.40–0.59 (2)	0.012	(1)	0.32	0.18–0.45 (2)		
Tilsiter			0.015	(1)			0.029	(1)
Trappist[e]								

(Continued)

Cheese, Vitamin Content (Continued)

TABLE 2.C.29 (Continued)

Cheese variety[b]	Vitamin B6 Average	Vitamin B6 Range	Biotin Average	Biotin Range	Folic Acid Average	Folic Acid Range	Vitamin B12[c] Average	Vitamin B12[c] Range
Ripened principally by blue mold in the interior								
Blue[e]	1.81	1.12–2.30 (3)	0.046	0.016–0.076 (2)	0.48	0.36–0.59 (2)	0.014	(1)
Gorgonzola	1.06	(1)	0.019	(1)	0.31	(1)	0.012	(1)
Roquefort[f]	1.00	0.97–1.04 (2)	0.025	0.015–0.036 (2)	0.46	0.43–0.49 (2)	0.013	0.006–0.027 (3)
Soft								
Ripened								
Brie[e]	3.71	1.52–5.9 (2)	0.062	0.045–0.080 (2)	0.65	(1)	0.016	(1)
Brinza[e]	2.06	1.3–2.50 (4)	0.045	0.023–0.057 (3)	0.62	0.62–0.62 (2)	0.002	(1)
Camembert	0.60	(1)					0.013	0.012–0.014 (3)
Coulommiers	0.75	(1)						
Reblochon					0.37	(1)	0.011	(1)
Unripened								
Carré	0.60	(1)						
Cottage	0.54	(1)	0.020	(1)	0.30	0.29–0.33 (3)	0.0085	0.0059–0.0109 (4)
Cream	0.53	(1)	0.014	0.012–0.016 (2)	0.14	(1)	0.0021	0.002–0.0022 (2)
Demisel	0.72	(1)			0.29	(1)	0.0065	(1)
Double Crème[e]	0.56	(1)					0.0076[g]	(1)
Mozzarella[e]	0.64	(1)	0.016	(1)	0.099	(1)		
Neufchâtel			0.019	(1)	0.11	(1)		
Petit Suisse	0.63	(1)			0.19	(1)	0.0076[g]	(1)
Processed								
Cheddar	0.82	(1)	0.026	0.017–0.036 (2)	0.089	0.078–0.10 (2)		
Limburger			0.036	(1)			0.008	(1)
Swiss			0.011	(1)			0.012	(1)

[a] Mean and range of average values obtained from publications of various groups of workers.
[b] Classified primarily according to Sanders (935).
[c] Determined by microbial assay. By a hyperthyroid rat method, Cheddar cheese assayed 0.014 mg/kg (one reference). For values obtained by employment of an assay using the normal rat, see Table 10.
[d] Figures in parentheses indicate number of references consulted.
[e] May be made from milk of species other than the cow.
[f] Made from ewe's milk.
[g] Average includes both Double Crème and Petit Suisse.

Source: Hartman, A. M., and Dryden, L. P. Vitamins in milk and milk products. *J. Dairy Sci.,* American Dairy Science Association.

Chemical Poisoning

TABLE 2.C.30
Sources, prevention, and control of chemical poisoning

Disease	Reservoirs	Common Vehicle	Prevention and Control
Lead poisoning	Lead pipe, sprays, oxides, and utensils	Lead-contaminated food or acid drinks	Do not use lead pipe if water is acid; protect food; wash fruits.
Zinc poisoning	Galvanized iron pots	Acid food made in galvanized iron pots	Do not use galvanized utensils in preparation of food; or water with 15.0 ppm.
Sodium nitrite poisoning		Sodium nitrate taken for salt	Use U.S.P. sodium nitrate in curing meat.
Insecticides (rodenticides)			Protected storage.

Source: Food inspection specialist. Department of the Army, *TM 8-451* (1969). Reproduced by permission of the U.S. Department of the Army.

Cherries, Canned Weights

TABLE 2.C.31
Recommended minimum drained weights (in ounces) for pitted and unpitted canned sweet cherries

Container Size or Designation	In Extra Heavy Syrups and in Declared "Dietetic Packs" Whether or Not Packed in Water	In Heavy Syrups	In Light Syrup and in Slightly Sweetened Water or Juice	Other Than Declared "Dietetic Packs" Packed in Water
8Z tall	4¾	5	5¼	5¼
No. 1 tall	9¾	10	10¼	10¼
No. 303	9¾	10	10¼	10¼
No. 2	12	12½	12¾	12¾
No. 2½ metal	17½	18	18½	18½
No. 2½ glass	17¼	17¾	18¼	18¼
No. 10	66	68	70	70

Source: Marshall, R. E. Cherries and cherry products. In *Economic Crops*, Vol. 5. Z. I. Kertesz (editor). John Wiley & Sons, New York.

Cherry Brix

TABLE 2.C.32
Packing media and required Brix measurements for canned cherries

Media	Brix Measurement	
	Sweet Cherry	Red Sour Cherry
Water		
Cherry juice		
Slightly sweetened water	Less than 16°	Less than 18°
Light syrup	16–20°	18–23°
Heavy syrup	20–25°	22–28°
Extra heavy syrup	25–35°	28–45°
Slightly sweetened cherry juice	Less than 16°	Less than 18°
Light cherry juice syrup	16–20°	18–22°
Heavy cherry juice syrup	20–25°	22–28°
Extra heavy cherry juice syrup	25–35°	28–45°

Source: Marshall, R. E. Cherries and cherry products. In Economic Crops, Vol. 5.
Z. I. Kertesz (editor). John Wiley & Sons, New York.

Cherry Composition

TABLE 2.C.33
Proximate composition of some canned cherries (in percentage)

Description[1]	No. of Analyses	Total Solids	Ash	Fat (E.E.)	Protein (N × 6.25)	Crude Fiber	Carbohydrates by Difference	Cal per 100 g
Black, EP, WP	1	19.0	0.4	0.8	0.7	0.2	16.9	78
Black, JP	1	18.9	0.5	0.1	0.5	0.1	17.7	74
Napoleon, WP	2	12.3	0.3	0.3	0.6	0.2	10.8	48
Napoleon, JP	2	16.4	0.6	0.1	0.9	0.2	14.6	63
Napoleon, EP, SP	?	21.9	0.4	0.1	0.6	0.2	20.6	86
Red, pitted, WP	5	13.2	0.4	0.3	0.8	0.1	11.5	50
Red, pitted, JP	2	14.2	0.5	0.9	0.9	0.2	11.8	59
Red, pitted, SP	?	29.8	0.6	0.1	0.6	0.2	28.3	117

[1] The letters are to be interpreted as follows: EP, edible portion ; WP, water pack; JP, juice pack; SP, syrup pack.
Source: Marshall, R. E. Cherries and cherry products. In Economic Crops, Vol. 5. Z. I. Kertesz (editor). John Wiley & Sons, New York.

Chloride Salt, Injury

TABLE 2.C.34
Fruit rootstocks and varieties (When chloride salts predominate, the Cl⁻ concentration in the saturation extracts should not exceed the maximum permissible amounts shown below if leaf injury is to be avoided.)

	Crop	Specification	Max Permissible Cl⁻ (mEq/L)		Crop	Specification	Max Permissible Cl⁻ (mEq/L)
		Rootstocks				Varieties	
1	Avocado	West Indian	8	9	Berries[1]	Boysenberry; Olallie blackberry	10
2		Mexican	5	10		Indian Summer raspberry	5
3	Citrus	Rangpur lime; Cleopatra mandarin	25				
4		Rough lemon; tangelo; sour orange	15	11	Straw-	Lassen	8
				12	berry	Shasta	5
5		Sweet orange, citrange	10	13	Grape	Thompson Seedless; Perlette	25
6	Stone	Marianna	25	14		Cardinal; Black Rose	10
7	fruit	Lovell; Shalil	10				
8		Yunnan	7				

[1] Data available for single variety of each crop only.

Source: Altman, P. L., and Dittmer, D. S. (editors) (1966). *Environmental Biology*. Federation of American Societies for Experimental Biology, Bethesda, Maryland. Cited from Bernstein, L. (1965). USDA Agric. Inform. Bull. *292*.

Chlorine Availability

TABLE 2.C.35
Available chlorine in various preparations

Chemical	Equivalent Percentage Available Chlorine	Therefore a label stating:	
		This Percentage of Chemical	Contains this Percentage Avg Chlorine
Sodium hypochlorite	100	6.0	6.0
Calcium hypochlorite	100	50.0	50.0
Dichloroisocyanuric acid	70	5.8	4.0
Trichloroisocyanuric acid	90	10.0	9.0
Potassium dichloroisocyanurate	59	25.4	15.0
Sodium dichloroisocyanurate	60	18.0	10.8
Dichlorodimethyl hydantoin	66	25.0	16.5
Chloramine T	25	16.0	4.0

Source: Harper, W. J. (1972). Sanitation in dairy food plants. In *Food Sanitation*, R. K. Guthrie (editor). AVI Publishing Co., Westport, Connecticut.

Chlorine Compounds

TABLE 2.C.36
Chlorine compounds (classes of available chlorine compounds)

COMPOUND	STRUCTURE	SOLUBILITY
GASEOUS CHLORINE	Cl : Cl	0.716 GM/100 GM
CALCIUM HYPOCHLORITE	Ca⟨OCl / OCl	6.9 GM/100 GM (PRODUCES SLUDGE)
SODIUM HYPOCHLORITE	Na—OCl	
CHLORAMINE T	H_3C—⬡—S(=O)(=O)—N(H)(Cl)	15 GM/100 GM 1.2 GM/100 GM
DICHLORODIMETHYL HYDANTOIN		
DICHLOROCYANURIC ACID	Cl—N—Cl	2.6 GM/100 GM (SODIUM SALT IS ABOUT 10 X AS SOLUBLE)
TRICHLOROCYANURIC ACID	(Cl)	1.2 GM/100 GM

Source: Harper, W. J. (1972). Sanitation in dairy food plants. In *Food Sanitation*, R. K. Guthrie (editor). AVI Publishing Co., Westport, Connecticut.

Chlorine, Water Treatment

TABLE 2.C.37
Amounts of chlorine compound for charging chemical tank on water-treating equipment

Ppm Chlorine Desired in Water	Available Chlorine 5%	Available Chlorine 15%	Available Chlorine 50%	Available Chlorine 70%
	Weighed ounces of Compound Required for 1000 gal.			
4	9.6	3.2	1.0	0.7
6	14.0	4.8	1.5	1.0
8	19.2	6.4	2.0	1.4
10	24.0	8.0	2.6	1.8
12	29.0	9.6	3.1	2.2

Source: Woodroof, J. G., and Phillips, G. E. (editors) (1974). Water in beverages. In *Beverages: Carbonated and Noncarbonated*. AVI Publishing Co., Westport, Connecticut.

Cholesterol Control

TABLE 2.C.38
Cholesterol content of common measures of selected foods (in ascending order)[1]

Food	Amount	Cholesterol
		Milligrams
Milk, skim, fluid or reconstituted dry	1 cup	5
Cottage cheese, uncreamed	½ cup	7
Lard	1 tablespoon	12
Cream, light table	1 fluid ounce	20
Cottage cheese, creamed	½ cup	24
Cream, half and half	¼ cup	26
Ice cream, regular, approximately 10% fat	½ cup	27
Cheese, cheddar	1 ounce	28
Milk, whole	1 cup	34
Butter	1 tablespoon	35
Oysters, salmon	3 ounces, cooked	40
Clams, halibut, tuna	3 ounces, cooked	55
Chicken, turkey, light meat	3 ounces, cooked	67
Beef, pork, lobster, chicken, turkey, dark meat	3 ounces, cooked	75
Lamb, veal, crab	3 ounces, cooked	85
Shrimp	3 ounces, cooked	130
Heart, beef	3 ounces, cooked	230
Egg	1 yolk or 1 egg	250
Liver, beef, calf, hog, lamb	3 ounces, cooked	370
Kidney	3 ounces, cooked	680
Brains	3 ounces, raw	more than 1700

Source: USDA (1974). Fats in food and diet. USDA Agriculture Information Bull. *361*.

Citrus Fruit Storage

TABLE 2.C.39
Recommendations for storage of citrus fruits (relative humidity 87–92%)

Variety	Production area	Storage temperature	Length of storage period
		° F.	Weeks
Dancy tangerines	Florida	38–40	2–4
Tangelos	Florida	38–40	4
Temple oranges	Florida	38–40	4
Murcott Honey oranges	Florida	32–34	6–8
Valencia oranges	Florida	32–34	8–12
Do	Texas	32–34	8–12
Do	California	40–44	4–6
Navel oranges	California	40–44	4–6
Grapefruit	Florida	50	4–6
Do	Texas	50	4–6
Do	California	58–60	4–6
Do	Arizona	58–60	4–6
Limes	Florida	48–50	6–8
Lemons	California	58–60	12–24

Source: USDA (1971). Market diseases of citrus and other subtropical fruits. USDA Agriculture Handbook *398*.

Clouding Agents

TABLE 2.C.40
Advantages and limitations of clouding agents

Finished Product	Clouding Agent of Choice	Advantages	Limitations	Percentage in Finished Product
Bottled drinks	Neutral or citrus blenders	Improved flavor and shelf-life	Intensity of cloud limited	0.065-0.26
Canned drinks	Neutral or citrus blenders	Improved flavor and shelf-life	Cloud intensity limited if ringing undesirable	0.065-0.26
Dry drink powders	Spray-dried clouds	Easily incorporated in mix	None	0.1-0.25
Liquid alcoholic mixers	Non-stabilized blenders	Greater flavor stability and flexibility	Somewhat less cloud stability	0.1-0.2

Source: Woodroof, J. G., and Phillips, G. F. (editors) (1974). Beverage acids, flavors, colors, and emulsifiers. In *Beverages: Carbonated and Noncarbonated*. AVI Publishing Co., Westport, Connecticut.

Coatings

TABLE 2.C.41
Typical confectioner's coatings

Ingredient	Coating Type, Weight %			
	Milk Chocolate	Sweet Chocolate	Com-pounds	Pastel
Sugar	47.8	48.3	48.0	9.8
Chocolate liquor	16.0	31.0	...	...
Cocoa powder (10% fat)	...	...	8.0	...
Cocoa butter	18.2	19.2	...	...
Hard butter	...	...	30.7	31.7
Whole milk powder (26% fat)	16.5	...	...	...
Msnf	...	...	11.8	18.0
Lecithin	0.3	0.3	0.3	0.3
Sorbitan monostearate	0.6	0.6	0.6	0.6
Polysorbate 60	0.4	0.4	0.4	0.4
Salt	0.2	0.2	0.2	0.2

Flavor: vanillin, ethyl vanillin, heliotropin
Food colors are added to pastel coatings.

Source: Weiss, T. J. (editor) (1970). Confectionery coatings. In *Food Oils and Their Uses.* AVI Publishing Co., Westport, Connecticut.

Cocoa, Composition

TABLE 2.C.42
Analyses of unfermented West African cocoa

Constituent	Dried Beans (%)	Fat-free Material (%)
Cotyledons	89.60	—
Shell	9.63	—
Germ	0.77	—
Fat	53.05	—
Water	3.65	—
Ash (total)	2.63	6.07
Nitrogen		
Total nitrogen	2.28	5.27
Protein nitrogen	1.50	3.46
Ammonia nitrogen	0.028	0.065
Amide nitrogen	0.188	0.434
Theobromine	1.71	3.95
Caffeine	0.085	0.196
Carbohydrates		
Glucose	0.30	0.69
Sucrose	Nil	Nil
Starch	6.10	14.09
Pectins	2.25	5.20
Fiber	2.09	4.83
Cellulose	1.92	4.43
Pentosans	1.27	2.93
Mucilage and gums	0.38	0.88
Tannins	7.54	17.43
Acids		
Acetic (free)	0.014	0.032
Oxalic	0.29	0.67

Source: Rohan, T. A. *Processing of Raw Cocoa for the Market.* FAO, United Nations, Rome.

Cocoa Cultivation

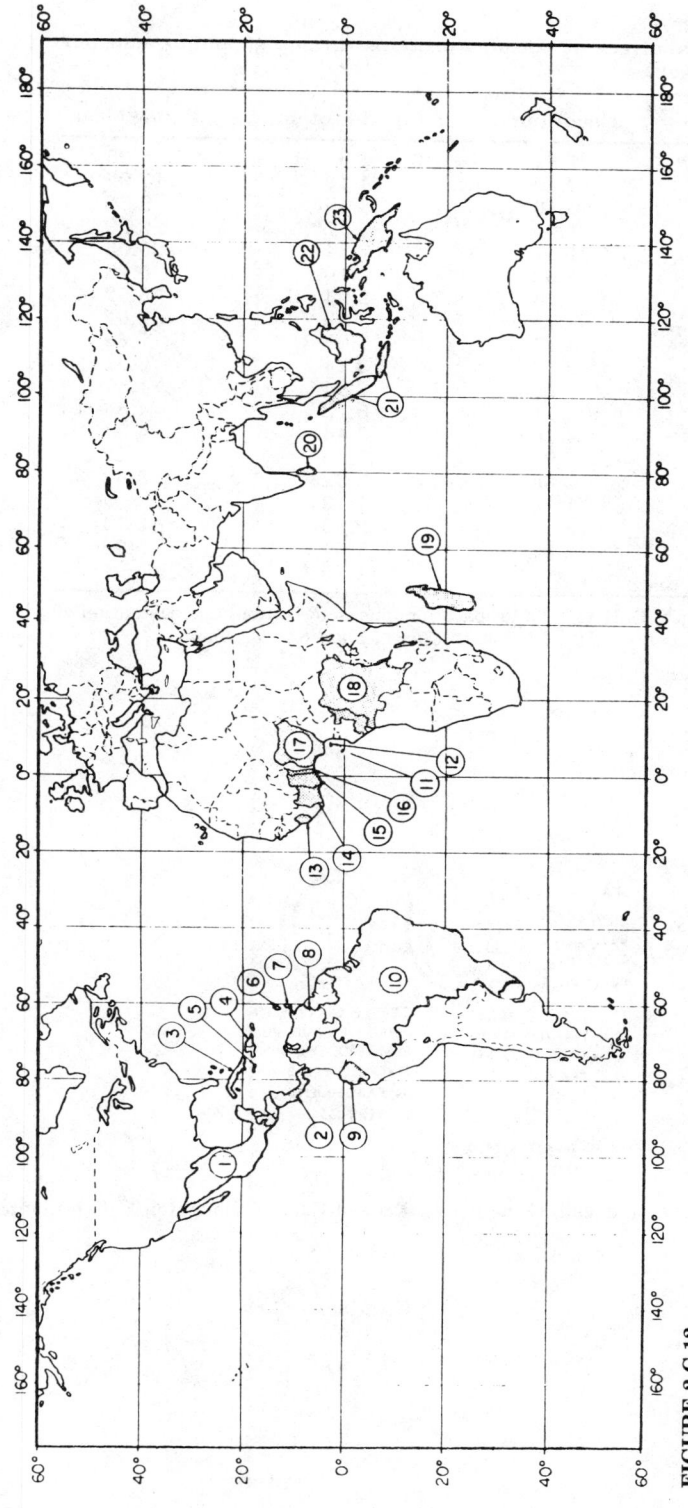

FIGURE 2.C.12

Geographical distribution of cocoa cultivation, showing only the more important areas: 1) Mexico; 2) Central America; 3) Cuba; 4) Dominican Republic; 5) Jamaica; 6) Grenada; 7) Trinidad; 8) Venezuela; 9) Equador; 10) Brazil; 11) São Tomé; 12) Fernando Po; 13) Sierra Leone; 14) Ivory Coast; 15) Ghana; 16) Togo; 17) Nigeria; 18) Zaire; 19) Mozambique; 20) Sri Lanka; 21) Indonesia; 22) Borneo; 23) New Guinea

Source: Rohan, T. A. *Processing of Raw Cocoa for the Market.* Food and Agriculture Organization, United Nations, Rome.

Coconut, Amino Acids

TABLE 2.C.43
Amino acid analyses of coconut proteins (grams of amino acid per 16 g of nitrogen)

Amino Acid	Cocoflour	Purified Protein[1]	Paring Meal
Ala	4.61	4.01	5.35
Arg	15.40	14.40	17.92
Asp	9.16	8.49	9.82
½ Cys	1.46	0.57	2.89
Glu	21.17	17.84	20.05
Gly	5.62	4.10	5.28
His	3.14	2.04	3.52
Iso	3.71	3.83	4.02
Leu	8.37	7.08	7.68
Lys	3.59	3.34	6.31
Met	1.63	2.34	1.57
Phe	5.11	5.13	4.84
Pro	4.10	3.44	4.34
Ser	4.95	5.46	5.22
Thr	3.65	3.32	3.84
Try	1.18	1.12	—
Tyr	3.14	2.93	3.14
Val	5.51	5.54	5.78
Ammonia	—	1.29	—

Source: Strength, D. R. (1971). Preparation, characterization, and evaluation of coconut protein. *Proc. Third Internat. Congr. Food Sci. Technol.*

Coffee Berry

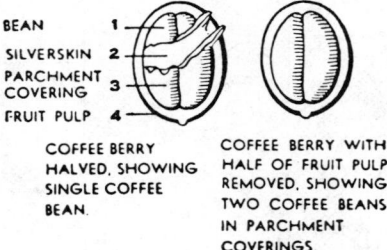

BEAN 1
SILVERSKIN 2
PARCHMENT COVERING 3
FRUIT PULP 4

COFFEE BERRY HALVED, SHOWING SINGLE COFFEE BEAN.

COFFEE BERRY WITH HALF OF FRUIT PULP REMOVED, SHOWING TWO COFFEE BEANS IN PARCHMENT COVERINGS.

FIGURE 2.C.13
Structure of the coffee berry

Source: Justin, M. M., Rust, L. O., and Vail, G. E. *Foods*, Revised Edition. Houghton Mifflin Company, Boston.

Coffee Composition

TABLE 2.C.44
Chemical composition of soluble and insoluble portions of roasted coffee (approximate dry basis)

	Solubles (%)	Insolubles (%)
Carbohydrates (53%)		
Reducing sugars	2	—
Caramelized sugars	17	—
Hemicellulose (hydrolyzable)	10	4
Fiber (not hydrolyzable)	—	22
Oils	—	15
Proteins ($N \times 6.25$); amino acids are soluble	2	11
Ash (oxide)	3	1
Acids, nonvolatile		
Chlorogenic	4.5	—
Caffeic	0.5	—
Quinic	0.5	—
Oxalic, malic, citric, tartaric	1.0	—
Volatile acids	0.35	—
Trigonelline	1.0	—
Caffeine (Arabicas 1.0%, Robustas 2.0%)	1.2	—
Phenolics (estimated)	2.0	—
Volatiles		
Carbon dioxide	Trace	2
Essence of aroma and flavor	0.04	—
Total	45	55

Source: Sivetz, M. (1974). Coffee. In *Encyclopedia of Food Technology*. A. H. Johnson and M. S. Peterson (editors). AVI Publishing Co., Westport, Connecticut.

Coffee Granule Designation

TABLE 2.C.45
Granule designation: size, number, and surface area per unit weight

Grind Designation	Approx Mesh (mm)	No. Particles per Gram	Relative No. Particles/Gram	Granule Area Exposed cm^2 per Gram Coffee
Whole bean	4/6.0	6	1 (basis)	8
Cracked bean	8/3.0	48	8	16
Regular grind	12/1.5	400	64	32
Fine grind	24/0.75	3,200	512	64
Vend grind	40/0.375	24,000	4,100	128

Source: Sivetz, M. (1974). *Coffee Origin and Use*. Coffee Publications, Corvallis, Oregon.

Coffee Particle Size

TABLE 2.C.46
Particle size analyses of roasted and ground coffee

Wire Meshes per Inch	Opening in Screen in.	Opening in Screen mm	Weight Percentage on Each Screen Size Commercial Regular	Commercial Drip	Commercial Fine	Vending Batch	Vending Single Cup
10	0.074	1.84	33	7	0	2	—
14	0.051	1.27					
20	0.034	0.86	55	73	70	33	0
28	0.020	0.51				40	<10
35	0.0176	0.45	—	—	—	15	35
48	0.011	0.28	—	—	—	—	35
Pan	—	—	12	20	30	10	>20
			100	100	100	100	100

Source: Sivetz, M. (1974). *Coffee Origin and Use*. Coffee Publications, Corvallis, Oregon.

Coffee Whitener, Composition

TABLE 2.C.47
Coffee whitener formulations

Ingredient	Weight % Liquid	Weight % Powder	Ingredient	Weight % Liquid	Weight % Powder
Sugar	1.0–3.0		Carrageenan	0.1–0.2	
Corn syrup solids (42 DE)	1.5–3.0	55.0–60.0	Dipotassium phosphate[2]	0.1–0.3	1.2–1.8
Fat	3.0–18.0	35.0–40.0	Flavor, color		
Sodium caseinate	1.0–3.0	4.5–5.5	Water to make 100%		
Mono-, diglycerides	0.3–0.5	0.2–0.5[1]	(liquid type)		

Source: Anon. (1966).
[1] Mono-, diglycerides 60%
Sorbitan monostearate 20% } 0.3–0.5%
Polysorbate 60 20%

or

Mono-, diglycerides 75%
Polysorbate 65 25% } 0.2–0.4%
[2] Disodium phosphate or sodium citrate may be substituted.

Source: Weiss, T. J. (editor) (1970). Imitation dairy products. In *Food Oils and Their Uses*. AVI Publishing Co., Westport, Connecticut.

Coffee Yield

TABLE 2.C.48
Yield of coffee of different strengths

Cup Size in Ounces	Usual Portion Ounces	Number of Cups Yield at: 2 Gal. per Lb	2¼ Gal. per Lb	2½ Gal. per Lb	2¾ Gal. per Lb	3 Gal. per Lb
5	4	56	64	72	80	88
6	4½	50	57	64	71	78
6½	5	45	51	57	64	70
7	5½	40	46	52	58	64
½ Gal. Equipment						
Coffee Weight Use		4 Oz	3½ Oz	3⅕ Oz	3 Oz	2¾ Oz
Beverage Yield of		56.0	56.0	57.0	60.0	60.0

Source: Sivetz, M. (1974). *Coffee Origin and Use*. Coffee Publications, Corvallis, Oregon.

Color Additives

TABLE 2.C.49
FAO/WHO classification and acceptable daily intakes of color additives permitted in the United States, exempt from certification

Name	Color Index No.	Toxicological Classification	Maximum Acceptable Daily Intake for Man mg/Kg Body Weight	U.S. Use Limits
Algae meal, dried[d]	—	c	—	Chicken feed only
Annatto extract	75120	A	1.25[a]	GMP
Beta-apo-8'-carotenal	—	A	2.5[f]	May not exceed 15 mg per pound or pint of the food
Beets, dehydrated (beet powder)	—	e	—	GMP
Canthaxanthine	—	A	12.5	May not exceed 30 mg per pound or pint of the food
Caramel	—	D	—	GMP
Carbon black	77266	c	—	g
Carotene (natural)	75130	c	—	GMP
Beta-carotene (synthetic)	—	A	2.5[f]	GMP
Carrot oil	—	e	—	GMP
Cochineal extract; carmine	75470	c	—	GMP
Corn endosperm oil[d]	—	c	—	Chicken feed only
Cottonseed flour, partially defatted, cooked, toasted	—	e	—	GMP
Ferrous gluconate	—	e	—	Ripe olives only
Fruit juice	—	e	—	GMP
Grape skin extract (Enocianina)	—	e	—	Still and carbonated drinks and ades, beverage bases and alcoholic beverages
Iron oxide, synthetic	77492	c	—	May not exceed 0.25% by weight of dog and cat food
Paprika	—	e	—	GMP
Paprika oleoresin	—	e	—	GMP
Riboflavin	—	A	0.5	GMP
Saffron	75100	c	—	GMP
Tagetes meal and extract[d]	—	c	—	Chicken feed only
Titanium dioxide	77891	A	GMP	May not exceed 1% by weight of the food
Turmeric	75300	A	0.5[b]	GMP
Turmeric oleoresin	75300	A	0.5[b]	GMP

(Continued)

Color Additives *(Continued)*

TABLE 2.C.49   *(Continued)*

Name	Color Index No.	Toxicological Classification	Maximum Acceptable Daily Intake for Man mg/Kg Body Weight	U.S. Use Limits
Ultramarine blue	77007,77013	c	—	May not exceed 0.5% by weight of salt intended for animal feed
Vegetable juice	—	e	—	GMP

[a] Temporary ADI. Further work required by June 1972: metabolic studies on the major carotenoids of annatto.
[b] Temporary ADI. Further work required by June 1974: studies on the metabolism of curcumin and a two-year study in a nonrodent mammalian species.
[c] No attempt was made at toxicological evaluation because the Expert Committee felt that, in the absence of specifications and experimental data, the principles set forth in previous reports precluded the possibility of making such evaluation. Meaningful specifications could not be established.
[d] These products are not listed as such in the FAO/WHO tabulation but are sources of xanthophylls which are listed but not classified toxicologically for the reason given above in footnote c.
[e] Not considered by the Expert Committee.
[f] Expressed as total carotenoids by weight.
[g] Provisionally listed.

Source: Schramm, A. T. (1971). Toxicological assessment of food colors. *Proc. Third Internat. Congr. Food Sci. Technol.*

Color, Meat

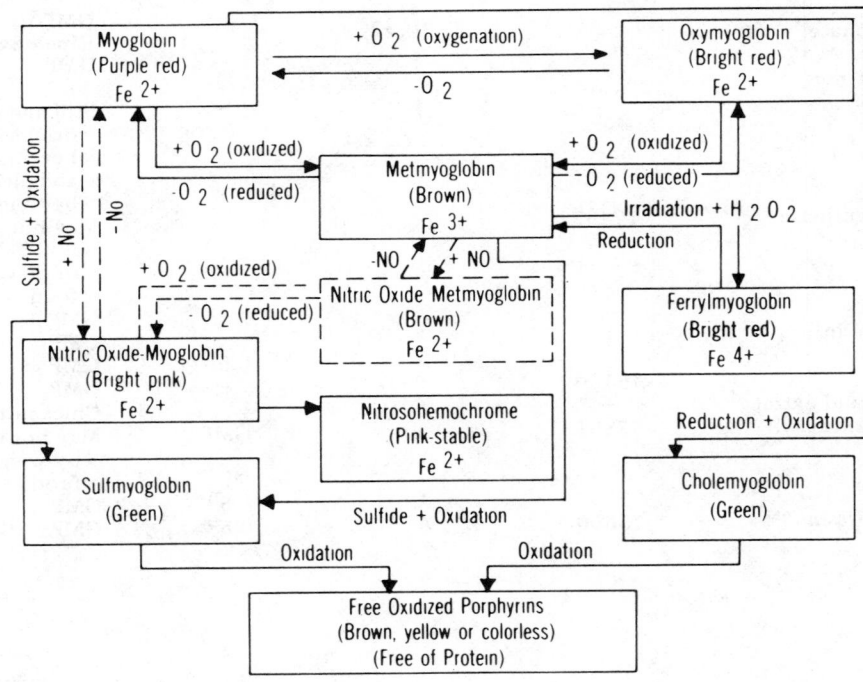

FIGURE 2.C.14
Heme pigments in muscle in relationship to fresh and cured meats (Broken lines indicate reactions and compounds possible but not definitely proven. Sulfmyoglobin and cholemyoglobin most frequently occur as a result of bacterial action.)

Source: Kramlich, W. E., Pearson, A. M., and Tauber, F. W. (editors) (1973). Curing. In *Processed Meats*. AVI Publishing Co., Westport, Connecticut.

Color, Organic

TABLE 2.C.50
Natural organic coloring matters

Name	Source	Color Principle	Color
Alkanet	Root: *Anchusa tinctoria*	Alkannin	Red
Annatto	Fruit of shrub: *Bixa orellana*	Bixin (main color)	Yellow
		Orellin (minor color)	Yellow
Brazilwood	Wood of tree: *Caesalpinia braziliensis*	Brazilin	Reddish-orange
Caramel	Heated sugar	High molecular weight carbohydrate	Reddish-brown
Carotene	Plants, carrots	α, β, γ, and K carotene	Yellow
Chlorophyll	Plant leaves	Chlorophyll α (62% of color)	Greenish-blue
		Chlorophyll β (23% of color)	Green
		Xanthophyll (10% of color)	Yellow
		Carotene (5% of color)	Yellow
Cochineal	Insect: *Coccus cacti*	Carminic acid	Red
Cocoa red	Cocoa beans	Cacaonin	Red
Fustic	Tree: *Morus tinctoria* or *Maclura tinctoria*	Morin (main color)	Yellow
		Maclurin (minor color)	Yellow
Indigo	Plant genus: *Indigofera*	Indigotin	Blue
Lac	Insect: *Coccus lacca*	Laccaic acid	Red
Litmus	Lichens	Azolitmin	Red
Logwood	Wood of tree: *Haematoxylon campechianum*	Haematoxylin	Red-brown
Madder	Root of herb: *Rubia tinctoria*	Alizarin (main color)	Red
		Purpurin (minor color)	Yellow
Orchil and cudbear	Lichens	Orecin	Red
Persian berries	Fruit of *Rhamnus amygdalinus*	Rhamnetin	Yellow
Quercitron	Inner bark of tree: *Quercus nigra* or *Q. tinctoria*	Quercetin	Yellow
Safflower	Flower: *Carthamus tinctoria*	Carthamin	Red
Saffron	Flower petals: *Crocus salivus*	Crocetin	Yellow
Turmeric	Underground stem: *Curcuma longa* or *C. tinctoria*	Curcumin	Yellow

Source: Roe, F. J. C. (1970). *Metabolic Aspects of Food Safety*. Blackwell Scientific Publications, Osney Media, Oxford, England.

Colors Permanently Listed

TABLE 2.C.51
Color additives permanently listed for food use, exempt from certification

Color	Use Limitation[1]
Algae meal, dried	For use in chicken feed to enhance the yellow color of chicken skin and eggs
Annatto extract	
β-Apo-8'-carotenal	Not to exceed 15 mg/lb, or pint, of food
Beets, dehydrated (beet powder)	
Canthaxanthine	Not to exceed 30 mg/lb, or pint, of food
Caramel	
β-Carotene	
Carrot oil	
Cochineal extract; carmine	
Corn endosperm oil	For use in chicken feed to enhance the yellow color of chicken skin and eggs
Cottonseed flour, partially defatted, cooked, toasted	
Ferrous gluconate	For coloring ripe olives
Fruit juice	
Grape skin extract	For coloring beverages
Iron oxide (synthetic)	For coloring pet food, not to exceed 0.25 percent by weight of the food
Paprika Paprika oleoresin	
Riboflavin	
Saffron	
Tagetes meal and extract (aztec marigold)	For use in chicken feed to enhance the yellow color of chicken skin and eggs
Titanium dioxide	Not to exceed 1% by weight of the food
Turmeric Turmeric oleoresin	
Ultramarine blue	For coloring salt intended for animal feed, not to exceed 0.5% by weight of the salt
Vegetable juice	

[1] Unless otherwise indicated, the color may be used for the coloring of food generally in amounts consistent with good manufacturing practice.

Source: Anon. (1971). Food Colors. Food and Nutrition Board, National Academy of Sciences—National Research Council, Washington, D.C.

Composition of Food

TABLE 2.C.52
Chemical composition of selected human foods (nutritive value of 100 g, edible portion)

Food Item	Water, %	Food Energy, Cal	Protein, g	Fat, g	Carbohydrate, g	Calcium, mg	Phosphorus, mg	Iron, mg	Vitamin A Value, I.U.	Thiamin, mg	Riboflavin, mg	Niacin, mg	Ascorbic Acid, mg
Milk, cream, ice cream, cheese													
Milk													
Dry whole	3.5	496	25.8	26.7	38.0	949	728	0.58	1,400	0.30	1.46	0.7	6
Evaporated, unsweetened	73.7	139	7.0	7.9	9.9	243	195	0.17	400	0.05	0.36	0.2	1
Fresh skim	90.5	35	3.5	0.1	5.1	118	93	0.07	Tr	0.04	0.18	0.1	1
Fresh whole	87.0	69	3.5	3.9	4.9	118	93	0.07	160	0.04	0.17	0.1	1
Cream, ice cream													
Cream (20%), sweet or sour	72.5	208	2.9	20.0	4.0	97	77	0.06	830	0.03	0.14	0.1	1
Ice cream, plain	62.0	210	4.0	12.3	20.8	132	104	0.10	540	0.04	0.19	0.1	Tr
Cheese													
Cheddar type	39	393	23.9	32.3	1.7	873	610	0.57	1,740	0.04	0.50	0.2	0
Cottage	74.0	101	19.2	0.8	4.3	82	263	0.46	30	0.02	0.29	0.1	0
Fats, oils													
Bacon, medium fat	10	626	9.1	65	1.1	13	108	0.8	0	0.42	0.10	2.1	0
Butter	15.5	733	0.6	81	0.4	16	16	0.2	3,300	Tr	0.01	0.1	0
Lard, other shortening	0	900	0	100	0	0	0	0	0	0	0	0	0
Margarine with vitamin A added	15.5	733	0.6	81	0.4	2	15	0.2	1,980	0	0	0	0
Salt pork, fat	8	781	3.9	85	0	2	42	0.6	0	0.18	0.04	0.9	0
Eggs													
Whole, dried	2	593	48.2	43.3	2.6	187	800	8.7	4,450	0.35	1.23	0.2	0
Whole, fresh	74.0	158	12.8	11.5	0.7	54	210	2.7	1,140	0.12	0.34	0.1	0
Meat, poultry, fish													
Beef													
Loin steaks (wholesale loin)	57	293	16.9	25	0	10	182	2.5	0	0.10	0.13	4.6	0
Round steak (wholesale round)	67	194	19.3	13	0	11	208	2.9	0	0.12	0.15	5.2	0
Lamb													
Leg roast (wholesale leg)	63.7	230	18.0	17.5	0	10	194	2.7	0	0.21	0.26	5.9	0
Sirloin chop (wholesale leg)	63.7	230	18.0	17.5	0	10	194	2.7	0	0.21	0.26	5.9	0
Pork													
Ham, fresh	53	340	15.2	31	0	9	164	2.3	0	0.96	0.19	4.1	0
Ham, smoked	42	384	16.9	35	0.3	10	182	2.5	0	0.78	0.19	3.8	0
Pork links, sausage	41.9	446	10.8	44.8	0	6	116	1.6	0	0.22	0.15	2.3	0
Poultry													
Chicken, roasters	66.0	194	20.2	12.6	0	16	218	1.9	Tr	0.11	0.18	8.6	—
Turkey, medium fat	58.3	262	20.1	20.2	0	23	320	3.8	Tr	0.12	0.19	7.9	—
Fish and shellfish													
Cod	82.6	70	16.5	0.4	0	18	189	0.9	0	0.04	0.05	2.3	2
Salmon, canned	67.4	169	20.6	9.6	0	67	286	1.3	80	0.03	0.18	6.5	0
Dry beans and peas, nuts													
Dry beans and peas													
Beans, canned, baked	71.0	117	5.7	2.0	19.0	40	154	3.4	70	0.05	0.05	0.8	4
Beans, lima, dry seed	12.6	341	20.7	1.3	61.6	68	381	7.5	0	0.60	0.24	2.1	2
Peas, split	10.0	354	24.5	1.0	61.7	73	397	6.0	370	0.87	0.29	3.9	2

(Continued)

Composition of Food   (Continued)

TABLE 2.C.52   (Continued)

Food Item	Water, %	Food Energy, Cal	Protein, g	Fat, g	Carbo-hydrate, g	Calcium, mg	Phos-phorus, mg	Iron, mg	Vitamin A Value, I.U.	Thia-min, mg	Ribo-flavin, mg	Niacin, mg	Ascorbic Acid, mg
Nuts													
Peanut butter	1.7	619	26.1	47.8	21.0	74	393	1.9	0	0.20	0.16	16.2	0
Peanuts, roasted	2.6	600	26.9	44.2	23.6	74	393	1.9	0	0.30	0.16	16.2	0
Fresh vegetables													
Asparagus	93.0	26	2.2	0.2	3.9	21	62	0.9	1,000	0.16	0.17	1.2	33
Beans, snap	88.9	42	2.4	0.2	7.7	65	44	1.1	630	0.08	0.10	0.6	19
Beets	87.6	46	1.6	0.1	9.6	27	43	1.0	20	0.03	0.05	0.4	10
Carrots	88.2	45	1.2	0.3	9.3	39	37	0.8	12,000	0.07	0.06	0.5	6
Corn, sweet, white, or yellow	73.9	108	3.7	1.2	20.5	9	120	0.5	390	0.15	0.14	1.4	12
Cucumbers	96.1	14	.7	0.1	2.7	10	21	0.3	0	0.04	0.09	0.2	8
Lettuce, headed	94.8	18	1.2	0.2	2.9	22	25	0.5	540	0.06	0.07	0.2	8
Onions, mature	87.5	49	1.4	0.2	10.3	32	44	0.5	50	0.03	0.02	0.1	9
Peas, green	74.3	101	6.7	0.4	17.7	22	122	1.9	680	0.36	0.18	2.1	26
Potatoes	77.8	85	2.0	0.1	19.1	11	56	0.7	20	0.11	0.04	1.2	17
Spinach	92.7	25	2.3	0.3	3.2	81	55	3.0	9,420	0.12	0.24	0.7	59
Sweet potatoes	68.5	125	1.8	0.7	27.9	30	49	0.7	7,700	0.10	0.06	0.7	22
Tomatoes	94.1	23	1.0	0.3	4.0	11	27	0.6	1,100	0.06	0.04	0.6	23
Turnips	90.9	35	1.1	0.2	7.1	40	34	0.5	Tr	0.06	0.06	0.5	28
Fresh fruit													
Apples	84.1	64	0.3	0.4	14.9	6	10	0.3	90	0.04	0.002	0.2	5
Bananas	74.8	99	1.2	0.2	23	8	28	0.6	430	0.09	0.06	0.6	10
Strawberries	90.0	41	0.8	0.6	8.1	28	27	0.8	60	0.03	0.07	0.3	60
Grapefruit	88.8	44	0.5	0.2	10.1	17	18	0.3	Tr	0.04	0.02	0.2	40
Lemons	89.3	44	0.9	0.6	8.7	14	10	0.1	0	0.04	Tr	0.1	45
Oranges	87.2	50	0.9	0.2	11.2	33	23	0.4	190	0.08	0.03	0.2	42
Peaches	86.9	51	0.5	0.1	12.0	8	22	0.6	880	0.02	0.05	0.9	8
Rhubarb	94.9	18	0.5	0.1	3.8	51	25	0.5	30	0.01	—	0.1	9
Grain products													
Flour													
Wheat, patent	12	355	10.8	0.9	75.9	19	93	0.7	0	0.07	0.03	0.8	0
Wheat, patent, enriched	12	355	10.8	0.9	75.9	19	93	2.9	0	0.44	0.26	3.5	0
Whole wheat	11	360	13.0	2.0	72.4	38	385	3.8	0	0.56	0.12	5.6	0
Breakfast cereals													
Corn flakes	9.3	359	7.9	0.7	80.3	10	56	1.0	0	0.16	0.08	1.6	0
Oatmeal	8.3	396	14.2	7.4	68.2	54	365	5.2	0	0.55	0.14	1.1	0
Shredded wheat	7.7	369	10.4	1.4	78.7	38	385	3.8	0	0.20	0.14	4.2	0
Other cereals													
Hominy	11.4	357	8.5	0.8	78.9	11	70	1.0	0	0.15	0.05	0.9	0
Macaroni, spaghetti	11	360	13	1.4	73.9	22	144	1.2	0	0.13	0.08	2.1	0
Sugars, sweets													
Honey	20	319	0.3	0	79.5	5	16	0.9	0	Tr	0.04	0.2	4
Sugar, granulated or powdered	0.5	398	0	0	99.5	0	0	0.1	0	0	0	0	0
Miscellaneous													
Cocoa	4.3	329	9.0	18.8	31.0	—	709	2.7	0	Tr	0.39	2.3	0
Yeast, dried, brewers'	7.0	348	46.1	1.6	37.4	106	1,893	18.2	0	9.69	5.45	36.2	0

Source: Mallette, M. F., Althouse, P. M., and Clagett, C. O. *Biochemistry of Plants and Animals.* John Wiley & Sons, New York.

Concentrated and Dried Milk Products

TABLE 2.C.53
Typical analyses of concentrated milks and dried products

Milk Products	Protein	Fat	Moisture	Carbohydrate Lactose	Sucrose	Ash	Calcium	Phosphorus	Lactic acid
	%	%	%	%	%	%	%	%	%
Concentrated									
Evaporated milk	7.0	7.9	73.8	9.7	0	1.6	0.252	0.205	0
Sweetened condensed, whole	8.1	8.7	27.1	11.4	44.3	1.8	0.262	0.206	0
Plain condensed skim	10.0	0.3	73.0	14.7	0	2.3	0.250	0.200	0
Sweetened condensed skim	10.0	0.3	28.4	16.3	42.0	2.3	0.300	0.230	0
Condensed buttermilk (acid)	9.9	1.5	72.0	12.0	0	2.2	—	—	5.7
Condensed skim (acid)	10.19	0.17	72.0	9.43	0	2.13	—	—	6.08
Condensed whey	7.0	2.4	48.1	38.5	0	4.0	—	—	2.4
Sweetened condensed whey	5.0	1.7	24.0	28.5	38.0	2.8	—	—	0
Dried									
Whole milk	26.4	27.5	2.0	38.2	0	5.9	0.909	0.708	0
Skim (conventional)	35.9	0.8	3.0	52.3	0	8.0	1.308	1.016	0
Skim (instant)	35.8	0.7	4.0	51.6	0	7.9	1.293	1.005	0
Buttermilk (sweet)	34.3	5.3	2.8	50.0	0	7.6	1.248	0.970	0
Buttermilk (acid)	37.6	5.7	4.8	38.8	0	7.4	—	—	5.7
Malted milk	14.7	8.3	2.6	20.0	50.5[a]	3.6	—	—	0
Cream	13.4	65.0	0.8	18.0	0	2.91	0.288	0.380	0
Whey (sweet) Cheddar	12.9	0.9	4.5	73.5	0	8.0	0.646	0.589	2.3
Whey (acid) cottage	13.0	0	3.2	66.5	0	10.2	1.44	1.17	8.6
Casein (commercial)	88.5	0.2	7.0	0	0	3.8	—	—	—
Casein (co-precipitate)	83.0	1.5	4.0	1.0	0	10.5	2.5	—	—

[a] 50.5% = maltose and dextrin.

Source: Hargrove, R. E., and Alford, J. A. (1974). Composition of milk products. In *Fundamentals of Dairy Chemistry*, 2d Edition. B. H. Webb, A. H. Johnson, and J. A. Alford (editors). AVI Publishing Co., Westport, Connecticut.

Concentration of Commercial Strengths of Acids and Bases

TABLE 2.C.54
Concentration of acids and bases (common commercial strengths)

	Molecular weight	Moles per liter	Grams per liter	Percent by weight	Specific gravity
acetic acid, glacial	60.05	17.4	1045	99.5	1.05
acetic acid	60.05	6.27	376	36	1.045
butyric acid	88.1	10.3	912	95	0.96
formic acid	46.02	23.4	1080	90	1.20
		5.75	264	25	1.06
hydriodic acid	127.9	7.57	969	57	1.70
		5.51	705	47	1.50
		0.86	110	10	1.1
hydrobromic acid	80.92	8.89	720	48	1.50
		6.82	552	40	1.38
hydrochloric acid	36.5	11.6	424	36	1.18
		2.9	105	10	1.05
hydrocyanic acid	27.03	25	676	97	0.697
		0.74	19.9	2	0.996
hydrofluoric acid	20.01	32.1	642	55	1.167
		28.8	578	50	1.155
hydrofluosilicic acid	144.1	2.65	382	30	1.27
hypophosphorous acid	66.0	9.47	625	50	1.25
		5.14	339	30	1.13
		1.57	104	10	1.04
lactic acid	90.1	11.3	1020	85	1.2
nitric acid	63.02	15.99	1008	71	1.42
		14.9	938	67	1.40
		13.3	837	61	1.37
perchloric acid	100.5	11.65	1172	70	1.67
		9.2	923	60	1.54
phosphoric acid	98	14.7	1445	85	1.70
sulfuric acid	98.1	18.0	1766	96	1.84
sulfurous acid	82.1	0.74	61.2	6	1.02
ammonia water	17.0	14.8	252	28	0.898
potassium hydroxide	56.1	13.5	757	50	1.52
		1.94	109	10	1.09
sodium carbonate	106.0	1.04	110	10	1.10
sodium hydroxide	40.0	19.1	763	50	1.53
		2.75	111	10	1.11

Source: The Merck Index, 8th Edition. (1968) Merck & Co., Rahway, New Jersey.

Condensed-Milk Dressing

TABLE 2.C.55

⅔ cup sweetened milk
¼ cup oil
¼ cup vinegar plus 1 tbsp
    lemon juice or 5 tbsp
    vinegar

½ tsp dry mustard
¼ tsp salt
1 tsp minced parsley
    (optional)

Procedure

Mix the ingredients and stir until the milk is throughly thickened. Refrigerate.

Source: Kintner, T. C., and Mangel, M. Vinegars and salad dressings. Univ. Missouri Agric. Expt. Sta. Bull. *631.*

Connective Tissue, Composition

TABLE 2.C.56
Percentage composition of white and yellow connective tissues

	Tendon of Achilles	Ligamentum Nuchae
Water	62.87	57.57
Ash	0.47	0.47
Fat	1.04	1.12
Albumin-globulin	0.22	0.62
Mucoid	1.28	0.53
Elastin	1.63	31.67
Collagen	31.59	7.23
Extractives	0.90	0.80

Source: Moulton, C. R., and Lewis, W. L. *Meat Through the Microscope,* Revised Edition. Institute of Meat Packing, University of Chicago, Chicago.

Connective Tissue Proteins

TABLE 2.C.57
Description of tissue proteins

Name	Shape	Size	Molecular Weight	Distinctive Composition	Reactions and Role
Collagen	Rod, coiled coil of three helices wound together	Polymer of tropocollagen	Indefinite	Hydroxy groups important in H-bonds, proline rings in shape of molecule. Vertebrate collagen contains about 0.5 percent carbohydrate—at least one galactose residue, often a glucose. Probably cross-linked both intra- and intermolecularly. Degree of cross-linking increases with age.	Shrink temperature, T, fiber shrinks to about 1/3 length. T, usually around 60° C—varies with pH, ions, solvent, rate of heating, stretching force. Major component of tissue supporting contractile fibers and connecting muscles to bones.
Tropocollagen	Rod, three chains, each left-handed helix, three wound together in right-handed superhelix	2800 A long, 14 A diameter	300,000–350,000	About 1/3 glycine, 1/8 proline, and 1/10 hydroxyproline. Small amount hydroxylysine. Configuration of single and triple chains determined by H-bonds and by proline rings.	Building blocks of collagen. Soluble in cold neutral salt solution. Heat to 30° C, triple chain separates into gelatin.
Elastin	Cross-linked three-dimensional gel		Indefinite	Very low in amino acids with hydrophilic side chains, small amount of hydroxyproline. Cross-linked by desmocine and isodesmocine.	Elastic component of connective tissue, found in small amounts in muscle. Mainly occurs in walls of blood vessels and in elastic ligaments.
Reticulin				Contains lipid, especially myristic acid.	More found in endomysium than in peri- or epimysium.
Ground substance: Protein, polysaccharides, glycoprotein, and the like				Protein bonded to polysaccharide is noncollagenous. Some glycoproteins—may contain glucose, galactose, mannose, hexosamine, fucose, and sialic acid.	Complexed with mucopolysaccharides.

Source: Paul, P. C., and Palmer, H. H. (1972). *Food Theory and Applications.* John Wiley & Sons, New York.

Constants, Fundamental

TABLE 2.C.58

Name	Value
Avogadro's number	$N_0 = 6.023 \times 10^{23}$ molecules/g mole
Base of natural logarithm	$e = 2.7183 \ldots$
Curie	$Ci = 3.7 \times 10^{10}$ disintegrations/sec
Electron charge	$e = 4.8 \times 10^{-10}$ statcoulomb $= 1.6 \times 10^{-19}$ coulomb
Energy equivalent of electron mass	$mc^2 = 0.51$ Mev
Faraday's constant	$F = 96{,}514$ coulombs/g equivalent (physical scale)
Gravitational acceleration	$g = 980.665$ cm/sec^2
Mass, alpha particle	$m_\alpha = 6.64 \times 10^{-24}$ g $= 4.002777\ mu$
Mass, electron	$m_e = 9.1066 \times 10^{-28}$ g $= 0.000548\ mu$
Mass, H atom	$m_H = 1.67339 \times 10^{-24}$ g $= 1.008142\ mu$
Mass, neutron	$m_n = 1.6751 \times 10^{-24}$ g $= 1.008982\ mu$
Mass, proton	$m_p = 1.67248 \times 10^{-24}$ g $= 1.007594\ mu$
Mass unit	$mu = 1.66035 \times 10^{-24}$ g $= 1.000\ mu$
Microcurie	$\mu Ci = 10^{-6}$ curie $= 3.7 \times 10^4$ disintegrations/sec
Micromicrocurie	$\mu\mu Ci = 10^{-12}$ curie $= 3.7 \times 10^{-2}$ disintegrations/sec
Millicurie	$mCi = 10^{-3}$ curie $= 3.7 \times 10^7$ disintegrations/sec
Pi	$\pi = 3.1416$
Planck's constant	$h = 6.624 \times 10^{27}$ erg-sec
Rad	rad = 100 ergs/g of tissue
Roentgen	$r = 1$ esu/0.001293 g of air
Rem	rem = rads $\times$ RBE
Rutherford	$rd = 10^6$ disintegrations/sec

Source: Wang, Y. (editor) (1969). *Handbook of Radioactive Nuclides*. CRC Press, Cleveland. Reproduced with permission of CRC Press.

Cooked Dressing

TABLE 2.C.59

Ingredients

2 tbsp fat	1 egg
2⅓ tbsp flour	¾ tsp salt
2⅓ tbsp sugar	¾ tsp dry mustard
½ cup water	⅛ tsp paprika
½ cup milk	3 tbsp vinegar

Procedure

Melt the fat in the top of the double boiler. Add the flour, and mix. Add the milk and water and cook in the double boiler for 10 min. Beat egg. Add to the starch mixture and cook until thickened. Remove from heat. Add spices and vinegar. Refrigerate.

Source: Kintner, T. C., and Mangel, M. Vinegars and salad dressings. Univ. Missouri Agric. Expt. Sta. Bull. *631*.

Cooking in Liquid, Time

TABLE 2.C.60
Time-table for cooking meat in liquid

Cut	Average Weight	Approx. Time Per Pound	Approx. Total Cooking Time
	Pounds	Minutes	Hours
Smoked ham (country cured)			
Large	12 to 16	20	
Small	10 to 12	25	
Half	5 to 8	30	
Smoked ham			
Shank or rump half	5 to 8	20-25	
Smoked arm picnic shoulder	5 to 8	45	
Fresh or corned beef	4 to 6	40-50	
Beef shank cross cuts	¾ to 1		2½ to 3½
Beef for stew			2½ to 3½
Veal for stew			2 to 3
Lamb for stew			1½ to 2

Source: Lessons on Meat. (1974). National Live Stock and Meat Board, Chicago.

Corn

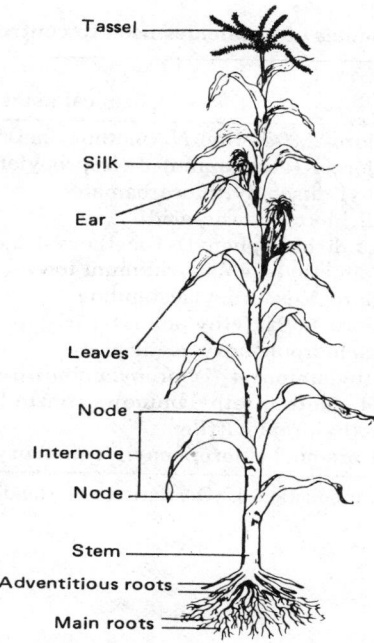

FIGURE 2.C.15
Nomenclature of a corn stalk

Source: Mittleider, J. R., and Nelson, A. N. (1970). *Food for Everyone*. Extension Division, Loma Linda University, California.

Corn, Amino Acids

TABLE 2.C.61
Amino acids in whole kernels of normal and Opaque-2 maize (grams per 100 g protein)

Amino Acid	Normal	*Opaque-2*
Lysine	3.0	4.8
Tryptophan	0.7	1.3
Histidine	2.6	3.3
Arginine	4.9	8.5
Aspartic acid	9.2	10.8
Glutamic acid	22.6	17.5
Threonine	4.1	4.0
Serine	5.6	4.8
Proline	9.6	7.6
Glycine	4.7	4.8
Alanine	9.2	6.6
Valine	5.7	5.1
Cystine	1.7	1.7
Methionine	1.3	2.1
Isoleucine	4.2	3.4
Leucine	14.6	9.1
Tyrosine	5.2	4.0
Phenylalanine	5.8	4.5
	Percent	Protein
	9.0	11.6

Source: Maize and maize diets. FAO Nutritional Studies *9*. FAO, United Nations, Rome.

Corn Herbicides

TABLE 2.C.62
Common and chemical names of herbicides used to control weeds in corn

Common name or designation	Chemical name
Alachlor	2-chloro-2′,6′-diethyl-*N*-(methoxymethyl)-acetanilide
Atrazine	2-chloro-4-(ethylamino)-6-(isopropylamino)-*s*-triazine
Butylate	*S*-ethyl diisobutylthiocarbamate
Dicamba	3,6-dichloro-*o*-anisic acid
Linuron	3-(3,4-dichlorophenyl)-1-methoxy-1-methylurea
Paraquat	1,1′-dimethyl-4,4′-bipyridinium ion
Propachlor	2-chloro-*N*-isopropylacetanilide
Simazine	2-chloro-4,6-bis(ethylamino)-*s*-triazine
2,4-D	2,4-dichlorophenoxy acetic acid
Ametryne	2-(ethylamino)-4-(isopropylamino)-6-(methylthio)-*s*-triazine
Cyanazine	2-[[4-chloro-6-(ethylamino)-*s*-triazin-2-yl]amino]-2-methylpropionitrile
Chlorobromuron	3-(4-bromo-3-chlorophenyl)-1-methoxy-1-methylurea

Source: USDA (1975). Corn production. USDA Agriculture Handbook *322*.

Corn Kernel

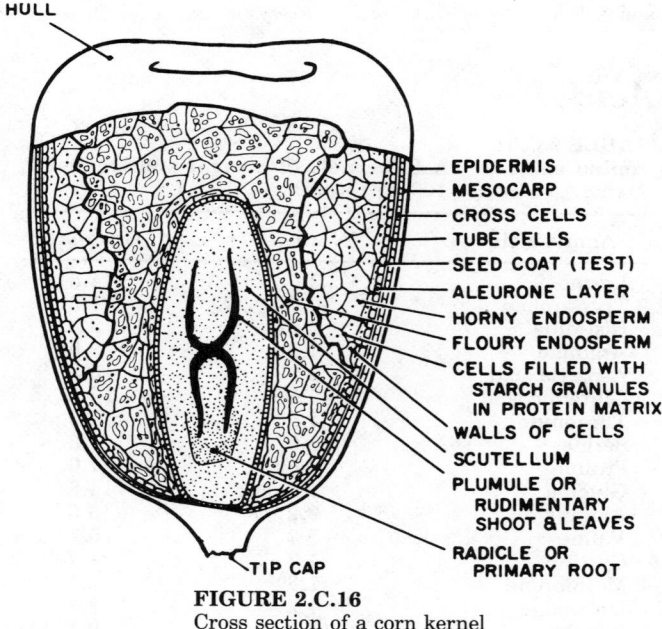

FIGURE 2.C.16
Cross section of a corn kernel

Source: Brooker, D. B., Bakker-Arkema, F. W., and Hall, C. W. (editors) (1974). Principles of grain drying. In *Drying Cereal Grains*. AVI Publishing Co., Westport, Connecticut.

Corn Kernel Composition

TABLE 2.C.63
Distribution of parts and chemical constituents in the maize kernel (moisture-free basis)

FRACTION	Composition of Fraction				% by weight of whole grain	% of Total in whole grain contained in specified fraction			
	Ash %	Protein (N × 6.25) %	Oil %	Carbohydrate (by dif) %		Ash	Protein	Oil	Carbohydrate (by dif.)
1. LOW PROTEIN EAR									
Tip cap	0.91	7.4	1.2	90.6	1.2	0.8	0.9	0.3	1.3
Hulls	0.82	5.0	0.9	93.3	5.5	3.3	2.7	1.2	6.0
Endosperm									
" Horny gluten "	0.92	19.2	4.0	75.9	11.6	8.0	22.6	11.1	10.4
" Horny starch "	0.18	8.1	0.2	91.5	37.1	5.0	30.5	1.4	40.2
" Crown starch " and " tip starch "	0.31	6.8	0.2	92.8	35.0	8.0	24.0	1.9	38.3
Germ	10.5	19.9	36.5	33.1	9.6	74.9	19.3	84.0	3.8
Whole grain, intact	1.4	9.3	4.2	85.1					
Calculated from parts	1.3	9.9	4.2	84.6	100.0	100.0	100.0	99.9	100.0
2. HIGH PROTEIN EAR:									
Tip cap	1.87	4.6	2.0	91.5	1.6	1.8	0.6	0.6	1.8
Hulls	1.10	3.8	0.8	94.3	6.1	3.9	1.8	0.9	7.1
Endosperm									
" Horny gluten "	1.74	24.6	4.6	69.1	13.3	13.5	25.9	12.3	11.4
" Horny starch "	0.21	11.0	0.2	88.6	44.9	5.5	39.0	2.0	49.3
" Crown starch " and " tip starch "	0.46	8.1	0.8	90.5	22.2	5.9	14.2	3.7	24.9
Germ	10.0	19.6	33.7	36.7	11.9	69.5	18.4	80.5	5.4
Whole grain, intact	1.7	12.8	5.4	80.1					
Calculated from parts	1.7	12.6	5.0	80.7	100.0	100.1	99.9	100.0	99.9

NOTE: Results obtained from fractions separated by hand from single ears of low-protein (9.3%) and high-protein (12.8%) maize.

Source: Maize and maize diets. FAO Nutritional Studies 9. FAO, United Nations, Rome.

Corn Plant Growth

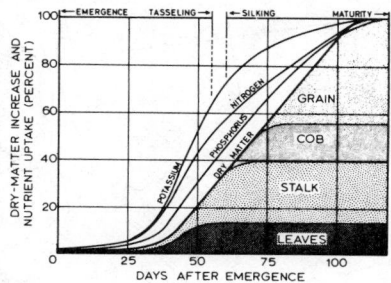

FIGURE 2.C.17
Dry-matter increase and nutrient uptake in developing corn plant.

Source: USDA (1975). Corn production. USDA Agriculture Handbook *322*.

Corn Production Area

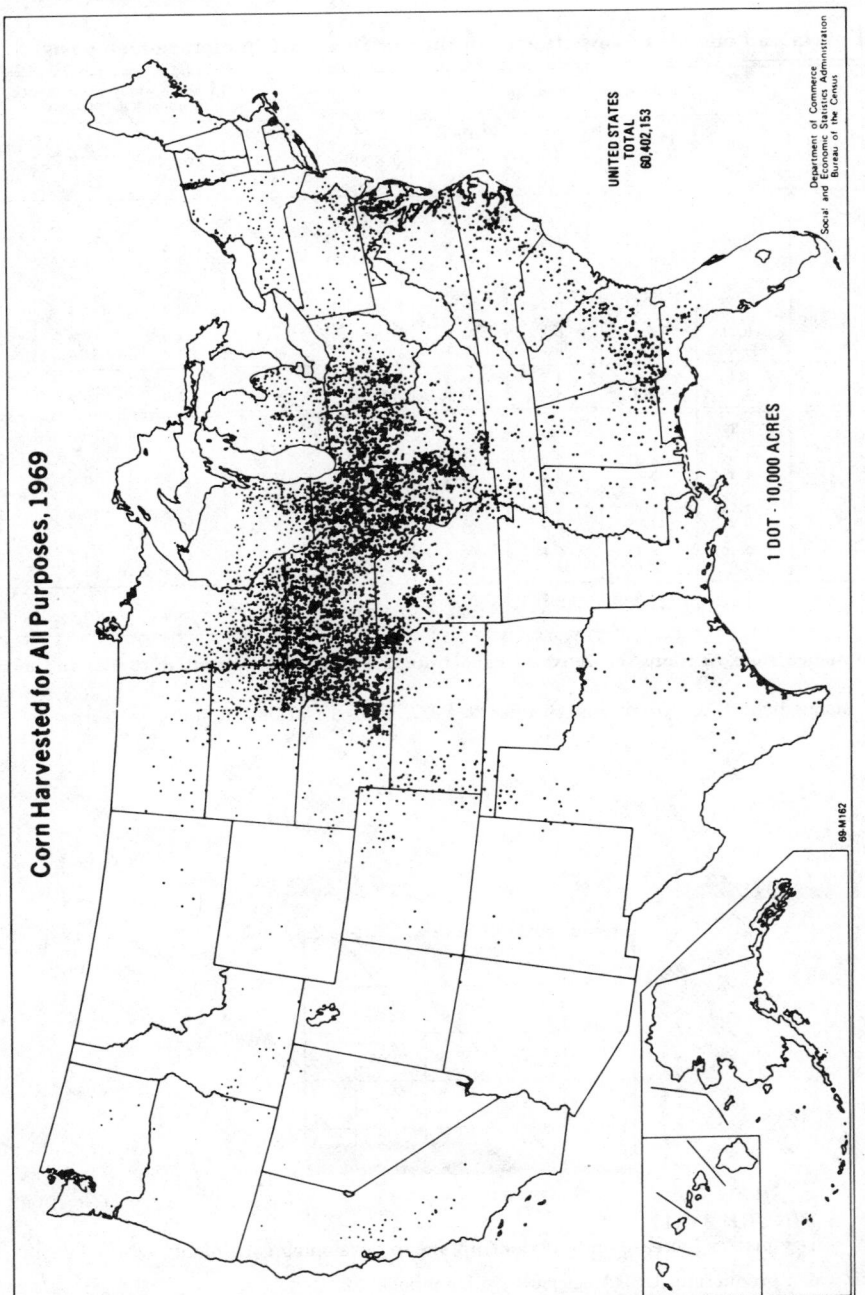

Corn Harvested for All Purposes, 1969

UNITED STATES
TOTAL
60,402,153

1 DOT · 10,000 ACRES

69-M162

Department of Commerce
Social and Economic Statistics Administration
Bureau of the Census

FIGURE 2.C.18
Corn acreage in the United States, 1969 (U.S. Bureau of Census). Corn Belt includes area where dots are thickest, extending from Ohio to Nebraska and from southern Minnesota to northern Missouri.

Source: USDA (1975). Corn production. USDA Agricultural Handbook *322.*

Cornstarch Pudding Variations

TABLE 2.C.64
Common variations of cornstarch pudding

Product	Liquid (cup)	Starchy Agent (tbsp)	Sugar (tbsp)	Other Ingredients
Plain blanc mange	1 milk	1½–2 cornstarch	2	½ tsp vanilla
Chocolate blanc mange	1 milk	1½–2 cornstarch	3	½ sq chocolate ¼ tsp vanilla
Chocolate cream pudding	1 milk	1½–2 cornstarch	3	1 stiffly beaten egg white ½ sq chocolate ¼ tsp vanilla
Coconut blanc mange	1 milk	1½–2 cornstarch	2	½ tsp vanilla ½–1 cup shredded coconut
Fruit blanc mange	1 milk	1½–2½ cornstarch	2	½ cup dates, pineapple, bananas, cherries, prunes, or other desired fruit
Nut blanc mange	1 milk	1½–2 cornstarch	2	½ tsp vanilla ¼–½ cup chopped nuts
Caramel blanc mange	1 milk	1½–2 cornstarch	2	½ tsp vanilla 2 tbsp caramel syrup
Maple blanc mange	1 milk	1½–2 cornstarch	2 maple sugar	
Fruit tapioca	1 fruit juice and water	2–2½ minute tapioca	3	½–1 cup fruit
Indian pudding	1 milk	1 cornmeal	1½–2 molasses	¼ tsp ginger

Source: Justin, M. M., Rust, L. O., and Vail, G. E. Foods, Revised Edition. Houghton Mifflin Co., Boston.

Correlation Significance

TABLE 2.C.65
Values of the correlation coefficient for different levels of significance

n	P = .1	.05	.02	.01	n	P = .1	.05	.02	.01
1	.98769	.996917	.9995066	.9998766	17	.3887	.4555	.5285	.5751
2	.90000	.95000	.98000	.990000	18	.3783	.4438	.5155	.5614
3	.8054	.8783	.93433	.95873	19	.3687	.4329	.5034	.5487
4	.7293	.8114	.8822	.91720	20	.3598	.4227	.4921	.5368
5	.6694	.7545	.8329	.8745					
6	.6215	.7067	.7887	.8343	25	.3233	.3809	.4451	.4869
7	.5822	.6664	.7498	.7977	30	.2960	.3494	.4093	.4487
8	.5494	.6319	.7155	.7646	35	.2746	.3246	.3810	.4182
9	.5214	.6021	.6851	.7348	40	.2573	.3044	.3578	.3932
10	.4973	.5760	.6581	.7079	45	.2428	.2875	.3384	.3721
					50	.2306	.2732	.3218	.3541
11	.4762	.5529	.6339	.6835	60	.2108	.2500	.2948	.3248
12	.4575	.5324	.6120	.6614	70	.1954	.2319	.2737	.3017
13	.4409	.5139	.5923	.6411	80	.1829	.2172	.2565	.2830
14	.4259	.4973	.5742	.6226	90	.1726	.2050	.2422	.2673
15	.4124	.4821	.5577	.6055	100	.1638	.1946	.2301	.2540
16	.4000	.4683	.5425	.5897					

For a total correlation, n is 2 less than the number of pairs in the sample; for a partial correlation, the number of eliminated variates also should be subtracted.

Source: Fisher, R. A. (1972). Statistical Methods for Research Workers, 14th Edition. Hafner Press, New York.

Cottage Cheese Shield

Cottage cheese may bear the USDA "Quality Approved" shield if it is of good quality and made under USDA supervision. During processing, a USDA inspector keeps constant check on all aspects of product quality, right down to a final check on the product in consumer packages.

FIGURE 2.C.19

Source: USDA (1979). How to buy dairy products. USDA Home and Garden Bull. *201*.

Creams, Butter, and Frozen Desserts

TABLE 2.C.66
Typical composition of market creams, butter, and frozen desserts[a]

	Moisture	Protein	Fat	Lactose	Ash	Calcium	Phosphorus
	%	%	%	%	%	%	%
Market creams							
Half and half	80.0	3.1	11.6	4.5	0.7	0.10	0.08
Light cream	73.0	2.9	19.3	4.2	0.6	0.10	0.08
Whipping, light	62.9	2.5	30.5	3.6	0.5	0.08	0.06
Whipping, heavy	57.3	2.2	36.8	3.2	0.5	0.07	0.05
Plastic	18.2	0.7	80.0	1.0	0.1	0.03	0.02
Butter, butter oil, ghee							
Butter	16.5	0.6	80.5	0.4	2.5	0.02	0.02
Butter oil	0.2	0.3	99.5	0.0	0.0	—	—
Ghee	0.1	0.1	99.8	0.0	0.0	—	—
Frozen desserts							
Ice cream	62.1	4.0	12.5	20.3[b]	0.8	0.12	0.10
Ice cream, low fat	63.2	4.5	10.6	20.8[b]	0.9	0.15	0.12
Ice cream, high fat	62.8	2.6	16.1	18.0[b]	0.5	0.08	0.06
Ice milk	66.7	4.8	5.1	22.4[b]	1.0	0.16	0.12
Sherbet	67.0	0.9	1.2	30.8[b]	0.1	0.02	0.01

[a] Salt concentration in butter ranges from 0.8–2.3%. The lower value is typical of most European countries, the higher value of the United States, New Zealand, and Australia.
[b] Carbohydrate other than lactose added.

Source: Hargrove, R. E., and Alford, J. A. (editors) (1974). Composition of milk products. In *Fundamentals of Dairy Chemistry*, 2d Edition. AVI Publishing Co., Westport, Connecticut.

Cucurbit Crops, Spacing and Depth of Planting

TABLE 2.C.67
Measurements are in inches

Crop	Spacing Between plants in row	Spacing Between rows	Planting Depth
Cucumber	12 [1] 24–36 [2]	48–72	1
Muskmelon	12 [1] 24–36 [2]	60–84	1–1½
Pumpkin	36–40	72–96	2–3
Squash (bush)	24–30	36	2–3
Squash (vining)	36–40	72–96	2–3
Gourd	36–40	72–96	2–3
Watermelon	24–36 [1] 72 [2]	72–84	1–2

[1] Single plants.
[2] Hills.

Source: USDA (1977). Growing your own vegetables. USDA Agricultural Information Bull. *409.*

Cultured Dairy Products, Composition

TABLE 2.C.68
Approximate composition of some cultured and special dairy products

Product	Water (%)	Fat (%)	Msnf (%)	Protein (%)	Carbohydrates (%)	Ash (%)	Lactic Acid (%)
Buttermilk sweet cream	90.83	0.55	8.25	3.45	4.40	0.73	0.04
Sour cream	91.3	0.65	8.25	3.40	3.40	0.65	0.60
Cultured cream	90.5	0.10	8.25	3.6	5.1	0.70	0.75
Plain yogurt	89.0	1.70	8.25	3.4	5.2	0.75	0.95
Flavored yogurt	91.0	1.5	8.25	3.2	12.8	0.70	0.95
Cultured sour cream	74.5	18.0	7.4	2.8	4.1	0.70	0.70
Flavored milk drink	86.0	2.0	8.25	2.8	8.0	0.65	—
Coffee creamer	83.0	5.0	12.00	3.5	5.4	0.80	—
Filled milk	87.0	3.5	8.5	3.5	5.0	0.7	—

Source: Arbuckle, W. S. (1973). Dairy products. In *Quality Control For The Food Industry*, Vol. 2, 3d Edition. A. Kramer and B. A. Twigg (editors). AVI Publishing Co., Westport, Connecticut.

Culture Media

TABLE 2.C.69
Summary of culture media for specific groups of microorganisms (*Note:* Those media that may be expected to give the most efficient results as evidenced by their ability to grow more species, or to grow them more rapidly, are indicated by asterisks)

Organisms	Isolation	Cultivation	Identification	Maintenance
Actinomycetes, aerobic Nocardia Streptomyces	Blood Agar Base Brain Heart Infusion Agar Emerson Media *Eugonagar *Mycophil Media Sabouraud Media *Thioglycollate Medium-135C *Trypticase Soy Media	Czapek Dox Media Emerson Media *Eugonagar *Eugonbroth *Mycophil Media Sabouraud Media Trypticase Soy Media	*C T A Media *Eugonagar Indole Nitrite Medium Nutrient Gelatin *Thiogel Medium Carbohydrate Taxo Discs	*C T A Medium *Trypticase Agar Base *Trypticase Soy Agar
Anaerobes, exclusive of clostridia, e.g. *A. bovis, israelii* Bacteroides Fusiforms *P. anaerobius* Sphaerophorus	Actinomyces Broth *Anaerobic Agars *Eugonagar *Forget-Fredette Agar *Thioglycollate Medium-135C Trypticase Soy Blood Agar Trypticase Soy Broth	Anaerobic Agar *C T A Medium Eugonagar *Eugonbroth Fluid Thioglycollate Medium *Thioglycollate Medium-135C Trypticase Soy Media	*Anaerobic Agar w/o Dextrose *C T A Medium with Carbohydrates *Indole Nitrite Medium Loeffler Medium *Thiogel Medium Thioglycollate Medium with proteins Carbohydrate Taxo Discs	Cooked Meat Medium *Cooked Meat Phytone Medium *C T A Medium Thioglycollate Medium-135C with $CaCO_3$
Bacillus	Nutrient Media Thermoacidurans Agar Trypticase Soy Media	A K Agar #2 Eugonagar and Eugonbroth Nutrient Media Trypticase Soy Media Trypticase Stratifying Agar 2%	D Nase Test Agar Litmus and other Skim Milk Media Thiogel Medium Trypticase Agar Base Urease Test Media Carbohydrate Taxo Discs	C T A Medium Trypticase Agar Base Trypticase Soy Agar
Bordetella	*Bordet Gengou Agars *Chocolate (Eugonagar) Agar *Trypticase Soy Agar with Yeast Hemin Extract G C Agar with IsoVitaleX and Hemoglobin	*Bordet Gengou Agars *Eugonagar with blood Trypticase Soy Agar with Yeast Hemin Extract	Litmus Milk	
Brucella	Biosate Agar + Crystal Violet Brucella Media *Eugonagar *Eugonbroth *Thioglycollate Medium-135C *Trypticase Soy Media	Biosate Agar Brucella Agar *Eugonagar *Eugonbroth Potato Infusion Agar *Thioglycollate Medium-135C *Trypticase Soy Media	*C T A Medium *Thiogel Medium *Trypticase Soy Agar with Fuchsin with Thionin Urease Test Agar *Urease Test Broth Carbohydrate Taxo Discs	*C T A Medium

(Continued)

Culture Media (Continued)

TABLE 2.C.69 (Continued)

Organisms	Isolation	Cultivation	Identification	Maintenance
Clostridium	Anaerobic Agars *Clostrisel Agar Cooked Meat Media Fluid Thioglycollate Medium Forget-Fredette Agar Reinforced Clostridial Media *Thioglycollate Medium-135C Trypticase Soy Media S P S Agar *T S N Agar	*Anaerobic Agars Eugonagar Eugonbroth Fluid Thioglycollate Medium *Thioglycollate Medium-135C with CaCO₃ *Trypticase Agar Base	*Anaerobic Agar w/o Dextrose *Indole Nitrite Medium Litmus, Purple or Ulrich Milks or Skim Milk Loeffler Medium Sulfite Agar *Thiogel Medium Thioglycollate Medium with proteins *Trypticase Agar Base *Trypticase Dextrose Agar *Trypticase Lactose Iron Agar Carbohydrate Taxo Discs	Cooked Meat Medium *Cooked Meat Phytone Medium *Thioglycollate Medium-135C with CaCO₃ *Trypticase Agar Base
Corynebacterium	Columbia Agar Loeffler Medium *Serum Tellurite Agar Thioglycollate Media Tinsdale Agar *Trypticase Soy Media *Trypticase Tellurite Agar	Blood Agar Base Brain Heart Infusion Media *Eugonagar Eugonbroth Infusion Broths Loeffler Medium Thioglycollate Media *Trypticase Soy Media	*C T A Media Indole Nitrite Medium *Thiogel Medium Tinsdale Agar *Trypticase Agar Base Carbohydrate and N Taxo Discs	*C T A Medium Trypticase Soy Agar
Enteric Bacilli	B D G Broth Buffered Glycerol Saline *Cary and Blair Transport Medium *Desoxycholate Agar *Desoxycholate Lactose Agar E M B Agars Endo Media Eugonagar *Eugonbroth *G N Broth *MacConkey Agars S B B A Agar *Sorbitol Agar Specimen Preservative Tergitol Media Thioglycollate Media Transport Media Trypticase Soy Media Violet Red Bile Agar	*Blood Agars *Eugonagar *Eugonbroth Extract Media Infusion Broths Nutrient Agars Nutrient Broths Sanders Media S B B A Agar Thioglycollate Media *Trypticase Soy Media	Carlquist Ninhydrin Broth Christensen Citrate Sulfide Agar D L I Slant Agar D L S I Agar Falkow Lysine Broth Gillies Media H Broth *Indole Nitrite Medium Kliger Iron Agar Koser Citrate Broth Krumwiede Triple Sugar Agar Levine E M B Agars *Lysine Iron Agar Malonate Broth Moeller Decarboxylase Broths Moeller K C N Broth Motility Test Medium *M R-V P (Clark and Lubs) Broth Nutrient Gelatin O F Medium Carbohydrate and N Taxo Discs	Eugonagar Infusion Agars Nutrient Agar *Trypticase Agar Base *Trypticase Soy Agar

(Continued)

Culture Media (Continued)

TABLE 2.C.69 (Continued)

Organisms	Isolation	Cultivation	Identification	Maintenance
Coliforms and Proteus	Boric Acid Broth *Brilliant Green Bile Media Crystal Violet Lactose Broth E C and Eijkman Broths Formate Ricinoleate Broth Fuchsin Lactose Broth H D Broth *Lactose Broth *Lauryl Sulfate Broth MacConkey Broth *M-Coliform Broth M-E M B and Endo Broths M-Endo Agar L E S M-F C Broth Purple Lactose Agar		Phenol Red Media Phenylalanine Media Purple Media Russell Double Sugar Agar Saccharose Mannitol Agar Sanders Agar + **Taxo Discs** Semisolid Medium of Edwards and Bruner Semisolid Medium for Enterics S I M Medium *Simmons Citrate Agar Sorbitol Iron Agar *Thiogel Medium *Trypticase Agar Base with **Taxo Discs** *Trypticase Lactose Iron Agar *T S I Agar⁹	
Salmonella and Shigella	*Bismuth Sulfite Agar (Wilson and Blair) Brilliant Green Agars Buffered Glycerol Saline Base D C L S Agar⁹ Desoxycholate-Citrate Agars E E Broth G N Broth M-Bismuth Sulfite and Brilliant Green Broths Salmonella Shigella Agar Sanders Booster Broth Selenite Media Specimen Preservative Tetrathionate Media Transport Media *X L D Agar		*Tryptophane Broth	
Desulfovibrio	Sulfate Reducer A P I Media			
Erysipelothrix	**Eugonagar** **Trypticase Soy Media** Thioglycollate Medium-135C	**Eugonagar** **Eugonbroth**	**C T A Medium** Indole Nitrite Medium **Thiogel Medium**	**C T A Medium**
Gram-Positive Cocci	*Anaerobic Agar Azide Blood Agar Blood Agar Base Brain Heart Media *B T B Lactose Agar Columbia Agar *Eugonagar **Eugonbroth** Mitis Salivarius Agar M N **Trypticase** Soy Agar Thioglycollate Media Transport Medium *Trypticase Soy Media	Blood Agar Base Brain Heart Media **Eugonagar** **Eugonbroth** Infusion Media Micro Assay Culture Agar **Trypticase** Soy Media	Ammonium Phosphate Agar *C T A Media *Indole Nitrite Medium *Thiogel Medium Litmus and other Milks *Trypticase Soy Media Urease Test Broth Carbohydrate **Taxo Discs**	*C T A Media *Thioglycollate Medium-135C with CaCO₃ **Trypticase Agar Base**

(Continued)

Culture Media (Continued)

Organisms	Isolation	Cultivation	Identification	Maintenance
Diplococcus *Streptococcus*	Columbia C N A Agar *Serum Tellurite Agar *Streptosel Agar *Thioglycollate Medium-135C Trypticase Tellurite Agar Veal Infusion Media		D Nase Test Agar	
Enterococci	Azide Dextrose Broth B A G G Broth Columbia C N A Agar Enterococcus Presumptive Broth Ethyl Violet Azide Broth K F Streptococcal Media MacConkey Agar w/o Crystal Violet Mead Agar *M-Enterococcus Media M-Slanetz Enterococcus Broth *Phenylethyl Alcohol Agar S F Broth *Streptosel Agar Thallous Acetate Agar		C T A Medium plus Sorbitol Ethyl Violet Azide Broth Infusion or Trypticase Soy Broth + 6.5% salt K F Streptococcal Media M-Enterococcus Media S F Broth Thiogel Medium Trypticase Soy Agar Blood Plates	
Staphylococci	Ammonium Phosphate Agar Baird-Parker Agar Chapman Stone Agar Cooked Meat Media *Mannitol Salt Agar Staphylococcus Agar #110 Tellurite Glycine Agar T P E Y Agar Vogel and Johnson Agar	Nutrient Agar Nutrient Broth	Baird-Parker Agar Casein Hydrolysate Broth Coagulase Mannitol Media C T A Medium + Mannitol D Nase Test Agar Mannitol Salt Agar Phenol Red Media Staphylococcus Agar #110 T P E Y Agar Carbohydrate Taxo Discs	C T A Media
Hemophilus	*Eugonagar Eugonbroth L B S Media M N Trypticase Soy Agar *Thioglycollate Medium-135C Transport Medium Trypticase Soy Agar with Yeast Hemin Extract G C Agar with IsoVitaleX and Hemoglobin	Eugonagar Eugonbroth *Trypticase Soy Media	Taxo Discs	*C T A Medium *Trypticase Soy Agar
Lactobacillus and *Leuconostoc*	*A P T Media *Eugonagar *L B S Media *Orange Serum Agar Snyder Agar Tomato Juice Agar	A P T Agar A P T Broth Eugonagar L Agar Micro Assay Culture Agar Micro Inoculum Broth Orange Serum Agar Peptonized Milk Agar Thioglycollate Medium-135C Tomato Juice Agar	C T A Media Indole Nitrite Medium L Agar Litmus Milk Purple Milk Skim Milk Thiogel Medium Ulrich Milk Carbohydrate Taxo Discs	Eugonagar *L Agar *Thioglycollate Medium-135C with CaCO3

Culture Media (Continued)

TABLE 2.C.69 (Continued)

Organisms	Isolation	Cultivation	Identification	Maintenance
Leptospira	Fletcher Medium Base or Stuart Broth Base with Leptospira Enrichment	Fletcher Medium Base or Stuart Broth Base with Leptospira Enrichment		
Listeria	•Biosate Agar Eugonagar •Serum Tellurite Agar •Thioglycollate Medium-135C •Trypticase Soy Media	Biosate Agar Eugonagar Eugonbroth Thioglycollate Media Trypticase Soy Media	C T A Media Indole Nitrite Medium Litmus and other Milks Simmons Citrate Agar Thiogel Medium Trypticase Agar Base T S I Agar Urease Test Broth Carbohydrate Taxo Discs	C T A Media Trypticase Soy Agar
Mima	Desoxycholate Lactose Agar Levine E M B Agar MacConkey Agar Trypticase Soy Agar Thioglycollate Medium-135C		Indole Nitrite Medium Litmus Milk Sellers Agar Simmons Citrate Agar Thiogel Medium Urea Agar Taxo Carbohydrate and N Taxo Discs	Trypticase Agar Base Trypticase Soy Agar
Mycobacterium	A T S Medium Blood Agar Base Cary and Blair Transport Medium Chocolate (Eugonagar) Agar •Lowenstein-Jensen Medium •Middlebrook 7H10 Agar Peizer T B Media Petragnani Medium Petroff Medium Tarshis Agar	A T S Medium Dubos Media Lowenstein-Jensen Medium Middlebrook 7H10 Agar Nutrient Agar 1.5% Petragnani Medium Petroff Medium Tarshis Agar T B Broth Media Thioglycollate Medium-135C	Dubos Media •Lowenstein-Jensen Media with Inhibitors MacConkey Agar Middlebrook 7H10 Agar T B Broth Media •Thioglycollate Medium-135C •Wayne Sulfatase Agar	•A-T S Medium •Dorset Medium Lowenstein-Jensen Medium Petroff Medium Tarshis Agar
Mycoplasma	B Y E Media •Columbia Agar •Mycoplasma Broth •Mycoplasma Agar •Mycoplasma Enrichment Broth	B Y E Media	B Y E Media Columbia Agar C T A Media Mycoplasma Agar •Taxo Mycoplasma Discs	Mycoplasma Media

(Continued)

Culture Media (Continued)

TABLE 2.C.69 (Continued)

Organisms	Isolation	Cultivation	Identification	Maintenance
Neisseria	**Eugonagar** G C Agar with **Iso. VitaleX** En-richment and Hemoglobin Mueller Hinton Media *Thayer-Martin Selective Agar *Thioglycollate Medium-135C **Trypticase Soy Media**	**Eugonagar and Eugonbroth** **Trypticase** Soy Media	**°C T A Medium** Carbohydrate and N **Taxo** Discs	**°C T A Medium**
Pasteurella	*Cary and Blair Transport Medium Cystine Heart Agar Desoxycholate and Desoxycholate-Citrate Agars **Eugonagar** G C A Agar with Thiamine Thioglycollate Medium-135C **Trypticase Soy Media**	**Eugonagar and Eugonbroth** Thioglycollate Medium-135C **Trypticase** Soy Media	**C T A Medium** Indole Nitrite Medium **Thiogel** Medium **T S I Agar** Carbohydrate **Taxo** Discs	*C T A Medium
Pseudomonas	**Eugonagar** **Pseudosel** Agar **Trypticase Soy Media**	**Eugonagar and Eugonbroth** Nutrient Media **Trypticase** Soy Media	D Nase Test Agar Flo Agar O F Medium· Sabouraud Maltose Agar Tech Agar **T S I Agar**	**Trypticase Agar Base** **Trypticase Soy Agar**
Streptobacillus	Thioglycollate Medium w/o Dextrose **Trypticase Soy Media**	Thioglycollate Medium w/o Dextrose **Trypticase** Soy Media	**C T A Medium**	C T A Medium
Treponema	*Spirolate Broth *Thioglycollate Medium-135C	Spirolate Broth Thioglycollate Medium-135C	C T A Media Indole Nitrite Medium **Thiogel** Medium	*Thioglycollate Medium-135C
Vibrio comma fetus and bulbulus	*Cary and Blair Transport Medium Chocolate Agar **D C L S Agar** **Desoxycholate-Citrate Agar** pH 8.4 **Eugonagar** **Eugonbroth** MacConkey Agar **Selenite-F** Broth T C B S Agar *Thioglycollate Medium-135C **Trypticase Soy Media**	**Eugonagar** **Eugonbroth** Thioglycollate Media **Trypticase** Soy Media	**C T A Medium** Indole Nitrite Medium Litmus Milk **Thiogel** Medium **Trypticase Lactose Iron Agar** **T S I Agar**	C T A Medium
Viruses			See Tissue Culture Manual for Media and Cell Lines	

(Continued)

Culture Media (Continued)

TABLE 2.C.69 (Continued)

Organisms	Isolation	Cultivation	Identification	Maintenance
Yeasts and Molds	BiGGY Agar Brain Heart Infusion Agars Dextrose Salt Agar *Eugonagar (Chocolate) Agar *Inhibitory Mold Agar Levine E M B Agar Littman Media Malt Media M-Yeast Media Mildew Test Agar *M-Green Yeast and Mold Broth M N Trypticase Soy Agar *Mycophil Media with Low pH *Mycosel Agar Orange Serum Agar *Phytone Yeast Extract Agar Potato Dextrose Agar Sabouraud Media *Serum Tellurite Agar Sugar-Free Agar *Thioglycollate Medium-135C *Trypticase Soy Media Trypticase Tellurite Agar W L Nutrient Agar Wort Media	A A T C C Mineral Salts Agar Antifungal Assay Agar Corn Meal Agar with Dextrose Czapek Dox Media Dextrose Agar Eugonagar Eugonbroth Malt Media Mycophil Agar Mycophil Broth Neurospora Culture Agar Sabouraud Media Trypticase Soy Media Wort Media	Chlamydospore Agar Corn Meal Agars C T A Media Cystine Heart Agar Levine E M B Agar Liu-Newton Agar Mycophil Agar Mycophil Broth *Rice Extract Agar *Trypticase Agar Media Trypticase Soy Broth Urea Agar Yeast Carbon Base Yeast Nitrogen Base Carbohydrate Taxo Discs Zein Agar	C T A Medium Eugonagar *Mycophil Agar Sabouraud Agars Trypticase Agar Base *Trypticase Soy Agar
Protozoa Entameba Trichomonas	*Hirsch Charcoal Agar with Rice Powder and Locke Solution Thioglycollate Medium-135C *Trichosel Broth	S T S Medium		

Source: BioQuest, Division of Becton, Dickinson & Company, Cockeysville, Maryland.

Dairy Cattle Breeds

TABLE 2.D.1
Origin and characteristics of dairy cattle breeds

Breed	Place of Origin	Color	Distinctive Head Characteristics	Other Distinguishing Characteristics	Disqualifications
Ayrshire	County of Ayr, in south-western Scotland.	Light to deep cherry red, mahogany, brown, or a combination of these colors, with white, or white alone. Black or brindle are objectionable.	Horns are wide-spread and tend to curve upward and outward. However, there is a polled strain.	The udders are especially symmetrical and well attached to the body. The breed is noted for its style and animation, good feet and legs, and grazing ability.	
Brown Swiss	The Alps of Switzerland.	Solid brown varying from very light to dark. White markings are objectionable.	The nose and tongue black, and there is a characteristic light-colored band around the muzzle. Medium length horns.	Strong and rugged, with some tendency toward the heavy muscling characteristic of the beef breeds. Calm and unexcitable.	
Guernsey	Isle of Guernsey.	Fawn with white markings clearly defined; preferably a clear (buff) muzzle.	Good length of head; horns incline forward, are refined and medium in length, and taper toward the tips.	The milk is especially yellow in color; golden yellow skin pigmentation; the un-haired portions of the body are light or pinkish in color (whereas in the Jersey they are near black); calves are relatively small at birth.	
Holstein-Friesian	Netherlands and Northern Germany.	Black and white markings, clearly defined.	Clean-cut, broad muzzle, open nostrils, strong jaw, broad and moderately dished fore-head, straight bridged nose.	Large angular animal; females should weigh 1,500 lbs. (mature); males in breeding condition 2,200 lbs.	Colors which bar registry: all black or all white, black in switch, black belly, black circling leg and touching hoof, black from hoof to knee or hock, black and white inter-mixed to give color other than distinct black and white.
Jersey	Island of Jersey.	Jerseys vary greatly in color, but the characteristic color is some shade of fawn, with or without white markings.	Forehead, broad and moderately dished with large, bright eyes. Clean-cut and proportionate to body.	Jerseys are especially known for their well-shaped udders and strong udder attachments. They are also very angular and refined.	Total blindness, permanent lameness that interferes with normal func-tion, blind quarter, free-martin heifers, and animals showing signs of being oper-ated upon or tampered with.

Source: Ensminger, M. E. (1969). *Animal Science*. Interstate Printers & Publishers, Danville, Illinois.

Dairy Products, Composition I

TABLE 2.D.2
Composition of milk and milk products

Material	Protein %	Mineral %	Lactose %	Fat %
Whole Milk	3.3	0.7	4.5	3.75
Evaporated Milk	7.0	1.5	9.9	7.9
Condensed (sweetened)	7.5	1.5	10.5	8.5
Dry Whole Milk	26.5	6.0	38.5	26.75
Malted Milk	7.3	1.6	9.9	8.25
Butter	0.6	0.2	0.4	80.5
Cream	2.9	0.6	4.0	20.0
Dry Cream	13.4	2.9	18.0	65.0
Ice Cream and Ice Cream Mix	3.8	0.9	5.3	12.0
Dry Ice Cream	10.5	2.3	15.0	27.0
Frozen Desserts	1.0	0.2	1.3	1.5
Cheese (fat min., all types)	24.5	3.4	1.8	32.0
Cheese (partially defatted)	39.0	5.4	2.8	15.0
Cheese (cottage, etc.)	19.2	1.7	4.3	0.8
Nonfat Dry Milk Solids	36.9	8.15	50.75	0.88
Dry Buttermilk Solids	34.0	8.0	48.0	5.8
Dry Whey Solids	13.0	8.0	73.0	1.0
Separated Condensed (sweetened)	8.8	2.0	12.7	0.5
Separated Condensed (plain)	7.3	1.6	10.8	0.3
Condensed Buttermilk	10.6	3.3	13.0	2.0
Cultured Buttermilk and Chocolate Drinks	3.5	0.7	4.6	2.0
Casein (commercial)	88.5	3.8	0.0	0.2
Dry Buttermilk	32.0	10.0	46.0	5.0
Dry Skim Milk	35.0	8.2	51.0	0.8
Dry Whey	13.0	9.5	71.0	0.5
Semi-Solid Buttermilk	10.6	3.3	13.0	2.0
Liquid Whey	0.8	0.6	4.5	0.05
Liquid Separated Milk	3.3	0.8	4.8	0.06
Lactose	0.0	0.0	99.5	0.0
Condensed Skim Milk (feed)	11.0	2.6	13.5	0.2
Partially defatted Dry Milk Solids	31.2	7.0	45.3	13.8

Source: Cook, H. L., and Day, G. H. (1967). The Dry Milk Industry. American Dry Milk Institute, Chicago.

Dairy Products, Composition II

TABLE 2.D.3
Nutritive values of the edible part of dairy products

DAIRY PRODUCTS (CHEESE, CREAM, IMITATION CREAM, MILK, RELATED PRODUCTS)

Butter. See Fats, oils; related products, items 103-108.

Item No. (A)	Foods, approximate measures, units, and weight (edible part unless footnotes indicate otherwise) (B)	Grams	Water (C) Per cent	Food energy (D) Calories	Protein (E) Grams	Fat (F) Grams	Saturated (total) (G) Grams	Oleic (H) Grams	Linoleic (I) Grams	Carbohydrate (J) Grams	Calcium (K) Milligrams	Phosphorus (L) Milligrams	Iron (M) Milligrams	Potassium (N) Milligrams	Vitamin A value (O) International units	Thiamin (P) Milligrams	Riboflavin (Q) Milligrams	Niacin (R) Milligrams	Ascorbic acid (S) Milligrams
	Cheese: Natural:																		
1	Blue — 1 oz	28	42	100	6	8	5.3	1.9	0.2	1	150	110	0.1	73	200	0.01	0.11	0.3	0
2	Camembert (3 wedges per 4-oz container) — 1 wedge	38	52	115	8	9	5.8	2.2	.2	Trace	147	132	.1	71	350	.01	.19	.2	0
	Cheddar: Cut pieces:																		
3	Cheddar, Cut pieces — 1 oz	28	37	115	7	9	6.1	2.1	.2	Trace	204	145	.2	28	300	.01	.11	Trace	0
4	Cheddar, Cut pieces — 1 cu in	17.2	37	70	4	6	3.7	1.3	.1	Trace	124	88	.1	17	180	Trace	.06	Trace	0
5	Shredded[1] — 1 cup	113	37	455	28	37	24.2	8.5	.7	1	815	579	.8	111	1,200	.03	.42	.1	0
	Cottage (curd not pressed down): Creamed (cottage cheese, 4% fat):																		
6	Large curd — 1 cup	225	79	235	28	10	6.4	2.4	.2	6	135	297	.3	190	370	.05	.37	.3	Trace
7	Small curd — 1 cup	210	79	220	26	9	6.0	2.2	.2	6	126	277	.3	177	340	.04	.34	.3	Trace
8	Low fat (2%) — 1 cup	226	79	205	31	4	2.8	1.0	.1	8	155	340	.4	217	160	.05	.42	.3	Trace
9	Low fat (1%) — 1 cup	226	82	165	28	2	1.5	.5	.1	6	138	302	.3	193	80	.05	.37	.3	Trace
10	Uncreamed (cottage cheese dry curd, less than 1/2% fat) — 1 cup	145	80	125	25	1	.4	.1	Trace	3	46	151	.3	47	40	.04	.21	.2	0
11	Cream — 1 oz	28	54	100	2	10	6.2	2.4	.2	1	23	30	.3	34	400	Trace	.06	Trace	0
	Mozzarella, made with—																		
12	Whole milk — 1 oz	28	48	90	6	7	4.4	1.7	.2	1	163	117	.1	21	260	Trace	.08	Trace	0
13	Part skim milk — 1 oz	28	49	80	8	5	3.1	1.2	.1	1	207	149	.1	27	180	.01	.10	Trace	0
	Parmesan, grated:																		
14	Cup, not pressed down — 1 cup	100	18	455	42	30	19.1	7.7	.3	4	1,376	807	1.0	107	700	.05	.39	.3	0
15	Tablespoon — 1 tbsp	5	18	25	2	2	1.0	.4	Trace	Trace	69	40	Trace	5	40	Trace	.02	Trace	0
16	Ounce — 1 oz	28	18	130	12	9	5.4	2.2	.1	1	390	229	.3	30	200	.01	.11	.1	0
17	Provolone — 1 oz	28	41	100	7	8	4.8	1.7	.1	1	214	141	.1	39	230	.01	.09	Trace	0
	Ricotta, made with—																		
18	Whole milk — 1 cup	246	72	428	28	32	20.4	7.1	.7	7	509	389	.9	257	1,210	.03	.48	.3	0
19	Part skim milk — 1 cup	246	74	340	28	19	12.1	4.7	.5	13	669	449	1.1	308	1,060	.05	.46	.2	0
20	Romano — 1 oz	28	31	110	9	8				1	302	215			160		.11	Trace	0
21	Swiss — 1 oz	28	37	105	8	8	5.0	1.7	.2	1	272	171	Trace	31	240	.01	.10	Trace	0
	Pasteurized process cheese:																		
22	American — 1 oz	28	39	105	6	9	5.6	2.1	.2	Trace	174	211	.1	46	340	.01	.10	Trace	0
23	Swiss — 1 oz	28	42	95	7	7	4.5	1.7	.1	1	219	216	.2	61	230	Trace	.08	Trace	0
24	Pasteurized process cheese food, American — 1 oz	28	43	95	6	7	4.4	1.7	.1	2	163	130	.2	79	260	.01	.13	Trace	0
25	Pasteurized process cheese spread, American — 1 oz	28	48	82	5	6	3.8	1.5	.1	2	159	202	.1	69	220	.01	.12	Trace	0
	Cream, sweet:																		
26	Half-and-half (cream and milk) — 1 cup	242	81	315	7	28	17.3	7.0	.6	10	254	230	.2	314	260	.08	.36	.2	2
27	Half-and-half — 1 tbsp	15	81	20	Trace	2	1.1	.4	Trace	1	16	14	Trace	19	20	.01	.02	Trace	Trace
28	Light, coffee, or table — 1 cup	240	74	470	6	46	28.8	11.7	1.0	9	231	192	.1	292	1,730	.08	.36	.2	2
29	Light, coffee, or table — 1 tbsp	15	74	30	Trace	3	1.8	.7	.1	1	14	12	Trace	18	110	Trace	.02	Trace	Trace

(Continued)

Dairy Products, Composition II *(Continued)*

TABLE 2.D.3 *(Continued)*

(A)	(B)	(grams)	(C)	(D)	(E)	(F)	(G)	(H)	(I)	(J)	(K)	(L)	(M)	(N)	(O)	(P)	(Q)	(R)	(S)
	Whipping, unwhipped (volume about double when whipped):																		
30	Light — 1 cup	239	64	700	5	74	46.2	18.3	1.5	7	166	146	.1	231	2,690	.06	.30	.1	1
31	— 1 tbsp	15	64	45	Trace	5	2.9	1.1	.1	Trace	10	9	Trace	15	170	Trace	.02	Trace	Trace
32	Heavy — 1 cup	238	58	820	5	88	54.8	22.2	2.0	7	154	149	.1	179	3,500	.05	.26	.1	Trace
33	— 1 tbsp	15	58	80	Trace	6	3.5	1.4	.1	Trace	10	9	Trace	11	220	Trace	.02	Trace	Trace
34	Whipped topping, (pressurized) — 1 cup	60	61	155	2	13	8.3	3.4	.3	7	61	54	Trace	88	550	Trace	.04	Trace	0
35	— 1 tbsp	3	61	10	Trace	1	.4	.2	Trace	Trace	3	3	Trace	4	30	Trace	Trace	Trace	0
36	Cream, sour — 1 cup	230	71	495	7	48	30.0	12.1	1.1	10	268	195	.1	331	1,820	.08	.34	.2	2
37	— 1 tbsp	12	71	25	Trace	3	1.6	.6	.1	1	14	10	Trace	17	90	Trace	.02	Trace	Trace
	Cream products, imitation (made with vegetable fat):																		
	Sweet:																		
	Creamers:																		
38	Liquid (frozen) — 1 cup	245	77	335	2	24	22.8	.3	Trace	28	23	157	.1	467	[1]220	0	0	0	0
39	— 1 tbsp	15	77	20	Trace	1	1.4	Trace	0	1	1	10	.1	29	[1]10	0	0	0	0
40	Powdered — 1 cup	94	2	515	5	33	30.6	.9	Trace	52	21	397	.1	763	[1]190	0	[1].16	0	0
41	— 1 tsp	2	2	10	Trace	1	.7	Trace	0	1	Trace	8	Trace	16	[1]Trace	0	[1]Trace	0	0
	Whipped topping:																		
42	Frozen — 1 cup	75	50	240	1	19	16.3	1.0	.2	17	5	6	.1	14	[1]650	0	0	0	0
43	— 1 tbsp	4	50	15	Trace	1	.9	.1	Trace	1	Trace	Trace	Trace	1	[1]30	0	0	0	0
44	Powdered, made with whole milk — 1 cup	80	67	150	3	10	8.5	.6	Trace	13	72	69	Trace	121	[1]290	.02	.09	Trace	1
45	— 1 tbsp	4	67	10	Trace	Trace	.4	Trace	Trace	1	4	3	Trace	6	[1]10	Trace	Trace	Trace	Trace
46	Pressurized — 1 cup	70	60	185	1	16	13.2	1.4	.2	11	4	13	Trace	13	[1]330	0	0	0	0
47	— 1 tbsp	4	60	10	Trace	1	.8	.1	Trace	1	Trace	1	Trace	1	[1]120	0	0	0	0
48	Sour dressing (imitation sour cream) made with nonfat dry milk — 1 cup	235	75	415	8	39	31.2	4.4	1.1	11	266	205	.1	380	[1]20	.09	.38	.2	2
	— 1 tbsp	12	75	20	Trace	2	1.6	.2	Trace	1	14	10	Trace	19	[1]Trace	.01	.02	Trace	Trace
49	Ice cream. See Milk desserts, frozen (items 75–80).																		
	Ice milk. See Milk desserts, frozen (items 81–83).																		
	Milk:																		
	Fluid:																		
50	Whole (3.3% fat) — 1 cup	244	88	150	8	8	5.1	2.1	.2	11	291	228	.1	370	[2]310	.09	.40	.2	2
51	Lowfat (2%): No milk solids added — 1 cup	244	89	120	8	5	2.9	1.2	.1	12	297	232	.1	377	500	.10	.40	.2	2
52	Milk solids added: Label claim less than 10 g of protein per cup. — 1 cup	245	89	125	9	5	2.9	1.2	.1	12	313	245	.1	397	500	.10	.42	.2	2
53	Label claim 10 or more grams of protein per cup (protein fortified). — 1 cup	246	88	135	10	5	3.0	1.2	.1	14	352	276	.1	447	500	.11	.48	.2	3
54	Lowfat (1%): No milk solids added — 1 cup	244	90	100	8	3	1.6	.7	.1	12	300	235	.1	381	500	.10	.41	.2	2
55	Milk solids added: Label claim less than 10 g of protein per cup. — 1 cup	245	90	105	9	2	1.5	.6	.1	12	313	245	.1	397	500	.10	.42	.2	2
56	Label claim 10 or more grams of protein per cup (protein fortified). — 1 cup	246	89	120	10	3	1.8	.7	.1	14	349	273	.1	444	500	.11	.47	.2	3
57	Nonfat (skim): No milk solids added — 1 cup	245	91	85	8	Trace	.3	.1	.1	12	302	247	.1	406	500	.09	.37	.2	2

[1]Vitamin A value is largely from beta-carotene used for coloring. Riboflavin value for items 40–41 apply to product with added riboflavin.

[2]Applies to product without added vitamin A. With added vitamin A, value is 500 International Units (I.U.).

(Continued)

Dairy Products, Composition II *(Continued)*

TABLE 2.D.3 *(Continued)*

Item No. (A)	Foods, approximate measures, units, and weight (edible part unless footnotes indicate otherwise) (B)	Grams	Water (C) Per cent	Food energy (D) Cal.	Protein (E) Grams	Fat (F) Grams	Saturated (total) (G) Grams	Unsat. Oleic (H) Grams	Unsat. Linoleic (I) Grams	Carbohydrate (J) Grams	Calcium (K) Mg	Phosphorus (L) Mg	Iron (M) Mg	Potassium (N) Mg	Vitamin A value (O) I.U.	Thiamin (P) Mg	Riboflavin (Q) Mg	Niacin (R) Mg	Ascorbic acid (S) Mg
	DAIRY PRODUCTS [CHEESE, CREAM, IMITATION CREAM, MILK; RELATED PRODUCTS]—Con.																		
	Milk—Continued																		
	Fluid—Continued																		
	Nonfat (skim)—Continued																		
	Milk solids added:																		
58	Label claim less than 10 g of protein per cup. 1 cup	245	90	90	9	1	0.4	0.1	Trace	12	316	255	0.1	416	500	0.10	0.43	0.2	2
59	Label claim 10 or more grams of protein per cup (protein fortified). 1 cup	246	89	100	10	1	.4	.1	Trace	14	352	275	.1	446	500	.11	.48	.2	3
60	Buttermilk 1 cup	245	90	100	8	2	1.3	.5	Trace	12	285	219	.	371	[3]80	.08	.38	.1	2
	Canned:																		
	Evaporated, unsweetened:																		
61	Whole milk 1 cup	252	74	340	17	19	11.6	5.3	0.4	25	657	510	.5	764	[3]610	.12	.80	.5	5
62	Skim milk 1 cup	255	79	200	19	1	.3	.1	Trace	29	738	497	.7	845	[4]1,000	.11	.79	.4	3
63	Sweetened, condensed 1 cup	306	27	980	24	27	16.8	6.7	.7	166	868	775	.6	1,136	[3]1,000	.28	1.27	.6	8
	Dried:																		
64	Buttermilk 1 cup	120	3	465	41	7	4.3	1.7	.2	59	1,421	1,119	.4	1,910	[5]260	.47	1.90	1.1	7
	Nonfat instant:																		
65	Envelope, net wt., 3.2 oz[5] 1 envelope	91	4	325	32	1	.4	.1	Trace	47	1,120	896	.3	1,552	[6]2,160	.38	1.59	.8	5
66	Cup[7] 1 cup	68	4	245	24	Trace	.3	.1	Trace	35	837	670	.2	1,160	[6]1,610	.28	1.19	.6	4
	Milk beverages:																		
	Chocolate milk (commercial):																		
67	Regular 1 cup	250	82	210	8	8	5.3	2.2	.2	26	280	251	.6	417	[3]300	.09	.41	.3	2
68	Lowfat (2%) 1 cup	250	84	180	8	5	3.1	1.3	.1	26	284	254	.6	422	500	.10	.42	.3	2
69	Lowfat (1%) 1 cup	250	85	160	8	3	1.5	.7	.1	26	287	257	.6	426	500	.10	.40	.2	2
70	Eggnog (commercial) 1 cup	254	74	340	10	19	11.3	5.0	.6	34	330	278	.5	420	890	.09	.48	.3	4
	Malted milk, home-prepared with 1 cup of whole milk and 2 to 3 heaping tsp of malted milk powder (about 3/4 oz):																		
71	Chocolate 1 cup of milk plus 3/4 oz of powder.	265	81	235	9	9	5.5	—	—	29	304	265	.5	500	330	.14	.43	.7	2
72	Natural 1 cup of milk plus 3/4 oz of powder.	265	81	235	11	10	6.0	—	—	27	347	307	.3	529	380	.20	.54	1.3	2
	Shakes, thick:[8]																		
73	Chocolate, container, net wt., 10.6 oz. 1 container	300	72	355	9	8	5.0	2.0	.2	63	396	378	.9	672	260	.14	.67	.4	0
74	Vanilla, container, net wt., 11 oz. 1 container	313	74	350	12	9	5.9	2.4	.2	56	457	361	.3	572	360	.09	.61	.5	0
	Milk desserts, frozen:																		
	Ice cream:																		
	Regular (about 11% fat):																		
75	Hardened 1/2 gal	1,064	61	2,155	38	115	71.3	28.8	2.6	254	1,406	1,075	1.0	2,052	4,340	.42	2.63	1.1	6
76	1 cup	133	61	270	5	14	8.9	3.6	.3	32	176	134	.1	257	540	.05	.33	.1	1
77	3-fl oz container	50	61	100	2	5	3.4	1.4	.1	12	66	51	Trace	96	200	.02	.12	.1	Trace
78	Soft serve (frozen custard) 1 cup	173	60	375	7	23	13.5	5.9	.6	38	236	199	.4	338	790	.08	.45	.2	1
79	Rich (about 16% fat), hardened. 1/2 gal	1,188	59	2,805	33	190	118.3	47.8	4.3	256	1,213	927	.8	1,771	7,200	.36	2.27	.9	5
80	1 cup	148	59	350	4	24	14.7	6.0	.5	32	151	115	.1	221	900	.04	.28	.1	1
	Ice milk:																		
81	Hardened (about 4.3% fat) 1/2 gal	1,048	69	1,470	41	45	28.1	11.3	1.0	232	1,409	1,035	1.5	2,117	1,710	.61	2.78	.9	6
82	1 cup	131	69	185	5	6	3.5	1.4	.1	29	176	129	.1	265	210	.08	.35	.1	1

(Continued)

Dairy Products, Composition II (Continued)

D.3 (Continued)

(A)	(B)	Grams	(C)	(D)	(E)	(F)	(G)	(H)	(I)	(J)	(K)	(L)	(M)	(N)	(O)	(P)	(Q)	(R)	(S)
83	Soft serve (about 2.6% fat)—— 1 cup	175	70	225	8	5	2.9	1.2	0.1	38	274	202	0.3	412	180	0.12	0.54	0.2	3
84	Sherbet (about 2% fat)—— 1/2 gal	1,542	66	2,160	17	31	19.0	7.7	.7	469	827	594	2.5	1,585	1,480	.26	.71	1.0	31
85	—— 1 cup	193	66	270	2	4	2.4	1.0	.1	59	103	74	.3	198	190	.03	.09	.1	4
86	Milk desserts, other: Custard, baked—— 1 cup	265	77	305	14	15	6.8	5.4	.7	29	297	310	1.1	387	930	.11	.50	.3	1
	Puddings: From home recipe: Starch base:																		
87	Chocolate—— 1 cup	260	66	385	8	12	7.6	3.3	.3	67	250	255	1.3	445	390	.05	.36	.3	1
88	Vanilla (blancmange)—— 1 cup	255	76	285	9	10	6.2	2.5	.2	41	298	232	Trace	352	410	.08	.41	.3	2
89	Tapioca cream—— 1 cup	165	72	220	8	8	4.1	2.5	.5	28	173	180	.7	223	480	.07	.30	.2	2
	From mix (chocolate) and milk:																		
90	Regular (cooked)—— 1 cup	260	70	320	9	8	4.3	2.6	.2	59	265	247	.8	354	340	.05	.39	.3	2
91	Instant—— 1 cup	260	69	325	8	7	3.6	2.2	.3	63	374	237	1.3	335	340	.08	.39	.3	2
	Yogurt: With added milk solids:																		
92	Made with lowfat milk—— 1 container, net wt., 8 oz	227	75	230	10	3	1.8	.6	.1	42	343	269	.2	439	[10]120	.08	.40	.2	1
93	Fruit-flavored[9]—— 1 container, net wt., 8 oz	227	85	145	12	4	2.3	.8	.1	16	415	326	.2	531	[10]150	.10	.49	.3	2
94	Plain—— 1 container, net wt., 8 oz	227	85	125	13	Trace	.3	.1	Trace	17	452	355	.2	579	[10]20	.11	.53	.3	2
	Without added milk solids:																		
95	Made with whole milk—— 1 container, net wt., 8 oz	227	88	140	8	7	4.8	1.7	.1	11	274	215	.1	351	280	.07	.32	.2	1
	EGGS																			
	Eggs, large (24 oz per dozen): Raw:																			
96	Whole, without shell—— 1 egg	50	75	80	6	6	1.7	2.0	.6	Trace	28	90	1.0	65	260	.04	.15	Trace	0
97	White—— 1 white	33	88	15	3	Trace	0	0	0	Trace	4	4	Trace	45	0	Trace	.09	Trace	0
98	Yolk—— 1 yolk	17	49	65	3	6	1.7	2.1	.6	Trace	26	86	.9	15	310	.04	.07	Trace	0
	Cooked:																			
99	Fried in butter—— 1 egg	46	72	85	5	6	2.4	2.2	.6	1	26	80	.9	58	290	.03	.13	Trace	0
100	Hard-cooked, shell removed—— 1 egg	50	75	80	6	6	1.7	2.0	.6	1	28	90	1.0	65	260	.04	.14	Trace	0
101	Poached—— 1 egg	50	74	80	6	6	1.7	2.0	.6	1	28	80	1.0	65	260	.04	.13	Trace	0
102	Scrambled (milk added) in butter. Also omelet.—— 1 egg	64	76	95	6	7	2.8	2.3	.6	1	47	97	.9	85	310	.04	.16	Trace	0
	FATS, OILS; RELATED PRODUCTS																			
	Butter: Regular (1 brick or 4 sticks per lb):																			
103	Stick (1/2 cup)—— 1 stick	113	16	815	1	92	57.3	23.1	2.1	Trace	27	26	.2	29	[13]3,470	.01	.04	Trace	0
104	Tablespoon (about 1/8 stick)—— 1 tbsp	14	16	100	Trace	12	7.2	2.9	.3	Trace	3	3	Trace	4	[11]430	Trace	Trace	Trace	0
105	Pat (1 in square, 1/3 in high; 90 per lb)—— 1 pat	5	16	35	Trace	4	2.5	1.0	.1	Trace	1	1		1	[11]150	Trace	Trace	Trace	0
	Whipped (6 sticks or two 8-oz containers per lb):																			
106	Stick (1/2 cup)—— 1 stick	76	16	540	1	61	38.2	15.4	1.4	Trace	18	17	.1	20	[12]2,310	Trace	.03	Trace	0
107	Tablespoon (about 1/8 stick)—— 1 tbsp	9	16	65	Trace	8	4.7	1.9	.2	Trace	2	2	Trace	2	[12]290	Trace	Trace	Trace	0
108	Pat (1 1/4 in square, 1/3 in high; 120 per lb)—— 1 pat	4	16	25	Trace	3	1.9	.8	.1	Trace	1	1	Trace	1	[11]120	0	Trace	Trace	0

[3] Applies to product without vitamin A added.
[4] Applies to product with added vitamin A. Without added vitamin A, value is 20 International Units (I.U.).
[5] Yields 1 qt of fluid milk when reconstituted according to package directions.
[6] Applies to product with added vitamin A.
[7] Weight applies to product with label claim of 1 1/3 cups equal 3.2 oz.
[8] Applies to products made from thick shake mixes and that do not contain added ice cream. Products made from milk shake mixes are higher in fat and usually contain added ice cream.
[9] Content of fat, vitamin A, and carbohydrate varies. Consult the label when precise values are needed for special diets.
[10] Applies to product made with milk containing no added vitamin A.
[11] Based on year-round average.

Source: Consumer and Food Economics Institute (1977). Nutritive value of foods. USDA Home and Garden Bull. 72.

Dairy Terms

TABLE 2.D.4

FRESH WHOLE MILK	
Whole milk	Grade A pasteurized milk sold for home use. At least 3.25 percent milkfat and 8.25 percent nonfat milk solids in most States.
Homogenized	Fat uniformly distributed through milk.
Cream-line	Layer of cream at top of container.
Vitamin D	Vitamin D increased to at least 400 U.S.P. or International Units per quart.
Fortified multiple-vitamin and/or mineral	Added vitamin A, vitamin D, riboflavin, thiamin, niacin, and/or iron, iodine.
Concentrated	Fresh milk with two-thirds water removed.
Skim milk or nonfat milk	Processed to remove most of the fat.
Fortified skim	Not more than 0.5 percent milkfat and at least 8.25 percent nonfat milk solids in most States. Added vitamin A and vitamin D, less than 0.5 percent milkfat, and at least 10 percent nonfat milk solids.
Lowfat	Between 0.5 and 2 percent milkfat.
2 percent	2 percent milkfat and—usually—10 percent nonfat milk solids.
Flavored milk	Flavoring and stabilizer added.
Chocolate milk	Made from whole milk with chocolate and sweetener.
Chocolate-flavored drink	Made from whole milk with cocoa and sweetener.
Chocolate drink (chocolate lowfat milk)	Made from skim or lowfat milk with chocolate and sweetener. Nonfat milk solids may be added.
Chocolate-flavored drink	Made from skim or lowfat milk with cocoa and sweetener. Nonfat milk solids may be added.
Other	Flavored milk: Strawberry, coffee, maple, or other flavoring combined with whole milk. Flavored drink or flavored lowfat milk: Flavoring combined with skim or lowfat milk.
CULTURED MILK	
Buttermilk	Made by adding bacterial culture to milk. Thick, smooth liquid. Usually made from skim milk; at least 8.25 percent nonfat milk solids.
Yogurt	Semisolid. Made from whole or skim milk. Fruit or other flavorings may be added.
CANNED MILK	
Evaporated milk	Concentrated by removing water from milk. Vitamin D added. Sterilized. At least 7.9 percent milkfat and 25.9 percent total milk solids.
Skim	Low milkfat—often 0.2 or 0.3 percent. At least 18 percent total milk solids. Vitamin A may be added.
Sweetened condensed milk	Sugar added to help preserve milk. At least 8.5 percent milkfat and 28 percent total milk solids.
DRY MILK	
Nonfat dry milk	Not more than 5 percent of moisture. Made from fluid skim milk. Usually "instantized." Not more than 1.25 percent milkfat in extra grade dry product. May have vitamins A and D added.
Whole dry milk	Made from fluid whole milk. At least 26 percent milkfat in the dry product.
HALF-AND-HALF	
Half-and-half	Mixture of milk and cream. Pasteurized, Grade A. At least 10.5 percent milkfat; generally homogenized.
Sour half-and-half	Made by adding bacterial culture to fresh half-and-half; 0.2 percent acidity. Fluid or semifluid. Pasteurized, Grade A.
CREAM	
Table cream (coffee or light cream)	At least 18 percent milkfat; generally homogenized.
Sour cream	Made by adding bacterial culture to fresh table cream; 0.2 percent acidity. Fluid or semifluid.
Light whipping cream	At least 30 percent milkfat.
Heavy whipping cream	At least 36 percent milkfat.
Pressurized whipped cream	Liquid containing fresh table or whipping cream, sugar, stabilizer, emulsifier in aerosol can.
FROZEN DESSERTS	
Ice cream	Hard or soft frozen, pasteurized during processing. Made from cream, milk, sugar, stabilizers. At least 10 percent milkfat and 20 percent total milk solids.
Frozen custard (French or New York ice cream)	Made from the usual ingredients for ice cream, plus egg yolks. At least 10 percent milkfat and 20 percent total milk solids.
Ice milk	Made from milk, stabilizers, sweeteners. Between 2 and 7 percent milkfat and at least 11 percent total milk solids.
Fruit sherbet	Made from milk, fruit or fruit juice, stabilizers, sweeteners. From 1 to 2 percent milkfat, and between 2 and 5 percent total milk solids.

Based on recommendations in "Grade 'A' Pasteurized Milk Ordinance," Public Health Service Publication 229 (1967 revision). "Federal and State Standards for the Composition of Milk Products," Agriculture Handbook No. 51 (Jan. 1968), and Federal standards of identity as published in the Federal Register. A few States have set slightly lower minimums than those listed for milkfat and nonfat milk solids for some products.

Source: Anonymous (1974). Milk in family meals. USDA Home and Garden Bull. *127.*

Defectives in Lot

TABLE 2.D.5
Probable defectives in processed food lots (Probabilities for use when the sample size n is less than 10% of the lot size N†)

Probability of being right if, based on a sample of n which contains c defectives, one assumes there is X% or less defective in the lot

n	c	\multicolumn{15}{c}{X(%)}
		1	2	3	4	5	6	7	8	9	10	12	14	16	18	20
3	0	3	6	9	12	14	17	20	22	25	27	32	36	41	45	49
	1	°	°	°	°	1	1	1	2	2	3	4	5	7	9	10
	2															1
6	0	6	11	17	22	26	31	35	39	43	47	54	60	65	70	74
	1	°	1	1	2	3	5	6	8	10	11	16	20	25	30	34
	2		°	°	°	°	°	1	1	1	2	3	4	6	8	10
	3												°	1	1	2
	4													°	°	°
13	0	12	23	33	41	49	55	61	66	71	75	81	86	90	92	95
	1	1	3	6	9	14	18	23	28	33	38	47	56	64	71	77
	2	°	°	1	1	2	4	6	8	11	13	20	27	35	42	50
	3		°	°	°	°	1	1	2	2	3	6	10	14	19	25
	4							°	°	°	1	1	3	4	7	10
	5										°	°	1	1	2	3
	6												°	°	°	1
	7															°
21	0	19	35	47	58	66	73	78	83	86	89	93	96	97	98	99
	1	2	7	13	20	28	36	44	51	58	64	74	81	87	91	94
	2	•	1	2	5	8	13	18	23	29	35	47	58	68	76	82
	3	•	•	•	1	2	3	6	8	11	15	24	34	44	54	63
	4		•	°	•	•	1	1	2	4	5	10	16	24	32	41
	5						•	•	1	1	1	3	6	11	16	23
	6								•	°	°	1	2	4	7	11
	7											•	1	1	2	4
	8												°	°	1	1
	9														°	°

(Continued)

Defectives in Lot (Continued)

TABLE 2.D.5 (Continued)

n	c	X(%) 1	2	3	4	5	6	7	8	9	10	12	14	16	18	20
20	0	25	44	59	69	77	83	88	91	94	95	98	99	99	100	100
	1	3	11	22	32	43	53	61	69	75	80	88	93	96	98	99
	2	•	2	6	11	15	25	33	41	49	57	69	79	86	91	95
	3		•	1	3	5	9	14	20	26	33	47	59	70	79	86
	4			•	1	1	3	5	8	11	16	26	38	50	62	72
	5				•	•	1	1	3	4	6	13	21	32	43	54
	6						•	•	1	1	2	5	10	17	26	36
	7								•	•	1	2	4	8	14	21
	8										•	1	1	3	6	11
	9											•	•	1	3	5
	10													•	1	2
	11														•	1
	12															•
30	0	32	54	69	79	86	90	94	96	97	98	99	100	100	100	100
	1	5	18	32	45	57	67	76	82	87	90	95	98	99	100	99
	2	1	4	10	19	30	40	50	60	68	75	85	92	96	98	96
	3	•	1	3	6	12	19	27	36	45	54	68	80	88	93	90
	4		•	1	2	4	8	12	18	25	33	49	63	75	84	80
	5			•	•	1	2	5	8	12	17	30	44	58	70	66
	6					•	1	1	3	5	8	16	28	41	54	50
	7						•	•	1	2	3	8	15	26	37	34
	8								•	1	1	3	8	14	23	22
	9									•	•	1	3	7	13	12
	10											•	1	3	7	6
	11												•	1	3	3
	12													•	1	1
	13														•	•
	14															
48	0	38	62	77	86	91	95	97	98	99	99	100	100	100	100	100
	1	8	25	42	58	70	79	86	91	94	96	98	99	100	100	100
	2	1	7	17	30	43	56	66	75	82	87	94	97	99	98	99
	3	•	2	6	12	22	33	44	54	64	72	84	92	96	95	98
	4		•	1	4	9	16	24	34	44	53	70	82	90	89	94
	5			•	1	3	6	12	18	26	35	52	68	80	78	87
	6				•	1	2	5	9	14	20	35	52	67	65	77
	7					•	1	2	4	6	10	21	36	51		

†When the sample size is more than 10% of the lot size, the probabilities in this table will be changed. The extent of change depends on the value of n/N.

Source: Thatcher, F. S., and Clark, D. S. (1968). Microorganisms in Foods. University of Toronto Press, Toronto, Canada.

Defrosting Time

TABLE 2.D.6
Timetable for defrosting frozen meat

Meat	In Refrigerator (36°–40°F)
Large roast	4–7 hr per lb
Small roast	3–5 hr per lb
1-in. steak	12–14 hr

NOTE: Refreezing meat is not a recommended practice because of possible variation in the history and treatment of meat before freezing, during freezing and/or during defrosting prior to refreezing. When refreezing may seem necessary to prevent spoilage, some loss in juiciness can be expected.

Source: Lessons on Meat. (1974). National Live Stock and Meat Board, Chicago.

Detergent Properties

TABLE 2.D.7
Properties of various detergent materials

DETERGENT MATERIALS	CORROSIVENESS	DISSOLVING OR NEUTRALIZING POWER	WATER CONDITIONING PROPERTIES FOR MAGNESIUM	WATER CONDITIONING PROPERTIES FOR CALCIUM	DEFLOCCULATING OR DISPERSING POWER .15% Soln–75°C	EMULSIFYING POWER .15% Soln.	RINSING PROPERTIES	WETTING OR PENETRATING ACTION
CAUSTIC SODA (LYE) NaOH			PPT	PPT				
SODA ASH Na₂CO₃			PPT	PPT				
SODIUM METASILICATE Na₂SiO₃·5H₂O								
SODIUM SESQUISILICATE (1.5-L6)Na₂O·(1)SiO₂·(5.5)H₂O								
SODIUM ORTHOSILICATE 2Na₂O·SiO₂·(5.5)H₂O								
TRISOD. ORTHOPHOSPHATE TSP–Na₃PO₄ 10 H₂O								
TETRASOD. PYROPHOSPHATE PYRO–TSPP–Na₄P₂O₇								
SOD. TRIPOLYPHOSPHATE Na₅P₃O₁₀								
SOD. TETRAPHOSPHATE QUADRAFOS–Na₆P₄O₁₃								
SOD. DECAPHOSPHATE Na₁₂P₁₀O₃₁								
SOD. HEXAMETAPHOSPHATE CALGON–(NaPO₃)₆								
SULFONIC ACID GROUPS ALKYL ARYL SULFONATES NACCONAL, SANTOMERSE, ETC.								
SULFURIC ESTERS SULFATED FATTY ALCOHOLS DUPONOLS, DREFT, ETC.								

Note: Degree scales across columns range LOW / AVG. / HIGH (Corrosiveness, Dissolving or Neutralizing Power, Deflocculating or Dispersing Power, Emulsifying Power); POOR / AVG. / GOOD (Water Conditioning Properties, Rinsing Properties, Wetting or Penetrating Action). Emulsifying Power: "HIGHEST IN .1% SOLN." / "HIGHER IF FATTY ACIDS PRESENT – HIGHEST IN .1% SOLN. – NO VALUE ABOVE 2%." Rinsing Properties and Wetting or Penetrating Action: "HIGHER IF FATTY ACIDS PRESENT."

Source: Kramer, A., and Twigg, B. A. (editors) (1973). Sanitation, national canners association. In *Quality Control For The Food Industry*, Vol. 2, 3rd Edition. AVI Publishing Co., Westport, Connecticut.

Detergents

TABLE 2.D.8
Properties of detergents

	Strong Alkalis	Mild Alkalis	Poly-phosphates	Mild Acids	Strong Acids	Sur-factants
Sequestering	0	+	++++	0	0	0
Wetting	+	++	+	+	0	++++
Emulsifying, suspending	+	++	++	0	0	++++
Dissolving	++++	+++	++	+++	++++	+
Saponifying	++++	+++	0	0	0	+
Peptizing	++++	+++	+	++	+++	0
Dispersion	++	+++	+	+	0	+++
Rinsing	+++	+++	++	+	0	++++
Corrosion	++++	++,+++	0	++	++++	0

Degrees of Activity: extreme ++++, high +++, medium ++, low +, none 0.

Source: Harper, W. J. (1972). Sanitation in dairy food plants. In *Food Sanitation*. R. K. Guthrie (editor). AVI Publishing Co., Westport, Connecticut.

Diseases, Food-Borne

TABLE 2.D.9
Food-borne diseases

Disease	Etiologic Agent	Foods Usually Involved
1. Botulism	*Cl. botulinum* toxins	Canned and bottled food improperly processed
2. *Staphylococcus*	Staphylococci enterotoxin	Custard pastries, cooked ham, hollandaise sauce
3. Salmonellosis	A variety of members of the *Salmonella* group	"Hand-made" salads, sliced cooked meats, "warmed over" foods
4. Typhoid fever	Typhoid bacillus	Contaminated food, water, milk, shellfish
5. Dysentery, Bacillary	Various species of genus *Shigella*	Contaminated food, water, by contact with excreta
6. Dysentery, Amoebic	*Endamoeba histolytica*	Cold moist foods, contaminated drinking water
7. Tularemia	*Pasteurella tularensis*	Wild rabbits (by handling)
8. Brucellosis	*Brucella melitensis, Brucella abortus, Brucella suis*	Ingestion of infected milk and dairy products. Direct contact with infected animals or animal products
9. Q fever	*Coxiella burnetii*	Milk, contact, or exposure to infected livestock
10. Trichinosis	*Trichinella spiralis*	Insufficiently cooked pork or pork products

(Continued)

TABLE 2.D.9 *(Continued)*

Average Time of Onset	Symptoms	Preventive Procedure
1. 1–2 days	Difficulty in swallowing and speech, double vision	Careful canning procedure. Cooking to detoxify toxins.
2. 3–6 hours	Nausea, vomiting, abdominal cramps	Prompt refrigeration of foods; pasteurization of custard-filled pastries.
3. 6–18 hours	Diarrhea, abdominal cramps, vomiting	Strict attention to cleanliness of hands of food handlers. Protection of foods during processing and storage. Refrigeration of food.
4. 7–14 days	Fever	Pasteurization of milk, safe water supply; approved source of shellfish; isolation of carrier from food handling.
5. 1–7 days	Diarrhea, fever	Protection of water supply; handwashing.
6. Several days to 4 weeks	Diarrhea	Handwashing. Prevention of cross connections.
7. 1–10 days	Sudden chills and fever	Avoid handling of rabbits or use protective gloves.
8. 6–30 days	Undulating fever; pains in joints and muscles	Pasteurization of milk and dairy products; care in handling meat and meat products.
9. 2–3 weeks	Sudden chills, headaches, severe sweats, malaise	Pasteurization of milk.
10. 2–28 days	Nausea, diarrhea, soreness in muscles, fever	Thorough cooking of pork and pork products. Antigen testings of hogs. Prevent feeding of raw garbage to hogs. Freezing of pork.

Source: Weiser, H. H., Mountney, G. J., and Gould, W. A. (editors) (1971). Food poisoning. In *Practical Food Microbiology.* AVI Publishing Co., Westport Connecticut.

Dryer Types

TABLE 2.D.10
Common dryer types used for liquid and solid foods

Drier Type	Usual Food Type
Air Convection Driers	
kiln	pieces
cabinet, tray, or pan	pieces, purées, liquids
tunnel	pieces
continuous conveyor belt	purées, liquids
belt trough	pieces
air lift	small pieces, granules
fluidized bed	small pieces, granules
spray	liquids, purées
Drum or Roller Driers	
atmospheric	purées, liquids
vacuum	purées, liquids
Vacuum Driers	
vacuum shelf	pieces, purées, liquids
vacuum belt	purées, liquids
freeze driers	pieces, liquids

Source: Potter, N. N. (editor) (1973). Food dehydration and concentration. In *Food Science,* 2nd Edition. AVI Publishing Co., Westport, Connecticut.

Edible Meat and Chilled Carcass (or M. Biceps Femoris)

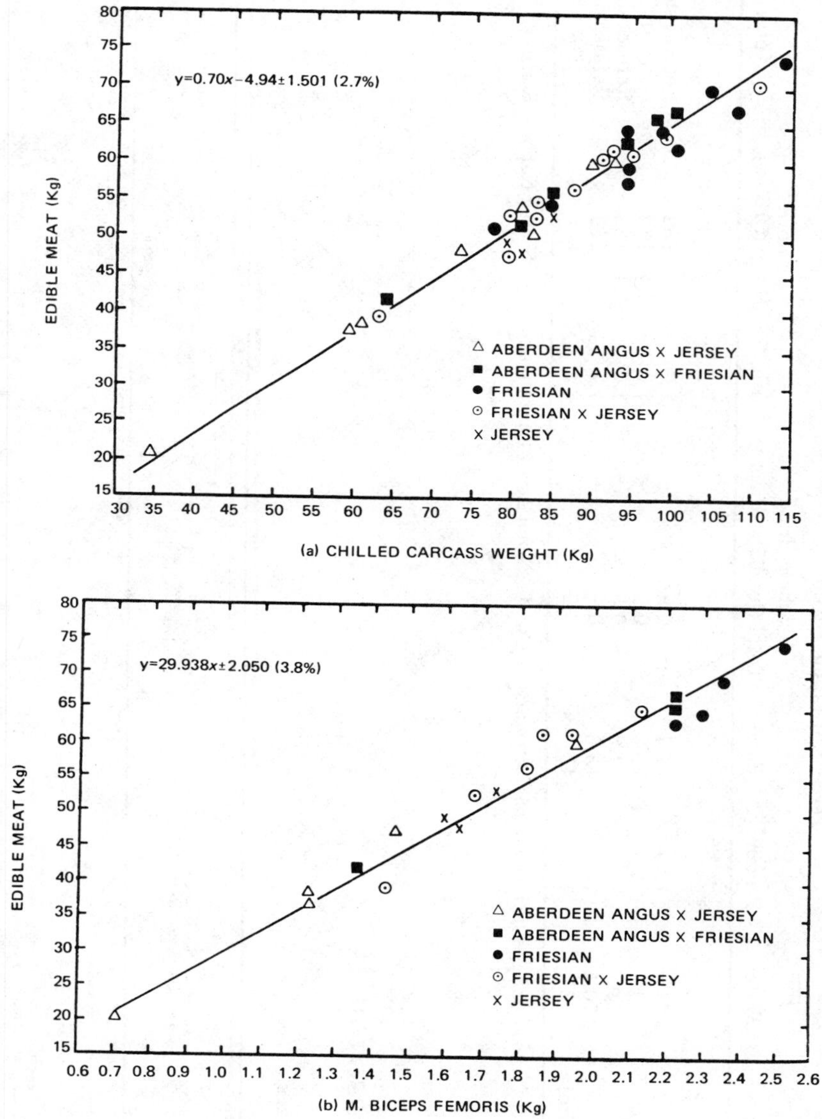

FIGURE 2.E.1

The relation of the yield of edible meat from breeds and crosses of calves at 10 months of age with (a) chilled carcass weight and (b) the weight of the right biceps femoris muscle

Source: Tribe, D. E. (editor). *Carcass Composition and Appraisal of Meat Animals*. CSIRO, Australia.

Egg Composition I

TABLE 2.E.1
Composition of the edible portion (EP) and refuse in the material as purchased (AP)

Commodity and Description	Percent of Edible Portion						Calories (No. per 100 g)	Notes	Refuse in AP (%)
	Water	Protein	Fat	Carbohydrate Total (by dif)	Fiber	Ash			
EGGS									
Fresh									
Hen	74	12.4	11.7	0.9	—	1.0	163	Refuse: shell	11
—liquid, whole	74	12.4	11.7	0.9	—	1.0	163		0
Duck	71	13	14.5	0.5	—	1.0	189	Refuse: shell	13
Goose	70.5	14	13.6	0.8	—	1.1	187	Refuse: shell	13
Dehydrated, whole	3	47	43	3.2	—	3.8	605		0

Source: Chatfield, C. Food Composition Tables for International Use. Food and Agriculture Organization, United Nations, Rome.

Egg Composition II

TABLE 2.E.2
Composition of eggs

(Dashes (—) denote lack of reliable data for a constituent believed to be present in measurable amount)

Item No.	Foods, approximate measures, units, and weight (edible part unless footnotes indicate otherwise)		Water	Food energy	Protein	Fat	Fatty Acids			Carbohydrate	Calcium	Phosphorus	Iron	Potassium	Vitamin A value	Thiamin	Riboflavin	Niacin	Ascorbic acid
							Saturated (total)	Unsaturated Oleic	Linoleic										
(A)	(B)		(C)	(D)	(E)	(F)	(G)	(H)	(I)	(J)	(K)	(L)	(M)	(N)	(O)	(P)	(Q)	(R)	(S)
		Grams	Percent	Calories	Grams	Grams	Grams	Grams	Grams	Grams	Milligrams	Milligrams	Milligrams	Milligrams	International units	Milligrams	Milligrams	Milligrams	Milligrams
	EGGS																		
	Eggs, large (24 oz per dozen):																		
	Raw:																		
96	Whole, without shell-----	1 egg-----	50	75	80	6	6	1.7	2.0	.6	1	28	90	1.0	65	260	.04	.15	Trace	0
97	White-----	1 white-----	33	88	15	3	Trace	0	0	0	Trace	4	4	Trace	45	0	Trace	.09	Trace	0
98	Yolk-----	1 yolk-----	17	49	65	3	6	1.7	2.1	.6	Trace	26	86	.9	15	310	.04	.07	Trace	0
	Cooked:																			
99	Fried in butter-----	1 egg-----	46	72	85	5	6	2.4	2.2	.6	1	26	80	.9	58	290	.03	.13	Trace	0
100	Hard-cooked, shell removed-	1 egg-----	50	75	80	6	6	1.7	2.0	.6	1	28	90	1.0	65	260	.04	.14	Trace	0
101	Poached-----	1 egg-----	50	74	80	6	6	1.7	2.0	.6	1	28	90	1.0	65	260	.04	.13	Trace	0
102	Scrambled (milk added) in butter. Also omelet.	1 egg-----	64	76	95	6	7	2.8	2.3	.6	1	47	97	.9	85	310	.04	.16	Trace	0

Source: Consumer and Food Economics Institute (1977). Nutritive value of foods. USDA Home and Garden Bull. 72.

Egg, Dried Equivalents

TABLE 2.E.3
Amounts of dried egg product and water to replace specified numbers of whole
eggs, egg yolks, or egg whites

| If a recipe calls for— | You may use— | |
	Dried egg product, sifted	Lukewarm water
Whole eggs: [1]		
1	2½ tablespoons.	2½ tablespoons.
6	1 cup.	1 cup.
Egg yolks:		
1	2 tablespoons.	2 teaspoons.
6	¾ cup.	¼ cup.
Egg whites:		
1	2 teaspoons.	2 tablespoons.
6	¼ cup.	¾ cup.

[1] Large eggs weighing 24 ounces per dozen.

Source: USDA (1970). Eggs in family meals. USDA Home and Garden Bull. *103.*

Egg Equivalents

TABLE 2.E.4
Guide for using whole eggs of various sizes in recipes

| Number of Large Eggs | In Recipe Use Equivalent to: | | | Approximate Volume |
	Extra Large Eggs	Medium Eggs	Small Eggs	
1	1	1	1	3 Tbsp
2	2	2	3	¼ cup + 2 Tbsp
3	3	4	4	½ cup + 2 Tbsp
4	3	5	6	¾ cup
5	4	6	7	1 cup
6	5	7	8	1 cup + 2 Tbsp
8	6	10	11	1½ cups
10	8	12	14	2 cups
12	10	14	17	2½ cups

Source: Van Egmond, D. (editor) (1974). Food preparation. In *School Food Service.*
AVI Publishing Co., Westport, Connecticut.

Egg Incubation Periods

TABLE 2.E.5
Incubation periods

Domestic Birds	Days	Caged and Game Birds	Days
Chicken	20–22	Budgerigar	17–31
Duck	26–28	Dove	12–19
Muscovy duck	33–35	Finch	11–14
Goose	30–33	Parrot	17–31
Guinea fowl	26–28	Pheasant	21–28
Turkey	26–28	Pigeon	16–18
		Quail	21–28
		Swan	21–35

Source: The Merck Veterinary Manual, 4th Edition. (1973). Merck & Co., Rahway, New Jersey.

Egg Products, Nutritive Value

TABLE 2.E.6
Nutritive value of egg products (Nutrients per 100 grams of product)

	Whole Egg Liquid	Whole Egg Dry	White Liquid	White Dry	Yolk Liquid	Yolk Dry		Whole Egg Liquid	Whole Egg Dry	White Liquid	White Dry	Yolk Liquid	Yolk Dry
Calories	193	592	51	372	312	664.	Minerals (ash)—gm	1.0	3.7	0.7	5.7	1.6	3
Water—gm	75.3	5.0	89.0	8.0	57.0	5.0	Calcium—mg	54.0	201.0	6.0	48.4	147.0	309.
Protein—gm	12.0	45.0	10.0	81.0	14.0	32.0	Chlorine—mg	100.0	372.0	131.0	1057.0	67.0	141.
Amino acids							Copper—mg	0.17	0.63	0.04	0.32	0.25	0.
Alanine—gm	0.64	2.59	0.83	5.34	0.79	1.83	Fluorine—mg	0.06	0.22	0.22	0.16	0.12	0.
Arginine—gm	0.78	3.03	0.73	5.03	1.08	2.29	Iodine—mg	12.0	45.0	6.8	54.9	16.0	34.
Aspartic acid—gm	0.95	2.61	0.75	6.94	1.04	2.43	Iron—mg	2.1	7.8	0.3	0.24	5.6	11
Cystine—gm	0.27	1.01	0.28	2.35	0.25	0.64	Magnesium—mg	9.0	33.5	11.0	89.0	13.0	27.
Glutamic acid—gm	1.48	5.73	1.24	10.93	1.75	3.88	Manganese —mg	0.04	0.15	—	—	0.11	0
Glycine—gm	0.42	1.61	0.42	3.21	0.49	1.05	Phosphorous—mg	210.0	731.0	17.0	137.0	586.0	1231
Histidine—gm	0.30	1.09	0.25	1.94	0.41	0.81	Potassium—mg	149.0	554.0	149.0	1202.0	110.0	231.
Isoleucine—gm	0.72	2.72	0.61	5.09	0.89	1.88	Sodium—mg	111.0	413.0	175.0	1412.0	78.0	164
Leucine—gm	1.01	3.82	0.83	6.94	1.29	2.68	Sulfur—mg	233.0	867.0	211.0	1702.0	214.0	449
Lysine—gm	0.84	2.17	0.65	5.67	1.11	2.36	Zinc—mg	1.3	4.8	0.01	0.8	3.8	8.
Methionine—gm	0.40	1.51	0.40	3.40	0.36	0.85	Vitamins						
Phenylalanine—gm	0.61	2.41	0.58	5.00	0.63	1.43	A-IU	1140.0	4240.0	—	—	3210.0	6741
Serine—gm	0.92	3.63	0.66	5.94	1.27	2.82	B₁₂—mcg	0.28	1.04	0.01	0.08	0.83	1
Threonine—gm	0.63	2.35	0.48	4.03	0.83	1.73	Biotin—mcg	22.5	83.7	7.0	56.5	52.0	109
Tryptophane—gm	0.22	0.81	0.18	1.46	0.24	0.49	Choline—gm	0.53	1.97	—	—	1.49	3
Tyrosine—gm	0.54	1.94	0.43	3.40	0.68	1.38	D-IU	50.0	186.0	—	—	150.0	315
Valine—gm	0.88	3.27	0.85	6.38	0.98	2.09	E—mg	2.0	7.4	—	—	6.0	12
Lipids—gm	10.5	40.0	—	—	28.0	60.7	Folic acid—mg	9.4	35.0	1.6	12.9	23.2	48.
Total saturated fatty acids—gm	3.0	11.4	—	—	8.0	17.7	Niacin—mg	0.1	0.37	—	—	—	
Total unsaturated fatty acids—gm	6.0	22.8	—	—	16.0	35.4	Pantothenic acid—mg	2.7	10.0	0.13	1.05	6.0	12
Oleic—gm	4.0	15.2	—	—	10.7	23.7	Pyridoxine—mg	0.25	0.93	0.22	1.78	0.31	0
Linoleic—gm	0.9	3.4	—	—	2.4	5.3	Riboflavin—mg	0.29	1.08	0.26	2.1	0.35	0
Cholesterol—gm	0.42	1.60	—	—	1.12	2.5	Thiamin —mg	0.1	0.37	—	—	0.27	0
Phospholipids—gm	3.3	12.5	—	—	8.6	19.1	Inositol—mg	33.0	122.8	—	—	—	—
							Carbohydrates—gm	0.7	—	0.8	—	0.7	

Source: Cotterill, O. J. (1974). *A Scientist Speaks About Egg Products.* (Revised). Technical Advisory Committe American Egg Board, Park Ridge, Illinois.

Egg Quality

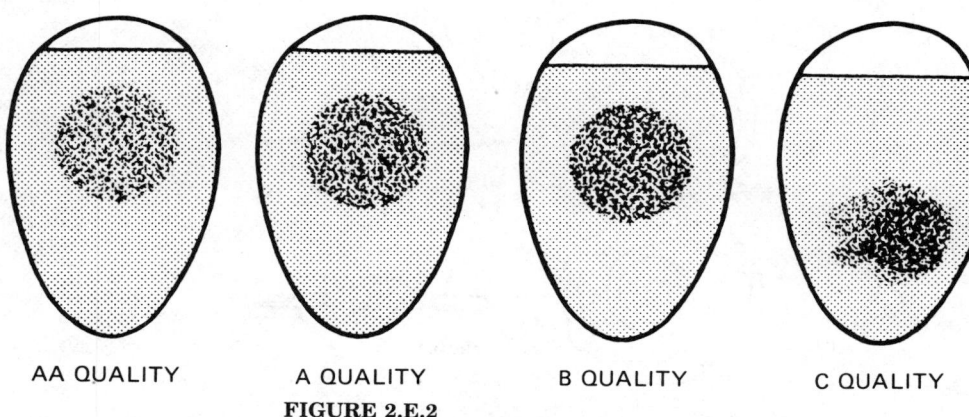

AA QUALITY A QUALITY B QUALITY C QUALITY

FIGURE 2.E.2
Candled appearance of eggs denoting quality

Source: U.S. Department of the Army (1969). Food inspection specialist. *TM 8-451.*

Egg Quality and Size Label

LOOK FOR THE USDA GRADE SHIELD

It tells you:

● The quality of the eggs.
● That the eggs have been certified for quality under USDA supervision.
● That the eggs were packed in a plant which meets USDA's rigid sanitary requirements.

Check for size:
Eggs that are officially graded are also checked for size.
The size must be shown on the main panel of the egg carton. Occasionally the size is shown within the grade shield.

Eggs packed according to U.S. grade are checked for quality and weight. Grading service is provided by USDA and cooperating State agencies on a voluntary basis to those who request and pay a fee for it.

FIGURE 2.E.3

Source: USDA (1977). How to buy eggs. *USDA Home and Garden Bull. 144.*

Egg Quality, Broken

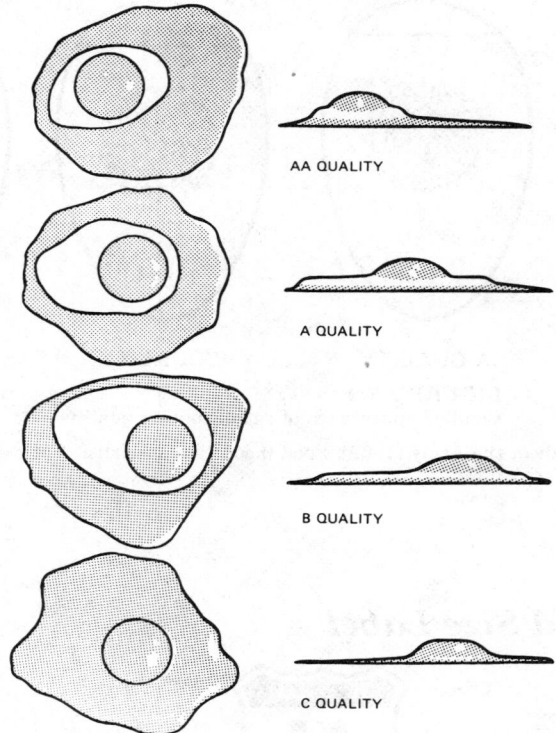

FIGURE 2.E.4
Appearance of broken eggs denoting quality

Source: U.S. Department of the Army (1969). Food inspection specialist. *TM 8-451.*

Egg Specifications

TABLE 2.E.7
Specifications for various egg products

Specification	Liquid or frozen			Solids						
				Whites		Whole		Yolk		
	White	Yolk[a]	Whole	Spray Dried	Pan Dried	Plain	Free[b] Flowing	Plain	Free Flowing	Scram. Egg
Moisture—%	—	—	—	8.0	14.0	5.0	3.0	5.0	3.0	2.5
Total solids—%	11.0	43.0	24.7	80.0	74.0	45.0	45.0	30.0	30.0	34.3
Crude protein—%	10.0	14.0	12.0	80.0	74.0	40.0	40.0	56.0	56.0	36.5
Total lipids—%	nil	28.0	10.5	<.02	nil	40.0	40.0	56.0	56.0	—
pH	8.9±.3	6.2±.1	7.3±.3	7.0±.5	5.5±.5	8.3±.3	8.3±.3	6.4±.3	6.4±.3	—
Carbohydrates[c]—%	—	—	—	glu. free	glu. free	SOP	SOP	SOP	SOP	17
Total microbial count—gm	<5,000	<5,000	<5,000	<10,000	<10,000	<10,000	<10,000	<10,000	<10,000	<10,000
Yeast—gm	10 max.	10 max.	10 max.	10 max.	10 max.	10 max.	10 max.	10 max.	10 max.	—
Mold—gm	10 max.	10 max.	10 max.	10 max.	10 max.	10 max.	10 max.	10 max.	10 max.	—
Coliform—gm	10 max.	10 max.	10 max.	10 max.	10 max.	10 max.	10 max.	10 max.	10 max.	—
Salmonellae—gm	Neg.[d]	Neg.	Neg.	Neg.	Neg.	Neg.	Neg.	Neg.	Neg.	Neg.
Granulation	—	—	—	100%[e]	SOP	100%	100%	100%	100%	—
Others[f]	—	—	—	USBS-60	—	USBS-16	USBS-16	USBS-16	USBS-16	—

a Egg yolk contains 17% egg white; Natural egg yolk contains about 52% solids.
b Free flowing products contain less than 2% sodium silicoaluminate.
c Most egg white solids are desugared. Whole egg and yolk products are desugared if specified on purchase (SOP).
d Negative by approved testing procedures.
e U.S. Bureau of Standard Screens No. 80.
f Additives and performance specifications may be specified on purchase.

Source: Cotterill, O. J. (1974). *A Scientist Speaks About Egg Products.* (Revised). Technical Advisory Committee, American Egg Board, Park Ridge, Illinois.

Egg Structure

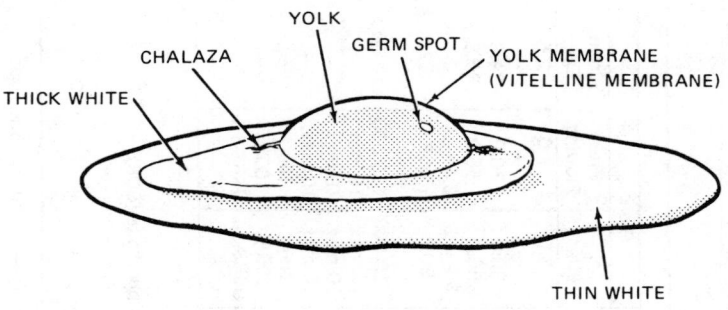

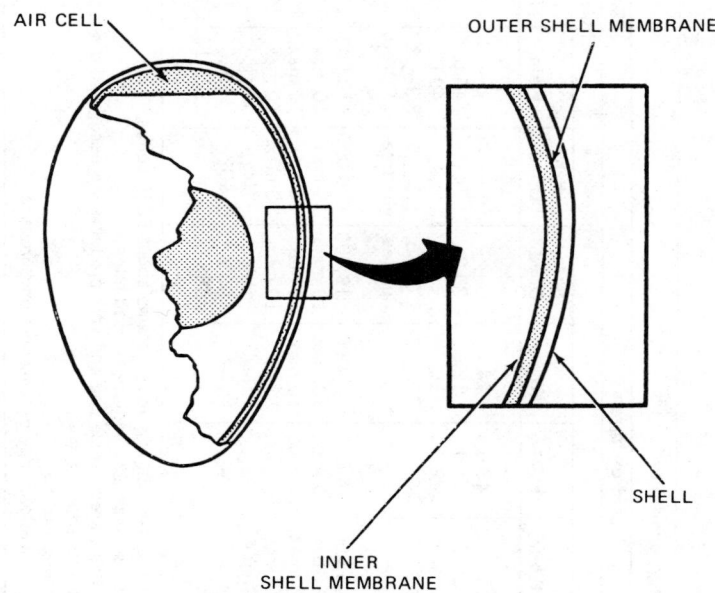

FIGURE 2.E.5

Source: U.S. Department of the Army (1969). Food inspection specialist. *TM 8-451.*

Egg Volume

TABLE 2.E.8

The following shows the approximate number of whole eggs needed to make 1 cup:

Egg Size	No. of Whole Eggs
Small	7
Medium	6
Large	5
Extra large	4

The following shows the approximate number of whites or yolks needed to make 1 cup:

Egg Size	Whites	Yolks
Small	10	18
Medium	8	16
Large	7	14
Extra large	6	12

Source: USDA (1970). Eggs in family meals. USDA Home and Garden Bull. *103.*

Elements

FISHER SCIENTIFIC / PERIODIC CHART OF THE ELEMENTS

IA	IIA	IIIA	IVA	VA	VIA	VIIA	VIIIA			IB	IIB	IIIB	IVB	VB	VIB	VIIB	NOBLE GASES
1 H 1.0079																	2 He 4.00260
3 Li 6.941†	4 Be 9.01218											5 B 10.81	6 C 12.011	7 N 14.0067	8 O 15.9994†	9 F 18.998403	10 Ne 20.179†
11 Na 22.98977	12 Mg 24.305											13 Al 26.98154	14 Si 28.0855†	15 P 30.97376	16 S 32.06	17 Cl 35.453	18 Ar 39.948†
19 K 39.0983†	20 Ca 40.08	21 Sc 44.9559	22 Ti 47.90†	23 V 50.9414†	24 Cr 51.996	25 Mn 54.9380	26 Fe 55.847†	27 Co 58.9332	28 Ni 58.70	29 Cu 63.546†	30 Zn 65.38	31 Ga 69.72	32 Ge 72.59†	33 As 74.9216	34 Se 78.96†	35 Br 79.904	36 Kr 83.80
37 Rb 85.4678†	38 Sr 87.62	39 Y 88.9059	40 Zr 91.22	41 Nb 92.9064	42 Mo 95.94	43 Tc (97)	44 Ru 101.07†	45 Rh 102.9055	46 Pd 106.4	47 Ag 107.868	48 Cd 112.41	49 In 114.82	50 Sn 118.69†	51 Sb 121.75†	52 Te 127.60†	53 I 126.9045	54 Xe 131.30
55 Cs 132.9054	56 Ba 137.33	57 *La 138.9055†	72 Hf 178.49†	73 Ta 180.9479†	74 W 183.85†	75 Re 186.207	76 Os 190.2	77 Ir 192.22	78 Pt 195.09†	79 Au 196.9665	80 Hg 200.59†	81 Tl 204.37†	82 Pb 207.2	83 Bi 208.9804	84 Po (209)	85 At (210)	86 Rn (222)
87 Fr (223)	88 Ra 226.0254	89 ¹Ac (227)	104 (260)	105 (260)													

*Lanthanides

58 Ce 140.12	59 Pr 140.9077	60 Nd 144.24†	61 Pm (145)(147)	62 Sm 150.4	63 Eu 151.96	64 Gd 157.25†	65 Tb 158.9254	66 Dy 162.50†	67 Ho 164.9304	68 Er 167.26†	69 Tm 168.9342	70 Yb 173.04†	71 Lu 174.97

¹Actinides

90 Th 232.0381	91 Pa 231.0359	92 U 238.029	93 Np 237.0482	94 Pu (244)	95 Am (243)	96 Cm (247)	97 Bk (247)	98 Cf (251)	99 Es (254)	100 Fm (257)	101 Md (258)	102 No (259)	103 Lr (260)

FIGURE 2.E.6

FISHER SCIENTIFIC COMPANY
CAT. NO 5-702-10

†The International Union for Pure and Applied Chemistry has not adopted official names or symbols for these elements.

¹ These weights are considered reliable to ±3 in the last place. Other weights are reliable to ±1 in the last place.

Atomic weights corrected to conform to the 1976 values of the Commission on Atomic Weights.

Data in this chart have been checked by the National Bureau of Standards Office of Standard Reference Data.

*Copyright 1977
Fisher Scientific Company

Enzymes, Food Industry

TABLE 2.E.9
Classification of enzymes significant in food and in the food industry

Trivial Name	Systematic Name	Enzyme Commission No.	Reaction (As Significant in Food Material)
Oxidoreductases			
Glucose oxidase	β-D-Glucose: O_2 oxidoreductase	1.1.3.4	β-D-Glucose + O_2 → D-glucono-δ-lactone + H_2O_2
Phenolase (polyphenol oxidase)	o-Diphenol: O_2 oxidoreductase	1.10.3.1	2 o-Diphenol + O_2 → 2 o-quinone + 2 H_2O
Ascorbic acid oxidase	L-Ascorbate: O_2 oxidoreductase	1.10.3.3	2 L-ascorbate + O_2 → 2 dehydroascorbate + 2 H_2O
Catalase	H_2O_2: H_2O_2 oxidoreductase	1.11.1.6	H_2O_2 + H_2O_2 → O_2 + 2 H_2O
Peroxidase	Donor: H_2O_2 oxidoreductase	1.11.1.7	Donor + H_2O_2 → oxidized donor + 2 H_2O
Lipoxidase (lipoxygenase)	—	1.99.2.1	Unsaturated fat + O_2 → a peroxide of the unsaturated fat
Hydrolases			
Lipase	Glycerol ester hydrolase	3.1.1.3	Triglyceride + H_2O → glycerol + fatty acids
Pectin methylesterase	Pectin pectyl-hydrolase	3.1.1.11	Pectin + n H_2O → pectic acid + n MeOH
Chlorophyllase	Chlorophyll chlorophyllido-hydrolase	3.1.1.14	Chlorophyll + H_2O → phytol + chlorophyllide
Phosphatase (acid or alkaline)	Orthophosphoric monoester phosphohydrolase	3.1.3 (1,2)	An orthophosphoric monoester + H_2O → an alcohol + H_3PO_4
α-Amylase	α-1,4-Glucan 4-glucanohydrolase	3.2.1.1	Internal random hydrolysis
β-Amylase	α-1,4-Glucan maltohydrolase	3.2.1.2	Hydrolysis of { Successive maltose units removed
Glucoamylase	α-1,4-Glucan glucohydrolase	3.2.1.3	α-1,4-glucan links Successive glucose units removed
Cellulase	β-1,4-Glucan 4-glucanohydrolase	3.2.1.4	Hydrolyses β-1,4-glucan links in cellulose
Amylopectin-1,6-glucosidase (R-enzyme)	Amylopectin 6-glucanohydrolase	3.2.1.9	Hydrolyses α-1,6-glucan links in amylopectin
Polygalacturonase	Polygalacturonide glucanohydrolase	3.2.1.15	Pectic acid + (x − 1) H_2O → x α-D-galacturonic acid
Maltase (α-glucosidase)	α-D-Glucoside glucohydrolase	3.2.1.20	Maltose + H_2O → 2 α-D-glucose
Lactase	β-D-Galactoside galactohydrolase	3.2.1.23	Lactose + H_2O → α-D-glucose + β-D-galactose
Invertase (sucrase)	β-D-Fructofuranoside fructohydrolase	3.2.1.26	Sucrose + H_2O → α-D-glucose + β-D-fructose
Pepsin	—	3.4.4.1	
Rennin	—	3.4.4.3	
Trypsin	—	3.4.4.4	
Chymotrypsin	—	3.4.4.5	
Elastase	—	3.4.4.7	Hydrolysis of peptide linkages
Papain	—	3.4.4.10	
Chymopapain	—	3.4.4.11	
Ficin	—	3.4.4.12	
Bromelain	—	3.4.4.c	
Bacterial protease	—	3.4.4.16	
Fungal protease	—	3.4.4.17	
Collagenase	—	3.4.4.19	

Source: Eskin, N. A. M., Henderson, H. M., and Townsend, R. J. (1971). *Biochemistry of Foods.* Academic Press, New York.

Equivalent Weights

TABLE 2.E.10
Equivalent combining weights and their reciprocals based on international atomic weights, 1973

Neg. Radicals	Equiv. Combining Wts	Reciprocals of Equiv. Combining Wts	Pos. Radicals	Equiv. Combining Wts	Reciprocals of Equiv. Combining Wts
NO_3	62.0049	0.01613	NH_4	18.0383	0.05544
BO_2	42.81	0.02336	Li	6.941	0.14407
AsO_4	46.3064	0.02160	K	39.098	0.02558
I	126.9045	0.00788	Na	22.98977	0.04350
Br	79.904	0.01252	Mg	12.153	0.08228
PO_4	31.6571	0.03159	Ca	20.04	0.04990
HS	33.07	0.03024	Sr	43.81	0.02283
S	16.03	0.06238	Ba	68.67	0.01456
SiO_3	38.042	0.02629	Mn	27.4690	0.03640
O	7.9997	0.12500	Fe^{++}	27.924	0.03581
Cl	35.453	0.02821	Fe^{+++}	18.616	0.05372
SO_4	48.03	0.02082	Al	8.9938	0.11119
CO_3	30.005	0.03333	Cu	31.773	0.03147
HCO_3	61.017	0.01639			

Salts	Equiv. Combining Wts	Reciprocals of Equiv. Combining Wts	Salts	Equiv. Combining Wts	Reciprocals of Equiv. Combining Wts
NH_4Cl	53.491	0.01869	$MgCl_2$	47.606	0.02101
LiCl	42.394	0.02359	$MgSO_4$	60.18	0.01662
Li_2SO_4	54.97	0.01819	$MgCO_3$	42.157	0.02372
Li_2CO_3	36.946	0.02707	$Mg(HCO_3)_2$	73.170	0.01367
$LiHCO_3$	67.958	0.01471	$Mg(NO_3)_2$	74.157	0.01348
KCl	74.551	0.01341	$CaCl_2$	55.49	0.01802
K_2SO_4	87.13	0.01148	$CaSO_4$	68.07	0.01469
K_2CO_3	69.103	0.01447	$CaCO_3$	50.04	0.01998
$KHCO_3$	100.115	0.00999	$Ca(HCO_3)_2$	81.06	0.01234
KI	166.003	0.00602	$CaSiO_3$	58.08	0.01722
KBr	119.002	0.00840	$Ca_3(PO_4)_2$	51.70	0.01934
NaCl	58.443	0.01711	$SrSO_4$	91.84	0.01089
NaBr	102.894	0.00972	$SrCO_3$	73.81	0.01355
NaI	149.8942	0.00667	$Sr(HCO_3)_2$	104.83	0.00954
Na_2SO_4	71.02	0.01408	$BaSO_4$	116.70	0.00857
Na_2CO_3	52.994	0.01887	$Ba(HCO_3)_2$	129.69	0.00771
$NaHCO_3$	84.007	0.01190	$MnSO_4$	75.50	0.01325
$NaNO_2$	68.9952	0.01449	$MnCO_3$	57.474	0.01740
$NaNO_3$	84.9946	0.01177	$Mn(HCO_3)_2$	88.486	0.01130
$NaBO_2$	65.80	0.01520	$FeSO_4$	75.95	0.01317
Na_3AsO_4	69.2961	0.01443	$Fe_2(SO_4)_3$	66.64	0.01501
NaF	41.9881	0.02382	$FeCO_3$	57.928	0.01726
NaHS	56.06	0.01784	$Fe(HCO_3)_2$	88.941	0.01124
Na_3PO_4	54.6468	0.01830	Fe_2O_3	26.615	0.03757
Na_2S	39.02	0.02563	$Al_2(SO_4)_3$	57.02	0.01754
Na_2SiO_3	61.032	0.01638	Al_2O_3	16.9935	0.05885

Source: AOAC (1975). *Official Methods of Analysis*, 12th Edition. Editorial Board (Editors). Association of Official Analytical Chemists.

Essential Oils

TABLE 2.E.11
Details of some of the essential oils to show how diverse odors and flavors are derived from the vegetable world

Oil of—	Distilled or extracted from—	Chief odorous components	Remarks
Allspice (Pimento)	Fruit of *Pimenta officinalis*, W. Indies	Eugenol, cineol	Odour recalls nutmeg, pepper and cinnamon. Used in bay rum
Angelica	Root or seed of *Angelica Archangelica*, Saxony	Exaltolide and Δ^7 hexadeceno-lactone	Musky odour. Used for liqueurs
Angostura bark	Bark of *Galipea cusparia*, Venezuela	Cadinene	Used for liqueurs
Asafœtida	Gum resin of *Ferula narthex*, Afghanistan	Terpenes, foul sulphur compounds, diallyl sulphide	Foul-smelling
Balsam of Peru	Oleo-resinous exudation of *Myroxylon Balsamum β-Pereiræ*, San Salvador	Benzyl benzoate, benzyl cinnamate	The resin itself is more commonly used than the oil from it
Balsam of Tolu	Exudation of *Myroxylon Balsamum gennimum*, New Granada, Venezuela	Benzyl benzoate, benzyl cinnamate, farnesol	Hyacinth odour
Bay	Leaves of *Pimenta acris*, W. Indies	Eugenol and its methyl ether, pinene, myrcene	Used in preparation of bay rum
Bergamot	Peel of Bergamot, *Citrus aurantium Bergamot*, Calabria	Linalyl acetate, 40 per cent, linalool, limonene, bisabolene, pinene	Perfumes
Bitter almonds	Kernels of bitter almond, *Prunus amygdalis*, all parts of the world	Benzaldehyde, hydrocyanic acid	
Camphor	Twigs of *Cinnamomum Camphora*, Formosa	Camphor, terpenes	Household and medical uses. Also a source of synthetic safrol for art. oil of sassafras
Cananga			Inferior grade of ylang-ylang (*q.v.*)
Caraway	Seeds of *Carum carui* Holland, etc.	*l*-carvone, carveol, *d*-limonene	Medicine. Perfumes. Used in soaps of Brown Windsor type
Carrot seed	Seed of carrot *Daucus carota*	Pinene	
Cassia	Leaves and twigs of *Cinnamomum cassia*, China	Cinnamic aldehyde, 80 to 90 per cent	Spice and perfumery. Used in Brown Windsor type soap
Cedar wood	Pencil shavings of cedar wood, *Juniperus virginiana*, Florida	Cedrene, cedrol, cedrenol	Oil used for fine soap and perfumes. Powdered wood used for incense
Celery seed	Common celery seed, *Apium graveolens*	Selinene, sedanolide (tetrahydrobutyl phthalide)	

(Continued)

Essential Oils (*Continued*)

TABLE 2.E.11 (*Continued*)

Oil of—	Distilled or extracted from—	Chief odorous components	Remarks
Chamomile	Flowers of *Anthemis nobilis*, Germany	Esters of angelic and tiglic acids	Medicine
Cinnamon	Bark and leaves of *Cinnamomum Zeylanicum*, Ceylon, E. Indies	Bark oil—cinnamic aldehyde; leaf oil —eugenol	Similar to oil of cassia but more delicate in odour. Used for dentifrices and also in Oriental type perfumes
Citronella	Citronella grass, several varieties, Ceylon, Java	Geraniol, citronellol, camphene	Cheap perfumery
Clary sage	Leaves and twigs of *Salvia sclarea*, Dalmatia	Pinene, cineol, linalool	Odour recalls ambergris. Used as a fixative
Cloves	Dried flower-buds of *Eugenia caryophyllata*, E. Indies, Zanzibar	Eugenol, 80 per cent	Source of vanillin (via isoeugenol). Also used for dentifrices and soaps
Coriander	Fruit of *Coriandrum sativum*, many parts of the world	Linalool, pinene	
Cubebs	Dried fruits of *Piper cubeba*, Singapore	*dl*-Limonene, pinene, cadinene	Used in medicine
Dill	Fruit of *Anethum graveolens*, Europe, India	Carvone, limonene	Used as a carminative
Elemi	Exudation of *Canarium luzonicum*, Philippines	Phellandrene, *d*-limonene	
Eucalyptus	Leaves of *Eucalyptus globulus*, Australia, etc.	Cineol, pinene	Used medicinally
Fennel	Fruit of *Fœniculum vulgare*, Mediterranean countries	Anethol; 60 per cent, fenchone	Anethole is a source of Aubepine or anisaldehyde
Frankincense	Exudation of *Boswellia Carterii* and *B. serrata*, India	Pinene, Camphene, *dl*-limonene	Balsamic odour
Gardenia	Flowers of *Gardenia grandiflora*	Benzyl acetate, linalool, methyl anthranilate	
Garlic	Entire plant, *Allium sativum*	Diallyl disulphide	Flavours
Geranium	Leaves of varieties of *Pelargonium*, France, Algeria, etc.	Geraniol, Citronellol	Used for floral bouquets
Ginger	Rhizome of *Zingiber officinale*, Asia, W. Indies	Zingiberene, Zingerone, Camphene, Cineol, Borneol, citral	Flavour
Jasmine	Flowers of *Jasminum grandiflorum*, Asia chiefly	Jasmone, indole, Methyl anthranilate	Perfume
Lavender	Flowers of *Lavandula vera*, England, France	Cineol, limonene, linalyl acetate, linalool, geraniol and esters	Perfumery

(*Continued*)

Essential Oils (*Continued*)

TABLE 2.E.11 (*Continued*)

Oil of—	Distilled or extracted from—	Chief odorous components	Remarks
Lemon	Peel of lemon, *Citrus limonum*, Mediterranean countries	*d*-limonene, 90 per cent; citral	
Lemon-grass	Lemon-grass, Varieties of *Cymbopogon*, E. Indies	Citral, 80 per cent	Source of citral from which ionone is made for violet perfumes
Limes	Fruit of *Citrus medica acida*, W. Indies	Citral, limonene	
Linaloe	Wood and fruit of *Bursera Delpechiana*, Mexico	Linalool	Soft sweet odour. Used for perfumes and soaps
Mignonette	Flowers of mignonette, *Reseda odorata*	Aldehydes, eugenol caprylic acid	Yield only 0·002 per cent. Powerful odour. Floral extract generally used instead of oil
Musk-seed	Seeds of *Hibiscus abelmoschus*, Java	Farnesol, Δ^7 hexadecenolactone	Known also as oil of ambrette seeds. Musky odour.
Mustard	Seeds of *Brassica nigra*	Allyl thiocarbimide	
Myrrh	Oleo-resin secreted in the bark of various *Commiphora*, Arabia, Somaliland	Cuminic aldehyde, bisabolene, pinene, *dl*-limonene, eugenol, *m*-cresol	
Myrtle	Leaves of *Myrtus communis*, Mediterranean countries	Pinene, cineol, camphene	
Nepeta	Catmint, *Nepeta cataria*, Sicily	Menthol and its caprylic and valeric esters	
Neroli	Orange-flowers, *Citrus aurantium*, France	Nerol, geraniol, linalool, Phenyl ethyl alcohol methyl anthranilate	Perfumes. Used for eau-de-Cologne
Opoponax	Exudation of varieties of *Commiphora*, Arabia, Somaliland	Bisabolene	Similar to oil of myrrh
Orange	Peel of orange, *Citrus aurantium*, Mediterranean countries	*d*-limonene, 90 per cent; decylic aldehyde	
Orris-root	Iris rhizomes, varieties of *Iris*, Italy	Irone, aldehydes	Odour develops after roots are dried. Powdered roots used in violet powder. Pure oil used in highest quality violet perfumes; as a fixative for ionone in cheaper qualities
Parsley	All parts of common parsley, *Petroselinum sativum*, France, Germany	Pinene, apiol	

(*Continued*)

Essential Oils (*Continued*)

TABLE 2.E.11 (*Continued*)

Oil of—	Distilled or extracted from—	Chief odorous components	Remarks
Parsnip	Chiefly parsnip seed, *Pastinaca sativa*	Octyl butyrate, octyl propionate	
Patchouli	Dried leaves of *Pogostemon patchouli*, Singapore, Java	Terpenes, eugenol	Used for face powder and perfumes. Thick liquid with powerful and persistent odour. Good fixative
Pennyroyal	Leaves of *Mentha pulegium*, Europe	Pulegone, 85 per cent	
Pepper	Unripe berries of *Piper nigrum*	Piperine, *dl*-limonene	
Peppermint	Flowering tops of mint herb, *Mentha piperita*, England, America, Japan	Menthol, 50 per cent menthyl acetate, menthone, cadinene, *l*-limonene	Flavouring sweetmeats and dentifrices
Perilla	Leaves of *Perilla nankinensis*, Japan	Perillic aldehyde	Peculiar hay-like odour. Used in perfumes
Petitgrain	Leaves and young shoots of orange, *Citrus aurantium*, Paraguay	Pinene, geraniol, linalool, Methyl anthranilate	Used for making eau-de-Cologne
Roses	Flowers of *Rosa damascena*, Bulgaria, France	Citronellol, 30 per cent, geraniol, 40 per cent, phenylethyl alcohol, nerol	Perfumes
Rose-geranium	Mixture of roses and pelargonium leaves, France		
Rosemary	Flowering tops of *Rosemarina officinalis*, S. Europe	Camphor, borneol, pinene, cineol	Used in cheap perfumes, soaps and hair-washes
Rue	Herb, *Ruta graveolens*, France	Methyl nonyl ketone, methyl heptyl ketone	
Sandalwood	Wood or roots of *Santalum album*, India	Santalenes, santalone, cadinene, diacetyl	Used as a fixative for Oriental type perfumes. Also used in soaps and face powders
Sassafras	Bark and roots of *Sassafras officinale*, N. America	Safrol, 80 per cent, Pinene	Used in soap perfumery
Shaddock	Grape-fruit, *Citrus decumana*, W. Indies	Limonene	
Spearmint	Herb, *Mentha viridis*, America chiefly	*l*-carvone, phellandrene, limonene and esters	Used for flavouring sweetmeats
Spikenard	Root of *Nardostachys jatamansi*, India	Sesquiterpenes	Valued in the East as a perfume. Disliked by Western people as a rule. Largely replaced by oil of valerian.

(*Continued*)

Essential Oils (Continued)

TABLE 2.E.11 (Continued)

Oil of—	Distilled or extracted from—	Chief odorous components	Remarks
Star Aniseed (Badiane)	Fruit of *Illicium verum*, China	Pinene, anethol, phellandrene	Flavouring
Storax	Oleo-resin from bark of *Liquidamber orientale*, Asia Minor	Phenyl ethylene (oil of styrol)	
Sweet Basil	Herb, *Oceum basilicum*, Europe, Algeria	Ocimene, cineol, pinene	Used in mignonette perfumes, etc.
Tansy	Herb, *Tanacetum vulgare*, England, France, America	Thujone, borneol	
Tea	Leaves of tea plant, *Thea chinensis*, China		Yield only 0·006 per cent
Thyme	Herb, *Thymus vulgaris*, France, Spain	Borneol, thymol, carvacrol, bornyl acetate	Used medicinally. Also in soap
Tropæolum	Leaves of nasturtium, *Tropæolum majus*	Benzyl thiocarbimide, 80 per cent (benzyl mustard oil)	
Tuberose	Flowers of *Polyanthus tuberosa*, France	Methyl anthranilate, methyl benzoate	Made by enfleurage
Turpentine	Pine-wood exudations, Europe, India	Pinene, limonene	Ordinary turpentine is a solution of resins, e.g. colophony in the oil of turpentine. Source of terpincol
Valerian	Roots of *Valeriana officinalis*, Europe, Japan	Borneol, bornyl acetate, camphene isovalerianic esters	Used in medicine, also as a soap perfume
Verbena	Herb, *Lippia citriodora*, France, etc.	Citral	Perfumes. Lemon-grass oil also consists chiefly of citral and is often called verbena
Vetivert	Roots of Khas-khas grass, *Vetiveria zizanioides*, India	Sesquiterpenes, esters	Heavy liquid used as a fixative. Perfume suggests myrrh
Wallflower	Wallflowers, *Cheiranthus cheiri*	Nerol, geraniol, indol, methyl anthranilate	Yield only 0·06 per cent
Wintergreen	Originally from leaves of *Gaultheria procumbens*, later bark of sweet birch. *Betula lenta*	99 per cent methyl salicylate	Used for flavouring dentifrices, etc.
Ylang-ylang	Flowers of *Cananga odorata*, Philippines	Benzyl benzoate alcohols, esters	Over 30 components already isolated. Used for fine perfumes

Source: Moncrieff, R. W. (1967). *The Chemical Senses.* Leonard Hill Books, London, England.

Fat and Body Weight

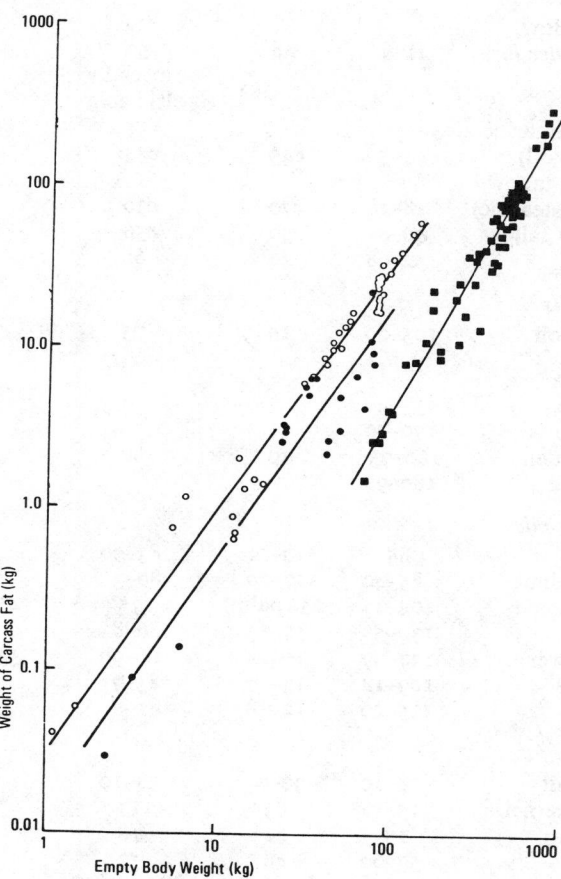

FIGURE 2.F.1
Weight of dissected fat in a carcass (excluding kidney fat) compared with empty body weight for sheep (●), cattle
(■), and pigs (○).

Source: Tribe, D. E. (editor). Carcass Composition and Appraisal of Meat Animals. CSIRO, Australia.

Fats and Oils, Characteristics

TABLE 2.F.1
Main edible fats used as raw materials in the manufacture of margarine together with their characteristic figures

Name	Iodine number	Saturated fatty acids %	Unsaturated fatty acids %	Polyunsaturated fatty acids %
Animal fats				
Beef tallow (*premier jus*)	42–8	48	52 especially oleic acid	
Oleomargarine (oleo oil)	44–5	c45	c55	
Pressed tallow (oleostearine)	18–28	c70	c30	
Mutton tallow	40–8	c50	c50	
Lard	52–68	40	60	
Animal oils				
Whale oil	105–20	25	75	
Fish oils				
Herring	135–40			
Sardine	170–90			
Menhaden	160–75	20	80	
Pilchard	180–90			
Vegetable oils				
Olive	85	10–12	83–90	7
Groundnut	85–40	17–20	80–3	20–40
Cottonseed	104–12	25 (palm)	75	45 (linol)
Soya	130–5	12–15	86–8	60
Sunflower	127–37	10–14	86–90	55 (linol)
Sesame	109–14	13–17	83–7	38–48
Maize	115–20	12–18	82–8	40
Vegetable fats				
Coconut	8–10	90–2	8–10	
Palm kernel	15–18	83	17	
Babassu	15	82	18	
Palm	53–60	48	52	
Shea	±60	46	54	

Source: Van Stuyvenberg, J. H. (1969). *Margarine*. Liverpool University Press, Liverpool, England.

Fats and Oils, Composition I

TABLE 2.F.2
Composition of fats and oils

(Dashes (—) denote lack of reliable data for a constituent believed to be present in measurable amount)

Item No. (A)	Foods, approximate measures, units, and weight (edible part unless footnotes indicate otherwise) (B)		Grams	Water (C) Percent	Food energy (D) Calories	Protein (E) Grams	Fat (F) Grams	Saturated (total) (G) Grams	Unsaturated Oleic (H) Grams	Unsaturated Linoleic (I) Grams	Carbohydrate (J) Grams	Calcium (K) Milligrams	Phosphorus (L) Milligrams	Iron (M) Milligrams	Potassium (N) Milligrams	Vitamin A value (O) International units	Thiamin (P) Milligrams	Riboflavin (Q) Milligrams	Niacin (R) Milligrams	Ascorbic acid (S) Milligrams
	FATS, OILS; RELATED PRODUCTS																			
	Butter:																			
	Regular (1 brick or 4 sticks per lb):																			
103	Stick (1/2 cup)	1 stick	113	16	815	1	92	57.3	23.1	2.1	Trace	27	26	.2	29	¹3,470	.01	.04	Trace	0
104	Tablespoon (about 1/8 stick).	1 tbsp	14	16	100	Trace	12	7.2	2.9	.3	Trace	3	3	Trace	4	¹430	Trace	Trace	Trace	0
105	Pat (1 in square, 1/3 in high; 90 per lb).	1 pat	5	16	35	Trace	4	2.5	1.0	.1	Trace	1	1	Trace	1	¹150	Trace	Trace	Trace	0
	Whipped (6 sticks or two 8-oz containers per lb).																			
106	Stick (1/2 cup)	1 stick	76	16	540	1	61	38.2	15.4	1.4	Trace	18	17	.1	20	¹2,310	Trace	.03	Trace	0
107	Tablespoon (about 1/8 stick).	1 tbsp	9	16	65	Trace	8	4.7	1.9	.2	Trace	2	2	Trace	2	¹290	Trace	Trace	Trace	0
108	Pat (1 1/4 in square, 1/3 in high; 120 per lb).	1 pat	4	16	25	Trace	3	1.9	.8	.1	Trace	1	1	Trace	1	¹120	0	Trace	Trace	0
109	Fats, cooking (vegetable shortenings).	1 cup	200	0	1,770	0	200	48.8	88.2	48.4	0	0	0	0	0	—	0	0	0	0
110		1 tbsp	13	0	110	0	13	3.2	5.7	3.1	0	0	0	0	0	—	0	0	0	0
111	Lard	1 cup	205	0	1,850	0	205	81.0	83.8	20.5	0	0	0	0	0	0	0	0	0	0
112		1 tbsp	13	0	115	0	13	5.1	5.3	1.3	0	0	0	0	0	0	0	0	0	0
	Margarine:																			
	Regular (1 brick or 4 sticks per lb):																			
113	Stick (1/2 cup)	1 stick	113	16	815	1	92	16.7	42.9	24.9	Trace	27	26	.2	29	²3,750	.01	.04	Trace	0
114	Tablespoon (about 1/8 stick).	1 tbsp	14	16	100	Trace	12	2.1	5.3	3.1	Trace	3	3	Trace	4	²470	Trace	Trace	Trace	0
115	Pat (1 in square, 1/3 in high; 90 per lb).	1 pat	5	16	35	Trace	4	.7	1.9	1.1	Trace	1	1	Trace	1	²170	Trace	Trace	Trace	0
116	Soft, two 8-oz containers per lb.	1 container	227	16	1,635	1	184	32.5	71.5	65.4	Trace	53	52	.4	59	²7,500	.01	.08	.1	0
117		1 tbsp	14	16	100	Trace	12	2.0	4.5	4.1	Trace	3	3	Trace	4	²470	Trace	Trace	Trace	0
	Whipped (6 sticks per lb):																			
118	Stick (1/2 cup)	1 stick	76	16	545	Trace	61	11.2	28.7	16.7	Trace	18	17	.1	20	²2,500	Trace	.03	Trace	0
119	Tablespoon (about 1/8 stick).	1 tbsp	9	16	70	Trace	8	1.4	3.6	2.1	Trace	2	2	Trace	2	²310	Trace	Trace	Trace	0
	Oils, salad or cooking:																			
120	Corn	1 cup	218	0	1,925	0	218	27.7	53.6	125.1	0	0	0	0	0	—	0	0	0	0
121		1 tbsp	14	0	120	0	14	1.7	3.3	7.8	0	0	0	0	0	—	0	0	0	0
122	Olive	1 cup	216	0	1,910	0	216	30.7	154.4	17.7	0	0	0	0	0	—	0	0	0	0
123		1 tbsp	14	0	120	0	14	1.9	9.7	1.1	0	0	0	0	0	—	0	0	0	0
124	Peanut	1 cup	216	0	1,910	0	216	37.4	98.5	67.0	0	0	0	0	0	—	0	0	0	0
125		1 tbsp	14	0	120	0	14	2.3	6.2	4.2	0	0	0	0	0	—	0	0	0	0
126	Safflower	1 cup	218	0	1,925	0	218	20.5	25.9	159.8	0	0	0	0	0	—	0	0	0	0
127		1 tbsp	14	0	120	0	14	1.3	1.6	10.0	0	0	0	0	0	—	0	0	0	0
128	Soybean oil, hydrogenated (partially hardened).	1 cup	218	0	1,925	0	218	31.8	93.1	75.6	0	0	0	0	0	—	0	0	0	0
129		1 tbsp	14	0	120	0	14	2.0	5.8	4.7	0	0	0	0	0	—	0	0	0	0
130	Soybean-cottonseed oil blend, hydrogenated.	1 cup	218	0	1,925	0	218	38.2	63.0	99.6	0	0	0	0	0	—	0	0	0	0
131		1 tbsp	14	0	120	0	14	2.4	3.9	6.2	0	0	0	0	0	—	0	0	0	0

Source: Consumer and Food Economics Institute (1977). Nutritive value of foods. USDA Home and Garden Bull. 72.

Fats and Oils, Composition II

TABLE 2.F.3
Composition of principal classes of food, animal, and vegetable fats and oils

Composition and Analytical Characteristics of Principal Classes of Food Fats and Oils of the U.S.A.

	Household Shortenings		Commercial Bulk shortenings		Margarine oils	Cottonseed salad oils	Liquid shortenings
	Vegetable fat	Meat fat and vegetable fat	Vegetable fat	Meat fat and vegetable fat			
Composition							
Oleic acid (%)[a]	53-75	37-57	45-76	40-65	42-79	17-36	18-45
Linoleic acid (%)[b]	3-14	6-13	3-13	3-13	2-18	42-55	30-47
Linolenic acid (%)[b]	0-0.5	0-0.6	0-0.7	0-0.8	0-0.4	0-0.7	0-1.0
Arachidonic acid (%)[b]	0	0-0.5	0	0-0.5	0	0	0
Total saturated acids (%)	16-31	30-50	15-40	28-40	12-24	18-30	17-36
Analytical characteristics							
Iodine value	70-81	54-74	65-90	55-67	68-83	107-117	90-104
Melting point (FAC) (°F)	108-125	114-129	103-124	110-125	96-106	—	86-126
Solids index at 70°F	15-30	16-28	16-26	19-30	11-21	—	2-7
Solids index at 90°F	10-20	10-22	7-21	7-21	1-7	—	0.5-5

[a] Total monounsaturated acids.   [b] By spectrophotometric analysis.

Composition and Analytical Characteristics of the Principal Animal and Vegetable Fats and Oils Used in Foods in the U.S.A.

	Beef fat	Butter fat	Coco butter	Coconut oil	Corn oil	Cotton-seed oil	Lard	Olive oil	Peanut oil	Soybean oil
Composition										
Oleic acid (%)[a]	35-45	30-32	34-38	6-9	25-37	17-37	47-83	62-83	30-58	16-47
Linoleic acid (%)[b]	0.5-3	1.0-2.5	3-3.5	1-4	50-56	44-55	7-13	8-15	21-37	39-53
Linolenic acid (%)[b]	0.2-0.6	0.2-0.5	0.1-0.2	0-0.1	0.1-0.7	0-0.6	0.2-1.4	0.5-0.7	0-0.5	4-9
Arachidonic acid (%)[b]	0.05-0.2	0.2-0.4	—	—	—	—	0.2-0.4	—	—	—
Total saturated acids (%)	45-58	63-68	57-61	86-91	9-15	17-31	29-37	9-22	16-26	5-24
Analytical characteristics										
Iodine value	38-44	30-40	37-44	8-15	122-125	103-112	63-69	76-88	90-99	125-131
Melting point (FAC) (°F)	116-121	97-100	86-95	79-82	—	—	99-112	—	—	—
Solids index at 70°F	23-30	11-13	47-49	19-27	—	—	17-21	—	—	—
Solids index at 90°F	18-24	2.5-4	0	0	—	—	4-6	—	—	—

[a] Total monounsaturated acids.   [b] By spectrophotometric analysis.

Composition and Analytical Characteristics of Some Other Vegetable Oils Not Normally Used in Foods in the U.S.A.

	Linseed oil	Palm oil	Palm kernel oil	Rape-seed oil	Saf-flower oil	Sesame oil			Linseed oil	Palm oil	Palm kernel oil	Rape-seed oil	Saf-flower oil	Sesame oil
Composition								**Analytical characteristics**						
Oleic acid (%)[a]	31-36	34-56	14[c]	59-62[d]	10-23	35-47		Iodine value	181-192	51-58	16-18	103-109	141-150	109-115
Linoleic acid (%)[b]	8-21	10-11	2-3[c]	15	69-78	40-44		Melting point (FAC)(°F)	—	—	103-105	84-86	—	—	—
Linolenic acid (%)[b]	42-50	0.1-0.4	—	9-10	0-2	0-0.3		Solids index at 70°F	—	11-13	31-33	—	—	—
Arachidonic acid (%)[b]	—	—	—	—	—	—		Solids index at 90°F	—	6-8	—	—	—	—
Total saturated acids (%)	0-6	34-50	84[c]	14-16	5-13	12-16								

[a] Total monounsaturated acids.   [b] By spectrophotometric analysis.   [c] Only one analysis available.   [d] Mostly erucic.

Source: Anonymous (1969). *The Wecobee Handbook.* PVO International, Boonton, New Jersey.

Fats and Oils, Fatty Acid Composition

TABLE 2.F.4
Fatty acid composition of common fats and oils as determined by gas chromatography

Acid (Commonly referred to ..name of.. predominant specie)	G.C. Common Designation	Babassu	Butter Fat (1)	Cocoa Butter	Coconut	Corn	Cottonseed	Lard (1)	Ouri-Curi	Palm	Palm Kernel
Caprylic	C8:0	7	1.5	—	8	—	—	—	10	—	4
Capric	C10:0	5	3	—	7	—	0.1	—	9	—	4
Lauric	C12:0	45	4	—	48.2	—	0.1	0.1	46	—	50
Myristic	C14:0	15	12	0.5	18	0.2	0.9	1	9	1	16
Palmitic	C16:0	9	25	25	8.5	12	23.5	23	8	46	8
Stearic	C18:0	3	9	35	2.3	2.2	2.5	9	2	4	2.5
Oleic	C18:1	13	—	37.5	6	27	18	46	13	37	12
Linoleic	C18:2	2	—	2	2	57	54	14	3	10	3
Arachidic	C20:0	0.1	1	—	—	0.3	0.3	0.2	—	0.4	0.1
Linolenic	C18:3	—		—	—	1	0.3	—	—	0.3	0.1
Gadoleic	C20:1	—		—	—		0.3	1	—		
Behenic	C22:0	—		—	—	—	—	Trace	—	—	—
Lignoceric	C24:0	—	—	—	—	—	—	—	—	—	—
Others	C4:0		3	—	—						
	C6:0		1								
	C12:1		0.4								
	C14:1		1.5								
	C16:1		4								
Iodine No. (Wijs) Typical		16	30	40	9	125	110	73	15	50	17
Iodine No. (Wijs) Range		15-19	25-35	35-43	8-12	120-128	105-116	65-80	12-18	45-55	16-20
Sap. Value Range		247-250	216-240	190-200	254-262	189-193	189-198	190-198	255-260	196-200	244-255
Wiley Melting Pt. °F.		79	82-95	79-99	76	—	—	88-110		104-110	80

Acid (Commonly referred to ..name of.. predominant specie)	G.C. Common Designation	Peanut (1)	Rapeseed (1)	Rice-Bran	Safflower	Soybean	Sunflower	Tallow Beef	Tallow Mutton
Caprylic	C8:0	—	—	—	—	—	—	—	—
Capric	C10:0	—	—	—	—	—	—	—	—
Lauric	C12:0	0.2	—	—	—	—	—	—	—
Myristic	C14:0	0.1	—	0.5	—	—	—	2	1
Palmitic	C16:0	11	3	17	8	11	8	35	21
Stearic	C18:0	3	1.5	2.5	3	4	3	16	30
Oleic	C18:1	46	32	46	13	25	20	44	43
Linoleic	C18:2	31	19	32	75	50	67.8	2	5
Arachidic	C20:0	1.5	—	0.5	trace	0.4	0.5	—	—
Linolenic	C18:3	1.5	10	1	1	8	0.5	0.4	—
Gadoleic	C20:1	1.5	10						
Behenic	C22:0	3.3	0.5	—	—	0.3	0.2	—	—
Lignoceric	C24:0	1.3	—	—	—	0.3	0.2	—	—
Others	C22:1	23.5	—	—	—	—	—	—	—
Iodine No. (Wijs) Typical		100	101	145	132	130		40	40
Iodine No. (Wijs) Range		90-110	95-108	135-150	127-140	125-140		35-45	35-45
Sap. Value Range		170-180	183-194	188-192	190-194	188-194		196-200	193-195
Wiley Melting Pt. °F.		—	—	—	—	—		—	—

(1) Large variation normally encountered.

Source: Anonymous (1969). *The Wecobee Handbook*. PVO International, Boonton, New Jersey.

Fats and Oils, Physical and Chemical Properties

TABLE 2.F.5
Properties of land and marine animals and plants

PROPERTIES OF LAND AND MARINE ANIMALS AND PLANTS

Specific Gravity was calculated at the specified temperature and referred to water at the same temperature, unless otherwise indicated. Refractive Index was measured at 40°C, unless otherwise specified, using the D-line of sodium (589 nm). Data in brackets refer to the column heading in brackets.

	Fat or Oil	Source (Synonym)	Melting [Solidification] Point, °C	Specific Gravity 1/ [Temp, °C]	Refractive Index [Temp, °C]	Iodine Value	Saponification Value
			Land Animals				
1	Butterfat	*Bos taurus*	32.2	0.911 [40]2/	1.4548	36.1	227
2	Depot fat	*Homo sapiens*	[15]	0.918 [15]	1.4602	67.6	196.2
3	Lard oil	*Sus scrofa*	[30.5]	0.919 [15]	1.4615	58.6	198.5
4	Neat's-foot oil	*Bos taurus*	....	0.910 [25]	1.464 [25]	69-76	190-199
5	Tallow, beef	*Bos taurus*	....	....	....	49.5	197
6	mutton	*Ovis aries*	[42.0]	0.945 [15]	1.4565	40	194
			Marine Animals				
7	Cod-liver oil	*Gadus morhua*	....	0.925 [25]	1.481 [25]	165	186
8	Herring oil	*Clupea harengus*	....	0.900 [60]	1.4610 [60]	140	192
9	Menhaden oil	*Brevoortia tyrannus*	....	0.903 [60]	1.4645 [60]	170	191
10	Sardine oil	*Sardinops caerulea*	....	0.905 [60]	1.4660 [60]	185	193
11	Sperm oil, body	*Physeter catodon (P. macrocephalus)*	....	....	....	76-88	122-130
12	head	*Physeter catodon (P. macrocephalus)*				70	140-144
13	Whale oil	*Balaena mysticetus*	....	0.892 [60]	1.460 [60]	120	195
			Plants				
14	Babassu oil	*Attalea funifera*	22-26	0.893 [60]3/	1.443 [60]	15.5	247
15	Castor oil	*Ricinus communis*	[−18.0]	0.961 [15]	1.4770	85.5	180.3
16	Cocoa butter	*Theobroma cacao*	34.1	0.964 [15]	1.4568	36.5	195
17	Coconut oil	*Cocos nucifera*	25.1	0.924 [15]	1.4493	10.4	257
18	Corn oil	*Zea mays*	[−20.0]	0.922 [15]	1.4734	122.6	190
19	Cottonseed oil	*Gossypium hirsutum*	[−1.0]	0.917 [25]	1.4735	105.7	194.3
20	Linseed oil	*Linum usitatissimum*	[−24.0]	0.938 [15]	1.4782 [25]	178.7	190.3
21	Mustard oil	*Brassica hirta*	....	0.914 [15]	1.475	102	174
22	Neem oil	*Melia azedarach*	−3	0.917 [15]	1.4615	71	194.5
23	Niger-seed oil	*Guizotia abyssinica*	....	0.925 [15]	1.471	128.5	190
24	Oiticica oil	*Licania rigida*	....	0.974 [25]	1.514 [25]	140-180	190.5
25	Olive oil	*Olea europaea sativa*	[−6.0]	0.918 [15]	1.4679	81.1	192
26	Palm oil	*Elaeis guineensis*	35.0	0.915 [15]	1.4578	54.2	199.1
27	Palm-kernel oil	*Elaeis guineensis*	24.1	0.923 [15]	1.4569	37.0	250
28	Peanut oil	*Arachis hypogaea*	[3.0]	0.914 [15]	1.4691	93.4	192.1
29	Perilla oil	*Perilla frutescens*	....	0.935 [15]3/	1.481 [25]	195	192
30	Poppy-seed oil	*Papaver somniferum*	[−15]	0.925 [15]	1.4685	135	197.5
31	Rapeseed oil	*Brassica campestris*	[−10]	0.915 [15]	1.4706	98.6	174.7
32	Safflower oil	*Carthamus tinctorius*	....	0.900 [60]3/	1.462 [60]	145	192
33	Sesame oil	*Sesamum indicum*	[−6.0]	0.919 [25]	1.4646	106.6	191.5
34	Soybean oil	*Glycine max (G. soja)*	[−16.0]	0.927 [15]	1.4729	130.0	190.6
35	Sunflower-seed oil	*Helianthus annuus*	[−17.0]	0.923 [15]	1.4694	125.5	188.7
36	Tung oil	*Aleurites fordii*	[−2.5]	0.934 [15]	1.5174 [25]	168.2	193.1
37	Wheat-germ oil	*Triticum aestivum*	....	0.929 [25]	1.4745	125	174.5

1/ Unless otherwise indicated.   2/ Referred to water at 15°C.   3/ Density, measured at the specified temperature.

Source: Altman, P. L., and Dittmer, D. S. (editors) (1972). *Biology Data Book*, Vol. 1. Federation of American Societies for Experimental Biology, Bethesda, Maryland.

Fatty Acids

TABLE 2.F.6
Common fatty acids and their structural formulas

Common Name	Systematic Name	Structural Formula
	Saturated Acids	
Butyric	n-Butanoic	$CH_3(CH_2)_2COOH$
Isovaleric	3-Methyl-n-Butanoic	$(CH_3)_2CH\ CH_2COOH$
Caproic	n-Hexanoic	$CH_3(CH_2)_4COOH$
Caprylic	n-Octanoic	$CH_3(CH_2)_6COOH$
Capric	n-Decanoic	$CH_3(CH_2)_8COOH$
Lauric	n-Dodecanoic	$CH_3(CH_2)_{10}COOH$
Myristic	n-Tetradecanoic	$CH_3(CH_2)_{12}COOH$
Palmitic	n-Hexadecanoic	$CH_3(CH_2)_{14}COOH$
Stearic	n-Octadecanoic	$CH_3(CH_2)_{16}COOH$
Arachidic	n-Eicosanoic	$CH_3(CH_2)_{18}COOH$
Behenic	n-Docosanoic	$CH_3(CH_2)_{20}COOH$
Lignoceric	n-Tetracosanoic	$CH_3(CH_2)_{22}COOH$
	Unsaturated Acids	
Palmitoleic	Hexadec-9-enoic	$CH_3(CH_2)_5CH:CH(CH_2)_7COOH$
Oleic	Octadec-9-enoic	$CH_3(CH_2)_7CH:CH(CH_2)_7COOH$
Linoleic	Octadeca-9,12-dienoic	$CH_3(CH_2)_4CH:CH\ CH_2CH:CH(CH_2)_7COOH$
Linolenic	Octadeca-9,12,15-trienoic	$CH_3CH_2CH:CHCH_2CH:CHCH_2CH:CH(CH_2)_7COOH$
Arachidonic	Eicosa-5,8,11,14-tetraenoic	$CH_3(CH_2)_4CH:CHCH_2CH:CHCH_2CH:CHCH_2CH:CH(CH_2)_3COOH$

Source: Paul, P. C., and Palmer, H. H. (1972). *Food Theory and Applications.* John Wiley & Sons, New York.

Fatty Acids and Their Properties

TABLE 2.F.7
Properties of various fatty acids

Acid	Formula	Molecular Weight	Neutralization Value	Iodine Value	Melting Pt. °C.	Boiling Pt. °C. @ 5 mm Hg	Boiling Pt. °C. @ 10 mm Hg	Number Double Bonds
Butyric	$C_4H_8O_2$	88.10	636.82	0	− 8.0	50.0	—	0
Caproic	$C_6H_{12}O_2$	116.16	483.03	0	− 3.5	86.5	99	0
Caprylic	$C_8H_{16}O_2$	144.21	389.07	0	16.5	113.5	124	0
Capric	$C_{10}H_{20}O_2$	172.26	325.71	0	31.3	137.0	152	0
Lauric	$C_{12}H_{24}O_2$	200.31	280.08	0	43.6	158.0	170	0
Lauroleic	$C_{12}H_{22}O_2$	198.29	282.94	128.01	—	—	—	1
Myristic	$C_{14}H_{28}O_2$	228.36	245.69	0	53.8	178.0	190	0
Myristoleic	$C_{14}H_{26}O_2$	226.34	247.87	112.14	− 4.5	—	—	1
Pentadecanoic	$C_{15}H_{30}O_2$	242.40	231.46	0	52.3	187.0	—	0
Palmitic	$C_{16}H_{32}O_2$	256.42	218.80	0	62.9	197.0	210	0
Palmitoleic	$C_{16}H_{30}O_2$	254.40	220.53	99.78	1.5	—	—	1
Margaric	$C_{17}H_{34}O_2$	270.45	207.45	0	61.3	206.0	—	0
Stearic	$C_{18}H_{36}O_2$	284.47	197.23	0	69.9	214.0	226	0
Oleic	$C_{18}H_{34}O_2$	282.44	198.64	89.87	13.4	209.0	—	1
Linoleic	$C_{18}H_{32}O_2$	280.43	200.07	181.03	− 5.0	—	—	2
Linolenic	$C_{18}H_{30}O_2$	278.40	201.51	273.51	−11.0	—	—	3
Hydnocarpic	$C_{16}H_{28}O_2$	252.22	222.6	100.65	—	—	—	1

(Continued)

Fatty Acids and Their Properties (Continued)

TABLE 2.F.7 (Continued)

	Formula							
Gorlic	$C_{18}H_{30}O_2$	278.24	201.7	181.16	—	—	—	2
Chaulmoogric	$C_{18}H_{32}O_2$	280.25	200.4	90.58	—	—	—	1
Ricinoleic	$C_{18}H_{34}O_3$	298.44	187.98	85.05	5.0	—	—	1
Satvic	$C_{18}H_{36}O_6$	348.29	161.6	0	—	—	—	0
Linusic	$C_{18}H_{36}O_8$	380.29	147.6	0	—	—	—	0
Dihydroxystearic	$C_{18}H_{36}O_4$	316.47	177.20	0	141.0	—	—	0
Licanic	$C_{18}H_{28}O_3$	292.40	191.87	260.43	99.5	—	—	3
Eleostearic	$C_{18}H_{30}O_2$	278.42	201.51	273.51	48.5	—	—	3
Arachidic	$C_{20}H_{40}O_2$	312.52	179.52	0	75.2	233.0	240	0
Gadoleic	$C_{20}H_{38}O_2$	310.50	180.69	81.75	24.5	—	—	1
Arachidonic	$C_{20}H_{32}O_2$	304.5	185	333.5	−45.5	—	—	4
Behenic	$C_{22}H_{44}O_2$	340.56	164.73	0	80.2	233.0	257	0
Erucic	$C_{22}H_{42}O_2$	338.54	165.72	74.98	34.7	—	—	1
Clupanodonic	$C_{22}H_{34}O_2$	332.5	169	384.0	—	—	—	5
Lignoceric	$C_{24}H_{48}O_2$	368.61	152.22	0	84.2	255.0	272	0
Tetracosenoic	$C_{24}H_{46}O_2$	366.59	153.04	69.24	—	—	—	1
Nisinic	$C_{24}H_{38}O_2$	358.51	156.49	354.02	—	—	—	5

Source: Anonymous (1969). *The Wecobee Handbook.* PVO International, Boonton, New Jersey.

Fatty Acids, Fats, and Oils

TABLE 2.F.8
Fatty acid composition of common animal and vegetable fats and oils

SECTION 1

Systematic Name	Common Name	No. of Carbon Atoms	Cottonseed	Kapok	Soybean	Sesame	Coconut	Palm Kernel	Babassu
n-Tetranoic	Butyric	4							
n-Hexanoic	Caproic	6					0-0.8		0-0.2
n-Octanoic	Caprylic	8					5.5-9.9	3-4	4-6.5
n-Decanoic	Capric	10					4.5-9.5	3-7	2.7-7.6
n-Dodecanoic	Lauric	12					44-52	46-52	44-46
n-Tetradecanoic	Myristic	14	0.5	10.5	14	0.1	13-19	14-17	15-20
n-Hexadecanoic	Palmitic	16	21.9	8.6		8.2-9.4	7.5-10.5	6.5-9	6-9
n-Octadecanoic	Stearic	18	1.9			3.6-5.7	1-3	1-2.5	3-6
n-Eicosanoic	Arachidic	20	0.1	1.3		0.8-1.2	0-0.4		0.2-0.7
n-Docosanoic	Behenic	22							
n-Tetracosanoic	Lignoceric	24							
9-Tetradecenoic	Myristoleic	14							
9-Hexadecenoic	Palmitoleic	16				0.5	0-1.3		
9-Octadecenoic	Oleic	18	30.7	46.1	23.0	35-45.4	5-8	13-19	12-18
9-Eicosenoic	Gadoleic	20							
13-Docosenoic	Erucic	22							
9,12-Octadecadienoic	Linoleic	18	44.9	33.5	55.0	40.4-48.4	1.5-2.5	0.5-2	1.4-2.8
9,12,15-Octadecatrienoic	Linolenic	18			8.0				
9,11,13-Octadecatrienoic	Eleostearic	18							
5,8,11,14-Eicosatetraenoic	Arachidonic	20							
4,8,12,15,19-Docosapentaenoic	Clupanodonic	22							
Docosadienoic		22							

(Continued)

Fatty Acids, Fats, and Oils (Continued)

TABLE 2.F.8 (Continued)

SECTION 2

Fatty Acid Systematic Name	Common Name	No. of Carbon Atoms	Palm	Rapeseed	Mustard		Ravison	Sunflower	Safflower
					White	Black			
n-Tetranoic	Butyric	4							
n-Hexanoic	Caproic	6							
n-Octanoic	Caprylic	8							
n-Decanoic	Capric	10							
n-Dodecanoic	Lauric	12							
n-Tetradecanoic	Myristic	14	1.1–2.5						
n-Hexadecanoic	Palmitic	16	40–46	1.9–2.8	0.4	0.8	4.3	7–14.2	6.4
n-Octadecanoic	Stearic	18	3.6–4.7	0.4–3.5	1.5	0.7	2.1		3.1
n-Eicosanoic	Arachidic	20		0.5–2.4	0.4	0.5	1.8		0.2
n-Docosanoic	Behenic	22		0.6–2.1	2.0	2.3	0.5		
n-Tetracosanoic	Lignoceric	24		0.5–0.8	1.0	1.8	0.6		
9-Tetradecenoic	Myristoleic	14							
9-Hexadecenoic	Palmitoleic	16	0–1.2	0.1–2.9			0.6		
9-Octadecenoic	Oleic	18	39–45	12.3–16.0	22.0	20.7	15.5	14.1–43.1	13.4
9-Eicosenoic	Gadoleic	20		3.5–6.0	7.0	8.1	4.1		
13-Docosenoic	Erucic	22		45–54	44.2	40.6	38.7		
9,12-Octadecadienoic	Linoleic	18	7–11	12–16	14.2	18.0	20.9	44.2–75.4	76.9
9,12,15-Octadecatrienoic	Linolenic	18		7.0–9.9	6.8	0.5	9.9		
9,11,13-Octadecatrienoic	Eleostearic	18							
5,8,11,14-Eicosatetraenoic	Arachidonic	20							
4,8,12,15,19-Docosapentaenoic	Clupanodonic	22		0.9–2.3					
Docosadienoic		22					1.0		

(Continued)

Fatty Acids, Fats, and Oils   (Continued)

TABLE 2.F.8 (Continued)

SECTION 3

Systematic Name	Common Name	No. of Carbon Atoms	Olive	Teaseed	Walnut	Peanut	Perilla	Linseed	Butterfat
n-Tetranoic	Butyric	4							3.5–3.7
n-Hexanoic	Caproic	6							1.4–2.0
n-Octanoic	Caprylic	8							0.5–1.7
n-Decanoic	Capric	10							1.9–2.6
n-Dodecanoic	Lauric	12							2.5–4.5
n-Tetradecanoic	Myristic	14	0.5–1.2		0.01–0.4	←17.1–21.9→		←5.9–16.5→	8.1–14.6
n-Hexadecanoic	Palmitic	16	9.7–15.6	4.9	3.5–4.6		←6–12→		25.9–30.2
n-Octadecanoic	Stearic	18	1.0–3.3	1.2	0.9–1.9				9.2–11.2
n-Eicosanoic	Arachidic	20	0.1–0.9						←1.2–2.4→
n-Docosanoic	Behenic	22							
n-Tetracosanoic	Lignoceric	24							
9-Tetradecenoic	Myristoleic	14							
9-Hexadecenoic	Palmitoleic	16				0.9			3.4–5.7
9-Octadecenoic	Oleic	18	64.6–79.8	86.7	17.8–36.4	42.3–71.5	← →	13–28.6	18.7–32.8
9-Eicosenoic	Gadoleic	20							
13-Docosenoic	Erucic	22							
9,12-Octadecadienoic	Linoleic	18	7.5–15.0	6.8	50–73.4	13.0–33.4	83–88	15.2–22.4	2.1–3.7
9,12,15-Octadecatrienoic	Linolenic	18			3.3–7.7			46.8–54	
9,11,13-Octadecatrienoic	Eleostearic	18							
5, 8, 11, 14-Eicosatetraenoic	Arachidonic	20						C20 & C22	0.9–1.7
4, 8, 12, 15, 19-Docosapentaenoic									
Docosadienoic	Clupanodonic	22							

(Continued)

Fatty Acids, Fats, and Oils   (Continued)

TABLE 2.F.8 (Continued)
SECTION 4

Fatty Acid Systematic Name	Common Name	No. of Carbon Atoms	Lard	Beef Tallow	Mutton Tallow	Corn	Castor	Tung	Cacao Butter
n-Tetranoic	Butyric	4							
n-Hexanoic	Caproic	6							
n-Octanoic	Caprylic	8							
n-Decanoic	Capric	10	← Trace to 1.1	← 2–8.2 →	1–4				
n-Dodecanoic	Lauric	12					Saturated acids 2.4 ← ... →		
n-Tetradecanoic	Myristic	14				0.2–1.7			
n-Hexadecanoic	Palmitic	16	26–32	24–33	20–28	8–12			26.2
n-Octadecanoic	Stearic	18	12–16	14–29	25–32	2.5–4.5		5.5	34.4
n-Eicosanoic	Arachidic	20							
n-Docosanoic	Behenic	22							
n-Tetracosanoic	Lignoceric	24							
9-Tetradecenoic	Myristoleic	14							
9-Hexadecenoic	Palmitoleic	16	2–5	1.9–2.7		0.2–1.6			
9-Octadecenoic	Oleic	18	41–51	39–50	26–47	19–49	7.4	4.0	37.3
9-Eicosenoic	Gadoleic	20							
13-Docosenoic	Erucic	22							
9,12-Octadecadienoic	Linoleic	18	3–14	1–4	3–5	34–62	3.1	8.5	2.1
9,12,15-Octadecatrienoic	Linolenic	18		Trace to 0.5	0.5				
9,11,13-Octadecatrienoic	Eleostearic	18						82	
5,8,11,14-Eicosatetraenoic	Arachidonic	20	0.4–3	Trace to 0.5	1.5				
Dihydroxystearic	Dihydroxy-stearic	18					0.6		
12-OH, 9-octadecanoic	Ricinoleic	18					87.0		

Source: Mahlenbacher, C. V. The Analysis of Fats and Oils. Garrard Publishing Co., Champaign, Illinois.

F-Distribution, Upper 5% (0.05 or 95% Level)

TABLE 2.F.9
If a calculated F value is equal to or greater than the table value, the calculated F value is significant

df of Lesser Mean Square ν_2	df of Greater Mean Square ν_1								
	1	2	3	4	5	6	7	8	9
1	161.45	199.50	215.71	224.58	230.16	233.99	236.77	238.88	240.54
2	18.513	19.000	19.164	19.247	19.296	19.330	19.353	19.371	19.385
3	10.128	9.5521	9.2766	9.1172	9.0135	8.9406	8.8867	8.8452	8.8123
4	7.7086	6.9443	6.5914	6.3882	6.2561	6.1631	6.0942	6.0410	5.9988
5	6.6079	5.7861	5.4095	5.1922	5.0503	4.9503	4.8759	4.8183	4.7725
6	5.9874	5.1433	4.7571	4.5337	4.3874	4.2839	4.2067	4.1468	4.0990
7	5.5914	4.7374	4.3468	4.1203	3.9715	3.8660	3.7870	3.7257	3.6767
8	5.3177	4.4590	4.0662	3.8379	3.6875	3.5806	3.5005	3.4381	3.3881
9	5.1174	4.2565	3.8625	3.6331	3.4817	3.3738	3.2927	3.2296	3.1789
10	4.9646	4.1028	3.7083	3.4780	3.3258	3.2172	3.1355	3.0717	3.0204
11	4.8443	3.9823	3.5874	3.3567	3.2039	3.0946	3.0123	2.9480	2.8962
12	4.7472	3.8853	3.4903	3.2592	3.1059	2.9961	2.9134	2.8486	2.7964
13	4.6672	3.8056	3.4105	3.1791	3.0254	2.9153	2.8321	2.7669	2.7144
14	4.6001	3.7389	3.3439	3.1122	2.9582	2.8477	2.7642	2.6987	2.6458
15	4.5431	3.6823	3.2874	3.0556	2.9013	2.7905	2.7066	2.6408	2.5876
16	4.4940	3.6337	3.2389	3.0069	2.8524	2.7413	2.6572	2.5911	2.5377
17	4.4513	3.5915	3.1968	2.9647	2.8100	2.6987	2.6143	2.5480	2.4943
18	4.4139	3.5546	3.1599	2.9277	2.7729	2.6613	2.5767	2.5102	2.4563
19	4.3807	3.5219	3.1274	2.8951	2.7401	2.6283	2.5435	2.4768	2.4227
20	4.3512	3.4928	3.0984	2.8661	2.7109	2.5990	2.5140	2.4471	2.3928
21	4.3248	3.4668	3.0725	2.8401	2.6848	2.5727	2.4876	2.4205	2.3660
22	4.3009	3.4434	3.0491	2.8167	2.6613	2.5491	2.4638	2.3965	2.3419
23	4.2793	3.4221	3.0280	2.7955	2.6400	2.5277	2.4422	2.3748	2.3201
24	4.2597	3.4028	3.0088	2.7763	2.6207	2.5082	2.4226	2.3551	2.3002
25	4.2417	3.3852	2.9912	2.7587	2.6030	2.4904	2.4047	2.3371	2.2821
26	4.2252	3.3690	2.9752	2.7426	2.5868	2.4741	2.3883	2.3205	2.2655
27	4.2100	3.3541	2.9604	2.7278	2.5719	2.4591	2.3732	2.3053	2.2501
28	4.1960	3.3404	2.9467	2.7141	2.5581	2.4453	2.3593	2.2913	2.2360
29	4.1830	3.3277	2.9340	2.7014	2.5454	2.4324	2.3463	2.2783	2.2229
30	4.1709	3.3158	2.9223	2.6896	2.5336	2.4205	2.3343	2.2662	2.2107
40	4.0847	3.2317	2.8387	2.6060	2.4495	2.3359	2.2490	2.1802	2.1240
60	4.0012	3.1504	2.7581	2.5252	2.3683	2.2541	2.1665	2.0970	2.0401
120	3.9201	3.0718	2.6802	2.4472	2.2899	2.1750	2.0868	2.0164	1.9588
∞	3.8415	2.9957	2.6049	2.3719	2.2141	2.0986	2.0096	1.9384	1.8799

(Continued)

F-Distribution, Upper 5% (Continued)

TABLE 2.F.9 *(Continued)*

df of Lesser Mean Square	df of Greater Mean Square ν_1									
ν_2	10	12	15	20	24	30	40	60	120	∞
1	241.88	243.91	245.95	248.01	249.05	250.10	251.14	252.20	253.25	254.31
2	19.396	19.413	19.429	19.446	19.454	19.462	19.471	19.479	19.487	19.496
3	8.7855	8.7446	8.7029	8.6602	8.6385	8.6166	8.5944	8.5720	8.5494	8.5264
4	5.9644	5.9117	5.8578	5.8025	5.7744	5.7459	5.7170	5.6877	5.6581	5.6281
5	4.7351	4.6777	4.6188	4.5581	4.5272	4.4957	4.4638	4.4314	4.3985	4.3650
6	4.0600	3.9999	3.9381	3.8742	3.8415	3.8082	3.7743	3.7398	3.7047	3.6680
7	3.6365	3.5747	3.5107	3.4445	3.4105	3.3758	3.3404	3.3043	3.2674	3.2298
8	3.3472	3.2839	3.2184	3.1503	3.1152	3.0794	3.0428	3.0053	2.9669	2.9276
9	3.1373	3.0729	3.0061	2.9365	2.9005	2.8637	2.8259	2.7872	2.7475	2.7067
10	2.9782	2.9130	2.8450	2.7740	2.7372	2.6996	2.6609	2.6211	2.5801	2.5379
11	2.8536	2.7876	2.7186	2.6464	2.6090	2.5705	2.5309	2.4901	2.4480	2.4045
12	2.7534	2.6866	2.6169	2.5436	2.5055	2.4663	2.4259	2.3842	2.3410	2.2962
13	2.6710	2.6037	2.5331	2.4589	2.4202	2.3803	2.3392	2.2966	2.2524	2.2064
14	2.6022	2.5342	2.4630	2.3879	2.3487	2.3082	2.2664	2.2229	2.1778	2.1307
15	2.5437	2.4753	2.4034	2.3275	2.2878	2.2468	2.2043	2.1601	2.1141	2.0658
16	2.4935	2.4247	2.3522	2.2756	2.2354	2.1938	2.1507	2.1058	2.0589	2.0096
17	2.4499	2.3807	2.3077	2.2304	2.1898	2.1477	2.1040	2.0584	2.0107	1.9604
18	2.4117	2.3421	2.2686	2.1906	2.1497	2.1071	2.0629	2.0166	1.9681	1.9168
19	2.3779	2.3080	2.2341	2.1555	2.1141	2.0712	2.0264	1.9795	1.9302	1.8780
20	2.3479	2.2776	2.2033	2.1242	2.0825	2.0391	1.9938	1.9464	1.8963	1.8432
21	2.3210	2.2504	2.1757	2.0960	2.0540	2.0102	1.9645	1.9165	1.8657	1.8117
22	2.2967	2.2258	2.1508	2.0707	2.0283	1.9842	1.9380	1.8894	1.8380	1.7831
23	2.2747	2.2036	2.1282	2.0476	2.0050	1.9605	1.9139	1.8648	1.8128	1.7570
24	2.2547	2.1834	2.1077	2.0267	1.9838	1.9390	1.8920	1.8424	1.7896	1.7330
25	2.2365	2.1649	2.0889	2.0075	1.9643	1.9192	1.8718	1.8217	1.7684	1.7110
26	2.2197	2.1479	2.0716	1.9898	1.9464	1.9010	1.8533	1.8027	1.7488	1.6906
27	2.2043	2.1323	2.0558	1.9736	1.9299	1.8842	1.8361	1.7851	1.7306	1.6717
28	2.1900	2.1179	2.0411	1.9586	1.9147	1.8687	1.8203	1.7689	1.7138	1.6541
29	2.1768	2.1045	2.0275	1.9446	1.9005	1.8543	1.8055	1.7537	1.6981	1.6376
30	2.1646	2.0921	2.0148	1.9317	1.8874	1.8409	1.7918	1.7396	1.6835	1.6223
40	2.0772	2.0035	1.9245	1.8389	1.7929	1.7444	1.6928	1.6373	1.5766	1.5089
60	1.9926	1.9174	1.8364	1.7480	1.7001	1.6491	1.5943	1.5343	1.4673	1.3893
120	1.9105	1.8337	1.7505	1.6587	1.6084	1.5543	1.4952	1.4290	1.3519	1.2539
∞	1.8307	1.7522	1.6664	1.5705	1.5173	1.4591	1.3940	1.3180	1.2214	1.0000

$F = s_1^2/s_2^2 = (S_1/\nu_1)/(S_2/\nu_2)$, where $s_1^2 = S_1/\nu_1$ and $s_2^2 = S_2/\nu_2$ are independent mean square estimators of a common variance σ^2, based on ν_1 and ν_2 degrees of freedom, respectively.

Source: Pearson, E. S., and Hartley, H. O. (1972). *The Biometrika Tables for Statisticians*, Vol. II. University Press, Cambridge, England.

F-Distribution, Upper 1% (0.01 or 99% Level)

TABLE 2.F.10
If a calculated F value is equal to or greater than the table value, the calculated F value is significant

df of Lesser Mean Square ν_2	df of Greater Mean Square ν_1								
	1	2	3	4	5	6	7	8	9
1	4052.2	4999.5	5403.4	5624.6	5763.6	5859.0	5928.4	5981.1	6022.5
2	98.503	99.000	99.166	99.249	99.299	99.333	99.356	99.374	99.388
3	34.116	30.817	29.457	28.710	28.237	27.911	27.672	27.489	27.345
4	21.198	18.000	16.694	15.977	15.522	15.207	14.976	14.799	14.659
5	16.258	13.274	12.060	11.392	10.967	10.672	10.456	10.289	10.158
6	13.745	10.925	9.7795	9.1483	8.7459	8.4661	8.2600	8.1017	7.9761
7	12.246	9.5466	8.4513	7.8466	7.4604	7.1914	6.9928	6.8400	6.7188
8	11.259	8.6491	7.5910	7.0061	6.6318	6.3707	6.1776	6.0289	5.9106
9	10.561	8.0215	6.9919	6.4221	6.0569	5.8018	5.6129	5.4671	5.3511
10	10.044	7.5594	6.5523	5.9943	5.6363	5.3858	5.2001	5.0567	4.9424
11	9.6460	7.2057	6.2167	5.6683	5.3160	5.0692	4.8861	4.7445	4.6315
12	9.3302	6.9266	5.9525	5.4120	5.0643	4.8206	4.6395	4.4994	4.3875
13	9.0738	6.7010	5.7394	5.2053	4.8616	4.6204	4.4410	4.3021	4.1911
14	8.8616	6.5149	5.5639	5.0354	4.6950	4.4558	4.2779	4.1399	4.0297
15	8.6831	6.3589	5.4170	4.8932	4.5556	4.3183	4.1415	4.0045	3.8948
16	8.5310	6.2262	5.2922	4.7726	4.4374	4.2016	4.0259	3.8896	3.7804
17	8.3997	6.1121	5.1850	4.6690	4.3359	4.1015	3.9267	3.7910	3.6822
18	8.2854	6.0129	5.0919	4.5790	4.2479	4.0146	3.8406	3.7054	3.5971
19	8.1849	5.9259	5.0103	4.5003	4.1708	3.9386	3.7653	3.6305	3.5225
20	8.0960	5.8489	4.9382	4.4307	4.1027	3.8714	3.6987	3.5644	3.4567
21	8.0166	5.7804	4.8740	4.3688	4.0421	3.8117	3.6396	3.5056	3.3981
22	7.9454	5.7190	4.8166	4.3134	3.9880	3.7583	3.5867	3.4530	3.3458
23	7.8811	5.6637	4.7649	4.2636	3.9392	3.7102	3.5390	3.4057	3.2986
24	7.8229	5.6136	4.7181	4.2184	3.8951	3.6667	3.4959	3.3629	3.2560
25	7.7698	5.5680	4.6755	4.1774	3.8550	3.6272	3.4568	3.3239	3.2172
26	7.7213	5.5263	4.6366	4.1400	3.8183	3.5911	3.4210	3.2884	3.1818
27	7.6767	5.4881	4.6009	4.1056	3.7848	3.5580	3.3882	3.2558	3.1494
28	7.6356	5.4529	4.5681	4.0740	3.7539	3.5276	3.3581	3.2259	3.1195
29	7.5977	5.4204	4.5378	4.0449	3.7254	3.4995	3.3303	3.1982	3.0920
30	7.5625	5.3903	4.5097	4.0179	3.6990	3.4735	3.3045	3.1726	3.0665
40	7.3141	5.1785	4.3126	3.8283	3.5138	3.2910	3.1238	2.9930	2.8876
60	7.0771	4.9774	4.1259	3.6490	3.3389	3.1187	2.9530	2.8233	2.7185
120	6.8509	4.7865	3.9491	3.4795	3.1735	2.9559	2.7918	2.6629	2.5586
∞	6.6349	4.6052	3.7816	3.3192	3.0173	2.8020	2.6393	2.5113	2.4073

(Continued)

F-Distribution, Upper 1%   (Continued)

TABLE 2.F.10   (Continued)

df of Lesser Mean Square ν_2	df of Greater Mean Square ν_1									
	10	12	15	20	24	30	40	60	120	∞
1	6055.8	6106.3	6157.3	6208.7	6234.6	6260.6	6286.8	6313.0	6339.4	6365.9
2	99.399	99.416	99.433	99.449	99.458	99.466	99.474	99.482	99.491	99.499
3	27.229	27.052	26.872	26.690	26.598	26.505	26.411	26.316	26.221	26.125
4	14.546	14.374	14.198	14.020	13.929	13.838	13.745	13.652	13.558	13.463
5	10.051	9.8883	9.7222	9.5526	9.4665	9.3793	9.2912	9.2020	9.1118	9.0204
6	7.8741	7.7183	7.5590	7.3958	7.3127	7.2285	7.1432	7.0567	6.9690	6.8800
7	6.6201	6.4691	6.3143	6.1554	6.0743	5.9920	5.9084	5.8236	5.7373	5.6495
8	5.8143	5.6667	5.5151	5.3591	5.2793	5.1981	5.1156	5.0316	4.9461	4.8588
9	5.2565	5.1114	4.9621	4.8080	4.7290	4.6486	4.5666	4.4831	4.3978	4.3105
10	4.8491	4.7059	4.5581	4.4054	4.3269	4.2469	4.1653	4.0819	3.9965	3.9090
11	4.5393	4.3974	4.2509	4.0990	4.0209	3.9411	3.8596	3.7761	3.6904	3.6024
12	4.2961	4.1553	4.0096	3.8584	3.7805	3.7008	3.6192	3.5355	3.4494	3.3608
13	4.1003	3.9603	3.8154	3.6646	3.5868	3.5070	3.4253	3.3413	3.2548	3.1654
14	3.9394	3.8001	3.6557	3.5052	3.4274	3.3476	3.2656	3.1813	3.0942	3.0040
15	3.8049	3.6662	3.5222	3.3719	3.2940	3.2141	3.1319	3.0471	2.9595	2.8684
16	3.6909	3.5527	3.4089	3.2587	3.1808	3.1007	3.0182	2.9330	2.8447	2.7528
17	3.5931	3.4552	3.3117	3.1615	3.0835	3.0032	2.9205	2.8348	2.7459	2.6530
18	3.5082	3.3706	3.2273	3.0771	2.9990	2.9185	2.8354	2.7493	2.6597	2.5660
19	3.4338	3.2965	3.1533	3.0031	2.9249	2.8442	2.7608	2.6742	2.5839	2.4893
20	3.3682	3.2311	3.0880	2.9377	2.8594	2.7785	2.6947	2.6077	2.5168	2.4212
21	3.3098	3.1730	3.0300	2.8796	2.8010	2.7200	2.6359	2.5484	2.4568	2.3603
22	3.2576	3.1209	2.9779	2.8274	2.7488	2.6675	2.5831	2.4951	2.4029	2.3055
23	3.2106	3.0740	2.9311	2.7805	2.7017	2.6202	2.5355	2.4471	2.3542	2.2558
24	3.1681	3.0316	2.8887	2.7380	2.6591	2.5773	2.4923	2.4035	2.3100	2.2107
25	3.1294	2.9931	2.8502	2.6993	2.6203	2.5383	2.4530	2.3637	2.2696	2.1694
26	3.0941	2.9578	2.8150	2.6640	2.5848	2.5026	2.4170	2.3273	2.2325	2.1315
27	3.0618	2.9256	2.7827	2.6316	2.5522	2.4699	2.3840	2.2938	2.1985	2.0965
28	3.0320	2.8959	2.7530	2.6017	2.5223	2.4397	2.3535	2.2629	2.1670	2.0642
29	3.0045	2.8685	2.7256	2.5742	2.4946	2.4118	2.3253	2.2344	2.1379	2.0342
30	2.9791	2.8431	2.7002	2.5487	2.4689	2.3860	2.2992	2.2079	2.1108	2.0062
40	2.8005	2.6648	2.5216	2.3689	2.2880	2.2034	2.1142	2.0194	1.9172	1.8047
60	2.6318	2.4961	2.3523	2.1978	2.1154	2.0285	1.9360	1.8363	1.7263	1.6006
120	2.4721	2.3363	2.1915	2.0346	1.9500	1.8600	1.7628	1.6557	1.5330	1.3805
∞	2.3209	2.1847	2.0385	1.8783	1.7908	1.6964	1.5923	1.4730	1.3246	1.0000

$F = s_1^2/s_2^2 = (S_1/\nu_1)/(S_2/\nu_2)$, where $s_1^2 = S_1/\nu_1$ and $s_2^2 = S_2/\nu_2$ are independent mean square estimators of a common variance σ^2, based on ν_1 and ν_2 degrees of freedom, respectively.

Source: Pearson, E. S., and Hartley, H. O. (1972). *The Biometrika Tables for Statisticians*, Vol. II. University Press, Cambridge, England.

F-Distribution, Upper 0.5% (0.005 or 99.5% Level)

TABLE 2.F.11
If a calculated F value is equal to or greater than the table value, the calculated F value is significant

df of Lesser Mean Square ν_2	df of Greater Mean Square ν_1								
	1	2	3	4	5	6	7	8	9
1	16211	20000	21615	22500	23056	23437	23715	23925	24091
2	198.50	199.00	199.17	199.25	199.30	199.33	199.36	199.37	199.39
3	55.552	49.799	47.467	46.195	45.392	44.838	44.434	44.126	43.882
4	31.333	26.284	24.259	23.155	22.456	21.975	21.622	21.352	21.139
5	22.785	18.314	16.530	15.556	14.940	14.513	14.200	13.961	13.772
6	18.635	14.544	12.917	12.028	11.464	11.073	10.786	10.566	10.391
7	16.236	12.404	10.882	10.050	9.5221	9.1553	8.8854	8.6781	8.5138
8	14.688	11.042	9.5965	8.8051	8.3018	7.9520	7.6941	7.4959	7.3386
9	13.614	10.107	8.7171	7.9559	7.4712	7.1339	6.8849	6.6933	6.5411
10	12.826	9.4270	8.0807	7.3428	6.8724	6.5446	6.3025	6.1159	5.9676
11	12.226	8.9122	7.6004	6.8809	6.4217	6.1016	5.8648	5.6821	5.5368
12	11.754	8.5096	7.2258	6.5211	6.0711	5.7570	5.5245	5.3451	5.2021
13	11.374	8.1865	6.9258	6.2335	5.7910	5.4819	5.2529	5.0761	4.9351
14	11.060	7.9216	6.6804	5.9984	5.5623	5.2574	5.0313	4.8566	4.7173
15	10.798	7.7008	6.4760	5.8029	5.3721	5.0708	4.8473	4.6744	4.5364
16	10.575	7.5138	6.3034	5.6378	5.2117	4.9134	4.6920	4.5207	4.3838
17	10.384	7.3536	6.1556	5.4967	5.0746	4.7789	4.5594	4.3894	4.2535
18	10.218	7.2148	6.0278	5.3746	4.9560	4.6627	4.4448	4.2759	4.1410
19	10.073	7.0935	5.9161	5.2681	4.8526	4.5614	4.3448	4.1770	4.0428
20	9.9439	6.9865	5.8177	5.1743	4.7616	4.4721	4.2569	4.0900	3.9564
21	9.8295	6.8914	5.7304	5.0911	4.6809	4.3931	4.1789	4.0128	3.8799
22	9.7271	6.8064	5.6524	5.0168	4.6088	4.3225	4.1094	3.9440	3.8116
23	9.6348	6.7300	5.5823	4.9500	4.5441	4.2591	4.0469	3.8822	3.7502
24	9.5513	6.6609	5.5190	4.8898	4.4857	4.2019	3.9905	3.8264	3.6949
25	9.4753	6.5982	5.4615	4.8351	4.4327	4.1500	3.9394	3.7758	3.6447
26	9.4059	6.5409	5.4091	4.7852	4.3844	4.1027	3.8928	3.7297	3.5989
27	9.3423	6.4885	5.3611	4.7396	4.3402	4.0594	3.8501	3.6875	3.5571
28	9.2838	6.4403	5.3170	4.6977	4.2996	4.0197	3.8110	3.6487	3.5186
29	9.2297	6.3958	5.2764	4.6591	4.2622	3.9831	3.7749	3.6131	3.4832
30	9.1797	6.3547	5.2388	4.6234	4.2276	3.9492	3.7416	3.5801	3.4505
40	8.8279	6.0664	4.9758	4.3738	3.9860	3.7129	3.5088	3.3498	3.2220
60	8.4946	5.7950	4.7290	4.1399	3.7599	3.4918	3.2911	3.1344	3.0083
120	8.1788	5.5393	4.4972	3.9207	3.5482	3.2849	3.0874	2.9330	2.8083
∞	7.8794	5.2983	4.2794	3.7151	3.3499	3.0913	2.8968	2.7444	2.6210

(Continued)

F-Distribution, Upper 0.5%   (Continued)

TABLE 2.F.11   (Continued)

df of Lesser Mean Square ν_2	df of Greater Mean Square ν_1									
	10	12	15	20	24	30	40	60	120	∞
1	24224	24426	24630	24836	24940	25044	25148	25253	25359	25464
2	199.40	199.42	199.43	199.45	199.46	199.47	199.47	199.48	199.49	199.50
3	43.686	43.387	43.085	42.778	42.622	42.466	42.308	42.149	41.989	41.828
4	20.967	20.705	20.438	20.167	20.030	19.892	19.752	19.611	19.468	19.325
5	13.618	13.384	13.146	12.903	12.780	12.656	12.530	12.402	12.274	12.144
6	10.250	10.034	9.8140	9.5888	9.4742	9.3582	9.2408	9.1219	9.0015	8.8793
7	8.3803	8.1764	7.9678	7.7540	7.6450	7.5345	7.4224	7.3088	7.1933	7.0760
8	7.2106	7.0149	6.8143	6.6082	6.5029	6.3961	6.2875	6.1772	6.0649	5.9506
9	6.4172	6.2274	6.0325	5.8318	5.7292	5.6248	5.5186	5.4104	5.3001	5.1875
10	5.8467	5.6613	5.4707	5.2740	5.1732	5.0706	4.9659	4.8592	4.7501	4.6385
11	5.4183	5.2363	5.0489	4.8552	4.7557	4.6543	4.5508	4.4450	4.3367	4.2255
12	5.0855	4.9062	4.7213	4.5299	4.4314	4.3309	4.2282	4.1229	4.0149	3.9039
13	4.8199	4.6429	4.4600	4.2703	4.1726	4.0727	3.9704	3.8655	3.7577	3.6465
14	4.6034	4.4281	4.2468	4.0585	3.9614	3.8619	3.7600	3.6552	3.5473	3.4359
15	4.4235	4.2497	4.0698	3.8826	3.7859	3.6867	3.5850	3.4803	3.3722	3.2602
16	4.2719	4.0994	3.9205	3.7342	3.6378	3.5389	3.4372	3.3324	3.2240	3.1115
17	4.1424	3.9709	3.7929	3.6073	3.5112	3.4124	3.3108	3.2058	3.0971	2.9839
18	4.0305	3.8599	3.6827	3.4977	3.4017	3.3030	3.2014	3.0962	2.9871	2.8732
19	3.9329	3.7631	3.5866	3.4020	3.3062	3.2075	3.1058	3.0004	2.8908	2.7762
20	3.8470	3.6779	3.5020	3.3178	3.2220	3.1234	3.0215	2.9159	2.8058	2.6904
21	3.7709	3.6024	3.4270	3.2431	3.1474	3.0488	2.9467	2.8408	2.7302	2.6140
22	3.7030	3.5350	3.3600	3.1764	3.0807	2.9821	2.8799	2.7736	2.6625	2.5455
23	3.6420	3.4745	3.2999	3.1165	3.0208	2.9221	2.8197	2.7132	2.6015	2.4837
24	3.5870	3.4199	3.2456	3.0624	2.9667	2.8679	2.7654	2.6585	2.5463	2.4276
25	3.5370	3.3704	3.1963	3.0133	2.9176	2.8187	2.7160	2.6088	2.4961	2.3765
26	3.4916	3.3252	3.1515	2.9685	2.8728	2.7738	2.6709	2.5633	2.4501	2.3297
27	3.4499	3.2839	3.1104	2.9275	2.8318	2.7327	2.6296	2.5217	2.4079	2.2867
28	3.4117	3.2460	3.0727	2.8899	2.7941	2.6949	2.5916	2.4834	2.3690	2.2470
29	3.3765	3.2110	3.0379	2.8551	2.7594	2.6600	2.5565	2.4479	2.3331	2.2102
30	3.3440	3.1787	3.0057	2.8230	2.7272	2.6278	2.5241	2.4151	2.2998	2.1760
40	3.1167	2.9531	2.7811	2.5984	2.5020	2.4015	2.2958	2.1838	2.0636	1.9318
60	2.9042	2.7419	2.5705	2.3872	2.2898	2.1874	2.0789	1.9622	1.8341	1.6885
120	2.7052	2.5439	2.3727	2.1881	2.0890	1.9840	1.8709	1.7469	1.6055	1.4311
∞	2.5188	2.3583	2.1868	1.9998	1.8983	1.7891	1.6691	1.5325	1.3637	1.0000

Source: Pearson, E. S., and Hartley, H. O. (1972). *The Biometrika Tables for Statisticians*, Vol. II. University Press, Cambridge, England.

Fermented Ingredients

TABLE 2.F.12
Examples of formulas for fermented foods

Ingredient	Pastry		Crackers				Bagel	Pretzel
	Sweet Dough Mellow Br.	Danish Bread	Soda Cracker	Cheese Cracker	Sprayed Cracker	Graham Cracker	H. Glut	Cracker
Flour	46.8	35.8	70.3	66.1	69.0	43.5	64.0	71.6
Water	23.3	18.0	20.5	15.1	20.7	13.3	28.8	25.0
Salt	0.7	0.6	1.1	0.8	1.0	0.9	1.2	1.1
Yeast	2.9	2.2	0.1	0.2	0.1		1.8	0.2
Shortening	8.7	22.5*	7.0	4.0	5.9	7.0		2.1
Yeast food				0.1	0.1			
Malt			0.6	0.3	0.3		4.2	
Sugar	8.7	9.0			1.7	12.1		
Nonfat milk solids	2.9	2.2			0.9			
Whole egg	5.8	9.0						
Sodium bi-carbonate			0.4	0.2	0.3	0.7		
Ammonium bi-carbonate						0.3		
Cheese				13.2				
Invert syrup						2.9		
Molasses						2.4		
Graham meal						2.4		
Graham flour						14.5		
Mace	0.2							
Vanilla		0.6						
Cardamom		0.1						

*Approximately 80.0% of this shortening is comprised of "roll in" shortening.

Data based on 100 parts of wet dough or batter.

Source: Cotton, R. H., and Ponte, J. G. (1973). Baking industry. In *Wheat: Production and Utilization*. G. E. Inglett (editor). AVI Publishing Co., Westport, Connecticut.

Fertilizer

TABLE 2.F.13
Examples of grade formulas

Pounds	Ingredient	Analysis	Nitrogen (N)	Available phosphoric acid (APA)	Potassium oxide (K_2O)	Pounds input	Ammonia capacity	Water	Residual acidity
			5-10-5 (including organic N)						
200	Tankage	8.0 N	0.80	—	—	—	—	0.80	—
424	Sulfate of ammonia	20.8 N	4.41	—	—	—	—	—	458
1,020	Superphosphate	20.0 APA	—	10.20	—	—	61	3.32	—
174	Muriate of potash	60.0 K_2O	—	—	5.22	—	—	—	
182	Limestone or sand	—	—	—	—	—	—	—	182+
2,000			5.21	10.20	5.22	0	61	4.12	276
			5-10-5						
254	Nitrogen solution 410 (22-65-0)	41.0 N	5.21	—	—	56	—	1.59	188
1,020	Superphosphate	20.0 APA	—	10.20	—	—	61	3.32	
174	Muriate of potash	60.0 K_2O	—	—	5.22				
552	Limestone or sand	—	—	—	—	—	—	—	552+
2,000			5.21	10.20	5.22	56	61	4.91	364+
			8-16-8						
304	Nitrogen solution 410 (22-65-0)	41.0 N	6.23	—	—	67	—	1.90	224
200	Sulfate of ammonia	20.8 N	2.08	—	—	—	—	—	225
392	Triple superphosphate	46.0 APA	—	9.02	—	—	32	0.88	
730	Superphosphate	20.0 APA	—	7.30	—	—	44	2.37	
274	Muriate of potash	60.0 K_2O	—	—	8.22				
100	Conditioner	—							
2,000			8.31	16.32	8.22	67	76	5.15	449
			10-20-10						
274	Nitrogen solution 410 (19-72-0)	41.0 N	5.62	—	—	52	—	1.16	202
300	Diammonium phosphate	18.0 N 46.0 APA	2.70	6.90	—	—	—	0.30	

(Continued)

Fertilizer   (Continued)

TABLE 2.F.13   (Continued)

Pounds	Ingredient	Analysis	Nitrogen (N)	Available phosphoric-acid (APA)	Potassium oxide (K_2O)	Pounds input	Ammonia capacity	Water	Residual acidity
200	Sulfate of ammonia	20.8 N	2.08	—	—	—	—		225
434	Triple superphosphate	46.0 APA	—	9.98	—	—	35	0.98	
352	Superphosphate	20.0 APA	—	3.52	—	—	21	1.14	
340	Muriate of potash	60.0 K_2O	—	—	10.20				
100	Conditioner	—							
2,000			10.40	20.40	10.20	52	56	3.59	427

0-20-20

Pounds	Ingredient	Analysis	Nitrogen (N)	Available phosphoric-acid (APA)	Potassium oxide (K_2O)	Pounds input	Ammonia capacity	Water	Residual acidity
570	Triple superphosphate	46.0 APA	—	13.11	—	—	—	1.28	
730	Superphosphate	20.0 APA	—	7.30	—	—	—	2.37	
680	Muriate of potash	60.0 K_2O	—	—	20.40				
20	Hydrated lime (or 5 lb of ammonia)	—							
2,000			0	20.41	20.40	0	0	3.65	0

20-0-20

Pounds	Ingredient	Analysis	Nitrogen (N)	Available phosphoric-acid (APA)	Potassium oxide (K_2O)	Pounds input	Ammonia capacity	Water	Residual acidity
1,220	Ammonium nitrate	33.5 N	20.44	—					
680	Muriate of potash	60.0 K_2O	—	—	20.40				
100	Conditioner	—							
2,000			20.44	0	20.40	0	0	0	0

Source: Sauchelli, V. (editor). *Chemistry and Technology of Fertilizers.* Van Nostrand Reinhold Co., New York.

Fertilizer Materials

TABLE 2.F.14
Composition of principal fertilizer materials[1]

Material	Nitrogen %	Available Phosphate %P_2O_5	Potash %K_2O	Calcium %	Magnesium %	Sulfur %	Chlorine %	Copper %	Manganese %	Zinc %	Boron %	Approximate Calcium Carbonate Equiv.[2] Lb./per Ton
						Nitrogen						
Ammonia, anhydrous	82	—	—	—	—	—	—	—	—	—	—	-2,960
Ammonia, aqua	16–25	—	—	—	—	—	—	—	—	—	—	-720 to -1,080
Ammonium nitrate	33.5	—	—	—	—	—	—	—	—	0.01	—	-1,180
Ammonium nitrate-limestone mixtures	20.5	—	—	7.3	4.4	0.4	0.4	—	—	—	—	0
Ammonium sulfate	21	—	—	0.3	—	23.7	0.5	0.3	—	0.1	—	-2,200
Ammonium sulfate-nitrate	26	—	—	—	—	15.1	—	—	—	—	—	-1,700
Calcium cyanamide	21	—	—	38.5	.06	0.3	0.2	0.02	0.04	—	—	+1,260
Calcium nitrate	15	—	—	19.4	1.5	0.02	0.2	—	—	—	—	+400
Nitrogen solutions	21–49	—	—	—	—	—	—	—	—	—	—	-750 to -1,760
Sodium nitrate	16	—	0.2	0.1	0.05	0.07	0.4	0.07	—	—	0.01	+580
Urea	46	—	—	—	—	—	—	—	—	—	—	-1,680
Urea-form	38	—	—	—	—	—	—	—	—	—	—	-1,360
						Organics						
Castor pomace	5	1.8	1.1	0.4	0.3	0.04	0.3	—	0.04	0.05	0.01	-100
Cottonseed meal	6	2.6	1.4	0.2	0.4	0.3	0.06	—	—	0.02	—	-200
Dried cattle manure	2	1.5	2.2	3.3	0.9	0.4	0.6	0.01	0.03	0.03	0.01	+300
Sewage sludge, activated	5–6	2.9	0.6	1.3	0.7	0.5	0.6	0.07	0.07	0.10	—	-200
Sewage sludge, digested	2	1.4	0.8	2.1	0.5	0.1	0.2	0.30	0.3	0.4	—	-100
Tankage, Process	7–9	1	0.1	0.8	0.01	0.9	0.8	—	—	—	0.03	-320

(Continued)

Fertilizer Materials   (Continued)

TABLE 2.F.14 (Continued)

Basic slag, open hearth	—	8-12[3]	—	29.0	3.4	0.3	—	—	—	2.2	—	+1,000
Bone meal	2-4.5	22-28[4]	0.2	20-25	0.4	0.1	0.2	—	—	—	0.02	+400 to 500
Phosphoric acid	—	52-54[5]	—	—	—	0.3	0.1	—	0.03	—	—	−1000 to −1400
Rock phosphate	—	—	—	33.2	0.2	—	0.3	—	—	—	0.01	+200
Superphosphate, normal	—	18-20	0.2	20.4	0.2	11.9	—	0.01	0.01	—	—	0
Superphosphate, concentrated	—	42-50	0.4	13.6	0.3	1.4	—	—	—	—	0.01	0
Superphosphoric acid	—	76	—	—	—	—	—	0.01	0.01	—	—	—
Potash												
Potassium chloride (muriate)	—	—	60-62	0.1	0.1	0.1	47.0	—	—	—	0.03	0
Potassium magnesium sulfate	—	—	22	—	11.2	22.7	1.5	—	—	—	—	0
Potassium sulfate	—	—	50	0.7	1.2	17.6	2.1	0.001	0.03	—	0.002	0
Tobacco stems	2	0.7	6.0	3.6	0.4	0.4	1.2	0.01	0.03	—	0.02	+400
Multiple Nutrient												
Ammoniated super-phosphate	3-6	18-20	—	17.2	—	12	—	—	—	—	—	−140
Ammonium phosphate-nitrate	27	15	—	—	—	—	—	—	—	—	—	−1240
Ammonium phosphate-sulfate	13-16	20-39	0.2	0.3	0.1	15.4	0.1	0.02	0.2	0.02	0.03	−1520 to −2260
Cotton hull ashes	—	4-7	22-30	6.8	3.1	1.0	1.9	0.04	0.06	0.07	—	+
Diammonium phosphate	16-21	48-53	—	—	—	2.2	0.1	0.02	0.03	0.03	0.02	−1250 to −1,550
Monoammonium phosphate	11	48	0.2	1.1	0.3	2.2	0.1	0.02	0.03	0.03	0.02	−1,300
Nitric phosphates	14-22	10-22	—	8-10	0.1	0.2-3.6	1.-12.0	0.02	0.2	0.02	0.03	−300 to −500
Nitrate of soda-potash	15	—	14	—	0.4	—	0.5	—	—	—	0.13	+550
Potassium nitrate	13	—	45	0.6	0.4	0.2	1.1	0.12	0.76	0.20	0.10	+520
Wood ashes	—	1.8	5.5	23.3	2.2	0.4	0.2	—	—	0.20	0.16	+

(Continued)

Fertilizer Materials   (Continued)

TABLE 2.F.14 (Continued)

| Material | Nitrogen % | Available Phosphate %P₂O₅ | Potash %K₂O | Secondary Nutrient | | | Chlorine % | Copper % | Manganese % | Zinc % | Boron % | Approximate Calcium Carbonate Equiv.[2] Lb/per Ton |
				Calcium %	Magnesium %	Sulfur %						
Blast furnace slag	—	1.7	0.6	29.3	3.8	1.4	—	—	1.02	0.001	0.01	+
Chats	—	—	—	21.2	9.3	0.2	—	0.001	0.55	0.2	—	+1,800
Dolomite	—	—	—	21.5	11.4	0.3	—	0.001	0.11	—	0.01	+1,960
Gypsum	—	—	0.5	22.5	0.4	16.8	0.3	—	—	—	—	0
Kieserite (emjeo)	—	—	—	1.6	18.2	—	—	—	—	—	—	0
Limestone	—	—	0.3	31.7	3.4	0.1	—	0.004	0.48	0.05	0.003	+1,800
Lime-sulfur solution	—	—	—	6.7	—	23.8	—	—	—	—	—	
Magnesium sulfate (epsom salt)	—	—	—	2.2	10.5	14.0	0.4	—	—	—	—	0
Sulfur	—	—	—	—	—	30–99.6	—	—	—	—	—	−1900 to −6,320

[1] Most of the percentages larger than one of N, P₂O₅ and K₂O are the usual guarantees. Where more than one grade is sold, the range is indicated by two numbers separated by a dash. The rest of the percentages are averages compiled by A. L. Mehring from many published analyses.

[2] Ind. Eng. Chem. Anal. Ed. 5, 229–34 and other sources. A minus sign indicates the number of pounds of calcium carbonate needed to neutralize acid formed when 1 ton of the material is added to the soil. A plus sign indicates basic materials, and a zero physiologically neutral materials.

[3] By the 2% citric acid method.

[4] Total P₂O₅. All of the P₂O₅ in natural organics is considered available.

[5] 30–36% total P₂O₅, which is relatively unavailable in some soils.

Micro Nutrient Materials. Some commercial grades have the following average compositions:

Borax   11.6% B
Copper oxide   75% Cu
Copper sulfate   24.9% Cu, 12.8% S, and 0.5% Zn
Hydrated Iron sulfate   19.7% iron
Manganese sulfate   25.1% Mn, 0.5% Cu, 0.08% Zn, 0.3% B, and 14.5% S
White copperas   34.4% iron
Zinc oxide   77.2% Zn
Zinc sulfate   27.8% Zn, 0.02% Cu, and 13.6% S

Source: Garman, W. H. (editor). The Fertilizer Handbook, 2nd Edition. Fertilizer Institute.

Film Gauge

TABLE 2.F.15

A film gauge is the number indicative of the thickness of packaging films. (1) For films other than cellophane the gauge number is a numerical prefix and is the last figures of the 5-digit decimal fraction of the thickness in inches, thus 88-gauge = 0.00088 in. (2) Cellophane is designated by the first three digit numbers to indicate yield (square inches per pound). Example: 250 indicates a film with 25,000 sq in. per lb. Typical weights and yields are:

	Approx Thickness, In.	Approx No. Sq In. Per Lb
215 plain	0.0009	21,500
195 plain	0.0010	19,500
150 plain	0.0013	15,000
250 moistureproof	0.0008	25,000
210 moistureproof	0.0009	21,000
195 moistureproof	0.0010	19,500
140 moistureproof	0.0014	14,000

(3) Film thickness is sometimes expressed in mils which is equivalent to 0.001 in.

Source: F. W. Greene Co. (editors) (1967). *Glossary of Packaging Terms*, 4th Edition. Packaging Institute, New York.

Fish and Shellfish, Composition I

TABLE 2.F.16
Composition of fish and shellfish

(Dashes (—) denote lack of reliable data for a constituent believed to be present in measurable amount)

Foods, approximate measures, units, and weight (edible part unless footnotes indicate otherwise)							Fatty Acids												
		Water	Food energy	Protein	Fat	Saturated (total)	Unsaturated Oleic	Linoleic	Carbohydrate	Calcium	Phosphorus	Iron	Potassium	Vitamin A value	Thiamin	Riboflavin	Niacin	Ascorbic acid
	Grams	Percent	Calories	Grams	Grams	Grams	Grams	Grams	Grams	Milligrams	Milligrams	Milligrams	Milligrams	International units	Milligrams	Milligrams	Milligrams	Milligrams
FISH, SHELLFISH, MEAT, POULTRY; RELATED PRODUCTS																		
Fish and shellfish:																		
Bluefish, baked with butter or margarine. 3 oz	85	68	135	22	4	—	—	—	0	25	244	0.6	—	40	0.09	0.08	1.6	—
Clams:																		
Raw, meat only 3 oz	85	82	65	11	1	—	—	—	2	59	138	5.2	154	90	.08	.15	1.1	8
Canned, solids and liquid, 3 oz	85	86	45	7	1	0.2	Trace	Trace	2	47	116	3.5	119	—	.01	.09	.9	—
Crabmeat (white or king), canned, not pressed down. 1 cup	135	77	135	24	3	.6	0.4	0.1	1	61	246	1.1	149	—	.11	.11	2.6	—
Fish sticks, breaded, cooked, frozen (stick, 4 by 1 by 1/2 in). 1 fish stick or 1 oz	28	66	50	5	3	—	—	—	2	3	47	.1	—	0	.01	.02	.5	—
Haddock, breaded, fried[14] 3 oz	85	66	140	17	5	1.4	2.2	1.2	5	34	210	1.0	296	—	.03	.06	2.7	2
Ocean perch, breaded, fried[14] 1 fillet	85	59	195	16	11	2.7	4.4	2.3	6	28	192	1.1	242	—	.10	.10	1.6	—
Oysters, raw, meat only (13–19 medium Selects). 1 cup	240	85	160	20	4	1.3	.2	.1	8	226	343	13.2	290	740	.34	.43	6.0	—
Salmon, pink, canned, solids and liquid. 3 oz	85	71	120	17	5	.9	.8	.1	0	[15]167	243	.7	307	60	.03	.16	6.8	—
Sardines, Atlantic, canned in oil, drained solids. 3 oz	85	62	175	20	9	3.0	2.5	.5	0	372	424	2.5	502	190	.02	.17	4.6	—
Scallops, frozen, breaded, fried, reheated. 6 scallops	90	60	175	16	8	—	—	—	9	—	—	—	—	—	—	—	—	—
Shad, baked with butter or margarine, bacon. 3 oz	85	64	170	20	10	—	—	—	0	20	266	.5	320	30	.11	.22	7.3	—
Shrimp:																		
Canned meat 3 oz	85	70	100	21	1	.1	.1	Trace	1	98	224	2.6	104	50	.01	.03	1.5	—
French fried[16] 3 oz	85	57	190	17	9	2.3	3.7	2.0	9	61	162	1.7	195	—	.03	.07	2.3	—
Tuna, canned in oil, drained solids. 3 oz	85	61	170	24	7	1.7	1.7	.7	0	7	199	1.6	—	70	.04	.10	10.1	—
Tuna salad[17] 1 cup	205	70	350	30	22	4.3	6.3	6.7	7	41	291	2.7	—	590	.08	.23	10.3	2

14 Dipped in egg, milk or water, and breadcrumbs; fried in vegetable shortening.
15 If bones are discarded, value for calcium will be greatly reduced.
16 Dipped in egg, breadcrumbs, and flour or batter.
17 Prepared with tuna, celery, salad dressing (mayonnaise type), pickle, onion, and egg.

Source: Consumer and Food Economics Institute (1977). Nutritive value of foods. USDA Home and Garden Bull. 72.

Fish and Shellfish, Composition II

TABLE 2.F.17
Composition of the edible portion (EP) and refuse in the material as purchased (AP).

Item No.	Commodity and Description	Water	Protein	Fat	Carbohydrate		Ash	Calories (No. per 100 g)	Notes	Refuse in AP (%)
					Total (by dif)	Fiber				
		Percent of Edible Portion								
	Fish, fresh									
	Fat-rich—fillet	68.6	20	10	0	—	1.4	176	Herring and similar sp., tuna, mackerel (all types), salmon, trout, jacks, pompanos	0
220										
221	—round	68.6	20	10	0	—	1.4	176		50
	Fish and shellfish									
222	Cod and related species—fillet	81.8	16.4	0.5	0	—	1.3	75	Hake, haddock, cusk, saithe	0
223	—round	81.8	16.4	0.5	0	—	1.3	75		55
224	Others—fillet	77.2	19	2.5	0	—	1.3	104	Incl flatfish, sharks, barracudas, mullets, perch, bream, freshwater species	0
225	—round	77.2	19	2.5	0	—	1.3	104		55
226	All, unspecified—fillet	74.1	18.8	5.7	0	—	1.4	132		0
227	—round	74.1	18.8	5.7	0	—	1.4	132		53
	Crustaceans and molluscs, fresh									
228	Crustaceans, in shell	76.0	17.8	2.1	2.0	—	2.1	103	Lobster, crawfish, crab, shrimp, etc.	63
229	Molluscs, in shell	81.0	13.0	1.5	2.9	—	1.6	80	Oysters, mussels, clams, squids, etc.	75
230	Both, unspecified, in shell	79.3	14.6	1.7	2.6	—	1.8	88		72
	Fish, cured—salted, smoked, dried									
	Fat-rich kinds								Herring, sardines, salmon, mackerel Brined: kippers, bloaters	
	Light cure:									
231	Only flesh considered as edible	58	21	11	0	0	10	189		31
232[1]	Eaten whole	58	21	11	0	0	10	189	Refuse: bones	0
	Medium cure:									
233	Only flesh considered as edible	41	40	10	0	0	9	261		31
234[1]	Eaten whole	41	40	10	0	0	9	261		0

(Continued)

Fish and Shellfish, Composition II   (Continued)

TABLE 2.F.17   (Continued)

Item No.	Commodity and Description	Water	Protein	Fat	Carbohydrate Total (by dif)	Fiber	Ash	Calories (No. per 100 g)	Notes	Refuse in AP (%)
			Percent of Edible Portion							
	Hard, heavy cure:									
235	Only flesh considered as edible	25	55	14	0	0	6	361		31
236[1]	Eaten whole	25	55	14	0	0	6	361		0
237	Dried—fish eaten whole Fat-poor kinds	4	60	21	0	0	15	446	Very dry; Haddock, cod, sea bream, sapsap, maigre	0
	Light cure:									
238	Only flesh considered as edible	54	27.5	2	0	0	16.5	135	Brined	45
239[1]	Eaten whole	54	27.5	2	0	0	16.5	135	Refuse: bones	0
	Medium cure:									
240	Only flesh considered as edible	37	46	3	0	0	14	223		45
241[1]	Eaten whole	37	46	3	0	0	14	223	Refuse: bones	0
	Hard, heavy cure:									
242	Only flesh considered as edible	21	62	5	0	0	12	310		45
243[1]	Eaten whole	21	62	5	0	0	12	310	Refuse: bones	0
244	Fully dried, boneless flesh; fish meal	10	75	5	0	0	10	365	Very dry	0
	Fish, canned									
245	All kinds in oil	51	22	24	1	0	2	314		0
246	Fat-rich kinds, not in oil	65	20	11	1	0	3	188	Refuse: bones	0
247	Fat-poor kinds, not in oil	75	21	2	0	0	1.5	108		0
	Shellfish, canned									
248	Crustaceans, canned	78	17.5	1.5	1	0	2	92	Lobster, crawfish, crab, shrimp, etc.	0
249	Molluscs, canned	88	7	1	2	0	2	47	Oysters, mussels, clams, squid, etc.	0

[1] More information required.

Source: Chatfield, C. Food Composition Tables for International Use. Food and Agriculture Organization, United Nations, Rome.

Fish Cross Section

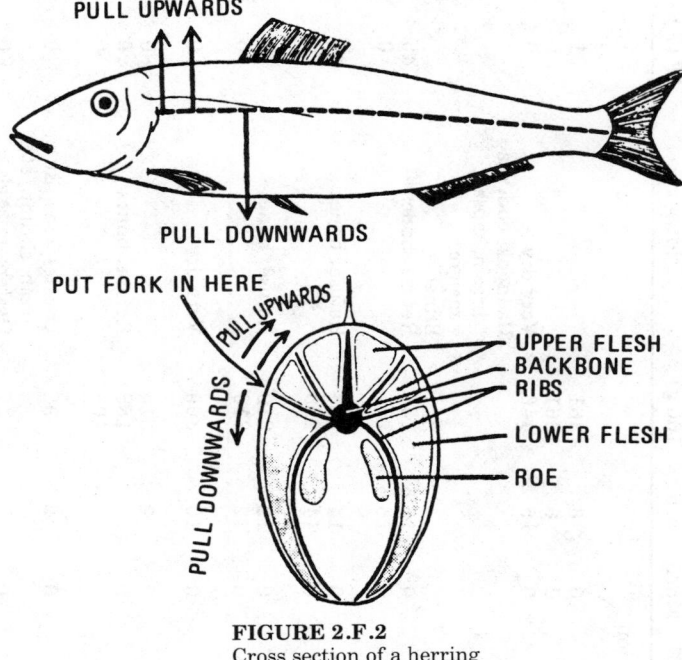

FIGURE 2.F.2
Cross section of a herring

Source: Callow, A. B. *Cooking and Nutritive Value*. Oxford University Press, Fairlawn, New Jersey.

Fish, Drawn (Eviscerated)

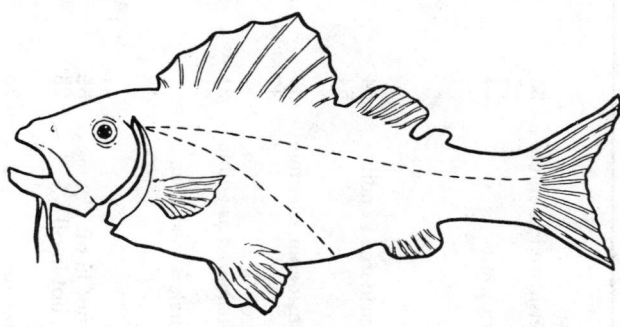

FIGURE 2.F.3

Source: U.S. Department of the Army (1969). Food inspection specialist. *TM 8-451*.

Fish, Dressed

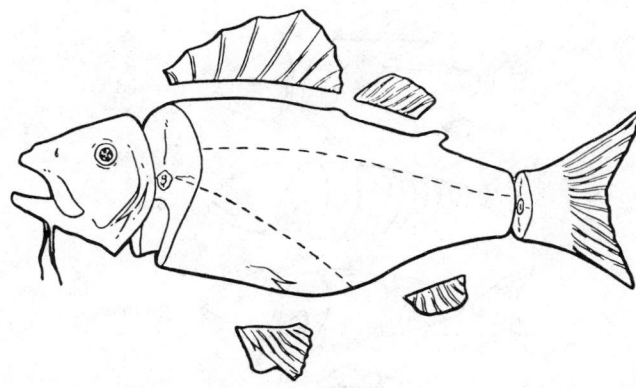

FIGURE 2.F.4

Source: U.S. Department of the Army (1969). Food inspection specialist. *TM 8-451.*

Fish Fillets

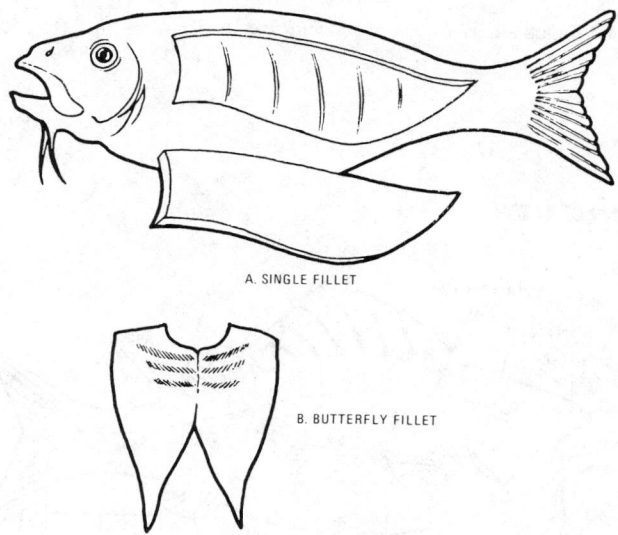

A. SINGLE FILLET

B. BUTTERFLY FILLET

FIGURE 2.F.5

Single fillet (A) is cut from only one side of fish; butterfly fillet is cut from both sides of fish and not separated
Source: U.S. Department of the Army (1969). Food inspection specialist. *TM 8-451.*

Fish Forms

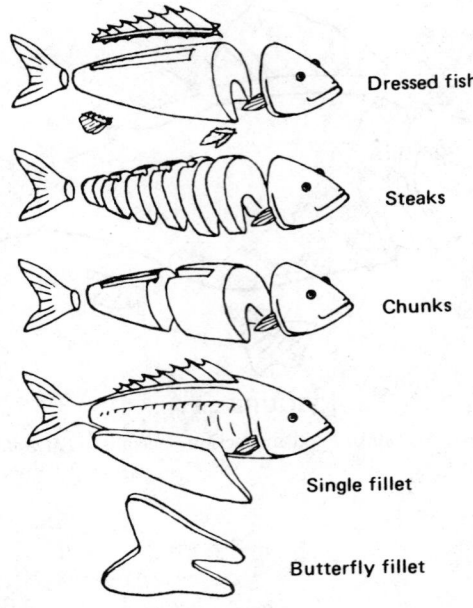

Dressed fish

Steaks

Chunks

Single fillet

Butterfly fillet

FIGURE 2.F.6
Market forms of fish

Source: USDA (1969). Food for us all. *Yearbook of Agriculture*.

Fish Nomenclature

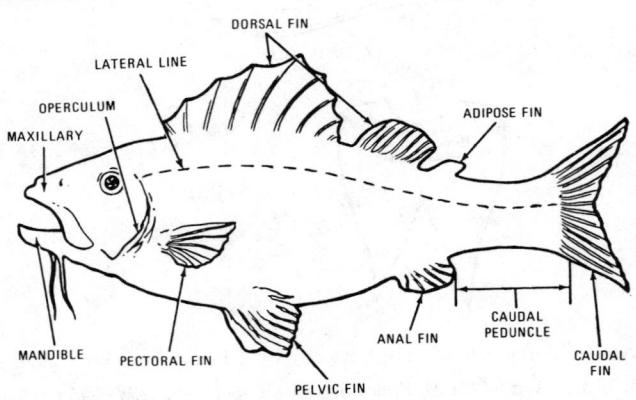

DORSAL FIN

LATERAL LINE

OPERCULUM

MAXILLARY

ADIPOSE FIN

MANDIBLE   PECTORAL FIN

PELVIC FIN

ANAL FIN

CAUDAL
PEDUNCLE

CAUDAL
FIN

FIGURE 2.F.7
Showing names and location of various parts of fish

Source: U.S. Department of the Army (1969). Food inspection specialist. *TM 8-451*.

Fish, Smoke-Cured

TABLE 2.F.18
Chief types of smoke-cured fish

Product	Species Usually Used	Pretreatment	Method of Salting	Smoking				
				Type	Time (hr)		Weight Loss by Drying (%)	Final Salt Concentration (g/100 g Fish)
					Traditional Kilns	Torry Kiln		
"Finnans"	Haddocks	Headed, split up belly, second cut made into flesh, blood and black lining removed.	Brined for 10–15 min, depending on size, in 70–80% saturated brine.	Cold-smoked.	6-12	4-6	15-18	2-3
Fillets (single)	Cod, large Haddocks	Cut from the gutted fish, sometimes skinned and "lugs" (belly-walls) removed.	Brined for 10–15 min, according to size; usually with dye.	Cold-smoked.	6-12	4-6	10-15	2-3
Fillets ("block")	Smaller Haddocks or Whiting	Head and bone removed; skin on or off, double fillet.	Brined for about 4 min.	Cold-smoked.	4-6	2-3	12-14	2-3
"Smokies"	Small Haddocks or Whitings	Whole gutted fish headed and cleaned; tied in pairs by tails with string.	Brined for about 1 hr.	Hot-smoked in a dense smoke without excessive drying.	2-3	1½	30	2-3
"Reds"	Herring	Whole, ungutted.	Dry-salted in vats with about 1 salt: 2 fish for 7-8 days (if salted longer, require partial desalting before smoking).	Cold-smoked intermittently.	a	b	20-25	14
Kippers	Herring	Split along back and gills, and viscera removed and washed.	Brined for 20-25 min, usually with dye.	Cold-smoked.	6-18	4-6	15-20	2-3
Buckling	Herring	Whole, usually ungutted.	Dry-salted overnight.	Hot-smoked in a dense smoke.	3-4	2-3	20-25	2-3
Smoked Salmon	Salmon	Gutted and cleaned and backbone taken out but head left on; flesh scored in order to let salt in.	Dry-salted 16-40 hr, depending on size.	Cold-smoked.	24-36	9-12	10	5

[a] Smoked on alternate nights for a week.
[b] Smoked nightly for 3-4 days.

Source: Herschdoerfer, S. M. (editor) (1968). Quality Control in the Food Industry, Vol. 2. Academic Press, New York.

Fish Steaks

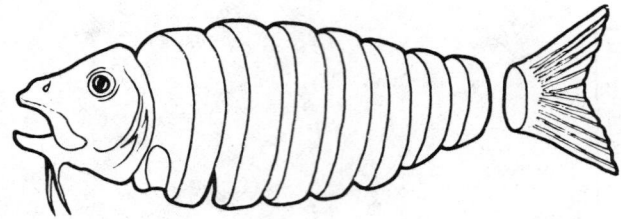

FIGURE 2.F.8
Steaks ($\frac{5}{8}$ to $\frac{3}{4}$ inch thick) are cut crosswise from fish as illustrated

Source: U.S. Department of the Army (1969). Food inspection specialist. *TM-8451*.

Fish, Storage

TABLE 2.F.19
Approximate storage times for packaged and glazed fish and shellfish[1]

Product[2]	Storage Time in Months at 0°F. (−18°C.)	
	(A)[3]	(B)[4]
Fatty fish		
Mackerel	2–3	4–6
Salmon	2–3	4–6
Sea herring	2–3	4–6
Smelt	2–3	4–6
Sprat	2–3	4–6
Trout	2–3	4–6
Lean and medium fatty fish		
Cod fillets	3–4	7–10
Haddock fillets	3–4	7–10
Fish sticks	3–4	7–10
Flounder fillets	3–4	7–10
Ocean perch fillets	3–4	7–10
Plaice	3–4	7–10
Pollock fillets	3–4	7–10
Sole	3–4	7–10
Shellfish		
Shrimp	3–4	6–8
Scallops	3–4	6–8
Clams	2–3	4–6
Lobster (cooked)	2–3	4–6
Oysters	2–3	4–6

[1] The storage times at a designated temperature will vary with the quality of the fish prior to freezing.
[2] Values for fish up to three days in ice before freezing.
[3] (A) Hardly detectable changes in quality occur; product is still of good acceptability.
[4] (B) Very significant changes in quality occur, and product is of low acceptability.

Source: Slavin, J. W. (1968). Frozen fish: Characteristics and factors affecting quality during freezing and storage. In *The Freezing Preservation of Foods*, Vol. 2, 4th Edition. D. K. Tressler, W. B. Van Arsdel, and M. J. Copley (editors). AVI Publishing Co., Westport, Connecticut.

Fish Yields

FISH YIELDS (APPROX)

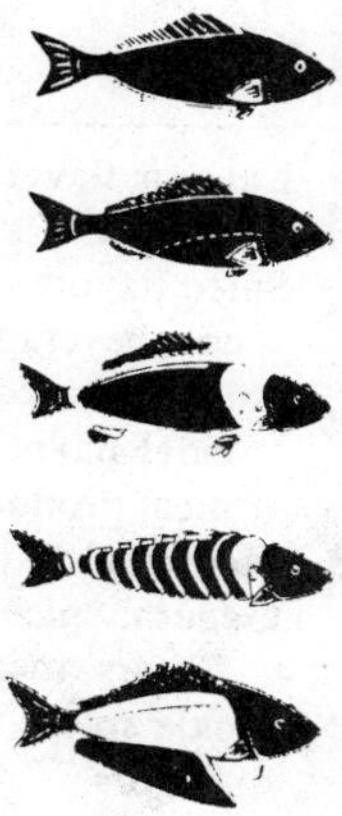

		Edible Portion %
Whole	----------------	45
Drawn	----------------	48
Dressed or pan dressed	--	67
Steaks	----------------	84
Fillets	----------------	100

FIGURE 2.F.9

Source: USDA (1982). Freezing meat and fish in the home. USDA Home and Garden Bull. *93*.

Flavoring Agents, Natural

TABLE 2.F.20
Natural flavoring agents

Name	Chemical Component Eliciting Flavor	Flavor Contributed	Use
Anise	Anethole	Anise	Licorice-anise flavor
Basil	Methyl chavicol, cineole, linalool	Medicinal, herby, slight licorice	Spicy flavors, meat products
Bergamot	Limonene	Bitter orange	Citrus flavor, orange, cola
Betula	Methyl salicylate	Wintergreen	Mint-type flavors
Caraway	d-Carvone	Caraway	Spice flavor, bakery products
Cardamom	Terpineol, cineole	Spicy, slight lemon citrus	Processed meats
Cassia	Cinnamic aldehyde	Cinnamon, bite	Hot, spicy, candy, bakery products
Celery Seed	Limonene, sedenene	Celery, spicy	Spice blends, carbonated beverages, meat products

(Continued)

Flavoring Agents, Natural (Continued)

TABLE 2.F.20 (Continued)

Name	Chemical Component Eliciting Flavor	Flavor Contributed	Use
Chamomile		Pungent aromatic	Liqueur flavor
Cinnamon	Cinnamic aldehyde	Spicy, hot	Spice flavors, cola beverages
Clove	Eugenol	Warm, pungent, spicy clove	Spice and medi- cinal flavors, meat products
Copaiba	Caryophyllene	Bitter balsamic	Medicinal flavor
Coriander	d-Linalool	Spicy	General spice flavors, meats
Dill (weed)	Phellandrene, carvone	Herby, bitter	Pickle spice flavors
Fennel	Anethole	Anise	Liqueur, salad dressing
Grapefruit	Limonene	Grapefruit	Citric products (beverages)
Hops	Humulone	Fatty, green, oily	Beverage flavors
Horseradish	Allyl isothiocyanate	Hot, bite, pene- trating	Hot sauces
Lavandin	Linalyl acetate	Pungent lavender	Dentrifices, chewing gum
Mace	d-Pinene, myristicin, d-Camphene	Nutmeg, aro- matic, pine	Spice flavors
Marjoram	Terpinene	Spicy, pungent	Spice flavors
Mustard	Allyl isothiocyanate	Pungent, sharp	Relish flavors, salad dress- ings
Nutmeg	Pinene, myristicin	Spicy, hot, nutmeg	General spice flavors, baked goods
Orris root	Methyl ionone	Violet	Raspberry flavors
Patchouly		Earthy, slight woody	Cola beverages
Pepper	Piperidine	Warm, spicy	General spice flavors, pre- pared meats
Rosemary	Pinene, borneol, cineole	Slight medi- cinal, woody	Herb blends, mouthwashes
Sage	Thujone	Spicy, warm, tea-like	Meat flavors, poultry
Thyme	Thymol	Medicinal, burnt	Medicinal flavors
Ylang ylang	Benzyl alcohol, linalool, cresol methyl ether	Fragrant, slight orange	Beverage flavors

Source: Berarde, M. A. (1971). The chemicals we eat. McGraw-Hill Book Co., New York.

Flavor Ingredients, Taste and Flavor Type

TABLE 2.F.21
Classification of flavor ingredients by primary taste and flavor type

Flavor ingredient	Taste			Flavor type
	Sweet	Bittersweet	Bitter	
Acetophenone			x	—
Allyl anthranilate		x		Green leaves
Allyl benzoate		x		Cherry
Allyl butyrate		x		Apple, apricot
Allyl caproate		x		Pineapple
Allyl cyclohexylacetate		x		Pineapple
Allyl cyclohexylbutyrate		x		Pineapple
Allyl cyclohexylcaproate		x		Peach, apricot
Allyl cyclohexylpropionate		x		Pineapple
Allyl cyclohexylvalerate		x		Peach, apricot, apple
Allyl formate				Mustard
Allyl isovalerate		x		Apple, cherry
Allyl 2-nonylenate				Pineapple
Allyl pelargonate		x		Cognac, pineapple
Allyl phenoxyacetate		x		Pineapple, honey
Allyl phenylacetate			x	Honey
Allyl propionate		x		Apple, apricot
Allyl salicylate		x		Wintergreen, grape
Allyl undecylate		x		Coconut, peach
n-Amyl butyrate		x		Cherry, apple
Amyl phenylacetate	x			Apricot, peach
Anethol	x			Anise
Anisyl alcohol	x			Peach
Anisyl butyrate		x		Cherry, peach
Anisyl formate	x			Strawberry
Anisyl propionate		x		Cherry
Benzyl acetate			x	—
Benzyl butyrate	x			Pear
Benzyl cinnamate	x			Honey
Benzyl formate	x			Apricot, pineapple
Benzyl isobutyrate	x			Strawberry
Benzyl isovalerate	x			Apple
Benzyl propionate	x			Apricot, peach
Benzyl salicylate	x			Raspberry
Bornyl acetate	x			Pineapple
n-Butyl acetate	x			Pineapple
Butyl formate				Plum
Butyl isobutyrate	x			Pineapple
Butyl isovalerate	x			Apple
Butyl propionate	x			Apricot
Butyl valerate				Apple

(Continued)

Flavor Ingredients, Taste and Flavor Type   (Continued)

TABLE 2.F.21   (Continued)

Flavor ingredient	Taste			Flavor type
	Sweet	Bittersweet	Bitter	
Carvacryl acetate		x		Honey
Cinnamaldehyde		x		Cinnamon, melon
Cinnamic acid	x			Apricot
Cinnamyl acetate	x			Pineapple
Cinnamyl alcohol			x	—
Cinnamyl anthranilate		x		Grape
Cinnamyl butyrate	x			Honey
Cinnamyl formate		x		Apple
Cinnamyl isobutyrate	x			Apple
Citral				Lemon
l-Citronellol	x			Peach
Citronellyl acetate	x			Apricot
Citronellyl butyrate	x			Plum
Citronellyl formate	x			Plum
Citronellyl isovalerate	x			Apple
Citronellyl propionate		x		Plum
Coumarin			x	—
p-Cresyl acetate				Honey
p-Cresyl ethyl ether	x			Honey
m-Cresyl phenylacetate	x			Honey
p-Cresyl phenylacetate	x			Honey
Cuminic alcohol		x		Strawberry
Cyclohexyl acetate		x		Apple, banana
Cyclohexyl butyrate		x		Banana, apple, currant
Cyclohexyl caproate		x		Peach, cognac
Cyclohexyl cinnamate				Peach, cherry
Cyclohexyl formate		x		Cherry
Cyclohexyl isovalerate		x		White apple
Cyclohexyl phenylacetate		x		Honey
Cyclohexyl propionate		x		Apple, banana
γ-Decalactone		x		Plum, apricot, peach
Decanal dimethyl acetal			x	Citrus
Decyl acetate	x			Pineapple
Decyl formate	x			Grape
Diacetyl	x			Butter
Dimethylbenzylcarbinol			x	—
Dimethyl hydroquinone			x	—
Dimethyl phenethyl carbinyl acetate			x	—
Dimethyl phenethyl carbinyl propionate	x			Rose-like
Diphenyl ether	x			Black currant
γ-Dodecalactone		x		Apricot, peach
Ethyl acetate		x		Wine

(Continued)

Flavor Ingredients, Taste and Flavor Type (Continued)

TABLE 2.F.21 (Continued)

Flavor ingredient	Taste			Flavor type
	Sweet	**Bittersweet**	**Bitter**	
2-Ethylbutyl acetate		x		Pear
Ethyl butyrate	x			Pineapple
Ethyl cinnamate	x			Apricot, peach
Ethyl formate			x	Rum
2-Ethyl-3-furylacrolein		x		Cola
Ethyl heptylate	x			Wine, pear
Ethyl hexadienoate		x		Pineapple, melon
Ethyl isovalerate	x			Apple
Ethyl methylphenylglycidate	x			Strawberry
Ethyl-2-octynoate	x			—
Ethyl phenoxyacetate		x		Pineapple, honey
Ethyl phenylacetate		x		Honey
Ethyl phenylglycidate	x			Strawberry
Ethyl undecylate		x		Coconut
Ethyl undecynoate			x	—
Ethyl valerate		x		Apple, banana
Ethyl vanillin		x		Vanilla
Eugenol			x	Clove buds
Geraniol			x	Rose-like
Geraniol ''palmarosa''	x			Peach, apricot
Geranyl acetate			x	—
Geranyl anthranilate			x	—
Geranyl butyrate	x			Apricot
Geranyl formate			x	—
Geranyl isobutyrate	x			Apricot
Geranyl isovalerate	x			Apricot
Geranyl propionate			x	—
Guaiol acetate	x			Black currant, grape
Guaiol butyrate	x			Plum
Guaiol phenylacetate	x			Honey
Heptyl acetate	x			Apricot
Heptyl formate				Plum
Heptyl propionate		x		Apricot
Hexyl acetate		x		Pear
Hexyl butyrate	x			Pineapple
Hexyl formate	x			Plum
Hexyl furan carboxylate		x		Pear, mushroom
α-Ionone	x			Raspberry
Isoamyl acetate		x		Pear
Isoamyl formate	x			Plum
Isoamyl isobutyrate				Pineapple
Isoamyl propionate		x		—

(Continued)

Flavor Ingredients, Taste and Flavor Type (Continued)

TABLE 2.F.21   (Continued)

Flavor ingredient	Sweet	Bittersweet	Bitter	Flavor type
Isoamyl salicylate		x		Strawberry
Isobutyl acetate			x	—
Isobutyl anthranilate		x		Strawberry, grape
Isobutyl butyrate	x			Rum
Isobutyl cinnamate	x			Raspberry
Isobutyl formate	x			Rum
Isobutyl phenylacetate	x			Honey
Isobutyl propionate			x	—
Isobutyl salicylate			x	—
Isopropyl acetate	x			Apple
Isopropyl benzyl carbinol		x		Peach
Isopropyl formate	x			Plum
Isopropyl isovalerate	x			Apple
Isopropyl propionate		x		Plum
Isopropyl valerate		x		Apple
Isovalerophenone		x		Grape
Linalool	x			Plum
Linalyl acetate	x			Black currant
Linalyl anthranilate	x			Orange
Linalyl butyrate	x			Honey
Linalyl formate		x		Pineapple
Linalyl isobutyrate	x			Black currant
Linalyl isovalerate			x	—
Linalyl propionate	x			Black currant
Methyl acetate			x	—
Methylacetophenone	x			Strawberry
2-Methylallyl butyrate		x		Apple, plum
2-Methylallyl caproate		x		Pineapple
Methyl amyl ketone			x	Pear
Methyl anisate	x			Melon
Methyl anthranilate			x	—
Methylbenzyl propionate		x		Cherry
Methyl butyrate	x			Apple
Methyl cinnamate	x			Strawberry
Methyl eugenol			x	Clove
Methylheptenone			x	Pear
Methyl ionone	x			Raspberry, black currant
Methyl isobutyrate	x			Apricot
Methyl isoeugenol			x	Clove
Methyl isovalerate			x	—
Methyl methylanthranilate		x		Peach
Methyl-β-methylpropionate		x		Pineapple
Methyl naphthyl ketone		x		Strawberry

(Continued)

Flavor Ingredients, Taste and Flavor Type (Continued)

TABLE 2.F.21 (Continued)

Flavor ingredient	Taste			Flavor type
	Sweet	Bittersweet	Bitter	
Methyl nonyl ketone	x			Peach
Methyl octine carbonate	x			Peach
Methyl phenylacetate	x			Honey
Methyl phenyl carbinyl acetate				—
Methyl propionate	x			Black currant
Methyl undecylate				Pineapple
Methyl undecyl ketone		x		Coconut
Musk ambrette	x			Peach
Nerol			x	Rose-like
Nerolin	x			Strawberry
Neryl acetate	x			Raspberry
Neryl butyrate	x			Cocoa
Neryl formate			x	—
Neryl isobutyrate	x			Strawberry
Neryl isovalerate			x	—
Neryl propionate	x			Plum
γ-Nonalactone		x		Coconut
Nonyl acetate			x	—
Nonyl alcohol			x	—
γ-Octalactone		x		Peach, coconut, walnut
Octyl acetate	x			Peach
Octyl butyrate	x			Melon
Octyl formate		x		—
Octyl isobutyrate	x			Grape
2-Octynoate	x			—
Phenethyl acetate		x		Honey
Phenethyl alcohol			x	Peach, rose
Phenethyl butyrate	x			Honey
Phenethyl cinnamate			x	—
Phenethyl dimethyl carbinol	x			Apricot
Phenethyl dimethyl carbinyl isovalerate		x		Rose
Phenethyl formate		x		Green plum
Phenethyl isobutyrate		x		Green plum
Phenethyl isovalerate		x		Peach
Phenethyl phenylacetate	x			Honey
Phenethyl propionate				Honey
Phenethyl salicylate	x			Peach
Phenylacetaldehyde dimethyl acetal		x		—
Phenylacetic acid	x			Honey
Phenylallyl alcohol		x		Plum, peach
Phenylglycidate	x			Strawberry
Phenylpropyl acetate		x		Grape
Phenylpropyl alcohol	x			Apricot
Phenylpropyl butyrate	x			Plum

(Continued)

Flavor Ingredients, Taste and Flavor Type *(Continued)*

TABLE 2.F.21 *(Continued)*

Flavor ingredient	Taste			Flavor type
	Sweet	Bittersweet	Bitter	
Phenylpropyl cinnamate	x			Cocoa
Phenylpropyl ether		x		Grape
Phenylpropyl isobutyrate		x		Peach
Propenyl guaethol	x			Vanilla
Propyl acetate		x		Pear
Propyl cinnamate		x		Peach, apricot
Propyl formate		x		Plum
Propyl isobutyrate	x			Pineapple
Propyl phenylacetate	x			Honey
Propyl propionate			x	—
Rhodinol			x	Rose
Rhodinyl acetate			x	—
Rhodinyl butyrate	x			Whortleberry
Rhodinyl formate		x		Cherry
Rhodinyl isobutyrate	x			Peach
Rhodinyl isovalerate		x		Cherry
Santalol	x			Woody, raspberry
Santalyl acetate		x		Apricot
Santalyl phenylacetate	x			Honey
Styralyl acetate			x	Grapefruit
Terpenyl acetate	x			Raspberry
Terpenyl anthranilate			x	—
Terpenyl butyrate		x		Plum
Terpenyl cinnamate			x	—
Terpenyl formate				—
Terpenyl isovalerate	x			Apple
Terpenyl propionate		x		—
Terpineol		x		Peach
Tetrahydrofurfuryl propionate		x		Apricot, chocolate
Tetrahydrogeraniol			x	
Tolualdehyde (*o,m,p*)		x		Cherry, almond
γ-Undecalactone	x			Apricot, peach
Undecynoate			x	—
Vanillin			x	Vanilla
Vanillylidene acetone		x		Vanilla
Yara yara	x			Strawberry

Source: Furia, T. E., and Bellanca, N. (editors) (1971). *Fenaroli's Handbook of Flavor Ingredients*. CRC Press, Cleveland.

Flavors, Beverage

TABLE 2.F.22
Handy guide for choosing beverage flavors

Flavor	Best Type	Best Form	Recommended Strength	Remarks
Birch beer	Natural	Extract or emulsion	1 oz	Because of faint color desired in finished drink, an extract is somewhat better than an emulsion.
Cherry	Natural	Extract-concentrate	4 oz	The 4-oz strength is best for all-round economy and flavor quality. Extract-concentrate gives longest shelf-life.
Cola	Natural	Extract or emulsion	4 oz	Necessary flavor and color can be incorporated in a 4-oz strength. Some additional acid may be needed, however. Because of deep color, either extract or emulsion can be used.
Cream soda	Imitation	Extract	1 oz or 2 oz	A very satisfactory product can be made with aromatic chemicals. Extract affords better, easier dispersion.
Ginger ale	Natural	Extract	4 oz or 2 oz	Flavor bouquet composed mainly of citrus oils, with some flower and spice oils. Extract needed to produce a clear beverage.
Grape	Imitation	Extract	2 oz	Combination of grape extractives, juice, wine, and aromatic chemicals gives excellent flavor with 2 oz.
Grapefruit	Natural	Concentrate Emulsion	1-10 1-17 or 2 oz.	Acceptable flavor obtainable without juice, but juices give added appeal.
Lemon (table beverage)	Natural	Concentrate Emulsion	1-17	Should contain juice and show deep cloud.

(Continued)

Flavors, Beverage *(Continued)*

TABLE 2.F.22 *(Continued)*

Lemon mixer ("UP" tang type)	Natural	Extract	2 oz or ½ oz	Due to solubility of lemon and lime oils, a superior product can be produced in the 2 oz strength.
Lemon and lime (table beverage)	Natural	Emulsion	2 oz 1-10	An emulsion necessary to produce deep cloud.
Orange	Natural	Concentrate Emulsion	1-17 or 2 oz	If economy is prime consideration, 2 oz recommended. There is marked difference, however, in flavor quality of a juice orange and one that contains no juice.
Punch	Natural and imitation	Concentrate Emulsion	1-17 2 oz	In general, there are two types—citrus and berry base. Citrus punch should contain juice and be no more conc. than 1-17. Berry punch can be part artificial with conc. as high as 2 oz.
Raspberry	Natural and imitation	Extract-Concentrate	4 oz 2 oz	There are some good imitation raspberry flavors available using natural extractions and imitation fortifiers, but best flavor is obtained with true fruit.
Root beer	Natural and imitation	Extract or emulsion	4 oz	Root beer is made from oils of sassafras, sweet birch, wintergreen, cassia, spice, citrus, vanillin, and other materials. Finished product is deeply colored with caramel, which occupies volume in extract.
Strawberry	Natural and imitation	Extract-Concentrate	2 oz 4 oz	A mixture of true fruit and imitation flavors has a slight edge over straight true fruit flavor.
Tom Collins	Natural	Emulsion Concentrate	1-10 1-17	Best flavor base is made with heavy emulsion of lemon and lime oils in liberal quantity of concentrated juice.

Source: Phillips, G. F., and Woodroof, J. G. (editors) (1974). Beverage acids, flavors, colors, and emulsifiers. In *Beverages: Carbonated and Noncarbonated.* AVI Publishing Co., Westport, Connecticut.

Flour, Extraction Rates

TABLE 2.F.23
Composition of flours of different extraction rates

Extraction Rate (%)	Protein (g/100g)	Fat (g/100g)	Carbohydrate (g/100g)	Fiber (g/100g)	Calories (per 100g)
100	12.2	2.4	64.1	2.0	327
85	12.1	1.6	69.8	0.40	342
80	11.7	1.4	70.2	0.21	341
70/72	11.3	1.1	72.0	0.10	343
Patent flour (about 40)	10.0	0.8	74.5	Tr	345

Extraction Rate (%)	Thiamin (mg/100g) Mean	Range	Riboflavin (mg/100g) Mean	Range	Nicotinic Acid (mg/100g) Mean	Range	Iron (mg/100g) Mean
100	0.37	0.28–0.46	0.12	0.09–0.15	5.70	4.2–7.2	3.50
85	0.29	0.22–0.36	0.07	0.05–0.09	2.00	1.5–2.5	2.10
80	0.24	0.18–0.39	0.06	0.045–0.075	1.60	1.2–2.0	1.65
70/72	0.08	0.06–0.10	0.05	0.04–0.06	0.80	0.6–1.0	1.25
Patent flour (about 40)	0.05	0.04–0.06	0.03	0.02–0.04	0.70	0.5–0.9	0.90

Source: Aykroyd, W. R., and Doughty, J. (1970). *Wheat in Human Nutrition*. Food and Agriculture Organization, United Nations, Rome.

Flower, Imperfect

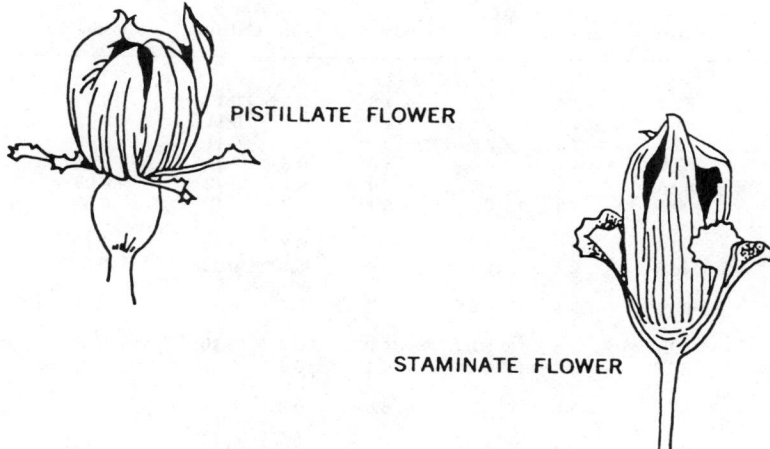

PISTILLATE FLOWER

STAMINATE FLOWER

FIGURE 2.F.10
The flowers of squash, pumpkins, cucumbers, muskmelons, and watermelons are imperfect, each flower having only one type of sex organ

Source: USDA (1973). Handbook for the home. *Yearbook of Agriculture*.

Flower, Perfect

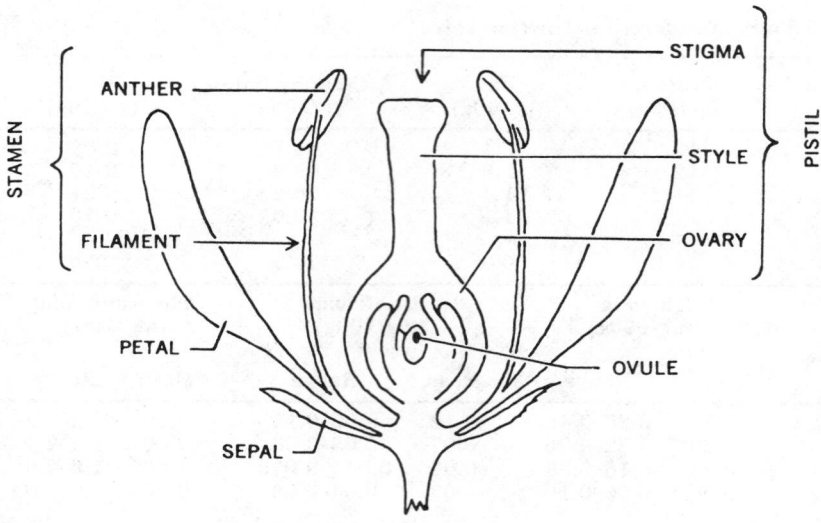

FIGURE 2.F.11

Showing the parts of a perfect flower with both male and female reproductive organs; stamen is the male organ, pistil is the female organ

Source: USDA (1973). Handbook for the home. *Yearbook of Agriculture.*

Fluid and Fermented Milks, Composition

TABLE 2.F.24

Typical composition of fluid and fermented milks

	Moisture	Protein	Fat	Lactose	Ash	Calcium	Phosphorus	Lactic acid	Ethyl alcohol
	%	%	%	%	%	%	%	%	%
Whole milk	87.4	3.5	3.5	4.8	0.7	0.1	0.09		
Chocolate milk	81.5	3.4	3.4	11.0[a]	0.7	0.11	0.09		
Chocolate drink	82.8	3.3	2.3	10.9[a]	0.7	0.11	0.09		
10—2 Milk	87.0	4.2	2.0	6.0	0.8	0.14	0.11		
Low fat, 1%, milk	89.5	3.5	1.0	4.9	0.7	0.12	0.09		
Skim milk	90.5	3.6	0.1	5.1	0.7	0.12	0.09		
Cultured buttermilk	90.5	3.6	0.1[b]	4.3	0.7	0.12	0.10	0.8	
Sour cream	74.5	2.8	18.0	3.4	0.5	0.10	0.08	0.6	
Acidophilus skim milk	90.1	3.5	0.5	4.4	0.7	0.12	0.09	0.7	
Kefir, part skim	89.4	3.5	2.0	4.0	0.7	0.10	0.09	0.6	1.0
Yoghurt, plain	87.2	3.4	3.4	4.1	0.6	0.12	0.09	0.9	
Yoghurt, solids added	83.1	5.0	4.8	6.0	0.8	0.18	—	0.9	
Yoghurt, part skim	89.0	3.4	1.7	5.2	0.7	0.11	0.09	0.9	
Yoghurt, full skim	91.0	3.4	—	4.0	0.7	0.12	0.09	0.9	
Yoghurt, fruit	c	3.4	1.7	12.5[b]	—	0.14	0.10	0.8	

a Carbohydrate other than lactose added.   b Additional fat may be added.   c Varies with solids content of added fruit.

Source: Hargrove, R. E., and Alford, J. A. (1974). Composition of milk products. In *Fundamentals of Dairy Chemistry*, 2nd Edition. B. H. Webb, A. H. Johnson, and J. A. Alford (editors). AVI Publishing Co., Westport, Connecticut.

Food, Composition

TABLE 2.F.25
Nutrients in foods per pound of dry matter

Food Item	Water Originally Present (%)	Energy (Cal)	Protein (g)	Fat (g)	Carbohydrate (g)	Calcium (mg)	Phosphorus (mg)	Iron (mg)	Vitamin A (IU)	Thiamin (mg)	Riboflavin (mg)	Niacin (mg)
Liquid milk	87.0	2400	122.3	136.1	170.8	4123	3246	2.3	5,538	1.23	6.00	3.84
Nonfat dry milk solids	3.23	1681	173.0	4.3	248.3	6040	4784	2.7	196	1.65	9.58	4.33
Dry whole milk	2.03	2294	123.5	124.5	179.3	4387.7	3619	2.7	6,490	1.32	6.54	3.27
Cottage cheese	74.0	1765	335.4	13.8	75.0	1430	4592	8.0	577	0.31	5.07	1.92
Cheddar cheese	39.0	2924	177.8	240.3	12.6	6496	4539	4.2	12,983	0.33	3.75	1.47
Ice cream, plain	62.0	2507	47.8	146.8	248.4	1576	1242	1.3	6,447	0.45	2.21	1.31
Butter	15.5	3937	3.2	435.1	2.1	86	86	1.1	17,751	0.01	0.06	0.59
Bacon sliced (medium fat)	20.0	3550	51.6	3.7	6.2	74	612	4.5		2.38	0.59	11.75
Mayonnaise	16.0	3890	8.1	421.4	16.2	102	323	5.3	1,130	0.19	0.19	0
Eggs, whole fresh	74.0	2446	198.8	178.8	10.7	838	3261	41.9	17,653	1.80	5.19	1.15
Beef, chopped	54.0	3217	158.9	286.9	0	89	1717	23.7	0	0.98	1.26	42.8
Beef, roasting (boned)	67.0	2648	260.0	178.7		151	2806	38.4	0	1.60	2.06	70.3
Lamb, leg	63.7	2385	187.0	181.8		104	2013	28.0	0	2.20	2.75	61.7
Pork, ham smoked	42.0	2610	115.1	237.9	2.0	69	1239	17.0	0	5.31	1.31	26.0
Pork, loin chops	58.0	2547	143.8	219.0		88	1550	21.9	0	9.07	1.78	38.8
Veal, cutlet	70.0	2410	295.0	136.6		167	3176	44.0	0	2.66	4.17	97.6
Frankfurters	64.3	2554	193.2	179.3	42.0	115	2087	29.1	0	2.41	2.91	30.0
Liver, fresh	70.9	2051	308.9	65.6	56.0	123	5817	188.6	298,969	4.22	43.74	250.8
Chicken, roaster	66.0	1582	164.7	111.4	0	129	1776	15.6	Trace	0.91	1.44	70.0
Fish, steaks	77.2	1644	317.5	41.6		350	3644	16.6	—	1.09	1.09	69.3
Salmon, canned	67.4	2349	286.8	149.0	0	932	3981	18.1	113	0.46	2.45	90.8
Beans, dry	10.5	1774	111.6	7.6	314.9	750	2348	52.3	0	3.03	1.19	10.7
Pecans	3.0	1816	22.8	177.6	31.6	180	788	5.9	124	1.74	0.28	2.2
Beans, snap	88.9	1549	88.3	7.2	283.8	2396	1621	40.5	23,063	2.88	3.69	22.5
Beets	87.6	1250	43.5	2.4	262.9	742	1177	27.4	645	0.88	1.37	11.3
Broccoli	89.9	1020	90.1	5.9	150.5	3564	2089	35.6	96,040	2.57	5.84	24.7

(Continued)

Food Composition   (*Continued*)

TABLE 2.F.25 (*Continued*)

Food												
Cabbage	92.4	1250	60.5	9.2	230.2	2000	1355	22.3	3,552	3.02	2.76	11.8
Corn on cob, edible portion	73.9	712	24.5	8.0	136.0	61	796	3.4	2,605	1.03	0.92	9.2
Carrots	88.2	1517	40.6	10.1	315.2	1322	1254	27.1	40,678	2.28	2.20	16.9
Lettuce, head	94.8	1096	73.0	11.5	175.0	1326	1500	30.7	32,884	3.84	4.03	9.6
Mustard greens	92.2	1179	97.4	12.8	169.2	9333	1615	123.0	27,397	3.97	8.71	35.9
Peas, fresh	74.3	801	53.3	3.1	140.4	175	968	15.1	5,408	2.80	1.44	16.3
Potatoes	77.8	1464	34.2	1.8	327.9	189	959	12.1	315	1.80	0.67	19.8
Spinach	92.7	1260	117.8	15.0	163.0	4127	2808	153.4	480,000	6.02	12.30	35.6
Tomatoes	94.1	1542	67.7	20.3	271.1	745	1830	40.6	74,237	4.06	2.70	42.3
Apples	84.1	1622	7.5	10.0	374.8	151	251	7.5	2,264	0.94	0.50	6.3
Bananas	74.8	1186	14.3	2.3	277.3	95	337	7.1	5,158	1.07	0.75	6.7
Strawberries	90.0	1790	35.0	26.0	353.0	1220	1180	35.0	2,500	1.30	2.90	13.0
Grapefruit	88.8	1187	13.3	5.3	270.5	455	482	8.0	625	0.98	0.53	5.3
Oranges	87.2	1281	22.6	5.4	285.9	844	586	10.1	4,840	1.95	0.62	6.2
Peaches	86.9	1557	15.2	3.0	366.4	244	671	18.3	26,946	0.61	1.45	27.4
Cantaloupe	94.0	800	21.6	6.6	163.3	600	566	15.0	121,500	2.00	1.33	28.3
Prunes	24.0	1517	11.7	3.0	360.9	273	431	19.7	9,605	0.50	0.84	8.7
Raisins	24.0	1782	13.7	3.0	425.2	465	771	19.7	302	0.90	0.48	2.9
Corn meal, white	12	1831	38.6	5.6	406.6	51	722	5.1	0	0.82	0.47	4.8
Corn meal, yellow	12	1835	42.8	6.1	402.3	51	722	5.1	1,545	0.77	0.31	4.6
Wheat flour (patent)	12	1831	55.6	4.6	391.6	97	479	15.0	0	2.27	1.36	18.2
Bread, white (enriched)	35.9	1850	60.2	14.2	370.3	396	708	12.8	0	1.71	1.11	15.6
Bread, whole wheat	37	1884	68.4	25.2	345.8	431	2666	18.7	0	2.03	1.11	25.5
Bread, rye	37.6	1913	46.6	24.6	376.1	160	698	5.7	0	1.13	0.29	8.0
Corn flakes	9.3	1798	39.5	3.5	402.0	49	280	4.9	0	0.79	0.43	7.9
Oatmeal	8.3	1962	70.3	36.6	337.6	267	1807	25.7	0	2.71	0.69	5.6
Farina	11	1832	58.6	5.0	388.2	106	638	4.0	0	0.31	0.28	4.9
Whole grain (uncooked)	8.7	1830	58.1	9.9	376.8	189	1914	18.9	0	2.21	0.64	22.6
Macaroni	11	1838	66.3	7.2	376.9	112	734	6.0	0	0.66	0.40	10.6
Rice (white)	12.3	1816	39.3	1.6	411.0	46	476	3.6	0	0.27	0.14	7.2
Molasses	24	1434	0	0	358.4	1630	305	4.0	0	0.47	0.95	16.9
Sugar (Gran.)	0.5	1816	0	0	453.9	0	0	0.5	0	0	0	0
Cocoa	4.3	1562	42.7	89.2	147.0	758	3363	12.8	0	0	1.84	10.8
Olives, green	75.2	2080	21.7	195.5	580.6	1463	217	29.0	6,048	0	0	0
Pickles	95.2	1083	47.9	18.7	179.1	2270	2083	85.4	18,125	0.62	2.29	4.1

Source: Cook, H. L., and Day, G. H. *The Dry Milk Industry.* American Dry Milk Institute, Chicago.

Food Guide

TABLE 2.F.26

SERVINGS RECOMMENDED	WHAT COUNTS AS A SERVING *
MEAT GROUP 2 OR MORE	2 TO 3 OUNCES OF LEAN COOKED MEAT, POULTRY, OR FISH. As alternates: 1 egg, ½ cup cooked dry beans or peas, or 2 tablespoons of peanut butter may replace ½ serving of meat.
MILK GROUP CHILD, under 9 _____ 2 TO 3 CHILD, 9 to 12 _____ 3 OR MORE TEENAGER _____ 4 OR MORE ADULT _____ 2 OR MORE PREGNANT WOMAN ____ 3 OR MORE NURSING WOMAN _____ 4 OR MORE	ONE 8-OUNCE CUP OF FLUID MILK—whole, skim, buttermilk—or evaporated or dry milk, reconstituted. As alternates: 1-inch cube cheddar-type cheese, ¾ cup cottage cheese, ice milk, or ice cream, or ½ cup plain yogurt may replace ½ cup of fluid milk.
VEGETABLE — FRUIT GROUP 4 OR MORE, INCLUDING:	½ CUP OF VEGETABLE OR FRUIT; OR A PORTION, for example, 1 medium apple, banana, or potato, half a medium grapefruit or cantaloup.
1 GOOD OR 2 FAIR SOURCES OF VITAMIN C DAILY	*Good sources:* Grapefruit or grapefruit juice, orange or orange juice, cantaloup, guava, mango, papaya, raw strawberries, broccoli, brussels sprouts, green pepper, sweet red pepper. *Fair sources:* Honeydew melon, lemons, tangerine or tangerine juice, watermelon, asparagus, cabbage, cauliflower, collards, garden cress, kale, kohlrabi, mustard greens, potatoes and sweetpotatoes, cooked in the jacket, rutabagas, spinach, tomatoes or tomato juice, turnip greens.
1 GOOD SOURCE OF VITAMIN A—AT LEAST EVERY OTHER DAY	*Good sources:* Dark-green and deep-yellow vegetables and a few fruits, namely: Apricots, broccoli, cantaloup, carrots, chard, collards, cress, kale, mango, persimmon, pumpkin, spinach, sweetpotatoes, turnip greens and other dark-green leaves, winter squash.
BREAD — CEREAL GROUP 4 OR MORE	COUNT ONLY IF WHOLE-GRAIN OR ENRICHED: 1 slice of bread or similar serving of baked goods made with whole-grain or enriched flour, 1 ounce ready-to-eat cereal, ½ to ¾ cup cooked cereal, cornmeal, grits, spaghetti, macaroni, noodles, or rice.
OTHER FOODS AS NEEDED TO ROUND OUT MEALS AND MEET ENERGY REQUIREMENTS	Refined unenriched cereals and flours and products made from them; sugars; butter, margarine, other fats. Try to include some vegetable oil among the fats used.

* *Amounts actually served may differ—small for young children, extra large (or seconds) for very active adults or teenagers.*

Source: USDA (1979). Your money's worth in foods. USDA Home and Garden Bull. *183.*

Food Poisoning, Bacteria

TABLE 2.F.27
Characteristics of food poisoning

Disease	Onset of Symptoms	Type of Food Commonly Involved	Symptoms and Other Characteristics
Botulism	6 hours to 8 days; avg 12–30 hr	Home-canned low-acid vegetables.	Difficulty in swallowing, speech, and respiration; double vision. Death from paralysis of muscles of repiration.
Staphylococcus poisoning	1 to 6 hr; avg 2½–3 hr	Processed meat, potato salad, cream-filled bakery products, dairy products.	Nausea, vomiting, abdominal cramps, diarrhea, and acute prostration and circulatory collapse in occasional severe cases. Usually no fever. No secondary cases.
Salmonellosis	5 to 72 hr	Poultry and poultry products, processed meat.	Abdominal pain, diarrhea, chills, fever, frequent vomiting, and prostration. Secondary cases may occur. Leukocytosis.
Streptococcus faecalis poisoning		Ground meats, dressing.	
Clostridium perfringens poisoning	2 to 18 hr; usually 11–15 hr	Reheated meats, meat pies, and pasties, cold meats, stews, and made-up dishes.	Nausea, seldom vomiting, usually abdominal cramps and diarrhea. Symptoms seldom persist longer than 8–12 hr. No secondary cases. Fever and prostration absent.
Bacillus cereus poisoning		Foods containing cereal products, e.g., vanilla pudding.	

Source: Albertsen, V. E. et al. Meat hygiene. Agricultural Studies *34*. Food and Agriculture Organization, United Nations.

Food, Water Intake

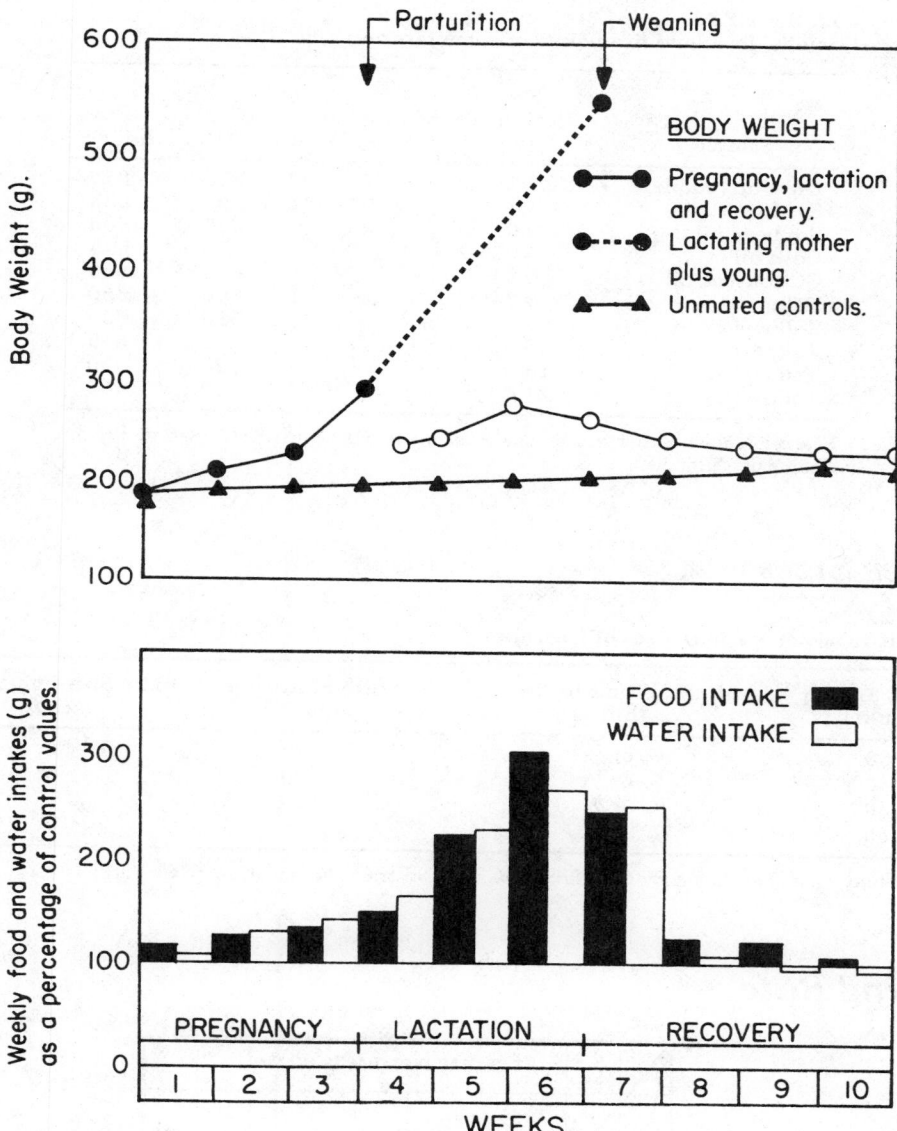

FIGURE 2.F.12

Mean body weight, food, and water consumption of female rats during reproduction and subsequent recovery

Source: Roe, F. J. C. *Metabolic Aspects of Food Safety*. Blackwell Scientific Publications, Oxford, England.

Free Fatty Acids, Smoke, Flash, and Fire Points

TABLE 2.F.28
Smoke, flash and fire points of some fats and oils

Sample	Free Fatty Acids (%)	Smoke (°F)	Flash (°F)	Fire (°F)
Olive oil (edible)	2.1	280	550	670
Safflower oil	1.7	318	603	683
Soybean oil	0.01	443	625	685
Corn oil	0.065	400	618	675
Cottonseed oil	0.04	428	613	680
Tallow (1)	0.34	—	600	650
Tallow (2)	5.3	—	510	650
Tallow (3)	8.0	—	495	615
Tallow (4)	18.0	—	420	500
Tallow (5)	21.0	—	400	475

Source: Mahlenbacher, C. V. *The Analysis of Fats and Oils.* Garrard Press, Champaign, Illinois.

Freezer Sizes

TABLE 2.F.29
Size unit to use on various sizes of freezers

Size of Freezer (cu ft)	Min Size Unit to Use (hp)	Size of Freezer (cu ft)	Min Size Unit to Use (hp)
30	⅕ or ¼	80	⅓ or ½
40	¼ or ⅓	100	½ or ¾
50	¼ or ⅓	150	¾
60	⅓		

Source: Stout, G. J. *The Home Freezer Handbook.* Van Nostrand Reinhold Co., New York.

Freezing Rate

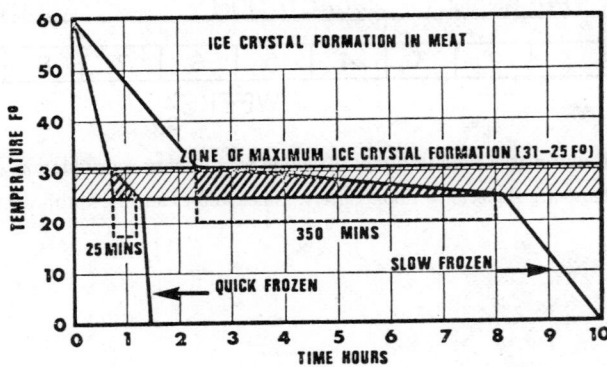

FIGURE 2.F.13
Zone of maximum ice formation

Source: Geary, D., and Gerrard, F. (1968). Meat and refrigeration. Meat Trades J., London, England.

French Dressings

TABLE 2.F.30

French Dressing

½ cup salad oil   1 tsp sugar
2 tbsp vinegar   ¼ tsp paprika
1 tsp salt   ¼ celery seed

Procedure

Mix the dry ingredients, add vinegar and oil. Shake thoroughly before using. Keep in the refrigerator.

Honey French Dressing

½ cup sugar   1 tsp paprika
⅓ cup strained honey   6 tbsp vinegar or use
1 tsp salt   3 tbsp vinegar with
1 tsp dry mustard   3 tbsp lemon juice
1 tsp celery seed   1 cup salad oil

Procedure

Mix the dry ingredients, add the honey, vinegar and oil. Store in refrigerator. Shake well before using. This is a rather sweet dressing.

Red French Dressing

½ small onion   ½ tsp salt
½ clove of garlic   ½ tsp paprika
2 tbsp vinegar   ½ tsp celery salt
¼ cup lemon juice   ¼ cup tomato catsup
⅔ cup white corn syrup ½ cup salad oil

Procedure

Chop the garlic and onion and let stand 10 min in the vinegar and lemon juice. Strain. Add the spices, catsup, syrup and oil. Store in the refrigerator. Shake well before using.

Sweet Mustard French Dressing

⅔ cup sugar   1 cup vinegar
2 tsp salt   1 cup oil
2 tsp dry mustard

Procedure

Mix the dry ingredients, add the oil and vinegar. Shake well before using. This is a good general purpose French dressing. Refrigerate.

Tomato Soup French Dressing

1 can tomato soup   1 tsp paprika
½ cup salad oil   1 chopped green pepper
¾ cup vinegar   (optional)
½ cup sugar   1 chopped onion
1 tsp dry mustard   (optional)

Procedure

Combine all the ingredients in a jar. Shake well before using. Keep refrigerated.

Thick French Dressing
(Will Not Separate)

½ cup sugar   1½ cups salad oil
1 pkg prepared pectin 1 tsp Worcestershire sauce
1 tsp paprika   1 tsp minced onion
1 tsp dry mustard   1 can tomato soup
2 tsp salt   1 clove garlic chopped
⅔ cup vinegar (or less   (optional)
  if preferred)

Procedure

Mix all ingredients and beat with an egg beater. This dressing will not separate. Keep in the refrigerator.

Source: Kintner, T. C., and Mansel, M. Vinegars and salad dressings. Univ. Missouri Agric. Exp. Sta. Bull. *631.*

French Dressing Variations

TABLE 2.F.31
Suggested variations to be made with french dressing

Kind	Amount of Dressing	Suggested Additions	Suggested Uses
Cocktail Sauce	1 cup	1 cup chili sauce	Fish sauce
Russian	1 cup	2 tbsp chili sauce 1 tbsp chopped onion	Green or vegetable salads
Red	1 cup	2 tbsp tomato catsup 2 tbsp chopped olives or pickles Sweeten if desired	Green salads Sauces
Roquefort	1 cup	2–4 tbsp crumbled Roquefort or blue cheese Few drops Worcestershire sauce	Green salads
Martinique	1 cup	2 tbsp chopped parsley 2 tbsp green pepper	Green salads
Chiffonade	1 cup	2 tbsp chopped olives 1 tbsp chopped green pepper 1 tbsp chopped onion 1 chopped hard cooked egg	Lettuce or greens
Creamy	1 cup	2–3 tbsp cream (shake well)	Greens
Sweet French	1 cup	4 tbsp confectioner's sugar or 4 tbsp honey	Fruit salads

Source: Kintner, T. C., and Mangel, M. Vinegars and salad dressings. Univ. Missouri Agric. Exp. Sta. Bull. 631.

Frost Date, Autumn

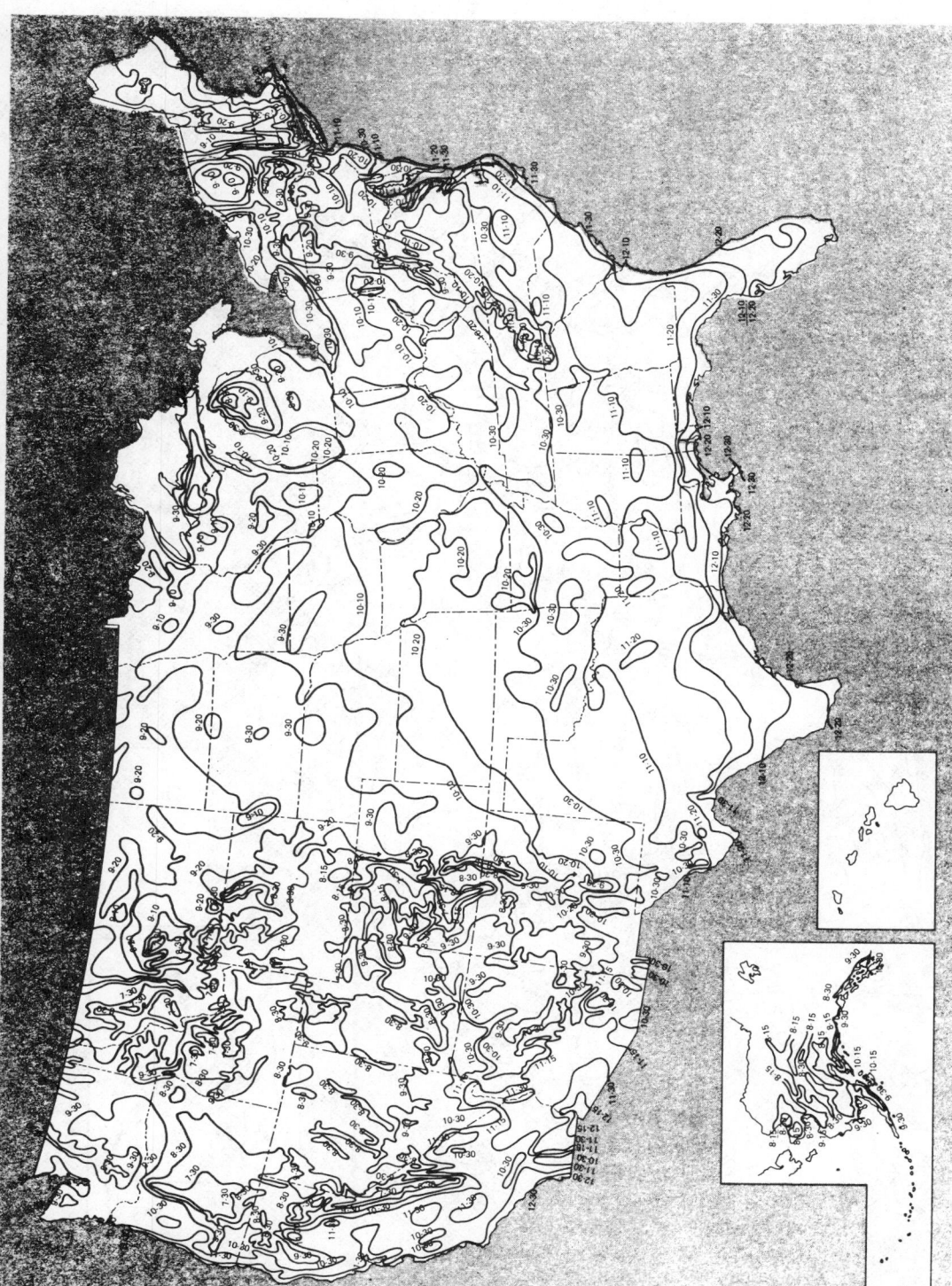

FIGURE 2.F.14
Average dates of the first killing frost in fall

Source: USDA (1972). Growing vegetables in the home garden. USDA Home and Garden Bull. 202.

Frost Date, Spring

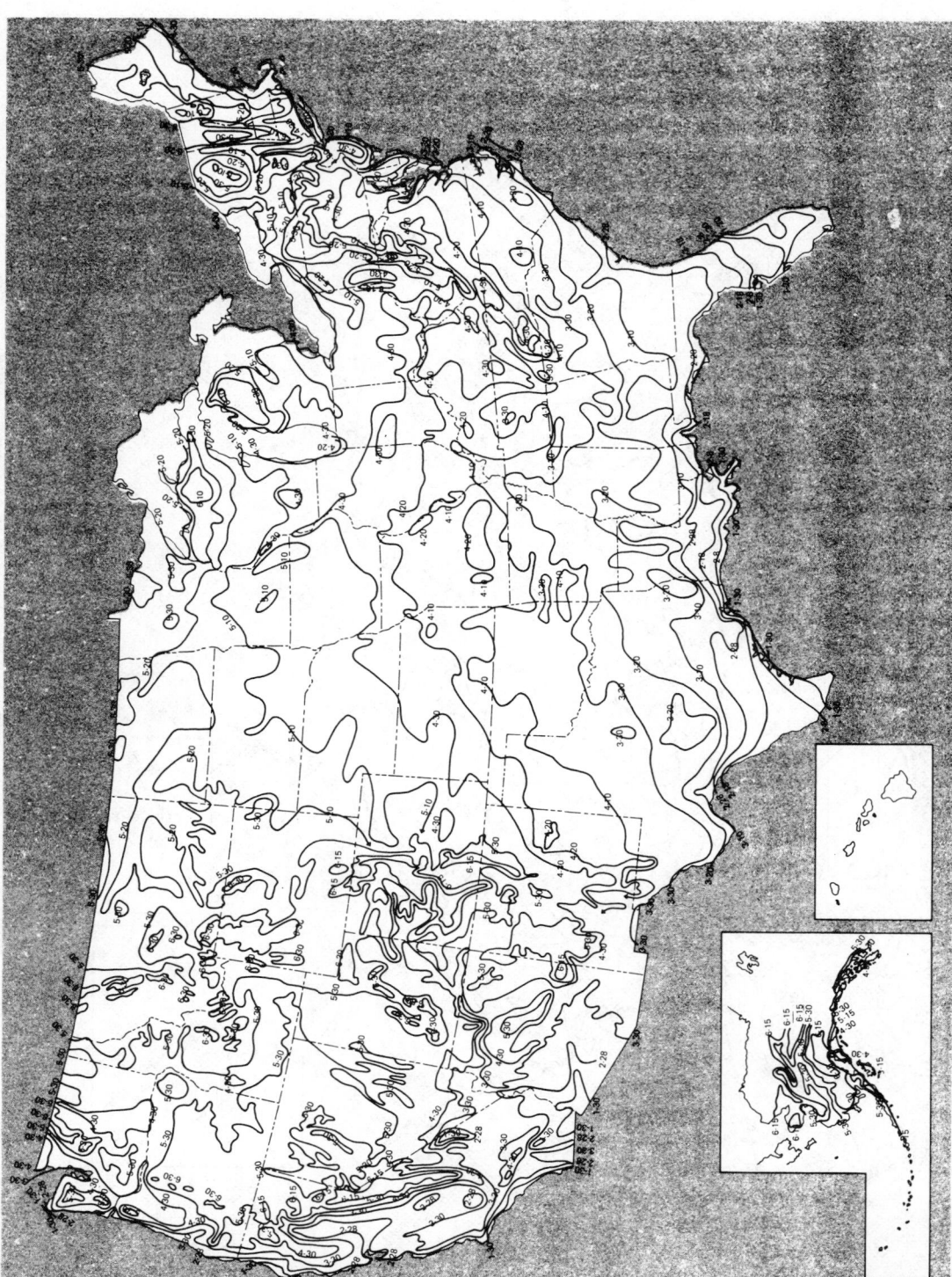

MEAN DATE OF LAST 32° (F.) TEMPERATURE IN SPRING

FIGURE 2.F.15

Average dates of the last killing frost in spring

Frozen Food Containers

TABLE 2.F.32
Frozen food containers

	Cellophane Bag or Wrapper (Heat Sealed)	Carton with Cellophane Liner (Heat Sealed)	Carton with Thermoplastic Liner (Heat Sealed)	Carton, No Liner (Thermoplastic Seal)	Tin-tie Bag (Single)	Tin-tie (Bag) (Double)	Waxed Paper Cup or "Tub"	Round Sealright Paper Container	Tin Can Standard Flange	Tin Can Friction Top	Special Rect "Can", Tin Ends, Paper Sides	Glass Jars
Inexpensive	Yes	No	No	No	Yes	No	No	No	No	No	?	No
Liquid, moisture, and vapor tight	Yes	Yes	Yes	?	No	Yes	Yes	?	Yes	Yes	Yes	Yes
Easily and securely sealed	Yes	Yes	Securely but not easily	No	Easily but not securely	Yes	Yes	Easily, not so securely	?	Yes	No	Yes
Special filling or closing devices required	No	No	?	No	No	No	No	No	Yes	No	Yes	No
Substantial—not broken by usual handling	No	Yes	Yes	Yes	Yes	Yes	Yes	Yes	Yes	Yes	Yes	No
Economical of space	No	Yes	Yes	Yes	No	No	No	No	No	No	Yes	No
Readily emptied without thawing	?	?	Yes	Yes	Yes	Yes	Yes	Yes	Yes	No	Yes	No
Transparent	Yes	Yes	No	No	No	No	No	No	No	No	No	Yes
Easy to mark on or label	No	Yes	Yes	No	Yes	Yes	Yes	Yes	Yes	Yes	Yes	Yes
Readily obtainable	?	?	?	?	Yes	Yes	?	?	Yes	No	No	Yes
Re-usable	No	Carton yes	Carton yes	?	?	?	Yes	Yes	Yes	Yes	No	Yes
Heat conductivity good (a questionable virtue)	Yes	No	No	No	No	No	No	No	Yes	Yes	?	Yes
Use: F—fruits V—vegetables M—meats L—liquids	FVM	FV	VF	V	V	VF	Anything	Anything	Anything	Anything	FVM	VFL

Source: Stout, G. J. *The Home Freezer Handbook.* Van Nostrand Reinhold Co., New York.

Frozen Food Storage I

TABLE 2.F.33
Maximum home-storage periods to maintain good quality in purchased frozen foods

Food	Approximate holding period at 0° F.	Food	Approximate holding period at 0° F.
Fruits and vegetables		*Meat—Continued*	
Fruits:	*Months*	Cooked meat:	*Months*
Cherries	12	Meal dinners	3
Peaches	12	Meat pie	3
Raspberries	12	Swiss steak	3
Strawberries	12	*Poultry*	
Fruit juice concentrates:		Chicken:	
Apple	12	Cut-up	9
Grape	12	Livers	3
Orange	12	Whole	12
Vegetables:		Duck, whole	6
Asparagus	8	Goose, whole	6
Beans	8	Turkey:	
Cauliflower	8	Cut up	6
Corn	8	Whole	12
Peas	8	Cooked chicken and turkey:	
Spinach	8	Chicken or turkey din-	
Baked goods		ners (sliced meat	
Bread and yeast rolls:		and gravy)	6
White bread	3	Chicken or turkey pies	6
Cinnamon rolls	2	Fried chicken	4
Plain rolls	3	Fried chicken dinners	4
Cakes:		*Fish and shellfish*	
Angel	2	Fish:	
Chiffon	2	Fillets:	
Chocolate layer	4	Cod, flounder, had-	
Fruit	12	dock, halibut,	
Pound	6	pollack	6
Yellow	6	Mullet, ocean	
Danish pastry	3	perch, sea trout,	
Doughnuts:		striped bass	3
Cake type	3	Pacific Ocean perch	2
Yeast raised	3	Salmon steaks	2
Pies (unbaked):		Sea trout, dressed	3
Apple	8	Striped bass, dressed	3
Boysenberry	8	Whiting, drawn	4
Cherry	8	Shellfish:	
Peach	8	Clams, shucked	3
Meat		Crabmeat:	
Beef:		Dungeness	3
Hamburger or chipped		King	10
(thin) steaks	4	Oysters, shucked	4
Roasts	12	Shrimp	12
Steaks	12	Cooked fish and shellfish:	
Lamb:		Fish with cheese sauce	3
Patties (ground meat)	4	Fish with lemon butter	
Roasts	9	sauce	3
Pork, cured	2	Fried fish dinner	3
Pork, fresh:		Fried fish sticks, scallops,	
Chops	4	or shrimp	3
Roasts	8	Shrimp creole	3
Sausage	2	Tuna pie	3
Veal:		*Frozen desserts*	
Cutlets, chops	9	Ice cream	1
Roasts	9	Sherbet	1

Source: (1982). Purchased frozen foods. 1975 Home and Garden Bull. *69.*

Frozen Food Storage II

TABLE 2.F.34
Approximate storage life of some frozen foods at various temperatures[1]

	+10°F Months	0°F Months	−10°F Months
Fish			
Fish, fatty	4	6-8	10-12
Fish, lean	6	10-12	14-16
Fruit			
Apricots, with ascorbic acid	6-8	18-24	24
Apricots, without ascorbic acid	3-4	8-10	12-14
Peaches, with ascorbic acid	6-8	18-24	24
Peaches, without ascorbic acid	3-4	8-10	12-14
Raspberries, sugared	8-10	18	24
Raspberries, without sugar or syrup	6-8	12	18
Strawberries, sliced	8-10	18	24
Meat			
Beef, roasts	6-8	16-18	18-24
Lamb	5-7	14-16	16-18
Pork, roasts	4	8-10	12-15
Pork, sausage	2	4-6	8-10
Poultry			
Poultry, giblets	1	3-5	8-10
Poultry, roasting	4	8-10	12-15
Shellfish			
Lobsters	3-4	8-10	10-12
Shrimp, raw	6	12	16-18
Vegetables			
Asparagus	4-6	8-12	16-18
Beans, snap	4-6	8-12	16-18
Beans, lima	6-8	14-16	24 or longer
Broccoli	6-8	14-16	24 or longer
Brussels sprouts	4-6	8-12	16-18
Cauliflower	6-8	14-16	24 or longer
Corn, on the cob	4-6	8-10	12-14
Corn, cut	12	24	36 or longer
Carrots	12	24	36 or longer
Mushrooms	3-4	8-10	12-14
Peas	6-8	14-16	24 or longer
Pumpkin	12	24	36 or longer
Spinach	6-8	14-16	24 or longer
Squash	12	24	36 or longer

[1]Data compiled by D. K. Tressler (1946A and B) and presented at the First Regional Training Conference, The Refrigeration Research Foundation, Hershey, Pa., 1946. Published in The Refrigeration Research Foundation, Commodity Storage Manual, p. 23, (Appendix C) 1953.

Source: Tressler, D. K., and Evers, C. F. *The Freezing Preservation of Foods,* Vol. 1, 3rd Edition. AVI Publishing Co., Westport, Connecticut.

Frozen Meat Storage Time

TABLE 2.F.35
Suggested storage times for meat at 0°F

	Months
Beef	8-12
Lamb	8-12
Pork, fresh	4-8
Ground beef and lamb	3-4
Pork Sausage	1-3

Source: USDA (1969). How to buy meat for your freezer. USDA Home and Garden Bull. *166.*

Fruit and Nut Rootstock

TABLE 2.F.36
Data for rootstocks for fruits and nuts

Common Name	Latin Name	Approx Seeds per Ounce	After-ripening Needed for Germination (days)	Speed of Germination at Optimum Temp (days)	Length of Viability (yr)
Almond	*Prunus amygdalus*	12–15	50	15	5
Apple	*Malus domestica*	600–1000	75–100	30	2–3
Apple (crab)	*Malus pumila*	1000	75	30	2–3
Apricot	*Prunus armeniaca*	18–20	60	15	5
Cherry (Mahaleb)	*Prunus mahaleb*	300–350	100	15	1–3 cool-dry
Cherry (sweet) (Mazzard)	*Prunus avium*	150–160	100–120	15	1–2 cool-dry
Cherry (sour)	*Prunus cerasus*	200–250	100–120	15	1–2 cool-dry
Citranges	*Poncirus trifoliata* X *Citrus sinensis*	200–300	None	10–15 at 55°F	Up to 1 yr in polyethylene bag at 45°
Citrus macrophylla	*Citrus macrophylla*	200–300	None	(Same)	(Same)
Fig	*Ficus carica*		Propagated by cuttings		
Filbert	*Corylus maxima*		Propagated by cuttings		
Grapefruit	*Citrus paradisi*	150–200	None	10–15 at 55°F	(Same)
Lemon (rough)	*Citrus limon*	200–300	None	(Same)	(Same)
Lime (sweet)	*Citrus aurantifolia*	300–400	None	(Same)	(Same)
Orange (sweet)	*Citrus sinensis*	200–300	None	(Same)	(Same)
Orange (sour)	*Citrus aurantium*	200–300	None	(Same)	(Same)
Orange (trifoliate)	*Poncirus trifoliata*	200–300	None	(Same)	(Same)
Peach	*Prunus persica*	8–10	100	15	5
Peach (David)	*Prunus davidiana*	10–14	100	15	5
Pear	*Pyrus communis*	750	60–90	45	2–3 dry
Pear (Oriental)	*Pyrus calleryana*	1000	60–90	45	3
Pear (Oriental)	*Pyrus serotina*	1000	60–90	45	3
Pear (Oriental)	*Pyrus ussuriensis*	1000	60–90	45	3
Pecan	*Carya pecan*	8–10	30–90	20	1–3
Plum (American)	*Prunus americana*	50–55	150	30	4–6
Plum (Bessey)	*Prunus besseyi*	160–170	80–100	15	4–6
Plum (Damson)	*Prunus insititia*	100–120	100–120	30	4–6
Plum (Japanese)	*Prunus salicina*	20–40	60–100	15	4–6
Plum (domestic)	*Prunus domestica*	26–30	120	30	4–6
Plum (Myrobalan) (cherry plums)	*Prunus cerasifera*	60–70	80–100	30	4–6
Plum (Marianna)	*Prunus cerasifera*	50–70	100	30	4–6
Plum (Wild Goose)	*Prunus munsoniana*	120–140	80–100	15	4–6
Quince	*Cydonia oblonga*		Propagated by cuttings		
Tangelo	*Citrus reticulata* X *Citrus paradisi*	200–300	None	10–15 at 55°F	Up to 1 yr in polyethylene bag at 45°
Tangerine (Mandarin)	*Citrus reticulata*	300–400	None	(Same)	(Same)
Tung	*Aleurites fordii*	10–15	30–60	10	1–3
Walnut (Eastern black)	*Fuglans nigra*	3	60–120	30	3–5
Walnut (Northern Calif. black)	*Fuglans hindsii*	2–4	60–120	30	3–5
Walnut (Persian)	*Fuglans regia*	2	30–60	20	1–3
Walnut (Paradox hybrid)	*Fuglans hindsii* X *F. regia*	3–4	60–80	25	3–5
Walnut (Royal hybrid)	*Fuglans hindsii* X *F. nigra*	3–5	60–100	25	3–5

Source: USDA. Seeds. *Yearbook of Agriculture.*

Fruit and Vegetables, Composition

TABLE 2.F.37

Composition of selected fruits and vegetables, 100 grams edible portion[1]

Food Description	Iron (mg)	Vitamin A Value (IU)	Thiamin (mg)	Ribo-flavin (mg)	Ascorbic Acid (mg)	Sodium (mg)	Potassium (mg)
Apricots							
Raw	0.5	2,700	0.03	0.04	10	1	281
Canned	0.3	1,830	0.02	0.02	4	1	246
Asparagus							
Raw spears	1.0	900	0.18	0.20	33	2	278
Cooked spears, boiled and drained	0.6	900	0.16	0.18	26	1	183
Green, canned spears, regular pack, drained solids	1.9	800	0.06	0.10	15	236	166
Lima beans							
Raw	2.8	290	0.24	0.12	29	2	650
Cooked, boiled, drained	2.5	280	0.18	0.10	17	1	422
Canned, drained solids	2.4	190	0.03	0.05	6	236	222
Frozen, cooked, boiled, drained	1.7	230	0.07	0.05	17	101	426
Green snap beans							
Raw	0.8	600	0.08	0.11	19	7	243
Cooked, boiled and drained	0.6	540	0.07	0.09	12	4	151
Canned, drained solids	1.5	470	0.03	0.05	4	236	95
Frozen, cooked, boiled, drained	0.7	580	0.07	0.09	5	1	152
Cauliflower							
Raw	1.1	60	0.11	0.10	78	13	295
Cooked, boiled, drained	0.7	60	0.09	0.08	55	9	206
Frozen, cooked, boiled, drained	0.5	30	0.04	0.05	41	10	207
Cherries							
Raw, sour, red	0.4	1,000	0.05	0.06	10	2	191
Canned, sour, red, water pack	0.3	680	0.03	0.02	5	2	130
Sweet corn							
Raw	0.7	400	0.15	0.12	12	Tr	280
Cooked, boiled, drained, cut off cob	0.6	400	0.11	0.10	7	Tr	165
Canned, cream style	0.6	330	0.03	0.05	5	Tr	196
Frozen, cooked, boiled, drained	0.8	350	0.09	0.06	5	1	184
Grapefruit							
Raw, all varieties	0.4	20	0.04	0.02	38	1	135
Canned, water pack	0.3	10	0.03	0.02	30	4	144
Peaches							
Raw	0.5	1,330	0.02	0.05	7	1	202
Canned, water pack	0.3	450	0.01	0.03	3	2	137
Peas							
Raw	1.9	640	0.35	0.14	27	2	316
Cooked, boiled, drained	1.8	540	0.28	0.11	20	1	196
Canned, regular pack, drained solids	1.9	690	0.09	0.06	8	236	96
Frozen, cooked, boiled, drained	1.9	600	0.27	0.09	13	115	135
Potatoes							
Raw	0.6	Tr	0.10	0.04	20	3	407
French fried from raw	1.3	Tr	0.13	0.08	21	6	853
Mashed from raw	0.4	170	0.08	0.05	9	331	331
Dehydrated, mashed, prepared	0.5	110	0.04	0.05	3	290	290
Frozen French fries, heated	1.8	Tr	0.14	0.02	21	4	652

[1] The data shown here provide an indication of what may be expected when processed forms are substituted for fresh on an equal weight basis. It is not a measure of the effect of processing on nutritive values. Some differences may be attributed to a difference in the selection of varieties used for the fresh market and for the processed product. In the case of fruit items, the dilution with sirup in the canned product also contributes to the difference between the values for the fresh and canned products.

Source: White, P. L., and Selvey, N. (editors) (1974). *Nutritional Qualities of Fresh Fruits and Vegetables.* Futura Publishing Co., Mt. Kisco, New York.

Fruit and Vegetables, Cost per Serving

The net weight of various foods in the same size can (or glass jar) will vary with the density of the food. Net weight of a No. 10 can of vegetables, for instance, will vary from 6 lb 2 oz for spinach to 6 lb 12 oz for kidney beans. Corn weighs 6 lb 10 oz, peas 6 lb 9 oz, etc. Similarly, No. 10 fruits vary from approximately 6 lb for certain apples to 6 lb 14 oz for peaches in heavy syrup; 7 lb 5 oz for cranberry sauce, all the way up to 7 lb 8 oz for pitted cherries.

Pieces (depends on size) in 1 No. 10 can:
Can contains 3 qt of juice
Can contains 12–13 cups
Can contains 50–60 medium size whole apricots
Can contains 95–130 medium size apricot halves
Can contains 45–65 peach or pear halves
Can contains 28–50 pineapple slices
Can contains 40–60 plums or prunes
Can contains 70–90 figs
Can contains 115–145 asparagus spears
Can contains 55–65 small whole white potatoes

Approx equivalents of other can sizes:
1 No. 10 Can equals 7 No. 303 (1 lb) cans
1 No. 10 Can equals 5 No. 2 (1 lb 4 oz) cans
1 No. 10 Can equals 4 No. 2-½ (1 lb 13 oz) cans
1 No. 10 Can equals 2 No. 3 cyl. (46–50 oz) cans

TABLE 2.F.38
Cost per serving chart for no. 10 cans of fruits & vegetables

Cost per Case of 6/10	Cost Per Can	Number of Servings			
		20	25[1]	33	50
		5/8 cup 5 fl oz	1/2 cup 4 fl oz	3/8 cup 3 fl oz	1/4 cup 2 fl oz
$2.00	$0.33	0.016	0.013	0.010	0.007
2.25	0.38	0.019	0.015	0.012	0.008
2.50	0.42	0.021	0.017	0.013	0.008
2.75	0.46	0.023	0.018	0.014	0.009
3.00	0.50	0.025	0.020	0.015	0.010
3.25	0.54	0.027	0.022	0.016	0.011
3.50	0.58	0.029	0.023	0.017	0.012
3.75	0.63	0.032	0.025	0.019	0.013
4.00	0.67	0.034	0.027	0.020	0.013
4.25	0.71	0.036	0.028	0.022	0.014
4.50	0.75	0.038	0.030	0.023	0.015
4.75	0.79	0.040	0.032	0.024	0.016
5.00	0.83	0.042	0.033	0.025	0.017
5.25	0.88	0.044	0.035	0.027	0.018
5.50	0.92	0.046	0.037	0.028	0.018
5.75	0.96	0.048	0.038	0.029	0.019
6.00	1.00	0.050	0.040	0.030	0.020
6.25	1.04	0.052	0.042	0.032	0.021
6.50	1.08	0.054	0.043	0.033	0.022
6.75	1.13	0.057	0.045	0.034	0.023
7.00	1.17	0.059	0.047	0.035	0.023
7.50	1.25	0.063	0.050	0.038	0.025
8.00	1.33	0.067	0.053	0.040	0.027
8.50	1.42	0.071	0.057	0.043	0.028
9.00	1.50	0.075	0.060	0.045	0.030
9.50	1.58	0.079	0.063	0.048	0.032
10.00	1.67	0.083	0.067	0.051	0.033
10.50	1.75	0.087	0.070	0.053	0.035
11.00	1.83	0.091	0.073	0.055	0.037
11.50	1.92	0.096	0.077	0.058	0.038
12.00	2.00	0.100	0.080	0.061	0.040
12.50	2.08	0.104	0.083	0.063	0.042

(Continued)

TABLE 2.F.38 *(Continued)*

Cost per Case of 6/10	Cost Per Can	Number of Servings			
		20	25[1]	33	50
		5/8 cup 5 fl oz	1/2 cup 4 fl oz	3/8 cup 3 fl oz	1/4 cup 2 fl oz
13.00	2.17	0.108	0.087	0.066	0.043
13.50	2.25	0.112	0.090	0.068	0.045
14.00	2.33	0.116	0.093	0.071	0.047
14.50	2.42	0.121	0.097	0.073	0.048
15.00	2.50	0.125	0.100	0.076	0.050
15.50	2.58	0.129	0.103	0.078	0.052
16.00	2.67	0.133	0.107	0.081	0.053
16.50	2.75	0.137	0.110	0.083	0.055
17.00	2.83	0.141	0.113	0.086	0.057
17.50	2.92	0.146	0.117	0.088	0.058
18.00	3.00	0.150	0.120	0.091	0.060
18.50	3.08	0.154	0.123	0.093	0.062
19.00	3.17	0.158	0.127	0.096	0.063
19.50	3.25	0.162	0.130	0.098	0.065
20.00	3.33	0.166	0.133	0.101	0.067
21.00	3.50	0.175	0.140	0.106	0.070
22.00	3.67	0.183	0.147	0.111	0.073
23.00	3.83	0.191	0.153	0.116	0.077
24.00	4.00	0.200	0.160	0.121	0.080
25.00	4.17	0.208	0.167	0.126	0.083
26.00	4.33	0.216	0.173	0.131	0.087
27.00	4.50	0.225	0.180	0.136	0.090
28.00	4.67	0.233	0.187	0.141	0.093
29.00	4.83	0.241	0.193	0.146	0.097
30.00	5.00	0.250	0.200	0.151	0.100
31.00	5.17	0.258	0.207	0.157	0.103
32.00	5.33	0.266	0.213	0.162	0.107
33.00	5.50	0.275	0.220	0.167	0.110
34.00	5.67	0.283	0.227	0.172	0.113
35.00	5.83	0.291	0.233	0.177	0.117
36.00	6.00	0.300	0.240	0.182	0.120
37.00	6.17	0.308	0.247	0.187	0.123
38.00	6.33	0.316	0.253	0.192	0.127
39.00	6.50	0.325	0.260	0.197	0.130
40.00	6.67	0.333	0.267	0.202	0.133
41.00	6.83	0.341	0.273	0.207	0.137
42.00	7.00	0.350	0.280	0.212	0.140
43.00	7.17	0.358	0.287	0.217	0.143
44.00	7.33	0.366	0.293	0.222	0.147
45.00	7.50	0.375	0.300	0.227	0.150
46.00	7.67	0.383	0.307	0.232	0.153
47.00	7.83	0.391	0.313	0.237	0.157
48.00	8.00	0.400	0.320	0.242	0.160
49.00	8.17	0.408	0.327	0.247	0.163
50.00	8.33	0.416	0.333	0.252	0.167

[1]25 servings per can (1/2 cup each) is the average serving for most fruits and vegetables. *Source:* Wisconsin Canners Association.

Source: (1973). *The Almanac of the Canning, Freezing, Preserving Industries*, 58th Edition. E. E. Judge & Son, Baltimore.

Fruit and Vegetables, Diseases

TABLE 2.F.39
Diseases and conditions common to fruits and vegetables

Apples

Internal breakdown
Internal browning
Watercore
Jonathan spot
Scab (storage)
Scale
Blue mold rot
Bullseye rot

Bananas

Black rot
Anthracnose
Chilling injury
Scars
Freeze injury
Overripe

Cabbage

Alternaria leaf spot
Aphids
Black leaf speck
Bursting
Leaf separation from stem
Yellowing of outer leaves

Cantaloupes

Coal dust damage
Fresh cracks
Ground color
Low temperature breakdown
Mold in stem scar
Surface mold

Carrots

Broken roots
Brown, black, or yellow tops
New top growth
Wilting and flabbiness of roots
Wilting of tops

Cauliflower

Alternaria leaf spot
Aphids
Black leaf speck
Curd discoloration

Fuzziness
Riciness
Ring spot

Celery

Bacterial soft rot
Bacterial blight
Black heart
Brown stem
Early blight
Late blight on leaves or stems
Pithiness
Wilting
Watery soft rot

Citrus

Stem and rot
Skin breakdown
Softness
Watery breakdown
Water spot
Blue and green mold

Cucumbers

Bacterial spot
Flabbiness
Scab

Lettuce

Bacterial soft rot
Broken midribs
Brown blight
Downy mildew
Red butts or midribs
Russet
Tipburn
Watery soft rot

Melons
(Honeydew and Honeyball)

Brown discoloration of rind
Coal dust damage
Low temperature breakdown
Cracks, unhealed
Surface mold
Free liquid and loose seeds

Onions

Black mold
Breakdown
Gray mold
Fusarium rot
Scalding
Sun scale

Peaches

California blight
Discoloration around pit
Discoloration from brushing
  injury
Ground color
Brown rot

Peppers

Anthracnose
Dark discoloration
Flabbiness
Shriveling
Ripe rot

Potatoes

Greening
Air cracks
Black heart
Late blight
Southern bacterial wilt
Ring rot
Internal browning
Scald
Bacterial soft rot
Sprouts
Wet breakdown
Fusarium rot

Tomatoes

Blossom end rot
Radial cracks
Sun scald
Late blight
Rhizopus
Catface
Alternaria
Fusarium rot

Source: U.S. Department of the Army (1969). Food inspection specialist. TM 8-451.

Fruit, Availability

TABLE 2.F.40
Availability of fresh fruit (G = good supply, F = fair supply, S = small supply)

	Jan-uary	Feb-ruary	March	April	May	June	July	August	Sep-tember	Octo-ber	Novem-ber	Decem-ber
Apples	G	G	G	G	F	S	S	S	G	G	G	G
Apricots					S	G	G	S				
Avocados	G	G	G	G	G	F	F	F	F	F	G	G
Bananas	G	G	G	G	G	G	G	G	G	G	G	G
Berries (misc)						G	G	G	S	S	S	
Blueberries					S	G	G	G	S			
Cantaloup		S	S	S	F	G	G	G	G	S	S	
Cherries				S	G	G	S	S				
Cranberries	S								F	F	G	G
Dates	G	F	F	S	S	S	S	S	S	G	G	G
Figs						F	G	G	F			
Grapefruit	G	G	G	G	G	F	S	S	S	G	G	G
Grapes	S	S	S	S	S	F	G	G	G	G	G	F
Honeydews		F	G	F	F	G	G	G	G	G	S	S
Lemons	G	G	G	G	G	G	G	G	G	G	G	G
Limes	S	S	S	S	G	G	G	F	F	F	S	G
Mangoes			S	F	G	G	G	F	S			
Nectarines	S	S				F	G	G	G	S		
Oranges	G	G	G	G	G	F	S	S	S	F	G	G
Papayas	S	S	S	S	F	S	S	S	S	F	S	S
Peaches					S	G	G	G	G	S		
Pears	F	F	F	F	F	S	S	G	G	G	G	F
Pineapple	S	F	G	G	G	G	F	F	S	F	F	F
Plums-prunes						G	G	G	G	S		
Strawberries	S	S	F	G	G	G	G	S	S	S	S	S
Tangelos	F	S							S	F	G	G
Tangerines	G	S	S	S	S	S				S	G	G
Watermelons	S	S	S	S	F	G	G	G	S	S	S	S

NOTE: Each year's production will vary. This chart is an estimate of probable availability.

Source: USDA (1969). Food for us all. *Yearbook of Agriculture.*

Fruit Classification, I

TABLE 2.F.41
Chart showing classification of fruits

Fleshy							Dry
Simple					Multiple	Aggregate	
Berry	Pepo	Hesperidium	Drupe	Pome			
Cranberry	Cucumber	Orange	Cherry	Apple	Pineapple	Blackberry	Legumes
Blueberry	Squash	Grapefruit	Peach	Pear	Fig	Dewberry	Nuts
Gooseberry	Pumpkin	Lemon	Plum	Quince	Mulberry	Loganberry	Grains
Huckleberry	Muskmelon	Lime	Apricot			Raspberry	
Currant	Watermelon	Tangerine	Nectarine			Strawberry	
Grape		Kumquat	Prune				
Banana			Olive				
Tomato			Coconut[1]				
Eggplant			Date				

[1] The coconut is a somewhat modified fruit, the edible portion being a part of the food storage inside the hard seed, often called the endosperm.

Source: Justin, M. M., Rust, L. O., and Vail, G. E. *Foods*, Revised Edition. Houghton Mifflin Co., Boston.

Fruit Classification, II

TABLE 2.F.42
Classification of fruits and vegetables according to systematic position, type, and use

Family	Fruit/Vegetable	Scientific Name	Type	Description
			A. Fruits	
Anarcardiaceae	Cashew	*Anacardium occidentale* L.	Nut	The woody achene is borne on a fleshy receptacle.
	Mango	*Mangifcra indica* L.	Fleshy drupe	Tough rind, extensive fleshy mesocarp with a stony outer endocarp and inner papyraceous membrane.
Annonaceae	Sugar apple	*Annona squamosa* L.	Aggregate	Each fruitlet is a small berry.
	Soursop	*Annona muricata* L.	Aggregate	Large, fleshy with soft, spiny rind. Multiple accessory fruit. Fruitlets (berries) fused together with associated bracts and floral axis.
Bromeliaceae	Pineapple	*Ananas comosus* Merr.	Sorosis	Multiple accessory fruit.
Bombacaceae	Durian	*Durio zibethinus* L.	Berry	Thick, bony dehiscent rind covered with hard sharp spines.
Caricaceae	Papaya	*Carica papaya* L.	Berry	Fleshy pericarp with large central cavity; derived from superior ovary.
Cucurbitaceae	Watermelon	*Citrullus vulgaris* Schrad	Pepo	Modified berry formed from an inferior ovary with well-developed carpel wall including some receptacle tissue.
	Melon	*Cucumis Melo* L.	Pepo	–ditto–
Guttiferae	Mangosteen	*Garcinia mangostana* L.	Berry	Thick, tough skin with sweet flesh adhering to the seeds.
Lauraceae	Avocado	*Persea americana* Mill	Berry	Thick exocarp, fleshy mesocarp and a very thin layer of endocarp next to the outer seed coat. Testa is hard.
Meliaceae	Lanzones, Langsat	*Lansium domesticum* Correa	Berry	Leathery exocarp, thin mesocarp and fleshy endocarp.
	Santol	*Sandoricum koetjape* M.	Berry	Exocarp fused with mesocarp with fleshy fibrous aril adhering to seeds.
Moraceae	Fig	*Ficus carica* L.	Synconium	Multiple accessory fruit, mainly a fleshy hollow receptacle bearing numerous small achenes.
	Jackfruit	*Artocarpus integra* L.	Multiple	Very large, fruit with sharp protruberances, thick endocarp fused with the mesocarp, aromatic, and rich in latex.
Musaceae	Banana	*Musa paradisiaca* L. var. *sapientum*	Berry	Fruits borne in bunches bearing fingers.
Myrtaceae	Duhat	*Syzygium cumini* Skeels	Drupe	Dark purple fruit, clustered, high in tannins and anthocyanins.
	Guava	*Psidium guajava* L.	Berry	Pericarp is not distinct.
	Makopa	*Eugenia javanica* Lam.	Berry	Cone-shaped fruit with porous pericarp.
Passifloraceae	Passion fruit	*Passiflora edulis* Sims.	Berry	Thick pericarp with shell-like, brittle rind.
Rosaceae	Strawberry	*Fragaria vesca* L.	Etaenio	Aggregate accessory fruit, mainly a large fleshy receptacle bearing externally numerous small achenes.
Rutaceae	Orange	*Citrus sinensis* Osbeck	Hesperidium	Modified berry with well-developed endocarp.
Sapindaceae	Rambutan	*Nephellium lappaceum* L.	Berry	Fruit covered with soft spines, leathery rind and juicy aril.
Sapotaceae	Cainito	*Chrysophyllum cainito* L.	Berry	Very fleshy, juicy endocarp, rich in latex.
	Chico	*Achras sapota* L.	Berry	Mesocarp fused with endocarp.

Source: Pantastico, E. B. (editor) (1975). Structure of fruits and vegetables. In *Postharvest Physiology, Handling and Utilization of Tropical and Subtropical Fruits and Vegetables*. AVI Publishing Co., Westport, Connecticut.

Fruit Composition, Part I

TABLE 2.F.43
Nutritive values of the edible part of fruits and fruit products

(Dashes (—) denote lack of reliable data for a constituent believed to be present in measurable amount)

Foods, approximate measures, units, and weight (edible part unless footnotes indicate otherwise)	Weight (Grams)	Water (Per cent)	Food energy (Calories)	Protein (Grams)	Fat (Grams)	Fatty Acids Saturated (total) (Grams)	Fatty Acids Unsaturated Oleic (Grams)	Fatty Acids Unsaturated Linoleic (Grams)	Carbohydrate (Grams)	Calcium (Milligrams)	Phosphorus (Milligrams)	Iron (Milligrams)	Potassium (Milligrams)	Vitamin A value (International units)	Thiamin (Milligrams)	Riboflavin (Milligrams)	Niacin (Milligrams)	Ascorbic acid (Milligrams)
FRUITS AND FRUIT PRODUCTS																		
Apples, raw, unpeeled, without cores: 2 3/4-in diam. (about 3 per lb with cores), 1 apple	138	84	80	Trace	1	—	—	—	20	10	14	.4	152	120	.04	.03	.1	6
3 1/4-in diam. (about 2 per lb with cores), 1 apple	212	84	125	Trace	1	—	—	—	31	15	21	.6	233	190	.06	.04	.2	8
Applejuice, bottled or canned[24], 1 cup	248	88	120	Trace	Trace	—	—	—	30	15	22	1.5	250	—	.02	.05	.2	2[25]
Applesauce, canned: Sweetened, 1 cup	255	76	230	1	Trace	—	—	—	61	10	13	1.3	166	100	.05	.03	.1	3[26]
Unsweetened, 1 cup	244	89	100	Trace	Trace	—	—	—	26	10	12	1.2	190	100	.05	.02	.1	2[26]
Apricots: Raw, without pits (about 12 per lb with pits), 3 apricots	107	85	55	1	Trace	—	—	—	14	18	25	.5	301	2,890	.03	.04	.6	11
Canned in heavy sirup (halves and sirup), 1 cup	258	77	220	2	Trace	—	—	—	57	28	39	.8	604	4,490	.05	.05	1.0	10
Dried: Uncooked (28 large or 37 medium halves per cup), 1 cup	130	25	340	7	1	—	—	—	86	87	140	7.2	1,273	14,170	.01	.21	4.3	16
Cooked, unsweetened, fruit and liquid, 1 cup	250	76	215	4	1	—	—	—	54	55	88	4.5	795	7,500	.01	.13	2.5	8
Apricot nectar, canned, 1 cup	251	85	145	1	Trace	—	—	—	37	23	30	.5	379	2,380	.03	.03	.5	36[26]
Avocados, raw, whole, without skins and seeds: California, mid- and late-winter (with skin and seed, 3 1/8-in diam.; wt., 10 oz), 1 avocado	216	74	370	5	37	5.5	22.0	3.7	13	22	91	1.3	1,303	630	.24	.43	3.5	30
Florida, late summer and fall (with skin and seed, 3 5/8-in diam.; wt., 1 lb), 1 avocado	304	78	390	4	33	6.7	15.7	5.3	27	30	128	1.8	1,836	880	.33	.61	4.9	43
Banana without peel (about 2.6 per lb with peel), 1 banana	119	76	100	1	Trace	—	—	—	26	10	31	.8	440	230	.06	.07	.8	12
Banana flakes, 1 tbsp	6	3	20	Trace	Trace	—	—	—	5	2	6	.2	92	50	.01	.01	.2	Trace
Blackberries, raw, 1 cup	144	85	85	2	1	—	—	—	19	46	27	1.3	245	290	.04	.06	.6	30
Blueberries, raw, 1 cup	145	83	90	1	1	—	—	—	22	22	19	1.5	117	150	.04	.09	.7	20
Cantaloup. See Muskmelons (item 271).																		
Cherries: Sour (tart), red, pitted, canned, water pack, 1 cup	244	88	105	2	Trace	—	—	—	26	37	32	.7	317	1,660	.07	.05	.5	12
Sweet, raw, without pits and stems, 10 cherries	68	80	45	1	Trace	—	—	—	12	15	13	.3	129	70	.03	.04	.3	7
Cranberry juice cocktail, bottled, sweetened, 1 cup	253	83	165	Trace	Trace	—	—	—	42	13	8	.8	25	Trace	.03	.03	.1	81[27]
Cranberry sauce, sweetened, canned, strained, 1 cup	277	62	405	Trace	1	—	—	—	104	17	11	.6	83	60	.03	.03	.1	6

(Continued)

[24]Also applies to pasteurized apple cider.
[25]Applies to product without added ascorbic acid. For value of product with added ascorbic acid, refer to label.
[26]Based on product with label claim of 45% of U.S. RDA in 6 fl oz.
[27]Based on product with label claim of 100% of U.S. RDA in 6 fl oz.

Fruit Composition, Part I (Continued)

TABLE 2.F.43 (Continued)

(Dashes (—) denote lack of reliable data for a constituent believed to be present in measurable amount)

Foods, approximate measures, units, and weight (edible part unless footnotes indicate otherwise)	Weight (Grams)	Water (Percent)	Food energy (Calories)	Protein (Grams)	Fat (Grams)	Fatty Acids: Saturated (total) (Grams)	Fatty Acids: Unsaturated Oleic (Grams)	Fatty Acids: Unsaturated Linoleic (Grams)	Carbohydrate (Grams)	Calcium (Milligrams)	Phosphorus (Milligrams)	Iron (Milligrams)	Potassium (Milligrams)	Vitamin A value (International units)	Thiamin (Milligrams)	Riboflavin (Milligrams)	Niacin (Milligrams)	Ascorbic acid (Milligrams)
FRUITS AND FRUIT PRODUCTS																		
Dates:																		
Whole, without pits — 10 dates	80	23	220	2	Trace	—	—	—	58	47	50	2.4	518	40	.07	.08	1.8	0
Chopped — 1 cup	178	23	490	4	1	—	—	—	130	105	112	5.3	1,153	90	.16	.18	3.9	0
Fruit cocktail, canned, in heavy sirup — 1 cup	255	80	195	1	Trace	—	—	—	50	23	31	1.0	411	360	.05	.03	1.0	5
Grapefruit:																		
Raw, medium, 3 3/4-in diam. (about 1 lb 1 oz):																		
Pink or red — 1/2 grapefruit with peel[28]	241	89	50	1	Trace	—	—	—	13	20	20	.5	166	540	.05	.02	.2	44
White — 1/2 grapefruit with peel[28]	241	89	45	1	Trace	—	—	—	12	19	19	.5	159	10	.05	.02	.2	44
Canned, sections with sirup — 1 cup	254	81	180	2	Trace	—	—	—	45	33	36	.8	343	30	.08	.05	.5	76
Grapefruit juice:																		
Raw, pink, red, or white — 1 cup	246	90	95	1	Trace	—	—	—	23	22	37	.5	399	(29)	.10	.05	.5	93
Canned, white:																		
Unsweetened — 1 cup	247	89	100	1	Trace	—	—	—	24	20	35	1.0	400	20	.07	.05	.5	84
Sweetened — 1 cup	250	86	135	1	Trace	—	—	—	32	20	35	1.0	405	30	.08	.05	.5	78
Frozen, concentrate, unsweetened:																		
Undiluted, 6-fl oz can — 1 can	207	62	300	4	1	—	—	—	72	70	124	.8	1,250	60	.29	.12	1.4	286
Diluted with 3 parts water by volume — 1 cup	247	89	100	1	Trace	—	—	—	24	25	42	.2	420	20	.10	.04	.5	96
Dehydrated crystals, prepared with water (1 lb yields about 1 gal). — 1 cup	247	90	100	1	Trace	—	—	—	24	22	40	.2	412	20	.10	.05	.5	91
Grapes, European type (adherent skin), raw:																		
Thompson Seedless — 10 grapes	50	81	35	Trace	Trace	—	—	—	9	6	10	.2	87	50	.03	.02	.2	2
Tokay and Emperor, seeded types — 10 grapes[30]	60	81	40	Trace	Trace	—	—	—	10	7	11	.2	99	60	.03	.02	.2	2
Grapejuice:																		
Canned or bottled — 1 cup	253	83	165	1	Trace	—	—	—	42	28	30	.8	293	—	.10	.05	.5	[25]Trace
Frozen concentrate, sweetened:																		
Undiluted, 6-fl oz can — 1 can	216	53	395	1	Trace	—	—	—	100	22	32	.9	255	40	.13	.22	1.5	[31]32
Diluted with 3 parts water by volume — 1 cup	250	86	135	1	Trace	—	—	—	33	8	10	.3	85	10	.05	.08	.5	[31]10
Grape drink, canned — 1 cup	250	86	135	Trace	Trace	—	—	—	35	8	10	.3	88	—	[32].03	[32].03	.3	[32]
Lemon, raw, size 165, without peel and seeds (about 4 per lb with peels and seeds). — 1 lemon	74	90	20	1	Trace	—	—	—	6	19	12	.4	102	10	.03	.01	.1	39
Lemon juice:																		
Raw — 1 cup	244	91	60	1	Trace	—	—	—	20	17	24	.5	344	50	.07	.02	.2	112
Canned, or bottled, unsweetened — 1 cup	244	92	55	1	Trace	—	—	—	19	17	24	.5	344	50	.07	.02	.2	102
Frozen, single strength, unsweetened, 6-fl oz can. — 1 can	183	92	40	1	Trace	—	—	—	13	13	16	.5	258	40	.05	.02	.2	81
Lemonade concentrate, frozen:																		
Undiluted, 6-fl oz can — 1 can	219	49	425	Trace	Trace	—	—	—	112	9	13	.4	153	40	.05	.06	.7	66
Diluted with 4 1/3 parts water by volume — 1 cup	248	89	105	Trace	Trace	—	—	—	28	2	3	.1	40	10	.01	.02	.2	17

(Continued)

[28] Weight includes peel and membranes between sections. Without these parts, the weight of the edible portion is 123 g for item 246 and 118 g for item 247.
[29] For white-fleshed varieties, value is about 20 International Units (I.U.) per cup; for red-fleshed varieties, 1,080 I.U.
[30] Weight includes seeds. Without seeds, weight of the edible portion is 57 g.
[31] Applies to product without added ascorbic acid. With added ascorbic acid, based on claim that 6 fl oz of reconstituted juice contain 45% or 50% of the U.S. RDA, value in milligrams is 108 or 120 for a 6-fl oz can (item 258), 36 or 40 for 1 cup of diluted juice (item 259).
[32] For products with added thiamin and riboflavin but without added ascorbic acid, values in milligrams would be 0.60 for thiamin, 0.80 for riboflavin, and trace for ascorbic acid. For products with only ascorbic acid added, value varies with the brand. Consult the label.

Fruit Composition, Part I (Continued)

TABLE 2.F.43 (Continued)

(Dashes (—) denote lack of reliable data for a constituent believed to be present in measurable amount)

Foods, approximate measures, units, and weight (edible part unless footnotes indicate otherwise)	Water	Food energy	Protein	Fat	Fatty Acids Saturated (total)	Unsaturated Oleic	Linoleic	Carbohydrate	Calcium	Phosphorus	Iron	Potassium	Vitamin A value	Thiamin	Riboflavin	Niacin	Ascorbic acid
	Grams	Per-cent	Cal-ories	Grams	Grams	Grams	Grams	Grams	Grams	Milli-grams	Milli-grams	Milli-grams	Milli-grams	Inter-national units	Milli-grams	Milli-grams	Milli-grams	Milli-grams
FRUITS AND FRUIT PRODUCTS—Con.																		
Limeade concentrate, frozen:																		
Undiluted, 6-fl oz can —— 1 can	218	50	410	Trace	Trace	—	—	—	108	11	13	0.2	129	Trace	0.02	0.02	0.2	26
Diluted with 4 1/3 parts water by volume —— 1 cup	247	89	100	Trace	Trace	—	—	—	27	3	3	Trace	32	Trace	Trace	Trace	Trace	6
Limejuice:																		
Raw —— 1 cup	246	90	65	1	Trace	—	—	—	22	22	27	.5	256	20	.05	.02	.2	79
Canned, unsweetened —— 1 cup	246	90	65	1	Trace	—	—	—	22	22	27	.5	256	20	.05	.02	.2	52
Muskmelons, raw, with rind, without seed cavity:																		
Cantaloup, orange-fleshed (with rind and seed cavity, 5-in diam., 2 1/3 lb) —— 1/2 melon with rind[33]	477	91	80	2	Trace	—			20	38	44	1.1	682	9,240	.11	.08	1.6	90
Honeydew (with rind and seed cavity, 6 1/2-in diam., 5 1/4 lb) —— 1/10 melon with rind[33]	226	91	50	1	Trace	—			11	21	24	.6	374	60	.06	.04	.9	34
Oranges, all commercial varieties, raw:																		
Whole, 2 5/8-in diam., without peel and seeds (about 2 1/2 per lb with peel and seeds) —— 1 orange	131	86	65	1	Trace	—			16	54	26	.5	263	260	.13	.05	.5	66
Sections without membranes —— 1 cup	180	86	90	2	Trace	—			22	74	36	.7	360	360	.18	.07	.7	90
Orange juice:																		
Raw, all varieties —— 1 cup	248	88	110	2	Trace	—			26	27	42	.5	496	500	.22	.07	1.0	124
Canned, unsweetened —— 1 cup	249	87	120	2	Trace	—			28	25	45	1.0	496	500	.17	.05	.7	100
Frozen concentrate:																		
Undiluted, 6-fl oz can —— 1 can	213	55	360	5	Trace	—			87	75	126	.9	1,500	1,620	.68	.11	2.8	360
Diluted with 3 parts water by volume —— 1 cup	249	87	120	2	Trace	—			29	25	42	.2	503	540	.23	.03	.9	120
Dehydrated crystals, prepared with water (1 lb yields about 1 gal) —— 1 cup	248	88	115	1	Trace	—			27	25	40	.5	518	500	.20	.07	1.0	109
Orange and grapefruit juice:																		
Frozen concentrate:																		
Undiluted, 6-fl oz can —— 1 can	210	59	330	4	1	—			78	61	99	.8	1,308	800	.48	.06	2.3	302
Diluted with 3 parts water by volume —— 1 cup	248	88	110	1	Trace	—			26	20	32	.2	439	270	.15	.02	.7	102
Papayas, raw, 1/2-in cubes —— 1 cup	140	89	55	1	Trace	—			14	28	22	.4	328	2,450	.06	.06	.4	78
Peaches:																		
Raw:																		
Whole, 2 1/2-in diam., peeled, pitted (about 4 per lb with peels and pits) —— 1 peach	100	89	40	1	Trace	—			10	9	19	.5	202	[34]1,330	.02	.05	1.0	7
Sliced —— 1 cup	170	89	65	1	Trace	—			16	15	32	.9	343	[34]2,260	.03	.09	1.7	12
Canned, yellow-fleshed, solids and liquid (halves or slices):																		
Syrup pack —— 1 cup	256	79	200	1	Trace	—			51	10	31	.8	333	1,100	.03	.05	1.5	8
Water pack —— 1 cup	244	91	75	1	Trace	—			20	10	32	.7	334	1,100	.02	.07	1.5	7
Dried:																		
Uncooked —— 1 cup	160	25	420	5	1	—			109	77	187	9.6	1,520	6,240	.02	.30	8.5	29
Cooked, unsweetened, halves and juice —— 1 cup	250	77	205	3	1	—			54	38	93	4.8	743	3,050	.01	.15	3.8	5

[33] Weight includes rind. Without rind, the weight of the edible portion is 272 g for item 271 and 149 g for item 272.

[34] Represents yellow-fleshed varieties. For white-fleshed varieties, value is 50 International Units (I.U.) for 1 peach, 90 I.U. for 1 cup of slices.

(Continued)

Fruit Composition, Part I (Continued)

TABLE 2.F.43 (Continued)

(Dashes (—) denote lack of reliable data for a constituent believed to be present in measurable amount)

Foods, approximate measures, units, and weight (edible part unless footnotes indicate otherwise)		Water	Food energy	Pro-tein	Fat	Fatty Acids Saturated (total)	Fatty Acids Unsaturated Oleic	Fatty Acids Unsaturated Lino-leic	Carbo-hydrate	Calcium	Phos-phorus	Iron	Potas-sium	Vitamin A value	Thiamin	Ribo-flavin	Niacin	Ascorbic acid
	Grams	Per-cent	Cal-ories	Grams	Grams	Grams	Grams	Grams	Grams	Milli-grams	Milli-grams	Milli-grams	Milli-grams	Inter-national units	Milli-grams	Milli-grams	Milli-grams	Milli-grams
FRUITS AND FRUIT PRODUCTS—Con.																		
Frozen, sliced, sweetened:																		
10-oz container—— 1 container	284	77	250	1	Trace	—	—	—	64	11	37	1.4	352	1,850	0.03	0.11	2.0	35,116
Cup—— 1 cup	250	77	220	1	Trace	—	—	—	57	10	33	1.3	310	1,630	.03	.10	1.8	35,103
Pears:																		
Raw, with skin, cored:																		
Bartlett, 2 1/2-in diam. (about 2 1/2 per lb with cores and stems)—— 1 pear	164	83	100	1	1	—	—	—	25	13	18	.5	213	30	.03	.07	.2	7
Bosc, 2 1/2-in diam. (about 3 per lb with cores and stems)—— 1 pear	141	83	85	1	1	—	—	—	22	11	16	.4	83	30	.03	.06	.1	6
D'Anjou, 3-in diam. (about 2 per lb with cores and stems)—— 1 pear	200	83	120	1	1	—	—	—	31	16	22	.6	260	40	.04	.08	.2	8
Canned, solids and liquid, sirup pack, heavy (halves or slices)—— 1 cup	255	80	195	1	1	—	—	—	50	13	18	.5	214	10	.03	.05	.3	3
Pineapple:																		
Raw, diced—— 1 cup	155	85	80	1	Trace	—	—	—	21	26	12	.8	226	110	.14	.05	.3	26
Canned, heavy sirup pack, solids and liquid:																		
Crushed, chunks, tidbits—— 1 cup	255	80	190	1	Trace	—	—	—	49	28	13	.8	245	130	.20	.05	.5	18
Slices and liquid:																		
Large—— 1 slice; 2 1/4 tbsp liquid	105	80	80	Trace	Trace	—	—	—	20	12	5	.3	101	50	.08	.02	.2	7
Medium—— 1 slice; 1 1/4 tbsp liquid	58	80	45	Trace	Trace	—	—	—	11	6	3	.2	56	30	.05	.01	.1	4
Pineapple juice, unsweetened, canned—— 1 cup	250	86	140	1	Trace	—	—	—	34	38	23	.8	373	130	.13	.05	.5	2,80
Plums:																		
Raw, without pits:																		
Japanese and hybrid (2 1/8-in diam., about 6 1/2 per lb with pits)—— 1 plum	66	87	30	Trace	Trace	—	—	—	8	8	12	.3	112	160	.02	.02	.3	4
Prune-type (1 1/2-in diam., about 15 per lb with pits)—— 1 plum	28	79	20	Trace	Trace	—	—	—	6	3	5	.1	48	80	.01	.01	.1	1
Canned, heavy sirup pack (Italian prunes), with pits and liquid:																		
Cup—— 1 cup[36]	272	77	215	1	Trace	—	—	—	56	23	26	2.3	367	3,130	.05	.05	1.0	5
Portion—— 3 plums; 2 3/4 tbsp liquid[36]	140	77	110	1	Trace	—	—	—	29	12	13	1.2	189	1,610	.03	.03	.5	3

[27]Based on product with label claim of 100% of U.S. RDA in 6 fl oz.

[35]Value represents products without added ascorbic acid. For products with added ascorbic acid, value in milligrams is 116 for a 10-oz container, 103 for 1 cup.

[36]Weight includes pits. After removal of the pits, the weight

(Continued)

Fruit Composition, Part I (Continued)

TABLE 2.F.43 (Continued)

(Dashes (—) denote lack of reliable data for a constituent believed to be present in measurable amount)

Foods, approximate measures, units, and weight (edible part unless footnotes indicate otherwise)	Grams	Water (Percent)	Food energy (Calories)	Protein (Grams)	Fat (Grams)	Fatty Acids: Saturated (total) (Grams)	Unsaturated Oleic (Grams)	Linoleic (Grams)	Carbohydrate (Grams)	Calcium (Milligrams)	Phosphorus (Milligrams)	Iron (Milligrams)	Potassium (Milligrams)	Vitamin A value (International units)	Thiamin (Milligrams)	Riboflavin (Milligrams)	Niacin (Milligrams)	Ascorbic acid (Milligrams)
FRUITS AND FRUIT PRODUCTS—Con.																		
Prunes, dried, "softenized," with pits:																		
Uncooked—4 extra large or 5 large prunes.[36]	49	28	110	1	Trace	—	—	—	29	22	34	1.7	298	690	.04	.07	.7	1
Cooked, unsweetened, all sizes, fruit and liquid—1 cup[36]	250	66	255	2	1	—	—	—	67	51	79	3.8	695	1,590	.07	.15	1.5	2
Prune juice, canned or bottled—1 cup	256	80	195	1	Trace	—	—	—	49	36	51	1.8	602	—	.03	.03	1.0	5
Raisins, seedless:																		
Cup, not pressed down—1 cup	145	18	420	4	Trace	—	—	—	112	90	146	5.1	1,106	30	.16	.12	.7	1
Packet, 1/2 oz (1 1/2 tbsp)—1 packet	14	18	40	Trace	Trace	—	—	—	11	9	14	.5	107	Trace	.02	.01	.1	Trace
Raspberries, red:																		
Raw, capped, whole—1 cup	123	84	70	1	1	—	—	—	17	27	27	1.1	207	160	.04	.11	1.1	31
Frozen, sweetened, 10-oz container—1 container	284	74	280	2	1	—	—	—	70	37	48	1.7	284	200	.06	.17	1.7	60
Rhubarb, cooked, added sugar:																		
From raw—1 cup	270	63	380	1	Trace	—	—	—	97	211	41	1.6	548	220	.05	.14	.8	16
From frozen, sweetened—1 cup	270	63	385	1	1	—	—	—	98	211	32	1.9	475	190	.05	.11	.5	16
Strawberries:																		
Raw, whole berries, capped—1 cup	149	90	55	1	1	—	—	—	13	31	31	1.5	244	90	0.04	0.10	0.9	88
Frozen, sweetened:																		
Sliced, 10-oz container—1 container	284	71	310	1	1	—	—	—	79	40	48	2.0	318	90	.06	.17	1.4	151
Whole, 1-lb container (about 1 3/4 cups)—1 container	454	76	415	2	1	—	—	—	107	59	73	2.7	472	140	.09	.27	2.3	249
Tangerine, raw, 2 3/8-in diam., size 176, without peel (about 4 per lb with peels and seeds).—1 tangerine	86	87	40	1	Trace	—	—	—	10	34	15	.3	108	360	.05	.02	.1	27
Tangerine juice, canned, sweetened—1 cup	249	87	125	1	Trace	—	—	—	30	44	35	.5	440	1,040	.15	.05	.2	54
Watermelon, raw, 4 by 8 in wedge with rind and seeds (1/16 of 32 2/3-lb melon, 10 by 16 in).[37]—1 wedge with rind and seeds[37]	926	93	110	2	1	—	—	—	27	30	43	2.1	426	2,510	.13	.13	.9	30

[37] Weight includes rind and seeds. Without rind and seeds, weight of the edible portion is 426 g.

Source: Consumer and Food Economics Institute (1977). Nutritive value of foods. USDA Home and Garden Bull. 72.

Fruit Composition, Part II

TABLE 2.F.44
Composition of the edible portion (EP) and refuse in the material as purchased (AP)

Commodity and Description	Water	Protein	Fat	Carbohydrate Total (by dif.)	Fiber	Ash	Calories (per 100 g)	Notes	Refuse in A.P. (%)
		Percent of edible portion							
Bananas and plantains, fresh									
Bananas (*Musa sapientum*)	73.5	1.3	0.4	24.0	0.5	0.8	94	Edible raw when ripe; can apply in all areas	29
Plantains (*Musa paradisiaca*)	68.2	1.2	0.5	29.2	0.4	0.9	113	Require cooking; can apply in producing areas	34
Both, unspecified (*Musa spp.*)	71.0	1.2	0.4	26.5	0.5	0.9	103	Can apply in producing areas	31
Citrus, fresh									
Grapefruit (*Citrus grandis*)	89.0	0.6	0.2	9.8	0.5	0.4	39		36
Lemons (*C. limonia*)	88.7	0.8	0.5	9.5	0.9	0.5	41		38
Limes (*C. aurantifolia*)	86.8	0.9	0.4	11.2	1.3	0.7	47		(65)
Oranges (*C. sinensis*)	87.1	0.9	0.2	11.3	0.8	0.5	45	Juice only	28
Oranges, Mandarin type (*C. nobilis*)	87.4	0.8	0.3	10.9	0.6	0.6	44		29
Other fruits, fresh									
Apples (*Malus sylvestris*)	84.0	0.3	0.4	15.0	0.9	0.3	58		16
Apricots (*Prunus armeniaca*)	85.3	0.9	0.2	12.9	1.0	0.7	51		9
Avocados (*Persea spp.*), all types	75	1.7	16	6.1	1.5	1.2	162		32
Low fat types	82.9	1.4	8.3	6.5	1.5	0.9	98		33
High fat types	67.1	1.8	23.4	6.3	1.7	1.4	225		30
Berries									
Blackberries (*Rubus spp.*)	84.9	1.2	1.0	12.4	3.8	0.5	57		0
Blueberries (*Vaccinium spp.*)	85.0	0.7	0.7	13.3	1.9	0.3	56		0
Cranberries (*Oxycoccus macrocarpus*)	87.3	0.4	0.7	11.4	1.4	0.2	48		0
Currants (*Ribes spp.*)	83.7	1.4	0.4	13.9	3.2	0.6	58		3
Gooseberries (*Ribes spp.*)	88.4	1.0	0.4	9.8	2.0	0.4	42		1
Raspberries (*Rubus spp.*)	82.7	1.3	1.3	14.2	3.9	0.5	66		0
Strawberries (*Fragaria spp.*)	89.9	0.8	0.5	8.3	1.2	0.5	37		4
All, unspecified	86.5	1.0	0.7	11.3	2.4	0.5	50		2
Breadfruit, jackfruit, monkey fruit (*Artocarpus spp.*)	76.2	1.1	0.4	21.3	1.8	1.0	84		45
Cherimoya, custard apple, sweetsop (*Annona cherimola, A. reticulata, A. squamosa*)	73.3	1.9	0.5	23.5	2.9	0.8	95		40
Cherries (*Prunus spp.*)	83.4	1.1	0.4	14.6	0.5	0.5	60		9
Figs (*Ficus carica*)	81.7	1.2	0.4	16.1	1.4	0.6	65		3
Grapes (*Vitis spp.*)	81.5	0.8	0.4	16.8	0.5	0.5	67		8
Guavas (*Psidium spp.*)	80.6	1.0	0.4	17.3	6.2	0.7	69		22
Mangoes (*Mangifera indica*)	81.7	0.7	0.2	17.0	0.8	0.4	65		38

(Continued)

Fruit Composition, Part II (Continued)

Commodity and Description	Water	Protein	Fat	Carbohydrate Total (by dif.)	Fiber	Ash	Calories (per 100 g)	Notes	Refuse in A.P. (%)
		Percent of edible portion							
Melons:									
Muskmelons (*Cucumis melo*)	92.6	0.7	0.2	6.0	0.5	0.5	26		44
Watermelons (*Citrullus vulgaris*)	92.9	0.5	0.2	6.1	0.2	0.3	25		47
Both, unspecified	92.8	0.6	0.2	6.0	0.3	0.4	25		46
Papayas (*Carica papaya*)	88.6	0.6	0.1	10.1	0.9	0.6	39		34
Passion fruit or granadillo (*Passiflora* spp.)	80.0	0.6	(0)	18.9	(0)	0.5	70	Juice only	67
Peaches (*Amygdalus persica*)	86.6	0.8	0.2	11.8	0.6	0.6	47		12
Pears (*Pyrus communis*)	83.2	0.5	0.4	15.5	1.5	0.4	61		18
Persimmons, Japanese (*Diospyros kaki*)	79.6	0.8	0.3	18.7	1.2	0.6	73		20
Pineapples (*Ananas sativus*)	86.7	0.5	0.2	12.2	0.5	0.4	47		36
Plums (*Prunus* spp.)	82.0	0.8	0.2	16.5	0.5	0.5	64	Includes fresh prunes	6
Pomegranates (*Punica granatum*)	81.3	0.6	0.3	17.2	0.3	0.6	66		52
Quinces (*Cydonia oblonga*)	83.2	0.7	0.3	14.9	2.4	0.9	59		22
Sapodilla or sapote (*Achras sapota*)	75.8	0.6	1.1	22.0	2.4	0.5	90		23
Sapote or marmalade plum (*Calocarpum mammosum*)	67.9	1.3	0.5	29.3	2.5	1.0	114		26
Soursop (*Annona muricata*)	80.2	0.8	0.4	18.0	1.0	0.6	71		34
Unspecified (group figures)[1] Temperate areas	84.6	0.6	0.3	14.1	0.9	0.4	55	Other than citrus fruits, bananas, and plantains	17
Subtropical areas	83.2	0.8	0.9	14.6	1.1	0.5	63		21
Tropical areas	83.4	0.8	1.1	14.1	1.5	0.6	63		35
All regions	84.0	0.7	0.7	14.1	1.1	0.5	59		24
Fruits, canned									
General (excluding sugar)	90	0.5	0.2	9	0.7	0.3	36	Applies to net weight of canned fruit	0
Orange juice, unsweetened	86	0.6	0.1	12.9	—	0.4	49		0
Grapefruit juice, unsweetened	89.4	0.5	0.2	9.4	—	0.5	37		0
Fruits, dried									
Figs, dates, prunes, raisins, jujubes	21.1	3.1	0.8	73.0	3.4	2	280		11
Apples, apricots, peaches, pears	20	3	0.6	73.8	4.5	2.6			0
All, unspecified	20.4	3	0.7	73.6	4	2.3	281		5
Olives									
Processed (green)	75	1	14	4	0.9	6	135	Ordinary cure	20
Greek process (ripe)	43.4	2.1	32.3	14.9	3.8	7.3	331	Heavy brine	27

[1] Group figures are unsatisfactory because the proportions of different kinds vary widely within areas and the fruits are dissimilar in many respects (for example, compare apples, avocados, and watermelons). Thus, group figures should be applied only to quantities of unspecified kinds, i.e., the residual supply, after making separate estimates for the principal kinds.

Source: Chatfield, C. *Food Composition Tables for International Use.* Food and Agriculture Organization, United Nations, Rome.

Fruit, Cooking

TABLE 2.F.45
Cooking guide for fresh fruit

Kind of Fruit	Amount[1] of Fruit	How to Prepare	Amount of Water	Amount of Sugar	Cooking Time After Adding Fruit
			Cups	Cups	Minutes
Apples	8 medium-size	Pare and slice	½	¼	8–10, for slices / 12–15, for sauce
Apricots	15	Halve, pit, peel if desired.	½	¾	5
Cherries	1 qt	Remove pits	1	⅔	5
Cranberries	1 lb	Sort	1 or 2, as desired[2]	2	5
Peaches	6 medium-size	Peel, pit, halve, or slice.	¾	¾	5
Pears	6 medium-size	Pare, core, halve, or slice.	⅔	⅓	10, for soft varieties / 20–25, for firm varieties
Plums	8 large	Halve, pit	½	⅔	5
Rhubarb	1½ lb	Slice	¾	⅔	2–5

[1] Makes 6 servings, about ½ cup each.
[2] Cranberries make 6 servings with 1 cup water; 8 servings with 2 cups water.

Source: USDA (1969). Food for us all. *Yearbook of Agriculture.*

Fruit Dressing

TABLE 2.F.46

Clear Fruit Dressing

½ cup salad oil
2 tbsp vinegar
3 tbsp sugar

½ tsp salt
¼ tsp dry mustard (optional)

Procedure

Mix the dry ingredients, add vinegar and oil and shake thoroughly. Keep refrigerated.

Source: Kintner, T. C., and Mangel, M. Vinegars and salad dressings. Univ. Missouri Agric. Exp. Sta. Bull. *631.*

Fruit, Dried, Simmering

TABLE 2.F.47
Guide to simmering dried fruits

Guide to Simmering Dried Fruits

Kind of fruit	Amount of fruit	Amount of water	Amount of sugar	Cooking time	Approximate number of ½-cup servings [1]
	Ounces	*Cups*	*Cups*	*Minutes*	
Apples -------	8	3½	⅓	10	8
Apricots ------ {	8	2¼	⅓	10	6
	11	3	½	10	8
Mixed fruits -- {	8	2¼	¼	20	5
	11	3	⅓	20	7
Peaches ------ {	8	3	⅓	25	6
	11	4	½	25	8
Pears -------- {	8	2	⅛	25	4
	11	3	¼	25	6
Prunes, unpitted ---- {	16	4	¼	25	9
	32	8	½	25	19

[1] Fruit and liquid.

Source: USDA (1975). Fruits in family meals: A guide for consumers. USDA Home and Garden Bull. *125*.

Fruit, Frozen Yield

TABLE 2.F.48
Approximate yield of frozen fruits from fresh

Fruit	Fresh, as Purchased or Picked	Frozen
Apples	1 bu. (48 lb.)	32 to 40 pt.
	1 box (44 lb.)	29 to 35 pt.
	1 ¼ to 1 ½ lb.	1 pt.
Apricots	1 bu. (48 lb.)	60 to 72 pt.
	1 crate (22 lb.)	28 to 33 pt.
	⅔ to ⅘ lb.	1 pt.
Berries [1]	1 crate (24 qt.)	32 to 36 pt.
	1⅓ to 1½ pt.	1 pt.
Cantaloups	1 dozen (28 lb.)	22 pt.
	1 to 1¼ lb.	1 pt.
Cherries, sweet or sour	1 bu. (56 lb.)	36 to 44 pt.
	1¼ to 1½ lb.	1 pt.
Cranberries	1 box (25 lb.)	50 pt.
	1 peck (8 lb.)	16 pt.
	½ lb.	1 pt.
Currants	2 qt. (3 lb.)	4 pt.
	¾ lb.	1 pt.

(Continued)

Fruit, Frozen Yield (*Continued*)

TABLE 2.F.48 (*Continued*)

Fruit	Fresh, as Purchased or Picked	Frozen
Peaches	1 bu. (48 lb.)	32 to 48 pt.
	1 lug box (20 lb.)	13 to 20 pt.
	1 to 1½ lb.	1 pt.
Pears	1 bu. (50 lb.)	40 to 50 pt.
	1 western box (46 lb.)	37 to 46 pt.
	1 to 1¼ lb.	1 pt.
Pineapple	5 lb.	4 pt.
Plums and prunes	1 bu. (56 lb.)	38 to 56 pt.
	1 crate (20 lb.)	13 to 20 pt.
	1 to 1½ lb.	1 pt.
Raspberries	1 crate (24 pt.)	24 pt.
	1 pt.	1 pt.
Rhubarb	15 lb.	15 to 22 pt.
	⅔ to 1 lb.	1 pt.
Strawberries	1 crate (24 qt.)	38 pt.
	⅔ qt.	1 pt.

[1] Includes blackberries, blueberries, boysenberries, dewberries, elderberries, gooseberries, huckleberries, loganberries, and youngberries.

Source: USDA (1976). Home freezing of fruits and vegetables. USDA Home and Garden Bull. *10*.

Fruit Grade Uses

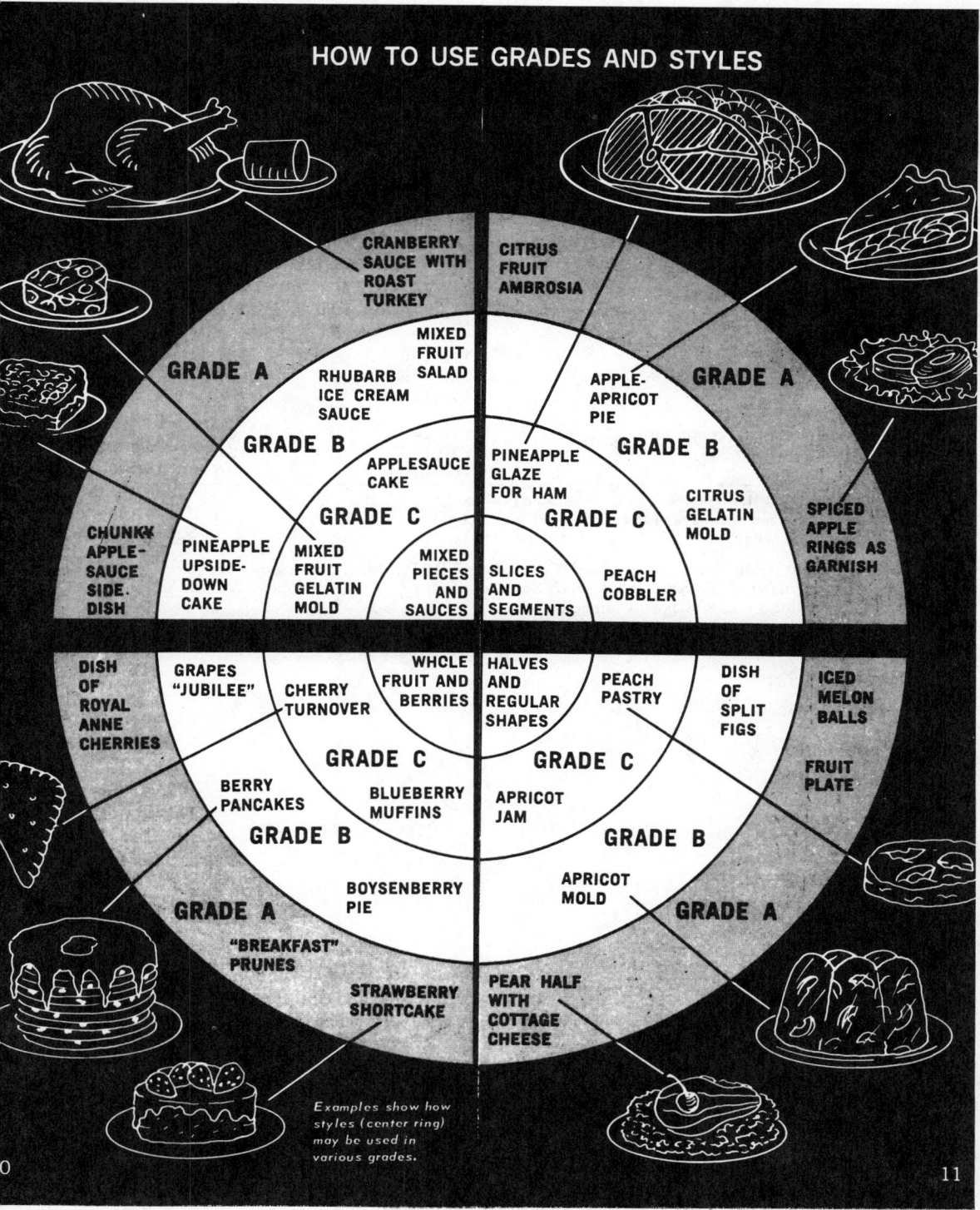

HOW TO USE GRADES AND STYLES

Examples show how styles (center ring) may be used in various grades.

FIGURE 2.F.16

rce: USDA (1977). How to buy canned and frozen fruits. USDA Home and Garden Bull. *191*.

Fruit, Growing Season, Storage Life

TABLE 2.F.49
Growing season for fruits in relation to storage life

Fruit	Full Bloom to Harvest	Normal Storage Life[1]
	Days	Days
Strawberries[2]		
Klondlike and others	24-28	5-7
Cherries[3]		
Black Tartarian	57	14
Bing	71	14
Napoleon	68	14
Apricots[4]		
Royal	100	7-21
Peaches[3]		
Belle of Georgia	122	14
Elberta	128	21-28
Pears[5]		
Bartlett	110-130	75-90
Bosc	130-145	90-105
Anjou	145-150	120-180
Apples[6]		
Yellow Transparent	70-75	0-7
Jonathan	140-145	60-90
Winesap	160-170	150-180

[1] Lutz and Hardenburg (1968) [4] Brown (1952)
[2] Wilson and Giamalva (1954) [5] Ryall, et al (1941)
[3] Tukey (1942) [6] Magness (1941)

Source: Ryall, A. L., and Pentzer, W. T. (editors) (1974). Fruit physiology after harvest. In *Handling, Transportation and Storage of Fruits and Vegetables*, Vol. 2. AVI Publishing Co., Westport, Connecticut.

Fruit Harvest Dates

TABLE 2.F.50
Opening and closing canning dates

| States and Territories | Apples | Apricots | Berries | | | | | | | Cherries | Figs |
			Black	Blue	Cran	Goose	Logan	Rasp	Straw		
Arkansas	Aug. 15 Nov. 15		June 1 July 15						Apr. 1 Oct. 1		
California		June 8 Aug. 15								May 10 July 10	Aug. 15 Oct. 31
Colorado	Oct. 15 Dec. 15	July 10 Aug. 1								June 15 July 15	
Delaware	Oct. 1 Nov. 10										
Kansas	Aug. 1 Nov. 1										
Louisiana			June 1 July 31								May 1 July 31
Maine				Aug. 10 Sept. 15							
Maryland	Aug. 25 Dec. 1										
Massachu-setts					Sept. 1 Dec. 31						
Michigan	Aug. 1 Nov. 30		July 25 Aug. 10	July 25 Sept. 15		July 20 Aug. 20		July 5 July 20	June 10 July 10	July 1 Aug. 15	
Missis-sippi			June 1 July 31								May 1 July 31
Missouri	Aug. 15 Dec. 1		June 20 Aug. 1								
Montana										July 14 Aug. 15	
New Jersey			June 10 July 10	June 20 Aug. 20	Sept. 1 Dec. 31			July 15 Aug. 15	June 10 July 10		
New York	Sept. 15 Dec. 31	Aug. 1 Aug. 15						July 10 Aug. 20	June 14 July 17	June 25 Aug. 15	
Ohio	Sept. 15 Dec. 31									July 5 Aug. 15	
Okla-homa	Aug. 15 Oct. 15		June 1 July 1								
Oregon	Sept. 15 Dec. 31	Aug. 15 Sept. 15	Aug. 1 Oct. 10			May 15 June 15	June 20 Aug. 1	June 25 Aug. 1	May 20 June 25	June 20 July 31	
Pennsyl-vania	Aug. 15 Dec. 31									June 30 July 31	
Texas			June 10 July 31								May 1 July 1
Utah	Oct. 15 Dec. 15	July 10 Aug. 1						July 1 July 20	June 15 July 15	June 15 July 15	
Virginia	Aug. 15 Dec. 31										
Washing-ton	Sept. 15 Dec. 31	Aug. 25 Sept. 20	Aug. 15 Oct. 15	Oct. 1 Oct. 30		May 15 June 15	June 25 Aug. 1	July 1 Aug. 1	June 1 July 1	June 25 July 31	
West Virginia	Aug. 15 Nov. 30										
Wisconsin				June 10 Aug. 30	Oct. 1 Nov. 20	June 25 Aug. 1			June 10 July 20	June 25 Aug. 20	
Ontario, Canada	Sept. 15 Dec. 31		Aug. 1 Sept. 1					July 10 Aug. 17	June 14 July 17	July 1 Aug. 10	
Quebec, Canada	Sept. 15 Nov. 30			Aug. 15 Sept. 15							
Van-couver, B. C.	Sept. 1 Dec. 1	July 15 Aug. 30	Sept. 1 Oct. 30				July 1 Aug. 30	July 1 Aug. 30	June 1 July 30	July 1 July 30	

(Continued)

Fruit Harvest Dates   (Continued)

TABLE 2.F.50   (Continued)

OPENING AND CLOSING CANNING DATES—Continued
FRUITS—Continued

States and Territories	Grapes	Grape-fruit	Lemons	Olives	Oranges	Peaches	Pears	Pineapple	Plums	Prunes
Alabama						June 10 Aug. 1				
Arizona		Nov. 1 May 1								
Arkansas	Aug. 15 Oct. 1					July 10 Sept. 1				
California	Aug. 1 Sept. 25		All Year	Oct. 15 Feb. 15	July 1 Nov. 15	July 10 Sept. 20	July 18 Sept. 15		July 15 Sept. 30	All Year
Colorado						Aug. 25 Sept. 25	Sept. 15 Oct. 20			
Delaware						Aug. 1 Sept. 1	Oct. 1 Nov. 1			
Florida		Oct. 15 June 15			Dec. 1 June 1					
Georgia						June 10 Aug. 1				
Hawaii								Jan. 1– Mar. 15 June 15– Sept. 30		
Idaho										Sept. 15 Oct. 15
Maryland						Aug. 1 Sept. 15	Oct. 1 Nov. 15			
Michigan	Sept. 1 Oct. 30					Sept. 1 Oct. 15	Sept. 1 Dec. 30		Aug. 1 Aug. 30	
Missouri	Aug. 25 Oct. 15					July 25 Sept. 1				
New Jersey						Aug. 1 Sept. 15	Sept. 20 Nov. 15			
New York	Oct. 1 Nov. 1					Sept. 1 Oct. 5	Sept. 15 Nov. 10		Aug. 10 Oct. 7	Sept. 10 Oct. 5
North Carolina						July 15 Aug. 15				
Oregon						Aug. 15 Oct. 1	Aug. 10 Nov. 1		Aug. 15 Sept. 30	Sept. 1 Sept. 30
Pennsylvania	Sept. 20 Nov. 1					Aug. 15 Sept. 15				
Puerto Rico		Nov. 15 Apr. 30						May 1 June 30		
South Carolina						July 15 Aug. 15				
Texas		Dec. 1 May 1				June 10 Aug. 1				
Utah						Aug. 25 Sept. 25	Sept. 15 Oct. 20			Sept. 15 Oct. 15
Washington						Aug. 15 Sept. 20	Aug. 10 Nov. 1		Aug. 15 Sept. 30	Sept. 1 Sept. 30
Ontario, Canada						Sept. 1 Oct. 5	Sept. 15 Dec. 15		Sept. 15 Oct. 7	
Vancouver, B. C.						Aug. 15 Sept. 30	Aug. 15 Oct. 10		Aug. 15 Oct. 15	Aug. 15 Oct. 15

Source: (1973). *The Almanac of the Canning, Freezing, Preserving Industries*, 58th Edition. E. E. Judge & Son, Inc.

Fruit Inspection Labels

The grade name, such as "Grade A," is sometimes shown without "U.S." in front of it. If the grade name alone appears on a container, the contents should meet the quality for the grade shown, even though the product has not been officially inspected for grade.

FIGURE 2.F.17

Source: USDA (1977). How to buy canned and frozen fruits. USDA Home and Garden Bull. *191*.

Fruit Juice Flavors

TABLE 2.F.51
Ranges in PPM of different flavors used in imitation fruit juice drinks

Flavor Compound	Usage Level in ppm
Lime oil	10–150
Lemon oil	10–200
Orange oil	10–150
Grapefruit oil	10–150
Allyl heptanoate	1–4
Benzaldehyde	10–30
Benzyl butyrate	1–6
Citral	5–15
Cognac	3–8
Geraniol	1–2
Isoamyl acetate	10–25
Isoamyl butyrate	10–15
Isoamyl formate	5–10
Ethyl acetate	30–50
Ethyl butyrate	10–30
Linalool	1–3
Methyl anthranilate	5–20

Source: Phillips, G. F. (1971). Imitation fruit flavored beverages and fruit juice bases. In *Fruit and Vegetable Juice Processing Technology*, 2nd Edition. D. K. Tressler and M. A. Joslyn (editors). AVI Publishing Co., Westport, Connecticut.

Fruit Label

Federal regulations require that the following information be included on the front panel of the label of a can or package.

The common or usual name of the fruit.

The form (or style) of fruit, such as whole, slices, or halves. If the form is visible through the package, it need not be stated.

For some fruits, the variety or color.

Sirups, sugar, or liquid in which a fruit is packed must be listed near the name of the product.

The total contents (net weight) must be stated in ounces for containers holding 1 pound or less. From 1 pound to 4 pounds, weight must be given in both total ounces and pounds and ounces (or pounds and fractions of a pound).

FIGURE 2.F.18

Source: USDA (1977). How to buy canned and frozen fruits. USDA Home and Garden Bull. *191.*

Fruit Salad Dressing

TABLE 2.F.52

Ingredients	
2 egg yolks	2 tbsp vinegar
2 tbsp sugar	¼ cup pineapple or other fruit juice
1 tbsp butter	

Procedure

Beat the egg until fluffy. Add the other ingredients, and blend. Cook in the top of the double boiler until thick. Cool. Combine with an equal quantity of whipped cream just before using. Refrigerate.

Source: Kintner, T. C., and Mangel, M. Vinegars and salad dressings. Univ. Missouri Agric. Exp. Sta. Bull. *631.*

Fruit Sauces

TABLE 2.F.53
Guide to making fresh fruit sauces

Kind of fruit	Amount of fruit, as purchased	Amount of water	Amount of sugar [1]	Cooking time after adding fruit	Approximate yield
	Pounds	*Cups*	*Cups*	*Minutes*	*Cups*
Apples...........	2	⅓	¼	12–15	3
Cherries..........	1	⅔	½	5	2
Cranberries.......	1	2	2	15	4 (whole) 3 (strained)
Peaches..........	1	⅔	½	5–8	2
Rhubarb..........	1½	¾	⅔	2–5	3

[1] For fruits of medium tartness. For very tart fruits, add more sugar.

Source: USDA (1972). Fruits in family meals. USDA Home and Garden Bull. *125.*

Fruit, Servings per pound (or Package)

TABLE 2.F.54
Servings per pound of fruit

	Servings per Market Unit [1]		Servings per Can (1 lb)
Fresh Fruit		**Canned Fruit**	
Apples ⎤		Served with liquid	4
Bananas ⎮		Drained	2 or 3
Peaches ⎬ 3 or 4 per lb			
Pears ⎮			**Servings per Package (8 oz)**
Plums ⎦			
Apricots ⎤		**Dried Fruit**	
Cherries, sweet ⎬ 5 or 6 per lb		Apples	8
Grapes, seedless ⎦		Apricots	6
Blueberries ⎤ 4 or 5 per pt		Mixed fruits	5
Raspberries ⎦		Peaches	6
Strawberries 5 or 6 per pint		Pears	4
		Prunes	4 or 5

[1] As purchased.

	Servings per Package (10 or 12 oz)
Frozen Fruit	
Blueberries	3 or 4
Peaches	2 or 3
Raspberries	2 or 3
Strawberries	2 or 3

Source: USDA (1978). Nutrition, food at work for you. USDA Home and Garden Bull. *1.*

Fruit, Simmering

TABLE 2.F.55
Guide to simmering fresh fruits

Kind of Fruit	Amount of fruit, as purchased	Amount of water	Amount of sugar [1]	Cooking time after adding fruit	Approximate number of ½-cup servings
	Pound	*Cup*	*Cup*	*Minutes*	
Apples _____	2	½	¼	8–10	6
Apricots _____	1½	½	¾	5	6
Peaches _____	1½	¾	¾	5	6
Pears:					
Soft varieties __	2	⅔	⅓	10	6
Firm varieties __	2	⅔	⅓	20–25	6
Plums _____	1	½	⅔	5	6

[1] For fruit of medium tartness.   For very tart fruit, add more sugar.

Source: USDA (1975). Fruits in family meals: A guide for consumers. USDA Home and Garden Bull. *125.*

Fruit Storage I

TABLE 2.F.56
Recommended cold storage conditions, heat of respiration, and loss in weight of fruits grown in the tropics

Fruits	Temp. °F	Relative Humidity %	Storage Life Wk	Heat Evolution[a] BTU/ton-day	Weight Loss[b] %
Acerola	32	85–90	8		
Avocado, West Indian	55	85–90	2	10,400	6.3
Avocado, Guatemalan	42–45	85–90	4	4,440–7,700	10.0
Banana					
'Lacatan', green	55–60	85–90	4	5,280–6,600	6.2
'Lacatan', ripe	55	85–90	1.5	9,282	
'Latundan', green	58–60	85–90	3–4	5,500–6,600	5.8
'Latundan', ripe	55–58	85–90	1		
'Cavendish', green	55–58	85–90	3–4	6,600	5.2
'Cavendish', ripe	55	85–90	1.5	11,200	
'Plantain', green	50	85–90	5	3,960	6.0
'Plantain', ripe	45–50	85–90	1.5		
'Poovan', green	55	85–90	2–3	3,520–5,500	6.7
Caimito, ripe	37–42	90	3	1,600–4,400	
Cashew	32–35	85–90	5	6,600–7,600	22.0
Citrus					
Calamondin	48–50	90	2	5,500	6.5
'Coorg' mandarin (main crop)	42–45	85–90	8	4,400	13.0
'Coorg' mandarin (rainy season)	42–45	85–90	6	2,200–3,300	15.8
'Valencia' orange	40–43	88–92	5–6	2,545	12.0
'Swikom' orange	48–50	85–90	4–5	3,300	8.0
'Ponkan' orange	40	85–90	3–4	2,200	7.5
'Sathgudi' orange	42–45	85–90	16	1,760–2,229	15.0

(Continued)

Fruit Storage I (Continued)

TABLE 2.F.56 (Continued)

Fruits	Temp. °F	Relative Humidity %	Storage Life Wk	Heat Evolution[a] BTU/ton-day	Weight Loss[b] %
Lime, yellow	52–55	85–90	8	1,760–2,640	15.0
Lime, green	52–55	85–90	7	880–1,760	18.0
Lemon	42–45	85–90	6	1,600–2,680	
Grapefruit	42–45	85–90	8–12	1,200–1,530	
Pomelo	45–48	85–90	12	1,800	
Custard apple	41	85–90	6		
Date	44	85–90	2		
Durian	39–42	85–90	6–8		
Fig	32–35	85–90	7	800–1,400	11.5
Guava	47–50	85–90	2–5	7,040–7,700	14.0
Indian Gooseberry	32–35	85–90	8		
Jackfruit	52–55	85–90	6		15.6
Langsat	52–58	85–90	2	15,400–16,000	24.3
Lychee	35	85–90	8–12		
Mango					
'Carabao'	45–50	85–90	2.5–3.5	6,700	5.1
'Pico'	45–50	85–90	2.5	6,700	6.2
'Badami'	47–50	85–90	4	11,000–13,200	6.8
'Raspuri'	42–45	85–90	6	11,000–13,200	6.8
Mangosteen	39–42	85–90	7		
Papaya, green	50	85–90	3–4	2,500	5.8
Papaya, turning	47	85–90	2–3		
Passion fruit, purple	42–45	85–90	3		32.0
Persimmon	32–35	85–90	7		
Pineapple, all green	47–50	85–90	4–6	1,700	4.0
Pineapple, 25% yellow	40–44	85–90	1–2		
Plum					
'Alu Bokharo'	32–35	85–90	2	1,700–1,920	5.2–9.6
'Gaviotaa' and 'Rubio'	32–35	85–90	3	1,700–1,920	5.2–7.8
'Shiro' and 'Hale'	32–35	85–90	4	1,760–1,920	5.2–12.9
Pomegranate, 'Khandari'	32–35	85–90	11		
Rambutan	50	90–95	1–2.5	13,200	6.0–12.0
Santol, 'Bangkok'	45–48	85–90	3		
Sapota, turning	67–70	85–90	2.5	3,300–5,500	12.0
Sapota, ripe	32–36	85–90	2		
Sugar apple, turning	45	85–90	4		
Sugar apple, ripe	34–37	85–90	2		

Source: Authors' unpublished data.

[a]Represents steady state heat production during storage at indicated temperatures.
[b]Loss in weight upon removal from storage at indicated storage periods.

Source: Pantastico, E. B., Chattopadhyay, T. K., and Subramanyam, H. (1975). Storage and commercial storage operations. In *Postharvest Physiology, Handling and Utilization of Tropical and Subtropical Fruits and Vegetables.* E. B. Pantastico (editor). AVI Publishing Co., Westport, Connecticut.

Fruit Storage II

TABLE 2.F.57

Hold at room temperature until ripe; then refrigerate, uncovered:

Apples	Grapes	Peaches
Apricots	Melons, except watermelons	Pears
Avocados	Nectarines	Plums
Berries		Tomatoes
Cherries		

Store in cool room or refrigerate, uncovered:

Grapes
Grapefruit   Limes
Lemons   Oranges

Source: USDA (1978). Nutrition, food at work for you. USDA Home and Garden Bull. *1.*

Frying Time

TABLE 2.F.58
Approximate frying times for conventional fryers

Food Item	Frying Time (Min)
Chicken	
Raw pieces	10–15
Fritters	3–4
Sea foods	
Fish fillets	3–5
Clams	3–4
Scallops	3–5
Shrimp	3–4
Oysters	3–5
Vegetables	
Potatoes, $\frac{1}{4}$ in. cut	4–6
Potatoes, $\frac{3}{8}$ in. cut	5–7
Potatoes, $\frac{1}{2}$ in. cut	6–8
Cauliflower	2–4
Eggplant	5–7
Onions	2–3
Miscellaneous	
Doughnuts	2–3
Corn on the cob	3–4
Meat turnovers	5–7
French toast	2–3

Source: Kazarian, E. A. (editor) (1975). Equipment requirements. In *Food Service Facilities Planning.* AVI Publishing Co., Westport, Connecticut.

Fuel, Heating Value

TABLE 2.F.59
Heating value of typical fuels

Fuel	High heating value Btu/lb
Coal	11,000–14,000
Oil	18,000–19,500
Natural gas	700–1,000
Saturated hydrocarbons ($C_n H_{2n+2}$)	21,000–23,000
Unsaturated hydrocarbons ($C_n H_{2n}$)	18,000–21,000
Lignite (dry)	6,000–7,000
Bagasse (dry)	8,000–9,000
Gasoline	20,200
Kerosene	19,900
Fuel oil	18,500
Hardwoods	8,100–8,900
Softwoods	8,400–11,000

Source: Hall, C. W., Farrall, A. W., and Rippen, A. L. (editor) (1971). Energy. In *Encyclopedia of Food Engineering.* AVI Publishing Co., Westport, Connecticut.

Fumigants

TABLE 2.F.60
Fumigants and amounts used per 1000 cu ft of air space

Fumigant	Amount	Comment
Carbon disulfide	20 lb	Explosive, inflammable
Hydrogen cyanide	8 oz	Very toxic to man, leaves residue
Methyl bromide	1 lb	Toxic to man
Ethylene dichloride-carbon tetrachloride	15–20 lb	Anesthetic to man
Ethylene oxide-ethylene dichloride	10–15 lb	Anesthetic to man
Ethyl formate	5–10 lb	
Ethylene oxide	2–4 lb	
Chloropicrin	1 lb	Lachrymator
Sulfur dioxide	Burning sulfur fumes	Inexpensive

Source: Jacobs, M. B. (editor). *The Chemistry and Technology of Food and Food Products*, Vol. 1, 2nd Edition. Interscience Publishers, New York.

Fungi Food Products

TABLE 2.F.61
Some common oriental foods which are produced by processes in which filamentous fungi are used

Food Type	Consistency	Raw Materials	Fungus Employed
Miso	Paste	Soybeans and rice	*Aspergillus oryzae*
Shoyu	Liquid	Soybeans and rice or wheat	*Aspergillus oryzae*
Tempeh	Solid	Soybeans or coconut meat	*Rhizopus oligosporus*
Ang-khak	Solid	Rice	*Monascus purpureus*
Ontjom	Solid	Peanut press cake	*Neurospora sitophila*
Sufu	Moist solid	Soybean "milk"	*Actinomucor elegans*
Meitauza	Solid	Residuum from preparation of soybean "milk"	*Actinomucor elegans*
Ketjap	Liquid	Black soybeans	*Aspergillus oryzae*
Katsuobushi	Solid	Bonito fish	*Aspergillus glaucus*

Source: Gray, W. D. (1974). Fungi as food. In *Encyclopedia of Food Technology*. A. H. Johnson and M. S. Peterson (editors). AVI Publishing Co., Westport, Connecticut.

Gestation Periods

TABLE 2.G.1
Gestation periods of domestic and wild animals

	Days		Days	Months
Domestic Animals		**Wild Animals**		
Ass	365	Ape, Barbary	210	
Cat	63–65	Bear, black		7
Cattle		Bison		9
Aberdeen-Angus	281	Camel	410	
Ayrshire	279	Coyote	60–64	
Brown Swiss	290	Deer, Virginia	197–220	
Charolais	289	Elephant		20–22
Guernsey	283	Elk, Wapiti		8½
Hereford	285	Giraffe		14–15
Holstein-Friesian	279	Hare	38	
Jersey	279	Hippopotamus	225–250	
Red Poll	285	Kangaroo, red	32–34[1]	
Shorthorn, beef	282	Leopard	92–95	
Shorthorn, milking	282	Lion	108	
Simmental	289	Llama		11
Dog	58–63	Marmoset	140–150	
Goat	151	Moose	240–250	
Horse		Muskrat	28–30	
Heavy	333–345	Otter		9–10
Light	330–337	Panther	90–93	
Pig	112–115	Porcupine	112	
Sheep		Pronghorn	230–240	
Mutton breeds	144–147	Raccoon	63	
Wool breeds	148–151	Reindeer		7–8
		Rhinoceros,		
Laboratory and Fur Animals		African	530–550	
Chinchilla	105–128	Seal		11
Ferret	42	Shrew	20	
Fisher	338–358	Skunk	62–65	
Fox	49–55	Squirrel, gray	44	
Marten, European	236–274	Tapir	390–400	
Pine Marten	220–265	Tiger	105–113	
Mink	40–75	Walrus		12
Monkey, macaque	150–180	Whale, sperm		16
Mouse	18–20	Woodchuck	31–32	
Nutria (coypu)	120–134	Wolf	60–63	

[1] Delayed development as long as a "joey" is in the pouch.

Source: (1973). *The Merck Veterinary Manual*, 4th Edition, Merck & Co., Rahway, New Jersey.

Gland Weights

TABLE 2.G.2
Weights of important glands or tissues of meat-producing animals (weights in grams, ounces, or pounds)

Portion	Beef Animal	Sheep	Hog
Pineal body	0.32 g	0.04–0.12 g	0.10 g
Pituitary gland	3.0 g	0.37–0.55 g	0.33–0.78 g
Ovary	5.7 g	0.76 g	3.15 g
Testis	$\frac{1}{2}$ lb	2 oz	3–4 oz
Suprarenal	11–15 g	1.5–2 g	3–5 g
Thyroid	1–$1\frac{1}{2}$ oz	2–9 g	4–10 g
Thymus	$\frac{1}{3}$–$\frac{1}{2}$ lb	15–25 g	9–35 g
Pancreas	$\frac{1}{2}$–1 lb	1 oz	$1\frac{1}{2}$–2 oz
Stomach	16–20 lb	1–2 lb	2–4 lb
Spleen	1–2 lb	$\frac{1}{6}$–$\frac{1}{2}$ lb	$\frac{1}{3}$–$\frac{3}{4}$ lb
Kidney	$\frac{1}{2}$–$1\frac{1}{2}$ lb	3–4 oz	$\frac{1}{3}$–$1\frac{1}{8}$ lb
Heart	$3\frac{1}{2}$–$4\frac{1}{2}$ lb	$\frac{3}{8}$–$\frac{5}{8}$ lb	$\frac{1}{2}$–$\frac{3}{4}$ lb
Lungs	4–5 lb	$\frac{1}{2}$–1 lb	1–$1\frac{1}{2}$ lb
Brain and cord	20–26 oz	6–9 oz	10–16 oz
Liver	10 lb	1–2 lb	2–4 lb
Blood	30–40 lb	3–5 lb	5–10 lb
Skin, vessels, etc.	65–75 lb	12–14 lb	Not Removed
Bones and muscles	560–600 lb	37–43 lb	160–175 lb
Total	1,000 lb	85–90 lb	215–225 lb

Source: Moulton, C. R., and Lewis, W. L. *Meat Through the Microscope*, Revised Edition. Institute of Meat Packaging, University of Chicago, Chicago.

Glass Jar Tops

FIGURE 2.G.1
Components of two kinds of tops for glass jars for home canning

Source: USDA (1977). Home canning of fruits and vegetables. USDA Home and Garden Bull. *8.*

Glutamate

TABLE 2.G.3
The glutamate content of foods

Product	Percentage of Protein[1] in Food	Percentage of Glutamate[1] in Protein	Total Glutamate[1] (g/100 g)	Free Glutamate[2] (g/100 g)
Milk				
Cow	3.5	23.4	0.819	0.004 [5]
Human	1.4	16.4	0.229	0.020 [5]
Milk Products				
Casein	100.0	23.0	23.052	—
Buttermilk	3.5	17.7	0.620	0.004 [6]
Cheese				
Camembert	17.5	27.4	4.787	ca. 0.600 [6, 7]
Parmesan	36.0	27.4	9.847	ca. 0.600 [6, 7]
Poultry Products				
Eggs	12.8	12.4	1.583	0.023 [3]
Chicken	20.6	16.1	3.309	0.044 [2]
Duck	21.4	17.0	3.636	0.069 [3]
Meat				
Beef	18.8	15.1	2.846	0.033 [2]
Lamb	18.0	15.2	2.730	0.020 [4]
Pork	15.2	15.3	2.325	0.023 [2]
Fish				
Cod	16.5	12.7	2.101	0.009 [3]
Mackerel	18.7	12.7	2.382	0.036 [2]
Salmon	17.4	12.7	2.216	0.020 [4]
Vegetables				
Peas	23.8	23.5	5.583	0.200 [4]
Corn	10.0	17.7	1.765	0.130 [4]
Beets	1.6	16.0	0.256	0.030 [4]
Carrots	1.2	18.2	0.218	0.033 [2]
Onions	1.4	14.9	0.208	0.018 [2]
Spinach	2.3	12.6	0.289	0.039 [2]
Tomatoes	1.0	23.8	0.238	0.140 [2]

1–Orr, M. L. and Watt, B. K., "Amino Acid Content of Foods", Home Economics Research Report #4, U.S. Government Printing Office, 1957.

2–Maeda, S., et al, Journal of Home Economics (Japan) 9 163 (1968).

3–Ibid, 12 105 (1969).

4–Hac, L. R., et al, Food Technology 3 351 (1949).

5–Private Communication. Research Laboratories, Ajinomoto Company, Inc., Tokyo, Japan.

6–Private Communication, Research Laboratories, C.O.F.A.G., Paris, France.

7–Müller, H. Z., Ernährungswissenschaft 10 83 (1970).

Source: International Glutamate Technical Committee (1974). The Remarkable Story of Monosodium Glutamate.

Glutamate Addition

TABLE 2.G.4
Comparison of glutamate ingested in foods with glutamate added to foods as a flavor enhancer

Food	Total Glutamate Naturally Present %	Free Glutamate Naturally Present %	Recommended Addition of MSG* %	MSG in Proportion to Total Glutamate %
Beef	2.846	0.033	0.4	14.1
Chicken	3.309	0.044	0.3	9.1
Pork	2.325	0.023	0.4	17.2
Peas	5.583	0.200	0.2	3.6
Corn	1.765	0.130	0.2	11.3

*General Guideline: Use ½ teaspoon MSG per pound of meat or per 4 to 6 servings of vegetables.

Source: International Glutamate Technical Committee (1974). *The Remarkable Story of Monosodium Glutamate.*

Gluten-Free Diet

TABLE 2.G.5
Foods included and excluded in gluten-free diet

Type of Food	Foods Included	Foods Excluded
Beverage	Carbonated beverages, cocoa powder, coffee, tea, whole milk (not > 2½ cups/day)	Cereal beverages; cocoa mixes; malted milks, drinks made with malt or other excluded cereals; ale, beer
Bread	Bread and muffins made with arrowroot, corn, potato, rice, or soybean flour	Any made with wheat, barley, rye, or oat flour; crackers; pretzels; rusk; pancakes; prepared mixes
Cereal	Ready-to-eat corn and rice cereals, cornmeal, rice, hominy	Any made with wheat, oats, rye, bran, malt flavoring, barley, buckwheat; macaroni, noodles, spaghetti
Dessert	Blancmange, custards, and puddings made with allowable flours or starches; gelatin desserts; sherbert; tapioca; home-made ice cream; special cookies made without wheat, rye, or oat flour	Any containing wheat, rye, barley, or oat products, as commercial cakes, cookies, ice cream, pastries, pies, puddings, or those made from commercial mixes

(Continued)

Gluten-Free Diet (Continued)

TABLE 2.G.5 (Continued)

Type of Food	Foods Included	Foods Excluded
Fat	Butter, margarine, pure mayonnaise, cooking oils, shortening	Commercial salad dressings, wheat germ oil
Fruit	Any	
Meat, egg, or cheese	Any meat, fish, or fowl except those excluded; natural cheese; eggs	Meat, fish, or chicken loaf or croquettes made with bread or bread crumbs; cheese spreads; canned meat dishes, cold cuts unless pure meat; bread stuffings; gravy thickened with flour
Soup	Broth or bouillon; vegetable soup and cream soups made from allowable foods, thickened with cornstarch or potato flour only	Any containing excluded flours or starches
Sweets	Any except those prepared with excluded grain products	Candy containing wheat, rye, oats, barley
Vegetable	Any except those prepared with excluded grain products	
Miscellaneous	Salt, spices, vinegar, herbs, pickles, baking chocolate, olives, nuts, peanut butter	All gravies or sauces thickened with wheat flour; flavoring syrups, bottled meat sauces, malt extract

Source: Holvey, D. N. (1972). *The Merck Manual*, 12th Edition. Merck & Co., Rahway, New Jersey.

Goats, Milk Breeds

TABLE 2.G.6
Breeds of milk goats and their characteristics

Breed	Place of Origin	Color; Face, Ears, and Legs	Head Characteristics	Disqualification
French-Alpine	France; but from Swiss foundation stock.	Multicolored coats, with no standard markings.	Some have horns at birth and are disbudded, others are hornless; erect ears; straight nose.	Pendulous ears.
La Mancha	Spain	Any color or combination of colors.	Short ears; straight nose; hornless or neatly disbudded.	Anything other than gopher ears in males. Ears other than true La Mancha type in females.
Nubian	Nubia, in northeastern Africa.	Black and whites, tan and whites, red and whites are common, but they may be any of these colors without white markings.	Some born with horns and disbudded, others are hornless. Long drooping ears. Roman nose and prominent forehead. Does are beardless.	Upright ears.
Rock Alpine	United States.	Multicolored coats, with no standard markings.	Some have horns at birth and are disbudded, others are hornless; erect ears; straight nose.	
Saanen	Switzerland, in the Saanen Valley.	Pure white or creamy white.	Hornless animals preferred; straight nose; erect ears.	Large (1½" diameter or more) dark spot in hair; pendulous ears.
Swiss Alpine	Switzerland.	Chamoise; solid brown, ranging from light to a deep-red bay. Black points.	Hornless or neatly disbudded. Erect ears.	
Toggenburg	Switzerland, in the Toggenburg Valley.	Brown, with 2 white stripes on the face and white on the legs below the knees.	Hornless or debudded; straight or dished nose; erect ears.	Tricolor or piebald; large (1½" or more) white spot in males; pendulous ears.

In addition to the specific breed disqualifications given in the right-hand column, the American Dairy Goat Association lists the following as disqualifications in any breed: total blindness; permanent lameness or difficulty in walking; blind or non-functioning half of udder; blind teat; double teats; extra teats that interfere with milking; hermaphrodism; navel hernia; crooked face in bucks; and extra teats, teats cut off, or double orifice in bucks.

Source: Ensminger, M. E. (1969). *Animal Science.* Interstate Printers & Publishers, Danville, Illinois.

Grades, Meat

TABLE 2.G.7
Government grades for beef, veal, lamb, and pork

Beef Quality	Cutability	Veal	Lamb	Pork
Prime	1	Prime	Prime	U.S. No. 1
Choice	2	Choice	Choice	U.S. No. 2
Good	3	Good	Good	U.S. No. 3
Standard	4	Standard	Utility	U.S. No. 4
Commercial	5	Utility	Cull	Utility
Utility		Cull		
Cutter				
Canner				

Source: Lessons on Meat. (1974). National Live Stock and Meat Board, Chicago.

Grain Analysis

TABLE 2.G.8
Comparative nutrient analysis of wheat and corn

	Wheat		Corn[1]
	Hard	Soft	
Protein, % (N x 5.7)	11.93	10.48	7.84
Ash, %	1.54	1.41	1.03
Moisture, %	12.34	13.88	11.00
Crude fat, %	1.60	1.68	3.78
Crude fiber, %	2.28	1.91	1.89
Starch, %	57.13	57.49	
Gross energy, kcal/kg	3910	3782	3786
Lysine, %	0.33	0.34	0.17
Histidine, %	0.28	0.29	0.17
Arginine, %	0.57	0.59	0.44
Aspartic acid, %	0.63	0.61	
Threonine, %	0.36	0.35	0.34
Serine, %	0.59	0.58	
Glutamic acid, %	4.07	3.86	
Proline, %	1.31	1.21	
Glycine, %	0.53	0.50	
Alanine, %	0.45	0.44	
Cystine, %	0.29	0.32	0.09
Valine, %	0.54	0.52	0.34
Methionine, %	0.20	0.19	0.09
Isoleucine, %	0.45	0.41	0.44
Leucine, %	0.85	0.81	0.95
Tyrosine, %	0.38	0.35	
Phenylalanine, %	0.59	0.56	0.44
Minerals:			
Ca, %	0.035	0.026	
P, %	0.36	0.35	
K, %	0.37	0.39	
Na, %	0.007	0.006	
Mg, %	0.11	0.10	
Zn, ppm	42	31	
Fe, ppm	25	26	
Mn, ppm	30	26	
Cu, ppm	4.2	4.2	
Se, ppm	0.34	0.04	
B, ppm	1.3	2.0	
Sr, ppm	0.64	0.48	
Al, ppm	25.0	>5.0	
Ba, ppm	5.8	4.9	
Co, ppm	0.13	0.12	
Niacin, ppm	54.2	47.5	25.3
Pantothenic acid, ppm	9.3	8.5	3.8
Folic acid, ppm	0.385	0.391	
Thiamine, ppm	3.85	4.11	3.4
Riboflavin, ppm	1.57	1.43	1.3
Pyridoxine, ppm	2.39	1.86	
α-Tocopherol, ppm	13.3	14.9	
Betaine, ppm	716.7	1234.3	
Choline, ppm	1096.5	1060.4	

[1] Yellow U.S. #2

Source: Saunders, R. M., Walker, Jr., H. G., and Kohler, G. O. (1973). Feed uses of wheat and its products. In *Wheat: Production and Utilization*. G. E. Inglett (editor). AVI Publishing Co., Westport, Connecticut.

Grain Products, Composition

TABLE 2.G.9 (Continued)

Foods, approximate measures, units, and weight (edible part unless footnotes indicate otherwise)	Grams	Water Percent	Food energy Calories	Protein Grams	Fat Grams	Fatty Acids Saturated (total) Grams	Unsaturated Oleic Grams	Unsaturated Linoleic Grams	Carbohydrate Grams	Calcium Milligrams	Phosphorus Milligrams	Iron Milligrams	Potassium Milligrams	Vitamin A value International units	Thiamin Milligrams	Riboflavin Milligrams	Niacin Milligrams	Ascorbic acid Milligrams
GRAIN PRODUCTS—Con.																		
Bagel, 3-in diam.:																		
Egg---------- 1 bagel	55	32	165	6	2	0.5	0.9	0.8	28	9	43	1.2	41	30	.14	.10	1.2	0
Water-------- 1 bagel	55	29	165	6	1	.2	.4	.6	30	8	41	1.2	42	0	.15	.11	1.4	0
Barley, pearled, light, uncooked-- 1 cup	200	11	700	16	2	.3	.2	.8	158	32	378	4.0	320	0	.24	.10	6.2	0
Biscuits, baking powder, 2-in diam. (enriched flour, vegetable shortening):																		
From home recipe---- 1 biscuit	28	27	105	2	5	1.2	2.0	1.2	13	34	49	.4	33	Trace	.08	.08	.7	Trace
From mix---- 1 biscuit	28	29	90	2	3	.6	1.1	.7	15	19	65	.6	32	Trace	.09	.08	.8	Trace
Breadcrumbs (enriched):[38]																		
Dry, grated---- 1 cup	100	7	390	13	5	1.0	1.6	1.4	73	122	141	3.6	152	Trace	.35	.35	4.8	Trace
Breads:																		
Soft. See White bread (items 349-350).																		
Boston brown bread, canned, slice 3 1/4 by 1/2 in.[38]-- 1 slice	45	45	95	2	1	.1	.2	.2	21	41	72	.9	131	[39]0	.06	.04	.7	0
Cracked-wheat bread (3/4 enriched wheat flour, 1/4 cracked wheat):[38]																		
Loaf, 1 lb---- 1 loaf	454	35	1,195	39	10	2.2	3.0	3.9	236	399	581	9.5	608	Trace	1.52	1.13	14.4	Trace
Slice (18 per loaf)---- 1 slice	25	35	65	2	1	.1	.2	.2	13	22	32	.5	34	Trace	.08	.06	.8	Trace
French or vienna bread, enriched:[38]																		
Loaf, 1 lb---- 1 loaf	454	31	1,315	41	14	3.2	4.7	4.6	251	195	386	10.0	408	Trace	1.80	1.10	15.0	Trace
Slice:																		
French (5 by 2 1/2 by 1 in)-- 1 slice	35	31	100	3	1	.2	.4	.4	19	15	30	.8	32	Trace	.14	.08	1.2	Trace
Vienna (4 3/4 by 4 by 1/2 in)-- 1 slice	25	31	75	2	1	.2	.3	.3	14	11	21	.6	23	Trace	.10	.06	.8	Trace
Italian bread, enriched:																		
Loaf, 1 lb---- 1 loaf	454	32	1,250	41	4	.6	.3	1.5	256	77	349	10.0	336	0	1.80	1.10	15.0	0
Slice, 4 1/2 by 3 1/4 by 3/4 in.-- 1 slice	30	32	85	3	Trace	Trace	Trace	.1	17	5	23	.7	22	0	.12	.07	1.0	0
Raisin bread, enriched:[38]																		
Loaf, 1 lb---- 1 loaf	454	35	1,190	30	13	3.0	4.7	3.9	243	322	395	10.0	1,057	Trace	1.70	1.07	10.7	Trace
Slice (18 per loaf)---- 1 slice	25	35	65	2	1	.2	.3	.2	13	18	22	.6	58	Trace	.09	.06	.6	Trace
Rye Bread:																		
American, light (2/3 enriched wheat flour, 1/3 rye flour):[38]																		
Loaf, 1 lb---- 1 loaf	454	36	1,100	41	5	0.7	0.5	2.2	236	340	667	9.1	658	0	1.35	0.98	12.9	0
Slice (4 3/4 by 3 3/4 by 7/16 in)-- 1 slice	25	36	60	2	Trace	Trace	Trace	.1	13	19	37	.5	36	0	.07	.05	.7	0
Pumpernickel (2/3 rye flour, 1/3 enriched wheat flour):																		
Loaf, 1 lb---- 1 loaf	454	34	1,115	41	5	.7	.5	2.4	241	381	1,039	11.8	2,059	0	1.30	0.93	8.5	0
Slice (5 by 4 by 3/8 in)-- 1 slice	32	34	80	3	Trace	Trace	Trace	.2	17	27	73	.8	145	0	.09	.07	.6	0
White bread, enriched:[38]																		
Soft-crumb type:																		
Loaf, 1 lb---- 1 loaf	454	36	1,225	39	15	3.4	5.3	4.6	229	381	440	11.3	476	Trace	1.80	1.10	15.0	Trace
Slice (18 per loaf)---- 1 slice	25	36	70	2	1	.3	.3	.3	21	21	24	.6	26	Trace	.10	.06	.8	Trace
Slice, toasted---- 1 slice	22	25	70	2	1	.3	.3	.3	21	21	24	.6	26	Trace	.08	.06	.8	Trace
Slice (22 per loaf)---- 1 slice	20	36	55	2	1	.2	.2	.2	17	19	21	.5	21	Trace	.08	.05	.7	Trace
Slice, toasted---- 1 slice	17	25	55	2	1	.2	.2	.2	17	17	19	.5	21	Trace	.06	.05	.7	Trace

[38] Made with vegetable shortening.
[39] Applies to product made with white cornmeal. With yellow cornmeal, value is 30 International Units (I.U.).

(Continued)

Grain Products, Composition (Continued)

TABLE 2.G.9 (Continued)

Foods, approximate measures, units, and weight (edible part unless footnotes indicate otherwise)		Water	Food energy	Protein	Fat	Saturated (total)	Unsaturated Oleic	Linoleic	Carbohydrate	Calcium	Phosphorus	Iron	Potassium	Vitamin A value	Thiamin	Riboflavin	Niacin	Ascorbic acid
	Grams	Percent	Calories	Grams	Grams	Grams	Grams	Grams	Grams	Milligrams	Milligrams	Milligrams	Milligrams	International units	Milligrams	Milligrams	Milligrams	Milligrams
GRAIN PRODUCTS—Con.																		
Loaf, 1 1/2 lb------- 1 loaf	680	36	1,835	59	22	5.2	7.9	6.9	343	571	660	17.0	714	Trace	2.70	1.65	22.5	Trace
Slice (24 per loaf)--- 1 slice	28	36	75	2	1	.2	.3	.3	14	24	27	.7	29	Trace	.11	.07	.9	Trace
Slice, toasted------- 1 slice	24	25	75	2	1	.2	.3	.3	14	24	27	.7	29	Trace	.09	.07	.9	Trace
Slice (28 per loaf)--- 1 slice	24	36	65	2	1	.2	.2	.2	12	20	23	.6	25	Trace	.10	.06	.8	Trace
Slice, toasted------- 1 slice	21	25	65	2	1	.2	.3	.2	12	20	23	.6	25	Trace	.08	.06	.8	Trace
Cubes-------------- 1 cup	30	36	80	3	1	.2	.3	.3	15	25	29	.8	32	Trace	.12	.07	1.0	Trace
Crumbs------------- 1 cup	45	36	120	4	1	.3	.5	.5	23	38	44	1.1	47	Trace	.18	.11	1.5	Trace
Firm-crumb type:																		
Loaf, 1 lb-------- 1 loaf	454	35	1,245	41	17	3.9	5.9	5.2	228	435	463	11.3	549	Trace	1.80	1.10	15.0	Trace
Slice (20 per loaf)-- 1 slice	23	35	65	2	1	.2	.3	.3	12	22	23	.6	28	Trace	.09	.06	.8	Trace
Slice, toasted----- 1 slice	20	24	65	2	1	.2	.3	.3	12	22	23	.6	28	Trace	.07	.06	.8	Trace
Loaf, 2 lb-------- 1 loaf	907	35	2,495	82	34	7.7	11.8	10.4	455	871	925	22.7	1,097	Trace	3.60	2.20	30.0	Trace
Slice (34 per loaf)-- 1 slice	27	35	75	2	1	.2	.3	.3	14	26	28	.7	33	Trace	.11	.06	.9	Trace
Slice, toasted----- 1 slice	23	24	75	2	1	.2	.3	.5	14	26	28	.7	33	Trace	.09	.06	.9	Trace
Whole-wheat bread:																		
- Soft-crumb type:[38]																		
Loaf, 1 lb-------- 1 loaf	454	36	1,095	41	12	2.2	2.9	4.2	224	381	1,152	13.6	1,161	Trace	1.37	.45	12.7	Trace
Slice (16 per loaf)-- 1 slice	28	36	65	3	1	.1	.2	.2	14	24	71	.8	72	Trace	.09	.03	.8	Trace
Slice, toasted----- 1 slice	24	24	65	3	1	.1	.2	.2	14	24	71	.8	72	Trace	.07	.03	.8	Trace
Firm-crumb type:[38]																		
Loaf, 1 lb-------- 1 loaf	454	36	1,100	48	14	2.5	3.3	4.9	216	449	1,034	13.6	1,238	Trace	1.17	.54	12.7	Trace
Slice (18 per loaf)-- 1 slice	25	36	60	3	1	.1	.2	.3	12	25	57	.8	68	Trace	.06	.03	.7	Trace
Slice, toasted----- 1 slice	21	24	60	3	1	.1	.2	.3	12	25	57	.8	68	Trace	.05	.03	.7	Trace
Breakfast cereals:																		
Hot type, cooked:																		
Corn (hominy) grits, degermed:																		
Enriched---------- 1 cup	245	87	125	3	Trace	Trace	Trace	.1	27	2	25	.7	27	[40]Trace	.10	.07	1.0	0
Unenriched-------- 1 cup	245	87	125	3	Trace	Trace	Trace	.1	27	2	25	.2	27	[40]Trace	.05	.02	.5	0
Farina, quick-cooking, en- riched. 1 cup	245	89	105	3	Trace	Trace	Trace	.1	22	147	[41]113	(42)	25	0	.12	.07	1.0	0
Oatmeal or rolled oats--- 1 cup	240	87	130	5	2	.4	.8	.9	23	22	137	1.4	146	0	.19	.05	.2	0
Wheat, rolled----- 1 cup	240	80	180	5	1	---	---	---	41	19	182	1.7	202	0	.17	.07	2.2	0
Wheat, whole-meal--- 1 cup	245	88	110	4	1	---	---	---	23	17	127	1.2	118	0	.15	.05	1.5	0
Ready-to-eat:																		
Bran flakes (40% bran), added sugar, salt, iron, vitamins. 1 cup	35	3	105	4	1	---	---	---	28	19	125	12.4	137	1,650	.41	.49	4.1	12
Bran flakes with raisins, add- ed sugar, salt, iron, vita- mins. 1 cup	50	7	145	4	1	---	---	---	40	28	146	17.7	154	2,350	.58	.71	5.8	18
Corn flakes:																		
Plain, added sugar, salt, iron, vitamins. 1 cup	25	4	95	2	Trace	---	---	---	21	(43)	9	0.6	30	1,180	0.29	0.35	2.9	9
Sugar-coated, added salt, iron, vitamins. 1 cup	40	2	155	2	Trace	---	---	---	37	1	10	1.0	27	1,880	.46	.56	4.6	14
Corn, puffed, plain, added sugar, salt, iron, vita- mins. 1 cup	20	4	80	2	1	---	---	---	16	4	18	2.3	---	940	.23	.28	2.3	7
Corn, shredded, added sugar, salt, iron, thiamin, niacin. 1 cup	25	3	95	2	Trace	---	---	---	22	1	10	.6	---	0	.11	.05	.5	0

(Continued)

[40] Applies to white varieties. For yellow varieties, value is 150 International Units (I.U.).
[41] Applies to products that do not contain di-sodium phosphate. If di-sodium phosphate is an ingredient, value is 162 mg.
[42] Value may range from less than 1 mg to about 8 mg depending on the brand. Consult the label.
[43] Value varies with the brand. Consult the label.

Grain Products, Composition (*Continued*)

Foods, approximate measures, units, and weight (edible part unless footnotes indicate otherwise)		Water	Food energy	Protein	Fat	Saturated (total)	Oleic	Linoleic	Carbohydrate	Calcium	Phosphorus	Iron	Potassium	Vitamin A value	Thiamin	Riboflavin	Niacin	Ascorbic acid
	Grams	Percent	Calories	Grams	Grams	Grams	Grams	Grams	Grams	Milligrams	Milligrams	Milligrams	Milligrams	International units	Milligrams	Milligrams	Milligrams	Milligrams
GRAIN PRODUCTS																		
Oats, puffed, added sugar, salt, minerals, vitamins. 1 cup	25	3	100	3	1	—	—	—	19	44	102	2.9	—	1,180	.29	.35	2.9	9
Rice, puffed:																		
Plain, added iron, thiamin, niacin. 1 cup	15	4	60	1	Trace	—	—	—	13	3	14	.3	15	0	.07	.01	.7	0
Presweetened, added salt, iron, vitamins. 1 cup	28	3	115	1	0	—	—	—	26	3	14	[44]1.1	43	1,250	.38	.43	5.0	[45]515
Wheat flakes, added sugar, salt, iron, vitamins. 1 cup	30	4	105	3	Trace	—	—	—	24	12	83	([43])	81	1,410	.35	.42	3.5	11
Wheat, puffed:																		
Plain, added iron, thiamin, niacin. 1 cup	15	3	55	2	Trace	—	—	—	12	4	48	.6	51	0	.08	.03	1.2	0
Presweetened, added salt, iron, vitamins. 1 cup	38	3	140	3	Trace	—	—	—	33	7	52	[44]1.6	63	1,680	.50	.57	6.7	[45]520
Wheat, shredded, plain. 1 oblong biscuit or 1/2 cup spoon-size biscuits	25	7	90	2	1	—	—	—	20	11	97	.9	87	0	.06	.03	1.1	0
Wheat germ, without salt and sugar, toasted. 1 tbsp	6	4	25	2	1	—	—	—	3	3	70	.5	57	10	.11	.05	.3	1
Buckwheat flour, light, sifted. 1 cup	98	12	340	6	1	—	—	—	78	11	86	1.0	314	0	.08	.04	.4	0
Bulgur, canned, seasoned. 1 cup	135	56	245	8	4	0.2	0.4	0.4	44	27	263	1.9	151	0	.08	.05	4.1	0
Cake icings. See Sugars and Sweets (items 532–536).																		
Cakes made from cake mixes with enriched flour:[46]																		
Angelfood:																		
Whole cake (9 3/4-in diam. tube cake). 1 cake	635	34	1,645	36	1	—	—	—	377	603	756	2.5	381	0	.37	.95	3.6	0
Piece, 1/12 of cake. 1 piece	53	34	135	3	Trace	—	—	—	32	50	63	.2	32	0	.03	.08	.3	0
Coffeecake:																		
Whole cake (7 3/4 by 5 5/8 by 1 1/4 in). 1 cake	430	30	1,385	27	41	11.7	16.3	8.8	225	262	748	6.9	469	690	.82	.91	7.7	1
Piece, 1/6 of cake. 1 piece	72	30	230	5	7	2.0	2.7	1.5	38	44	125	1.2	78	120	.14	.15	1.3	Trace
Cupcakes, made with egg, milk, 2 1/2-in diam.:																		
Without icing. 1 cupcake	25	26	90	1	3	.8	1.2	.7	14	40	59	.3	21	40	.05	.05	.4	Trace
With chocolate icing. 1 cupcake	36	22	130	2	5	2.0	1.6	.6	21	47	71	.4	42	60	.05	.06	.4	Trace
Devil's food with chocolate icing:																		
Whole, 2 layer cake (8- or 9-in diam.). 1 cake	1,107	24	3,755	49	136	50.0	44.9	17.0	645	653	1,162	16.6	1,439	0	1.06	1.65	10.1	1
Piece, 1/16 of cake. 1 piece	69	24	235	3	8	3.1	2.8	1.1	40	41	72	1.0	90	100	.07	.10	.6	Trace
Cupcake, 2 1/2-in diam. 1 cupcake	35	24	120	2	4	1.6	1.4	.5	20	21	37	.5	46	50	.03	.05	.3	Trace
Gingerbread:																		
Whole cake (8-in square). 1 cake	570	37	1,575	18	39	9.7	16.6	10.0	291	513	570	8.6	1,562	Trace	0.84	1.00	7.4	Trace
Piece, 1/9 of cake. 1 piece	63	37	175	2	4	1.1	1.8	1.1	32	57	63	.9	173	Trace	.09	.11	.8	Trace
White, 2 layer with chocolate icing:																		
Whole cake (8- or 9-in diam.). 1 cake	1,140	21	4,000	44	122	48.2	46.4	20.0	716	1,129	2,041	11.4	1,322	680	1.50	1.77	12.5	2
Piece, 1/16 of cake. 1 piece	71	21	250	3	8	3.0	2.9	1.2	45	70	127	.7	82	40	.09	.11	.8	Trace
Yellow, 2 layer with chocolate icing:																		
Whole cake (8- or 9-in diam.). 1 cake	1,108	26	3,735	45	125	47.8	47.8	20.3	638	1,008	2,017	12.2	1,208	1,550	1.24	1.67	10.6	2
Piece, 1/16 of cake. 1 piece	69	26	235	3	8	3.0	3.0	1.3	40	63	126	.8	75	100	.08	.10	.7	Trace
Cakes made from home recipes using enriched flour:[47]																		
Boston cream pie with custard filling:																		
Whole cake (8-in diam.). 1 cake	825	35	2,490	41	78	23.0	30.1	15.2	412	553	833	8.2	[48]734	1,730	1.04	1.27	9.6	2
Piece, 1/12 of cake. 1 piece	69	35	210	3	6	1.9	2.5	1.3	34	46	70	.7	[48]861	140	.09	.11	.8	Trace

(Continued)

[44]Value varies with the brand. Consult the label.
[45]Applies to product with added ascorbic acid. Without added ascorbic acid, value is trace.
[46]Applies to product with added ascorbic acid. Without added ascorbic acid, value would be higher.
[47]Excepting angelfood cake, cakes were made from mixes containing vegetable shortening; icings, with butter.
[48]Excepting spongecake, vegetable shortening used for cake portion; butter, for icing. If butter or margarine used for cake portion, vitamin A values would be higher.
[49]Applies to product made with a sodium aluminum-sulfate type baking powder. With a low-sodium type baking powder containing potassium, value would be about twice the amount shown.

Grain Products, Composition (Continued)

TABLE 2.G.9 (Continued)

Foods, approximate measures, units, and weight (edible part unless footnotes indicate otherwise)		Water	Food energy	Protein	Fat	Fatty Acids Saturated (total)	Unsaturated Oleic	Linoleic	Carbohydrate	Calcium	Phosphorus	Iron	Potassium	Vitamin A value	Thiamin	Riboflavin	Niacin	Ascorbic acid
		Grams / Percent	Calories	Grams	Grams	Grams	Grams	Grams	Grams	Milligrams	Milligrams	Milligrams	Milligrams	International units	Milligrams	Milligrams	Milligrams	Milligrams
GRAIN PRODUCTS																		
Fruitcake, dark:																		
Loaf, 1-lb (7 1/2 by 2 by 1 1/2 in).	1 loaf	454 / 18	1,720	22	69	14.4	33.5	14.8	271	327	513	11.8	2,250	540	.72	.73	4.9	2
Slice, 1/30 of loaf	1 slice	15 / 18	55	1	2	.5	1.1	.5	9	11	17	.4	74	20	.02	.02	.2	Trace
Plain, sheet cake:																		
Without icing:																		
Whole cake (9-in square)	1 cake	777 / 25	2,830	35	108	29.5	44.4	23.9	434	497	793	8.5	[48]614	1,320	1.21	1.40	10.2	2
Piece, 1/9 of cake	1 piece	86 / 25	315	4	12	3.3	4.9	2.6	48	55	88	.9	[48]68	150	.13	.15	1.1	Trace
With uncooked white icing:																		
Whole cake (9-in square)	1 cake	1,096 / 21	4,020	37	129	42.2	49.5	24.4	694	548	822	8.2	[48]669	2,190	1.22	1.47	10.2	2
Piece, 1/9 of cake	1 piece	121 / 21	445	4	14	4.7	5.5	2.7	77	61	91	.8	[48]74	240	.14	.16	1.1	Trace
Pound:[49]																		
Loaf, 8 1/2 by 3 1/2 by 3 1/4 in.	1 loaf	565 / 16	2,725	31	170	42.9	73.1	39.6	273	107	418	7.9	345	1,410	.90	.99	7.3	0
Slice, 1/17 of loaf	1 slice	33 / 16	160	2	10	2.5	4.3	2.3	16	6	24	.5	20	80	.05	.06	.4	0
Spongecake:																		
Whole cake (9 3/4-in diam. tube cake).	1 cake	790 / 32	2,345	60	45	13.1	15.8	5.7	427	237	885	13.4	687	3,560	1.10	1.64	7.4	Trace
Piece, 1/12 of cake	1 piece	66 / 32	195	5	4	1.1	1.3	.5	36	20	74	1.1	57	300	.09	.14	.6	Trace
Cookies made with enriched flour:[50] [51]																		
Brownies with nuts:																		
Home-prepared, 1 3/4 by 1 3/4 by 7/8 in:																		
From home recipe	1 brownie	20 / 10	95	1	6	1.5	3.0	1.2	10	8	30	.4	38	40	.04	.03	.2	Trace
From commercial recipe	1 brownie	20 / 11	85	1	4	.9	1.4	1.3	13	9	27	.4	34	20	.03	.02	.2	Trace
Frozen, with chocolate icing,[52] 1 1/2 by 1 3/4 by 7/8 in.	1 brownie	25 / 13	105	1	5	2.0	2.2	.7	15	10	31	.4	44	50	.03	.03	.2	Trace
Chocolate chip:																		
Commercial, 2 1/4-in diam., 3/8 in thick.	4 cookies	42 / 3	200	2	9	2.8	2.9	2.2	29	16	48	1.0	56	50	.10	.17	.9	Trace
From home recipe, 2 1/3-in diam.	4 cookies	40 / 3	205	2	12	3.5	4.5	2.9	24	14	40	.8	47	40	.06	.06	.5	Trace
Fig bars, square (1 5/8 by 1 5/8 by 3/8 in) or rectangular (1 1/2 by 1 3/4 by 1/2 in).	4 cookies	56 / 14	200	2	3	.8	1.2	.7	42	44	34	1.0	111	60	.04	.14	.9	Trace
Gingersnaps, 2-in diam., 1/4 in thick.	4 cookies	28 / 3	90	2	2	.7	1.0	.6	22	20	13	.7	129	20	.08	.06	.7	0
Macaroons, 2 3/4-in diam., 1/4 in thick.	2 cookies	38 / 4	180	2	9	—	—	—	25	10	32	.3	176	0	.02	.06	.2	0
Oatmeal with raisins, 2 5/8-in diam., 1/4 in thick.	4 cookies	52 / 3	235	3	8	2.0	3.3	2.0	38	11	53	1.4	192	30	.15	.10	1.0	Trace
Plain, prepared from commercial chilled dough, 2 1/2-in diam., 1/4 in thick.	4 cookies	48 / 5	240	2	12	3.0	5.2	2.9	31	17	35	.6	23	30	0.10	0.08	0.9	0
Sandwich type (chocolate or vanilla), 1 3/4-in diam., 3/8 in thick.	4 cookies	40 / 2	200	2	9	2.2	3.9	2.2	28	10	96	.7	15	0	.06	.10	.7	0
Vanilla wafers, 1 3/4-in diam., 1/4 in thick.	10 cookies	40 / 3	185	2	6	—	—	—	30	16	25	.6	29	50	.10	.09	.8	0

[49] Equal weights of flour, sugar, eggs, and vegetable shortening.
[50] Products are commercial unless otherwise specified.
[51] Made with enriched flour and vegetable shortening except for macaroons which do not contain flour or shortening.
[52] Icing made with butter.

(Continued)

Grain Products, Composition (Continued)

Foods, approximate measures, units, and weight (edible part unless footnotes indicate otherwise)		Water	Food energy	Protein	Fat	Fatty Acids Saturated (total)	Fatty Acids Unsaturated Oleic	Fatty Acids Linoleic	Carbohydrate	Calcium	Phosphorus	Iron	Potassium	Vitamin A value	Thiamin	Riboflavin	Niacin	Ascorbic acid
	Grams	Percent	Calories	Grams	Grams	Grams	Grams	Grams	Grams	Milligrams	Milligrams	Milligrams	Milligrams	International units	Milligrams	Milligrams	Milligrams	Milligrams
GRAIN PRODUCTS																		
Cornmeal:																		
Whole-ground, unbolted, dry form.———1 cup	122	12	435	11	5	.5	1.0	2.5	90	24	312	2.9	346	[53]620	.46	.13	2.4	0
Bolted (nearly whole-grain), dry form.———1 cup	122	12	440	11	4	.5	.9	2.1	91	21	272	2.2	303	[53]590	.37	.10	2.3	0
Degermed, enriched:																		
Dry form———1 cup	138	12	500	11	2	.2	.4	.9	108	8	137	4.0	166	[53]610	.61	.36	4.8	0
Cooked———1 cup	240	88	120	3	Trace	Trace	.1	.2	26	2	34	1.0	38	[53]140	.14	.10	1.2	0
Degermed, unenriched:																		
Dry form———1 cup	138	12	500	11	2	.2	.4	.9	108	8	137	1.5	166	[53]610	.19	.07	1.4	0
Cooked———1 cup	240	88	120	3	Trace	Trace	.1	.2	26	2	34	.5	38	[53]140	.05	.02	.2	0
Crackers:[58]																		
Graham, plain, 2 1/2-in square———2 crackers	14	6	55	1	1	.3	.5	.3	10	6	21	.5	55	0	.02	.08	.5	0
Rye wafers, whole-grain, 1 7/8 by 3 1/2 in.———2 wafers	13	6	45	2	Trace				10	7	50	.5	78	0	.04	.03	.2	0
Saltines, made with enriched flour.———4 crackers or 1 packet	11	4	50	1	1	.3	.5	.4	8	2	10	.5	13	0	.05	.05	.4	0
Danish pastry (enriched flour), plain without fruit or nuts:[54]																		
Packaged ring, 12 oz———1 ring	340	22	1,435	25	80	24.3	31.7	16.5	155	170	371	6.1	381	1,050	.97	1.01	8.6	Trace
Round piece, about 4 1/4-in diam. by 1 in.———1 pastry	65	22	275	5	15	4.7	6.1	3.2	30	33	71	1.2	73	200	.18	.19	1.7	Trace
Ounce———1 oz	28	22	120	2	7	2.0	2.7	1.4	13	14	31	.5	32	90	.08	.08	.7	Trace
Doughnuts, made with enriched flour:[38]																		
Cake type, plain, 2 1/2-in diam., 1 in high.———1 doughnut	25	24	100	1	5	1.2	2.0	1.1	13	10	48	.4	23	20	.05	.05	.4	Trace
Yeast-leavened, glazed, 3 3/4-in diam., 1 1/4 in high.———1 doughnut	50	26	205	3	11	3.3	5.8	3.3	22	16	33	.6	34	25	.10	.10	.8	0
Macaroni, enriched, cooked (cut lengths, elbows, shells):																		
Firm stage (hot)———1 cup	130	64	190	7	1				39	14	85	1.4	103	0	.23	.13	1.8	0
Tender stage:																		
Cold macaroni———1 cup	105	73	115	4	Trace				24	8	53	.9	64	0	.15	.08	1.2	0
Hot macaroni———1 cup	140	73	155	5	1				32	11	70	1.3	85	0	.20	.11	1.5	0
Macaroni (enriched) and cheese:																		
Canned[55]———1 cup	240	80	230	9	10	4.2	3.1	1.4	26	199	182	1.0	139	260	.12	.24	1.0	Trace
From home recipe (served hot)[56]———1 cup	200	58	430	17	22	8.9	8.8	2.9	40	362	322	1.8	240	860	.20	.40	1.8	Trace
Muffins made with enriched flour:[38]																		
From home recipe:																		
Blueberry, 2 3/8-in diam., 1 1/2 in high.———1 muffin	40	39	110	3	4	1.1	1.4	.7	17	34	53	.6	46	90	.09	.10	.7	Trace
Bran———1 muffin	40	35	105	3	4	1.2	1.4	.8	17	57	162	1.5	172	90	.07	.10	1.7	Trace
Corn (enriched degermed cornmeal and flour), 2 3/8-in diam., 1-1/2 in high.———1 muffin	40	33	125	3	4	1.2	1.6	.9	19	42	68	.7	54	[57]120	.10	.10	.7	Trace
Plain, 3-in diam., 1 1/2 in high.———1 muffin	40	38	120	3	4	1.0	1.7	1.0	17	42	60	.6	50	40	.09	0.12	0.9	Trace
From mix, egg, milk:																		
Corn, 2 3/8-in diam., 1 1/2 in high.[58]———1 muffin	40	30	130	3	4	1.2	1.7	.9	20	96	152	.6	44	[57]100	.08	.09	.7	Trace
Noodles (egg noodles), enriched, cooked.———1 cup	160	71	200	7	2				37	16	94	1.4	70	110	.22	.13	1.9	0
Noodles, chow mein, canned.———1 cup	45	1	220	6	11				26									
Pancakes, (4-in diam.):[38]																		
Buckwheat, made from mix (with buckwheat and enriched flours), egg and milk added.———1 cake	27	58	55	2	2	.8	.9	.4	6	59	91	.4	66	60	.04	.05	.2	Trace

[53] Applies to yellow varieties; white varieties contain only a trace.
[54] Contains vegetable shortening and butter.
[55] Made with corn oil.
[56] Made with regular margarine.
[57] Applies to product made with yellow cornmeal.
[58] Made with enriched degermed cornmeal and enriched flour.

(Continued)

Grain Products, Composition (Continued)

TABLE 2.G.9 (Continued)

Foods, approximate measures, units, and weight (edible part unless footnotes indicate otherwise)	Grams	Water (Per cent)	Food energy (Calories)	Protein (Grams)	Fat (Grams)	Saturated (total) (Grams)	Unsat. Oleic (Grams)	Linoleic (Grams)	Carbohydrate (Grams)	Calcium (Milligrams)	Phosphorus (Milligrams)	Iron (Milligrams)	Potassium (Milligrams)	Vitamin A value (International units)	Thiamin (Milligrams)	Riboflavin (Milligrams)	Niacin (Milligrams)	Ascorbic acid (Milligrams)
GRAIN PRODUCTS—Con.																		
Plain:																		
Made from home recipe using enriched flour. 1 cake	27	50	60	2	2	.5	.8	.5	9	27	38	.4	33	30	.06	.07	.5	Trace
Made from mix with enriched flour, egg and milk added. 1 cake	27	51	60	2	2	.7	.7	.3	9	58	70	.3	42	70	.04	.06	.2	Trace
Pies, piecrust made with enriched flour, vegetable shortening (9-in diam.):																		
Apple:																		
Whole — 1 pie	945	48	2,420	21	105	27.0	44.5	25.2	360	76	208	6.6	756	280	1.06	.79	9.3	9
Sector, 1/7 of pie — 1 sector	135	48	345	3	15	3.9	6.4	3.6	51	11	30	.9	108	40	.15	.11	1.3	2
Banana cream:																		
Whole — 1 pie	910	54	2,010	41	85	26.7	33.2	16.2	279	601	746	7.3	1,847	2,280	.77	1.51	7.0	9
Sector, 1/7 of pie — 1 sector	130	54	285	6	12	3.8	4.7	2.3	40	86	107	1.0	264	330	.11	.22	1.0	1
Blueberry:																		
Whole — 1 pie	945	51	2,285	23	102	24.8	43.7	25.1	330	104	217	9.5	614	280	1.03	.80	10.0	28
Sector, 1/7 of pie — 1 sector	135	51	325	3	15	3.5	6.2	3.6	47	15	31	1.4	88	40	.15	.11	1.4	4
Cherry:																		
Whole — 1 pie	945	47	2,465	25	107	28.2	45.0	25.3	363	132	236	6.6	992	4,160	1.09	.84	9.8	Trace
Sector, 1/7 of pie — 1 sector	135	47	350	4	15	4.0	6.4	3.6	52	19	34	.9	142	590	.16	.12	1.4	Trace
Custard:																		
Whole — 1 pie	910	58	1,985	56	101	33.9	38.5	17.5	213	874	1,028	8.2	1,247	2,090	.79	1.92	5.6	0
Sector, 1/7 of pie — 1 sector	130	58	285	8	14	4.8	5.5	2.5	30	125	147	1.2	178	300	.11	.27	.8	0
Lemon meringue:																		
Whole — 1 pie	840	47	2,140	31	86	26.1	33.8	16.4	317	118	412	6.7	420	1,430	.61	.84	5.2	25
Sector, 1/7 of pie — 1 sector	120	47	305	4	12	3.7	4.8	2.3	45	17	59	1.0	60	200	.09	.12	.7	4
Mince:																		
Whole — 1 pie	945	43	2,560	24	109	28.0	45.9	25.2	389	265	359	13.3	1,682	20	.96	.86	9.8	9
Sector, 1/7 of pie — 1 sector	135	43	365	3	16	4.0	6.6	3.6	56	38	51	1.9	240	Trace	.14	.12	1.4	1
Peach:																		
Whole — 1 pie	945	48	2,410	24	101	24.8	43.7	25.1	361	95	274	8.5	1,408	6,900	1.04	.97	14.0	28
Sector, 1/7 of pie — 1 sector	135	48	345	3	14	3.5	6.2	3.6	52	14	39	1.2	201	990	.15	.14	2.0	4
Pecan:																		
Whole — 1 pie	825	20	3,450	42	189	27.8	101.0	44.2	423	388	850	25.6	1,015	1,320	1.80	.95	6.9	Trace
Sector, 1/7 of pie — 1 sector	118	20	495	6	27	4.0	14.4	6.3	61	55	122	3.7	145	190	.26	.14	1.0	Trace
Pumpkin:																		
Whole — 1 pie	910	59	1,920	36	102	37.4	37.5	16.6	223	464	628	7.3	1,456	22,480	.78	1.27	7.0	Trace
Sector, 1/7 of pie — 1 sector	130	59	275	5	15	5.4	5.4	2.4	32	66	90	1.0	208	3,210	.11	.18	1.0	Trace
Piecrust (home recipe) made with enriched flour and vegetable shortening, baked. 1 pie shell, 9-in diam.	180	15	900	11	60	14.8	26.1	14.9	79	25	90	3.1	89	0	.47	.40	5.0	0
Piecrust mix with enriched flour and vegetable shortening, 10-oz pkg. prepared and baked. Piecrust for 2-crust pie, 9-in diam.	320	19	1,485	20	93	22.7	39.7	23.4	141	131	272	6.1	179	0	1.07	.79	9.9	0
Pizza (cheese) baked, 4 3/4-in sector; 1/8 of 12-in diam. pie.[19] 1 sector	60	45	145	6	4	1.7	1.5	0.6	22	86	89	1.1	67	230	.16	0.18	1.6	4
Popcorn, popped:																		
Plain, large kernel — 1 cup	6	4	25	1	Trace	Trace	.1	.2	5	1	17	.2	—	—	—	.01	.1	0
With oil (coconut) and salt added, large kernel. 1 cup	9	3	40	1	2	1.5	.2	.2	5	1	19	.2	—	—	—	.01	.2	0
Sugar coated — 1 cup	35	4	135	2	1	.5	.2	.4	30	2	47	.5	—	—	.02	—	.4	0

(Continued)

Grain Products, Composition   (Continued)

TABLE 2.G.9 (Continued)

Foods, approximate measures, units, and weight (edible part unless footnotes indicate otherwise)		Grams	Water Per-cent	Food energy Cal-ories	Pro-tein Grams	Fat Grams	Satu-rated (total) Grams	Unsaturated Oleic Grams	Linoleic Grams	Carbo-hydrate Grams	Calcium Milli-grams	Phos-phorus Milli-grams	Iron Milli-grams	Potas-sium Milli-grams	Vitamin A value International units	Thiamin Milli-grams	Ribo-flavin Milli-grams	Niacin Milli-grams	Ascorbic acid Milli-grams
GRAIN PRODUCTS																			
Pretzels, made with enriched flour:																			
Dutch, twisted, 2 3/4 by 2 5/8 in.	1 pretzel	16	5	60	2	1	—	—	—	12	4	21	.2	21	0	.05	.04	.7	0
Thin, twisted, 3 1/4 by 2 1/4 by 1/4 in.	10 pretzels	60	5	235	6	3	—	—	—	46	13	79	.9	78	0	.20	.15	2.5	0
Stick, 2 1/4 in long	10 pretzels	3	5	10	Trace	Trace	—	—	—	2	1	4	Trace	4	0	.01	.01	.1	0
Rice, white, enriched:																			
Instant, ready-to-serve, hot	1 cup	165	73	180	4	Trace	Trace	Trace	Trace	40	5	31	1.3	—	0	.21	([59])	1.7	0
Long grain:																			
Raw	1 cup	185	12	670	12	1	.2	.2	.2	149	44	174	5.4	170	0	.81	.06	6.5	0
Cooked, served hot	1 cup	205	73	225	4	Trace	.1	.1	.1	50	21	57	1.8	57	0	.23	.02	2.1	0
Parboiled:																			
Raw	1 cup	185	10	685	14	1	.2	.1	.2	150	111	370	5.4	278	0	.81	.07	6.5	0
Cooked, served hot	1 cup	175	73	185	4	Trace	.1	.1	.1	41	33	100	1.4	75	0	.19	.02	2.1	0
Rolls, enriched:[38]																			
Commercial:																			
Brown-and-serve (12 per 12-oz pkg.), browned.	1 roll	26	27	85	2	2	.4	.7	.5	14	20	23	.5	25	Trace	.10	.06	.9	Trace
Cloverleaf or pan, 2 1/2-in diam., 2 in high.	1 roll	28	31	85	2	2	.4	.6	.4	15	21	24	.5	27	Trace	.11	.07	.9	Trace
Frankfurter and hamburger (8 per 11 1/2-oz pkg.).	1 roll	40	31	120	3	2	.5	.8	.6	21	30	34	.8	38	Trace	.16	.10	1.3	Trace
Hard, 3 3/4-in diam., 2 in high.	1 roll	50	25	155	5	2	.4	.6	.5	30	24	46	1.2	49	Trace	.20	.12	1.7	Trace
Hoagie or submarine, 11 1/2 by 3 by 2 1/2 in.	1 roll	135	31	390	12	4	.9	1.4	1.4	75	58	115	3.0	122	Trace	.54	.32	4.5	Trace
From home recipe:																			
Cloverleaf, 2 1/2-in diam., 2 in high.	1 roll	35	26	120	3	3	.8	1.1	.7	20	16	36	.7	41	30	.12	.12	1.2	Trace
Spaghetti, enriched, cooked:																			
Firm stage, "al dente," served hot.	1 cup	130	64	190	7	1	—	—	—	39	14	85	1.4	103	0	.23	.13	1.8	0
Tender stage, served hot.	1 cup	140	73	155	5	1	—	—	—	32	11	70	1.3	85	0	.20	.11	1.5	0
Spaghetti (enriched) in tomato sauce with cheese:																			
From home recipe	1 cup	250	77	260	9	9	2.0	5.4	.7	37	80	135	2.3	408	1,080	.25	.18	2.3	13
Canned	1 cup	250	80	190	6	2	.5	.3	.4	39	40	88	2.8	303	930	.35	.28	4.5	10
Spaghetti (enriched) with meat balls and tomato sauce:																			
From home recipe	1 cup	248	70	330	19	12	3.3	6.3	.9	39	124	236	3.7	665	1,590	.25	.30	4.0	22
Canned	1 cup	250	78	260	12	10	2.2	3.3	3.9	29	53	113	3.3	245	1,000	.15	.18	2.3	5
Toaster pastries	1 pastry	50	12	200	3	6	—	—	—	36	[59]54	[60]67	1.9	[60]74	500	.16	.17	2.1	([60])
Waffles, made with enriched flour, 7-in diam.:[38]																			
From home recipe	1 waffle	75	41	210	7	7	2.3	2.8	1.4	28	85	130	1.3	109	250	.17	.23	1.4	Trace
From mix, egg and milk added	1 waffle	75	42	205	7	8	2.8	2.9	1.2	27	179	257	1.0	146	170	.14	.22	.9	Trace
Wheat flours:																			
All-purpose or family flour, enriched:																			
Sifted, spooned	1 cup	115	12	420	12	1	0.2	0.1	0.5	88	18	100	3.3	109	0	0.74	0.46	6.1	0
Unsifted, spooned	1 cup	125	12	455	13	1	.2	.1	.1	95	20	109	3.6	119	0	.80	.50	6.6	0
Cake or pastry flour, enriched, sifted, spooned.	1 cup	96	12	350	7	1	.1	.1	.3	76	16	70	2.8	91	0	.61	.38	5.1	0
Self-rising, enriched, unsifted, spooned.	1 cup	125	12	440	12	1	.2	.1	.5	93	331	583	3.6	—	0	.80	.50	6.6	0
Whole-wheat, from hard wheats, stirred.	1 cup	120	12	400	16	2	.4	.2	1.0	85	49	446	4.0	444	0	.66	.14	5.2	0

[59] Product may or may not be enriched with riboflavin. Consult the label.
[60] Value varies with the brand. Consult the label.

Source: Consumer and Food Economics Institute (1977). Nutritive value of foods. USDA Home and Garden Bull. 72.

Gram Stain

TABLE 2.G.10

FORMULA

1. Crystal violet stain (Hucker's Modification)
   Solution A:
   Crystal violet (85% dye content)   20 g
   Ethyl alcohol (95%)   200 ml
   Solution B:
   Ammonium oxalate   8 g
   Distilled water   800 ml
   Mix Solutions A and B
   Filter

2. Iodine solution
   a. Resublimed iodine   20 g
   b. N 1 Sodium hydroxide solution   100 ml
      (4 g per 100 ml distilled H_2O)
   c. Distilled water   900 ml
      Note: Dissolve iodine in NaOH
      and add water to make 1000 ml

3. Safranin Counterstain
   a. Ethyl alcohol solution of safranin   10 ml
      (Use 3.4 g per 100 ml of 95%
      alcohol)
   b. Distilled water   90 ml

Source: BioQuest, Division of Becton, Dickinson and Co., Rutherford, New Jersey.

Grapefruit Oil, Composition

TABLE 2.G.11
Chemical composition of cold-pressed grapefruit oil

TERPENES:
α-pinene
sabinene
β-myrcene
d-limonene
γ-α-terpinene
β-ocimene
α-β-cubebene
α-β-copaene
b-elemene
carophyllene
   ?
α,β-humulene
cadinene
   ?
△-cadinene
$C_{15}H_{24}$
auraptene

ALDEHYDES:
heptanal
octanal
nonanal
citronellal
decanal
undecanal

dodecanal
citral { geranial
        { neral

PHENOLS:
o-phenylphenol

ACIDS:
acetic acid
caprylic acid
capric acid

ALCOHOLS:
methyl heptenol
linalool
octanol
nonanol
decanol
α-terpineol
nerol
geraniol
nerolidol
elemol
trans-2-8-p-menthadiene-1-ol
cis-2-8-p-menthadiene-1-ol

citronellol
trans-carveol
cis-carveol
dodecanol
1-8-p-menthadiene-9-ol
8-p-menthene-1,2-diol

TRITERPENOIDS:
b-sitosterol
citrostadienol
campesterol
stigmasterol
cycloartenol
24-methylene
   cycloartenol
24-methylene lophenol

ESTERS:
octyl acetate
linalyl acetate
nonyl acetate
geranyl acetate
decyl acetate
neryl acetate
citronellyl acetate
geranyl butyrate

OXIDES:
trans-linalool oxide
cis-linalool oxide

COUMARINS & PSORALENS:
bergamottin
7-geranyloxycoumarin
osthol
limettin (citroptene)
bergapten
bergaptol
7-methoxy-8-(2-formyl-2-methylpropyl)-coumarin
7-((6,7-dihydroxy-3,7-dimethyl-2-octenyl)oxy)-coumarin
5-((3,6-dimethyl-6-formyl-2-heptenyl)oxy)-psoralen
Umbelliferone

KETONES:
nootkatone
methyl heptenone
carvone

Source: Kesterson, J. W., Hendrickson, R., and Braddock, R. J. (1971). Florida citrus oils. Florida Agric. Exp. Sta. Tech. Bull. *749*.

Grapefruit Oil, Properties

TABLE 2.G.12
Maximum and minimum values for the properties of cold-pressed grapefruit oil produced by various methods

Method of Extraction No. of Samples	Pipkin Roll 4		Screw Press 13		Fraser-Brace 32		FMC Rotary 5		FMC In-Line 36		AMC Scarifier 4		Brown Shaver 6	
Property	Max.	Min.	Max.	Min.	Max.	Min.	Max.	Min.	Max.	Min.	Max.	Min.	Max.	Min.
Sp. grav. 25°C/25°C	0.8537	0.8508	0.8552	0.8483	0.8610	0.8539	0.8649	0.8515	0.8576	0.8476	0.8715	0.8520	0.8583	0.8531
Ref. ind. η_D^{20}	1.4767	1.4746	1.4769	1.4749	1.4785	1.4764	1.4777	1.4752	1.4784	1.4751	1.4836	1.4762	1.4775	1.4766
Ref. ind. 10% dist. η_D^{20}	1.4714	1.4702	1.4721	1.4713	1.4716	1.4706	1.4713	1.4698	1.4722	1.4715	1.4719	1.4714	1.4721	1.4713
Difference	0.0053	0.0038	0.0051	0.0030	0.0072	0.0052	0.0064	0.0054	0.0068	0.0033	0.0117	0.0048	0.0062	0.0047
Opt. rot. α_D^{25}	+92.96	+92.03	+95.56	+91.07	+90.68	+85.14	+91.97	+88.92	+93.95	+90.60	+93.74	+87.02	+93.04	+90.49
Opt. rot. 10% dist. α_D^{25}	+97.77	+96.29	+98.53	+96.60	+98.05	+96.03	+98.14	+95.52	+98.91	+96.55	+98.82	+97.86	+98.28	+97.33
Difference	+4.81	+3.68	+6.10	+2.96	+11.29	+5.99	+6.60	+4.03	+6.40	+3.44	+14.56	+4.12	+6.88	+4.60
Aldehyde content %	1.61	1.49	1.57	1.30	2.06	1.01	1.67	1.12	1.75	0.74	1.91	1.02	1.56	1.17
Ester content %	4.38	2.77	3.68	2.48	5.25	2.91	4.66	2.11	—	—	—	—	—	—
Evaporation residue %	7.72	2.82	8.24	4.57	14.59	9.59	10.12	7.85	9.39	5.22	18.16	7.18	10.45	7.23

Source: Kesterson, J. W., Hendrickson, R., and Braddock, R. J. (1971). Florida citrus oils. Florida Agric. Exp. Sta. Tech. Bull. 749.

Gum Characteristics

TABLE 2.G.13
Characteristics of edible gums

Popular Name	Raw Material	Chemical Remarks	Main Residue	Viscosity
Agar-agar	Seaweed	Mixture of poly-saccharides	D-galactose, sulfate 3,6-anhydro-L-galactose	Gel
Algin	Brown algae	Polyuronic acid	D-mannuronic acid, L-glucuronic acid	1,800
Carrageenan	Red algae	Polysaccharide ester sulfate	D-galactose, sulfate 3,6-anhydro-D-galactose	225
Guar gum	Seed of bean family	Polyhexose	D-mannose, D-galactose	3,000
Gum acacia	Secretion from a tree	Ca, Mg, and K salts of arabic acid	D-galactose, L-arabinose, L-rhamnose, D-glucuronic acid	Low
Gum traga-canth	Secretion from a shrub	Mixture of complex acid, polysaccharide and neutral araban	L-arabinose, D-xylose, L-fucose, D-galactose	3,200
Karaya gum	Secretion from a tree	Complex acid of polysaccharide	D-galacturonic acid, L-rhamnose, D-galactose	2,300
Locust bean gum	Seed of a tree	Galactomannan	D-galactose, D-mannose	2,750

Source: Sone, T. (1972). Consistency of Foodstuffs. D. Reidel Publishing Co., Dordrecht, The Netherlands.

Gum Distribution

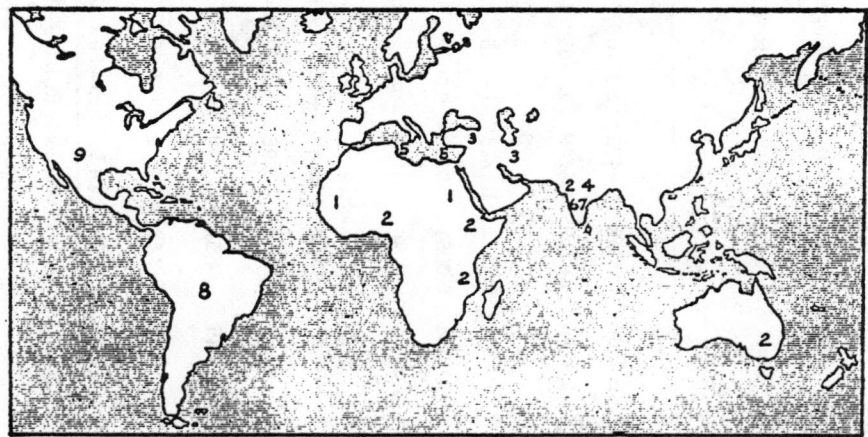

FIGURE 2.G.2
Map showing the distribution of the more important vegetable gums: (1) Gum Arabic (*Acacia senegal* Willd.); (2) other Acacia Gums; (3) Gum Tragacanth (*Astragalus* spp.); (4) Indian Tragacanth or Karaya Gum (*Sterculia urens* Roxb.); (5) Carob Seed Gum (*Ceratonia siliqua* L.); (6) Kutira Gum (*Cochlospermum gossypium* DC.); (7) Ghatti Gum (*Anogeissus latifolia* Wall.); (8) Angico Gum (*Piptadenia* spp.); (9) Mesquite Gum (*Prosopis juliflora* DC.).

Source: Howes, F. N. *Vegetable Gums and Resins*. Ronald Press Company, New York.

Gums and Gelling Agents

TABLE 2.G.14
Properties of gelling agents and gums

Agent	pH	Solubility Cold	Solubility Hot	Heat	Stability Acid	Storage	Viscosity (aq soln)	Gel Formation
Agar agar	at 1%–:7	Insoluble (swells)	Soluble	Fairly stable	Fairly stable	Weakens	Viscous	Forms firm gel at 0.5% conc. Gels show syneresis. Swell less in acid media.
Alginate	Varies with type	Na salt soluble	Na salt soluble	Fairly stable	Stable	Stable	Very viscous	Compatible with alkalis up to pH 11. Gels formed by divalent salts, the setting time controlled by phosphate.
Arabic gum	at 10%–:4.6	Truly soluble up to 50%	Truly soluble	Degrades	Fairly stable	Weakens	Viscous at at high conc.	Gelling power low. Electrolytes reduce consistency.
Carob gum	at 1%–:5.3	Slightly soluble (swells)	Soluble	Fairly stable	Fairly stable	Stable	Viscous	Useful with agar. Gelling by addition of alkali.
Carrageenan	at 1%–:7.9	Fairly soluble (swells)	Soluble	Stable	Stable	Stable	Viscous	Forms firm gel with added K+ —hence regulation of gel strength by K+ salt. Gel thermally reversible.
Gelatin	Varies with type	Insoluble (swells)	Soluble	Degrades	Degrades	Stable	Viscous at low conc.	Gel thermally reversible its rigidity depending on pH, conc., temp, and additives.

(Continued)

Gums and Gelling Agents (Continued)

TABLE 2.G.14 (Continued)

Agent	pH	Solubility Cold	Solubility Hot	Stability Heat	Stability Acid	Storage	Viscosity (aq soln)	Gel Formation
Ghatti gum	at 1%: ~4.5	Slightly soluble	Soluble	Fairly stable	Fairly stable	Stable	Viscous	Mainly used as an emulsification agent for oil-in-water emulsions.
Guar gum	at 1%: ~5.5–6.1	Slightly soluble (swells)	Soluble	Stable	Stable	Stable	Viscous	Gel resistant to heat shock for long periods.
Karaya gum	at 1%: ~4.6	Slightly soluble	Soluble	Not very stable	Stable	Stable	Viscous	Normally 3–4% conc. max for uniform gel by cold water hydration.
Pectin	Varies with esterification	Slightly soluble	Soluble	Stable	Stable	Stable	Very viscous	High degree of esterification or methoxylation gives rapid-set gels.
Starch: Unmodified	5.0–6.5	Slightly soluble	Soluble	Stable	Degrades	Stable	Viscous	Can be modified for many gels and textures.
Modified	Neutral or adjusted for acid conditions	Slightly soluble	Soluble	Stable	Stable	Stable	Viscosity controlled	Many starches when cooked have a low viscosity but form a rigid gel on cooling.
Tragacanth	at 1%: 5.1–5.9	Slightly soluble	Disperses	Highly stable	Stable	Stable	Very viscous	2–4% of gum gives thick gel when thoroughly dispersed.

Source: Lees, R., and Jackson, E. B. (1973). *Sugar Confectionery & Chocolate Manufacture.* Leonard Hill Books, London, England.

Gums and Gelling Agents, Characteristics

TABLE 2.G.15
Characteristics

	Gum Arabic	Starch	Gelatin	Agar	Pectin
Usage Levels for Gelling Agents in Confectionery Products	35%-45%	9%-12%	5%-12½%	1%-1½%	1%-1½%
Percentage of gelling agent to water to effect solution water/agent	50/50	10/1	2/1	50/1	40/1
Temperature of solution required to bring about solution	25°C 77°F	71°-82°C 160°-180°F	60°-65°C 140°-150°F	87°-93°C 190°-200°F	93°-100°C 200°-212°F
Sweetener ratio sucrose/glucose syrup	66/33-50/50	66/33-50/50	66/33-50/50	66/33-60/40	50/50-60/40
Temperature of acid addition	82°C 180°F	93°C 200°F	71°-82°C 160°-180°F	76°C 170°F	93°C 200°F
Depositing temperature	71°-82°C 160°-180°F	82°-93°C 180°-200°F	71°-82°C 160°-180°F	65°-76°C 150°-170°F	82°-93°C 180°-200°F
Setting temperature	20°-37°C 68°-100°F	20°-37°C 68°-100°F	20°-37°C 68°-100°F	35°-37°C 95°-100°F	71°-82°C 160°-180°F
Setting time	24 hr +	12 hr +	4 hr +	3 hr +	1 hr +
Time in starch moulds	36-72 hr	12-36 hr	12-24 hr	12-24 hr	6-12 hr
Starch moisture (%)	5%-8%	5%-8%	5%-8%	5%-8%	5%-10%
Starch temperature	26°-37°C 80°-100°F	37°-49°C 100°-120°F	26°-37°C 80°-100°F	26°-43°C 80°-110°F	37°-49°C 100°-120°F
Total solids: Depositing	68%-70%	72%-78%	72%-78%	76%-80%	76%-78%
Final	85% +	78% +	78% +	80% +	78% +

(Continued)

Gums and Gelling Agents, Characteristics   (Continued)

TABLE 2.G.15   (Continued)

	Gum Arabic	Starch	Gelatin	Agar	Pectin
Usage Levels for Gelling Agents in Confectionery Products	35%–45%	9%–12%	5%–12½%	1%–1½%	1%–1½%
Texture	Smooth Malleable Hard bite	Short	Tough, long	Short, soft, some insolubility	Short, ridged, clean bite
Complementary gelling agents	Starch Gelatin	Gum arabic Agar pectin	Agar-starch	Starch Gelatin	Starch
Temperature at final solid atmospheric pressure	124°C 256°F	108°C 228°F	115°C 240°F	107°C 226°F	108°C 228°F
Effect of cooking or holding time on gel strength	Decrease in strength due to extended time and low pH	Prolonged cooking at low pH decreases gel strength	Prolonged time in liquid state and low pH causes loss of gel strength	Lengthy cooking causes weak gel with discoloration	Prolonged boiling causes some degradation
pH during cooking recommended	pH 5.0–6.0	pH 5.0–6.0	pH 5.0–6.0	pH 5.0–6.0	pH 4.0–5.0
Percentage of acid for flavoring	0.3%–0.45%	0.2%–0.4%	0.2%–0.3%	0.2%–0.3%	0.4%–0.7%
Buffer salt recommended	Only required for low pH products	Not normally required	0.1% if acid is added	0.1% to prevent degradation of agar at high temperatures and low pH	0.1%–0.2% to retard setting
Final pH of product	pH 4.2–5.0	pH 4.2–5.0	pH 4.5–5.0	pH 4.8–5.6	pH 3.2–3.5
Shelf-life—Approx	6 months +	5 months +	4 months +	3 months +	5 months +
Flavor carrying performance	Good	Good	Poor	Fair	Very good
Ease of manufacture	Good	Excellent particularly continuous production	Good	Fair	Fair
Preparation of reclaimed waste material for re-use	Good	Fair	Good	Fair	Difficult

Source: Lees, R., and Jackson, E. B. (1973). Sugar Confectionery and Chocolate Manufacture. Leonard Hill Books, London, England.

Gums, Physicochemical Properties

TABLE 2.G.16
Physicochemical properties of edible gums

| Popular Name | pH | Gelation | Effect of Reagents | | | Thermal Effect |
			HCl	NaOH	Salts	
Agar-agar	7	Yes	Decrease of viscosity	Increase of viscosity up to pH 8.5, then decrease	Little affected	Rigid gel up to 92°C
Carrageenan	7	Yes	Decrease of viscosity	Decrease of viscosity	Prompt gelation	Sol ⇄ Gel at 38°C
Guar gum	7	No	Little affected	Little affected	Gelation	Decrease of viscosity
Gum acacia	5	No	Decrease of viscosity	Increase of viscosity up to pH 7	Gelation	Decrease of viscosity
Gum tragacanth	5.5	Yes	Decrease of viscosity	Increase of viscosity up to pH 8, then decrease	Little affected	Decrease of viscosity
Karaya gum	4.6	No	Decrease of viscosity	Increase of viscosity	Decrease of viscosity	Decrease of viscosity
Locust bean gum	5.3	No	Increase of viscosity	Decrease of viscosity at low concentration. Increase of viscosity at high concentration	Gelation	Increase of viscosity up to 70°C

Source: Sone, T. (1972). *Consistency of Foodstuffs.* D. Reidel Publishing Co., Dordrecht, The Netherlands.

H

Ham Beetle, Red-Legged (Enlarged)

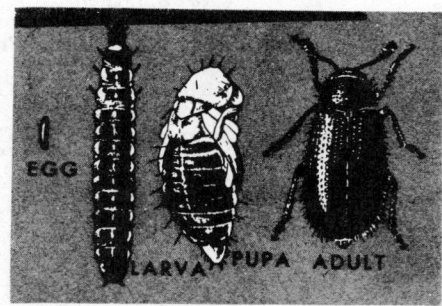

FIGURE 2.H.1

Source: USDA (1974). Protecting home cured meat from insects. USDA Home and Garden Bull. *109*.

Ham, Carving (Whole)

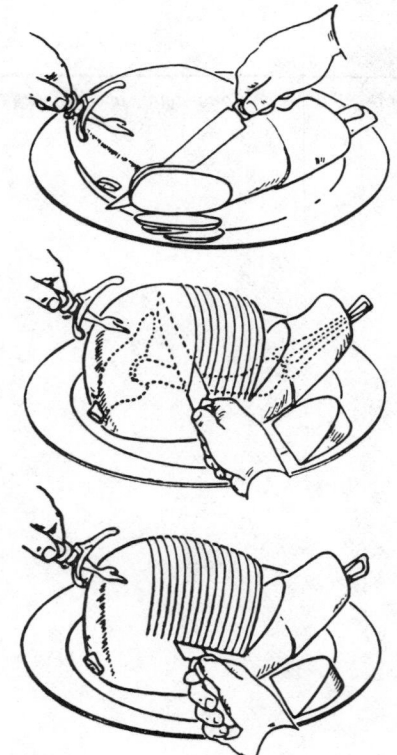

Place the ham on the platter with the decorated side up and the shank to the carver's right. Remove several slices from the thin side to form a solid base on which to set the ham.

Turn the ham on its base. Starting at the shank end, a small wedge cut is removed; then carve perpendicular to the leg bone as shown at right.

Release slices by cutting under them and along the leg bone, starting at the shank end. For additional servings, turn ham over to the original position and make slices to the bone, release and serve.

FIGURE 2.H.2

Source: Carving Meat. National Live Stock and Meat Board, Chicago.

Ham, Curing

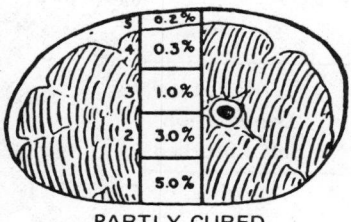 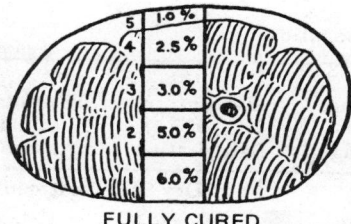 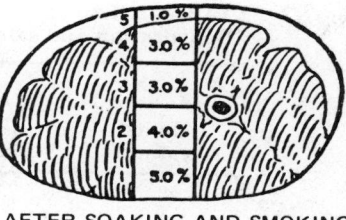

PARTLY CURED   FULLY CURED   AFTER SOAKING AND SMOKING

FIGURE 2.H.3
Analytical control of ham curing (dry curing) showing sections sampled and typical analysis for salt

Source: Moulton, C. R., and Lewis, W. L. *Meat Through The Microscope*, Revised Edition. Institute of Meat Packing, The University of Chicago, Chicago.

Herb Vinegars

TABLE 2.H.1

Bring to the boiling point 1 pt of cider vinegar and pour it over one of the following:

½ tsp of dried herbs
    rosemary   tarragon
    basil   dill seed
2 tbsp of fresh herbs
    rosemary   sorrel
    sage
½ cup of chopped mint leaves
    chives
1 head dill seed
1 small clove garlic (slashed)

  Some prefer a mixed spice herb vinegar. Here is one combination. To 1 qt of boiling clear vinegar add:

½ tsp clove buds   1 stick cinnamon
½ tsp peppercorn   1 small clove garlic, slashed

  Let the above infusion stand for about 10 days, then strain and store covered or bottled for future use.

Source: Kintner, T. C., and Mangel, M. Vinegars and salad dressings. Univ. Missouri Agric. Exp. Sta. Bull. *631*.

Hide Curing

TABLE 2.H.2
Dehydration and salt absorption

Hours Treatment	Percentage of Shrinkage	Percentage of Dehydration	Percentage of Salt Absorbed	Ratio: Dehydration / Salt Absorbed
		Dry-Salt Treatment		
1	5.37	6.91	+1.54	4.49
3	10.45	13.81	+3.36	4.11
4	12.79	16.69	+3.89	4.29
5	16.45	20.76	+4.31	4.81
24	23.85	30.51	+6.66	4.58
		Brining in 25% Salt Solution		
1	5.76	8.15	+2.39	3.41
2	8.96	11.62	+2.66	4.37
3	9.63	13.12	+3.49	3.76
4	10.90	15.06	+4.16	3.62
5	11.81	16.48	+4.67	3.53
24	13.45	21.21	+7.76	2.74

Source: Moulton, C. R., and Lewis, W. L. *Meat Through the Microscope*, Revised Edition. Institute of Meat Packing, University of Chicago, Chicago.

Hide, Layers

TABLE 2.H.3
Percentage of water and salt in various hide layers

Layer		When Fresh	After 1 hr in Salt	After 4.5 hr in Salt	After 24 hr in Salt
Epidermal layer	Water	74.35	74.00	71.75	54.75
	Salt	—	0.42	0.85	1.10
Corium	Water	61.00	57.25	58.85	45.30
	Salt	—	0.80	2.09	3.78
Adipose tissue	Water	54.10	50.00	46.60	22.30
	Salt	—	0.28	0.37	1.03
Total hide	Water	61.66	60.41	57.07	40.78
	Salt	—	1.50	3.31	5.90

Source: Moulton, C. R., and Lewis, W. L. *Meat Through the Microscope*, Revised Edition. Institute of Meat Packing, University of Chicago, Chicago.

Hides, Salt Absorption

TABLE 2.H.4
Absorption of salt from flesh and hair sides

Side	Hours	Percentage of Salt Absorbed	Percentage of Total Salt in		
			Epidermis	Corium	Adipose Tissue
Hair side only	1.0	None	—	—	—
	4.5	None	—	—	—
	24.0	0.227	23	59	18
Flesh side only	1.0	1.20	28	62	10
	4.5	2.97	23	66	11
	24.0	5.70	18	67	15
Both sides	1.0	1.05	28	53	19
	4.5	2.86	26	53	11
	24.0	5.45	19	64	17

Source: Moulton, C. R., and Lewis, W. L. *Meat Through the Microscope*, Revised Edition. Institute of Meat Packing, University of Chicago, Chicago.

Histochemical Tests

TABLE 2.H.5
Preparation and methods for histochemical tests. Abbreviations: conc. = concentrated; sat. = saturated; sol. = solution.

Substance	Preparation of Tissue	Preparation of Reagents	Test Method	Result
Lipids	Fix in 4% formaldehyde containing 1% calcium chloride. Cut frozen sections, if necessary, after embedding in gelatin.	Digest 1 g Sudan black B in 100 ml 60% triethyl phosphate at 100°C for 5 min with constant agitation. Cool, then filter.	Stain section 2-5 min. Wash in 60% triethyl phosphate. Wash in H_2O and stain carmine-light green. Mount in aqueous medium.	Lipid granules, black; nuclei, red; cytoplasm, green.
Cholesterol	Cut frozen sections of fresh or formaldehyde-fixed material.		Strand section on slide. Drain well. Cover with 2 drops conc. H_2SO_4 for 10 sec. Add 2 drops acetic anhydride, wait 10 sec, then wash thoroughly with acetic anhydride. Place cover slip on section.	Cholesterol shows green, or blue-green. Preparation cannot be preserved.
Glycogen	Fix in ethanol at 0°C. Cut 10-μ paraffin sections and mount on slide; deparaffinize in xylene. Rinse in equal parts ethanol and ether. Dip in collodion U.S.P.	Boil 2 g carmine, 1 g potassium carbonate, and 5 g potassium chloride in 60 ml H_2O for 5 min. Cool, then add 20 ml ammonium hydroxide. For use, dilute 10 ml of this stock sol. with 15 ml ammonium hydroxide and 15 ml ethanol.	Stain collodionized sections in celestin blue B. Wash thoroughly in water. Stain in carmine 15 min. Rinse thoroughly in methanol, dehydrate in acetone, clear in xylene, and mount in balsam.	Nuclei, black; glycogen granules, scarlet.
Starch	Fix in any dichromate--chromic acid--formaldehyde fixative. Cut paraffin sections.	Saturate hot anilin with acid fuchsin. Shake well, separate, and retain water fraction.	Pour acid fuchsin stain on sections; heat to steaming for 1 min. Rinse in H_2O and place in 5% aurantia in ethanol until no color comes away. Rinse in 70% ethanol and transfer to 2% tannic acid for 15 min. Transfer directly to 1% methyl green for 10 min. Differentiate in ethanol until starch grains are sharply distinct.	Plastids, proplastids, and mitochondria, red; starch, green. The standard iodine test for starch does not yield permanent preparations.
Mucin	Cut paraffin sections of material fixed in any mercuric chloride or dichromate fixative.		Stain 10-40 sec in 1% Alcian Blue. Rinse quickly in H_2O and transfer for 2 hr to 0.5% borax in 80% ethanol. Dehydrate and mount in balsam.	Mucin, bright blue. Stained sections may be counterstained in hematoxylin-eosin if further histological detail is desired.
Celluloses	Sections of plant tissues, or teased fibers.	Dissolve 2 g iodine and 5 g potassium iodide in a small amount of H_2O. Dilute to 100 ml. Add 10 ml iodine sol. and 0.25 ml glycerol to 90 ml H_2O.	Cover specimen with iodine sol. for 15 sec. Blot dry. Add 1 drop of sat. aqueous sol. lithium carbonate. Apply cover slip.	Pure cellulose, blue; impure celluloses, various shades of green, yellow, and brown.
Lignin	Sections of plant tissues, or teased fibers.		Place in 1% phloroglucinol for 2 min. Blot and add 1 drop of HCl.	Lignin, red.
Chitin	Sections of tissues.	Dissolve 10 g anilin hydrochloride in 100 ml 1% HCl. Stain sections 5 min.	Transfer to 7.5% potassium dichromate for 1 min. Rinse in H_2O and place in alkaline tap water until color changes from green to blue.	Chitin, blue.

(Continued)

Histochemical Tests (Continued)

TABLE 2.H.5 (Continued)

Substance	Preparation of Tissue	Preparation of Reagents	Test Method	Result
DNA	Sections or smears of either animal or plant material.	Boil 1 g magenta ("basic" fuchsin) in 100 ml H_2O. Add 20 ml N HCl. Cool, filter, and add 5 ml 10% sodium bisulfite. Leave in dark 24 hr.	Hydrolyze material 20 min in N HCl. Stain 2 hr in dark. Bleach cytoplasm 1-2 min in freshly made 100 ml H_2O, 5 ml 10% sodium bisulfite, 5 ml N HCl. Counterstain in light green if desired. Dehydrate, clear, and mount in balsam.	
RNA	10-μ paraffin sections of tissues.	Shake 0.5 g methyl green with successive batches of chloroform until all chloroform-soluble color is removed. Add 13 ml of purified dye sol. to 50 ml pH 4.8 acetate buffer and 37 ml 0.5% pyroam G.	Take sections to H_2O. Blot. Stain 30 min. Blot. Pass to acetone 1 min, and 50:50 acetone-xylene 1 min. Clear in xylene and mount in balsam.	RNA, blue to blue-green; DNA, red.
Proteins	10-μ sections of neutral formaldehyde-fixed material.	Mix 95 ml ethanol with 0.5 ml 0.2 N sodium hydroxide. Add 0.5 g 2,4-dinitro-fluorobenzene.	Take sections to H_2O. Stain 24 hr. Rinse thoroughly in ethanol, then H_2O. Bleach in 5% sodium thiosulfate 40 min at 37°C. Rinse in H_2O. Add 5 ml ice-cold $4N$ H_2SO_4 to 100 ml ice-cold 5% sodium nitrate. Soak bleached sections 4-5 min. Rinse in H_2O. Transfer to 2% H-acid in barbitone-acetate pH 9.2 buffer for 15 min. Rinse in H_2O, dehydrate, clear, and mount in balsam.	Protein, purple-red.
Iron	10-μ, or thicker, sections of tissues fixed in iron-free, neutral formaldehyde.		Take sections to H_2O. Place in 2% potassium ferrocyanide with equal volume of 0.2 N HCl and stain 20 min. Dehydrate, clear, mount in balsam.	Reactive iron, blue. Non-reactive iron (e.g., in hemoglobin) may be rendered reactive by treating sections for 30 min, before staining, in alkaline H_2O_2.
Hemoglobin	10-μ, or thicker, sections of tissues fixed in neutral formaldehyde.	Dissolve 1-2 g benzidine in 100 ml methanol with 1.2 ml acetic acid. Add 0.12 g sodium nitroprusside.	Deparaffinize sections in xylene. Remove xylene completely in several changes of methanol. Stain 10 min. Wash in 50 ml methanol, 25 ml ether, 25 ml 3% H_2O_2. Dehydrate, clear, and mount in balsam.	Hemoglobin, bright blue.
Carotene	Immerse plant tissues in 20 ml sat. aqueous sol. potassium hydroxide, 15 ml ethanol, 85 ml H_2O in dark until all green removed.		Wash pieces thoroughly in H_2O. Place fragment on slide, blot, and cover with H_2SO_4.	Areas of dark blue crystals indicate carotene locations.

Source: Altman, P. L., and Dittmer, D. S. (editors). *Biology Data Book*. Federation of American Societies for Experimental Biology, Bethesda, Maryland.

Honey Composition

TABLE 2.H.6
Average composition of U.S. honey and range of values[1]

Characteristic or constituent		Floral Honey	
		Average values	Range of Values
Color[2]		Dark half of white	Light half of water white to dark
Granulating tendency[3]		Few clumps of crystals, 1/8- to 1/4-inch layer	Liquid to complete hard granulation
Moisture	percent	17.2	13.4 - 22.9
Fructose	,,	38.19	27.45 - 44.26
Glucose	,,	31.28	22.03 - 40.75
Sucrose	,,	1.31	0.25 - 7.57
"Maltose"[4]	,,	7.31	2.74 - 15.98
Higher sugars	,,	1.50	0.13 - 8.49
Undetermined		3.1	0 - 13.2
pH		3.91	3.42 - 6.10
Free acidity[5]		22.03	6.75 - 47.19
Lactone[5]		7.11	0 - 18.76
Total acidity[5]		29.12	8.68 - 59.49
Lactone ÷ free acid		0.335	0 - 0.950
Ash	percent	0.169	0.02 - 1.028
Nitrogen	,,	0.041	0 - 0.133
Diastase[6] (270 samples)		20.8	2.1 - 61.2

[1] Based on 490 samples of floral honey.
[2] Expressed in terms of USDA color classes.
[3] Extent of granulation for heated samples after 6 months' undisturbed storage.
[4] Reducing disaccharides as maltose.
[5] Milliequivalent per kilogram.
[6] Grams of starch converted by enzyme in 100 gm honey in 1 hr under assay conditions.

Source: White, Jr., J., and Underwood, J. C. (1974). Maple syrup and honey. In *Symposium: Sweeteners.* G. E. Inglett (editor). AVI Publishing Co., Westport, Connecticut.

Humidity, Solutions

TABLE 2.H.7
Constant humidity solutions. A saturated aqueous solution in contact with an excess of the solute when kept in an enclosed space will maintain a constant humidity at a given temperature.

Substance Dissolved and Solid Phase	Temp (°C)	Humidity (%)
Lead nitrate, $Pb(NO_3)_2$	20	98
Dibasic sodium phosphate, $Na_2HPO_4 \cdot 12H_2O$	20	95
Monobasic ammonium phosphate, $NH_4H_2PO_4$	20–25	93
Zinc sulfate, $ZnSO_4 \cdot 7H_2O$	20	90
Potassium chromate, K_2CrO_4	20	88
Potassium bisulfate, $KHSO_4$	20	86
Potassium bromide, KBr	20	84
Ammonium sulfate, $(NH_4)_2SO_4$	20	81
Ammonium chloride, NH_4Cl	20–25	79
Sodium acetate, $NaC_2H_3O_2 \cdot 3H_2O$	20	76
Sodium chlorate, $NaClO_3$	20	75
Sodium nitrite, $NaNO_2$	20	66
Sodium bromide, $NaBr \cdot 2H_2O$	20	58
Magnesium nitrite, $Mg(NO_3)_2 \cdot 6H_2O$	18.5	56
Sodium dichromate, $Na_2Cr_2O_7 \cdot 2H_2O$	20	52
Potassium thiocyanate, KSCN	20	47
Zinc nitrate, $Zn(NO_3)_2 \cdot 6H_2O$	20	42
Chromium trioxide, CrO_3	20	35
Calcium chloride, $CaCl_2 \cdot 6H_2O$	24.5	31
Potassium acetate, $KC_2H_3O_2$	20	20
Lithium chloride, $LiCl \cdot H_2O$	20	15

Source: (1968). *The Merck Index*, 8th Edition. Merck & Co., Rahway, New Jersey.

Hydrochloric Acid Solution

TABLE 2.H.8
Various strengths of hydrochloric acid solutions. Hydrochloric acid solutions: Specification requires not less than 35% HCl by weight; sp. gr. = 1.778 at 15°. Mix with H_2O and dilute to 1 liter.

HCl Strength Desired	HCl Required		
g per liter	g	ml	
5	14.29	12.13	
10	28.57	24.26	
15	42.85	36.39	
20	57.14	48.52	
36.46	104.17	88.45	1N soln
50	142.86	121.29	
100	285.71	242.58	
150	428.57	363.88	
200	571.43	485.17	
222.6	636.00	539.99	Constant boiling
278.4	795.43	675.35	Sp gr 1.125
300	857.14	727.75	

Source: Editorial Board, AOAC (1975). *Official Methods of Analysis of the Association of Official Analytical Chemists*, 12th Edition. Association of Official Analytical Chemists, Washington, D.C.

I

Ice, Vapor Pressure

TABLE 2.I.1
Vapor pressure of ice

Pressure of Aqueous Vapor over Ice in mm Hg at Various Temperatures							
Temperature		Vapor Pressure		Temperature		Vapor Pressure	
°C	°F	mm Hg	μ	°C	°F	mm Hg	μ
0	32.0	4.579	4579.0	−36	−32.8	0.1507	150.7
−2	28.4	3.880	3880.0	−40	−40.0	0.0966	96.6
−4	24.8	3.280	3280.0	−44	−47.2	0.0609	60.9
−6	21.2	2.765	2765.0	−48	−54.4	0.0378	37.8
−8	17.6	2.326	2326.0	−52	−61.6	0.02300	23.00
−10	14.0	1.950	1950.0	−56	−68.8	0.01380	13.80
−12	10.4	1.632	1632.0	−60	−76.0	0.00808	8.08
−14	6.8	1.361	1361.0	−64	−83.2	0.00464	4.64
−16	3.2	1.132	1132.0	−68	−90.4	0.00261	2.61
−18	−0.4	0.939	939.0	−72	−97.6	0.00143	1.43
−20	−4.0	0.776	776.0	−76	−104.8	0.00077	0.77
−22	−7.6	0.640	640.0	−80	−112.0	0.00040	0.40
−24	−11.2	0.526	526.0	−84	−119.2	0.00020	0.20
−26	−14.8	0.430	430.0	−88	−126.4	0.00010	0.10
−28	−18.4	0.351	351.0	−92	−133.6	0.000048	0.048
−30	−22.0	0.2859	285.9	−96	−140.8	0.000022	0.022
−32	−25.6	0.2318	231.8	−98	−144.4	0.000015	0.015
−34	−29.2	0.1873	187.3	—	—	—	—

Source: Copson, D. A. (editor) (1975). Derivation of the theory of microwave freeze-drying. In *Microwave Heating*, 2nd Edition. AVI Publishing Co., Westport, Connecticut.

Illness From Food

TABLE 2.I.2
Classification of illness attributable to foods

Type of Illness	Causative agent	Food Usually Involved	Incubation Period	Symptoms
		A. Bacterial Food Infections		
Shigellosis Bacillary Dysentery	Members of the genus *Shigella*	Moist prepared foods, milk and other dairy products, contaminated with excreta	Usually 2–3 days	Diarrhea, bloody stools, fever in severe cases
Cholera	*Vibrio Comma*	Fecally contaminated food and water	2–5 days	Nausea, vomiting, diarrhea and abdominal cramps
Brucellosis, Undulant Fever or Bang's Disease	*Brucella abortus, B. melitensis,* or *B. Suis*	Raw milk or dairy products contaminated with raw milk, animal contact (meat)	3–21 days sometimes several months	Chills, sweats, weakness, malaise, headache, fever, muscle and joint pains, and loss of weight
Diphtheria	*Corynebacterium diphtheriae*	Milk contaminated from human sources	3–7 days	Insidious onset, inflammation of throat and nose
Hemolytic streptococci, scarlet fever and septic sore throat	Beta hemolytic streptococci	Food contaminated with nasal or oral discharges and milk from cows having udder infections	1–7 days	Fever, sore throat, sometimes rash
Streptococcal food infections	*Enterococcus coccus fecalis*	Food contaminated with excreta or human carrier	2–18 days	Nausea, vomiting, pains, and diarrhea
Salmonellosis a. Typhoid Fever	*Salmonella typhi*	Any food contaminated with excreta from human case or carrier	Usually 7–21 days	Malaise, lack of appetite, headache, fever
b. Paratyphoid A.	*Salmonella paratyphi* A.	Same as for typhoid fever	1–10 days	Same as for typhoid fever

(Continued)

Illness From Food (*Continued*)

TABLE 2.I.2 (Continued)

Type of Illness	Causative agent	Food Usually Involved	Incubation Period	Symptoms
c. Other Types	*Salmonella typhimurium*, *Salmonella enteritis*, *Salmonella cholera suis*, *Salmonella newport*	Meat, poultry salads, and egg products	12–72 hours	Abdominal pain, diarrhea, chills, fever, vomiting, and prostration
Tuberculosis	*Mycobacterium tuberculosis*, human and bovine types A and B	Raw contaminated milk and other dairy products	Variable	Depends on part of body affected
Tularemia	*Pasteurella tularensis*	Wild game animals	3–10 days	Sudden onset, headache, chills, body pains, fever, vomiting, swollen lymph glands, and loss of appetite
Trichinosis	*Trichinella spiralis*	Raw pork or similar products	36–72 hours	
B. Bacterial Food Intoxications				
Staphylococcal intoxication	Staphylococcus producing Enterotoxin	Meats, food rich in carbohydrates, especially salads and warmed over foods	2–11 hours	Nausea, vomiting, diarrhea, and abdominal cramps
Botulism	Exotoxin *Clostridium botulinum* and *C. parabotulinum*	Home processed foods and contaminated canned foods with pH over 4.5	12 hours to 6 days	Dizziness, double vision, muscular weakness, difficulty in swallowing, speech and respiration
Clostridium perfringens (*welchii*)	*Cl. welchii* Type A. Exotoxin Alpha type	Cold and reheated meats, water, milk, salt rising bread. Found in intestinal tract of man and animals	8–22 hours (variable)	Acute abdominal pains, diarrhea, nausea, and vomiting rare

NOTE: *Clostridium perfringens* and *Bacillus cereus* may cause symptoms identical to *Streptococcus fecalis*, providing they are present in the food product in large numbers.

Source: Weiser, H. H., Mountney, G. J., and Gould, W. A. (editors) (1971). Food poisoning. In *Practical Food Microbiology and Technology*, 2nd Edition. AVI Publishing Co., Westport, Connecticut.

Indicators: pH and Acid–Base

TABLE 2.I.3
Acid–base indicators

Indicator	Approximate pH range	Color-change	Preparation
Methyl Violet	0.0–1.6	yel to bl	0.01–0.05% in water
Crystal Violet	0.0–1.8	yel to bl	0.02% in water
Ethyl Violet	0.0–2.4	yel to bl	0.1 g in 50 ml of MeOH + 50 ml of water
Malachite Green	0.2–1.8	yel to bl grn	water
Methyl Green	0.2–1.8	yel to bl	0.1% in water
2-(p-dimethylaminophenylazo)pyridine	0.2–1.8	yel to bl	0.1% in EtOH
	4.4–5.6	red to yel	
o-Cresolsulfonephthalein (Cresol Red)	0.4–1.8	yel to red	0.1 g in 26.2 ml 0.01N
	7.0–8.8	yel to red	NaOH + 223.8 ml water
Quinaldine Red	1.0–2.2	col to red	1% in EtOH
p-(p-dimethylaminophenylazo)-benzoic acid, Na-salt (Paramethyl Red)	1.0–3.0	red to yel	EtOH
m-(p-anilnophenylazo)benzene sulfonic acid, Na-salt (Metanil Yellow)	1.2–2.4	red to yel	0.01% in water
4-Phenylazodiphenylamine	1.2–2.6	red to yel	0.01 g in 1 ml 1N HCl + 50 ml EtOH + 49 ml water
Thymolsulfonephthalein (Thymol Blue)	1.2–2.8	red to yel	0.1 g in 21.5 ml
	8.0–9.6	yel to bl	0.01N NaOH + 229.5 ml water
m-Cresolsulfonephthalein (Metacresol Purple)	1.2–2.8	red to yel	0.1 g in 26.2 ml
	7.4–9.0	yel to purp	0.01N NaOH + 223.8 ml water
p-(p-anilinophenylazo)benzenesulfonic acid, Na-salt (Orange IV)	1.4–2.8	red to yel	0.01% in water
4-o-Tolylazo-o-toluidine	1.4–2.8	or to yel	water
Erythrosine, disodium salt	2.2–3.6	or to red	0.1% in water
Benzopurpurine 48	2.2–4.2	vt to red	0.1% in water
N,N-dimethyl-p-(m-tolylazo)aniline	2.6–4.8	red to yel	0.1% in water
4,4'-Bix(2-amino-1-naphthylazo)2,2'-stilbenedisulfonic acid	3.0–4.0	purp to red	0.1 g in 5.9 ml 0.05N NaOH + 94.1 ml water
Tetrabromophenolphthaleinethyl ester, K-salt	3.0–4.2	yel to bl	0.1% in EtOH
3',3'',5',5''-tetrabromophenol-sulfonephthalein (Bromophenol Blue)	3.0–4.6	yel to bl	0.1 g in 14.9 ml 0.01N NaOH + 235.1 ml water
2,4-Dinitrophenol	2.8–4.0	col to yel	saturated water solution
N,N-Dimethyl-p-phenylazoaniline (p-Dimethylaminoazobenzene)	2.8–4.4	red to yel	0.1 g in 90 ml in EtOH + 10 ml water
Congo Red	3.0–5.0	blue to red	0.1% in water
Methyl Orange-Xylene Cyanole solution	3.2–4.2	purp to grn	ready solution
Methyl Orange	3.2–4.4	red to yel	0.01% in water
Ethyl Orange	3.4–4.8	red to yel	0.05–0.2% in water or aqueous EtOH
4-(4-Dimethylamino-1-naphthylazo)-3-methoxybenzenesulfonic acid	3.5–4.8	vt to yel	0.1% in 60% EtOH
3',3'',5',5''-Tetrabromo-m-cresol-sulfonephthalein (Bromocresol Green)	3.8–5.4	yel to blue	0.1 g in 14.3 ml 0.01N NaOH + 235.7 ml water
Resazurin	3.8–6.4	or to vt	water
4-Phenylazo-1-naphthylamine	4.0–5.6	red to yel	0.1% in EtOH
Ethyl Red	4.0–5.8	col to red	0.1 g in 50 ml MeOH + 50 ml water
2-(p-Dimethylaminophenylazo)-pyridine	0.2–1.8	yel to red	0.1% in EtOH
	4.4–5.6	red to yel	
4-(p-ethoxyphenylazo)-m-phenylenediamine monohydrochloride	4.4–5.8	or to yel	0.1% in water
Lacmoid	4.4–6.2	red to bl	0.2% in EtOH
Alizarin Red S	4.6–6.0	yel to red	dilute solution in water
Methyl Red	4.8–6.0	red to yel	0.02 g in 60 ml EtOH + 40 ml water

(Continued)

Indicators, pH and Acid–Base (Continued)

TABLE 2.I.3 (Continued)

Indicator	Approximate pH range	Color-change	Preparation
Propyl Red	4.8–6.6	red to yel	EtOH
5′,5″-Dibromo-o-cresolsulfone-phthalein (Bromocresol Purple)	5.2–6.8	yel to purp	0.1 g in 18.5 ml 0.01N NaOH + 231.5 ml water
3′,3″-Dichlorophenolsulfonephthalein (Chlorophenol Red)	5.2–6.8	yel to red	0.1 g in 23.6 ml 0.01N NaOH + 226.4 ml water
p-Nitrophenol	5.4–6.6	col to yel	0.1% in water
Alizarin	5.6–7.2	yel to red	0.1% in MeOH
	11.0–12.4	red to purp	
2-(2,4-Dinitrophenylazo)-1-naphthol-3, 6-disulfonic acid, di-Na salt	6.0–7.0	yel to bl	0.1% in water
3′,3″-Dibromothymolsulfonephthalein (Bromothymol Blue)	6.0–7.6	yel to bl	0.1 g in 16 ml 0.01N NaOH + 234 ml water
6,8-Dinitro-2,4-(1H)quinazolinedione (m-Dinitrobenzoylene urea)	6.4–8.0	col to yel	25 g in 115 ml M NaOH + 50 ml boiling water 0.292 g of NaCl in 100 ml water
Brilliant Yellow	6.6–7.8	yel to or	1% in water
Phenolsulfonephthalein (Phenol Red)	6.6–8.0	yel to red	0.1 g in 28.2 ml 0.01N NaOH + 221.8 ml water
Neutral Red	6.8–8.0	red to amb	0.01 g in 50 ml EtOH + 50 ml water
m-Nitrophenol	6.8–8.6	col to yel	0.3% in water
o-Cresolsulfonephthalein (Cresol Red)	0.0–1.0	red to yel	0.1 g in 26.2 ml 0.01N NaOH + 223.8 ml water
	7.0–8.8	yel to red	
Curcumin	7.4–8.6	yel to red	EtOH
	10.2–11.8		
m-Cresolsulfonephthalein (Metacresol Purple)	1.2–2.8	red to yel	0.1 g in 26.2 ml 0.01N NaOH + 223.8 ml water
	7.4–9.0	yel to purp	
4,4′-Bis(4-amino-1-naphthylazo) 2,2′stilbene disulfonic acid	8.0–9.0	bl to red	0.1 g in 5.9 ml 0.05N NaOH + 94.1 ml water
Thymolsulfonephthalein (Thymol Blue)	1.2–2.8	red to yel	0.1 g in 21.5 ml 0.01N NaOH + 228.5 ml water
	8.0–9.6		
o-Cresolphthalein	8.2–9.8	col to red	0.04% in EtOH
p-Naphtholbenzene	8.2–10.0	or to bl	1% in dil. alkali
Phenolphthalein	8.2–10.0	col to pink	0.05 g in 50 ml EtOH + 50 ml water
Ethyl-bis(2,4-dimethylphenyl)acetate	8.4–9.6	col to bl	saturated solution in 50% acetone alcohol
Thymolphthalein	9.4–10.6	col to bl	0.04 g in 50 ml EtOH + 50 ml water
5-(p-Nitrophenylazo)salicylic acid, Na-salt (Alizarin Yellow R)	10.1–12.0	yel to red	0.01% in water
p-(2,4-Dihydroxyphenylazo)benzene-sulfonic acid, Na-salt	11.4–12.6	yel to or	0.1% in water
5,5′-Indigodisulfonic acid, di-Na-salt	11.4–13.0	bl to yel	water
2,4,6-Trinitrotoluene	11.5–13.0	col to or	0.1–0.5% in EtOH
1,3,5-Trinitrobenzene	12.0–14.0	col to or	0.1–0.5% in EtOH
Clayton Yellow	12.2–13.2	yel to amb	0.1% in water

Source: Weast, R. C. (editor) (1974–1975). *Handbook of Chemistry and Physics*, 55th Edition. CRC Press, Cleveland.

Infectious Agents

TABLE 2.I.4
Disease from ingestion of infectious agents

Disease	Reservoirs	Common Vehicle	Prevention and Control
Salmonellosis (salmonella infection)	Hogs, cattle and other livestock, poultry, pets, eggs, powdered eggs, carriers.	Contaminated cooked meat; infected meats; salads; warmed over foods; milk; milk products.	Thoroughly cook food; eliminate rodents, pets and carriers; similar measures as in staphylococcus, plant sanitation.
Typhoid fever	Feces and urine of typhoid carrier or patient.	Contaminated water; milk and milk products; shellfish and foods; flies.	Protect and purify water supply; pasteurize milk and milk products; educate food handlers; provide food, fly, shellfish control, and sanitary sewage disposal; supervise carriers; immunize.
Streptococcal infections	Human mouth, nose, throat, respiratory tract.	Contaminated meats; milk; croquettes; cheese; dressing.	Provide control measures similar to those for Staphylococcus; pasteurize milk and milk products.
Shigellosis (bacillary dysentery)	Bowel discharges of carriers and infected persons.	Contaminated water or foods; milk and milk products; flies.	Provide food, water, sewage sanitation as in typhoid; pasteurize milk (boil for infants); control flies; supervise carriers.

Source: U.S. Department of the Army (1969). Food inspection specialist. *TM 8-451.*

Infectious Diseases, Food-Borne

TABLE 2.I.5
Some common infectious diseases according to most usual mode of transmission (common food-borne)

Disease	Synonym	Causative Agent	Mode of Transmission	Methods of Prevention	Treatments Available
Food poisoning	Staph food poisoning	Soluble enterotoxin produced by the growth of *Staphylococcus aureus* in foods	Ingestion of contaminated foods	1. Prevent contamination 2. Refrigeration	Supportive
Food poisoning		Growth of *Clostridium perfringens* in foods, most often meats	Ingestion of contaminated foods	1. Prevent contamination 2. Serve foods hot without delay 3. Adequate cooking 4. Refrigeration	Supportive
Botulism		Soluble toxins produced by growth of *Clostridium botulinum* in anaerobic nonacid foods	Ingestion of contaminated foods	1. Prevent contamination 2. Proper heat preservation 3. Heat to boiling for 15 min before eating	Specific antitoxin

(Continued)

Infectious Diseases, Food-Borne (Continued)

TABLE 2.1.5 (Continued)

Disease	Synonym	Causative Agent	Mode of Transmission	Methods of Prevention	Treatments Available
Salmonellosis	Food poisoning	Anyone of many species or types of *Salmonella*	Ingestion of live organisms in contaminated foods	1. Prevent contamination 2. Cleaning raw foods 3. Thorough cooking 4. Refrigeration 5. Detect and eliminate carriers	Antibiotic treatment has irregular success
Typhoid fever, Paratyphoid fever	Enteric fever	*Salmonella typhi, Salmonella paratyphi* A, *Salmonella paratyphi* B, *Salmonella paratyphi* C	Ingestion of live organisms in contaminated foods or water	1. Chlorination of water 2. Detection and elimination of carriers 3. Proper cooking of foods 4. Immunization 5. General sanitation	Antibiotic treatment
Shigellosis	Bacillary dysentery	Any one of many species or types of *Shigella*	Ingestion of live organisms in contaminated foods or water	1. Chlorination of water 2. Proper cooking and handling of foods 3. General sanitation	Antibiotic treatment plus fluid maintenance
Streptococcal Pharangitis	Strep throat Septic sore throat	*Streptococcus pyogenes,* many types	Ingestion of live organisms in contaminated food or milk. Also contact and respiratory	1. General sanitation 2. Pasteurization of milk 3. Proper food cooking, handling, storage	Antibiotic treatment
Diphtheria		*Corynebacterium diphtheriae*	Ingestion of live organisms in milk or food. Also contact and respiratory	1. Immunization 2. Pasteurization of milk 3. Proper food handling and refrigeration 4. General sanitation	Antibiotic treatment and antitoxin treatment
Brucellosis	Undulant fever, milk fever, malta fever	*Brucella abortus B. melitensis* or *B. suis*	Ingestion of live organisms in milk or meat products. Also contact	1. Pasteurization of milk 2. Proper cooking of milk and meat products 3. General sanitation	Antibiotic treatment
Infectious hepatitis	Epidemic jaundice Catarrhal jaundice	Virus	Ingestion of virus in contaminated water, milk and food. Also direct contact	1. General sanitation 2. Isolation of cases	Gamma globulin
Amebiasis	Amebic dysentery	*Entamoeba histolytica*	Ingested cysts of organism in contaminated water, food	1. General sanitation 2. Water filtration	Antibiotic and chemical therapy

(Continued)

Infectious Diseases, Food-Borne (Continued)

TABLE 2.I.5 (Continued)

Disease	Synonym	Causative Agent	Mode of Transmission	Methods of Prevention	Treatments Available
Trichinosis	Trichiniasis Trichinellosis	Larva of *Trichinella spiralis*	Ingested meat containing viable larva of organisms	1. Adequate processing of pork 2. Adequate cooking of pork	
Acute diarrheal disease	Summer complaint Travelers diarrhea Infant diarrhea	*Escherichia coli, Shigella* sp., *Salmonella* sp., *Giardia lamblia, Staphylococcus* sp., *Pseudomonas aeruginosa, Proteus vulgaris,* others	Ingestion of live organisms in contaminated water, food. Also direct contact	1. Chlorination of water 2. General sanitation	Antibiotic and supportive therapy. Especially fluid balance in children.
Epidemic gastroenteritis	The Virus	One of several viruses	Ingestion of virus in contaminated water, food. Also contact	1. Treatment of water 2. General sanitation	Supportive therapy
Poliomyelitis	Infantile paralysis Polio	One of three types of poliovirus	Direct contact. Contaminated water. Foods possible but not proven	1. General sanitation 2. Immunization	Supportive therapy
Tularemia		*Pasteurella tularensis*	Direct contact. Bite of insects. Ingestion of organisms.	1. Properly cooking meat, especially rabbit	Antibiotic therapy
Tuberculosis	TB	*Mycobacterium tuberculosis*	Contact. Respiratory. Consumption of organism in milk from infected cows.	1. General sanitation 2. Pasteurization of milk and milk products 3. Elimination of infected cattle	Antibiotic and supportive therapy

Source: Guthrie, R. K. (editor) (1972). In *Food Sanitation*. AVI Publishing Co., Westport, Connecticut.

Ingestion and Inhalation

TABLE 2.I.6
Daily rates of ingestion and inhalation of water and air

Water intake in food	700 cm^3
Water intake in fluids	1,500 cm^3
Water of oxidation	300 cm^3
Total water consumption	2,500 cm^3
Air inhaled during 8-hr working day	10^7 cm^3
Air inhaled during 16 hr not at work	10^7 cm^3
Total air inhaled	2 × 10^7 cm^3

Source: Wang, Y. (editor) (1969). *Handbook of Radioactive Nuclides*. CRC Press, Cleveland.

Insect Control

TABLE 2.I.7
Insecticides for insect control

	5% Sevin	4% or 5% Malathion	1.5% Lindane	1% Rotenone
Aphids		X	X	
Armyworms	X			X
Budworms	X			
Cabbage worms	X	X		X
Col. potato beetle	X			
Cucumber beetle		X	X	
Earworms	X			X
Fleabeetle	X			X
Fruit, horn, pinworms	X			X
Leaf-hopper	X	X	X	X
Leaf-roller	X	X		X
Melon pickle worms		X	X	X
Mexican bean beetle	X	X		
Pameras	X	X		
Pea weevils	X	X	X	
Red spiders		X		
Stink bugs	X	X	X	
Thrips	X	X	X	Diazinon 2%
Leafminers			X	Diazinon 2%

Source: Vegetable Gardening Guide. (1975). Florida Coop. Ext. Serv. Circ. *104K*, Gainesville, Florida.

Insulating Value

TABLE 2.I.8
Insulating slabs or boards

Material	Density Lb per Cu Ft	Average Btu Passing per Hr Through a Plate of Material 1 Sq Ft in Area, 1 In. Thick, per °F Difference in the Two Faces
Cellular glass	9	0.41
Glass fiber	7	0.21
Polyurethane (exp.)	3	0.17
Rubber (exp.)	4.5	0.22
Polystyrene (extruded)	1.9	0.22
Expandable polystyrene	1.0	0.24

Source: Woolrich, W. R., and Hallowell, E. R. (editors) (1970). Insulation for, and heat transfer through cold and freezer storage walls and ceilings. In *Cold and Freezer Storage Manual*. AVI Publishing Co., Westport, Connecticut.

Insulation

TABLE 2.I.9
Thermal conductivities and densities

Insulating Materials	Density, lb/cu. ft.	Thermal Conductivity[1] for Thickness of 1 in., B.t.u./sq ft/hr. per °F.
Air cell ½ in.	8.80	0.458
Asbestos fibers packed	44	1.6
Asphalt roofing	55	0.70
Balsa wood	7–9	0.31–0.38
Balsam-wool	3.6	0.250
Brick, soft	87	5.0
Brick, hard	140	9.2
Concrete, $1:2:5$[2]	170	6.3
Concrete, cinder aggregate	97	4.9
Celotex	13.8	0.300
Corkboard, various grades	8–10	0.28–0.32
Cork, granulated	5	0.32
Cotton	5	0.42
Cottonseed hulls	5	0.31
Dry-Zero	2.0	0.250
Eel brass mats	14	0.34
Ferro-Therm (steel)	—	0.226
Foamglas	—	0.450
Glass wool	4	0.29
Hair felt	17	0.25
Insulite	11.9	0.296
Kapok fibers	1	0.24
Magnesia, 85%	17	0.50
Masonite	15.0	0.330
Mineral wool (slag or rock wool)	12	0.26
Mineral wool board, asphaltic binder	16	0.33
Oak lumber, cross grain	38	1.0
Redwood bark, fiber	6	0.28
Rock cork	14.5	0.326
Rock wool	14	0.28
Sand, river dried	95	2.3
Sawdust, pine	12	0.40
Stone masonry	170	12.0
Styrofoam	1.7	0.250
Sugar cane fiberboard	15	0.33
Tar roofing	55.0	0.707
Vermiculite	6.2	0.32
White pine lumber, cross grain	31	0.78
Wood fiber board	14	0.33
Wool, pure	5	0.26

[1] British thermal units per hr. passing through 1 sq. ft. of a plate of material 1 in. thick, per °F difference in temperature between the two faces.
[2] Mix 1 part Portland cement, 2 parts sand, 5 parts limestone.

Source: Woolrich, W. R. (1968). Design of above ground refrigerated storages. In *The Freezing Preservation of Foods*, Vol. 1, 4th Edition. D. K. Tressler, W. B. Van Arsdel, M. J. Copley, and W. R. Woolrich (editors). AVI Publishing Co., Westport, Connecticut.

Insulation, Conductivity Values

TABLE 2.I.10
Comparison of heat conductivity values

	Btu
Expanded ebonite	0.20
Regranulated cork	0.238
Cork slab	0.25
Slag wool	0.25–0.28
Granulated cork	0.328–0.345
Charcoal	0.369
Polystyrene	0.23
Alfol	0.22–0.36
Glass wool	0.26–0.40
Expanded slate concrete	1.9
Bricks (Flettons)	6.3
Concrete;	
Gravel (4), sand (2), cement (1)	7.0

Based upon the above, the equivalent thickness in inches to give a similar insulating effect would be:

Expanded ebonite 1 in.
Cork slab 1.25 in.
Expanded polystyrene 1.15 in.
Bricks 31.5 in. and concrete 35 in.

Source: Geary, D., and Gerrard, F. (1968). Meat and refrigeration. Meat Trades J., London, England.

Insulation, Thickness

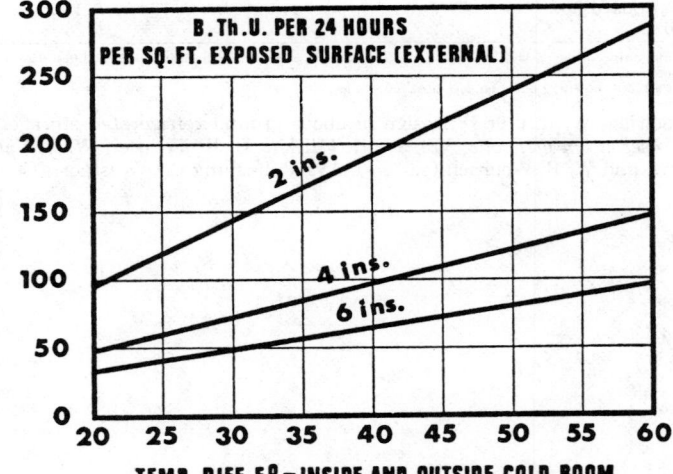

FIGURE 2.I.1
Effect of insulation thickness on cold room temperature

Source: Geary, D., and Gerrard, F. (1968). Meat and refrigeration. Meat Trades J., London, England.

Intestinal Microorganisms in Triple-Sugar Agar

TABLE 2.I.12
Reactions and suggested microorganisms indicated

Reaction on Slant[1]	Butt[2]	H₂S Production	Abbreviated Recording	Microorganisms Suggested	Indicated Procedure for Organisms Isolated from Faeces
Alk	Acid	−	A−	*Shigella, S. typhosa, Proteus*, paracolon, alkalescens-dispar group	Screen and identify as indicated
Alk	Acid	+	A+	*S. typhosa, Proteus*, paracolon, anaerogenic *Salmonella*	Screen and identify as indicated
Alk	Acid and gas	+	AG+	*Salmonella, Proteus*, paracolon (including Arizona)	Screen and identify as indicated (ordinarily many pathogens)
Alk	Acid and gas	−	AG−	Paracolon, *Proteus*, occasionally *Salmonella*	Screen and identify as indicated (ordinarily very few pathogens)
Acid	Acid	−	A/A−	Streptococci, staphylococci, occasionally *S. typhosa*, other Gram-negative rods	Screen and identify as indicated if a Gram-negative rod; discard others
Alk (spreading growth)	Acid and gas	+ or −	Sp[3]	*Proteus*	Discard
Acid	Acid and gas	−	−	"Coli-aerogenes"	Examine serologically for entero-pathogenic *E. coli* when indicated; otherwise discard
Alk	Alk	−	−	*Alcaligenes, Mimae, Pseudomonas*	Discard
Purplish	Alk	−	−	*Pseudomonas* species	Discard

[1] Alk slant indicates lactose and sucrose not fermented; acid slant indicates lactose and or sucrose fermented.
[2] Alk butt indicates dextrose not fermented; acid butt indicates dextrose fermented.
[3] Sp indicates spreader.

Source: Albertson, V. E. et al. Meat hygiene. FAO Agricultural Studies *34*, United Nations, Rome.

Intestinal Microorganisms

TABLE 2.I.11
Character of growth of enteric organisms on selective plating media

Group of Microorganisms	Shigella Salmonella (SS) Agar	Plain Desoxycholate, MacConkey's, or Eosin Methylene-blue Agar (EMB)	Bismuth Sulfite Wilson-Blair (WB) Agar	Brilliant-green (BG) Agar
Shigella	Colorless, some slightly pink; translucent, varying to transparent or to moderate opacity; round; raised; 1- to 5-mm diameter, some larger. *S. sonnei* may be large, flat, and irregular.	Colorless; transparent, 2- to 7-mm diameter; generally round. *S. sonnei* may be large, flat, and irregular.	Large, inhibited, occasionally develop as small colorless or greenish colonies with depressed centers.	No significant growth.
Salmonella typhosa	Similar to *Shigella*.	Similar to *Shigella*.	Isolated surface colonies; black, with surrounding brownish-black zone; a characteristic metallic sheen by reflected light. With congested growth; small, light green, often with darker center. Sub-surface colonies; jet black, well-defined; no sheen. Size 1-4 mm.	Largely inhibited.
Salmonella group (other than *S. typhosa*)	Similar to *Shigella*; occasionally some darkening of center of colonies.	Similar to *Shigella*.	Variable; many types markedly inhibited, a few simulate *S. typhosa*, others develop as flat greenish to brownish colonies.	Isolated surface colonies, pink to fuchsia surrounded by red medium, occasionally brownish with little change in medium.
Alkalescens-dispar group	Similar to *Shigella*; tend to be more opaque.	Similar to *Shigella*.	Light to dark green, smooth, glistening.	Largely inhibited; rarely may simulate *Salmonella* group.
"Coliform-aerogenes groups"	Largely inhibited; pink to red; opaque; may be mucoid; size variable.	On desoxycholate and MacConkey's: red; opaque; on EMB: characteristic sheen by reflected light; 2- to 7-mm diameter; may be mucoid with dark centers.	Quite marked inhibition; some develop as dark, brown, or greenish colonies.	Largely inhibited; may be yellowish-green.
Proteus group	Growth in discrete colonies; colorless, some with black centers, transparent to water-clear; irregular edge.	Often a spreading growth on EMB or MacConkey's; usually discrete colonies on plain desoxycholate; may simulate *Shigella* or *Salmonella*.	Marked inhibition; some green with darker centers.	Largely inhibited; may be small reddish colony.
Paracolon groups	Variable; may be similar to *Shigella* or may approach coli-aerogenes group.	Variable; may be similar to *Shigella* or may approach coliforms.	Similar to coliform group.	Similar to coliform.
Pseudomonas group	Variable; usually colorless, often greyish-brown.	Variable; may simulate *Proteus*.	Variable.	Pink to purplish; irregular edges; may closely simulate *Salmonella* group.

Source: Albertson, V. E. et al. Meat hygiene. FAO Agricultural Studies *34*, United Nations, Rome.

Iodine and Saponification Values

TABLE 2.I.13
Iodine values and saponification values of natural fats and oils

Fat	Saponification Value	Iodine Value	Fat	Saponification Value	Iodine Value
Babassu kernel oil	247–251	14–18	Rice bran oil	183–194	92–109
Borneo tallow	189–200	29–38	Safflower oil	188–194	140–150
Cacao butter	190–200	35–40	Sesame oil	188–195	103–116
Cashew nut oil	187–195	79–85	Sheanut butter oil	178–190	56–67
Castor oil	176–187	81–91	Soybean oil	189–195	120–141
Chinese vegetable tallow	200–209	20–29	Stillingia oil	203–212	169–187
Coconut oil	250–264	7.5–10.5	Sunflower oil	188–194	125–136
Cohune nut oil	252–260	9–14	Teaseed oil	188–196	80–90
Corn oil	187–193	103–128	Tung oil	189–195	160–175
Cottonseed oil	189–198	99–113	Walnut oil	189–198	140–152
Hempseed oil	190–193	150–166	Butterfat	210–233	26–42
Illipe butter	188–204	53–70	Bone grease	186–198	48–56
Jaboty tallow	228–236	5–9	Chicken fat	194–204	64–76
Kapok oil	189–197	86–110	Horse fat	195–199	72–86
Linseed oil	188–196	170–204	Lard	190–202	52–77
Mustard seed oil—black	176–184	106–113	Neatsfoot oil	190–199	69–76
Mustard seed oil—white	170–178	94–106	Tallow (beef)	190–199	40–48
Oiticica oil	186–193	140–160	Tallow (mutton)	192–197	35–46
Olive oil	188–196	80–88	Ghee	225–235	28–32
Palm oil	195–205	44–54	Cod-liver oil	180–190	140–170
Peanut oil	188–195	84–100	Herring oil	179–194	124–128
Perilla oil	188–197	193–208	Menhaden oil	189–193	148–160
Rapeseed oil (Calza)	170–180	97–108	Salmon oil	183–186	141–166
Ravison oil	173–181	109–122	Sardine oil	189–193	170–193
			Shark oil	158–164	115–139
			Shark-liver oil	160–196	112–136
			Whale oil	185–194	110–135
			Sperm oil (wax)	120–129	76–88

Source: Mahlenbacher, C. W. *The Analysis of Fats and Oils*. Garrard Press, Champaign, Illinois.

Iron

TABLE 2.I.14
Iron content of foods

	mg/100 g		mg/100 g
Spinach	3.1	Snap beans	0.8
Lima beans	2.8	Corn	0.7
Peas	1.9	Bananas	0.7
Brussels sprouts	1.5	Potatoes	0.6
Artichokes	1.3	Watermelon	0.6
Broccoli	1.1	Tomatoes	0.5
Cauliflower	1.1	Lettuce	0.5
Strawberries	1.0	Apples	0.3
Asparagus	1.0	Oranges	0.2

Source: White, P. L., and Selvey, N. (editors) (1974). *Nutritional Qualities of Fresh Fruits and Vegetables*. Futura Publishing Co., Mt. Kisco, New York.

Intestine, Cross Section

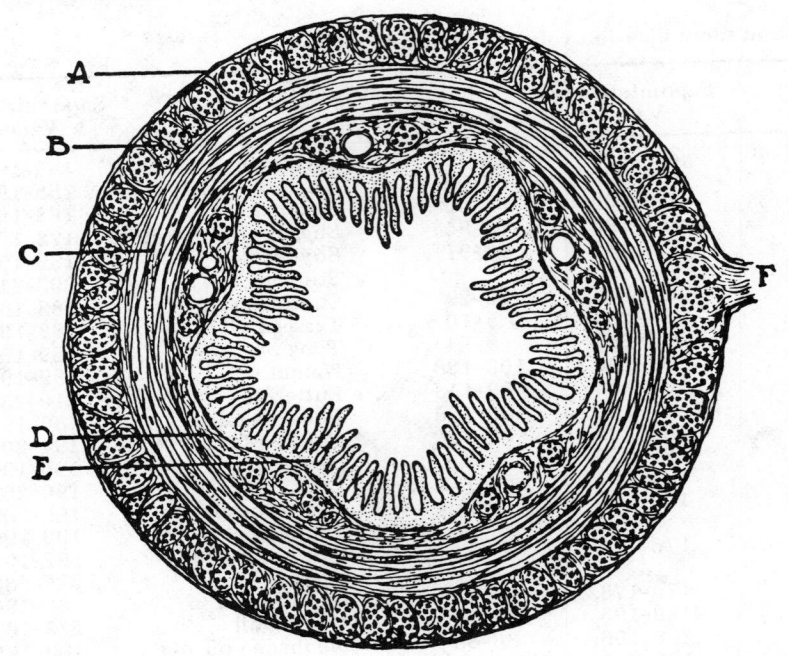

FIGURE 2.I.2
Diagrammatic cross section of small intestine (after sobotta). (A) serous coat, (B) longitudinal muscle layer, (C) circular muscle layer, (D) submucous layer, (E) mucous membrane, (F) mesentery attachment

Source: Moulton, C. R., and Lewis, W. L. *Meat Through the Microscope*, Revised Edition. Institute of Meat Packing, The University of Chicago, Chicago.

Iron, Daily Recommendations

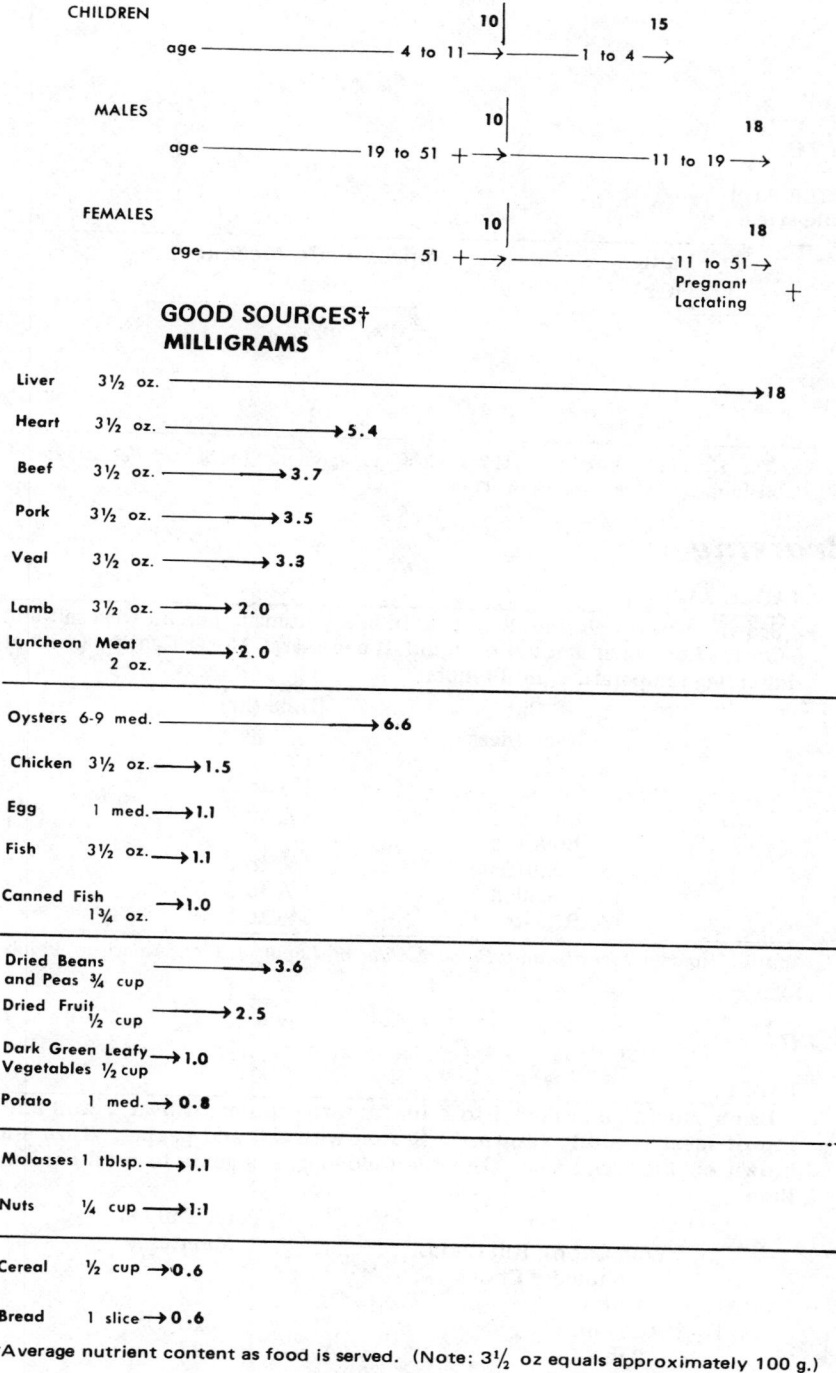

MILLIGRAMS

CHILDREN

age ——————————— 4 to 11 →——————— 1 to 4 →
10   15

MALES

age ——————————— 19 to 51 + →——————— 11 to 19 →
10   18

FEMALES

age——————————— 51 + →——————— 11 to 51 →
10   18
Pregnant
Lactating   +

GOOD SOURCES†
MILLIGRAMS

Liver   3½ oz. ————————————————————→ 18

Heart   3½ oz. —————————→ 5.4

Beef   3½ oz. —————————→ 3.7

Pork   3½ oz. —————————→ 3.5

Veal   3½ oz. —————————→ 3.3

Lamb   3½ oz. —————→ 2.0

Luncheon Meat
2 oz. —————→ 2.0

Oysters 6-9 med. —————————→ 6.6

Chicken   3½ oz. ————→ 1.5

Egg   1 med. ————→ 1.1

Fish   3½ oz. ————→ 1.1

Canned Fish
1¾ oz. ———→ 1.0

Dried Beans
and Peas ¾ cup —————→ 3.6

Dried Fruit
½ cup —————→ 2.5

Dark Green Leafy
Vegetables ½ cup ———→ 1.0

Potato   1 med. —→ 0.8

Molasses 1 tblsp. ———→ 1.1

Nuts   ¼ cup ———→ 1:1

Cereal   ½ cup —→ 0.6

Bread   1 slice —→ 0.6

†Average nutrient content as food is served. (Note: 3½ oz equals approximately 100 g.)

FIGURE 2.1.3

Source: Lessons on Meat. (1974). National Live Stock and Meat Board, Chicago.

L

Ladle Size

TABLE 2.L.1
Ladle sizes

Ladles (Oz)	Approximate Measure (Cup)
2	$1/4$
4	$1/2$
6	$3/4$
8	1

Source: Van Egmond, D. (editor) (1974). Cost management. In *School Food Service.* AVI Publishing Co., Westport, Connecticut.

Lamb Braising

TABLE 2.L.2

Brown meat on all sides in hot fat in heavy utensil. Season with salt and pepper. Add small amount of liquid, if necessary. Cover tightly. Cook at simmering temperature until tender.

Cut	Time (hr)
Neck slices	
¾ in.	1
Shanks	1½ to 2
Cubes	1½ to 2
Breast	
Stuffed	1½ to 2
Rolled	1½ to 2
Riblets	1½ to 2

Source: How to Identify and Prepare Cuts of Lamb. (1971). American Lamb Council.

Lamb Broiling

TABLE 2.L.3

Lamb should be broiled 3 to 4 in. from the source of heat. Broil until top of meat is nicely browned. Season with salt and pepper. Turn and brown on the other side. Use the following as a guide to total cooking time.

Cut	Total Time in Minutes
Loin Chops, Rib Chops, Shoulder Chops	
1 in.	12
1½ in.	18
2 in.	22
Lamb Patties	
1 in. × 3 in.	18

Source: How to Identify and Prepare Cuts of Lamb. (1971). American Lamb Council.

Lamb Chart

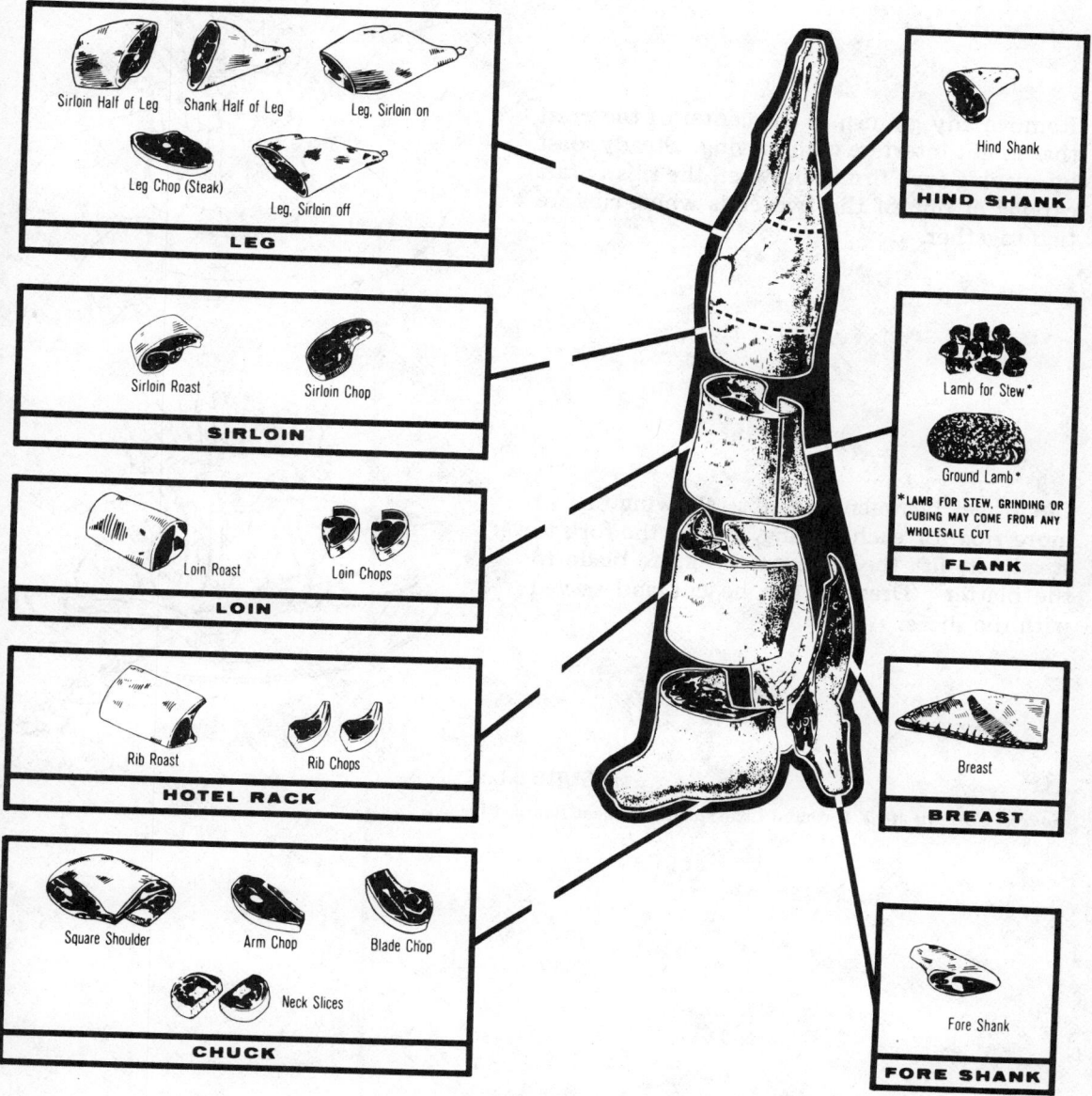

FIGURE 2.L.1

Source: USDA (1969). How to buy meat for your freezer. USDA Home and Garden Bull. *166*.

Lamb Crown Roast Carving

Remove any garnish in the center of the roast that might interfere with carving. Steady roast by placing fork firmly between the ribs. Start carving at one of the two ends where ribs are tied together.

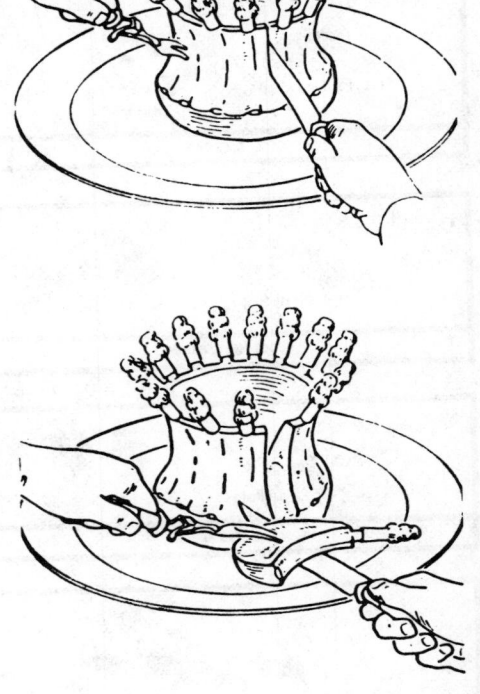

Cut down between the ribs, allowing one or more ribs for each serving. Using the fork to steady it, lift the slice on the knife blade to the platter. Dressing can be cut and served with the slices.

FIGURE 2.L.2

Source: Carving Meat. National Live Stock and Meat Board, Chicago.

Lamb Cuts

TABLE 2.L.4
Characteristics and cooking methods for lamb cuts

WHOLESALE CUTS	RETAIL CUTS	CHARACTERISTICS	COOKING METHODS
Leg	Frenched Leg	Shank bone is "frenched", that is, meat is removed to expose one inch or more of lower end of shank bone.	*Roast*
	American Leg	Shank meat is removed at stifle joint. Shank meat is tucked into pocket under fell and pinned into place	*Roast*
	Half of Leg	Either the shank half or the loin half.	*Roast*
	Leg Chops (*Steaks*)	May contain cross section of back bone and aitch bone. Center cut steaks look like miniature beef round steaks.	*Broil; panbroil; panfry*
	Sirloin Chops	Correspond to beef sirloin steaks. Pinbone chops have considerable bone.	*Broil; panbroil; panfry*
	Boneless Sirloin Roast	Small boneless roll weighing from 2 to 3½ pounds.	*Roast*
Loin	Loin Roast	Corresponds to beef short loin. It can be the unsplit loin but is usually one side of the split loin.	*Roast*
	Rolled Loin Roast	Boned and rolled loin.	*Roast*
	Loin Chops	Contain T-shaped bones; correspond to porterhouse, T-bone, and club beef steaks.	*Broil; panbroil; panfry*
	English Chops	Cut across the unsplit loin. Back bone removed and boneless chop skewered into shape.	*Broil; panbroil; panfry*
Rack	Rib (Rack) Roast	Contains rib bones and rib eye muscle.	*Roast*
	Crown Roast	Ribs are "frenched," that is, meat is removed from rib ends, then two or more rib sections are shaped and tied into a "crown".	*Roast*
	Rib Chops	Contain rib bone and rib eye muscle.	*Broil; panbroil; panfry*
	Frenched Chops	Same as rib chops except meat is removed from ends of ribs.	*Broil; panbroil; panfry*

(Continued)

Lamb Cuts (Continued)

TABLE 2.L.4 (Continued)

WHOLESALE CUTS	RETAIL CUTS	CHARACTERISTICS	COOKING METHODS
Shoulder	Square Cut Shoulder	Thickest part of forequarter, with shank, breast, rib (rack), and neck removed.	Roast
	Cushion Shoulder	Boned and left flat. Sewed on two sides. One side may be left open for stuffing, then skewered or sewed.	Roast
	Rolled Shoulder	Boneless roll made from square cut shoulder.	Roast
	Boneless Shoulder Chops	Cut from boneless rolled shoulder.	Broil; panbroil; panfry; braise
	Mock Duck	Made from outside of shoulder. Shaped like a duck.	Roast
	Arm Chops	Contain small round bone and usually the cross sections of 4 or 5 rib bones.	Broil; panbroil; panfry; braise
	Blade Chops	Contain portions of rib, back and blade bones.	Broil; panbroil; panfry; braise
	Saratoga Chops	Boneless chops made from the inside shoulder muscle.	Broil; panbroil; panfry; braise
	Neck Slices	Round slice with neck vertebrae in center.	Braise; cook in liquid
Breast	Breast	Corresponds to veal breast and to short plate and brisket of beef. Narrow strip of meat containing breast bone and ends of 12 ribs.	Roast; braise; cook in liquid
	Breast with Pocket	Same as above but with pocket between ribs and lean.	Roast; braise
	Rolled Breast	Small boneless roll. Alternating layers of lean and fat.	Roast; braise
	Riblets	Breast bone removed and breast cut between ribs. Each small piece contains part of a rib bone.	Braise; cook in liquid
Shank	Shank	Contains shank and elbow bones.	Braise; cook in liquid
Ground Lamb	Loaf	Usually made from flank, breast, shank, and neck. May be straight ground lamb or combined with varying amounts of beef, pork or veal.	Roast (bake)
	Patties	Ground lamb formed into patties. May be encircled with sliced bacon.	Broil; panbroil; panfry

Source: Meat Manual, 6th Edition. National Live Stock and Meat Board, Chicago.

Lamb Cuts and Uses

TABLE 2.L.5
Lamb cuts and how to use them

CUT	DESCRIPTION	RETAIL CUTS	LAMB SPECIALTIES
LEG	Solid meat, fine quality	Roasts, steaks	Brains— Cream, braise, scramble with eggs
LOIN	Tender, high quality, small amount of bone	Chops, English chops, roast	Heart— Braise, cook in water
RACK	Tender, high quality; contains rib bones	Chops, roasts, crown roast	Kidney— Fry, broil, cook in water
SHOULDER	Tender, well-flavored; often boned and rolled or made into cushion style roast	Roasts, chops, stews, loaf	Liver— Fry, broil, braise
BREAST (including flank)	Meat tender, but not so fine in grain as other sections	Stews; boned and rolled for roast; pocket for stuffing	Tongue— Cook in water

Source: Meat Buying Manual. National Live Stock and Meat Board, Chicago.

Lamb Leg Carving

Place the roast on the platter with the shank to the carver's right and the tip section on the near side. From this, remove two or three slices lengthwise to form a base.

Turn the roast up on the base and, starting at the shank end, make slices perpendicular to the leg bone as shown in the illustration.

After reaching the aitch bone, loosen the slices by cutting under them, following the top of the leg bone. Remove slices to platter and then serve.

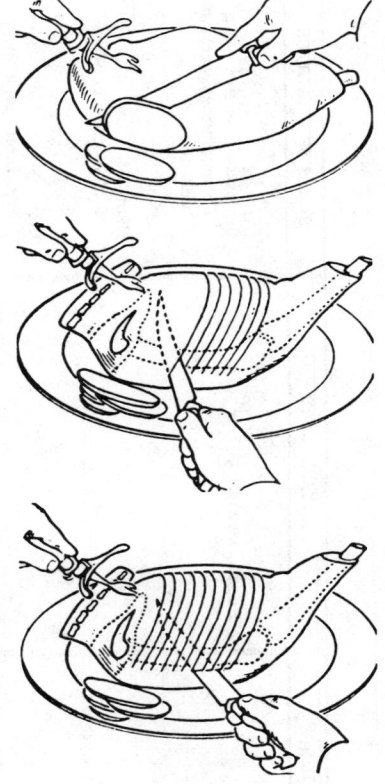

FIGURE 2.L.3

Source: Carving Meat. National Live Stock and Meat Board, Chicago.

Lamb, Percentages of Daily Recommended Allowances

TABLE 2.L.6
Percentages of daily recommended allowances[1] (based on $3\frac{1}{2}$ oz cooked lean lamb)

	Age	Pro-tein	Calo-ries	Iron	Phos-phorus	Mag-nesium	Thiamin	Ribo-flavin	Niacin	Vit. B-6	Vit. B-12
Children	1–3	116	20	13	26	15	31	40	84	53	280
	4–6	87	14	20	26	11	24	29	63	36	187
	7–10	74	11	20	26	9	18	27	48	27	140
Males	11–14	60	9	11	18	6	16	21	42	20	93
	15–18	49	9	11	18	6	15	18	38	16	93
	19–22	49	9	20	26	6	15	18	38	16	93
	23–50	47	10	20	26	6	16	20	42	16	93
	51+	47	11	20	26	6	18	21	48	16	93
Females	11–14	60	11	11	18	8	18	25	48	20	93
	15–18	55	12	11	18	8	20	23	54	16	93
	19–22	58	12	11	26	8	20	23	54	16	93
	23–50	58	13	11	26	8	22	27	58	16	93
	51+	58	14	20	26	8	22	29	63	16	93

[1] Figures based on 1974 National Research Council Recommended Dietary Allowances.

Source: Facts About Lamb. (1974). National Live Stock and Meat Board, Chicago.

Lamb Quality Guide

LOOK FOR THE GRADE

Each USDA lamb grade is a measure of a distinct level of quality. Five grades span the range of quality — Prime, Choice, Good, Utility, and Cull. The two lower grades are seldom, if ever, sold as retail cuts.

USDA Prime is the highest quality grade, but the grade most widely sold at retail is USDA Choice. Choice lamb is produced in the greatest volume and retailers have found that this quality pleases most of their customers.

FIGURE 2.L.4

Source: USDA (1971). How to buy lamb. USDA Home and Garden Bull. *195.*

Lamb Roasting I

TABLE 2.L.7

To roast lamb, place fat side up on a rack in an open roasting pan. Add no water. Do not cover. Baste only if a glaze or flavor-adding sauce is used. Lamb is best when it roasts at an oven temperature of 325°F. The meat is well done when it reaches an internal temperature of 175°–180°F.

Tip: Try lamb a little rare—slightly pink and extra juicy in the middle.

Cut	Min per Lb
Leg	
Bone-in	30 to 35
Boneless, rolled or netted	35 to 40
Shoulder	
Bone-in	30 to 35
Boneless, rolled or netted	40 to 45
Cushion roast	30 to 35
Breast	
Stuffed	30 to 35
Rolled	30 to 35
Lamb loaf	30 to 35
Crown roast	40 to 45
Rack	40 to 45

Source: How to Identify and Prepare Cuts of Lamb. (1971). American Lamb Council.

Lamb Roasting II

TABLE 2.L.8
Time-table for roasting lamb

Cut	Approx. Wt. of Single Roasts	No. of Roasts in Oven	Approx. Total Wt. of Roasts in Oven	Oven Temperature	Interior Temperature of Roast When Removed from Oven	Minutes per Pound Based on One Roast	Minutes per Pound Based on Total Wt. of Roasts in Oven	Approximate Total Time
	pounds		*pounds*					
Leg		2	16	300° F.	180° F.		15	4 hours
Leg	6½ to 7½	1		300° F.	180° F.	30 to 35		3 to 4 hours
Cushion shoulder (with stuffing)	4½ to 5½	1		300° F.	180° F.	30 to 35		2 to 3 hours
Rolled shoulder	3 to 4	1		300° F.	180° F.	40 to 45		2½ to 3 hours
Rolled shoulder		5	29	300° F.	180° F.		10	5 hours
Square cut shoulder		8	40	300° F.	180° F.		7	4 to 5 hours

Source: Cooking Meat in Quantity. National Live Stock and Meat Board, Chicago.

Lamb Simmering

TABLE 2.L.9

Brown meat on all sides in hot fat. Season with salt and pepper. Cover with water, then cover kettle tightly. Cook slowly. Allow meat to simmer, not boil, until tender. Add vegetables just long enough before serving to be cooked.

Cut	Time (hr)
Cubes	
1 to 1½ in.	1½ to 2
Larger cuts	
Riblets, neck, shanks	1½ to 2

Source: How to Identify and Prepare Cuts of Lamb. (1971). American Lamb Council.

Lamb Wholesale Cuts

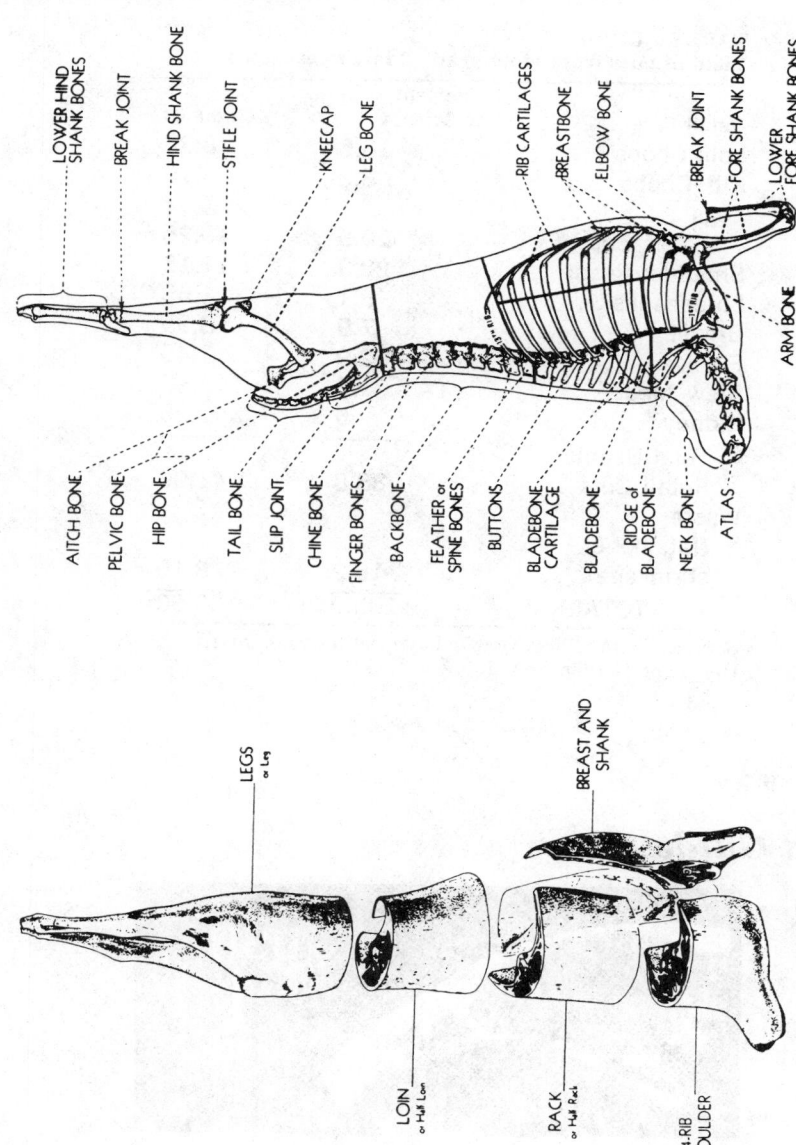

FIGURE 2.L.5
Wholesale cuts of lamb (left); structure, location, and names of carcass bones (right)

Source: Cooking Meat In Quantity. National Live Stock and Meat Board, Chicago.

Lamb Yield

TABLE 2.L.10
Yield of cuts from yield grade 3 lamb carcasses

Retail Cuts	Percent of Carcass	Pounds
Loin Chops	16.5	8.25
Rib Chops	8.2	4.10
Legs		
(Short Cut)	20.5	10.25
Shoulder Roast . . .	22.3	11.15
Foreshanks	3.1	1.55
Breast	7.9	3.95
Flank	2.9	1.45
Stew Meat	1.9	.95
Kidney	.5	.25
Total Usable Retail Cuts	83.8	41.90
Waste (fat, bone, shrinkage)	16.2	8.10
TOTAL	100.0	50.00

Source: USDA (1969). How to buy meat for your freezer. USDA Home and Garden Bull. *166.*

Lamb Yield Guide

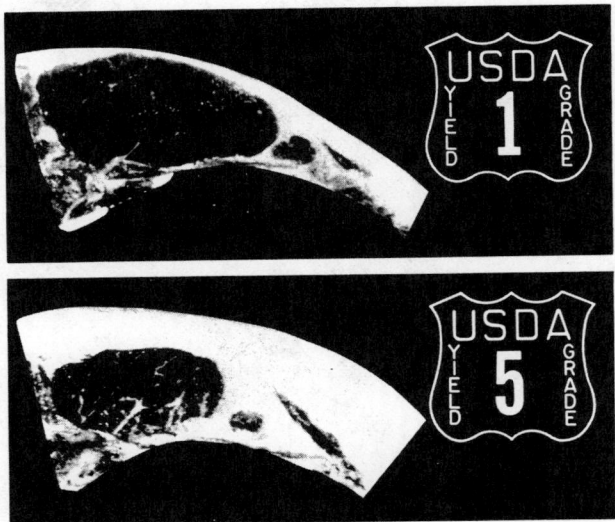

FIGURE 2.L.6

Source: USDA (1971). How to buy lamb. USDA Home and Garden Bull. *195.*

Larder Beetle (Enlarged)

FIGURE 2.L.7

Source: USDA (1974). Protecting home cured meat from insects. Home and Garden Bull. *109*.

Lard, Triglyceride Mole Percent Composition

TABLE 2.L.11
Percentage of moles of triglycerides in lard

0 Double Bonds				3 Double Bonds	
PMP	0.1	StMO	0.7	OOO	11.7
PMSt	0.4	MPO	0.8	PLO	0.2
StMSt	0.4	PPO	7.9	StLO	0.6
PPP	0.5	StPO	12.8	OML	0.6
PPSt	2.0	PStO	0.9	OPL	7.2
StPSt	2.0	StStO	1.6	OStL	1.2
PStP	0.1	Remaining ones	0.6	Remaining ones	0.3
PStSt	0.4				
StStSt	0.4	**2 Double Bonds**			
Remaining ones	0.3	POO	5.2		
		StOO	6.1	**4 or More Double Bonds**	
1 Double Bond		OMO	1.6	OLL	1.4
POP	0.6	OPO	18.4	OLO	1.5
POSt	1.9	OStO	1.2	LPL	0.5
StOSt	1.5	PPL	1.8	LStL	0.1
PMO	0.4	StPL	2.1	OPLe	0.3
		Remaining ones	1.5	Remaining ones	0.2

Source: Boekenoogen, H. A. (editor) (1968). *Oil, Fats and Fat Products*, Vol. 2. John Wiley & Sons, New York.

Lemon Juice, Composition

TABLE 2.L.12
Composition of lemon juice

Constituent	Source of Juice[1]	Number of Samples	Content per 100 Grams			
			Range		Average	
Protein (total N × 6.25)	C, X	26	0.26–0.77	gm	0.42	gm
Amino nitrogen	C	31	0.019–0.046	gm	0.035	gm
Fat (ether extract)	C, X	...	None—0.6	gm	0.2	gm
Soluble solids, total (°Brix)	C	2746	7.1–11.9	gm	9.3	gm
Acid, total, as anhyd. citric	C	3123	4.20–8.33	gm	5.97	gm
Malic acid	C	15	0.15–0.41	gm	0.26	gm
Sugar, total, as invert	C, X	368	0.77–4.08	gm	2.16	gm
Reducing sugar	C	95	0.78–2.63	gm	1.67	gm
Sucrose	C	47	0.03–0.63	gm	0.18	gm
Minerals, total ash	C, X	50	0.15–0.35	gm	0.25	gm
Calcium	C, X	26	5.6–27.9	mg	9.88	mg
Phosphorus	C, X	27	5.3–16.6	mg	9.35	mg
Iron	C, X	20	0.14–0.69	mg	0.23	mg
Magnesium	C, X	19	5.8–11.3	mg	6.7	mg
Potassium	C	24	99–128	mg	103	mg
Sodium	C, X	19	1.0–5.0	mg	1.3	mg
Sulfur	C, X	20	2.0–8.0	mg	3.36	mg
Chlorine	C, X	4	2.3–4.0	mg	3	mg
Vitamin A (as carotene)	C, X	...	None or trace		None	
Thiamine (B₁)	C, X	34[2]	0.004–0.125	mg	0.043	mg
Riboflavin (B₂)	C, X	30[3]	0.005–0.073	mg	0.0183	mg
Niacin	C, X	26	0.056–0.196	mg	0.089	mg
Inositol	C	17	56–76	mg	66.5	mg
Folic acid	C	17	0.00082–0.00094	mg	0.00091	mg
Flavanones	C	2	46–54	mg	50	mg
Ascorbic acid (vitamin C)	C	357	31–61	mg	45	mg
pH	C	93	2.11–2.48		2.30[1]	

[1] C denotes juice from California-Arizona fruit; X, juice from fruit of other or unknown sources.
[2] Includes 8 samples of edible portion (excluding peel and seeds).
[3] Includes 6 samples of edible portion.
[4] Representative value.
Note: Original references used, weighted with data from the Wisconsin Alumni Research Foundation, W.A.R.F.

Source: Swisher, H. E., and Swisher, L. H. (1971). Lemon and lime juices. In *Fruit and Vegetable Juice Processing Technology*, 2nd Edition. Donald K. Tressler and Maynard A. Joslyn (editors). AVI Publishing Co., Westport, Connecticut.

Lemon Oil, Composition

TABLE 2.L.13
The chemical composition of cold-pressed lemon oil

TERPENES:	ACIDS:	KETONES:
α-terpinene	acetic acid	methyl heptenone
α-pinene	caprylic acid	d-carvone
β-pinene	capric acid	
β-myrcene		**ESTERS:**
d-limonene	**ALCOHOLS:**	citronellyl acetate
γ-terpinene	octanol	neryl acetate
p-cymene	nonanol	geranyl acetate
α-terpinolene	linalool	n-propyl benzoate
sabinene	terpinene-1-ol	octyl acetate
camphene	terpinene-4-ol	decyl acetate
β-phellandrene	α-terpineol	nonyl acetate
α-phellandrene	citronellol	geranyl butyrate
tetradecane	nerol	
?	geraniol	
?	decanol	
pentadecane	1,8-methadiene-9-ol	**COUMARINS:**
$C_{15}H_{24}$		5-geranoxy psoralen
α-bergamotene	**ALDEHYDES:**	7-methoxy-5-geranoxy-
caryophyllene	hexanal	coumarin
?	heptanal	5-allyloxypsoralen
$C_{15}H_{24}$	octanal	7-methoxy-5-allyloxy-
α, β-humulene	nonanal	psoralen
β-bisabolene	decanal	8-geranoxy psoralen
$C_{15}H_{24}$	undecanal	5,7-dimethoxy coumarin
$C_{15}H_{24}$	citral { neral / geranial }	(limettin)
α-thujene	citronellal	5-methoxy-8-psoralen
Δ-3-carene	dodecanal	(byakangelicin)
p-isopropenyltoluene		Bergamotene

Source: Kesterson, J. W., Hendrickson, R., and Braddock, R. J. (1971). Florida citrus oils. Florida Agric. Exp. Sta. Tech. Bull. *749*.

Lemon Oil, Properties

TABLE 2.L.14
Physical and chemical properties used as a criterion of purity for cold-pressed lemon oil

Property	U.S.P. xvii Min.	U.S.P. xvii Max.	Italian Min.	Italian Max.	California Min.	California Max.
Specific gravity 25C°/25°C	0.849	0.855	0.849	0.855	0.849	0.855
Refractive index η_D^{20}	1.4739	1.4755	1.4742	1.4755	1.4742	1.4755
Difference	Not less than 0.0010 and not more than 0.0027 lower than original oil.		—	—	—	—
Optical rotation α_D^{25}	+57°	+65.6°	+57°	+65.36°	+57°	+65.36°
Difference	Not more than 6° less than original oil.		—	—	—	—
Aldehyde content % Calif.	2.2	3.8			2.3	2.8
Italian	3.0	5.5	3.7	5.0		
Evaporation residue %	—	—	1.5	2.2	1.5	1.8
U. V. spectrum 315 mμ log E $\frac{0.25g}{100 cc}$ CD Calif.	0.20	—			0.23	0.74
Italian	0.49	—	0.49	0.96		
Peak	—	—	1.00	1.70	0.53	1.50

Source: Kesterson, J. W., Hendrickson, R., and Braddock, R. J. (1971). Florida citrus oils. Florida Agric. Exp. Sta. Tech. Bull. *749*.

Lettuce Types

TABLE 2.L.15

Type	Subtype	Cultivars	Area of culture	Harvest season	Use
	New York	New York	---------	---------	Obsolete.
		New York 515	---------	---------	Do.
	Imperial	615	Desert	Winter	Nearly obsolete.
		101	----do----	----do----	Do.
		152	---------	---------	Obsolete.
Crisphead	Great Lakes	Calmar	Coast	Spring	Distance transportation.
		Great Lakes 659	Interior / Desert	Summer / Winter	
		Merit	Coast / Desert	Spring / Fall	
		Empire	Desert	Fall	
		Great Lakes 118	Coast	Summer / Fall	
		Minetto	East	Summer	
		Fulton	----do----	----do----	
	Other	Vanguard	Desert	Winter	
		Climax	----do----	----do----	
		Golden State C, D	----do----	----do----	
		Valverde	Lower Rio Grande	----do----	
Butterhead		Bibb / Big Boston	---------	---------	Local market.
Cos or romaine		Parris Island / Dark Green / Valmaine	---------	---------	Local market and some distance transportation.
Looseleaf		Grand Rapids / Prize Head	---------	---------	Local market.
Latin		Fordhook / Gallega	---------	---------	Not grown in United States.
Stem		Celtuce	---------	---------	Local market.

Source: (1974). Lettuce production in the United States. Agriculture Handbook 221.

Lime Juice, Composition

TABLE 2.L.16
Composition of lime juice

Constituent	Number of Samples	Content per 100 Grams	
		Range	Average
Protein (total N × 6.25)	11	0.3–0.7 gm	0.4 gm
Fat	...	0.0–0.11 gm	Trace
Soluble solids, total (°Brix)	93	8.3–14.1 gm	10.0 gm
Acid, total, as anhyd. citric	129	4.94–8.32 gm	5.97 gm
Sugar, total, as invert	13	0.0–1.74 gm	0.72 gm
Non-reducing sugar	7	0.02–0.26 gm	0.14 gm
Ash, total	5	0.25–0.4 gm	0.35 gm
Calcium	2	4.5–10.4 mg	7 mg
Phosphorus	2	9.3–11.2 mg	10 mg
Iron	2	0.19–0.92 mg	0.6 mg
Carotene	2	0.003–0.005 mg	0.004 mg
Thiamine (B_1)	2	0.011–0.028 mg	0.020 mg
Riboflavin (B_2)	2	0.011–0.018 mg	0.015 mg
Niacin	5	0.090–0.275 mg	0.19 mg
Ascorbic acid (vitamin C)	13	23.6–32.7 mg	29 mg
pH	20	1.7–3.2	...
Food energy (calories)	...	24–33	...

Source: Swisher, H. E., and Swisher, L. H. (1971). Lemon and lime juices. In *Fruit and Vegetable Juice Processing Technology*, 2nd Edition. Donald K. Tressler and Maynard A. Joslyn (editors). AVI Publishing Co., Westport, Connecticut.

Lime Oil, Composition

TABLE 2.L.17
Chemical composition of cold-pressed "persian" lime oil

TERPENES:

α-pinene
β-pinene
β-myrcene
d-limonene
γ-terpinene
p-cymene
camphene
terpinolene
tetradecane
△-elemene
$C_{15}H_{24}$
pentadecane
$C_{15}H_{24}$
α-bergamotene
caryophyllene
α-elemene
$C_{15}H_{24}$
α,β-humulene
$C_{15}H_{24}$
β-bisabolene
$C_{15}H_{24}$
$C_{15}H_{24}$

ALCOHOLS:

octanol
nonanol
α-terpineol
linalool
β-terpineol
borneol
geraniol
bergaptol
decanol

OXIDE:

(2) monoterpene-oxides $C_{10}H_{17}O$

ALDEHYDES:

nonanal
decanal
dodecanal
citral { neral { geranial

PHENOLS:

1,4-cineole
1,8-cineole

ESTERS:

Methyl anthranilate

ACIDS:

acetic
octylic
decylic

COUMARINS:

5,7-dimethoxy coumarin (limettin)
5,8-dimethoxyfurano-2',3',6,7-coumarin (isopimpinellin)
7-methoxy-5-geranoxy coumarin
5-hydroxy-7-methoxy coumarin
4,6-dimethoxy-2-geranoxycinnamic acid
5,-Hydroxyfurano-2',3',6,7-coumarin (Bergaptol)

Source: Kesterson, J. W., Hendrickson, R., and Braddock, R. J. (1971). Florida citrus oils. Florida Agric. Exp. Sta. Tech. Bull. *749*.

Lime Oil, Properties

TABLE 2.L.18
Comparison of commercial cold-pressed "persian" lime oils made by three different processes

Property	Pipkin roll (11)[*]		Fraser-Brace (4)		FMC in-line (15)	
	Max.	Min.	Max.	Min.	Max.	Min.
Sp. grav. 20°C/20°C	0.8823	0.8769	0.8792	0.8786	0.8947	0.8533
Ref. ind. η_D^{20}	1.4853	1.4834	1.4849	1.4841	1.4907	1.4744
Ref. ind. 10% dist. η_D^{20}	1.4732	1.4729	1.4734	1.4724	1.4734	1.4730
Difference	0.0122	0.0103	0.0122	0.0110	0.0177	0.0053
Opt. rot. α_D^{20}	+43.36	+38.60	**	**	+49.01	+39.85
Opt. rot. 10% dist. α_D^{20}	+52.20	+47.60	+54.60	+49.32	+51.71	+48.33
Difference	+9.88	+6.20	**	**	+10.27	+689
Aldehyde (citral), %	6.14	3.66	5.20	4.46	6.66	4.30
Ester content, %	8.08	4.95	7.28	6.78	—	—
Evap. res., %	14.67	11.01	13.24	12.62	16.67	11.50

[*] No. of samples.
** Too dark to read in 25 mm tube.

Source: Kesterson, J. W., Hendrickson, R., and Braddock, R. J. (1971). Florida citrus oils. Florida Agric. Exp. Sta. Tech. Bull. *749*.

Liming Materials I

TABLE 2.L.19
Relative neutralizing values of pure liming materials

Liming Materials	Relative Neutralizing Values	Pounds of Liming Materials Equivalent to 1 Ton	
		Calcium Carbonate	Calcium Oxide
Calcium carbonate	100	2,000	3,570
Magnesium carbonate	119	1,680	3,000
Calcium oxide	178	1,120	2,000
Magnesium oxide	250	800	1,430
Calcium hydrate	135	1,480	2,640
Magnesium hydrate	172	1,160	2,070
Dolomite	108	1,850	3,330
Dolomitic hydrate	175	1,145	2,040

Source: Sauchelli, V. (editor). *Chemistry and Technology of Fertilizers.* Van Nostrand Reinhold Co., New York.

Liming Materials II

TABLE 2.L.20
Common liming materials

Common Names	Neut[1] Equiv	Approx Analyses	Pounds of Liming Material Equiv to 1 Ton Calcium Carbonate
Ground dolomitic limestone[2]	95–108	52% $CaCO_3$ 42% $MgCO_3$	2105–1852
Ground agricultural limestone[2] Air slacked lime	85–100	80–95% $CaCO_3$	2353–2000
Precipitated lime Lump lime Builders lime Caustic lime	150–175	85% CaO	1333–1143
Hydrated lime Water slacked lime	120–135	65% CaO	1667–1481
Burned oyster shells	90–110	55% CaO; 5% MgO	2222–1818
Baked oyster shells	80–90	85% $CaCO_3$	2500–2222
Marl	50–90	60% $CaCO_3$	4000–2222
Basic Slag 8–10% P_2O_5	50–70	45% CaO; 6% MgO	4000–2857
Wood Ashes	40–50	45% $CaCO_3$	5000–4000
Land Plaster	None	70–75% $CaSO_4$	None

[1] Neutralizing equivalent given is percent in comparison to $CaCO_3$ as 100.
[2] Fineness of grinding is important. For practical purposes a limestone ground so that 65 to 80% passes a 48 mesh screen is satisfactory providing the 100 mesh and finer materials have not been removed.

Source: Agronomy Extension Handbook of N.C. and Bulletin A-60 University of Maryland. Reproduced in The Fertilizer Handbook, 2nd Edition. Fertilizer Institute, Washington, D.C.

Liquid Cooking of Meat

TABLE 2.L.21

Recommended procedure for cooking meats in liquid are:

1. If you prefer, brown meat on all sides in own fat or lard.
2. Season with salt and pepper if desired.
3. Cover with liquid, cover kettle, cook below boiling point until tender.
4. Add vegetables just long enough before serving to be cooked.

Source: Be a Smarter Shopper ... a Better Cook. (1973). National Live Stock and Meat Board, Chicago.

Liver

TABLE 2.L.22
The average weight and color of the liver and the length of the gallbladder in meat animals

Animal (Market Weight)	Liver				Gallbladder
	Weight of Liver	Percentage of Body Weight	Color	Lobes	
Beef	10–14 lb	1.1	Reddish brown	2	4–6 in. long
Veal	2–2½ lb	1.5	Reddish brown	2	3–4 in. long
Lamb	1½ lb	1.5	Reddish brown	2	4 in. long
Pork	2 lb	1.7	Reddish brown	4	3 in. long
Sow	7 lb	1.7	Reddish brown	4	3–5 in. long
Horse	10–12 lb	0.8–1.5	Purplish brown	3	Absent
Chicken (3–4 lb)	31–50 g	1.6–2.3	Chocolate	2	0.8 in. long
Rabbit (3¾ lb)	95 g	5.5	Reddish brown	4–5	1 in. long

Source: Ockerman, H. W. (1975). Comparative anatomy of meat animals. In *Meat Hygiene*. J. A. Libby (editor). Lea & Febiger, Philadelphia.

Lobster

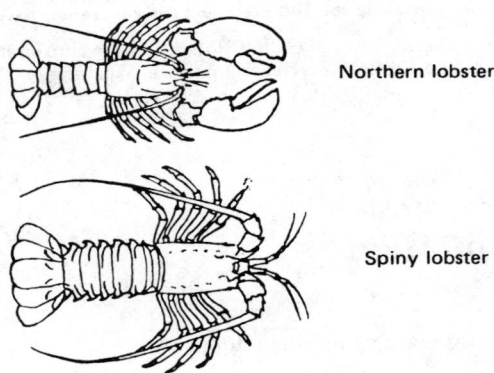

Northern lobster

Spiny lobster

FIGURE 2.L.8
How to identify northern and spiny lobsters

Source: USDA (1969). Food for us all. Yearbook of Agriculture.

Lymph Nodes, Ox

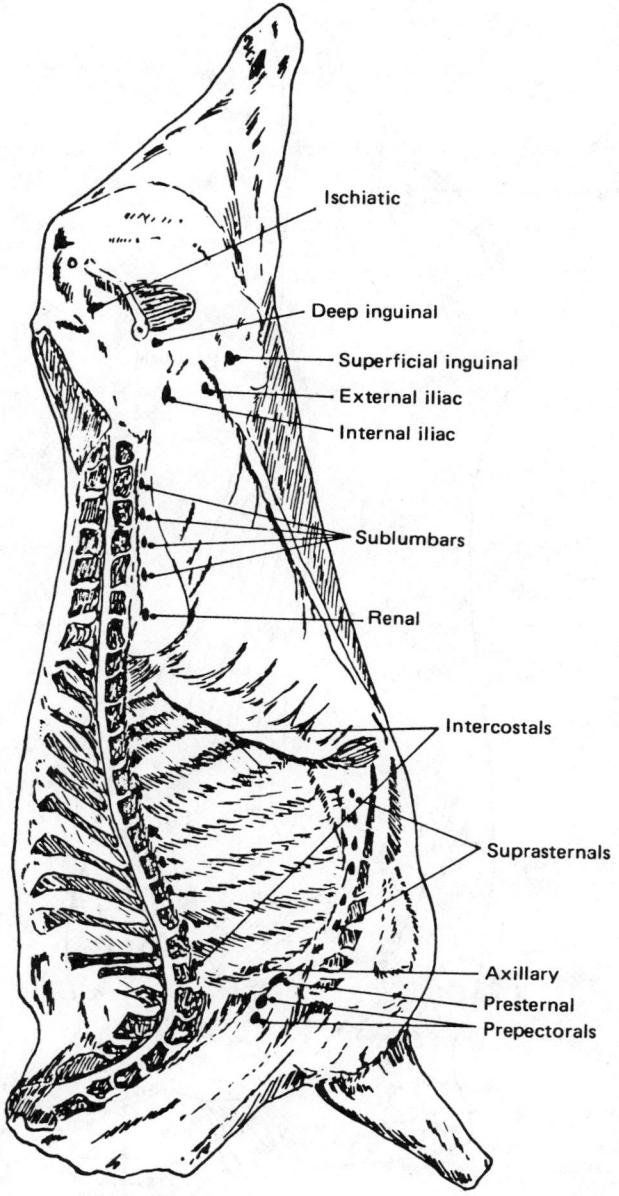

FIGURE 2.L.9
Showing location of lymph nodes on ox carcass

Source: Wilson, A. (1968). *Practical Meat Inspection*. Blackwell Scientific Publications, Ltd., Osney Media, Oxford, England.

Lymph Nodes, Ox, Lateral

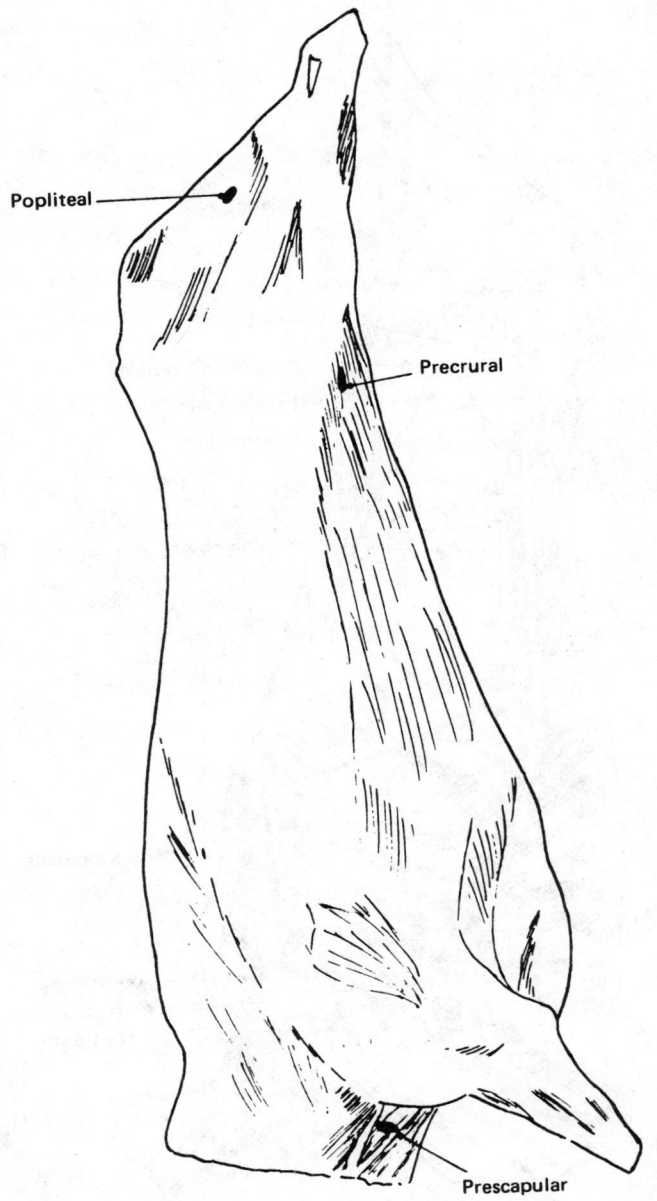

FIGURE 2.L.10
Showing location of lymph nodes on exterior of ox carcass

Source: Wilson, A. (1968). *Practical Meat Inspection*. Blackwell Scientific Publications, Ltd., Osney Media, Oxford, England.

Lymph Nodes, Pig

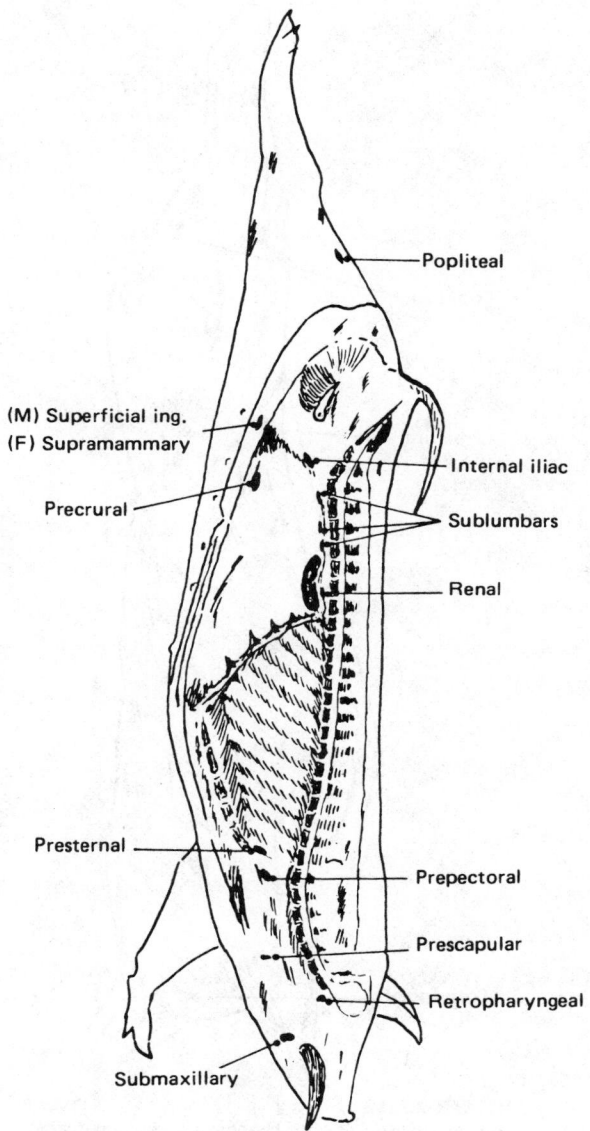

FIGURE 2.L.11
Showing location of lymph nodes on hog carcass

Source: Wilson, A. (1968). *Practical Meat Inspection*. Blackwell Scientific Publications, Ltd., Osney Media, Oxford, England.

Lymph Nodes, Sheep

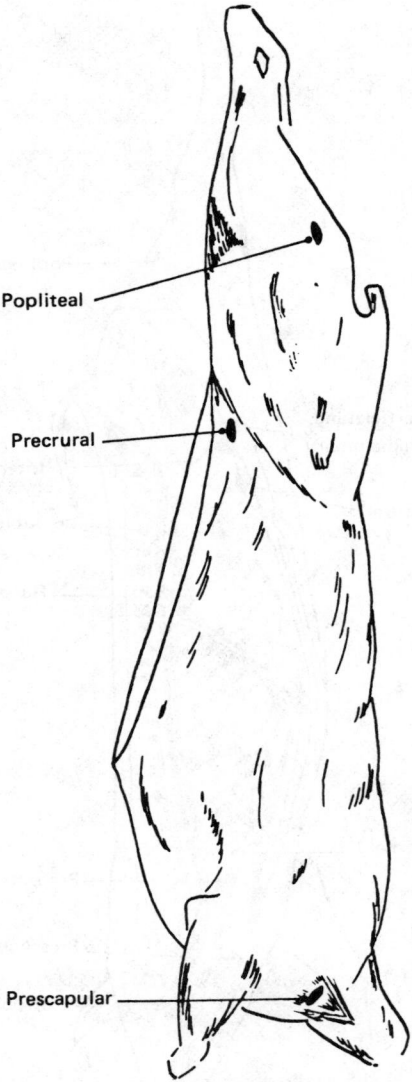

Popliteal

Precrural

Prescapular

FIGURE 2.L.12
Showing location of lymph nodes on sheep carcass

Source: Wilson, A. (1968). *Practical Meat Inspection*. Blackwell Scientific Publications, Ltd., Osney Media, Oxford, England.

Macaroni and Noodles, Composition

TABLE 2.M.1
Composition of macaroni and noodles

Food[1]	Energy, Cal/100 Gm	Major Constituents[2]					Minerals, Mg/100 Gm						Vitamins/100 Gm			
		Proteins (%)	Carbohydrates (%)	Crude Fiber (%)	Fat (%)	Moisture (%)	Na	K	Ca	Mg	P	Fe	Thiamin (Mg)	Riboflavin (Mg)	Niacin (Mg)	A (IU)
Macaroni, enriched dry	368	12.5	74.0	0.3	1.2	12.0	2.0	197	27	48	161	2.9	0.88	0.37	6.0	0
Macaroni, enriched cooked	107	3.4	23.0	0.1	0.4	73.1	0.7	60	8	18	50	0.9	0.14	0.08	1.1	0
Macaroni, not enriched dry	386	12.5	74.0	0.3	1.2	12.0	2.0	197	27	48	161	1.3	0.09	0.06	1.7	0
Macaroni, not enriched cooked	107	3.4	23.0	0.1	0.4	73.1	0.7	60	8	18	50	0.4	0.01	0.01	0.3	0
Egg noodles, enriched dry	388	15.5	67.8	0.3	4.4	12.0	6.0	133	33	48	183	2.8	0.89	0.39	6.1	220
Egg noodles, enriched cooked	125	4.1	23.3	0.1	1.5	71.0	2.0	44	10	14	59	0.9	0.14	0.08	1.2	70

[1] All products as defined by FDA Definitions and Standards, no optional ingredients included.
[2] All data reported on an "as is" basis.

Source: Walsh, D. E., and Gilles, K. A. (1974). Macaroni products. In *Encyclopedia of Food Technology.* A. H. Johnson, and M. S. Peterson (editors). AVI Publishing Co., Westport, Connecticut.

Manure Analysis

TABLE 2.M.2
Analysis of typical manure (dry matter basis)

Proximate Analysis	%	lb/ton
Crude protein	12.9	258
Fat	1.0	20
Fiber	33.1	662
NFE	47.8	956
Ash	5.2	104
Minerals		
Carbon	50.0	1,000
Nitrogen (organic)	2.1	42
Phosphorus	0.4	8
Potassium	1.0	20
Calcium	1.0	20
Magnesium	0.4	8
Sodium	1.0	20
Sulfur	0.3	6
Iron	0.4	8
Amino Acids		
Alanine	0.47	9.4
Valine	0.27	5.4
Glycine	0.32	6.4
Isoleucine	0.20	4.0
Leucine	0.48	9.6
Proline	0.32	6.4
Threonine	0.26	5.2
Serine	0.25	5.0
Methionine	0.12	2.4
Hydroxyproline	0.03	0.6
Phenylalanine	0.27	5.4
Aspartic acid	0.53	10.6
Glutamic acid	0.82	16.4
Tyrosine	0.18	3.6
Lysine	0.18	3.6
Histidine	0.10	2.0
Arginine	0.15	3.0
Tryptophan	—	—
Cystine/2	0.05	1.0
Diaminopimelic acid	—	—
Total Amino Acid	5.00	100.0
Amino Acid/Crude Protein	0.39	—

Source: Coe, W. B., and Turk, M. (1973). Processing animal waste by anaerobic fermentation. In *Processing Agricultural and Municipal Wastes*. G. E. Inglett (editor). AVI Publishing Co., Westport, Connecticut.

Maple Syrup Composition

TABLE 2.M.3
Composition of maple syrup[1]

Component	Amount %	Component	Amount %
Water	34.0	Soluble ash	0.30-0.81
Sucrose	58.2-65.5	Insoluble ash	0.08-0.67
Hexoses	0.0-7.9	Calcium	0.07
Malic acid	0.093	Silica	0.02
Citric acid	0.010	Manganese	0.005
Succinic acid	0.008	Sodium	0.003
Fumaric acid	0.004		

[1] Willits 1965; Hart and Fisher 1971.

Source: White, Jr., J. W., and Underwood, J. C. (1974). Maple syrup and honey. In *Symposium: Sweeteners.* G. E. Inglett (editor). AVI Publishing Co., Westport, Connecticut.

Margarine Formulae

TABLE 2.M.4
The composition of the fatty phase of margarine may be varied *ad infinitum* and allows for the properties required of the product as well as the raw materials available. These formulae were collected from the literature from the late 19th Century up to 1967.

1. Formulae for animal fats (table margarine)

	%		%
Oleomargarine	60	Oleomargarine	40
Lard	30	Premier jus	20
Liquid oil	10	Lard	15
		Liquid oil	25

2. Formulae for coconut and palm kernel oils

	%		%
Coconut oil	50	Palm oil	50
Vegetable oil hydrogenated (P.F. 42°C.)	25	Palm oil hydrogenated (P.F. 44°C.)	20
Liquid oil	25	Liquid oil	30

3. Formulae for hydrogenated oils

	%		%
Groundnut hydrogenated (P.F. 32–4°C.)	70	Palm kernel hydrogenated (P.F. 34°C.)	70
Coconut	10	Coconut	15
Liquid oil	20	Liquid oil	15

4. 'Single oil' formulae

	%		%
Cottonseed hydrogenated (P.F. 28°C.)	85	Sunflower hydrogenated (P.F. 44°C.)	20
Cottonseed hydrogenated (P.F. 42–4°C.)	15	Sunflower hydrogenated (P.F. 32°C.)	60
		Sunflower liquid	20

(Continued)

Margarine Formulae *(Continued)*

TABLE 2.M.4 *(Continued)*

5. Formulae for bakery margarines

	%		%
Premier jus	25	Groundnut hydrogenated	
Palm oil hydrogenated		(P.F. 42°C.)	30
(P.F. 46°C.)	25	Coconut oil	20
Groundnut hydrogenated		Palm kernel oil	20
(P.F. 34°C.)	10	Liquid oil	30
Liquid oil	40	(For biscuits and	
(For puff pastry)		raised pastry)	

6. Standard margarine made in the United Kingdom during the 1939–45 war

	%
Coconut oil	
Palm kernel oil }	40
Palm oil	7
Groundnut oil hydrogenated (P.F. 34°C.)	13
Whale oil hydrogenated (P.F. 46–8°C.)	20
Groundnut oil	20

7. Recent formulae for products with special characteristics

   (a) Margarine rich in essential fatty acids

	%
Coconut oil	30
Palm oil	10
Palm kernel oil	15
Palm oil hydrogenated (P.F. 42°C.)	10
Liquid sunflower oil hydrogenated	35

   (b) Margarine very rich in polyunsaturated fatty acids

	%
Liquid sunflower oil	88
Palm kernel oil hydrogenated	6
Palm oil hydrogenated	6

   (c) Margarine using a mixture of interesterified oils

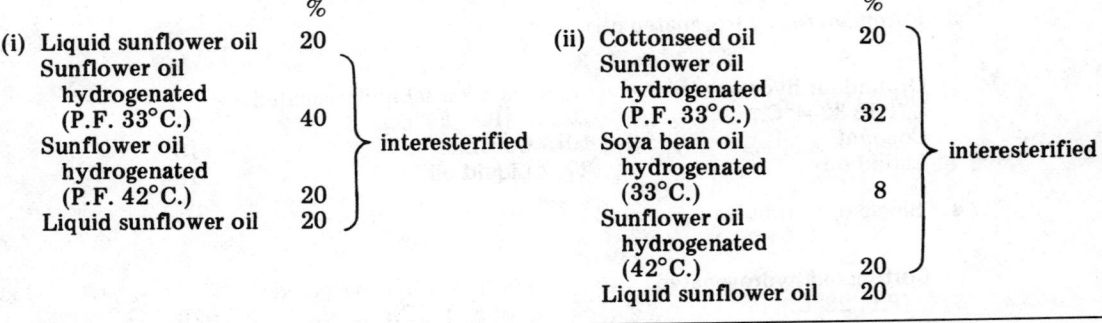

(i)	%		(ii)	%	
Liquid sunflower oil	20		Cottonseed oil	20	
Sunflower oil hydrogenated (P.F. 33°C.)	40	interesterified	Sunflower oil hydrogenated (P.F. 33°C.)	32	interesterified
Sunflower oil hydrogenated (P.F. 42°C.)	20		Soya bean oil hydrogenated (33°C.)	8	
Liquid sunflower oil	20		Sunflower oil hydrogenated (42°C.)	20	
			Liquid sunflower oil	20	

Source: Stuyvenberg, J. H. (1969). *Margarine.* Liverpool University Press, United Kingdom.

Margarine Production

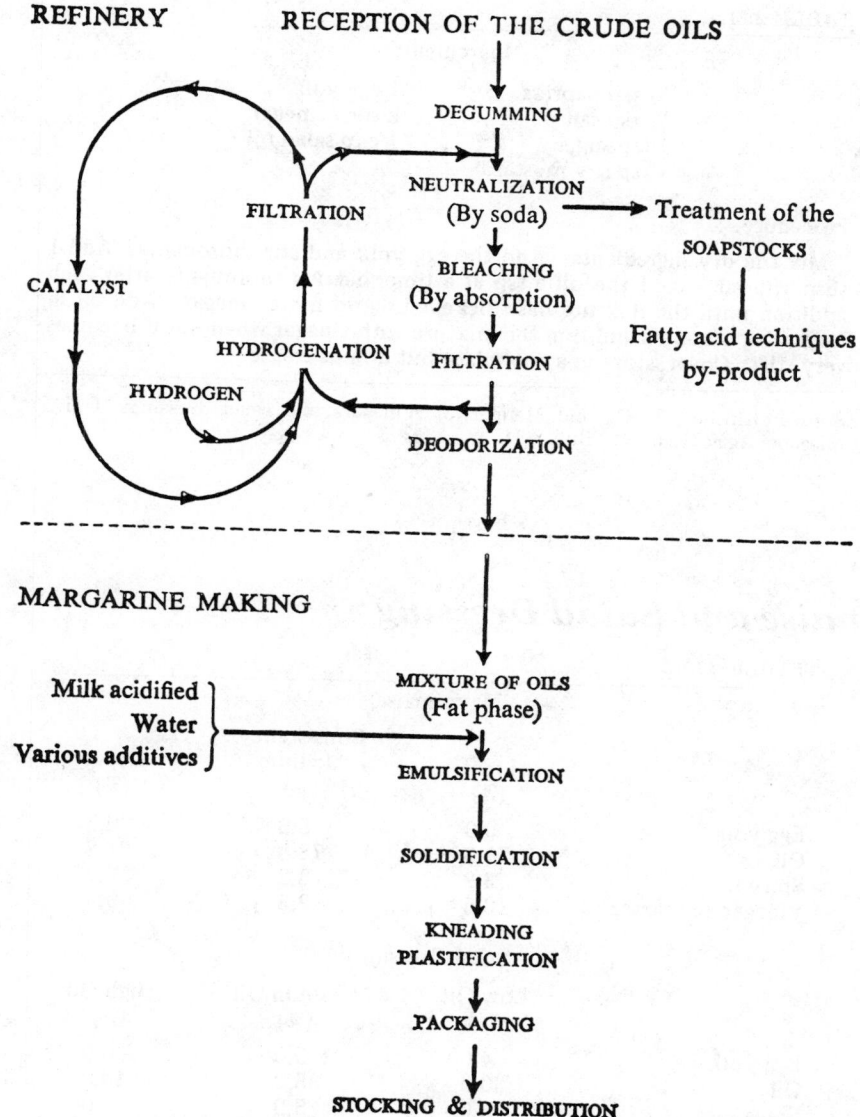

REFINERY   RECEPTION OF THE CRUDE OILS

DEGUMMING

FILTRATION   NEUTRALIZATION
(By soda)   → Treatment of the
                      SOAPSTOCKS

CATALYST   BLEACHING
(By absorption)

Fatty acid techniques
by-product

HYDROGENATION   FILTRATION

HYDROGEN

DEODORIZATION

MARGARINE MAKING

Milk acidified ⎫
Water   ⎬   MIXTURE OF OILS
Various additives ⎭   (Fat phase)

EMULSIFICATION

SOLIDIFICATION

KNEADING
PLASTIFICATION

PACKAGING

STOCKING & DISTRIBUTION

FIGURE 2.M.1
Flow sheet showing stages in the production of margarine

Source: Stuyvenberg, J. H. (1969). *Margarine*. Liverpool University Press, United Kingdom.

Mayonnaise

TABLE 2.M.5

Ingredients

½ tsp paprika	1 egg yolk
½ tsp salt	2 tbsp vinegar
1 tsp sugar	1 cup salad oil
1 tsp dry mustard	

Procedure

Mix the dry ingredients. Add the egg yolk and stir thoroughly. Add 1 tbsp vinegar. Add the oil a tsp at a time, beating thoroughly after each addition until the mixture has thickened. Add more vinegar. Add oil in increasing amounts and thin the mixture with vinegar whenever it becomes very stiff. Cover, store in a cool place but do not freeze.

Source: Kintner, T. C., and Mangel, M. Vinegars and salad dressings. Univ. Missouri Agric. Exp. Sta. Bull. *631.*

Mayonnaise and Salad Dressing

TABLE 2.M.6

	Mayonnaise		
		Consistency	
	Light (%)	Medium (%)	Heavy (%)
Egg yolk	9.0	8.5	6.3
Oil	77.3	78.8	81.2
Spice mix	3.2	3.2	3.2
Vinegar and water	10.5	9.5	9.3

	Salad Dressing		
	Low Oil (%)	Medium Oil (%)	High Oil (%)
Egg yolk	4.0	5.0	6.0
Oil	30.0	35.0	40.0
Spice mix	6.0	5.0	4.0
Sugar	10.0	9.0	8.0
Starch paste	50.0	46.0	42.0

Source: Binsted, R., Devey, J. D., and Dakin, J. C. (1971). *Pickle & Sauce Making*, 3rd Edition. Food Trade Press, London, England.

Meat and Meat Products, Composition

TABLE 2.M.7
Composition of the edible portion (EP) and refuse in the material as purchased (AP)

Item No.	Commodity and Description	Water	Protein	Fat	Carbohydrate Total (by dif)	Fiber	Ash	Calories No. per 100 g	Wt (kg) Live	Wt (kg) Carc	Notes	Corres U.S. Grade	Refuse in AP (%)
				(Percent of edible portion)									
	Meat and Meat Products												
	Beef, carcasses[1]												
172	Thin—incl kidney fat (0.9%)	66	18.8	14	0	0	1.0	207	375	119		Utility	19
173	—excl kidney fat	67	19.0	13	0	0	1.0	198					19
174	Medium—incl kidney fat	60	17.5	22	0	0	0.9	273	408	220		Commercial	16
175	—excl kidney fat (1.8%)	61	17.8	20	0	0	0.9	256					16
176	Fat—incl kidney fat	55	16.3	28	0	0	0.8	322	446	250		Good	15
177	—excl kidney fat (2.5%)	56	16.8	26	0	0	0.8	306					15
178	Very fat—incl kidney fat	47	13.7	39	0	0	0.7	410	487	290		Choice and Prime	12
179	—excl kidney fat (3.4%)	48	14.2	37	0	0	0.7	394					
180	Beef, or veal, very thin carcasses[1]	69	19.6	10	0	0	1.0	174			Use in exceptional cases only		20
	Veal, carcasses[1]												
181	Thin—incl kidney fat	70	19.4	10	0	0	1.0	173					22
182	—excl kidney fat (2.3%)	71	19.7	8	0	0	1.0	156					23
183	Medium—incl kidney fat	66	18.8	14	0	0	1.0	207					21
184	—excl kidney fat (2.4%)	68	19.1	12	0	0	1.0	190					21
185	Fat—incl kidney fat	62	18.0	19	0	0	0.9	248					19
186	—excl kidney fat (2.7%)	65	18.5	16	0	0	0.9	223					19
	Pork, carcasses[2]												
187	Thin—shipper's carcass (head on)	50	14.1	35	0	0	0.8	376	75	54			22.6
188	—packer's carcass (head off)	50	14.1	35	0	0	0.8	376	75	50			16.4
189	Medium—shipper's carcass (head on)	42	11.9	45	0	0	0.6	457	100	74			17.5
190	—packer's carcass (head off)	42	11.9	45	0	0	0.6	457	100	70			12.5
191	Fat—shipper's carcass (head on)	35	9.8	55	0	0	0.5	538	125	96			14.5
192	—packer's carcass (head off)	35	9.8	55	0	0	0.5	538	125	92			10.5
	Mutton and Lamb, carcasses[2]												
193	Thin, young, incl kidney fat	71.1	18.0	10.0	0	0	0.9	167	20	9		Cull and Utility	29
194	Medium, incl kidney fat	56	15.7	27.7	0	0	0.8	317	32	15		Commercial and Good	24

(Continued)

Meat and Meat Products, Composition (Continued)

TABLE 2.M.7 (Continued)

Item No.	Commodity and Description	Water	Protein	Fat	Carbohydrate Total (by dif)	Fiber	Ash	Calories No. per 100 g	Notes	Refuse in AP (%)
195	Fat, incl kidney fat	46.5	13.0	39.8	0	0	0.7	415	46 22.5 Choice and Prime	19
196	Offal, all species	74	16.0	7.8	1	0	1.2	143	Liver, heart, kidney, tongue, brains, pancreas, etc.	0
	Other Meats									
197	Horsemeat, carcass	74	20	4	1		1	125		25
198	Goat meat, carcass	71	18.7	9.4	0		0.9	165		25
199²	Buffalo, carcass, very lean Carabao, carcass, very lean } *Camel—use No. 172	74	20	4	1		1	125		36
	*Reindeer—use No. 172									
200	Rabbit, domestic, dressed and drawn	71	21.8	6.1	0		1.2	148	1.2 kg (drawn weight) AP	20
201	Whale meat, lean only, edible portion	74	20	4	1		1	125		0
	Game									
202	Mammals, dressed	73.8	21.4	3.6	0		1.2	124	Deer, wild rabbit, wild boar, etc.	16
203	Birds, dressed, not drawn	71.3	22.4	5.2	0		1.1	143	Wt dressed, not drawn (AP) (Kilograms)	42
	Poultry (total edible—flesh, skin, giblets, and fat)									
204	Chickens	66	20.2	12.6	0		1.0	200	1.4	39
205	Ducks } Geese }	52.8	16.2	30	0		1.0	340	(2.2) (5.3)	39
206	Turkeys	58.3	20.1	20.2	0		1.0	268	7.5	33
207	Poultry, unspecified, group figure	65	20	14	1		1.0	212	1.5	39
	Meats, canned									
208	Roast beef, corned beef	58	25	14	0		3	233		0
209	Luncheon meats (chiefly pork)	57	16	22	1		4	271		0
	Meats, cured									
210	Corned beef	57	22	17	0		4	247		0
211	Pork (ham, shoulder)	44	17.2	33	0		5.3	371		13
212	Bacon (smoked belly)	21	9	65	1		4	629		6
	Meats, dehydrated									
213	Beef or pork (lean with some fat)	9	60	28	0		3	509		0
214	Lean beef	9	82	5	0		4	395		0

¹These factors are for the edible portion of the entire *untrimmed* carcass, except for Nos. 173, 175, 177, 179, 182, 184, and 186 where allowances have been made for the removal of small proportions of fat. When fat has been trimmed in excess of the indicated percentages separate calculations are needed.

²These factors are for the edible portion of the entire *untrimmed* carcass, *including kidney fat*. When meat fat has been removed (domestic production of pork or mutton fat), these figures are not directly applicable; separate calculations are required.

³More information required.

Source: Chatfield, C. *Food Composition Tables for International Use.* Food and Agriculture Organization, United Nations, Rome.

Meat Composition

TABLE 2.M.8
Composition of meat

(Dashes (—) denote lack of reliable data for a constituent believed to be present in measurable amount)

Foods, approximate measures, units, and weight (edible part unless footnotes indicate otherwise)	Weight (Grams)	Water (Percent)	Food energy (Calories)	Protein (Grams)	Fat (Grams)	Saturated (total) (Grams)	Oleic (Grams)	Linoleic (Grams)	Carbohydrate (Grams)	Calcium (Milligrams)	Phosphorus (Milligrams)	Iron (Milligrams)	Potassium (Milligrams)	Vitamin A value (International units)	Thiamin (Milligrams)	Riboflavin (Milligrams)	Niacin (Milligrams)	Ascorbic acid (Milligrams)
FISH, SHELLFISH, MEAT, POULTRY; RELATED PRODUCTS—Con.																		
Meat and meat products:																		
Bacon, (20 slices per lb, raw), broiled or fried, crisp. — 2 slices	15	8	85	4	8	2.5	3.7	.7	Trace	2	34	.5	35	0	.08	.05	.8	—
Beef,[18] cooked:																		
Cuts braised, simmered or pot roasted:																		
Lean and fat (piece, 2 1/2 by 2 1/2 by 3/4 in) — 3 oz	85	53	245	23	16	6.8	6.5	.4	0	10	114	2.9	184	30	.04	.18	3.6	—
Lean only from item 162 — 2.5 oz	72	62	140	22	5	2.1	1.8	.2	0	10	108	2.7	176	10	.04	.17	3.3	—
Ground beef, broiled:																		
Lean with 10% fat — 3 oz or patty 3 by 5/8 in	85	60	185	23	10	4.0	3.9	.3	0	10	196	3.0	261	20	.08	.20	5.1	—
Lean with 21% fat — 2.9 oz or patty 3 by 5/8 in	82	54	235	20	17	7.0	6.7	.4	0	9	159	2.6	221	30	.07	.17	4.4	—
Roast, oven cooked, no liquid added:																		
Relatively fat, such as rib:																		
Lean and fat (2 pieces, 4 1/8 by 2 1/4 by 1/4 in). — 3 oz	85	40	375	17	33	14.0	13.6	.8	0	8	158	2.2	189	70	.05	.13	3.1	—
Lean only from item 166 — 1.8 oz	51	57	125	14	7	3.0	2.5	.3	0	6	131	1.8	161	10	.04	.11	2.6	—
Relatively lean, such as heel of round:																		
Lean and fat (2 pieces, 4 1/8 by 2 1/4 by 1/4 in). — 3 oz	85	62	165	25	7	2.8	2.7	.2	0	11	208	3.2	279	10	.06	.19	4.5	—
Lamb, cooked:																		
Chop, rib (cut 3 per lb with bone), broiled:																		
Lean and fat — 3.1 oz	89	43	360	18	32	14.8	12.1	1.2	0	8	139	1.0	200	—	.11	.19	4.1	—
Lean only from item 182 — 2 oz	57	60	120	16	6	2.5	2.1	.2	0	6	121	1.1	174	—	.09	.15	3.4	—
Leg, roasted:																		
Lean and fat (2 pieces, 4 1/8 by 2 1/4 by 1/4 in). — 3 oz	85	54	235	22	16	7.3	6.0	.6	0	9	177	1.4	241	—	.13	.23	4.7	—
Lean only from item 184 — 2.5 oz	71	62	130	20	5	2.1	1.8	.2	0	9	169	1.4	227	—	.12	.21	4.4	—
Shoulder, roasted:																		
Lean and fat (3 pieces, 2 1/2 by 2 1/2 by 1/4 in). — 3 oz	85	50	285	18	23	10.8	8.8	.9	0	9	146	1.0	206	—	.11	.20	4.0	—
Lean only from item 186 — 2.3 oz	64	61	130	17	6	3.6	2.3	.2	0	8	140	1.0	193	—	.10	.18	3.7	—
Liver, beef, fried[20] (slice, 6 1/2 by 2 3/8 by 3/8 in). — 3 oz	85	56	195	22	9	2.5	3.5	.9	5	9	405	7.5	323	[21]45,390	.22	3.56	14.0	23
Pork, cured, cooked:																		
Ham, light cure, lean and fat, roasted (2 pieces, 4 1/8 by 2 1/4 in).[22] — 3 oz	85	54	245	18	19	6.8	7.9	1.7	0	8	146	2.2	199	0	.40	.15	3.1	—
Luncheon meat:																		
Boiled ham, slice (8 per 8-oz pkg.). — 1 oz	28	59	65	5	5	1.7	2.0	.4	0	3	47	.8	—	0	.12	.04	.7	—
Canned, spiced or unspiced: Slice, approx. 3 by 2 by 1/2 in. — 1 slice	60	55	175	9	15	5.4	6.7	1.0	1	5	65	1.3	133	0	.19	.13	1.8	—

[18] Outer layer of fat on the cut was removed to within approximately 1/2 in of the lean. Deposits of fat within the cut were not removed.
[19] Crust made with vegetable shortening and enriched flour.
[20] Regular-type margarine used.
[21] Value varies widely.
[22] About one-fourth of the outer layer of fat on the cut was removed. Deposits of fat within the cut were not removed.

(Continued)

Meat Composition *(Continued)*

TABLE 2.M.8 *(Continued)*

Foods, approximate measures, units, and weight (edible part unless footnotes indicate otherwise)		Water	Food energy	Protein	Fat	Saturated (total)	Oleic	Linoleic	Carbohydrate	Calcium	Phosphorus	Iron	Potassium	Vitamin A value	Thiamin	Riboflavin	Niacin	Ascorbic acid
Roast, oven cooked, no liquid added—Continued																		
Relatively lean such as heel of round—Continued																		
Lean only from item 168	2.8 oz	78	125	24	3	1.2	1.0	0.1	0	10	199	3.0	268	Trace	0.06	0.18	4.3	—
Steak:																		
Relatively fat-sirloin, broiled:																		
Lean and fat (piece, 2 1/2 by 2 1/2 by 3/4 in)	3 oz	44	330	20	27	11.3	11.1	.6	0	9	162	2.5	220	50	.05	.15	4.0	—
Lean only from item 170	2.0 oz	59	115	18	4	1.8	1.6	.2	0	7	146	2.2	202	10	.05	.14	3.6	—
Relatively lean—round, braised:																		
Lean and fat (piece, 4 1/8 by 2 1/4 by 1/2 in)	3 oz	55	220	24	13	5.5	5.2	.4	0	10	213	3.0	272	20	.07	.19	4.8	—
Lean only from item 172	2.4 oz	61	130	21	4	1.7	1.5	.2	0	9	182	2.5	238	10	.05	.16	4.1	—
Beef, canned:																		
Corned beef	3 oz	59	185	22	10	4.9	4.5	.2	0	17	90	3.7		—	.01	.20	2.9	—
Corned beef hash	1 cup	67	400	19	25	11.9	10.9	.5	24	29	147	4.4	440	—	.02	.20	4.6	—
Beef, dried, chipped	2 1/2-oz jar	48	145	24	4	2.1	2.0	.1	0	14	287	3.6	142	—	.05	.23	2.7	0
Beef and vegetable stew	1 cup	82	220	16	11	4.9	4.5	.2	15	29	184	2.9	613	2,400	.15	.17	4.7	17
Beef potpie (home recipe), baked, piece, 1/3 of 9-in diam. pie)	1 piece	55	515	21	30	7.9	12.8	6.7	39	29	149	3.8	334	1,720	.30	.30	5.5	6
Chili con carne with beans, canned	1 cup	72	340	19	16	7.5	6.8	.3	31	82	321	4.3	594	150	.08	.18	3.3	—
Chop suey with beef and pork (home recipe)	1 cup	75	300	26	17	8.5	6.2	.7	13	60	248	4.8	425	600	.28	.38	5.0	33
Heart, beef, lean, braised	3 oz	61	160	27	5	1.5	1.1	.6	1	5	154	5.0	197	20	.21	1.04	6.5	1
Pork, fresh, [18] cooked:																		
Chop, loin (cut 3 per lb with bone), broiled:																		
Lean and fat	2.7 oz	42	305	19	25	8.9	10.4	2.2	0	9	209	2.7	216	0	.75	.22	4.5	—
Lean only from item 192	2 oz	53	150	17	9	3.1	3.6	.8	0	7	181	2.2	192	0	.63	.18	3.8	—
Roast, oven cooked, no liquid added:																		
Lean and fat (piece, 2 1/2 by 2 1/2 by 3/4 in)	3 oz	46	310	21	24	8.7	10.2	2.2	0	9	218	2.7	233	0	.78	.22	4.8	—
Lean only from item 194	2.4 oz	55	175	20	10	3.5	4.1	.8	0	9	211	2.6	224	0	.73	.21	4.4	—
Shoulder cut, simmered:																		
Lean and fat (3 pieces, 2 1/2 by 2 1/2 by 1/4 in)	3 oz	46	320	20	26	9.3	10.9	2.3	0	9	118	2.6	158	0	.46	.21	4.1	—
Lean only from item 196	2.2 oz	60	135	18	6	2.2	2.6	.6	0	8	111	2.3	146	0	.42	.19	3.7	—

[18] Outer layer of fat on the cut was removed to within approximately 1/2 in of the lean. Deposits of fat within the cut were not removed.
[19] Crust made with vegetable shortening and enriched flour.

(Continued)

Meat Composition (Continued)

TABLE 2.M.8 (Continued)

(Dashes (—) denote lack of reliable data for a constituent believed to be present in measurable amount)

Foods, approximate measures, units, and weight (edible part unless footnotes indicate otherwise)		Water	Food energy	Pro-tein	Fat	Fatty Acids			Carbo-hydrate	Calcium	Phos-phorus	Iron	Potas-sium	Vitamin A value	Thiamin	Ribo-flavin	Niacin	Ascorbic acid
						Satu-rated (total)	Unsaturated											
							Oleic	Lino-leic										
	Grams	Per-cent	Cal-ories	Grams	Grams	Grams	Grams	Grams	Grams	Milli-grams	Milli-grams	Milli-grams	Milli-grams	Inter-national units	Milli-grams	Milli-grams	Milli-grams	Milli-grams
Sausages (see also Luncheon meat (items 190-191)):																		
Bologna, slice (8 per 8-oz pkg.). 1 slice	28	56	85	3	8	3.0	3.4	.5	Trace	2	36	.5	65	—	.05	.06	.7	—
Braunschweiger, slice (6 per 6-oz pkg.). 1 slice	28	53	90	4	8	2.6	3.4	.8	1	3	69	1.7	—	1,850	.05	.41	2.3	—
Brown and serve (10-11 per 8-oz pkg.), browned. 1 link	17	40	70	3	6	2.3	2.8	.7	Trace	—	—	—	—	—	—	—	—	—
Deviled ham, canned. 1 tbsp	13	51	45	2	4	1.5	1.8	.4	0	1	12	.3	—	0	.02	.01	.2	—
Frankfurter (8 per 1-lb pkg.), cooked (reheated). 1 frankfurter	56	57	170	7	15	5.6	6.5	1.2	1	3	57	.8	—	—	.08	.11	1.4	—
Meat, potted (beef, chicken, turkey), canned. 1 tbsp	13	61	30	2	2	—	—	—	0	—	—	—	—	—	Trace	.03	.2	—
Pork link (16 per 1-lb pkg.), cooked. 1 link	13	35	60	2	6	2.1	2.4	.5	Trace	1	21	.3	35	0	.10	.04	.5	—
Salami:																		
Dry type, slice (12 per 4-oz pkg.). 1 slice	10	30	45	2	4	1.6	1.6	.1	Trace	1	28	.4	—	—	.04	.03	.5	—
Cooked type, slice (8 per 8-oz pkg.). 1 slice	28	51	90	5	7	3.1	3.0	.2	Trace	3	57	.7	—	—	.07	.07	1.2	—
Vienna sausage (7 per 4-oz can). 1 sausage	16	63	40	2	3	1.2	1.4	.2	Trace	1	24	.3	—	—	.01	.02	.4	—
Veal, medium fat, cooked, bone removed:																		
Cutlet (4 1/8 by 2 1/4 by 1/2 in), braised or broiled. 3 oz	85	60	185	23	9	4.0	3.4	.4	0	9	196	2.7	258	—	.06	.21	4.6	—
Rib (2 pieces, 4 1/8 by 2 1/4 by 1/4 in), roasted. 3 oz	85	55	230	23	14	6.1	5.1	.6	0	10	211	2.9	259	—	.11	.26	6.6	—

Source: Consumer and Food Economics Institute (1977). Nutritive value of foods. USDA Home and Garden Bull. 72.

Meat Curing Ingredients

TABLE 2.M.9
Liquid pickle for curing large pieces of meats using either salt or brine

| Ingredients | Quantity To Be Used When Various Percentages are To Be Pumped | | | | | |
	10%	12%	14%	16%	18%	20%
When using salt (lb)	167	140	130	111	95	83.50
Bring volume up to 100 gal. with water						
or						
When using 100° salinometer brine (gal.)	63	53	49	42	36	31.50
Bring volume up to 100 gal. with water						
Make up pickle with these ingredients:						
Sodium nitrite (lb)	2.0	1.67	1.43	1.25	1.11	1.0
Sodium nitrate (lb)	2.0	1.67	1.43	1.25	1.11	1.0
Food grade phosphate (lb)[1]	50.0	41.66	35.71	31.25	27.78	25.0
Sodium erythorbate (lb)	5.51	4.55	3.90	3.42	3.04	2.75
Sodium carbonate or bicarbonate	Use sufficient amount to stabilize sodium erythorbate and sodium nitrite to pH of 7.6 at pickle temperature of 40°F					
Cane sugar (lb)	30.0	25.0	21.5	18.75	16.5	15.0
If flavoring ingredients are desired add:						
Monosodium glutamate (oz)	24.0	24.0	20.0	20.0	16.0	16.0
Plant protein hydrolyzate (oz)	15.0	12.50	10.75	9.50	8.25	7.50
Smoke flavor (optional)	Depending on the concentrate desired					

[1] It is now permissible to use sodium hydroxide in combination with food grade phosphate. It may be used only in combination with food grade phosphate in the ratio of 4 parts of phosphate to 1 part of sodium hydroxide. The combination should not exceed 5% pickle at 10% pump, or 0.5% to products. Instead of using the quantities indicated above of the food grade phosphate, the following combined percentages may be used:

	10%	12%	14%	16%	18%	20%
Food grade phosphate (lb)	40.0	33.33	28.57	25.00	22.23	20.0
Sodium hydroxide (lb)	10.0	8.33	7.14	6.25	5.55	5.0

Source: Komarik, S. L., Tressler, D. K., and Long, L. (editors) (1974). Cured meats. In *Food Products Formulary*, Vol. 1. AVI Publishing Co., Westport, Connecticut.

Meat, Frozen Storage

TABLE 2.M.10
Recommended length of storage for frozen meats

Meat	Maximum Number of Months at 0°F
Beef	
Roasts, steaks	6-12
Ground	2-3
Veal	
Roasts	4-8
Cutlets, chops	3-4
Ground meat	2-3
Lamb	
Chops	3-4
Roasts	6-12
Pork	
Roasts	4-6
Chops	3-4
Sausage, without salt	1-2
Ham, cured	1-2
Bacon	Less than 1
Poultry	6-12

Source: Simonds, L. A., and Vanstavern, B. D. (1975). *Buying Meat for Locker or Home Freezer*. Ohio State Univ. Coop. Ext. Serv.

Meat Grade (Quality) Stamps

USDA Prime
Prime grade beef is the ultimate in tenderness, juiciness, and flavor. It has abundant marbling —flecks of fat within the lean— which enhances both flavor and juiciness. Steaks of this grade are the best for broiling.

USDA Standard
Standard grade beef has a high proportion of lean meat and very little fat. Because it comes from young animals, beef of this grade is fairly tender. But because it lacks marbling, it is mild in flavor and most cuts will be somewhat dry unless prepared with moist heat.

USDA Choice
Most USDA Choice steaks are good for broiling and pan-broiling, too—they will be very tender, juicy, and flavorful. Choice grade beef has slightly less marbling than Prime, but still is of very high quality.

USDA Commercial
Commercial grade beef is produced only from mature animals —the top four grades are restricted to young animals. It has abundant marbling (compare it with the Prime grade), and will have the rich, full flavor characteristic of mature beef. However, Commercial grade beef requires long, slow cooking with moist heat to make it tender. When prepared in this manner it can provide delicious and economical meat dishes.

USDA Good
Good grade beef often pleases thrifty shoppers because it is somewhat more lean than the higher grades. It is relatively tender, but because it has less marbling it lacks some of the juiciness and flavor of the higher grades. Some stores sell this quality of beef under a "house" brand name rather than under the USDA grade name.

FIGURE 2.M.2

Source: USDA (1968). How to buy beef steaks. USDA Home and Garden Bull. *145.*

Meat Identification

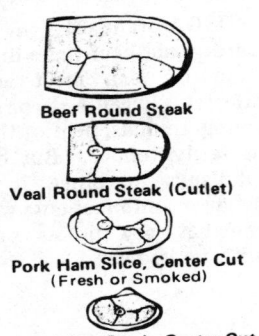

Beef Round Steak

Veal Round Steak (Cutlet)

Pork Ham Slice, Center Cut
(Fresh or Smoked)

Lamb Leg Steak, Center Cut

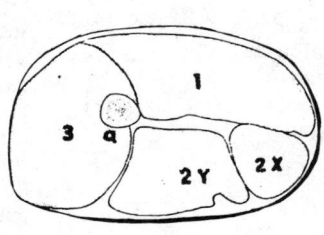

Bone
  a. Round or leg (smallest in center cuts)
Muscles
  1. Top (inside) round or leg
  2. Bottom (outside) round or leg
    (X) Eye of round or leg
    (Y) Bottom round or leg
  3. Tip (knuckle)
Other Features
  Oval shape
  Separating lines of connective tissue and
    fat between muscles.

Beef Sirloin Steak

Veal Sirloin Steak

Pork Sirloin Chop

Lamb Sirloin Chop

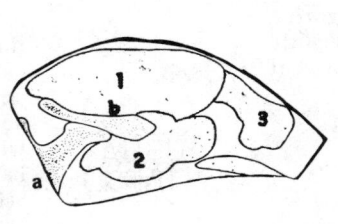

Bones
  a. Back ⎫ wide variation in shape
  b. Hip ⎬
Muscles
  1. Top sirloin
  2. Tenderloin ⎬ wide variation in shape
  3. Tip (knuckle)
    Tip muscle (3) is replaced by flank in
    steaks and chops cut across forward
    end of hip bone.
Other Features
  Muscles in area (3), in some steaks and
    chops, appear to have been cut with
    grain of meat.

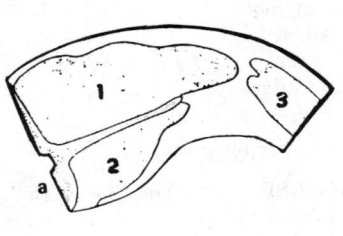

Beef Porterhouse or T-Bone Steak

Veal Loin Chop

Pork Loin Chop

Lamb Loin Chop

Bone
  a. Back (T shape)
Muscles
  1. Loin eye or strip
  2. Tenderloin (larger in Porterhouse than
    in T-Bone)
  3. Flank (tail of steaks and chops)
Other Features
  Beef club steak looks very much like
    Porterhouse or T-Bone except that it
    contains no tenderloin.

FIGURE 2.M.3
Characteristics and typical cuts of meats

(Continued)

Meat Identification   (Continued)

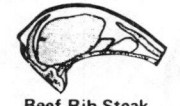

Beef Rib Steak

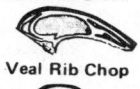

Veal Rib Chop

Pork Rib (Loin) Chop

Lamb Rib Chop

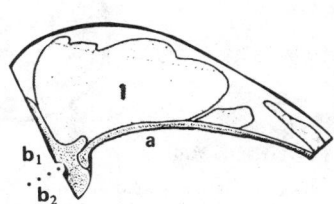

Bones
　a. Rib (steaks and chops cut between ribs do not have this bone).
　b. Back
　　(b₁) Feather
　　(b₂) Chine

Muscles
　1. Rib eye (continuation of loin eye muscle.)

Other Features
　Steaks and chops near chuck or shoulder have thin layer of meat over rib eye called rib cover.

Beef Arm Steak

Veal Arm Steak (Chop)

Pork Arm Steak (Chop)

Lamb Arm Chop

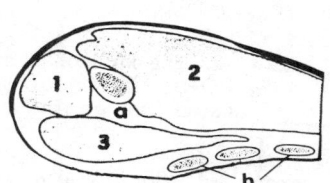

Bones
　a. Arm
　b. Rib cross cuts (in all cuts except pork)

Muscles
　1. Small round forearm muscle completely surrounded with connective tissue
　2. Arm (thick end of clod or outside shoulder)
　3. Brisket or middle rib

Other Features
　Although cuts from round and arm look somewhat alike, a close comparison shows a wide difference in muscle structure. Cuts from round contain no cross cut rib bones.

Beef Blade Steak

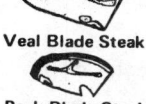

Veal Blade Steak

Pork Blade Steak

Lamb Blade Chop

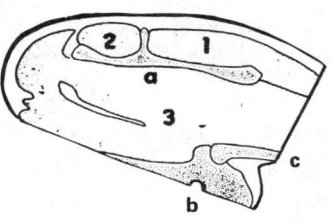

Bones
　a. Blade
　b. Back (in all cuts except pork)
　c. Rib (in all cuts except pork, unless made between ribs)

Muscles
　1. Outside chuck (thin end of clod or outside shoulder)
　2. Chuck tender
　3. Inside chuck

Other Features
　Muscles of inside chuck (3) run in different directions.

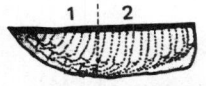

Beef Brisket (1) and Short Plate (2)

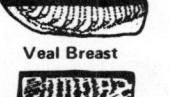

Veal Breast

Pork (Side Pork and Bacon)

Lamb Breast

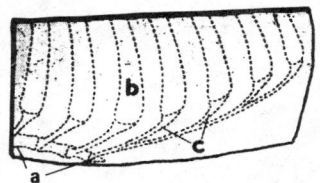

Bones
　a. Breast (except in pork)
　b. Ribs (except in pork)
　c. Rib cartilages (except in pork)

Muscles
　1. Alternating layers of lean and fat.

Other Features
　Breasts of veal and lamb are comparable to plate and brisket sections of beef.
　Side pork (bacon before curing and smoking) comes from same area in pork as preceding cuts come from in beef, lamb and veal.
　Side pork and bacon are sold boneless. Bones (spareribs) were removed in packing plant.

FIGURE 2.M3   (*Continued*)

Source: Meat Manual, 6th Edition, National Live Stock and Meat Board, Chicago.

Meat Inspection (Wholesomeness) Stamp

Inspection for
Wholesomeness

FIGURE 2.M.4

Source: USDA (1968). How to buy beef steaks. USDA Home and Garden Bull. *145.*

Meat Label

1 The kind of meat — BEEF, PORK, LAMB or VEAL. It's listed first on every label.

2 The primal (wholesale) cut —CHUCK, RIB, LOIN or ROUND —tells where the meat comes from on the animal.

3 The retail cut — BLADE ROAST, SPARERIBS, LOIN CHOPS, etc.—tells what part of the primal cut the meat comes from.

FIGURE 2.M.5
How to identify the label on retail meat packages

Source: Be a Smarter Shopper . . . a Better Cook. (1973). National Live Stock and Meat Board, Chicago.

Meat, Nutritive Value

TABLE 2.M.11
Nutritive value of cooked meats

	Beef[1]	Veal[1]	Lamb[1]	Pork[1]
		(3½ oz Cooked Lean Meat)		
Protein (g)	29.6	32.7	26.6	28.5
Calories/100 g	265.8	213	258	240
Fat (g)	15.4	8.1	16.1	13.1
Carbohydrate (gm)	0	0	0	0
Iron (mg)[2]	3.7	3.3	2.0	3.5
Calcium (mg)	9.6	9.7	8.2	8.1
Phosphorus (mg)	191.1	260	210.8	228
Potassium (mg)	442	543	499	496
Magnesium (mg)	21.3	21.7	22.6	22.7
Zinc (mg)[3]	5.8[4]	4.1[4]	4.3[4]	3.8[4]
	(6.2)[5]	(4.2)[5]	(5)[5]	
Thiamin (mg)	0.10	0.18	0.22	1.03
Riboflavin (mg)	0.39	0.35	0.32	0.29
Niacin (mg)	4.5	7.2	7.6	4.4
B-6 (mg)	0.37	0.48	0.32	0.46
B-12 (mcg)	2.056	2.53	2.8	1.2
Vitamin A (IU)	0	0	0	0
Vitamin C (mg)	0	0	0	0

[1] LEVERTON, RUTH M. and ODELL, G. V. 1958. The nutritive value of cooked meat. Stillwater, Oklahoma: Oklahoma Agric. Expt. Sta., Misc. Publ. MP-49, Oklahoma State Univ.
[2] WATT, BERNICE K. and MERRILL, ANNABEL L. Revised 1963. Composition of Foods—Raw, Processed, Prepared. USDA Agriculture Handbook 8.
[3] MURPHY, E. W., WILLIS, B. W. and WATT, BERNICE K. 1975. Provisional tables on zinc content of foods. J. Am. Diet. Assoc. 66, 345.
[4] Dry heat.
[5] Moist heat.

Source: Nutritive Value of Cooked Meat (1975). National Live Stock and Meat Board, Chicago.

Meat Pigment

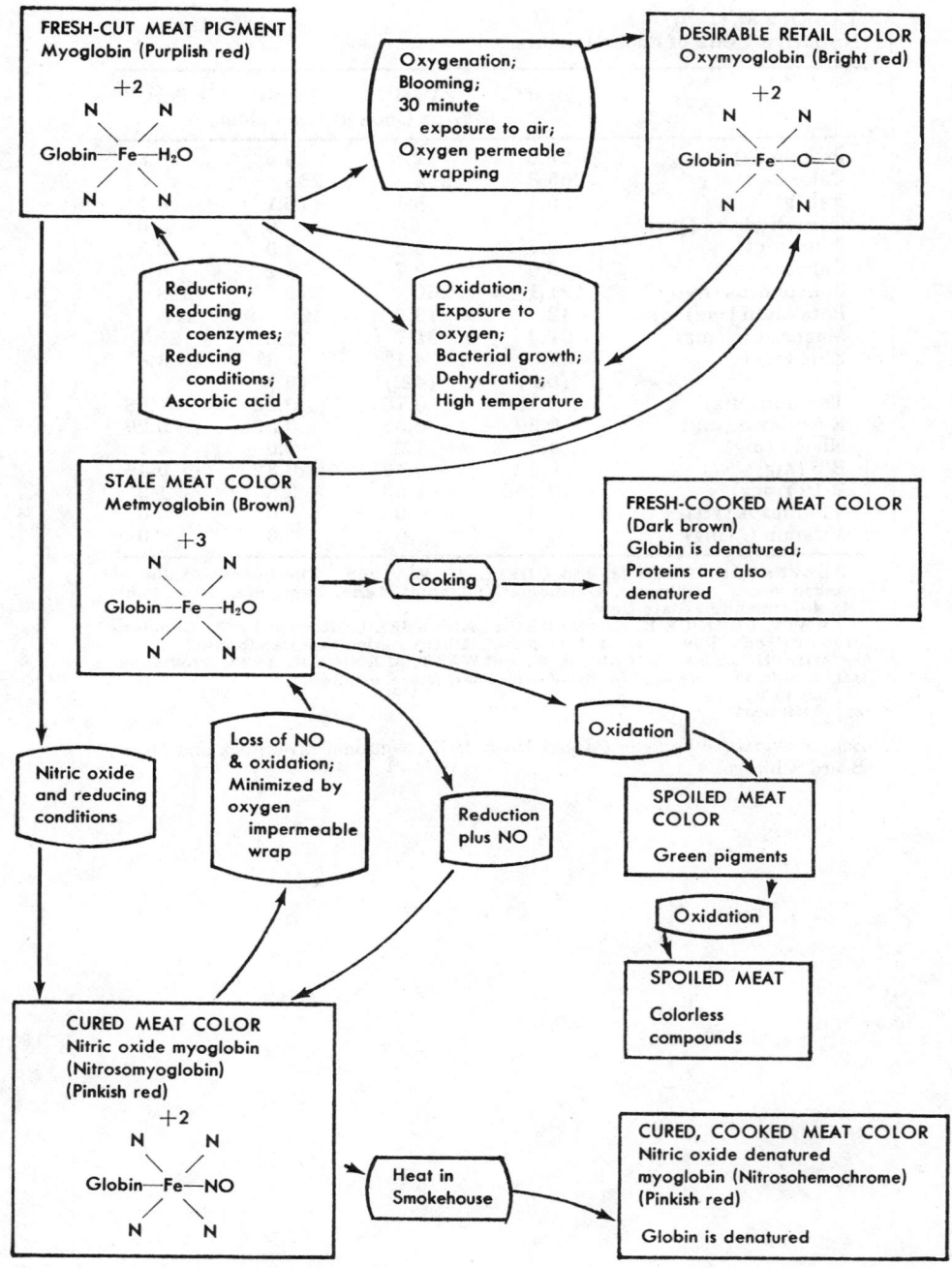

FIGURE 2.M.6
Fresh and cured meat pigment alterations

Source: Ockerman, H. W. (1975). Chemistry of muscle and major organs. In *Meat Hygiene*. J. A. Libby (editor). Lea & Febiger, Philadelphia.

Meat, Servings per Pound I

TABLE 2.M.12
Average number of servings from one pound of different retail cuts of meat and poultry[1]

Meat Cut	Servings Per Pound	Meat Cut	Servings Per Pound
Beef		**Pork, fresh**	
Sirloin steak	2½	Center cut or rib chops	4
Porterhouse, T-bone,		Loin or rib roasts	2½
rib steak	2	Ham roast	2½
Round steak	3½	Boston butt, bone in	3
Flank steak	4	Boston butt, boneless	4
Chuck steak	2	Blade steak	3
Chuck roast, bone in	2	Spareribs	1-⅓
Rib roast, boneless	2½	Liver	5
Chuck roast, boneless	3	**Pork, cured**	
Rib roast, bone in	2	Picnic:	
Rump roast, sirloin roast	3	Bone in	2
Ground beef	4	Boneless	3
Short ribs	2	Canned	5
Heart, liver or kidney	5	Center slice	3
Tongue	3	Ham, ready-to-eat:	
Frankfurters	4	Bone in	3½
Stew meat, boneless	5	Boneless	5
Dried, chipped	8	Shankless	4½
Lamb		Center slice	5
Loin, rib or shoulder chops	3	Ham, cook-before-eating:	
Breast and shank	2	Bone in	2½
Shoulder roast	2½	Boneless	3½
Leg of lamb	3	Shankless	3
Stew meat, boneless	5		

[1] From 2½ to 3½ oz of cooked, lean meat is considered a standard serving.

Source: Potts, B. (1975). *Meat Buying "Know-How."* Ohio State Univ. Coop. Ext. Serv.

Meat, Servings per Pound II

TABLE 2.M.13
Meat, poultry, and fish

	Servings per Lb[1]
Meat	
Much bone or gristle	1–2
Medium amounts of bone	2–3
Little or no bone	3–4
Poultry (Ready-To-Cook)	
Chicken	2–3
Turkey	2–3
Duck and goose	2
Fish	
Whole	1–2
Dressed or pan-dressed	2–3
Portions or steaks	3
Fillets	3–4

[1] Three ounces of cooked lean meat, poultry, or fish per serving.

Source: USDA (1978). Nutrition, food at work for you. USDA Home and Garden Bull. *1.*

Meat Storage

TABLE 2.M.14
Maximum meat storage time

Meat	Refrigerator (36°–40°F)	Freezer (at 0°F or lower)
Beef (fresh)	2–4 days	6–12 months
Veal (fresh)	2–4 days	6–9 months
Pork (fresh)	2–4 days	3–6 months
Lamb (fresh)	2–4 days	6–9 months
Ground beef, veal and lamb	1–2 days	3–4 months
Ground pork	1–2 days	1–3 months
Variety meats	1–2 days	3–4 months
Luncheon meats	1 week	Not recommended
Sausage, fresh pork	1 week	60 days
Sausage, smoked	3–7 days	
Sausage, dry and semi-dry (unsliced)	2–3 weeks	
Frankfurters	4–5 days	1 month
Bacon	5–7 days	1 month
Smoked ham, whole	1 week	60 days
Ham slices	3–4 days	60 days
Beef, corned	1 week	2 weeks
Leftover cooked meat	4–5 days	2–3 months

Source: Be a Smarter Shopper . . . a Better Cook. (1973). National Live Stock and Meat Board, Chicago.

Melting Points, Fats and Oils

TABLE 2.M.15
Melting points of some fats and oils[1]

Oil or Fat	Melting Point (°C)
Coconut	23–26
Palm	27–43
Palm kernel	24–26
Babassu	24–26
Butter	28–35
Tallow (beef)	43–48
Tallow (mutton)	44–47
Lard	36–45
Horse fat	36–43
Cacao butter	28–36
Borneo tallow	34–39

[1] Closed capillary tube method.

Source: Mahlenbacher, C. V. The Analysis of Fats and Oils. Garrard Press, Champaign, Illinois.

Mesh Sizes

TABLE 2.M.16

Mesh reference: wire and nylon cloth. (Below are some of the most widely used mesh sizes. British and U.S. standard sizes differ only slightly. Special metal meshes with fine wires which provide greater percentage open area are available for higher outputs.)

Mesh No.	Size of Opening (in.)	Open Area (%)	Wire Diam (in.)	Closest Equiv Nylon Cloth (No.)	Aperture Size (μ)	Open Area (%)
20	.0340	46.2	.016	860	860	57
30	.0198	35.3	.0135	505	505	51
40	.0150	36.0	.010	390	390	47
60	.0087	27.2	.008	223	223	45
80	.0070	31.4	.0055	183	183	47
100	.0055	30.3	.0045	130	130	44
120	.0046	30.7	.0037	116	116	43
150	.0041	37.4	.0026	102	102	39
180	.0033	34.7	.0023	86	86	35
200	.0029	33.6	.0021	73	73	33
250	.0024	36.0	.0016	64	64	30
325	.0017	30.0	.0014	44	44	17

Source: Slade, F. H. (1967). Food Processing Plant, Vol. 1. International Textbook Co., London, England.

Microbial Toxins

TABLE 2.M.17

Intoxication from microbial toxins

Disease	Reservoirs	Common Vehicle	Prevention and Control
Clostridial intoxication (Botulism).	Soil, dust, fruits, vegetables, and other foods.	Improperly processed canned and bottled foods containing toxin.	Boil home-canned nonacid food 5 minutes; thoroughly cook meat, fish and dried foods held over; do not taste suspected food.
Staphylococcal intoxication.	Skin, mucous membranes, pus, dust, air, sputum, and throat.	Contaminated custard pastries, cooked or processed meats, poultry, dairy products, hollandaise sauce, salads, and milk.	Refrigerate prepared food in shallow container at a temperature below 45°F; avoid handling food; educate food handlers in personal hygiene and sanitation.
Clostridium welchii type A.	Meat animal species, soil, and man.	Meat and meat products.	Avoid storage of large pieces of cooked meat; refrigerate so that temperature at the center of the meat cut is below 45°F; reheat thoroughly meat cuts or gravy immediately prior to serving.

Source: U.S. Department of the Army (1969). Food inspection specialist. TM 8-451.

Microbiological Examination of Dairy Products

TABLE 2.M.18
Microbiological examination of dairy products

APHA Designation	Used For
AK medium No. 2	Spore production
Antibiotic medium No. 1	Detection of inhibitory substances
Aureomycin-rose	Yeast and mold counts
Bengal agar	
Brilliant green lactose	Detection of coliforms
Bile broth, 2%	
Casein soy peptone agar	Quantitative surface sampling by the RODAC® plate method
Casein soy peptone agar with Polysorbate 80[1] and lecithin	Surface sampling by the RODAC plate method
Citrate azide agar	Enterococcus count for butter
Endo agar	Isolation of coliforms
Eosine methylene blue agar, levine	Isolation of coliforms
Lactose broth	Detection of coliforms
MF-endo broth	Coliform determination with membrane filters
Mueller hinton agar	Detection of inhibitory substances in milk
Nutrient agar	
Nutrient broth	Surface sampling by the Rinse Solution Method
Potato glucose agar (acidified)	Yeast and mold counts
Standard methods agar	Standard plate count
Standard methods agar with Polysorbate 80[1] and lecithin	Surface sampling by the RODAC plate method
Violet red bile agar	Isolation of coliforms

[1] TWEEN 80® Atlas Chemical Industries.

Source: BioQuest. Division of Becton, Dickinson and Co., Rutherford, New Jersey.

Microbiological Media

TABLE 2.M.19

Organisms and media for examination of foods, water, and other materials of sanitary and public health importance (note: those media which may be expected to give the most efficient results as evidenced by their ability to grow more species, or to grow them more rapidly, are indicated by asterisks)

Organisms	Media
CANNED FOODS	
Clostridia	Clostrisel Agar
C. perfringens	T S N Agar
Enteric Bacilli	Desoxycholate Lactose Agar
	E E Broth
Lactobacilli	A P T Agar and Eugonagar
	L Agar
	Thioglycollate Medium-135C
Pseudomonas	Pseudosel Agar
Thermophiles	Dextrose Tryptone Agar
Total Aerobes	Eugonagar or Standard Methods Agar
Yeasts and Molds	Mycophil Agar with Low pH or Potato Dextrose Agar
FROZEN FOODS	
These present new problems in evaluation of sanitary quality and safety.	
Total Aerobes	Eugonagar
	Trypticase Soy Agar
Staphylococci	
Total	
Coagulase +	Mannitol Salt Agar
Streptococci	Vogel and Johnson Agar
especially enterococci	Azide Blood Agar Base
Total	*M*-Enterococcus Agar
Yeasts and Molds	Streptosel Agar
	Mycophil Agar with Low pH or Potato Dextrose Agar
MILK AND OTHER DAIRY PRODUCTS	
Total Aerobes	Standard Methods Agar
	Dextrose Salt Agar
Brucella	Trypticase Soy Agar
	Brucella or Biosate Agars
Coliforms	Brilliant Green Bile Broth 2%
	Desoxycholate Lactose Agar or
	Levine E M B Agar
Plant Contaminants	Eugonagar
Salmonella	Desoxycholate Lactose Agar
	D C L S Agar® or
	Brilliant Green Agar
	E E Broth
	Selenite-F Broth
	X L D Agar
Staphylococci	
Total	
Coagulase +	Mannitol Salt Agar
Streptococci	Vogel and Johnson Agar
Yeasts and Molds	Trypticase Soy Media
	Mycophil Agar with Low pH or
	Potato Dextrose Agar
	Sugar-Free Agar

(Continued)

Microbiological Media   (Continued)

TABLE 2.M.19   (Continued)

Organisms	Media

SUGARS, SYRUPS, CITRUS, CARBONATED AND OTHER BEVERAGES

Organisms	Media
Aerobes—Total Also for plant control studies	*Eugonagar or Standard Methods Agar
Coliforms	*Desoxycholate Lactose or Levine E M B Agar
Lactobacilli, etc.	*Orange Serum Agar
Thermophiles—Aerobic	*Dextrose Tryptone Agar
Anaerobic	Sulfite Agar
Yeasts and Molds	*M-Green Yeast and Mold Broth
	*Mycophil Agar with Low pH or Potato Dextrose Agar
(For BEER, the above media may be used; the bracketed media are particularly recommended.)	{ Eugonagar W L Differential Agar W L Nutrient Agar

WATER AND WASTEWATER

Organisms	Media
Clostridia	Clostrisel Agar
Coliforms	Brilliant Green Bile Broth 2%
	*Desoxycholate Lactose or Levine E M B Agars
	*Lauryl Sulfate Broth or Lactose Broth
	M-Coliform Broth
	*M-Endo Agar L E S
Enterococci	*Azide Dextrose Broth
	*Ethyl Violet Azide Broth
	Mead Agar
	*M-Enterococcus Agar
	*S F Broth

DISINFECTANT TESTING

AOAC NAME	BBL NAME
Nutrient Broth	F D A Broth
Synthetic Broth	Wright and Mundy Broth
Nutrient Agar	F D A Agar
Letheen Broth	Letheen Broth
Cystine Trypticase Agar	C T A Medium
Fluid Thioglycollate Medium	Fluid Thioglycollate Medium

Source: BioQuest. Division of Becton, Dickinson and Company, Cockeysville, Maryland.

Microbiological Standards, Dairy

TABLE 2.M.20
Quality control guidelines for microbiological standards in dairy foods

Product	SPC	Coliform	Psychrotrophic SPC After (5 Days at 70°C)	Yeast and Mold	*Staphylococci*	*Salmonella*
Raw milk–bulk tankers	<1000-50,000	<100-<1000	<10,000-<100,000			
Comingled raw milk at pasteurizer	<50,000-30,000	<100-<1000	<100,000-<800,000		<5,000-<100,000	
Pasteurized milk	<1,000-<10,000	<1-<5	<20,000-<6000			
Cottage cheese (dry)	<1,000-<20,000	<1-<5	<10,000-<100,000	<5-<10	<1	<1
Butter	<5,000-<20,000		<50,000	<5-<10	<1	<1
Milk powder	<20,000-<50,000	NS	NS	<10	<1	<1

Source: Harper, W. J. (1972). Sanitation in dairy food plants. In *Food Sanitation*. R. K. Guthrie (editor). AV
Publishing Co., Westport, Connecticut.

Microorganism, Culture Media, Dairy and Food Products

TABLE 2.M.21

Culture media used for the examination of dairy and other food products:

Plate Counts
Tryptone Glucose Extract Agar
Proteose Tryptone Agar
Beef Lactose Agar
Nutritive Caseinate Agar
Heart Infusion Agar
Plate Count Agar
Antibiotic Medium No. 1
Nutrient Agar
Brucella
Tryptose Agar
Lactobacilli
Tomato Juice Agar
Trypsin Digest Agar
Peptonized Milk
Skim Milk
Micro Assay Culture Agar
Micro Inoculum Broth
Snyder Test Agar
Hemolytic Streptococci
Heart Infusion Agar

Coliform Organisms
Brilliant Green Bile 2%
Formate Ricinoleate Broth
Violet Red Bile Agar
Desoxycholate Agar
Desoxycholate Lactose Agar
MacConkey Agar
Lactose Broth
Endo Agar
Levine EMB Agar
Bacto—Tryptone
MR-VP Medium
Koser Citrate Medium
Thermophiles
Dextrose Tryptone Agar
Thermoacidurans Agar
Molds and Yeasts
Potato Dextrose Agar
Malt Agar

Source: Difco Laboratories, Detroit.

Microorganism, Culture Media, Water and Sewage, Standard Methods

TABLE 2.M.22

Culture Media used for the examination of water and sewage "Standard Methods" procedures:

Plate Counts	Presumptive	Tests for Coliform Organisms Confirmed	Completed
Nutrient Agar	Lactose Broth	Endo Agar	Nutrient Agar
Nutrient Gelatin	Lauryl Tryptose Broth	Levine EMB Agar	Lactose Broth
Tryptone Glucose Extract Agar	Azide Dextrose Broth	Brilliant Green Bile 2%	
Plate Count Agar	Ethyl Violet Azide Broth	Formate Ricinoleate Broth	
	m Enterococcus Agar	Lauryl Tryptose Broth	
	KF Streptococcus Agar	EC Medium	
		Boric Acid Broth	
		m Endo Agar LES	
		m Endo Broth MF	
		m FC Broth Base	
		m Coliform Holding Broth	

Source: Difco Laboratories, Detroit.

Microorganism, Media

TABLE 2.M.23

Media for growth of microorganisms:

Microorganism

Organism	Process	Media
Actinomyces (aerobic)	Isolation	Actinomyces Agar; Actinomycete Isolation Agar; Casitone Starch Agar; Fluid Sabouraud Medium; Sabouraud Dextrose/Maltose Agar; Tryptic Soy Agar/Broth
	Differentiation	Nutrient Gelatin
	Propagation	Actinomyces Agar/Broth/Medium; Actinomycete Isolation Agar; Fluid Sabouraud Medium; Sabouraud Dextrose Agar; Sabouraud Maltose Agar; Tryptic Soy Agar
Algae	Isolation	Algae Culture Agar/Broth; Chlorella Agar/Broth; Euglena Agar/Broth; Euglena Broth BM
	Propagation	Algae Culture Broth; Chlorella Broth; Euglena Broth; Euglena Broth BM
Brucella	Isolation	Brain Heart Infusion w/PAB & Agar; Brucella Agar/Broth; Columbia Blood Agar Base; Eugon Agar + Supplement B or C; Potato Infusion Agar; Tryptose Agar; Tryptose Agar w/Crystal Violet; Tryptose Broth
	Differentiation	Tryptic Soy Agar w/Thionin or Basic Fuchsin
	Propagation	Brain Heart Infusion w/PAB & Agar; Brucella Agar/Broth; Liver Infusion Agar/Broth; Potato Infusion Agar; Tryptose Agar/Broth
	Serological Identification	Brucella Abortus Antiserum; Brucella AMS Antiserum Poly; Brucella Melitensis Antiserum; Brucella Suis Antiserum; Corresponding Antigens Also Available; FA Brucella Abortus
Candida albicans	Isolation	BiGGY Agar (Nickerson Medium); Candida BCG Agar; Chlamydospore Agar; Levine EMB Agar; Rice Extract Agar; Wolin Bevis Agar
	Differentiation	Chlamydospore Agar; Corn Meal Agar; Pagano Levin Agar; Rice Extract Agar; Wolin Bevis Agar
	Propagation	ABY Agar; BiGGY Agar (Nickerson Medium); Candida BCG Agar; Corn Meal Agar; Sabouraud Dextrose Agar; Sabouraud Maltose Agar
	Serological Identification	Candida Albicans Antiserum; F A C. Albicans
Clostridia	Isolation	Brewer Anaerobic Agar; Columbia Blood Agar Base; Cooked Meat Medium; Fluid Thioglycollate Medium; Forget Fredette Agar; LM Agar; Liver Veal Agar; Liver Veal Agar w/o Dext.; McClung Toabe Agar Base; Proteose No. 3 Agar w/Hemoglobin; SFP Agar Base w/Egg Yolk Enrichment 50% and Antimicrobic Vials; K & P; SPS Agar; Tryptose Blood Agar Base
Coliform Group	Isolation	BDG Broth; m BG Endo Broth; Cled Agar; Desoxycholate Agar; Desoxycholate Lactose Agar; Endo Agar; m Endo Agar LES; m Endo Broth w/BG; m Endo Broth MF; m FC Broth Base; m HD Endo Broth; Hektoen Enteric Agar; Levine EMB Agar; MacConkey Agar; MacConkey Agar w/o Salt; Sorbitol 7 Agar (Path. E. Coli); Tergitol 7 Agar; Tryptose Blood Agar Base w/Blood; XL Agar Base; XLD Agar

(Continued)

Microorganism, Media (Continued)

Differentiation

- LM Agar
- Loeffler Blood Serum
- Nutrient Gelatin
- Peptone Colloid Medium
- Phenol Red Broth Base w/Carbohydrates under anaerobic conditions
- Sulfite Agar
- Tryptone

- Acetate Differential Agar
- Christensen Agar
- Christensen Iron Agar
- Citrate Mannitol Agar
- Decarboxylase Base Moeller
- Decarboxylase Medium Base
- Differentiation Disks Lysine, ONPG, Ornithine, Urea
- F35M Hajna
- H_2S Test Strips
- Indole Nitrite Medium
- Indole Test Strips
- KCN Broth Base
- Kligler Iron Agar
- Koser Citrate Medium
- Krumweide Tri Sugar Agar
- Levine EMB Agar
- Lysine Decarboxylase Broth
- Lysine Iron Agar
- Lysine Lactose Broth
- MIO Medium
- MR–VP Medium
- Malonate Broth
- Motility Medium S
- Motility Sulfide Medium

- Motility Test Medium
- Nitrite Test Strips
- OF Basal Medium
- Phenol Red Agar/Broth w/Carbohydrates or w/Diff. Disks, Carbohydrates
- Phenol Red Tartrate Agar
- Phenylalanine Agar
- Phenylalanine Malonate Broth
- Purple Agar/Broth w/Carbohydrates or w/Diff. Disks, Carbohydrates
- Purple Lactose Agar
- Russell Double Sugar Agar
- Sanders Agar w/Differentiation Disks Carbohydrates
- Simmons Citrate Agar
- Sorbitol Iron Agar
- TSU Agar
- Triple Sugar Iron Agar
- Tryptone Solution 1% (Indole Test)
- Urea Agar/Broth
- Urea R Broth

Propagation

- AC Medium
- Brain Heart Infusion w/PAB & Agar
- Columbia Blood Agar Base
- Cooked Meat Medium

- Egg Meat Medium
- Liver Veal Agar w/o Dext.
- Veal Infusion Medium

- Brain Heart Infusion w/PAB & Agar
- Cooked Meat Medium
- Nutrient Agar/Broth
- Plate Count Agar
- Tryptic Soy Broth
- Tryptone Glucose Extract Agar

Serological Identification

- Arizona Antiserum Poly Monophasic or Diphasic
- Bethesda–Ballerup Antiserum Poly (Citrobacter Antiserum)
- E Coli OB & OK Antisera 20 Serogroups and 3 Polyvalent
- E Coli O Antisera 51 Serogroups

- E Coli OB Antigens 11 Serogroups
- E Coli O Antigens 11 Serogroups
- Fluorescent E Coli Conjugates 20 F A E Coli Serogroups 3 F A E Coli Polyvalent

Corynebacterium

Isolation

- Columbia Blood Agar Base w/Tinsdale Enrichment
- Dextrose Proteose No. 3 Agar w/Tellurite Blood Solution
- Loeffler Blood Serum

- Mueller Tellurite Base w/Mueller Tellurite Serum
- Pai Egg Medium, Tubes
- Tinsdale Base & Enrichment

Differentiation

- Columbia Blood Agar Base w/Tinsdale Enrichment
- Dextrose Proteose No. 3 Agar w/Tellurite Blood Solution
- Mueller Tellurite Base w/Mueller Tellurite Serum

- Phenol Red Agar/Broth w/Carbohydrates or w/Diff. Disks, Carbohydrates
- Tinsdale Base and Enrichment
- Tryptic Tellurite Agar Base

Endamoeba histolytica

- Balamuth Medium
- Endamoeba Medium w/Horse Serum
- Saline 1 : 6 & Rice Powder

(Continued)

Microorganism, Media (Continued)

TABLE 2.M.23 (Continued)

Corynebacterium (Continued)

Propagation
- Brain Heart Infusion w/PAB & Agar
- Loeffler Blood Serum
- Tryptic Soy Agar
- Tryptose Blood Agar Base

Serological Identification
- C Acnes 554 & 605 Antisera
- FA C Diphtheriae
- KL Antitoxin Strips
- KL Virulence Agar
- KL Virulence Enrichment

Endamoeba histolylica (Continued)

Propagation
- Balamuth Medium
- Endamoeba Medium w/Horse Serum
- Saline 1:6 and Rice Powder

Hemophilus or Bordetella

Isolation
- Bordet Gengou Agar Base w/Fresh Blood (Pertussis only)
- Brain Heart Infusion w/Supp. B, C, or VX
- Casman Medium Base
- Charcoal Agar
- Columbia Blood Agar Base w/Blood (Chocolated) and Supplement B
- Eugon Agar w/Supplement B or C
- Heart Infusion Agar/Broth w/Fildes Enrichment
- Proteose No. 3 Agar or GC Med. Base w/Hemo. and Supp. A, B, C, or VX

Differentiation
- Brain Heart Infusion Agar
- Heart Infusion Agar
- Proteose No. 3 Agar or GC Med. Base w/Hemo. and Supp. A, B, C, or VX
- Tryptic Soy Agar w/Differentiation Disks BV, BVX, BX

Propagation
- Bordet Gengou Agar Base w/Blood
- Brain Heart Infusion w/Supp. B
- Casman Broth Base
- Charcoal Agar
- Eugon Broth w/Supp. A or B
- Proteose No. 3 Agar w/Hemo. and Supp. A, B, or VX

Serological Identification
- B. Parapertussis Antiserum
- B. Pertussis Antiserum
- B. Pertussis Antigen
- FA Bordetella Parapertussis
- FA Bordetella Pertussis
- FA H. Influenzae A, B, C, D, E, F
- H. Influenzae Antisera Type A, B, C, D, E, F. Poly

Fungi

Isolation
- Actinomycete Isolation Agar
- Brain Heart CC Agar
- Brain Heart Infusion Agar
- Cooke Rose Bengal Agar
- DTM Agar
- Emerson YpSs Agar
- Eugon Agar w/Blood
- Georg Fungus Medium
- Ink Blue Agar
- Littman Oxgall Agar
- Malt Agar
- Mycobiotic Agar
- Potato Dextrose Agar
- SABHI Agar
- Sabouraud Agar Modified
- Sabouraud Dextrose Agar
- Sabouraud Maltose Agar

Differentiation
- Brain Heart CC Agar
- Corn Meal Agar
- SABHI Agar
- Sabouraud Agar Modified
- Sabouraud Dextrose Agar
- Sabouraud Maltose Agar
- Trichophyton Agars 1, 2, 3, 4, 5, 6, 7
- Vitamin Free Yeast Base
- Yeast Carbon Base
- Yeast Morphology Agar
- Yeast Nitrogen Base

Propagation
- Actinomycete Isolation Agar
- Brain Heart Infusion Agar
- Cantino PYG Agar/Broth
- Dextrose Neopeptone Broth
- Fluid Sabouraud Medium
- Lima Bean Agar
- Malt Extract Broth
- Mycological Agar & Broth
- Neurospora Culture Agar
- Potato Dextrose Agar
- Potato Maltose Agar
- SABHI Agar
- Sabouraud Agar Modified
- Sabouraud Dextrose Agar
- Sabouraud Maltose Agar/Broth
- Stoddard Oat Agar
- WL Nutrient Broth
- Wort Agar/Broth (Cult. of yeasts)
- YM Agar/Broth

Serological Identification
- Candida Albicans Antiserum
- FA C. Albicans

Klebsiella

Isolation
- Bismuth Sulfite Agar
- m Bismuth Sulfite Broth
- Brilliant Green Agar
- m Brilliant Green Broth
- EMB Agar
- Endo Agar
- Hektoen Enteric Agar
- MacConkey Agar
- MacConkey Agar w/o CV
- MacConkey Agar w/o Salt
- XL Agar Base
- XLD Agar

Lactobacilli

Isolation
- APT Agar/Broth
- Elliker Broth
- Eugon Broth
- Lactobacilli MRS Broth
- Orange Serum Agar
- Orange Serum Broth Conc. 10X
- Rogosa SL Agar/Broth
- Tomato Juice Agar/Broth
- Trypsin Digest Agar
- Whey Agar/Broth

(Continued)

Microorganism, Media   (Continued)

Purpose	Media
Differentiation	Capsule Ink; Decarboxylase Medium Base; Differentiation Disks Lysine, ONPG, Ornithine, Urea; F 35M Hajna; H₂S Test Strips; Indole Test Strips; KCN Broth Base; Kligler Iron Agar; Lysine Decarboxylase Broth; Lysine Iron Agar; Lysine Lactose Broth; MIO Medium; Nitrite Test Strips; Phenol Red Agar/Broth w/Carbohydrates or w/Diff. Disks, Carbohydrates; Phenol Red Tartrate Agar; Purple Agar/Broth w/Carbohydrates w/Diff. Disks, Carbohydrates; Russell Double Sugar Agar; SIM Medium; Triple Sugar Iron Agar; Tryptone Solution 1% (Indole Test); Worfel Ferguson Agar/Broth; Litmus Milk; Purple Milk; Snyder Test Agar
Propagation	Brain Heart Infusion w/PAB & Agar; Cooked Meat Medium; Nutrient Agar/Broth; APT Agar/Broth; Elliker Broth; L Agar; Lactobacilli Agar AOAC; Litmus Milk; Micro Assay Culture Agar; Micro Inoculum Broth; Orange Serum Agar/Broth; Peptonized Milk Agar; Purple Milk; Skim Milk; Tomato Juice Agar/Broth; Tryptic Digest Agar; Ulrich Milk; Whey Agar/Broth
Serological Identification	Capsule Ink; FA Klebsiella Type 1; FA Klebsiella Type 2; FA Klebsiella Poly (1–6); Klebsiella Antisera Types 1 through 72 and Poly (1–6)

Leptospira

Purpose	Media
Isolation	Fletcher Medium Base w/Leptospira Enrichment; Leptospira Medium Base EMJH w/Lepto Enrichment EMJH; Stuart Medium Base w/Leptospira Enrichment; Stuart Medium Base w/o Phenol Red w/Leptospira Enrichment
Propagation	Fletcher Medium Base w/Leptospira Enrichment; Leptospira Medium EMJH w/Leptospira Enrichment EMJH; Stuart Medium Base w/Leptospira Enrichment; Stuart Medium Base w/o Phenol Red w/Leptospira Enrichment
Serological Identification	**LEPTOSPIRA ANTIGENS** — Pool 1: L. Ballum, L. Canicola, L. Icterohemorrhagiae; Pool 2: L. Bataviae, L. Grippotyphosa, L. Pyrogenes; Pool 3: L. Autumnalis, L. Pomona, L. Wolffi; Pool 4: L. Australis, L. Hyos, L. Mini, Georgia (LT 117); Pool 5: L. Cynopteri, L. Ce Iedoni, L. Javanica; Pool 6: L. Cynopteri, L. Panama, L. Shermani; Leptospira Ictero Kremastos Antigen Pool. Individual Antigens and Antisera Listed in Pools also Available, plus L. Andamana, L. Medanensis, L. Sejroe, L. Biflexa, Patoc and L. Hardjo.

Listeria

Purpose	Media
Isolation	McBride Listeria Agar; Tryptose Blood Agar Base w/Blood; Cystine Heart Agar w/Hemoglobin and Supplement B; Eugon Agar/Broth
Differentiation	Phenol Red Broth w/1% Carbohydrates; Tryptone Solution 1% (Indole Test); Urea R Broth; Indole Nitrite Medium; Indole Test Strips; MR–VP Medium; Motility GI Medium; Motility Medium S
Propagation	Tryptose Blood Agar Base; Tryptose Agar/Broth; Brain Heart Infusion; Thiol Medium; Tryptic Soy Agar/Broth
Serological Identification	FA Listeria Type 1; FA Listeria Type 4; FA Listeria Poly; Listeria O Antiserum Type 1; Listeria O Antiserum Type 4; Listeria O Antiserum Poly; Corresponding Slide and Tube Antigens Available

(Continued)

Microorganism, Media (Continued)

TABLE 2.M.23 (Continued)

	Mima-Herellea		Mycobacterium tuberculosis	
Isolation	Blood Agar Base w/Blood Brain Heart Infusion Agar EMB Agar	Hektoen Enteric Agar Herellea Agar Tryptose Blood Agar Base w/Blood	ATS Medium Bovine TB Medium Dubos Oleic Agar IUTM Base Lowenstein Medium Gruft Lowenstein Jensen Medium	Middlebrook 7H9 Agar/7H10 Agar Middlebrook 7H10 Agar w/WR1339 Mycobacteria 7H11 Agar Peizer TB Medium Petragnani Medium
Differentiation	p-Aminodimethylaniline Oxalate (Oxidase Reagent) Differentiation Disks Oxidase F 35M Hajna Indole Test Strips Motility GI Medium	Motility Medium S Nitrite Test Strips OF Basal Medium Phenol Red Agar/Broth Base w/1% & 10% Carbohydrates Simmons Citrate Agar Tryptone Solution 1% (Indole Test)	Differentiation Disks Auramine Dubos Medium Albumin Lowenstein Medium Gruft Lowenstein Jensen Medium Deeps (for Catalase) Mycobacteria 7H11 Agar	Nitrite Test Strips Proskauer Beck Medium TB Niacin Test Base TB Niacin Test Strips & Control TB Stain Sets K & ZN TB Fluorescent Stain Sets M, & T
Propagation	Brain Heart Infusion Brain Heart Infusion w/PAB & Agar Nutrient Agar/Broth Tryptic Soy Broth		ATS Medium Bovine TB Medium Dubos Media IUTM Base Kirchner Medium Lowenstein Jensen Medium	Middlebrook 7H9 Broth Mycobacteria 7H11 Agar Peizer TB Medium Petragnani Medium TB Egg Agar
Serological Identification	Mima Polymorpha Antiserum Poly Herellea Vaginicola Antiserum		H-37 Ra Antigen & Antiserum	

	Neisseriae		Pasteurella	
Isolation	Brain Heart Infusion w/PAB & Agar Casman Medium Base Chocolate Agar Columbia Blood Agar Base w/Hemoglobin 2% w/Supp. B, C, or VX	Eugon Agar/Broth w/Supp. B, C, or VX GC Med. Base or Proteose No. 3 Agar enriched w/Hemoglobin and Supplement A, B, C, or VX Thayer Martin Medium Transgrow Medium Tryptose Blood Agar Base w/Blood	Civil Defense Agar Cystine Heart Agar w/Hemo. and Supplement B Tryptose Agar Tryptose Blood Agar Base	Eugon Agar/Broth w/Supp. B or C Tryptose Agar Tryptose Blood Agar Base
Differentiation	p-Aminodimethylaniline Oxalate (Oxidase Reagent) Cystine Tryptic Agar w/Carbohydrates Differentiation Disks Oxidase	Phenol Red Agar/Broth Base w/Carbohydrates	Indole Nitrite Medium Indole Test Strips Motility GI Medium Motility Medium S	Phenol Red Broth w/1% Carbohydrates Tryptone Solution 1% (Indole Test)
Propagation	Brain Heart Infusion Agar/Broth Chocolate Agar (tubes) Dextrose Broth Dextrose Starch Agar Eugon Broth w/Supp. B, C, or VX	GC Medium Base or Proteose No. 3 Agar enriched w/Hemoglobin or Hemoglobin Solution 2% and Supplement B, C, or VX Tryptose Phosphate Broth	Brain Heart Infusion w/PAB & Agar Civil Defense Agar	Cystine Heart Agar w/Hemoglobin or Hemoglobin Solution 2% Tryptose Agar/Broth YPC Broth
Serological Identification	FA N. Gonorrhoeae FA Meningococcus Poly	Meningococcus Antisera Groups A, B, C, D, X, Y, Z, Poly & Poly 2	P. Tularensis Antigen (Slide) P. Tularensis Antigen (Tube)	P. Tularensis Antiserum

(Continued)

Microorganism, Media (Continued)

TABLE 2.M.23 (Continued)

	PPLO Pleuropneumonia-Like Organisms (Mycoplasma)	Pneumococci
Isolation	Heart Infusion Agar or Broth w/* { Enriched with PPLO Serum Fraction or *Mycoplasma Supplement or *Mycoplasma Supplement S } PPLO Agar PPLO Broth w/CV PPLO Broth w/o CV	Blood Agar Base w/Blood Blood Agar Base No. 2 w/Blood Brain Heart Infusion Agar Columbia Blood Agar Base w/Blood Eugon Agar GC Medium Base w/Hemoglobin Tryptic Soy Agar w/Blood Tryptose Blood Agar Base w/Blood
Differentiation		Bile Salts No. 3 Blood Agar Base Media Differentiation Disks Optochin Hiss Capsule Stain + Copper Sulfate
Propagation	Heart Infusion Agar or Broth w/* { Enriched with PPLO Serum Fraction or *Mycoplasma Supplement or *Mycoplasma Supplement S } PPLO Agar PPLO Broth w/CV PPLO Broth w/o CV	Brain Heart Infusion Agar/Broth Brain Veal Agar Tryptic Soy Agar/Broth
Serological Identification		PNEUMOCOCCUS ANTISERA (Diplococcus Pneumoniae) Pool A: Types 1, 2, 7 Pool B: Types 3, 4, 5, 6, 8 Pool C: Types 9, 12, 14, 15, 17, 33 Pool D: Types 10, 11, 13, 20, 22, 24 Pool E: Types 16, 18, 19, 21, 28 Pool F: Types 23, 25, 27, 29, 31, 32 Individual Types 1, 2, 3, 4, 5, 6, 7, 8, 14, 18 & 19 Also Available. FA Pneumococcus Poly

	Proteus	Pseudomonas
Isolation	Bismuth Sulfite Agar m Bismuth Sulfite Broth Brilliant Green Agar m Brilliant Green Broth Cled Agar EMB Agar Endo Agar Hektoen Enteric Agar MacConkey Agar MacConkey Agar w/o CV MacConkey Agar w/o Salt XL Agar Base XLD Agar	BDG Broth Bismuth Sulfite Agar Cetrimide Agar Base Cled Agar EMB Agar Endo Agar Hektoen Enteric Agar MacConkey Agar MacConkey Agar w/o CV MacConkey Agar w/o Salt Pseudomonas Isolation Agar Tryptic Soy Agar Tryptose Blood Agar Base w/Blood XL Agar Base XLD Agar
Differentiation	Decarboxylase Base Moeller Decarboxylase Medium Base Differentiation Disks Lysine ONPG, Ornithine, Urea F35M Hajna H_2S Test Strips Indole Test Strips Kligler Iron Agar Lysine Iron Agar MIO Medium Motility Medium S Motility Sulfide Medium Motility Test Medium Nitrite Test Strips Phenol Red Agar/Broth w/Carbohydrates or w/Diff. Disks, Carbohydrates Phenylalanine Agar Purple Agar/Broth w/Carbohydrates or w/Diff. Disks, Carbohydrates Sanders Agar w/Diff. Disks Carbohydrates TSU Agar Triple Sugar Iron Agar Tryptone Solution, 1% (Indole Test) Urea Agar/Broth Urea R Broth	Decarboxylase Medium Base Differentiation Disks Lysine, ONPG, Ornithine, Oxidase, Urea Indole Test Strips Kligler Iron Agar Lysine Decarboxylase Broth Lysine Iron Agar MIO Medium Motility GI Medium Motility Medium S Motility Sulfide Medium Motility Test Medium N Broth OF Basal Medium Pseudomonas Agar F & P SIM Medium Sellers Differential Agar TSU Agar Tryptone Solution 1% (Indole Test)

(Continued)

Microorganism, Media   (Continued)

TABLE 2.M.23 (Continued)

	Proteus (Continued)		Pseudomonas (Continued)	
Propagation	Brain Heart Infusion w/PAB & Agar Cooked Meat Medium Nutrient Agar	Nutrient Broth Tryptic Soy Agar/Broth	Brain Heart Infusion w/PAB & Agar Cooked Meat Medium Nutrient Agar/Broth Tryptic Soy Agar/Broth	
Serological Identification	Proteus OX2 Antigen (Slide) Proteus OX19 Antigen (Slide) Proteus OXK Antigen (Slide)	Corresponding Antigens Also Available for Tube Test Corresponding Antisera Also Available	FA Pseudomonas Pseudomallei Pseudomonas Pseudomallei Antiserum	

	Salmonella typhosa		Salmonella other than Typhosa	
Isolation	ENRICHMENTS FAS Broth GN Broth Hajna SBG Enrichment SBG Sulfa Enrichment Selenite Broth Selenite Cystine Broth Tetrathionate Broth Base m Tetrathionate Broth Base TT Broth Base PLATING MEDIA BCP-D Agar BG Sulfa Agar Bismuth Sulfite Agar m Bismuth Sulfite Broth	Brilliant Green Agar m Brilliant Green Broth Cled Agar Desoxycholate Citrate Agar EMB Agar m EMB Broth Endo Agar Hektoen Enteric Agar MacConkey Agar MacConkey Agar w/o CV MacConkey Agar w/o Salt SS Agar m Urease Test Reagent XL Agar Base XLD Agar	ENRICHMENTS FAS Broth GN Broth Hajna M Broth SBG Enrichment SBG Sulfa Enrichment Selenite Broth Selenite Cystine Broth Tetrathionate Broth Base m Tetrathionate Broth Base TT Broth Base	PLATING MEDIA BCP-D Agar BG Sulfa Agar Bismuth Sulfite Agar m Bismuth Sulfite Broth Brilliant Green Agar m Brilliant Green Broth Cled Agar Desoxycholate Citrate Agar EMB Agar m EMB Broth Endo Agar Hektoen Enteric Agar MacConkey Agar MacConkey Agar w/o CV MacConkey Agar w/o Salt SS Agar m Urease Test Reagent XL Agar Base XLD Agar
Differentiation	Decarboxylase Base Moeller Decarboxylase Medium Base Differentiation Disks Lysine, ONPG, Ornithine, Urea F35M Hajna H Broth H$_2$S Test Strips Hemmes 7-In Medium Indole Test Strips KCN Broth Base KP Organic Acid Base Kligler Iron Agar Lysine Decarboxylase Broth Lysine Iron Agar Lysine Lactose Broth	MIO Medium Motility Test Medium Nitrite Test Strips Phenol Red Tartrate Agar Purple Agar/Broth w/Carbohydrates or w/Diff. Disks, Carbohydrates Russell Double Sugar Agar SIM Medium Sanders Agar w/Diff. Disks, Carbohydrates TSU Agar Triple Sugar Iron Agar Tryptone Solution 1% (Indole Test) Urea Agar/Broth Urea R Broth	Decarboxylase Base Moeller Decarboxylase Medium Base Differentiation Disks Lysine, ONPG, Ornithine, Urea F35M Hajna H Broth H$_2$S Test Strips Hemmes 7-In Medium Indole Test Strips KCN Broth Base KP Organic Acid Base Kligler Iron Agar Krumweide Tri Sugar Agar Lysine Decarboxylase Broth Lysine Iron Agar Lysine Lactose Broth MIO Medium Motility GI Medium	Motility Medium S Motility Sulfide Medium Motility Test Medium Nitrite Test Strips OF Basal Medium w/Carbohydrates Phenol Red Tartrate Agar Purple Agar/Broth w/Carbohydrates or w/Diff. Disks, Carbohydrates Russell Double Sugar Agar SIM Medium Sanders Agar w/Diff. Disks, Carbohydrates TSU Agar Triple Sugar Iron Agar Tryptone Solution 1% (Indole Test) Urea Agar/Broth Urea R Broth Wilson Blair Base

(Continued)

TABLE 2.M.23 (*Continued*)

Microorganism, Media (*Continued*)

Category				
Propagation	Brain Heart Infusion w/PAB & Agar Cooked Meat Medium	Nutrient Agar/Broth Tryptic Soy Agar/Broth	Brain Heart Infusion w/PAB & Agar Cooked Meat Medium	Nutrient Agar/Broth Tryptic Soy Agar/Broth
Serological Identification	Salmonella H Antiserum Group d Salmonella O Antiserum Group D Salmonella O Antiserum Poly A-I and Vi Salmonella O Antiserum Poly A Corresponding Antigens Also Available		POLYVALENT ANTISERA Salmonella O Antiserum Poly A-I and Vi Salmonella O Antisera Poly A, B, C, D, E, F, and G Salmonella H Antiserum Poly a-z Salmonella H Antisera Poly A, B, C, D, E, and F Salmonella H Antisera Spicer Edwards 1, 2, 3, 4, and EN, Z_4, L and 1 Complexes FA Salmonella Panvalent FA Salmonella Poly	SALMONELLA O ANTISERA Groups A, B, C_1, C_2, D, E, E_1, E_2, E_3, E_4, F, G, H, I, J, K, L, M, N, O, P, Q, R, S, T, U, V, W, X, Y, Z and 51–61 and Salmonella Vi Antiserum SALMONELLA H ANTISERA Salmonella H Antisera a-z SALMONELLA ANTIGENS Salmonella O Antisera A-I and Vi Salmonella H Antigens a, b, c, d, eh, g, i and 1 Complex

Shigella

Category		
Isolation	BCP-D Agar Cled Agar Desoxycholate Agar Desoxycholate Citrate Agar EMB Agar Hektoen Enteric Agar MacConkey Agar MacConkey Agar w/o CV MacConkey Agar w/o Salt SS Agar XL Agar Base XLD Agar	
Differentiation	Acetate Differential Agar Decarboxylase Base Moeller Decarboxylase Medium Base Differentiation Disks Lysine, ONPG, Ornithine, Urea H Broth Hemmes 7-In Medium H_2S Test Strips Indole Test Strips KCN Broth Base KP Organic Acid Base Kligler Iron Agar Lysine Decarboxylase Broth Lysine Iron Agar Lysine Lactose Broth MIO Medium Motility GI Medium	Motility Medium S Motility Test Medium Nitrite Test Strips Phenol Red Tartrate Agar Purple Agar/Broth w/Carbohydrates or w/Diff. Disks, Carbohydrates Russell Double Sugar Agar SIM Medium Sanders Agar w/Diff. Disks, Carbohydrates TSU Agar Triple Sugar Iron Agar Tryptone Solution 1% (Indole Test) Urea Agar/Broth Urea R Broth Wilson Blair Base
Propagation	Brain Heart Infusion w/PAB & Agar Cooked Meat Medium Nutrient Agar/Broth Tryptic Soy Agar/Broth	

Staphylococci

Category		
Isolation	Baird Parker Agar Base w/EY Tellurite Enrichment Blood Agar Base w/Blood Chapman Stone Medium Coagulase Agar Base Colbeck EY Agar Base/Broth Columbia CNA Agar w/Blood DNase Test Agar DNase Test Agar w/Methyl Green Mannitol Neomycin Agar Mannitol Salt Agar	Mannitol Salt Broth Phenylethanol Agar Staphylococcus Medium 110 Staphylococcus Medium 110 w/Azide m Staphylococcus Broth TMM Broth Tellurite Glycine Agar TPEY Agar w/TPEY Enrichment & Antimicrobic Vial P Tryptose Blood Agar Base
Differentiation	Blood Agar Base w/Blood Chapman Stone Medium Coagulase Agar Base Coagulase Plasma Coagulase Plasma EDTA Colbeck EY Agar Base/Broth DNase Test Agar DNase Test Agar w/Methyl Green Mannitol Salt Agar Mannitol Salt Broth	OF Basal Medium w/Carbohydrates Staphylococcus Medium 110 Staphylococcus Medium 110 w/Azide Tellurite Glycine Agar TPEY Agar w/TPEY Enrichment and Antimicrobic Vial P Tryptose Blood Agar Base w/Blood VJ Agar
Propagation	Brain Heart Infusion Agar/Broth Cooked Meat Medium Dextrose Starch Agar Phenylethanol Agar	Tryptic Soy Agar/Broth Tryptose Agar Tryptose Phosphate Broth

Microorganism, Media   (Continued)

TABLE 2.M.23 (Continued)

	Shigella (Continued)	Streptococci including Enterococci	Trichomonas	Staphylococci (Continued)	Thermophilic Flat Sour Organisms
Serological Identification	Alkalescens-Dispar Antisera Types 1, 2, 3, 4 and Poly Shigella Antisera Poly Groups A, A_1, B, C_1, C_2, D Shigella Boydii Antisera Types 1-15 Shigella Dysenteriae Antisera Types 1-10 Shigella Flexneri Antisera Types 1-6			FA Staphylococcus Aureus	Dextrose Tryptone Agar m Dextrose Tryptone Broth
Isolation		Azide Blood Agar Base Azide Dextrose Broth m Azide Broth BAGG Broth Columbia CNA Agar w/Blood m Enterococcus Agar EVA Broth Heart Infusion Agar KF Streptococcus Agar/Broth Mannitol Neomycin Agar Mitis Salivarius Agar Phenylethanol Agar Pike Streptococcal Broth SF Medium Tryptose Blood Agar Base w/Blood Tryptose Blood Agar Base w/Hemo. and Supp. A or B			
Differentiation		Bile Esculin Agar (entero) Bile Esculin Azide Agar (entero) Blood Agar Base w/Blood Blood Agar Base No. 2 w/Blood Differentiation Disks Bacitracin EVA Broth Enterococcus Confirmatory Agar Enterococcus Presumptive Broth Heart Infusion 6.5% NaCl Broth (entero) Phenol Red Broth Base w/Carbohydrates SR Medium Base Tryptose Blood Agar Base w/Blood			Dextrose Tryptone Agar m Dextrose Tryptone Broth
Propagation		AC Medium Brain Heart Infusion Agar/Broth Brain Veal Agar Cooked Meat Medium Dextrose Agar Dextrose Broth Todd Hewitt Broth Tryptic Soy Agar/Broth Tryptose Agar Tryptose Phosphate Broth			
Serological Identification		AHT Kit FA Streptococcus Group A, Streptolysin O Reagents Streptococcus Antisera Groups A, B, C, D, E, F, G, H, K, L, M, N, O, P, Q, R, S, T, MG Streptococcus MG Suspension			
Isolation			Kupferberg Trichomonas Base Kupferberg Trichomonas Broth Lash Serum Medium (tubes)		
Propagation			Kupferberg Trichomonas Base Kupferberg Trichomonas Broth Lash Serum Medium (tubes)		

Source: Difco Product Selection Guide. 0229. (1974). Difco Laboratories, Detroit.

Microorganism Reactions on Differential Tube Media

TABLE 2.M.24
Microorganism reactions on differential tube media

Organism[1]	Xylose	Dextrose	Maltose	Saccharose	Lactose	Rhamnose	Mannitol	Dulcitol	Salicin	Indol	Motility	H₂S	Bacto Urea Broth	Urea Agar Butt	Urea Agar Slant	Bacto Simmons Citrate Agar
Shigella dysenteriae (Shiga)	NC	Y	NC	NC	NC	NC	NC	NC	NC	−	−	−	−	−	−	−
Shigella ambigua (Schmitz)	NC	Y	NC	NC	NC	Y	NC	NC	NC	+	−	−	−	−	−	−
Shigella sonnei	NC or Y	Y	NC or Y	Y	Y slow	Y	Y	NC	NC	−	−	−	−	−	−	−
Shigella paradysenteriae—Boyd and Flexner	NC	Y	NC or Y	NC	NC	NC	Y	NC	NC	±	−	−	−	−	−	−
Shigella paradysenteriae—Newcastle	NC	YG	Y	NC	NC	NC	YG	Y	NC	−	−	−	−	−	−	−
Shigella alkalescens	Y	Y	Y	NC or Y	NC	Y	Y	Y	NC	+	−	−	−	−	−	−
Shigella madampensis	Y	Y	Y	Y	Y	Y	Y	NC	NC	−	−	−	−	−	−	−
Shigella ceylonensis (dispar)	Y	Y	Y	Y	Y	NC	Y	NC	NC	+	−	−	−	−	−	−
Salmonella typhosa (Eberthella typhosa)	NC	Y	YG	NC	NC	NC	Y	NC	NC	−	+	+	−	−	−	−
Salmonella paratyphi	YG	YG	YG	NC	NC	YG	YG	YG	NC	−	+	−	−	−	−	−
Salmonella schottmuelleri	YG	YG	YG	NC	NC	YG	YG	YG	NC	−	+	+	−	−	−	+
Salmonella typhimurium	YG	YG	YG	NC	NC	YG	YG	YG	NC	−	+	+	−	−	−	+
Salmonella choleraesuis	YG	YG	YG	NC	NC	YG	YG	NC	NC	−	+	±	−	−	−	+
Salmonella enteritidis	YG	YG	YG	NC	NC	YG	YG	YG	NC	−	+	+	−	−	−	+
Salmonella pullorum	Y	YG	YG	NC	NC	YG	YG	YG	NC	−	−	+	−	−	−	+
Salmonella gallinarum	YG	Y	Y	NC	NC	YG	Y	Y	NC	−	−	+	−	−	−	+
Aerobacter aerogenes	YG	YG	YG	NC or YG	YG	NC or Y	YG	NC or YG	YG	−	−	−	−	−	−	+
Aerobacter cloacae	YG	YG	YG	YG	YG	NC	YG	NC	YG	−	+	−	−	−	−	+
Escherichia coli	YG	YG	YG	NC or YG	YG	YG	YG	NC or YG	NC or YG	+	+	−	−	−	−	−
Escherichia freundii	YG	YG	YG	NC or YG	YG	YG	YG	NC or YG	NC or YG	−	+	±	R	−	R	+
Escherichia intermedium	YG	YG	YG	NC or YG	YG	YG	YG	NC or YG	NC or YG	±	±	±	R	−	−	+
Proteus vulgaris	YG	YG	YG	YG	NC		NC		NC or YG	+	+	+	R	R	R	−
Proteus mirabilis	YG	YG	YG	YG	NC	NC	NC		NC	−	+	+	R	R	R	+
Proteus morganii	NC or Y	Y or YG	NC	NC	NC		Y or YG	NC	NC	+	+	−	R	R	R	±
Proteus rettgeri	Y or YG	Y or YG	NC or YG	NC or YG	NC or YG	NC	NC or YG	NC	NC or YG	+	±	−	R	R	R	+
Klebsiella pneumoniae	Y or YG	NC or YG	NC	NC	NC		NC		NC	−	−	−	−	−	−	±
Pseudomonas aeruginosa	NC	NC or Y	NC	NC	NC	NC	NC	NC	NC	−	+	−	−	−	−	+
Alcaligenes faecalis	NC	NC	NC	NC	NC	NC	NC	NC	NC	−	+	−	−	−	−	+

(*Continued*)

Microorganism Reactions on Differential Tube Media

(Continued)

TABLE 2.M.24 *(Continued)*

Organism[1]	Bacto Russell Double Sugar Agar		Bacto-Kligler Iron Agar			Bacto Kramwiede Triple Sugar Agar			Bacto Triple Sugar Iron Agar			Bacto Friewer Shaughnessy Medium		
	Butt	Slant	Butt	Slant	H₂S	Butt	Slant	H₂S	Butt	Slant	H₂S	Fermentation	Motility	H₂S
Shigella dysenteriae (Shiga)	Y	NC	Y	NC	−	Y	NC	−	Y	NC	−	NC	−	−
Shigella ambigua (Schmitz)	Y	NC	Y	NC	−	Y	NC	−	Y	NC	−	NC	−	−
Shigella sonnei	Y	NC	Y	NC	−	Y	NC	−	Y	NC	−	NC	−	−
Shigella paradysenteriae—Boyd and Flexner	Y or YG	NC	Y or YG	NC	−	Y or YG	NC	−	Y or YG	NC	−	NC	−	−
Shigella paradysenteriae—Newcastle	Y	NC	Y	NC	−	Y	NC	−	Y	NC or Y	−	NC	−	−
Shigella alkalescens	Y	Y	Y	Y	−	Y	Y	−	Y	Y	−	Y	−	−
Shigella madampensis	Y	Y	Y	Y	−	Y	NC or Y	−	Y	Y	−	Y	−	−
Shigella ceylonensis (dispar)	Y	Y	Y	Y	−	Y	Y	−	Y	Y	−	NC	−	−
Salmonella typhosa (Eberthella typhosa)	Y	NC	Y	NC	+	Y	NC	+	Y	NC	+	NC	+	+
Salmonella paratyphi	YG	NC	YG	NC	−	YG	NC	−	YG	NC	−	YG	+	−
Salmonella schottmuelleri	YG	NC	YG	NC	+	YG	NC	+	YG	NC	+	YG	+	+
Salmonella typhimurium	YG	NC	YG	NC	+	YG	NC	+	YG	NC	+	YG	+	+
Salmonella choleraesuis	YG	NC	YG	NC	−	YG	NC	−	YG	NC	−	YG	+	−
Salmonella enteritidis	YG	NC	YG	NC	+	YG	NC	+	YG	NC	+	YG	+	+
Salmonella pullorum	Y	NC	Y	NC	+	Y	NC	+	Y	NC	+	YG	−	+
Salmonella gallinarum	YG	NC	YG	NC	±	YG	NC	±	YG	NC	±	YG	−	±
Aerobacter aerogenes	YG	Y	YG	Y	−	YG	Y	−	YG	Y	−	YG	−	−
Aerobacter cloacae	YG	Y	YG	Y	−	YG	Y	−	YG	Y	−	YG	+	−
Escherichia coli	YG	Y	YG	Y	−	YG	Y	−	YG	Y	−	YG	±	−
Escherichia freundii	YG	Y	YG	Y	−	YG	Y	−	YG	Y	−	YG	±	±
Escherichia intermedium	YG	Y	YG	Y	−	YG	Y	−	YG	Y	−	YG	±	−
Proteus vulgaris	YG	NC	YG	NC	+	YG	NC or Y	+	YG	NC or Y	+	NC	+	+
Proteus mirabilis	YG	NC	YG	NC	+	YG	NC or Y	+	YG	NC or Y	+	NC	+	+
Proteus morganii	Y or YG	NC	Y or YG	NC	−	Y or YG	NC	−	Y or YG	NC	+	NC	+	+
Proteus rettgeri	Y or YG	NC	Y or YG	NC	−	Y or YG	NC	−	Y or YG	NC	−	NC	±	−
Klebsiella pneumoniae	Y or YG	NC	Y or YG	NC	−	Y or YG	NC	−	Y or YG	NC	−	YG	−	−
Pseudomonas aeruginosa	NC	NC	NC	NC	−	NC	NC	−	NC	NC	−	NC	+	−
Alcaligenes faecalis	NC	NC	NC	NC	−	NC	NC	−	NC	NC	−	NC	+	−
Paracolobactrum aerogenoides	Reactions are the same as those of Aerobacter aerogenes except that the fermentation of lactose is consistently delayed.													
Paracolobactrum intermedium	Reactions are the same as those of Escherichia freundii or E. intermedium except that the fermentation of lactose is consistently delayed.													
Paracolobactrum coliforme	Reactions are the same as those of Escherichia coli except that the fermentation of lactose is consistently delayed.													

NC=No change or alkaline reaction.
Y=Yellow—acid formation.
YG=Acid and gas formation.
R=Red—urea hydrolyzed.

+=Positive for a given reaction.
−=Negative.
±=Variable.

[1] Names of organisms according to Bergey's "Manual of Determinative Bacteriology," Sixth Edition, 1948.

Source: Difco Manual, 9th Edition. (1973). Difco Laboratories, Detroit.

Microorganism, Selective and Differential Broths and Media, Water Filtration Plant

TABLE 2.M.25
Selective and differential broths and media used for control of water filtration plant operation

Selective Broths	Selective Agars	Differential Test Media
Fuchsin Lactose Broth	MacConkey Agar	Bacto-Tryptone
Brilliant Green Bile 2%	Violet Red Bile Agar	MR-VP Medium
MB-BCP	Desoxycholate Lactose Agar	Koser Citrate Medium
Formate Ricinoleate Broth	Brilliant Green Bile Agar	Simmons Citrate Agar
Crystal Violet Broth	Levine EMB Agar	Decarboxylase w/Lysine
Eijkman Lactose Medium	Brilliant Green Agar	Decarboxylase w/Arginine
EC Medium	Bismuth Sulfite Agar	Decarboxylase w/Ornithine
MacConkey Broth	Desoxycholate Citrate Agar	TSI
Tetrathionate Broth	XLD Agar	KCN Broth
Selenite Broth		SIM Medium
GN Broth, Hajna		m Bismuth Sulfite Broth
		Purple Broth Base w/Carbohydrates

Source: Difco Laboratories, Detroit.

Microwave Cooking, Fresh Vegetables

TABLE 2.M.26
Microwave cooking of fresh vegetables. These vegetables require cooking in a 3-qt casserole with $\frac{1}{2}$ tsp of salt added. Times are average and may need adjustments according to taste (power input, 0.8 kW)

Vegetable	Weight (Oz)	Water (Cups)	Cooking Time (Min)	Preparation Notes
Asparagus	16	½	12	—
Beans (green or waxed)	16	1	9	—
Parsnip	16	1	8	Peel and slice
Peas	16	½	6½	Shell
Potatoes	16	None	3½	Skins on
Squash				
Acorn	16	None	6	Halve and remove seeds
Butternut	16	½	6	Peeled 1-in. cubes
Hubbard	16	½	6	Peeled 1-in. cubes
Summer	16	¼	6	Quarter and slice
Turnip	16	1	15	Cut into 8 pieces
Spinach	10	None	4	Wash and drain
Onions	12	2	15	—

Source: Copson, D. A. (editor) (1975). Guide to domestic microwave cooking. In Microwave Heating, 2nd Edition. AVI Publishing Co., Westport, Connecticut.

Microwave Cooking, Frozen Vegetables

TABLE 2.M.27
Microwave cooking of frozen vegetables. These vegetables require cooking in a casserole with $\frac{1}{2}$ tsp of salt added (power input, 0.8 kW)

Vegetable	Weight (oz)	Water (Cups)	Cooking Time (Min)
Asparagus	10	⅓	6½
Beans (green)	12	⅔	12-14
Beans (wax)	10	1	12
Broccoli	10	½	9
Brussels sprouts	10	½	10
Cauliflower	10	½	4½
Corn-on-cob	8 (2 ears)	¼	5
Corn (whole kernel)	10	½	4
Lima beans (baby)	10	1½	15
Lima beans (fordhook)	10	1	10
Peas	12	⅓	8
Peas and carrots	10	½	8
Spinach (chopped)	12	None	8
Spinach (whole)	12	⅓	9
Squash	12	None	4

Source: Copson, D. A. (editor) (1975). Guide to domestic microwave cooking. In *Microwave Heating*, 2nd Edition. AVI Publishing Co., Westport, Connecticut.

Microwave Cooking, Fruit

TABLE 2.M.28
Preparation and heating times in minutes for cooking fruit

Fruit	Amount	Time (min)	Preparation
Apples	4 medium	6	Remove core, pare around top, fill, and sprinkle with sugar.
Apple sauce	6 medium	6-8	Wash and core. Cook with ½ cup water. Strain. Add ¼ cup sugar.
Apricots (dried)	11 oz	9	Cook in 2 cups boiling water. Covered casserole.
Bananas	2 large	1½	Quarter, space well in dish, brush with melted butter. Heat.
Cranberry sauce	1 lb	8	Cook until skins burst in 2 cups sugar, 1½ cups water.
Grapefruit	4 halves	8	Brush fruit with hot mixture of 2 tsp butter, 2 tbsp honey, ⅛ tsp nutmeg. Cook until hot.
Peaches (fresh)	8 medium	5	Mix 2 tbsp lemon juice and ¼ cup water. Pour over sliced, peeled fruit. Make smooth mixture and pour over fruit; ¾ cup flour, 1 cup brown sugar, ¼ tsp salt. Heat.
Prunes	1 lb	8	Place in 2 cups of water and soak over night. Cook.
Rhubarb sauce	2 cups	4	Mix rhubarb with 1 cup sugar, 2 tbsp water and dash of salt.

Source: Copson, D. A. (editor) (1975). Guide to domestic microwave cooking. In *Microwave Heating*, 2nd Edition. AVI Publishing Co., Westport, Connecticut.

Microwave Processing Time

TABLE 2.M.29
Approximate processing times for microwave ovens

Food Item	Processing Time (Min)
Meat, precooked and cooled	
Ham steak	3
Short ribs of beef	2
Poultry, precooked and cooled	
Fried chicken, disjointed	2½
Fried chicken, half	2½
Seafood, raw to done	2
Vegetables, canned	
Corn, green beans, peas	½
Baked beans	¾
Potatoes	1¼
Vegetables, fresh	
Corn on the cob	2
Broccoli	8
Spinach	3
Asparagus	9
Potatoes	5
Vegetables, frozen	
Corn	5
Asparagus	7
Cauliflower	12
Casseroles, precooked and cooled	
Chicken a la king	1½
Stuffed cabbage	2
Macaroni and cheese	1¾
Spanish rice	1½
Spaghetti	1½
Beef Stew	2
Ravioli	2
Chili con carne	1¾
Meat pie	1¾
Chop suey	2

Source: Kazarian, E. A. (editor) (1975). Equipment requirements. In *Food Service Facilities Planning.* AVI Publishing Co., Westport, Connecticut.

Milk, Amino Acids

TABLE 2.M.30
Amino acids essential to man in cow's milk products (gr per 100 gm)

	Casein	Lactalbumin	Dried Nonfat Milk	Dried Whey
Tryptophan	1.3	2.2	0.50	0.15
Threonine	4.3	5.2	1.6	0.68
Isoleucine	6.6	6.2	2.3	0.73
Leucine	10.0	12.3	3.5	1.04
Lysine	8.0	9.1	2.8	0.77
Methionine	3.1	2.3	0.87	0.19
Cystine	0.38	3.4	0.32	0.25
Phenylalanine	5.4	4.4	1.7	0.32
Tyrosine	5.8	3.8	1.8	0.13
Valine	7.4	5.7	2.4	0.64

Source: Gordon, W. G., and Kalan, E. B. (1974). Proteins of milk. In *Fundamentals of Dairy Chemistry*, 2nd Edition. B. H. Webb, A. H. Johnson, and J. A. Alford (editors). AVI Publishing Co., Westport, Connecticut.

Milk and Cheese Composition

TABLE 2.M.31
Composition of the edible portion (EP) and refuse in the material as purchased (AP)

(Percent of Edible Portion)

Item No.	Commodity and Description	Water	Protein	Fat	Carbohydrate Total (by dif)	Fiber	Ash	Calories (No./100 g)	Notes	Refuse in AP (%)
	Milk and Cheese									
	Milk (cow's)									
250	Whole, fluid—3.5% fat	87.3	3.5	3.5	5.0	0	0.7	65		0
251	3.0% fat	88.0	3.3	3.0	5.0	0	0.7	60		0
252	3.2% fat	87.7	3.4	3.2	5.0	0	0.7	62		0
253	3.9% fat	87.0	3.5	3.9	4.9	0	0.7	68		0
254	Skim, fluid, or buttermilk	90.2	3.6	0.4	5.1	0	0.7	39		0
255	Cream (20% butterfat)	72.4	2.9	20	4.1	0	0.6	204		0
	Other milk									
256	Goat's, whole, fluid	86.4	3.8	4.5	4.5	0	0.8	73		0
257	Sheep's, whole, fluid	82.3	5.8	6.5	4.5	0	0.9	99		0
258	Buffalo's, whole, fluid	83	4	7.5	4.7	0	0.8	101		0
259	Carabao's, whole, fluid	80	5.8	9	4.4	0	0.8	121		0
	Camel's—Use No. 256									
	Processed milk (cow's)									
260	Whole, evaporated, unsweetened	73.7	7	7.9	9.9	0	1.5	138	Use for U.S.A., Canada	0
261	Whole, evaporated, unsweetened	69	8.3	9.0	12.0	0	1.7	161	Use for U.K., prewar (Currently composition is similar to No. 260)	0
262	Whole, condensed, sweetened	27	8.1	8.4	54.8	0	1.7	320	Use for U.S.A. Canada	0
263	Whole, condensed, sweetened	25	8.2	10	55	0	1.8	336	Use for U.K.	0
264	Skim, condensed, sweetened	28	9.6	0.4	59.9	0	2.1	276		0

(Continued)

Milk and Cheese Composition (Continued)

TABLE 2.M.31 (Continued)

Item No.	Commodity and Description	Water	Protein	Fat	Carbohydrate Total (by dif)	Fiber	Ash	Calories (No./100 g)	Notes	Refuse in AP (%)
					(Percent of Edible Portion)					
265	Whole, dried	4	26	27	37	0	6	492	Use for U.S.A., Canada	0
266	Whole, dried	4	26	30	34	0	6	506	Use for Australia	0
267	Skim, dried	4	36	1	51	0	8	360		
	Cheese									
268[1]	Hard, whole milk[1]	37	25	31	2	0	5	387	Cheddar, Gruyere, Roquefort, Gorgonzola, Caciocavallo	0
269[1]	Hard, "3/4 fat"[1]	36	34	21	3	0	6	341	Edam, Parmesan	0
270[1]	Hard, skim milk[1]	40	46	4	4	0	6	247		0
271[1]	Semi-soft, whole milk[1]	51	18	24	3	0	4	299	Camembert, Limburger, Feta, and cheeses from buffalo or carabao milk	0
272[1]	Semi-soft, skim milk[1]	55	35	3	3	0	4	187	Topfen, Petit Suisse, fromage à la pie	0
273[1]	Soft, fresh, partly whole milk[1]	70	15	7	5	0	3	145		0
274[1]	Soft, fresh, skim milk[1]	74	19	1	4	0	2	105	Quark, cottage cheese, fromage blanc	0
	Whey cheeses									
275[1]	Hard, low fat type[1]	30	9	3	52	0	6	266	Mysost	0
276[1]	Soft[1]	75	14	3	5	0	3	106	Ziger, Mizithra	0

[1] More information required.

Source: Chatfield, C. *Food Composition Tables for International Use.* Food and Agriculture Organization, United Nations, Rome.

Milk and Milk Products, Vitamin Content

TABLE 2.M.32
Vitamin content of milk and milk products (content of thiamin, riboflavin, nicotinic acid, and pantothenic acid in milk and milk products[a])

Milk or milk product	Thiamin Avg	Thiamin Range	Riboflavin Avg	Riboflavin Range	Nicotinic Acid Avg	Nicotinic Acid Range	Pantothenic Acid Avg	Pantothenic Acid Range
				(mg/kg)[b]				
Whole milk:								
Fluid	0.44	0.20–0.80 (48)[c]	1.75	0.81–2.58 (73)	0.94[d]	0.30–2.00 (34)	3.46	2.60–4.90 (23)
Condensed	1.1	0.8–1.5 (5)	3.6	2.6–4.0 (4)	2.1	1.6–2.4 (3)	8.7	7.5–10.4 (3)
Evaporated	0.56	0.40–0.82 (6)	3.8	2.8–4.8 (6)	2.0	1.8–2.3 (5)	7.0	5.8–8.0 (4)
Dried	3.4	2.5–5.1 (9)	15.5	9.8–25.6 (9)	7.3	6.1–9.0 (7)	27.3	22.7–39.0 (7)
Skimmilk:								
Fluid	0.40	0.20–0.53 (6)	1.7	1.5–1.8 (4)	0.86	0.74–1.1 (4)	3.6	2.8–4.0 (6)
Dried	3.6	2.2–4.6 (14)	18.9	13.0–25.4 (25)	10.6	8.2–18.3 (8)	38.8	22.9–77.0 (12)
Chocolate milk:								
Fluid	0.30	0.28–0.31 (2)	1.7	1.5–1.8 (4)				
Malted milk:								
Dried	3.3	(1)	5.4	(1)				
Buttermilk:								
Fluid	0.42	(1)	1.7	1.6–1.8 (2)	0.55	0.27–0.82 (2)	3.8	2.9–4.7 (2)
Condensed			14.3					
Dried	3.5	(1)	32.0	29–35 (10)	8.6	(1)	28.0	27.0–30.1 (3)
Kefir			0.7	(1)	1.3	0.8–1.9 (2)		
Yoghurt	0.37		1.4	0.8–1.8 (3)				
Cream:								
Half and half	0.3	(1)	1.5	(1)	0.4	(1)		
Light table	0.3	(1)	1.4	1.4–1.5 (2)	0.4	(1)		
Medium whipping	0.25	(1)	1.3	(1)	0.4	(1)		
Heavy whipping	0.2	(1)	1.2	(1)	0.4	(1)		
Butter	0.03		0.16	0.08–0.37 (4)	0.5	0–1.0 (2)	2.6	(1)
Ice cream	0.48	0.38–0.65 (3)	2.3	2.0–2.6 (6)	1.1	1.0–1.2 (2)	2.3	0–4.6 (2)
Whey:								
Fluid	0.4		1.2	0.5–1.6 (3)	0.85	0.72–1.03 (3)	3.4	2.1–4.1 (5)
Condensed	3.3	(1)	16.3	(1)	3.5	(1)	15.1	(1)
Dried	3.7	1.7–4.9 (5)	23.4	20.0–29.7 (8)	9.6	8.0–11.2 (2)	47.3	42.4–56.0 (4)
Casein, crude	0.82	0.44–1.2 (2)	2.6	1.5–3.6 (2)	2.4	1.3–3.4 (2)	3.6	2.6–4.5 (2)
Milk albumin:								
Dried	0.7	(1)	8.8	(1)	2.0	(1)	7.3	(1)

(Continued)

Milk and Milk Products, Vitamin Content (Continued)

TABLE 2.M.32 (Continued)

Content of vitamin B-6, biotin, folic acid, and vitamin B-12 in milk and milk products[a]

Units: (mg/kg)[b]

Milk or milk product	Vitamin B6		Biotin		Folic Acid		Vitamin B12	
	Avg	Range	Avg	Range	Avg	Range	Avg	Range
Whole milk								
Fluid	0.64	0.22-1.90[e] (42)[c]	0.031	0.012-0.060 (21)	0.0028	0.0004-0.0062 (12)[f]	0.0043	0.0024-0.0074 (44)
Condensed	0.56	0.52-0.59 (2)	0.040	0.032-0.047 (2)			0.0039	0.0031-0.0054 (3)
Evaporated	0.74	0.55-1.37 (5)	0.056	0.031-0.090 (3)	0.014	(1)[g]	0.0014	0.0010-0.0019 (3)
Dried	3.9	1.7-7.0 (7)	0.30	0.10-0.47 (5)	0.018	0.014-0.022 (2)[g]	0.026	0.018-0.038 (6)
Skimmilk:								
Fluid	0.45	0.26-0.56 (3)	0.016	0.015-0.016 (2)	0.012	0.008-0.016 (2)[h]	0.0038	0.0031-0.0047 (4)
Dried	4.5	2.8-6.8 (6)	0.27	0.14-0.35 (3)	0.044	0.029-0.059 (2)[h]	0.034	0.022-0.045 (9)
Malted milk:								
Dried							0.022	(1)
Buttermilk:								
Fluid	0.39	0.38-0.40 (2)	0.011	(1)	0.11	(1)[i]	0.0023	
Dried	2.4	(1)	0.29	(1)	0.40	(1)[i]	0.019	0.018-0.02 (1)
Kefir							0.0021	0.0017-0.0024 (2)
Yoghurt			0.012	(1)			0.0012	0.0007-0.0018 (5)
Cream:								
Half and half	0.38	(1)						
Light table	0.40	(1)						
Medium whipping	0.35	(1)						
Butter	0.04	(1)						
Whey:								
Fluid	0.42	0.21-0.77 (3)	0.014	0.013-0.015 (2)			0.0020	0.0015-0.0024 (4)
Condensed	1.8	(1)	0.29	(1)	0.89	0.88-0.90 (2)[j]		
Dried	4.0	(1)	0.37		0.34	0.16-0.51 (2)		
Casein, crude	2.7	0.4-7.0 (3)	0.052	0.044-0.060 (2)			0.021	0.017-0.025 (3)
Milk albumin:								
Dried	1.2	(1)					0.071	0.043-0.104 (4)

(Continued)

Milk and Milk Products, Vitamin Content (Continued)

TABLE 2.M.32 *(Continued)*

Content of choline, vitamin C, and vitamin E in milk and milk products[a]

Milk or milk product	Choline Avg	Choline Range	Vitamin C Avg	Vitamin C Range	Vitamin E Avg	Vitamin E Range
			(mg/kg)[b]			
Whole milk:						
Fluid	121	43–218 (9)[c]	21.1[k]	16.5–27.5 (46)	0.98	0.20–1.84 (14)
Condensed	344	(1)	26	4–58 (7)		
Evaporated	246		11	4–18 (6)	2.6	2.2–3 (2)
Dried	862	394–1,070 (4)	81	26–120 (7)	7.5	5–10 (2)
Skimmilk:						
Fluid	48	(1)	19	9–25 (4)		
Dried	1,182	410–1,700 (6)	98	53–170 (3)	4.8	0.5–9.1 (2)
Chocolate milk:						
Fluid	13			(1)		
Buttermilk:						
Fluid			12	9–14 (2)		
Dried	2,059	1,808–2,310 (2)	0	(1)		
Kefir			8	(1)		
Yoghurt	6	(1)	6.2	0–10.9 (5)		
Cream:						
Half and half			9	(1)		
Butter	183	20–400 (3)	0	0–0 (4)	24	17–31 (10)
Ice Cream	24	(1)	3	0–11 (4)	3	(1)
Whey:						
Fluid			13	11–15 (2)		
Dried	1,356	700–2,011 (2)				
Casein, crude	210	209–210 (2)				
Cheese:[l]						
Very hard:						
Parmesan	220	(1)				
Hard:						
Cantal			0	0–0 (1)	10	(1)
Cheddar	335	190–480 (2)	0	(3)		
Cheshire			0	(1)		
Edam			0	(1)	3.1	(1)
Gruyère			0	(1)	3.0	(1)
Swiss			0			

(Continued)

Milk and Milk Products, Vitamin Content (Continued)

TABLE 2.M.32 (Continued)

Milk or milk product	Choline Avg	Choline Range	Vitamin C Avg (mg/kg)[b]	Vitamin C Range	Vitamin E Avg	Vitamin E Range
Semisoft:						
Blue[m]			0			
Münster			8.5	(1)		
Roquefort[n]			0	(1)		
Stilton			0	(1)	6.5	(1)
Soft:						
Ripened:						
Bel Paese			0	(1)		
Brie			4.0	(1)		
Camembert			4.0	(1)		
Reblochon			8.8	(1)		
Unripened:						
Cottage			0	(1)		
Cream			0	(1)		
Processed:						
Cheddar			0	(1)		
Gruyère	470	(1)				

[a] Mean and range of average values obtained from publications of various groups of workers.
[b] Milligram per liter for products designated fluid.
[c] Figures in parentheses indicate number of references consulted.
[d] This average is based on determinations made by both microbiological and chemical assays, but some of the early values obtained by chemical means were extremely high (3.0, 4.5, and 8.2 mg per liter) and have been omitted.
[e] Three figures outside this range, one much higher (6.5) and two much lower (each 0.06) have been omitted.
[f] One high value of 0.024 mg per liter has been excluded.
[g] Obtained by microbiological assay; rat assay gave 0.500 (1).
[h] Obtained by microbiological assay; chick assay gave 0.585 (0.570–0.600) (2); other assays of unstated type gave 0.616 (1).
[i] Type of assay not stated.
[j] One value obtained by chick assay; the other, by assay of unstated type.
[k] Fresh milk; average for market milk (18 references); 10.5 (2.4–20.5) mg per liter.
[l] Classified primarily according to Sanders.
[m] May be made from milk of species other than the cow.
[n] Made from ewe's milk.

Source: Hartman, A. M., and Dryden, L. P. Vitamins in milk and milk products. J. Dairy Sci.

Milk Breeds, Composition

TABLE 2.M.33
Typical composition (percent) of the milks of cows of six breeds

Breed	in Milk							in Total Solids				
	Water	Fat	Protein	Lactose	Ash	Nonfat Solids	Total Solids	Fat	Protein	Lactose	Ash	Nonfat Solids
Guernsey	85.35	5.05	3.90	4.96	0.74	9.60	14.65	34.47	26.62	33.86	5.05	65.53
Jersey	85.47	5.05	3.78	5.00	0.70	9.48	14.53	34.75	26.02	34.41	4.82	65.25
Ayrshire	86.97	4.03	3.51	4.81	0.68	9.00	13.03	30.93	26.94	36.91	5.22	69.07
Brown Swiss	86.87	3.85	3.48	5.08	0.72	9.28	13.13	29.32	26.50	38.69	5.48	70.68
Shorthorn	87.43	3.63	3.32	4.89	0.73	8.94	12.57	28.88	26.41	38.82	5.81	71.12
Holstein	87.72	3.41	3.32	4.87	0.68	8.87	12.28	27.77	27.03	39.66	5.54	72.23

Source: Webb, B. H., Johnson, A. H., and Alford, J. A. (1974). Fundamentals of Dairy Chemistry, 2nd Edition. AVI Publishing Co., Westport, Connecticut.

Milk Composition I

TABLE 2.M.34
Composition[1] of whole and skim cow's milk, in liquid, concentrated and dried forms, and losses in nutrients in treatment

	Water	Protein (N × 6.38)	Fat	Carbo-hydrate	Calcium	Vitamin A (retinol) activity		Vitamin D		Thiamine	
						Amount (μg/ 100 g)	Loss (%)	Amount (IU/ 100 g)	Loss (%)	Amount (μg/ 100 g)	Loss (%)
	. . . *Percent* . . .										
WHOLE											
Raw	87.6	3.3	3.6	4.7	0.12	50	—	2	—	45	—
HTST treated	87.6	3.3	3.6	4.7	0.12	50	None	2	None	42	<10
Sterilized (in-bottle process)	87.6	3.3	3.6	4.7	0.12	50	None	2	None	30	35
UHT treated	87.6	3.3	3.6	4.7	0.12	50	None	2	None	42	<10
Evaporated											
(1)	68.5	8.4	9.2	12.0	0.30	125	None	5	None	67	40
(2)	73.0	7.0	8.0	10.0	0.26	105	None	4	None	57	40
Sweetened condensed											
(1)	25.0	8.4	9.2	55.4	0.30	125	None	5	None	103	10
(2)	29.0	7.3	8.0	53.9	0.27	110	None	4	None	90	10
Dried											
Roller	3.0	25.0	27.5	37.5	0.91	383	None	15	None	290	15
Spray	3.0	25.0	27.5	37.5	0.91	383	None	15	None	310	10
SKIM											
Raw	90.8	3.4	0.1	4.9	0.12	1	—	0	—	47	—
Evaporated	80.0	7.4	0.2	10.7	0.26	3	None	0	—	61	40
Sweetened condensed	29.0	9.6	0.3	58.8	0.34	4	None	0	—	120	10
Dried	3.0	36.0	1.0	50.5	1.26	13	None	1	None	450	10

? indicates possible slight loss.   (*Continued*)

[1] For simplicity, rounded-off values have been taken for raw milk and all other forms are assumed to sweetened condensed whole milk to represent two different degrees of concentration current on the raw milk: 2 mg/100 g is for milk as it leaves the udder. — [3] Appreciable loss of biological availability.

Milk Composition I (Continued)

TABLE 2.M.34 (Continued)

Riboflavin		Pantothenic acid		Nicotinic acid		Vitamin B$_6$		Biotin		Vitamin B$_{12}$		Vitamin C [2]	
Amount (µg/100 g)	Loss (%)	Amount (µg/100 g)	Loss (%)	Amount (µg/100 g)	Loss (%)	Amount (µg/100 g)	Loss (%)	Amount (µg/100 g)	Loss (%)	Amount (µg/100 g)	Loss (%)	Amount (µg/100 g)	Loss (%)
150	—	350	—	100	—	25	—	1.5	—	0.30	—	2.0	—
150	None	350	?	100	None	25	None	1.5	None	0.30	<10	1.8	10
150	None	350	?	100	None	25	[3]	1.5	None	Trace	>90	1.0	50
150	None	350	?	100	None	25	None	1.5	None	0.24	20	1.8	10
375	None	875	?	250	?	63	[3]	3.4	10	<0.10	90	2.0	60
315	None	735	?	210	?	53	[3]	2.8	10	<0.10	90	1.7	60
375	None	875	?	250	None	63	None	3.4	10	0.53	30	4.3	15
330	None	775	?	220	None	55	None	3.0	10	0.47	30	3.8	15
1 150	None	2 700	?	760	?	190	None	10.0	10	1.60	30	11.0	30
1 150	None	2 700	?	760	?	190	None	10.0	10	1.60	30	13.0	20
145	[4]—	360	—	103	—	26	—	1.5	—	0.30	—	2.0	—
315	None	780	?	225	?	57	[3]	2.9	10	<0.10	90	1.7	60
410	None	1 000	?	290	None	73	None	3.8	10	0.60	30	4.8	15
1 530	None	3 800	?	1 100	?	275	None	14.0	10	2.20	30	17.0	20

have been derived from that particular milk. Two separate values are given for evaporated and for international market. — [2] Survival of vitamin C would depend on the amount originally present in the — [4] Loss of riboflavin in the fat-globule membrane.

Source: Kon, S. K. (1972). *Milk and Milk Products in Human Nutrition.* Food and Agriculture Organization, United Nations, Rome.

Milk Composition II

TABLE 2.M.35
Composition of cow's milk

Composition	Mean	Normal Variations	Breed Means					Minimum Requirements	
			Holstein	Jersey	Guernsey	Ayrshire	Brown Swiss	States	USPH
Fat	4.00	2.60–8.37	3.40	5.37	4.95	4.00	4.01	3.25	3.25
Protein	3.50	2.44–6.48	3.32	3.92	3.91	3.58	3.61	—	—
Casein	2.90	1.60–4.50	2.30	3.00	2.90	2.50	2.60	—	—
Lactose	4.90	2.41–6.11	4.87	4.93	4.93	4.67	5.04	—	—
Ash	0.70	0.56–0.936	0.68	0.71	0.74	0.73	0.68	—	—
Milk-solids-not-fat (msnf)	9.10	7.20–11.90	8.86	9.54	9.66	8.90	9.40	8.50	8.00
Total solids	13.10	10.56–17.90	12.26	14.93	14.61	12.90	13.41	11.75	11.25

Source: Arbuckle, W. S. (1973). Dairy products. In *Quality Control For The Food Industry*, Vol. 2, 3rd Edition. A. Kramer, and B. A. Twigg (editors). AVI Publishing Co., Westport, Connecticut.

Milk, Concentrated Products

TABLE 2.M.36
Approximate composition of concentrated milk products

Product	Water (%)	Fat (%)	Protein (%)	Lactose (%)	Sucrose (%)	Ash (%)
Evaporated milk	73.00	8.30	7.50	9.70	—	1.40
Plain condensed milk	70.00	8.50	7.80	11.90	—	1.80
Condensed skim milk	71.50	0.50	8.80	12.70	—	2.00
Sweetened condensed whole	27.47	9.28	7.42	13.35	40.60	1.88
Sweetened condensed skim	29.00	0.06	10.32	15.60	42.27	2.25
Condensed buttermilk	72.00	1.95	10.61	13.01	—	3.33
Condensed whey	70.00	0.30	3.60	21.60	—	3.33

Source: Arbuckle, W. S. (1973). Dairy products. In *Quality Control For The Food Industry*, Vol. 2, 3rd Edition. A. Kramer, and B. A. Twigg (editors). AVI Publishing Co., Westport, Connecticut.

Milk, Dry Products

TABLE 2.M.37
Approximate composition of dry milk products

Product	Water (%)	Fat (%)	Protein (%)	Lactose (%)	Ash (%)	Lactic Acid (%)
Dried whole milk	2.00	27.00	26.50	38.00	6.05	—
Nonfat dry milk	3.23	0.88	36.89	50.52	8.15	1.40
Dry buttermilk	3.90	4.68	35.88	47.84	7.80	1.55
Dried whey	6.10	0.90	12.50	72.25	8.90	7.00
Dried malted milk	3.29	7.55	13.19	72.40[1]	3.66	—
Dry cream	0.66	65.15	13.42	17.86	2.91	—

[1] Lactose, maltose, and dextrin.

Source: Arbuckle, W. S. (1973). Dairy products. In *Quality Control For The Food Industry*, Vol. 2, 3rd Edition. A. Kramer, and B. A. Twigg (editors). AVI Publishing Co., Westport, Connecticut.

Milk, Fatty Acids, Seasonal

TABLE 2.M.38
Seasonal variation (weight percent) of component acids of milkfat

Acid	Stall-Fed Winter	Silage-Fed Winter	June Pasture	August Pasture
Butyric	3.0	3.6	3.7	3.5
Caproic	1.4	2.0	1.7	1.9
Caprylic	1.5	0.5	1.0	0.7
Capric	2.7	2.3	1.9	2.1
Lauric	3.7	2.5	2.8	1.9
Myristic	12.1	11.1	8.1	7.9
Palmitic	25.3	29.0	25.9	25.8
Stearic	9.2	9.2	11.2	12.7
As Arachidic	1.3	2.4	1.2	1.5
9-Decenoic	0.3	0.1	0.1	0.1
9-Dodecenoic	0.4	0.1	0.2	0.2
9-Tetradecenoic	1.6	0.9	0.6	0.6
9-Hexadecenoic	4.0	4.6	3.4	2.4
Oleic	29.6	26.7	32.8	34.0
As Octadecadienoic	3.6	3.6	3.7	3.7
As C_{20-22} unsaturated	0.3	1.4	1.7	1.0

Source: Kurtz, F. E. (1974). The lipids of milk: composition and properties. In *Fundamentals of Dairy Chemistry*, 2nd Edition. B. H. Webb, A. H. Johnson, and J. A. Alford (editors). AVI Publishing Co., Westport, Connecticut.

Milk, Mammals, Composition

TABLE 2.M.39
Average composition (percent) of milks of various mammals[1]

Species	in Milk							in Total Solids				
	Water	Fat	Protein	Lactose	Ash	Nonfat Solids	Total Solids	Fat	Protein	Lactose	Ash	Nonfat Solids
Woman	87.43	3.75	1.63	6.98	0.21	8.82	12.57	29.83	12.97	55.53	1.67	70.17
Cow	87.2	3.7	3.5	4.9	0.7	9.1	12.8	28.9	27.34	38.28	5.47	71.1
Cow	86.61	4.14	3.58	4.96	0.71	9.25	13.39	30.91	26.76	37.04	5.30	69.09
Goat	87.00	4.25	3.52	4.27	0.86	8.75	13.00	32.69	27.08	32.85	6.62	67.31
Ewe	80.71	7.90	5.23	4.81	0.90	11.39	19.29	40.96	27.11	24.94	4.67	59.05
Egyptian buffalo	82.09	7.96	4.16	4.86	0.78	9.95	17.91	44.44	23.23	27.14	4.36	55.56
Chinese buffalo	76.80	12.60	6.04	3.70	0.86	10.60	23.20	54.31	26.03	15.94	3.71	45.69
Philippine cara-bao	78.46	10.35	5.88	4.32	0.84	11.19	21.54	48.05	27.30	20.06	3.90	51.95
Indian buffalo	82.76	7.38	3.60	5.48	0.78	9.86	17.24	42.81	20.88	31.78	4.52	57.19
Camel	87.61	5.38	2.98	3.26	0.70	7.01	12.39	43.42	24.05	26.31	5.65	56.58
Mare	89.04	1.59	2.69	6.14	0.51	9.37	10.96	14.51	24.54	56.02	4.65	85.49
Ass	89.03	2.53	2.01	6.07	0.41	8.44	10.97	23.06	18.32	55.33	3.74	76.94
Reindeer	63.30	22.46	10.30	2.50	1.44	14.24	36.70	61.20	28.06	6.81	3.92	38.80
Llama	86.55	3.15	3.90	5.60	0.80	10.30	13.45	23.42	29.00	41.63	5.95	76.58

[1] Ed. note. An unpublished survey (1973) of over one million commercial cow milk samples indicates an average composition of: fat 3.68%, protein 3.14%, nonfat solids 8.48%, lactose 4.64%, ash .7%.

Source: Johnson, A. H. (1974). The composition of milk. In Fundamentals of Dairy Chemistry, 2nd Edition. B. H. Webb, A. H. Johnson, and J. A. Alford (editors). AVI Publishing Co, Westport, Connecticut.

Milk, Physical Properties

TABLE 2.M.40
Physical properties of milk

Acidity (%)	0.16±0.02
pH	6.6±0.2
Surface tension (dynes)	55.3
Specific gravity	1.032±0.004
Freezing point (°C)	−0.55
Boiling point (°C)	100.17
Specific heat at	
0°C	0.920
15°C	0.938
40°C	0.930
Coefficient of expansion at	
10°C	0.9975
15.6°C	0.9985
21.1°C	1.0000
Viscosity (centipoise)	1.6314
Electrical conductivity (mho)	45–48 × 10^{-4}

Source: Arbuckle, W. S. (1973). Dairy products. In
Quality Control For The Food Industry, Vol. 2, 3rd
Edition. A. Kramer, and B. A. Twigg (editors). AVI
Publishing Co., Westport, Connecticut.

Milk, Species

TABLE 2.M.41
Composition of milk of different species

Component	Cow	Human	Goat	Sheep
Fat (%)	4.0	3.7	4.25	7.92
Protein (total %)	3.5	1.6	3.52	5.2
Casein (%)	2.9	0.9	2.8	3.6
Albumin (%)	0.5	0.7	0.7	1.3
Lactose (%)	4.9	7.0	4.2	4.8
Ash (%)	0.7	0.21	0.73	0.93
Specific gravity	1.032	1.029	1.035	1.034
Total solids (%)	13.1	12.5	13.0	19.29

Source: Arbuckle, W. S. (1973). Dairy products. In Quality Control For The Food
Industry, Vol. 2, 3rd Edition. A. Kramer, and B. A. Twigg (editors). AVI Publishing Co.,
Westport, Connecticut.

Milk, Total Solids

TABLE 2.M.42

The following data show the percentages of total solids in milk corresponding to the percentage of fat and Quevenne lactometer reading.[1] To use the data, first find in the column at the extreme left the number corresponding to the percentage of butterfat, then in the same line with this and in the same column as the observed lactometer reading as given across the top will be found the percentage of total solids.

Per Cent Fat	Quevenne Lactometer Reading at 15.56°C (60°F)																						
	25.0	25.5	26.0	26.5	27.0	27.5	28.0	28.5	29.0	29.5	30.0	30.5	31.0	31.5	32.0	32.5	33.0	33.5	34.0	34.5	35.0	35.5	36.0
2.6	9.5	9.6	9.8	9.9	10.0	10.1	10.3	10.4	10.5	10.6	10.8	10.9	11.0	11.1	11.3	11.4	11.5	11.6	11.8	11.9	12.0	12.1	12.3
2.7	9.6	9.8	9.9	10.0	10.1	10.3	10.4	10.5	10.6	10.8	10.9	11.0	11.1	11.3	11.4	11.5	11.6	11.8	11.9	12.0	12.1	12.3	12.4
2.8	9.8	9.9	10.0	10.1	10.3	10.4	10.5	10.6	10.8	10.9	11.0	11.1	11.3	11.4	11.5	11.6	11.8	11.9	12.0	12.1	12.3	12.4	12.5
2.9	9.9	10.0	10.1	10.2	10.4	10.5	10.6	10.7	10.9	11.0	11.1	11.2	11.4	11.5	11.6	11.7	11.9	12.0	12.1	12.2	12.4	12.5	12.6
3.0	10.0	10.1	10.2	10.4	10.5	10.6	10.7	10.9	11.0	11.1	11.2	11.4	11.5	11.6	11.7	11.9	12.0	12.1	12.2	12.4	12.5	12.6	12.7
3.1	10.1	10.2	10.4	10.5	10.6	10.7	10.9	11.0	11.1	11.2	11.4	11.5	11.6	11.7	11.9	12.0	12.1	12.2	12.4	12.5	12.6	12.7	12.9
3.2	10.2	10.4	10.5	10.6	10.7	10.9	11.0	11.1	11.2	11.4	11.5	11.6	11.7	11.9	12.0	12.1	12.2	12.4	12.5	12.6	12.7	12.9	13.0
3.3	10.4	10.5	10.6	10.7	10.9	11.0	11.1	11.2	11.4	11.5	11.6	11.7	11.9	12.0	12.1	12.2	12.4	12.5	12.6	12.7	12.9	13.0	13.1
3.4	10.5	10.6	10.7	10.8	11.0	11.1	11.3	11.4	11.5	11.6	11.8	11.9	12.0	12.1	12.2	12.3	12.5	12.6	12.7	12.8	13.0	13.1	13.2
3.5	10.6	10.7	10.8	11.0	11.1	11.2	11.3	11.5	11.6	11.7	11.8	12.0	12.1	12.2	12.3	12.5	12.6	12.7	12.8	13.0	13.1	13.2	13.3
3.6	10.7	10.8	11.0	11.1	11.2	11.3	11.5	11.6	11.7	11.8	12.0	12.1	12.2	12.3	12.5	12.6	12.7	12.8	13.0	13.1	13.2	13.3	13.5
3.7	10.8	11.0	11.1	11.2	11.3	11.5	11.6	11.7	11.8	12.0	12.1	12.2	12.3	12.5	12.6	12.7	12.8	13.0	13.1	13.2	13.3	13.5	13.6
3.8	11.0	11.1	11.2	11.3	11.5	11.6	11.7	11.8	12.0	12.1	12.2	12.3	12.5	12.6	12.7	12.8	13.0	13.1	13.2	13.3	13.5	13.6	13.7
3.9	11.1	11.2	11.3	11.4	11.6	11.7	11.8	11.9	12.1	12.2	12.3	12.4	12.6	12.7	12.8	12.9	13.1	13.2	13.3	13.4	13.6	13.7	13.8
4.0	11.2	11.3	11.4	11.6	11.7	11.8	11.9	12.1	12.2	12.3	12.4	12.6	12.7	12.8	12.9	13.1	13.2	13.3	13.4	13.6	13.7	13.8	13.9
4.1	11.3	11.4	11.6	11.7	11.8	11.9	12.1	12.2	12.3	12.4	12.6	12.7	12.8	12.9	13.1	13.2	13.3	13.4	13.6	13.7	13.8	13.9	14.1
4.2	11.4	11.6	11.7	11.8	11.9	12.1	12.2	12.3	12.4	12.6	12.7	12.8	12.9	13.1	13.2	13.3	13.4	13.6	13.7	13.8	13.9	14.1	14.2
4.3	11.6	11.7	11.8	11.9	12.1	12.2	12.3	12.4	12.6	12.7	12.8	12.9	13.1	13.2	13.3	13.4	13.6	13.7	13.8	13.9	14.1	14.2	14.3
4.4	11.7	11.8	11.9	12.0	12.2	12.3	12.4	12.5	12.7	12.8	12.9	13.0	13.2	13.3	13.4	13.5	13.7	13.8	13.9	14.0	14.2	14.3	14.4
4.5	11.8	11.9	12.0	12.2	12.3	12.4	12.5	12.7	12.8	12.9	13.0	13.2	13.3	13.4	13.5	13.7	13.8	13.9	14.0	14.2	14.3	14.4	14.5
4.6	11.9	12.0	12.2	12.3	12.4	12.5	12.7	12.8	12.9	13.0	13.2	13.3	13.4	13.5	13.7	13.8	13.9	14.0	14.2	14.3	14.4	14.5	14.7
4.7	12.0	12.2	12.3	12.4	12.5	12.7	12.8	12.9	13.0	13.2	13.3	13.4	13.5	13.7	13.8	13.9	14.0	14.2	14.3	14.4	14.5	14.7	14.8
4.8	12.2	12.3	12.4	12.5	12.7	12.8	12.9	13.0	13.2	13.3	13.4	13.5	13.7	13.8	13.9	14.0	14.2	14.3	14.4	14.5	14.7	14.8	14.9
4.9	12.3	12.4	12.5	12.6	12.8	12.9	13.0	13.1	13.3	13.4	13.5	13.6	13.8	13.9	14.0	14.1	14.3	14.4	14.5	14.6	14.8	14.9	15.0
5.0	12.4	12.5	12.6	12.8	12.9	13.0	13.1	13.3	13.4	13.5	13.6	13.8	13.9	14.0	14.1	14.3	14.4	14.5	14.6	14.8	14.9	15.0	15.1
5.1	12.5	12.6	12.8	12.9	13.0	13.1	13.3	13.4	13.5	13.6	13.8	13.9	14.0	14.1	14.3	14.4	14.5	14.6	14.8	14.9	15.0	15.1	15.3
5.2	12.6	12.8	12.9	13.0	13.1	13.3	13.4	13.5	13.6	13.8	13.9	14.0	14.1	14.3	14.4	14.5	14.6	14.8	14.9	15.0	15.1	15.3	15.4
5.3	12.8	12.9	13.0	13.1	13.3	13.4	13.5	13.6	13.8	13.9	14.0	14.1	14.3	14.4	14.5	14.6	14.8	14.9	15.0	15.1	15.3	15.4	15.5
5.4	12.9	13.0	13.1	13.2	13.4	13.5	13.6	13.7	13.9	14.0	14.1	14.2	14.4	14.5	14.6	14.7	14.9	15.0	15.1	15.2	15.4	15.5	15.6
5.5	13.0	13.1	13.2	13.4	13.5	13.6	13.7	13.9	14.0	14.1	14.2	14.4	14.5	14.6	14.7	14.9	15.0	15.1	15.2	15.4	15.5	15.6	15.7
5.6	13.1	13.2	13.4	13.5	13.6	13.7	13.9	14.0	14.1	14.2	14.4	14.5	14.6	14.7	14.9	15.0	15.1	15.2	15.4	15.5	15.6	15.7	15.9
5.7	13.2	13.4	13.5	13.6	13.7	13.9	14.0	14.1	14.2	14.4	14.5	14.6	14.7	14.9	15.0	15.1	15.2	15.4	15.5	15.6	15.7	15.9	16.0
5.8	13.4	13.5	13.6	13.7	13.9	14.0	14.1	14.2	14.4	14.5	14.6	14.7	14.9	15.0	15.1	15.2	15.4	15.5	15.6	15.7	15.9	16.0	16.1
5.9	13.5	13.6	13.7	13.8	14.0	14.1	14.2	14.3	14.5	14.6	14.7	14.8	15.0	15.1	15.2	15.3	15.5	15.6	15.7	15.8	16.0	16.1	16.2
6.0	13.6	13.7	13.8	14.0	14.1	14.2	14.3	14.5	14.6	14.7	14.8	15.0	15.1	15.2	15.3	15.5	15.6	15.7	15.8	16.0	16.1	16.2	16.3

[1]The percentage of total milk solids may be calculated from the following expression: $(A + B + 0.14) = \%$ total solids; where A = % butter fat × 1.2; and B = Quevenne lactometer reading × 0.25.

Source: Lange, N. A. (editor) (1967). *Lange's Handbook of Chemistry*, 10th Edition. McGraw-Hill Book Co., New York.

Minerals (Major), Food

TABLE 2.M.43
Percentages of major mineral elements in the edible portion of foods
(fresh basis)

Food	Cal-cium	Mag-nesium	Potas-sium	Sodium	Phos-phorus	Chlorine	Sul-fur
Almonds	.228	.275	.756	.024	.465	.037	.164
Apples, fresh	.011	.006	.116	.015	.011	.004	.004
dried	.053	.029	.557	.072	.053	.019	.019
Apricots, fresh	.028	.012	.370	.021	.038	.004	.006
dried	.146	.062	1.924	.109	.198	.021	.031
Asparagus	.020	.015	.200	.008	.055	.047	.051
Bananas	.008	.024	.412	.023	.029	.163	.013
Barley, entire	.058	.126	.495	.070	.343	.139	.152
Beans, dried	.164	.165	1.284	.189	.495	.007	.224
Lima, fresh	.030	.067	.606	.089	.128	:009	.068
dried	.078	.181	1.899	.282	.367	.025	.156
string or green	.066	.032	.288	.012	.050	.045	.024
Beef	.014	.032	.382	.066	.198	.056	.221
Beets	.023	.027	.235	.053	.040	.040	.017
Beet greens	.158	.097	.390	*	.040	*	.035
Brains	.008	.016	.269	.160	.385	.155	.130
Bread, white	.036	.034	.110	.517	.080	.602	.083
Broccoli	.146	.024	.352	.030	.086	.076	.126
Brussels sprouts	.033	.015	.375	*	.051	*	.098
Butter	.022	.002	.019	(a)	.004	(a)	.009
Cabbage	.054	.016	.217	.038	.031	.034	.074
celery	.040	.011	.400	.028	.041	.023	.013
Cantaloupe	.019	.016	.243	.048	.016	.048	.016
Carrots	.044	.020	.219	.050	.037	.035	.019
Cauliflower	.036	.023	.292	.048	.068	.038	.074
Celery	.098	.025	.320	.101	.041	.225	.021
Cheese, hard	.703	.031	.116	.900	.547	.972	.214
Cherries	.016	.012	.125	.015	.031	.004	.018
Chestnuts	.029	.048	.415	.037	.081	.010	.049
Chicken	.015	.047	.402	.054	.218	.034	.303
Chocolate	.067	.082	.400	.019	.285	.009	.114
Cocoa	.065	.192	.534	.060	.476	.050	.197
Coconut, fresh	.020	.040	.360	.040	.118	.120	.044
Collards	.205	.017	*	*	.078	*	*
Corn, field, mature	.013	.142	.300	.110	.341	.041	.124
sweet, fresh	.008	.047	.278	*	.117	*	.037
mature	.021	.121	.415	.148	.349	.050	.146
Cowpeas, dried	.060	.265	1.305	.036	.390	.019	.250
Crabs	.126	.117	.271	.366	.261	.570	.255
Cranberries	.013	.005	.056	.002	.008	.004	.008

(Continued)

Minerals (Major), Food (Continued)

TABLE 2.M.43 (Continued)

Food	Calcium	Magnesium	Potassium	Sodium	Phosphorus	Chlorine	Sulfur
Cream...............	.073	.006	.112	.031	.048	.067	.033
Cucumbers........	.027	.020	.170	.026	.037	.028	.011
Currants, fresh.....	.036	.031	.208	.015	.044	.010	.021
dried............	.180	.155	1.040	.075	.220	.050	.105
Dates.............	.065	.065	.580	.040	.059	.253	.048
Eel..............	.039	.018	.241	.032	.177	.035	.133
Eggplant...........	.018	.015	.260	.026	.037	.063	.020
Eggs.............	.059	.009	.149	.111	.166	.100	.233
Egg white.........	.012	.011	.149	.175	.014	.131	.211
yolk...........	.146	.013	.110	.078	.577	.067	.214
Figs, fresh........	.060	.020	.205	.043	.021	.037	.017
dried............	.207	.068	.709	.151	.074	.126	.060
Fish (all kinds).....	.031	.024	.375	.064	.221	.137	.199
Flour, wheat, white.	.021	.021	.137	.053	.096	.079	.155
Frog..............	.016	.024	.308	.055	.196	.040	.163
Garlic.............	.006	.008	.130	.009	.090	.004	.318
Goose.............	.012	.031	.406	*	.197	*	.326
Gooseberries.......	.020	.009	.150	.010	.036	.009	.015
Grapefruit.........	.019	.007	.164	.006	.035	.007	.005
Grapes............	.040	.004	.267	.011	.018	.002	.009
Haddock...........	.022	.017	.334	.099	.137	.241	.225
Heart............	.025	.035	.329	.102	.313	.204	.151
Honey.............	.004	.004	.051	.006	.015	.015	.003
Horseradish........	.160	.028	.550	.094	.059	.013	.234
Kale.............	.340	.055	.486	.050	.089	.120	.160
Kidney............	.014	.019	.240	.238	.233	.376	.148
Kohlrabi...........	.059	.052	.370	.050	.060	.050	.039
Lamb—See mutton							
Leeks.............	.091	.037	.380	.036	.049	.110	.056
Lemons...........	.030	.006	.152	.009	.018	.006	.012
Lentils, dried.......	.064	.082	.662	.754	.392	.062	.123
Lettuce...........	.047	.015	.256	.028	.032	.085	.014
Liver............	.011	.021	.255	.021	.327	.091	.258
Lobster...........	.027	.022	.258	*	.395	*	*
Macaroni..........	.027	.038	.054	.010	.130	.077	.119
Milk, cow, fresh....	.123	.019	.129	.047	.088	.114	.031
evaporated.....	.260	.038	.258	.094	.176	.228	.067
powder........	.934	.118	.955	.348	.580	1.029	.229
goat...........	*	*	*	.026	.118	.163	*
human.........	.032	.005	.055	*	.017	.058	.142
Mushrooms........	.008	.012	.280	.013	.083	.026	.025
Mustard greens.....	.194	.016	.330	.020	.053	.090	.142
Mutton............	.020	.033	.260	.070	.212	.069	.187

(Continued)

Minerals (Major), Food   (Continued)

TABLE 2.M.43   (Continued)

Food	Calcium	Magnesium	Potassium	Sodium	Phosphorus	Chlorine	Sulfur
Oatmeal (rolled oats)	.098	.143	.365	.072	.351	.027	.207
Oats, entire	.094	.150	.450	.168	.318	.089	.187
Onions	.040	.016	.200	.020	.039	.053	.065
Oranges	.036	.011	.177	.014	.027	.006	.011
Orange juice	.017	.014	.200	.006	.017	.008	.005
Parsnips	.060	.038	.396	.010	.094	.038	.025
Peaches, fresh	.007	.015	.174	.012	.019	.006	.005
dried	.041	.087	1.009	.070	.110	.035	.029
Peanuts	.111	.169	.706	.052	.394	.040	.276
Pears	.005	.005	.110	.010	.008	.004	.010
Peas, green	.033	.035	.259	.024	.124	.049	.035
mature	.091	.121	.943	.072	.369	.034	.178
Peppers, green	.016	.025	.270	.015	.039	.031	.030
red	.035	.013	.120	.006	.042	.014	.030
Persimmons	.010	.005	.170	.013	.019	.009	.011
Pike	.040	.031	.416	.029	.213	.032	.218
Pineapple	.014	.014	.230	.008	.033	.038	.003
Plums	.007	.010	.212	.003	.022	.002	.004
Pork	.014	.027	.415	.081	.262	.040	.216
Potatoes	.012	.027	.498	.030	.053	.048	.033
Prunes, dried	.047	.032	.845	.101	.068	.004	.024
Pumpkins	.029	.021	.198	.011	.026	.025	.016
Rabbit	.018	.029	.415	.047	.244	.051	.184
Radishes	.035	.014	.166	.083	.032	.056	.038
Raisins	.040	.017	.796	.120	.126	.068	.043
Raspberries	.021	.018	.141	.007	.013	.010	.012
Rhubarb	.066	.015	.392	.010	.044	.070	.008
Rice, entire	.079	.141	.334	.068	.310	.066	.121
polished	.013	.033	.046	.012	.113	.056	.114
Rutabagas	.054	.015	.210	.052	.035	.031	.069
Rye, entire	.104	.136	.477	.060	.333	.043	.152
Sardines, fresh	.900	.035	*	*	.550	*	*
Shrimps, dried, salted	.860	.327	.760	(a)	.480	(a)	.183
Soybeans, mature	.225	.287	1.693	.280	.633	.007	.269
Spaghetti—See macaroni							
Spinach	.098	.048	.416	.093	.053	.118	.027
Squash	.034	.006	.161	.011	.038	.018	.029
Strawberries	.035	.019	.205	*	.020	*	.013
Sugar beets	.030	.041	.440	.130	.049	.180	.021
Sweet potatoes	.024	.035	.381	.031	.039	.022	.014

(Continued)

Minerals (Major), Food   (Continued)

TABLE 2.M.43   (Continued)

Food	Cal-cium	Mag-nesium	Potas-sium	Sodium	Phos-phorus	Chlorine	Sul-fur
Tomatoes..........	.012	.016	.277	.013	.033	.048	.017
Turkey............	.023	.028	.367	.130	.205	.123	.234
Turnips...........	.042	.019	.193	.104	.032	.054	.048
Turnip greens......	.317	.079	.300	.260	.040	.390	.051
Veal..............	.014	.030	.380	.086	.235	.073	.199
Venison...........	.010	.029	.336	.070	.249	.041	.211
Walnuts...........	.108	.132	.606	.013	.309	.030	.120
Watercress........	.072	.010	.100	.031	.044	.059	.071
Watermelon........	.008	.006	.071	.012	.010	.006	.005
Wheat, entire......	.055	.163	.409	.106	.342	.088	.175
Wheat bran........	.065	.420	1.252	.007	1.430	.042	.245
Yams..............	.041	.015	.290	.015	.042	.037	.013

(a) Variable.

Source: Peterson, W. H., Skinner, J. T., and Strong, F. M. *Elements of Food Biochemistry.* Prentice-Hall, Englewood Cliffs, New Jersey.

Minerals (Trace), Food

TABLE 2.M.44
Trace elements in foods (fresh basis)

Food	Milligrams per 100 grams of edible portion				Micrograms per 100 grams of edible portion
	Fe	Cu	Mn	Zn	Iodine
Abalone	*	0.88	*	2.5	105.3
Almonds	4.1	1.2	1.2	1.9	*
Apples	0.36	0.1	0.11	0.07	6.6
Apricots, fresh	0.54	0.15	*	0.04	*
dried	6.5	0.32	0.28	*	*
Artichokes	2.2	0.32	0.38	*	*
Asparagus	1.3	0.11	0.19	0.34	6.9
Avocados	0.58	0.21	0.29	*	*
Bacon	1.7	0.41	0.08	*	16.0 cooked
Bananas	0.62	0.21	1.1	0.26	20.0
Barley, whole	8.9	1.2	1.6	2.3	9.1
pearled	1.3	0.26	*	*	*
Bass	0.26	0.14	*	*	15.5
Beans, navy, dried	9.9	0.98	1.9	3.1	4.8
kidney, dried	7.6	0.92	1.6	5.2	1.8
Lima, dried	9.1	0.86	1.1	*	*
Lima, fresh	3.2	0.53	0.6	1.5	*
string	1.3	0.13	0.37	0.09	6.9
Beef, chuck	2.8	0.1	*	*	*
heart	4.2	*	*	*	30.0
kidney	11.0	0.11	1.0	2.4	9.0
liver	7.4	2.0	0.32	3.5	14.0
"lean"	4.2	0.05	0.02	1.5	3.5
loin	2.8	0.1	*	*	*
steak	3.7	0.11	0.02	*	9.1
sweetbreads	6.0	0.08	0.07	2.0	*
Beets	1.3	0.12	0.62	0.65	3.3

(Continued)

Minerals (Trace), Food   (Continued)

TABLE 2.M.44   (Continued)

Food	Milligrams per 100 grams of edible portion				Micrograms per 100 grams of edible portion
	Fe	Cu	Mn	Zn	Iodine
Beet greens	4.2	0.12	1.2	0.02	8.0
Blackberries	0.89	0.15	0.57	*	*
Blueberries	0.64	0.11	3.4	*	*
Bluefish	0.9	0.23	*	*	26.0
Brazil nuts	3.6	1.3	0.94	*	*
Bread, rye	1.8	0.28	1.3	*	9.0
white	0.86	0.25	0.42	3.3	11.3
whole wheat	2.5	0.33	3.2	*	11.0
Broccoli	1.8	0.20	0.26	*	15.0
Brussels sprouts	1.9	0.11	0.30	*	6.2
Butter	0.18	0.04	0.04	*	8.6
Buttermilk	0.28	0.05	*	*	*
Butternuts	6.8	1.2	*	*	*
Cabbage	0.66	0.11	0.21	0.20	2.3
Calf's liver	5.2	6.3	0.37	3.0	*
Cantaloupe	0.58	0.05	0.05	0.09	2.3
Carrots	0.91	0.12	0.37	0.35	4.4
Catfish	0.36	0.17	*	12.4	9.4
Cauliflower	1.2	0.27	0.15	0.22	1.6
Celery	0.68	0.12	0.17	0.21	12.3
Celery cabbage	0.6	0.06	0.12	*	*
Chard	3.7	0.11	0.8	*	11.0
Cheese, hard	1.0	0.09	0.11	*	10.0
cottage	0.98	*	0.05	*	6.4
Cherries	0.54	0.13	0.03	0.15	0.6
Chestnuts	2.2	0.39	1.7	0.19	*
Chicken	2.0	0.54	*	0.46	*
Chocolate	3.0	2.1	3.2	2.6	*
Citron	5.0	0.57	*	*	2.1
Clams	4.3	0	*	3.6	124.0
Cocoa	8.2	2.4	3.5	2.6	*
Coconut, dried	2.8	0.62	*	*	*
fresh	1.9	0.53	1.3	0.84	1.8
Codfish	0.65	0.55	0.01	*	31.4
Cod-liver oil	*	*	0	0.9	860.0
Coffee, beans	5.4	1.3	*	0.5	8.6
water extract	0.46	*	*	*	4.0
Collards	3.1	*	2.0	*	1.0
Corn	3.1	0.71	1.1	2.2	12.0
Corn germ	25.0	0.91	3.6	9.4	*
Corn meal, yellow	1.1	0.19	0.22	1.8	*
Corn, sweet	0.64	0.08	0.31	*	3.3
Cow peas	2.7	0.17	1.5	*	5.7
Crab	2.0	1.3	0.3	2.5	30.2
Cranberries	0.57	0.11	0.38	*	3.3
Cream	0.23	0.15	*	*	5.7
Cucumber	0.31	0.13	0.13	0.12	0.83
Currants, dried	3.3	0.8	0.31	*	*
fresh	0.74	0.13	*	0.2	*
Dandelion greens	5.5	0.17	0.34	1.2	*
Dates	3.5	0.23	2.6	0.32	*
Duck	2.0	0.46	0.03	0.34	*
Eggplant	0.61	0.09	0.23	0.28	0.8
Eggs, hen	2.6	0.17	0.04	1.3	12.0
Egg white	0.1	0.04	*	0.01	6.8
Egg yolk	7.0	0.25	0.11	3.8	16.0
Endive	2.9	0.09	0.23	0.12	3.7

(Continued)

Minerals (Trace), Food *(Continued)*

TABLE 2.M.44 *(Continued)*

Food	Milligrams per 100 grams of edible portion				Micrograms per 100 grams of edible portion
	Fe	Cu	Mn	Zn	Iodine
Escarole (chicory)	1.1	0.14	*	0.19	*
Figs, dried	3.5	0.34	0.34	0.36	*
fresh	0.42	0.06	*	0.12	1.5
Filberts	4.1	1.2	*	1.0	*
Fish, general	0.61	0.33	0.02	0.80	66.5 salt water
					7.0 fresh water
Flounder	0.73	0.22	*	0.82	30.9
Flour, buckwheat	1.2	0.72	2.1	1.0	*
graham or					
whole wheat	3.8	0.47	4.3	1.9	*
rye	2.1	0.43	2.0	*	2.3
white	1.2	0.14	0.54	1.2	3.6
Garlic	*	0.26	0.46	0.92	2.7
Goose	2.2	0.33	0.05	*	*
Gooseberries	0.49	0.10	0.05	0.1	*
Grapefruit	0.28	0.45	0.01	*	1.3
Grapes	0.80	0.11	0.08	0.17	*
Grape juice	0.3	0.02	*	*	0.9
Haddock	0.71	0.28	0.02	*	83.4
Halibut	0.97	0.23	*	*	27.7
Hazelnuts	4.3	1.2	3.6	0.97	1.4
Herring	1.1	0.27	*	3.6	21.4
Hickory nuts	2.6	1.4	*	*	*
Hominy	0.73	0.18	0.11	*	*
Honey	0.75	0.15	0.03	*	*
Huckleberries					
See blueberries					
Kale	3.1	0.52	0.86	*	*
Kidney—See beef,					
lamb					
Kohlrabi	0.65	0.14	0.12	*	*
Kumquats	0.55	0.09	0.07	*	*
Lamb	2.4	0.42	*	*	*
chop	3.3	0.42	0.04	*	15.0
kidney	12.0	0.31	*	1.9	*
Lard	0.1	0.02	*	*	9.3
Leeks	1.3	0.17	*	0.23	*
Lemons	0.6	0.04	0.35	*	0.5
Lemon juice	0.15	0.13	*	0.17	5.2
Lentils (dried)	8.1	0.59	3.3	5.4	*
Lettuce, head	0.58	0.11	1.0	0.39	2.9
leaf	2.0	0.14	0.82	0.44	2.7
Liver—See beef, etc.					
Lobster	0.67	1.5	0.04	0.24	80.1
Loganberries	1.4	0.14	*	0.45	2.7
Macaroni	1.3	0.07	*	*	*
Mackerel	0.98	0.27	0.02	*	16.3
Mangoes	0.3	0.04	*	*	1.6
Milk, cow's	0.24	0.04	0.03	0.36	3.8
Milk powder	0.64	0.34	*	*	32.0
Molasses	8.2	1.4	0.44	*	*
Mushrooms	1.5	1.0	0.12	0.4	0.0
Muskmelon—See					
cantaloupe					
Mussels	*	0.35	0.46	4.5	80.2
Mustard greens	4.9	0.12	1.2	*	5.4

(Continued)

Minerals (Trace), Food   (Continued)

TABLE 2.M.44   (Continued)

| Food | Milligrams per 100 grams of edible portion | | | | Micrograms per 100 grams of edible portion |
	Fe	Cu	Mn	Zn	Iodine
Mutton, leg	4.8	0.4	*	2.2	1.8
chop	1.0	0.16	*	*	*
liver	*	1.6	*	4.1	3.3
Nectarines	0.46	0.06	*	*	*
Oatmeal	4.0	0.38	3.3	*	4.2
Oats	7.2	1.4	5.0	2.9	5.2
Okra	1.2	0.14	0.56	*	5.6
Oleomargarine	0.3	0.04	*	*	7.4
Olives	2.0	0.25	0.12	0.3	*
Onions	0.68	0.11	0.38	1.3	3.6
Oranges	0.42	0.18	0.03	0.17	0.6
Orange juice	0.24	0.05	*	0	1.5
Oysters	5.9	3.4	0.13	46.0	74.2
Oyster plant— See salsify					
Parsley	13.0	0.23	1.2	*	*
Parsnips	1.1	0.12	0.04	*	3.6
Peaches	0.38	0.07	*	0.02	1.3
dried	6.3	0.27	0.68	*	*
Peanuts	2.2	1.1	0.86	1.6	0.7
Pears	0.47	0.16	0.05	0.16	0.4
Peas, dried	5.5	1.1	1.8	4.0	*
fresh	2.0	0.23	0.3	1.1	2.1
Pecans	2.6	1.4	3.5	*	*
Peppers, green	0.49	0.11	0.15	0.06	*
red	0.6	*	0.19	*	2.3
Perch	0.74	0.37	*	*	5.3
Pickerel	0.8	0.34	*	*	7.0
Pike	0.34	0.17	*	*	*
Pimentos	*	0.60	*	0.23	0.2
Pineapple	0.38	0.09	1.5	0.28	16.0
Pistachio nuts	7.9	1.2	0.67	*	*
Plums	0.71	0.14	0.11	0.03	4.7
Pork, general	1.5	1.5	*	1.4	7.6
chop	2.0	0.31	0.06	*	*
liver	25.0	1.3	0.38	0.79	14.0
Potatoes	1.3	0.17	0.41	0.31	3.9
Prunes, dried	3.6	0.29	0.16	0.05	0.12
Pumpkin	0.81	0.07	0.04	0.21	1.4
Quinces	0.85	0.13	0.04	*	*
Radishes	1.5	0.22	0.17	0.16	6.4
Raisins	2.7	0.23	0.34	0.20	*
Raspberries	0.96	0.16	0.67	0.35	*
Red snapper	0.40	0.16	0.01	0.28	31.0
Rhubarb	0.90	0.09	0.16	0.16	26.0
Rice, entire	4.4	0.26	1.9	2.1	25.0
polished	0.93	0.2	1.1	0.22	5.1
Rutabagas	0.64	0.12	0.12	0.30	6.7
Rye, whole	4.2	0.63	9.0	1.8	6.7
flour	2.1	0.43	2.0	*	6.8
Salsify (oyster plant)	1.4	0.3	0.41	0.22	*
Salmon	1.2	0.23	*	0.8	29.1
Sardines	3.3	0.04	0.26	0.94	27.0
Scallops	3.0	0.23	3.9	*	47.5
Shrimp	2.7	1.2	0.23	1.4	35.5
Soybeans	7.2	1.1	2.9	1.8	6.3

(Continued)

Minerals (Trace), Food (Continued)

TABLE 2.M.44 (Continued)

Food	Milligrams per 100 grams of edible portion				Micrograms per 100 grams of edible portion
	Fe	Cu	Mn	Zn	Iodine
Soybean flour	7.4	1.2	*	*	*
Spinach	4.7	0.11	0.73	0.62	41.0
Squash, summer	0.53	0.08	0.14	*	2.3
winter	0.77	0.10	0.22	0.21	*
Strawberries	0.75	0.07	0.23	0.09	*
Sweet potatoes	1.0	0.15	0.3	0.23	2.4
Syrup	1.5	0.09	*	*	*
Tangerines	0.46	0.09	0.04	*	*
Tapioca	0.96	0.07	*	0.04	*
Tea extract	0.72	*	*	*	16.0
Tomatoes	0.50	0.09	0.13	0.24	1.5
Trout	0.89	0.33	0.06	1.0	3.1
Tuna fish	1.6	0.5	*	*	30.5
Turkey	3.0	0.17	0.03	*	*
Turnips	0.61	0.08	0.16	0.08	7.5
Turnip greens	6.1	0.08	1.9	0.28	2.4
Veal, medium, lean	2.6	0.20	0.03	3.5	5.0
Vinegar	0.47	0.04	1.0	*	*
Walnuts, black	6.0	3.2	*	*	*
English	2.6	0.88	2.4	2.3	*
Watercress	4.4	0.1	0.42	0.56	3.6
Watermelon	0.41	0.07	0.02	*	*
Wheat	6.0	0.8	4.2	5.4	7.6
Wheat bran	13.7	1.3	10.2	12.0	*
Wheat germ	24.0	2.7	13.0	14.3	*
Whitefish	0.42	0.19	*	*	3.0
Yams	8.4	*	0.05	*	4.7

Source: Peterson, W. H., Skinner, J. T., and Strong, F. M. *Elements of Food Biochemistry*. Prentice-Hall, Englewood Cliffs, New Jersey.

Minerals (Trace), Limits

TABLE 2.M.45
Limits for trace elements in foods

General Limits in Parts per Million	
(a) Statutory—Lead 2 ppm —Arsenic 1 ppm	(b) Recommended—Copper 20 ppm —Zinc 50 ppm —Tin 250 ppm (canned foods only)

Specific Limits in Parts per Million

Foods	Lead	Statutory Arsenic	Fluorine	Recommended Copper	Zinc
Agar	10				
Alcoholic cordials	1.0			7.0	
Alginic acid and alginates	10				
Apples	3.0				
Baking powder			15		
Beer	0.5			7.0	
Beer: black beer or black beer and rum		0.5			
Beverages: alcoholic	1.0	0.2			
Beverages: nonalcoholic: prepared from cider				7.0	
Beverages: nonalcoholic: ready-to-drink	0.2	0.1			
Beverages: ready-to-drink				2.0	5.0
Brandy	0.5				
Caramel	5.0				
Carrageen	10				
Chemicals	10				
Chemicals: excluding synthetic colorings		2.0			
Chemicals: for which arsenic limits are specified in the British Pharmacopoeia or the British Pharmaceutical Codex, excluding synthetic colors		2.0[1]			
Chemicals: for which lead limits are specified in the British Pharmacopoeia or the British Pharmaceutical Codex	—[2]				
Chicory: dried and roasted		4.0		30	
Cider	0.5			7.0	
Cocktails	1.0			7.0	
Cocoa nib, mass and liquor				70[3]	
Cocoa powder	5.0[4]			70[3]	
Coffee beans				30	
Colors				30[5]	
Colors: excluding caramel	20[5]				
Colors: excluding synthetic colors		5.0[3]			
Curry powder	20				
Dextrose: anhydrous or monohydrate	0.5				
Fats	0.5				
Finings and clearing agents		5.0			
Fish: canned	5.0				
Fish paste: canned	5.0				
Flavorings	10			30	
Flour: self-rising; containing a farinaceous substance and an acidic phosphate			3.0		
Frozen confections	0.5	0.5			
Fruit juices: concentrated	2.0				
Fruit juices: excluding lime or lemon	0.5				
Fruit juices: undiluted		0.5			
Gelatine: edible	5.0	2.0		30	100
Geneva	0.5				

(Continued)

Minerals (Trace), Limits (Continued)

TABLE 2.M.45 (Continued)

Foods	Lead	Statutory Arsenic	Fluorine	Recommended Copper	Zinc
Gin	0.5				
Glucose: liquid or solid; sulphated ash content greater than 1%	5.0				
Golden raising powder					
Herbs: dried	10	5.0	15		
Hop concentrates: excluding those for commercial brewing		5.0			
Hops: dried: excluding those for commercial brewing		2.0			
Ice cream		0.5			
Ice cream: excluding water ices	1.0				
Iron: reduced iron; used in the preparation of flour		5.0			
Lecithin	5.0				
Lemon juice	2.0				
Licorice: dried extract		2.0			
Lime juice	2.0				
Liqueurs	1.0				
Meat: canned	5.0			7.0	
Meat extract	5.0				
Meat paste: canned	5.0				
Milk beverages: ready-to-drink; prepacked	1.0				
Molasses: edible	5.0				
Mustard		5.0			
Mustard: ground	20				
Oils: edible	0.5				
Onions: dehydrated	10	2.0			
Pears	3.0				
Pectin: liquid	10	2.0		30	
Pectin: solid	50	5.0		300	
Perry	0.5				
Phosphates: acidic; for use as food ingredients			30[6]		
Protein: hydrolyzed	5.0				
Rum	0.5				
Seaweed: products derived from seaweed	10				
Soft drink concentrates: for use in the manufacture of soft drinks	2.5	0.5		20	
Soft drinks: concentrated	1.0	0.5		7.0	
Soft drinks: ready-to-drink	0.2				
Spices		5.0			
Spices: excluding ground	10				
Spices: ground	20				
Starch conversion products: sulphated ash content greater than 1%	5.0				
Sugar: raw: for the manufacture of refined sugar	5.0				
Sugar: white: refined; ash content less than 0.03%	0.5				
Sugars and sugar syrups: sulphated ash content greater than 1%	5.0				
Tea	10				
Tomato catsup				150	
Tomato juice				20	
Tomato juice beverages	1.0			100[7]	
Tomato juice cocktails				100[7]	
Tomato paste	1.0				
Tomato paste: total solids between 15 and 25%	3.0			100[7]	
Tomato paste: total solids greater than 25%	5.0				

(Continued)

Minerals (Trace), Limits   (Continued)

TABLE 2.M.45   (Continued)

Foods	Lead	Statutory Arsenic	Fluorine	Recommended Copper	Zinc
Tomato powder				100[7]	
Tomato powder: total solids between 15 and 25%	3.0[8]				
Tomato powder: total solids greater than 25%	5.0				
Tomato purée				100[7]	
Tomato purée: total solids between 15 and 25%	3.0				
Tomato purée: total solids more than 25%	5.0			6	
Tomato relish				20	
Tomato sauce				20	
Vegetable juices: excluding tomato juice and tomato juice cocktail	0.5				
Vegetables: dehydrated or dried, excluding onions	5.0				
Water ices	0.5				
Whisky	0.5				
Wines				7.0	
Wines: excluding vintage port	1.0				
Yeast: brewers' yeast: for the manufacture of yeast products	10[9]	5.0[9]			
Yeast and yeast products				120[9]	
Yeast and yeast products: excluding brewers' yeast for the manufacture of yeast products	7.0[9]	2.0[9]			

[1]—Note: 2.0 ppm or the limit specified in the BP or the BPC, whichever is the higher.
[2]—Limit specified in the BP or the BPC.
[3]—Calculated on the fat-free substance.
[4]—Calculated on the dry fat-free substance.
[5]—Calculated on the dry coloring matter.
[6]—Of the acidic phosphate present.
[7]—Calculated on dried tomato solids.
[8]—See notes about lead regulations above.
[9]—Calculated on dry matter.

Source: Davis, M. S. U.K. Regulations on Trace Elements in Foods. Food Trade Review, Vol. 36, No. 3. Food Trade Press Ltd., London, England.

Minerals, Plant or Animal Tissue

TABLE 2.M.46
Some specific organic compounds of mineral elements known to exist in plant or animal materials

Element	Compound Name	Compound Formula	Contained in
Potassium	Acid salt of tartaric acid	$KHC_4H_4O_6$	Grapes, cucumbers
	Salts of citric acid	$K_2HC_6H_5O_7$	Fruits, vegetables
	Salts of malic acid	$KHC_4H_4O_5$	Fruits, vegetables
Calcium	Acid salt of tartaric acid	$Ca(HC_4H_4O_6)_2$	Grapes
	Salts of phytic acid	$C_6H_6(CaPO_4)_6$	Bran of wheat, rye, etc.
	Calcium caseinate	Not known	Milk
Magnesium	Salts of phytic acid	$C_6H_6(MgPO_4)_6$	Bran of wheat, rye, etc.
	Chlorophyll	$C_{55}H_{72}N_4MgO_5$	Green plants
Iron	Hematin	$C_{34}H_{33}N_4FeO_5$	Hemoglobin of blood
Sulfur	Cystine	$C_6H_{12}N_2S_2O_4$	Proteins
	Glutathione	$C_{10}H_{17}N_3SO_6$	Animal tissues
	Insulin	$(C_{45}H_{69}N_{11}SO_{14})_n$	A hormone, secreted by Isles of Langerhans
	Thiamin chloride	$C_{12}H_{17}N_4SCl$	Yeast, pork muscle, etc.
	Allyl isothiocyanate	C_3H_5NCS	Mustard, onions
	Allyl sulfide	$(C_3H_5)_2S$	Garlic, radishes, cabbage, turnips, etc.
Phosphorus	Lecithins	*e.g.*, $C_{44}H_{88}NPO_9$	Egg yolk, brain, nerves, etc.
	Cephalins	*e.g.*, $C_{41}H_{80}NPO_8$	Blood
	Nucleic acids	*e.g.*, $C_{29}H_{45}N_5PO_{26}$	Nuclear tissue, *e.g.*, thymus
	Phosphoproteins	Not known	Egg yolk, milk
	Hexosemonophosphate	$C_6H_{11}O_5(H_2PO_4)$	Yeast, muscle
	Hexosediphosphate	$C_6H_{10}O_4(H_2PO_4)_2$	Yeast
	Phytic acid	$C_6H_6(H_2PO_4)_6$	Bran of wheat, rye, etc.
	Creatine phosphate	$C_4H_{10}N_3PO_5$	Muscle
Iodine	Thyroxine	$C_{15}H_{11}I_4O_4N$	A hormone secreted by thyroid gland
Copper	Hemocyanins	Not known	Respiratory protein in lower animals (*e.g.*, lobster)
Zinc	Carbonic anhydrase	Not known	Red blood cells

Source: Peterson, W. H., Skinner, J. T., and Strong, F. M. *Elements of Food Biochemistry.* Prentice-Hall, Englewood Cliffs, New Jersey.

Mite (Enlarged)

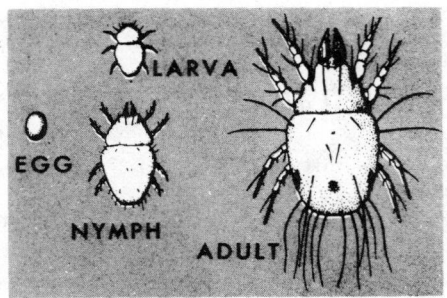

FIGURE 2.M.7

Source: USDA (1974). Protecting home cured meat from insects. USDA Home and Garden Bull. *109.*

Moisture, Drying

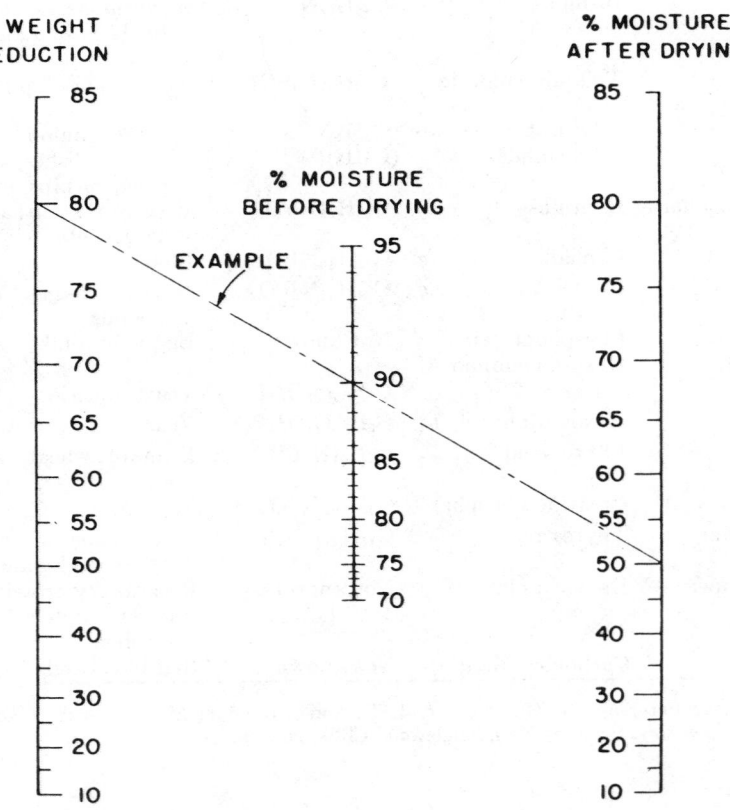

FIGURE 2.M.8
Moisture and weight relationship due to drying

Source: Tressler, D. K., VanArsdel, W. B., and Copley, M. J. (1968). *The Freezing Preservation of Foods,* Vol. 3. AVI Publishing Co., Westport, Connecticut.

Moisture in Biological Materials

TABLE 2.M.47
Water content of some important biological materials

Material	Water per cent
Human body	65
Brain, white matter	68
Brain, gray matter	84
Liver	76
Muscle	73
Blood	80
Bone	10–40
Saliva	99.5
Protoplasm	70–93
Fish, muscle	80
Milk	87
Vegetables	90
Fruits	85
Seeds	10–20
Larvae of clothes-moth	58
Wool, hair (food of larvae of clothes-moth)	4–9

Source: Peterson, W. H., Skinner, J. T., and Strong, F. M. *Elements of Food Biochemistry.* Prentice-Hall, Englewood Cliffs, New Jersey.

Mold, Food

TABLE 2.M.48
Molds affecting foods

Product	Organism	Common Name, or Type of Rot
Dairy products	Alternaria sp.	
	Oospora lactis	
	Cladosporium sp.	
	Penicilium sp.	
Stone fruits	Sclerotinia fructicola	Brown rot
	Rhizopus nigricans	Soft rot
	Cladosporium sp.	Green mold
	Penicillium sp.	Blue mold rot
	Aspergillus sp.	Black rot
	Botrytis sp.	Gray mold rot
Pome fruits	Glomerella cingulata	Bitter rot
	Physalospora cydoniae	Black rot
	Penicillium expansum	Blue mold rot
Tomatoes	Colletotricum phomoides	Anthracnose
	Alternaria sp.	Alternaria rot
	Oospora sp.	Machine mold
	Fusarium sp.	
	Phoma destructiva	
	Phytophthora sp.	Buckeye rot
	Rhizopus nigricans	
Other vegetable crops	Sclerotiorum sp.	Watery rot
	Rhizopus nigricans	Soft, mushy rot
	Colletotricum lindimuthianum	Anthracnose
	Diaportha batatis	Dry rot
	Sclerotium bataticola	Dry rot
	Botrytis sp.	Gray mold
	Rhizoctonia	Soil rot

Source: Kramer, A., and Twigg, B. A. (editors) (1970). Microanalytical and microbiological methods. In *Quality Control For The Food Industry*, Vol. 1, 3rd Edition. AVI Publishing Co., Westport, Connecticut.

Molds, Mycotoxins

TABLE 2.M.49
Mycotoxinogenic molds

Species	Clinical effect	Susceptible species
Group 1, Producers of well-defined mycotoxins		
Alternaria tenuis	ATA	man
A. sp.	haemorrhages	mouse
Aspergillus amstelodami	emaciation	poultry
Asp. candidus	cf. *Pen. citrinum*	
Asp. clavatus	haemorrhages	poultry
Asp. flavus	hepatic carcinoma	poultry, man
	tremors	mouse
	haemorrhages	swine
Asp. fumigatus	perirenal oedema	swine
Asp. glaucus	haemorrhages and diarrhoea	poultry
Asp. niger	cf. *Asp. flavus*	
Asp. ochraceus	hepatic injury	poultry
		rat
Asp. oryzae	hepatic necrosis	various
Asp. ostianus	cf. *Asp. ochraceus*	
Asp. parasiticus	cf. *Asp. flavus*	
Asp. ruber	cf. *Asp. flavus*	
Asp. terreus	cf. *Pen. citrinum*	
Asp. wentii	emaciation	poultry
Chaetomium globosum	haemorrhages and paralysis	rat
Cladosporium epiphyllum	ATA	man
Fusarium culmorum	anorexia	bovine
Fus. nivale	emaciation and gangrene	bovine
Fus. roseum (Syn. Gibberella saubinetti)	hepatic necrosis	swine
Fus. sporotrichioides	ATA	man
Gibberella zeae	oestromimetic response	swine
Mucor hiemalis	ATA	man
Penicillium brevicompactum	ATA	man
Pen. citreoviride	ascending paralyses	various
Pen. citrinum	haemorrhages and renal damage	poultry
		mouse
Pen. cyclopium	tremors	mouse
Pen. islandicum	hepatic atrophia cirrhosis	various
Pen. puberulum	cf. *Asp. flavus*	
Pen. rubrum	haemorrhages and hepatic injury	swine
Pen. rugulosum	cf. *Pen. citrinum*	
Pen. tardum	cf. *Pen. citrinum*	
Pen. variabile	cf. *Asp. flavus*	
Pen. viridicatum	renal damage	swine, rat
Pen. sp.	cf. *Asp. ochraceus*	
Pithomyces chartarum	angiocholecystitis	sheep
	facial oedema	bovine
Rhizopus sp.	cf. *Asp. flavus*	
Stachyobotrys atra	haemorrhages	horse

Group 2. Producers of less well-defined orally active toxins
Asp. avenaceus, carneus, chevalieri, nidulans and *niveus*
Cladosporium fragi
Fusarium moniliforme
Paecilomyces varioti (Syn. Byssochlamys fulva)
Pen. oxalicum, piceum, purpurogenum, urticae
Trichoderma lignorum

Source: Mossel, D. A. A. (1970). Microbial spoilage of proteinaceous foods. In *Proteins as Human Food*. R. A. Lawrie (editor). AVI Publishing Co., Westport, Connecticut.

Most Probable Number

TABLE 2.M.50
Most probable number calculations (MPN index and 95% confidence limits for various combinations of positive and negative results when five 10-ml portions, five 1-ml portions, and five 0.1-ml portions are used.)

Number of tubes giving positive reaction out of			MPN index per 100 ml	95% confidence limits	
5 of 10 ml each	5 of 1 ml each	5 of 0.1 ml each		Lower	Upper
0	0	1	2	<0.5	7
0	1	0	2	<0.5	7
0	2	0	4	<0.5	11
1	0	0	2	<0.5	7
1	0	1	4	<0.5	11
1	1	0	4	<0.5	11
1	1	1	6	<0.5	15
1	2	0	6	<0.5	15
2	0	0	5	<0.5	13
2	0	1	7	1	17
2	1	0	7	1	17
2	1	1	9	2	21
2	2	0	9	2	21
2	3	0	12	3	28
3	0	0	8	1	19
3	0	1	11	2	25
3	1	0	11	2	25
3	1	1	14	4	34
3	2	0	14	4	34
3	2	1	17	5	46
3	3	0	17	5	46
4	0	0	13	3	31
4	0	1	17	5	46
4	1	0	17	5	46
4	1	1	21	7	63
4	1	2	26	9	78
4	2	0	22	7	67
4	2	1	26	9	78
4	3	0	27	9	80
4	3	1	33	11	93
4	4	0	34	12	93
5	0	0	23	7	70
5	0	1	31	11	89
5	0	2	43	15	114
5	1	0	33	11	93
5	1	1	46	16	120
5	1	2	63	21	150
5	2	0	49	17	130
5	2	1	70	23	170
5	2	2	94	28	220
5	3	0	79	25	190
5	3	1	109	31	250
5	3	2	141	37	340
5	3	3	175	44	500
5	4	0	130	35	300
5	4	1	172	43	490
5	4	2	221	57	700
5	4	3	278	90	850
5	4	4	345	120	1000
5	5	0	240	68	750
5	5	1	348	120	1000
5	5	2	542	180	1400
5	5	3	918	300	3200
5	5	4	1609	640	5800

Source: Thatcher, F. S., and Clark, D. S. (1968). *Microorganisms in Foods*. University of Toronto Press, Toronto, Canada.

Most Probable Number, Bacterial

TABLE 2.M.51
Values for the most probable number (MPN) for five tubes inoculated from each of three successive tenfold dilutions[1]

No. of Positive Tubes Observed			MPN of Inoculum of First Dilution	No. of Positive Tubes Observed			MPN of Inoculum of First Dilution
0	1	0	0.18	5	0	0	2.3
1	0	0	0.20	5	0	1	3.1
1	1	0	0.40	5	1	0	3.3
2	0	0	0.45	5	1	1	4.6
2	0	1	0.68	5	2	0	4.9
2	1	0	0.68	5	2	1	7.0
2	2	0	0.93	5	2	2	9.5
3	0	0	0.78	5	3	0	7.9
3	0	1	1.1	5	3	1	11.0
3	1	0	1.1	5	3	2	14.0
3	2	0	1.4	5	4	0	13.0
4	0	0	1.3	5	4	1	17.0
4	0	1	1.7	5	4	2	22.0
4	1	0	1.7	5	4	3	28.0
4	1	1	2.1	5	5	0	24.0
4	2	0	2.2	5	5	1	35.0
4	2	1	2.6	5	5	2	54.0
4	3	0	2.7	5	5	3	92.0
				5	5	4	160.0

[1] Example 1. Suppose 1 ml was inoculated from the 10^0, 10^{-1} and 10^{-2} dilutions of culture into 5 tubes for each dilution, and that the numbers of turbid tubes observed after incubation were 4-2-1. The table shows that the MPN = 2.6 per inoculum taken from the 10^0 dilution.

Example 2. Suppose the same results were obtained with tubes inoculated from 10^{-3}, 10^{-4} and 10^{-5} dilutions. The MPN is then 2.6 per inoculum taken from the 10^{-3} dilution, or 2.6×10^{-3} per inoculum of undiluted culture.

Source: Sulzbacher, W. L. (1973). Meat and meat products. In *Quality Control For The Food Industry*, Vol. 2, 3rd Edition. A. Kramer, and B. A. Twigg (editors). AVI Publishing Co., Westport, Connecticut.

Muscle and Body Weight

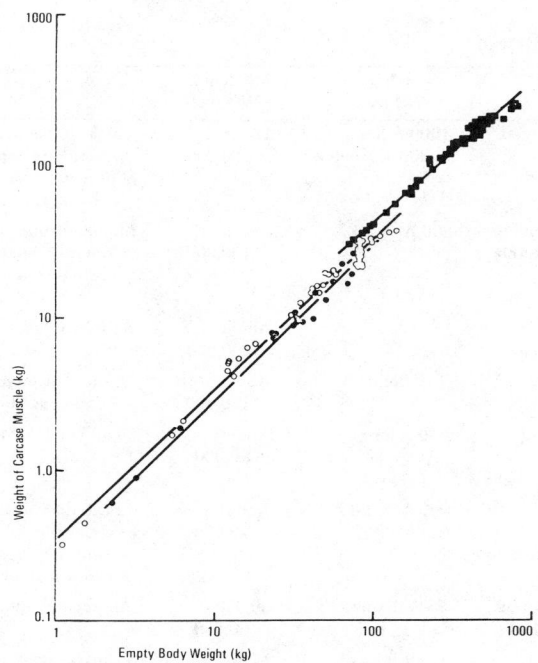

FIGURE 2.M.9
Weight of dissected muscle in a carcass compared with empty body weight for sheep (●), cattle (■), and pigs (○)

Source: Tribe, D. E. (editor). *Carcass Composition and Appraisal of Meat Animals.* CSIRO, Australia.

Mustard, French

TABLE 2.M.52
Prepared french mustard

Prepared French Mustard	
Distilled malt vinegar (4% acetic acid)	60 gal. (U.S.)
White mustard farina	60 lb
Salt	16½ lb
Ground turmeric	2½ lb
Ground cayenne pepper	1 lb
Ground cloves	1 lb
Ground pimiento	½ lb

Source: Binsted, R., Devey, J. D., and Dakin, J. C. (1971). *Pickle & Sauce Making,* 3rd Edition. Food Trade Press, London, England.

Myofibrillar Proteins of Muscle

TABLE 2.M.53
Description of proteins of muscle

Protein	Shape	Size	Molecular Weight	Makeup and Role
Myosin	Rod with enlarged "head," 57 percent α-helix	1600 Å long, 30Å diameter	About 500,000	Thick filaments of A band; major role in contraction-relaxation; contains about 7-SH groups per 10^5; made up of subunits, LMM + HMM, ratio 2:1; ATPase
Light meromyosin (LMM)	Rod, 76 percent α-helix, probably 2-stranded coiled-coil	850 Å × 15 Å	About 150,000	Major portion of "tail" of myosin molecule; noncovalently bonded to HMM so that two subunits are easily separated
Heavy meromyosin (HMM)	"Tadpole," 43 percent α-helix		About 200,000	ATPase; "head" and part of "tail" of myosin
HMMS₁	Globular, 27 percent α-helix	70 Å long	About 120,000	"Head" of myosin; contains four times as much proline as "tail" portion
HMMS₂	Rod, 2-stranded coiled-coil, 73 percent α-helix	450 Å long	About 60,000	"Tail" of HMM
Tropomyosin	Rod, 2-chain coiled-coil, 91 percent α-helix	400 Å × 20 Å	About 70,000	Located in Z line and thin filaments; possibly responsible for structure of Z line; highly charged molecule; resistant to denaturation; may act as core for double helix of F-actin
Actin-G form	Globular, about 30 percent helical	55 Å diameter	50,000–60,000	Aggregates into F-actin of thin filaments
Actin-F form	Double chain of spheres coiled together	Length approximates that of thin filaments	Many millions	Primary structural units of thin filaments; major role in contraction-relaxation; sensitive to Ca++ when complexed with tropomyosin and troponin, so may be trigger mechanism for contraction
Actomyosin (myosin B)				Complex of myosin +1 actin doublet, formed and broken in contraction-relaxation
Troponin A and B				Found in thin filaments; troponin A binds Ca++
α-actinin				Influences cross linking of actin; found in Z line and in thin filaments adjacent to Z line
β-actinin			6500 to 300,000 depending on solvent used	May occur in thin filaments; may act by influencing natural filament length; deterrent to interaction among actin strands, which otherwise tend to form gel
M-protein				Located in middle of H-zone; accelerates lateral aggregation of myosin; holds thick filaments in position in A band

Source: Paul, P. C., and Palmer, H. H. (1972). *Food Theory and Applications.* John Wiley & Sons, New York.

Niacin

TABLE 2.N.1
Niacin content of foods

	mg/100 g		mg/100 g
Peas	2.9	Brussels sprouts	0.9
Corn	1.7	Cauliflower	0.7
Potatoes	1.5	Tomatoes	0.7
Asparagus	1.5	Bananas	0.7
Lima beans	1.4	Carrots	0.6
Peaches	1.0	Watermelon	0.5
Artichokes	1.0	Oranges	0.4
Broccoli	0.9	Lettuce	0.3

Source: White, P. L., and Selvey, N. (editors) (1974). *Nutritional Qualities of Fresh Fruits and Vegetables.* Futura Publishing Co., Mt. Kisco, New York.

Niacin, Daily Recommendations

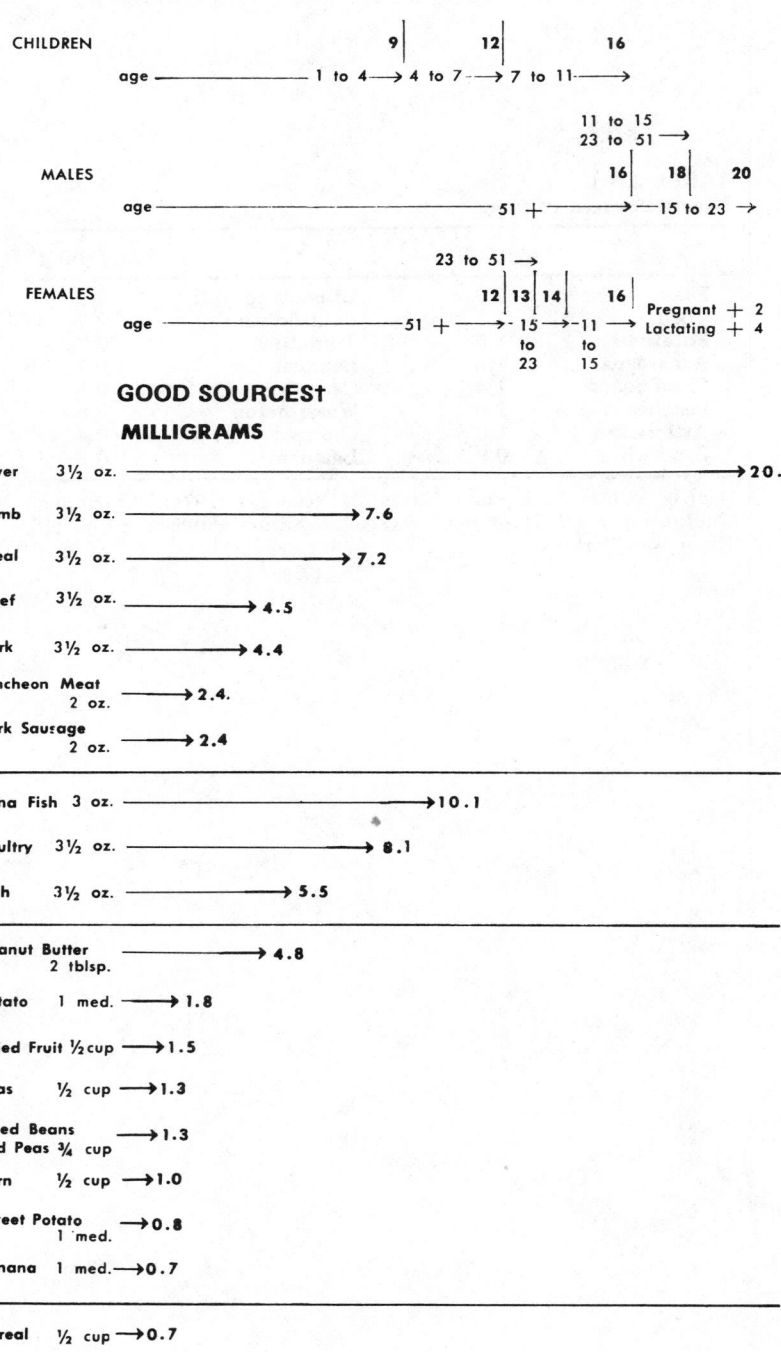

MILLIGRAMS

CHILDREN

| | 9 | 12 | 16 |
age ——————————— 1 to 4 ——→ 4 to 7 ——→ 7 to 11 ——→

MALES

11 to 15
23 to 51 ——→
| 16 | 18 | 20 |
age ———————————————————————— 51 + ——————→ —15 to 23 →

FEMALES

23 to 51 ——→
| 12 | 13 | 14 | 16 |
age ———————————————————————— 51 + ——→ -15 —→-11 —→ Pregnant + 2
                                            to   to   Lactating + 4
                                            23   15

GOOD SOURCES†

MILLIGRAMS

Liver   3½ oz. ————————————————————————→ 20.1

Lamb   3½ oz. ——————————→ 7.6

Veal   3½ oz. ——————————→ 7.2

Beef   3½ oz. ——————→ 4.5

Pork   3½ oz. ——————→ 4.4

Luncheon Meat
        2 oz. ——→ 2.4.

Pork Sausage
        2 oz. ——→ 2.4

Tuna Fish 3 oz. ——————————————→ 10.1

Poultry   3½ oz. ——————————————→ 8.1

Fish   3½ oz. ——————→ 5.5

Peanut Butter
        2 tblsp. ——————→ 4.8

Potato   1 med. ——→ 1.8

Dried Fruit ½ cup ——→ 1.5

Peas   ½ cup ——→ 1.3

Dried Beans
and Peas ¾ cup ——→ 1.3

Corn   ½ cup ——→ 1.0

Sweet Potato ——→ 0.8
        1 med.

Banana 1 med.——→ 0.7

Cereal   ½ cup ——→ 0.7

Bread   1 slice ——→ 0.7

†Average nutrient content as food is served. (Note: 3½ oz equals approximately 100 g.)

FIGURE 2.N.1

Source: Lessons on Meat. (1974). National Live Stock and Meat Board, Chicago.

Nicotinic Acid, Food

TABLE 2.N.2
Nicotinic acid content of foods (mg/100 g)

Cereals and Cereal Products		Beverages	
Bread, white	1.7	Beer	0.7
wholemeal	3.5	Chocolate	1.0
Maize	1.0	Tea	6.0
Oats	1.0	Vegetables and Nuts	
Rice, milled	1.5	Asparagus	1.2
parboiled and milled	3.8	Beans, broad	4.0
Eggs	0.07	Cabbage	0.3
Fish		Carrot	0.25
Herring	3.5	Kale	1.0
White	3.0	Peas	2.6
Fruits		Peanut	16.0
Apples	0.1	Potato	1.2
Tomatoes	0.6	Spinach	0.6
Meats		Sprouts	0.7
Beef	5.0	Swede	1.2
Heart	7.0	Yeast	
Kidney	6.0	Baker's moist	10.0
Liver	13.0	Brewer's moist	10.0
Tongue	6.0		
Milk	0.08		
Dried	0.7		
Dried, skimmed	0.8		

Source: Sinclair, H. M., and Hollingsworth, D. F. (1969). *Hutchison's Food and the Principles of Nutrition.* Edward Arnold (Publishers), London, England.

Nitrate, Meat Curing

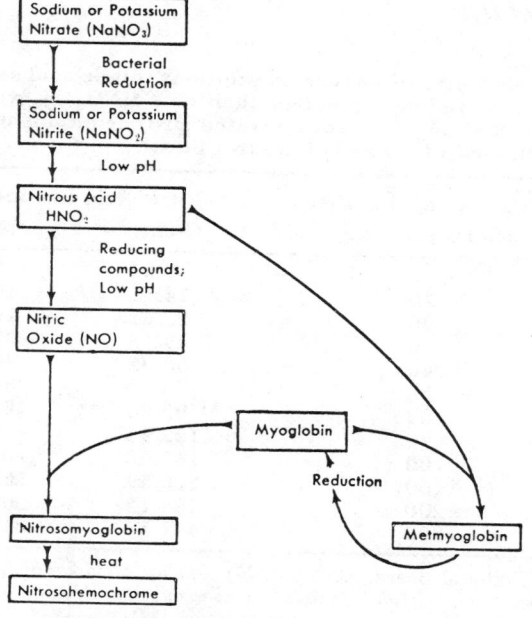

FIGURE 2.N.2
Nitrate and nitrite pathway in meat curing

Source: Ockerman, H. W. (1975). Comparative anatomy of meat animals. In *Meat Hygiene.* J. A. Libby (editor). Lea & Febiger, Philadelphia.

Nitrate, Vegetables

TABLE 2.N.3
Nitrate content of vegetables grown in 1963 and 1964 and vegetables purchased in Columbia, Missouri, stores in 1964[a]

| | NO$_3$-N Content (% dry weight) | | |
	Field Grown[b] (1963)	Field Grown[b] (1964)	Purchased[c] (1964 range)
Vegetable			
Radishes (red)	0.53–1.2	0.8 –1.9	0.39–1.50
Beets (red)	–	0.19–0.78	0.09–0.84[d]
Turnips, tops	0.25–0.85	–	0.03–0.76
Carrots	0.02–0.05	0.02–0.05	0.0 –0.13
Lettuce, leaf	0.08–0.5	0.09–0.60	0.02–1.06
Spinach	–	0.09–0.24	0.07–0.66
Kale	0.30–1.02	–	–
Mustard	0.46–0.98	–	
Sweet corn	–	–	0.01
Cabbage	–	–	0.01–0.09
Broccoli	–	–	0.01–0.09
Cauliflower	–	–	0.0 –0.31
Celery	–	–	0.11–1.12
Green beans	–	–	0.04–0.25
Squash	–	–	0.09–0.43
Cucumbers	–	–	0.0 –0.16
Tomatoes	–	–	0.0 –0.11

[a] From Brown and Smith (1967).
[b] Low values were from plants grown on soil receiving no nitrogen fertilizer, and high values were from plants grown in soil receiving 400 lb N/acre (450 kg/ha).
[c] Includes both locally grown and shipped-in supplies.
[d] Baby foods.

Source: Anonymous (1972). *Accumulation of Nitrate.* Publ. *2038,* Agric. Board, Nat. Acad. Sci.—Nat. Res. Council.

Nitric Acid Solution

TABLE 2.N.4
Various strengths of nitric acid solutions (nitric acid solutions: specification requires not less than 68% HNO$_3$ by weight sp gr = 1.4146 at 15°. 1 ml concentrated HNO$_3$ contains ca 0.96 g HNO$_3$. Mix with H$_2$O and dilute to 1 liter.)

HNO$_3$ Strength Desired Grams per Liter	Nitric Acid Required	
	Grams	Ml
5	7.35	5.2
10	14.71	10.4
20	29.41	20.8
30	44.12	31.2
40	58.82	41.6
50	73.53	52.0
63	92.65	65.5
70	102.94	72.8
100	147.06	104.0
150	220.59	156.0
200	294.12	207.9
300	441.18	312.9

Source: Editorial Board, AOAC (1975). *Official Methods of Analysis of the Association of Official Analytical Chemists,* 12th Edition. Association of Official Analytical Chemists, Washington, D.C.

Normal Curve

TABLE 2.N.5
Areas under the normal probability curve. Area to the right of z (or to the left of −z), or the probability of a random value of z exceeding the marginal value

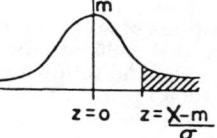

z	.00	.01	.02	.03	.04	.05	.06	.07	.08	.09
.0	.5000	.4960	.4920	.4880	.4840	.4801	.4761	.4721	.4681	.4641
.1	.4602	.4562	.4522	.4483	.4443	.4404	.4364	.4325	.4286	.4247
.2	.4207	.4168	.4129	.4090	.4052	.4013	.3974	.3936	.3897	.3859
.3	.3821	.3783	.3745	.3707	.3669	.3632	.3594	.3557	.3520	.3483
.4	.3446	.3409	.3372	.3336	.3300	.3264	.3228	.3192	.3156	.3121
.5	.3085	.3050	.3015	.2981	.2946	.2912	.2877	.2843	.2810	.2776
.6	.2743	.2709	.2676	.2643	.2611	.2578	.2546	.2514	.2483	.2451
.7	.2420	.2389	.2358	.2327	.2296	.2266	.2236	.2206	.2177	.2148
.8	.2119	.2090	.2061	.2033	.2005	.1977	.1949	.1922	.1894	.1867
.9	.1841	.1814	.1788	.1762	.1736	.1711	.1685	.1660	.1635	.1611
1.0	.1587	.1562	.1539	.1515	.1492	.1469	.1446	.1423	.1401	.1379
1.1	.1357	.1335	.1314	.1292	.1271	.1251	.1230	.1210	.1190	.1170
1.2	.1151	.1131	.1112	.1093	.1075	.1056	.1038	.1020	.1003	.0985
1.3	.0968	.0951	.0934	.0918	.0901	.0885	.0869	.0853	.0838	.0823
1.4	.0808	.0793	.0778	.0764	.0749	.0735	.0721	.0708	.0694	.0681
1.5	.0668	.0655	.0643	.0630	.0618	.0606	.0594	.0582	.0571	.0559
1.6	.0548	.0537	.0526	.0516	.0505	.0495	.0485	.0475	.0465	.0455
1.7	.0446	.0436	.0427	.0418	.0409	.0401	.0392	.0384	.0375	.0367
1.8	.0359	.0351	.0344	.0336	.0329	.0322	.0314	.0307	.0301	.0294
1.9	.0287	.0281	.0274	.0268	.0262	.0256	.0250	.0244	.0239	.0233
2.0	.0228	.0222	.0217	.0212	.0207	.0202	.0197	.0192	.0188	.0183
2.1	.0179	.0174	.0170	.0166	.0162	.0158	.0154	.0150	.0146	.0143
2.2	.0139	.0136	.0132	.0129	.0125	.0122	.0119	.0116	.0113	.0110
2.3	.0107	.0104	.0102	.0099	.0096	.0094	.0091	.0089	.0087	.0084
2.4	.0082	.0080	.0078	.0075	.0073	.0071	.0069	.0068	.0066	.0064
2.5	.0062	.0060	.0059	.0057	.0055	.0054	.0052	.0051	.0049	.0048
2.6	.0047	.0045	.0044	.0043	.0041	.0040	.0039	.0038	.0037	.0036
2.7	.0035	.0034	.0033	.0032	.0031	.0030	.0029	.0028	.0027	.0026
2.8	.0026	.0025	.0024	.0023	.0023	.0022	.0021	.0021	.0020	.0019
2.9	.0019	.0018	.0018	.0017	.0016	.0016	.0015	.0015	.0014	.0014
3.0	.0013	.0013	.0013	.0012	.0012	.0011	.0011	.0011	.0010	.0010
3.1	.0010	.0009	.0009	.0009	.0008	.0008	.0008	.0008	.0007	.0007
3.2	.0007	.0007	.0006	.0006	.0006	.0006	.0006	.0005	.0005	.0005
3.3	.0005	.0005	.0005	.0004	.0004	.0004	.0004	.0004	.0004	.0003
3.4	.0003	.0003	.0003	.0003	.0003	.0003	.0003	.0003	.0003	.0002
3.6	.0002	.0002	.0001	.0001	.0001	.0001	.0001	.0001	.0001	.0001
3.9	.0000									

Source: Amerine, M. A., Pangborn, R. M., and Roessler, E. B. *Principles of Sensory Evaluation of Food.* Academic Press, New York.

Normal Solutions

TABLE 2.N.6
Decinormal solutions of salts and other reagents (Atomic and molecular weights in the following table are based upon the 1965 atomic weight scale and the isotope C-12. The weight in grams of the compound in 1 cc of the following decinormal solutions is found by dividing the H equivalent in the last column by 1000.)

Name	Formula	Atomic or molecular weight	Hydrogen equivalent	0.1 Hydrogen equivalent in g
Acetic acid	$HC_2H_3O_2$	60.0530	$HC_2H_3O_2$	6.0053
Ammonia	NH_3	17.0306	NH_3	1.7031
Ammonium ion	NH_4^+	18.0386	NH_4	1.8039
Ammonium chloride	NH_4Cl	53.4916	NH_4Cl	5.3492
Ammonium sulfate	$(NH_4)_2SO_4$	132.1388	$\frac{1}{2}(NH_4)_2SO_4$	6.6069
Ammonium thiocyanate	NH_4CNS	76.1204	NH_4CNS	7.6120
Barium	Ba	137.34	$\frac{1}{2}Ba$	6.867
Barium carbonate	$BaCO_3$	197.3494	$\frac{1}{2}BaCO_3$	9.8675
Barium chloride hydrate	$BaCl_2 \cdot 2H_2O$	244.2767	$\frac{1}{2}BaCl_2 \cdot 2H_2O$	12.2138
Barium hydroxide	$Ba(OH)_2$	171.3547	$\frac{1}{2}Ba(OH)_2$	8.5677
Barium oxide	BaO	153.3394	$\frac{1}{2}BaO$	7.6670
Bromine	Br	79.909	Br	7.9909
Calcium	Ca	40.08	$\frac{1}{2}Ca$	2.004
Calcium carbonate	$CaCO_3$	100.0894	$\frac{1}{2}CaCO_3$	5.0045
Calcium chloride	$CaCl_2$	110.9860	$\frac{1}{2}CaCl_2$	5.5493
Calcium chloride hydrate	$CaCl_2 \cdot 6H_2O$	219.0150	$\frac{1}{2}CaCl_2 \cdot 6H_2O$	10.9508
Calcium hydroxide	$Ca(OH)_2$	74.0947	$\frac{1}{2}Ca(OH)_2$	3.7047
Calcium oxide	CaO	56.0794	$\frac{1}{2}CaO$	2.8040
Chlorine	Cl	35.453	Cl	3.5453
Citric acid	$C_6H_8O_7 \cdot H_2O$	210.1418	$\frac{1}{3}C_6H_8O_7 \cdot H_2O$	7.0047
Cobalt	Co	58.9332	$\frac{1}{2}Co$	2.9466
Copper	Cu	63.54	$\frac{1}{2}Cu$	3.177
Copper oxide (cupric)	CuO	79.5394	$\frac{1}{2}CuO$	3.9770
Copper sulfate hydrate	$CuSO_4 \cdot 5H_2O$	249.6783	$\frac{1}{2}CuSO_4 \cdot 5H_2O$	12.4839
Cyanogen	$(CN)_2$	26.0179	CN	2.6018
Hydrochloric acid	HCl	36.4610	HCl	3.6461
Hydrocyanic acid	HCN	27.0258	HCN	2.7026
Iodine	I	126.9044	I	12.6904
Lactic acid	$C_3H_6O_3$	90.0795	$C_3H_6O_3$	9.0080
Malic acid	$C_4H_6O_5$	134.0894	$\frac{1}{2}C_4H_6O_5$	6.7045
Magnesium	Mg	24.312	$\frac{1}{2}Mg$	1.2156
Magnesium carbonate	$MgCO_3$	84.3214	$\frac{1}{2}MgCO_3$	4.2161
Magnesium chloride	$MgCl_2$	95.2180	$\frac{1}{2}MgCl_2$	4.7609
Magnesium chloride hydrate	$MgCl_2 \cdot 6H_2O$	203.2370	$\frac{1}{2}MgCl_2 \cdot 6H_2O$	10.1623
Magnesium oxide	MgO	40.3114	$\frac{1}{2}MgO$	2.0156
Manganese	Mn	54.938	$\frac{1}{2}Mn$	2.7469
Manganese sulfate	$MnSO_4$	150.9996	$\frac{1}{2}MnSO_4$	7.5500
Mercuric chloride	$HgCl_2$	271.4960	$\frac{1}{2}HgCl_2$	13.5748
Nickel	Ni	58.71	$\frac{1}{2}Ni$	2.9356
Nitric acid	HNO_3	63.0129	HNO_3	6.3013
Nitrogen	N	14.0067	N	1.4007
Nitrogen pentoxide	N_2O_5	108.0104	$\frac{1}{2}N_2O_5$	5.4005
Oxalic acid	$H_2C_2O_4$	90.0358	$\frac{1}{2}H_2C_2O_4$	4.5018
Oxalic acid hydrate	$H_2C_2O_4 \cdot 2H_2O$	126.0665	$\frac{1}{2}H_2C_2O_4 \cdot 2H_2O$	6.3033

(Continued)

Normal Solutions   (Continued)

TABLE 2.N.6   (Continued)

Name	Formula	Atomic or molecular weight	Hydrogen equivalent	0.1 Hydrogen equivalent in g
Oxalic acid anhydride	C_2O_3	72.0205	$\frac{1}{2}C_2O_3$	3.6010
Phosphoric acid	H_3PO_4	97.9953	$\frac{1}{3}H_3PO_4$	3.2665
Potassium	K	39.102	K	3.9102
Potassium bicarbonate	$KHCO_3$	100.1193	$KHCO_3$	10.0119
Potassium carbonate	K_2CO_3	138.2134	$\frac{1}{2}K_2CO_3$	6.9106
Potassium chloride	KCl	74.5550	KCl	7.4555
Potassium cyanide	KCN	65.1199	KCN	6.5120
Potassium hydroxide	KOH	56.1094	KOH	5.6109
Potassium oxide	K_2O	94.2034	$\frac{1}{2}K_2O$	4.7102
Potassium permanganate for Co estimation	$KMnO_4$	158.0376	$\frac{1}{6}KMnO_4$	2.6339
Potassium permanganate for Mn estimation	$KMnO_4$	158.0376	$\frac{1}{3}KMnO_4$	5.2678
Potassium tartrate	$K_2H_4C_4O_6$	226.2769	$\frac{1}{2}K_2H_4C_4O_6$	11.3139
Silver	Ag	107.87	Ag	10.787
Silver nitrate	$AgNO_3$	169.8749	$AgNO_3$	16.9875
Sodium	Na	22.9898	Na	2.2990
Sodium bicarbonate	$NaHCO_3$	84.0071	$NaHCO_3$	8.4007
Sodium carbonate	Na_2CO_3	105.9890	$\frac{1}{2}Na_2CO_3$	5.2995
Sodium chloride	NaCl	58.4428	NaCl	5.8443
Sodium hydroxide	NaOH	39.9972	NaOH	3.9997
Sodium oxide	Na_2O	61.9790	$\frac{1}{2}Na_2O$	3.0990
Sodium sulfide	Na_2S	78.0436	$\frac{1}{2}Na_2S$	3.9022
Succinic acid	$H_2C_4H_4O_4$	118.0900	$\frac{1}{2}H_2C_4H_4O_4$	5.9045
Sulfuric acid	H_2SO_4	98.0775	$\frac{1}{2}H_2SO_4$	4.9039
Sulfur trioxide	SO_3	80.0622	$\frac{1}{2}SO_3$	4.0031
Tartaric acid	$C_4H_6O_6$	150.0888	$\frac{1}{2}C_4H_6O_6$	7.5044
Zinc	Zn	65.37	$\frac{1}{2}Zn$	3.269
Zinc sulfate	$ZnSO_4 \cdot 7H_2O$	287.5390	$\frac{1}{2}ZnSO_4 \cdot 7 \cdot H_2O$	14.3769

Source: Weast, R. C. (editor) (1974–1975). *Handbook of Chemistry and Physics*, 55th Edition. CRC Press, Cleveland.

Nut, Grades

TABLE 2.N.7
U.S. grade standards for nuts

Kind of Nut	Grade	Description of quality
in-shell		
Almonds	U.S. No. 1	Best quality.
Brazils	"	" "
English walnuts	"	" "
Filberts	"	" "
Pecans	"	" "
Mixed nuts (almonds, brazils, filberts, pecans, and English walnuts).	U.S. Extra Fancy	Best quality and largest sizes. At least 10 percent but not over 40 percent of each kind in the mixture.
	U.S. Fancy	Same quality and mixture, but permits smaller sizes of some kinds.
Shelled, raw		
Almonds	U.S. Fancy	Best quality.
	U.S. Extra No. 1	Almost the best—permits a few doubles and broken.
	U.S. No. 1	Very good quality—permits more doubles and broken.
English walnuts	U.S. No. 1	Best quality.
Pecans	U.S. No. 1	" "
Peanut butter	U.S. Grade A	" "

Source: USDA (1969). Food for us all. Yearbook of Agriculture.

Nutrients in Crops

TABLE 2.N.8
Approximate pounds per acre of nutrients contained in portion of the size of crop (will vary with variety, soil type, season and fertility of soil)

Crop Kind	Part	Acre Yield Bushels	Acre Yield Tons	Nitrogen	Phosphorus as P$_2$O$_5$	Potassium as K$_2$O	Calcium	Magnesium	Sulfur	Boron	Copper	Manganese	Zinc
Grains													
Barley	Grain	40	0.96	35	15	10	1	2	3	0.04	0.03	0.03	0.06
	Straw		1	15	5	30	8	2	4		.01	.32	.05
Corn	Grain	100	3.5	90	36	26	10	14	9	.08	.04	.06	.10
	Stover		3	67	24	96	18	12	7		.03	1.00	.20
Oats	Grain	80	1.28	50	20	15	2	3	5		.03	.12	.05
	Straw		2	25	15	80	8	8	9		.03		.29
Rice	Rough grain	100	2.25	60	24	12	4	5	4		.01	.10	.08
	Straw		3	36	12	80	11	6				1.89	
Rye	Grain	30	0.84	35	10	10	2	3	7		.02	.22	.03
	Straw		1.5	15	8	25	8	2	3		.01	.14	.07
Sorghum	Grain	80	2	65	35	20	4	18	5			.04	.04
	Straw		3	85	25	125	29						
Wheat	Grain	40	1.2	50	25	15	1	6	3	.04	.03	.09	.14
	Straw		1.5	20	5	35	6	3	5		.01	.16	.05
Hay													
Alfalfa[1]			4	180	40	180	112	21	19	.06	.06	.44	.42
Bluegrass			2	60	20	60	16	7	5		.02	.30	.08
Cowpea[1]			2	120	25	80	55	15	13	.21		.65	
Peanut[1]			2	91	22	83	39	15	14		.03	.20	.28
Red Clover[1]			2	80	20	80	55	14	6	.05	.04	.44	.15
Soybean[1]			2	90	20	50	40	18	10	.01	.02	.46	.16
Timothy			2	48	20	76	14	5	4			.25	
Fruits and Vegetables													
Apples		500	12	30	10	45	8	5	10	.01	.03	.03	.03
Beans, dry		30	0.9	75	25	25	2	2	5	.12	.02	.03	.06
Cabbage	Heads		20	130	35	130	20	8	44	.09	.04	.10	.08
Onions			15	90	40	80	22	4	16		.06	.16	.62
Oranges		(800-70-lb. boxes)	28	85	30	140	33	12	9	.14	.20	.06	.24
Peaches		600	14.4	35	20	65	4	8	8	.05	.04		.01
Potatoes	Tubers	400	12	80	30	150	3	6	6	.05	.02	.09	.05
Spinach			5	50	15	30	12	5	4			.10	.10
Sweet Potatoes	Roots		8.25	45	15	75	4	9	6	.05	.03	.06	.03
Tomatoes	Fruit	300	20	120	40	160	7	11	14	.14	.07	.13	.16
Other Crops													
Cotton	Seed & lint		.75	40	20	15	2	4	2		.06	.11	.32
	Stalks, leaves & burs			35	10	35	28	8					
Peanuts[1]	Nuts	40	1	68	8	11	1	2	4	.03	.02	.01	
Soybeans[1]	Grain		1.2	150	35	55	7	7	4		.04	.05	.04
Sugar Beets	Roots		20	80	27	66	44	32	13		.04	1.00	
Sugar Cane			30	96	54	270	28	24	24			.55	
Tobacco	Leaves		1	75	15	120	75	18	14	.05	.03		.07

[1] Legumes normally get the greater part of their nitrogen from the air. Computed from data in USDA Misc. Publ. 369. Morrison's Feed and Feeding, from a Spec. USDA rept. by Lowe. USDA Tech. Bull. 1009, Our Land and Its Care. American Potash Institute, and other sources, by A. L. Mehring.

Source: Garman, W. H. (editor) (19xx). *The Fertilizer Handbook,* 2nd Edition. Fertilizer Institute.

Nutritional Labeling

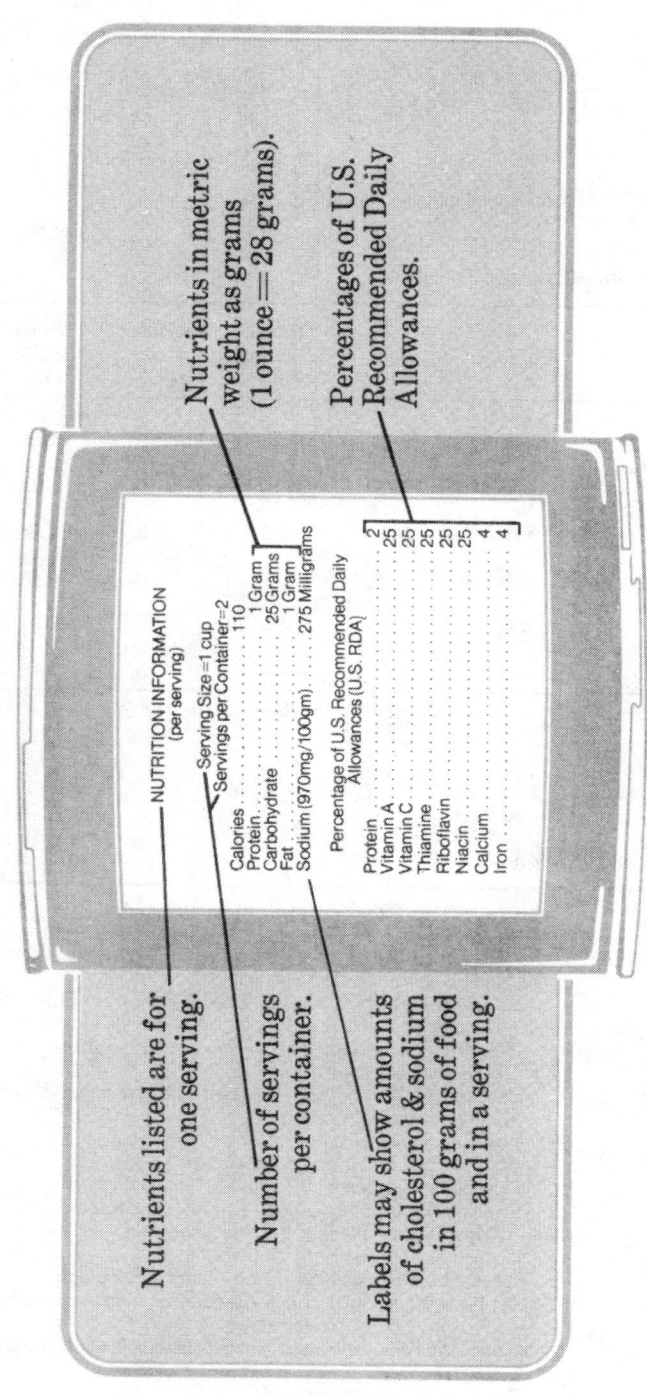

FIGURE 2.N.3.

Source: FDA (1980). Read the label, set a better table. FDA DHHS Publication No. 76-2049.

Oil Meals, Composition

TABLE 2.O.1
Composition of the common oil meals

Feeding Stuff	Dry Matter (%)	Ash (%)	Crude Protein (%)	Crude Fiber (%)	Crude Lipide (%)	N-free Extract (%)
Soybean meal (solvent process)	90.4	6.1	45.7	5.9	1.3	31.4
Cottonseed meal (hydraulic) (Texas analyses)	92.6	5.6	42.1	10.5	6.1	28.3
Linseed meal (solvent process)	91.0	5.8	36.6	9.3	1.0	38.3
Peanut meal (hydraulic) (hulls)	92.3	4.8	41.1	15.0	6.6	24.8
Safflower (hydraulic) (hulled)	90.5	6.4	42.5	8.5	6.7	26.4
Sunflower (hydraulic) (hulled)	94.3	5.9	49.5	5.4	4.9	28.6

Source: Mallette, M. F., Althouse, P. M., and Clagett, C. O. *Biochemistry of Plants and Animals.* John Wiley & Sons, New York.

Oil or Fat, Characteristics

TABLE 2.O.2
Characteristics of oil or fat

Oil or Fat	Identifiable Characteristics
Babassu kernel oil	High saponification value, low iodine value, contains lauric acid
Castor oil	Solubility characteristics, high hydroxyl value, high viscosity
Coconut oil	High saponification value—low iodine value—contains lauric acid
Cottonseed oil	Positive Halphen test—not reliable for heated or hydrogenated oils
Kapok oil	Positive Besson test
Linseed oil	Bromo-derivatives of unsaturated fatty acid
Olive oil	Contains squalene
Peanut oil	Positive Bellier test—contains arachidic acid
Perilla oil	Bromo-derivatives of unsaturated fatty acids
Rape seed oil	Contains erucic acid
Ravison oil	Resembles rapeseed oil—contains erucic acid
Sesame oil	Positive Baudouin and Villavecchia tests—not destroyed by hydrogenation
Soybean oil	Contains linolenic acid but no reliable specific tests available
Teaseed oil	Positive Fitelson test
Butterfat	Contains butyric and other low molecular weight fatty acids
Fish oils	Contain squalene, also bromo-derivatives of unsaturated fatty acids

Source: Mahlenbacher, C. V. *The Analysis of Fats and Oils.* Garrard Press, Champaign, Illinois.

Oils and Fats, Composition

TABLE 2.O.3
Composition of the edible portion (EP) and refuse in the material as purchased (AP)

Item No.	Commodity and Description	Water	Protein	Fat	Carbohydrate Total (By Dif)	Fiber	Ash	Cal (No./100 g)	Notes	Refuse in AP (%)
		Percent of Edible Portion								
	Vegetable									
277	Oils, pure			100	0			884	Cottonseed, sesame, coconut, olive, etc.	0
278	Shortening (hardened)			100	0			884		0
279	Margarine (either vegetable or animal)	15.5	0.6	81	0.4		2.5	720		0
	Marine									
280	Liver oils, body oils			100	0			902		0
	Animal fats									
281	Butter	15.5	0.6	81	0.4		2.5	716	Butter, "fat basis"	0
282	Ghee			100	0			879		0
283	Lard, leaf fat	5	2	93	0		0.1	847		0
284	Pork fat, other	12	4	84	0		0.2	775	Fat trimmed from pork carcasses	0
285	Pork fat, all	8	3	89	0		0.1	816		0
286	Suet, tallow (kidney fat)	5	2	93	0		0.1	847	Fat trimmed from beef, veal, mutton or lamb	0
287	Meat fat, rendered			100	0			902	Lard or tallow, "fat basis"	0

Source: Chatfield, C. *Food Composition Tables for International Use.* Food and Agriculture Organization, United Nations, Rome.

Oils, Seed and Fruit

TABLE 2.O.4
Oil content and composition of some seeds and fruits

Tissue and Species	Fat, %, Dry-weight Basis	Lauric	My-ristic	Pal-mitic	Stearic	Oleic	Lin-oleic	Lin-olenic	α-Eleo-stearic	Ricin-oleic
Nut or seed										
Peanut	45			8.3	3.1	56.0	26.0			
Cotton (whole seed)	20		0.5	21.9	1.9	30.7	44.9			
Soybean	18		0.1	9.8	2.4	28.4	50.7	6.5		
Flaxseed	38		0.2	5.4	3.5	19.0	24.0	47.0		
Palm	50		1.5	42.9	4.7	39.8	11.3			
Coconut (copra)	67	46.4	18.0	9.0	1.0	7.6	1.6			
Castor bean	48					7.4	3.1			87.0
Tung (kernel)	58			5.5		4.0	8.5		82.0	
Seed germ										
Corn	35		0.5	10.0	3.5	33.0	53.0			
Fruit										
Olive	30–65		1.2	15.6	2.0	64.6	15.0			

Source: Mallette, M. F., Althouse, P. M., and Clagett, C. O. *Biochemistry of Plants and Animals*. John Wiley & Sons, New York.

Oil, Triglyceride Mole Percent Composition

TABLE 2.0.5
Analysis of glycerides [triglyceride composition (mole %) of oils]

Triglyceride	Corn Oil	Cottonseed Oil	Groundnut Oil (Argentine)	Safflower seed Oil	Sesame Oil	Soyabean Oil	Sunflower seed Oil
0 double bonds							
SSS		0.5					
1 double bond							
SOS	} 2.5	4.5	2.3	} 1.7	} 3.1	1.1	0.3
SSO		0.8	0.7			0.3	0.2
2 double bonds							
SOO	6.0	4.8	8.7	} 1.2	} 8.1	2.9	2.3
OSO	0.3	0.3	0.8			0.4	0.1
SLS	5.0	12.4	5.3	} 2.2	} 3.4	2.8	2.2
SSL	0.1	0.6	0.6			0.6	0.3
3 double bonds							
OOO	4.0	0.8	6.2	0.2	7.7	1.5	1.3
SOL	6.6	9.4	5.0			4.1	4.4
SLO	7.0	8.4	15.7	} 8.1	} 16.7	5.0	5.0
OSL	0.7	0.6	1.0			0.4	0.5
SSLe						0.1	
SLeS							
4 double bonds							
OOL	8.4	4.1	7.8	} 1.7	} 21.8	6.7	8.1
OLO	4.2	1.6	8.7			2.5	3.1
SLL	13.8	22.5	10.7	} 20.1	} 9.2	13.9	13.2
LSL	0.4	1.1	1.2			0.9	1.3
SOLe	} 0.1					0.2	
SLeO						0.2	
OSLe							
5 double bonds							
OLL	15.3	6.4	17.8	} 21.3	} 19.8	13.5	20.4
LOL	4.8	6.5	2.2			5.1	8.4
OOLe	} 0.3		} 0.2			0.2	
OLeO						0.6	
SLeL		} 0.4				0.4	
SLLe	} 1.0		} 0.7			0.3	
LSLe						0.5	
6 double bonds							
LLL	16.3	13.0	3.9	43.5	10.2	} 35.8	28.1
Remaining with 6 or more double bonds	3.2	1.3	0.5				0.8

Source: Boekenoogen, H. A. (1968). Oils, Fats and Fat Products, Vol. 2. John Wiley & Sons, New York.

Olives and Pickles, Composition

TABLE 2.0.6

(Dashes (—) denote lack of reliable data for a constituent believed to be present in measurable amount)

Foods, approximate measures, units, and weight (edible part unless footnotes indicate otherwise)		Water	Food energy	Pro-tein	Fat	Fatty Acids			Carbo-hydrate	Calcium	Phos-phorus	Iron	Potas-sium	Vitamin A value	Thiamin	Ribo-flavin	Niacin	Ascorbic acid
						Satu-rated (total)	Unsaturated Oleic	Lino-leic										
	Grams	Per-cent	Cal-ories	Grams	Grams	Grams	Grams	Grams	Grams	Milli-grams	Milli-grams	Milli-grams	Milli-grams	Inter-national units	Milli-grams	Milli-grams	Milli-grams	Milli-grams
Olives, pickled, canned:																		
Green—— 4 medium or 3 extra large or 2 giant.[69]	16	78	15	Trace	2	.2	1.2	.1	Trace	8	2	.2	7	40	—	—	—	—
Ripe, Mission—— 3 small or 2 large[69]	10	73	15	Trace	2	.2	1.2	.1	Trace	9	1	.1	2	10	Trace	Trace	—	—
Pickles, cucumber:																		
Dill, medium, whole, 3 3/4 in long, 1 1/4-in diam.—— 1 pickle	65	93	5	Trace	Trace	—	—	—	1	17	14	.7	130	70	Trace	.01	Trace	4
Fresh-pack, slices 1 1/2-in diam., 1/4 in thick.—— 2 slices	15	79	10	Trace	Trace	—	—	—	3	5	4	.3	—	20	Trace	Trace	Trace	1
Sweet, gherkin, small, whole, about 2 1/2 in long, 3/4-in diam.—— 1 pickle	15	61	20	Trace	Trace	—	—	—	5	2	2	.2	—	10	Trace	Trace	Trace	1
Relish, finely chopped, sweet—— 1 tbsp	15	63	20	Trace	Trace	—	—	—	5	3	2	.1	—	—	—	—	—	—

[69]Weight includes pits. Without pits, weight is 13 g for item 701, 9 g for item 702.

Source: Consumer and Food Economics Institute (1977). Nutritive value of foods. USDA Home and Garden Bull. 72.

Orange Essence Oils

TABLE 2.O.7
Physicochemical properties of orange essence oils

Property	Max	Min	Avg
Sp gr 25°C/25°C	0.8428	0.8403	0.8415
Ref ind η_D^{20}	1.4725	1.4721	1.4723
Opt rot α_D^{25}	+99.16	+97.68	+98.42
Aldehyde (%)	1.86	1.28	1.57
Evap res (%)	1.29	0.34	0.81
Acid No.	0.22	0.11	0.16
Free acid (%)	0.06	0.03	0.04
Ester No. before acetylation	3.08	2.94	3.00
% ester before acetylation	1.08	1.03	1.05
Ester No. after acetylation	6.50	5.43	6.06
% ester after acetylation	2.27	1.90	2.12
Free alcohol (%)	0.97	0.64	0.84
Total alcohol (%)	1.78	1.49	1.66

Source: Kesterson, J. W., Hendrickson, R., and Braddock, R. J. (1971). Florida citrus oils. Florida Agric. Exp. Sta. Tech. Bull. *749*.

Orange Oil Composition

TABLE 2.O.8
Chemical composition of cold-pressed valencia orange oil

TERPENES:

α-thujene
α-pinene
camphene
2,4-p-menthadiene
sabinene
myrcene
δ-3-carene
α-phellandrene
α-terpinene
d-limonene
β-terpinene
p-cymene
α-terpinolene
α-β-cubebene
α-β-copaene
β-elemene
caryophyllene
farnesene
α-β-humulene
valencene
δ-cadinene

ALDEHYDES:

formaldehyde
acetaldehyde
n-hexanal
n-heptanal
n-octanal
n-nonanal
n-decanal
n-undecanal
n-dodecanal
citral ⎰ neral
⎱ geranial
citronellal
α-sinensal
β-sinensal
trans-hexen-2-al-1
dodecene-2-al-1
furfural
perillyldehyde
Aldehyde A
B
C
D
E

OXIDES:

trans-limonene oxide
cis-limonene oxide

ALCOHOLS:

methyl alcohol
ethyl alcohol
amyl alcohol
n-octanol
n-decanol
linalool
citronellol
α-terpineol
n-nonanol
trans-carveol
geraniol
nerol
heptanol
undecanol
dodecanol
elemol
cis-trans-2,8-p-menthadiene-1-ol
cis-carveol
1-p-methene-9-ol
1,8-p-menthadiene-9-ol
8-p-methene-1,2-diol
isopulegol
borneol
methyl heptenol
hexanol-1
terpinen-4-ol

ESTERS:

perillyl acetate
n-octyl acetate
bornyl acetate
geranyl formate
terpinyl acetate
linalyl acetate
linalyl propionate
geranyl acetate
nonyl acetate
decyl acetate
neryl acetate
citronellyl acetate
ethyl isovalerate
geranyl butyrate
1,8-p-menthadiene-9-yl-acetate

ACIDS:

formic
acetic
caprylic
capric

KETONES:

carvone
methyl heptenone
α-ionone
acetone
piperitenone
6-methyl-5-hepten-2-one
nootkatone

α,β-DIALKYL ACROLEINS:

α-hexyl-β-heptyl acrolein
α-hexyl-β-octyl acrolein
α-heptyl-β-heptyl acrolein
α-octyl-β-heptyl acrolein
α-hexyl-β-nonyl acrolein
α-octyl-β-octyl acrolein

α-heptyl-β-nonyl acrolein

PARAFIN WAXES:

n-$C_{21}H_{44}$

2-methyl-$C_{21}H_{43}$

n-$C_{22}H_{46}$

2-methyl-$C_{22}H_{45}$

n-$C_{23}H_{48}$

3-methyl-$C_{23}H_{47}$

n-$C_{24}H_{30}$

2-methyl-$C_{24}H_{49}$

n-$C_{25}H_{52}$

3-methyl-$C_{25}H_{51}$

n-$C_{26}H_{54}$

2-methyl-$C_{26}H_{53}$

n-$C_{27}H_{56}$

3-methyl-$C_{27}H_{55}$

n-$C_{28}H_{58}$

2-methyl-$C_{28}H_{57}$

n-$C_{29}H_{60}$

Source: Kesterson, J. W., Hendrickson, R., and Braddock, R. J. (1971). Florida citrus oils. Florida Agric. Exp. Sta. Tech. Bull. *749.*

Orange Oil Properties

TABLE 2.O.9
Maximum and minimum values for the properties of cold-pressed orange oil produced by various methods

Method of Extraction	Pipkin Roll		Screw Press		Fraser-Brace		FMC Rotary		FMC In-Line		AMC Scarifier		Brown Shaver	
No. of Samples	21		123		52		112		237		2		4	
Yield, lbs. oil/ton fruit	0.75 to 1.0		3.5 to 5.0		4.5 to 7.5		2.0 to 3.0		3.0 to 4.5		3.0 to 5.0		3.5 to 6.0	
Property	Max.	Min.	Max.	Min.	Max.	Min.	Max.	Min.	Max.	Min.	Max.	Min.	Max.	Min.
Sp. grav. 25°C/25°C	0.8432	0.8420	0.8426	0.8416	0.8458	0.8441	0.8443	0.8420	0.8438	0.8424	0.8449	0.8433	0.8435	0.8427
Ref. ind. η^{20}_D	1.4734	1.4718	1.4733	1.4719	1.4743	1.4730	1.4737	1.4722	1.4731	1.4725	1.4731	1.4728	1.4730	1.4730
Ref. ind. 10% dist. η^{20}_D	1.4722	1.4708	1.4723	1.4707	1.4724	1.4703	1.4727	1.4707	1.4717	1.4715	1.4716	1.4716	1.4723	1.4719
Difference	0.0013	0.0007	0.0015	0.0007	0.0031	0.0016	0.0015	0.0010	0.0014	0.0010	0.0015	0.0012	0.0011	0.0007
Opt. rot. α^{25}_D	+98.05	+96.64	+97.80	+96.53	+96.30	+94.54	+97.57	+94.98	+97.08	+95.32	+96.70	+96.36	+97.32	+97.18
Opt. rot. 10% dist. α^{25}_D	+98.31	+97.30	+98.65	+97.24	+98.70	+96.96	+98.73	+96.49	+97.92	+95.74	+98.16	+97.47	+99.11	+98.09
Difference	+1.28	+0.01	+1.41	+0.03	+3.70	+1.51	+2.00	+0.00	+1.51	+0.11	+1.80	+0.77	+1.89	+0.80
Aldehyde content, %	2.02	1.63	1.85	0.92	1.65	0.93	2.04	1.17	1.96	1.54	1.86	1.86	1.66	0.86
Ester content, %	1.01	0.15	1.09	0.04	1.63	0.35	1.34	0.08	—	—	—	—	—	—
Evaporation residue, %	2.42	1.07	2.23	1.37	4.93	3.12	3.22	1.85	3.08	2.45	4.00	2.80	2.56	2.17

Source: Kesterson, J. W., Hendrickson, R., and Braddock, R. J. (1971). Florida citrus oils. Florida Agric. Exp. Sta. Tech. Bull. 749.

Orange Structure

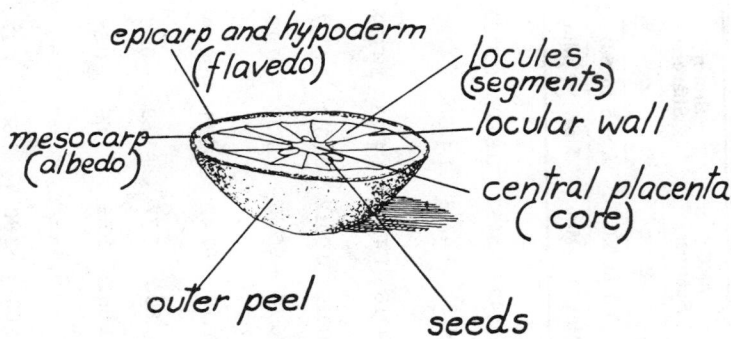

FIGURE 2.0.1
Macroscopic structure of halved orange

Source: Veldhuis, M. K. (1971). Orange and tangerine juices. In *Fruit and Vegetable Juice Processing Technology,* 2nd Edition. Donald K. Tressler, and Maynard A. Joslyn (editors). AVI Publishing Co., Westport, Connecticut.

Organic Acids in Fruits and Vegetables

TABLE 2.0.10
Natural acids found in fruits and vegetables

Acid	Chemical Formula	Product
Malic	$C_4H_6O_5$	Apples, cherries, plums, cauliflower
Citric	$C_6H_8O_7$	Apricots, bananas, lemons, lima beans
Oxalic	$C_4H_8O_8$	Sorrel, rhubarb, apricots, blueberries
Tartaric	$C_4H_6O_6$	Grapes, apples, cherries
Benzoic	$C_6H_5CO_2HC_7H_6O_2$	Cranberries, benzoin, Peru and Tolu balsams
Succinic	$C_4H_6O_4$	Currants, cranberries
Quinic	$C_7H_{12}O_7$	Cranberries, carrot leaves, quinine, pears
Isocitric	$C_6H_8O_7$	Blueberries
Fumaric	$C_4H_4O_4$	Gooseberries, apples, watermelon

Source: Berarde, M. A. (1971). *The Chemicals We Eat.* McGraw-Hill Book Company, New York.

Organ Weights

TABLE 2.O.11
Weights of organs in the human body (conventional standard man)

Organ	Mass (g)	Organ	Mass (g)
Total body	70,000	Lungs (2)	1,000
Muscle	30,000	Lymphoid tissue	700
Skin and subcutaneous tissue	6,100	Kidneys (2)	200
Skin only	2,000	Heart	300
Fat	10,000	Spleen	150
Skeleton		Urinary bladder	150
Without bone marrow	7,000	Pancreas	70
Red marrow	1,500	Salivary glands (6)	50
Yellow marrow	1,500	Testes (2)	40
Blood	5,400	Spinal cord	30
Gastrointestinal tract	2,000	Eyes (2)	30
Contents of gastrointestinal tract		Thyroid gland	20
Stomach	250	Teeth	20
Small intestine	1,000	Prostate gland	20
Upper large intestine	135	Adrenal glands or suprarenal (2)	20
Lower large intestine	150	Thymus	10
Liver	1,700	Miscellaneous (blood vessels,	
Brain	1,500	cartilage, nerves, etc.)	390

Source: Wang, Y. (editor) (1969). *Handbook of Radioactive Nuclides.* CRC Press, Cleveland.

Packinghouse By-products Composition

TABLE 2.P.1
Composition of some typical packinghouse by-products

Feeding Stuff	Dry Matter (%)	Ash (%)	Crude Protein (%)	Crude Fiber (%)	Crude Lipid (%)	N-free Extract (%)
Blood meal	92.2	4.7	84.7	1.1	1.0	0.7
Fish meal	92.9	17.6	63.9	0.6	6.8	4.0
Meat scraps	93.9	25.4	55.8	2.1	9.3	1.3
No. 1 tankage	93.1	20.2	60.6	2.0	8.5	1.8

Source: Mallette, M. F., Althouse, P. M., and Clagett, C. O. *Biochemistry of Plants and Animals.* John Wiley & Sons, New York.

Paired Comparisons

TABLE 2.P.2
Paired comparison-number of correct selections required to indicate significant differences

Total Number of Comparisons	Number of Correct Choices for Odds: 19:1 (5 Per cent Level)	99:1 (1 Per cent Level)	999:1 (.1 Per cent Level)
6	6	. .	. .
8	7	8	. .
10	9	10	. .
12	10	11	. .
14	11	12	14
16	13	14	15
18	14	15	17
20	15	16	18
25	18	20	22
30	21	23	25
35	24	26	28
40	27	29	32
45	30	32	35
50	33	35	38
60	38	41	44
70	44	46	50
80	50	52	56
90	55	58	62
100	60	63	67
200	113	116	121
300	165	169	175
400	218	223	230
500	270	276	284
600	332	338	347
700	374	480	490
800	427	434	445
900	479	487	499
1000	531	539	552

Source: Kramer, A., and Twigg, B. A. (1968). Statistical quality control. In *The Freezing Preservation of Foods*, Vol. 3, 4th Edition, D. K. Tressler, W. B. Van Arsdel, and M. J. Copley (editors). AVI Publishing Co., Westport, Connecticut.

Paired Taste Tests

TABLE 2.P.3
Significance in paired taste tests ($p = \frac{1}{2}$)

No. of Tasters or Tastings	Minimum Agreeing Judgments Necessary to Establish Significant Differentiation (Two-tail Test)			Minimum Correct Answers Necessary to Establish Significant Differentiation (One-tail Test)		
	Probability Level			Probability Level		
	0.05	0.01	0.001	0.05	0.01	0.001
5	—	—	—	5	—	—
6	—	—	—	6	—	—
7	7	—	—	7	7	—
8	8	8	—	7	8	—
9	8	9	—	8	9	—
10	9	10	—	9	10	10
11	10	11	11	9	10	11
12	10	11	12	10	11	12
13	11	12	13	10	12	13
14	12	13	14	11	12	13
15	12	13	14	12	13	14
16	13	14	15	12	14	15
17	13	15	16	13	14	16
18	14	15	17	13	15	16
19	15	16	17	14	15	17
20	15	17	18	15	16	18
21	16	17	19	15	17	18
22	17	18	19	16	17	19
23	17	19	20	16	18	20
24	18	19	21	17	19	20
25	18	20	21	18	19	21
26	19	20	22	18	20	22
27	20	21	23	19	20	22
28	20	22	23	19	21	23
29	21	22	24	20	22	24
30	21	23	25	20	22	24
31	22	24	25	21	23	25
32	23	24	26	22	24	26
33	23	25	27	22	24	26
34	24	25	27	23	25	27
35	24	26	28	23	25	27
36	25	27	29	24	26	28
37	25	27	29	24	27	29
38	26	28	30	25	27	29
39	27	28	31	26	28	30
40	27	29	31	26	28	31
41	28	30	32	27	29	31
42	28	30	32	27	29	32
43	29	31	33	28	30	32
44	29	31	34	28	31	33
45	30	32	34	29	31	34
46	31	33	35	30	32	34
47	31	33	36	30	32	35
48	32	34	36	31	33	36
49	32	34	37	31	34	36
50	33	35	37	32	34	37
60	39	41	44	37	40	43
70	44	47	50	43	46	49
80	50	52	56	48	51	55
90	55	58	61	54	57	61
100	61	64	67	59	63	66

Source: Roessler, E. B., Baker, G. A., and Amerine, M. A. One-tailed and two-tailed tests in organoleptic comparisons. Food Res. 21, 117.

Pan Broiling Meat

TABLE 2.P.4
Recommendations for pan broiling meats

1. Place meat in heavy frying pan.
2. Do not add fat or water. Do not cover.
3. Cook slowly, turning occasionally.
4. Pour fat from pan as it accumulates.
5. Brown meat on both sides.
6. Cook to desired doneness. Season if desired. Serve at once.

Source: Be a Smarter Shopper...a Better Cook. (1973). National Live Stock and Meat Board, Chicago.

Pan Frying Meat

TABLE 2.P.5
Recommendations for pan frying meats

1. Brown meat on both sides in small amount of fat.
2. Season with salt and pepper if desired.
3. Do not cover.
4. Cook at moderate temperature until done, turning occasionally
5. Remove from pan and serve at once.

Source: Be a Smarter Shopper...a Better Cook. (1973). National Live Stock and Meat Board, Chicago.

Pantothenic Acid Content

TABLE 2.P.6
The daily amount in a normal diet is more than adequate. The following shows the pantothenic acid content of some foods which are good sources.

Brewer's dry yeast	200 γ/g	Spinach (fresh)	26 γ/g
Beef liver	76 γ/g	Wheat bran	30 γ/g
Egg yolk	63 γ/g	Roasted peanuts	25 γ/g
Kidney	35 γ/g	Whole milk powder	24 γ/g
Buckwheat	26 γ/g	Bread	5 γ/g

Source: Braverman, J. B. S. *Introduction to the Biochemistry of Foods.* ASP Biological and Medical Press (Elsevier Division), New York.

Pear Firmness

TABLE 2.P.7

Variety	Firmness[1]		
	Maximum	Optimum	Minimum
	Pounds	*Pounds*	*Pounds*
Anjou	15	13	10
Bartlett	19	17	15
Bosc	16	13	11
Comice	13	11	9
Hardy	11	10	9
Kieffer	15	14	12
Seckel	18	16	14
Winter Nelis	15	12	11

[1] As measured by a Magness-Taylor pressure tester with a 5/16-inch plunger tip.

Source: USDA (1978). Pear production. USDA Agriculture Handbook Number 526.

Pecan Varieties

TABLE 2.P.8

Variety	State of origin	Pollination type*	Relative production	Kernel quality	Disease resistance
		Southeast			
Chickasaw	Tex.	II	excellent	fair	good
Desirable	Fla.	I	good	good	fair
Elliott	Fla.	II	good	fair	good
Farley	—	I	fair	excellent	fair
Kernodle	Fla.	II	fair	good	fair
Mahan	Miss.	II	fair	poor	poor
Schley	Miss.	II	good	excellent	poor
Stuart	Miss.	II	good	good	good
		Southwest			
Ideal	—	II	good	good	poor
San Saba Imp.	Tex.	I	good	good	poor
Sioux	Tex.	II	good	excellent	poor
Western	Tex.	I	excellent	good	poor
Wichita	Tex.	II	excellent	excellent	poor

Variety	State of origin	Pollination type*	Kernel quality	Remarks
		Midwest		
Colby	Ill.	II	poor	Retains foliage late in fall
Fritz	Ill.	II	—	Hardy tree for extreme north
Greenriver	Ky.	II	good	Susceptible to spring frost
Major	Ky.	I	good	Good producer; susceptible to aphids
Perque	Mo.	I	good	Susceptible to aphids, squirrels and birds

* I. Pollen shed before females are receptive. II. Pollen shed after females are receptive. Interplant at least one tree from each group for best pollination.

Source: USDA (1977). Growing fruits and nuts. USDA Agriculture Information Bull. *408.*

Pectic Acid Formula

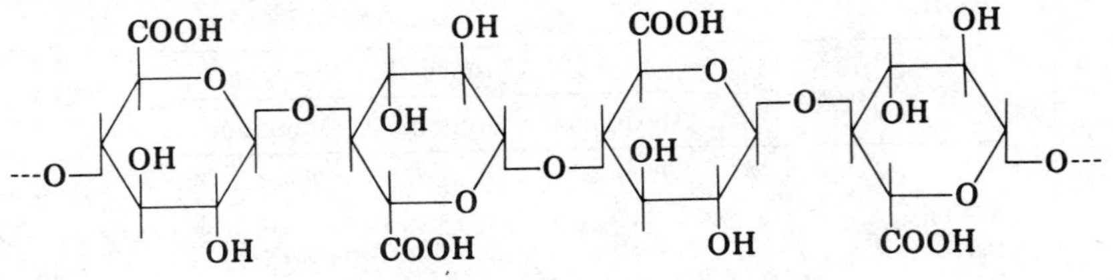

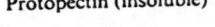

FIGURE 2.P.1
Structure of pectic acid

Source: Braverman, J. B. S. *Introduction to the Biochemistry of Foods.* ASP Biological and Medical Press (Elsevier Division), New York.

Pectin

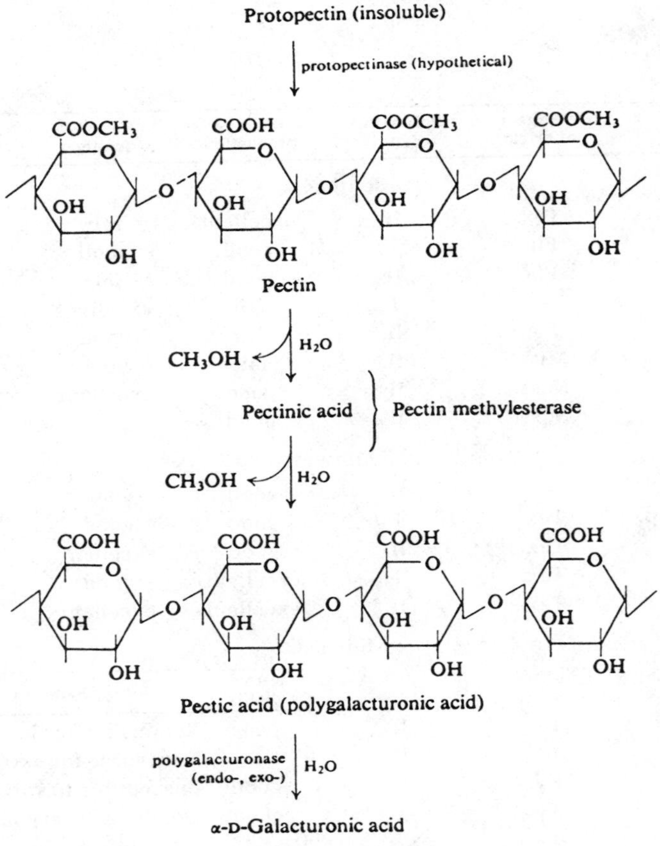

Protopectin (insoluble)

↓ protopectinase (hypothetical)

Pectin

CH_3OH ← H_2O

Pectinic acid } Pectin methylesterase

CH_3OH ← H_2O

Pectic acid (polygalacturonic acid)

polygalacturonase (endo-, exo-) H_2O ↓

α-D-Galacturonic acid

FIGURE 2.P.2
Structure of pectin

Source: Eskin, N. A. M., Henderson, H. M., and Townsend, R. J. (1971). *Biochemistry of Foods.* Academic Press, New York.

Pectin Content

TABLE 2.P.9
Pectin content of several plant tissues

Tissue	Pectin (%)
Potato	2.5
Tomato	3
Apple	5-7
Apple pomace	15-20
Carrot	10
Sunflower heads	25
Sugar beet pulp	15-20
Citrus albedo	30-35

Source: Schultz, H. W., Cain, R. F., and Wrolstad, R. W. (editors) (1969). *Symposium on Foods; Carbohydrates and Their Roles*. AVI Publishing Co., Westport, Connecticut.

Pectin Formula

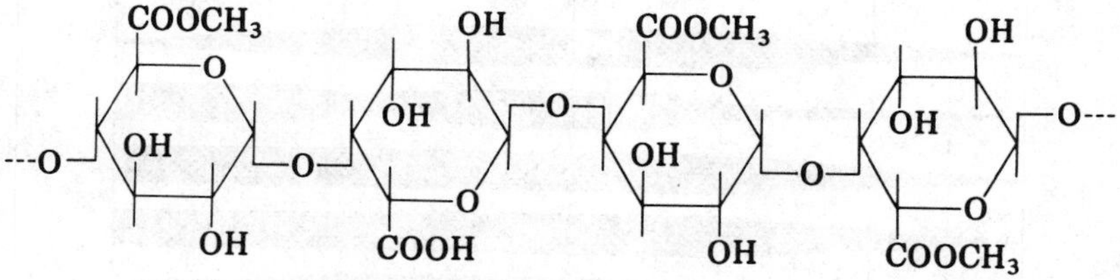

FIGURE 2.P.3
Structure of a portion of the pectin molecule

Source: Braverman, J. B. S. *Introduction to the Biochemistry of Foods*. ASP Biological and Medical Press (Elsevier Division), New York.

Pentosans

TABLE 2.P.10
Pentosans in plant materials (undried basis)

	(%)		(%)
Navy bean	8.4	Cabbage	1.0
Corn meal	5.0	Wheat bran	22.0
Corn (whole)	7.4	Wheat straw	27.1
Dried peas	7.2	Corn fodder	21.8
Barley (whole)	11.1	Corn cobs	35.0
Cottonseed flour	5.6	Gum arabic	26.0
Beets	1.7	Cherry gum	52.0
Spinach	1.0		

Source: Peterson, W. H., Skinner, J. T., and Strong, F. M. *Elements of Food Biochemistry*. Prentice-Hall, Englewood Cliffs, New Jersey.

pH and Availability of Plant Nutrients

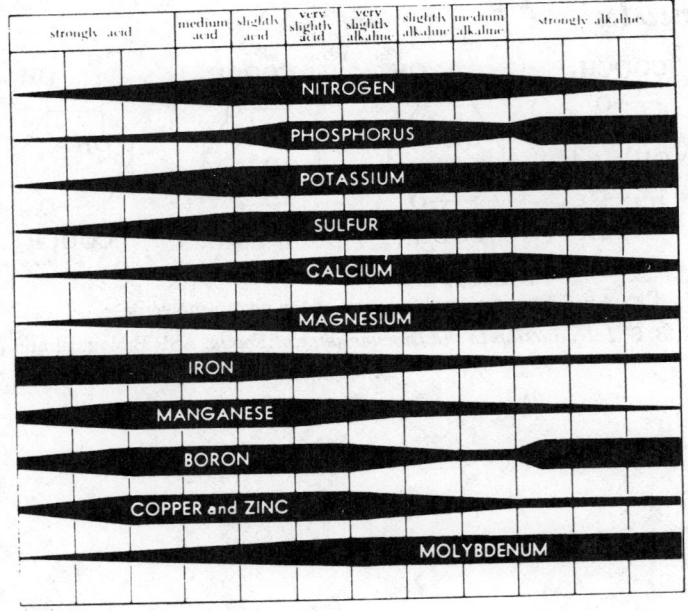

FIGURE 2.P.4
High soil pH affects availability of plant nutrients; the wider the bar, the greater the availability.

Source: Mittleider, J. R., and Nelson, A. N. (1970). *Food for Everyone*. Extension Division, Loma Linda University, Loma Linda, California.

pH, Buffer Solutions

TABLE 2.P.11
Buffer solutions for indicator measurements and pH control

25 ml 0.2 M KCl, x ml 0.2 M HCl, diluted to 100 ml				50 ml 0.1 M KH Phthalate, x ml 0.1 M HCl, diluted to 100 ml			
pH	x	pH	x	pH	x	pH	x
1.00	67.0	1.50	20.7	2.20	49.5	3.20	15.7
1.10	52.8	1.60	16.2	2.30	45.8	3.30	12.9
1.20	42.5	1.70	13.0	2.40	42.2	3.40	10.4
1.30	33.6	1.80	10.2	2.50	38.8	3.50	8.2
1.40	26.6	1.90	8.1	2.60	35.4	3.60	6.3
—	—	2.00	6.5	2.70	32.1	3.70	4.5
—	—	2.10	5.1	2.80	28.9	3.80	2.9
—	—	2.20	3.9	2.90	25.7	3.90	1.4
				3.00	22.3	4.00	0.1
				3.10	18.8	—	—

50 ml 0.1 M KH Phthalate, x ml 0.1 M NaOH, diluted to 100 ml				50 ml 0.1 M KH₂PO₄, x ml 0.1 M NaOH, diluted to 100 ml			
pH	x	pH	x	pH	x	pH	x
4.10	1.3	5.10	25.5	5.80	3.6	6.80	22.4
4.20	3.0	5.20	28.8	5.90	4.6	6.90	25.9
4.30	4.7	5.30	31.6	6.00	5.6	7.00	29.1
4.40	6.6	5.40	34.1	6.10	6.8	7.10	32.1
4.50	8.7	5.50	36.6	6.20	8.1	7.20	34.7
4.60	11.1	5.60	38.8	6.30	9.7	7.30	37.0
4.70	13.6	5.70	40.6	6.40	11.6	7.40	39.1
4.80	16.5	5.80	42.3	6.50	13.9	7.50	41.1
4.90	19.4	5.90	43.7	6.60	16.4	7.60	42.8
5.00	22.6	—	—	6.70	19.3	7.70	44.2
				—	—	7.80	45.3
				—	—	7.90	46.1
				—	—	8.00	46.7

50 ml 0.1 M Tris(hydroxmethyl)-aminomethane, x ml 0.1 M HCl, diluted to 100 ml				50 ml of a mixture 0.1 M with respect to both KCl and H₃BO₃, x ml 0.1 M NaOH, diluted to 100 ml			
pH	x	pH	x	pH	x	pH	x
7.00	46.6	8.00	29.2	8.00	3.9	9.00	20.8
7.10	45.7	8.10	26.2	8.10	4.9	9.10	23.6
7.20	44.7	8.20	22.9	8.20	6.0	9.20	26.4
7.30	43.4	8.30	19.9	8.30	7.2	9.30	29.3
7.40	42.0	8.40	17.2	8.40	8.6	9.40	32.1
7.50	40.3	8.50	14.7	8.50	10.1	9.50	34.6
7.60	38.5	8.60	12.4	8.60	11.8	9.60	36.9
7.70	36.6	8.70	10.3	8.70	13.7	9.70	38.9
7.80	34.5	8.80	8.5	8.80	15.8	9.80	40.6
7.90	32.0	8.90	7.0	8.90	18.1	9.90	42.2
—	—	9.00	5.7	—	—	10.00	43.7
				—	—	10.10	45.0
				—	—	10.20	46.2

(Continued)

pH, Buffer Solutions   (Continued)

TABLE 2.P.11   (Continued)

50 ml 0.025 M Borax, x ml 0.1 M HCl, diluted to 100 ml				50 ml 0.025 M Borax, x ml 0.1 M NaOH, diluted to 100 ml			
pH	x	pH	x	pH	x	pH	x
8.00	20.5	8.50	15.2	9.20	0.9	10.20	20.5
8.10	19.7	8.60	13.5	9.30	3.6	10.30	21.3
8.20	18.8	8.70	11.6	9.40	6.2	10.40	22.1
8.30	17.7	8.80	9.4	9.50	8.8	10.50	22.7
8.40	16.6	8.90	7.1	9.60	11.1	10.60	23.3
—	—	9.00	4.6	9.70	13.1	10.70	23.80
—	—	9.10	2.0	9.80	15.0	10.80	24.25
				9.90	16.7	—	—
				10.00	18.3		
				10.10	19.5		

50 ml 0.05 M NaHCO₃, x ml 0.1 M NaOH, diluted to 100 ml				50 ml 0.05 M Na₂HPO₄, x ml 0.1 M NaOH, diluted to 100 ml			
pH	x	pH	x	pH	x	pH	x
9.60	5.0	10.60	19.1	10.90	3.3	11.40	9.1
9.70	6.2	10.70	20.2	11.00	4.1	11.50	11.1
9.80	7.6	10.80	21.2	11.10	5.1	11.60	13.5
9.90	9.1	10.90	22.0	11.20	6.3	11.70	16.2
10.00	10.7	11.00	22.7	11.30	7.6	11.80	19.4
10.10	12.2	—	—	—	—	11.90	23.0
10.20	13.8	—	—	—	—	12.00	26.9
10.30	15.2	—	—				
10.40	16.5	—	—				
10.50	17.8	—	—				

25 ml 0.2 M KCl, x ml 0.2 M NaOH, diluted to 100 ml			
pH	x	pH	x
12.00	6.0	12.50	20.4
12.10	8.0	12.60	25.6
12.20	10.2	12.70	32.2
12.30	12.8	12.80	41.2
12.40	16.2	12.90	53.0
—	—	13.00	66.0

Source: Sober, H. A. (editor) (1968). *Handbook of Biochemistry: Selected Data for Molecular Biology.* CRC Press, Cleveland.

Phosphate

TABLE 2.P.12
Comparison of phosphate nomenclatures

Na_2HPO_4	
Disodium phosphate	Industry
Disodium hydrogen orthophosphate	Scientific
Sodium phosphate, dibasic	FCC
Disodium monophosphate	Codex Alimentarius
$Na_2H_2P_2O_7$	
Sodium acid pyrophosphate	Industry
Disodium dihydrogen phosphate	Scientific
Sodium acid pyrophosphate	FCC
Disodium diphosphate	Codex Alimentarius
$Na_5P_3O_{10}$	
Sodium tripolyphosphate	Industry
Pentasodium triphosphate	Scientific
Sodium tripolyphosphate	FCC
Pentasodium triphosphate	Codex Alimentarius
Glass	
Sodium hexametaphosphate	Industry
Glassy sodium polyphosphate	
$XNa_2O : yP_2O_5$ [1]	Scientific
Sodium metaphosphate	FCC
Sodium polyphosphate	Codex Alimentarius

[1] Suggested.

Source: Bell, R. N. (1971). The nomenclature and manufacture of phosphates. In *Phosphates in Food Processing, Symposium*. J. M. deMan and P. Melnychyn (editors). AVI Publishing Co., Westport, Connecticut.

Phosphorus

TABLE 2.P.13
Phosphorus content of foods

	mg/100 g		mg/100 g
Lima beans	142	Cauliflower	56
Peas	116	Potatoes	53
Corn	111	Onions	36
Artichoke	88	Cabbage	29
Brussels sprouts	80	Tomatoes	27
Broccoli	78	Bananas	26
Watermelon	69	Lettuce	22
Asparagus	62	Oranges	17

Source: White, P. L., and Selvey, N. (editors) (1974). *Nutritional Qualities of Fresh Fruits and Vegetables*. Futura Publishing Co., Mt. Kisco, New York.

pH, Post Mortem

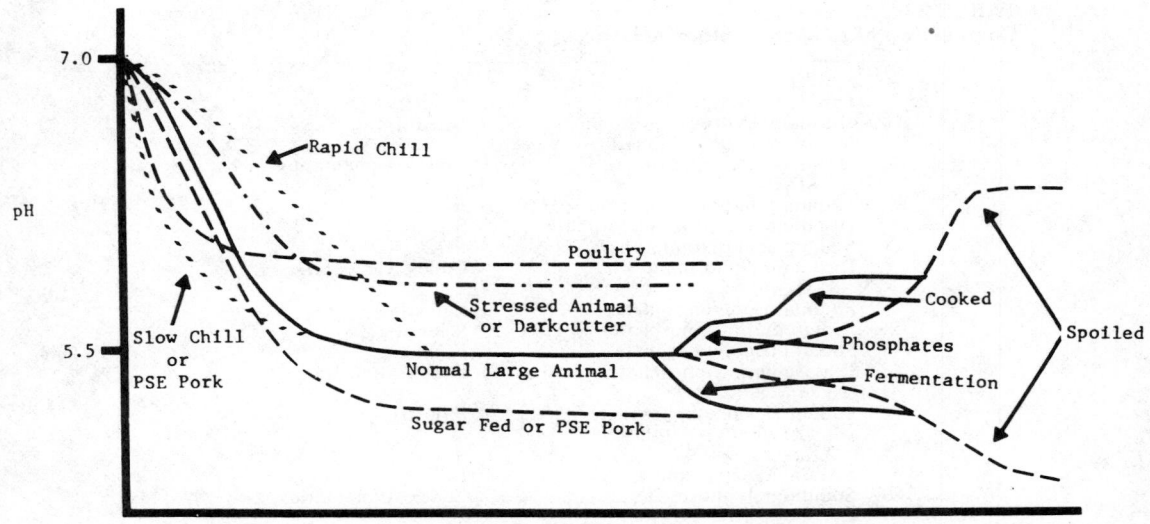

FIGURE 2.P.5

Alteration of pH plotted against time post mortem for a variety of tissues and conditions

Source: Ockerman, H. W. (1975). Chemistry of muscle and major organs. In *Meat Hygiene*. J. A. Libby (editor). Lea & Febiger, Philadelphia.

pH, Standard Solutions

TABLE 2.P.14
pH values of standard solutions

Normality	pH values			
	HCl	CH₃COOH	NaOH	NH₃
1	0.10	2.37	14.05	11.77
0.1	1.07	2.87	13.07	11.27
0.01	2.02	3.37	12.12	10.77
0.001	3.01	3.87	11.13	10.27
0.0001	4.01			

Source: The Merck Index, 8th Edition. (1968).
Merck & Co., Rahway, New Jersey.

pH, Universal Indicators

TABLE 2.P.15
For approximate pH determinations

pH	Color		pH	Color	
	No. 1	No. 2		No. i	No. 2
1	cherry-red	red	7	yellowish-green	greenish-yellow
2	rose	red	8	green	green
3	red-orange	red	9	bluish-green	greenish-blue
4	orange-red	deeper red	10	blue	violet
5	orange	orange-red	11	—	reddish-violet
6	yellow	orange-yellow			

No. 1. Dissolve 60 mg methyl yellow, 40 mg methyl red, 80 mg bromthymol blue, 100 mg thymol blue and 20 mg phenolphthalein in 100 ml of ethanol and add enough 0.1N NaOH to produce a yellow color.

No. 2. Dissolve 18.5 mg methyl red, 60 mg bromthymol blue and 64 mg phenolphthalein in 100 ml of 50% ethanol and add enough 0.1N NaOH to produce a green color.

Source: The Merck Index, 8th Edition. (1968). Merck & Co., Rahway, New Jersey.

pH, Values of Biological Materials

TABLE 2.P.16
pH values of representative biological materials

Material	pH Value	Material	pH Value
Blood, normal limits	7.3–7.5	Gastric juice, adult	0.9–1.6
Blood, extreme limits	7.0–7.8	Milk, cows, limits	6.2–7.3
Enzymes, activity range of		Milk, human	7.0–7.2
Amylopsin, optimum	7.0	Muscle juice	6.8
Erepsin, optimum	7.8	Plants (extracted juice)	
Invertase, optimum	5.5	Alfalfa tops	5.9
Lipase, pancreatic	7.0–8.0	Carrot	5.2
Maltase, optimum	6.1–6.8	Cucumber	5.1
Pepsin, optimum	1.5–2.4	Peas, field	6.8
Trypsin, optimum	8–9	Potato	6.1
Fruit juices		Rhubarb, stalks	3.4
Apple	3.8	String beans	5.2
Banana	4.6	Saliva	6.2–7.6
Grapefruit	3.0–3.3	Sweat	4.5–7.1
Orange	3.1–4.1	Tears	7.2
Tomato	4.2	Urine, human, limits	4.2–8.0

Source: Peterson, W. H., Skinner, J. T., and Strong, F. M. Elements of Food Biochemistry. Prentice-Hall, Englewood Cliffs, New Jersey.

Plant and Animal Poisoning

TABLE 2.P.17
Plant and animal poisoning

Disease	Reservoirs	Common Vehicle	Prevention and Control
Mushroom poisoning		Poisonous mushrooms (*Amanita phalloides*, *Amanita muscaria*, others).	Do not eat wild mushrooms. Amanita very poisonous when raw or cooked.
Fish poisoning	Pike, carp, sturgeon roe in breeding season.	Fish-Tedrodon, Meletta, Clupea, pickerel eggs.	Avoid eating roe during breeding season; heed local warnings concerning edible fish.
Shellfish poisoning	Probably plankton, food of mussels.	Mussels	Avoid eating shellfish during spawning season (July through September); toxin appears to be heat stable.

Source: U.S. Department of the Army (1969). Food inspection specialist. *TM 8-451.*

Plant Foods, Composition

TABLE 2.P.18
Foods of plant origin: composition

Values are per 100 g of edible portion of fresh, uncooked food, unless otherwise specified.   Values based on inadequate evidence are enclosed in parentheses.

	Food	Water	Food Energy	Protein	Fat	Carbohydrate Total	Carbohydrate Fiber	Ash	Ca	Fe	P	Vitamin A	Ascorbic Acid	Niacin	Riboflavin	Thiamine
		g	Cal	g	g	g	g	g	mg	mg	mg	I.U.	mg	mg	mg	mg
1	Apple (Pyrus malus)	84.1	58	0.3	0.4	14.9	1.0	0.3	6	0.3	10	90	5	0.2	0.03	0.04
2	Apricot (Prunus armeniaca)	85.4	51	1.0	0.1	12.9	0.6	0.6	16	0.5	23	2790	7	0.8	0.05	0.03
3	Asparagus (Asparagus officinalis)	93.0	21	2.2	0.2	3.9	0.7	0.7	21	0.9	62	1000	33	1.4	0.19	0.16
4	Avocado (Persea gratissima)	65.4	245	1.7	26.4	5.1	1.8	1.4	10	0.6	38	290	16	1.1	0.13	0.06
5	Banana (Musa paradisiaca sapientum)	74.8	88	1.2	0.2	23.0	0.6	0.8	28	8	0.6	430	10	0.7	0.05	0.04
6	Barley, pearled, dry (Hordeum vulgare)	11.1	349	8.2	1.0	78.8	0.5	0.9	189	16	(2.0)	(0)	0	3.1	0.08	0.12
7	Bean, common, dried (Phaseolus vulgaris)	12.2	336	23.1	1.7	59.4	3.5	3.6	163	6.9	437	(0)	2	2.5	0.22	0.57
8	Bean, lima, immature (P. lunatus mac.)	66.5	128	7.5	0.8	23.5	1.5	1.7	63	2.3	158	280	32	1.4	0.11	0.21
9	Bean, lima, mature (P. lunatus macrocarpus)	12.6	333	20.7	1.3	61.6	4.3	3.8	68	7.5	381	0	2	2.0	0.18	0.48
10	Bean, snap, green and yellow (P. vulgaris)	88.9	35	2.4	0.2	7.7	1.4	0.8	65	1.1	44	630[1]	19	0.5	0.11	0.08
11	Beet, garden (Beta vulgaris)	87.6	42	1.6	0.1	9.6	0.9	1.1	27	1.0	43	20	10	0.4	0.05	0.02
12	Blackberry (Rubus spp)	84.8	57	1.2	1.0	12.5	4.2	0.5	32	0.9	32	200	21	0.4	0.04	0.04
13	Blueberry (Vaccinium corymbosum)	83.4	61	0.6	0.6	15.1	1.2	0.3	16	0.8	13	280	16	(0.3)	(0.02)	(0.02)
14	Brazil nut (Bertholletia excelsa)	5.3	646	14.4	65.9	11.0	2.1	3.4	186	3.4	693	Trace				0.86
15	Broccoli (Brassica oleracea botrytis)	89.9	29	3.3	0.2	5.5	1.3	1.1	130	1.3	76	3500	118	1.1	0.2	0.10
16	Brussels sprouts (B. oleracea gemmifera)	84.9	47	4.4	0.5	8.9	1.3	1.3	34	1.3	78	400	94	0.7	0.16	0.08
17	Cabbage (B. oleracea capitata)	92.4	24	1.4	0.2	5.3	1.0	0.8	46	0.5	31	80	50	0.5	0.04	0.05
18	Cantaloupe (Cucumis melo cantalupensis)	94.0	20	0.6	0.2	4.6	0.6	0.6	17	0.4	16	3420	33	0.5	0.06	0.06
19	Carrot (Daucus carota)	88.2	42	1.2	0.3	9.3	1.1	1.0	39	0.8	37	12000		0.6	0.10	0.11
20	Cauliflower (Brassica oleracea botrytis)	91.7	25	2.4	0.2	4.9	0.9	0.8	22	1.1	72	90	69	0.4	0.04	0.05
21	Celery (Apium graveolens)	93.7	18	1.3	0.2	3.7	0.7	1.1	50	0.5	40	0	7	0.4	0.06	0.05
22	Cherry, sour and sweet (Prunus spp)	83.0	61	1.1	0.5	14.8	0.3	0.6	18	0.4	20	620	8	0.2	0.01	0.10
23	Coconut (Cocos nucifera)	46.9	359	3.4	34.7	14.0	3.2	1.0	21	2.0	98	0	2	0.4	0.03	0.10
24	Collard (Brassica acephala)	86.6	40	3.9	0.6	7.2	1.2	1.7	249	1.6	58	6870	100	(2.0)	0.27	0.11
25	Corn, sweet, white and yellow (Zea mays)	73.9	92	3.7	1.2	20.5	0.8	0.7	9	0.5	120	390	12	1.7	0.12	0.15
26	Cranberry (Vaccinium macrocarpon)	87.4	48	0.4	0.7	11.3	1.4	0.2	14	0.6	11	40	12	0.1	(0.02)	(0.03)
27	Cucumber (Cucumis sativus)	96.1	12	0.7	0.1	2.7	0.5	0.4	10	0.3[2]	21	0[2]	8	0.2	0.04	0.03
28	Currant, red (Ribes rubrum)	84.4	55	1.2	0.2	13.6	4.0	0.6	36	0.9	33	120	36		0.04	0.04
29	Date, dried (Phoenix dactylifera)	20.0	284	2.2	0.6	75.4	2.4	1.8	72	2.1	60	60	(0)	2.2	0.10	0.09
30	Eggplant (Solanum melongena)	92.7	24	1.1	0.2	5.5	0.9	0.5	15	0.4	37	30	5	0.6	0.05	0.04

(Continued)

Plant Foods, Composition (Continued)

TABLE 2.P.18 (Continued)

Values are per 100 g of edible portion of fresh, uncooked food, unless otherwise specified. Values based on inadequate evidence are enclosed in parentheses.

Food	Water g	Food Energy Cal	Protein g	Fat g	Carbohydrate Total g	Carbohydrate Fiber g	Ash g	Ca mg	Fe mg	P mg	Vitamin A I.U.	Ascorbic Acid mg	Niacin mg	Riboflavin mg	Thiamine mg
31 Fig, dried (Ficus carica)	24.0	270	4.0	1.2	68.4	5.8	2.4	186	3.0	111	80	(0)	1.7	0.12	0.16
32 Grape, American (Vitis spp)[3]	81.9	70	1.4	1.4	14.9	0.5	0.4	17	0.6	21	80	4	0.2	0.04	0.06
33 Grapefruit (Citrus paradisi)	88.8	40	0.5	0.2	10.1	0.3	0.4	22	0.2	18	Trace	40	0.2	0.02	0.04
34 Guava (Psidium guajava)	80.6	70	1.0	0.6	17.1	5.5	0.7	30	0.7	29	250	302	1.2	0.04	0.07
35 Kale (Brassica oleracea acephala)	86.6	40	3.9	0.6	7.2	1.2	1.7	225	2.2	62	7540	115	2.0	0.26	0.10
36 Lemon (Citrus limonia)	89.3	32	0.9	0.6	8.7	0.9	0.5	40	0.6	22	0	50	0.1	Trace	0.04
37 Lettuce (Lactuca sativa)	94.8	15	1.2	0.2	2.9	0.6	0.9	22	0.5	25	540	8	0.2	0.08	0.04
38 Mango (Mangifera indica)	81.4	66	0.7	0.2	17.2	1.0	0.5	9	0.2	13	6350	41	0.9	0.06	0.06
39 Mushroom (Agaricus campestris)	91.1	16	2.4	0.3	4.0	0.9	1.1	9	1.0	115	0	5	4.9	0.44	0.10
40 Mustard greens (Brassica japonica)	92.2	22	2.3	0.3	4.0	0.8	1.2	220	2.9	38	6460	102	0.8	0.20	0.09
41 Oats, rolled (Avena sativa)	8.3	390	14.2	7.4	68.2	1.2	1.9	53	4.5	405	(0)	(0)	1.0	0.14	0.60
42 Okra (Hibiscus esculentus)	89.8	32	1.8	0.2	7.4	1.0	0.8	82	0.7	62	740	30	1.1	0.07	0.08
43 Onion, immature, green (Allium cepa)	87.6	35	1.0	0.2	10.6	1.8	0.6	135	0.9	24	(50)	24	(0.2)	(0.04)	(0.03)
44 Onion, mature (A. cepa)	87.5	45	1.4	0.2	10.3	0.8	0.6	32	0.5	44	50	9	0.2	0.04	0.03
45 Orange (Citrus spp)	87.2	45	0.9	0.2	11.2	0.6	0.5	33	0.4	23	(190)	49	0.2	0.03	0.08
46 Papaya (Carica papaya)	88.7	39	0.6	0.1	10.0	0.9	0.6	20	0.3	16	1750	56	0.3	0.04	0.03
47 Parsnip (Pastinaca sativa)	78.6	78	1.5	0.5	18.2	2.2	0.9	57	0.7	80	0	18	0.2	0.12	0.08
48 Pea, garden, immature (Pisum sativum)	74.3	98	6.7	0.4	17.7	2.2	0.9	22	1.9	122	680	26	2.7	0.16	0.34
49 Pea, garden, mature, dried (P. sativum)	11.6	339	23.8	1.4	60.2	5.4	3.0	57	4.7	388	370	2	3.1	0.28	0.77
50 Peach (Prunus persica)	86.9	46	0.5	0.1	12.0	0.6	0.5	8	0.6	22	880	8	0.9	0.05	0.02
51 Peanut, roasted (Arachis hypogaea)	2.6	559	26.9	44.2	23.6	2.4	2.7	74	1.9	393	0	(0)	16.2	0.13	0.30
52 Pear (Pyrus communis)	82.7	63	0.7	0.4	15.8	1.4	0.4	13	0.3	16	20	4	0.1	0.04	0.02
53 Pecan (Carya illinoensis)	3.0	696	9.4	73.0	13.0	2.2	1.6	74	2.4	324	50	2	0.9	0.11	0.72
54 Pepper, green (Capsicum annuum)	92.4	25	1.2	0.2	5.7	1.4	0.5	11	0.4	25	630	120	0.4	0.07	0.04
55 Pineapple (Ananas sativus)	85.3	52	0.4	0.2	13.7	0.4	0.4	16	0.3	11	130	24	0.2	0.02	0.08
56 Plantain (Musa paradisiaca)	66.4	119	1.1	0.4	31.2	0.4	0.9	7	0.7	30	10[4]	14	0.6	0.04	0.06
57 Plum (Prunus spp)	85.7	50	0.7	0.2	12.9	0.4	0.5	17	0.5	20	350	5	0.5	0.04	0.06
58 Potato (Solanum tuberosum)	77.8	83	2.0	0.1	19.1	0.4	1.0	11	0.7	56	20	17[5]	1.2	0.04	0.11
59 Prune (Prunus spp)	24.0	268	2.3	0.6	71.0	1.6	2.1	54	3.9	85	1890	3	1.7	0.16	0.10
60 Pumpkin (Cucurbita pepo)	90.5	31	1.2	0.2	7.3	1.3	0.8	21	0.8	44	(3400)	8	(0.6)	(0.08)	(0.05)
61 Radish (Raphanus sativus)	93.6	20	1.2	0.1	4.2	0.7	1.0	37	1.0	31	30	24	0.3	0.02	0.03
62 Raisin (Vitis vinifera)	24.0	268	2.3	0.5	71.2		2.0	78	3.3	129	50	Trace	0.5	0.08	0.15
63 Rice, brown (Oryza sativa)	12.0	360	7.5	1.7	77.7	0.6	1.1	39	2.0	303	(0)	(0)	4.6	0.05	0.32
64 Rice, white (O. sativa)	12.3	362	7.6	0.3	79.4	0.2	0.4	24	0.8	136	(0)	(0)	1.6	0.03	0.07
65 Rutabaga (Brassica campestris)	89.1	38	1.1	0.1	8.9	1.3	0.8	55	0.4	41	330	36	0.9	0.08	0.07
66 Rye (Secale cereale)	11.0	321	12.1	1.7	73.4	2.0	1.8	(38)	3.7	376	(0)	(0)	1.6	0.22	0.43
67 Soybean, mature, dried (Glycine soja)	7.5	331	34.9	18.1	34.8	5.0	4.7	227	8.0	586	110	Trace	2.3	0.31	1.07
68 Soybean, sprouts (G. soja)	86.3	46	6.2	1.4	5.3	0.8	0.8	48	1.0	67	180	13	0.8	0.20	0.23
69 Spinach (Spinacia oleracea)	92.7	20	2.3	0.3	3.2	0.6	1.5	81	3.0	55	9420	59	0.6	0.20	0.11
70 Squash, summer (Cucurbita pepo)	95.0	16	0.6	0.1	3.9	0.5	0.4	15	0.4	15	260	17	0.8	0.09	0.05
71 Squash, winter (C. maxima)	88.6	38	1.5	0.3	8.8	1.4	0.8	19	0.6	28	4950	8	0.5	0.12	0.05
72 Strawberry (Fragaria spp)	89.9	37	0.8	0.5	8.3	1.4	0.5	28	0.8	27	60	60	0.3	0.07	0.03
73 Sweetpotato (Ipomoea batatas)	68.5	123	1.8	0.4	27.9	1.0	1.1	30	0.7	49	7700	22	0.6	0.05	0.09
74 Tangerine (Citrus reticulata)	87.3	44	0.8	0.3	10.9	1.0	0.7	(33)	(0.4)	(23)	(420)	31	(0.2)	(0.03)	0.07
75 Tomato (Lycopersicon esculentum)	94.1	20	1.0	0.3	4.0	0.6	0.6	11	0.6	27	1100	23	0.5	0.04	0.06
76 Turnip (Brassica rapa)	90.9	32	1.1	0.2	7.1	1.1	0.7	40	0.5	34	Trace	28	0.5	0.07	0.05
77 Turnip greens (B. rapa)	89.5	30	2.9	0.4	5.4	1.2	1.8	259	2.4	50	9540	136	0.8	0.46	0.09
78 Walnut, English (Juglans regia)	3.3	654	15.0	64.4	15.6	2.1	1.7	83	2.1	380	30	3	1.2	0.13	0.48
79 Watermelon (Citrullus vulgaris)	92.1	28	0.5	0.2	6.9	0.3	0.3	7	0.2	12	590	6	0.2	0.05	0.05
80 Wheat (Triticum aestivum)	12.5	330	12.3	1.8	71.7	2.3	1.7	46	3.4	354	(0)		4.3	0.12	0.52

/1/ For yellow varieties, 150 I. U. /2/ Applicable to pared cucumber; for unpared, 1.2 mg iron and 260 I. U. vitamin A. /3/ Data also applicable to European grapes with the following modifications; food energy, 66 cal.; protein, 0.8 g; fat, 0.4 g; ash, 0.5 g. /4/ Applicable to white varieties; for yellow varieties, 1200 I. U. /5/ Year-round average. Recently harvested potatoes, 24 mg; after storage of 3 mo, 12 mg; after storage of 6 mo, 8 mg.

Source: Spector, W. S. (editor). Handbook of Biological Data. Federation of American Societies for Experimental Biology, Bethesda, Maryland.

Planting Density

TABLE 2.P.19
Quantity of seed and number of plants required for 100 feet of row, depths of planting, and distances apart for rows and plants

Crop	Requirement for 100 feet of row		Depth for planting seed	Distance apart		
				Rows		Plants in the row
	Seed	Plants		Horse- or tractor-cultivated	Hand-cultivated	
			Inches	*Feet*		
Asparagus	1 ounce	75	1 -1½	4 -5	1½ to 2 feet	18 inches.
Beans:						
Lima, bush	½ pound		1 -1½	2½-3	2 feet	3 to 4 inches.
Lima, pole	½ pound		1 -1½	3 -4	3 feet	3 to 4 feet.
Snap, bush	½ pound		1 -1½	2½-3	2 feet	3 to 4 inches.
Snap, pole	4 ounces		1 -1½	3 -4	2 feet	3 feet.
Beet	2 ounces		1	2 -2½	14 to 16 inches	2 to 3 inches.
Broccoli:						
Heading	1 packet	50- 75	½	2½-3	2 to 2½ feet	14 to 24 inches.
Sprouting	1 packet	50- 75	½	2½-3	2 to 2½ feet	14 to 24 inches.
Brussels sprouts	1 packet	50- 75	½	2½-3	2 to 2½ feet	14 to 24 inches.
Cabbage	1 packet	50- 75	½	2½-3	2 to 2½ feet	14 to 24 inches.
Cabbage, Chinese	1 packet		½	2 -2½	18 to 24 inches	8 to 12 inches.
Carrot	1 packet		½	2 -2½	14 to 16 inches	2 to 3 inches.
Cauliflower	1 packet	50- 75	½	2½-3	2 to 2½ feet	14 to 24 inches.
Celeriac	1 packet	200-250	⅛	2½-3	18 to 24 inches	4 to 6 inches.
Celery	1 packet	200-250	⅛	2½-3	18 to 24 inches	4 to 6 inches.
Chard	2 ounces		1	2 -2½	18 to 24 inches	6 inches.
Chervil	1 packet		½	2 -2½	14 to 16 inches	2 to 3 inches.
Chicory, witloof	1 packet		½	2 -2½	18 to 24 inches	6 to 8 inches.
Chives	1 packet		½	2½-3	14 to 16 inches	In clusters.
Collards	1 packet		½	3 -3½	18 to 24 inches	18 to 24 inches.
Cornsalad	1 packet		½	2½-3	14 to 16 inches	1 foot.
Corn, sweet	2 ounces		2	3 -3½	2 to 3 feet	Drills, 14 to 16 inches; hills, 2½ to 3 feet.
Cress Upland	1 packet		⅛- ¼	2 -2½	14 to 16 inches	2 to 3 inches.
Cucumber	1 packet		½	6 -7	6 to 7 feet	Drills, 3 feet; hills, 6 feet.
Dasheen	5 to 6 pounds	50	2 -3	3½-4	3½ to 4 feet	2 feet.
Eggplant	1 packet	50	½	3	2 to 2½ feet	3 feet.
Endive	1 packet		½	2½-3	18 to 24 inches	12 inches.
Fennel, Florence	1 packet		½	2½-3	18 to 24 inches	4 to 6 inches.
Garlic	1 pound		1 -2	2½-3	14 to 16 inches	2 to 3 inches.
Horseradish	Cuttings	50-75	2	3 -4	2 to 2½ feet	18 to 24 inches.
Kale	1 packet		½	2½-3	18 to 24 inches	12 to 15 inches.
Kohlrabi	1 packet		½	2½-3	14 to 16 inches	5 to 6 inches.
Leek	1 packet		½-1	2½-3	14 to 16 inches	2 to 3 inches.
Lettuce, head	1 packet	100	½	2½-3	14 to 16 inches	12 to 15 inches.
Lettuce, leaf	1 packet		½	2½-3	14 to 16 inches	6 inches.
Muskmelon	1 packet		1	6 -7	6 to 7 feet	Hills, 6 feet.
Mustard	1 packet		½	2½-3	14 to 16 inches	12 inches.
Okra	2 ounces		1 -1½	3 -3½	3 to 3½ feet	2 feet.
Onion:						
Plants		400	1 -2	2 -2½	14 to 16 inches	2 to 3 inches.
Seed	1 packet		½-1	2 -2½	14 to 16 inches	2 to 3 inches.
Sets	1 pound		1 -2	2 -2½	14 to 16 inches	2 to 3 inches.
Parsley	1 packet		⅛	2 -2½	14 to 16 inches	4 to 6 inches.
Parsley, turnip-rooted	1 packet		⅛- ¼	2 -2½	14 to 16 inches	2 to 3 inches.
Parsnip	1 packet		½	2 -2½	18 to 24 inches	2 to 3 inches.
Peas	½ pound		2 -3	2 -4	1½ to 3 feet	1 inch.
Pepper	1 packet	50-70	½	3 -4	2 to 3 feet	18 to 24 inches.
Physalis	1 packet		½	2 -2½	1½ to 2 feet	12 to 18 inches.
Potato	5 to 6 pounds, tubers		4	2½-3	2 to 2½ feet	10 to 18 inches.
Pumpkin	1 ounce		1 -2	5 -8	5 to 8 feet	3 to 4 feet.
Radish	1 ounce		½	2 -2½	14 to 16 inches	1 inch.
Rhubarb		25-35		3 -4	3 to 4 feet	3 to 4 feet.
Salsify	1 ounce		½	2 -2½	18 to 26 inches	2 to 3 inches.
Shallots	1 pound (cloves)		1 -2	2 -2½	12 to 18 inches	2 to 3 inches.
Sorrel	1 packet		½	2 -2½	18 to 24 inches	5 to 8 inches.
Soybean	½ to 1 pound		1 -1½	2½-3	24 to 30 inches	3 inches.
Spinach	1 ounce		½	2 -2½	14 to 16 inches	3 to 4 inches.
Spinach, New Zealand	1 ounce		1 -1½	3 -3½	3 feet	18 inches.

(*Continued*)

Planting Density   (Continued)

TABLE 2.P.19   (Continued)

Crop	Requirement for 100 feet of row		Depth for planting seed	Distance apart		
	Seed	Plants		Rows		Plants in the row
				Horse- or tractor-cultivated	Hand-cultivated	
Squash:						
Bush	½ ounce		1 –2	4 –5	4 to 5 feet	Drills, 15 to 18 inches; hills, 4 feet.
Vine	1 ounce		1 –2	8 –12	8 to 12 feet	Drills, 2 to 3 feet; hills, 4 feet.
Sweetpotato	5 pounds, bedroots	75	2 –3	3 –3½	3 to 3½ feet	12 to 14 inches.
Tomato	1 packet	35–50	½	3 –4	2 to 3 feet	1½ to 3 feet.
Turnip greens	1 packet		¼– ½	2 –2½	14 to 16 inches	2 to 3 inches.
Turnips and rutabagas	½ ounce		¼– ½	2 –2½	14 to 16 inches	2 to 3 inches.
Watermelon	1 ounce		1 –2	8 –10	8 to 10 feet	Drills, 2 to 3 feet; hills, 8 feet.

Source: USDA (1972). Growing vegetables in the home garden. USDA Home and Garden Bull. *202*.

Plastic Permeability

TABLE 2.P.20
Permeability of selected plastics at indicated temperatures

Material	T ($^\circ$F)	Permeability Coefficient[a] (cc) (cm^{-2})/(sec) (cm Hg) (cm^{-1})
Cellulose nitrate	68	450
Cellulose acetate	75	6210
Polyvinylbutyral	77	185
Polyvinyl chloride (PVC)	88	15
Polystyrene	77	97
	122	107
Polyethylene (den = 0.922)	75	9
(den = 0.038)	75	2.5
(den = 0.96)	75	1.2
Polyethylene	68	3.2
	104	7.9
	176	50
Polystyrene	75	83.5 × 10^{-9}
	100	83.0
Polyvinyl chloride	75	11.6–12.3
	95	15.5
	131	20.3
Polyvinylidene chloride	75	0.20
	91	0.52
	100	0.82

[a](cc) (cm^{-2})/(sec) (cm^{-1}) (cm Hg) = (cc) (cm)/(sec) (sq cm) (cm Hg).

Source: Hall, C. W., Hardenburg, R. E., and Pantastico, E. B. (1975). Principles of packaging. Part II. Consumer packaging with plastics. In *Postharvest Physiology, Handling and Utilization of Tropical and Subtropical Fruits and Vegetables*. E. B. Pantastico (editor). AVI Publishing Co., Westport, Connecticut.

Poisonous Plants

TABLE 2.P.21
Poisonous plants of North America

Dangerous Season	Scientific Name	Common Name	Habitat and Distribution	Affected Animals	Important Characteristics	Toxic Principle and Effects	Remarks and Treatment
SPRING	Hymenoxys spp.	Bitterweed, Rubberweed, Pingue	Roadways, lakebeds, flooded areas, overgrazed range; western.	Sheep, also cattle	Much-branched annual or perennial up to 2 ft. high. Yellow flower head. Leaves divided into narrow glandular segments.	Depression, loss of appetite, abdominal pain, green nasal discharge, salivation, prostration.	Fresh or dry. Remove from pasture. Avoid overgrazing.
	Nolina texana	Sacahuista, Beargrass	Open areas on rolling hills and slopes; southwest.	Sheep, cattle and goats	Perennial with many clustered, long, narrowed leaves. Several flower stems with many small white flowers in clusters.	Toxin in buds, flowers and fruit. Photosensitization. Anorexia, icterus, prostration.	Remove animals from range during blooming season. (See PHOTOSENSITIZATION, p. 6.)
	Cicuta spp.	Water hemlock	Open, moist to wet situations.	All	White flower, umbels. Veins of leaflets ending at notches. Stems hollow except at nodes. Tuberous roots from chambered rootstock.	A higher alcohol—excessive salivation, violent convulsions, dilation of pupils, diaphragm contractions, pain.	Death usually rapid. Use sedatives to control spasm and heart action. Intestinal evacuation followed by astringents may help.
	Delphinium	Larkspurs	Either cultivated or wild. Usually in open foothills or meadows; mostly western.	All grazing animals, mostly cattle	Annual or perennial herbs. Flowers each with one spur, in racemes. Perennial with tuberous roots. Leaves palmately lobed or divided.	Alkaloid delphinine and others—straddled stance, repeated falling, nausea, rapid pulse and respiration, constipation, bloating.	Use R 486.
	Phytolacca americana	Pokeweed, Poke	Recent clearings, pastures, waste areas; eastern.	Cattle, swine	Tall, glabrous, green, red-purplish perennial herbs. Berries black-purple, staining, in drooping racemes.	More than one—vomiting, spasms, respiratory paralysis, ulcerative gastritis.	Roots most poisonous. 10 ml nikethamide (cattle).
(and occasionally fall)	Xanthium spp.	Cocklebur	Fields, waste places, exposed shores of ponds or rivers.	All animals, more common in swine	Coarse annual herb. Fruit one solid mass, 2 beaked, with 2 cavities, armed with hooked spines.	Hydroquinone—anorexia, depression, incoordination, twitching, paralysis, inflammation of mucous membranes.	Only cotyledons poisonous. Eaten after emerging from seed. Milk, vegetable oil and fats may be beneficial.
	Peganum harmala	African rue	Arid to semiarid ranges; southwest.	Cattle and sheep	Much-branched, leafy, perennial, bright green, succulent herb; leaves divided; flowers white.	Alkaloids—weakness of hind limbs, listlessness, subserous edema and hemorrhage of small intestine.	Unpalatable. Eaten only under drought conditions.
	Sarcobatus vermiculatus	Greasewood	Alkaline or saline bottom soils, not in higher mountains; western.	Sheep	Large shrub with spiny stems; fleshy, alternate cross-section. Flowers inconspicuous.	Oxalates—kidney lesions, weakness, depression, prostration, coma.	Poisoning occurs only on steady diet of greasewood leaves. Provide other forage.
	Veratrum spp.	False hellebore	Low, moist woods and pastures, and high mountain valleys.	Cattle, sheep and fowl	Erect herbs; leafy throughout, leaves large and plaited. Flowers small and white or greenish.	Steroid alkaloids—salivation, prostration, depressed heart action, dyspnea, "Monkey-face" in lambs.	Remove animals from range. Provide other forage.
	Tetradymia spp.	Horsebrush	Arid foothills and higher desert and sagebrush ranges; western.	Sheep	Shrubs with yellow flowers in spring, not later. Leaves spiny, silvery white, early deciduous.	Resinous substances—weakness, "bighead" photosensitization; liver injury, death.	Cumulative. Remove animals from range and light. Antihistaminics. (See PHOTOSENSITIZATION, p. 6.)
	Zygadenus spp.	Death camas	Foothill grazing lands, occasionally boggy grasslands, low open woods.	Sheep, cattle and horses	Perennial bulbous herbs with basal flat grass-like leaves; flowers greenish, yellow or pink, in racemes or panicles. No onion odor.	Steroid alkaloids of the veratrum group—salivation, vomiting, staggering or prostration, coma and death.	Hay with dried camas is poisonous. 2 to 3 subcut. injections of 2 mg atropine sulfate and 8 mg picrotoxin in 5 ml of water per 100 lb body wt.

(Continued)

Poisonous Plants (Continued)

TABLE 2.P.21 (Continued)

Dangerous Season	Scientific Name	Common Name	Habitat and Distribution	Affected Animals	Important Characteristics	Toxic Principle and Effects	Remarks and Treatment
SPRING and SUMMER	Aesculus spp.	Buckeyes	Woods and thickets; Eastern U.S.A. and California.	All grazing animals	Trees or shrubs. Leaves opposite and palmately compound. Seeds large, glossy brown, with large white scar.	Glycoside, aesculin and possibly others—depression, incoordination, twitching, paralysis, inflammation of mucous membranes.	Young shoots and seeds especially poisonous. Use stimulants and purgatives.
	Amianthium muscaetoxicum	Fly-poison, Staggergrass	Open woods, fields, and acid bogs; eastern.	All grazing animals	Bulbous perennial herb. Leaves basal, linear white flowers in a compact raceme, the pedicels subtended by short brownish bracts.	Alkaloid, of the veratrum group—salivation, vomiting, rapid and irregular respiration, weakness, death by respiratory failure.	No practical treatment. Especially dangerous for animals new to pasture. Keep animals well fed.
	Lantana spp.	Lantana	Ornamentals and wild in lower coastal plain of southeast, and southern California.	All grazing animals	Shrubs. Young stems 4-angled. Leaves opposite. Flowers in flat-topped clusters. Berries black.	Lantadene A, a polycyclic triterpenoid—erythema, pruritus, edematous suffusions and usually sloughing of skin, gastroenteritis, bloody watery feces.	Remove plants from pasture. Keep animals out of light sources after eating plant.
	Quercus spp.	Oaks	In most deciduous woods.	All grazing animals	Mostly deciduous trees, rarely shrubs, with 2 to 4 leaves clustered at tip of all twigs.	Tannic acid—anorexia, constipation, dry muzzle, black pelleted feces followed by diarrhea with blood and mucus, frequent urination, thin rapid pulse.	Remove animals from oak source. Treat symptomatically.
SUMMER and FALL	Prosopis juliflora	Mesquite	Dry ranges, washes, draws; southwest.	Cattle	Deciduous shrub or small tree with smooth or furrowed gray bark, paired spines; leaves divided. Legume pod long, constricted between seeds.	Malnutrition, excessive salivation, stasis of rumen; sublingual or submaxillary edema, loss of weight.	Believed that high-sucrose content of beans alters bacterial flora to extent that cellulose cannot be digested and B-vitamins synthesized.
	Centaurea solstitialis	Yellow star thistle	Waste areas, roadsides, pastures; mostly western.	Horses	Annual weed. Leaves densely covered with cottony hair. Terminal spreading cluster of bright yellow flowers with spines below. Branches winged.	Involuntary chewing movements, twitching of lips, flicking of tongue. Mouth commonly held open. Unable to eat. Eventual death from starvation or thirst.	Force food far back into mouth
	Oxytenia acerosa	Copperweed	Arid, alkaline soils in foothills, and sagebrush plains; western.	Cattle, also sheep	Tall, perennial herb with leaflets; flowers in many heads resembling goldenrod.	Stupor, loss of appetite, coma, death without struggling.	Supplement diet.
	Eupatorium rugosum	White snakeroot	Woods, cleared areas, waste places, usually the more moist and richer soils; eastern.	Cattle and sheep	Perennial herb; leaves 3-nerved, taper-pointed, opposite; flowers small, white, many.	An alcohol, tremetol—trembling, depression, vomiting, labored respiration, death.	"Milk sickness." "Trembles." Cathartics and stimulants may help.
	Solanum spp.	Nightshades, Jerusalem cherry, potato, Horsenettle	Fence rows, waste areas, grain and hay fields.	All	Fruits small, when ripe yellow, red, or black; structurally like tomatoes; clustered on stalk arising from stem between leaves.	Glycoalkaloids—weakness, trembling, dyspnea, nausea, constipation or diarrhea, death.	Leaves, shoots and berries may be poisonous. In cattle repeated doses of 2 to 3 mg carbachol or of injection of 15 mg strychnine may be useful.
FALL or WINTER	Haplopappus heterophyllus	Rayless goldenrod	Dry plains, grasslands, open woodlands and along irrigation canals; western.	Cattle, sheep and horses	Bushy perennial 2 to 4 ft. tall with many yellow flower heads. Leaves alternate, sticky.	An alcohol, tremetol—trembling, depression, vomiting, labored respiration, coma, death.	"Milk sickness." Keep animals away by fencing.

(Continued)

Poisonous Plants (Continued)

TABLE 2.P.21 (Continued)

	Scientific name	Common name	Habitat	Animals affected	Description	Symptoms	Control / Remedy
	Halogeton glomeratus	Halogeton	Deserts, overgrazed areas, winter ranges, alkaline soils; western.	Sheep, also cattle	Annual herb. Leaves fleshy, round in cross-section, tip with stiff hair. Axillary flowers inconspicuous. Fruits bracted and conspicuous.	Oxalates—dyspnea followed by rapid death.	Alfalfa hay or dicalcium phosphate, fed free-choice when added to 3 parts salt, is effective preventive in sheep. Avoid dense growths of weeds.
	Sophora secundiflora	Mescal bean	Hills and canyons, limestone soils; southwestern Texas into Mexico.	Cattle, also sheep and goats	Evergreen shrub or small tree. Leaves alternate, divided and leathery; flowers violet-blue, fragrant; seeds large and bright red with hard seed coat, in legume pod.	Alkaloid sophorine—trembling, stiff gait, falling after exercise; recumbent for few minutes, then arise alert and fall again if exercised.	Not cumulative. Provide supplemental feed.
	Notholaena sinuata var. *cochisensis*	Jimmy fern, Cloak fern	Dry rocky slopes and crevices, chiefly limestone areas; southwest.	Sheep, goats and cattle	Evergreen, perennial, erect fern with divided leaves, folding when dry.	After exercise by walking, will have arched back, stilted movement of hind legs, and usually increased respiration. Continued walking induced violent trembling and death if not allowed to rest.	Avoid driving during danger period. Provide ample watering, placed to avoid long walks.
	Glottidium vesicarium, Sesbania spp.	Bladder pod, Rattlebox, Sesbane, Coffeebean	Mostly open low ground, abandoned cultivated fields; southeast.	All	Tall annual. Legume pods flat, tapered at both ends, 2-seeded. Leaves pinnate-divided. Flowers yellow.	Saponins—intense inflammation of gastrointestinal tract, yellowish diarrhea, frequent urination, shallow and accelerated respiration, death.	Seeds poisonous. Remove plants from pasture. Keep animals off pasture after seed pods form.
	Daubentonia punicea	Rattlebox, Purple sesbane	Cultivated and escaped in waste places; southeastern coastal plain.	All	Shrub. Flowers orange. Legume pods longitudinally four-winged.	A saponin—rapid pulse, weak respiration, diarrhea, death.	Seeds poisonous. Keep seeds from animals. Use saline purgative followed by stimulants and soft food.
FALL, WINTER and SPRING	*Melia azedarach*	Chinaberry	Fence rows, brush, waste places; southeast.	Swine, cattle	Tree. Leaves 2 to 3 pinnate; fruit cream or yellow with a furrowed globose stone, persisting on tree through winter.	Nausea, constipation, excitement or depression, often weakened heart action and death.	Fruit most poisonous. Use stimulants and cathartics followed by easily digestible diet.
ALL SEASONS	*Baccharis* spp.	Silverling, Baccharis, Yerba-de-pasmo	Open areas, often moist; eastern and southwestern.	All grazing cattle	Shrubs; numerous small, whitish flowers; leaves resin-dotted, and persistent southward.	Glucosidal saponin having digitaloidal properties—paralysis and death soon after ingestion. Depression and weakness in chronic cases.	Most dangerous during new growth in spring or root sprouts in fall.
	Pteridium aquilinum	Bracken fern	Dry poor soil, open woods, sandy ridges.	All grazing animals	Leaves firm, leathery, thrice pinnate.		(See BRACKEN FERN POISONING, p. 977.)
	Prunus spp.	Chokecherries, Wild cherries, Peaches	Waste areas, fence rows, woods, orchards, prairies, dry slopes.	All grazing animals	Large shrubs or trees. Flowers white or pink. Cherries or peach. (Crushed twigs with strong odor.)	Prussic acid—slobbering, increased respiration rate, dyspnea, rapid weak pulse, convulsions, rapid death.	(See CYANIDE POISONING, p. 938.)
	Acacia berlandieri	Guajillo	Semiarid range lands; southwestern Texas into Mexico.	Sheep, also goats	Deciduous shrub or small tree; leaf divided; flowers white to yellowish in dense heads; fruit a legume with margins thickened.	Amine, N-methyl beta phenyl-ethylamine—after eating for 6 to 9 months, may have locomotor ataxia called "limber leg." Mortality as high as 50% in extreme drought.	Dominates vegetation in some areas. Valuable to sheep industry due to high nutritive value and dominance. Supplemental feeding.

(Continued)

Poisonous Plants (Continued)

TABLE 2.P.21 (Continued)

Dangerous Season	Scientific Name	Common Name	Habitat and Distribution	Affected Animals	Important Characteristics	Toxic Principle and Effects	Remarks and Treatment
(especially spring)	Agave lechuguilla	Lechuguilla	Low limestone hills, dry valleys and canyons; southwest.	Sheep, goats, rarely cattle	Perennial stemless, with thick fleshy tapered leaves having sharply serrated margins. Flowering infrequently with tall terminal panicle.	A photodynamic agent; also a saponin that is hepatonephrotoxic—photosensitization, generalized icterus, listlessness, progressive weakness, coma, death.	Remove animals from range and provide shade. (See Photosensitization, p. 6.)
	Asclepias spp.	Milkweeds	Dry areas, usually waste places, roadsides, streambeds.	All	Perennial herbs with milky sap; seeds very silky-hairy from elongated pods.	Resinoid and others—loss of control, spasms, bloating, pulse rapid and weak, rapid breathing, coma, death.	Mainly due to drought or overgrazing.
(especially spring)	Astragalus spp. Oxytropis spp.	Locoweeds, Poison vetch	Nearly all habitats; mostly western.	All	Perennial stemmed or stemless herbs. Leaves with many small leaflets. Flowers like garden peas, in racemes.	Selenium or "locoine" in different species. Weakness, trembling, ataxia, or paralysis.	Cumulative. (See Selenium Poisoning, p. 947 as one type.)
(especially spring)	Stanleya pinnata	Prince's plume	Foothills or deserts; western.	All	Perennial herb, woody at base and coarse; leaves divided; flowers yellow in showy spike.	May not be eaten but does accumulate selenium.	(See Selenium Poisoning, p. 947.)
	Drymaria pachyphylla	Inkweed, Drymary	Heavy alkaline clay soil in low areas or dry overgrazed pastures; southwest.	Cattle, sheep; also goats	Much-branched, succulent, prostrate annual with opposite leaves and small white flowers.	Diarrhea, lack of appetite, arched back, coma, death.	Occurs after rain. Avoid overstocking to improve range.
	Gutierrezia microcephala	Broomweed, Snakeweed, Slinkweed, Turpentine weed	Widespread over dry range and desert; overgrazed lands; western.	Cattle, sheep, goats and swine	Much-branched, perennial, resinous shrub, with many yellow-flowered heads.	Saponin. Loss of appetite, listlessness, hematuria in severe cases. Abortion with retained placenta in cattle.	Supplement diet.
	Psilostrophe spp.	Paperflowers	Open range lands and pastures; southwest.	Sheep	Perennial composite with erect, woolly stems branching from base. Many small heads of yellow flowers.	Sluggishness, stumbling, coughing, vomiting, depression, death.	About 2 weeks of grazing before signs appear. Pasture rotation, or placing animals on other feed.
	Senecio spp.	Groundsel, Senecio	Grassland areas; mostly western.	Cattle, horses and sheep	Perennial or annual herbs; heads of yellow flowers with whorl of bracts below.	Alkaloids—aimless walking, slight staggering, staring expression, and running into fences or other objects. Hepatic cirrhosis, edema of visceral peritoneum and distension of gallbladder.	Cumulative, fresh or dry. Supplemental feeding. Treat symptoms. (See Senecio Poisoning, p. 1003.)
(especially dry season)	Triglochin spp.	Arrowgrass	Salt marshes, wet alkaline soils, lake shores.	Sheep and cattle	Grass-like, except leaves are thick; heads of fruits globular on erect raceme. Flowers inconspicuous.	Prussic acid in leaves—abnormal breathing, trembling, and jerking, convulsions. Rapid poisoning.	(See Cyanide Poisoning, p. 938.)
	Hypericum perforatum	St. Johnswort, Goatweed, Klamath weed	Dry soil, roadsides, pastures, ranges.	Sheep, cattle, horses and goats	Perennial herb or woody below; leaves opposite, dotted; flowers many, yellow, with many stamens.	Primary photosensitizer; skin lesions in white skin, itching, blindness, convulsions, death.	Fresh or dry. Remove animals from infested areas. (See Photosensitization, p. 6.)
	Agrostemma githago	Corn cockle	Weed, grain fields and waste areas.	All	Green winter annual with silky white hairs, opposite leaves, purple flowers, black seeds.	Sapogenin, githagenin—irritation of mucosa, vomiting, vertigo, diarrhea.	Toxin in seeds. Avoid grain screenings containing seed. Give oils, demulcents, cardiac stimulants.

(Continued)

Poisonous Plants (Continued)

TABLE 2.P.21 (Continued)

		Location	Animals affected	Description	Symptoms	Remarks
Helenium hoopesii	Sneezeweed	Moist slopes and well-drained mountain meadows; western.	Sheep, also cattle	Perennial herb with orange sunflower-like heads or yellow flowers. Leaves alternate.	Glycoside dugaldin—salivation, "spewing sickness," vomiting, weakness.	Cumulative. Cathartics may help. Avoid dense areas of weed.
Lupinus spp.	Lupines, Bluebonnet	Dry to moist soils, roadsides, fields, and mountains; mostly western.	Sheep, also cattle, goats, horses and swine	Perennials; leaves simple or palmately divided; flowers in terminal raceme.	Alkaloids D-lupanine, sparteine and others, nervousness, convulsions or coma.	Fresh or dry. Eating of pods with seeds frequent cause of poisoning. Not cumulative. (See MYCOTOXIC LUPINOSIS, p. 998.)
Contium maculatum	Poison hemlock	Roadside ditches, damp waste areas, especially northward.	All	Purple-spotted hollow stem; leaves resemble parsley, parsnip odor when crushed; tap root; flowers white, in umbels.	Alkaloid coniine and others—loss of appetite, salivation, bloating, feeble pulse, paralysis.	Vegetative parts, later the seeds most poisonous. Give stimulants.
Crotalaria spp.	Crotalaria, Rattlebox	Fields and roadsides; Eastern and Central States.	All	Annual legume with yellow flowers in racemes; pods inflated; bracts at base of pedicels of flowers and fruits persistent; leaves simple or divided.	Alkaloid monocrotaline—diarrhea, abnormally light or dark comb in fowl. Diarrhea, stupor alternating with apparent improvement, walking in circles in horse and mule. Bloody feces, anorexia, weakness in others. In all death.	Cumulative. All parts, especially seeds, poisonous. Seeds often found in combined corn. No treatment known. Keep plant from fields and hay.
Datura stramonium	Jimsonweed	Fields, barn lots, trampled pastures, and waste places on rich bottom soils.	All	Leaves wavy; flower large (4 in.) white, tubular; fruit a spiny pod, 2 in. long.	Alkaloids atropine, hyoscyamine and hyoscine—nausea, vertigo, thirst, dilated pupils convulsions, death.	Rapid death. KI or tannic acid per os; cardiac and respiratory stimulants.
Gelsemium sempervirens	Yellow jessamine	Open woods, thickets; eastern.	All	Climbing or trailing vines with evergreen, entire, opposite leaves; yellow tubular flowers, very fragrant.	Alkaloids gelsemine and gelsemine—weakness, convulsions rigid extremities, lowered respiration and temperature; death; "limp-neck" in fowl	Use relaxing agents, sedatives; repeat as required.
Kalmia spp. (especially winter and spring)	Laurel, Ivybush, Lambkill	Rich moist woods, meadows; or acid bogs; eastern and northwestern.	All, often sheep	Woody shrub with evergreen glossy leaves; flowers pink to rose, showy.	Andromedotoxin—salivation, nasal discharge, emesis paralysis, coma, death.	Laxatives, demulcents nerve stimulants.
Nerium oleander	Oleander	Common ornamental in southern regions.	All	Evergreen shrub. Leaves whorled and prominently finely pinnately veined beneath. Flowers showy, white to deep pink.	Cardiac glucosides—nausea, depression, increased pulse rate, mydriasis, bloody diarrhea, later weak and irregular heart beat, death.	Fresh, clipped or dried leaves most dangerous.
Prunus caroliniana (especially winter and spring)	Laurel cherry, Cherrylaurel	Woods, fence rows and often escaped from cultivation; southern regions.	All grazing animals	Leaves evergreen, shiny, leathery. Broken twigs with strong cherry bark odor.	Prussic acid—slobbering, increased respiration rate, dyspnea, rapid weak pulse, convulsions, rapid death.	Wilted parts most poisonous. (See CYANIDE POISONING, p. 938.)
Ricinus communis	Castor bean	Cultivated in southern regions.	All	Large palmately lobed leaves; seeds resembling engorged ticks, usually 3 in somewhat spiny pod.	Ricin, irritant blood poison—nausea, vomiting, diarrhea, thirst, cessation of rumination, death.	Seeds and "press-cakes" most dangerous. Gastric lavage, warmth, sedation.
Sorghum vulgare	Sorghum, Sudan grass, Kafir, Durra, Milo, Broomcorn, Schrock, etc.			Coarse grasses with terminal flower cluster. Some to 8 ft tall.	Prussic acid—slobbering, increased respiration rate, dyspnea, rapid weak pulse, convulsions, rapid death.	Dark green, short (2 ft) second-growth or stunted by dry weather most dangerous. (See CYANIDE POISONING, p. 938.)

(Continued)

Poisonous Plants (*Continued*)

TABLE 2.P.21 (*Continued*)

Dangerous Season	Scientific Name	Common Name	Habitat and Distribution	Affected Animals	Important Characteristics	Toxic Principle and Effects	Remarks and Treatment
	Sorghum halepense	Johnson grass	Weed of open fields and waste places in south; scattered north to New York and Iowa.	All grazing animals	Coarse grass with large rhizomes and white midvein on leaf. Topped by large, open panicle.	Prussic acid—slobbering, dyspnea, increased respiration rate, rapid weak pulse, convulsions, rapid death.	Dark green second growth or stunted by dry weather most dangerous. (*See* CYANIDE POISONING, p. 938.)
ALL SEASONS (especially winter)	*Pinus ponderosa*	Western yellow pine	Coniferous forests of Rocky Mountains at moderate elevations; western.	Cattle	Tree, 150 to 180 ft; leaves in groups of 3, yellowish green, 7 to 11 in. long; barky platy, reddish orange.	Toxin in leaves; browsing cattle predisposed to abortion.	Remove from western yellow pine stands in later stages of gestation.

Source: Merck & Co. (1973). *The Merck Veterinary Manual*, 4th Edition. Merck & Company, Rahway, New Jersey.

Population

TABLE 2.P.22

(in 1,000)

Country	1950	1955	1960	1965	1970	1975	1980	1985	1990	1995	2000
Africa	218,833	243,316	272,753	308,701	351,594	401,138	460,686	531,407	613,714	707,994	813,119
Eastern Africa	61,878	68,807	77,193	87,727	99,818	114,498	131,992	152,868	177,581	206,659	239,861
Ethiopia	16,675	18,202	20,024	22,231	24,855	27,975	31,522	35,739	40,708	46,673	53,665
Kenya	6,018	7,001	8,115	9,527	11,247	13,251	15,688	18,605	22,102	26,263	31,020
Uganda	5,969	6,687	7,551	8,578	9,806	11,353	13,222	15,423	17,996	20,932	24,160
Middle Africa	26,258	28,758	31,775	35,766	40,446	45,310	51,201	58,356	66,735	76,485	87,732
Zaire	13,055	14,468	16,151	18,651	21,638	24,485	27,952	32,139	37,061	42,809	49,450
Northern Africa	51,806	58,051	65,732	74,268	85,627	98,185	113,055	130,334	149,748	170,525	191,824
Algeria	8,753	9,715	10,800	11,923	14,330	16,792	19,828	23,501	27,741	32,226	36,663
Egypt	20,461	22,990	25,929	29,389	33,329	37,543	42,144	47,191	52,640	58,438	64,588
Morocco	8,953	10,132	11,640	13,139	15,126	17,504	20,384	23,788	27,633	31,752	35,904
Sudan	9,067	10,210	11,770	13,540	15,695	18,268	21,420	25,147	29,425	34,321	38,977
Southern Africa	14,354	16,123	18,164	20,779	24,202	27,678	31,950	36,848	42,321	48,591	55,669
South Africa	12,458	14,065	15,925	18,337	21,500	24,663	28,533	32,955	37,881	43,539	49,951
Western Africa	64,331	71,578	79,889	90,160	101,501	115,469	132,488	153,000	177,329	205,734	238,034
Nigeria	34,331	38,241	42,947	48,676	55,073	62,925	72,596	84,400	98,497	115,258	134,924
Latin America	163,925	187,627	215,577	247,324	283,020	324,092	371,631	425,635	485,585	550,603	619,929
Caribbean	16,725	18,314	20,226	22,489	24,616	27,116	30,016	33,272	36,847	40,662	44,504
Middle America	35,835	41,538	48,689	57,202	67,003	78,652	92,631	109,180	128,160	149,315	172,670
Mexico	26,606	30,949	36,369	42,859	50,313	59,204	69,965	82,803	97,585	114,055	132,244
Temperate South America	25,437	28,065	30,821	33,493	36,073	38,747	41,564	44,407	47,152	49,719	52,078
Argentina	17,150	18,928	20,611	22,179	23,748	25,384	27,064	28,678	30,189	31,584	32,861
Chile	6,091	6,743	7,585	8,510	9,369	10,253	11,235	12,303	13,379	14,405	15,355
Tropical South America	85,928	99,709	115,841	134,139	155,328	179,578	207,421	238,774	273,426	310,907	350,676
Brazil	52,901	61,864	71,539	82,541	95,204	109,730	126,389	145,082	165,757	188,273	212,507
Colombia	11,689	13,593	15,905	18,691	22,075	25,890	30,215	35,050	40,324	45,874	51,464
Peru	7,915	8,775	9,993	11,440	13,248	15,326	17,711	20,424	23,478	26,871	30,561
Venezuela	5,145	6,073	7,635	9,105	10,559	12,213	14,134	16,326	18,706	21,143	23,552
Northern America	166,073	181,741	198,662	214,040	226,389	236,841	248,833	262,344	275,136	286,163	296,199
Canada	13,737	15,736	17,909	19,644	21,406	22,801	24,576	26,511	28,357	30,000	31,613
United States	152,271	165,932	180,671	194,303	204,879	213,925	224,133	235,701	246,639	256,015	264,430
East Asia	674,821	728,914	787,980	854,003	926,221	1,005,665	1,087,008	1,164,108	1,232,719	1,301,064	1,369,069
China	558,190	605,081	654,488	710,324	771,840	838,803	907,609	973,155	1,031,142	1,089,572	1,147,987
Japan	83,625	89,815	94,096	98,881	104,331	111,120	117,546	122,445	126,213	129,567	132,929
Other East Asia	33,005	34,018	39,396	44,799	50,050	55,742	61,853	68,508	75,363	81,925	88,153
Korea	30,096	30,524	35,221	39,814	44,613	49,800	55,370	61,439	67,707	73,726	79,456
Korea, Dem. People's Republic of	9,740	9,100	10,526	12,100	13,892	15,852	17,926	20,179	22,581	25,022	27,457
Korea, Rep. of	20,356	21,424	24,695	27,714	30,721	33,949	37,444	41,260	45,126	48,704	51,998
South Asia	692,916	762,815	855,711	970,157	1,101,199	1,249,793	1,426,843	1,624,722	1,836,258	2,053,610	2,267,266
Eastern South Asia	173,228	191,741	216,986	247,747	282,969	323,836	370,855	423,221	478,712	535,640	591,622
Burma	18,380	20,166	22,254	24,754	27,748	31,240	35,195	39,687	44,573	49,701	54,902
Indonesia	75,449	82,791	92,701	105,070	119,467	136,044	154,869	175,471	196,576	217,623	237,507
Malaysia	6,187	6,934	7,908	9,080	10,466	12,093	13,998	16,076	18,260	20,239	22,054
Philippines	20,988	23,913	27,561	32,030	37,604	44,437	52,203	60,842	70,119	79,876	89,707
Thailand	20,010	22,762	26,392	30,641	35,745	42,093	49,473	57,784	66,752	76,135	85,618
Vietnam	24,600	26,495	30,200	34,835	39,106	43,451	48,634	54,612	61,302	68,491	75,802

(Continued)

Population (Continued)

TABLE 2.P.22 (Continued)

(in 1,000)

Country	1950	1955	1960	1965	1970	1975	1980	1985	1990	1995	2000
Vietnam Dem.	12,973	14,080	16,100	18,711	21,154	23,798	26,901	30,455	34,431	38,729	43,141
Vietnam, Rep. of	11,627	12,415	14,100	16,124	17,952	19,653	21,733	24,157	26,871	29,762	32,661
Middle South Asia	475,345	520,353	580,563	655,811	741,710	837,799	953,997	1,083,462	1,221,669	1,362,961	1,501,213
Afghanistan	11,660	12,552	13,736	15,097	16,978	19,280	22,038	25,207	28,739	32,598	36,654
Bangladesh	41,037	45,607	51,446	58,795	67,692	73,746	84,803	98,003	112,694	128,298	144,347
India	352,664	384,235	427,802	482,365	543,132	613,217	694,309	782,890	876,051	969,748	1,059,429
Iran	16,913	19,020	21,554	24,662	28,359	32,923	38,492	44,904	51,897	59,221	66,593
Nepal	8,000	8,590	9,180	10,100	11,232	12,572	14,231	16,186	18,348	20,771	23,196
Pakistan	36,450	40,609	45,851	52,415	60,449	70,560	82,952	97,354	113,239	129,877	146,924
Sri Lanka	7,678	8,723	9,889	11,164	12,514	13,986	15,465	16,922	18,530	20,002	21,339
Western South Asia	44,343	50,721	58,161	66,599	76,520	88,158	101,992	118,039	135,877	155,009	174,432
Iraq	5,180	5,940	6,847	7,976	9,356	11,067	13,125	15,578	18,277	21,242	24,445
Turkey	20,809	23,859	27,509	31,151	35,232	39,882	45,363	51,692	58,656	65,843	72,588
Europe	391,968	407,616	425,154	444,990	459,085	473,128	486,611	500,090	513,779	526,994	539,812
Eastern Europe	88,500	92,967	96,709	100,055	102,942	106,297	109,717	112,889	115,780	118,645	121,749
Czechoslovakia	12,389	13,093	13,654	14,159	14,339	14,757	15,189	15,579	15,941	16,329	16,807
German, Dem. Rep.	18,387	17,944	17,240	17,019	17,058	17,193	17,358	17,553	17,761	17,977	18,233
Hungary	9,338	9,825	9,984	10,153	10,338	10,534	10,721	10,841	10,907	10,972	11,069
Poland	24,824	27,281	29,561	31,496	32,473	33,841	35,316	36,685	37,824	38,822	39,846
Romania	16,311	17,325	18,403	19,027	20,244	21,178	22,057	22,908	23,793	24,755	25,758
Northern Europe	72,477	73,832	75,834	78,566	80,309	81,975	83,740	85,501	87,424	89,355	91,320
United Kingdom	50,616	51,199	52,559	54,520	55,480	56,427	57,519	58,667	59,993	61,363	62,794
Southern Europe	108,552	113,120	118,098	123,357	127,696	132,354	137,106	141,875	146,669	151,293	155,685
Italy	46,769	48,200	50,223	51,944	53,565	55,023	56,319	57,508	58,677	59,801	60,876
Spain	27,868	29,056	30,303	31,913	33,779	35,433	37,209	39,080	41,041	43,008	44,924
Yugoslavia	16,346	17,519	18,402	19,434	20,371	21,322	22,299	23,236	24,107	24,908	25,653
Western Europe	122,439	127,697	134,513	143,012	148,137	152,503	156,049	159,825	163,906	167,702	171,058
France	41,736	43,428	45,684	48,758	50,670	52,913	55,103	57,052	58,816	60,508	62,131
German, Fed. Rep. of	49,989	52,382	55,433	59,012	60,700	61,682	62,023	62,858	64,188	65,370	66,242
Netherlands	10,114	10,751	11,480	12,292	13,032	13,599	14,107	14,614	15,116	15,588	16,010
Oceania	12,632	14,139	15,771	17,507	19,323	21,308	23,482	25,777	28,109	30,431	32,715
Australia and New Zeland	10,127	11,376	12,687	14,015	15,371	16,840	18,403	19,997	21,549	23,038	24,512
Australia	8,219	9,240	10,315	11,387	12,552	13,809	15,140	16,490	17,796	19,034	20,245
U.S.S.R.	180,075	196,159	214,329	230,936	242,768	255,038	268,115	281,540	293,742	304,607	315,027
World Total	2,501,243	2,722,326	2,985,937	3,287,657	3,609,600	3,967,005	4,373,210	4,815,621	5,279,041	5,761,465	6,253,135
More developed region	857,305	914,772	975,748	1,036,355	1,084,018	1,131,715	1,181,072	1,230,823	1,277,570	1,320,089	1,360,557
Less developed region	1,643,938	1,807,554	2,010,189	2,251,302	2,525,582	2,835,290	3,192,138	3,584,798	4,001,471	4,441,376	4,892,579

Source: USDA (1977). World population growth: Analysis and new projections of the United Nations. USDA Foreign Agricultural Report *129.*

Pork Carcass, Retail Yield

TABLE 2.P.23
Retail yield of a side of pork carcass [pork carcass (side) = 70 lb]

Retail Cut	% of Carcass	Lb
Fresh ham	18–23	13–16
Trimmed loin	14–20	10–14
Fresh picnic	8–11	6–8
Fresh Boston butt	7–9	5–6
Fresh side	11–16	8–11
Spareribs and neckbones	4–6	3–4
Jowl	1½–4	1–3
Sausage	3–7	2–5
Hocks	3–4	2–3
Trimmed fat (for lard)	11–24	8–17

Source: Simonds, L. A., and Vanstavern, B. D. (1975). Buying meat for locker or home freezer. Ohio State Univ. Coop. Ext. Serv. Bull.

Pork Chart

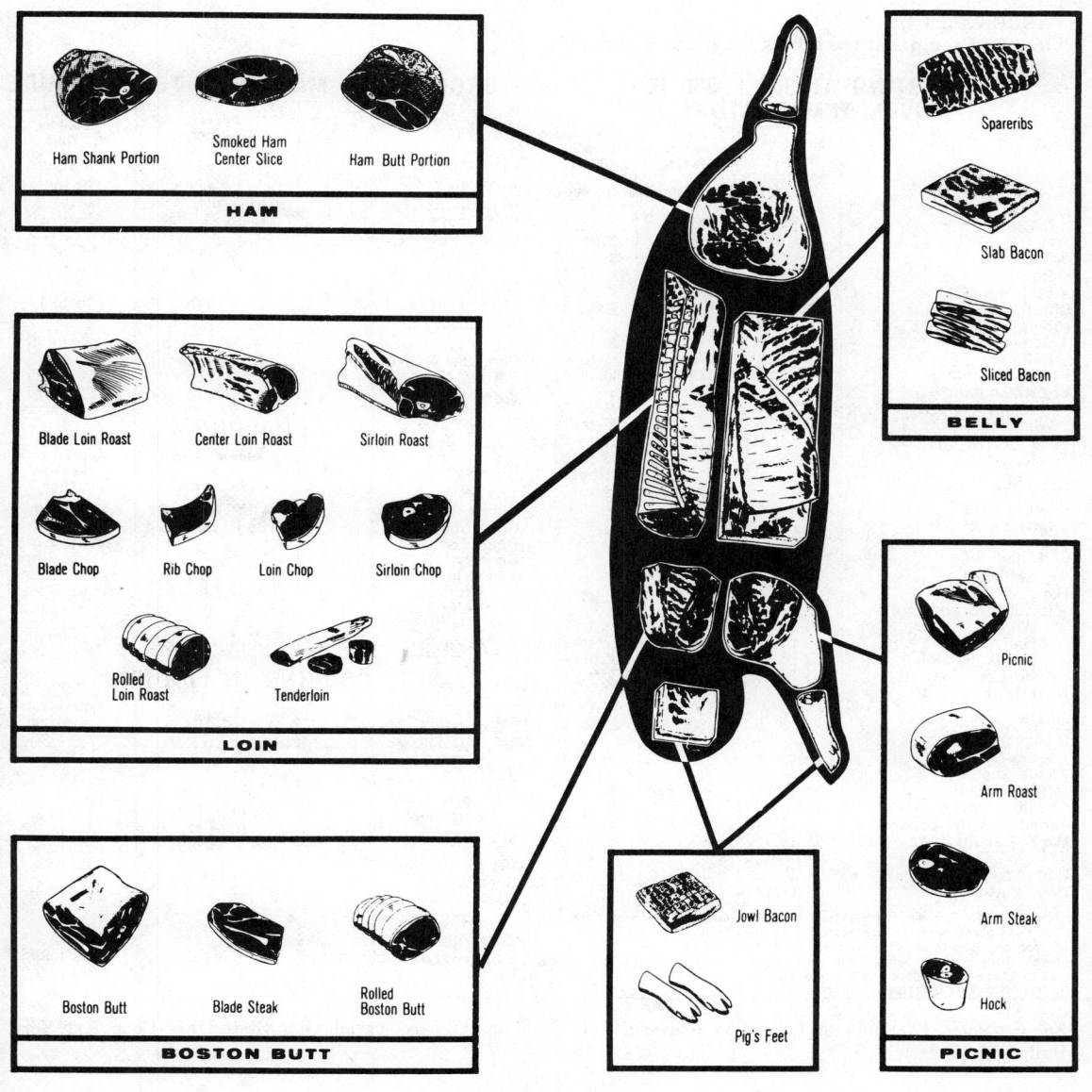

FIGURE 2.P.6

Source: USDA (1969). How to buy meat for your freezer. USDA Home and Garden Bull. *166.*

Pork, Cooking

TABLE 2.P.24
Time and temperature tables for pork cookery

ROASTING AT 300°F.-350°F.* OVEN TEMPERATURE

CUT	Approximate Weight	Meat Thermometer Reading	Approximate[1] Cooking Time
FRESH	**Pounds**	**Degrees F.**	**Min. Per Lb.**
Loin			
Center	3 to 5	170° F.	30 to 35
Half	5 to 7	170° F.	35 to 40
End	3 to 4	170° F.	40 to 45
Roll	3 to 5	170° F.	35 to 40
Boneless Top	2 to 4	170° F.	30 to 35
Crown	4 to 6	170° F.	35 to 40
Picnic Shoulder			
Bone-In	5 to 8	170° F.	30 to 35
Rolled	3 to 5	170° F.	35 to 40
Boston Shoulder	4 to 6	170° F.	40 to 45
Leg (fresh ham)			
Whole (boneless)	10 to 14	170° F.	24 to 28
Whole (bone-in)	12 to 16	170° F.	22 to 26
Half (bone-in)	5 to 8	170° F.	35 to 40
Tenderloin	½ to 1		45 to 60
			Hours
Back ribs		Cooked	1½ to 2½
Country-style		Well	
backbones		Done	1½ to 2½
Spareribs			1½ to 2½
Pork loaf	2		1¾
SMOKED			
Ham			
(cook-before-eating)			
Whole	10 to 14	160° F.	18 to 20
Half	5 to 7	160° F.	22 to 25
Shank Portion	3 to 4	160° F.	35 to 40
Butt Portion	3 to 4	160° F.	35 to 40
Ham (fully-cooked)[2]			
Half	5 to 7	140° F.	18 to 24
Loin	3 to 5	160° F.	25 to 30
Picnic Shoulder			
(cook-before-eating)	5 to 8	170° F.	30 to 35
Picnic Shoulder			
(fully-cooked)	5 to 8	140° F.	25 to 30
Shoulder roll (butt)	2 to 4	170° F.	35 to 40
Canadian-style bacon	2 to 4	160° F.	35 to 40
Ham Kabobs	1" to 1½"		
	cubes		45 to 60
Ham loaf	2	160° F.	1½ hrs.
Ham Patties	1" thick	160° F.	45 to 60

*325°F. to 350°F. oven temperature is recommended for fresh pork and 300°F. to 325°F. oven temperature for smoked pork.
[1] Based on meat taken directly from the refrigerator.
[2] Heat "fully-cooked" whole hams to 140°F. internal temperature. Allow 15 to 18 minutes per pound for heating.
Source: National Livestock and Meat Board.

BROILING AT MODERATE TEMPERATURE

CUT	Approx. Thickness	Approx. Total Cooking Time
SMOKED		**Minutes**
Ham Slice	½ inch	10 to 12
Ham Slice	1 inch	16 to 20
Loin Chops	½ to ¾ inch	15 to 20
Canadian-Style Bacon		
Sliced	¼ inch	6 to 8
Sliced	½ inch	8 to 10
Bacon		4 to 5
Ham Patties	1 inch	16 to 20
FRESH		
Rib or loin chops	¾ to 1 inch	20 to 25
Shoulder Steaks	½ to ¾ inch	20 to 22
Patties	1 inch	20 to 25
Pork Kabobs	1½x1½x¾ to 1 inch	22 to 25

BRAISING

CUT	Approx. Weight or Thickness	Approx. Total Cooking Time
Chops, fresh	¾ to 1½ inches	45 to 60 min.
Spareribs	2 to 3 pounds	1½ hrs.
Backribs		1½ to 2 hrs.
Country-style backbones		1½ to 2 hrs.
Tenderloin		
Whole	¾ to 1 pound	45 to 60 min.
Fillets	½ inch	30 min.
Shoulder steaks	¾ inch	45 to 60 min.
Cubes	1 to 1¼ inches	45 to 60 min.

COOKING IN LIQUID

CUT	Approx. Weight	Approx. Total Cooking Time
SMOKED	**Pounds**	**Hours**
Ham (old style and		
country-cured		
Large	12 to 16	4½ to 5
Small	10 to 12	4½ to 5
Half	5 to 8	3 to 4
Picnic Shoulder	5 to 8	3½ to 4
Shoulder roll	2 to 4	1½ to 2
Hocks		2 to 2½
FRESH		
Spareribs		2 to 2½
Country-style backbones		2 to 2½
Hocks		2½ to 3

Source: Potts, B., Simonds, L., and Vanstavern, B. D. Meat specials are special. Ohio State Univ. Coop. Ext. Serv. Bull. *574.*

Pork, Cooking Cured Products

TABLE 2.P.25
Roasting and broiling cured ham products

Label instructions should be followed. When not available, one of the following cooking methods should be used.

Roasting (Baking)

Place meat on a rack in a shallow roasting pan. Insert meat thermometer so the bulb is centered in the thickest part but does not rest in fat or on bone. Do not add water or cover. Roast (bake) in a slow oven (325°F) until done—internal temperature of 140°F is recommended for fully-cooked or canned hams and arm picnic shoulders; 160°F for cook-before-eating hams, loins and Canadian-style bacon; and 170°F for cook-before-eating arm picnic shoulders and shoulder rolls (butts). If ham is to be glazed, brush glaze on the ham 15 to 30 min before the end of the cooking time.

Broiling

Set oven regulator for broiling. Broil meat 2 to 3 in. from heat until meat is lightly browned on one side. Turn meat and cook until done.

Panbroiling

Cuts cooked by broiling can also be panbroiled. Allow about half as much cooking time as for broiling.

Cooking in Liquid

Cook-before-eating arm picnic shoulders and shoulder rolls can also be cooked in liquid. Follow cooking instructions on the package label. In case of no instructions, simmer in water just to cover in a covered utensil, allowing 1½ hr for the shoulder roll and 3½ to 4 hr for the picnic.

Cut	Weight or Approx Thickness	Approx Total Cooking Time[1] at 325°F	Cut	Weight or Approx Thickness	Approx Total Cooking Time[1] at 325°F
		For Roasting (Baking)			
	(lb)	(hr)		(lb)	(hr)
Boneless ham, fully-cooked	3-4 (portion)	1½-1¾	Bone-in ham, cook-before-eating		
	5-7 (half)	2-2¼		3-4 (portion)	2½-2¾
	7-10	2½-3		5-7 (half)	3-3¼
	10-12	3-3½		10-12	3½-4
	12-14	3½-4		12-15	4-4½
Bone-in ham, fully-cooked				15-18	4½-5
	10-13	3-3½		18-22	5-6
	13-16	3½-4			
Semi-boneless ham, fully-cooked			Loin, cook-before-eating		
	4-6 (half)	1¾-2½		3-5	1-2
	10-12	3-3½			
Canned hams	1½-3	1-1½	Canadian-style bacon		
	3-7	1½-2		2-4	1¼-2¼
	7-10	2-2½			
	10-13	2½-3	Arm picnic shoulder, cook-before-eating		
Arm picnic shoulder, fully-cooked	4-8	1¾-2¾		4-8	2½-4
Boneless ham, cook-before-eating			Shoulder roll (butt), cook-before-eating		
	8-11	2½-3¼		2-3	1½-2
	11-14	3¼-4			

(Continued)

Pork Cooking Cured Products   (Continued)

TABLE 2.P.25   (Continued)

Cut	Approx Thickness (in.)	Approx Total Cooking Time (min)
For Broiling at Moderate Temp[2]		
Ham slice	½	10–12
Ham slice	1	16–20
Smoked loin chops	½–¾	15–20
Canadian-style bacon		
Sliced	¼	6–8
Sliced	½	8–10
Ham kabobs	1–1½	16–20
Ham patties	1	16–20

[1] Cooking times are for (1) heating fully-cooked or canned cuts to 140°F internal temperature as registered on a meat thermometer; (2) cooking cook-before-eating ham and loin cuts to 160°F; and (3) cooking cook-before-eating picnics and shoulder rolls to 170°F.
[2] Temperature that results from broiling ½ to 1-in. thick cuts 2 to 3 in. from the heat.

Source: Pork Industry Group. National Live Stock & Meat Board, Chicago.

Pork, Cooking Methods

TABLE 2.P.26
Suggested cooking methods

For fresh pork	
Arm or blade shoulder chop or steak	Pan fry, pan broil, or braise
Ham	Roast
Hocks	Simmer
Loin or rib roast	Roast
Loin or rib chops	Pan fry, pan broil, or braise
Shoulder roast (picnic) or shoulder butt roast (Boston butt)	Roast
Spareribs	Roast or braise
Tenderloin	Pan fry, pan broil, or braise
For cured pork	
Bacon	Broil, pan broil, or pan fry
Canadian bacon	Roast, broil, pan broil, or pan fry
Ham, whole or part	Roast or simmer
Ham slices	Broil,[1] pan broil, pan fry, or braise
Ham shanks	Simmer or braise
Shoulder (picnic) or shoulder butt (Boston butt)	Roast or simmer

[1] Thin slices only.

Source: USDA (1969). Pork in family meals. USDA Home and Garden Bull. *160.*

Pork, Cooking Yield

TABLE 2.P.27
Yield of boneless cooked meat from retail pork cuts

Cut of pork	Approximate yield of cooked lean and some fat from one pound of pork as purchased [1]	
	3-ounce servings	Volume, chopped or diced
	Number	*Cups*
Fresh:		
Ham:		
Bone-in	2½	1½
Boneless	3	2
Heart	2 to 2½	1½ to 2
Liver	3	
Loin chops, bone-in	2½	
Loin roast:		
Bone-in	2 to 2½	1 to 1½
Boneless	3 to 3½	2
Rib chops, bone-in	2 to 2½	
Shoulder roast (picnic):		
Bone-in	2	1 to 1½
Boneless	3	1½ to 2
Shoulder butt roast (Boston butt):		
Bone-in	3	1½ to 2
Boneless	3 to 3½	2
Spareribs	1½ to 2	
Cured (mild):		
Ham:		
Canned, boneless:		
Served cold	4½	2½ to 3
Heated before serving	4	2½
Cook-before-eating:		
Bone-in	3½	2
Boneless	4	2½
Fully cooked:		
Bone-in	3½	2
Boneless	4	2½
Shoulder (picnic):		
Bone-in	2½	1½
Boneless	3 to 3½	2
Shoulder butt (Boston butt):		
Bone-in	3	1½ to 2
Boneless	3½	2

[1] These figures allow no more than 10 percent fat on a cooked bone-in cut and no more than 15 percent fat on a cooked boneless cut.

Source: USDA (1969). Pork in family meals. USDA Home and Garden Bull. *160.*

Pork Cuts

TABLE 2.P.28
Characteristics and cooking methods for pork cuts

WHOLESALE CUTS	RETAIL CUTS	CHARACTERISTICS	COOKING METHODS
Ham Fresh Pickled, or Smoked	Ham, Whole	Corresponds to beef round with tail bone and portion of backbone removed. Outer skin or rind is left on the regular ham but it is removed, with excess fat, from the skinned ham.	Roast (bake); cook in liquid
	Ham, Shank Half	Lower half of ham. Includes shank and ½ of center section.	Roast (bake); cook in liquid
	Ham Shank	Cone-shaped, rind-covered piece containing shank bones.	Cook in liquid
	Ham, Butt Half	Upper half of ham. Includes butt and ½ of center section.	Roast (bake); cook in liquid
	Ham Butt	Same as above minus most of center section.	Roast (bake); cook in liquid
	Ham, Center Baking Piece	Center section of ham. Both cut surfaces look like center slices.	Roast (bake); cook in liquid
	Ham, Center Slice	Oval shape, small round bone, four separate muscles.	Broil, panbroil, panfry
	Ham, Boneless	Boneless roll. Fresh, pickled, or smoked.	Roast (bake); cook in liquid
Loin Also Tenderloin, Boneless Back Strip and Canadian Style Bacon	Tenderloin	Long tapering round muscle. Weighs ½ to 1 pound.	Roast; braise
	Frenched Tenderloin	Piece cut from tenderloin and flattened.	Braise; panfry
	Boneless Loin Roast	Boneless back strip. Two pieces sometimes tied together.	Roast
	Canadian Style Bacon	Boneless back strip, cured and smoked.	Roast; broil; panbroil; panfry
	Butterfly Chop	Double chop, hinged together, cut from boneless loin strip.	Braise; panfry
	Sirloin Roast	Ham end of loin containing hip bone.	Roast
	Blade Loin Roast	Shoulder end of loin containing rib bones and blade bone.	Roast
	Loin Chop	T-shaped bone and two muscles (back strip and tenderloin).	Braise; panfry
	Rib Chop	Alternate chops have rib bone. May be "frenched".	Braise; panfry
	Crown Roast	Rib sections "frenched" and formed in shape of crown.	Roast

(Continued)

Pork Cuts (Continued)

TABLE 2.P.28 (Continued)

WHOLESALE CUTS	RETAIL CUTS	CHARACTERISTICS	COOKING METHODS
Picnic Shoulder Fresh, Pickled, or Smoked	Picnic Shoulder	Includes arm and shank sections of the shoulder.	Roast (bake); cook in liquid
	Rolled Picnic Shoulder	Boneless roll. Fresh, pickled or smoked.	Roast (bake); cook in liquid
	Cushion Picnic Shoulder	Arm section of fresh picnic with pocket for stuffing.	Roast
	Arm Steak	Oval at one end, squared off at other. Small round bone.	Braise; panfry
	Pork Hock	Round, tapering, skin-covered piece containing shank bones.	Braise; cook in liquid
Boston Butt Also Smoked Shoulder Butt	Boston Butt	Upper half of shoulder. Contains part of blade bone.	Roast
	Blade Steak	Cut from Boston butt. Most steaks have section of blade bone.	Braise; panfry
	Smoked Shoulder Butt	Eye of Boston butt. Cured and smoked boneless roll.	Roast (bake); cook in liquid
	Sm. Sh. Butt Slices	Round boneless slices. Lean and fat intermixed.	Broil; panbroil; panfry
Side (Belly) Fresh, Salt Pickled, or Smoked	Fresh Side Pork	Usually sliced. Alternating layers of lean and fat.	Braise; panfry
	Pickled Side Pork	Same as above but cured in a sweet pickle solution.	Braise; panfry
	Salt Side Pork	Same as above but cured with dry salt.	Panfry; cook in liquid
	Sliced Bacon	Same as above but cured, dry or in pickle, then smoked.	Broil; panbroil; panfry
Spareribs	Spareribs	Ribs and breastbone which have been removed from the bacon strip.	Roast; braise; cook in liquid
Jowl	Jowl Bacon Square	Jowl, trimmed square, then cured and smoked. High percentage of fat. May be sliced.	Cook in liquid; broil; panbroil; panfry
Feet	Pig's Feet, Fresh	Contain bones and tendons of foot and ankle. Little lean meat.	Cook in liquid
	Pig's Feet, Pickled	Pickled, cooked and ready to eat.	No cooking necessary

Source: Meat Manual, 6th Edition. National Live Stock and Meat Board, Chicago.

Pork Cuts and Uses

TABLE 2.P.29
Pork cuts and how to use them

WHOLESALE CUT	DESCRIPTION OF CUT	RETAIL CUTS	PORK SPECIALTIES
FEET	Bone, skin, not much meat, but this is delicate.	Pig's feet	Brains— Fry, scramble with eggs
HAM OR LEG OF PORK	Solid meat, very little bone. Fresh or smoked.	Roasts, steaks	Lungs— Braise
BACON	Cured and smoked, fat streaked with lean.	Breakfast bacon	Head— Head cheese
LOIN	Tender, lean meat. May be boned and cured as Canadian style bacon.	Roasts, chops, tenderloin	Heart— Braise
PICNIC SHOULDER	Well flavored, largely lean meat, fresh or smoked.	Roasts, steaks	Liver— Fry, broil, braise, roast whole or as loaf
BOSTON BUTT	Higher in lean than any pork cut, very little bone	Boston butt, steaks, smoked shoulder butt	Tongue— Cook in water
SPARERIBS	Lean and fat, good flavor.	Spareribs	Tails— Cook in water with vegetables
			Ears and snouts— Cook in water with vegetables

Source: Meat Buying Manual. National Live Stock and Meat Board, Chicago.

Pork Loin Carving

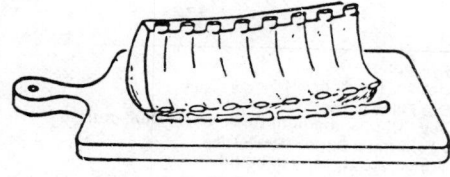

Have retailer saw backbone free from ribs for easier carving. Saw cut should not cut into meaty center.

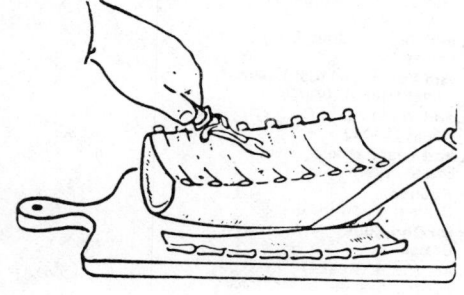

Before the roast is brought to the table, remove the backbone. Do this by cutting close along the bone, leaving as much meat on roast as possible. Place roast with bone side facing carver.

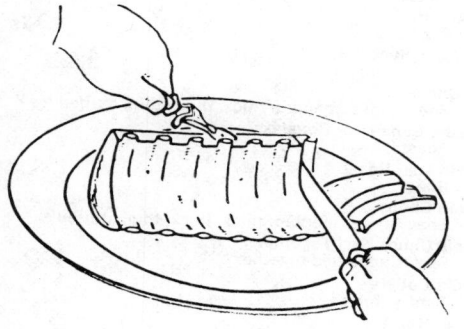

Insert the fork in the top of the roast. Make slices by cutting close along each side of the rib bone. One slice will contain the rib, the next will be boneless.

FIGURE 2.P.7

Source: Carving Meat. National Live Stock and Meat Board, Chicago.

Pork Loin Cooking

TABLE 2.P.30
How to cook cuts from the pork loin

Back Ribs
Braise, cook in liquid, roast
Back Ribs, Meaty
Braise, roast, cook in liquid
Blade/Bladeless Loin Chops
See "Chops, medium thick, thick, thin, stuffed"
Blade/Bladeless Loin Chops Tied Together
See "Chops tied together"
Blade/Bladeless Loin Roast
Roast
Blade Pieces
Cook in liquid, braise
Boneless Crown Roast
Roast
Brown and Serve (Breakfast) Chops
Panfry
Butterfly Chops
See "Chops, medium thick, thick, thin, stuffed"
Butterfly Cutlets
Braise, Panfry
Butterfly Top Loin
Braise, roast, broil
Canadian Style Bacon, Piece
Roast (Bake)
Canadian Style Bacon, Sliced
Broil, panbroil, panfry
Center Chops (Loin, Rib, Strip, Top Loin)
See "Chops, medium thick, thick, thin, stuffed"
Center Roast (Loin, Rib, Strip, Top Loin)
Roast
Chops, Medium Thick (½" to ¾")
Braise, panfry, broil, panbroil
Chops, Thick (1" to 2")
Braise, roast, broil
Chops, Thin (¼" to ⅜")
Braise, panfry
Chops, Stuffed
Braise, roast
Chops Tied Together
Best results when chops are separated and
cooked as regular chops
Combination Loaf (Pork, Beef, Veal)
Roast (Bake)
Country Style Back Bones
Braise, roast, cook in liquid
Cradle Roast
Roast
Crown Roast, Bone-In or Boneless
Roast
Cube Steak (Porklets)
Panfry, braise
Cutlets, Regular (about ¼")
Braise, panfry
Cutlets, Wafer (⅛" to 3/16")
Panfry, braise
Frenched Rib Chops
See "Chops, medium thick, thick, thin, stuffed"
Frenched Rib Roast
Roast
Ground Pork, Individual Loaves (or Pork with Veal/Beef)
Roast (Bake), braise
Ground Pork, Loaf (or Pork with Veal/Beef)
Roast (Bake)
Ground Pork, Patties
Braise, panfry
Loin Back Bones
Cook in liquid
Loin Back Bones, Meaty
Braise, roast, cook in liquid
Loin Chops
See "Chops, medium thick, thick, thin, stuffed"

Loin Eye Fillet
Braise, roast, broil
Loin Eye Fillet Slices
See "Chops, medium thick, thick, thin, stuffed"
Meaty Loin Back Bones/Back Ribs
Braise, roast, cook in liquid
Pork and Ham Loaf
Roast (Bake)
Pork and Veal Cube Steaks
Panfry, braise
Pork and Veal for Chop Suey
Braise
Pork and Veal Individual Loaves
Roast (Bake), braise
Pork and Veal Loaf
Roast (Bake)
Pork and Veal Patties
Braise, panfry
Pork Kabobs
Braise, roast, broil
Pork for Chop Suey
Braise
Porklets (Cube Steaks)
Panfry, braise
Pork Mates
Braise, roast
Pork Patties
Braise, panfry
Rib Back Bones
Cook in liquid
Rib Chops
See "Chops, medium thick, thick, thin, stuffed"
Roasts, Bone-In or Boneless
Roast
Rolled Loin Roast
Roast
Sirloin Chops
See "Chops, medium thick, thick, thin, stuffed"
Sirloin Chops Tied Together
See "Chops tied together"
Sirloin Cutlets
Panfry, braise
Sirloin Roast
Roast
Strip Loin Chops
See "Chops, medium thick, thick, thin, stuffed"
Strip Loin Roast
Roast
Stuffed Chops (All Kinds)
Braise, roast
Tenderloin, Frenched or Butterflied
Braise, panfry
Tenderloin Kabobs
Braise, roast, broil, panfry
Tenderloin Roll
Roast
Tenderloin Roundels
Roast, braise, broil, panfry
Tenderloin Tips
Braise, panfry
Tenderloin, Whole
Braise, roast, broil
Tipless Tenderloin
Braise, roast, broil
Top Loin Chops
See "Chops, medium thick, thick, thin, stuffed"
Top Loin Roast
Roast
Top Loin Wafer Cutlets
Panfry
Wafer Cutlets
Panfry

Source: Merchandising Pork Loins. National Live Stock and Meat Board, Chicago.

Pork Loin Nomenclature

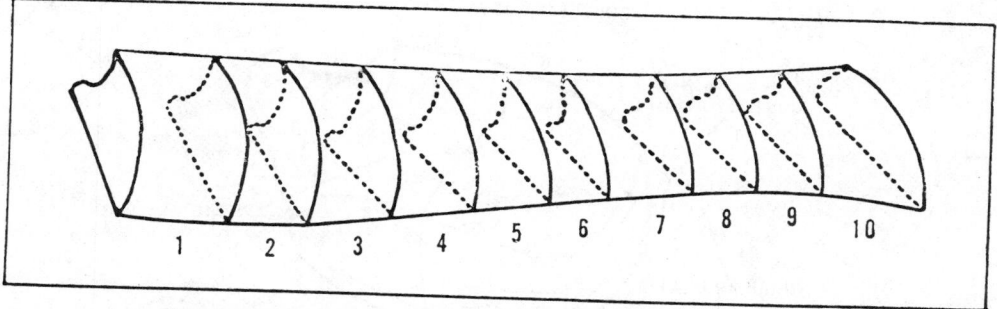

Recommended Name	Descriptive Information
(1) Pork loin blade roast	3-rib (blade/bladeless) loin roast
(1-2) Pork loin blade roast	5-rib (blade/bladeless) loin roast
(1-3) Pork loin blade roast	7-rib (blade/bladeless) loin roast
(1-4) Pork loin blade roast	9-rib (blade/bladeless) loin roast
(1-5) Pork loin blade half	Rib half (blade/bladeless) pork loin
(10) Pork loin sirloin roast	Pork sirloin (hip only)
(9-10) Pork loin sirloin roast	7 in. sirloin roast
(8-10) Pork loin sirloin roast	9 in. sirloin roast (or portion)
(6-10) Pork loin sirloin half	Loin half of pork loin
(2-9) Pork loin center loin roast or chops	Pork center loin roast or chops

FIGURE 2.P.8

Source: Uniform Retail Meat Identity Standards. (1973). National Live Stock and Meat Board, Chicago.

Pork, Percentages of Daily Recommended Allowances

TABLE 2.P.31

Percentages of daily recommended allowances* (based on $3\frac{1}{2}$ oz cooked lean pork)

	Age	Protein	Calories	Iron	Phosphorus	Magnesium	Thiamin	Riboflavin	Niacin	Vit. B$_6$	Vit. B$_{12}$
CHILDREN	1-3	124	18	23	30	16	147	36	49	69	110
	4-6	95	13	35	30	12	114	26	37	46	73
	7-10	79	10	35	30	10	86	24	28	35	55
MALES	11-14	65	9	19	20	7	74	19	24	26	37
	15-18	53	8	19	20	6	69	16	22	21	37
	19-22	53	8	35	30	7	69	16	22	21	37
	23-50	51	9	35	30	7	74	18	24	21	37
	51+	51	10	35	30	7	86	19	28	21	37
FEMALES	11-14	65	10	19	20	8	86	22	28	26	37
	15-18	59	11	19	20	8	94	21	31	21	37
	19-22	62	11	19	30	8	94	21	31	21	37
	23-50	62	12	19	30	8	103	24	34	21	37
	51+	62	13	35	30	8	103	26	37	21	37

*Figures based on 1974 National Research Council Recommended Dietary Allowances.

Source: Facts About Pork. (1974). National Live Stock and Meat Board, Chicago.

Pork Shoulder

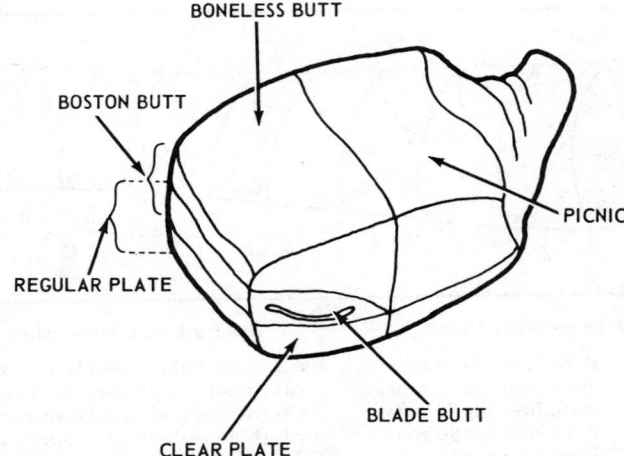

FIGURE 2.P.9
Breakdown of pork shoulder showing retail cuts

Source: U.S. Department of the Army (1969). Food inspection specialist. *TM 8-451.*

Pork Storage

TABLE 2.P.32
Suggested home storage periods to maintain high quality in pork

	Storage period	
Product	Refrigerator, 35° to 40° F.	Freezer, 0° F.
Fresh raw pork:		
Chops	3 to 5 days	3 to 4 months
Roasts	3 to 5 days	4 to 8 months
Sausage	1 to 2 days	1 to 2 months
Variety meats	1 to 2 days	3 to 4 months
Cured or processed pork:		
Bacon	7 days	1 month or less [1]
Frankfurters	7 days	2 weeks
Ham:		
Whole	7 days	1 to 2 months [1]
Half	3 to 5 days	1 to 2 months [1]
Slices	3 days	1 to 2 months [1]
Large canned, unopened	Several months	
Luncheon meat	3 to 5 days	Not recommended
Sausage:		
Smoked	7 days	Not recommended
Dry and semi-dry	2 to 3 weeks	Not recommended
Cooked pork:		
Cooked pork and pork dishes	1 to 2 days	2 to 3 months
Gravy and meat broth	1 to 2 days	2 to 3 months

[1] Frozen cured meat loses quality rapidly and should be used as soon as possible.

Source: USDA (1969). Pork in family meals. USDA Home and Garden Bull. *160.*

Pork Wholesale Cuts

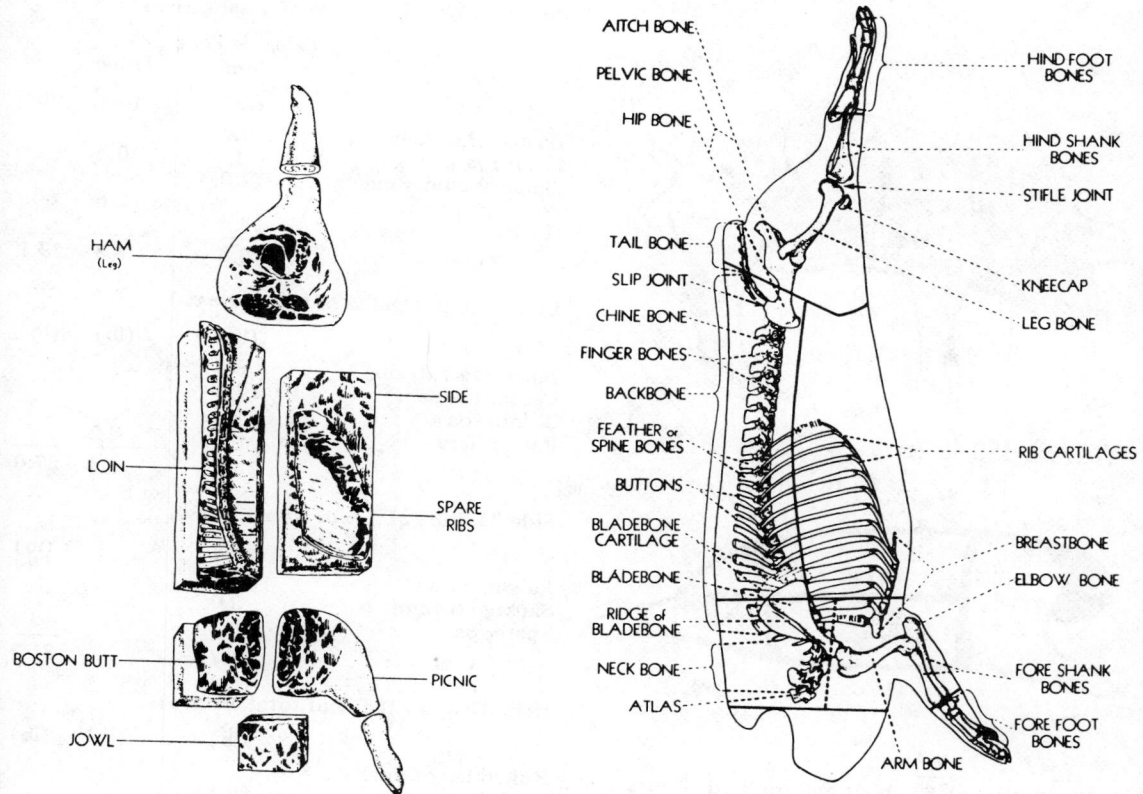

FIGURE 2.P.10
Wholesale cuts of pork (left); structure, location, and names of carcass bones (right)
Source: Cooking Meat in Quantity. National Live Stock and Meat Board, Chicago.

Pork Yield

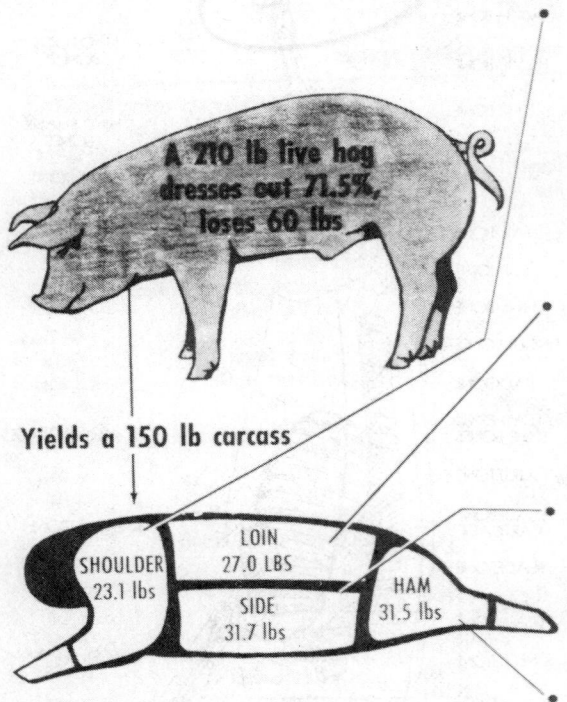

Yields a 150 lb carcass

An additional 30 lb of fat for lard, bones and waste further reduces this 150-lb carcass to only 120 lb of saleable retail cuts—chops, hams, bacon, ribs and sausage—that the retailer wraps and puts on display in the meat case.

Figures are averages taken from actual cut-out tests. Carcass data vary, depending on cutting method and type of hog.

Shoulder 23.1 lb (15.4% of total carcass)

	Saleable Pork		
	Cuts	Other	
	(lb)	(lb)	(lb)
Boston shoulder	9.4		
Fat for lard		0.5	
Picnic shoulder cubes	7.0		
Bone		2.8	
Hocks	3.4		
Total	19.8	3.3	23.1

Loin 27.0 lb (18.0% of total carcass)

	(lb)	(lb)	(lb)
Blade roast (5 rib)	6.3		
Center chops	13.3		
Sirloin roast	4.2		
Fat for lard		3.2	
Total	23.8	3.2	27.0

Side 31.7 lb (21.1% of total carcass)

	(lb)		(lb)
Bacon, cured	24.0		
Sausage trimmings	2.0		
Spareribs	5.7		
Total	31.7		31.7

Ham 31.5 lb (21.0% of total carcass)

	(lb)	(lb)	(lb)
Rolled leg of pork roast, boneless	19.8		
Sausage trimmings	2.8		
Skin	2.2		
Fat for lard		3.2	
Bone and shrink		3.5	
Total	24.8	6.7	31.5

Miscellaneous 36.7 lb (24.5% of total carcass)

	(lb)	(lb)	(lb)
Jowl, trimmed	4.5		
Feet, tail, neckbones	9.0		
Sausage trimmings	6.4		
Fat for lard		16.8	
Total	19.9	16.8	36.7

	(lb)
Total saleable pork cuts	120.0
Total fat for lard	23.7
Bone and shrink	6.3
Total carcass weight	150.0

FIGURE 2.P.11

Source: A Hog's Not All Chops. (1972). National Live Stock and Meat Board, Chicago.

Portion Size

TABLE 2.P.33
Typical portion sizes for menu items

Beverages		Beef		Sandwiches (excluding bread)	
Coffee	4 oz	Roasts	6 oz	Beef	4 oz
Tea	4 oz	Steaks		Cheese	2 oz
Milk	½ pt	Chateaubriand	16 oz	Chicken	2 oz
Soft drinks	4–6 oz	Filet mignon	6 oz	Ham	2 oz
Breads, rolls, cereals		Minute	6 oz	Hamburgers	2–4 oz
Bread	2 oz	Porterhouse	16 oz	Turkey	2 oz
Cream of wheat	4 oz	Salisbury	8 oz	Seafood	
Hot rolls	2 oz	Sirloin	8 oz	Clams (Little Neck)	12
Muffins (cakes)	2	T-bone	12 oz	Crabs, soft-shell	2
Cereals, flaked	4 oz	Ham	6 oz	Fish	6–7 oz
Cereals, puffed	2 oz	Lamb chops	10 oz	Frogs' legs	8 oz
Toast	4 oz	Liver	4 oz	Lobster, half	12 oz
Casseroles, stews, etc.		Pork chops	7 oz	Oysters	6
Baked beans	6 oz	Sausage	6 oz	Shrimp	6 oz
Chili con carne	6 oz	Veal chops	8 oz	Soups	
Corned beef	6 oz	Veal cutlets	5 oz	Cup	6 oz
Corned beef hash	6 oz	Pastries, desserts, etc.		Bowl	8 oz
Goulash	6 oz	Cakes	2 oz	Vegetables	
Ham a la king	4 oz	Ice cream	4 oz	Asparagus, fresh	
Macaroni and		Pies, fruit	8 oz	pieces	7
cheese	5 oz	Puddings	5 oz	Asparagus, tips	5 oz
Meat loaf	5 oz	Poultry		Beans, green	4 oz
Short ribs	12 oz	Chicken, fried	8 oz	Beans, lima	4 oz
Spaghetti	5 oz	Chicken, broiled	8 oz	Beets	5 oz
Spanish rice	5 oz	Duck	10 oz	Cauliflower	5 oz
Stews	7 oz	Turkey	7 oz	Carrots	5 oz
Stuffed cabbage	4 oz	Salads		Corn, cob (ears)	2
Fruits		Cole slaw	3 oz	Corn, kernel	5 oz
Canned	4 oz	Chicken salad	4 oz	Potatoes	6 oz
Fresh	4–6 oz	Mixed vegetable	4 oz	Peas	4 oz
Meats		Potato	4 oz	Spinach	6 oz
Bacon	5 oz	Waldorf	4 oz	Squash	4 oz
				Tomatoes	5 oz

Source: Kazarian, E. A. (1975). *Food Service Facilities Planning*. AVI Publishing Co., Westport, Connecticut.

Potassium

TABLE 2.P.34
Potassium content of foods

	mg/100 g		mg/100 g
Lima beans	650	Carrots	341
Watermelon	600	Celery	341
Spinach	470	Corn	280
Artichokes	430	Tomatoes	244
Potatoes	407	Peaches	202
Brussels sprouts	390	Oranges	200
Broccoli	382	Lettuce	175
Bananas	370	Apples	110

Source: White, P. L., and Selvey, N. (editors) (1974). *Nutritional Qualities of Fresh Fruits and Vegetables*. Futura Publishing Co., Mt. Kisco, New York.

Potassium-Rich Foods

TABLE 2.P.35
Foods that are rich in potassium

Foods	Average Portion	Potassium (mg)	Calories
Fruits			
Orange	1 medium	360	95
Grapefruit	1 cup	380	75
Banana	1 medium	630	130
Strawberries	1 cup	270	55
Avocado	½ medium	380	275
Apricots	3 medium	500	55
Dates	1 cup	1390	500
Watermelon	½ slice	380	95
Cantaloupe	½ medium	880	75
Raisins	1 cup	1150	425
Prunes	4 large	240	90
Juices			
Orange	8-oz glass	440	105
Grapefruit	8-oz glass	370	130
Prune	8-oz glass	620	170
Pineapple	8-oz glass	340	120
Meats			
Hamburger	3 oz	290	310
Beef chuck	3 oz	310	260
Beef round	3 oz	340	200
Rib roast	3 oz	290	270
Turkey	4 oz	350	300
Vegetables			
Tomato	1 medium	340	30
Artichoke	1 medium	210	30
Brussels sprouts	1 cup	300	35

Source: Holvey, D. N. (1972). *The Merck Manual*, 12th Edition. Merck & Co., Rahway, New Jersey.

Poultry Breeds and Varieties

TABLE 2.P.36
Some breeds and varieties of poultry and their characteristics

Breed and Variety	Plumage	Standard Weight Cock (lb)	Hen (lb)	Comb Type	Ear Lobe Color	Skin Color	Shank Color	Shanks Feathered?	Egg Color
American:									
White Plymouth Rock	White	9½	7½	Single	Red	Yellow	Yellow	No	Brown
White Wyandotte	White	8½	6½	Rose	Red	Yellow	Yellow	No	Brown
Rhode Island Red	Red	8½	6½	Single and rose	Red	Yellow	Yellow	No	Brown
New Hampshire	Red	8½	6½	Single	Red	Yellow	Yellow	No	Brown
Asiatic:									
Brahma (light)	Columbian pattern	12	9½	Pea	Red	Yellow	Yellow	Yes	Brown
Cochin (buff)	Buff	11	8½	Single	Red	Yellow	Yellow	Yes	Brown
English:									
Australorp	Black	8½	6½	Single	Red	White	Dark slate	No	Brown
White Cornish	White	10½	8	Pea	Red	Yellow	Yellow	No	Brown
Mediterranean:									
White Leghorn	White	6	4½	Single and rose	White	Yellow	Yellow	No	White

Source: Ensminger, M. E. (1969). Animal Science. Interstate Printers & Publishers, Danville, Illinois.

Poultry Class

TABLE 2.P.37
The following are cooking recommendations and identification labeling for classes of poultry

The following are cooking recommendations and identification labeling for classes of poultry:

Young tender-meated classes are most suitable for barbecuing, frying, broiling, or roasting.

Young chickens may be labeled: young chicken, Rock Cornish game hen, broiler, fryer, roaster, or capon.

Young turkeys may be labeled: young turkey, fryer-roaster, young hen, or young tom.

Young ducks may be labeled: duckling, young duckling, broiler duckling, fryer duckling, or roaster duckling.

Mature, less-tender meated classes may be preferred for stewing, baking, soups, or salads.

Mature chickens may be labeled: mature chicken, old chicken, hen, stewing chicken, or fowl.

Mature turkeys may be labeled: mature turkey, yearling turkey, or old turkey.

Mature ducks, geese, and guineas may be labeled: mature or old.

Source: USDA (1968). How to buy poultry. USDA Home and Garden Bull. 157.

Poultry Composition

TABLE 2.P.38
Composition of poultry products

(Dashes (–) denote lack of reliable data for a constituent believed to be present in measurable amount)

Foods, approximate measures, units, and weight (edible part unless footnotes indicate otherwise)	Grams	Water (Percent)	Food energy (Calories)	Protein (Grams)	Fat (Grams)	Fatty Acids Saturated (total) (Grams)	Fatty Acids Unsaturated Oleic (Grams)	Fatty Acids Unsaturated Linoleic (Grams)	Carbohydrate (Grams)	Calcium (Milligrams)	Phosphorus (Milligrams)	Iron (Milligrams)	Potassium (Milligrams)	Vitamin A value (International units)	Thiamin (Milligrams)	Riboflavin (Milligrams)	Niacin (Milligrams)	Ascorbic acid (Milligrams)
Poultry and poultry products:																		
Chicken, cooked:																		
Breast, fried,[2,3] bones removed, 2.8 oz 1/2 breast (3.3 oz with bones).	79	58	160	26	5	1.4	1.8	1.1	1	9	218	1.3	—	70	.04	.17	11.6	—
Drumstick, fried,[2,3] bones removed (2 oz with bones). 1.3 oz	38	55	90	12	4	1.1	1.3	.9	Trace	6	89	.9	—	50	.03	.15	2.7	—
Half broiler, broiled, bones removed (10.4 oz with bones). 6.2 oz	176	71	240	42	7	2.2	2.5	1.3	0	16	355	3.0	483	160	.09	.34	15.5	—
Chicken, canned, boneless 3 oz	85	65	170	18	10	3.2	3.8	2.0	0	18	210	1.3	117	200	.03	.11	3.7	3
Chicken a la king, cooked (home recipe). 1 cup	245	68	470	27	34	2.7	14.3	3.3	12	127	358	2.5	404	1,130	.10	.42	5.4	12
Chicken and noodles, cooked (home recipe). 1 cup	240	71	365	22	18	5.9	7.1	3.5	26	26	247	2.2	149	430	.05	.17	4.3	Trace
Chicken chow mein:																		
Canned 1 cup	250	89	95	7	Trace	—	—	—	18	45	85	1.3	418	150	.05	.10	1.0	13
From home recipe 1 cup	250	78	255	31	10	2.4	3.4	3.1	10	58	293	2.5	473	280	.08	.23	4.3	10
Chicken potpie (home recipe), baked,[19] piece (1/3 or 9-in diam. pie). 1 piece	232	57	545	23	31	11.3	10.9	5.6	42	70	232	3.0	343	3,090	.34	.31	5.5	5
Turkey, roasted, flesh without skin:																		
Dark meat, piece, 2 1/2 by 1 5/8 by 1/4 in. 4 pieces	85	61	175	26	7	2.1	1.5	1.5	0	—	—	2.0	338	—	.03	.20	3.6	—
Light meat, piece, 4 by 2 by 1/4 in. 2 pieces	85	62	150	28	3	.9	.6	.7	0	—	—	1.0	349	—	.04	.12	9.4	—
Light and dark meat:																		
Chopped or diced 1 cup	140	61	265	44	9	2.5	1.7	1.8	0	11	351	2.5	514	—	.07	.25	10.8	—
Pieces (1 slice white meat, 4 by 2 by 1/4 in with 2 slices dark meat, 2 1/2 by 1 5/8 by 1/4 in). 3 pieces	85	61	160	27	5	1.5	1.0	1.1	0	7	213	1.5	312	—	.04	.15	6.5	—

[1,9] Crust made with vegetable shortening and enriched flour.
[2,3] Vegetable shortening used.

Source: Consumer and Food Economics Institute (1977). Nutritive value of foods. USDA Home and Garden Bull. 72.

Poultry, Dressing Percentage

TABLE 2.P.39
Dressing percentages of the several kinds of poultry processed at Ontario commercial processing plants

Kind	Sex	As a Percentage of Live Weight				Giblets						As a Percentage of Dressed Weight			
		Hot Dressed	Heads	Legs	Carcass and Neck	Heart	Liver	Gizzard	Total	Total Ready-to-Cook	Chilled Carcass and Neck	Carcass and Neck	Total Giblets	Total Ready-to-Cook	Chilled Carcass
		%	%	%	%	%	%	%	%	%	%	%	%	%	%
Chicken Broilers	Male	92.1	2.7	5.3	72.2	0.5	2.1	1.9	4.6	76.7	72.8	78.3	4.9	83.3	79.0
	Female	91.8	2.9	4.8	71.5	0.5	2.2	2.3	5.1	76.7	72.9	77.9	5.6	83.5	79.5
	Male	94.5	2.6	4.7	74.2	0.4	1.9	1.6	3.9	78.2	76.4	78.5	4.2	82.7	80.9
	Female	92.6	2.5	3.9	73.8	0.4	1.9	2.3	4.7	78.5	74.8	79.7	5.1	84.8	80.7
Capons		90.3	2.4	3.9	68.9	0.4	1.7	2.0	4.0	75.7	71.5	79.3	4.5	83.8	79.1
Turkeys B.B.W.	Male	92.6	1.8	1.7	77.0	0.4	1.9	1.2	3.6	80.6	80.1	83.2	3.8	87.1	86.6
	Female	92.0	1.5	2.7	75.8	0.4	1.7	1.6	3.6	79.4	78.7	82.4	4.0	86.3	85.5
Turkey Broilers B.B.W.	Male	89.9	3.7	3.1	75.8	0.4	1.3	1.4	3.2	79.0	81.5	84.3	3.5	87.8	89.5
	Female	92.8	2.8	2.6	77.0		1.7[2]	1.5	3.2	80.1	80.5	83.0	3.4	86.3	86.8
Pekin Ducks	Male	85.8	4.3	2.1	64.4	0.7	3.3	1.8	5.7	70.1	67.9	75.1	6.6	81.7	79.1
	Female	84.8	4.0	2.0	64.7	0.6	3.0	1.9	5.5	70.3	64.7	76.3	6.5	82.9	76.3
Pheasants	Male	91.7	3.0	2.4	76.8	0.5	1.9	1.8	4.3	81.1	78.9	83.7	4.7	88.4	86.0
	Female	90.8	2.8	2.1	75.1	0.5	1.8	2.2	4.5	79.6	78.8	82.7	4.9	87.6	86.8

Note:
(2) Hearts and livers

Poultry Products Lab.
Ontario Agricultural College
1962-63

Source: Snyder, E. S., and Orr, H. L. (1964). Poultry meat. Dep. Agric. Publ. 9, Can. Dep. Agric., Ottawa.

Poultry Grade Stamp

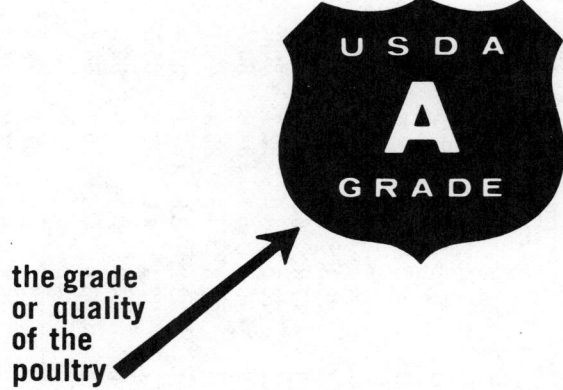

FIGURE 2.P.12

Source: USDA (1968). How to buy poultry. USDA Home and Garden Bull. *157*.

Poultry Inspection and Grade Stamp

FIGURE 2.P.13

Source: USDA (1968). How to buy poultry. USDA Home and Garden Bull. *157*.

Poultry Inspection Stamp

**Assurance
of wholesomeness**

FIGURE 2.P.14

Source: USDA (1968). How to buy poultry. USDA Home and Garden Bull. *157*.

Poultry Roasting

TABLE 2.P.40
Roasting guide for poultry

Kind	Ready-to-cook weight [1]	Approximate total roasting time at 325° F.[2]	Internal temperature of poultry when done
Chickens, whole:	*Pounds*	*Hours*	*Degrees F.*
Broilers, fryers, or roasters	1½ to 2½	1 to 2	
	2½ to 4½	2 to 3½	
Capons	5 to 8	2½ to 3½	
Ducks	4 to 6	2 to 3	
Geese	6 to 8	3 to 3½	
	8 to 12	3½ to 4½	
Turkeys:			
Whole	6 to 8	3 to 3½	180 to 185 in thigh.
	8 to 12	3½ to 4½	180 to 185 in thigh.
	12 to 16	4½ to 5½	180 to 185 in thigh.
	16 to 20	5½ to 6½	180 to 185 in thigh.
	20 to 24	6½ to 7	180 to 185 in thigh.
Halves, quarters, and pieces	3 to 8	2 to 3	
	8 to 12	3 to 4	
Boneless turkey roasts	3 to 10	3 to 4	170 to 175 in center.

[1] Weight of giblets and neck included for whole poultry.

[2] Cooking time suggested is for stuffed poultry (except for turkey parts and boneless roasts). Unstuffed whole poultry may take slightly less time than stuffed poultry.

Cooking time is only approximate; a meat thermometer can be used to help determine doneness of whole turkeys. Stuffing temperature should reach at least 165° F.

Cooking time is based on chilled poultry or poultry that has just been thawed—temperature not above 40° F. Unstuffed poultry cooked from the frozen state will take longer. Do not use this table for frozen commercially stuffed poultry

Source: USDA (1974). Poultry in family meals. USDA Home and Garden Bull. *110.*

Poultry, Time and Temperature, Cooking (Frozen)

TABLE 2.P.41
Recommended cooking times for frozen commercially stuffed poultry [1]

Kind and class	Weight as purchased	Approximate time, uncovered, at 325° F.	Approximate time, covered, at 400° F.
	Pounds	*Hours*	*Hours*
Turkeys	5 to 7	4½ to 6	2½ to 3½.
	7 to 9	6 to 6¾	3½ to 4.
	9 to 11	6¾ to 7¼	4 to 4½.
	11 to 13	7¼ to 8	4½ to 5.
	13 to 15	8 to 8½	5 to 5½.
	15 to 17	8½ to 10	5½ to 6.
Chickens:			
Rock Cornish game hens	2 to 2½	2½ to 3½	
Rock Roasters	4 to 5		2¾ to 3.
	5 to 6		3 to 3¼.
	6 and over		3¼ to 3½.

[1] Do not thaw before cooking.

Source: USDA (1974). Poultry in family meals. USDA Home and Garden Bull. *110.*

Poultry Yield

TABLE 2.P.42
Percentage relationship of cooked edible portion, parts and bones to live weight of various kinds of poultry processed in Ontario commercial plants

Kind	Sex	Method of Cooking	Cooked Carcass[2] and Neck %	White Meat %	Dark Meat %	Skin %	Neck Meat %	Total Edible Meat %	Carcass Bones %	Neck Bones %	Total Bones %	Total Loss[3] in Deboning %
Chicken Broilers	Male	Combined	51.9	15.3	13.5	4.2	1.3	36.8	10.9	0.7	11.6	3.5
	Female	Combined	52.7	17.0	13.8	5.1	1.4	37.4	11.0	0.8	11.7	3.6
Chicken Broilers	Male	Combined	51.8	16.9	14.4	4.1	1.2	36.6	11.0	0.7	11.8	3.4
	Female	Combined	51.2	17.2	13.6	4.5	1.4	36.8	10.2	0.7	10.8	2.7
Capons		Combined	47.9	17.6	14.7	3.5		35.8	8.7			3.4
Turkey Broilers	Male	Roasted	54.8	21.8	14.1	3.4	1.4	40.6	11.0	0.7	11.7	2.5
	Female	Roasted	57.7	22.3	15.1	3.5	1.3	42.2	10.7	0.7	11.4	3.6
Pekin Ducks	Male	Roasted	34.2	10.7[4]	9.0	4.3		24.1	7.8			2.6
	Female	Roasted	33.2	10.1	8.7	4.2		23.0	7.1			3.0
Pheasants	Male	Roasted	57.7	26.0	13.7	3.2	1.2	44.1	7.9	0.5	8.4	5.1
	Female	Roasted	52.7	24.0	12.3	3.0	1.0	40.4	6.8	0.4	7.2	5.0

Poultry Products Lab.
Ontario Agricultural College
1962-63

Note (2) For capons and ducks—carcass only, necks not included
(3) Includes waste + evaporation
(4) Breast meat

Source: Snyder, E. S., and Orr, H. L. (1964). Poultry meat. Dep. Agric. Publ. 9, Can. Dep. Agric., Ottawa.

Protein and Amino Acids, Color Reactions

TABLE 2.P.43

Some color reactions of proteins and amino acids

Test	Reagents	Linkage, group, or amino acid giving positive reaction	Color
Biuret reaction	Strong alkali, dilute copper sulfate	$HN\begin{cases} CO{-}NH_2 \\ CO{-}NH_2 \end{cases}$; $H_2C\begin{cases} CO{-}NH_2 \\ CO{-}NH_2 \end{cases}$; $\begin{matrix} CO{-}NH_2 \\ \mid \\ CO{-}NH_2 \end{matrix}$; $H_2N{-}\overset{\mid}{C}{-}CO{-}NH{-}\overset{\mid}{C}{-}$; three or more amino acids joined by peptide linkage; histidine	Reddish violet to violet
Millon reaction	Mercurous and mercuric nitrate in a solution of nitric acid	Hydroxyphenyl group; among amino acids specific for tyrosine	Brick-red
Xanthoproteic reaction	Concentrated nitric acid	Phenyl group; among amino acids, tyrosine and tryptophan give test most readily	Yellow, deepens to orange on addition of alkali
Glyoxylic or Hopkins-Cole reaction	Glyoxylic acid	Indole ring; among amino acids specific for tryptophan	Violet
Ninhydrin reaction	Triketohydrindene hydrate	α-Amino acids; proline; hydroxyproline	Blue
Ehrlich benzaldehyde reaction	p-Dimethylaminobenzaldehyde	Indole ring	Blue[a]
Sakaguchi reaction	α-Naphthol, sodium hypochlorite	Guanidine group; among amino acids specific for arginine	Red
Sullivan reaction	1,2-Naphthoquinone-4-sodium sulfonate; sodium sulfite; sodium hydrosulfite; sodium cyanide	Cysteine, cystine	Red

[a] Proteins or a mixture of amino acids containing tryptophan yield a blue color when treated with Ehrlich's reagent in the presence of concentrated hydrochloric acid. Indole yields a red color. With p-dimethylaminobenzaldehyde in sulfuric acid, tryptophan gives a red-violet color

Source: Jacobs, M. B. (editor). The Chemistry and Technology of Food and Food Products, 2nd Edition, Vol. 1. John Wiley & Sons, New York.

Protein Factors

TABLE 2.P.44
Factors suggested for use in converting percentages of nitrogen in various substances into percentages of protein[1]

Substance	Factor Suggested	Substance	Factor Suggested
Cereal grains		Brazil nut	5.46
Wheat, endosperm	5.70	Hazelnut	5.30
Wheat, embryo	5.80	Walnut	5.30
Wheat, bran	6.31	Peanut	5.46
Wheat, whole kernel	5.83	Soybean	5.71
Rye	5.83	Butternut	5.30
Barley	5.83	Castor bean	5.30
Oats	5.83		
Rice	5.95	Substances of animal origin	
Corn (maize)	5.26	Milk	6.38
		Eggs	6.25
Oilseeds and nuts		Meats	6.25
Hempseed	5.30	Gelatin	5.55
Cottonseed	5.30		
Sunflower seed	5.30		
Flaxseed	5.30	Leguminous seeds	
Squash seed	5.30	Navy bean	6.25
Pumpkin seed	5.30	Lima bean	6.25
Sesame seed	5.30	Mung bean	6.25
Cantaloupe seed	5.30	Velvet bean	6.25
Almonds	5.18	Adzuki bean	6.25
Coconut	5.30	Jack bean	6.25

[1] D. B. Jones, *U.S. Dept. Agr., Circ.* 183 (1941).

Source: Jacobs, M. B. (editor). *The Chemistry and Technology of Food and Food Products*, 2nd Edition, Vol. 1. John Wiley & Sons, New York.

Pulses, Nuts, and Seeds, Composition

TABLE 2.P.45
Composition of the edible portion and refuse in the material as purchased

Commodity and Description Pulses, Nuts, and Seeds	Water	Protein	Fat	Carbohydrate Total (by Dif.)	Fiber	Ash	Calories (No. per 100 g)	Notes	Refuse (%)
				Percent of edible portion					
Groundnuts, peanuts—in shell	5.2	25.6	43.3	23.4	3.3	2.5	546		29
—shelled	5.2	25.6	43.3	23.4	3.3	2.5	546		0
Soybeans and soybean products								Yield from 1 kg soybeans (kg)	
Whole seeds, dry	8	38	18	31.3[1]	4.8	4.7	335	1.0	0
Flour, full fat (seed coat removed)	8	39	21	27.4[1]	2.4	4.6	357	0.95	0
Flour, low fat; grits, flakes (partially defatted)	8	46	5	35.2[1]	2.3	5.8	261	0.84	0
Curd, tofu	87.4	6.3	3.1	2.5	0.1	0.7	58	3.5	0
Fermented beans, Japanese *natto*	61	17	9	11[1]	3	2	153	2.0	0
Fermented beans, Chinese *tsiang*	45	17	10	6[1]	3	22	153	2.0	0
Soybean milk	92	3.2	2.0	2.3	0.4	0.5	37	7.5	0
Paste, miso (made with small amounts of rice or other starchy materials)	52	11.0	5.8	16.5[1]	2.9	14.7	114	2.5	0
Shouyu sauce	67	5.5	0.5	8	(0)	19	56	3.5	0
Other dry beans and peas, unspecified	11	22.2	2.1	61.6	4.4	3.1	345	Beans, grams, peas, chickpea, fava, cowpea, lentils	0
Treenuts									
Coconuts, meat, fresh									
Old, ripe	48	4.2	34	12.8	3.3	1	351	As purchased: in shell, outer husk removed	54
Young, under-ripe	70	4	15	10	3	1	180	As purchased: in shell, outer husk removed	66
Chestnuts									
Fresh	48	3.4	1.9	45.6	1.3	1.1	213		21
Dry	9	6.3	4.0	78.5	2.5	2.2	375		18
Treenuts, other	7	16	58	17	2.6	2	610	Almonds, Brazil nuts, filberts, pecans, pistachios, walnuts	57
Treenuts, other shelled	7	16	58	17	2.6	2	610		0
Seeds									
Squash, watermelon, sunflower	5	27.4	43.0	19.7	2.7	4.9	535		47
Sesame, whole or decorticated	6	18.1	51.3	20.0	3.7	4.6	574		0

[1] In these products, only a small part of the carbohydrate, approximately 40%, is in sugar, starch, and dextrin. In calculating the calories it is assumed that the digestibility quotient is 40%.

Source: Chatfield, C. *Food Composition Tables for International Use.* Food and Agriculture Organization, United Nations, Rome.

Radiation Preservation

TABLE 2.R.1
Required dosages of radiation

Purpose	Dose Range (1000 rad)
Sterilization	1000–5000
Pasteurization	50–1000
Insect disinfestation	5–100
Sprout-depressing	5–100

Source: Borgstrom, G. (1968). *Principles of Food Science*, Vol. 1. Macmillan Publishing Co., New York.

Rapeseed Oil, Triglyceride Mole Percent Composition

TABLE 2.R.2

1 Double Bond

SOS	0.2
SSEr[1]	0.2

2 Double Bonds

SOO	0.1
SOEr	3.9
SErEr	0.2
ErSEr	1.0
SLS	0.3

3 Double Bonds

OOEr	0.9
ErOEr	18.1
ErErEr	0.9
SOL	0.4
SLO	0.1
SLEr	5.2
ErSL	0.2
SLeS	0.2

4 Double Bonds

OOL	0.1
OLEr	1.2
ErOL	3.4
ErErL	0.2
ErLEr	24.3
SLL	0.5
SLeO	0.1
SOLe	0.2
SLeEr	3.4
ErSLe	0.1

5 Double Bonds

LOL	0.2
OLL	0.1
ErLL	4.5
OOLe	0.1
OLeEr	0.8
ErOLe	2.2
ErErLe	0.1
ErLeEr	16.3

5 Double Bonds (Cont.)

SLLe	0.3
SLeL	0.3

6 Double Bonds

LLL	0.2
OLLe	0.1
OLeL	0.1
LOLe	0.2
ErLLe	3.0
ErLeL	3.0
SLeLe	0.2

7 Double Bonds

LLLe	0.3
LLeL	0.1
OLeLe	0.1
ErLeLe	2.0
LLeLe	0.2
LeLLe	0.2

[1] Er = Erucic acid.

Source: Boekenoogen, H. A. (editor) (1968). *Oil, Fats and Fat Products*, Vol. 2. John Wiley & Sons, New York.

Reagents, Normal Solutions

TABLE 2.R.3
Weights of typical reagents in representative standard solutions

Reagent	Molecular Weight	Hydrogen Equivalent	Equivalent Weight	Grams of Reagent	
				Per Liter of Normal Solution	Per cc of Normal Solution
HCl	36.5	1	36.5	36.5	0.0365
$HC_2H_3O_2$	60	1	60	60	0.060
H_2SO_4	98	2	49	49	0.049
$H_2C_2O_4 \cdot 2H_2O$	126	2	63	63	0.063
$H_2C_4H_4O_6$	150	2	75	75	0.075
H_3PO_4	98	3	32.7	32.7	0.0327
$H_3C_6H_5O_7$	192	3	64	64	0.064
NaOH	40	1	40	40	0.040
$Ca(OH)_2$	74	2	37	37	0.037
NH_4OH	35	1	35	35	0.035
NaCl	58.5	1	58.5	58.5	0.0585
$Ba(NO_3)_2$	261.4	2	130.7	130.7	0.1307
$Al_2(SO_4)_3$	342	6	57	57	0.057
$K_2C_4H_4O_6$	226.2	2	113.1	113.1	0.1131
$KHC_4H_4O_6$	188.1	1	188.1	188.1	0.1881
$NaHCO_3$	84	1	84	84	0.084

Source: Peterson, W. H., Skinner, J. T., and Strong, F. M. *Elements of Food Biochemistry.* Prentice-Hall, Englewood Cliffs, New Jersey.

Recommended Daily Dietary Allowances

TABLE 2.R.4
Food and nutrition board, national academy of sciences—national research council recommended daily dietary allowances, revised 1974 (designed for the maintenance of good nutrition of practically all healthy people in the U.S.A.)

	Age (yr)	Weight (kg)	Weight (lb)	Height (cm)	Height (in.)	Energy (kcal)[2]	Protein (gm)	Vitamin A Activity (RE)[3]	Vitamin A Activity (IU)	Vitamin D (IU)	Vitamin E Activity[5] (IU)	Ascorbic Acid (mg)	Folacin[6] (μg)	Niacin[7] (mg)	Riboflavin (mg)	Thiamin (mg)	Vitamin B-6 (mg)	Vitamin B-12 (μg)	Calcium (mg)	Phosphorus (mg)	Iodine (μg)	Iron (mg)	Magnesium (mg)	Zinc (mg)
Infants	0.0–0.5	6	14	60	24	kg X 117	kg X 2.2	420[4]	1400	400	4	35	50	5	0.4	0.3	0.3	0.3	360	240	35	10	60	3
	0.5–1.0	9	20	71	28	kg X 108	kg X 2.0	400	2000	400	5	35	50	8	0.6	0.5	0.4	0.3	540	400	45	15	70	5
Children	1–3	13	28	86	34	1300	23	400	2000	400	7	40	100	9	0.8	0.7	0.6	1.0	800	800	60	15	150	10
	4–6	20	44	110	44	1800	30	500	2500	400	9	40	200	12	1.1	0.9	0.9	1.5	800	800	80	10	200	10
	7–10	30	66	135	54	2400	36	700	3300	400	10	40	300	16	1.2	1.2	1.2	2.0	800	800	110	10	250	10
Males	11–14	44	97	158	63	2800	44	1000	5000	400	12	45	400	18	1.5	1.4	1.6	3.0	1200	1200	130	18	350	15
	15–18	61	134	172	69	3000	54	1000	5000	400	15	45	400	20	1.8	1.5	2.0	3.0	1200	1200	150	18	400	15
	19–22	67	147	172	69	3000	54	1000	5000	400	15	45	400	20	1.8	1.5	2.0	3.0	800	800	140	10	350	15
	23–50	70	154	172	69	2700	56	1000	5000		15	45	400	18	1.6	1.4	2.0	3.0	800	800	130	10	350	15
	51+	70	154	172	69	2400	56	1000	5000		15	45	400	16	1.5	1.2	2.0	3.0	800	800	110	10	350	15
Females	11–14	44	97	155	62	2400	44	800	4000	400	12	45	400	16	1.3	1.2	1.6	3.0	1200	1200	115	18	300	15
	15–18	54	119	162	65	2100	48	800	4000	400	12	45	400	14	1.4	1.1	2.0	3.0	1200	1200	115	18	300	15
	19–22	58	128	162	65	2100	46	800	4000	400	12	45	400	14	1.4	1.1	2.0	3.0	800	800	100	18	300	15
	23–50	58	128	162	65	2000	46	800	4000		12	45	400	13	1.2	1.0	2.0	3.0	800	800	100	18	300	15
	51+	58	128	162	65	1800	46	800	4000		12	45	400	12	1.1	1.0	2.0	3.0	800	800	80	10	300	15
Pregnant						+300	+30	1000	5000	400	15	60	800	+2	+0.3	+0.3	2.5	4.0	1200	1200	125	18+[8]	450	20
Lactating						+500	+20	1200	6000	400	15	80	600	+4	+0.5	+0.3	2.5	4.0	1200	1200	150	18	450	25

[1] The allowances are intended to provide for individual variations among most normal persons as they live in the United States under usual environmental stresses. Diets should be based on a variety of common foods in order to provide other nutrients for which human requirements have been less well defined. See text for more detailed discussion of allowances and of nutrients not tabulated. See Table I (p. 6) for weights and heights by individual year of age.

[2] Kilojoules (kJ) = 4.2 X kcal.

[3] Retinol equivalents.

[4] Assumed to be all as retinol in milk during the first six months of life. All subsequent intakes are assumed to be half as retinol and half as β-carotene when calculated from international units. As retinol equivalents, three fourths are as retinol and one fourth as β-carotene.

[5] Total vitamin E activity, estimated to be 80 percent as α-tocopherol and 20 percent other tocopherols. See text for variation in allowances.

[6] The folacin allowances refer to dietary sources as determined by *Lactobacillus casei* assay. Pure forms of folacin may be effective in doses less than one fourth of the recommended dietary allowance.

[7] Although allowances are expressed as niacin, it is recognized that on the average 1 mg of niacin is derived from each 60 mg of dietary tryptophan.

[8] This increased requirement cannot be met by ordinary diets; therefore, the use of supplemental iron is recommended.

Source: Pennington, J. A. (editor) (1976). A food guide critique. In *Dietary Nutrient Guide.* AVI Publishing Co., Westport, Connecticut.

Refractive Indices, Fats and Oils

TABLE 2.R.5
Refractive indices of some common fats and oils

Fat or Oil	Refractive Index at 40°C	Fat or Oil	Refractive Index at 40°C
Cottonseed	1.4643–1.4679	Palm	1.4531–1.4580
Coconut	1.4477–1.4495	Palm kernel	1.4492–1.4517
Corn	1.4765–1.4768	Linseed	1.4742–1.4754
Castor	1.4659–1.4730	Walnut	1.469 –1.471–
Kapok	1.4605–1.4657	Mustard seed (white)	1.4704 at 20°C
Peanut	1.4600–1.4643	Mustard seed (black)	1.4720–1.4733
Sunflower	1.4663–1.4680	Tung	1.5100–1.5200
Safflower	1.4679–1.4693		at 20°C
Perilla	1.4735–1.4785	Oiticica	1.4942–1.5062
Soybean	1.4675–1.4736	Borneo tallow	1.4561–1.4573
Sesame	1.4698–1.4731	Cacao butter	1.4565–1.4570
Teaseed	1.4619–	Shea butter	1.4635–1.4668
Olive	1.4606–1.4633	Illipé butter	1.4577–1.4610

Source: Mahlenbacher, C. V. The Analysis of Fats and Oils. Garrard Press, Champaign, Illinois.

Refrigerants I

TABLE 2.R.6
Refrigerant performance per standard american ton at 86°F (30°C) condensation, 5°F (−15°C) suction

Refrigerant	No.	Evaporator Pressure, p.s.i.g.	Condensing Pressure, p.s.i.g.	Refrigerant Circulated, lb./min.	Net Refrigerating Effect, B.t.u. lb.	Coefficient of Performance	Horse-Power per Ton	Compressor Discharge Temp., °F	Compression Ratio	Compressor Discharge Temp., °C
Ethane	170	221.3	661.1	3.41	58.6	2.41	1.953	1.22	2.86	50
Nitrous oxide	744A	294.3	922.3	2.35	85.2	3.60	1.310	—	3.03	—
Carbon dioxide	744	317.5	1031.0	3.62	55.5	2.56	1.840	151	3.15	66.11
Propane	290	27.2	140.5	1.65	121.0	4.58	1.030	97	3.70	36.11
22/115 azeotrope	502	36.0	175.1	4.38	45.7	4.37	1.079	99	3.75	37.22
Monochlorodifluoromethane	22	28.2	158.2	2.86	70.0	4.66	1.011	128	4.03	53.33
Ammonia	717	19.6	154.5	0.422	474.4	4.76	0.989	210	4.94	98.89
12/152a azeotrope	500	16.4	113.4	3.27	61.1	4.61	1.022	105	4.12	40.56
Dichlorodifluoromethane	12	11.8	93.3	4.00	50.0	4.70	1.002	101	4.08	38.33
Methyl chloride	40	6.5	80.0	1.33	150.2	4.90	0.962	172	4.48	77.78
Isobutane	601	3.3	44.8	1.79	111.5	4.36	1.083	80	4.54	26.67
Sulfur dioxide	764	5.9	51.8	1.41	141.4	4.87	0.968	191	5.63	88.33
Methylamine	630	9.9	46.8	0.66	304.0	4.81	0.978	—	6.13	—
Butane	600	13.2	26.9	1.56	128.6	4.95	0.953	88	5.07	31.11
Dichlorotetrafluoroethane	114	16.1	22.0	4.64	43.1	4.49	1.049	86	5.42	30.00
Dichloromonofluoromethane	21	19.2	16.5	2.24	89.4	5.01	0.941	142	5.96	61.11
Ethyl chloride	160	20.5	12.4	1.45	142.3	5.21	0.906	106	5.83	41.11
Ethylamine	631	23.1	10.0	0.89	225.5	5.52	0.855	—	7.40	—
Trichloromonofluoromethane	11	24.0	3.6	2.98	67.3	5.05	0.933	109	6.24	42.7
Methyl formate	611	26.3	1.6	1.06	189.2	—	—	—	7.74	—
Ethyl ether	610	26.9	4.9	1.58	126.3	5.74	0.822	—	8.20	—
Trichlorotrifluoroethane	113	27.9	13.9	3.73	53.7	4.84	0.973	86	8.02	30.00
Dichloroethylene	1130	28.3	15.8	1.75	114.3	4.83	0.973	—	8.42	—
Trichloroethylene	1120	29.6	26.2	2.18	91.7	4.80	0.980	—	11.65	—

Source: Woolrich, W. R. (1968). Principles of refrigeration. In *The Freezing Preservation of Foods*, Vol. 1, 4th Edition. D. K. Tressler, W. B. Van Arsdel, and M. J. Copley (editors). AVI Publishing Co., Westport, Connecticut.

Refrigerants II

TABLE 2.R.7
Chemical formulas of refrigerants

Group I

Carbon dioxide (Refrigerant 744)	CO_2
Dichlorodifluoromethane (Refrigerant 12)	CCl_2F_2
Dichlorodifluoromethane, 73.8%	CCl_2F_2
and ethylidene, 26.2%	CH_3CHF_2
(Refrigerant 500)	
Dichloromethane (Methylene Chloride)	CH_2Cl_2
(Refrigerant 30)	
Dichloromonofluoromethane (Refrigerant 21)	$CHCl_2F$
Dichlorotetrafluoroethane (Refrigerant 114)	$C_2Cl_2F_4$
Monochlorodifluoromethane (Refrigerant 22)	$CHClF_2$
Monochlorotrifluoromethane (Refrigerant 13)	$CClF_3$
Trichloromonofluoromethane (Refrigerant 11)	CCl_3F
Trichlorotrifluoroethane (Refrigerant 113)	$C_2Cl_3F_3$

Group II

Ammonia	NH_3
Dichloroethylene	$C_2H_2Cl_2$
Ethyl chloride	C_2H_5Cl
Methyl chloride	CH_3Cl
Methyl formate	$HCOOCH_3$
Sulfur dioxide	SO_2

Group III

Butane	C_4H_{10}
Ethane	C_2H_6
Ethylene	C_2H_4
Isobutane	$(CH_3)_3CH$
Propane	C_3H_8

Group I has the greater usefulness because these refrigerants possess low toxicity, explosiveness and flammability.

Group II is next in preference, while Group III refrigerants must be handled with the most discretion and caution.

Source: Woolrich, W. R., and Hallowell, E. R. (editors) (1970). Safety of workmen in cold and freezer storage rooms. In *Cold and Freezer Storage Manual*. AVI Publishing Co., Westport, Connecticut.

Relative Humidity

DRY BULB TEMPERATURE °F

WET BULB TEMPERATURE °F	21	22	23	24	25	26	27	28	29	30	31	32	33	34	35	36	37	38	39	40	41	42	43	44	45	46	47	48	49	50	51	52	53	54	55	56	57	58	59	60
14	1																																							
15	15	4																																						
16	28	17	7																																					
17	42	31	20	10	1																																			
18	56	44	33	22	13	4																																		
19	71	58	46	35	25	16	7																																	
20	85	71	59	47	37	27	18	10	3																															
21	100	86	72	60	49	39	29	21	13	6																														
22		100	86	73	62	51	41	32	23	16	8	2																												
23			100	87	74	63	52	43	34	26	18	11	5																											
24				100	87	75	64	54	44	36	28	20	14	8	2																									
25					100	87	76	65	55	46	37	30	23	16	10	5																								
26						100	88	76	66	56	47	39	32	25	19	13	7	2																						
27							100	88	77	67	58	49	41	34	27	21	15	10	5																					
28								100	88	78	68	59	51	43	36	29	23	17	12	7	3																			
29									100	89	78	69	60	52	45	38	31	25	20	15	10	5																		
30										100	89	79	70	62	54	46	40	33	27	22	17	12	8	4																
31											100	89	80	71	63	55	48	42	35	29	24	19	14	10	6															
32												100	90	81	72	64	57	50	43	37	31	26	21	16	12	8	5	1												
33													100	90	81	73	65	58	51	45	39	33	28	23	18	14	10	7	3											
34														100	91	82	74	66	59	52	46	40	35	30	25	20	16	12	9	5										
35															100	91	83	75	67	60	54	47	42	36	31	26	22	18	14	10	7	4	1							
36																100	91	83	75	68	61	55	48	43	38	32	28	23	19	16	12	9	6	3						
37																	100	91	83	75	69	62	55	49	44	39	34	29	25	21	17	14	10	8	5	2				
38																		100	92	83	76	69	63	56	51	45	40	35	31	27	23	19	16	12	9	7	4	1		
39																			100	92	84	77	70	63	57	52	46	41	36	32	28	24	20	17	14	11	8	6	3	1
40																				100	92	85	77	71	64	58	52	47	42	38	34	29	26	22	19	16	13	10	7	5
41																					100	92	85	78	71	65	59	54	48	43	39	35	31	27	23	20	17	14	11	9
42																						100	92	85	78	72	66	60	54	49	45	40	36	32	28	25	22	18	16	13
43																							100	93	86	79	72	66	61	55	50	46	41	37	33	30	26	23	20	17
44																								100	93	86	79	73	67	61	56	51	47	42	38	34	31	27	24	21
45																									100	93	86	79	73	67	62	57	52	48	43	39	35	32	29	26
46																										100	93	86	80	74	68	63	58	53	49	44	40	37	33	30
47																											100	93	86	80	75	69	63	59	54	50	45	41	38	34
48																												100	93	87	81	75	69	64	59	55	50	46	42	39
49																													100	93	87	81	75	70	65	60	55	51	47	43
50																														100	94	87	81	76	70	65	61	56	52	48
51																															100	94	87	82	76	71	66	61	57	53
52																																100	94	88	82	76	71	66	62	58
53																																	100	94	88	82	77	72	67	63
54																																		100	94	88	82	77	72	68

Taylor Relative Humidity Tables

These values are correct for air velocity of not less than 600 ft. per minute.

In using wall or standing type hygrometers when greatest accuracy is desired the instrument must be fanned vigorously until the column of the wet-bulb thermometer no longer recedes.

Printed by
Taylor Instrument Companies
Rochester, N. Y.

DRY BULB TEMPERATURE °F

FIGURE 2.R.1

(*Continued*)

Relative Humidity (Continued)

WET BULB TEMPERATURE °F

DRY BULB TEMPERATURE °F

DRY BULB TEMPERATURE °F

Printed by
Taylor Instrument Companies
Rochester, N. Y.

WET BULB TEMPERATURE °F

(Continued)

Relative Humidity (Continued)

WET BULB TEMPERATURE °F

DRY BULB TEMPERATURE °F

Taylor Relative Humidity Tables

The values on this chart are for air velocity of not less than 600 ft. per minute. It is cautioned that values above 140° (Dry Bulb) are extrapolated.

In using wall or standing type hygrometers when greatest accuracy is desired the instrument must be fanned vigorously until the column of the wet-bulb thermometer no longer recedes.

Printed by
Taylor Instrument Companies
Rochester, N. Y.

DRY BULB TEMPERATURE °F

WET BULB TEMPERATURE °F

(Continued)

Relative Humidity (Continued)

WET BULB TEMPERATURE °F

DRY BULB TEMPERATURE °F

Printed by
Taylor Instrument Companies
Rochester, N. Y.

WET BULB TEMPERATURE °F

DRY BULB TEMPERATURE °F

(Continued)

Source: Relative Humidity Tables. (1933). Taylor Instrument Co., Arden, N. Carolina.

Reproductive Cycle

TABLE 2.R.8
Features of the reproductive cycle

Species	Age at Puberty	Cycle Type	Cycle Length	Duration of Heat	Best Breeding Time	First Heat after Parturition	Remarks
Cattle*	4 to 8 months. Usually first bred about 15 months.	Polyestrous, all year.	21 days (18 to 24).	18 hours (10 to 24).	Insemination, from mid-heat until 6 hours after end.	Varies,* best to breed at 60 to 90 days.	Ovulation 10 to 12 hours after end of heat. Uterine bleeding about 24 hours after ovulation in most.
Horse	1 year.	Seasonally polyestrous. Early spring on.	Very variable, about 22 days.	6 days (2 to 11).	Last few days; should be bred at 3-day intervals.	4 to 14 days.	Ovulation 1 to 2 days before end of heat. Twins are usually aborted.
Sheep	7 to 8 months.	Seasonally polyestrous. Early fall to winter. Prolonged seasons in Dorsets and Merinos.	16½ days (14 to 19).	30 to 36 hours.	Little significance.	Next fall.	Ovulation near end of heat.
Swine	5 to 8 months.	Polyestrous, all year.	20 to 22 days.	2 to 3 days.	Little significance.	About 7 days after weaning.	Ovulation usually about 36 hours after beginning of heat.
Goat	7 to 8 months.	Seasonally polyestrous from early fall to late winter.	20 to 22 days.	2 to 3 days.		Next fall.	Many intersexes born in hornless strains.
Dog	6 to 8 months or later.	Monestrous. All year, but mostly late winter and summer.		About 1 week.		Several months.	Proestrous bleeding 7 to 10 days. Ovulation usually 1 to 3 days after first acceptance. Ova shed before 1st polar body has been extruded. Pseudopregnancy (pseudocyesis) usually ends between 60 and 70 days.
Cat	6 to 15 months.	Provoked ovulation. Seasonally polyestrous spring and early fall.	15 to 21 days.	9 to 10 days in absence of male. Four days if mated.		4 to 6 weeks.	Ovulation 24 to 56 hours after coitus. Pseudopregnancy lasts 36 days.
Fox	10 months.	Monestrous. December to March, but mostly late January to February.		2 to 4 days.		Next winter.	Ovulation usually on 1st or 2nd day of receptivity. Ova shed before 1st polar body has been extruded. No proestrous bleeding.
Mink	10 months.	Provoked ovulation. Seasonally polyestrous. Mid-February to early April.	Waves of follicles at intervals of a few days.			Next spring.	Ovulation begins 47 hours after coitus which must last ½ hour at least.
Chinchilla	4 months.	Polyestrous, all year.	24 days.	2 days. Mate at night.		12 hours.	
Nutria	5 to 8 months.	Polyestrous, all year.	24 to 29 days.	2 to 4 days.		48 hours.	

(Continued)

Reproductive Cycle   (Continued)

TABLE 2.R.8   (Continued)

Species	Age at Puberty	Cycle Type	Cycle Length	Duration of Heat	Best Breeding Time	First Heat after Parturition	Remarks
Rabbit	5 to 9 months.	Provoked ovulation. Breed all year, more or less.		To 1 month.	When vulva is enlarged and hyperemic.	Immediately, but blastocysts die if doe suckles large litter.	In United States do not breed well in summer. Ovulation 10½ hours after coitus. Pseudopregnancy lasts 14 to 16 days.
Rhesus Monkey (*Macaca mulatta*)	3 years.	Polyestrous all year; tendency to anovulatory cycles in summer in United States.	27 to 28 days (23 to 33).	Most matings near ovulation time.	Near ovulation.		Menstruation lasts 4 to 6 days. Ovulation usually about 13 days after onset.
Rat	37 to 67 days.	Polyestrous, all year.	4 to 5 days.	About 14 hours (12 to 18). Usually begins about 7 p.m.	Near ovulation.	Within 24 hours.	Ovulation a little after midnight. Cervical stimulation causes pseudopregnancy lasting 12 to 14 days.
Mouse	35 days (28 to 49).	Polyestrous, all year.	4 or 5 days, usually.	A few hours from 10 p.m. on.		Within 24 hours.	Ovulation soon after midnight. Stimulation of cervix causes pseudopregnancy lasting 10 to 12 hours.
Guinea pig	55 to 70 days.	Polyestrous, all year.	16½ days.	6 to 11 hours. Begins usually in evening.	Mid-heat on.	Usually immediately.	Ovulation about 10 hours after onset of heat.
Hamster	7 to 8 weeks.	Polyestrous, all year. Few pregnancies in winter.	4 days.	At night.		After weaning.	Ovulation about 1 a.m. Pseudopregnancy lasts 7 to 13 days.

* Many normal cows ovulate as early as 8 to 12 days after parturition with or without detectable external signs of estrus.

Source: Merck & Co. (1973). *The Merck Veterinary Manual*, 4th Edition. Merck & Company, Rahway, New Jersey.

Riboflavin

TABLE 2.R.9
Riboflavin content of foods

	mg/100 g		mg/100 g
Broccoli	0.23	Peppers	0.08
Spinach	0.20	Lettuce	0.06
Asparagus	0.20	Bananas	0.06
Brussels sprouts	0.16	Peaches	0.05
Peas	0.14	Potatoes	0.04
Corn	0.12	Tomatoes	0.04
Lima beans	0.12	Oranges	0.03
Snap beans	0.11	Apples	0.02
Cauliflower	0.10		

Source: White, P. L., and Selvey, N. (editors) (1974). *Nutritional Qualities of Fresh Fruits and Vegetables*. Futura Publishing Co., Mt. Kisco, New York.

Riboflavin, Daily Recommendations

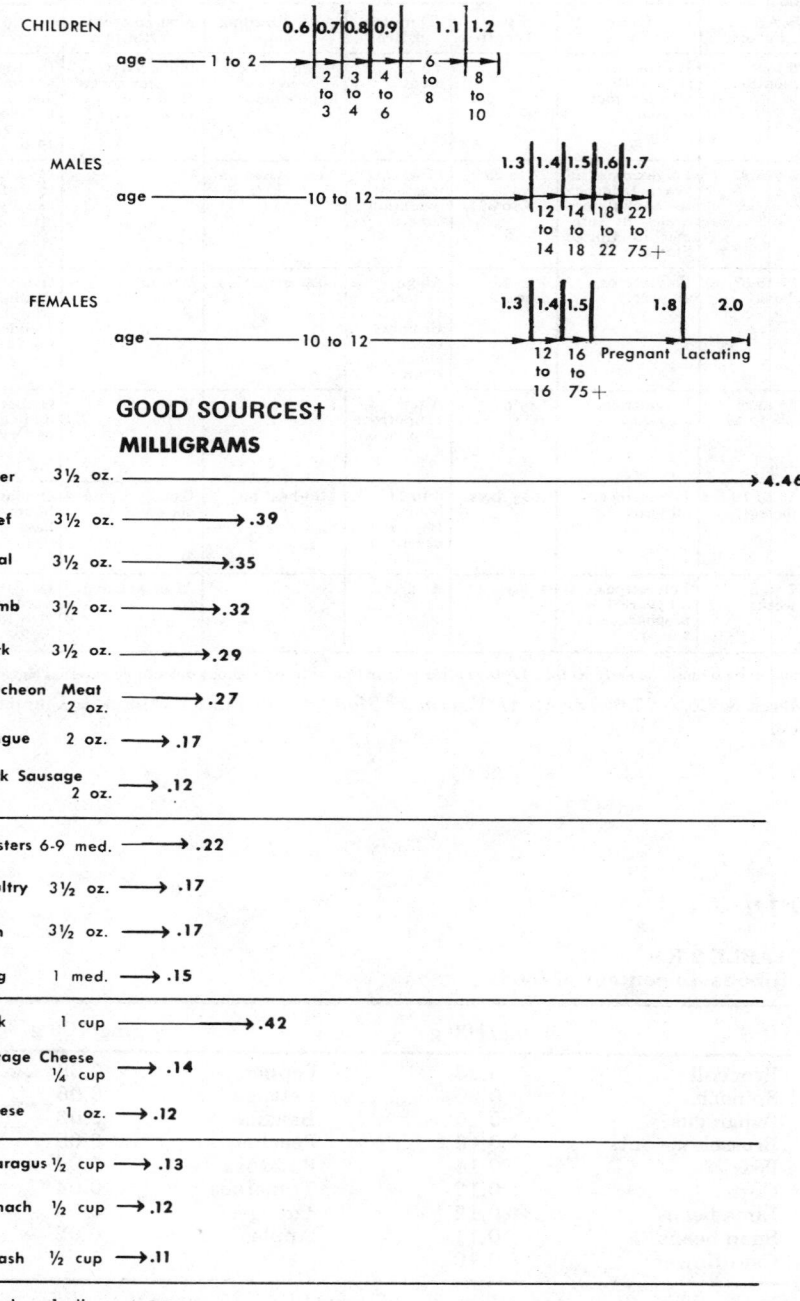

MILLIGRAMS

CHILDREN

age —— 1 to 2 —— | 0.6 | 0.7 | 0.8 | 0.9 | 1.1 | 1.2 |

2 to 3 · 3 to 4 · 4 to 6 · 6 to 8 · 8 to 10

MALES

age —————— 10 to 12 —————— | 1.3 | 1.4 | 1.5 | 1.6 | 1.7 |

12 to 14 · 14 to 18 · 18 to 22 · 22 to 75+

FEMALES

age —————— 10 to 12 —————— | 1.3 | 1.4 | 1.5 | 1.8 | 2.0 |

12 to 16 · 16 to 75+ · Pregnant · Lactating

GOOD SOURCES†

MILLIGRAMS

Liver	3½ oz.	4.46
Beef	3½ oz.	.39
Veal	3½ oz.	.35
Lamb	3½ oz.	.32
Pork	3½ oz.	.29
Luncheon Meat	2 oz.	.27
Tongue	2 oz.	.17
Pork Sausage	2 oz.	.12

Oysters	6-9 med.	.22
Poultry	3½ oz.	.17
Fish	3½ oz.	.17
Egg	1 med.	.15

Milk	1 cup	.42
Cottage Cheese	¼ cup	.14
Cheese	1 oz.	.12

Asparagus	½ cup	.13
Spinach	½ cup	.12
Squash	½ cup	.11

| Bread | 1 slice | .04 |
| Cereal | ½ cup | .03 |

†Average nutrient content as food is served. (*Note: 3½ oz equals approximately 100 g.*)

FIGURE 2.R.2

Source: Lessons on Meat. (1974). National Live Stock and Meat Board, Chicago.

Riboflavin, Food

TABLE 2.R.10
Riboflavin content of foods (mg/100 g)

Cereals		**Dairy Products, etc. (Cont.)**	
Flour,		Milk	0.15
White	0.04	Milk powder	
Wholemeal	0.16	Skim	1.6
Fish		Whole	1.2
Cod	0.10	**Vegetables**	
Herring	0.30	Asparagus	0.15
Soft roe	0.50	Beans, broad	0.05
Kipper	0.30	Lettuce	0.08
Sardines in oil	0.20	Onions	0.05
Turbot	0.15	Peas	0.15
Meat		Potatoes	0.04
Beef		Spinach	0.20
Brisket	0.20	Tomatoes	0.04
Corned	0.20	**Fruits**	
Lean	0.20	Apple	0.02
Ham	0.20	Currants	0.06
Liver		Gooseberries	0.03
Ox	3.0	**Nuts**	
Pig	3.0	Nuts	0.10
Mutton	0.25	**Sundries**	
Meat Extract	2.0	Beer	0.05
Juice (conc)	1.5	Honey	0.05
Dairy Products, etc.		Tea	0.90
Cheese		Yeast	
Dutch	0.40	Bakers	3.0
Whole milk	0.50	Brewer's	2.5
Eggs	0.35		

Source: Sinclair, H. M., and Hollingsworth, D. F. (1969). *Hutchison's Food and the Principles of Nutrition.* Edward Arnold (Publishers), London, England.

Rice Kernel

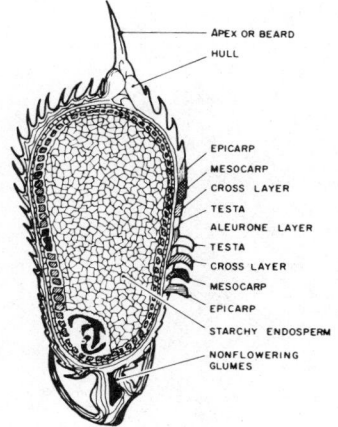

FIGURE 2.R.3
Cross section of a rice kernel

Source: Brooker, D. B., Bakker-Arkema, F. W., and Hall, C. J. (editors) (1974). Principles of grain drying. In *Drying Cereal Grains.* AVI Publishing Co., Westport, Connecticut.

Roasting Meat I

TABLE 2.R.11
Recommendations for roasting procedures for meats

1. Season with salt and pepper if desired.
2. Place meat fat side up on rack in open roasting pan.
3. Insert meat thermometer.
4. Do not add water. Do not cover. Do not baste.
5. Roast in slow oven (325°F) until done as shown on meat thermometer.

Roasts permitted to stand 15–20 min before carving will carve more easily.

Source: Be a Smarter Shopper ... a Better Cook. (1973). National Live Stock and Meat Board, Chicago.

Roasting Meat II

TABLE 2.R.12
Estimated times for roasting meat at 325°F

Kind of meat and cut	Ready-to-cook weight Pounds	Time required for center of meat to reach a given temperature					
		°F.	Hours	°F.	Hours	°F.	Hours
Beef roasts	5	140	2 to 3	160	2½	170	3 to 3¾
Veal roasts	3 to 5					170	2½ to 3½
Lamb roasts	5			150	2½ to 3	180	2¾ to 3¼
Fresh pork roasts	5			170	2¾ to 3½	185	3½ to 4
Spareribs	3						1½
Stuffed pork chops							¾
Mild cured ham	6	130	1½ to 2	160	2½		
Mild cured pork shoulder	6					170	3½

Source: USDA (1969). Food for us all. Yearbook of Agriculture.

Roasting, Time and Temperature

TABLE 2.R.13
Roasting guide for meats

Cut	Approx. Wt (lb)	Oven Temp Constant (°F)	Interior Temp When Removed From Oven (°F)	Approx. Cooking Time (Min. per lb.)
Beef				
Rib[1]	6–8	300–325	140 (rare)	23–25
			160 (med)	27–30
			170 (well)	32–35
	4–6	300–325	140 (rare)	26–32
			160 (med)	34–38
			170 (well)	40–42
Rolled rib	5–7	300–325	140 (rare)	32
			160 (med)	38
			170 (well)	48
Rib eye (Delmonico)	4–6	350	140 (rare)	18–20
			160 (med)	20–22
			170 (well)	22–24
Tenderloin, Whole	4–6	425	140 (rare)	45–60 (total)
Tenderloin, Half	2–3	425	140 (rare)	45–60 (total)
Boneless rolled rump (high quality)	4–6	300–325	150–170	25–30
Tip (high quality)	3½–4	300–325	140–170	35–40
	4–6	300–325	140–170	30–35
Veal				
Leg	5–8	300–325	170	25–35
Loin	4–6	300–325	170	30–35
Rib (rack)	3–5	300–325	170	35–40
Boneless shoulder	4–6	300–325	170	40–45
Pork, fresh				
Loin				
Center	3–5	325–350	170	30–35
Half	5–7	325–350	170	35–40
Blade loin or sirloin	3–4	325–350	170	40–45
Boneless double	3–5	325–350	170	35–45
Arm picnic shoulder	5–8	325–350	170	30–35
Boneless	3–5	325–350	170	35–40
Cushion	3–5	325–350	170	30–35
Blade Boston shoulder	4–6	325–350	170	40–45
Leg (fresh ham)				
Whole (bone in)	12–16	325–350	170	22–26
Whole (boneless)	10–14	325–350	170	24–28
Half (bone in)	5–8	325–350	170	35–40
Spareribs		325–350	Well done	1½–2½ (hr total)
Pork, smoked				
Ham (cook before eating)				
Whole	10–14	300–325	160	18–20
Half	5–7	300–325	160	22–25
Shank or rump portion	3–4	300–325	160	35–40
Ham (fully cooked)[2]				
Half	5–7	325	140	18–24
Arm picnic shoulder	5–8	300–325	170	35
Shoulder roll	2–3	300–325	170	35–40
Canadian-style bacon	2–4	325	160	35–40
Lamb				
Leg	5–8	300–325	175–180	30–35
Shoulder	4–6	300–325	175–180	30–35
Boneless	3–5	300–325	175–180	40–45
Cushion	3–5	300–325	175–180	30–35
Rib	1½–3	375	170–180	35–45

[1] Ribs which measure 6 to 7 in. from chine bone to tip of rib.
[2] Allow approximately 15 min per lb for heating whole ham to serve hot.

Source: Lessons on Meat. (1974). National Live Stock and Meat Board, Chicago.

Root-Crop Characteristics

TABLE 2.R.14

	Optimum monthly average growing temperature (Fahrenheit)		Optimum soil temperatures range for germination (Fahrenheit)	Frost tolerance	Spacing suggested in inches		Days to maturity	Time and frequency of planting	Harvest duration for each planting
	Min.	Max.			In row	Between rows			
Beets	40°	65°	50°–85°	Moderate	2–4	16–24	55–80	Early spring and early summer	2–3 months
Celeriac	45°	70°	60°–70°	Good	4–6	23–30	100–110 (56–84 for transplants)	Early spring only	3–6 weeks
Carrots	45°	70°	45°–85°	Moderate	1–3	16–24	60–85	Early spring and early summer	2–4 months
Parsnips	40°	75°	50°–70°	Good	3–6	18–30	100–130	Early spring only	3–4 months
Salsify	45°	85°	50°–90°	Good	2–4	18–30	150–155	Early spring only	1–2 months
Radishes (spring)	40°	75°	45°–90°	Good	½–1	9–18	25–30	Early spring and weekly	1 week
(winter)	40°	75°	45°–90°	Good	½–1	9–18	52–56	Early fall	3–5 weeks
Turnips	40°	75°	60°–95°	Good	2–6	12–30	45–75	Early spring and late summer	2–3 weeks
Rutabagas	40°	75°	50°–90°	Good	5–8	18–36	90–95	Early spring and midsummer	1–2 months

Source: USDA (1977). Growing Your Own Vegetables. USDA Agricultural Information Bull. 409.

Rot Spoilage

TABLE 2.R.15
Organisms associated with soft rot spoilage

Fruit or Vegetable	Spoilage	Microorganism
Apples	Soft rot	*Bacillus polymyxa*
Pears	Brown rot	*Penicillium expansum,*
		Aspergillus niger,
		A. foetidus
Oranges	Black rot	*Alternaria* spp.
Lemons	Dry rot	*Penicillium digitatum*
Citrus fruits	Soft rot	*P. italicum,*
		P. herbarum,
		P. glaucum
Grapes	Soft rot	*Rhizopus nigricans*
Raspberries	Soft rot	*R. stolonifer*
Plum	Soft rot	Yeasts
Strawberries	Soft rot	*Bacillus cereus*
Tomato	Soft rot	*Byssochlamys fulva*
Carrots	Soft rot	*Erwinia carotovora*
Cabbage	Soft rot	*Botrytis cinerea*
Celery	Pink rot	*Sclerotinia sclerotiorum,*
		Mucor racemosus

Source: Eskin, N. A. M., Henderson, H. M., and Townsend, R. J. (1971). *Biochemistry of Foods.* Academic Press, New York.

S

Salad Dressing or Mayonnaise Variations

TABLE 2.S.1
Variations to be made with mayonnaise or salad dressing

Kind	Amount of Dressing	Suggested Additions	Suggested Uses
Appetizer	1 cup	1 cup French dressing	Vegetable salads
Thousand Island	1 cup	1/3 cup chili sauce 1 T. chopped olives 1 T. chopped pickles 1 chopped hard cooked egg	Lettuce
Russian	1 cup	2 T. chili sauce 1 t. sugar	Lettuce Greens
Roquefort	1 cup	2 T. mashed Roquefort cheese 1 T. lemon juice	Lettuce or Greens
Cream	1 cup	1/3 cup cream or canned milk 1 T. sugar 1/2 t. salt	All types vegetables
Herb	1 cup	2 T. chopped chive 1 T. chopped parsley 2 T. milk	Fish Meat Cabbage
Tart	1 cup	2 T. horseradish 1 T. prepared mustard	Potato or starchy vegetable salads
Red	1 cup	4 T. tomato paste Sugar) to taste Salt)	Fish Salad or sauces
Fluffy	1 cup	2 T. sugar 1/2 cup cream, whipped	Fruit or sweet salads
Fruit	1 cup	1/4 cup fruit juice 1/2 cup cream, whipped	Fruit
Party	1 cup	2 T. Maraschino cherry sirup 4 T. Maraschino cherries 1/4 cup cream, whipped	Fruit
Hawaiian	1 cup	1/2 cup crushed pineapple (slightly drained)	Fruit
Cranberry	1 cup	1/2 cup cranberry jelly 1/4 cup cream, whipped	Turkey, chicken, banana salads
Peanut Butter	1 cup	1/3 cup peanut butter 1 T. sugar 3 T cream	Apple or fruit
Gelatin	1 cup	1/2 cup stiff gelatin - beaten 2 T. sugar	Fruit or gelatin salads
Cream cheese	1 cup	6 oz. cream cheese 1 T. sugar 1/2 t. salt	Fruit or gelatin salads (excellent as spread)

Source: Kintner, T. C., and Mangel, M. (19xx). Vinegars and salad dressings. Univ. Missouri Agric. Exp. Sta. Bull. *631.*

Salmon and Trout

TABLE 2.S.2
Description of different species of pacific salmon and of steelhead trout after canning

Common Name	Normal Oil Color	Normal Flesh Color	Normal Flesh Texture	Normal Flake Size	Normal Vertebrae Size	Normal Scale Size
Chinook (King)	Deep red through orange to almost white	Bright red to white	Soft	Large, thick	Large	Large
Red (Sockeye) (Blueback)	Deep red	Deep red	Very firm	Small, thin	Small	Medium
Medium red (Silver) (Coho)	Light red to yellowish pink	Light red w/orange	Very firm	Large, medium, thick	Large	Large
Pink (Humpback)	Deep pink to light yellow	Pink	Tendency to be soft	Small, thin	Small	Small
Chum (Fall), (Dog), or (Keta)	Light pink w/orange shade to yellow	Light pink to grayish white	Firm	Medium	Medium	Medium
Steelhead trout	Light orange to yellow	Pink w/ orange shade	Rather soft	Large, thick	Large	Large

Source: U.S. Department of the Army (1969). Food inspection specialist. *TM 8-451.*

Salt, Brine

TABLE 2.S.3
Sodium chloride brines—gallon basis [Gerlach salimeter scale (26.395 g NaCl/100 g brine)]

A	B	C	D	E		F	G
	%	Degrees	Lbs NaCl per Gal. of Brine	Water Required to Make 1 Gal. of Brine		Wt per Gal. of Brine in Lbs at 60°/60°F	Lbs of Salt per Gal. of Water
Sp Gr	Salt by Wt	Salimeter[1]	(BXF)	(Lb)	(Gal.)	(Sp Gr × 8.32823)	
1.000	0.00	0	0.00	8.32823	1.000	8.32823	0.000
1.019	2.64	10	0.22	8.27	0.992	8.49	0.226
1.038	5.28	20	0.46	8.18	0.983	8.64	0.464
1.058	7.92	30	0.70	8.11	0.974	8.81	0.716
1.078	10.56	40	0.95	8.03	0.964	8.98	0.983
1.098	13.20	50	1.20	7.94	0.953	9.14	1.266
1.118	15.84	60	1.47	7.84	0.941	9.31	1.568
1.139	18.48	70	1.75	7.74	0.929	9.49	1.888
1.149	19.80	75	1.89	7.68	0.922	9.57	2.057
1.160	21.12	80	2.04	7.62	0.915	9.66	2.229
1.171	22.44	85	2.19	7.56	0.908	9.75	2.409
1.179	23.31	88.3	2.29	7.53	0.904	9.82	2.531
1.182	23.76	90	2.34	7.50	0.901	9.84	2.594
1.193	25.08	95	2.49	7.45	0.894	9.94	2.787
1.204	26.40	100	2.65	7.38	0.886	10.03	2.987

(Continued)

Salt, Brine (Continued)

TABLE 2.S.3 (Continued)
Sodium choride brine-liter basis [Gerloch salimeter scale (26.395 g NaCl / 100 g H₂0)]

A	B	C		H	I	J	K
	%	Degrees		G NaCl per Liter of Brine	G H₂O Needed to Make 1 Liter of Brine	Wt per Liter of Brine at 20°C (or 68°F)	Freezing Point
Sp Gr	Salt by Wt	Salimeter[1]	Baumé	(BXJ)	(J-H)	(Sp Gr × 997.18 g)	(°F)
1.000	0.00	0	0.00	0.00	997.18	997.18	+32.0
1.019	2.640	10	2.7	26.83	989.30	1016.1	+29.3
1.038	5.279	20	5.3	54.64	980.43	1035.1	+26.4
1.058	7.919	30	7.9	83.55	971.47	1055.0	+23.0
1.078	10.558	40	10.5	113.49	961.47	1075.0	+19.4
1.098	13.197	50	12.9	144.49	950.41	1094.9	+15.4
1.118	15.837	60	15.3	176.57	938.28	1114.9	+10.9
1.139	18.477	70	17.7	209.86	925.93	1135.8	+5.7
1.149	19.796	75	18.9	226.81	918.95	1145.8	+2.8
1.160	21.116	80	20.0	244.26	912.47	1156.7	-0.4
1.171	22.436	85	21.2	261.99	905.71	1167.7	-3.7
1.179	23.307	88.3	22.0	274.02	901.66	1175.7	-6.0
1.182	23.756	90	22.3	280.00	898.67	1178.7	-1.1
1.193	25.075	95	23.5	298.30	891.34	1189.6	+14.4
1.204	26.395	100	24.6	316.90	883.70	1200.6	+60.0

[1] Temperature correction: Subtract 0.116° Salimeter for each degree Fahrenheit below 60°.

Source: Ockerman, H. W. (1976). *Quality Control of Post-Mortem Muscle Tissue*, Vol. II. Ohio State University, Columbus.

Salt, Brine Table

TABLE 2.S.4
Sodium chloride brine table

Salometer°	Sp Gr	Baumé°	Sodium Chloride by Wt (%)	Lb per Gal. Brine		Gal. Water per Gal. Brine	Lb Salt per Gal. Water	Freezing Point (F°)
				NaCl	Water			
0	1.000	0.0	.000	.000	8.328	1.000	.0	+32.0
2	1.004	0.6	.528	.044	8.318	.999	.044	+31.5
4	1.007	1.1	1.056	.089	8.297	.996	.089	+31.1
6	1.011	1.6	1.584	.133	8.287	.995	.134	+30.5
8	1.015	2.1	2.112	.178	8.275	.993	.179	+30.0
10	1.019	2.7	2.640	.224	8.262	.992	.226	+29.3
12	1.023	3.3	3.167	.270	8.250	.990	.273	+28.8
14	1.026	3.7	3.695	.316	8.229	.988	.320	+28.2
16	1.030	4.2	4.223	.362	8.216	.987	.367	+27.6
18	1.034	4.8	4.751	.409	8.202	.985	.415	+27.0
20	1.038	5.3	5.279	.456	8.188	.983	.464	+26.4
22	1.042	5.8	5.807	.503	8.175	.982	.512	+25.7
24	1.046	6.4	6.335	.552	8.159	.980	.563	+25.1

(Continued)

Salt, Brine Table (Continued)

TABLE 2.S.4 (Continued)

Salometer°	Sp Gr	Baume°	Sodium Chloride by Wt (%)	Lb per Gal. Brine		Gal. Water per Gal. Brine	Lb Salt per Gal. Water	Freezing Point (F°)
				NaCl	Water			
26	1.050	6.9	6.863	.600	8.144	.978	.614	+24.4
28	1.054	7.4	7.391	.649	8.129	.976	.665	+23.7
30	1.058	7.9	7.919	.698	8.113	.974	.716	+23.0
32	1.062	8.5	8.446	.747	8.097	.972	.768	+22.3
34	1.066	9.0	8.974	.797	8.081	.970	.821	+21.6
36	1.070	9.5	9.502	.847	8.064	.968	.875	+20.9
38	1.074	10.0	10.030	.897	8.047	.966	.928	+20.2
40	1.078	10.5	10.558	.948	8.030	.964	.983	+19.4
42	1.082	11.0	11.086	.999	8.012	.962	1.039	+18.7
44	1.086	11.5	11.614	1.050	7.994	.960	1.094	+17.9
46	1.090	12.0	12.142	1.102	7.976	.958	1.151	+17.1
48	1.094	12.5	12.670	1.154	7.957	.955	1.208	+16.2
50	1.098	12.9	13.198	1.207	7.937	.953	1.266	+15.4
52	1.102	13.4	13.725	1.260	7.918	.951	1.325	+14.5
54	1.106	13.9	14.253	1.313	7.898	.948	1.385	+13.7
56	1.110	14.4	14.781	1.366	7.878	.946	1.444	+12.8
58	1.114	14.8	15.309	1.420	7.858	.943	1.505	+11.8
60	1.118	15.3	15.837	1.475	7.836	.941	1.568	+10.9
62	1.122	15.8	16.365	1.529	7.815	.938	1.629	+9.9
64	1.126	16.2	16.893	1.584	7.794	.936	1.692	+8.9
66	1.130	16.7	17.421	1.639	7.772	.933	1.756	+7.9
68	1.135	17.2	17.949	1.697	7.755	.931	1.822	+6.8
70	1.139	17.7	18.477	1.753	7.733	.929	1.888	+5.7
72	1.143	18.1	19.004	1.809	7.710	.926	1.954	+4.6
74	1.147	18.6	19.532	1.866	7.686	.923	2.022	+3.4
76	1.152	19.1	20.060	1.925	7.669	.921	2.091	+2.2
78	1.156	19.6	20.588	1.982	7.645	.918	2.159	+1.0
80	1.160	20.0	21.116	2.040	7.620	.915	2.229	-.4
82	1.164	20.4	21.644	2.098	7.596	.912	2.300	-1.6
84	1.169	21.0	22.172	2.158	7.577	.910	2.372	-3.0
86	1.173	21.4	22.700	2.218	7.551	.907	2.446	-4.4
88	1.178	21.9	23.228	2.279	7.531	.904	2.520	-5.8
88.3	1.179	22.0	23.310	2.288	7.528	.904	2.531	-6.0
90	1.182	22.3	23.755	2.338	7.506	.901	2.594	-1.1
92	1.186	22.7	24.283	2.398	7.479	.898	2.670	+4.8
94	1.191	23.3	24.811	2.459	7.460	.896	2.745	+11.1
95	1.193	23.5	25.075	2.491	7.444	.894	2.787	+14.4
96	1.195	23.7	25.339	2.522	7.430	.892	2.827	+18.0
97	1.197	23.9	25.603	2.552	7.417	.891	2.865	+21.6
98	1.200	24.2	25.867	2.585	7.409	.890	2.906	+25.5
99	1.202	24.4	26.131	2.616	7.394	.888	2.947	+29.8
100	1.204	24.6	26.395	2.647	7.380	.886	2.987	

Source: Ion Exchange Calculator, Morton Salt Co., Chicago (1958).

Salt Penetration Rate

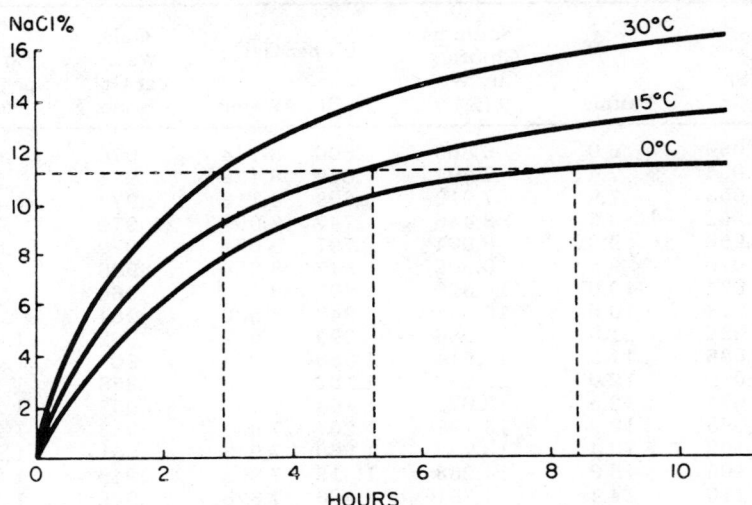

FIGURE 2.S.1
Rate of salt penetration as affected by temperature

Source: Borgstrom, G. (1968). *Principles of Food Science*, Vol. 1. Macmillan Publishing Co., New York.

Salt Solution, Freezing

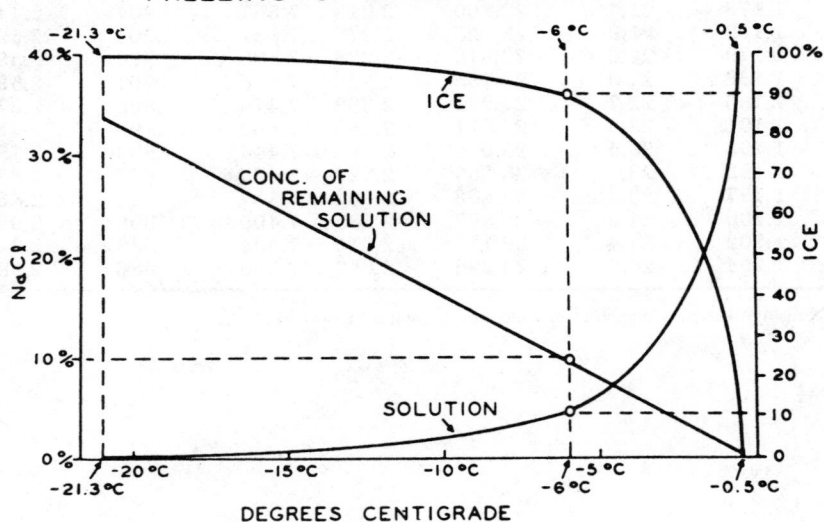

FIGURE 2.S.2
Freezing curve for sodium chloride solution—the eutectic temperature: $-21.3°C$

Source: Borgstrom, G. (1968). *Principles of Food Science*, Vol. 1, Macmillan Publishing Co., New York.

Sanitizers

TABLE 2.S.5

Manufacturers' recommendations for concentration and time of exposure

Chemical	Concentration Soak and Circulation (Ppm)	Spray and Fog (Ppm)	Exposure Time	Temp (°F)
Chlorine				
Sodium hypochlorite	100	200	1–2	75
Calcium hypochlorite	100	200	1–2	75
Dichloroisocyanuric acid	100	200	1–2	75
Trichloroisocyanuric acid	100	200	1–2	75
Potassium dichloroisocyanurate	100	200	1–2	75
Sodium dichloroisocyanurate	100	200	1–2	75
Chloramine T (pH 7.0)	250	400–500	2	
Chloramine T (pH 8.5)	250	400–500	20	
Hydantoin (acid pH)	200	400	2	
Quaternary Ammonium Compounds pH 6.0 or higher at 75°F				
or higher	200	400	2	
Iodine				
nonionic wetting agents				
plus iodine	12.5	25	2	
Bromine-chlorine	25	75	2	
Acid-anionic	200	400	2	

Source: Harper, W. J. (1972). Sanitation in dairy food plants. In *Food Sanitation*. R. K. Guthrie (editor). AVI Publishing Co., Westport, Connecticut.

Sanitizing Chemicals

TABLE 2.S.6

Relative comparative properties of selected chemical sanitizing agents

	Relative Effectiveness Chlorine	Iodine	Quaternary Ammonium
Gram + bacteria	2nd in effectiveness	Most effective	3rd in effectiveness
Gram − bacteria	Most effective	2nd in effectiveness	Poor
Spores	Most effective	2nd in effectiveness	Least effective
Thermoduric organisms	2nd in effectiveness	Least effective	Most effective
Bacteriophage	Most effective	2nd in effectiveness	Not effective
Affected by hard water	2nd	Least	Most
Corrosiveness	Most corrosive	Slightly corrosive	Noncorrosive
Cause of off-flavors	+ (10 ppm)	++ (7 ppm)	± (15 ppm)
Affected by organic matter	Most	2nd	Least

Source: Harper, W. J. (1972). Sanitation in dairy food plants. In *Food Sanitation*. R. K. Guthrie (editor). AVI Publishing Co., Westport, Connecticut.

Saturated Fatty Acids

TABLE 2.S.7
Name, formula, and source of saturated fatty acids

Common Name	Systematic Name	Formula	Source
Butyric	n-Butanoic	$CH_3(CH_2)_2COOH$	Butter fat
Caproic	n-Hexanoic	$CH_3(CH_2)_4COOH$	Butter fat, coconut oil, babassu fat, palm oil
Caprylic	n-Octanoic	$CH_3(CH_2)_6COOH$	Butter fat, coconut oil, palm oil, seed oils
Capric	n-Decanoic	$CH_3(CH_2)_8COOH$	Butter fat, head oil of sperm whale, coconut oil
Lauric	n-Dodecanoic	$CH_3(CH_2)_{10}COOH$	Laurel kernel oil, seed fats of laurel family and Palmae; milk fat, coconut oil
Myristic	n-Tetradecanoic	$CH_3(CH_2)_{12}COOH$	Nutmeg fat, most animal and vegetable fats; nutmeg butter, fatty acids of Myristicaceae
Palmitic	n-Hexadecanoic	$CH_3(CH_2)_{14}COOH$	Lard, in practically all animal and vegetable fats
Stearic	n-Octadecanoic	$CH_3(CH_2)_{16}COOH$	Mutton tallow, usually wherever palmitic acid is present
Arachidic	n-Eicosanoic	$CH_3(CH_2)_{18}COOH$	Peanut oil, rambutan tallow, macassar nut fat, fish oils
Behenic	n-Docosanoic	$CH_3(CH_2)_{20}COOH$	Behen oil from horseradish tree (Moringa oleifera Lam.), peanut, rapeseed, and mustard oils
Lignoceric	n-Tetracosanoic	$CH_3(CH_2)_{22}COOH$	Beech-tar paraffin, peanut oil; most natural fats in small amounts; seed oil of Adenanthera pavonina ("Circassian seeds" from red sandalwood)
Cerotic	n-Hexacosanoic	$CH_3(CH_2)_{24}COOH$	Chinese insect wax (Coccus ceriferus), beeswax, wool wax, flax wax
Montanic	n-Octacosanoic	$CH_3(CH_2)_{26}COOH$	Beeswax, most waxes including montan wax
Melissic	n-Triacontanoic	$CH_3(CH_2)_{28}COOH$	Beeswax, various vegetable, insect, and mineral waxes
Lacceroic	n-Dotriacontanoic	$CH_3(CH_2)_{30}COOH$	Stick-lac wax (Tachardia lacca), natural waxes

Source: Mahlenbacher, C. V. The Analysis of Fats and Oils. Garrard Publishing Co., Champaign, Illinois.

Sauce, Barbecue

TABLE 2.S.8

Ingredients	Amount
Water	85 gal. (U.S.)
Butter	80 lb
Vinegar (10% acetic acid)	4.8 gal. (U.S.)
Prepared mustard	10 lb
Locust bean gum	10 lb
Sugar	8 lb
Tomato paste	8 lb
Salt	4 lb
Paprika	2½ lb
Worcester sauce	2½ lb
Chilli powder	2½ lb
Tabasco sauce	1½ lb
Red pepper	15 oz
Black pepper	15 oz
Garlic powder	4 oz
Onion powder	4 oz

Source: Binsted, R., Devey, J. D., and Dakin, J. C. (1971). Pickle & Sauce Making, 3rd Edition. Food Trade Press, London, England.

Sauce, Beef Steak

TABLE 2.S.9

Ingredients	Amount
Vinegar (2.4% acetic acid)	30 gal. (U.S.)
Soy	5 gal. (U.S.)
Mushroom ketchup	5 gal. (U.S.)
Tamarinds	30 lb
Sugar	10 lb
Salt	5 lb
Onions	4 lb
Horseradish	3 lb
Ground mustard	3 lb
Ground cayenne pepper	½ lb
Garlic	½ lb
Caramel	4 oz

Source: Binsted, R., Devey, J. D., and Dakin, J. C. (1971). *Pickle & Sauce Making*, 3rd Edition. Food Trade Press, London, England.

Sauce, Thick

TABLE 2.S.10

Ingredients	Amount
Vinegar (20-grain)	43 gal. (U.S.)
Onions	36 lb
Molasses	25 lb
Tapioca	18 lb
Dates	6½ lb
Salt	4½ lb
Garlic (chopped)	4¼ lb
Caramel	4¼ lb
Lemon pulp	2½ lb
Ground ginger	1 lb
Ground coriander	½ lb
Ground nutmeg	½ lb

Source: Binsted, R., Devey, J. D., and Dakin, J. C. (1971). *Pickle & Sauce Making*, 3rd Edition. Food Trade Press, London, England.

Sauce, Tomato

TABLE 2.S.11

Ingredients	Amount
Tomato paste (single strength)	120 gal. (U.S.)
Vinegar	14.5 gal. (U.S.)
Acetic acid	1.2 gal. (U.S.)
Sugar	123 to 125 lb
Salt	27 to 29 lb
Onions (chopped)	25 lb
Paprika	2 lb
Cinnamon (bark)	24 oz
Allspice	15 oz
Cloves (ground)	13 oz
Mace (ground)	3½ oz
Cayenne pepper	3 oz
Garlic (chopped)	4 oz

Source: Binsted, R., Devey, J. D., and Dakin, J. C. (1971). *Pickle & Sauce Making*, 3rd Edition. Food Trade Press, London, England.

Sauce, Worcester

TABLE 2.S.12

Ingredients	Amount
Vinegar (20-grain)	21 gal. (U.S.)
Walnut ketchup	13 gal. (U.S.)
Mushroom ketchup	12 gal. (U.S.)
Sherry (or equiv non-alcoholic flavor)	6 gal. (U.S.)
Soy sauce	5.5 gal. (U.S.)
Hogs' livers (ground)	21 lb
Salt	11 lb
Tamarinds	10 lb
Brandy (or equiv essence)	1.2 gal. (U.S.)
Sugar	2½ lb
Ground cayenne pepper	1 lb
Ground black pepper	1 lb
Ground pimiento	1 lb
Ground coriander	1 lb
Ground mace	7 oz

Source: Binsted, R., Devey, J. D., and Dakin, J. C. (1971). *Pickle & Sauce Making*, 3rd Edition. Food Trade Press, London, England.

Sausage Composition

TABLE 2.S.13
Composition of sausage

Food, Approximate Measure, and Weight (in Grams)	Water (%)	Food Energy (Cal)	Protein (g)	Fat (Total Lipid) (g)	Saturated (Total) (g)	Oleic (g)	Lin-oleic (g)	Carbohy-drate (g)	Calcium (mg)	Iron (mg)	Vitamin A Value (IU)	Thiamin (mg)	Riboflavin (mg)	Niacin (mg)	Ascorbic Acid (mg)
					Fatty Acids										
						Unsat-urated									
Sausage:															
Bologna, slice 4.1 by 0.1 in. 8 slices (227 g)	56	690	27	62	26	27	3	2	16	4.1	—	0.36	0.49	6.0	—
Frankfurter, cooked 1 frankfurter (51 g)	58	155	6	14	6	6	1	1	3	0.8	—	0.08	0.10	1.3	—
Pork, bulk, canned 4 oz (113 g)	55	340	18	29	10	12	3	0	10	2.6	0	0.23	0.27	3.4	—

Source: Institute of Home Economics. Nutritive value of foods. USDA Home and Garden Bull. 72.

Sausage Identification

TABLE 2.S.14

Fresh Sausage

Fresh sausage is made from selected cuts of fresh meats, principally pork and beef that have not previously been cured. Being neither cooked nor smoked, it should be stored under refrigeration and always thoroughly cooked before serving. Some of the varieties of fresh sausage are:

Fresh Pork Sausage	Fresh Bockwurst
Bratwurst	Italian Pork Sausage
Fresh Thuringer	Fresh Beef Sausage
Fresh Country Style Pork Sausage	

Fresh Smoked Sausage

As the name implies, fresh smoked sausage has been smoked, but has not been cooked. Like fresh sausage, it should always be refrigerated and thoroughly cooked before serving. Included in the fresh smoked sausage family are:

Country-Style Pork Sausage   Mettwurst
Roumanian Sausage

Cooked Sausage

Cooked sausages are prepared basically from fresh meats, although occasionally some cured meats are used. They are thoroughly cooked and ready to serve. Like all sausages, this group also must be refrigerated. Examples of the cooked sausage group are:

Liver Sausage	Blutwurst
Beer Salami	Veal Sausage
Braunschweiger	

Cooked Smoked Sausage

Cooked smoked sausages are prepared from fresh meats and are both cooked and smoked. Although they are ready to eat, some of the products in this group are improved in flavor if heated before serving. The two most popular members of this family are the wiener or frankfurter and bologna. Included in this classification are:

Knackwurst	Bologna
Mortadella	Berliner
Wiener or Frankfurter	Vienna Sausage
Kielbasa	Smoked Links

Dry and Semidry Sausage

Made from selected meats and prepared in a complicated and carefully controlled drying process, the dry and semidry sausages are ready to eat. They will keep for a long period of time if refrigerated. Included are:

Summer Sausage	Chorizos
Cappicola	Frizzes
Cervelat	German Salami
Italian Salami	Hungarian Salami

Ready-to-Serve Meats

The ready-to-serve meats, commonly called luncheon meats, are fully cooked and most are available in the presliced form. Examples of ready-to-serve meats are:

Peppered Loaf	Olive Loaf
Honey Loaf	Head Cheese
Meat Loaf	Pickle and Pimiento Loaf

Source: Facts About Sausage. (1974). National Live Stock and Meat Board, Chicago.

Sausage, Nutritive Value

TABLE 2.S.15
Nutritive value of selected sausages and ready-to-serve meats

TYPE OF SAUSAGE	PROTEIN (gm/100gm)	CALORIES (cal/100gm)	IRON (mg/100gm)	THIAMINE (mg/100gm)	RIBOFLAVIN (mg/100gm)	NIACIN (mg/100gm)
Bologna	14.8	220	0.8	.31	.30	3.1
Braunschweiger	15.2	280	5.9	.13	1.40	8.1
Dutch Loaf	15.0	190	1.8	.31	.17	3.2
Frankfurters	15.2	200	2.3	.23	.24	2.7
Head Cheese	15.1	240	2.3	.08	.12	1.1
Kolbassie	13.5	310	2.4	.34	.19	3.1
Liver Sausage	16.7	260	5.4	.20	1.30	5.7
Pork Sausage Links	10.8	450	1.6	.40	.15	2.3
Salami	23.9	430	3.6	.25	.21	2.9
Country-Style Sausage	16.2	310	1.6	.22	.19	3.1
Summer Sausage	23.5	410	2.8	.46	.36	4.1
Thuringer	17.7	290	2.8	.12	.23	4.2

Source: Facts About Sausage. (1974). National Live Stock and Meat Board, Chicago.

Sausage, Types

TABLE 2.S.16
Characteristics and storage conditions for sausages

Type	Characteristics	Examples	Storage
Fresh sausages	Made of chopped, uncured meat. Usually not smoked. They are sold uncooked and must be cooked thoroughly before eating.	Fresh pork sausage Country-style sausage Bratwurst Fresh thuringer Bockwurst	Refrigerate and use within a day or two for finest flavor. Freezing is not generally recommended because product will lose some of its delicate flavor.
Uncooked smoked sausages	Similar to fresh sausage but contain a mild cure and are smoked. Must be cooked before eating.	Country-style sausage Mettwurst Italian and Polish sausage	Same as above. Use within a week.
Cooked smoked sausages	Include a large variety of table-ready meat thought of broadly as "baloney." Usually made from smoked meat. Completely cooked; can be eaten cold. Require heating only to enhance flavor.	Frankfurters Bologna Cooked thuringer Vienna sausage	Wrap well and refrigerate. Use within a week. Freeze only if necessary to prevent waste of product, and freeze for the shortest time possible. Freezing adversely affects flavor and texture.
Dry sausages	Processed by long continuous air drying. During this time the products undergo a bacterial fermentation which gives characteristic "tanginess." Some are smoked. They are ready-to-serve.	Dry salami Pepperoni Farmer cervelat Cappicola Mortodella	Wrap loosely and refrigerate. Will keep several weeks. Freezing is not recommended.
Semidry sausages	Similar to dry sausages. Usually cooked and then dried a relatively short time. Contain more moisture than fully dry sausages. They are ready-to-eat.	Cooked salami Lebanon bologna Kosher salami Cervelat	Same as above.
Cooked specialities	Made from fresh or cured meat; may be smoked. Cooked or baked and are ready-to-serve.	Luncheon meat Liver loaf Jellied corned beef Tongue loaf Head cheese or souse	Wrap well and refrigerate. Use within a week. Freezing is not recommended because the flavor of salted and spiced meat is adversely affected by freezing.

Source: Franks, E. B. When you buy sausage. Ohio State Univ. Coop. Ext. Serv. Leaflet *45*.

Scoop Size

TABLE 2.S.17
Measures and weights of scoop sizes

Scoop Number	Measure	Equivalent Weight (Oz)
6	$\frac{2}{3}$ cup (10 Tbsp+)	6
8	$\frac{1}{2}$ cup (8 Tbsp)	4–5
10	$\frac{2}{5}$ cup (6 Tbsp)	3–4
12	$\frac{1}{3}$ cup (5 Tbsp +)	$2\frac{1}{2}$–3
16	$\frac{1}{4}$ cup (4 Tbsp)	2–$2\frac{1}{4}$
20	$3\frac{1}{5}$ Tbsp	$1\frac{3}{4}$–2
24	$2\frac{2}{3}$ Tbsp	$1\frac{1}{2}$–$1\frac{3}{4}$
30	$2\frac{1}{5}$ Tbsp	1–$1\frac{1}{2}$
40	$1\frac{3}{5}$ Tbsp	$\frac{3}{4}$–1

Source: Van Egmond, Dorothy (editor) (1974). Cost management. In *School Food Service*. AVI Publishing Co., Westport, Connecticut.

Seed, Chemical Composition

TABLE 2.S.18
Seeds: chemical composition (values, except as otherwise indicated, are g or mg per 100 g seeds)

Species	Gross Composition					Amino Acids (g/100g)											Fatty Acids (g/100g fat[1])					Vitamins (mg/100g)			
	Water	Protein	Fat	Carbohydrate	Ash	Arginine	Histidine	Isoleucine	Leucine	Lysine	Methionine	Phenylalanine	Threonine	Tryptophan	Tyrosine	Valine	Palmitic	Stearic	Oleic	Linoleic	Linolenic	Niacin	Pantothenic Acid	Riboflavin	Thiamin
Barley (Hordeum vulgare)	11.1	8.2	1.0	78.8	0.9	0.61	0.26	0.51	0.84	0.42	0.19	0.62	0.48	0.19	0.66	0.61	9	3	33	54		3.1	0.66	0.08	0.12
Bean, lima (Phaseolus vulgaris mac.)	12.6	20.7	1.3	61.6	3.8																	2.0	0.84	0.18	0.48
Bean, mung (P. aureus)	9.8	23.3	1.0	62.0	3.9																	2.0		0.21	0.68
Chick-pea (Cicer arietinum)	10.6	20.8	4.7	60.9	3.0	0.30	0.21	0.12	3.2	0.74	0.25	1.2	0.60	0.17		1.9						1.6		0.18	0.49
Corn (Zea mays)	13.0	8.8	4.0	73.0	1.2												28	8	18	40	3	2.8		0.10	0.49
Cotton (Gossypium hirsutum)[2]	7.3	23.1	22.9	43.2	3.5	0.45	0.24	0.36	1.1	0.29	0.21	0.46	0.34	0.08	0.6	0.50	10.2	3.0	50	34		4.4	0.64	0.31	
Cowpea (Vigna sinensis)	10.6	22.9	1.4	61.6	3.5	3.0	1.1	1.8	2.2	1.5	0.5	2.2	1.1	0.4		1.8	27		19	54		2.2		0.16	0.92
Flax (Linum usitatissimum)[2]	6.2	24.0	35.9	30.3	3.6																				
Gingko (Gingko biloba)	7.3	7.2	1.6	41.2	3.6																				
Hemp (Cannabis sativa)	7.0	28	37	13.2	1.7	3.6	0.65	1.8	2.3	1.4	0.35	2.2	1.3	0.63		2.2	10.1		16	46	28	2.2		0.24	0.56
Lentil (Lens culinaris)	11.2	25.0	1.0	59.5	3.3																				
Lotus (Nelumbium nelumbo)	9.6	16.5	2.3	63.9	3.6																				
Oat (Avena sativa)	9.8	12.0	4.6	69.6	4.0	0.99	0.23	0.80	0.87	0.51	0.23	0.72	0.54	0.20	0.50	0.99	10		59	31		1.0		0.13	0.92
Pea (Pisum sativum)	11.6	23.8	1.4	60.2	3.0	2.6	0.4	1.2	1.9	1.5	0.1	1.4	1.2	0.2		1.2						3.1		0.28	0.77
Peanut (Arachis hypogaea)[2]	4.0	26.2	42.8	24.3	2.7	6.9	1.3	2.6	4.1	1.9	0.6	3.1	1.6	0.8		2.8	6.3	4.9	61	21.8		15.6	0.63	0.13	1.09
Pigeon-pea (Cajanus cajan)	13.1	21.9	1.6	59.9	3.5																	2.0	1.01	0.18	0.47
Popcorn (Zea mays praecox)	9.8	11.9	4.7	72.1	1.5																	2.1	3.50	0.11	0.39
Pumpkin (Cucurbita pepo)	2.4	22.9	31.9	13.2	3.6												1		32	15		1.5		0.10	0.18
Rape (Brassica napus)	9.5	20.4	43.6	22.3	4.2	0.54	0.14	0.28	0.51	0.28	0.14	0.31	0.22	0.10		0.40	13.2	1.9	44	39	6				
Rice (Oryza sativa)	12.0	7.5	1.7	77.7	1.1	0.59	0.25	0.44	0.67	0.45	0.18	0.47	0.37	0.14		0.56									
Rye (Secale cereale)	11.0	12.1	1.7	73.4	1.8												21		18	61		4.6	1.01	0.05	0.32
Safflower (Carthamus tinctorius)	6.0	12.7	30.8		3.0												5.8		16	78		1.6	0.92	0.22	0.43
Sesame (Sesamum indicum)	5.8	19.3	51.1	18.1	5.7	4.1	1.3	2.6	4.3	3.1	0.5	3.1	2.3	0.7		2.7	8.5								
Sorghum (Sorghum vulgare)	10.0	11.2	3.5	73.8	1.5																	4.5		0.22	0.93
Soybean (Glycine soja)[2]	7.5	34.9	18.1	34.8	4.7	5.46	1.43	2.78	3.71	1.45	1.61	2.39	1.64	1.14		2.70	15		27	52	6	4.5	1.04	0.13	1.07
Sunflower (Helianthus annuus)[2]	5.0	18.5	27.8		3.3												11.3		30	60		2.3	1.56	0.31	
Wheat (Triticum esculentum)	12.5	12.3	1.8	71.7	1.7	0.63	0.31	0.58	0.91	0.35	0.22	0.70	0.38	0.19		0.64	13.8	1.0	30	49	6	4.3	1.39	0.12	0.52

[1] Component fatty acids are expressed as percent by weight of the total fatty acids of the seed.
[2] Values for amino acids are applicable to meal or flour.

Source: Spector, W. S. (editor). *Handbook of Biological Data.* Federation of American Societies for Experimental Biology. Bethesda, Maryland.

Seed Composition

TABLE 2.S.19
Chemical composition of seeds

Kind of Seed	Water (%)	Ash (%)	Crude Protein (%)	Crude Fiber (%)	N-free Extract (%)	Lipids (%)
Barley	10.6	2.8	12.7	5.4	66.6	1.9
Corn, dent No. 1	13.0	1.2	8.8	2.1	70.9	4.0
Cottonseed	9.4	4.6	19.5	22.6	24.9	19.0
Flaxseed	6.2	3.6	24.0	6.3	24.0	35.9
Oats	9.8	4.0	12.0	11.0	58.8	4.6
Peanut kernels	5.4	2.3	30.4	2.5	11.7	47.7
Soybeans	10.0	4.6	37.9	5.0	24.5	18.0
Wheat	10.5	1.9	13.2	2.6	69.9	1.9

Source: Mallette, M. F., Althouse, P. M., and Clagett, C. O. *Biochemistry of Plants and Animals.* John Wiley & Sons, New York.

Seed, Germination

TABLE 2.S.20
Average quality, amount needed for a test, and days for germination

Kind	Pure seed (percent)	Germination (percent)	Weed seed (percent)	Size sample	Days for germination
Alfalfa	99	90	0.50	⅓ cup	7
Bahiagrass	72	70	.50	1 cup	21–28
Barley	99	90	.50	1 qt.	7
Bean	99	90	.00	3 cups	7–10
Beet, field	97	75	.00	1½ qts.	14
Bentgrass	95	90	.50	¼ cup	21–28
Bermudagrass	97	85	1.00	½ cup	21
Bluegrass:					
Kentucky	85	80	1.00	½ cup	21–28
Rough	85	80	1.00	½ cup	21–28
Brome:					
Smooth	92	85	1.00	1 cup	14
Broomcorn	98	85	.50	3 cups	10
Buckwheat	97	85	1.00	3 cups	6
Canarygrass, Reed	96	80	.50	¼ cup	21
Carpetgrass	92	90	.50	½ cup	21
Chickpea	99	90	.00	1 qt.	7
Clovers:					
Alsike	97	90	1.00	¼ cup	7
Alyce	98	90	1.00	⅓ cup	21
Berseem	98	90	.50	⅓ cup	7
Bur (in bur)	90	90	.50	1½ qts.	14
Bur (out of bur)	98	90	.50	⅓ cup	14
Cluster	95	85	1.00	¼ cup	10
Crimson	98	85	.80	⅓ cup	7
Ladino and white	95	90	1.00	¼ cup	7
Persian	95	85	1.00	¼ cup	7
Red	98	90	.50	⅓ cup	7
Sour	98	90	.50	⅓ cup	14
Strawberry	97	90	1.00	⅓ cup	7
Subterranean	99	90	.50	1 cup	14
Sweet	95	90	1.00	¼ cup	7
Corn	99	90	.00	3 cups	7
Cotton	99	85	:00	1¼ qts.	12
Cowpea	98	85	.00	3 cups	8
Crotalaria: Slender leaf	99	80	.50	⅓ cup	10
Dallisgrass	70	70	1.00	1 cup	21

(Continued)

Seed, Germination   (Continued)

TABLE 2.S.20   (Continued)

Kind	Pure seed (percent)	Germination (percent)	Weed seed (percent)	Size sample	Days for germination
Fescue:					
Meadow	97	90	2.00	1 cup	14
Red, Chewings	97	80	.50	¾ cup	21–28
Tall	97	90	2.00	1 cup	14
Flax	97	85	.50	¾ cup	7
Johnsongrass	98	85	.50	½ cup	35
Kudzu	99	70	.50	1 cup	14
Lespedeza:					
Sericea or Chinese	98	90	1.00	⅔ cup	28
Common and Kobe	96	90	1.00	⅔ cup	14
Korean	97	90	1.00	⅔ cup	14
Lupine	99	90	.00	3 cups	10
Meadow foxtail	90	80	.50	½ cup	14
Medic, Black	98	90	.50	⅓ cup	7
Millet:					
Browntop	96	70	.50	⅔ cup	14
Foxtail, German, Hungarian, or Golden	98	90	.50	⅔ cup	10
Japanese	97	90	.50	⅔ cup	10
Pearl	98	85	.50	1 cup	7
Proso	98	85	.50	1 cup	7
Oats	98	90	.10	1¼ qts.	10
Oatgrass, Tall	85	80	1.00	1 cup	14
Orchardgrass	85	85	1.50	1 cup	21
Peanuts	99	80	.00	1¼ qts.	10
Peas, Field	99	90	.00	3 cups	8
Rape, Dwarf Essex, Winter	99	90	.50	½ cup	7–10
Redtop	92	90	1.00	½ cup	10
Rescuegrass	95	85	1.00	¾ cup	28
Rhodesgrass	60	60	1.00	½ cup	14
Rice	99	90	.50	1 qt.	14
Rough pea	98	90	.00	3 cups	14
Rye	97	85	.10	3 cups	7
Ryegrass	98	90	.50	⅔ cup	14
Sainfoin	98	70	.50	2 cups	14
Sesbania	99	90	.25	¾ cup	7
Sorghum	98	85	.50	⅔ cup	10
Soybean	98	85	.00	3 cups	8
Sudangrass	98	80	.50	1¼ cups	10
Sunflower (Cult)	99	90	.00	1¾ qts.	7
Timothy	99	90	.50	⅓ cup	10
Trefoil, Big	98	80	1.00	¼ cup	10
Trefoil, Birdsfoot	96	90	1.00	¼ cup	10
Velvetgrass	95	85	.50	½ cup	14
Vetch	97	90	.50	3 cups	10–14
Wheat	99	90	.10	3 cups	7–10
Wheatgrass:					
Crested	95	85	.50	⅔ cup	14
Slender	95	85	.50	⅔ cup	14
Western	80	80	2.00	⅔ cup	28

Source: Anonymous (19xx). Seeds. The Yearbook of Agriculture, U.S. Dep. Agric.

Sheep Breeds

TABLE 2.S.21
Breeds of sheep and their characteristics

Breed	Place of origin	Color; face, ears, and legs	Head characteristics	Other distinguishing characteristics	Disqualifications
(Classified by type of wool produced)[1] Fine-Wool Breeds:					
American Merino	Spain	White. Reddish-brown spots may occasionally appear on lips, ears, and pasterns.	Most rams have horns, but there are some polled strains.	Distinguished from the Delaine Merinos by more skin wrinkles; the more wrinkled American Merinos being the "A" and "B" types. Strong flocking instinct. Ewes will breed out of season.	
Debouillet	On the Amos Dee Jones ranches of Roswell and Tatum, New Mexico. Ass'n organized in 1954.	White	Rams may have horns, but there are also polled strains; open face.	Comparatively smooth body; long staple.	Failure to pass inspection.
Delaine Merino	Spain	White. Reddish-brown spots may occasionally appear on lips, ears, and pasterns.	Most rams have horns, but there are some polled strains.	Comparatively smooth bodied; of the "C" type. Strong flocking instinct. Ewes will breed out of season.	
Rambouillet	France	White, brownish, or black spots are sometimes present, but discriminated against.	Most rams have horns, but there are some polled strains. Ewes are hornless.	The largest fine wool breed. Strong flocking instinct. Ewes will breed out of season.	Less than 2 normal sized testicles descended in the scrotum, short or long jaws, rolled eyelids, inverted teats, black spots or black fibers in the fleece, excess pigmentation in the hooves, broken-down pasterns, any serious bone deformity, or any other defect which will limit the animal's usefulness.
Medium-Wool Breeds:					
Cheviot	Scotland; in the Cheviot Hills between Scotland and England.	White face with a black nose. Often black spots are on the ears.	Both sexes are polled.	Stylish, alert, and active. Head and legs free from wool.	Black spots other than ears. Overshot or undershot jaw.

(Continued)

Sheep Breeds (Continued)

eed	Place of origin	Color; face, ears, and legs	Head characteristics	Other distinguishing characteristics	Disqualifications
et	England; especially in the southern countries of Dorset and Sumerset.	White and practically free from wool.	There are horned and polled strains, both of which are registered by The Continental Dorset Club. Except for the presence or absence of horns, the two strains are identical.	Ewes will breed out of season.	Black spots on body, legs, and face.
pshire	England; in the south-central country of Hampshire.	Rich deep brown, approaching black.	Both sexes are hornless, although rams sometimes have scurs.	Large size; early maturity.	Horns; short or long jaw; abnormal testicles; inverted eyelids.
adale lumbia Chev-	U.S.; by E.H. Mattingly. St. Louis, Missouri.	White	Both sexes are polled.	Face and legs free from wool.	Horns. Brown hair or spots on face, ears or legs. Black spots in the wool.
n ntry eviot	In Scotland, from the old Long Hill sheep, but with infusion of Merino, Ryeland, and Southdown blood in formative period.	White	Nose straight to slightly Roman. Rams are sometimes horned.	Wool grades 50's to 56's mature rams weigh up to 300 pounds and mature ewes up to 200 pounds.	
d	England; in the south-central county of Oxford.	Variable, from gray to brown.	Both sexes are polled. Topknot of wool.	Largest of the Down breeds.	Black fiber; stub horns.
shire	England; in the central western counties of Shropshire and Stafford.	Dark face, but a gray nose is not objectionable.	Both sexes are polled, although rams frequently have scurs.	Covering of dense wool well over the poll.	Such lack of type as to render the identity of the breed doubtful; horns or stubs (not scurs); overshot or undershot jaws.
down	England; in the southeastern county of Sussex.	Light or mouse brown color preferred.	Both sexes are polled, although rams sometimes have scurs.	Superior conformation and quality of carcass.	Horns; dark poll; speckled markings on face, ears, and legs; one testicle only; black or brown
lk	England; in the southeastern counties of Suffolk, Essex, and Norfolk.	Very black head, ears, and legs.	Both sexes are polled, although rams frequently have scurs.	The head and ears are entirely free from wool.	

(Continued)

Sheep Breeds *(Continued)*

TABLE 2.S.21 *(Continued)*

Breed	Place of origin	Color; face, ears, and legs	Head characteristics	Other distinguishing characteristics	Disqualifications
Tunis (or American Tunis)	Asia; in Tunis.	Reddish brown to bright tan.	Both sexes are polled; long, drooping ears, head free from wool.	Originally, it was a fat-tailed sheep, which means that the tail was distinctly broad and fat. However, breeders have selected away from this trait. Pendulous ears. Will mate almost any season of the year.	Horns; red or black wool; one testicle; undershot or overshot jaw.
Long-Wool Breeds:					
Cotswold	England; in the Cotswold hills of Gloucestershire.	White, although grayish specks and bluish tinge are common.	Both sexes are polled, although rams frequently have scurs.	The natural wavy ringlets or curls in which the fleece hangs all over the body. The tuft of wool on the forehead. Second only to the Lincoln in size.	
Leicester	England; in the central county of Leicester.	White, but may have a bluish tinge or black spots.	Both sexes are polled.		
Lincoln	England; along the eastern coast of England and bordering the North Sea, in Lincolnshire.	White. Black spots may be present but are discriminated against.	Both sexes are polled.	The largest of all breeds of sheep. Produces the heaviest fleece of any mutton breed.	
Romney	England; in the Romney Marsh region of the County of Kent.	White	Both sexes are polled.	In comparison with other long-wool breeds; the Romney is shorter legged, more rugged, and its fleece is shorter, finer, and less open.	
Crossbred Wool Breeds[1]					
Columbia (Lincoln rams, Rambouillet ewes)	United States; in Wyoming and Idaho.	White	Both sexes are polled.	Open-faced, with no tendency to wool blindness.	Horns or scurs; wool blindness; uneven light fleece; overshot or undershot jaw; colored wool; excessive folds.
Corriedale (Lincoln and Leicester rams, Merino ewes)	New Zealand	White, although black spots are sometimes present.	Both sexes are polled.		Black or brown spots. Wool blindness. Malformed mouth. Horns.

(Continu

Sheep Breeds *(Continued)*

ABLE 2.S.21 *(Continued)*

Breed	Place of origin	Color; face, ears, and legs	Head characteristics	Other distinguishing characteristics	Disqualifications
anama (Rambouil-let rams, Lincoln ewes)	United States; by Laidlaw and Brockie of Muldoon, Idaho.	White	Both sexes are polled.		Horns, scurs, or knobs; overshot or undershot mouth; excessive folds or wrinkles; colored wool; colored spots larger than 3/4 in. in diameter on clear areas; any un-sound hereditary fac-tor.
illess (or No Tail)	South Dak. Agric. Expt. Sta.	White	Both sexes are polled.	Usually produce tail-less offspring.	
rghee Rambou-llet rams, Lincoln-Rambouil-et-Corrie-dale ewes)	United States; by the USDA at Dubois, Idaho.	White	Both sexes are polled.	Open-faced.	Marked scurs or horns. Noticeable coarseness of wool on the britch or tail. Noticeable defects.
pet-Wool Breed:					
ck-faced Highland or Scott-sh Black ace)	Scotland; in the highland country.	Black or mottled.	Both sexes have horns.	Striking stylish appear-ance. Fleece consists of long coarse outer-coat and a finer inner-coat.	
-Sheep Breed:					
akul	Asia; in the county of Bokhara USSR).	Black or brown.	Rams have horns, but ewes are hornless.	Drooping ears. A fat-tailed sheep. Lamb pelts suitable for fur production.	

e listing of the crosses which produced each of the "crossbred-wool breeds" is given for breed history purposes only, and does not
ly any lack of purity of the respective breeds. Nor does it indicate that all of them are new breeds: for example, the Corriedale,
ch is an old breed, was originated in New Zealand about 1880.

rce: Ensminger, M. E. (1969). *Animal Science.* Interstate Printers and Publishers, Danville, Illinois.

Sheep Market Classes and Grades

TABLE 2.S.22
Market classes and grades of sheep

Use Selection	Sex Classes	Age	Wt Division	(Pounds)	(Kilograms)	Commonly Used Grades
Sheep — Slaughter sheep	Ewes	Yearling	Light	90 down	40.9 down	Prime, Choice, Good, Utility, Cull[1]
			Medium	90 to 100	40.9–45.4	
			Heavy	100 up	45.4-up	
		Mature (2-year-old or older)	Light	120 down	54.5 down	Choice, Good, Utility, Cull[1]
			Medium	120–140	54.5–63.6	
			Heavy	140 up	63.6 up	
	Wethers	Yearling	Light	100 down	45.5 down	Prime, Choice, Good, Utility, Cull[1]
			Medium	100–110	45.4–49.9	
			Heavy	110 up	49.9 up	
		Mature (2-year-old or older)	Light	115 down	52.2 down	Choice, Good, Utility, Cull[1]
			Medium	115–130	52.2–59.0	
			Heavy	130 up	59.0 up	
	Rams	Yearling	All weights			Prime, Choice, Good, Utility, Cull[1]
		Mature (2-year-old or older)	All weights			Choice, Good, Utility, Cull[1]
Feeder sheep	Ewes and wethers	Yearlings	All weights			Fancy, Choice, Good, Medium, Cull
	Ewes	Mature (2-year-old or older)	All weights			Choice, Good, Medium, Cull
Breeding sheep	Ewes (rams occasionally purchased as breeders, but not listed in market reports)	Yearlings, 2-, 3-, or 4-yr.- olds and older	All weights			Fancy, Choice, Good, Medium, Cull
Lambs — Slaughter lambs	Ewes, wethers, and rams	Hothouse lambs	60 down			Prime, Choice, Good, Utility, Cull[1]
	Ewes, wethers, and rams	Spring lambs	Light	70 down	31.8 down	Prime, Choice, Good, Utility, Cull[1]
			Medium	70–90	31.8–40.9	
			Heavy	90 up	40.9 up	
	Ewes, wethers, and rams	Lambs	Light	75 down	34.0 down	Prime, Choice, Good, Utility, Cull[1]
			Medium	75–95	34.0–43.1	
			Heavy	95 up	43.1 up	
Feeder lambs	Ewes and wethers	All ages	All weights			Fancy, Choice, Good, Medium, Cull
Shearer lambs	Ewes and wethers	All ages	All weights			Choice, Good, Medium

[1] In addition to the above quality grades the following yield grades became effective March 1, 1969: Yield Grade 1, Yield Grade 2, Yield Grade 3, Yield Grade 4, and Yield Grade 5. Thus, slaughter sheep and lambs may be graded for (1) quality alone, (2) yield grade alone, or (3) both quality and yield grades.

Source: Ensminger, M. E. (1969). *Animal Science.* Interstate Printers & Publishers, Danville, Illinois.

Shrimp

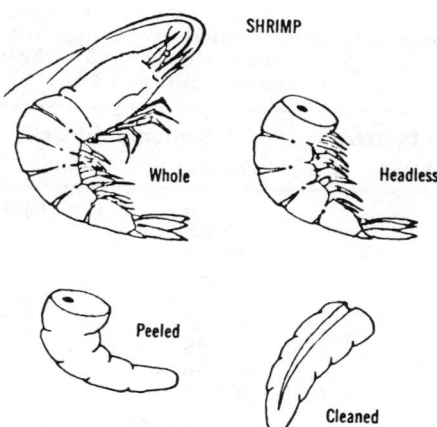

FIGURE 2.S.3
Forms in which shrimp are marketed
Source: USDA (1969). Food for us all. Yearbook of Agriculture.

Simmering Meat

TABLE 2.S.23
Simmering times (cooking in water) for large cuts and stews

Cut	Average Size or Average Weight	Approximate Cooking Time	
		minutes per pound	*total hours*
Fresh beef	4 to 8 pounds	40 to 50	3 to 4
Corned beef	6 to 8 pounds	40 to 50	4 to 6
Fresh pork	Weight desired	30	
Smoked whole ham	12 to 16 pounds	18 to 20	4 to 5
Smoked half ham	6 to 8 pounds	25	2½ to 3½
Smoked picnic	4 to 8 pounds	35 to 45	3 to 4½
Stew, lamb or veal	1 to 2 inch cubes		1½ to 2*
Stew, beef	1 to 2 inch cubes		2 to 3*

* If cooking in pressure pans, follow time-table of manufacturer.

Source: Cooking Meat in Quantity. National Live Stock and Meat Board, Chicago.

Sodium Hydroxide Solution

TABLE 2.S.24
Amount of sodium hydroxide needed for strength desired (sodium hydroxide solutions: specification requires 95% NaOH in sticks or pellets of caustic soda. Dissolve and dilute to 1 l)

NaOH Strength Desired Grams per Liter	Sodium Hydroxide Required Grams	
12.5	13.16	For crude fiber
30	31.58	
40	42.11	1N soln
50	52.63	
75	78.95	
100	105.26	
150	157.89	
200	210.53	
250	263.16	
300	315.79	

Source: Editorial Board, AOAC (1975). *Official Methods of Analysis of the Association of Official Analytical Chemists*, 12th Edition. Association of Official Analytical Chemists.

Sodium-Restricted Diet

TABLE 2.S.25
Food lists for sodium-restricted diets

List 1—Milk Products

	List 1	*List 1A*
For Mild Na Restriction	1,800 or Unrestricted Calorie Diet	1,200-Calorie Diet
	Each unit contains approx: carbohydrate 12, protein 8, fat 10 g; cal 170; Na 120 mg	Each unit contains approx: carbohydrate 12, protein 8 g, fat negligible; cal 85; Na 120 mg
	1 unit =	1 unit =
	1 cup Whole milk	1 cup Skim milk
	1 cup Whole milk buttermilk	1 cup Evaporated skin milk (reconstituted)
	1 cup Evaporated whole milk (reconstituted)	1 cup Nonfat buttermilk
	2 Fat units plus	3 tbsp Nonfat dry milk (powder) (or amt specified on package for making 1 cup)
	1 cup Nonfat buttermilk	1 cup Nonfat dry milk (reconstituted)
	2 Fat units plus	
	3 tbsp Nonfat dry milk (powder) (or amt specified on package for making 1 cup)	
	2 Fat units plus	
	1 cup Nonfat dry milk (reconstituted)	
	2 Fat units plus	
	1 cup Skim milk	
	N.B.: 2 units from the meat list may be substituted for not >1 milk unit/day.	N.B.: 1 unit from the meat list may be substituted for not >1 milk unit/day.
	AVOID: Any commercial foods made of milk—ice cream, sherbet, milk shakes, chocolate milk, malted milk, milk mixes, condensed milk, etc.	AVOID: Whole milk or any commercial foods made of milk—ice cream, sherbet, milk shakes, chocolate milk, malted milk, milk mixes, condensed milk, etc.

(Continued)

Sodium-Restricted Diet *(Continued)*

TABLE 2.S.25 *(Continued)*

For Moderate & Strict Na Restriction	As above except that buttermilk must be unsalted. Where <500 mg of Na is necessary, use special low-Na milk products.	As above except that buttermilk must be unsalted. Where <500 mg of Na is necessary, use special low-Na dry milk products; avoid buttermilk products.

List 2—Vegetables

	Group A	*Group B*	*Group C*
For Mild Na Restriction	Each unit contains: carbohydrate, protein, fat, and cal negligible; Na varies	Each unit contains approx: carbohydrate 7, protein 2, fat 0 g; cal 35, Na 9 mg	Each unit contains approx: carbohydrate 15, protein 2, fat 0 g; cal 70; Na 5 mg
	1 unit = ½ cup	1 unit = ½ cup	1 unit =
	Artichoke	Beets	¼ cup Beans, baked (no pork)
	Asparagus	Carrots	½ cup cooked Beans, Lima or navy (fresh or dried)
	Beet greens	Onions	
	Broccoli	Peas	
	Brussels sprouts	Pumpkin	⅓ cup or
	Cabbage	Rutabaga (yellow turnip)	½ small ear Corn
	Cauliflower	Squash, winter (acorn, Hubbard, etc.)	½ cup Hominy
	Celery		½ cup cooked Lentils (dried)
	Chard, Swiss	Turnip, white	
	Chicory		⅔ cup Parsnips
	Cucumber		½ cup cooked Peas, split green or yellow, cowpeas, etc. (dried)
	Dandelion greens		
	Eggplant		
	Endive		1 small Potato, white
	Escarole		½ cup Potatoes, mashed
	Green beans		¼ cup or
	Kale		½ small Sweet potato
	Lettuce		
	Mushrooms		
	Mustard greens		
	Okra		
	Peppers, green or red		
	Radishes		
	Spinach		
	Squash, summer (yellow, zucchini, etc.)		
	Tomato juice	*N.B.:* 2 units from Group A may be substituted for 1 unit from Group B.	*N.B.:* 1 unit from the bread list may be substituted for 1 unit from Group C.
	Tomatoes		
	Turnip greens		
	Wax beans		
For Moderate & Strict Na Restriction	All of the above, except artichokes, beet greens, celery, chard, dandelion greens, kale, mustard greens, spinach.	All of the above, except beets, carrots, turnips.	All of the above, except hominy.

Canned vegetables and tomato juice should be of low-Na dietetic type. Frozen vegetables must be processed without salt. (Check labels.)

(Continued)

Sodium-Restricted Diet (Continued)

TABLE 2.S.25 (Continued)

List 3—Fruit Products

For all Na-Restricted Diets	Includes fresh, frozen, canned, or dried fruit
	Each unit contains approx:
	carbohydrate 10 g; protein and fat negligible; cal 40; Na 2 mg

1 unit =

1 cup	Blackberries, raspberries, strawberries, watermelon
⅔ cup	Blueberries
⅓ cup	Apple juice or cider, cranberry juice (sweetened), pineapple juice
½ cup	Applesauce, fruit cup or mixed fruits, diced pineapple; orange, tangerine, or grapefruit juice
¼ cup	Apricot nectar, grape juice, prune juice
1	Apple, fig, pear, tangerine, orange, peach
2	Apricots (fresh or dried), dates, plums, prunes
½	Banana, grapefruit, mango
10	Cherries
12	Grapes
⅓	Papaya
¼	Cantaloupe
⅛	Honeydew melon
1 tbsp	Cranberries (sweetened)
2 tbsp	Raisins, rhubarb (sweetened)

Fresh lemons and limes, unsweetened cranberries, cranberry juice, and rhubarb: Use as desired; do not count as a unit.

On 1,200- and 1,800-cal diets, do not use glazed or sweetened fruits or those packed in sugar syrup.

List 4—Bread and Cereal Products

| For Mild Na Restriction | Each unit contains approx: |
| | carbohydrate 15, protein 2 g; fat negligible; cal 70; Na 5 mg |

| 1 unit = | N.B.: 1 unit from the vege-table list, group C, may be substituted for 1 bread unit. |

1 slice	Bread
4 pieces (3½ × 1½ × ⅛ in.)	Melba toast
1 medium	Roll, biscuit, or muffin
1 cube (1½ in.)	Cornbread
2 (3 in.)	Griddle cakes
½ cup cooked	Farina, grits, oatmeal, rolled wheat, wheat meal (lightly salted)
⅔ biscuit	Shredded wheat
¾ cup	Other dry cereal
1½ tbsp	Uncooked barley
2 tbsp	Cornmeal
5 (2 in. sq)	Crackers (low-Na dietetic)
2½ tbsp	Flour or cornstarch
2	Graham crackers
½ cup cooked	Macaroni, rice (brown or white), noodles, or spaghetti
1 (5 in. sq)	Matzo (plain, unsalted)
1½ cup	Popcorn
2 tbsp uncooked	Tapioca
1 (3 in. sq section)	Waffle, yeast

(Continued)

Sodium-Restricted Diet (*Continued*)

TABLE 2.S.25 (*Continued*)

For Moderate & Strict Na Restriction	As above except that yeast bread and rolls, quick breads, and cooked cereals must be made without salt or monosodium glutamate; all breads must be made with Na-free baking powder or low-Na dietetic mix, and the dry cereal used must have not >6 mg of Na/100 g of cereal (check the label). Avoid self-rising cornmeal; graham crackers; salted popcorn, potato chips, pretzels, and crackers.

List 5—Meat or Meat Substitutes

For Mild Na Restriction

Each unit contains approx:
  carbohydrate negligible; protein 7, fat 5 g; cal 75; Na 25 mg

1 unit =

1 oz, cooked

Beef	Lamb	Rabbit
Brain	Liver (beef, calf,	Tongue
Chicken	chicken, pork)	Turkey
Duck	Pork	Veal
Kidney	Quail	
Bass	Eels	Salmon
Bluefish	Flounder	Scallops
Catfish	Halibut	Shrimp
Clams	Lobster	Sole
Cod	Oyster	Trout
Crab	Rockfish	Tuna

1 oz	American cheddar or Swiss cheese
¼ cup	Cottage cheese (lightly salted)
1	Egg
2 tbsp	Low-Na dietetic peanut butter

AVOID: Salty or smoked meats or fish (e.g., bacon, luncheon meats, chipped or corned beef, ham, frankfurters, salt pork, smoked tongue, sausage; anchovies, caviar, salted and dried cod, herring, sardines, etc.), processed cheese, cheese spreads, Roquefort, Camembert, Gorgonzola.

For Moderate & Strict Na Restriction

As above except that (1) brain, kidney, and shellfish are to be avoided. (2) Canned meat, poultry, and fish are to be of low-Na dietetic type. (3) Cottage cheese should be unsalted; other cheeses are to be of low-Na dietetic type. (4) Fish, except as noted under (2), to be fresh only. (5) Eggs are limited to 1/day.

List 6—Fats

For Mild Na Restriction

Each unit contains approx:
  fat 5 g; cal 45; Na negligible

1 unit =

⅛ (4 in. diam)	Avocado
1 tsp (1 pat)	Butter or margarine
1 tbsp	Cream, heavy (sweet or sour)
2 tbsp	Cream, light (sweet or sour)
1 tsp	Fat or oil, cooking
1 tbsp	French dressing
1 tsp	Mayonnaise
6 small	Nuts, unsalted

AVOID: Salted nuts, bacon and bacon fat, olives, salt pork.

(*Continued*)

Sodium-Restricted Diet (*Continued*)

TABLE 2.S.25 (*Continued*)

For Moderate & Strict Na Restriction	As above except that salted butter and margarine are to be avoided; commercial salads and dressings are to be of low-Na dietetic type.

List 7—Free Choice

For Mild Na Restriction	1 unit from	List 4—Breads
	75 cal	Candy (made without salted nuts)
	2 units from	List 6—Fats
	2 units from	List 3—Fruits
	4 tsp	Sugar (white or brown)
	4 tsp	Syrup, honey, jelly, jam, or marmalade
	1 unit from	List 2—Vegetables, group C

Flavorings and seasonings may be used as desired except that barbecue sauce, bouillon, catsup, celery salt, chili sauce, garlic salt, prepared horseradish, meat extracts or tenderizers, monosodium glutamate, prepared mustard, olives, onion salt, pickles, relishes, soy sauce, Worcestershire sauce, and cooking wines are to be avoided.

For Moderate & Strict Na Restriction	As above except that candy is to be home-made, salt-free, or low-Na dietetic.

Source: Holvey, D. N. (1972). *The Merck Manual*, 12th Edition. Merck & Co., Rahway, New Jersey.

Soil Classes

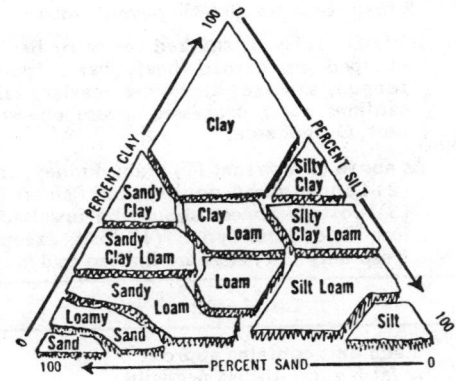

FIGURE 2.S.4

The texture triangle shows the percentage of sand, silt, and clay in each of the textural classes

Source: USDA (1957). Soil. Yearbook of Agriculture.

Sorghum Diseases

TABLE 2.S.26

Common name	Causal organism	Common name	Causal organism
Anthracnose	Colletotrichum graminicola (Ces). G. W. Wils.	Head smut	Sphacelotheca reiliana (Kuehn) Clint.
Bacterial spot	Pseudomonas syringae v. Hall	Leaf blight	Helminthosporium turcicum Pass.
Bacterial streak	Xanthomonas holcicola (Elliott) Starr & Burkh.	Loose kernel smut	Sphacelotheca cruenta (Kuehn) Potter
Bacterial stripe	Pseudomonas andropogoni (E. F. Sm.) Stapp	Maize dwarf mosaic	aphid-transmitted virus
Charcoal rot	Macrophomina phaseoli (Maubl.) Ashby	Milo disease	Periconia circinata (Mangin) Sacc.
Covered kernel smut	Sphacelotheca sorghi (Lk.) Clint.	Rhizoctonia stalk rot	Rhizoctonia solani Kuehn
Crazy top	Sclerophthora macrospora (Sacc.) Thrim., Shaw, & Naras	Rough spot	Ascochyta sorghina Sacc.
Downy mildew	Sclerospora sorghi Weston & Uppal	Rust	Puccinia purpurea Cke.
Fusarium stalk rot	Fusarium moniliforme Sheldon	Sooty stripe	Ramulispora sorghi (Ell. & Ev.) L. S. Olive & Lefebvre
Gray leaf spot	Cercospora sorghi Ell. & Ev.	Target spot	Helminthosporium sorghicola Lefebvre & Sherwin
		Zonate leaf spot	Gloeocercospora sorghi D. Bain & Edg.

Source: USDA (1979). Culture and use of grain sorghum. USDA Agriculture Handbook 385.

Soups, Composition

TABLE 2.S.27

(Dashes (—) denote lack of reliable data for a constituent believed to be present in measurable amount)

NUTRIENTS IN INDICATED QUANTITY

Foods, approximate measures, units, and weight (edible part unless footnotes indicate otherwise)		Water	Food energy	Pro-tein	Fat	Fatty Acids			Carbo-hydrate	Calcium	Phos-phorus	Iron	Potas-sium	Vitamin A value	Thiamin	Ribo-flavin	Niacin	Ascorbic acid
						Satu-rated (total)	Unsaturated Oleic	Lino-leic										
	Grams	Per-cent	Cal-ories	Grams	Grams	Grams	Grams	Grams	Grams	Milli-grams	Milli-grams	Milli-grams	Milli-grams	Inter-national units	Milli-grams	Milli-grams	Milli-grams	Milli-grams
MISCELLANEOUS ITEMS—Con.																		
Soups:																		
Canned, condensed:																		
Prepared with equal volume of milk:																		
Cream of chicken———— 1 cup————	245	85	180	7	10	4.2	3.6	1.3	15	172	152	0.5	260	610	0.05	0.27	0.7	2
Cream of mushroom———— 1 cup————	245	83	215	7	14	5.4	2.9	4.6	16	191	169	.5	279	250	.05	.34	.7	1
Tomato———— 1 cup————	250	84	175	7	7	3.4	1.7	1.0	23	168	155	.8	418	1,200	.10	.25	1.3	15
Prepared with equal volume of water:																		
Bean with pork———— 1 cup————	250	84	170	8	6	1.2	1.8	2.4	22	63	128	2.3	395	650	.13	.08	1.0	3
Beef broth, bouillon, consomme. 1 cup————	240	96	30	5	0	0	0	0	3	Trace	31	.5	130	Trace	Trace	.02	1.2	—
Beef noodle———— 1 cup————	240	93	65	4	3	.6	.7	.8	7	7	48	1.0	77	50	.05	.07	1.0	Trace
Clam chowder, Manhattan type (with tomatoes, without milk). 1 cup————	245	92	80	2	3	.5	.4	1.3	12	34	47	1.0	184	880	.02	.02	1.0	—
Cream of chicken———— 1 cup————	240	92	95	3	6	1.6	2.3	1.1	8	24	34	.5	79	410	.02	.05	.5	Trace
Cream of mushroom———— 1 cup————	240	90	135	2	10	2.6	1.7	4.5	10	41	50	.5	98	70	.02	.12	.7	Trace
Minestrone———— 1 cup————	245	90	105	5	3	1.1	.9	1.3	14	37	59	1.0	314	2,350	.07	.05	1.0	—
Split pea———— 1 cup————	245	85	145	9	3	1.1	1.2	.4	21	29	149	1.5	270	440	.25	.15	1.5	1
Tomato———— 1 cup————	245	91	90	2	3	.5	.5	1.0	16	15	34	.7	230	1,000	.05	.05	1.2	12
Vegetable beef———— 1 cup————	245	92	80	5	2	—	—	—	10	12	49	.7	162	2,700	.05	.05	1.0	—
Vegetarian———— 1 cup————	245	92	80	2	2	—	—	—	13	20	39	1.0	172	2,940	.05	.05	1.0	—
Dehydrated:																		
Bouillon cube, 1/2 in———— 1 cube————	4	4	5	1	Trace	—	—	—	Trace	—	—	—	4	—	—	—	—	—
Mixes:																		
Unprepared:																		
Onion———— 1 1/2-oz pkg————	43	3	150	6	5	1.1	2.3	1.0	23	42	49	.6	238	30	.05	.03	.3	6
Prepared with water:																		
Chicken noodle———— 1 cup————	240	95	55	2	1	—	—	—	8	7	19	.2	19	50	.07	.05	.5	Trace
Onion———— 1 cup————	240	96	35	1	1	—	—	—	6	10	12	.2	58	Trace	Trace	Trace	Trace	2
Tomato vegetable with noodles. 1 cup————	240	93	65	1	1	—	—	—	12	7	19	.2	29	480	.05	.02	.5	5

Source: Consumer and Food Economics Institute (1977). Nutritive value of foods. USDA Home and Garden Bull. 72.

Sour-Cream Dressing

TABLE 2.S.28

Ingredients

1 cup cream
2 tbsp vinegar & 1 tbsp lemon juice or
3 tbsp vinegar

1 tbsp sugar
1 tsp salt

Procedure

Mix the dry ingredients and add the acid. Add the cream. Stir thoroughly. Store in the refrigerator.

Source: Kintner, T. C., and Mangel, M. Vinegars and salad dressings. Univ. Missouri Agric. Exp. Sta. Univ. Bull. *631*.

Soybean Composition

TABLE 2.S.29
Proximate analyses of commercial soybean flours and grits[a]

Product	Moisture %	Protein (N×6.25) %	Fat %	Crude fiber %	Ash %
Full-fat flour	5.0	41.5	21.0	2.1	5.2
Low-fat flour	5.5	46.0	6.5	3.0	5.5
Defatted flour[b]	5.0	53.0	0.9	2.9	6.0
Lecithinated flour[c]	5.5	45.2	16.4	2.4	5.3

[a]These analyses are not product standards, but are values typical for product.
[b]Available in a variety of moist-heat treatments.
[c]Available with lower lecithin contents.

Source: Meyer, E. W. (1971). Soybean flours and grits. Proc. 3rd Intern. Congr. Food Science Technol.

Specific Gravities, Fats and Oils

TABLE 2.S.30
Specific gravities of some fats and oils

Fat or Oil	99°/15°C	Specific Gravity 15°/15°C	25°/25°C
Babassu			0.916-0.918
Castor		0.958-0.968	
Coconut	0.869-0.874		
Corn		0.922-0.926	0.915-0.920
Cottonseed		0.921-0.924	0.916-0.918
Kapok		0.920-0.923	
Linseed		0.931-0.938	0.924-0.931
Olive		0.914-0.919	0.909-0.915
Palm	0.849-0.856	0.921-0.925	0.914-0.918
Palm kernel	0.863-0.872		
Peanut		0.917-0.921	0.910-0.915
Safflower		0.925-0.928	
Sesame		0.920-0.926	
Soybean		0.924-0.928	
Sunflower		0.922-0.926	
Lard	0.858-0.864	0.934-0.938	0.908-0.913
Tallow (beef)	0.860-0.870	0.943-0.952	0.903-0.907
Tallow (mutton)	0.857-0.860	0.937-0.952	
Neatsfoot	0.860-0.865		
Horse		0.916-0.921	

Source: Mahlenbacher, C. V. The Analysis of Fats and Oils. Garrard Press, Champaign, Illinois.

Specific Heat, Meat

TABLE 2.S.31
Average specific heat of meats and poultry

	Fresh	Frozen
Beef (lean)	0.77	0.40
Beef (fat)	0.60	0.35
Pork (ave)	0.55	0.32
Mutton (ave)	0.65	0.36
Poultry (ave)	0.80	0.48

Source: Geary, D., and Gerrard, F. (1968). Meat and refrigeration. Meat Trades J., London, England.

Spices, Microbial Content

TABLE 2.S.32
Microbial content of untreated spices

Kind of Spice or Herb	Untreated Spice Suspensions Incubated at: 37°C (98.6°F) Total Micro-organisms per Gram Bacteria	Room Temp Molds
Whole allspice	1,000,000	70,000
Ground allspice	64,000	50,000
Sweet basil	525,000	50
Whole cloves	4,400	100
Whole Zanzibar cloves	190	0
Ground China cinnamon	36,000	60,000
Crushed cinnamon	8,000	600
Ground ginger	60,000	2,000
Bay leaves	15,000	350
Ground Bandamace	2,800	400
Ground mustard	1,800	0
Ground East Indian nutmeg	1,200	700
Ground paprika	680,000	5,000
Ground red pepper	2,190,000	1,220,000
Ground white pepper	42,000	9,000
Decorticated pepper	1,780,000	70,000
Ground black pepper	10,400,000	1,300,000
Savory	4,000	450
Ground sage	270,000	20,000
Whole thyme	2,700,000	12,000
Ground thyme	35,000	30,000
Miscellaneous:		
Celery seed	1,150,000	10,000
Onion powder	6,000	0
Garlic cloves	200	20,000
Onion juice	30,000,000	100
Ground garlic powder	90,000	200
Liquid garlic	10,000	10,000
Emulsified spice oil	10	10

Source: Weiser, H. H., Mountney, G. J., and Gould, W. A. (editors) (1971). Microbiology of spices. In *Practical Food Microbiology and Technology*. AVI Publishing Co., Westport, Connecticut.

Spoilage, Carbohydrate Foods

TABLE 2.S.33
Types of food spoilage associated with the fermentation and metabolism of carbohydrates in foods

Type of Food	Spoilage	Organism
Fruit juices	Souring, CO_2	*Lactobacillus* spp.
Fruit juice	Acetification	*Acetobacter* spp.
concentrates	Slime formation, ropy and viscous	*Leuconostoc* spp.
Canned fruit	Souring, CO_2	*Lactobacillus* spp.
Bottled fruit	Alcohol, butyric acid	Osmophilic yeasts, *Clostridia* spp.
Chocolate creams	Alcoholic, CO_2	Osmophilic yeasts, *Escherichia coli*
Wines	Acetification	*Acetobacter* spp., *Acetomonas* spp.
	Slimes and off-flavors	*Leuconostoc* spp., *Lactobacillus* spp.
Beers	Off-flavors	*Saccharomyces* spp.
	Gassing and slimes	*S. lactis*
		S. fragilis
Fruits	Souring, soft rots, and bitter flavors	*Streptococcus faecalis*, *Byssochlamys fulva*, *Penicillium italicum*, *P. citrinum*, *P. digitatum*
Cucumber	Souring	*Bacillus polymyxa*
	Soft rots	*Erwinia carotovora*
Carrots and vegetables	Off-flavors	*Sclerotinia sclerotiorum*
Milk	Souring	*Lactobacillus* spp.
	Acidity and gassing	*Streptococcus* spp.
Bread	Sour flavor	*Bacillus mesentericus*
	Ropy	*Rhizopus oryzae*
Cereals	Discoloration	*R. nigricans*
	Moldy flavor	*Penicillium glacum*, *Serratia marcescens*
Vinegar	Loss of acidity	*Acetobacter*
	Slimes	*Monilia acetobutans*
Sauerkraut	Slimes	*Lactobacillus plantarum*

Source: Eskin, N. A. M., Henderson, H. M., and Townsend, R. J. (1971). *Biochemistry of Foods*. Academic Press, New York.

Spoilage, Fat in Food

TABLE 2.S.34
Types of food spoilage associated with the microbial degradation of fats in foods

Type of food	Spoilage	Spoilage organism
Milk	Souring	*Streptococcus lactis*
Cream	Rancidity, free fatty acid	*S. cremoris, Oidium lactis*
Butter	Free fatty acid	*Cladosporium suaveolens*
Margarine	Rancidity, methyl ketones	*C. butyri, Candida lipolytica*
Lard	Free fatty acid	*Paecilomyces aureocinnamoneum*
Palm oil	Rancidity	
Coconut oil	Methyl ketones	*Margarinomyces bubaki*
Groundnut oil		*Staphylococcus aureus*
Cottonseed oil	Rancidity	*Lactosaprophiticus*
Corn oil	Free fatty acid	*Aspergillus tamarii*
Rapeseed oil	Lipoxidation	*A. niger*
Olive oil	Rancidity	*A. repens*
Oats	Bitterness	*A. restrictus*
Wheat	Soapiness	*Paecilomyces variotii*
Barley		*Monilia acremonium*
Biscuits		*Serratia marcescens, Pseudomonas hydrophila*

Source: Eskin, N. A. M., Henderson, H. M., and Townsend, R. J. (1971). *Biochemistry of Foods.* Academic Press, New York.

Spoilage, Protein Foods

TABLE 2.S.35
Types of food spoilage associated with the microbial degradation of proteins in foods

Type of food	Spoilage	Spoilage organism
Milk	Coagulation of caseins, off-flavors, rancidity, putrefaction, cadaverine	*Bacillus subtilis*, *B. cereus* *Pseudomonas putrefaciens*, *P. ichthyosmia* *Proteus vulgaris*, *Streptococcus liquefaciens*, *S. lactis*
Meats and meat products	Surface slimes, liquefaction, collagen degradation, elastin degradation, keratin degradation, putrefaction, cadaverine, putrescine, indole, amines, NH_3, H_2S, and bone taint	*Clostridium perfringens*, *Cl. welchii*, *Cl. histolyticum*, *Cl. sporogenes*, *Flavobacterium elastolyticum*, *Aeromonas* spp., *Achromobacter* spp., *Proteus* spp., *Pseudomonas* spp.
Fish, fish sausage, and fish cakes	Fishy odors, trimethylamine, dimethylamine, indole, cadaverine, putrescine, H_2S, surface slimes	*Achromobacter* spp., *Pseudomonas* spp., *Flavobacterium* spp., *Micrococcus* spp., *Sarcina* spp., *Proteus* spp., *Bacillus* spp.
Hams	Greening	*Lactobacillus viridescens*
Bacon	Putrefaction	*Clostridium sporogenes*
Chicken and turkey	Liquefaction, bone taint, rancidity	*Cl. aerofoetidum* *Cl. bifermentans* *Cl. histolyticum* *Cl. putrefaciens* *Cl. perfringens* *Pseudomonas fluorescens* *Vibrio costicolus* *Micrococcus candidus* *M. luteus*
Eggs	White rot, black rot, mixed rot, and fungal infections	*Clostridium sporogenes* *Cl. putrificum* *Cladosporium herbarum* *Penicillium glaucum*
Cheese	Moldy	*P. glaucum* *P. expansum* *Monilia sitophila*

Source: Eskin, N. A. M., Henderson, H. M., and Townsend, R. J. (1971). *Biochemistry in Foods.* Academic Press, New York.

Stabilizers, Thickeners

TABLE 2.S.36
Functions and uses of stabilizers and thickeners

Additive	Function	Type of Food
Agar agar	Thickener	Frozen candied sweet potatoes, ice cream, frozen custard, sherbet
Sodium alginate (algins)	Water retainers	Condiments, salad dressing, cake icing, chocolate milk, dessert toppings
Carrageenan	Stabilizer	Chocolate milk, syrups for frozen products, evaporated milk, pressure-dispersed whipped cream, cottage cheese
Sodium carboxymethyl cellulose	Stabilizer, bodying agent	Ice cream, icing for baked goods, cheese spreads, dietetic canned fruit products, fruited ham glaze
Dextrin	Stabilizer	Beer, baked goods, gelatin desserts
Gelatin	Thickener	Fruit gelatins and puddings, cream cheese, cheese spreads, cheese foods
Cellulose gums	Thickener, suspender, bodying agent	Dessert mixes, cake mixes, salad dressing
Gum acacia (gum arabic)	Thickener, stabilizer	Beer, soft drinks, ice cream, imitation fruit juice drinks
Locust bean gum	Thickener, stabilizer	Cream cheese, fruit sherbert, salad dressing
Guar gum	Thickener, stabilizer, binder	Cheese spreads, baked goods, meat products
Gum tragacanth	Thickener	Pickle relish, icings, fruit juices, salad dressings

Source: Berarde, M. A. (1971). *The Chemicals We Eat.* McGraw-Hill Book Company, New York.

Stainless Steel

TABLE 2.S.37
Composition and properties of some types of stainless steel[1]

Part I—Composition of Some Stainless Steels

Composition	Type 302	Type 304	Type 316	Type 430	Type 440C	Type 502
Carbon	0.08–0.20	0.08	0.10	0.12	0.95	0.10
Manganese	2.00	2.00	2.00	1.00	1.00	1.00
Phosphorus	0.04	0.04	0.04	0.04	0.04	0.04
Sulfur	0.03	0.03	0.03	0.03	0.03	0.03
Silicon	1.00	1.00	1.00	1.00	1.00	1.00
Nickel	8.00–10.00	8.00–10.00	10.00–14.00	0.00	0.00	0.00
Chromium	17.00–19.00	18.00–20.00	16.00–18.00	14.00–18.00	16.00–18.00	4.00–6.00
Molybdenum	0.00	0.00	2.00–3.00	0.00	0.75	0.00

Part II—Properties of Some Types of Stainless Steel

Mechanical Properties	Types 302 and 304		Type 316		Type 430 Ann. and		Type 440C Ann. and		Type 502
	Annealed	Cold Drawn	Annealed	Cold Drawn	Annealed	Cold Drawn	Annealed	Cold Drawn	Annealed Bars
Tensile strength	75,000	100,000	80,000	90,000	75,000	85,000	110,000	125,000	65,000
Yield strength	35,000	60,000	30,000	60,000	45,000	70,000	65,000	100,000	25,000
Brinnel hardness	150	212	149	190	155	185	230	260	150
Rockwell hardness		C-33	78				B.97	C.24	B.75
Scaling temp., °F	1,650	1,650	1,650	1,650	1,550	1,550			1,150
Annealing temp., °F	1,900–2,000 and quench		1,900–2,050 and quench		Air cool from		Cool slowly		Furnace Cool
	1,650	1,650	1,650	1,650	1,500–1,400°F		1,550–1,650		1,600–1,525
Hardenable	No	No					Yes	Yes	Yes
Magnetic							Yes	Yes	Yes

[1] Percent iron not shown.

Source: Hall, C. W., Farrall, A. W., and Rippen, A. L. (editors) (1971). Stainless steel. In *Encyclopedia of Food Engineering.* AVI Publishing Co., Westport, Connecticut.

Standards, Processed Fruit and Vegetable Products

TABLE 2.S.38

Relative importance of factors involved in USDA standards for processed fruit and vegetable products

Product	Absence of Defects	Color	Flavor	Char-acter	Consist-ency	Uni-formity	Tex-ture	Tender-ness and Ma-turity	Clear-ness of Liquor
Apples	20	20	..	40	..	20 siz.	..	..	..
Apple Butter	20	20	20	20 fin.	20	..	..	..	..
Apple Juice	20	20	60	..	..	..	..	..	..
Apple Sauce	20	20	20	20 fin.	20	..	..	..	..
Apricots	30	20	..	30	..	20 siz.	..	..	..
Asparagus	30	20	..	..	..	..	..	40	10
Green & Wax Beans	35	15	..	..	..	..	..	40	10
Dried Beans	40	..	..	40	20	..	..	..	..
Lima Beans	25	35	..	30	..	..	..	..	..
Beets	30	25	..	..	..	15	30	..	10
Berries	30	20	..	30	..	20	..	..	..
Blueberries	40	20	..	40	..	..	..	..	..
Carrots	30	25	..	..	shape	15 siz.	30	..	..
Cherries, Sweet	30	30	..	20	..	20 siz.	..	..	..
Cherries, Sour	30	20	..	30	..	20 pits	..	..	..
Corn, Cream	20	10	20	..	20	..	..	30	..
Corn, Whole	20	10	20	..	..	..	..	40	10
Cranberry Sauce	20	20	20	..	40	..	..	..	..
Figs, Kadota	30	20	..	35	..	15 siz.	..	..	..
Frozen Apples	20	20	..	40	..	20	..	..	..
Fruit Cocktail	20	20	..	20	..	20	..	..	20
Fruit Jelly	..	20	40	..	40	..	..	..	..
Fruit Preserv. (Jam)	20	20	40	..	20	..	..	..	..
Fruit Salad	30	20	..	30	..	20 siz.	..	..	..
Grapefruit	20	20	..	20 (Wholeness 20) (Drained Wt. 20)					
Grapefruit Juice	40	20	40	..	..	..	..	..	..
Grape Juice	20	40	40	..	..	..	..	..	..
Lemon Juice	35	35	30	..	..	..	..	..	..
Mushroom	30	30	..	20	..	20 siz.	..	..	..
Olives, Green	30	30	..	20	..	20 siz.	..	..	..
Olives, Ripe	10	15	30	25	..	20	..	..	..
Orange Juice	20	40	40	..	..	..	..	..	..
Orange Juice con.	20	40	40	..	..	..	..	..	..
Orange Marm.	20	20	40	..	20	..	..	..	..
Okra	20	15	15	..	..	10	..	35	5
Peaches	30	20	..	30	..	20 siz.	..	..	..
Peanut Butter	30	20	30	..	20	..	..	..	..
Pears	30	20	..	30	..	20 siz.	..	..	..
Peas	30	10	..	..	..	..	..	50	10
Peas, Field	40	20	..	40	..	..	..	..	..
Cucumber Pick.	30	20	..	..	..	20	30	..	..
Pimientos	40	30	..	10	..	20 siz.	..	..	..
Pineapples	30	20	..	30	..	20	..	..	..
Pineapple Juice	40	20	40	..	..	..	..	..	..
Plums	30	20	..	30	..	20 siz.	..	..	..
Potatoes, peeled	40	20	..	..	..	20	20	..	..
Prunes, dr.	30	20	..	35	..	15	..	..	..
Pumpkins & Squash	30	20	..	20 fin.	30	..	..	..	..
Raspberries	20	25	..	35	..	20 siz.	..	..	..
Sauerkraut	10	15	45	15 crisp	..	..	..	..	15
Sauerkraut, bulk	10	15	45	15 crisp	..	..	..	..	15
Spinach	40	30	..	30	..	..	..	..	..
Sw. Potatoes	40	20	..	20	..	20 siz.	..	..	..
Tomatoes	30	30	..	..	(Wholeness 20) (Drained Wt. 20)				
Tomato Juice	15	30	..	..	15	..	..	..	..
Tomato Paste	40	60	..	..	..	..	..	..	..
Tomato Pulp—pure	50	50	..	..	..	..	..	..	..
Tom. Sauce-Catsup	25	25	25	..	25	..	..	..	..
Chili Sauce	20	20	20	20	20	..	..	..	..

Source: Kramer, A., and Twigg, B. A. (editors) (1970). In *Quality Control for the Food Industry*, Vol. 1, 3rd Edition. AVI Publishing Co., Westport, Connecticut.

Starch

TABLE 2.S.39
Types of starches used in sugar confectionery

Type	Use and Characteristics
Unmodified maize starch	Filler for cheap cream paste, toffee cigarettes, licorice paste. Dusting powder. Can be mixed with fat for release agents; with icing sugar for Turkish Delight dusting.
Acid modified thin boiling starches Fluidity Nos. 30, 40	Used in gums and jellies. Generally used for open pan cooking; can also be used for continuous processes where acid is present during cooking process.
Nos. 50, 60, 70, 85	Enable high solids production, good depositing capability, can be used in combination with other gelling agents. Produce gels of high rigidity, clarity and short texture and are capable of producing a wide range of textures (soft to hard); good shelf life.
Oxidized modified thin boiling starches	Similar range of fluidity available. Produce gels of increased clarity but lack the rigidity of acid-modified starches. Produces soft eating products; can be used in combination with other starches and gelling agents.
Molding starches Oil bound molding starch (contains 0.12%–0.2% mineral oil) Oil bound 0.75%	Provides good molding characteristics at low moisture percentages. Reduces explosion hazard by suppressing dust. Oil used is not susceptible to rancidity. Can be mixed with oil-free starch in mogul plant to improve molding. Increase total oil content to suitable range 0.2%.
Oil-free molding starches	Can be mixed with heavy molding starch to rejuvenate after extended use. Excellent water absorption properties. (Molding starches based on di-glycerides as binders are also available.)
Amylopectin thin boiling (range of fluidities)	Produces gels of excellent clarity with no setback. Can be used at high concentration to produce hard texture; with other gelling agents, to provide a variety of textures. Also for continuous licorice paste production.
Modified waxy maize starches	Similar viscosity to gum arabic at same concentration. Excellent clarity, very soluble, low gelatinization temperature.
Soluble dextrin starches (range of fluidities; manufactured from maize or tapioca starches.)	For adhesive coatings and glazes. Used in panning operation as a seal. In some cases can replace natural gums. Good sheen and clarity.
Pregelatinized maize starch	Cold-water soluble; used as a tablet binder.
Physical modified oxidized starch	Cold-water soluble, easily dispersible, smooth texture, good film former, bland flavor. Used as tablet binder. Replaces gums and gelling agents in lozenge pastes, etc. Good seal for nuts, etc., in panning.

(Continued)

Starch   (Continued)

TABLE 2.S.39   (Continued)

Type	Use and Characteristics
Modified waxy maize starches cross bonded	For use in caramel and caramel coating, gives body with a soft eating texture, good clarity and flavor, acid-stable and resistant to long storage. Also used as a gelling agent in deposited and extruded marshmallow. Acid, heat, and shear stable.
Pregelatinized cross bonded acetylated waxy maize starches	Used where moisture is a restriction, dissolves readily in cold water even in high concentrations to form a clear smooth short texture. Gel resistant to freezing and thawing.
High amylose starches	Very high gelatinization temperature with strong set back used for quick-setting starch jellies. (High amylose can be blended with thin boiling maize starches to produce different amylopectin/amylose ratio.)

Source: Lees, R., and Jackson, E. B. (1973). *Sugar Confectionery and Chocolate Manufacture.* Leonard Hill Books, International Textbook Co., London, England.

Starch, Microappearance

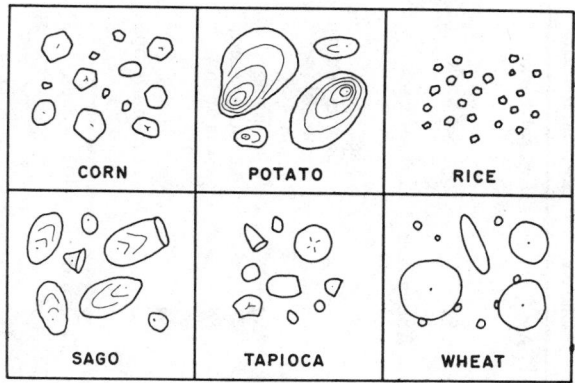

FIGURE 2.S.5
Microappearance of various granular starches

Source: Schoch, T. J. (1969). Starches in foods. In *Carbohydrates and Their Roles, Symposium on Foods.* H. W. Schultz, R. F. Cain, and R. W. Wrolstad (editors). AVI Publishing Co., Westport, Connecticut.

Starch, Modified

TABLE 2.S.40
Properties of modified starches

Type of Modified Starch	Texture	Clarity	To Retrogradation	Terminal Viscosity	Stability				Gelatinization Temp in Water
					Shear	Acid	Heat	Freeze Thaw	
Roll dried maize	Short Granular	Avg	High set back	Instant cold water soluble; thick	Good	Fair	Fair	Poor	Cold water soluble
Acid modified maize	Short Smooth	Avg	High set back	Thick	Fair	Fair	Fair	Poor	63°–73°C in Water
Oxidized maize	Short Smooth	Above Avg	Soft set back	Thin	Poor	Fair	Fair	Poor	54°–64°C in Water
Moderately cross bonded waxy maize	Short Smooth	Avg	No set back at room temp; some at low temp	Thick	Good	Good	Good	Mod.	67°–77°C
Medium cross bonded waxy maize	Short Smooth	Avg	No set back at room temp; some at low temp	Thick	V. good	V. good	V. good	Fair	69°–79°C
High cross bonded waxy maize	Short Smooth	Avg	No set back at room temp; set back at low temp	Thick	Exc.	Exc.	Exc.	Poor	73°–83°C
Cross bonded acetylated waxy maize	Short Smooth	V. good	No set back	Thick	Exc.	Exc.	Exc.	Exc.	60°–72°C
Roll dried cross bonded acetylated waxy maize	Short Smooth	Above Avg	No set back	Instant cold water soluble	Exc.	Exc.	Exc.	Exc.	Cold water soluble

Source: Lees, R., and Jackson, E. B. (1973). *Sugar Confectionery and Chocolate Manufacture.* Leonard Hill Books, International Textbook Co, London, England.

Starchy Roots, Composition

TABLE 2.S.41
Composition of the edible portion (EP) and refuse in the material as purchased (AP)

Commodity and Description	Water	Protein	Fat	Carbohydrate Total (By Dif)	Fiber	Ash	Calories (No./100 g)	Notes	Refuse in AP (%)
	(Percent of Edible Portion)								
Potatoes									
Potato (*Solanum tuberosum*)	78	2.0	0.1	18.9	0.4	1.0	82		15
Potato flour	7	8.5	0.4	80.0	1.7	4.1	349		0
Sweet potatoes (*Ipomoea batatas*)	70	1.3	0.4	27.3	0.8	1.0	117		17
Cassava									
Fresh (*Manihot* spp.)	62.5	1.2	0.3	34.7	1.3	1.3	146	Manioc, yuca	25
Meal and flour	14	1.5	0.6	81.5		2.4	338		0
Yautia (*Xanthosoma* spp.)[1]	65	2.1	0.4	31.5	0.8	1.0	136	Also called tanier, malanga	20
Taro (*Colocasia* spp.)[1]	72.5	1.9	0.2	24.2	0.9	1.2	104		18
Yam (*Dioscorea* spp.)[1]	72.4	2.4	0.2	24.1	0.9	0.9	105		14
Arracacha (*Arracacia xanthorrhiza*)[2]	72	1.7	0.3	24.9	0.6	1.1	108		30
Starches, pure dry	12	0.5	0.3	86.9	0.2	0.3	362	Arrowroot, corn-starch, sago, tapioca, etc.	0

[1] More information needed.
[2] More information needed, especially on refuse.

Source: Chatfield, C. *Food Composition Tables for International Use.* Food and Agriculture Organization, United Nations, Rome.

Steam, Properties

TABLE 2.S.42
Properties of saturated steam, 0 to 200 PSI gauge

Psig	Temp, °F	Specific Volume, Cu Ft per Lb	Heat of the Liquid	Latent Heat, Btu/Lb	Total Heat of Steam, Btu/Lb	Psig	Temp, °F	Specific Volume, Cu Ft per Lb	Heat of the Liquid	Latent Heat, Btu/Lb	Total Heat of Steam, Btu/Lb
0	212.0	26.79	180.0	970.4	1,150.3	76	320.9	4.86	291.1	893.4	1,184.5
1	215.3	25.23	183.4	967.2	1,151.6	78	322.4	4.76	292.7	892.2	1,184.9
2	218.5	23.80	186.6	966.3	1,152.8	80	323.9	4.67	294.3	891.0	1,185.3
3	221.5	22.53	189.6	964.3	1,153.9	82	325.4	4.57	295.9	889.5	1,185.7
4	224.4	21.40	192.5	962.4	1,154.9	84	326.9	4.48	297.4	888.7	1,186.1
5	227.2	20.38	195.3	960.4	1,155.9	86	328.4	4.400	298.9	887.5	1,186.4
6	229.8	19.45	198.0	958.8	1,156.8	88	329.8	4.319	300.4	886.4	1,186.8
7	232.4	18.61	200.6	957.2	1,157.8	90	331.2	4.241	301.8	885.3	1,187.1
8	234.8	17.85	203.1	955.5	1,158.6	92	332.5	4.166	303.2	884.3	1,187.5
9	237.1	17.14	205.4	954.0	1,159.4	94	333.9	4.093	304.6	883.2	1,187.8
10	239.4	16.49	207.7	952.5	1,160.2	96	335.2	4.023	306.0	882.4	1,188.1
11	241.6	15.89	209.9	951.1	1,161.0	98	336.0	3.955	307.4	881.1	1,188.5
12	243.7	15.34	212.1	949.6	1,161.7	100	337.0	3.890	308.8	880.0	1,188.8
13	245.8	14.82	214.2	948.2	1,162.4	102	339.2	3.826	310.1	879.0	1,189.1
14	247.8	14.33	216.2	946.8	1,163.0	104	340.4	3.765	311.4	878.0	1,189.4
15	249.7	13.88	218.2	945.5	1,163.7	106	341.7	3.706	313.5	876.2	1,189.7
16	251.6	13.45	220.1	944.2	1,164.3	108	343.0	3.648	314.1	875.8	1,189.9
17	253.5	13.05	222.0	942.9	1,164.9	110	344.2	3.591	315.3	874.9	1,190.2
18	255.3	12.68	223.9	941.6	1,165.5	112	345.4	3.538	316.6	873.9	1,190.5
19	257.1	12.33	225.7	940.4	1.166.1	114	346.6	3.486	317.8	873.0	1,190.8
20	258.8	11.99	227.4	939.3	1,166.7	116	347.8	3.435	319.1	872.0	1,191.1
21	260.5	11.67	229.1	938.1	1,167.2	118	348.9	3.385	320.3	871.0	1,191.3
22	262.1	11.38	230.8	936.9	1,167.7	120	350.1	3.338	321.5	870.5	1,191.6
23	263.7	11.09	232.4	935.8	1,168.2	122	351.2	3.292	322.7	869.1	1,191.8
24	265.3	10.82	234.0	934.8	1,168.8	124	352.4	3.248	323.8	868.8	1,192.1
25	266.9	10.67	235.6	933.7	1,169.3	126	353.5	3.204	325.0	867.3	1,192.3
26	268.3	10.32	237.2	932.5	1.169.7	128	354.6	3.160	326.2	866.4	1,192.6
27	269.8	10.00	238.7	931.5	1.170.2	130	355.7	3.118	327.3	865.5	1,192.8
28	271.3	9.86	240.1	930.5	1,170.6	132	356.7	3.078	328.4	864.6	1,193.0
29	272.7	9.65	241.6	929.5	1,171.1	134	357.8	3.039	329.5	863.8	1,193.3
30	274.1	9.45	243.0	928.5	1,171.5	136	358.9	2.999	330.6	862.8	1,193.5
32	276.8	9.07	245.7	926.6	1,172.3	138	359.9	2.961	331.8	861.9	1,193.7
34	279.4	8.72	248.4	924.7	1,173.1	140	360.9	2.925	332.8	861.1	1,193.9
36	281.9	8.40	251.0	922.9	1,173.9	142	362.0	2.890	333.9	860.3	1,194.2
38	284.3	8.10	253.5	921.1	1,174.6	144	363.0	3.856	335.0	859.4	1,194.4
40	286.7	7.82	255.9	919.4	1,175.3	146	364.0	2.823	336.0	858.6	1,194.6
42	289.0	7.56	258.3	917.6	1,175.9	148	365.0	2.790	337.1	857.7	1,194.8
44	291.3	7.32	260.6	916.0	1,176.6	150	365.9	2.758	338.1	856.9	1,195.0
46	293.5	7.09	262.9	914.3	1,177.2	152	366.9	2.726	339.1	856.1	1,195.2
48	295.6	6.88	265.1	912.7	1,177.8	154	367.9	2.695	340.1	855.3	1,195.4
50	297.7	6.68	267.2	911.2	1,178.4	156	368.8	2.665	341.1	854.4	1,195.5
52	299.7	6.50	269.3	909.6	1,178.9	158	369.8	2.635	342.1	853.6	1,195.7
54	301.7	6.32	271.3	908.2	1,179.5	160	370.7	2.606	343.1	852.8	1,195.9
56	303.6	6.14	273.3	906.7	1,180.0	162	371.6	2.578	344.1	852.0	1,196.1
58	305.5	5.98	275.2	905.3	1,180.5	164	372.6	2.551	345.1	851.2	1,196.3
60	307.3	5.83	277.1	903.9	1,181.0	166	373.5	2.524	346.0	850.5	1,196.5
62	309.1	5.69	279.0	902.5	1,181.5	168	374.4	2.498	347.0	849.7	1,196.7
64	310.9	5.56	280.8	901.2	1,182.0	170	375.3	2.472	347.9	848.9	1,196.8
66	312.6	5.43	282.6	999.8	1,182.4	172	376.2	2.447	348.9	848.1	1,197.0
68	314.4	5.30	284.4	998.5	1,182.9	174	377.1	2.422	349.8	847.4	1,197.2
70	316.0	5.18	286.1	897.2	1,183.3	176	377.9	2.397	350.7	846.6	1,197.3
72	317.7	5.07	287.8	895.9	1,183.7	178	378.8	2.373	351.6	845.9	1,197.5
74	319.3	4.97	289.5	894.6	1,184.1						

Source: Hall, C. W., Farrall, A. W., and Rippen, A. L. (editors) (1971). Steam. In *Encyclopedia of Food Engineering*. AVI Publishing Co., Westport, Connecticut.

Steroids

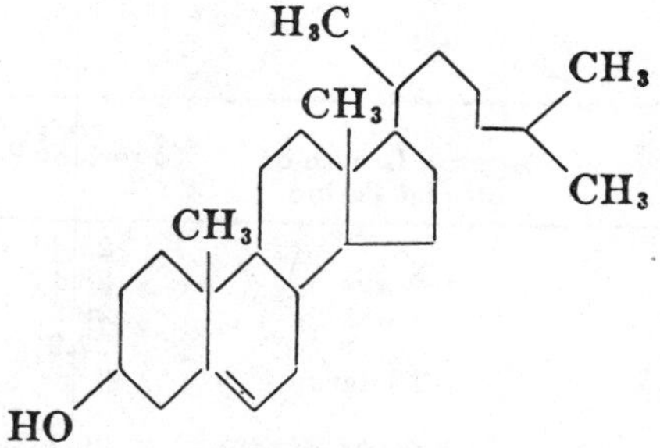

Cholesterol

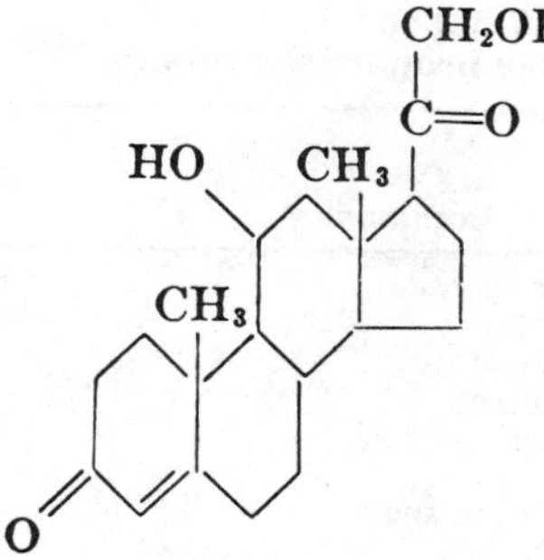

Corticosterone

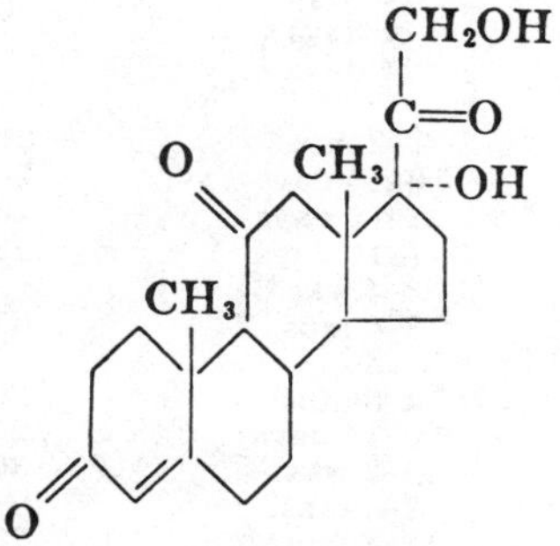

Cortisone

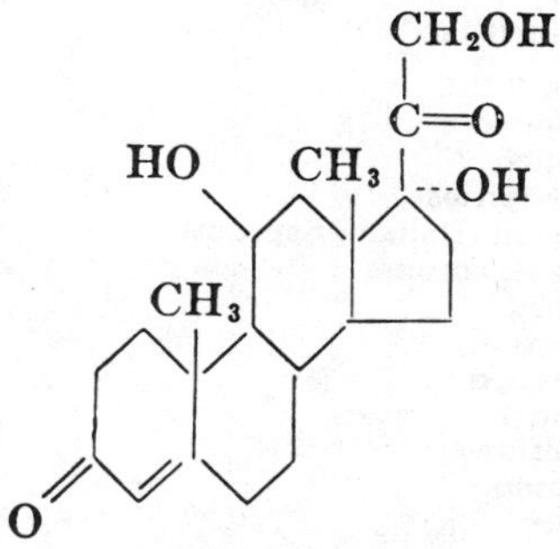

Cortisol

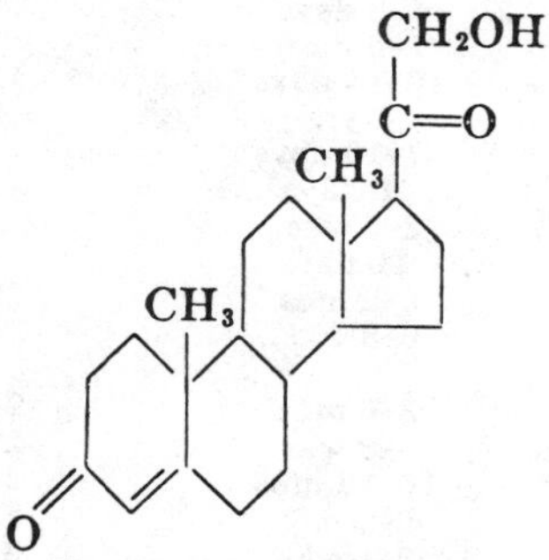

Desoxycorticosterone

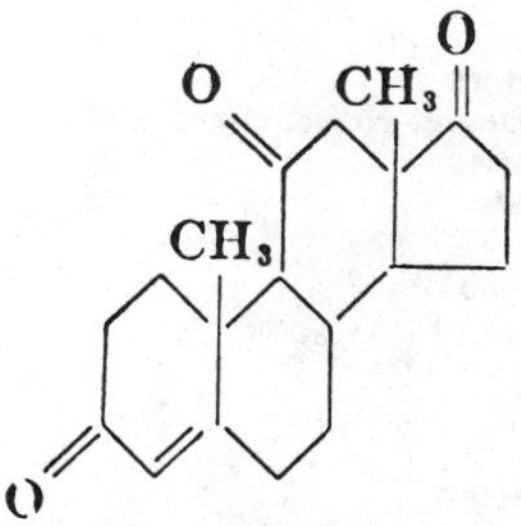

Adrenosterone

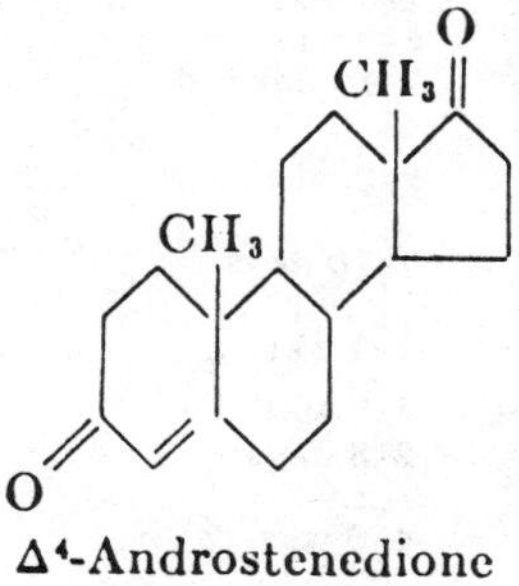

Δ^4-Androstenedione

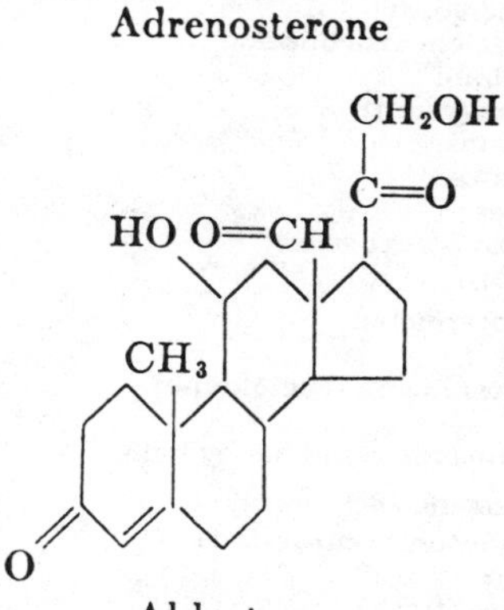

Aldosterone

FIGURE 2.S.6
Diagram of the cholesterol molecule showing close family resemblance of steroid derivatives

Source: Shideman, F. E. (1967). *Take as Directed—Our Modern Medicines*. Chemical Rubber Co., Cleveland.

Storage

TABLE 2.S.43
Storage properties of foods

Commodity	Temp (°F)	Relative Humidity (%)	Approx Length of Storage Period	Avg. Freezing Point (°F)
Apples	30–32	85–88	—	28.4
Apricots	31–32	80–85	1–2 wks.	28.1
Asparagus	32	85–90	3–4 wks.	29.8
Avocados	—	85–90	—	27.2
Bananas	56–60	90–95	7–10 days	—
Beans				
Green, or snap	32–40	85–90	2–4 wks.	29.7
Lima				
Unshelled	{32 / 40	85–90 / 85–90	2–4 wks.} / 10 days }	
Shelled	{32 / 40	85–90 / 85–90	15 days } / 4 days }	30.1
Beets				
Topped	32	95–98	1–3 mos.	26.9
Bunch	32	85–90	10–14 days	26.9
Blackberries	31–32	80–85	7–10 days	28.9
Broccoli (Italian or sprouting)	32–35	90–95	7–10 days	29.2
Brussels sprouts	32–35	90–95	3–4 wks.	—
Cabbage	32	90–95	3–4 mos.	31.2
Carrots				
Topped	32	95–98	4–5 mos.	29.6
Bunch	32	85–90	10–14 days	29.6
Cauliflower	32	85–90	2–3 wks.	30.1
Celeriac	32	95–98	3–4 mos.	—
Celery	31–32	90–95	2–4 mos.	29.7
Cherries	31–32	80–85	10–14 days	—
Coconuts	32–35	80–85	1–2 mos.	25.5
Corn (green)	31–32	85–90	4–8 days	28.9
Cranberries	36–40	85–90	1–3 mos.	27.3
Cucumbers	45–50	85–95	10–14 days	30.5
Dates, Deglet Noor, cured	0–24	—	1 yr.	-4.1
Dewberries	31–32	80–85	7–10 days	—
Eggplants	45–50	85–90	10 days	30.4
Endive	32	90–95	2–3 wks.	30.9
Figs (fresh)	31–32	85–90	10 days	—
Garlic (dry)	32	70–75	6–8 mos.	25.4
Grapefruit		85–90	6–8 wks.	28.4
Grapes				
Vinifera	30–31	85–90	3–6 mos.	24.9
American	31–32	80–85	3–8 wks.	27.5
Horseradish	32	95–98	10–12 mos.	26.4
Jerusalem artichokes	31–32	90–95	2–5 mos.	27.5
Kohlrabi	32	95–98	2–4 wks.	30.0
Leeks (green)	32	85–90	1–3 mos.	29.2
Lemons	55–58	85–90	1–4 mos.	28.1
Lettuce	32	90–95	2–3 wks.	31.2
Limes	45–48	85–90	6–8 wks.	29.3
Logan blackberries	31–32	80–85	7–10 days	29.5
Melons				
Watermelon	36–40	75–85	2–3 wks.	{29.2 flesh / 28.8 rind
Muskmelon (cantaloupe)	32–34	75–78	7–10 days	{29.0 flesh / 28.4 rind
Honeydew and honey ball	36–38	75–85	2–4 wks.	{29.0 flesh / 28.8 rind
Cassaba and Persian	36–40	75–85	4–6 wks.	
Mushrooms (cultivated)	32–35	80–85	2–3 days	30.2
Okra	50	85–95	2 wks.	30.1
Olives (fresh)	45–50	85–90	4–6 wks.	28.5

(Continued)

Storage (Continued)

TABLE 2.S.43 (Continued)

Commodity	Temp (°F)	Relative Humidity (%)	Approx Length of Storage Period	Avg. Freezing Point (°F)
Onions	32	70–75	6–8 mos.	30.1
Onion sets	32	70–75	5–8 mos.	29.5
Oranges		85–90	8–10 wks.	{28.0 flesh / 27.4 peel
Parsnips	32	90–95	2–4 mos.	28.9
Peaches	31–32	80–85	2–4 wks.	29.4
Pears				
Bartlett	29–31	85–90		28.5
Fall and winter varieties	29–31	85–90	—	—
Peas (green)	32	85–90	1–2 wks.	30.0
Peppers				
Chili (dry)	—	70–75	6–9 mos.	—
Sweet	32	85–90	4–6 wks.	30.1
Pineapples				
Mature green	50–60	85–90	3–4 wks.	29.1
Ripe	40–45	85–90	2–4 wks.	29.9
Plums (including prunes)	31–32	80–85	3–8 wks.	28.0
Potatoes				
Early		85–90		—
Late	38–50	85–90	—	28.9
Pumpkins	50–55	70–75	2–6 mos.	30.1
Quinces	31–32	80–85	2–3 mos.	28.1
Radishes (winter)	32	95–98	2–4 mos.	—
Raspberries	31–32	80–85	7–10 days	29.9
Rhubarb	32	90–95	2–3 wks.	28.4
Rutabagas	32	95–98	2–4 mos.	29.5
Salsify	32	95–98	2–4 mos.	28.4
Spinach	32	90–95	10–14 days	30.3
Squashes				
Summer	40–50	85–95	2–3 wks.	—
Winter	50–55	70–75	4–6 mos.	29.3
Strawberries	31–32	80–85	7–10 days	29.9
Sweet potatoes	50–55	80–85	4–6 mos.	28.5
Tomatoes				
Ripe	40–50	80–85	7–10 days	30.4
Mature green	55–70	80–85	3–5 wks.	30.4
Turnips	32	95–98	4–5 mos.	30.5
Dried fruits		—	9–12 mos.	—
Nuts	32–45	65–75	8–12 mos.	—

Source: Rose, D. H., Wright, R. C., and Whitman, T. M., *The Commercial Storage of Fruits, Vegetables and Florists' Stocks*, U.S. Dep. Agric. Circ. *278.*

Storage, Dry

TABLE 2.S.44
The following are recommended dry storage times for various foods

6–12 Months
Canned Fruits and Vegetables
Honey and Peanut Butter

3–6 Months
Dry Milk Solids
Macaroni
Dry Beans and Peas
Cereals (corn meal)

3–6 Months (Cont.)
Flour
Sugar
Spices
Rice

3 Months
Dried Fruit

7–30 Days
Potatoes
Root Vegetables
Onions

7–10 Days
Oranges
Apples
Pears

Source: Food Storage. Ohio Department of Health, Columbus.

Storage Times (°F)

TABLE 2.S.45
Recommended temperature and storage life of various foods

Food	Suggested Maximum Temperature °F	Recommended Maximum Storage Life	Remarks
Candy (chocolate)	70	3 months	Wrapped or in original carton – may be frozen
Canned Goods.	70	12 months	In original containers
Cereals	70	6 months	In original package
Beans, flour, rice.	70	6 months	In original container or covered galvanized can
Cream filled pastries	36	serve day prepared	Spoil readily; must be served the day prepared
Cream pies, custards, Cream puffs, etc.			
Dairy products			
Milk – Fluid.	40	5 days	In original container, tightly covered
Milk – Dried.	70	3 months	In original package – If open, 38° in tight can
Milk – Evaporated	70	12 months	In cans – invert every 30 days
Butter.	40	2 weeks	In waxed cartons
Cheese (hard)	40	6 months	Tightly wrapped
Cheese (soft)	40	7 days	In tightly covered container
Ice cream and ices.	10	3 months	In original container, covered
Eggs	45	7 days	Unwashed – never in cardboard carton
Eggs (dried)	70	6 months	In original carton – if open, 45° in tight can
Egg whites.	45	2 days	In tight container
Egg yolks	45	2 days	In tight container – cover with water
Fish (fresh).	36	5 days	Wrap loosely
Shellfish	36	5 days	In covered container

(Continued)

Storage Times (°F) (Continued)

TABLE 2.S.45 (Continued)

Food	Suggested Maximum Temperature °F	Recommended Maximum Storage Life	Remarks
Fruits			
Peaches, Plums, Berries	45	7 days	Unwashed
Apples, pears, citrus	70	2 weeks	In original containers
Dried	70	3 months	In original containers
Gravies, sauces	36	2 days	In covered containers
Left-overs	36	2 days	In covered containers
Meat			
Ground	38	2 days	Loosely wrapped
Fresh meat cuts	38	5 days	Loosely wrapped
Liver & variety meats	38	2 days	Loosely wrapped
Cold cuts (sliced)	38	5 days	Wrap in semi-moistureproof (waxed paper)
Cured bacon (sliced)	38	1 to 2 weeks	May wrap tightly
Ham (tender cured)	38	1 to 2 weeks	May wrap tightly
Ham (canned)	38	6 weeks	In original container, unopened
Tongue (smoked)	38	7 weeks	May wrap tightly
Dried beef	38	6 weeks	May wrap tightly
Poultry	36	3 days	Wrap loosely
Processed foods made with eggs, meat, milk, fish or poultry	36	serve day prepared	In covered container. Spoils rapidly Must serve day prepared
Sugar – Spices	70	3 to 6 months	In original package – or covered galvanized can
Vegetables			
Leafy	45	5 days	Unwashed
Potatoes, onions and root vegetables	70	7 to 30 days	Dry in ventilated container or bags

Source: Food Storage. Ohio Department of Health, Columbus.

Sugar Beet Yield

TABLE 2.S.46
Changes in the value of the crop from increases in nitrogen fertilizer application in Great Britain

N dressing	Root yield	Sugar	Payment		Total sugar	Juice purity	Extractable white sugar
(cwt/acre)	(ton/acre)	(%)	(£/ton roots)	(£/acre)	(cwt/ acre)	(%)	(cwt/acre)
0·0	12·34	17·30	8·45	104·27	42·7	93·1	33·5
0 to 0·6	+3·40	−0·10	−0·05	+27·95	+11·4	−0·5	+8·8
0·6 to 1·2	+1·24	−0·45	−0·20	+7·02	+2·7	−0·4	+0·9
1·2 to 1·8	+0·06	−0·63	−0·35	−5·48	−1·9	+0·6	−2·8
(kg/ha)	(t/ha)	(%)	(£/t roots)	(£/ha)	(t/ha)	(%)	(t/ha)
0	30·99	17·30	8·59	257·44	5·36	93·1	4·20
0 to 75	+8·54	−0·10	−0·05	+69·01	+1·43	−0·5	+1·10
75 to 150	+3·11	−0·45	−0·20	+17·33	+0·34	−0·4	+0·11
150 to 225	+0·15	−0·63	−0·36	−13·53	−0·24	−0·6	−0·35

Source: Draycott, A. P. (1972). *Sugar-Beet Nutrition*. Applied Science Publishers, Essex, England.

Sugar Cane Composition

TABLE 2.S.47
Vegetative composition of cane plant based on average tons of millable cane reaped annually in Natal for 12 years, 1940–41 to 1951–52, compared with Hawaiian data

Portion of Plant	Green Weight			Dry Material			Hawaii
	Tons per Acre	Percent Millable Cane	Percent Total Plant	Percent of Green Weight	Tons Acre	Percent Total Dry Weight	Percent Total Dry Weight
Millable cane	33.35	100	57.80	32	10.72	49.02	45.23
Tops	8.38	25	14.44	26	2.18	9.95	14.60
Trash	5.04	15	8.68	85	4.28	19.53	20.59
Stubble	8.38	25	14.44	35	2.93	13.37	11.65
Roots	2.69	8	4.64	66	1.78	8.13	7.30
Young shoots	—	—	—	—	—	—	0.63
Total plant	58.04	173	100	37.75	21.91	100.00	100.00
Plant residues	24.49	73	42.2	45.6	11.17	50.98	54.77

Source: Barnes, A. C. (1974). *The Sugar Cane*. Leonard Hill Books, London, England.

Sugar, D-Aldehydo

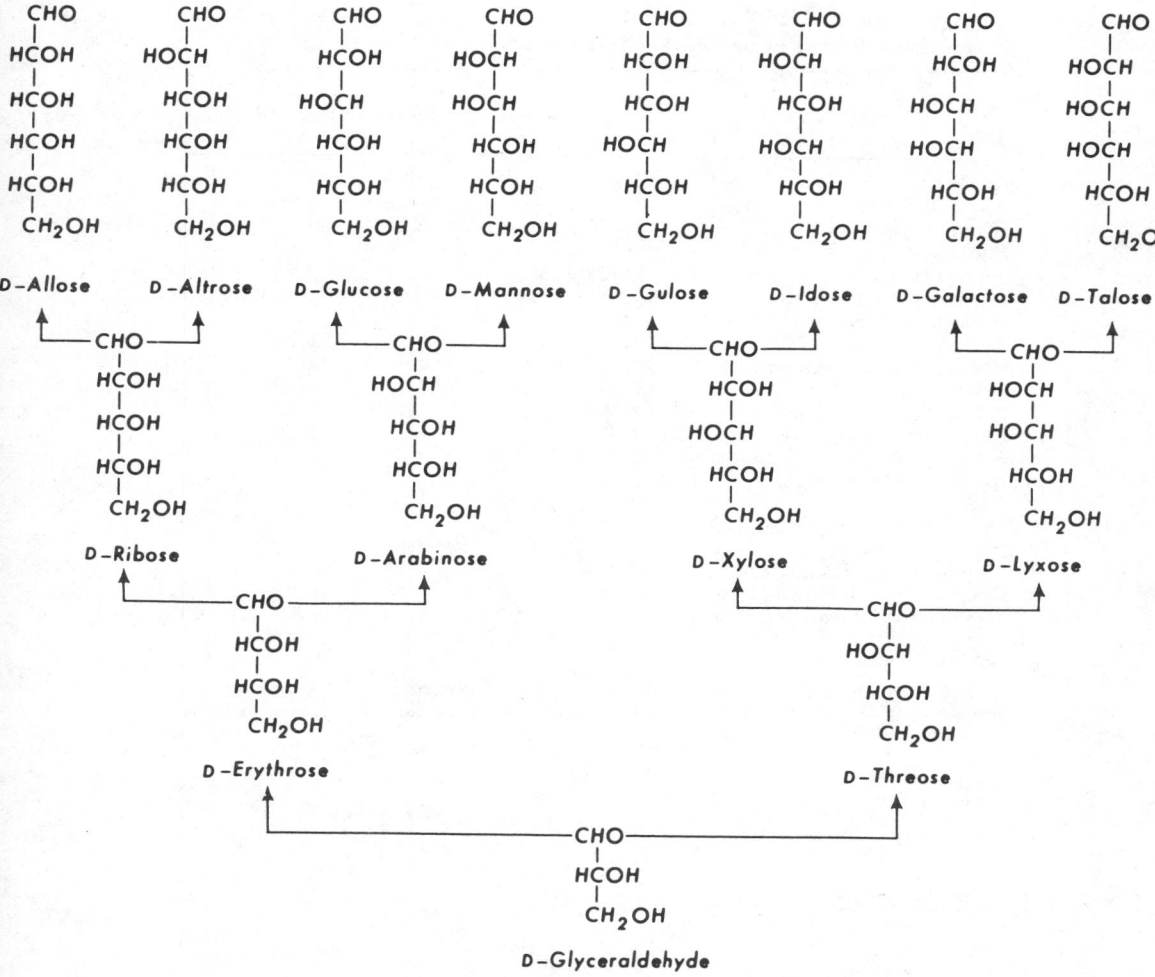

FIGURE 2.S.7
Family tree of D-aldehydo sugars

Source: Shallenberger, R. S., and Birch, G. G. (editors) (1975). Structure of monosaccharides. In *Sugar Chemistry*. AVI Publishing Co., Westport, Connecticut.

Sugar, Fruit

TABLE 2.S.48
Free sugars in fruit as percentage fresh basis

Fruit	Total Solids %	Glucose %	Fructose %	Sucrose %	Maltose %
Apple, *Pyrus Malus*	15.96	1.17	6.04	3.78	Trace
Apricot, *Prunus Armeniaca*	14.44	1.73	1.28	5.84	
Blackberry, *Rubus*	15.28	2.48	2.15	0.59	0.66
Blueberry, *Vaccinium corymbosum*	15.89	3.76	3.82	0.19	0.08
Currant, *Ribes sativum*	17.68	3.33	3.68	0.95	0.64
Gooseberry, *Ribes grossularia*	14.81	3.29	3.90	1.21	
Grape, *Vitis Labruscana*	19.13[1]	6.86	7.84	2.25	1.58
Grape, *Vitis vinifera*	17.97[1]	5.35	5.33	1.32	2.19
Peach, *Prunus Persica*	12.79	0.91	1.18	6.92	0.12
Pear, *Pyrus communis*	13.58	0.95	6.77	1.61	0.31
Plum, *Prunus domestica*	17.97	3.49	1.53	4.94	0.15
Raspberry (red), *Rubus idaeus*	20.67	2.40	1.58	3.68	
Raspberry (black), *Rubus occidentalis*	28.22	4.56	4.84	1.90	
Cherry (sour), *Prunus cerasus*	15.05	4.30	3.28	0.40	
Cherry (sweet), *Prunus avium*	22.39	6.49	7.38	0.22	
Strawberry, *Fragaria chiloensis*	9.45	2.09	2.40	1.03	0.07

[1] Soluble solids.

Source: Shallenberger, R. S., and Birch, G. G. (editors) (1975). Occurrence and properties of sugars. In *Sugar Chemistry*. AVI Publishing Co., Westport, Connecticut.

Sugar, Legumes

TABLE 2.S.49
Free sugars in legumes

Legume	Total Solids	Glucose	Fructose	Sucrose	Raffinose	Stachyose
Fava bean,[1] *Vicia faba*	16.61		0.18	3.36	0.66	
Lima bean,[1] *Phaseolus lunatus*	26.74	0.04	0.08	2.59	0.20	0.59
Pole Lima bean[1], *Phaseolus lunatus*	24.58	0.18		2.26	0.32	0.60
Pole snap bean,[1] *Phaseolus lunatus*	10.21	0.48	1.30	0.28	0.26	
Snap bean,[1] *Phaseolus vulgaris*	7.79	1.08	1.20	0.25	0.11	0.19
Pea (Alaska)[1] *Pisum sativum*	25.54		0.08	3.00	0.06	0.06
(Wrinkled)[1] *Pisum sativum*	22.77	0.32	0.23	5.27	0.58	0.49
Cow Pea,[1] *Vigna sinensis*	39.30	0.08	0.06	1.86	0.10	1.66
Dry bean,[2] *Phaseolus vulgaris*				2.40	0.80	3.40
Mung bean,[2] *Phaseolus aureus*				1.19	0.40	1.75
Pea bean,[2] *Phaseolus vulgaris*				2.55	0.65	3.06
Pea seed,[2] *Pisum sativum*		0.24		4.11	1.75	7.96
Soybean,[2] *Glycine Max*				4.53	0.73	2.73

[1] Sugars as % fresh basis.
[2] Sugars as % total bean weight.

Source: Shallenberger, R. S., and Birch, G. G. (editors) (1975). Occurrence and properties of sugars. In *Sugar Chemistry*. AVI Publishing Co., Westport, Connecticut.

Sugars and Sweets, Composition

TABLE 2.S.50
Composition of sugars and sweets

(Dashes (—) denote lack of reliable data for a constituent believed to be present in measurable amount)

Foods, approximate measures, units, and weight (edible part unless footnotes indicate otherwise)		Water	Food energy	Pro-tein	Fat	Fatty Acids Satu-rated (total)	Unsaturated Oleic	Unsaturated Lino-leic	Carbo-hydrate	Calcium	Phos-phorus	Iron	Potas-sium	Vitamin A value	Thiamin	Ribo-flavin	Niacin	Ascorbic acid
SUGARS AND SWEETS	Grams	Per-cent	Cal-ories	Grams	Grams	Grams	Grams	Grams	Grams	Milli-grams	Milli-grams	Milli-grams	Milli-grams	Inter-national units	Milli-grams	Milli-grams	Milli-grams	Milli-grams
Cake icings:																		
Boiled, white:																		
Plain—— 1 cup	94	18	295	1	0	0	0	0	75	2	2	Trace	17	0	Trace	0.03	Trace	0
With coconut—— 1 cup	166	15	605	3	13	11.0	.9	Trace	124	10	50	0.8	277	0	0.02	.07	0.3	0
Uncooked:																		
Chocolate made with milk and butter—— 1 cup	275	14	1,035	9	38	23.4	11.7	1.0	185	165	305	3.3	536	580	.06	.28	.6	1
Creamy fudge from mix and water—— 1 cup	245	15	830	7	16	5.1	6.7	3.1	183	96	218	2.7	238	Trace	.05	.20	.7	Trace
White—— 1 cup	319	11	1,200	2	21	12.7	5.1	.5	260	48	38	Trace	57	860	Trace	.06	Trace	Trace
Candy:																		
Caramels, plain or chocolate—— 1 oz	28	8	115	1	3	1.6	1.1	.1	22	42	35	.4	54	Trace	.01	.05	.1	Trace
Chocolate:																		
Milk, plain—— 1 oz	28	1	145	2	9	5.5	3.0	.3	16	65	65	.3	109	80	.02	.10	.1	Trace
Semisweet, small pieces (60 per oz)—— 1 cup or 6-oz pkg	170	1	860	7	61	36.2	19.8	1.7	97	51	255	4.4	553	30	.02	.14	.9	0
Chocolate-coated peanuts—— 1 oz	28	1	160	5	12	4.0	4.7	2.1	11	33	84	.4	143	Trace	.10	.05	2.1	Trace
Fondant, uncoated (mints, candy corn, other)—— 1 oz	28	8	105	Trace	1	.1	.3	.1	25	4	2	.3	1	0	Trace	Trace	Trace	0
Fudge, chocolate, plain—— 1 oz	28	8	115	1	3	1.3	1.4	.6	21	22	24	.3	42	Trace	.01	.03	.1	Trace
Gum drops—— 1 oz	28	12	100	Trace	Trace	—	—	—	25	2	Trace	.1	1	0	0	Trace	Trace	0
Hard—— 1 oz	28	1	110	0	Trace	—	—	—	28	6	2	.5	1	0	0	0	0	0
Marshmallows—— 1 oz	28	17	90	1	Trace	—	—	—	23	5	2	.5	2	0	0	Trace	Trace	0
Chocolate-flavored beverage powders (about 4 heaping tsp per oz):																		
With nonfat dry milk—— 1 oz	28	2	100	5	1	.5	.3	Trace	20	167	155	.5	227	10	.04	.21	.2	1
Without milk—— 1 oz	28	2	100	1	1	.4	.2	Trace	25	9	48	.6	142	—	.01	.03	.1	0
Honey, strained or extracted—— 1 tbsp	21	17	65	Trace	0	0	0	0	17	1	1	.1	11	0	Trace	.01	.1	Trace
Jams and preserves—— 1 tbsp	20	29	55	Trace	Trace	—	—	—	14	4	2	.2	18	Trace	Trace	.01	Trace	Trace
—— 1 packet	14	29	40	Trace	Trace	—	—	—	10	3	1	.1	12	Trace	Trace	Trace	Trace	Trace
Jellies—— 1 tbsp	18	29	50	Trace	Trace	—	—	—	13	4	1	.3	14	Trace	Trace	.01	Trace	1
—— 1 packet	14	29	40	Trace	Trace	—	—	—	10	3	1	.2	11	Trace	Trace	Trace	Trace	Trace
Syrups:																		
Chocolate-flavored sirup or topping:																		
Thin type—— 1 fl oz or 2 tbsp	38	32	90	1	1	.5	.3	Trace	24	6	35	.6	106	Trace	.01	.03	.2	0
Fudge type—— 1 fl oz or 2 tbsp	38	25	125	2	5	3.1	1.6	.1	20	48	60	.5	107	60	.02	.08	.2	Trace
Molasses, cane:																		
Light (first extraction)—— 1 tbsp	20	24	50	—	—	—	—	—	13	33	9	.9	183	—	.01	.01	Trace	—
Blackstrap (third extraction)—— 1 tbsp	20	24	45	—	—	—	—	—	11	137	17	3.2	585	—	.02	.04	Trace	—
Sorghum—— 1 tbsp	21	23	55	—	—	—	—	—	14	35	5	2.6	—	—	—	.02	—	—
Table blends, chiefly corn, light and dark—— 1 tbsp	21	24	60	0	0	0	0	0	15	9	3	.8	1	0	0	0	0	0
Sugars:																		
Brown, pressed down—— 1 cup	220	2	820	0	0	0	0	0	212	187	42	7.5	757	0	.02	.07	.4	0
White:																		
Granulated—— 1 cup	200	1	770	0	0	0	0	0	199	0	0	.2	6	0	0	0	0	0
—— 1 tbsp	12	1	45	0	0	0	0	0	12	0	0	Trace	Trace	0	0	0	0	0
—— 1 packet	6	1	23	0	0	0	0	0	6	0	0	Trace	Trace	0	0	0	0	0
Powdered, sifted, spooned into cup—— 1 cup	100	1	385	0	0	0	0	0	100	0	0	.1	3	0	0	0	0	0

Source: Consumer and Food Economics Institute (1977). Nutritive value of foods. USDA Home and Garden Bull. 72.

Sugars and Syrups, Composition

TABLE 2.S.51
Composition of the edible portion (EP) and refuse in the material as purchased (AP)

Commodity and Description	Water	Protein	Fat	Carbohydrate Total (By Dif)	Fiber	Ash	Calories (No./100 g)	Notes	Refuse in AP (%)
				(Percent of Edible Portion)					
Sugars and Syrups									
Sugars									
Sugar, refined				100			387	Cane or beet	0
Crude sugars from cane, palm, coconut, maple	7	1		90		2	351	Jaggery, ghur, panela, marena, piloncillo	0
Syrups									
Molasses (by-product of cane sugar)	24			(60)		4.5	232		0
Sorghum syrup (concentrated juice)	23			(67)		2.5	259	From sweet sorghum (*Sorghum saccharatum*)	0
Cane syrup (concentrated cane juice)	27			(67)		1.5	259		0
Maple syrup	34			(64)		0.7	248		0
Syrups, miscellaneous, incl. corn syrup	20			(80)		0.5	310		0
Honey	21			(75)		0.2	290		0

Source: Chatfield, C. *Food Composition Tables for International Use.* Food and Agriculture Organization, United Nations, Rome.

Sugar Solutions I

TABLE 2.S.52
Degrees brix, degrees baumé, refractive index, and specific gravity of sugar (sucrose) solutions

Degrees Brix[1]	Refractive Index at 20°C	Degrees Baumé[2]	Specific Gravity 20°/20°C[3]	Degrees Brix[1]	Refractive Index at 20°C	Degrees Baumé[2]	Specific Gravity 20°/20°C[3]
0.0	1.3330	0.00	1.0000	8.2	1.3451	4.58	1.0326
0.2	1.3333	0.11	1.0008	8.4	1.3454	4.69	1.0334
0.4	1.3336	0.22	1.0016	8.6	1.3457	4.80	1.0343
0.6	1.3339	0.34	1.0023	8.8	1.3460	4.91	1.0351
0.8	1.3341	0.45	1.0031	9.0	1.3463	5.02	1.0359
1.0	1.3344	0.56	1.0039	9.2	1.3466	5.13	1.0367
1.2	1.3347	0.67	1.0047	9.4	1.3469	5.24	1.0376
1.4	1.3350	0.79	1.0055	9.6	1.3472	5.35	1.0384
1.6	1.3353	0.90	1.0062	9.8	1.3475	5.46	1.0392
1.8	1.3356	1.01	1.0070	10.0	1.3478	5.57	1.0400
2.0	1.3359	1.12	1.0078	10.2	1.3481	5.68	1.0408
2.2	1.3362	1.23	1.0086	10.4	1.3485	5.80	1.0416
2.4	1.3365	1.34	1.0094	10.6	1.3488	5.91	1.0425
2.6	1.3368	1.46	1.0102	10.8	1.3491	6.02	1.0433
2.8	1.3370	1.57	1.0109	11.0	1.3494	6.13	1.0441
3.0	1.3373	1.68	1.0117	11.2	1.3497	6.24	1.0450
3.2	1.3376	1.79	1.0125	11.4	1.3500	6.35	1.0458
3.4	1.3379	1.90	1.0133	11.6	1.3503	6.46	1.0466
3.6	1.3382	2.02	1.0141	11.8	1.3506	6.57	1.0475
3.8	1.3385	2.13	1.0149	12.0	1.3509	6.68	1.0483
4.0	1.3388	2.24	1.0157	12.2	1.3512	6.79	1.0492
4.2	1.3391	2.35	1.0165	12.4	1.3516	6.90	1.0500
4.4	1.3394	2.46	1.0173	12.6	1.3519	7.02	1.0508
4.6	1.3397	2.57	1.0181	12.8	1.3522	7.13	1.0517
4.8	1.3400	2.68	1.0189	13.0	1.3525	7.24	1.0525
5.0	1.3403	2.79	1.0197	13.2	1.3528	7.35	1.0534
5.2	1.3406	2.91	1.0205	13.4	1.3531	7.46	1.0542
5.4	1.3409	3.02	1.0213	13.6	1.3534	7.57	1.0551
5.6	1.3412	3.13	1.0221	13.8	1.3538	7.68	1.0559
5.8	1.3415	3.24	1.0229	14.0	1.3541	7.79	1.0568
6.0	1.3418	3.35	1.0237	14.2	1.3544	7.90	1.0576
6.2	1.3421	3.46	1.0245	14.4	1.3547	8.01	1.0585
6.4	1.3424	3.57	1.0253	14.6	1.3550	8.12	1.0593
6.6	1.3427	3.69	1.0261	14.8	1.3554	8.23	1.0602
6.8	1.3430	3.80	1.0269	15.0	1.3557	8.34	1.0610
7.0	1.3433	3.91	1.0277	15.2	1.3560	8.45	1.0619
7.2	1.3436	4.02	1.0285	15.4	1.3563	8.56	1.0628
7.4	1.3439	4.13	1.0294	15.6	1.3566	8.67	1.0636
7.6	1.3442	4.24	1.0302	15.8	1.3570	8.78	1.0645
7.8	1.3445	4.35	1.0310	16.0	1.3573	8.89	1.0653
8.0	1.3448	4.46	1.0318	16.2	1.3576	9.00	1.0662

(Continued)

Sugar Solutions I (Continued)

TABLE 2.S.52 (Continued)

Degrees Brix[1]	Refractive Index at 20°C	Degrees Baumé[2]	Specific Gravity 20°/20°C[3]	Degrees Brix[1]	Refractive Index at 20°C	Degrees Baumé[2]	Specific Gravity 20°/20°C[3]
16.4	1.3579	9.11	1.0671	25.2	1.3726	13.95	1.1064
16.6	1.3582	9.22	1.0679	25.4	1.3730	14.06	1.1074
16.8	1.3586	9.33	1.0688	25.6	1.3733	14.17	1.1083
17.0	1.3589	9.45	1.0697	25.8	1.3737	14.28	1.1092
17.2	1.3592	9.56	1.0706	26.0	1.3740	14.39	1.1101
17.4	1.3596	9.67	1.0714	26.2	1.3744	14.49	1.1111
17.6	1.3599	9.78	1.0723	26.4	1.3747	14.60	1.1120
17.8	1.3602	9.89	1.0732	26.6	1.3751	14.71	1.1129
18.0	1.3605	10.00	1.0740	26.8	1.3754	14.82	1.1139
18.2	1.3609	10.11	1.0749	27.0	1.3758	14.93	1.1148
18.4	1.3612	10.22	1.0758	27.2	1.3761	15.04	1.1157
18.6	1.3615	10.33	1.0767	27.4	1.3765	15.15	1.1167
18.8	1.3618	10.44	1.0776	27.6	1.3768	15.26	1.1176
19.0	1.3622	10.55	1.0784	27.8	1.3772	15.37	1.1186
19.2	1.3625	10.66	1.0793	28.0	1.3775	15.48	1.1195
19.4	1.3628	10.77	1.0802	28.2	1.3779	15.59	1.1204
19.6	1.3632	10.88	1.0811	28.4	1.3782	15.69	1.1214
19.8	1.3635	10.99	1.0820	28.6	1.3786	15.80	1.1223
20.0	1.3638	11.10	1.0829	28.8	1.3789	15.91	1.1233
20.2	1.3642	11.21	1.0838	29.0	1.3793	16.02	1.1242
20.4	1.3645	11.32	1.0847	29.2	1.3797	16.13	1.1252
20.6	1.3648	11.43	1.0855	29.4	1.3800	16.24	1.1261
20.8	1.3652	11.54	1.0864	29.6	1.3804	16.35	1.1271
21.0	1.3655	11.65	1.0873	29.8	1.3807	16.46	1.1280
21.2	1.3658	11.76	1.0882	30.0	1.3811	16.57	1.1290
21.4	1.3662	11.87	1.0891	30.2	1.3815	16.67	1.1299
21.6	1.3665	11.98	1.0903	30.4	1.3818	16.78	1.1309
21.8	1.3668	12.09	1.0909	30.6	1.3822	16.89	1.1319
22.0	1.3672	12.20	1.0918	30.8	1.3825	17.00	1.1328
22.2	1.3675	12.31	1.0927	31.0	1.3829	17.11	1.1338
22.4	1.3679	12.42	1.0936	31.2	1.3833	17.22	1.1347
22.6	1.3682	12.52	1.0945	31.4	1.3836	17.33	1.1357
22.8	1.3685	12.63	1.0955	31.6	1.3840	17.43	1.1367
23.0	1.3689	12.74	1.0964	31.8	1.3843	17.54	1.1376
23.2	1.3692	12.85	1.0973	32.0	1.3847	17.65	1.1386
23.4	1.3696	12.96	1.0982	32.2	1.3851	17.76	1.1396
23.6	1.3699	13.07	1.0991	32.4	1.3854	17.87	1.1406
23.8	1.3703	13.18	1.1000	32.6	1.3858	17.98	1.1415
24.0	1.3706	13.29	1.1009	32.8	1.3861	18.08	1.1425
24.2	1.3709	13.40	1.1018	33.0	1.3865	18.19	1.1435
24.4	1.3713	13.51	1.1028	33.2	1.3869	18.30	1.1445
24.6	1.3716	13.62	1.1037	33.4	1.3872	18.41	1.1454
24.8	1.3720	13.73	1.1046	33.6	1.3876	18.52	1.1464
25.0	1.3723	13.84	1.1055	33.8	1.3879	18.63	1.1474

(Continued)

Sugar Solutions I (Continued)

TABLE 2.S.52   (Continued)

De-grees Brix[1]	Refractive Index at 20°C	Degrees Baumé[2]	Specific Gravity 20°/20°C[3]	De-grees Brix[1]	Refractive Index at 20°C	Degrees Baumé[2]	Specific Gravity 20°/20°C[3]
34.0	1.3883	18.73	1.1484	43.2	1.4060	23.68	1.1952
34.2	1.3887	18.84	1.1494	43.4	1.4064	23.78	1.1962
34.4	1.3891	18.95	1.1503	43.6	1.4068	23.89	1.1973
34.6	1.3894	19.06	1.1513	43.8	1.4072	24.00	1.1983
34.8	1.3898	19.17	1.1523	44.0	1.4076	24.10	1.1994
35.0	1.3902	19.28	1.1533	44.2	1.4080	24.21	1.2004
35.2	1.3906	19.38	1.1543	44.4	1.4084	24.32	1.2015
35.4	1.3909	19.49	1.1553	44.6	1.4088	24.42	1.2025
35.6	1.3913	19.60	1.1563	44.8	1.4092	24.53	1.2036
35.8	1.3916	19.71	1.1573	45.0	1.4096	24.63	1.2047
36.0	1.3920	19.81	1.1583	45.2	1.4100	24.74	1.2057
36.2	1.3924	19.92	1.1593	45.4	1.4104	24.85	1.2068
36.4	1.3928	20.03	1.1603	45.6	1.4109	24.95	1.2079
36.6	1.3931	20.14	1.1613	45.8	1.4113	25.06	1.2089
36.8	1.3935	20.25	1.1623	46.0	1.4117	25.17	1.2100
37.0	1.3939	20.35	1.1633	46.2	1.4121	25.27	1.2111
37.2	1.3943	20.46	1.1643	46.4	1.4125	25.38	1.2122
37.4	1.3947	20.57	1.1653	46.6	1.4129	25.48	1.2132
37.6	1.3950	20.68	1.1663	46.8	1.4133	25.59	1.2143
37.8	1.3954	20.78	1.1673	47.0	1.4137	25.70	1.2154
38.0	1.3958	20.89	1.1683	47.2	1.4141	25.80	1.2165
38.2	1.3962	21.00	1.1693	47.4	1.4145	25.91	1.2176
38.4	1.3966	21.11	1.1704	47.6	1.4150	26.01	1.2186
38.6	1.3970	21.21	1.1714	47.8	1.4154	26.12	1.2197
38.8	1.3974	21.32	1.1724	48.0	1.4158	26.23	1.2208
39.0	1.3978	21.43	1.1734	48.2	1.4162	26.33	1.2219
39.2	1.3982	21.54	1.1744	48.4	1.4166	26.44	1.2230
39.4	1.3986	21.64	1.1755	48.6	1.4171	26.54	1.2241
39.6	1.3989	21.75	1.1765	48.8	1.4175	26.65	1.2252
39.8	1.3993	21.86	1.1775	49.0	1.4179	26.75	1.2263
40.0	1.3997	21.97	1.1785	49.2	1.4183	26.86	1.2274
40.2	1.4001	22.07	1.1796	49.4	1.4187	26.96	1.2284
40.4	1.4005	22.18	1.1806	49.6	1.4192	27.07	1.2295
40.6	1.4008	22.29	1.1816	49.8	1.4196	27.18	1.2306
40.8	1.4012	22.39	1.1827	50.0	1.4200	27.28	1.2317
41.0	1.4016	22.50	1.1837	50.2	1.4204	27.39	1.2328
41.2	1.4020	22.61	1.1847	50.4	1.4208	27.49	1.2340
41.4	1.4024	22.72	1.1858	50.6	1.4213	27.60	1.2351
41.6	1.4028	22.82	1.1868	50.8	1.4217	27.70	1.2362
41.8	1.4032	22.93	1.1878	51.0	1.4221	27.81	1.2373
42.0	1.4036	23.04	1.1889	51.2	1.4225	27.91	1.2384
42.2	1.4040	23.14	1.1899	51.4	1.4229	28.02	1.2395
42.4	1.4044	23.25	1.1910	51.6	1.4234	28.12	1.2406
42.6	1.4048	23.36	1.1920	51.8	1.4238	28.23	1.2417
42.8	1.4052	23.46	1.1931	52.0	1.4242	28.33	1.2428
43.0	1.4056	23.57	1.1941	52.2	1.4246	28.44	1.2440

(Continued)

Sugar Solutions I (Continued)

TABLE 2.S.52   (Continued)

Degrees Brix[1]	Refractive Index at 20°C	Degrees Baumé[2]	Specific Gravity 20°/20°C[3]	Degrees Brix[1]	Refractive Index at 20°C	Degrees Baumé[2]	Specific Gravity 20°/20°C[3]
52.4	1.4251	28.54	1.2451	61.6	1.4455	33.31	1.2982
52.6	1.4255	28.65	1.2462	61.8	1.4459	33.41	1.2994
52.8	1.4260	28.75	1.2473	62.0	1.4464	33.51	1.3006
53.0	1.4264	28.86	1.2484	62.2	1.4468	33.61	1.3018
53.2	1.4268	28.96	1.2496	62.4	1.4473	33.72	1.3030
53.4	1.4272	29.06	1.2507	62.6	1.4477	33.82	1.3042
53.6	1.4277	29.17	1.2518	62.8	1.4482	33.92	1.3054
53.8	1.4281	29.27	1.2530	63.0	1.4486	34.02	1.3066
54.0	1.4285	29.38	1.2541	63.2	1.4491	34.12	1.3078
54.2	1.4289	29.48	1.2552	63.4	1.4495	34.23	1.3090
54.4	1.4294	29.59	1.2564	63.6	1.4500	34.33	1.3102
54.6	1.4298	29.69	1.2575	63.8	1.4504	34.43	1.3114
54.8	1.4303	29.80	1.2586	64.0	1.4509	34.53	1.3126
55.0	1.4307	29.90	1.2598	64.2	1.4514	34.63	1.3138
55.2	1.4311	30.00	1.2609	64.4	1.4518	34.74	1.3150
55.4	1.4316	30.11	1.2620	64.6	1.4523	34.84	1.3162
55.6	1.4320	30.21	1.2632	64.8	1.4527	34.94	1.3175
55.8	1.4325	30.32	1.2643	65.0	1.4532	35.04	1.3187
56.0	1.4329	30.42	1.2655	65.2	1.4537	35.14	1.3199
56.2	1.4333	30.52	1.2666	65.4	1.4541	35.24	1.3211
56.4	1.4338	30.63	1.2678	65.6	1.4546	35.34	1.3223
56.6	1.4342	30.73	1.2689	65.8	1.4550	35.45	1.3235
56.8	1.4347	30.83	1.2701	66.0	1.4555	35.55	1.3248
57.0	1.4351	30.94	1.2712	66.2	1.4560	35.65	1.3260
57.2	1.4355	31.04	1.2724	66.4	1.4565	35.75	1.3272
57.4	1.4360	31.15	1.2736	66.6	1.4569	35.85	1.3284
57.6	1.4364	31.25	1.2747	66.8	1.4574	35.95	1.3297
57.8	1.4369	31.35	1.2759	67.0	1.4579	36.05	1.3309
58.0	1.4373	31.46	1.2770	67.2	1.4584	36.15	1.3321
58.2	1.4378	31.56	1.2782	67.4	1.4589	36.25	1.3334
58.4	1.4382	31.66	1.2794	67.6	1.4593	36.35	1.3346
58.6	1.4387	31.76	1.2805	67.8	1.4598	36.45	1.3358
58.8	1.4391	31.87	1.2817	68.0	1.4603	36.55	1.3371
59.0	1.4396	31.97	1.2829	68.2	1.4607	36.66	1.3383
59.2	1.4400	32.07	1.2840	68.4	1.4612	36.76	1.3396
59.4	1.4405	32.18	1.2852	68.6	1.4617	36.86	1.3408
59.6	1.4409	32.28	1.2864	68.8	1.4622	36.96	1.3421
59.8	1.4414	32.38	1.2876	69.0	1.4627	37.06	1.3433
60.0	1.4418	32.49	1.2887	69.2	1.4631	37.16	1.3446
60.2	1.4423	32.59	1.2899	69.4	1.4636	37.26	1.3458
60.4	1.4427	32.69	1.2911	69.6	1.4641	37.36	1.3471
60.6	1.4432	32.79	1.2923	69.8	1.4646	37.46	1.3483
60.8	1.4436	32.90	1.2935	70.0	1.4651	37.56	1.3496
61.0	1.4441	33.00	1.2946	70.2	1.4656	37.66	1.3508
61.2	1.4446	33.10	1.2958	70.4	1.4661	37.76	1.3521
61.4	1.4450	33.20	1.2970	70.6	1.4666	37.86	1.3533

(Continued)

Sugar Solutions I (Continued)

TABLE 2.S.52 (Continued)

Degrees Brix[1]	Refractive Index at 20°C	Degrees Baumé[2]	Specific Gravity 20°/20°C[3]	Degrees Brix[1]	Refractive Index at 20°C	Degrees Baumé[2]	Specific Gravity 20°/20°C[3]
70.8	1.4671	37.96	1.3546	78.0	1.4850	41.50	1.4010
71.0	1.4676	38.06	1.3559	78.2	1.4855	41.60	1.4023
71.2	1.4681	38.16	1.3571	78.4	1.4860	41.70	1.4036
71.4	1.4685	38.26	1.3584	78.6	1.4865	41.79	1.4049
71.6	1.4690	38.35	1.3596	78.8	1.4871	41.89	1.4063
71.8	1.4695	38.45	1.3609	79.0	1.4876	41.99	1.4076
72.0	1.4700	38.55	1.3622	79.2	1.4881	42.08	1.4089
72.2	1.4705	38.65	1.3635	79.4	1.4886	42.18	1.4102
72.4	1.4710	38.75	1.3647	79.6	1.4891	42.28	1.4116
72.6	1.4715	38.85	1.3660	79.8	1.4896	42.37	1.4129
72.8	1.4720	38.95	1.3673	80.0	1.4901	42.47	1.4142
73.0	1.4725	39.05	1.3686	80.2	1.4906	42.57	1.4155
73.2	1.4730	39.15	1.3698	80.4	1.4912	42.66	1.4169
73.4	1.4735	39.25	1.3711	80.6	1.4917	42.76	1.4182
73.6	1.4740	39.35	1.3724	80.8	1.4922	42.85	1.4196
73.8	1.4744	39.44	1.3737	81.0	1.4927	42.95	1.4209
74.0	1.4749	39.54	1.3750	81.2	1.4933	43.05	1.4222
74.2	1.4754	39.64	1.3763	81.4	1.4938	43.14	1.4236
74.4	1.4759	39.74	1.3775	81.6	1.4943	43.24	1.4249
74.6	1.4764	39.84	1.3789	81.8	1.4949	43.33	1.4263
74.8	1.4769	39.94	1.3801	82.0	1.4954	43.43	1.4276
75.0	1.4774	40.03	1.3814	82.2	1.4959	43.53	1.4289
75.2	1.4779	40.13	1.3827	82.4	1.4964	43.62	1.4303
75.4	1.4784	40.23	1.3840	82.6	1.4970	43.72	1.4316
75.6	1.4789	40.33	1.3853	82.8	1.4975	43.81	1.4330
75.8	1.4794	40.43	1.3866	83.0	1.4980	43.91	1.4343
76.0	1.4799	40.53	1.3879	83.2	1.4985	44.00	1.4357
76.2	1.4804	40.62	1.3892	83.4	1.4991	44.10	1.4371
76.4	1.4810	40.72	1.3905	83.6	1.4996	44.19	1.4384
76.6	1.4815	40.82	1.3918	83.8	1.5001	44.29	1.4398
76.8	1.4820	40.92	1.3931	84.0	1.5007	44.38	1.4411
77.0	1.4825	41.01	1.3944	84.2	1.5012	44.48	1.4425
77.2	1.4830	41.11	1.3957	84.4	1.5017	44.57	1.4439
77.4	1.4835	41.21	1.3970	84.6	1.5022	44.67	1.4452
77.6	1.4840	41.31	1.3984	84.8	1.5028	44.76	1.4466
77.8	1.4845	41.40	1.3997	85.0	1.5033	44.86	1.4479

Source: National Canners Assoc. (1968).

[1] Degrees Brix (or Balling) = the percent of sugar (sucrose) by weight at the temperature indicated on the instrument.

[2] Degrees Baumé = $145 - \dfrac{145}{Sp\ gr}$ (for materials heavier than water).

$= \dfrac{140}{Sp\ gr} - 130$ (for materials lighter than water).

[3] Accepted by International Commission for Uniform Methods of Sugar Analysis.

Source: Kramer, A., and Twigg, B. A. (editors) (1973). In *Quality Control For The Food Industry*. Vol. 2, 3rd Edition. AVI Publishing Co., Westport, Connecticut.

Sugar Solutions II

TABLE 2.S.53
Degrees brix, specific gravity, and degrees baumé of sugar solutions

Degrees Brix or percentage of sucrose by weight	Specific gravity at 20° 4° C	Specific gravity at 20° 20° C	Degrees Baumé (modulus 145)	Degrees Brix or percentage of sucrose by weight	Specific gravity at 20°/4° C	Specific gravity at 20°/20° C	Degrees Baumé (modulus 145)
0. 0	0. 99823	1. 00000	0. 00	5. 0	1. 01785	1. 01965	2. 79
. 1	. 99862	1. 00039	. 06	5. 1	1. 01825	1. 02005	2. 85
. 2	. 99901	1. 00078	. 11	5. 2	1. 01865	1. 02045	2. 91
. 3	. 99940	1. 00117	. 17	5. 3	1. 01905	1. 02085	2. 96
. 4	. 99979	1. 00155	. 22	5. 4	1. 01945	1. 02125	3. 02
. 5	1. 00017	1. 00194	. 28	5. 5	1. 01985	1. 02165	3. 07
. 6	1. 00056	1. 00233	. 34	5. 6	1. 02025	1. 02206	3. 13
. 7	1. 00095	1. 00272	. 39	5. 7	1. 02065	1. 02246	3. 18
. 8	1. 00134	1. 00311	. 45	5. 8	1. 02105	1. 02286	3. 24
. 9	1. 00173	1. 00350	. 51	5. 9	1. 02145	1. 02321	3. 30
1. 0	1. 00212	1. 00389	. 56	6. 0	1. 02186	1. 02366	3. 35
1. 1	1. 00251	1. 00428	. 62	6. 1	1. 02226	1. 02407	3. 41
1. 2	1. 00290	1. 00467	. 67	6. 2	1. 02266	1. 02447	3. 46
1. 3	1. 00329	1. 00506	. 73	6. 3	1. 02306	1. 02487	3. 52
1. 4	1. 00368	1. 00545	. 79	6. 4	1. 02346	1. 02527	3. 57
1. 5	1. 00406	1. 00584	. 84	6. 5	1. 02387	1. 02568	3. 63
1. 6	1. 00445	1. 00623	. 90	6. 6	1. 02427	1. 02608	3. 69
1. 7	1. 00484	1. 00662	. 95	6. 7	1. 02467	1. 02648	3. 74
1. 8	1. 00523	1. 00701	1. 01	6. 8	1. 02508	1. 02689	3. 80
1. 9	1. 00562	1. 00740	1. 07	6. 9	1. 02548	1. 02729	3. 85
2. 0	1. 00602	1. 00779	1. 12	7. 0	1. 02588	1. 02770	3. 91
2. 1	1. 00641	1. 00818	1. 18	7. 1	1. 02629	1. 02810	3. 96
2. 2	1. 00680	1. 00858	1. 23	7. 2	1. 02669	1. 02851	4. 02
2. 3	1. 00719	1. 00897	1. 29	7. 3	1. 02710	1. 02892	4. 08
2. 4	1. 00758	1. 00936	1. 34	7. 4	1. 02750	1. 02932	4. 13
2. 5	1. 00797	1. 00976	1. 40	7. 5	1. 02791	1. 02973	4. 19
2. 6	1. 00836	1. 01015	1. 46	7. 6	1. 02832	1. 03013	4. 24
2. 7	1. 00876	1. 01054	1. 51	7. 7	1. 02872	1. 03054	4. 30
2. 8	1. 00915	1. 01093	1. 57	7. 8	1. 02913	1. 03095	4. 35
2. 9	1. 00954	1. 01133	1. 62	7. 9	1. 02954	1. 03136	4. 41
3. 0	1. 00993	1. 01172	1. 68	8. 0	1. 02994	1. 03176	4. 46
3. 1	1. 01033	1. 01211	1. 74	8. 1	1. 03035	1. 03217	4. 52
3. 2	1. 01072	1. 01251	1. 79	8. 2	1. 03076	1. 03258	4. 58
3. 3	1. 01112	1. 01290	1. 85	8. 3	1. 03116	1. 03299	4. 63
3. 4	1. 01151	1. 01330	1. 90	8. 4	1. 03157	1. 03340	4. 69
3. 5	1. 01190	1. 01369	1. 96	8. 5	1. 03198	1. 03381	4. 74
3. 6	1. 01230	1. 01409	2. 02	8. 6	1. 03239	1. 03422	4. 80
3. 7	1. 01269	1. 01448	2. 07	8. 7	1. 03280	1. 03463	4. 85
3. 8	1. 01309	1. 01488	2. 13	8. 8	1. 03321	1. 03504	4. 91
3. 9	1. 01348	1. 01528	2. 18	8. 9	1. 03362	1. 03545	4. 96
4. 0	1. 01388	1. 01567	2. 24	9. 0	1. 03403	1. 03586	5. 02
4. 1	1. 01428	1. 01607	2. 29	9. 1	1. 03444	1. 03627	5. 07
4. 2	1. 01467	1. 01647	2. 35	9. 2	1. 03485	1. 03668	5. 13
4. 3	1. 01507	1. 01687	2. 40	9. 3	1. 03526	1. 03709	5. 19
4. 4	1. 01547	1. 01726	2. 46	9. 4	1. 03567	1. 03750	5. 24
4. 5	1. 01586	1. 01766	2. 52	9. 5	1. 03608	1. 03792	5. 30
4. 6	1. 01626	1. 01806	2. 57	9. 6	1. 03649	1. 03833	5. 35
4. 7	1. 01666	1. 01846	2. 63	9. 7	1. 03691	1. 03874	5. 41
4. 8	1. 01706	1. 01886	2. 68	9. 8	1. 03732	1. 03915	5. 46
4. 9	1. 01746	1. 01926	2. 74	9. 9	1. 03773	1. 03957	5. 52

(Continued)

Sugar Solutions **II** (*Continued*)

TABLE 2.S.53 (*Continued*)

Degrees Brix or percentage of sucrose by weight	Specific gravity at 20°/4° C	Specific gravity at 20°/20° C	Degrees Baumé (modulus 145)	Degrees Brix or percentage of sucrose by weight	Specific gravity at 20°/4° C	Specific gravity at 20°/20° C	Degrees Baumé (modulus 145)
10. 0	1. 03814	1. 03998	5. 57	15. 0	1. 05916	1. 06104	8. 34
10. 1	1. 03856	1. 04039	5. 63	15. 1	1. 05959	1. 06147	8. 40
10. 2	1. 03897	1. 04081	5. 68	15. 2	1. 06002	1. 06190	8. 45
10. 3	1. 03938	1. 04122	5. 74	15. 3	1. 06045	1. 06233	8. 51
10. 4	1. 03980	1. 04164	5. 80	15. 4	1. 06088	1. 06276	8. 56
10. 5	1. 04021	1. 04205	5. 85	15. 5	1. 06131	1. 06319	8. 62
10. 6	1. 04063	1. 04247	5. 91	15. 6	1. 06174	1. 06362	8. 67
10. 7	1. 04104	1. 04288	5. 96	15. 7	1. 06217	1. 06405	8. 73
10. 8	1. 04146	1. 04330	6. 02	15. 8	1. 06260	1. 06448	8. 78
10. 9	1. 04187	1. 04371	6. 07	15. 9	1. 06303	1. 06491	8. 84
11. 0	1. 04229	1. 04413	6. 13	16. 0	1. 06346	1. 06534	8. 89
11. 1	1. 04270	1. 04455	6. 18	16. 1	1. 06389	1. 06577	8. 95
11. 2	1. 04312	1. 04497	6. 24	16. 2	1. 06432	1. 06621	9. 00
11. 3	1. 04354	1. 04538	6. 30	16. 3	1. 06476	1. 06664	9. 06
11. 4	1. 04395	1. 04580	6. 35	16. 4	1. 06519	1. 06707	9. 11
11. 5	1. 04437	1. 04622	6. 41	16. 5	1. 06562	1. 06751	9. 17
11. 6	1. 04479	1. 04664	6. 46	16. 6	1. 06605	1. 06794	9. 22
11. 7	1. 04521	1. 04706	6. 52	16. 7	1. 06649	1. 06837	9. 28
11. 8	1. 04562	1. 04747	6. 57	16. 8	1. 06692	1. 06881	9. 33
11. 9	1. 04604	1. 04789	6. 63	16. 9	1. 06736	1. 06924	9. 39
12. 0	1. 04646	1. 04831	6. 68	17. 0	1. 06779	1. 06968	9. 45
12. 1	1. 04688	1. 04873	6. 74	17. 1	1. 06822	1. 07011	9. 50
12. 2	1. 04730	1. 04915	6. 79	17. 2	1. 06866	1. 07055	9. 56
12. 3	1. 04772	1. 04957	6. 85	17. 3	1. 06909	1. 07098	9. 61
12. 4	1. 04814	1. 04999	6. 90	17. 4	1. 06953	1. 07142	9. 67
12. 5	1. 04856	1. 05041	6. 96	17. 5	1. 06996	1. 07186	9. 72
12. 6	1. 04898	1. 05084	7. 02	17. 6	1. 07040	1. 07229	9. 78
12. 7	1. 04940	1. 05126	7. 07	17. 7	1. 07084	1. 07273	9. 83
12. 8	1. 04982	1. 05168	7. 13	17. 8	1. 07127	1. 07317	9. 89
12. 9	1. 05024	1. 05210	7. 18	17. 9	1. 07171	1. 07361	9. 94
13. 0	1. 05066	1. 05252	7. 24	18. 0	1. 07215	1. 07404	10. 00
13. 1	1. 05109	1. 05295	7. 29	18. 1	1. 07258	1. 07448	10. 05
13. 2	1. 05151	1. 05337	7. 35	18. 2	1. 07302	1. 07492	10. 11
13. 3	1. 05193	1. 05379	7. 40	18. 3	1. 07346	1. 07536	10. 16
13. 4	1. 05236	1. 05422	7. 46	18. 4	1. 07390	1. 07580	10. 22
13. 5	1. 05278	1. 05464	7. 51	18. 5	1. 07434	1. 07624	10. 27
13. 6	1. 05320	1. 05506	7. 57	18. 6	1. 07478	1. 07668	10. 33
13. 7	1. 05363	1. 05549	7. 62	18. 7	1. 07522	1. 07712	10. 38
13. 8	1. 05405	1. 05591	7. 68	18. 8	1. 07566	1. 07756	10. 44
13. 9	1. 05448	1. 05634	7. 73	18. 9	1. 07610	1. 07800	10. 49
14. 0	1. 05490	1. 05677	7. 79	19. 0	1. 07654	1. 07844	10. 55
14. 1	1. 05532	1. 05719	7. 84	19. 1	1. 07698	1. 07888	10. 60
14. 2	1. 05575	1. 05762	7. 90	19. 2	1. 07742	1. 07932	10. 66
14. 3	1. 05618	1. 05804	7. 96	19. 3	1. 07786	1. 07977	10. 71
14. 4	1. 05660	1. 05847	8. 01	19. 4	1. 07830	1. 08021	10. 77
14. 5	1. 05703	1. 05890	8. 07	19. 5	1. 07874	1. 08065	10. 82
14. 6	1. 05746	1. 05933	8. 12	19. 6	1. 07919	1. 08110	10. 88
14. 7	1. 05788	1. 05975	8. 18	19. 7	1. 07963	1. 08154	10. 93
14. 8	1. 05831	1. 06018	8. 23	19. 8	1. 08007	1. 08198	10. 99
14. 9	1. 05874	1. 06061	8. 29	19. 9	1. 08052	1. 08243	11. 04

(*Continued*)

Sugar Solutions II (Continued)

TABLE 2.S.53 (Continued)

Degrees Brix or percentage of sucrose by weight	Specific gravity at 20°/4° C	Specific gravity at 20°/20° C	Degrees Baumé (modulus 145)	Degrees Brix or percentage of sucrose by weight	Specific gravity at 20°/4° C	Specific gravity at 20°/20° C	Degrees Baumé (modulus 145)
20. 0	1. 08096	1. 08287	11. 10	25. 0	1. 10356	1. 10551	13. 84
20. 1	1. 08140	1. 08332	11. 15	25. 1	1. 10402	1. 10597	13. 89
20. 2	1. 08185	1. 08376	11. 21	25. 2	1. 10448	1. 10643	13. 95
20. 3	1. 08229	1. 08421	11. 26	25. 3	1. 10494	1. 10689	14. 00
20. 4	1. 08274	1. 08465	11. 32	25. 4	1. 10540	1. 10736	14. 06
20. 5	1. 08318	1. 08510	11. 37	25. 5	1. 10586	1. 10782	14. 11
20. 6	1. 08363	1. 08554	11. 43	25. 6	1. 10632	1. 10828	14. 17
20. 7	1. 08407	1. 08599	11. 48	25. 7	1. 10679	1. 10874	14. 22
20. 8	1. 08452	1. 08644	11. 54	25. 8	1. 10725	1. 10921	14. 28
20. 9	1. 08497	1. 08689	11. 59	25. 9	1. 10771	1. 10967	14. 33
21. 0	1. 08541	1. 08733	11. 65	26. 0	1. 10818	1. 11014	14. 39
21. 1	1. 08586	1. 08778	11. 70	26. 1	1. 10864	1. 11060	14. 44
21. 2	1. 08631	1. 08823	11. 76	26. 2	1. 10910	1. 11106	14. 49
21. 3	1. 08676	1. 08868	11. 81	26. 3	1. 10957	1. 11153	14. 55
21. 4	1. 08720	1. 08913	11. 87	26. 4	1. 11003	1. 11200	14. 60
21. 5	1. 08765	1. 08958	11. 92	26. 5	1. 11050	1. 11246	14. 66
21. 6	1. 08810	1. 09003	11. 98	26. 6	1. 11096	1. 11293	14. 71
21. 7	1. 08855	1. 09048	12. 03	26. 7	1. 11143	1. 11339	14. 77
21. 8	1. 08900	1. 09093	12. 09	26. 8	1. 11190	1. 11386	14. 82
21. 9	1. 08945	1. 09138	12. 14	26. 9	1. 11236	1. 11433	14. 88
22. 0	1. 08990	1. 09183	12. 20	27. 0	1. 11283	1. 11480	14. 93
22. 1	1. 09035	1. 09228	12. 25	27. 1	1. 11330	1. 11526	14. 99
22. 2	1. 09080	1. 09273	12. 31	27. 2	1. 11376	1. 11573	15. 04
22. 3	1. 09125	1. 09318	12. 36	27. 3	1. 11423	1. 11620	15. 09
22. 4	1. 09170	1. 09364	12. 42	27. 4	1. 11470	1. 11667	15. 15
22. 5	1. 09216	1. 09409	12. 47	27. 5	1. 11517	1. 11714	15. 20
22. 6	1. 09261	1. 09454	12. 52	27. 6	1. 11564	1. 11761	15. 26
22. 7	1. 09306	1. 09499	12. 58	27. 7	1. 11610	1. 11808	15. 31
22. 8	1. 09351	1. 09545	12. 63	27. 8	1. 11657	1. 11855	15. 37
22. 9	1. 09397	1. 09590	12. 69	27. 9	1. 11704	1. 11902	15. 42
23. 0	1. 09442	1. 09636	12. 74	28. 0	1. 11751	1. 11949	15. 48
23. 1	1. 09487	1. 09681	12. 80	28. 1	1. 11798	1. 11996	15. 53
23. 2	1, 09533	1. 09727	12. 85	28. 2	1. 11845	1. 12043	15. 59
23. 3	1. 09578	1. 09772	12. 91	28. 3	1. 11892	1. 12090	15. 64
23. 4	1. 09624	1. 09818	12. 96	28. 4	1. 11940	1. 12138	15. 69
23. 5	1. 09669	1. 09863	13. 02	28. 5	1. 11987	1. 12185	15. 75
23. 6	1. 09715	1. 09909	13. 07	28. 6	1. 12034	1. 12232	15. 80
23. 7	1. 09760	1. 09954	13. 13	28. 7	1. 12081	1. 12280	15. 86
23. 8	1. 09806	1. 10000	13. 18	28. 8	1. 12128	1. 12327	15. 91
23. 9	1. 09851	1. 10046	13. 24	28. 9	1. 12176	1. 12374	15. 97
24. 0	1. 09897	1. 10092	13. 29	29. 0	1. 12223	1. 12422	16. 02
24. 1	1. 09943	1. 10137	13. 35	29. 1	1. 12270	1. 12469	16. 08
24. 2	1. 09989	1. 10183	13. 40	29. 2	1. 12318	1. 12517	16. 13
24. 3	1. 10034	1. 10229	13. 46	29. 3	1. 12365	1. 12564	16. 18
24. 4	1. 10080	1. 10275	13. 51	29. 4	1. 12413	1. 12612	16. 24
24. 5	1. 10126	1. 10321	13. 57	29. 5	1. 12460	1. 12659	16. 29
24. 6	1. 10172	1. 10367	13. 62	29. 6	1. 12508	1. 12707	16. 35
24. 7	1. 10218	1. 10413	13. 67	29. 7	1. 12556	1. 12755	16. 40
24. 8	1. 10264	1. 10459	13. 73	29. 8	1. 12603	1. 12802	16. 46
24. 9	1. 10310	1. 10505	13. 78	29. 9	1. 12651	1. 12850	16. 51

(Continued)

Sugar Solutions II (Continued)

TABLE 2.S.53 (Continued)

Degrees Brix or percentage of sucrose by weight	Specific gravity at 20°/4° C	Specific gravity at 20°/20° C	Degrees Baumé (modulus 145)	Degrees Brix or percentage of sucrose by weight	Specific gravity at 20°/4° C	Specific gravity at 20°/20° C	Degrees Baumé (modulus 145)
30. 0	1. 12698	1. 12898	16. 57	35. 0	1. 15128	1. 15331	19. 28
30. 1	1. 12746	1. 12946	16. 62	35. 1	1. 15177	1. 15381	19. 33
30. 2	1. 12794	1. 12993	16. 67	35. 2	1. 15226	1. 15430	19. 38
30. 3	1. 12842	1. 13041	16. 73	35. 3	1. 15276	1. 15480	19. 44
30. 4	1. 12890	1. 13089	16. 78	35. 4	1. 15326	1. 15530	19. 49
30. 5	1. 12937	1. 13137	16. 84	35. 5	1. 15375	1. 15579	19. 55
30. 6	1. 12985	1. 13185	16. 89	35. 6	1. 15425	1. 15629	19. 60
30. 7	1. 13033	1. 13233	16. 95	35. 7	1. 15475	1. 15679	19. 65
30. 8	1. 13081	1. 13281	17. 00	35. 8	1. 15524	1. 15729	19. 71
30. 9	1. 13129	1. 13329	17. 05	35. 9	1. 15574	1. 15778	19. 76
31. 0	1. 13177	1. 13378	17. 11	36. 0	1. 15624	1. 15828	19. 81
31. 1	1. 13225	1. 13426	17. 16	36. 1	1. 15674	1. 15878	19. 87
31. 2	1. 13274	1. 13474	17. 22	36. 2	1. 15724	1. 15928	19. 92
31. 3	1. 13322	1. 13522	17. 27	36. 3	1. 15773	1. 15978	19. 98
31. 4	1. 13370	1. 13570	17. 33	36. 4	1. 15823	1. 16028	20. 03
31. 5	1. 13418	1. 13619	17. 38	36. 5	1. 15873	1. 16078	20. 08
31. 6	1. 13466	1. 13667	17. 43	36. 6	1. 15923	1. 16128	20. 14
31. 7	1. 13515	1. 13715	17. 49	36. 7	1. 15973	1. 16178	20. 19
31. 8	1. 13563	1. 13764	17. 54	36. 8	1. 16023	1. 16228	20. 25
31. 9	1. 13611	1. 13812	17. 60	36. 9	1. 16073	1. 16279	20. 30
32. 0	1. 13660	1. 13861	17. 65	37. 0	1. 16124	1. 16329	20. 35
32. 1	1. 13708	1. 13909	17. 70	37. 1	1. 16174	1. 16379	20. 41
32. 2	1. 13756	1. 13958	17. 76	37. 2	1. 16224	1. 16430	20. 46
32. 3	1. 13805	1. 14006	17. 81	37. 3	1. 16274	1. 16480	20. 52
32. 4	1. 13853	1. 14055	17. 87	37. 4	1. 16324	1. 16530	20. 57
32. 5	1. 13902	1. 14103	17. 92	37. 5	1. 16375	1. 16581	20. 62
32. 6	1. 13951	1. 14152	17. 98	37. 6	1. 16425	1. 16631	20. 68
32. 7	1. 13999	1. 14201	18. 03	37. 7	1. 16476	1. 16682	20. 73
32. 8	1. 14048	1. 14250	18. 08	37. 8	1. 16526	1. 16732	20. 78
32. 9	1. 14097	1. 14298	18. 14	37. 9	1. 16576	1. 16783	20. 84
33. 0	1. 14145	1. 14347	18. 19	38. 0	1. 16627	1. 16833	20. 89
33. 1	1. 14194	1. 14396	18. 25	38. 1	1. 16678	1. 16884	20. 94
33. 2	1. 14243	1. 14445	18. 30	38. 2	1. 16728	1. 16934	21. 00
33. 3	1. 14292	1. 14494	18. 36	38. 3	1. 16779	1. 16985	21. 05
33. 4	1. 14340	1. 14543	18. 41	38. 4	1. 16829	1. 17036	21. 11
33. 5	1. 14389	1. 14592	18. 46	38. 5	1. 16880	1. 17087	21. 16
33. 6	1. 14438	1. 14641	18. 52	38. 6	1. 16931	1. 17138	21. 21
33. 7	1. 14487	1. 14690	18. 57	38. 7	1. 16982	1. 17188	21. 27
33. 8	1. 14536	1. 14739	18. 63	38. 8	1. 17032	1. 17239	21. 32
33. 9	1. 14585	1. 14788	18. 68	38. 9	1. 17083	1. 17290	21. 38
34. 0	1. 14634	1. 14837	18. 73	39. 0	1. 17134	1. 17341	21. 43
34. 1	1. 14684	1. 14886	18. 79	39. 1	1. 17185	1. 17392	21. 48
34. 2	1. 14733	1. 14936	18. 84	39. 2	1. 17236	1. 17443	21. 54
34. 3	1. 14782	1. 14985	18. 90	39. 3	1, 17287	1. 17494	21. 59
34. 4	1. 14831	1. 15034	18. 95	39. 4	1. 17338	1. 17545	21. 64
34. 5	1. 14880	1. 15084	19. 00	39. 5	1. 17389	1. 17596	21. 70
34. 6	1. 14930	1. 15133	19. 06	39. 6	1. 17440	1. 17648	21. 75
34. 7	1. 14979	1. 15183	19. 11	39. 7	1. 17491	1. 17699	21. 80
34. 8	1. 15029	1. 15232	19. 17	39. 8	1. 17542	1. 17750	21. 86
34. 9	1. 15078	1. 15282	19. 22	39. 9	1. 17594	1. 17802	21. 91

(Continued)

Sugar Solutions II (Continued)

TABLE 2.S.53 (Continued)

Degrees Brix or percentage of sucrose by weight	Specific gravity at 20°/4° C	Specific gravity at 20°/20° C	Degrees Baumé (modulus 145)	Degrees Brix or percentage of sucrose by weight	Specific gravity at 20°/4° C	Specific gravity at 20°/20° C	Degrees Baumé (modulus 145)
40. 0	1. 17645	1. 17853	21. 97	45. 0	1. 20254	1. 20467	24. 63
40. 1	1. 17696	1. 17904	22. 02	45. 1	1. 20307	1. 20520	24. 69
40. 2	1. 17747	1. 17956	22. 07	45. 2	1. 20360	1. 20573	24. 74
40. 3	1. 17799	1. 18007	22. 13	45. 3	1. 20414	1. 20627	24. 79
40. 4	1. 17850	1. 18058	22. 18	45. 4	1. 20467	1. 20680	24. 85
40. 5	1. 17901	1. 18110	22. 23	45. 5	1. 20520	1. 20733	24. 90
40. 6	1. 17953	1. 18162	22. 29	45. 6	1. 20573	1. 20787	24. 95
40. 7	1. 18004	1. 18213	22. 34	45. 7	1. 20627	1. 20840	25. 01
40. 8	1. 18056	1. 18265	22. 39	45. 8	1. 20680	1. 20894	25. 06
40. 9	1. 18108	1. 18316	22. 45	45. 9	1. 20734	1. 20947	25. 11
41. 0	1. 18159	1. 18368	22. 50	46. 0	1. 20787	1. 21001	25. 17
41. 1	1. 18211	1. 18420	22. 55	46. 1	1. 20840	1. 21054	25. 22
41. 2	1. 18262	1. 18472	22. 61	46. 2	1. 20894	1. 21108	25. 27
41. 3	1. 18314	1. 18524	22. 66	46. 3	1. 20948	1. 21162	25. 32
41. 4	1. 18366	1. 18575	22. 72	46. 4	1. 21001	1. 21215	25. 38
41. 5	1. 18418	1. 18627	22. 77	46. 5	1. 21055	1. 21269	25. 43
41. 6	1. 18470	1. 18679	22. 82	46. 6	1. 21109	1. 21323	25. 48
41. 7	1. 18522	1. 18731	22. 88	46. 7	1. 21162	1. 21377	25. 54
41. 8	1. 18573	1. 18783	22. 93	46. 8	1. 21216	1. 21431	25. 59
41. 9	1. 18625	1. 18835	22. 98	46. 9	1. 21270	1. 21484	25. 64
42. 0	1. 18677	1. 18887	23. 04	47. 0	1. 21324	1. 21538	25. 70
42. 1	1. 18729	1. 18939	23. 09	47. 1	1. 21378	1. 21592	25. 75
42. 2	1. 18781	1. 18992	23. 14	47. 2	1. 21432	1. 21646	25. 80
42. 3	1. 18834	1. 19044	23. 20	47. 3	1. 21486	1. 21700	25. 86
42. 4	1. 18886	1. 19096	23. 25	47. 4	1. 21540	1. 21755	25. 91
42. 5	1. 18938	1. 19148	23. 30	47. 5	1. 21594	1. 21809	25. 96
42. 6	1. 18990	1. 19201	23. 36	47. 6	1. 21648	1. 21863	26. 01
42. 7	1. 19042	1. 19253	23. 41	47. 7	1. 21702	1. 21917	26. 07
42. 8	1. 19095	1. 19305	23. 46	47. 8	1. 21756	1. 21971	26. 12
42. 9	1. 19147	1. 19358	23. 52	47. 9	1. 21810	1. 22026	26. 17
43. 0	1. 19199	1. 19410	23. 57	48. 0	1. 21864	1. 22080	26. 23
43. 1	1. 19252	1. 19463	23. 62	48. 1	1. 21918	1. 22134	26. 28
43. 2	1. 19304	1. 19515	23. 68	48. 2	1. 21973	1. 22189	26. 33
43. 3	1. 19356	1. 19568	23. 73	48. 3	1. 22027	1. 22243	26. 38
43. 4	1. 19409	1. 19620	23. 78	48. 4	1. 22082	1. 22298	26. 44
43. 5	1. 19462	1. 19673	23. 84	48. 5	1. 22136	1. 22352	26. 49
43. 6	1. 19514	1. 19726	23. 89	48. 6	1. 22190	1. 22406	26. 54
43. 7	1. 19567	1. 19778	23. 94	48. 7	1. 22245	1. 22461	26. 59
43. 8	1. 19619	1. 19831	24. 00	48. 8	1. 22300	1. 22516	26. 65
43. 9	1. 19672	1. 19884	24. 05	48. 9	1. 22354	1. 22570	26. 70
44. 0	1. 19725	1. 19936	24. 10	49. 0	1. 22409	1. 22625	26. 75
44. 1	1. 19778	1. 19989	24. 16	49. 1	1. 22463	1. 22680	26. 81
44. 2	1. 19830	1. 20042	24. 21	49. 2	1. 22518	1. 22735	26. 86
44. 3	1. 19883	1. 20095	24. 26	49. 3	1. 22573	1. 22789	26. 91
44. 4	1. 19936	1. 20148	24. 32	49. 4	1. 22627	1. 22844	26. 96
44. 5	1. 19989	1. 20201	24. 37	49. 5	1. 22682	1. 22899	27. 02
44. 6	1. 20042	1. 20254	24. 42	49. 6	1. 22737	1. 22954	27. 07
44. 7	1. 20095	1. 20307	24. 48	49. 7	1. 22792	1. 23009	27. 12
44. 8	1. 20148	1. 20360	24. 53	49. 8	1. 22847	1. 23064	27. 18
44. 9	1. 20201	1. 20414	24. 58	49. 9	1. 22902	1. 23119	27. 23

(Continued)

Sugar Solutions II (Continued)

TABLE 2.S.53 (Continued)

Degrees Brix or percentage of sucrose by weight	Specific gravity at 20°/4° C	Specific gravity at 20°/20° C	Degrees Baumé (modulus 145)	Degrees Brix or percentage of sucrose by weight	Specific gravity at 20°/4° C	Specific gravity at 20°/20° C	Degrees Baumé (modulus 145)
50. 0	1. 22957	1. 23174	27. 28	55. 0	1. 25754	1. 25976	29. 90
50. 1	1. 23012	1. 23229	27. 33	55. 1	1. 25810	1. 26033	29. 95
50. 2	1. 23067	1. 23284	27. 39	55. 2	1. 25867	1. 26090	30. 00
50. 3	1. 23122	1. 23340	27. 44	55. 3	1. 25924	1. 26147	30. 06
50. 4	1. 23177	1. 23395	27. 49	55. 4	1. 25982	1. 26204	30. 11
50. 5	1. 23232	1. 23450	27. 54	55. 5	1. 26039	1. 26261	30. 16
50. 6	1. 23287	1. 23506	27. 60	55. 6	1. 26096	1. 26319	30. 21
50. 7	1. 23343	1. 23561	27. 65	55. 7	1. 26153	1. 26376	30. 26
50. 8	1. 23398	1. 23616	27. 70	55. 8	1. 26210	1. 26433	30. 32
50. 9	1. 23453	1. 23672	27. 75	55. 9	1. 26267	1. 26490	30. 37
51. 0	1. 23508	1. 23727	27. 81	56. 0	1. 26324	1. 26548	30. 42
51. 1	1. 23564	1. 23782	27. 86	56. 1	1. 26382	1. 26605	30. 47
51. 2	1. 23619	1. 23838	27. 91	56. 2	1. 26439	1. 26663	30. 52
51. 3	1. 23675	1. 23894	27. 96	56. 3	1. 26496	1. 26720	30. 57
51. 4	1. 23730	1. 23949	28. 02	56. 4	1. 26554	1. 26778	30. 63
51. 5	1. 23786	1. 24005	28. 07	56. 5	1. 26611	1. 26835	30. 68
51. 6	1. 23841	1. 24060	28. 12	56. 6	1. 26669	1. 26893	30. 73
51. 7	1. 23897	1. 24116	28. 17	56. 7	1. 26726	1. 26950	30. 78
51. 8	1. 23953	1. 24172	28. 23	56. 8	1. 26784	1. 27008	30. 83
51. 9	1. 24008	1. 24228	28. 28	56. 9	1. 26841	1. 27066	30. 89
52. 0	1. 24064	1. 24284	28. 33	57. 0	1. 26899	1. 27123	30. 94
52. 1	1. 24120	1. 24339	28. 38	57. 1	1. 26956	1. 27181	30. 99
52. 2	1. 24176	1. 24395	28. 44	57. 2	1. 27014	1. 27239	31. 04
52. 3	1. 24232	1. 24451	28. 49	57. 3	1. 27072	1. 27297	31. 09
52. 4	1. 24287	1. 34507	28. 54	57. 4	1. 27130	1. 27355	31. 15
52. 5	1. 24343	1. 24563	28. 59	57. 5	1. 27188	1. 27413	31. 20
52. 6	1. 24399	1. 24619	28. 65	57. 6	1. 27246	1. 27471	31. 25
52. 7	1. 24455	1. 24675	28. 70	57. 7	1. 27304	1. 27529	31. 30
52. 8	1. 24511	1. 24731	28. 75	57. 8	1. 27361	1. 27587	31. 35
52. 9	1. 24567	1. 24788	28. 80	57. 9	1. 27419	1. 27645	31. 40
53. 0	1. 24623	1. 24844	28. 86	58. 0	1. 27477	1. 27703	31. 46
53. 1	1. 24680	1. 24900	28. 91	58. 1	1. 27535	1. 27761	31. 51
53. 2	1. 24736	1. 24956	28. 96	58. 2	1. 27594	1. 27819	31. 56
53. 3	1. 24792	1. 25013	29. 01	58. 3	1. 27652	1. 27878	31. 61
53. 4	1. 24848	1. 25069	29. 06	58. 4	1. 27710	1. 27936	31. 66
53. 5	1. 24905	1. 25126	29. 12	58. 5	1. 27768	1. 27994	31. 71
53. 6	1. 24961	1. 25182	29. 17	58. 6	1. 27826	1. 28052	31. 76
53. 7	1. 25017	1. 25238	29. 22	58. 7	1. 27884	1. 28111	31. 82
53. 8	1. 25074	1. 25295	29. 27	58. 8	1. 27943	1. 28169	31. 87
53. 9	1. 25130	1. 25351	29. 32	58. 9	1. 28001	1. 28228	31. 92
54. 0	1. 25187	1. 25408	29. 38	59. 0	1. 28060	1. 28286	31. 97
54. 1	1. 25243	1. 25465	29. 43	59. 1	1. 28118	1. 28345	32. 02
54. 2	1. 25300	1. 25521	29. 48	59. 2	1. 28176	1. 28404	32. 07
54. 3	1. 25356	1. 25578	29. 53	59. 3	1. 28235	1. 28462	32. 13
54. 4	1. 25413	1. 25635	29. 59	59. 4	1. 28294	1. 28520	32. 18
54. 5	1. 25470	1. 25692	29. 64	59. 5	1. 28352	1. 28579	32. 23
54. 6	1. 25526	1. 25748	29. 69	59. 6	1. 28411	1. 28638	32. 28
54. 7	1. 25583	1. 25805	29. 74	59. 7	1. 28469	1. 28697	32. 33
54. 8	1. 25640	1. 25862	29. 80	59. 8	1. 28528	1. 28755	32. 38
54. 9	1. 25697	1. 25919	29. 85	59. 9	1. 28587	1. 28814	32. 43

(Continued)

Sugar Solutions II (Continued)

TABLE 2.S.53 (Continued)

Degrees Brix or percentage of sucrose by weight	Specific gravity at 20°/4° C	Specific gravity at 20°/20° C	Degrees Baumé (modulus 145)	Degrees Brix or percentage of sucrose by weight	Specific gravity at 20°/4° C	Specific gravity at 20°/20° C	Degrees Baumé (modulus 145)
60. 0	1. 28646	1. 28873	32. 49	65. 0	1. 31633	1. 31866	35. 04
60. 1	1. 28704	1. 28932	32. 54	65. 1	1. 31694	1. 31927	35. 09
60. 2	1. 28763	1. 28991	32. 59	65. 2	1. 31755	1. 31988	35. 14
60. 3	1. 28822	1. 29050	32. 64	65. 3	1. 31816	1. 32049	35. 19
60. 4	1. 28881	1. 29109	32. 69	65. 4	1. 31877	1. 32110	35. 24
60. 5	1. 28940	1. 29168	32. 74	65. 5	1. 31937	1. 32171	35. 29
60. 6	1. 28999	1. 29227	32. 79	65. 6	1. 31998	1. 32232	35. 34
60. 7	1. 29058	1. 29286	32. 85	65. 7	1. 32059	1. 32293	35. 39
60. 8	1. 29117	1. 29346	32. 90	65. 8	1. 32120	1. 32354	35. 45
60. 9	1. 29176	1. 29405	32. 95	65. 9	1. 32181	1. 32415	35. 50
61. 0	1. 29235	1. 29464	33. 00	66. 0	1. 32242	1. 32476	35. 55
61. 1	1. 29295	1. 29523	33. 05	66. 1	1. 32304	1. 32538	35. 60
61. 2	1. 29354	1. 29583	33. 10	66. 2	1. 32365	1. 32599	35. 65
61. 3	1. 29413	1. 29642	33. 15	66. 3	1. 32426	1. 32660	35. 70
61. 4	1. 29472	1. 29701	33. 20	66. 4	1. 32487	1. 32722	35. 75
61. 5	1. 29532	1. 29761	33. 26	66. 5	1. 32548	1. 32783	35. 80
61. 6	1. 29591	1. 29820	33. 31	66. 6	1. 32610	1. 32844	35. 85
61. 7	1. 29651	1. 29880	33. 36	66. 7	1. 32671	1. 32906	35. 90
61. 8	1. 29710	1. 29940	33. 41	66. 8	1. 32732	1. 32967	35. 95
61. 9	1. 29770	1. 29999	33. 46	66. 9	1. 32794	1. 33029	36. 00
62. 0	1. 29829	1. 30059	33. 51	67. 0	1. 32855	1. 33090	36. 05
62. 1	1. 29889	1. 30118	33. 56	67. 1	1. 32917	1. 33152	36. 10
62. 2	1. 29948	1. 30178	33. 61	67. 2	1. 32978	1. 33214	36. 15
62. 3	1. 30008	1. 30238	33. 67	67. 3	1. 33040	1. 33275	36. 20
62. 4	1. 30068	1, 30298	33. 72	67. 4	1. 33102	1. 33337	36. 25
62. 5	1. 30127	1. 30358	33. 77	67. 5	1. 33163	1. 33399	36. 30
62. 6	1. 30187	1. 30418	33. 82	67. 6	1. 33225	1. 33460	36. 35
62. 7	1. 30247	1. 30477	33. 87	67. 7	1. 33287	1. 33523	36. 40
62. 8	1. 30307	1. 30537	33. 92	67. 8	1. 33348	1. 33584	36. 45
62. 9	1. 30367	1. 30597	33. 97	67. 9	1. 33410	1. 33646	36. 50
63. 0	1. 30427	1. 30657	34. 02	68. 0	1. 33472	1. 33708	36. 55
63. 1	1. 30487	1. 30718	34. 07	68. 1	1. 33534	1. 33770	36. 61
63. 2	1. 30547	1. 30778	34. 12	68. 2	1. 33596	1. 33832	36. 66
63. 3	1. 30607	1. 30838	34. 18	68. 3	1. 33658	1. 33894	36. 71
63. 4	1. 30667	1. 30898	34. 23	68. 4	1. 33720	1. 33957	36. 76
63. 5	1. 30727	1. 30958	34. 28	68. 5	1. 33782	1. 34019	36. 81
63. 6	1. 30787	1. 31019	34. 33	68. 6	1. 33844	1. 34081	36. 86
63. 7	1. 30848	1. 31079	34. 38	68. 7	1. 33906	1. 34143	36. 91
63. 8	1. 30908	1. 31139	34. 43	68. 8	1. 33968	1. 34205	36. 96
63. 9	1. 30968	1. 31200	34. 48	68. 9	1. 34031	1. 34268	37. 01
64. 0	1. 31028	1. 31260	34. 53	69. 0	1. 34093	1. 34330	37. 06
64. 1	1. 31088	1 .31320	34. 58	69. 1	1. 34155	1. 34392	37. 11
64. 2	1. 31149	1. 31381	34. 63	69. 2	1. 34217	1. 34455	37. 16
64. 3	1. 31209	1. 31441	34. 68	69. 3	1. 34280	1. 34517	37. 21
64. 4	1. 31270	1. 31502	34. 74	69. 4	1. 34342	1. 34580	37. 26
64. 5	1. 31330	1. 31563	34. 79	69. 5	1. 34405	1. 34705	37. 36
64. 6	1. 31391	1. 31623	34. 84	69. 6	1. 34467	1. 34705	37. 36
64. 7	1. 31452	1. 31684	34. 89	69. 7	1. 34530	1. 34768	37. 41
64. 8	1. 31512	1. 31745	34. 94	69. 8	1. 34592	1. 34830	37. 46
64. 9	1. 31573	1. 31806	34. 99	69. 9	1. 34655	1. 34893	37. 51

(Continued)

Sugar Solutions II (Continued)

TABLE 2.S.53 (Continued)

Degrees Brix or percentage of sucrose by weight	Specific gravity at 20°/4° C	Specific gravity at 20°/20° C	Degrees Baumé (modulus 145)	Degrees Brix or percentage of sucrose by weight	Specific gravity at 20°/4° C	Specific gravity at 20°/20° C	Degrees Baumé (modulus 145)
70. 0	1. 34717	1. 34956	37. 56	75. 0	1. 37897	1. 38141	40. 03
70. 1	1. 34780	1. 35019	37. 61	75. 1	1. 37962	1. 38206	40. 08
70. 2	1. 34843	1. 35081	37. 66	75. 2	1. 38026	1. 38270	40. 13
70. 3	1. 34906	1. 35144	37. 71	75. 3	1. 38091	1. 38335	40. 18
70. 4	1. 34968	1. 35207	37. 76	75. 4	1. 38156	1. 38400	40. 23
70. 5	1. 35031	1. 35270	37. 81	75. 5	1. 38220	1. 38465	40. 28
70. 6	1. 35094	1. 35333	37. 86	75. 6	1. 38285	1. 38530	40. 33
70. 7	1. 35157	1. 35396	37. 91	75. 7	1. 38350	1. 38595	40. 38
70. 8	1. 35220	1. 35459	37. 96	75. 8	1. 38415	1. 38660	40. 43
70. 9	1. 35283	1. 35522	38. 01	75. 9	1. 38480	1. 38725	40. 48
71. 0	1. 35346	1. 35585	38. 06	76. 0	1. 38545	1. 38790	40. 53
71. 1	1. 35409	1. 35648	38. 11	76. 1	1. 38610	1. 38855	40. 57
71. 2	1. 35472	1. 35711	38. 16	76. 2	1. 38675	1. 38920	40. 62
71. 3	1. 35535	1. 35775	38. 21	76. 3	1. 38740	1. 38985	40. 67
71. 4	1. 35598	1. 35838	38. 26	76. 4	1. 38805	1. 39050	40. 72
71. 5	1. 35661	1. 35901	38. 30	76. 5	1. 38870	1. 39115	40. 77
71. 6	1. 35724	1. 35964	38. 35	76. 6	1. 38935	1. 39180	40. 82
71. 7	1. 35788	1. 36028	38. 40	76. 7	1. 39000	1. 39246	40. 87
71. 8	1. 35851	1. 36091	38. 45	76. 8	1. 39065	1. 39311	40. 92
71. 9	1. 35914	1. 36155	38. 50	76. 9	1. 39130	1. 39376	40. 97
72. 0	1. 35978	1. 36218	38. 55	77. 0	1. 39196	1. 39442	41. 01
72. 1	1. 36041	1. 36282	38. 60	77. 1	1. 39261	1. 39507	41. 06
72. 2	1. 36105	1. 36346	38. 65	77. 2	1. 39326	1. 39573	41. 11
72. 3	1. 36168	1. 36409	38. 70	77. 3	1. 39392	1. 39638	41. 16
72. 4	1. 36232	1. 36473	38. 75	77. 4	1. 39457	1. 39704	41. 21
72. 5	1. 36295	1. 36536	38. 80	77. 5	1. 39523	1. 39769	41. 26
72. 6	1. 36359	1. 36600	38. 85	77. 6	1. 39588	1. 39835	41. 31
72. 7	1. 36423	1. 36664	38. 90	77. 7	1. 39654	1. 39901	41. 36
72. 8	1. 36486	1. 36728	38. 95	77. 8	1. 39719	1. 39966	41. 40
72. 9	1. 36550	1. 36792	39. 00	77. 9	1. 39785	1. 40032	41. 45
73. 0	1. 36614	1. 36856	39. 05	78. 0	1. 39850	1. 40098	41. 50
73. 1	1. 36678	1. 36919	39. 10	78. 1	1. 39916	1. 40164	41. 55
73. 2	1. 36742	1. 36983	39. 15	78. 2	1. 39982	1. 40230	41. 60
73. 3	1. 36805	1. 37047	39. 20	78. 3	1. 40048	1. 40295	41. 65
73. 4	1. 36869	1. 37111	39. 25	78. 4	1. 40113	1. 40361	41. 70
73. 5	1. 36933	1. 37176	39. 30	78. 5	1. 40179	1. 40427	41. 74
73. 6	1. 36997	1. 37240	39. 35	78. 6	1. 40245	1. 40493	41. 79
73. 7	1. 37061	1. 37304	39. 39	78. 7	1. 40311	1. 40559	41. 84
73. 8	1. 37125	1. 37368	39. 44	78. 8	1. 40377	1. 40625	41. 89
73. 9	1. 37189	1. 37432	39. 49	78. 9	1. 40443	1. 40691	41. 94
74. 0	1. 37254	1. 37496	39. 54	79. 0	1. 40509	i. 40758	41. 99
74. 1	1. 37318	1. 37561	39. 59	79. 1	1. 40575	1. 40824	42. 03
74. 2	1. 37382	1. 37625	39. 64	79. 2	1. 40641	1. 40890	42. 08
74. 3	1. 37446	1. 37689	39. 69	79. 3	1. 40707	1. 40956	42. 13
74. 4	1. 37510	1. 37754	39. 74	79. 4	1. 40774	1. 41023	42. 18
74. 5	1. 37575	1. 37818	39. 79	79. 5	1. 40840	1. 41089	42. 23
74. 6	1. 37639	1. 37883	39. 84	79. 6	1. 40906	1. 41155	42. 28
74. 7	1. 37704	1. 37947	39. 89	79. 7	1. 40972	1. 41222	42. 32
74. 8	1. 37768	1. 38012	39. 94	79. 8	1. 41039	1. 41288	42. 37
74. 9	1. 37833	1. 38076	39. 99	79. 9	1. 41105	1. 41355	42. 42

(Continued)

Sugar Solutions II *(Continued)*

TABLE 2.S.53   *(Continued)*

Degrees Brix or percentage of sucrose by weight	Specific gravity at 20°,4° C	Specific gravity at 20°/20° C	Degrees Baumé (modulus 145)	Degrees Brix or percentage of sucrose by weight	Specific gravity at 20°/4° C	Specific gravity at 20°/20° C	Degrees Baumé (modulus 145)
80. 0	1. 41172	1. 41421	42. 47	85. 0	1. 44539	1. 44794	44. 86
80. 1	1. 41238	1. 41488	42. 52	85. 1	1. 44607	1. 44863	44. 91
80. 2	1. 41304	1. 41554	42. 57	85. 2	1. 44675	1. 44931	44. 95
80. 3	1. 41371	1. 41621	42. 61	85. 3	1. 44744	1. 45000	45. 00
80. 4	1. 41437	1. 41688	42. 66	85. 4	1. 44812	1. 45068	45. 05
80. 5	1. 41504	1. 41754	42. 71	85. 5	1. 44881	1. 45137	45. 09
80. 6	1. 41571	1. 41821	42. 76	85. 6	1. 44949	1. 45205	45. 14
80. 7	1. 41637	1. 41888	42. 81	85. 7	1. 45018	1. 45274	45. 19
80. 8	1. 41704	1. 41955	42. 85	85. 8	1. 45086	1. 45343	45. 24
80. 9	1. 41771	1. 42022	42. 90	85. 9	1. 45154	1. 45411	45. 28
81. 0	1. 41837	1. 42088	42. 95	86. 0	1. 45223	1. 45480	45. 33
81. 1	4. 41904	1. 42155	43. 00	86. 1	1. 45292	1. 45549	45. 38
81. 2	1. 41971	1. 42222	43. 05	86. 2	1. 45360	1. 45618	45. 42
81. 3	1. 42038	1. 42289	43. 10	86. 3	1. 45429	1. 45686	45. 47
81. 4	1. 42105	1. 42356	43. 14	86. 4	1. 45498	1. 45755	45. 52
81. 5	1. 42172	1. 42423	43. 19	86. 5	1. 45567	1. 45824	45. 57
81. 6	1. 42239	1. 42490	43. 24	86. 6	1. 45636	1. 45893	45. 61
81. 7	1. 42306	1. 42558	43. 29	86. 7	1. 45704	1. 45962	45. 66
81. 8	1. 42373	1. 42625	43. 33	86. 8	1. 45773	1. 46031	45. 71
81. 9	1. 42440	1. 42692	43. 38	86. 9	1. 45842	1. 46100	45. 75
82. 0	1. 42507	1. 42759	43. 43	87. 0	1. 45911	1. 46170	45. 80
82. 1	1. 42574	1. 42827	43. 48	87. 1	1. 45980	1. 46239	45. 85
82. 2	1. 42642	1. 42894	43. 53	87. 2	1. 46050	1. 46308	45. 89
82. 3	1. 42709	1. 42961	43. 57	87. 3	1. 46119	1. 46377	45. 94
82. 4	1. 42776	1. 43029	43. 62	87. 4	1. 46188	1. 46446	45. 99
82. 5	1. 42844	1. 43096	43. 67	87. 5	1. 46257	1. 46516	46. 03
82. 6	1. 42911	1. 43164	43. 72	87. 6	1. 46326	1. 46585	46. 08
82. 7	1. 42978	1. 43231	43. 77	87. 7	1. 46395	1. 46654	46. 13
82. 8	1. 43046	1. 43298	43. 81	87. 8	1. 46464	1. 46724	46. 17
82. 9	1. 43113	1. 43366	43. 86	87. 9	1. 46534	1. 46793	46. 22
83. 0	1. 43181	1. 43434	43. 91	88. 0	1. 46603	1. 46862	46. 27
83. 1	1. 43248	1. 43502	43. 96	88. 1	1. 46673	1. 46932	46. 31
83. 2	1. 43316	1. 43569	44. 00	88. 2	1. 46742	1. 47002	46. 36
83. 3	1. 43384	1. 43637	44. 05	88. 3	1. 46812	1. 47071	46. 41
83. 4	1. 43451	1. 43705	44. 10	88. 4	1. 46881	1. 47141	46. 45
83. 5	1. 43519	1. 43773	44. 15	88. 5	1. 46950	1. 47210	46. 50
83. 6	1. 43587	1. 43841	44. 19	88. 6	1. 47020	1. 47280	46. 55
83. 7	1. 43654	1. 43908	44. 24	88. 7	1. 47090	1. 47350	46. 59
83. 8	1. 43722	1. 43976	44. 29	88. 8	1. 47159	1. 47420	46. 64
83. 9	1. 43790	1. 44044	44. 34	88. 9	1. 47229	1. 47489	46. 69
84. 0	1. 43858	1. 44112	44. 38	89. 0	1. 47299	1. 47559	46. 73
84. 1	1. 43926	1. 44180	44. 43	89. 1	1. 47368	1. 47629	46. 78
84. 2	1. 43994	1. 44249	44. 48	89. 2	1. 47438	1. 47699	46. 83
84. 3	1. 44062	1. 44317	44. 53	89. 3	1. 47508	1. 47769	46. 87
84. 4	1. 44130	1. 44385	44. 57	89. 4	1. 47578	1. 47839	46. 92
84. 5	1. 44198	1. 44453	44. 62	89. 5	1. 47648	1. 47909	46. 97
84. 6	1. 44266	1. 44521	44. 67	89. 6	1. 47718	1. 47979	47. 01
84. 7	1. 44334	1. 44590	44. 72	89. 7	1. 47788	1. 48049	47. 06
84. 8	1. 44402	1. 44658	44. 76	89. 8	1. 47858	1. 48119	47. 11
84. 9	1. 44470	1. 44726	44. 81	89. 9	1. 47928	1. 48189	47. 15

(Continued)

Sugar Solutions II (Continued)

TABLE 2.S.53 (Continued)

Degrees Brix or percentage of sucrose by weight	Specific gravity at 20°/4° C	Specific gravity at 20°/20° C	Degrees Baumé (modulus 145)	Degrees Brix or percentage of sucrose by weight	Specific gravity at 20°/4° C	Specific gravity at 20°/20° C	Degrees Baumé (modulus 145)
90. 0	1. 47998	1. 48259	47. 20	95. 0	1. 51546	1. 51814	49. 49
90. 1	1. 48068	1. 48330	47. 24	95. 1	1. 51617	1. 51886	49. 53
90. 2	1. 48138	1. 48400	47. 29	95. 2	1. 51689	1. 51958	49. 58
90. 3	1. 48208	1. 48470	47. 34	95. 3	1. 51761	1. 52030	49. 62
90. 4	1. 48278	1. 48540	47. 38	95. 4	1. 51833	1. 52102	49. 67
90. 5	1. 48348	1. 48611	47. 43	95. 5	1. 51905	1. 52174	49. 71
90. 6	1. 48419	1. 48681	47. 48	95. 6	1. 51977	1. 52246	49. 76
90. 7	1. 48489	1. 48752	47. 52	95. 7	1. 52049	1. 52318	49. 80
90. 8	1. 48559	1. 48822	47. 57	95. 8	1. 52121	1. 52390	49. 85
90. 9	1. 48630	1. 48893	47. 61	95. 9	1. 52193	1. 52463	49. 90
91. 0	1. 48700	1. 48963	47. 66	96. 0	1. 52266	1. 52535	49. 94
91. 1	1. 48771	1. 49034	47. 71	96. 1	1. 52338	1. 52607	49. 98
91. 2	1. 48841	1. 49104	47. 75	96. 2	1. 52410	1. 52680	50. 03
91. 3	1. 48912	1. 49175	47. 80	96. 3	1. 52482	1. 52752	50. 08
91. 4	1. 48982	1. 49246	47. 84	96. 4	1. 52555	1. 52824	50. 12
91. 5	1. 49053	1. 49316	47. 89	96. 5	1. 52627	1. 52897	50. 16
91. 6	1. 49123	1. 49387	47. 94	96. 6	1. 52699	1. 52969	50. 21
91. 7	1. 49194	1. 49458	47. 98	96. 7	1. 52772	1. 53042	50. 25
91. 8	1. 49265	1. 49529	48. 03	96. 8	1. 52844	1. 53114	50. 30
91. 9	1. 49336	1. 49600	48. 08	96. 9	1. 52917	1. 53187	50. 34
92. 0	1. 49406	1. 49671	48. 12	97. 0	1. 52989	1. 53260	50. 39
92. 1	1. 49477	1. 49741	48. 17	97. 1	1. 53062	1. 53332	50. 43
92. 2	1. 49548	1. 49812	48. 21	97. 2	1. 53134	1. 53405	50. 48
92. 3	1. 49619	1. 49883	48. 26	97. 3	1. 53207	1. 53478	50. 52
92. 4	1. 49690	1. 49954	48. 30	97. 4	1. 53279	1. 53551	50. 57
92. 5	1. 49761	1. 50026	48. 35	97. 5	1. 53352	1. 53623	50. 61
92. 6	1. 49832	1. 50097	48. 40	97. 6	1. 53425	1. 53696	50. 66
92. 7	1. 49903	1. 50168	48. 44	97. 7	1. 53498	1. 53769	50. 70
92. 8	1. 49974	1. 50239	48. 49	97. 8	1. 53570	1. 53842	50. 75
92. 9	1. 50045	1. 50310	48. 53	97. 9	1. 53643	1. 53915	50. 79
93. 0	1. 50116	1. 50381	48. 58	98. 0	1. 53716	1. 53988	50. 84
93. 1	1. 50187	1. 50453	48. 62	98. 1	1. 53789	1. 54061	50. 88
93. 2	1. 50258	1. 50524	48. 67	98. 2	1. 53862	1. 54134	50. 93
93. 3	1. 50329	1. 50595	48. 72	98. 3	1. 53935	1. 54207	50. 97
93. 4	1. 50401	1. 50667	48. 76	98. 4	1. 54008	1. 54280	51. 02
93. 5	1. 50472	1. 50738	48. 81	98. 5	1. 54081	1. 54353	51. 06
93. 6	1. 50543	1. 50810	48. 85	98. 6	1. 54154	1. 54426	51. 10
93. 7	1. 50615	1. 50881	48. 90	98. 7	1. 54227	1. 54499	51. 15
93. 8	1. 50686	1. 50952	48. 94	98. 8	1. 54300	1. 54573	51. 19
93. 9	1. 50757	1. 51024	48. 99	98. 9	1. 54373	1. 54646	51. 24
94. 0	1. 50829	1. 51096	49. 03	99. 0	1. 54446	1. 54719	51. 28
94. 1	1. 50900	1. 51167	49. 08	99. 1	1. 54519	1. 54793	51. 33
94. 2	1. 50972	1. 51239	49. 12	99. 2	1. 54593	1. 54866	51. 37
94. 3	1. 51044	1. 51311	49. 17	99. 3	1. 54666	1. 54939	51. 42
94. 4	1. 51115	1. 51382	49. 22	99. 4	1. 54739	1. 55013	51. 46
94. 5	1. 51187	1. 51454	49. 26	99. 5	1. 54813	1. 55087	51. 50
94. 6	1. 51258	1. 51526	49. 31	99. 6	1. 54886	1. 55160	51. 55
94. 7	1. 51330	1. 51598	49. 35	99. 7	1. 54960	1. 55234	51. 59
94. 8	1. 51402	1. 51670	49. 40	99. 8	1. 55033	1. 55307	51. 64
94. 9	1. 51474	1. 51742	49. 44	99. 9	1. 55106	1. 55381	51. 68
				100. 0	1. 55180	1. 55454	51. 73

Source: Bates, F. J. Polarimetry, saccharimetry, and the sugars. Circ. *C440*, U.S. Dept. Comm.

Sugar, Vegetables

TABLE 2.S.54
Free sugars in vegetables as percentage fresh basis

Vegetable	Total Solids %	Glucose %	Fructose %	Sucrose %
Asparagus, *Asparagus officinalis*	9.15	0.92	1.30	0.28
Beet,[1] *Beta vulgarus*	11.19	0.18	0.16	6.11
Broccoli, *Brassica oleraceae (botrytis)*	11.84	0.73	0.67	0.42
Brussels sprout,[1] *Brassica oleracea (gemmifera)*	11.45	0.66	0.75	0.41
Cabbage, *Brassica oleracea (capitata)*	6.67	1.58	1.20	0.15
Cabbage, *Brassica oleracea (capitata)*, red	9.06	2.06	1.74	0.50
Carrot, *Daucus carota*	12.00	0.85	0.85	4.24
Cauliflower,[1] *Brassica oleracea (botrytis)*	8.05	0.83	0.74	0.67
Celery, *Apium graveolens*	8.29	0.49	0.43	0.31
Cucumber, *Cucumis sativus*	3.46	0.86	0.86	0.06
Eggplant, *Solanum melongena (esculentum)*	8.49	1.51	1.53	0.25
Endive, *Cichorum endivia*	5.60	0.07	0.16	0.07
Escarole, *Cichorum endivia*	6.15	0.16	0.32	0.10
Kale, *Brassica oleracea (acephala)*	9.74	0.27	0.21	
Kohlrabi, *Brassica oleracea (gongylodes)*	7.55	1.34	1.24	0.58
Leek,[1] *Allium porrum*	11.95	0.98	1.47	1.06
Lettuce, *Lactuca sativa*	4.97	0.25	0.46	0.10
Melon, Honeydew, *Cucumis melo*	12.74	2.56	2.62	5.86
Melon, Musk, *Cucumis melo (reticulatus)*	10.84	1.72	2.03	3.56
Melon, Water, *Citrullus vulgarus*	9.57	1.81	3.54	2.35
Okra, *Hibiscus esculentus*	10.70	1.03	1.06	0.75
Onion,[2] *Allium cepa*	11.56	2.07	1.09	0.89
Onion, green,[1] *Allium cepa*	9.59	0.56	0.76	0.86
Parsley, *Petroselinum hortense*	11.28	0.10		0.20
Parsnip,[1] *Pastinaca sativa*	20.99	0.18	0.24	2.98
Pepper, *Capsicum frutescens*	6.21	0.90	0.87	0.11
Potato, new, *Solanum tuberosum*	20.08	0.15	0.09	0.14
Potato, stored at 35°F[1]		1.04	1.15	1.69
Pumpkin,[1] *Cucurbita pepo*	7.13	1.69	1.43	1.30
Radish, white, *Raphanus sativus*	4.40	0.84	0.30	
Radish, red, *Raphanus sativus*	5.46	1.34	0.74	0.22
Rhubarb, *Rheum rhaponticum*	6.20	0.42	0.39	0.09
Rutabaga, *Brassica napobrassica*	6.69	0.38	0.34	0.07
Spinach, *Spinacia oleracea*	8.04	0.09	0.04	0.06
Squash, summer, *Cucurbita pepo*	5.55	0.77	0.82	0.09
Squash, winter, *Curcurbita pepo*	13.08	0.96	1.16	1.61
Sweet corn, *Zea mays*	22.69	0.34	0.31	3.03
Swiss Chard, *Beta vulgaris (cicla)*	9.20	0.17	0.09	0.06
Sweet Potato, *Ipomoea batatas Poir*	22.53	0.33	0.30	3.37
Tomato, *Lycopersicon esculentum*	5.23	1.12	1.34	0.01
Turnip, *Brassica rapa*	7.40	1.50	1.18	0.42

[1] Contains traces (0.02–0.20%) raffinose, stachyose, or both.
[2] Contains 0.24% to > 1.0% raffinose and stachyose.

Source: Shallenberger, R. S., and Birch, G. G. (editors) (1975). Occurrence and properties of sugars. In *Sugar Chemistry*. AVI Publishing Co., Westport, Connecticut.

Sulfuric Acid Solution

TABLE 2.S.55
Various strengths of sulfuric acid solutions (sulfuric acid solutions: specification requires not less than 94% H_2SO_4 by weight sp. gr. = 1.835 at 15°. Pour acid into excess of H_2O and dilute to 1 liter)

H_2SO_4 Strength Desired Grams per Liter	H_2SO_4 Required Grams	Ml	
5	5.32	3.0	
12.5	13.29	7.2	For crude fiber
20	21.28	11.6	
30	31.91	17.4	
40	42.55	23.2	
49	52.13	28.4	1N soln
100	106.38	58.0	
150	159.57	87.0	
250	265.96	144.9	
300	319.15	173.9	
400	425.53	231.9	

Source: Editorial Board, AOAC (1975). *Official Methods of Analysis of the Association of Official Analytical Chemists*, 12th Edition. Association of Official Analytical Chemists, Washington, D.C.

Sweetening Agents

TABLE 2.S.56
Composition of confectionery sweetening agents

Sugar Product	Total Sugar (%)	Sucrose (%)	Dextrose (%)	Levulose (%)	Invert sugar (%)	Maltose (%)	Dextrin (%)	Ash (%)	Water (%)	Sweetening Power Sucrose = 100[1]
Sucrose	100	100								100
Corn syrup	47.63		21.19			26.44	34.68		17.65	30[2]
Corn sugar (Cerelose)	91		87.5			3.5	0.5	0.04	9.1	66
Invert sugar (Nulomoline)	80	6			74				20	98
Golden syrup	68.5	31			37.5				22.5	77
Molasses	70.36	53.6	8.76	8				3.9	20	74
Honey	76.8	1.9	34.48	40.50				4.0	17.7	97
Maple syrup	64.07	62.6			1.47			0.18	35	64
Sorghum syrup	63	36			27			2.5	23	69
Saccharin[3]										30,000–50,000
Sucrol[3]										20,000

[1] Based on the composition of the sugar products and the relative sweetness values for the different sugars as determined by Biester.
[2] The sweetening power of corn syrup varies according to the grade of the syrup, *i.e.*, degree of hydrolysis: high purity syrup = 40–45; low purity syrup = 26–29; Sweetose = 56–64.
[3] See recent FDA rulings on use.

Source: Jacobs, M. B. (editor) *The Chemistry and Technology of Food and Food Products*, 2nd Edition, Vol. 2. Interscience Publishers, New York.

Sweetening Compounds

TABLE 2.S.57
Sweetening compounds used in meat processing

Sugar	Common Name	Type	Sweetening Value
Sucrose	Sugar	Disaccharide of glucose and fructose	100
Glucose	Dextrose	Monosaccharide	74–90
Fructose	Fruit sugar	Monosaccharide	173
Invert sugar		Mixture of monosaccharides; 50% glucose and 50% fructose	123–130
	Honey	65–80% invert sugar	125–173
Maltose		Disaccharide of glucose and glucose	33
	Corn syrup solids	Primarily maltose	30
Lactose	Milk sugar	Disaccharide of glucose and galactose	16
Glycogen	Animal starch	Polysaccharide	Little
Saccharin[1]	Nonnutritive sweeteners	$C_6H_4SO_2NHCO$	30,000–50,000

[1] See recent FDA rulings on use.

Source: Ockerman, H. W. (1975). Chemistry of muscle and major organs. In *Meat Hygiene*. J. A. Libby (editor). Lea & Febiger, Philadelphia.

Sweetness of Sweeteners

TABLE 2.S.58
Degree of sweetness of various sweeteners

Sugar	Degree of Sweetness
Sucrose	100
Fructose	173.3
Glucose	74.3
Corn syrup	30
Molasses	74
Honey	97
Sorghum syrup	69
Saccharin[1]	30,000–50,000
Dulcin (sucrol)	20,000

[1] See recent FDA rulings on use.

Source: Braverman, J. B. S. *Introduction to the Biochemistry of Foods*. ASP Biological and Medical Press (Elsevier Division), New York.

Sweet Potato and Irish Potato

FIGURE 2.S.8
Illustrating difference between a food storage tuber (A) and a food storage root (B)

Source: Mittleider, J. R., and Nelson, A. N. (1970). *Food for Everyone*. Extension Division, Loma Linda University, California.

Sweet Potato, Composition

TABLE 2.S.59
Proximate composition of edible portion of raw sweet potatoes[1]

Component	Percentage
Solids	31.5
Total carbohydrate	27.9
Protein	1.8
Mineral matter (ash)	1.1
Fat	0.7

[1] Calories per pound of peeled tuber—565.

Source: USDA (1971). Sweet potato culture and diseases. Agriculture Handbook *388*.

Sweet Potato, Forms

TABLE 2.S.60
Forms in which sweet potatoes are processed for food

Manner of preservation and type of product	Characterization
Canning:	
Sirup packs	Small whole roots, chunks, or mixed types packed and processed in sugar sirups of varying concentrations.
Vacuum packs	Roots, as above, processed under vacuum without addition of sirups.
Solid packs	Mashed stock packed solidly in cans and heat processed.
Purees	Comminuted, strained, precooked stocks, usually unflavored, heat processed.
Baby foods	Specially prepared and blended, heat-processed purees for infant and child feeding. Usually without additives.
Freezing:	
Strips, slices, dices, chunks.	Variously prepared from peeled or unpeeled potatoes, frozen with or without sirups, and with or without cooking or baking.
Mashed, souffle	Stock prepared as for solid-pack canning, but preserved by freezing.
Purees	Pureed product preserved by freezing.
Dehydration:	
Strips, dices	Prepared pieces blanched, dehydrated with heat and vacuum with or without antidarkening treatments.
Flakes	Peeled, preheated stock, sliced, cooked, pureed, double-drum dried, flaked, packaged in low-oxygen atmospheres.
Flours	Stock washed and dehydrated fresh or after cooking, ground and sifted.
"Alayam" and similar specialty products.	Prepared prebaked roots pulped, pureed, other additives incorporated, extruded onto trays, baked in ovens. Used directly as cookies, snacks, or confections; or ground to give "Alamalt" flour for use in ice creams or other products.
Cooking in oil:	
Chips	Prepared raw slices of suitable thickness and shapes immersed in hot cooking oils, drained, salted as desired, packaged in low-oxygen atmospheres.

Source: USDA (1971). Sweet potato culture and diseases. Agriculture Handbook *388*.

Sweet Potato, Nutritive Value

TABLE 2.S.61
Nutritive value of sweet potatoes prepared in various ways

Nutrient	Nature and size of prepared sweetpotato			
	Baked, peeled after baking 1 medium about 6 ounces (5 by 2 inches) 110 grams	Baked, peeled after boiling 1 medium about 6 ounces (5 by 2 inches) 147 grams	Candied, 1 (3½ by 2¼ inches) 175 grams	Canned, vacuum or solid pack 1 cup 218 grams
Food energy _____cal._____	155.0	170.0	295.0	235.0
Protein _____g._____	2	2	2	4
Fat _____g._____	1	1	6	Trace
Carbohydrates _____g._____	36	39	60	54
Calcium _____mg._____	44	47	65	54
Iron _____mg._____	1	1	1.6	1.7
Vitamins:				
A _____I.U._____	8,970	11,610	11,030	17,110
Thiamin _____mg._____	.10	.13	.10	.12
Riboflavin _____mg._____	.07	.09	.08	.09
Niacin _____mg._____	.7	.9	.8	1.1
C _____mg._____	24	25	17	30

Source: USDA Nutritive Value of Foods (1971). Sweet potato culture and diseases. Agriculture Handbook *388*.

Swine Breeds

TABLE 2.S.62
Breeds of swine and their characteristics

Breed	Place of Origin	Color	Distinctive Head Characteristics	Other Distinguishing Characteristics	Disqualifications
American Landrace	Denmark	White, although small black skin spots are common.	Medium lop ears, straight snout, and trim jowl.	Very long side.	Black in the hair coat. Fewer than six teats on either side. Erect ears, with no forward break.
Beltsville No. 1 (75% Landrace & 25% Poland China)	United States; by the USDA at Beltsville, Maryland, beginning in 1934.	Black with white spots.	Fairly long, narrow head with trim, light jowl and moderately large, drooping ears.		
Berkshire	England; chiefly in the south central counties of Berkshire and Wiltshire.	Black with 6 white points, 4 white feet, some white on the face, and a white switch on the tail. Any or all white points may be missing.	Medium short nose, medium dished face, and erect ears.	Striking style and carriage.	A swirl on upper half of body. More than 10% white.
Chester White	United States; chiefly in Chester and Delaware counties of Pennsylvania.	White. Small bluish spots are sometimes found on the skin, but are discriminated against.			Not two-thirds big enough for age, upright ears, off colored hair, spots on hide larger than a silver dollar, cryptorchidism in males, hernia in males or females, or swirls on body above flanks.

(Continued)

Swine Breeds (Continued)

TABLE 2.S.62 (Continued)

Breed	Place of Origin	Color	Distinctive Head Characteristics	Other Distinguishing Characteristics	Disqualifications
CPF No. 1 (Developed from San Pierre X Beltsville No. 1)	Conner Prairie Farm, Nobles-ville, Ind.; be-ginning in 1956, accepted for reg-istry in 1964.	Black and white.	Fairly long snout; trim jowl; moder-ate size, drooping ears.	Moderately long and well mus-cled.	
CPF No. 2 (25% Yorkshire, 25% Belts-ville No. 1, 50% Mary-land No. 1)	Conner Prairie Farm, Nobles-ville, Ind.; be-ginning in 1959, accepted for reg-istry in 1964.	Black and white.	Fairly short snout, small ears that jut forward.	Fairly long body and length of leg, trim mid-dle.	
Duroc	United States; chiefly in New York and New Jersey.	Red, varying from light to dark.	Medium size ear, tipping forward.		White feet or white spots on any part of body, any white on end of nose, black spots larger than 2 in. in diameter, swirls on upper half of the body or neck, ridgeling (one testicle) boars, or less than 6 udder sections on either side.
Hampshire	United States; in Boone County, Kentucky.	Black, with a white belt around the shoulders and body, including the front legs.	Longer and straight-er in the face than most breeds; ears carried erect.		Any white on head other than front of snout, white on hind legs high-er than bottom of ham, more than 2/3 of body white, solid black, white from belt running back on underline to meet white on hind quarters, an incomplete belt, one or both front legs black, a swirl, boar with one testicle, more than 2/3 undersize, or evidence of tampering to conceal faulty conformation or color markings.
Hereford	United States; by R. U. Webber of La Plata, Missouri.	Red body color, with white face, legs, and switch similar to Here-ford cattle.			A white belt extending over shoulders, back, or rump; more than 2/3 white markings; no white mark-ings on face; fewer than 2 white feet; a swirl; no marks or identification; boar with one testicle; or permanent deformities of any kind.
Kentucky Red Berkshire	United States; in Kentucky.	Red	Short upturned nose, dished face, and erect ears.		
Lacombe (55% Landrace, 23% Berk-shire, and 22% Chester White)	Canada; at the Experimental Farm La-combe, Alberta, beginning in 1947.	White	Medium-sized flop ears and a medi-um length, slight-ly dished face.	Of the 3 parent breeds, it re-sembles the Landrace most closely.	
Maryland No. 1 (62% Land-race X 38% Berkshire)	United States; by the USDA and the U. of Mary-land, beginning in 1941.	Black and white spotted.	The ears are erect or slightly droop-ing and interme-diate in size.		
Minnesota No. 1 (48% Land-race X 52% Tamworth)	United States; by the USDA and the U. of Min-nesota, begin-ning in 1936.	Red with occas-ional small black spots.	Long face, trim jowls, and fairly erect ears.	Long-bodied, short-legged, light shoulders, and a relatively straight back.	
Minnesota No. 2 (40% York-shire and 60% Poland China)	United States; by the U. of Min-nesota, begin-ning in 1941.	Black and white.	Ears of medium size, with erect carriage. Snout is shorter than Min-nesota No. 1.		

(Continued)

Swine Breeds *(Continued)*

TABLE 2.S.62 *(Continued)*

Breed	Place of Origin	Color	Distinctive Head Characteristics	Other Distinguishing Characteristics	Disqualifications
Minnesota No. 3 (From following 8 lines or breeds: Gloucester Old Spot, Welsh, Large White, C-Line Poland, Beltsville No. 2, Minnesota No. 1, Minnesota No. 2, and San Pierre)	Rosemount Experiment Station, Rosemount, Minn.; breeding stock first released in 1957.	Black and red spotted; or black and white.	Moderately dished face, trim jowl, ears tilted forward and slightly erect.	Noted for rapid growth and ruggedness.	
Montana No. 1 (55% Landrace X 45% Hampshire)	United States; in Montana, by the USDA and Montana State University, beginning in 1936.	Black	Drooping ears.		
OIC (Ohio Improved Chester)	United States; in Ohio, by L. B. Silver of Salem, Ohio.	White	Wide, short head and smooth dished face. Ears droop slightly.		Swirls on upper half of body, hernia, cryptorchidism, spots on skin with other than white hair, or inverted nipples.
Palouse (65% Landrace and 35% Chester White)	United States; by Washington State University, beginning in 1945.	White	Head is moderate in length; the ears are somewhat erect but inclined forward.		
Poland China	United States; in Ohio, in the Miami Valley of Warren and Butler Counties.	Black or black with white spots, with 6 white points—the feet, face, and tip of the tail.	Drooping ears.		Fewer than 6 teats on a side, a swirl on upper half of body, hernia, or cryptorchidism.
Spotted	United States, chiefly in Indiana.	Spotted black and white, 50% each.		Must have at least six prominent teats on each side to be eligible for show or sale.	Brown or sandy spots; less than 20% or more than 80% white on body; boar with a swirl; small upright ears; not over half normal size; cramped or deformed feet; seriously diseased, barren or blind; or if scoring fewer than 60 points.
Tamworth	England; in the central counties of Stafford, Leicester, Warwick, and Northampton.	Red, varying from light to dark. Black spots may occur, but are objectionable.	Wide between the ears, snout moderately long and straight, neat jowl, and medium size, erect ears.		Swirls.
Wessex Saddleback	Hampshire, England.	Black, with a white belt around the shoulders and body including the front legs.	Fairly long snout, medium sized ears with forward pitch, trim jowl.		
Yorkshire (known as the Large White in England)	England	White, although black "freckles" appear.	Slightly dished face, and erect ears.		Swirls on upper third of body, hernia, hair color other than white, cryptorchidism, hermaphrodite, blind or inverted teats, total blindness, or fewer than 6 teats on each side.

Source: Ensminger, M. E. (1969). *Animal Science.* Interstate Printers and Publishers, Danville, Illinois.

Swine, Market Classes and Grades

TABLE 2.S.63
Market classes and grades of hogs

Hogs or Pigs	Use Selection	Sex Class	Weight Divisions (lbs.)		Weight Divisions (kg)		Commonly Used Grades
Hogs	Slaughter hogs	Barrows and Gilts (often called butcher hogs)	120-140, 140-160, 160-180, 180-200, 200-220, 220-240	240-270, 270-300, 300-330, 330-360, 360-400, 400 lbs. up	55-64, 64-73, 73-82, 82-91, 91-100, 100-109	109-123, 123-136, 136-150, 150-163, 163-182, 182 up	U.S. No. 1, U.S. No. 2, U.S. No. 3, U.S. No. 4, U.S. Utility.
		Sows (or packing sows)	270-300, 300-330, 330-360, 360-400	400-450, 450-500, 500-600, 600 lbs. up	123-136, 136-150, 150-163, 163-182	182-204, 204-227, 227-272, 272 up	U.S. No. 1, U.S. No. 2, U.S. No. 3, U.S. Utility.
		Stags	All weights				Ungraded
		Boars	All weights				Ungraded
	Feeder hogs	Barrows and Gilts	120-140, 140-160, 160-180		55-64, 64-73, 73-82		U.S. No. 1, U.S. No. 2, U.S. No. 3, U.S. No. 4, U.S. Utility, Cull.
Pigs	Slaughter pigs	Barrows, Gilts, and Boars	Under 30, 30-60		13.6, 13.6-27.2		Ungraded
		Barrows and Gilts	60-80, 80-100, 100-120		27.2-36.3, 36.3-45.4, 45.4-54.5		Ungraded
	Feeder pigs	Barrows and Gilts	80-100, 100-120		36.3-45.4, 45.4-54.5		U.S. No. 1, U.S. No. 2, U.S. No. 3, U.S. No. 4, U.S. Utility, Cull.

Source: Ensminger, M. E. (1969). *Animal Science.* Interstate Printers and Publishers, Danville, Illinois.

Tallow, Beef, Triglyceride Mole Percent Composition

TABLE 2.T.1

0 *Double Bonds*		1 *trans Double Bond*—cont.		2 *cis Double Bonds*—cont.	
PMP	0.5	StPE	0.7	StOO	5.9
PMSt	1.0	PStE	0.6	OMO	0.5
StMSt	0.5	StStE	0.6	OPO	2.1
MPM	0.4	Remaining ones	0.8	OStO	0.5
MPP	0.5			PPL	0.3
MPSt	0.5			StPL	0.2
PPP	1.7	1 *cis Double Bond*		PLP	0.5
PPSt	3.6	MOP	0.5	PLSt	0.4
StPSt	1.8	MOSt	0.5	Transglycerides	2.3
MStM	0.3	POP	5.8	Remaining ones	0.4
MStP	0.4	POSt	10.5		
MStSt	0.5	StOSt	4.8	3 *cis Double Bonds*	
PStP	1.6	PMO	1.5	OOO	4.9
PStSt	3.2	StMO	1.4	POL	0.8
StStSt	1.6	PPO	3.9	StOL	0.4
Remaining ones	0.3	StPO	3.6	PLO	0.7
		PStO	1.6	StLO	0.3
		StStO	1.5	OPL	0.6
1 *trans Double Bond*		Transglycerides	4.5	OStL	0.2
PEP[1]	0.3	Remaining ones	0.2	PPLe	0.1
PESt	0.5			StPLe	0.1
PME	0.4	2 *cis Double Bonds*		PStLe	0.3
StME	0.4	MOO	0.6	Transglycerides	1.6
PPE	0.8	POO	12.1	Remaining ones	0.4

[1] E = Elaidic acid.

Source: Boekenoogen, H. A. (editor) (1968). *Oil, Fats and Fat Products*, Vol. 2. John Wiley & Sons, New York.

Tangerine Oil Composition

TABLE 2.T.2
Chemical composition of tangerine oil

TERPENES:	ALCOHOLS:	KETONES:
$\triangle_3$-carene	citronellol	carvone
$\triangle^3$-carene	heptanol	
α,β-phellandrene	octanol	**PHENOLS:**
α-pinene	nonanol	
β-pinene	decanol	1,8-cineol
β-myrcene	dodecanol	thymol
d-limonene	α,β-sabinol	o-phenylphenol
α-terpinene	linalool	
p-cymene	citronellol	**ACIDS:**
α-terpinolene	nerol	
α-thujene	benzyl	heptoic
camphene	trimethyl-benzyl	caprylic
$\triangle$-elemene	geraniol	pelargonic
copaene	terpinen-4-ol	citronellic
pentadecane	α-terpineol	capric
?	cis, trans-carveol	undecanoic
β-elemene	cis, trans-2,8-p-mentha-	lauric
caryophllene	diene-1-ol	
α-elemene	1,8-p-menthadiene-9-ol	**FLAVONE:**
α,β-humulene	elemol	
$C_{15}H_{24}$	thymol	tangeretin
$C_{15}H_{24}$	8-p-menthene-1,2-diol	
$\triangle$-cadinene	1-p-menthene-9-ol	
sabinene		
β-ocimene	**ESTERS:**	
	decyl acetate	
ALDEHYDES:	geranyl acetate	
	linalyl acetate	
octanal	terpinyl acetate	
decanal	methyl N-methylanthranilate	
undecanal		
dodecanal		
perilla		
citral { neral / geranial		

Source: Kesterson, J. W., Hendrickson, R., and Braddock, R. J. (1971). Florida citrus oils. Florida Agric. Exp. Sta. Tech. Bull. *749*.

Tangerine Oil Properties

TABLE 2.T.3
Maximum and minimum values for the physicochemical properties of tangerine oils

Type oil	Coldpressed						De-oiler
	Screw Press		FMC rotary		FMC in-line		
	Max.	Min.	Max.	Min.	Max.	Min.	
Number samples	4		3		20		1
Sp. grav. 25°C/25°C	0.8447	0.8445	0.8474	0.8454	0.8473	0.8449	0.8407
Ref. ind. η_D^{20}	1.4739	1.4738	1.4744	1.4734	1.4752	1.4736	1.4720
Ref. ind. 10% dist. η_D^{20}	1.4721	1.4720	1.4726	1.4711	1.4722	1.4713	—
Difference	0.0018	0.0018	0.0026	0.0018	0.0034	0.0015	—
Opt. rot. α_D^{25}	+93.31	+90.11	+91.18	+90.09	+93.75	+90.64	+93.67
Opt. rot. 10% dist. α_D^{25}	+94.86	+94.42	+94.21	+92.68	+96.26	+92.54	—
Difference	+4.75	+1.11	+4.12	+1.50	+4.00	+1.55	—
Aldehyde, %	1.02	0.96	1.08	0.95	1.23	1.09	1.24
Ester content, %	—	—	1.44	0.34	—	—	0.25
Evap. res., %	2.75	2.46	4.83	4.04	4.75	2.75	0.20
U.V. spectrum mμ log E 0.25 g/100 ml							
CD 1.	0.530	0.425	—	—	1.576	0.410	—
CD 2.	0.350	0.250	—	—	0.450	0.100	—
Peak 1.	1.130	0.920	—	—	3.580	0.810	—
Peak 2.	1.430	1.310	—	—	3.080	1.099	—
mμ 1.	325	324	—	—	328.8	322.0	—
mμ 2.	270	268	—	—	272.8	266.0	—

Source: Kesterson, J. W., Hendrickson, R., and Braddock, R. J. (1971). Florida citrus oils. Florida Agric. Exp. Sta. Tech. Bull. 749.

Taste Panel, Difference Tests

TABLE 2.T.4
Types of difference tests

Name	Method of presentation	Standard	Response	Probability
Single stimulus (A not A)	A │ ? ? ? ? . . .	One present and designated at onset of test and can be reintroduced	"A" or "not A"; "like A" or "not like A"	1/2
Paired comparison	A B or A A or B B or B A ? ? ? ? ? ? ? ?	Subjective	"Different" or "Not different"	1/2
Paired comparison	A B ? ?	Subjective	Which is saltier?, Which is tougher, etc.	1/2
Duo-trio	A │ A B │ ? ?	One present and designated	Which is the different sample? or Which is the same as A?	1/2
Triangle	A A B or A B B ? ? ? ? ? ?	None designated; criterion is within test	Which is the odd sample?	1/3
Triangle	A A B or A B B ? ? ? ? ? ?	None designated; criterion is within test	Which is sweeter? More acid? etc.	1/6
Dual standard	A B │ A B │ ? ?	Two present and designated	Which is A and which is B?	1/2
Multiple standard[a]	B ? A A A ? ? ?	None designated; criterion is within test	Which is *most* different?	1/4 (or less)
Multiple pairs	A B A B ? ? ? ? B A B A ? ? ? ?	None designated; criterion is within test	Which are A and which are B?	1/35[b]

[a] Used where standard is nonhomogeneous; all samples presented simultaneously.
[b] As shown for all correct; various higher probabilities for partially correct responses.
Adapted from Peryam (1958).

Source: Amerine, M. A., Pangborn, R. M., and Roessler, E. B. *Principles of Sensory Evaluation of Food.* Academic Press, New York.

Teeth Eruption

TABLE 2.T.5
Eruption of the teeth of animals

	Horse	Ox	Sheep, Goat	Swine	Dog	Cat
Di 1	Birth to 1 week	Before birth	Birth to 1 week	2-4 weeks	4-5 weeks	2-3 weeks
Di 2	4-6 weeks	Before birth	1-2 weeks	6-12 weeks	4-5 weeks	3-4 weeks
Di 3	6-9 months	Birth to 1 week	2-3 weeks	Before birth	5-6 weeks	3-4 weeks
I 1	$2\frac{1}{2}$ years	$1\frac{1}{2}$-2 years	1-$1\frac{1}{2}$ years	1 year	2-5 months	$3\frac{1}{2}$-4 months
I 2	$3\frac{1}{2}$ years	2-$2\frac{1}{2}$ years	$1\frac{1}{2}$-2 years	16-20 months	2-5 months	$3\frac{1}{2}$-4 months
I 3	$4\frac{1}{2}$ years	3 years	$2\frac{1}{2}$-3 years	8-10 months	4-5 months	4-$4\frac{1}{2}$ months
Dc	Does not erupt	Birth to 2 weeks[1]	3-4 weeks [1]	Before birth	3-4 weeks	3-4 weeks
C	$4\frac{1}{2}$-5 years	$3\frac{1}{2}$-4 years[1]	3-4 years [1]	6-10 months	5-6 months	5 months
Dp 2	Birth to 2 weeks	Birth to 3 weeks	Birth to 4 weeks	5-7 weeks	4-6 weeks	Upper: 2 months
						Lower: none
Dp 3	Birth to 2 weeks	Birth to 3 weeks	Birth to 4 weeks	1-4 weeks	4-6 weeks	4-5 weeks
Dp 4	Birth to 2 weeks	Birth to 3 weeks	Birth to 4 weeks	1-4 weeks	6-8 weeks	4-6 weeks
P 1	5-6 months					
	(wolf tooth)	None	None	5 months	4-5 months	None
P 2	$2\frac{1}{2}$ years	2-$2\frac{1}{2}$ years	$1\frac{1}{2}$-2 years	12-15 months	5-6 months	Upper: $4\frac{1}{2}$-5 mo.
						Lower: none
P 3	3 years	$1\frac{1}{2}$-$2\frac{1}{2}$ years	$1\frac{1}{2}$-2 years	12-15 months	5-6 months	5-6 months
P 4	4 years	$2\frac{1}{2}$-3 years	$1\frac{1}{2}$-2 years	12-15 months	4-5 months	5-6 months
M 1	9-12 months	5-6 months	3-5 months	4-6 months	5-6 months	4-5 months
M 2	2 years	1-$1\frac{1}{2}$ years	9-12 months	8-12 months	6-7 months	None
M 3	$3\frac{1}{2}$-4 years	2-$2\frac{1}{2}$ years	$1\frac{1}{2}$-2 years	18-20 months	6-7 months	None

[1] The canine tooth of domestic ruminants has commonly been accounted a fourth incisor.

Source: The Merck Veterinary Manual, 4th Edition. (1973). Merck & Co., Rahway, New Jersey.

Temperature

TABLE 2.T.6
Centigrade and fahrenheit conversion table

INTERPOLATION FACTORS

$$C = \frac{5}{9}(F - 32)$$

$$F = \frac{9}{5}C + 32$$

Kelvin (Absolute)
$$^{\circ}K = {}^{\circ}C + 273.15$$

C°		F°	C°		F°	C°		F°
0.56	1	1.8	2.22	4	7.2	3.89	7	12.6
1.11	2	3.6	2.78	5	9.0	4.44	8	14.4
1.67	3	5.4	3.33	6	10.8	5.00	9	16.2

Enter table at arrow with the temperature you have; Equivalent Fahrenheit is found 1 column to right and equivalent Centigrade temperature 1 column to the left.

C°		F°	C°		F°	C°		F°
-156.7	-250	-418.0	-112.2	-170	-274.0	-72.8	-99	-146.2
-151.1	-240	-400.0	-106.7	-160	-256.0	-72.2	-98	-144.4
-145.6	-230	-382.0	-101.1	-150	-238.0	-71.7	-97	-142.6
-140.0	-220	-364.0	-95.6	-140	-220.0	-71.1	-96	-140.8
-134.4	-210	-346.0	-90.0	-130	-202.0	-70.6	-95	-139.0
-128.9	-200	-328.0	-84.4	-120	-184.0	-70.0	-94	-137.2
-123.3	-190	-310.0	-78.9	-110	-166.0	-69.4	-93	-135.4
-117.8	-180	-292.0	-73.3	-100	-148.0	-68.9	-92	-133.6

(Continued)

Temperature (Continued)

TABLE 2.T.6 (Continued)

C°	↓	F°	C°	↓	F°	C°	↓	F°
-68.3	-91	-131.8	-34.4	-30	-22.0	-0.56	31	87.8
-67.8	-90	-130.0	-33.9	-29	-20.2	0.00	32	89.6
-67.2	-89	-128.2	-33.3	-28	-18.4	0.56	33	91.4
-66.7	-88	-126.4	-32.8	-27	-16.6	1.11	34	93.2
-66.1	-87	-124.6	-32.2	-26	-14.8	1.67	35	95.0
-65.6	-86	-122.8	-31.7	-25	-13.0	2.22	36	96.8
-65.0	-85	-121.0	-31.1	-24	-11.2	2.78	37	98.6
-64.4	-84	-119.2	-30.6	-23	-9.4	3.33	38	100.4
-63.9	-83	-117.4	-30.0	-22	-7.6	3.89	39	102.2
-63.3	-82	-115.6	-29.4	-21	-5.8	4.44	40	104.0
-62.8	-81	-113.8	-28.9	-20	-4.0	5.00	41	105.8
-62.2	-80	-112.0	-28.3	-19	-2.2	5.56	42	107.6
-61.7	-79	-110.2	-27.8	-18	-0.4	6.11	43	109.4
-61.1	-78	-108.4	-27.2	-17	1.4	6.67	44	111.2
-60.6	-77	-106.6	-26.7	-16	3.2	7.22	45	113.0
-60.0	-76	-104.8	-26.1	-15	5.0	7.78	46	114.8
-59.4	-75	-103.0	-25.6	-14	6.8	8.33	47	116.6
-58.9	-74	-101.2	-25.0	-13	8.6	8.89	48	118.4
-58.3	-73	-99.4	-24.4	-12	10.4	9.44	49	120.2
-57.8	-72	-97.6	-23.9	-11	12.2	10.00	50	122.0
-57.2	-71	-95.8	-23.3	-10	14.0	10.56	51	123.8
-56.7	-70	-94.0	-22.8	-9	15.8	11.11	52	125.6
-56.1	-69	-92.2	-22.2	-8	17.6	11.67	53	127.4
-55.6	-68	-90.4	-21.7	-7	19.4	12.22	54	129.2
-55.0	-67	-88.6	-21.1	-6	21.2	12.78	55	131.0
-54.4	-66	-86.8	-20.6	-5	23.0	13.33	56	132.8
-53.9	-65	-85.0	-20.0	-4	24.8	13.89	57	134.6
-53.3	-64	-83.2	-19.4	-3	26.6	14.44	58	136.4
-52.8	-63	-81.4	-18.9	-2	28.4	15.00	59	138.2
-52.2	-62	-79.6	-18.3	-1	30.2	15.56	60	140.0
-51.7	-61	-77.8	-17.78	0	32.0	16.11	61	141.8
-51.1	-60	-76.0	-17.22	1	33.8	16.67	62	143.6
-50.6	-59	-74.2	-16.67	2	35.6	17.22	63	145.4
-50.0	-58	-72.4	-16.11	3	37.4	17.78	64	147.2
-49.4	-57	-70.6	-15.56	4	39.2	18.33	65	149.0
-48.9	-56	-68.8	-15.00	5	41.0	18.89	66	150.8
-48.3	-55	-67.0	-14.44	6	42.8	19.44	67	152.6
-47.8	-54	-65.2	-13.89	7	44.6	20.00	68	154.4
-47.2	-53	-63.4	-13.33	8	46.4	20.56	69	156.2
-46.7	-52	-61.6	-12.78	9	48.2	21.11	70	158.0
-46.1	-51	-59.8	-12.22	10	50.0	21.67	71	159.8
-45.6	-50	-58.0	-11.67	11	51.8	22.22	72	161.6
-45.0	-49	-56.2	-11.11	12	53.6	22.78	73	163.4
-44.4	-48	-54.4	-10.56	13	55.4	23.33	74	165.2
-43.9	-47	-52.6	-10.00	14	57.2	23.89	75	167.0
-43.3	-46	-50.8	-9.44	15	59.0	24.44	76	168.8
-42.8	-45	-49.0	-8.89	16	60.8	25.00	77	170.6
-42.2	-44	-47.2	-8.33	17	62.6	25.56	78	172.4
-41.7	-43	-45.4	-7.78	18	64.4	26.11	79	174.2
-41.1	-42	-43.6	-7.22	19	66.2	26.67	80	176.0
-40.6	-41	-41.8	-6.67	20	68.0	27.22	81	177.8
-40.0	-40	-40.0	-6.11	21	69.8	27.78	82	179.6
-39.4	-39	-38.2	-5.56	22	71.6	28.33	83	181.4
-38.9	-38	-36.4	-5.00	23	73.4	28.89	84	183.2
-38.3	-37	-34.6	-4.44	24	75.2	29.44	85	185.0
-37.8	-36	-32.8	-3.89	25	77.0	30.00	86	186.8
-37.2	-35	-31.0	-3.33	26	78.8	30.56	87	188.6
-36.7	-34	-29.2	-2.78	27	80.6	31.11	88	190.4
-36.1	-33	-27.4	-2.22	28	82.4	31.67	89	192.2
-35.6	-32	-25.6	-1.67	29	84.2	32.22	90	194.0
-35.0	-31	-23.8	-1.11	30	86.0	32.78	91	195.8

(Continued)

Temperature (Continued)

TABLE 2.T.6 (Continued)

C°	↓	F°	C°	↓	F°	C°	↓	F°
33.33	92	197.6	67.22	153	307.4	101.11	214	417.2
33.89	93	199.4	67.78	154	309.2	101.67	215	419.0
34.44	94	201.2	68.33	155	311.0	102.22	216	420.8
35.00	95	203.0	68.89	156	312.8	102.78	217	422.6
35.56	96	204.8	69.44	157	314.6	103.33	218	424.4
36.11	97	206.6	70.00	158	316.4	103.89	219	426.2
36.67	98	208.4	70.56	159	318.2	104.44	220	428.0
37.22	99	210.2	71.11	160	320.0	105.00	221	429.8
37.78	100	212.0	71.67	161	321.8	105.56	222	431.6
38.33	101	213.8	72.22	162	323.6	106.11	223	433.4
38.89	102	215.6	72.78	163	325.4	106.67	224	435.2
39.44	103	217.4	73.33	164	327.2	107.22	225	437.0
40.00	104	219.2	73.89	165	329.0	107.78	226	438.8
40.56	105	221.0	74.44	166	330.8	108.33	227	440.6
41.11	106	222.8	75.00	167	332.6	108.89	228	442.4
41.67	107	224.6	75.56	168	334.4	109.44	229	444.2
42.22	108	226.4	76.11	169	336.2	110.00	230	446.0
42.78	109	228.2	76.67	170	338.0	110.56	231	447.8
43.33	110	230.0	77.22	171	339.8	111.11	232	449.6
43.89	111	231.8	77.78	172	341.6	111.67	233	451.4
44.44	112	233.6	78.33	173	343.4	112.22	234	453.2
45.00	113	235.4	78.89	174	345.2	112.78	235	455.0
45.56	114	237.2	79.44	175	347.0	113.33	236	456.8
46.11	115	239.0	80.00	176	348.8	113.89	237	458.6
46.67	116	240.8	80.56	177	350.6	114.44	238	460.4
47.22	117	242.6	81.11	178	352.4	115.00	239	462.2
47.78	118	244.4	81.67	179	354.2	115.56	240	464.0
48.33	119	246.2	82.22	180	356.0	116.11	241	465.8
48.89	120	248.0	82.78	181	357.8	116.67	242	467.6
49.44	121	249.8	83.33	182	359.6	117.22	243	469.4
50.00	122	251.6	83.89	183	361.4	117.78	244	471.2
50.56	123	253.4	84.44	184	363.2	118.33	245	473.0
51.11	124	255.2	85.00	185	365.0	118.89	246	474.8
51.67	125	257.0	85.56	186	366.8	119.44	247	476.6
52.22	126	258.8	86.11	187	368.6	120.00	248	478.4
52.78	127	260.6	86.67	188	370.4	120.56	249	480.2
53.33	128	262.4	87.22	189	372.2	121.11	250	482.0
53.89	129	264.2	87.78	190	374.0	121.67	251	483.8
54.44	130	266.0	88.33	191	375.8	122.22	252	485.6
55.00	131	267.8	88.89	192	377.6	122.78	253	487.4
55.56	132	269.6	89.44	193	379.4	123.33	254	489.2
56.11	133	271.4	90.00	194	381.2	123.89	255	491.0
56.67	134	273.2	90.56	195	383.0	124.44	256	492.8
57.22	135	275.0	91.11	196	384.8	125.00	257	494.6
57.78	136	276.8	91.67	197	386.6	125.56	258	496.4
58.33	137	278.6	92.22	198	388.4	126.11	259	498.2
58.89	138	280.4	92.78	199	390.2	126.67	260	500.0
59.44	139	282.2	93.33	200	392.0	127.22	261	501.8
60.00	140	284.0	93.89	201	393.8	127.78	262	503.6
60.56	141	285.8	94.44	202	395.6	128.33	263	505.4
61.11	142	287.6	95.00	203	397.4	128.89	264	507.2
61.67	143	289.4	95.56	204	399.2	129.44	265	509.0
62.22	144	291.2	96.11	205	401.0	130.00	266	510.8
62.78	145	293.0	96.67	206	402.8	130.56	267	512.6
63.33	146	294.8	97.22	207	404.6	131.11	268	514.4
63.89	147	296.6	97.78	208	406.4	131.67	269	516.2
64.44	148	298.4	98.33	209	408.2	132.22	270	518.0
65.00	149	300.2	98.89	210	410.0	132.78	271	519.8
65.56	150	302.0	99.44	211	411.8	133.33	272	521.6
66.11	151	303.8	100.00	212	413.6	133.89	273	523.4
66.67	152	305.6	100.56	213	415.4	134.44	274	525.2

(Continued)

Temperature   (Continued)

TABLE 2.T.6   (Continued)

C°	↓	F°	C°	↓	F°	C°	↓	F°
135.00	275	527.0	170.56	339	642.2	206.11	403	757.4
135.56	276	528.8	171.11	340	644.0	206.67	404	759.2
136.11	277	530.6	171.67	341	645.8	207.22	405	761.0
136.67	278	532.4	172.22	342	647.6	207.78	406	762.8
137.22	279	534.2	172.78	343	649.4	208.33	407	764.6
137.78	280	536.0	173.33	344	651.2	208.89	408	766.4
138.33	281	537.8	173.89	345	653.0	209.44	409	768.2
138.89	282	539.6	174.44	346	654.8	210.00	410	770.0
139.44	283	541.4	175.00	347	656.6	210.56	411	771.8
140.00	284	543.2	175.56	348	658.4	211.11	412	773.6
140.56	285	545.0	176.11	349	660.2	211.67	413	775.4
141.11	286	546.8	176.67	350	662.0	212.22	414	777.2
141.67	287	548.6	177.22	351	663.8	212.78	415	779.0
142.22	288	550.4	177.78	352	665.6	213.33	416	780.8
142.78	289	552.2	178.33	353	667.4	213.89	417	782.6
143.33	290	554.0	178.89	354	669.2	214.44	418	784.4
143.89	291	555.8	179.44	355	671.0	215.00	419	786.2
144.44	292	557.6	180.00	356	672.8	215.56	420	788.0
145.00	293	559.4	180.56	357	674.6	216.11	421	789.8
145.56	294	561.2	181.11	358	676.4	216.67	422	791.6
146.11	295	563.0	181.67	359	678.2	217.22	423	793.4
146.67	296	564.8	182.22	360	680.0	217.78	424	795.2
147.22	297	566.6	182.78	361	681.8	218.33	425	797.0
147.78	298	568.4	183.33	362	683.6	218.89	426	798.8
148.33	299	570.2	183.89	363	685.4	219.44	427	800.6
148.89	300	572.0	184.44	364	687.2	220.00	428	802.4
149.44	301	573.8	185.00	365	689.0	220.56	429	804.2
150.00	302	575.6	185.56	366	690.8	221.11	430	806.0
150.56	303	577.4	186.11	367	692.6	221.67	431	807.8
151.11	304	579.2	186.67	368	694.4	222.22	432	809.6
151.67	305	581.0	187.22	369	696.2	222.78	433	811.4
152.22	306	582.8	187.78	370	698.0	223.33	434	813.2
152.78	307	584.6	188.33	371	699.8	223.89	435	815.0
153.33	308	586.4	188.89	372	701.6	224.44	436	816.8
153.89	309	588.2	189.44	373	703.4	225.00	437	818.6
154.44	310	590.0	190.00	374	705.2	225.56	438	820.4
155.00	311	591.8	190.56	375	707.0	226.11	439	822.2
155.56	312	593.6	191.11	376	708.8	226.67	440	824.0
156.11	313	595.4	191.67	377	710.6	227.22	441	825.8
156.67	314	597.2	192.22	378	712.4	227.78	442	827.6
157.22	315	599.0	192.78	379	714.2	228.33	443	829.4
157.78	316	600.8	193.33	380	716.0	228.89	444	831.2
158.33	317	602.6	193.89	381	717.8	229.44	445	833.0
158.89	318	604.4	194.44	382	719.6	230.00	446	834.8
159.44	319	606.2	195.00	383	721.4	230.56	447	836.6
160.00	320	608.0	195.56	384	723.2	231.11	448	838.4
160.56	321	609.8	196.11	385	725.0	231.67	449	840.2
161.11	322	611.6	196.67	386	726.8	232.22	450	842.0
161.67	323	613.4	197.22	387	728.6	232.78	451	843.8
162.22	324	615.2	197.78	388	730.4	233.33	452	845.6
162.78	325	617.0	198.33	389	732.2	233.89	453	847.4
163.33	326	618.8	198.89	390	734.0	234.44	454	849.2
163.89	327	620.6	199.44	391	735.8	235.00	455	851.0
164.44	328	622.4	200.00	392	737.6	235.56	456	852.8
165.00	329	624.2	200.56	393	739.4	236.11	457	854.6
165.56	330	626.0	201.11	394	741.2	236.67	458	856.4
166.11	331	627.8	201.67	395	743.0	237.22	459	858.2
166.67	332	629.6	202.22	396	744.8	237.78	460	860.0
167.22	333	631.4	202.78	397	746.6	238.33	461	861.8
167.78	334	633.2	203.33	398	748.4	238.89	462	863.6
168.33	335	635.0	203.89	399	750.2	239.44	463	865.4
168.89	336	636.8	204.44	400	752.0	240.00	464	867.2
169.44	337	638.6	205.00	401	753.8	240.56	465	869.0
170.00	338	640.4	205.56	402	755.6	241.11	466	870.8

(Continued)

Temperature (Continued)

TABLE 2.T.6 (Continued)

C°	↓	F°	C°	↓	F°	C°	↓	F°
241.67	467	872.6	421.11	790	1454	765.56	1410	2570
242.22	468	874.4	426.67	800	1472	771.11	1420	2588
242.78	469	876.2	432.22	810	1490	776.67	1430	2606
243.33	470	878.0	437.78	820	1508	782.22	1440	2624
243.89	471	879.8	443.33	830	1526	787.78	1450	2642
244.44	472	881.6	448.89	840	1544	793.33	1460	2660
245.00	473	883.4	454.44	850	1562	798.89	1470	2678
245.56	474	885.2	460.00	860	1580	804.44	1480	2696
246.11	475	887.0	465.56	870	1598	810.00	1490	2714
246.67	476	888.8	471.11	880	1616	815.56	1500	2732
247.22	477	890.6	476.67	890	1634	821.11	1510	2750
247.78	478	892.4	482.22	900	1652	826.67	1520	2768
248.33	479	894.2	487.78	910	1670	832.22	1530	2786
248.89	480	896.0	493.33	920	1688	837.78	1540	2804
249.44	481	897.8	498.89	930	1706	843.33	1550	2822
250.00	482	899.6	504.44	940	1724	848.89	1560	2840
250.56	483	901.4	510.00	950	1742	854.44	1570	2858
251.11	484	903.2	515.56	960	1760	860.00	1580	2876
251.67	485	905.0	521.11	970	1778	865.55	1590	2894
252.22	486	906.8	526.67	980	1796	871.11	1600	2912
252.78	487	908.6	532.22	990	1814	876.67	1610	2930
253.33	488	910.4	537.78	1000	1832	882.22	1620	2948
253.89	489	912.2	543.33	1010	1850	887.78	1630	2966
254.44	490	914.0	548.89	1020	1868	893.33	1640	2984
255.00	491	915.8	554.44	1030	1886	898.89	1650	3002
255.56	492	917.6	560.00	1040	1904	904.44	1660	3020
256.11	493	919.4	565.56	1050	1922	910.00	1670	3038
256.67	494	921.2	571.11	1060	1940	915.56	1680	3056
257.22	495	923.0	576.67	1070	1958	921.11	1690	3074
257.78	496	924.8	582.22	1080	1976	926.67	1700	3092
258.33	497	926.6	587.78	1090	1994	932.22	1710	3110
258.89	498	928.4	593.33	1100	2012	937.78	1720	3128
259.44	499	930.2	598.89	1110	2030	943.33	1730	3146
260.00	500	932	604.44	1120	2048	948.89	1740	3164
265.56	510	950	610.00	1130	2066	954.44	1750	3182
271.11	520	968	615.56	1140	2084	960.00	1760	3200
276.67	530	986	621.11	1150	2102	965.56	1770	3218
282.22	540	1004	626.67	1160	2120	971.11	1780	3236
287.78	550	1022	632.22	1170	2138	976.67	1790	3254
293.33	560	1040	637.78	1180	2156	982.22	1800	3272
298.89	570	1058	643.33	1190	2174	987.78	1810	3290
304.44	580	1076	648.89	1200	2192	993.33	1820	3308
310.00	590	1094	654.44	1210	2210	998.89	1830	3326
315.56	600	1112	660.00	1220	2228	1004.44	1840	3344
321.11	610	1130	665.56	1230	2246	1010.00	1850	3362
326.67	620	1148	671.11	1240	2264	1015.56	1860	3380
332.22	630	1166	676.67	1250	2282	1021.11	1870	3398
337.78	640	1184	682.22	1260	2300	1026.67	1880	3416
343.33	650	1202	687.78	1270	2318	1032.22	1890	3434
348.89	660	1220	693.33	1280	2336	1037.78	1900	3452
354.44	670	1238	698.89	1290	2354	1043.33	1910	3470
360.00	680	1256	704.44	1300	2372	1048.89	1920	3488
365.56	690	1274	710.00	1310	2390	1054.44	1930	3506
371.11	700	1292	715.56	1320	2408	1060.00	1940	3524
376.67	710	1310	721.11	1330	2426	1065.56	1950	3542
382.22	720	1328	726.67	1340	2444	1071.11	1960	3560
387.78	730	1346	732.22	1350	2462	1076.67	1970	3578
393.33	740	1364	737.78	1360	2480	1082.22	1980	3596
398.89	750	1382	743.33	1370	2498	1087.78	1990	3614
404.44	760	1400	748.89	1380	2516	1093.33	2000	3632
410.00	770	1418	754.44	1390	2534	1648.89	3000	5432
415.56	780	1436	760.00	1400	2552	2760.00	5000	9632

Source: Ockerman, H. W. (1974). *Quality Control of Post-Mortem Muscle Tissue*, 9th Edition. Ohio State University, Columbus.

Temperature of Vaporization, Latent Heat of Vaporization, Boiling Point

TABLE 2.T.7
Relation between temperature of vaporization, latent heat of vaporization, and the boiling point of water

Temperature °F.	Inches of Vacuum (Hg)	Latent Heat B.t.u.
32	29.82	1073.4
50	29.64	1063.3
75	29.13	1049.4
100	28.07	1035.6
125	26.04	1021.6
150	22.42	1007.4
175	16.22	992.8
200	6.47	977.9
212	0.00	970.4

Source: Desrosier, N. W. (editor) (1970). In *The Technology of Food Preservation*, 3rd Edition. AVI Publishing Co., Westport, Connecticut.

Temperatures Corresponding to Gauge Pressure at Various Altitudes

TABLE 2.T.8
Guide to pressures above sea level

Temp. Deg. F.	Sea Level	500	1000	2000	3000	4000	5000	6000	Temp. Deg. C.
200	....	....	....	....	....	....	....	....	93.3
205	....	....	....	....	....	....	0.5	0.9	96.1
210	....	....	....	0.4	0.9	1.4	1.8	2.3	98.9
212	0.0	0.2	0.5	1.0	1.5	2.0	2.4	2.9	100.0
215	0.9	1.1	1.4	1.9	2.4	2.9	3.3	3.8	101.7
220	2.5	2.7	3.0	3.4	3.9	4.4	4.9	5.3	104.4
225	4.2	4.5	4.7	5.2	5.7	6.2	6.6	7.1	107.2
230	6.1	6.3	6.6	7.1	7.6	8.0	8.5	9.0	110.0
235	8.1	8.3	8.6	9.1	9.6	10.0	10.5	11.0	112.8
240	10.3	10.5	10.8	11.3	11.7	12.2	12.7	13.1	115.6
242	11.2	11.4	11.7	12.2	12.7	13.1	13.6	14.1	116.7
245	12.6	12.9	13.1	13.6	14.1	14.6	15.0	15.5	118.3
248	14.1	14.3	14.6	15.1	15.6	16.0	16.5	17.0	120.0
250	15.1	15.4	15.6	16.1	16.6	17.1	17.5	18.0	121.1
252	16.2	16.4	16.7	17.2	17.7	18.1	18.6	19.1	122.2
255	17.8	18.1	18.3	18.8	19.3	19.8	20.2	20.7	123.9
260	20.7	21.0	21.2	21.7	22.2	22.7	23.1	23.6	126.7

Source: Processes for Low-Acid Canned Foods in Metal Containers, 10th Edition. National Canners Association Research Laboratory Bull. *26L*.

Tenderness of Poultry

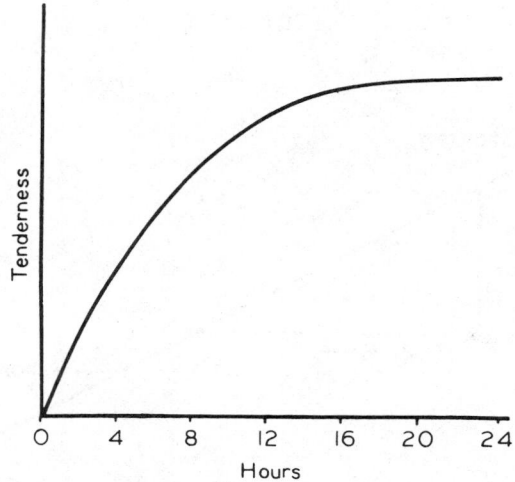

FIGURE 2.T.1

Effect of holding time on tenderness of poultry (the curve varies somewhat with size and kind of fowl and may vary with birds of the same lot and treatment. Maximum tenderness is reached usually at from 12 to 24 hr)

Source: Snyder, E. S., and Orr, H. L. (1964). Poultry meat. Dep. Agric. Publ. *9*, Can. Dep. Agric., Ottawa.

Thermal-Arrest Time

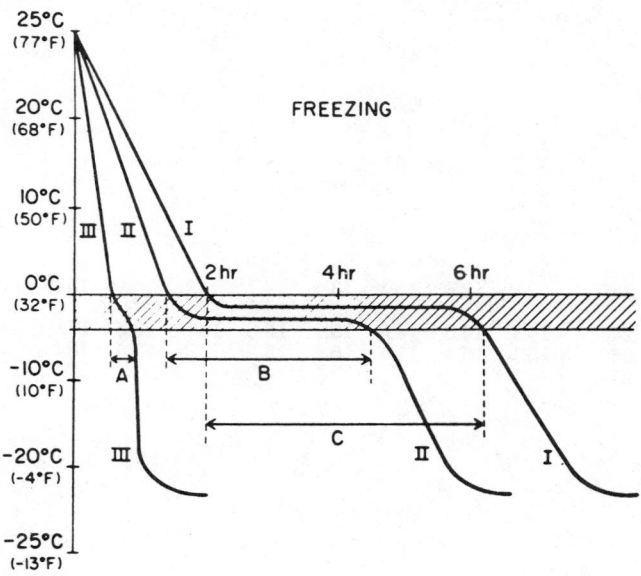

FIGURE 2.T.2

Thermal-arrest time indicated by A (15 min), B (155 min), and C (250 min) in the diagram

Source: Borgstrom, G. (1968). *Principles of Food Science*, Vol. 1. Macmillan Publishing Co., New York.

Thermal-Death-Time Curve

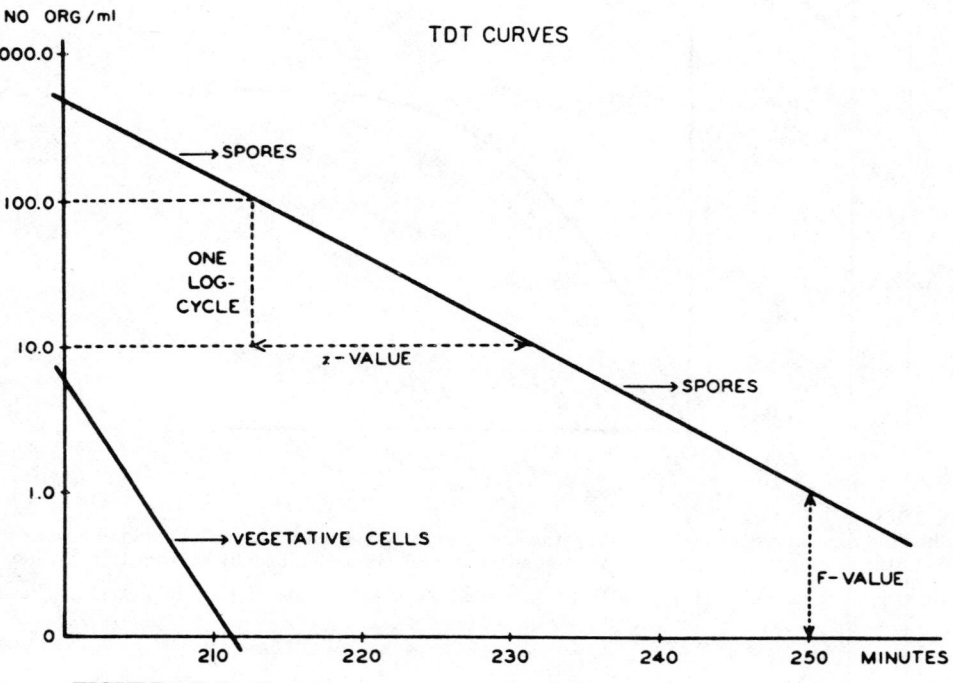

FIGURE 2.T.3
Thermal-death-time curves for spores and vegetative cells showing z and F values

Source: Borgstrom, G. (1968). *Principles of Food Science*, Vol. 1. Macmillan Publishing Co., New York.

Thermophiles

TABLE 2.T.9
Thermophiles of importance to the food industries

Name	Economic Importance	Heat-Resistant Spores	Growth Temperatures Optimum Degrees F.	Range Degrees F.	Oxygen Requirements
Streptococcus thermophilus	Grow during pasteurization of milk. Ripening agent in Swiss cheese.	None	120	77 –140	Facultative
Lactobacillus bulgaricus	Bulgaricus milk. Lactic acid manufacture.	None	120	77 –140	Facultative
Lactobacillus thermophilus	Grow during pasteurization of milk.	None	131	86 –150	Facultative
Lactobacillus delbruckii	Acidification of brewery mash. Lactic acid manufacture.	None	113	70 –140	Facultative
Bacillus calidolactis	Coagulates milk held at high temperatures.	Yes	131–149	113–167	Facultative
Bacillus thermoacidurans	Flat sour spoilage of tomato juice.	Yes	113	80 –140	Facultative
Bacillus stearothermophilus	Flat sour spoilage of canned foods.	Yes	122	113–169	Facultative
Clostridium thermosaccharolyticum	Hard swells of canned foods.	Yes	131–143	110–160	Anaerobic
Clostridium nigrificans	Sulfide-stinkers of canned foods	Yes	131	80 –158	Anaerobic

Source: Desrosier, N. W. (editor) (1970). Principles of food preservation by canning. In *The Technology of Food Preservation*, 3rd Edition. AVI Publishing Co., Westport, Connecticut.

Thiamin

TABLE 2.T.10
Thiamin content of foods

	Mg/100 g		Mg/100 g
Peas	0.35	Broccoli	0.10
Lima beans	0.24	Brussels sprouts	0.10
Asparagus	0.18	Oranges	0.09
Corn	0.15	Tomatoes	0.06
Cauliflower	0.11	Lettuce	0.06
Potatoes	0.10	Bananas	0.05
Watermelon	0.10	Grapefruit	0.04
Sweet potatoes	0.10	Apples	0.03
Spinach	0.10		

Source: White, P. L., and Selvey, N. (editors) (1974). *Nutritional Qualities of Fresh Fruits and Vegetables.* Futura Publishing Co., Mt. Kisco, New York.

Thiamin, Daily Recommendations

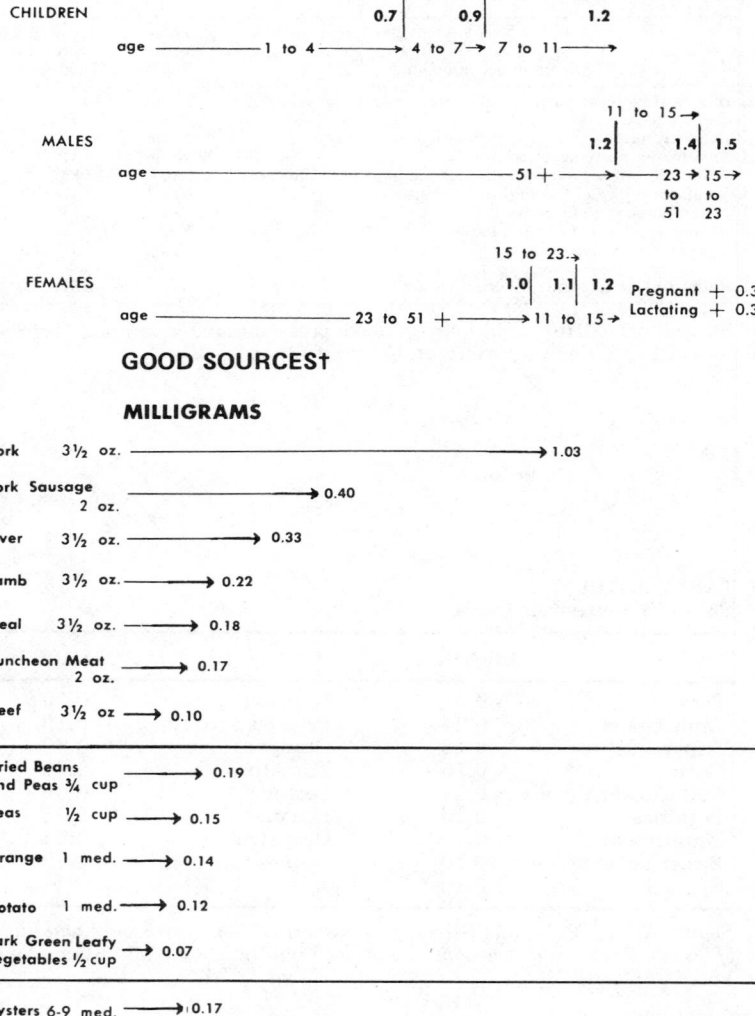

MILLIGRAMS

CHILDREN   0.7   0.9   1.2

age   1 to 4   4 to 7 → 7 to 11 →

                                                          11 to 15 →

MALES   1.2   1.4   1.5

age   51+   →   23 → 15 →
                                                to   to
                                                51   23

                                15 to 23 →

FEMALES   1.0   1.1   1.2   Pregnant + 0.3

age   23 to 51 +   → 11 to 15 →   Lactating + 0.3

GOOD SOURCES†

MILLIGRAMS

Pork	3½ oz.	→ 1.03
Pork Sausage 2 oz.		→ 0.40
Liver	3½ oz.	→ 0.33
Lamb	3½ oz.	→ 0.22
Veal	3½ oz.	→ 0.18
Luncheon Meat 2 oz.		→ 0.17
Beef	3½ oz	→ 0.10
Dried Beans and Peas ¾ cup		→ 0.19
Peas	½ cup	→ 0.15
Orange	1 med.	→ 0.14
Potato	1 med.	→ 0.12
Dark Green Leafy Vegetables ½ cup		→ 0.07
Oysters 6-9 med.		→ 0.17
Nuts	¼ cup	→ 0.17
Fish	3½ oz.	→ 0.09
Poultry	3½ oz.	→ 0.08
Egg	1 med.	→ 0.05
Cereal	½ cup	→ 0.09
Bread	1 slice	→ 0.06
Milk	1 cup	→ 0.08

†Average nutrient content as food is served. (*Note: 3½ oz equals approximately 100 g.*)

FIGURE 2.T.4

Source: Lessons on Meat. (1974). National Live Stock and Meat Board, Chicago.

Thiamin, Food

TABLE 2.T.11
Thiamin content of foods, as purchased (mg/100 g)

Cereal Products		Fruits	0.01–0.05
Biscuits	0.035–0.060	Meat	
Bread, white	0.18	Bacon	0.40
Bread, wholemeal	0.20	Beef	0.08
Cakes	0.085–0.160	Heart	0.60
Flour, white	0.40	Kidney	0.30
Flour, wholemeal	0.28	Liver	0.30
Macaroni	0.14	Mutton	0.15
Oatmeal	0.50	Pork	1.0
Rice (highly milled)	0.08	Sausages (pork)	0.17
Semolina	0.12	Veal	0.10
Dairy Products		Nuts	0.1–1.0
Cheese	0.03	Vegetables	
Milk	0.04	Peas (green)	0.32
Eggs	0.10	Potatoes	0.10
Fish, white	0.02–0.08	Vegetables (other)	0.02–0.10
Herring	0.03	Yeast Extracts	2.4–3.0
Cod roe	1.5		

Source: Sinclair, H. M., and Hollingsworth, D. F. (1969). *Hutchison's Food and the Principles of Nutrition.* Edward Arnold (Publishers), London, England.

Titer, Fats and Oils

TABLE 2.T.12
Titer points of some common fats and oils

Fat or Oil	Titer Point °C	Fat or Oil	Titer Point °C
Babassu	22–23	Safflower	15–18
Borneo tallow	51–53	Sesame	20–25
Cacao butter	45–50	Soybean	21–23
Coconut	20–24	Sunflower	16–20
Corn	14–20	Teaseed	13–18
Cottonseed	30–37	Tung	36–37
Hempseed	14–17	Walnut	14–16
Kapok	27–32	Butterfat	33–38
Linseed	19–21	Lard	32–43
Mustard (white)	8–10	Tallow-beef	40–47
Mustard (black)	6–8	Tallow mutton	43–48
Olive	17–26	Horse fat	34–38
Palm kernel	20–28	Cod liver	18–24
Palm	40–47	Sardine	27–28
Peanut	26–32	Whale	22–24
Rape	11–15	Sperm	8–14
Rice bran	26–28	Wool fat	38–40

Source: Mahlenbacher, C. V. *The Analysis of Fats and Oils.* Garrard Press, Champaign, Illinois.

Tocopherols

TABLE 2.T.13
Tocopherols in food (mg/100 gm)

Food	No. of Values Averaged	α-T	α-T-3	β-T	β-T-3	γ-T	γ-T-3	δ-T	δ-T-3
Nuts and grains									
Almond	2	27.4	0.5[1]	0.3[1]	—	0.9[1]	—	—	—
Barley	5	0.4	1.3	0.3	0.7[5]	0.05[4]	0.2[3]	0.01[1]	—
Corn	11	0.6	0.2[6]	—	0.4[1]	3.8	0.5[6]	tr	—
Millet	1	0.05	—	tr	—	1.3	—	0.4	—
Oats	6	0.7	0.7	0.2[4]	0.1[4]	0.3[4]	—	—	—
Peanuts	1	9.7	—	—	—	6.6	—	—	—
Peas	3	0.5	—	—	—	6.4[3]	—	0.6[1]	—
Pecans	1	1.2	—	—	—	19.1	—	—	—
Poppy seed	1	1.8	—	—	—	9.2	—	—	—
Rice	5	0.3	tr	—	—	0.3[4]	0.5[3]	0.04[5]	—
Rye	4	0.8	1.3[4]	0.4[4]	0.9	0.6[1]	—	—	—
Walnut, English	1	0.4	—	—	—	15.8	—	1.3	—
Wheat	9	1.0	0.4[8]	0.9	2.5[7]	—	—	0.08[1]	—
Vegetable oils									
Coconut	1	0.5	0.5	—	0.1	—	1.9	0.6	—
Corn	8	11.2	—	5.0[1]	—	60.2	—	1.8[3]	—
Cottonseed	9	38.9	—	—	—	38.7	—	—	—
Neem	1	—	—	—	—	58.0	—	59.0	—
Olive	4	5.1	—	—	—	—	—	—	—
Palm	4	25.6	14.3[1]	—	3.2[1]	31.6[2]	28.6[1]	7.0[1]	6.9[1]
Peanut	11	13.0	—	—	—	21.4	—	2.1[3]	—
Rapeseed	5	18.4	—	—	—	38.0	—	1.2[1]	—
Safflower	3	38.7	—	—	—	17.4	—	24.0[1]	—
Sesame	2	13.6	—	—	—	29.0	—	—	—
Soybean	14	10.1	—	—	—	59.3	—	26.4[9]	—
Sunflower	10	48.7	—	—	—	5.1	—	0.8[3]	—
Walnut	1	56.3	—	—	—	59.5	—	45.0	—
Wheat germ	3	133.0	2.6[1]	71.0	18.1[3]	26.0[1]	—	27.1[1]	—
Mustard seed	1	8.6	—	—	—	17.6	—	5.8	—
Asparagus (fresh weight)	—	1.8	—	0.05	—	0.07	—	—	—
Carrots (fresh weight)	—	0.51	0.04	0.01	0.08	—	—	—	—
Cucumber	—	8.4	—	—	—	—	—	—	—
Mango, flesh, green	—	0.26	—	—	—	—	—	0.27	—
Mango, flesh, ripe	—	0.98	—	—	—	—	—	—	—
Muskmelon	—	10.1	—	—	—	—	—	—	—
Tomato	—	18.2	—	—	—	—	—	—	—

[1] One value reported.
[2] Slover, unpublished data.
[3] Average of two values.
[4] Average of three values.
[5] Average of four values.
[6] Average of six values.
[7] Average of seven values.
[8] Average of eight values.
[9] Average of twelve values.

Source: Bauernfeind, J. C. (1975). Tocopherols. In *Encyclopedia of Food Technology.* A. H. Johnson, and M. S. Peterson (editors). AVI Publishing Co., Westport, Connecticut.

Tomato and Tomato Products, Composition

TABLE 2.T.14
Composition of tomato and tomato products, 100 g

	Tomato		Tomato Juice			Cocktail	Tomato Purée (pulp)	Catsup	Chili Sauce	Tomato Paste
	Fresh	Canned	Regular	Concentrated	Dehydrated					
Water (%)	93.5	93.7	93.6	75.0	1.0	93.0	87.0	68.6	68.0	75.0
Food energy (calories)	22	21	19	76	303	21	39	106	104	82
Protein, gm	1.1	1.0	0.9	3.4	11.6	0.7	1.7	2.0	2.5	3.4
Fat, gm	0.2	0.2	0.1	0.4	2.2	0.1	0.2	0.4	0.3	0.4
Carbohydrate:										
total, gm	4.7	4.3	4.3	17.1	68.2	5.0	8.9	25.4	24.8	18.6
fiber, gm	0.5	0.4	0.2	0.9	3.1	0.2	0.4	0.5	0.7	0.9
Ash, gm	0.5	0.8	1.1	4.1	17.0	1.2	2.2	3.6	4.4	2.6
Calcium, mg	13	6	7	27	85	10	13	22	20	27
Phosphorus, mg	27	19	18	70	279	18	34	50	52	70
Iron, mg	0.5	0.5	0.9	3.5	7.8	0.9	1.7	0.8	0.8	3.5
Sodium, mg	3	130	200	790	3934	200	399	1042	1338	38
Potassium, mg	244	217	227	888	3518	221	426	363	370	888
Vitamin A (I.U.)	900	900	800	3300	13100	800	1600	1400	1400	3300
Thiamine, mg	0.06	0.05	0.05	0.20	0.52	0.05	0.09	0.09	0.09	0.20
Riboflavin, mg	0.04	0.03	0.03	0.12	0.40	0.02	0.05	0.07	0.07	0.12
Niacin, mg	0.7	0.7	0.8	3.1	13.5	0.06	1.4	1.6	1.6	3.1
Ascorbic acid, mg	23	17	16	49	239	16	33	15	16	49

Source: Gould, W. A. (editor) (1974). Composition of tomatoes. In *Tomato Production, Processing and Quality Evaluation.* AVI Publishing Co., Westport, Connecticut.

Tomato Grades

TABLE 2.T.15
U.S. standards for grades of tomatoes for processing (3-1-73)

Factor	Category A	Category B	Category C	Culls
Firmness	Firm	Fairly firm	Fairly firm	Water soaked, soft, shriveled, or puffy over 20% waste
Any worm attached	Free from	Free from	Free from	
Freezing	Free from	Free from	Free from	Affected
Worm injury	Free from	Free from	Free from	Tomatoes Classed as Culls
Anthracnose	Free from	Free from	Not more than 2	

Source: Gould, W. A. (editor) (1974). Tomato grading practices. In *Tomato Production, Processing and Quality Evaluation*. AVI Publishing Co., Westport, Connecticut.

Tragacanth Species

TABLE 2.T.16
Geographical distribution of tragacanth species

Species	Geographical Distribution
A. gummifer	Northern Kurdistan, Armenia, Asia Minor and Syria
A. kurdicus	Southern Kurdistan to Asia Minor and Syria
A. brachycalyx	Iranian Kurdistan and Luristan
A. eriostylus	Luristan
A. pycnocladus	Kermanshab (Shahu and Avroman Mts.)
A. verus	Western Iran
A. leiocladus	Western and Central Iran
A. adscendens	South Western and Southern Iran
A. strobiliferus	Eastern Iran
A. heratensis	Khorasan to Afghanistan

Source: Howes, F. N. *Vegetable Gums and Resins*. Ronald Press Company, New York.

Transit Temperature

TABLE 2.T.17
Desirable transit temperatures for fruits and vegetables

Product	Temperature (°F)	Product	Temperature (°F)
Apples	32–40	Asparagus	32–36
Avocados			
Most varieties	45	Beans (snap)	45
West Indian varieties	55	Cantaloupe	35–40
Bananas (green)	56–60	Celery	32
Cherries (sweet)	32	Cucumbers	45–50
Cranberries	36–40	Honeydew melon	45–50
Dates	40–50	Lettuce	32
Grapefruit	50–60	Onions (dry)	32–40
Limes	48–50	Peppers (sweet)	45–50
Oranges		Potatoes	
Arizona & California	40–44	Early crop	50–60
Florida & Texas	32–40	Late crop	40–50

Source: White, P. L., and Selvey, N. (editors) (1974). *Nutritional Qualities of Fresh Fruits and Vegetables*. Futura Publishing Co., Mt. Kisco, New York.

Triangular Taste Test and Preference

TABLE 2.T.18
Significance in triangular taste tests ($p = \frac{1}{6}$)

No. of Tasters or Tastings	Minimum Agreeing Judgments Necessary to Establish Significant Differentiation (Two-tail Test)			Minimum Correct Answers Necessary to Establish Significant Differentiation (One-tail Test)		
	Probability Level			Probability Level		
	.05	.01	.001	.05	.01	.001
5	4	4	5	3	4	5
6	4	5	6	4	4	5
7	4	5	6	4	5	6
8	5	5	6	4	5	6
9	5	6	7	4	5	7
10	5	6	7	5	6	7
11	5	6	8	5	6	7
12	6	7	8	5	6	8
13	6	7	8	5	7	8
14	6	7	9	6	7	8
15	7	8	9	6	7	9
16	7	8	9	6	7	9
17	7	8	10	7	8	9
18	7	9	10	7	8	10
19	8	9	10	7	8	10
20	8	9	11	7	9	10
21	8	9	11	7	9	10
22	8	10	11	8	9	11
23	9	10	12	8	9	11
24	9	10	12	8	10	11
25	9	10	12	8	10	12
26	9	11	12	9	10	12
27	10	11	13	9	10	12
28	10	11	13	9	11	12
29	10	12	13	9	11	13
30	10	12	14	10	11	13
31	11	12	14	10	11	13
32	11	12	14	10	12	13
33	11	13	14	10	12	14
34	11	13	15	10	12	14
35	11	13	15	11	12	14
36	11	13	15	11	13	15
37	12	14	16	11	13	15
38	12	14	16	11	13	15
39	12	14	16	12	13	15
40	13	14	16	12	14	16
41	13	15	17	12	14	16
42	13	15	17	12	14	16
43	13	15	17	12	14	17
44	13	15	17	13	15	17
45	14	15	18	13	15	17
46	14	16	18	13	15	17
47	14	16	18	13	15	18
48	14	16	18	14	15	18
49	15	16	19	14	16	18
50	15	16	19	14	16	18
60	17	19	21	16	18	21
70	19	21	24	18	21	23
80	21	24	26	20	23	26
90	23	26	29	22	25	28
100	26	28	31	24	27	30

Source: Roessler, E. B., Baker, G. A., and Amerine, M. A. One-tailed and Two-tailed tests in organoleptic comparisons. Food Res. *21*, 117.

Triangular Taste Test Probability

TABLE 2.T.19
Probability in triangular taste tests

No. of Tasters or Tastings	No. of Correct Answers Necessary to Establish Significant Differentiation			No. of Tasters or Tastings	No. of Correct Answers Necessary to Establish Significant Differentiation		
	P = 0.05	P = 0.01	P = 0.001		P = 0.05	P = 0.01	P = 0.001
7	5	6	7	57	27	29	31
8	6	7	8	58	27	29	32
9	6	7	8	59	27	30	32
10	7	8	9	60	28	30	33
11	7	8	9	61	28	30	33
12	8	9	10	62	28	31	33
13	8	9	10	63	29	31	34
14	9	10	11	64	29	32	34
15	9	10	12	65	30	32	35
16	10	11	12	66	30	32	35
17	10	11	13	67	30	33	36
18	10	12	13	68	31	33	36
19	11	12	14	69	31	34	36
20	11	13	14	70	32	34	37
21	12	13	15	71	32	34	37
22	12	14	15	72	32	35	38
23	13	14	16	73	33	35	38
24	13	14	16	74	33	36	39
25	13	15	17	75	34	36	39
26	14	15	17	76	34	36	39
27	14	16	18	77	34	37	40
28	15	16	18	78	35	37	40
29	15	17	19	79	35	38	41
30	16	17	19	80	35	38	41
31	16	18	19	81	36	38	41
32	16	18	20	82	36	39	42
33	17	19	20	83	37	39	42
34	17	19	21	84	37	40	43
35	18	19	21	85	37	40	43
36	18	20	22	86	38	40	44
37	18	20	22	87	38	41	44
38	19	21	23	88	39	41	44
39	19	21	23	89	39	42	45
40	20	22	24	90	39	42	45
41	20	22	24	91	40	42	46
42	21	22	25	92	40	43	46
43	21	23	25	93	40	43	46
44	21	23	25	94	41	44	47
45	22	24	26	95	41	44	47
46	22	24	26	96	42	44	48
47	23	25	27	97	42	45	48
48	23	25	27	98	42	45	49
49	23	25	28	99	43	46	49
50	24	26	28	100	43	46	49
51	24	26	29	200	80	84	89
52	25	27	29	300	117	122	127
53	25	27	29	400	152	158	165
54	25	27	30	500	188	194	202
55	26	28	30	1,000	363	372	383
56	26	28	31	2,000	709	722	737

Source: Roessler, E. B., Warren, J., and Guymon, J. F. Significance in triangular taste tests. Food Res. *13*, 503.

Trichinosis

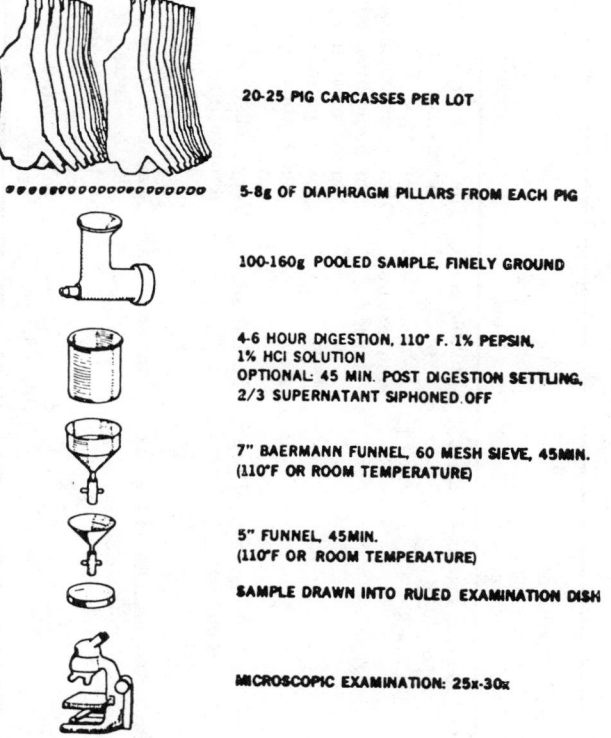

20-25 PIG CARCASSES PER LOT

5-8g OF DIAPHRAGM PILLARS FROM EACH PIG

100-160g POOLED SAMPLE, FINELY GROUND

4-6 HOUR DIGESTION, 110° F. 1% PEPSIN,
1% HCl SOLUTION
OPTIONAL: 45 MIN. POST DIGESTION SETTLING,
2/3 SUPERNATANT SIPHONED OFF

7" BAERMANN FUNNEL, 60 MESH SIEVE, 45MIN.
(110°F OR ROOM TEMPERATURE)

5" FUNNEL, 45MIN.
(110°F OR ROOM TEMPERATURE)

SAMPLE DRAWN INTO RULED EXAMINATION DISH

MICROSCOPIC EXAMINATION: 25x-30x

FIGURE 2.T.5
Schematic outline of modified pooled sample trichinosis diagnostic technique

Source: Zimmerman, W. F. (1975). Trichinosis. In *Meat Hygiene*. J. A. Libby (editor). Lea & Febiger, Philadelphia.

Turkey Composition

TABLE 2.T.20
Nutrient composition of cooked turkey meats

	Protein %	Food Energy Cal./100 gm.	Calorie-protein Cal./1% protein	Fat %	Moisture %	Ash %
Turkey, roasted and boned						
Breast (white meat)						
male	33.5	194	5.8	6.7	59	1.1
female	35.0	215	6.1	8.3	56	1.1
Leg (dark meat)						
male	30.8	224	7.3	11.2	57	1.0
female	30.3	230	7.6	12.1	56	1.0
Skin	17.7	375	21.2	33.8	45	1.0
Edible Viscera						
male	23.5	200	8.5	14.0	61	1.6
female	17.8	254	14.3	20.3	61	1.2
Smoked Turkey, bones						
Breast	31.0	207	6.7	9.2	57	2.8
Leg	30.2	221	7.3	11.1	56	2.8
Chicken, roasted and boned						
Breast	31.5	138	4.4	1.3	66	1.0
Leg	25.4	168	6.6	7.3	67	0.9

Source: Snyder, E. S., and Orr, H. L. (1964). Poultry meat. Dep.
Agric. Publ. *9*, Can. Dep. Agric., Ottawa.

Turkey Varieties

TABLE 2.T.21
Varieties of turkeys and their characteristics

Variety	Standard Weights		Plumage	Beak	Color of Throat Wattle	Beard	Shanks & Toes	Comments
	Adult tom (lb)	Adult hen (lb)						
Bronze	36	20	Black; with an iridescent sheen of red, green, bronze.	Light horn at tip, dark at base.	Red, changeable to bluish white.	Black	Dull black in young; smoky pink in mature birds.	The Broad-breasted Bronze is a sub-variety. Of all meat animals, the Broad-breasted Bronze most uniformly produces a well-fleshed carcass.
White Holland	33	18	Pure white.	Light pinkish horn.	Red, changeable to pinkish white.	Deep black	Pinkish white.	Very similar to Bronze; only white, and slightly higher in fertility.
Beltsville Small, white	23	13	Pure white.	Light pinkish horn.	Red, changeable to pinkish white.	Black	Pinkish white.	Developed by the USDA. These small turkeys are good egg producers of high hatchability.

Source: Ensminger, M. E. (1969). Animal Science. The Interstate Printers & Publishers, Inc., Danville, Illinois.

Unsaponifiable Matter

TABLE 2.U.1
Unsaponifiable content of some fats and oils

Oil or Fat	Unsaponifiable Matter %	Oil or Fat	Unsaponifiable Matter %
Babassu	0.2–0.8	Peanut	0.2–0.8
Cacao butter	0.2–1.0	Perilla	0.6–1.3
Castor	<1.0	Rapeseed	0.7–1.3
Chinese vegetable		Rice bran	3.0–5.0
tallow	0.5–1.5	Safflower	0.3–1.3
Coconut	<0.5	Sesame	0.9–2.3
Corn	0.8–2.0	Soybean	0.5–1.6
Cottonseed	<1.5	Sunflower	0.3–1.3
Hempseed	<1.5	Teaseed	<1.5
Kapok	0.5–1.0	Tung	<1.0
Linseed	<1.7	Lard	<0.8
Mustard seed		Neatsfoot	<0.8
(white)	0.7–1.5	Tallow (beef)	<1.0
(black)	0.7–1.5	Tallow (mutton)	<1.0
Olive	0.7–1.1	Whale	1.6–1.9
Palm	0.3–1.0	Cod	3.3–4.7
Palm kernel	0.2–0.8	Shark liver	13.0–20.0

Source: Mahlenbacher, C. V. *The Analysis of Fats and Oils.* Garrard Press, Champaign, Illinois.

Unsaturated Fatty Acids

TABLE 2.U.2
Name, formula, and source of unsaturated fatty acids

Common Name	Systematic Name	Formula	Source
Monoethenoid Fatty Acids			
Caproleic	9-Decenoic	$C_{10}H_{18}O_2$	Butter fat, milk fat of human, goat; sperm head oil.
Lauroleic	5-Dodecenoic	$C_{12}H_{22}O_2$	Herring oil, sperm blubber and head oil.
	9-Dodecenoic	$C_{12}H_{22}O_2$	Cochineal wax (*Coccus cacti*), cow's milk fat.
	5-Tetradecenoic	$C_{14}H_{26}O_2$	Sperm and dolphin oils, whale head oil, sardine.
Myristoleic	9-Tetradecenoic	$C_{14}H_{26}O_2$	Whale oil, shark liver oil, eel oil, turtle oil, human milk fat, depot fats.
Palmitoleic ("Physetoleic")	9-Hexadecenoic	$C_{16}H_{30}O_2$	Sperm head oil (*Physeter macrocephalus* Shaw), milk fat, seed oils, marine oils.
Petroselinic	6-Octadecenoic	$C_{18}H_{34}O_2$	Parsley seed oil, coriander, *Umbelliferae*.
Oleic	9-Octadecenoic	$C_{18}H_{34}O_2$	Olive oil, pork fat, most fats and oils.
Vaccenic	11-Octadecenoic	$C_{18}H_{34}O_2$	Butter, beef fat, mutton fat, lard.
Gadoleic	9-Eicosenoic	$C_{20}H_{38}O_2$	Cod-liver oil, many fish and marine oils.
	11-Eicosenoic	$C_{20}H_{38}O_2$	Jojoba oil.
Cetoleic	11-Docosenoic	$C_{22}H_{42}O_2$	Marine oil, shark liver, herring, sardine and other marine oils.
Erucic	13-Docosenoic	$C_{22}H_{42}O_2$	Mustard and rapeseed oils.
Diethenoid and Polyethenoid Fatty Acids			
Linoleic	9,12-Octadecadienoic	$C_{18}H_{32}O_2$	Linseed oil, most seed fats.
Hiragonic	6,10,14-Hexadecatrienoic	$C_{16}H_{26}O_2$	Sardine oil.
Linolenic	9,12,15-Octadecatrienoic	$C_{18}H_{30}O_2$	Hempseed oil, linseed oil, walnut oil, soybean oil, seed oils.
Eleostearic	9,11,13-Octadecatrienoic	$C_{18}H_{30}O_2$	Tung oil, bagilumbang nut, essang-seed oil.
Arachidonic	5,8,11,14-Eicosatetraenoic	$C_{20}H_{32}O_2$	Liver lipid, brain, egg lecithin, glandular organs.
	4,8,12,16-Eicosatetraenoic	$C_{20}H_{32}O_2$	Sardine oil, whale oil.
Clupanodonic	4,8,12,15,19—Docosapentaenoic	$C_{22}H_{34}O_2$	Sardine oil, sturgeon oil, white fish oil, pilchard oil, cod-liver oil, other fish oils.

Source: Mahlenbacher, C. V. *The Analysis of Fats and Oils*. Garrard Publishing Co., Champaign, Illinois.

Variety Meat, Cooking

TABLE 2.V.1
Timetable for cooking variety meats

Kind	Broiled	Braised	Cooked in Liquid
LIVER			
Beef			
3- to 4-pound piece		2 to 2½ hours	
Sliced		20 to 25 minutes	
Veal (Calf), sliced	8 to 10 minutes		
Pork			
Whole (3 to 3½ pounds)		1½ to 2 hours	
Sliced		20 to 25 minutes	
Lamb, sliced	8 to 10 minutes		
KIDNEY			
Beef		1½ to 2 hours	1 to 1½ hours
Veal (Calf)	10 to 12 minutes	1 to 1½ hours	¾ to 1 hour
Pork	10 to 12 minutes	1 to 1½ hours	¾ to 1 hour
Lamb	10 to 12 minutes	¾ to 1 hour	¾ to 1 hour
HEART			
Beef			
Whole		3 to 4 hours	3 to 4 hours
Sliced		1½ to 2 hours	
Veal (Calf)			
Whole		2½ to 3 hours	2½ to 3 hours
Pork		2½ to 3 hours	2½ to 3 hours
Lamb		2½ to 3 hours	2½ to 3 hours
TONGUE			
Beef			3 to 4 hours
Veal (Calf)			2 to 3 hours
Pork } usually sold			
Lamb { ready-to-serve			
TRIPE			
Beef	10 to 15 minutes[2]		1 to 1½ hours
SWEETBREADS	10 to 15 minutes[2]	20 to 25 minutes	15 to 20 minutes
BRAINS	10 to 15 minutes[2]	20 to 25 minutes	15 to 20 minutes

[1] On top of range or in a 300°F. to 325°F. oven.

[2] Time required after precooking in water.

Source: Lessons on Meat. (1974). National Live Stock and Meat Board, Chicago.

Variety Meat, Percentage of Daily Recommended Allowances

TABLE 2.V.2
Percentage of the daily recommended dietary allowances (1973) supplied by a $3\frac{1}{2}$-oz serving of variety meat[1] (for a 22 year-old male)

Food Constituent	Liver	Kidney	Heart	Brains	Sweetbreads	Tongue	Tripe
Protein	55	50	55	22	53	40	33
Calories	8	8	7	4	6	8	3
Calcium	2	2	1	16	26	2	16
Iron	176	130	51	21	31	18	16
Phosphorus	66	31	21	41	52	14	17
Magnesium	7		7				tr
Vitamin A	876	23	2	0	0	0	0
Ascorbic acid	68	27	tr	42	46	6	
Thiamin	22	34	16	7	4	4	tr
Riboflavin	248	268	75	12	9	16	8
Niacin	111	59	40	17	16	19	6
Vitamin B-6[2]	38	22	16	8	10	10	
Vitamin B-12[2]	2300	1070	224	133	307		

[1] Percentages are averages of representative values for beef, pork, lamb and veal.
[2] All values are for the cooked variety meats except vitamins B-6 and B-12 which are values for the raw product.

Source: Recipes for Variety Meats. (1974). National Live Stock and Meat Board, Chicago.

Variety Meat Preparation

TABLE 2.V.3
A guide for buying and preparing variety meats

Kind	Characteristics	Buying Guide		Preparation
		Avg Wt	Servings	
Liver (Beef, veal, pork, lamb)	Veal, lamb, pork livers more tender than beef. Veal and lamb livers milder in flavor than pork and beef.	1 beef—10 lb 1 veal—2½ lb 1 pork—3 lb 1 lamb—1 lb	¾–1 lb for four	Braise, fry, broil, grind for loaves or patties.
Kidney (Beef, veal, pork, lamb)	Veal, lamb and pork kidneys more tender than beef. Also milder in flavor. Veal and lamb kidney sometimes cut with chops.	1 beef—1 lb 1 veal—¾ lb 1 pork—¼ lb 1 lamb—⅛ lb	4–6 3–4 1–2 ½–1	Braise, broil, cook in liquid, grind for loaves or patties.
Heart (Beef, veal, pork, lamb)	Beef heart is least tender but all hearts must be made tender by proper cooking.	1 beef—4 lb 1 veal—½ lb 1 pork—½ lb 1 lamb—¼ lb	10–12 2–3 2–3 1	Braise, cook in liquid, grind for loaves or patties.
Tongue (Beef, veal, pork, lamb)	May be purchased fresh, pickled, corned or smoked. Must be made tender by proper cooking. Pork and lamb usually purchased ready-to-serve.	1 beef—3¾ lb 1 veal—1½ lb 1 pork—¾ lb 1 lamb—½ lb	12–16 3–6 2–4 2–3	Cook in liquid until tender. Remove skin, serve as desired.
Tripe (Beef)	Plain and honeycomb, latter preferred. Purchased fresh, pickled or canned. Often purchased precooked, requires further cooking.	Plain—7 lb Honey comb—1½ lb	¾–1 lb for four	Precook (unless purchased cooked) in water to make tender. Then braise, fry or broil.
Sweetbreads (Beef, veal, lamb)	Divided into two parts: heart and throat sweet breads. Tender and delicate in flavor.	⅛ lb	¾–1 lb for four	Precook in water to help keep and make firm. Broil, fry, braise or cream.
Brains (Beef, veal, pork, lamb)	Very tender and delicate to flavor.	⅜ lb	¾–1 lb for four	Precook in water to help keep and make firm. Broil, scramble, fry or cream.

Source: Recipes for Variety Meats. (1974). National Live Stock and Meat Board, Chicago.

Veal Chart

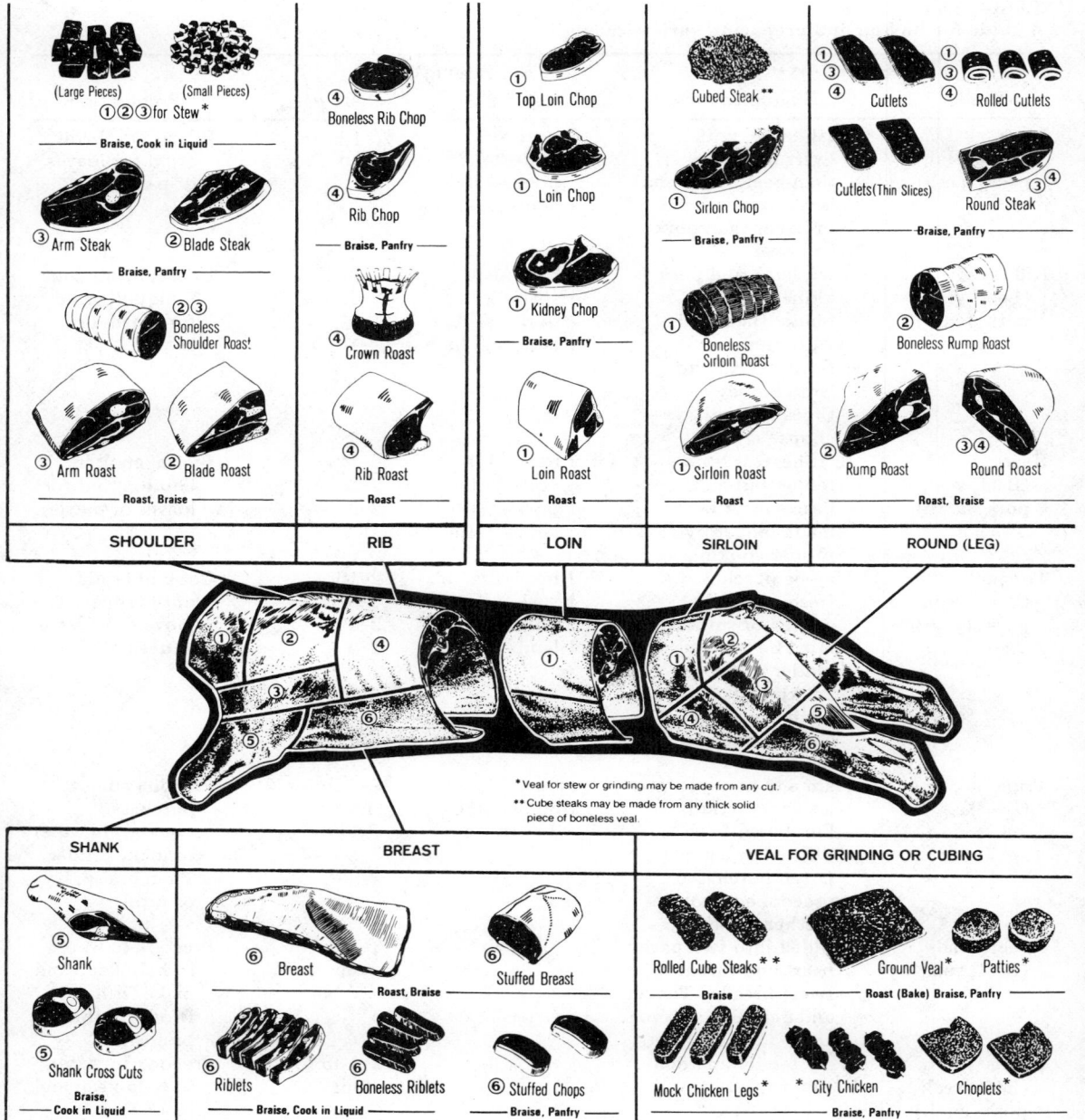

FIGURE 2.V.1
Retail cuts of veal, where they come from and how to cook them

Source: Be a Smarter Shopper . . . a Better Cook. (1973). National Live Stock and Meat Board, Chicago.

Veal Cuts

TABLE 2.V.4
Wholesale cuts, retail cuts, and their characteristics and cooking methods

WHOLESALE CUTS	RETAIL CUTS	CHARACTERISTICS	COOKING METHODS
Leg (Round)	Shank Half of Leg	Lower half of leg. Hock and part of shank bone usually removed.	Roast; braise
	Rump Half of Leg	Upper half of leg, including the rump.	Roast; braise
	Center Cut of Leg (Round)	Leg with rump and shank off.	Roast; braise
	Round Steak (Cutlet)	Same muscle and bone structure as beef round steaks.	Braise; panfry
	Standing Rump Roast	Contains aitch or rump bone, tail bone, and usually a part of leg bone.	Roast; braise
	Rolled Rump Roast	Boneless roll.	Roast; braise
	Heel of Round	Wedge-shaped boneless piece—same as in beef.	Braise; cook in liquid
	Hind Shank	Shank bone surrounded by varying amounts of shank meat.	Cook in liquid; braise
	Scallops	Thin boneless slices from any part of carcass.	Braise; panfry
	Rosettes	Solid boneless pieces or slices wrapped with bacon	Braise; panfry
Loin	Sirloin Roast	Corresponds to sirloin of beef. Contains hip and back bones.	Roast; braise
	Sirloin Steak	Same as above except cut into steaks.	Braise; panfry
	Loin Roast	Corresponds to beef short loin. Contains back bone and three separate muscles—loin eye, tenderloin and flank.	Roast; braise
	Loin Chop	Same as above except cut into chops. Corresponds to porterhouse, T-bone and club beef steaks.	Braise; panfry
	Kidney Chop	Cut to contain cross section of kidney. Made from rib end of loin.	Braise; panfry
Rib	Rib Roast	Similar to standing beef rib roast.	Roast
	Crown Roast	Rib sections "frenched" and formed into shape of crown.	Roast
	Rib Chop	Contains rib bone and rib eye, except chops cut between ribs have no rib bone.	Braise; panfry
Shoulder	Blade Roast	Includes that section of the shoulder which contains the blade bone.	Roast; braise
	Blade Steak (Chop)	Contains blade bone and rib bone except chops cut between ribs have no rib bone.	Braise; panfry
	Arm Roast	Includes arm section of shoulder. Contains arm bone and cross sections of 3 to 5 ribs.	Roast; braise
	Arm Steak (Chop)	Same as above except cut into slices.	Braise; panfry
	Rolled Shoulder Roast	Boneless roll.	Roast; braise
	City Chicken	Boneless cubes of veal fastened together on a wooden or metal skewer.	Braise
Breast	Breast	Corresponds to short plate and brisket of beef. Thin, flat cut containing rib ends and breast bone.	Braise; cook in liquid
	Breast with pocket	Same as above with pocket cut between ribs and lean.	Roast; braise
	Rolled Breast	Boned and rolled breast.	Roast; braise
	Riblets	Breast bone is removed (usually). Breast is separated into riblets by cutting between ribs.	Braise; cook in liquid
	Stew Meat	Small bone-in or boneless pieces of meat. Also made from the shoulder, shank and leg.	Braise; cook in liquid
Fore Shank	Fore Shank	Contains considerable bone and connective tissue. Varying amounts of lean. Rich in gelatin-forming substance.	Braise; cook in liquid
Ground Veal	Loaf and Patties	Usually made from flank, breast, shank and neck.	Roast; braise; panfry
	Mock Chicken Legs	Ground veal molded into shape of chicken legs with wooden skewer to represent leg bone.	Braise; panfry

(Continued)

Veal Cuts (*Continued*)

TABLE 2.V.4 (*Continued*)

WHOLESALE CUTS	RETAIL CUTS	CHARACTERISTICS	COOKING METHODS
Round (and Rump)	Round Steak (*full cut*)	Round or oval in shape with small round bone. One large muscle, three smaller ones.	*Braise*
	Top Round Steak or Pot-Roast	Most tender portion of round. Is one large muscle.	*Braise; roast; panfry*
	Bottom Round Steak or Pot-Roast	Not so tender as top round. Distinguished from top round by having two muscles.	*Braise*
	Tip Roast or Steak	Triangular cut; roast may contain kneecap. Steaks are boneless.	*Braise; roast; broil; panbroil; panfry*
	Standing Rump	Triangular in shape; contains portions of aitch (rump) bone and tail bone. Knuckle end of leg (round) bone usually removed.	*Braise: roast (high quality)*
	Rolled Rump	Boneless roll.	*Braise, roast (high quality)*
	Heel of Round	Boneless wedge-shaped cut from lower part of round. Weighs 4 to 8 pounds. Has very little fat and is least tender cut of round.	*Braise; cook in liquid*
	Hind Shank	Bony, considerable connective tissue, rich in extractives.	*Cook in liquid (soup)*
Sirloin	Sirloin Steak	Contains portions of back bone and hip bone. Wide variation in bone and muscle structure of the various steaks.	*Broil; panbroil; panfry*
	Pinbone Sirloin Steak	Lies next to the porterhouse. Contains pin bone which is the forward end of hip bone.	*Broil; panbroil; panfry*
	Boneless Sirloin Steak	Any boneless steak from the sirloin.	*Broil; panbroil; panfry*
Short Loin	Porterhouse Steak	Largest steak in short loin. Loin strip and tenderloin muscles. T-shaped bone. Tenderloin larger in porterhouse than in other short loin steaks.	*Broil; panbroil; panfry*
	T-Bone Steak	Same as porterhouse except tenderloin is smaller (porterhouse and T-bone used more or less interchangeably).	*Broil; panbroil; panfry*
	Club (Delmonico) Steak	Triangular-shaped; smallest steak in short loin. Tenderloin has practically disappeared.	*Broil; panbroil; panfry*
	Tenderloin Roast or Steak	Boneless tapering muscle. Most tender cut beef.	*Roast; broil; panbroil; panfry*
Flank	Flank Steak	Oval-shaped boneless steak weighing ¾ to 1½ pounds. Muscles run lengthwise; usually scored to shorten muscle fibers. Less tender cut.	*Braise*
	Flank Steak Fillets	Sections of flank steak rolled and fastened with skewers.	*Braise*
	Flank Meat	Boneless. Coarse fibers. May be rolled, cut into stew or ground.	*Braise; cook in liquid*
Rib	Standing Rib Roast (Short Cut)	Contains two or more ribs from which short ribs and chine bone have been removed. Comparable to rib roast served in restaurants.	*Roast*
	Rolled Rib Roast	Boneless roll. Outer cover of roll consists largely of thin plate meat wrapped around rib eye.	*Roast*
	Rib Steak	Contains rib eye and may contain rib bone.	*Broil; panbroil; panfry*
	Short Ribs	Cut from ends of ribs; layers of lean and fat.	*Braise; cook in liquid*
Short Plate	Plate "Boiling" Beef	Cut across plate parallel with ribs.	*Braise; cook in liquid*
	Rolled Plate	When rolled the absence of the rib eye distinguishes this cut from the rolled rib.	*Braise; cook in liquid*
	Short Ribs	Cut from ends of ribs; layers of lean and fat.	*Braise; cook in liquid*
Square-Cut Chuck	Arm Pot-roast or Steak	Has a round bone and cross sections of 3–5 ribs. A small round muscle near the round bone is surrounded by connective tissue.	*Braise*
	Blade Pot-roast or Steak	Pot-roast contains portions of rib and blade bones. Steaks cut between ribs will not contain rib bone.	*Braise*
	Boneless Chuck	Any part of the square-cut chuck (except the neck) from which the bones have been removed.	*Braise*
	Boneless Neck	Any part of the neck without the neck bone.	*Braise; cook in liquid*
	English (Boston) Cut	A rectangular piece cut across 2 or 3 chuck ribs.	*Braise*
Brisket	Brisket	Layers of lean and fat. Presence of breast bone sure indication that cut is from the brisket.	*Braise; cook in liquid*
	Boneless Brisket	Same as above with ribs and breast bone removed.	*Braise; cook in liquid*
Fore Shank	Shank Knuckle	Knuckle or upper end of fore shank.	*Cook in liquid, braise*
	Shank Cross-Cuts	Small pieces cut across shank bone.	*Braise; cook in liquid*
Ground Beef	Loaf and Patties	Usually made from flank, shank, plate and chuck.	*Roast (bake); broil; panbroil; panfry; braise*

Source: Meat Manual, 6th Edition. National Live Stock and Meat Board, Chicago.

Veal Cuts and Uses

TABLE 2.V.5
Veal cuts and how to use them

CUT	DESCRIPTION OF CUT	RETAIL CUTS	VEAL SPECIALTIES
LEG	Solid meat, small percentage of bone, little waste	Roasts, cutlets veal birds	Brains— Cream, scramble, fry
RUMP	Excellent quality; corresponds to rump of beef	Roast	Heart— Braise, cook in water
LOIN	Excellent quality, more bone than leg	Chops, roasts, kidney chops	Kidney— Broil, meat pie, fry, cook in water
RIB	Excellent quality	Chops, Frenched chops, roasts	Liver— Fry, broil, braise, roast whole or as loaf
BREAST	Narrow, thin strip of meat with breast bone and lower portion of ribs	Stuffed roast, stews, jellied veal	Tongue (Corned, smoked, fresh)— Cook in water
SHOULDER	Tender, juicy, and well flavored	Roast, boned and rolled roast, chops, pot-roasts	Sweetbreads— Cream, braise, broil, fry
SHANK	Little meat, fine flavor	Pressed veal, stock, stews,	
FLANK	Good flavor, no waste	Stews, pressed veal	

Source: Meat Buying Manual. National Live Stock and Meat Board, Chicago.

Veal Roasting

TABLE 2.V.6
Roasting times for veal

Cut	Approx. Wt. of Single Roast	No. of Roasts in Oven	Approx. Total Wt. of Roasts in Oven	Oven Temperature	Interior Temperature of Roast When Removed from Oven	Minutes per Pound Based on One Roast	Minutes per Pound Based on Total Wt. of Roasts in Oven	Approximate Total Time
	pounds		*pounds*					
Leg	7 to 8	1		300° F.	170° F.	25		3 to 3½ hours
Leg	16	1		300° F.	170° F.	22		6 hours
Leg	23	1		300° F.	170° F.	18 to 20		7 to 7½ hours
Loin	4½ to 5	1		300° F.	170° F.	30 to 35		2½ to 3 hours
Rack (4 to 6 ribs)	2½ to 3	1		300° F.	170° F.	30 to 35		1½ hours
Shoulder	7	1		300° F.	170° F.	25		3 hours
Shoulder	12 to 13	1		300° F.	170° F.	25		5 to 5½ hours
Cushion shoulder (with stuffing)	9 to 10	1		300° F.	170° F.	30 to 35		5 to 5½ hours
Cushion shoulder (with stuffing)		3	24	300° F.	170° F.		10 to 12	4 to 5 hours
Rolled shoulder	5	1		300° F.	170° F.	40 to 45		3½ to 4 hours
Rolled shoulder		3	20	300° F.	170° F.		14	5 hours
Rolled shoulder	9 to 10	1		300° F.	170° F.	35 to 40		6 to 7 hours
Round (rump and shank off)	20	1		300° F.	170° F.	20		6½ hours

Source: Cooking Meat in Quantity. National Live Stock and Meat Board, Chicago.

Veal Wholesale Cuts

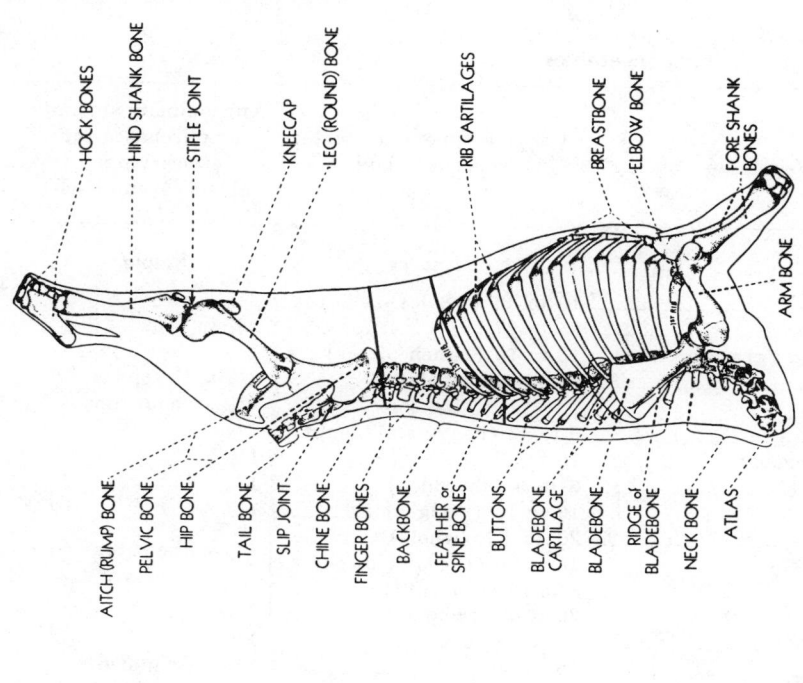

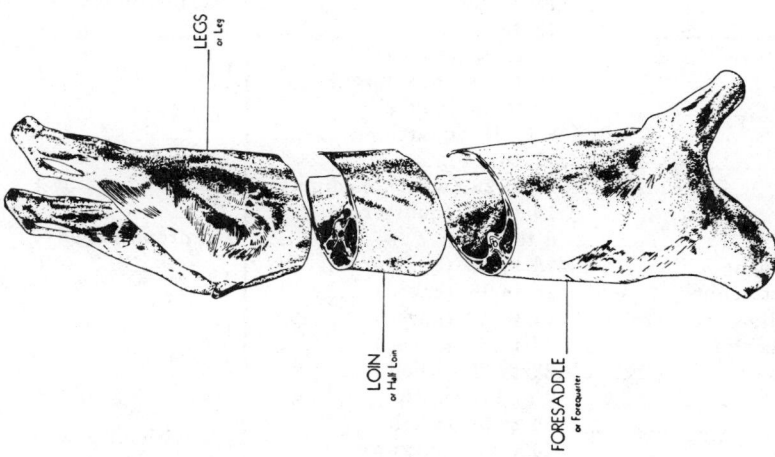

FIGURE 2.V.2

Veal wholesale cuts (left); location, structure, and names of carcass bones (right)

Source: Cooking Meat in Quantity. National Live Stock and Meat Board, Chicago.

Vegetable Boiling

TABLE 2.V.7
Boiling guide for fresh vegetables

Vegetable	Cooking time after water returns to boil	Approximate amount as purchased for six servings) (about ½ cup each)
	Minutes	*Pounds*
Asparagus	10 to 13 (whole)	2½
Beans, lima	25 to 27	2¾ in pods
Beans, snap (green or wax)	13 to 15 (1-inch pieces)	1
Beets	38 to 41 (whole)	2½ with tops or 1½ without tops
Broccoli	9 to 12 (heavy stalk, split)	2
Brussels sprouts	15 to 17	1½
Cabbage	6 to 8 (shredded)	1¼
	10 to 13 (wedges)	1½
Carrots	20 to 22 (whole) 18 to 20 (sliced or diced)	1½ without tops
Cauliflower	8 to 12 (separated) 20 to 24 (whole)	2
Celery	15 to 19 (cut-up)	1¼
Collards	15 to 20	1½ untrimmed
Corn	5 to 7 (on cob) 6 to 8 (whole kernel)	3 in husks
Kale	15 to 20	1¼ untrimmed
Okra	12 to 14	1¼
Onions, mature	11 to 15 (whole) 10 to 14 (quartered)	1¾
Parsnips	20 to 40 (whole) 8 to 15 (quartered)	1½
Peas	10 to 14	3 in pods
Potatoes	25 to 29 (whole, medium) 15 to 17 (quartered)	1½
Spinach	8 to 12	1½ prepackaged
Squash, acorn Squash, butternut	18 to 20 (quartered) 16 to 18 (cubed)	2½
Squash, yellow crookneck Squash, zucchini	11 to 13 (sliced) 13 to 15 (sliced)	1½
Sweetpotatoes	28 to 35 (whole)	2
Tomatoes	7 to 15 (cut-up)	1¼
Turnips	30 to 38 (whole) 10 to 12 (cut-up)	1¾ without tops

Source: USDA (1980). Vegetables in family meals. USDA Home and Garden Bull. *105.*

Vegetable Composition, Part I

Nutritive values of the edible part of vegetables and vegetable products

(Dashes (—) denote lack of reliable data for a constituent believed to be present in measurable amount)

Foods, approximate measures, units, and weight (edible part unless footnotes indicate otherwise)		Water	Food energy	Pro-tein	Fat	Fatty Acids Satu-rated (total)	Unsaturated Oleic	Lino-leic	Carbo-hydrate	Calcium	Phos-phorus	Iron	Potas-sium	Vitamin A value	Thiamin	Ribo-flavin	Niacin	Ascorbic acid
	Grams	Per cent	Cal-ories	Grams	Grams	Grams	Grams	Grams	Grams	Milli-grams	Milli-grams	Milli-grams	Milli-grams	Inter-national units	Milli-grams	Milli-grams	Milli-grams	Milli-grams
Asparagus, green:																		
Cooked, drained:																		
Cuts and tips, 1 1/2- to 2-in lengths:																		
From raw------ 1 cup	145	94	30	3	Trace	—	—	—	5	30	73	0.9	265	1,310	0.23	0.26	2.0	38
From frozen--- 1 cup	180	93	40	6	Trace	—	—	—	6	40	115	2.2	396	1,530	.25	.23	1.8	41
Spears, 1/2-in diam. at base:																		
From raw------ 4 spears	60	94	10	1	Trace	—	—	—	2	13	30	.4	110	540	.10	.11	.8	16
From frozen--- 4 spears	60	92	15	2	Trace	—	—	—	2	13	40	.7	143	470	.10	.08	.7	16
Canned, spears, 1/2-in diam. at base. 4 spears	80	93	15	2	Trace	—	—	—	3	15	42	1.5	133	640	.05	.08	.6	12
Beans:																		
Lima, immature seeds, frozen, cooked, drained:																		
Thick-seeded types (Fordhooks) 1 cup	170	74	170	10	Trace	—	—	—	32	34	153	2.9	724	390	.12	.09	1.7	29
Thin-seeded types (baby limas) 1 cup	180	69	210	13	Trace	—	—	—	40	63	227	4.7	709	400	.16	.09	2.2	22
Snap:																		
Green:																		
Cooked, drained:																		
From raw (cuts and French style). 1 cup	125	92	30	2	Trace	—	—	—	7	63	46	.8	189	680	.09	.11	.6	15
From frozen:																		
Cuts----- 1 cup	135	92	35	2	Trace	—	—	—	8	54	43	.9	205	780	.09	.12	.5	7
French style-- 1 cup	130	92	35	2	Trace	—	—	—	8	49	39	1.2	177	690	.08	.10	.4	9
Canned, drained solids (cuts). 1 cup	135	92	30	2	Trace	—	—	—	7	61	34	2.0	128	630	.04	.07	.4	5
Yellow or wax:																		
Cooked, drained:																		
From raw (cuts and French style). 1 cup	125	93	30	2	Trace	—	—	—	6	63	46	.8	189	290	.09	.11	.6	16
From frozen (cuts)- 1 cup	135	92	35	2	Trace	—	—	—	8	47	42	.9	221	140	.09	.11	.5	8
Canned, drained solids (cuts). 1 cup	135	92	30	2	Trace	—	—	—	7	61	34	2.0	128	140	.04	.07	.4	7
Beans, mature. See Beans, dry (items 509-515) and Blackeye peas, dry (item 516).																		
Bean sprouts (mung):																		
Raw-------- 1 cup	105	89	35	4	Trace	—	—	—	7	20	67	1.4	234	20	.14	.14	.8	20
Cooked, drained--- 1 cup	125	91	35	4	Trace	—	—	—	7	21	60	1.1	195	30	.11	.13	.9	8
Beets:																		
Cooked, drained, peeled:																		
Whole beets, 2-in diam.------- 2 beets	100	91	30	1	Trace	—	—	—	7	14	23	.5	208	20	.03	.04	.3	6
Diced or sliced----- 1 cup	170	91	55	2	Trace	—	—	—	12	24	39	.9	354	30	.05	.07	.5	10
Canned, drained solids:																		
Whole beets, small---- 1 cup	160	89	60	2	Trace	—	—	—	14	30	29	1.1	267	30	.02	.05	.2	5
Diced or sliced----- 1 cup	170	89	65	2	Trace	—	—	—	15	32	31	1.2	284	30	.02	.05	.2	5
Beet greens, leaves and stems, cooked, drained. 1 cup	145	94	25	2	Trace	—	—	—	5	144	36	2.8	481	7,400	.10	.22	.4	22
Blackeye peas, immature seeds, cooked and drained:																		
From raw------ 1 cup	165	72	180	13	1	—	—	—	30	40	241	3.5	625	580	.50	.18	2.3	28
From frozen--- 1 cup	170	66	220	15	1	—	—	—	40	43	286	4.8	573	290	.68	.19	2.4	15
Broccoli, cooked, drained:																		
From raw:																		
Stalk, medium size------ 1 stalk	180	91	45	6	1	—	—	—	8	158	112	1.4	481	4,500	.16	.36	1.4	162
Stalks cut into 1/2-in pieces- 1 cup	155	91	40	5	Trace	—	—	—	7	136	96	1.2	414	3,880	.14	.31	1.2	140
From frozen:																		
Stalk, 4 1/2 to 5 in long----- 1 stalk	30	91	10	1	Trace	—	—	—	1	12	17	.2	66	570	.02	.03	.2	22
Chopped------ 1 cup	185	92	50	5	1	—	—	—	9	100	104	1.3	392	4,810	.11	.22	.9	105
Brussels sprouts, cooked, drained:																		
From raw, 7-8 sprouts (1 1/4- to 1 1/2-in diam.). 1 cup	155	88	55	7	1	—	—	—	10	50	112	1.7	423	810	.12	.22	1.2	135
From frozen--- 1 cup	155	89	50	5	Trace	—	—	—	10	33	95	1.2	457	880	.12	.16	.9	126

(Continued)

Vegetable Composition, Part I (Continued)

TABLE 2.V.8 (Continued)

(Dashes (—) denote lack of reliable data for a constituent believed to be present in measurable amount)

Foods, approximate measures, units, and weight (edible part unless footnotes indicate otherwise)	Weight (Grams)	Water (Per cent)	Food energy (Calories)	Protein (Grams)	Fat (Grams)	Fatty Acids Saturated (total) (Grams)	Unsaturated Oleic (Grams)	Unsaturated Linoleic (Grams)	Carbohydrate (Grams)	Calcium (Milligrams)	Phosphorus (Milligrams)	Iron (Milligrams)	Potassium (Milligrams)	Vitamin A value (International units)	Thiamin (Milligrams)	Riboflavin (Milligrams)	Niacin (Milligrams)	Ascorbic acid (Milligrams)
Cabbage: Common varieties: Raw:																		
Coarsely shredded or sliced—1 cup	70	92	15	1	Trace	—	—	—	4	34	20	0.3	163	90	0.04	0.04	0.02	33
Finely shredded or chopped—1 cup	90	92	20	1	Trace	—	—	—	5	44	29	.4	210	120	.05	.05	.3	42
Cooked, drained—1 cup	145	94	30	2	Trace	—	—	—	6	64	29	.4	236	190	.06	.06	.4	48
Red, raw, coarsely shredded or sliced—1 cup	70	90	20	1	Trace	—	—	—	5	29	25	.6	188	30	.06	.04	.3	43
Savoy, raw, coarsely shredded or sliced—1 cup	70	92	15	2	Trace	—	—	—	3	47	38	.6	188	140	.04	.06	.2	39
Cabbage, celery (also called pe-tsai or wongbok), raw, 1-in pieces—1 cup	75	95	10	1	Trace	—	—	—	2	32	30	.5	190	110	.04	.03	.5	19
Cabbage, white mustard (also called bokchoy or pakchoy), cooked, drained—1 cup	170	95	25	2	Trace	—	—	—	4	252	56	1.0	364	5,270	.07	.14	1.2	26
Carrots: Raw, without crowns and tips, scraped:																		
Whole, 7 1/2 by 1 1/8 in, or strips, 2 1/2 to 3 in long—1 carrot or 18 strips	72	88	30	1	Trace	—	—	—	7	27	26	.5	246	7,930	.04	.04	.4	6
Grated—1 cup	110	88	45	1	Trace	—	—	—	11	41	40	.8	375	12,100	.07	.06	.7	9
Cooked (crosswise cuts), drained—1 cup	155	91	50	1	Trace	—	—	—	11	51	48	.9	344	16,280	.08	.08	.8	9
Canned: Sliced, drained solids—1 cup	155	91	45	1	Trace	—	—	—	10	47	34	1.1	186	23,250	.03	.05	.6	3
Strained or junior (baby food)—1 oz (1 3/4 to 2 tbsp)	28	92	10	Trace	Trace	—	—	—	2	7	6	.1	51	3,690	.01	.01	.1	1
Cauliflower: Raw, chopped—1 cup	115	91	31	3	Trace	—	—	—	6	29	64	1.3	339	70	.13	.12	.8	90
Cooked, drained: From raw (flower buds)—1 cup	125	93	30	3	Trace	—	—	—	5	26	53	.9	258	80	.11	.10	.8	69
From frozen (flowerets)—1 cup	180	94	30	3	Trace	—	—	—	6	31	68	.9	373	50	.07	.09	.7	74
Celery, Pascal type, raw: Stalk, large outer, 8 by 1 1/2 in, at root end—1 stalk	40	94	5	Trace	Trace	—	—	—	2	16	11	.1	136	110	.01	.01	.1	4
Pieces, diced—1 cup	120	94	20	1	Trace	—	—	—	5	47	34	.4	409	320	.04	.04	.4	11
Collards, cooked, drained: From raw (leaves without stems)—1 cup	190	90	65	7	1	—	—	—	10	357	99	1.5	498	14,820	.21	.38	2.3	144
From frozen (chopped)—1 cup	170	90	50	5	1	—	—	1	10	299	87	1.7	401	11,560	.10	.24	1.0	56
Corn, sweet: Cooked, drained: From raw, ear 5 by 1 3/4 in—1 ear[6]	140	74	70	2	1	—	—	1	16	2	69	.5	151	[6b]310	.09	.08	1.1	7
From frozen: Ear, 5 in long—1 ear[6]	229	73	120	4	1	—	—	1	27	4	121	1.0	291	[6b]440	.18	.10	2.1	9
Kernels—1 cup	165	77	130	5	1	—	—	1	31	5	120	1.3	304	[6b]580	.15	.10	2.5	8
Canned: Cream style—1 cup	256	76	210	5	2	—	—	2	51	8	143	1.5	248	[6b]840	.08	.13	2.6	13
Whole kernel: Vacuum pack—1 cup	210	76	175	5	1	—	—	1	43	6	153	1.1	204	[6b]740	.06	.13	2.3	11
Wet pack, drained solids—1 cup	165	76	140	4	1	—	—	1	33	8	81	.8	160	[6b]580	.05	.08	1.5	7
Cowpeas. See Blackeye peas. (Items 585-586).																		
Cucumber slices, 1/8 in thick (large, 2 1/8-in diam.; small, 1 3/4-in diam.): With peel—6 large or 8 small slices	28	95	5	Trace	Trace	—	—	—	1	7	8	.3	45	70	.01	.01	.1	3
Without peel—6 1/2 large or 9 small pieces	28	96	5	Trace	Trace	—	—	—	1	5	5	.1	45	Trace	.01	.01	.1	3
Dandelion greens, cooked, drained—1 cup	105	90	35	2	1	—	—	—	7	147	44	1.9	244	12,290	.14	.17	—	19
Endive, curly (including escarole), raw, small pieces—1 cup	50	93	10	1	Trace	—	—	—	2	41	27	.9	147	1,650	.04	.07	.3	5

[6] Weight includes cob. Without cob, weight is 77 g for item 612, 126 g for item 613.

[6b] Based on yellow varieties. For white varieties, value is trace.

Vegetable Composition, Part I *(Continued)*

TABLE 2.V.8 *(Continued)*

(Dashes (—) denote lack of reliable data for a constituent believed to be present in measurable amount)

Foods, approximate measures, units, and weight (edible part unless footnotes indicate otherwise)	Grams	Water (Per cent)	Food energy (Calories)	Protein (Grams)	Fat (Grams)	Saturated (total) (Grams)	Oleic (Grams)	Linoleic (Grams)	Carbohydrate (Grams)	Calcium (Milligrams)	Phosphorus (Milligrams)	Iron (Milligrams)	Potassium (Milligrams)	Vitamin A value (International units)	Thiamin (Milligrams)	Riboflavin (Milligrams)	Niacin (Milligrams)	Ascorbic acid (Milligrams)
Kale, cooked, drained:																		
From raw (leaves without stems and midribs): 1 cup	110	88	45	5	1	—	—	—	7	206	64	1.8	243	9,130	.11	.20	1.8	102
From frozen (leaf style): 1 cup	130	91	40	4	1	—	—	—	7	157	62	1.3	251	10,660	.08	.20	.9	49
Lettuce, raw:																		
Butterhead, as Boston types:																		
Head, 5-in diam.[3]: 1 head[3]	220	95	25	2	Trace	—	—	—	4	57	42	3.3	430	1,580	.10	.10	.5	13
Leaves: 1 outer or 2 inner or 3 heart leaves.	15	95	Trace	Trace	Trace	—	—	—	Trace	5	4	.3	40	150	.01	.01	Trace	1
Crisphead, as Iceberg:																		
Head, 6-in diam.[4]: 1 head[4]	567	96	70	5	1	—	—	—	16	108	118	2.7	943	1,780	.32	.32	1.6	32
Wedge, 1/4 of head: 1 wedge	135	96	20	1	Trace	—	—	—	4	27	30	.7	236	450	.08	.08	.4	8
Pieces, chopped or shredded: 1 cup	55	96	5	Trace	Trace	—	—	—	2	11	12	.3	96	180	.03	.03	.2	3
Looseleaf (bunching varieties including romaine or cos), chopped or shredded pieces: 1 cup	55	94	10	1	Trace	—	—	—	2	37	14	.8	145	1,050	.03	.04	.2	10
Mushrooms, raw, sliced or chopped: 1 cup	70	90	20	2	Trace	—	—	—	3	4	81	.6	290	Trace	.07	.32	2.9	2
Mustard greens, without stems and midribs, cooked, drained: 1 cup	140	93	30	3	1	—	—	—	6	193	45	2.5	308	8,120	.11	.20	.8	67
Okra pods, 3 by 5/8 in, cooked: 10 pods	106	91	30	2	Trace	—	—	—	6	98	43	.5	184	520	.14	.19	1.0	21
Onions:																		
Mature:																		
Raw:																		
Chopped: 1 cup	170	89	65	3	Trace	—	—	—	15	46	61	.9	267	[6]Trace	.05	.07	.3	17
Sliced: 1 cup	115	89	45	2	Trace	—	—	—	10	31	41	.6	181	[6]Trace	.03	.05	.2	12
Cooked (whole or sliced), drained: 1 cup	210	92	60	3	Trace	—	—	—	14	50	61	.8	231	[6]Trace	.06	.06	.4	15
Young green, bulb (3/8 in diam.) and white portion of top: 6 onions	30	88	15	Trace	Trace	—	—	—	3	12	12	.2	69	Trace	.02	.01	.1	8
Parsley, raw, chopped: 1 tbsp	4	85	Trace	Trace	Trace	—	—	—	Trace	7	2	.2	25	300	Trace	.01	Trace	6
Parsnips, cooked (diced or 2-in lengths): 1 cup	155	82	100	2	1	—	—	—	23	70	96	.9	587	50	.11	.12	.2	16
Peas, green:																		
Canned:																		
Whole, drained solids: 1 cup	170	77	150	8	1	—	—	—	29	44	129	3.2	163	1,170	.15	.10	1.4	14
Strained (baby food): 1 oz (1 3/4 to 2 tbsp)	28	86	15	1	Trace	—	—	—	3	3	18	.3	28	140	.02	.03	.3	3
Frozen, cooked, drained: 1 cup	160	82	110	8	Trace	—	—	—	19	30	138	3.0	216	960	.43	.14	2.7	21
Peppers, hot, red, without seeds, dried (ground chili powder, added seasonings): 1 tsp	2	9	5	Trace	Trace	—	—	—	1	5	4	.3	20	1,300	Trace	.02	.2	Trace
Peppers, sweet (about 5 per lb, whole), stem and seeds removed:																		
Raw: 1 pod	74	93	15	1	Trace	—	—	—	4	7	16	.5	157	310	.06	.06	.4	94
Cooked, boiled, drained: 1 pod	73	95	15	1	Trace	—	—	—	3	7	12	.4	109	310	.05	.05	.4	70
Potatoes, cooked:																		
Baked, peeled after baking (about 2 per lb, raw): 1 potato	156	75	145	4	Trace	—	—	—	33	14	101	1.1	782	Trace	.15	.07	2.7	31
Boiled (about 3 per lb, raw):																		
Peeled after boiling: 1 potato	137	80	105	3	Trace	—	—	—	23	10	72	.8	556	Trace	.12	.05	2.0	22
Peeled before boiling: 1 potato	135	83	90	3	Trace	—	—	—	20	8	57	.7	385	Trace	.12	.05	1.6	22
French-fried, strip, 2 to 3 1/2 in long:																		
Prepared from raw: 10 strips	50	45	135	2	7	1.7	1.2	3.3	18	8	56	.7	427	Trace	.07	.04	1.6	11
Frozen, oven heated: 10 strips	50	53	110	2	4	1.1	.8	2.1	17	5	43	.9	326	Trace	.07	.01	1.3	11
Hashed brown, prepared from frozen: 1 cup	155	56	345	3	18	4.6	3.2	9.0	45	28	78	1.9	439	Trace	.11	.03	1.6	12
Mashed, prepared from—																		
Raw:																		
Milk added: 1 cup	210	83	135	4	2	.7	.4	Trace	27	50	103	.8	548	40	.17	.11	2.1	21

(Continued)

Vegetable Composition, Part I (Continued)

TABLE 2.V.8 (Continued)

(Dashes (—) denote lack of reliable data for a constituent believed to be present in measurable amount)

NUTRIENTS IN INDICATED QUANTITY

Foods, approximate measures, units, and weight (edible part unless footnotes indicate otherwise)	Grams	Water (Per cent)	Food energy (Calories)	Protein (Grams)	Fat (Grams)	Fatty Acids — Saturated (total) (Grams)	Fatty Acids — Oleic (Grams)	Fatty Acids — Linoleic (Grams)	Carbohydrate (Grams)	Calcium (Milligrams)	Phosphorus (Milligrams)	Iron (Milligrams)	Potassium (Milligrams)	Vitamin A value (International units)	Thiamin (Milligrams)	Riboflavin (Milligrams)	Niacin (Milligrams)	Ascorbic acid (Milligrams)
Potatoes, cooked—Continued																		
Mashed, prepared from—Continued																		
Raw—Continued																		
Milk and butter added — 1 cup	210	80	195	4	9	5.6	2.3	0.2	26	50	101	0.8	525	360	0.17	0.11	2.1	19
Dehydrated flakes (without milk), water, milk, butter, and salt added — 1 cup	210	79	195	4	7	3.6	2.1	.2	30	65	99	.6	601	270	.08	.08	1.9	11
Potato chips, 1 3/4 by 2 1/2 in oval cross section — 10 chips	20	2	115	1	8	2.1	1.4	4.0	10	8	28	.4	226	Trace	.04	.01	1.0	3
Potato salad, made with cooked salad dressing — 1 cup	250	76	250	7	7	2.0	2.7	1.3	41	80	160	1.5	798	350	.20	.18	2.8	28
Pumpkin, canned — 1 cup	245	90	80	2	Trace	—	—	—	19	61	64	1.0	588	15,680	.07	.12	1.5	12
Radishes, raw (prepackaged) stem ends, rootlets cut off — 4 radishes	18	95	5	Trace	Trace	—	—	—	1	5	6	.2	58	Trace	.01	.01	.1	5
Sauerkraut, canned, solids and liquid — 1 cup	235	93	40	2	Trace	—	—	—	9	85	42	1.2	329	120	.07	.09	.5	33
Southern peas. See Blackeye peas (items 585-586).																		
Spinach:																		
Raw, chopped — 1 cup	55	91	15	2	Trace	—	—	—	2	51	28	1.7	259	4,460	.06	.11	.3	28
Cooked, drained: From raw — 1 cup	180	92	40	5	1	—	—	—	6	167	68	4.0	583	14,580	.13	.25	.9	50
From frozen: Chopped — 1 cup	205	92	45	6	1	—	—	—	8	232	90	4.3	683	16,200	.14	.31	.8	39
Leaf — 1 cup	190	92	45	6	1	—	—	—	7	200	84	4.8	688	15,390	.15	.27	1.0	53
Canned, drained solids — 1 cup	205	91	50	6	1	—	—	—	7	242	53	5.3	513	16,400	.04	.25	.6	29
Squash, cooked:																		
Summer (all varieties), diced, drained — 1 cup	210	96	30	2	Trace	—	—	—	7	53	53	.8	296	820	.11	.17	1.7	21
Winter (all varieties), baked, mashed — 1 cup	205	81	130	4	1	—	—	—	32	57	98	1.6	945	8,610	.10	.27	1.4	27
Sweetpotatoes:																		
Cooked (raw, 5 by 2 in; about 2 1/2 per lb.): Baked in skin, peeled — 1 potato	114	64	160	2	1	—	—	—	37	46	66	1.0	342	9,230	.10	.08	.8	25
Boiled in skin, peeled — 1 potato	151	71	170	3	1	—	—	—	40	48	71	1.1	367	11,940	.14	.09	.9	26
Candied, 2 1/2 by 2-in piece — 1 piece	105	60	175	1	3	2.0	.8	.1	36	39	45	.9	200	6,620	.06	.04	.4	11
Canned: Solid pack (mashed) — 1 cup	255	72	275	5	1	—	—	—	63	64	105	2.0	510	19,890	.13	.10	1.5	36
Vacuum pack, piece 2 3/4 by 1 in. — 1 piece	40	72	45	1	Trace	—	—	—	10	10	16	.3	80	3,120	.02	.02	.2	6
Tomatoes:																		
Raw, 2 3/5-in diam. (3 per 12 oz pkg.) — 1 tomato[66]	135	94	25	1	Trace	—	—	—	6	16	33	.6	300	1,110	.07	.05	.9	[67]28
Canned, solids and liquid — 1 cup	241	94	50	2	Trace	—	—	—	10	[68]14	46	1.2	523	2,170	.12	.07	1.7	41
Tomato catsup — 1 cup	273	69	290	5	1	—	—	—	69	60	137	2.2	991	3,820	.25	.19	4.4	41
Tomato catsup — 1 tbsp	15	69	15	Trace	Trace	—	—	—	4	3	8	.1	54	210	.01	.01	.2	2
Tomato juice, canned:																		
Cup — 1 cup	243	94	45	2	Trace	—	—	—	10	17	44	2.2	552	1,940	.12	.07	1.9	39
Glass (6 fl oz) — 1 glass	182	94	35	2	Trace	—	—	—	8	13	33	1.6	413	1,460	.09	.05	1.5	35
Turnips, cooked, diced — 1 cup	155	94	35	1	Trace	—	—	—	8	54	37	.6	291	Trace	.06	.08	.5	34
Turnip greens, cooked, drained:																		
From raw (leaves and stems) — 1 cup	145	94	30	3	Trace	—	—	—	6	252	49	1.5		8,270	.15	.33	.7	68
From frozen (chopped) — 1 cup	165	93	40	4	Trace	—	—	—	5	195	64	2.6	246	11,390	.08	.15	.7	31
Vegetables, mixed, frozen, cooked — 1 cup	182	83	115	6	1	—	—	—	24	46	115	2.4	348	9,010	.22	.13	2.0	15

[63] Weight includes refuse of outer leaves and core. Without these parts, weight is 163 g.

[64] Weight includes core. Without core, weight is 539 g.

[65] Value based on white-fleshed varieties. For yellow-fleshed varieties, value in International Units (I.U.) is 70 for item 633, 50 for item 634, and 80 for item 635.

[66] Weight includes cores and stem ends. Without these parts, weight is 123 g.

[67] Based on year-round average. For tomatoes marketed from November through May, value is about 12 mg; from June through October, 32 mg.

[68] Applies to product without calcium salts added. Value for products with calcium salts added may be as much as 63 mg for whole tomatoes, 241 mg for cut forms.

Vegetable Composition, Part II

Composition of the edible portion (EP) and refuse in fresh vegetables as purchased (AP)

Commodity and Description	Water	Protein	Fat	Carbohydrate Total (by dif.)	Fiber	Ash	Calories (per 100 g)	Notes	Refuse in A.P. (%)
		(Percent of edible portion)							
Tomatoes (*Lycopersicon esculentum*)	93.8	1.1	0.3	4.2	0.6	0.6	20		3
Roots, bulbs, and tubers									
Beets, common red (*Beta vulgaris*)	87.6	1.8	0.1	9.5	1.0	1.0	42	Refuse: A.P. without tops[1]	26
Jerusalem artichokes (*Helianthus tuberosus*)	80	2.2	0.1	16.5	0.8	1.2	70		30
Leeks and green onions (*Allium porrum, A. odorum, A. cepa*)	87.8	1.8	0.2	9.4	1.2	0.8	43		53
Oca (*Oxalis tuberosa*)	83.4	2.1	0.8	12.7	—	1.0	61		10
Onions, mature (*Allium cepa*)	88.8	1.4	0.2	9.0	0.8	0.6	40		7
Parsnips (*Pastinaca sativa*)	79.4	1.6	0.4	17.6	1.7	1.0	75		35
Radishes, common, small (*Raphanus sativus*)	93.7	1.1	0.1	4.2	0.7	0.9	20	Refuse: A.P. with tops	44
Radishes, large rooted (daikon) (*R. sativus*)	93.7	1.1	0.1	4.2	0.7	0.9	20	Refuse: A.P. without tops	5
Salsify and black salsify (*Tragopogon porrifolius, Scorzonera hispanica*)	79.0	3.2	0.6	16.4	1.8	0.8	77		23
Turnips and rutabagas or swedes (*Brassica rapa, B. campestris*)	91.3	1.1	0.1	6.8	1.1	0.7	80	Refuse: A.P. without tops[2]	5
Green and yellow vegetables									
Asparagus (*Asparagus officinalis*)	92.9	2.1	0.2	4.1	0.8	0.7	21		33
Beans, broad or fava (*Vicia faba*)	77.3	7.1	0.4	14.0	2.7	1.2	71		68
Beans, lima (*Phaseolus lunatus macrocarpus*)	66.3	7.5	0.9	23.6	1.4	1.7	110		61
Beans, snap or string, young in pods (haricots) (*P. vulgaris*)	89.1	2.4	0.2	7.6	1.5	0.7	35		9
Beet greens (*Beta vulgaris*)	89.8	2.1	0.5	6.5	1.5	2.1	29		(20)
Broccoli (*Brassica oleracea botrytis*)	85.7	4.3	0.3	8.7	1.3	1.0	44		42
Brussels sprouts (*B. oleracea gemmifera*)	84.8	4.7	0.5	8.7	1.2	1.3	47		24
Cabbage, Chinese (*B. chinensis and B. pekinensis*)	95	1.4	0.1	2.6	0.6	0.9	14		21
Cabbage, common, headed (*B. oleracea capitata*)	91.8	1.6	0.1	5.7	1.0	0.8	25		31
Carrots (*Daucus carota*)	88.6	1.1	0.2	9.1	1.0	1.0	40	Refuse: A.P. without tops[3]	8
Chard, silver beet (*Beta vulgaris*)	91.4	1.9	0.3	4.3	0.7	2.1	22		(20)
Chicory and endive (*Cichorium intybus, C. endivia*)	93.1	1.7	0.2	4.1	0.9	0.9	20		38
Dandelion greens (*Leontodon taraxacum*)	85.7	2.7	0.7	8.9	1.8	2.0	44		(10)

(Continued)

Vegetable Composition, Part II *(Continued)*

TABLE 2.V.9 *(Continued)*

Commodity and Description	Water	Protein	Fat	Carbohydrate Total (by dif.)	Fiber	Ash	Calories (per 100 g)	Notes	Refuse in A.P. (%)
		(Percent of edible portion)							
Ipomoea greens (*Ipomoea* spp.)	89.5	2.7	0.3	6.1	2.2	1.4	31		10
Kale (*Brassica oleracea acephala*)	85.9	3.9	0.6	7.8	1.3	1.8	42		37
Lettuce (*Lactuca sativa*)	94.8	1.3	0.2	2.8	0.6	0.9	15		31
Mustard greens (*Brassica juncea, B. lepidum*)	92.2	2.2	0.3	4.1	0.8	1.2	23		17
Peas, fresh (*Pisum sativum*)	75.0	6.7	0.4	17.0	0.2	0.9	80		56
Peas, edible-podded (*P. sativum*)	84.9	3.4	0.2	10.6	1.2	0.9	48		(9)
Peppers (*Capsicum annuum*), green	92.8	1.2	0.2	5.3	1.4	0.5	24	} Includes chilies	18
Peppers, red	89.5	1.5	0.3	8.0	1.5	0.7	36		18
Peppers, unspecified	91.2	1.4	0.3	6.5	1.4	0.6	29		18
Spinach (*Spinacia oleracea*)	92.1	2.2	0.3	3.9	0.7	1.5	22		19
Turnip and rutabaga tops (*Brassica rapa, B. campestris*)	89.3	3.1	0.4	5.4	1.2	1.8	30		25
Other vegetables									
Artichokes, French or globe (*Cynara scolymus*)	83.7	3	0.2	11.8	1.9	1.3	51		53
Cauliflower (*Brassica oleracea botrytis*)	91.5	2.4	0.2	5.0	1.0	0.9	25		47
Celery (*Celeri graveolens*)	93.3	1.1	0.2	4.3	0.9	1.1	20		38
Cucumbers (*Cucumis sativus*)	95.6	0.8	0.1	3.0	0.6	0.5	13		28
Eggplant (*Solanum melongena*)	92.7	1.2	0.2	5.4	0.9	0.5	24		18
Kohlrabi (*Brassica oleracea gongylodes*)	90.5	2.1	0.2	6.2	1.1	1.0	29		48
Maize (corn), green (*Zea mays*)	73.9	3.4	1.2	20.7	1.0	0.7	92		62
Pumpkins, squashes and gourds, mature (*Cucurbitaceae*, mainly *Cucurbita* spp.)	89.9	1.3	0.3	7.7	1.2	0.8	33	Winter types, squash, pumpkin	32
Pumpkins, squashes and gourds, immature (*Cucurbitaceae*, mainly *Cucurbita* spp.)	95	0.8	0.1	3.5	0.6	0.6	15	Summer squashes, vegetable marrow, zucchini, etc.	17
Unspecified fresh vegetables	91.3	1.8	0.2	5.8	1.0	0.9	27	Weighted average[4]	21

[1] Refuse, as purchased with tops is 48%.
[2] Refuse as purchased with tops is 35%.
[3] Refuse, as purchased with tops is 31%.
[4] Average of the kinds important in consumption; these figures are to be applied only when no information is available on each kind. In developing the averages for these values, the weights assigned to the groups were approximately as follows, in terms of the edible portion: tomatoes, 10%; roots, bulbs, and tubers, 16%; green and yellow, 56%; other vegetables, 18%.

Source: Chatfield, C. *Food Composition Tables for International Use.* Food and Agriculture Organization, United Nations, Rome.

Vegetable Cooking, Frozen

TABLE 2.V.10
Frozen vegetable cooking time chart[1]

Vegetable	In Open Kettle After Water Returns to Boiling Point	Vegetable	In Open Kettle After Water Returns to Boiling Point
	Min		Min
Asparagus, cuts and tips	5–8	Kale	20–25
Asparagus, spears	8–10	Kohlrabi	8–10
Beans, green, cut	12–15	Mixed vegetables	15–20
Beans, green, Frenched	8–10	Mushrooms (sauté—do	
Beans, lima, Fordhook	12–16	not cook in water)	10–15
Beans, lima, bush	16–20	Mustard greens	12–15
Beans, wax, cut	12–15	Okra	10–20
Beets, whole	18–20	Peas	6–8
Beets, cubed or sliced	Heat to serve	Peas and carrots	5–10
Beet greens	10–12	Rhubarb	10–12
Broccoli, chopped	4–6	Spinach, chopped	3–4
Broccoli	5–7	Spinach	4–6
Brussels sprouts	5–7	Succotash	8–10
Carrots	5–10	Squash, summer	10–12
Cauliflower	5–8	Squash, winter	Heat to serve
Corn, kernel	3–4	Swiss chard	8–10
Corn on the cob		Turnips	8–10
(defrost completely)	3–4	Turnip greens	15–20

[1] This information is based on retail size cartons and the approximate cooking times may vary with the maturity, size, and quality of the product.

Source: Tressler, D. K., and Evers, C. F. *The Freezing Preservation of Foods*, 3rd Edition, Vol. 1. AVI Publishing Co., Westport, Connecticut.

Vegetable Frozen Yield

TABLE 2.V.11
Approximate yield of frozen vegetables from fresh

VEGETABLE	FRESH, AS PURCHASED OR PICKED	FROZEN
Asparagus	1 crate (12 2-lb. bunches)	15 to 22 pt.
	1 to 1½ lb.	1 pt.
Beans, lima (in pods)	1 bu. (32 lb.)	12 to 16 pt.
	2 to 2½ lb.	1 pt.
Beans, snap, green, and wax	1 bu. (30 lb.)	30 to 45 pt.
	⅔ to 1 lb.	1 pt.
Beet greens	15 lb.	10 to 15 pt.
	1 to 1½ lb.	1 pt.
Beets (without tops)	1 bu. (52 lb.)	35 to 42 pt.
	1¼ to 1½ lb.	1 pt.
Broccoli	1 crate (25 lb.)	24 pt.
	1 lb.	1 pt.
Brussels sprouts	4 quart boxes	6 pt.
	1 lb.	1 pt.
Carrots (without tops)	1 bu. (50 lb.)	32 to 40 pt.
	1¼ to 1½ lb.	1 pt.
Cauliflower	2 medium heads	3 pt.
	1⅓ lb.	1 pt.
Chard	1 bu. (12 lb.)	8 to 12 pt.
	1 to 1½ lb.	1 pt.
Collards	1 bu. (12 lb.)	8 to 12 pt.
	1 to 1½ lb.	1 pt.
Corn, sweet (in husks)	1 bu. (35 lb.)	14 to 17 pt.
	2 to 2½ lb.	1 pt.
Kale	1 bu. (18 lb.)	12 to 18 pt.
	1 to 1½ lb.	1 pt.
Mustard greens	1 bu. (12 lb.)	8 to 12 pt.
	1 to 1½ lb.	1 pt.
Peas	1 bu. (30 lb.)	12 to 15 pt.
	2 to 2½ lb.	1 pt.
Peppers, sweet	⅔ lb. (3 peppers)	1 pt.
Pumpkin	3 lb.	2 pt.
Spinach	1 bu. (18 lb.)	12 to 18 pt.
	1 to 1½ lb.	1 pt.
Squash, summer	1 bu. (40 lb.)	32 to 40 pt.
	1 to 1¼ lb.	1 pt.
Squash, winter	3 lb.	2 pt.
Sweetpotatoes	⅔ lb.	1 pt.

Source: USDA (1976). Home freezing of fruits and vegetables. USDA Home and Garden Bull. 10.

Vegetable Planting and Maturity Chart

TABLE 2.V.12

Vegetables	Plants or seed per 100 feet	Spacing (Inches) Rows	Spacing (Inches) Plants	Number days ready for use
Asparagus	66 plants or 1 oz.	36–48	18	(2 years)
Beans, snap bush	½ lb.	24–36	3–4	45–60
Beans, snap pole	½ lb.	36–48	4–6	60–70
Beans, Lima bush	½ lb.	30–36	3–4	65–80
Beans, Lima pole	¼ lb.	36–48	12–18	75–85
Beets	1 oz.	15–24	2	50–60
Broccoli	* 40–50 pl. or ¼ oz.	24–36	14–24	60–80
Brussels sprouts	* 50–60 pl. or ¼ oz.	24–36	14–24	90–100
Cabbage	* 50–60 pl. or ¼ oz.	24–36	14–24	60–90
Cabbage, Chinese	* 60–70 pl. or ¼ oz.	18–30	8–12	65–70
Carrots	½ oz.	15–24	2	70–80
Cauliflower	* 50–60 pl. or ¼ oz.	24–36	14–24	70–90
Celeriac	200 pl.	18–24	4–8	120
Celery	200 pl.	30–36		125
Chard, Swiss	2 oz.	18–30	6	45–55
Collards and kale	¼ oz.	18–36	8–16	50–80
Corn, sweet	3–4 oz.	24–36	12–18	70–90
Cucumbers	½ oz.	48–72	24–48	50–70
Eggplant	⅛ oz.	24–36	18–24	80–90
Garlic (cloves)	1 lb.	15–24	2–4	140–150
Kohlrabi	½ oz.	15–24	4–6	55–75
Lettuce, head	¼ oz.	18–24	6–10	70–75
Lettuce, leaf	¼ oz.	15–18	2–3	40–50
Muskmelon (cantaloupe)	* 50 pl. or ½ oz.	60–96	24–36	85–100
Mustard	¼ oz.	15–24	6–12	30–40
Okra	2 oz.	36–42	12–24	55–65
Onions	400–600 plants or sets	15–24	3–4	80–120
Onions (seed)	1 oz.	15–24	3–4	90–120
Parsley	¼ oz.	15–24	6–8	70–90
Parsnips	½ oz.	18–30	3–4	120–170
Peas, English	1 lb.	18–36	1	55–90
Peas, southern	½ lb.	24–36	4–6	60–70
Peppers	⅛ oz.	24–36	18–24	60–90
Potatoes, Irish	6–10 lb. of seed tubers	30–36	10–15	75–100
Potatoes, sweet	75–100 pl.	36–48	12–16	100–130
Pumpkins	½ oz.	60–96	36–48	75–100
Radishes	1 oz.	14–24	1	25–40
Salsify	½ oz.	15–18	3–4	150
Soybeans	1 lb.	24–30	2	120
Spinach	1 oz.	14–24	3–4	40–60
Squash, summer	1 oz.	36–60	18–36	50–60
Squash, winter	½ oz.	60–96	24–48	85–100
Tomatoes	50 pl. or ⅛ oz.	24–48	18–36	70–90
Turnip greens	½ oz.	14–24	2–3	30
Turnip, roots	½ oz.	14–24	2–3	30–60
Watermelon	1 oz.	72–96	36–72	80–100

* Transplants

Source: USDA (1977). Growing your own vegetables. USDA Agricultural Information Bull. *409.*

Vegetable Planting Chart

TABLE 2.V.13

Crop	Depth to plant (inches)	Planting distances	
		Between rows (inches)	In the row (inches)
Cool Season Crops			
Asparagus (crowns)	6–8	36–60	12–18
Beets	1/4–1/2	15–24	2–3
Broccoli	1/4–1/2	24–36	12–18
Brussels sprouts	1/4–1/2	24–36	18–24
Cabbage	1/4–1/2	24–36	12–18
Cabbage, Chinese	1/4–1/2	18–30	8–12
Carrots	1/4–1/2	15–30	2–3
Cauliflower	1/4–1/2	24–36	18–24
Celery	1/8	18–36	4–6
Chard, Swiss	1/4–1/2	18–36	6–8
Chives	1/2	15–24	6–8
Collards	1/4–1/2	24–36	18–24
Cress, upland	1/4–1/2	15–30	2–3
Endive	1/4–1/2	18–36	12
Garlic (cloves)	1 1/2	18–24	3
Kale	1/4–1/2	18–36	8–12
Kohlrabi	1/4–1/2	18–36	4–6
Leeks	1/2	12–30	2–3
Lettuce, heading	1/4	18–30	12
Lettuce, leaf	1/4	12–18	4–6
Mustard	1/4–1/2	18–24	3–4
Onions, plants		15–24	3–4
Onions, seed	1/2	15–24	3–4
Onions, sets	1–2	15–24	3–4
Parsley	1/4	15–24	6–8
Parsnips	1/2	18–30	3–4
Peas	1–2	8–24	1
Potatoes	4	30–36	12
Radishes	1/2	12–24	1
Rhubarb, crowns		36–48	36–48
Rutabagas	1/4–1/2	18–30	3–4
Spinach	1/2	12–24	2–4
Turnips	1/4–1/2	18–30	2–3
Warm Season Crops			
Beans, lima	1–1 1/2	24–36	3–4
Beans, snap	1–1 1/2	24–36	1–2
Cantaloupes	1	48–72	24–30
Cucumbers	1	48–60	12–18
Eggplant	1/4	30–42	18–24
Okra	1	36–48	12–18
Peas, southern	1	24–36	4
Peppers	1/4	30–42	18–24
Pumpkins	1	60–96	36–48
Spinach, New Zealand	1/2–1	30–42	15–18
Squash, summer	1–1 1/2	48–60	18–24
Squash, winter	1–1 1/2	60–96	36–48
Sweet corn	1–2	30–36	10–12
Sweet potatoes		30–36	12–15
Tomatoes	1/4	36–60	18–24
Watermelons	1–1 1/2	60–96	36–60

Source: USDA (1977). Growing your own vegetables. USDA Agricultural Information Bull. *409.*

Vegetable Plants

TABLE 2.V.14
Habits and characteristics of vegetable plants

Common and Latin names	Plant habit[1]	Approximate seeds per ounce	Germination Time	At temperature	Notable characteristic or requirement
		Number	Days	Degrees F.	
Artichoke—*Cynara scolymus*........	P	700	7–21	68–86	Tolerates cool soil.
Asparagus—*Asparagus officinalis*....	P	700	7–21	68–86	Do.
Asparagusbean—*Vigna sesquipedalis*.	A	225	5–8	68–86	Requires warm soil.
Beans:					
Garden—*Phaseolus vulgaris*....	A	100–125	5–8	68–86	Do.
Dry edible—*Phaseolus vulgaris*..	A	100–125	5–8	68–86	Do.
Lima—*Phaseolus lunatus*.......	A	25–75	5–9	68–86	Do.
Runner—*Phaseolus coccineus*....	A	25–30	5–9	68–86	Do.
Beet—*Beta vulgaris*..............	B	1,600	3–14	68–86	Tolerates cool soil.
Broadbean—*Vicia faba*...........	A	20–50	4–14	68–86	Do.
Broccoli—*Brassica oleracea* var. *botrytis*.	A–B	9,000	3–10	68–86	Do.
Brussels sprouts—*Brassica oleracea* var. *gemmifera*.	B	9,000	3–10	68–86	Do.
Cabbage—*Brassica oleracea* var. *capitata*.	B	9,000	3–10	68–86	Do.
Cabbage, Chinese—*Brassica pekinensis*.	A–B	18,000	3–7	68–86	Do.
Cardoon—*Cynara cardunculus*.......	P	700	7–21	68–86	Do.
Carrot—*Daucus carota*............	B	23,000	6–21	68–86	Do.
Cauliflower—*Brassica oleracea* var. *botrytis*.	A–B	9,000	3–10	68–86	Do.
Celeriac—*Apium graveolens* var. *rapaceum*.	B	72,000	10–21	50–68	Requires cool soil.
Celery—*Apium graveolens* var. *dulce*..	B	72,000	10–21	50–68	Requires cool soil.
Chard, Swiss—*Beta vulgaris* var. *cicla*.	B	1,600	3–14	68–86	Tolerates cool soil.
Chicory—*Cichorium intybus*........	P	27,000	5–14	68–86	Do.
Citron—*Citrullus vulgaris*..........	A	300	7–14	68–86	Requires warm soil.
Collards—*Brassica oleracea* var. *acephala*.	B	9,000	3–10	68–86	Tolerates cool soil.
Corn, sweet—*Zea mays*...........	A	120–180	4–7	68–86	Requires warm soil.
Cornsalad (fetticus)—*Valerianella locusta* var. *olitoria*.	A–B	....	7–28	68	Tolerates cool soil.
Cowpea (southern pea)—*Vigna sinensis*.	A	225	5–8	68–86	Requires warm soil.
Cress:					
Garden—*Lepidium sativum*.....	A	12,000	4–10	68	Light sensitive.
Water—*Rorippa nasturtium-aquaticum*.	P	150,000	4–14	68–86	Tolerates cool soil.
Cucumber—*Cucumis sativus*........	A	1,100	3–7	68–86	Requires warm soil.
Dandelion—*Taraxacum officinale*....	B–P	35,000	7–21	68–86	Tolerates cool soil.
Eggplant—*Solanum melongena* var. *esculentum*.	A	6,500	7–14	68–86	Requires warm soil.
Endive—*Cichorium endivia*........	A–B	27,000	5–14	68–86	Tolerates cool soil.
Kale—*Brassica oleracea* var. *acephala*.	B	9,000	3–10	68–86	Do.
Kale, Chinese—*Brassica oleracea* var. *alboglabra*.	B	9,000	3–10	68–86	Do.
Kohlrabi—*Brassica oleracea* var. *gongylodes*.	B	9,000	3–10	68–86	Do.
Leek—*Allium porrum*............	B	11,000	6–14	68	Requires cool soil.

(Continued)

Vegetable Plants   (Continued)

TABLE 2.V.14   (Continued)

Common and Latin names	Plant habit [1]	Approximate seeds per ounce	Germination Time	Germination At temperature	Notable characteristic or requirement
		Number	Days	Degrees F.	
Lettuce—*Lactuca sativa*	A	25,000	7	68	Requires cool soil. Some varieties light sensitive.
Muskmelon (including cantaloup)— *Cucumis melo.*	A	1,300	4–10	68–86	Requires warm soil.
Mustard—*Brassica juncea*	A	18,000	3–7	68–86	Tolerates cool soil.
Mustard, spinach—*Brassica perviridis.*	A	15,000	3–7	68–86	Do.
Okra—*Hibiscus esculentus*	A	500	4–14	68–86	Requires warm soil.
Onion—*Allium cepa*	B	9,500	6–10	68	Requires cool soil.
Onion, Welsh—*Allium fistulosum* . . .	B	. . . .	6–12	68	Do.
Pak-choi—*Brassica chinensis*	A–B	18,000	3–7	68–86	Tolerates cool soil.
Parsley—*Petroselinum hortense (P. crispum).*	B	18,500	11–28	68–86	Do.
Parsnip—*Pastinaca sativa*	B	12,000	6–28	68–86	Do.
Pea—*Pisum sativum*	A	90–175	5–8	68	Requires cool soil.
Pepper—*Capsicum* spp	A	4,500	6–14	68–86	Requires warm soil.
Potato—*Solanum tuberosum*	P	. . . .	. . . . .	68	Tolerates cool soil.
Pumpkin—*Cucurbita pepo*	A	100–300	4–7	68–86	Requires warm soil.
Radish—*Raphanus sativus*	A	2–4,000	4–6	68	Requires cool soil.
Rhubarb—*Rheum rhaponticum*	P	1,700	7–21	68–86	Tolerates cool soil.
Rutabaga—*Brassica napus* var. *napobrassica.*	B	12,000	3–14	68–86	Do.
Salsify—*Tragopogon porrifolius*	B	1,900	5–10	68	Requires cool soil.
Sorrel—*Rumex acetosa*	P	30,000	3–14	68–86	Tolerates cool soil.
Soybean—*Glycine max*	A	175–350	5–8	68–86	Requires warm soil.
Spinach—*Spinacea oleracea*	A	2,800	7–21	59	Requires cool soil.
Spinach, New Zealand—*Tetragonia expansa.*	A	350	5–28	50–86	Germinates irregularly.
Sweetpotato—*Ipomoea batatas*	P	. . . .	. . . . .	77	Break or remove seedcoat.
Squash—*Cucurbita moschata* and *C. maxima.*	A	200–400	4–7	68–86	Requires warm soil.
Tomato—*Lycopersicon esculentum*	A	11,500	5–14	68–86	Do.
Tomato, husk—*Physalis pubescens* . . .	A	35,000	7–28	68–86	Do.
Turnip—*Brassica rapa*	B	15,000	3–7	68–86	Tolerates cool soil.
Watermelon—*Citrullus vulgaris*	A	200–300	4–14	68–86	Requires warm soil.

[1] This column shows the nature of the parent plant—whether it is an annual, a biennial, or a perennial species: A—annual, B—biennial, P—perennial. Plants shown as A-B or B-P may exhibit either of two kinds of behavior, depending on cultural conditions and management.

Source: USDA (1961). Seeds. The Yearbook of Agriculture.

Vegetables, Boiling Time, Frozen

TABLE 2.V.15
Boiling guide for home frozen vegetables

Vegetable	Cooking time after water returns to boil	Approximate amount of frozen vegetable for six servings (½ cup each)
	Minutes	*Ounces*
Asparagus, whole	8 to 10	24
Beans, lima	12 to 14	18
Beans, snap (green or wax), cut	7 to 9	16
Broccoli spears	6 to 8	22
Brussels sprouts	10 to 12	20
Carrots:		
Slices	6 to 8	18
Strips	7 to 9	18
Cauliflower	2 to 6	20
Corn:		
Whole kernel	7 to 9	20
On cob	4 to 8	32
Kale	8 to 10	25
Okra, whole	6 to 8	16
Peas	8 to 10	18
Spinach	2 to 6	25
Squash, summer, sliced	6 to 8	22

Source: USDA (1980). Vegetables in family meals. USDA Home and Garden Bull. *105*.

Vegetables, Canned Grades

| U.S. Grade A
or
Fancy | Grade A vegetables are carefully selected for color, tenderness, and freedom from blemishes. They are the most tender, succulent, and flavorful vegetables produced. |

U.S. Grade A
or
Fancy — Grade A vegetables are carefully selected for color, tenderness, and freedom from blemishes. They are the most tender, succulent, and flavorful vegetables produced.

U.S. Grade B
or
Extra Standard — Grade B vegetables are of excellent quality but not quite so well selected for color and tenderness as Grade A. They are usually slightly more mature and therefore have a slightly different taste than the more succulent vegetables in Grade A.

U.S. Grade C
or
Standard — Grade C vegetables are not so uniform in color and flavor as vegetables in the higher grades and they are usually more mature. They are a thrifty buy when appearance is not too important—for instance, if you're using the vegetables as an ingredient in soup or souffle.

Packed under continuous inspection of the U.S. Department of Agriculture — This statement may be given along with the grade name or it may be shown by itself. It provides assurance of a wholesome product of at least minimum quality.

The grade names and the statement, "Packed under continuous inspection of the U.S. Department of Agriculture," may also appear within shields.

FIGURE 2.V.3

Source: USDA (1977). Vegetables in family meals. USDA Home and Garden Bull. *105.*

Vegetables, Canning Dates

TABLE 2.V.16
Opening and closing canning dates

States and territories	Arti-chokes	Aspara-gus	Beans		Beets	Corn	Carrots	Kraut	Okra	Peas
			Lima	Snap						
Alabama				May 1–July 10 Oct. 1–Oct. 30					May 1 Sept. 1	
Arkansas			July 1 Nov. 15	May 5–July 5 Oct. 1–Nov. 15		July 1 July 31			June 1 Sept. 1	
California	Feb. 1 Apr. 30	Apr. 1 June 30	Sept. 1 Oct. 31	Aug. 1 Oct. 15	May 5 Dec. 20					Apr. 10 June 30
Colorado				July 15 Oct. 1	Aug. 1 Oct. 15			All year		June 15 Aug. 1
Delaware		Apr. 25 June 30	Aug. 5 Sept. 30	June 20–July 20 Sept. 5–Sept. 30		July 25 Sept. 15				May 25 June 20
Florida				Jan. 1–May 15 Nov. 1–Dec. 15						
Georgia				May 1–June 15 Aug. 20–Sept. 15					May 15 Sept. 1	
Idaho						Aug. 1 Sept. 15				June 1 July 20
Illinois		Apr. 20 June 25	Aug. 15 Sept. 30	July 5 Sept. 30		Aug. 1 Sept. 25				June 3 July 30
Indiana				July 1 Oct. 15		Aug. 1 Sept. 30		All year		June 1 July 30
Iowa		Apr. 25 June 25				Aug. 1 Oct. 1				June 10 July 15
Kentucky				June 1–July 15 Sept. 15–Oct. 15		June 1 July 15				
Louisiana						Aug. 20 Oct. 15		All year	May 1 Sept. 1	
Maine				Aug. 1–Sept. 15						
Maryland		Apr. 20 June 30	Aug. 5 Oct. 10	June 15 July 15	June 1 July 15	July 20 Sept. 15		All year		July 1 Aug. 30
Michigan		May 10 July 1	Sept. 1 Sept. 30	July 10 Sept. 15	Aug. 1 Nov. 20	Aug. 10 Sept. 20	Oct. 1 Nov. 25	All year		May 20 July 15
Minnesota		May 1 July 1	Aug. 15 Sept. 30	July 20 Sept. 20	July 20 Nov. 30	Aug. 5 Sept. 1				June 15 Aug. 15
Mississippi				May 1–July 31 Oct. 1–Nov. 1					May 1 Sept. 1	June 15 Aug. 1

(Continued)

Vegetables, Canning Dates (Continued)

TABLE 2.V.16 (Continued)

States and territories	Arti-chokes	Aspara-gus	Beans — Lima	Beans — Snap	Beets	Corn	Carrots	Kraut	Okra	Peas
Missouri				June 15 / Oct. 15						
Nebraska				July 10–Oct. 1		Aug. 10 / Oct. 1				May 20 / July 10
New Jersey		Apr. 20 / July 1	Aug. 1 / Oct. 1	July 1 / Oct. 1					Aug. 20 / Oct. 1	June 20 / Aug. 1
New York		May 10 / July 15		July 5 / Sept. 25	Aug. 1 / Dec. 31	Aug. 10 / Sept. 20	Sept. 15 / Dec. 31	All year		
North Carolina				June 1–July 10					June 1 / Sept. 15	
Ohio		May 5 / July 25		July 25 / Sept. 5	July 20 / Nov. 30	Aug. 1 / Sept. 25		All year		May 28 / Aug. 1
Oklahoma				May 15–July 10, Oct. 1–Nov. 15						
Oregon		Apr. 15 / July 1		Aug. 1 / Sept. 5	July 1 / Oct. 15	Aug. 15 / Sept. 30	Aug. 20 / Oct. 15	All year		June 10 / Aug. 20
Pennsylvania			July 1 / Oct. 1	July 15 / Sept. 20	July 25 / Oct. 1	Aug. 5 / Sept. 20		All year		June 1 / July 25
South Carolina				May 20–Aug. 10, Sept. 15–Oct. 30					June 1 / Sept. 15	Aug. 5 / Sept. 30
Tennessee			Aug. 1 / Sept. 20	July 15 / Sept. 20	July 10 / Aug. 15	July 25 / Aug. 30		All year		May 15 / June 15
Texas				Apr. 1–June 20, Nov. 1–Dec. 15	Nov. 15 / May 15		Nov. 15 / May 15			
Utah			Aug. 5 / Oct. 1	July 10 / Oct. 15	June 1 / Oct. 15	Aug. 15 / Sept. 25	Aug. 15 / Oct. 15	All year		June 10 / Aug. 10
Virginia			Aug. 1 / Oct. 10	June 10–July 15						May 15 / June 5
Washington		May 1 / July 1		Aug. 1 / Sept. 5	July 1 / Oct. 15	Aug. 15 / Sept. 30	Aug. 20 / Oct. 15	All year		June 10
Wisconsin			Aug. 20 / Sept. 20	July 10 / Oct. 1	July 20 / Nov. 30	Aug. 1 / Oct. 1	July 25 / Nov. 30	All year		June 10 / Aug. 20
Ontario, Canada		May 5 / June 30		July 15 / Sept. 25	Aug. 1 / Mar. 1	Aug. 10 / Oct. 1	Oct. 1 / Jan. 15	All year		June 25 / Aug. 20
Quebec, Canada				June 25 / Sept. 25	Oct. 1	Aug. 25 / Oct. 10	Oct. 1			July 1 / Aug. 5
Vancouver, B.C.		May 15 / June 15		Aug. 1 / Sept. 30	Dec. 1	Sept. 1 / Oct. 15	Dec. 1			June 20 / Aug. 1

(Continued)

Vegetables, Canning Dates (Continued)

TABLE 2.V.16 (Continued)

States and territories	Pickles	Pimientos	Pumpkin	Rhubarb	Spinach	Sprouts	Squash	Succotash	Sweet Potato	Tomatoes
Alabama		Aug. 1 Nov. 15			Feb. 20–May 30 Oct. 15–Dec. 31				Aug. 1 Feb. 1	Aug. 1–Sept. 15
Arkansas					Feb. 20–May 30 Oct. 15–Dec. 31					Aug. 1–Oct. 20
California	All year	Sept. 15 Dec. 15	Oct. 1 Nov. 15		Feb. 20–Apr. 20 Oct. 1–Dec. 15				Sept. 1 Dec. 31	July 10 Nov. 10
Colorado			Oct. 1 Nov. 15				Oct. 5 Nov. 15			Aug. 15 Oct. 15
Delaware					Nov. 10 Mar. 1		Oct. 1 Nov. 5		Sept. 15 Dec. 1	July 15 Oct. 1
Florida									Aug. 1 Feb. 1	Mar. 1 May 15
Georgia		Aug. 1 Nov. 15								Aug. 1–Feb. 1
Idaho										
Illinois			Sept. 10 Oct. 30							Aug. 1 Oct. 1
Indiana			Sept. 15 Nov. 15					Aug. 20 Sept. 15		Aug. 1 Oct. 15
Iowa				May 20 June 30						Aug. 10 Oct. 15
Kentucky								Aug. 10 Aug. 30		Aug. 1 Oct. 15
Louisiana		Oct. 1 Dec. 1								
Maryland			Oct. 1 Nov. 10		Apr. 1–May 15 Nov. 1–Nov. 30			Aug. 18 Oct. 1	July 20 Mar. 1	July 15 Oct. 15
Michigan	All year		Sept. 10 Oct. 30		June 10–July 1 Sept. 20–Oct. 20		Oct. 1 Nov. 10		Sept. 15 Dec. 1	Aug. 1 Sept. 30
Minnesota	All year		Sept. 10 Oct. 30		May 1 June 15		Sept. 5 Sept. 30			
Missouri									Aug. 15 Feb. 1	Aug. 10 Oct. 20
Nebraska			Oct. 1 Dec. 1							Aug. 1 Oct. 1

Vegetables, Canning Dates (Continued)

TABLE 2.V.16 (Continued)

States and territories	Pickles	Pimientos	Pumpkin	Rhubarb	Spinach	Sprouts	Squash	Succotash	Sweet Potato	Tomatoes
New Jersey			Oct. 1 Nov. 1		Apr. 1–May 31 Oct. 20–Nov. 30		Oct. 1 Nov. 15		Sept. 15 Nov. 15	July 15 Oct. 15
New York	All year	Aug. 10 Sept. 30	Sept. 20 Nov. 15	May 20 June 30	June 5–June 20 Sept. 25–Oct. 10		Sept. 15 Nov. 1	Sept. 1 Oct. 1		Aug. 5 Oct. 5
North Carolina									Sept. 1 Dec. 31	July 10 Sept. 1
Ohio			Sept. 10 Nov. 20							Aug. 1 Oct. 1
Oklahoma					Feb. 20–May 30 Oct. 15–Dec. 31					Aug. 1–Oct. 20
Oregon	All year		Oct. 1 Nov. 30	May 1 June 10			Oct. 10 Nov. 10			Aug. 15 Oct. 1
Pennsylvania								Aug. 20 Sept. 15		Aug. 5 Oct. 5
South Carolina										June 30 Aug. 15
Tennessee		Aug. 15 Nov. 15	Sept. 15 Nov. 15		Mar. 1–June 1 Sept. 15–Oct. 10			Aug. 10 Sept. 10	Sept. 1 Dec. 1	Apr. 25–June 1 Sept. 15–Oct. 10
Texas					Nov. 10 Mar. 20				Oct. 1 Feb. 1	May 15–June 20 Dec. 1–Jan. 15
Utah			Oct. 1 Nov. 15				Oct. 1 Nov. 15			Aug. 15 Oct. 15
Virginia					Apr. 1–May 25 Oct. 25–Nov. 30				Sept. 1 Dec. 15	July 15 Sept. 15
Washington	All year		Oct. 1 Nov. 30	May 1 June 10	Sept. 1 Oct. 15		Oct. 10 Nov. 10			Aug. 15 Oct. 1
West Virginia										Aug. 1 Sept. 30
Wisconsin	All year		Sept. 10 Nov. 20	May 10 May 30	June 1–June 20		Sept. 10 Nov. 20			Aug. 10 Oct. 10
Ontario, Canada			Oct. 1 Nov. 15	May 25 June 30	May 25–June 20 Sept. 20–Oct. 18					Aug. 10 Oct. 15
Quebec, Canada			Oct. 1 Oct. 15							Aug. 15 Oct. 10
Vancouver, B.C.			Oct. 1 Nov. 30	June 1 July 30						Aug. 1 Oct. 15

Source: The Almanac of the Canning, Freezing, Preserving Industries, 61th Edition. (1976). E. E. Judge & Son, Baltimore.

Vegetables, Classification

TABLE 2.V.17
Vegetable classification

Family	Fruit/Vegetable	Scientific Name	Type	Description
			Fruit Vegetables	
Cucurbitaceae	Chayote	*Sechium edule* (Jacq.) Sw.	Pepo	Outer wall is receptacle.
	Cucumber	*Cucumis sativus* L.	Pepo	Flesh of the fruit is mesocarp and endocarp. Derived from inferior ovary.
	Squash	*Cucurbita maxima* Duch.	Pepo	–Ditto–
Malvaceae	Okra	*Hibiscus esculentus* L.	Berry	Fibrous pericarp.
Leguminosae	Cowpea	*Vigna sinensis* (Stickm.) Savi ex Hassk	Legume	Derived from monocarpellary ovary; it splits along both sutures.
	Beans	*Phaseolus* sp. L.	Legume	–Ditto–
	Pea	*Pisum sativum* L.	Legume	–Ditto–
Solanaceae	Eggplant	*Solanum melongena* L. var. *esculentum*	Berry	Thin exocarp; mesocarp and exocarp fused.
	Sweet pepper	*Capsicum frutescens* L. var. *grossum*	Berry	Large internal cavity.
	Tomato	*Lycopersicon esculentum* Mill. var. *commune*	Berry	Seeds embedded in juicy flesh.
			Subterranean Vegetables	
Liliaceae	Garlic	*Allium sativum* L.	Modified skin	Compound bulb made of cloves; 3 kinds of scales.
	Leek	*Allium porum* L.	Leaves	Swollen, blanched bases but not a distinct bulb.
	Onion	*Allium cepa* L.	Bulb	Short stem with overlapping leaf bases, fleshy leaves.
Chenopodiaceae	Beet	*Beta vulgaris* L.	Storage root	Pigmented tissue.

(Continued)

Vegetables, Classification   (Continued)

TABLE 2.V.17   (Continued)

Family	Fruit/ Vegetable	Scientific Name	Type	Description
		Subterranean Vegetables		
Cruciferae	Radish	*Raphanus sativus* L.	Storage root	Fleshy root, porous when aged.
	Turnip	*Brassica rapa* L. var. *rapifera* Metz.	Modified root	Top-like organ.
Convolvulaceae	Sweet Potato	*Ipomoea batatas* (L.) Poir.	Root	Texture more rough than Irish potato.
Umbelliferae	Carrot	*Daucus carota* L. var. *sativa*	Modified root	Pigmented flesh.
Zingiberaceae	Ginger	*Zingiber officinale*	Rhizome	Bulky, underground, horizontal stem.
Solanaceae	Irish Potato	*Solanum tuberosum* L.	Tuber	Bulky, short terminal portion of stem.
		Leafy Vegetables (Including flower and stem)		
Liliaceae	Asparagus	*Asparagus officinalis* L. var. *altilis*	Stem	Fleshy shoot with spirally arranged scales.
Umbelliferae	Celery	*Apium graveolens* L. var. *dulce*	Leaf	Ridged petioles and compound leaves with 3 to 7 leaflets.
	Parsley	*Petroselinum crispum* (Mill.) Nym.	Stem and leaf	Lobed and curled leaves, pinnately compound.
Compositae	Lettuce	*Lactuca sativa* L.	Leaf	Curly tips.
Cruciferae	Brussels sprouts	*Brassica oleracea* var. *gemmifera*	Buds	Adventitious side shoots.
	Cabbage	*Brassica oleracea* var. *capitata*	Staminal bulb	Forms a head.
	Cauliflower	*Brassica oleracea* var. *botrytis* DC	Curd	Consists of short internodes, branched apices and bracts.
	Kohlrabi	*Brassica caulorapa*	Stem	Globular stem, thin rind.
	Mustard	*Brassica juncea* Coss.	Leaf	Leaves with notched margin and crepe-like surface.
	Petsai	*Brassica pekinensis*	Leaf	Spatulate leaves with broad midrib.

Source: Pantastico, E. B. (editor) (1975). Structure of fruits and vegetables. In *Postharvest Physiology, Handling and Utilization of*

Vegetables, Cooking Frozen

TABLE 2.V.18
Timetable for cooking frozen vegetables in a small amount of water[1]

VEGETABLE	Time to allow after water returns to boil [2] Minutes	VEGETABLE	Time to allow after water returns to boil [2] Minutes
Asparagus	5–10	Chard	8–10
Beans, lima:		Corn:	
Large type	6–10	Whole-kernel	3–5
Baby type	15–20	On-the-cob	3–4
Beans, snap, green, or wax:		Kale	8–12
1-inch pieces	12–18	Kohlrabi	8–10
Julienne	5–10	Mustard greens	8–15
Beans, soybeans, green	10–20	Peas, green	5–10
Beet greens	6–12	Spinach	4–6
Broccoli	5–8	Squash, summer	10–12
Brussels sprouts	4–9	Turnip greens	15–20
Carrots	5–10	Turnips	8–12
Cauliflower	5–8		

[1] Use ½ cup of lightly salted water for each pint of vegetable with these exceptions: Lima beans, 1 cup; corn-on-the-cob, water to cover.

[2] Time required at sea level; slightly longer time is required at higher altitudes.

Source: USDA (1976). Home freezing of fruits and vegetables. USDA Home and Garden Bull. *10*.

Vegetable Servings

TABLE 2.V.19
Approximate servings per can, pound, and package

Fresh vegetables	Servings per lb[1]		
Asparagus	2 or 3	Asparagus	2 or 3
Beans, lima[2]	2	Beans, lima	3 or 4
Beans, snap	5 or 6	Beans, snap	3 or 4
Beets, diced[3]	3 or 4	Broccoli	2 or 3
Broccoli	3 or 4	Brussels sprouts	3
Brussels sprouts	4	Cauliflower	3
Cabbage:		Corn, whole kernel	3
Raw, shredded	9 or 10	Kale	2 or 3
Cooked	4 or 5	Peas	3
Carrots:		Spinach	2 or 3
Raw, diced or shredded[3]	5 or 6		
Cooked[3]	4		
Cauliflower	3		

(Continued)

Vegetable Servings (Continued)

TABLE 2.V.19 (Continued)

Fresh vegetables	Servings per lb[1]		Canned vegetables	Servings per can (1 lb)
Celery:				
Raw, chopped or diced	5 or 6			
Cooked	4			
Kale[4]	5 or 6			
Okra	4 or 5		Most vegetables	3 or 4
Onions, cooked	3 or 4		Greens, such as kale	
Parsnips[3]	4		or spinach	2 or 3
Peas[2]	2			
Potatoes	4			
Spinach[5]	4		Dry vegetables	Servings per lb
Squash, summer	3 or 4			
Squash, winter	2 or 3		Dry beans	11
Sweet potatoes	3 or 4		Dry peas, lentils	10 or 11
Tomatoes, raw, diced or				
sliced	4			

[1]As purchased.
[2]Bought in pod.
[3]Bought without tops.
[4]Bought untrimmed.
[5]Bought prepackaged.

Source: USDA (1978). Nutrition, food at work for you. USDA Home and Garden Bull. *1.*

Vegetables, Panned

TABLE 2.V.20
Guide for cooking panned vegetables (6 servings, $\frac{1}{2}$ cup each)

Vegetable	Amount of—				Cooking time
	Vegetable	Fat	Salt	Water	
	Quarts	Table-spoons	Tea-spoons		Minutes
Beans, snap (green or wax), sliced in 1-inch pieces	1	1½	½	¾ cup	20 to 25.
Cabbage, finely shredded	1½	1½	¾	3 tablespoons	6 to 8.
Carrots, thinly sliced	1	2	½	3 tablespoons	10.
Corn, cut	1	1½	¼	⅓ cup	15 to 18.
Spinach, finely shredded	3	2	¼		6 to 8.
Summer squash, thinly sliced	1	1½	¼	3 tablespoons	12 to 15.

Source: USDA (1980). Vegetables in family meals. USDA Home and Garden Bull. *105.*

Vegetable Storage I

TABLE 2.V.21
Store in cool room, away from bright light

Store in cool room, away from bright light:

Onions, mature	Rutabagas	Sweetpotatoes
Potatoes	Squash, winter	

Refrigerate, covered:

Asparagus	Cauliflower	Parsnips
Beans, snap or wax	Celery	Peas, shelled
Beets	Corn, husked	Peppers, green
Broccoli	Cucumbers	Radishes
Cabbage	Greens	Squash, summer
Carrots	Onions, green	Turnips

Refrigerate, uncovered:

Beans, lima, in pods	Peas, in pods	Watermelons
Corn, in husks	Pineapples	

Source: USDA (1978). Nutrition, food at work for you. USDA Home and Garden Bull. 1.

Vegetable Storage II

TABLE 2.V.22
Recommended cold storage conditions, heat of respiration, and loss in weight of vegetables grown in the tropics

Vegetables	Temp. °F	Relative Humidity %	Storage Life Wk	Heat Evolution[a] BTU/ton-day	Weight Loss[b] %
Ampalaya	42–45	85–90	3		12.0
Asparagus	32	95	3–4	18,600	
Beans					
Bush sitao	42	88–92	4	6,881	14.0
Lima in pods	40–45	90–95	1.5–2	16,400	12.0
Lima, shelled	40	95	2	14,080	
Dolichos lablab, in pods	32–35	90	3	13,260–14,200	20.3
Snap	38–42	88	2–3	5,600	15.0
Winged	50	90	4	7,116	18.0
Beet, bunched	32	90	1.5	1,170	
Beet, topped	32–35	90–95	8–14	1,000	33.0
Betel leaves	42–45	85–90	1	13,200	2.8
Bitter Gourd	33–35	85–90	4		
Brinjal	47–50	85–90	4	4,400–6,600	17.7
Brussels Sprout	32–35	90–95	4–6		
Cabbage, wet season	32–35	92–95	4–6	3,600	
Cabbage, dry season	32–35	92–95	12	2,000–2,400	10.0
Carrot, bunched	32	90–95	4		25.0
Carrot, topped	32	95	20–24	810	20.0–35.0
Cauliflower, 'Snowball'	32–35	85–95	7	5,200–6,400	30.4
Celery	31–32	92–95	8	700	15.2
Chayote	45	85–90	4–6	1,271	4.9
Colocasia	52–55	85–90	21		
Condol	45	85	8		
Coriander leaves	32–35	90	5		
Corn, sweet	33–35	90–95	1	11,000–16,500	3.2
Corn, green	32	90–95	1.5		
Chow-Chow	52–55	90	3	5,500–6,600	10.0
Cucumber	50–53	92	2	3,960–5,500	7.2

(Continued)

Vegetable Storage II (Continued)

TABLE 2.V.22 (Continued)

Vegetables	Temp. °F	Relative Humidity %	Storage Life Wk	Heat Evolution[a] BTU/ton-day	Weight Loss[b] %
Eggplant	50–55	92	2–3	9,251–13,609	9.6
Garlic (bulbs), dry	32	65	28–36	800	12.6
Ginger	45–50	75	16–24		18.9
Gourd, bottle	45	85–90	4–6		3.2
Gourd, Snake	65–70	85–90	2		
Leek	32	90–95	4–12	2,500	
Lettuce, head	32	90–95	3	640	14.0
Lettuce, leaf	32	95	1		
Mushroom	32	95	1.5	10,800	7.8
Muskmelon, cantaloupe	35–38	85–90	1.5	3,960–4,640	7.2
Muskmelon, Honeydew	45	85	4–5		
Okra	48	90	2	10,670	6.8
Onion, white	34	70–75	16–20	1,000	14.2
Onion, red	32	70–75	20–24	660	16.3
Onion, green (immature)	32	90–95	2		
Patola (Trichosanthes)	42–45	85–90	3		11.3
Pea, green	32	88–92	2–3	5,000	8.0
Pepper, sweet (green)	45	85–90	3–5	5,200	7.1
Pepper, sweet (ripe)	42–45	90–95	2	2,200	
Petsai, Brassica	32	95	1.5–2.5	2,300	15.0
Potato, Irish (8 varieties)	38–40	85	34	800–2,200	4.9
Pumpkin	35–60	70–75	24–36		3.7
Radish, topped	32	88–92	3–5	4,200	8.0
Squash	55–60	70–75	8–24		4.0–15.0
Sweet potato	50–55	80–90	13–20	1,320–6,600	8.5
Tapioca root	32–35	85	23		
Tomato					
'VC-lines', mature green	48–50	85–90	4–5	3,216–4,156	5.2
'VC-lines', ripe	45	90	1	2,860	
'Oxheart', 'Hybrid-6',					
'Marathi', all green	35–38	85–90	6	3,300–4,400	4.8
'Ponderosa', yellow	42–45	85–90	3		
'Sioux', red	32–35	85–90	2	1,441–1,600	
Turnip	32	90–95	8–16	1,300	
Watermelon	45–60	80–90	2	2,400	2.0
Yam	80	60–70	3–5		

Source: Authors' unpublished data.

[a]Represents steady state heat production during storage at indicated temperatures.
[b]Loss in weight upon removal from storage at indicated storage periods. This may include trimming losses for leafy vegetables. Weight loss values are averages of several trials, some in commercial storage plants but mostly in experimental cold rooms.

Source: Pantastico, E. B., Chattopadhyay, T. K., and Subramanyam, H. (1975). Storage and commercial storage operations. In *Postharvest Physiology, Handling and Utilization of Tropical and Subtropical Fruits and Vegetables.* E. B. Pantastico (editor). AVI Publishing Co., Westport, Connecticut.

Vegetable Yield

TABLE 2.V.23
Amount of frozen product obtainable from 100-ft row

	Yield from 100-ft Row, (Avg)	Pounds of Frozen Product from 100-ft Row
Carrots	1 bu	40
Beets	1½ bu	60
Snap beans	1½ bu	20
Lima beans	12 qt shelled	18
Broccoli	75 lb	50
Spinach	40 lb	25
Peas	10 qt shelled	15
Sweet corn	60 ears	12
Cauliflower	25 heads	15
Asparagus	30 lb	20
Rhubarb	200 lb	175
Squash or pumpkin	150 lb	75

Source: Stout, G. J. *The Home Freezer Handbook.* Van Nostrand Reinhold Co., New York.

Vegetable Yields

TABLE 2.V.24

Vegetables	Average crop expected per 100 feet	Approximate planting per person	
		Fresh	Storage, canning or freezing
Asparagus	30 lb.	10–15 plants	10–15 plants
Beans, snap bush	120 lb.	15–16 feet	15–20 feet
Beans, snap pole	150 lb.	5–6 feet	8–10 feet
Beans, Lima bush	25 lb. shelled	10–15 feet	15–20 feet
Beans, Lima pole	50 lb. shelled	5–6 feet	8–10 feet
Beets	150 lb.	5–10 feet	10–20 feet
Broccoli	100 lb.	3–5 plants	5–6 plants
Brussels sprouts	75 lb.	2–5 plants	5–8 plants
Cabbage	150 lb.	3–4 plants	5–10 plants
Cabbage, Chinese	80 heads	3–10 feet	——
Carrots	100 lb.	5–10 feet	10–15 feet
Cauliflower	100 lb.	3–5 plants	8–12 plants
Celeriac	60 lb.	5 feet	5 feet
Celery	180 stalks	10 stalks	——
Chard, Swiss	75 lb.	3–5 plants	8–12 plants
Collards and kale	100 lb.	5–10 feet	5–10 feet
Corn, sweet	10 dozen	10–15 feet	30–50 feet
Cucumbers	120 lb.	1–2 hills	3–5 hills
Eggplant	100 lb.	2–3 plants	2–3 plants
Garlic	40 lb.	——	1–5 feet
Kohlrabi	75 lb.	3–5 feet	5–10 feet
Lettuce, head	100 heads	10 feet	——
Lettuce, leaf	50 lb.	10 feet	——
Muskmelon (cantaloupe)	100 fruits	3–5 hills	——
Mustard	100 lb.	5–10 feet	10–15 feet
Okra	100 lb.	4–6 feet	6–10 feet
Onions (plants or sets)	100 lb.	3–5 feet	30–50 feet
Onions (seed)	100 lb.	3–5 feet	30–50 feet

(Continued)

Vegetable Yields (Continued)

TABLE 2.V.24 (Continued)

| Vegetables | Average crop expected per 100 feet | Approximate planting per person | |
		Fresh	Storage, canning or freezing
Parsley	30 lb.	1–3 feet	1–3 feet
Parsnips	100 lb.	10 feet	10 feet
Peas, English	20 lb.	15–20 feet	40–60 feet
Peas, southern	40 lb.	10–15 feet	20–50 feet
Peppers	60 lb.	3–5 plants	3–5 plants
Potatoes, Irish	100 lb.	50–100 feet	—
Potatoes, sweet	100 lb.	5–10 plants	10–20 plants
Pumpkins	100 lb.	1–2 hills	1–2 hills
Radishes	100 bunches	3–5 feet	—
Salsify	100 lb.	5 feet	5 feet
Soybeans	20 lb.	50 feet	50 feet
Spinach	40–50 lb.	5–10 feet	10–15 feet
Squash, summer	150 lb.	2–3 hills	2–3 hills
Squash, winter	100 lb.	1–3 hills	1–3 hills
Tomatoes	100 lb.	3–5 plants	5–10 plants
Turnip greens	50–100 lb.	5–10 feet	—
Turnip, roots	50–100 lb.	5–10 feet	5–10 feet
Watermelon	40 fruits	2–4 hills	—

Source: USDA (1977). Growing your own vegetables. USDA Agricultural Information Bull. 409.

Vegetable Yield, Canned and Frozen

TABLE 2.V.25
Yield of vegetables processed in cans or frozen

| Vegetable | Approximate Amount of Cooked Vegetable Obtained From: | | | |
| | Canned (Drained) | | Frozen Packages | |
	Size of Container (oz)	Cups	Size of Container (oz)	Cups
Asparagus, cut	14	1⅓	10	1¼
Beans, green or wax, cut	15½	1¾	9	1⅔
Beans, lima	16	1¾	10	1⅔
Beets, sliced, diced or whole	16	1¾	—	—
Broccoli, cut	—	—	10	1½
Carrots, diced or sliced	16	1¾	10	1⅔
Cauliflower	—	—	10	1½
Corn, whole kernel	16	1⅔	10	1½
Kale	15	1⅓	10	1⅛
Okra	15½	1¾	10	1¼
Peas	16	1¾	10	1⅔
Potatoes, French fried	—	—	9	1⅔
Spinach	15	1⅓	10	1¼
Summer squash, sliced	—	—	10	1⅓
Tomatoes, undrained	16	1⅞	—	—

Source: Anonymous (1977). How to buy canned and frozen vegetables. USDA Home and Garden Bull. 167.

Vegetable Yield, Frozen, Canned, and Fresh

TABLE 2.V.26
Approximate amount of cooked vegetable obtained from frozen, canned, and fresh

Vegetable and style	Frozen vegetables		Canned vegetables (drained)		1 lb. of fresh vegetable as purchased—
	Size of container (ounces)	Cooked, Cups	Size of container (ounces)	Heated, Cups	Cups
Asparagus, cut	10	1¼	14	1⅓	1¾
Beans, green or wax, cut	9	1⅔	15½	1¾	2¾
Beans, lima	10	1⅔	16	1¾	1⅛
Beets, sliced, diced or whole	...	...	16	1¾	1⅞
Broccoli, cut	10	1⅓	...	...	1½
Brussels sprouts	10	1½	...	...	2¼
Cabbage, shredded	...	...	...	...	2⅓
Carrots, diced, or sliced	10	1⅔	16	1¾	2⅛
Cauliflower	10	1½	...	...	1½
Corn, whole kernel	10	1½	[1] 16	1⅔	...
Kale	10	1⅛	15	1⅓	2⅔
Okra	10	1¼	15½	1¾	2¼
Peas	10	1⅔	16	1¾	1
Potatoes	9	[2] 1⅔	...	...	[3] 1¾
Spinach	10	1¼	15	1⅓	2
Summer squash, sliced	10	1⅓	...	...	2
Tomatoes	...	...	[4] 16	1⅞	...

[1] Whole kernels with liquid; a 12 oz. can of whole kernels, vacuum pack, provides 1¾ cups.
[2] French fries.
[3] Mashed.
[4] Undrained.

Source: USDA (1969). Food for us all. Yearbook of Agriculture.

Vinegar, Spiced

TABLE 2.V.27

Ingredients	%
24's Vinegar	86.0
Chillies	3.4
Pimientos	2.4
Coriander seed	2.4
Cloves (whole)	1.7
Black pepper (whole)	1.7
Mustard seed	1.2
Root ginger	1.2
	100.0

Source: Binsted, R., Devey, J. D., and Dakin, J. C. (1971). *Pickle & Sauce Making*, 3rd Edition. Food Trade Press, London, England.

Vitamin A

TABLE 2.V.28
Vitamin A in some foods

	IU/100 g		IU/100 g
Carrots	11500	Cherries	1000
Sweet potatoes	8800	Tomatoes	900
Spinach	8100	Asparagus	900
Cantaloupe	3400	Peppers	420
Apricots	2700	Corn	400
Broccoli	2500	Lettuce	330
Peaches	1330	Oranges	200

Source: White, P. L., and Selvey, N. (editors) (1974). *Nutritional Qualities of Fresh Fruits and Vegetables*. Futura Publishing Co., Mt. Kisco, New York.

Vitamin A, Daily Recommendations

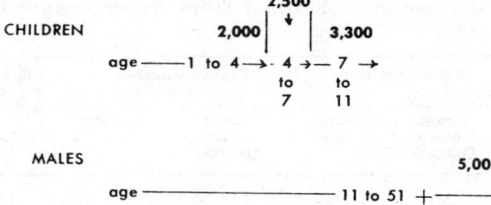

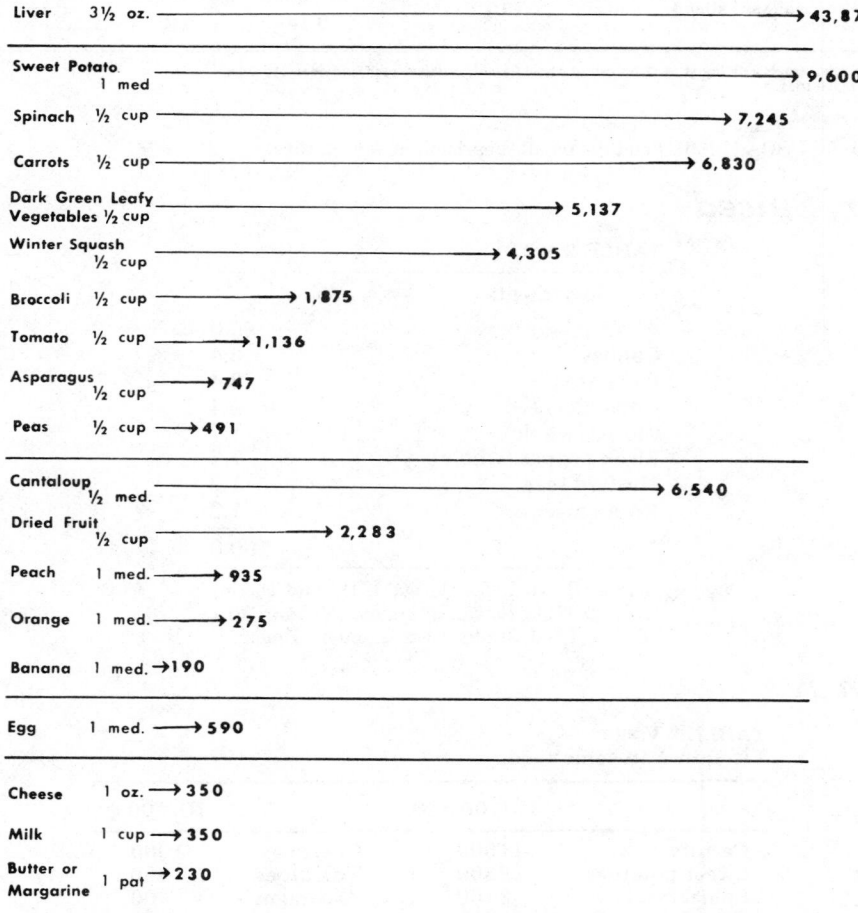

†Average nutrient content as food is served. (*Note: 3½ oz equals approximately 100 g.*)

FIGURE 2.V.4

Source: Lessons on Meat. (1974). National Live Stock and Meat Board, Chicago.

Vitamin A, Fish

TABLE 2.V.29
Vitamin A content of oils from fishery sources having commercial importance in the United States and Alaska[1]

Common Name	Area in Which Fish Are Caught	Source of Oil	Per Cent of Round Weight[2]	Oil Content, %	Vitamin A Content in U.S.P. Units Per Gram of Oil	
					Range	Average
Soupfin shark	Pacific (male)	Liver	10	55–68	45,000–200,000	120,000
"	(female)	"	10	65–72	15,000–40,000	32,000
Grayfish (dogfish)	" -Alaska	"	10	67–72	2,000–20,000	5,000
" "	" -Hecate Strait	"	10	65–70	7,000–15,000	10,000
" "	" -Wash.-Ore.	"	10	50–70	8,000–25,000	14,000
" "	" -N. Calif.	"	10	62–68	12,000–25,000	15,000
Halibut	Pacific-area 3[3]	Liver	1.5–3	8–21	40,000–160,000	87,000
"	" " 2[4]		1–1.75	17–27	20,000–65,000	40,000
Sablefish	Pacific	Viscera[5]	2.5–5	2–5	70,000–700,000	200,000
"	"	Liver	3–4	10–26	50,000–190,000	90,000
Lingcod	Pacific	Viscera	1–1.5	5–12	90,000–250,000	125,000
"	"	Liver	1.8–3	8–20	40,000–550,000	175,000
Sleeper shark	Pacific	Viscera	10–15	4–15	10,000–175,000	40,000
"	"	Liver	10–15	40–55	5,000–15,000	7,000
Mud shark		"		60–65	5,000–7,000	5,500
Great blue shark		"	6	30–45	7,000–27,000	20,000
Hammerhead shark	-Atlantic	"		30–40	30,000–120,000	50,000
" "	Atlantic	"		55–75	20,000–150,000	60,000
" "	Florida	"	6	6	5,000–140,000	40,000
Little black tip	Florida	"	6	6	10,000–125,000	50,000
Tiger shark		"		40–60	5,000–25,000	5,000
Sand-bar shark		"		45–60	2,000–5,000	3,000
Nurse shark		"	6	6	3,000–15,000	8,000
Dusky shark		"	6	6	1,000–10,000	3,000
Leopard shark	Pacific	"	6	6	5,000–60,000	25,000
Bay shark	"	"		40–50	1,000–5,000	3,000
Thresher shark	"	"		60–75	2,000–20,000	10,000
Mexican shark	"	"		45–55	1,000–5,000	3,000
Gray smooth hound	"	"		40–50	20,000–80,000	40,000
Cazon shark	Argentina-Brazil	"		50–60	10,000–25,000	20,000
Albacore tuna	Pacific	"	7–10	30–45	10,000–200,000	50,000
Bluefin tuna	"	"	1.5–2	7–20	25,000–100,000	25,000
Yellowfin tuna	"	"	6	4–6	25,000–60,000	75,000
Skipjack tuna	"	"		3–5	35,000–90,000	50,000
Bonito	"	"		4–6	30,000–60,000	40,000
Swordfish	Pacific-Atlantic	"	1.4–2.6	4–12	15,000–60,000	35,000
"	"	Viscera	3–6	8–35	20,000–400,000	250,000
				6–12	2,000–30,000	10,000

(Continued)

Vitamin A, Fish (Continued)

TABLE 2.V.29 (Continued)

Common Name	Area in Which Fish Are Caught	Source of Oil	Per Cent of Round Weight[2]	Oil Content, %	Vitamin A Content in U.S.P. Units Per Gram of Oil	
					Range	Average
Black sea bass	Pacific	Liver	6	13–20	100,000–1,000,000	300,000[6]
Totuava	Pacific	Liver	6	15–25	40,000–400,000	2,000
Cod	Atlantic	"	3–5	20–60	1,000–6,000	[6] "
Rosefish	"	Waste[7]	6	2–4	3,000–5,000	"
Halibut	"	Liver	1.5–2.5	15–25	40,000	"
Rockfish	Pacific	"	1–1.5	5–25	14,000–300,000	"
		Viscera	1.5–2.5	2–15	15,000–125,000	"
Petrale sole	Pacific	Liver	1–1.5	6–25	4,000–175,000	
Herring	"	Body	6	5–25	50–300	90
Pilchard	"	"	6	5–25	50–800	100
Menhaden	Atlantic	"	6	5–20	500	[6]

[1] These data compiled from reports of research at the laboratories of the Fish and Wildlife Service and of the Fisheries Research Board of Canada, and from articles published by representatives of commercial processors of fish livers and viscera. For the most part, the data are based on large lots of material or on samples taken over the normal season for the species.

[2] Per cent of round weight means the proportion of liver weight to the weight of the entire fish (undressed) expressed as per cent.

[3] Area 3 is defined by the International Halibut Commission regulations as follows: "Area 3 shall include all the convention waters off the coast of Alaska that are between Area 2 and a straight line running south from the southwestern extremity of Cape Sagak on Umnak Island, at a point approximately latitude 52°49'30" N., longitude 169°07'00" W., according to Chart 8802, published January, 1942, by the United States Coast and Geodetic Survey, and that are south of the Alaska Peninsula and of the Aleutian Islands and shall also include the intervening straits or passes of the Aleutian Islands."

[4] Area 2 includes: "all convention waters off the coasts of the United States of America and of the Dominion of Canada between Area 1B and a line running through the most westerly point of Glacier Bay, Alaska, to Cape Spenser Light as shown on Chart 8304, published in June, 1940, by the United States Coast and Geodetic Survey, which light is approximately latitude 58°11'57" N., longitude 136°38'18" W., thence south one-quarter east and is exclusive of the areas closed to all halibut fishing in Section 9 of these regulations."

[5] Viscera, unless otherwise designated, means the contents of the body cavity minus the liver, stomach, and gonads.

[6] The source from which information listed here was obtained did not supply data under this heading.

[7] Waste is the entire body of the rosefish minus the fillet or edible portion. It includes head, backbone, skin, and viscera.

Source: Brody, J. (editor). Non-fat components of fish oils. In *Fishery By-Products Technology.* AVI Publishing Co, Westport, Connecticut.

Vitamin A, Food

TABLE 2.V.30
Vitamin A potency (IU) of foods per 100 g (about $3\frac{1}{2}$ oz)

Cereals		**Fruits**	
Yellow maize (as carotene)	330–900	Apricots and peaches	750 (as carotene)
Flour, bread, cornflour, oatmeal, pearl barley, rice, rye, sago, etc.	} none	Tomatoes	3,000 (as carotene)
		Meats	
		Beef, veal, mutton, lamb	50
		Pork and pork products	none
Dairy foods		**Variety meats**	
Butter	3500	Heart	200
Cheddar cheese		Kidney	1,000
Winter milk	550	Liver	
Summer milk	1400	Pig	10,000
Eggs	1000	Cow	15,000
Milk		Rabbit	25,000
Winter	100	Sheep	60,000
Summer	150	Sperm whale	440,000
		Seal	1,300,000
Fish		**Vegetables**	
Herring		Beans, green	600–950
Fresh	150	Cabbage	900 (as carotene)
Canned	30	Carrots	9,000
Liver oil		Peas (green)	500 (as carotene)
Cod	10,000–400,000	Potatoes	none
Halibut	3–36 million	Sprouts	300 (as carotene)

Source: Sinclair, H. M., and Hollingsworth, D. F. (1969). *Hutchison's Food and the Principles of Nutrition.* Edward Arnold (Publishers), London, England.

Vitamin A, Milk and Milk Products

TABLE 2.V.31
Vitamin A content of milk and milk products[1]

Milk or Milk Product	Avg	Range (IU/100 g)[2]		Cheese Variety	Avg	Range (IU/100 g)	
Whole milk:				Very hard:			
Fluid	156	119–176		Parmesan	1410	—	(1)[3]
Condensed	276	141–352	(4)[3]	Hard:			
Evaporated	369	342–464	(4)	Cantal	1333	—	(1)
Dried	1100	600–1600	(6)	Cheddar	1169[4]	750–1985	(10)
Skimmilk:				Cheshire	970	—	(1)
Fluid	9	4–18	(4)	Edam	1203	733–1788	(4)
Dried	143	40–250	(3)	Gouda	1050	—	(1)
Malted milk:				Gruyère	822	267–1333	(3)
Dried	1020	—	(1)	Swiss	1592	954–2680	(3)
Buttermilk:				Semisoft:			
Fluid	12	4–20	(2)	Blue[5]	1935	1000–3502	(6)
Yoghurt	69	—	(1)	Brick	1626	853–2400	(2)
Cream:							
Half and half	480	—	(1)	Liederkranz	3437	—	(1)
Light table	880	—	(1)	Limburger	1280	—	(1)
Medium whipping	1336	—	(1)	Port Salut[5]	1333	—	(1)
Heavy whipping	1598	—	(1)	Roquefort[6]	1971	900–4012	(3)
Butter	3108	2374–3836		Stilton	1235	—	(1)
Ice cream	523	425–600	(4)	Tilsiter	1045	—	(1)
Whey:				Trappist[5]	742	—	(1)
Fluid	11	10–12	(2)	Soft:			
Dried	50	—	(1)	Ripened:			
				Brie	667	—	(1)
				Brinza[5]	483	—	(1)
				Camembert	2140	667–3612	(2)
				Unripened:			
				Cottage:			
				Creamed	291	185–397	(2)
				Uncreamed	42	9–60	(3)
				Cream	2194	1552–2819	(3)
				Neufchâtel	1495	—	(1)
				Pimento			
				Cream	3204	—	(1)
				Processed:			
				Brick	1407	—	(1)
				Cheddar	1705	1250–2160	(2)
				Limburger	1460	—	(1)
				Swiss	1680	1390–1970	(2)

[1] Mean and range of average values obtained from various publications.
[2] IU per 100 ml for products designated fluid.
[3] Figures in parentheses indicate the number of references consulted.
[4] One high value (5,500 IU/100 g) omitted.
[5] May be made from milk of species other than the cow.
[6] Made from ewe's milk.

Source: Hartman, A. M., and Dryden, L.P. Vitamins in milk and milk products. J. Dairy Sci., American Dairy Science Association.

Vitamin C

TABLE 2.V.32
Vitamin C in some foods

	mg/100 g		mg/100 g
Peppers	128	Grapefruit	38
Broccoli	113	Cantaloupe	33
Brussels sprouts	102	Asparagus	33
Cauliflower	78	Tomatoes	23
Strawberries	59	Potatoes	20
Spinach	51	Corn	12
Oranges	50	Bananas	10
Cabbage	47	Apples	7

Source: White, P. L., and Selvey, N. (editors) (1974). *Nutritional Qualities of Fresh Fruits and Vegetables.* Futura Publishing Co., Mt. Kisco, New York.

Vitamin D, Fish

TABLE 2.V.33
Vitamin D content of oils from fishery sources

Common Name	Area in Which Fish are Caught	Source of Oil	Vitamin D Content in International Units Per Gram of Oil
Albacore tuna	Pacific	Liver	25,000–250,000
Bluefin "	"	"	20,000–70,000
Yellowfin "	"	"	10,000–45,000
Skipjack "	"	"	25,000–250,000
Bonito	"	"	50,000
Swordfish	" -Atlantic	"	2,000–25,000
Mackerel, Pacific	Pacific	"	1,400
Albacore tuna	"	Waste[2]	67
Halibut	"	Liver	1,000–5,000
"	"	Viscera[3]	100–500
Sablefish	"	Liver	600–1,000
"	"	Viscera	100
Lingcod	"	Liver	1,000–6,000
"	"	Viscera	100–200
Rockfish	"	Liver	300–5,000
Cod	"	"	85–500
Ishinagi	"	"	3,800
Barracuda	"	"	2,000
Black sea bass	"	"	5,000
Beluga whale	"	"	50–100
Grayfish (dogfish)	"	"	5–25
" "	"	Body[4]	29
Ratfish	"	Liver	2–5
Soupfin shark	"	"	5–25
Herring	"	Body[5]	25–160
"	"	Liver	250
Pilchard	"	Body[5]	20–100
King salmon	"	Liver	100–500
" "	"	Offal[6]	50–150
Sockeye "	'	Liver	200–600
" "	"	Offal	100–300
Silver "	"	Liver	100–500
" "	"	Offal	100–200

(Continued)

Vitamin D, Fish   (*Continued*)

TABLE 2.V.33   (*Continued*)

Common Name	Area in Which Fish are Caught	Source of Oil	Vitamin D Content in International Units Per Gram of Oil
Pink "	"	Liver	100–600
" "	"	Offal	100–300
Chum "	"	Liver	100–500
" "	"	Offal	50–100
Starry flounder	"	Liver	1,000
Rex sole	"	"	150
Skate	"	"	25
Mud shark	"	"	20
Snoek	South Africa	"	500–6,000
"	" "	Viscera	85
Stonebass	" "	Liver	700–1,300
Stockfish	" "	"	50–380
"	" "	Viscera	3
Kingklip	" "	Liver	85–600
Halibut	" "	"	1,000–2,000
Cod	" "	"	100
Ling	New Zealand	"	500
Yellowtail	Australia	"	9,000–17,000
Halibut	Atlantic	"	2,000
Mackerel, common	"	"	750
Rosefish	"	Waste[7]	50
Dogfish	"	Liver	3

Table Courtesy of U. S. Fish and Wildlife Service.
[1] Data on vitamin A content of most of these fish are to be found in Tables 1 and 2.
[2] Waste indicates offal from the cannery fish cleaning tables.   The raw eviscerated fish is pre-cooked prior to this cleaning operation, hence some of the tuna body oil has been lost from this waste before it is made into meal and oil.
[3] Viscera indicates the contents of the body cavity minus the liver, stomach, and gonads.
[4] Body indicates the entire body of the fish minus the liver.
[5] Body indicates the entire body of the fish including the liver and viscera.
[6] Offal indicates the cannery trimmings, including heads, livers, and viscera but not eggs.
[7] Waste indicates the entire body of the rosefish minus the fillet or edible portion.   It includes head, backbone, skin, and viscera.

Source: Brody, J. (editor). Non-fat components of fish-oils. In *Fishery By-Products Technology*. AVI Publishing Co., Westport, Connecticut.

Vitamin D, Food

TABLE 2.V.34
Vitamin D content of foods

	IU per 100 g		IU per 100 g
Dairy foods		Fish	
Butter, Empire imported	60	Herrings	
Cheese	15	Fresh and cured	850
Dripping	30	Canned	170
Egg		Mackerel	700
Whole, fresh	60	Salmon, canned	600
Dried	240	Sardines, canned	1000
Margarine	200	Fish liver oils[1]	
		Cod	20,000

[1] Halibut liver oils, not included in this table, run from 20,000 to 400,000.

Source: Sinclair, H. M., and Hollingsworth, D. F. (1969). *Hutchison's Food and the Principles of Nutrition*. Edward Arnold (Publishers), London, England.

Vitamin Retention, Meat

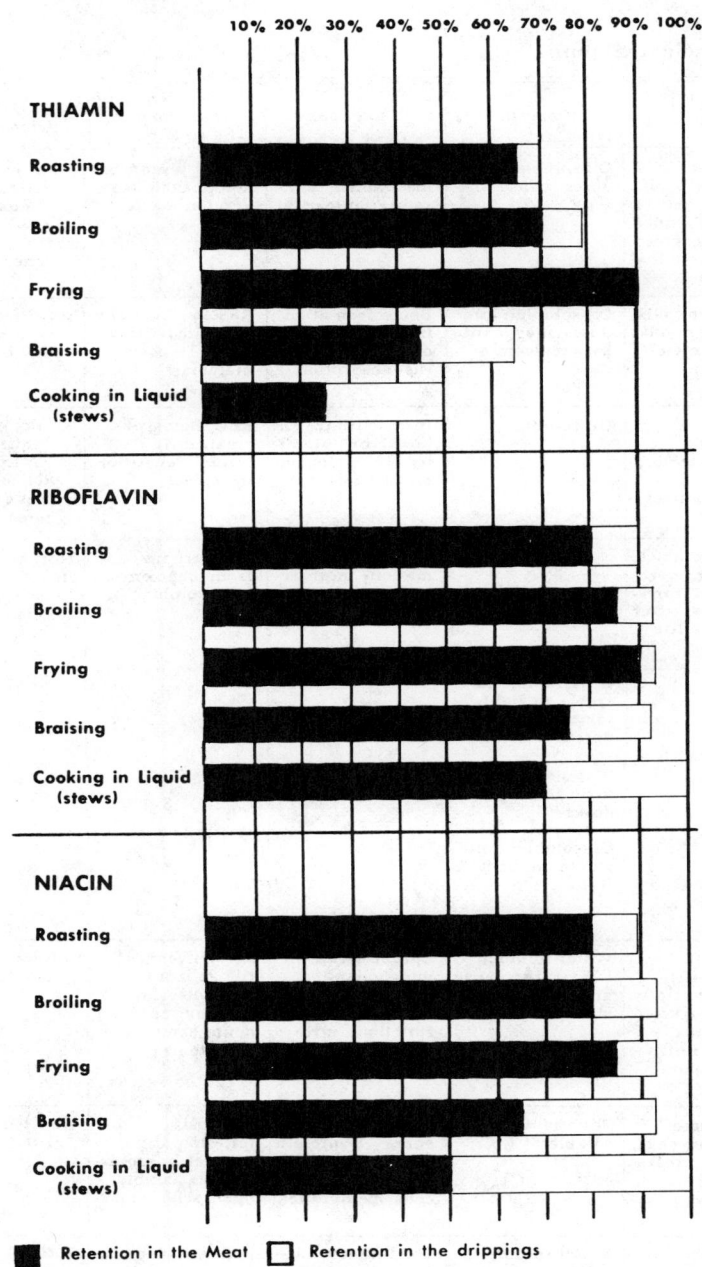

FIGURE 2.V.5

Source: Lessons on Meat. (1974). National Live Stock and Meat Board, Chicago.

Vitamins

TABLE 2.V.35
Data covering the principal vitamins

Vitamin	Principal Sources	Properties	Functions	Deficiency Symptoms in Man	Daily Allowances	Usual Therapeutic Dosage
Vitamin A (Retinol)	Fish liver oils, liver, egg yolk, butter, cream, vitamin A-fortified margarine, green leafy or yellow vegetables	Oil-soluble; large doses cause toxicity	Photoreceptor mechanism of retina, integrity of epithelia, lysosome stability	Night blindness; xerophthalmia; keratomalacia	*Adults:* 1.5 mg retinal (equals 5000 U.S.P. u. or 9 mg β-carotene)[b, c]	25,000–50,000 U.S.P. u./day[c] (*see* text for higher dosage)
Vitamin D Ergocalciferol (D_2) Cholecalciferol (D_3)	Fish liver oils, butter, egg yolk, liver, ultraviolet irradiation	Oil-soluble; large doses may cause hypercalcemia	Bone formation, increases calcium & phosphorus absorption	Rickets (tetany sometimes associated); osteomalacia	*Adults & children:* 400 U.S.P. u.[c]	400–1,600 U.S.P. u./day[c] (*see* text for higher dosage)
Vitamin E Group ($α$, $β$, $γ$, $δ$ tocopherol)	Vegetable oil, wheat germ, leafy vegetables, egg yolk, margarine, legumes	Oil-soluble	Intracellular antioxidant, stability of biological membranes	RBC hemolysis; creatinuria; ceroid deposition in muscle	*Adults:* 30 I.U. (equals 30 mg synthetic dl-α-tocopherol acetate)	50–300 I.U./day
Vitamin K (activity)	Leafy vegetables, pork liver, vegetable oils, intestinal flora after 4th day of life		Prothrombin formation; normal blood coagulation	Hemorrhage from deficient prothrombin	Not yet established; thought to be about 0.03 mg/kg	In situations conducive to neonatal hemorrhage, 2–5 mg during labor or daily for 1 wk prior; or 1–2 mg to newborn (*see* text for details)
Menadione		Oil-soluble; unstable to light; toxic in large doses				
Menadione sodium bisulfite		Water-soluble; toxic in large doses				
Phytonadione (Vitamin K_1)		Oil-soluble; unstable to heat & light				10–50 mg to counteract excessive anticoagulant (*see* text for details)
Thiamine (Vitamin B_1)	Dried yeast, whole grains; meat (especially pork, liver); enriched cereal products, nuts, legumes, potatoes	Water-soluble; I.V. may cause anaphylactoid shock	Carbohydrate metabolism; central & peripheral nerve cell function; myocardial function	Beriberi, infantile & adult (peripheral neuropathy; cardiac; acute cerebral symptoms)	*Adults:* 1.0–1.5 mg	5–30 mg/day
Riboflavin (Vitamin B_2)	Milk, cheese, liver, meat, eggs, enriched cereal products	Slightly water-soluble	Many aspects energy & protein metabolism; integrity of mucous membranes	Cheilosis, angular stomatitis, corneal vascularization, amblyopia, sebaceous dermatosis	*Adults:* 1.0–1.7 mg	10–30 mg/day
Niacin (Nicotinic acid) Niacinamide (Nicotinamide)	Dried yeast, liver, meat, fish, legumes, whole-grain enriched cereal products	Water-soluble; intolerance produces flushing, burning, itching (rare with niacinamide)	Oxidation-reduction reactions; carbohydrate & tryptophan metabolism	Pellagra (dermatosis, glossitis, GI & CNS dysfunction)	*Adults:* 15–20 mg equivalents[d]	Niacinamide 100–1000 mg/day

(*Continued*)

Vitamins   (*Continued*)

TABLE 2.V.35   (*Continued*)

Vitamin	Principal Sources	Properties	Functions	Deficiency Symptoms in Man	Daily Allowances	Usual Therapeutic Dosage
Vitamin B₆ Group (Pyridoxine, Pyridoxal, Pyridoxamine)	Dried yeast, liver, organ meats, whole-grain cereals, fish, legumes	Water-soluble	Essential for cellular function & for metabolism of certain amino & fatty acids	Convulsions in infancy, anemias, neuropathy, seborrhea-like skin lesions. Dependency states (*see text*)	*Adults:* 2 mg	25–100 mg/day
Pantothenic acid (Calcium pantothenate)	Dried yeast, liver, eggs, organ meats, legumes	Water-soluble	Involved in fat, protein, & carbohydrate metabolism by its relation to acetylation processes	Experimental deficiency in man characterized by fatigue, malaise, headache, sleep disturbances, nausea, abdominal & muscle cramps, vomiting, paresthesias, & impaired coordination	Not yet established; thought to be about 10 mg/day	Not known; not < 50 mg/day should be used for therapeutic trial
Folic acid (Folacin, Pteroylglutamic acid)	Fresh green leafy vegetables & fruit, organ meats, liver, dried yeast	Poorly water-soluble	Maturation of RBCs; synthesis of purines & pyrimidines	Pancytopenia, megaloblastosis (especially pregnancy, infancy, malabsorption)	*Adults:* 400 μg based on *L. casei* method or 100 μg synthetic folic acid	100 μg/day
Vitamin B₁₂ (Cyanocobalamin)	Liver, meats, (especially beef, pork, organ meats); eggs, milk & milk products	Water-soluble	Maturation of RBCs; neural function; DNA synthesis, related to folate coenzymes; methionine & acetate synthesis	Pernicious anemia; fish tapeworm & vegan anemias, some psychiatric syndromes, nutritional amblyopia	*Adults:* 5 μg; based on absorption of 30% or less	1–2 μg/day I.M. to maintain remission in pernicious anemia
Vitamin C (Ascorbic acid)	Citrus fruits, tomatoes, potatoes, cabbage, green pepper	Water-soluble	Essential to osteoid tissue, collagen formation, vascular function, tissue respiration, & wound healing	Scurvy (hemorrhages, loose teeth, gingivitis)	*Adults:* 60 mg *Children:* 40 mg	100–1000 mg/day

ᵇ One U.S.P. u. equals 0.3 μg of retinol. 1 μg of β-carotene is equivalent to 0.167 μg of retinol.

ᶜ One U.S.P. u. equals 1 I.U.

ᵈ 60 mg. of tryptophan is equivalent to 1 mg. of niacin.

Source: Holvey, D. N. (1972). *The Merck Manual*, 12th Edition. Merck & Co., Rahway, New Jersey.

Vitamin Sources, Functions, and Stability

TABLE 2.V.36
Vitamin sources, functions, and stability

	Food Sources	Functions	Effects of Processing[1]	Effects of Storage[2]
Fat-soluble vitamins				
Vitamin A and carotene	Liver, kidney, eggs, butter, whole milk, fortified skim milk, cream, cheese, dark green and deep yellow vegetables and deep yellow fruit.	Essential for healthy skin, eyes and hair; keeps mucous membranes firm and resistant to infection; prevents night blindness, and controls bone growth.	No appreciable loss by heating, freezing, preserving, or canning.	In the absence of air, stable. High storage temperatures in the presence of air result in loss.
Vitamin D (the sunshine vitamin)	Fish liver oils, sunshine on skin, vitamin D milk, egg yolk, margarine, mackerel, sardines, salmon, tuna, cod liver oil.	Necessary for teeth and bones, and normal utilization of calcium and phosphorus; prevents bone deformities.	Little or no loss unless oxidized.	Little or no loss unless oxidized.
Vitamin E	Whole grain cereal, pulses, wheat germ, soybean, cottonseed, peanut and corn oils, eggs, liver, butter, margarine.	Essential for normal muscle; antioxidant, preserving vitamins and unsaturated fatty acids in foods or the body; required for integrity of red blood cells.	Little or no loss unless food becomes rancid.	Little or no loss unless food becomes rancid.
Vitamin K	Cabbage, cauliflower, pork liver, soybean, spinach, wheat bran.	Essential for normal blood clotting.	Destroyed by irradiation.	No appreciable loss.
Water-soluble vitamins				
Vitamin B$_1$ (thiamin)	Liver, pork, poultry, fish, eggs, beans and peas, whole grain cereal, enriched bread, lean meat, potatoes, broccoli, collards, yeast.	Necessary for growth, fertility and lactation; promotes normal appetite; aids metabolic processes, releasing energy from food; keeps nervous system healthy and prevents irritability.	The higher and longer the heating period, the greater the loss. Loss is decreased in presence of acid and small amounts of water.	Refrigeration lessens destruction.
Vitamin B$_2$ (riboflavin)	Milk, cheese, ice cream, liver, meat, fish, poultry, eggs, yeast.	Assists in conversion of tryptophan to nicotinic acid; necessary for healthy skin; essential for building and maintaining body tissues and the use of oxygen by cells.	Stable to heat but may be dissolved and discarded in cooking water. Open vessels (or light) and use of sodium bicarbonate in cooking water will destroy riboflavin.	Relatively stable.

(Continued)

Vitamin Sources, Functions, and Stability *(Continued)*

TABLE 2.V.36 *(Continued)*

	Food Sources	Functions	Effects of Processing[1]	Effects of Storage[2]
Niacin	Liver, lean meats, eggs, peas, beans, nuts, peanut butter, enriched bread, whole grain cereal, yeast.	Prevents pellagra; necessary for growth and health of tissues; promotes appetite and good utilization of food in the body.	No loss during ordinary cooking processes, but may lose some in cooking water.	Relatively stable.
Pyridoxine hydrochloride	Barley, meat, cabbage, carrots, corn, cottonseed meal, milk, peanuts, peas, rice, wheat, brewers' yeast, lima beans.	Coenzyme, necessary for protein, tryptophan and fat metabolism; promotes normal red blood cell formation.	Loss occurs due to leaching of vitamin in cooking water (30%). Destroyed by high temperature, high irradiation dose, and exposure to light.	Loss increases with temperature and time of storage.
Pantothenic acid	Wheat, eggs, milk, meat, fish, yeast, molasses, oatmeal, broccoli, cabbage, cucumbers, corn, tomatoes, potatoes, peas, liver, nuts.	Essential for metabolism of carbohydrates and fats.	Fairly stable in moist heat, particularly in neutral solution; readily destroyed by prolonged dry heat in alkaline environment. Can be leached by water.	Relatively stable.
Biotin	Yeast, liver, peanuts, beans, eggs, kidney.	Important to intermediary metabolism-energy release mechanisms.	Stable to heat, but can be dissolved in cooking water.	Relatively stable.
Folic acid	Liver, dark green leafy vegetables; cauliflower, kidney, beef, veal, wheat breakfast foods, bran, blackeyed peas.	Prevents certain anemias; with vitamin C aids tyrosine metabolism in energy conversion cycles; aids in red blood cell formation.	High temperature processing is detrimental to folic acid stability.	Low temperatures of storage are preferred to room temperature to enhance stability.
Vitamin B_{12}	Liver, beef extract, dry milk, oysters, lean meat.	Prevents certain anemias and promotes good general nutrition by contributing to health of nervous system.	Very stable in neutral solutions, but loses potency in either acid or alkaline solutions. Cooking losses range from 24–90%.	More stable to storage than to processing; affected by presence of thiamin and nicotinamide in aqueous pharmaceutical preparations.
Ascorbic acid	Fresh fruits and vegetables, particularly citrus fruits and leafy vegetables.	Essential for healthy bones and strong teeth; helps to maintain body's resistance to infection; prevents capillary fragility; essential for growth and wound healing.	Most easily destroyed of all vitamins and should be processed in stainless steel or glass as a protective measure.	Foods can lose as much as 50% and more depending upon storage time and temperature. Storage at 0°F (−18°C) or below recommended for good retention.

[1] Loss of water-soluble vitamins may be large or small depending upon the processing and cooking techniques and methods that are employed.
[2] Vitamin losses in storage may be large or small depending on storage time and conditions, the product involved, and the vitamin in question.

Source: Thomas, M. H. (1975). Vitamins. In *Encyclopedia of Food Technology.* A. H. Johnson, and M. S. Peterson (editors). AVI Publishing Co., Westport, Connecticut.

Volume

TABLE 2.V.37
Liquid volume conversion table: gallons, quarts, pints, cups, and ounces to milliliters

U.S. Gallons	Milliliters	U.S. Quarts	Milliliters
1	3785.3	1	946.33
2	7570.6	2	1892.65
3	11355.9	3	2838.98
4	15141.2	4 (gal.)	3785.31
5	18926.5		
6	22711.8	**U.S. Pints**	**Milliliters**
7	26497.1		
8	30282.4		
9	34067.8	½	236.58
10	37853.1	1	473.16
11	41638.4	2 (1 qt)	946.33
12	45423.7	3	1419.49
13	49209.0	4 (2 qt)	1892.65
14	52994.3	5	2365.82
15	56779.6	6 (3 qt)	2838.98
16	60564.9	7	3312.14
17	64350.2	8 (gal.)	3785.31
18	68135.5		
19	71920.8	**Cups**	
20	75706.1	**½ pt; 8 oz**	**Milliliters**
21	79491.4		
22	83276.7	¼	59.15
23	87062.0	⅓	78.86
24	90847.3	½	118.29
25	94632.7	⅔	157.72
26	98417.0	¾	177.44
27	102203.3	1	236.58
28	105988.6		
29	109773.9	**Tablespoons (tbsp)**	
30	113559.2	**(3 tsp; ¹⁄₁₆ cup)**	**Milliliters**
31	117344.5		
32	121129.8	½	7.40
33	124915.1	1	14.79
34	128700.4		
35	132485.7	**Teaspoons (tsp)**	
36	136271.0	**(⅓ tbsp)**	**Milliliters**
37	140056.3		
38	143841.6	¼	1.23
39	147626.9	⅓	1.64
40	151412.2	½	2.46
41	155197.5	⅔	3.29
42	158982.9	¾	3.70
43	162768.2	1	4.93
44	166553.5		
45	170338.8		
46	174124.1		
47	177909.4		
48	181694.7		
49	185480.0		
50	189265.3		

(Continued)

Volume (Continued)

TABLE 2.V.37 (Continued)

U.S. Ounces	Milliliters	U.S. Ounces	Milliliters	U.S. Ounces	Milliliters
1	29.57	44	1301.20	87	2572.82
2 (¼ cup)	59.15	45	1330.77	88	2602.40
3	88.72	46	1360.34	89	2631.97
4 (½ cup)	118.29	47	1389.92	90	2661.54
5	147.86	48	1419.49	91	2691.12
6 (¾ cup)	177.44	49	1449.06	92	2720.69
7	207.01	50	1478.64	93	2750.26
8 (cup)	236.58	51	1508.21	94	2779.83
9	266.15	52	1537.78	95	2809.41
10	295.73	53	1567.35	96 (3 qt)	2838.98
11	325.30	54	1596.93	97	2868.55
12	354.87	55	1626.50	98	2898.12
13	384.44	56	1656.07	99	2927.70
14	414.02	57	1685.64	100	2957.27
15	443.59	58	1715.22	101	2986.84
16 (pt)	473.16	59	1744.79	102	3016.42
17	502.74	60	1774.36	103	3045.99
18	532.31	61	1803.93	104	3075.56
19	561.88	62	1833.51	105	3105.13
20	591.45	63	1863.08	106	3134.71
21	621.03	64 (2 qt)	1892.65	107	3164.28
22	650.60	65	1922.23	108	3193.85
23	680.17	66	1951.80	109	3223.42
24	709.74	67	1981.37	110	3253.00
25	739.32	68	2010.94	111	3282.57
26	768.89	69	2040.52	112	3312.14
27	798.46	70	2070.09	113	3341.72
28	828.04	71	2099.66	114	3371.29
29	857.61	72	2129.23	115	3400.86
30	887.18	73	2158.81	116	3430.43
31	916.75	74	2188.38	117	3460.01
32 (qt)	946.33	75	2217.95	118	3489.58
33	975.90	76	2247.53	119	3519.15
34	1005.47	77	2277.10	120	3548.72
35	1035.04	78	2306.67	121	3578.30
36	1064.62	79	2336.24	122	3607.87
37	1094.19	80	2365.82	123	3637.44
38	1123.76	81	2395.39	124	3667.02
39	1153.34	82	2424.96	125	3696.59
40	1182.91	83	2454.53	126	3726.16
41	1212.48	84	2484.11	127	3755.73
42	1242.05	85	2513.68	128 (1 gal.)	3785.31
43	1271.63	86	2543.25		

Example: 3 qt and 13 oz = 2838.98 ml + 384.44 ml = 3223.42 ml

Source: Ockerman, H. W. (1974). *Quality Control of Post-Mortem Muscle Tissue.* 9th Edition. Ohio State University, Columbus.

Volumetric Solutions, Temperature Corrections

This table gives the correction to various observed volumes of water, measured at the designated temperatures to give the volume at the standard temperature, 20°C. Conversely, by subtracting the corrections from the volume desired at 20°C, the volume that must be measured out at the designated temperatures in order to give the desired volume at 20°C will be obtained. It is assumed that the volumes are measured in a glass apparatus having a coefficient of cubical expansion of 0.000025 per degree centigrade. The table is applicable to dilute aqueous solutions having the same coefficient of expansion as water.

TABLE 2.V.38
Temperature correction for volumetric solutions

Temperature of Measurement, °C	Capacity of Apparatus in Milliliters at 20°C						
	2,000	1,000	500	400	300	250	150
	Correction in Milliliters to give volume of water at 20°C						
15	+1.54	+0.77	+0.38	+0.31	+0.23	+0.19	+0.12
16	+1.28	+0.64	+0.32	+0.26	+0.19	+0.16	+0.10
17	+0.99	+0.50	+0.25	+0.20	+0.15	+0.12	+0.07
18	+0.68	+0.34	+0.17	+0.14	+0.10	+0.08	+0.05
19	+0.35	+0.18	+0.09	+0.07	+0.05	+0.04	+0.03
21	-0.37	-0.18	-0.09	-0.07	-0.06	-0.05	-0.03
22	-0.77	-0.38	-0.19	-0.15	-0.12	-0.10	-0.06
23	-1.18	-0.59	-0.30	-0.24	-0.18	-0.15	-0.09
24	-1.61	-0.81	-0.40	-0.32	-0.24	-0.20	-0.12
25	-2.07	-1.03	-0.52	-0.41	-0.31	-0.26	-0.15
26	-2.54	-1.27	-0.64	-0.51	-0.38	-0.32	-0.19
27	-3.03	-1.52	-0.76	-0.61	-0.46	-0.38	-0.23
28	-3.55	-1.77	-0.89	-0.71	-0.53	-0.44	-0.27
29	-4.08	-2.04	-1.02	-0.82	-0.61	-0.51	-0.31
30	-4.62	-2.31	-1.16	-0.92	-0.69	-0.58	-0.35

Source: Weast, R. C. (editor) (1974–1975). Handbook of Chemistry and Physics, 55th Edition. CRC Press, Cleveland.

Walnut Varieties

TABLE 2.W.1

Old varieties	Danger of spring frost damage	Relative production	Kernel quality	best adapted to
Eureka	moderate	good	excellent	cool
Franquette	none	poor	good	cool
Hartley	slight	good	good	hot
Payne	great	excellent	excellent	cool
New varieties				
Amigo*	slight	good	fair	cool
Chico*	moderate	good	good	hot
Gustine	moderate	excellent	excellent	hot
Lompoc	moderate	good	good	cool
Midland	slight	good	good	cool
Pioneer	slight	good	fair	hot
Pedro*	slight to none	good	good	cool
Serr	moderate	good	excellent	hot
Tehema	slight to none	excellent	good	hot
Viva	moderate	excellent	excellent	hot

* Good pollen producers for cross pollination with other varieties.

Source: USDA (1977). Growing fruits and nuts. USDA Agriculture Information Bull. *408.*

Wastes, Agricultural and Industrial

TABLE 2.W.2
Composition of various industrial and agricultural organic wastes

Material	Moisture %	Ash %	N %	P_2O_5 %	K_2O %	N Availability[1]
		Industrial				
Antibiotic wastes						
Penicillin	75.3	29.5	3.85	4.13	1.08	0.4
Streptomycin	62.6	71.9	2.20	0.52	0.06	0.7
Botanical drug wastes						
Cascara bark	75.8	9.7	0.54	0.03	0.01	0.0
Licorice roots	—	—	2.20	0.11	1.12	0.1
Pryethrum flowers	25.0	12.1	1.07	0.58	2.58	0.0
Scammony roots	36.4	13.9	1.12	0.47	2.22	0.0
Cannery wastes						
Asparagus	93.8	12.5	3.96	0.91	3.54	0.6
Beet (red)	94.2	7.0	2.57	0.52	1.92	0.5
Spinach	85.7	58.4	3.21	1.14	1.07	0.9
Sweet potatoes	90.0	10.2	1.84	0.46	0.72	0.2
Spent spice mare						
Carolina chili	16.2	8.3	3.41	1.03	3.84	0.5
Ginger	11.8	5.5	1.74	0.35	1.80	0.1
Nutmeg	37.3	4.3	1.25	0.40	1.26	0.1
Patchouli leaves	11.0	19.5	3.34	0.60	3.96	0.7
Coffee wastes						
Chaff	3.0	5.5	2.58	0.19	2.10	0.0
Grounds, fresh	62.9	0.5	1.84	0.03	0.12	0.0
Grounds, composted	58.0	—	1.65	0.22	3.00	0.2
Snuff wastes						
Stem sand	7.5	38.8	2.81	0.77	4.54	0.2
Leaf sand	3.5	74.4	0.94	0.21	1.62	0.0
Sweepings	16.9	25.1	2.91	0.49	6.90	0.4
Cocoa shells	—	—	2.71	1.17	3.06	0.2
Seaweed	—	—	3.17	—	—	0.8
Spent hops	79.1	4.4	2.13	0.66	0.42	0.3
Tea leaves	86.0	3.2	4.41	0.29	0.24	0.2
		Agricultural				
Apple pomace	—	—	1.70	—	—	0.0
Cow manure	—	—	2.50	0.50	1.40	0.8
Duck manure	—	—	3.55	—	—	0.9
Horse manure	—	—	2.85	—	—	0.5
Poultry manure plus bedding	22.6	25.6	3.58	3.02	1.62	0.8
Sawdust						
Oak	45.6	2.1	0.12	0.002	0.12	0.0
Popular	43.3	2.5	0.13	0.001	0.15	0.0
Soybeans mash	84.0	15.1	4.81	1.49	0.78	0.8
Tobacco stems	20.0	21.5	1.96	0.63	10.80	0.4
Garbage	49.3	28.5	1.07	1.16	0.12	0.0
Garbage compost	10.0	55.0	1.00	2.7	0.69	0.0
Sewage sludge	38.0	15.0	2.00	1.7	0.10	0.0

[1] Based on $(NH_4)_2SO_4$ nitrification value of 1.0

Source: Toth, S. J. (1973). Composting agricultural and industrial organic wastes. In Symposium: Processing Agricultural and Municipal Wastes. G. E. Inglett (editor). AVI Publishing Co., Westport, Connecticut.

Water Activity, Organisms and Food

TABLE 2.W.3
Influence of a_w-values on the microbial spoilage of foods

a_w-range	Organisms inhibited by the lower value	Examples of foods having this lower a_w-value
1.00-0.95	Gram-negative rods; Spores of *Bacillaceae*	Foods containing *c.* 40 wt.% sucrose or *c.* 7 wt.% NaCl
		Bread crumb
		Some types of cooked sausage
0.95-0.91	Most cocci, lactobacilli and vegetative cells of *Bacillaceae*	Foods containing *c.* 55 wt.% sucrose or *c.* 12 wt.% NaCl
		Raw ham
0.91-0.88	Most yeasts	Foods containing *c.*65 wt.% sucrose or 15 wt.% NaCl
		Salami
		Fishmeal with *c.* 10% moisture
0.88-0.80	Most moulds; *Staph. aureus*	Flour, rice, pulses, etc. with *c.* 17% moisture
		Fruit cake
		Dry sausage
0.80-0.75	Most halophilic bacteria	Foods containing *c.* 26 wt.% NaCl
		Most jams and fondant creams
0.75-0.65	Xerophilic moulds	Marzipan, marshmallow
		Fishmeal with *c.* 5% moisture
0.65-0.60	Osmophilic yeasts	Liquorice, gums
		Medium salted cod with *c.* 12% moisture
<0.60	All micro-organisms	Toffees, boiled sweets
		Raisins

Source: Mossel, D. A. A. (1970). Microbial spoilage of proteinaceous foods. In *Proteins as Human Food*. R. A. Lawrie (editor). AVI Publishing Co., Westport, Connecticut.

Water Drinking Standards

TABLE 2.W.4
Comparison of standards for drinking water

	WHO Max Acceptable Concentration[1]	WHO Max Allowable Concentration[1]	U.S.PHS
Test			
Color (Hazen or platinum-cobalt scale units)	5	50	Not exceeding 15
Turbidity units	5	25	Not exceeding 3
Odor	Unobjectionable	—	Not exceeding threshold Odor number of 3 units
Taste	Unobjectionable	—	—
Iron (Fe)	0.3 mg/l	1.0 mg/l	Not exceeding 0.3 mg/l
Manganese (Mn)	0.1 mg/l	0.5 mg/l	Not exceeding 0.05 mg/l
Copper (Cu)	1.0 mg/l	1.5 mg/l	Not exceeding 1.0 mg/l
Zinc (Zn)	5.0 mg/l	15 mg/l	Not exceeding 5.0 mg/l
Calcium (Ca)	75 mg/l	200 mg/l	—
Magnesium (Mg)	50 mg/l	150 mg/l	—
Sulphate (SO_4)	200 mg/l	400 mg/l	Not exceeding 250 mg/l
Chloride (Cl)	200 mg/l	600 mg/l	Not exceeding 250 mg/l
Phenols	0.001 mg/l	0.002 mg/l	Not exceeding 0.001 mg/l
pH range	7.0–8.5	Less than 6.5 or greater than 9.2	—
Alkyl benzene sulphonates	0.5 mg/l	1.0 mg/l	Not exceeding 0.5 mg/l
Carbon chloroform extract	0.2 mg/l	0.5 mg/l	Not exceeding 0.2 mg/l
Nitrate (NO_3)	—	45 mg/l[2]	Not exceeding 45 mg/l
Fluoride (F)	1 mg/l	1.5 mg/l	1.7 mg/l (at average max daily air temp of 50–54°F) down to 0.8 mg/l (at temp of 79.3–90.5)
Toxic Substances			
Arsenic (As)		0.05 mg/l	0.05 mg/l[3]
Barium (Ba)		1.0 mg/l	1.0 mg/l
Cadmiun (Cd)		0.01 mg/l	0.01 mg/l
Chromium (Cr^{6+})		0.05 mg/l	0.05 mg/l
Cyanide (CN)		0.2 mg/l	0.01 mg/l
Lead (Pb)		0.05 mg/l	0.05 mg/l
Selenium (Se)		0.01 mg/l	0.01 mg/l
Silver (Ag)		—	0.05 mg/l

[1] "Maximum acceptable concentration" applies to a water generally acceptable by consumers. "Maximum allowable concentration": values greater than those listed would markedly impair the potability of the water.
[2] "May give rise to infantile methaemoglobinaemia."
[3] Arsenic should not be present in a water supply in excess of 0.01 mg/l where other more suitable supplies are or can be made available.

Source: Herschdoerfer, S. M. (editor) (1968). *Quality Control In the Food Industry*, Vol. 2. Academic Press, New York.

Water, Hardness

TABLE 2.W.5
U.S. geological water survey hardness classification

Class	Ppm	Gr/Gal.[1]
Soft	0–60	0–35
Moderately hard	60–120	3.5–7.0
Hard	120–180	7.0–10.5
Very hard	Over 180	Over 10.5

[1]17 ppm = 1 gr/gal.

Source: Harper, W. J. (1972). Sanitation in dairy food plants. In *Food Sanitation*. R. K. Guthrie (editor). AVI Publishing Co., Westport, Connecticut.

Water, Weight and Volume

TABLE 2.W.6
U.S. water weight and measure at 20°C or 68°F

One Gallon	
Weighs	8.322 lb
Weighs	3774.6 gm
Contains	3785 ml
Contains	128 fl oz
One Pint	
Weighs	1.0403 lb
Weighs	471.825 gm
Contains	16 fl oz
Contains	0.473 liters
One Liter	
Weighs	2.1987 lb
Contains	1.0569 qt
Contains	1000.00 ml

Source: Woodroof, J. G., and Phillips, G. F. (editors) (1974). In *Beverages: Carbonated and Noncarbonated*. AVI Publishing Co., Westport, Connecticut.

Waves, Energy-Producing

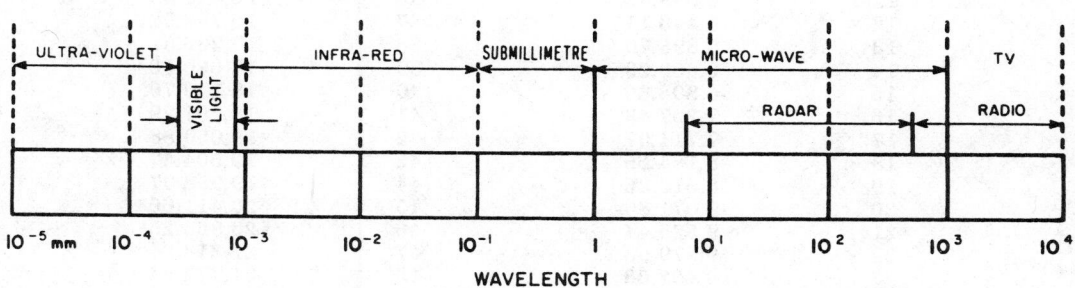

FIGURE 2.W.1
Wavelength spectrum of energy-producing waves

Source: Borgstrom, G. (1968). *Principles of Food Science*, Vol. 1. Macmillan Publishing Co., New York.

Wax

TABLE 2.W.7
Types and composition of waxes

Source	Examples	Composition
Mineral waxes	Paraffin	Straight-chain hydrocarbons, 26–30 C atoms/molecule
	Microcrystalline	Branched-chain hydrocarbons, 41–50 C atoms/molecule
	Oxidized microcrystalline	Hydrocarbons, esters, fatty acids
	Montan	Wax acids, alcohols, esters, ketones
	Hoechst waxes	Acids, esters (obtained by oxidizing montan)
	Ozokerite	Saturated and unsaturated high-mol-wt hydrocarbons
Vegetable waxes	Carnauba	Complex alcohols, hydrocarbons, resins
	Esparto	Mainly hydrocarbons
	Flax	Fatty-acid esters, hydrocarbons
	Sugarcane wax	Hydrocarbons, long straight-chain aldehydes, alcohols
	Candelilla	Hydrocarbons, acids, esters, alcohols, stearols, resins
Animal waxes	Beeswax	Hydrocarbons, acids, esters alcohols, lactones
Synthetic waxes	Fischer-Tropsch	Saturated and unsaturated hydrocarbons, oxygen compounds
	Polyethylene	Hydrocarbon

Source: Grant, J. (editor) (1969). *Hackh's Chemical Dictionary*, 4th Edition. McGraw-Hill Book Co., New York.

Weight

TABLE 2.W.8
Weight conversion table: pounds and ounces to grams

Pound	Grams	Pound	Grams
1	453.59	26	11,793.40
2	907.18	27	12,246.99
3	1,360.78	28	12,700.59
4	1,814.37	29	13,154.18
5	2,267.96	30	13,607.77
6	2,721.55	31	14,061.36
7	3,175.15	32	14,514.96
8	3,628.74	33	14,968.55
9	4,082.33	34	15,422.14
10	4,535.92	35	15,875.73
11	4,989.52	36	16,329.33
12	5,443.11	37	16,782.92
13	5,896.70	38	17,236.51
14	6,350.29	39	17,690.10
15	6,803.89	40	18,143.70
16	7,257.48	41	18,597.29
17	7,711.07	42	19,050.88
18	8,164.66	43	19,504.47
19	8,618.26	44	19,958.07
20	9,071.85	45	20,411.66
21	9,525.44	46	20,865.25
22	9,979.03	47	21,318.84
23	10,432.63	48	21,772.44
24	10,886.22	49	22,226.03
25	11,339.81	50	22,679.62

(Continued)

Weight   (Continued)

TABLE 2.W.8   (Continued)

Whole Ounces	Grams	Whole Ounces	Grams
1	28.35	9	255.15
2	56.70	10	283.50
3	85.05	11	311.84
4	113.40	12	340.19
5	141.75	13	368.54
6	170.10	14	396.89
7	198.45	15	425.24
8	226.80	16	453.59

Fractional Ounces	Grams	Fractional Ounces	Grams
$1/64$	0.44	$17/64$	7.53
$1/32$	0.89	$9/32$	7.97
$3/64$	1.33	$19/64$	8.42
$1/16$	1.77	$5/16$	8.86
$5/64$	2.21	$21/64$	9.30
$3/32$	2.66	$11/32$	9.75
$7/64$	3.10	$23/64$	10.19
$1/8$	3.54	$3/8$	10.63
$9/64$	3.99	$25/64$	11.07
$5/32$	4.43	$13/32$	11.52
$11/64$	4.87	$27/64$	11.96
$3/16$	5.32	$7/16$	12.40
$13/64$	5.76	$29/64$	12.85
$7/32$	6.20	$15/32$	13.29
$15/64$	6.64	$31/64$	13.73
$1/4$	7.09	$1/2$	14.17

Fractional Ounces	Grams	Fractional Ounces	Grams
$33/64$	14.62	$49/64$	21.71
$17/32$	15.06	$25/32$	22.15
$35/64$	15.50	$51/64$	22.59
$9/16$	15.95	$13/16$	23.03
$37/64$	16.39	$53/64$	23.48
$19/32$	16.83	$27/32$	23.92
$39/64$	17.28	$55/64$	24.36
$5/8$	17.72	$7/8$	24.81
$41/64$	18.16	$57/64$	25.25
$21/32$	18.60	$29/32$	25.69
$43/64$	19.05	$59/64$	26.13
$11/16$	19.49	$15/16$	26.58
$45/64$	19.93	$61/64$	27.02
$23/32$	20.38	$31/32$	27.46
$47/64$	20.82	$63/64$	27.91
$3/4$	21.26	1	28.35

Example: 6 lb and $14^3/4$ oz = 2,721.55 + 396.89 + 21.26 = 3,139.70 g.

Source: Ockerman, H. W. (1974). *Quality Control of Post-Mortem Muscle Tissue,* 9th Edition. Ohio State University, Columbus.

Weight, Human

TABLE 2.W.9
Weights of persons 20 to 30 years old

Height (Without Shoes) (ft) (in.)	Weight (Without Clothing)			Height (Without Shoes) (ft) (in.)	Weight (Without Clothing)		
	Low (lb)	Average (lb)	High (lb)		Low (lb)	Average (lb)	High (lb)
Men				Women			
5 3	118	129	141	5	100	109	118
5 4	122	133	145	5 1	104	112	121
5 5	126	137	149	5 2	107	115	125
5 6	130	142	155	5 3	110	118	128
5 7	134	147	161	5 4	113	122	132
5 8	139	151	166	5 5	116	125	135
5 9	143	155	170	5 6	120	129	139
5 10	147	159	174	5 7	123	132	142
5 11	150	163	178	5 8	126	136	146
6	154	167	183	5 9	130	140	151
6 1	158	171	188	5 10	133	144	156
6 2	162	175	192	5 11	137	148	161
6 3	165	178	195	6	141	152	166

Source: USDA (1969). Food for us all. Yearbook of Agriculture.

Wheat, Amino Acids

TABLE 2.W.10
Amino acids of wheat, flour, and bread (g per 16 g nitrogen)

	Wheat	Flour	Bread
Alanine	3.25	2.78	2.93
Arginine	4.69	3.80	3.56
Aspartic acid	5.09	4.14	4.60
Cystine	1.97	2.11	1.88
Glutamic acid	28.5	34.5	31.7
Glycine	3.88	3.22	3.21
Histidine	1.92	1.88	1.89
Isoleucine	3.90	4.26	4.32
Leucine	6.48	6.98	7.11
Lysine	2.74	2.08	2.48
Methionine	1.76	1.73	1.90
Phenylalanine	4.42	4.92	4.80
Proline	9.85	11.7	11.1
Serine	5.06	5.44	5.45
Threonine	3.02	2.82	3.01
Tryptophan	1.09	1.02	0.97
Tyrosine	3.10	3.25	3.32
Valine	4.50	4.54	4.68

Source: Pomeranz, Y. (editor) (1971). *Wheat Chemistry and Technology*, 2nd Edition. American Association of Cereal Chemists, St. Paul, Minnesota.

Wheat and Flour Composition

TABLE 2.W.11
Proximate chemical composition of a commercial mill mix of hard red spring wheat and its principal mill products[1]; chemical composition (13.5% M.B.)

Product	Proportion of Wheat (%)	Protein[2] (%)	Fat (%)	Ash (%)	Starch (%)	Pentosans (%)	Total Sugars[3] (%)	Undetermined (%)
Wheat	100.0	15.3	1.9	1.85	53.0	5.2	2.6	6.8
Patent flour	65.3	14.2	0.9	0.42	66.7	1.6	1.2	1.4
1st Clear flour	5.2	15.2	1.4	0.65	63.1	2.0	1.4	2.8
2nd Clear flour	3.2	18.1	2.4	1.41	56.3	2.6	2.1	3.6
Red dog flour	1.3	18.5	3.8	2.71	41.4	4.5	4.6	11.0
Shorts	8.4	18.5	5.2	5.00	19.3	13.8	6.7	18.0
Bran	16.4	16.7	4.6	6.50	11.7	18.1	5.5	23.5
Germ	0.2	30.9	12.6	4.30	10.0	3.7	16.6	8.4

[1] Compiled from USDA mimeographed publication ACE-189 (1942).
[2] Nitrogen X 5.7.
[3] Expressed as glucose.

Source: Pomeranz, Y. (editor) (1971). Wheat Chemistry and Technology, 2nd Edition. American Association of Cereal Chemists, St. Paul, Minnesota.

Wheat, Carbohydrate Composition

TABLE 2.W.12
Proximate carbohydrate composition of a French wheat and its principal mill products (% dry matter)

Product	Proportion of Wheat %	Ash	Starch	Crude Fiber	Pentosans	Sugars
Wheat	100.0	1.8	68.3	2.4	8.5	4.4
Flour	77.0	0.55	81.8	0.3	1.8	2.6
Red dog flour	2.4	2.4	54.8	1.1	7.9	7.75
Shorts	3.2	4.1	24.6	6.0	24.7	10.80
Bran fine	9.1	6.1	19.3	10.4	32.4	8.35
Bran coarse	7.7	7.5	14.7	12.3	34.7	7.15
Germ 1	0.4	4.7	20.8	4.5	13.5	16.90
Germ 2	0.2	4.6	20.8	3.3	8.2	20.55

Source: Cerning, J., and Guilbot, A. (1974). Carbohydrate composition of wheat. In Wheat: Production and Utilization. G. E. Inglett (editor). AVI Publishing Co., Westport, Connecticut.

Wheat, Fatty Acids

TABLE 2.W.13
Fatty acid composition of the total lipid and triglycerides from wheat, bran, germ, and endosperm

Fatty Acid Methyl Esters	Total Lipid				Triglycerides			
	From Whole Wheat (%)	From Bran (%)	From Germ (%)	From Endo-sperm (%)	From Whole Wheat (%)	From Bran (%)	From Germ (%)	From Endo-sperm (%)
Myristate (C-14:0)	0.1	tr	tr	tr	tr	tr	tr	tr
Palmitate (C-16:0)	24.5	18.3	18.5	18.0	16.7	17.9	19.4	12.9
Palmitoleate (C-16:1)	0.8	0.9	0.7	1.0	0.7	0.7	0.8	1.1
Stearate (C-18:0)	1.0	1.1	0.4	1.2	0.3	0.8	0.5	0.7
Oleate (C-18:1)	11.5	20.9	17.3	19.4	16.5	20.3	19.6	15.1
Linoleate (C-18:2)	56.3	57.7	57.0	56.2	59.0	56.2	52.5	65.1
Linolenate (C-18:3)	3.7	1.3	5.2	3.1	4.3	2.9	4.5	3.5
Arachidate (C-20:0)	0.8	tr	tr	tr	1.9	0.7	0.5	0.0
Other	1.1	tr	0.8	1.1	0.7	0.8	2.4	1.5

Source: Pomeranz, Y. (editor) (1971). Wheat Chemistry and Technology, 2nd Edition. American Association of Cereal Chemists, St. Paul, Minnesota.

Wheat Grades

TABLE 2.W.14
Grades and grade requirements for all classes of wheat except mixed wheat

Grade	Minimum test weight per bushel		Maximum limits of—					Wheat of other classes[1]	
	Hard Red Spring Wheat Or White Club	All other classes and sub-classes	Defects					Contrasting classes	Wheat of other classes (total)
			Heat-damaged kernels	Damaged kernels (total)	Foreign material	Shrunken and broken kernels	Defects (total)		
	Pounds	Pounds	Percent	Percent	Percent	Percent	Percent	Percent	Percent
U.S. No. 1	58.0	60.0	0.1	2.0	0.5	3.0	3.0	1.0	3.0
U.S. No. 2	57.0	58.0	0.2	4.0	1.0	5.0	5.0	2.0	5.0
U.S. No. 3	55.0	56.0	0.5	7.0	2.0	8.0	8.0	3.0	10.0
U.S. No. 4	53.0	54.0	1.0	10.0	3.0	12.0	12.0	10.0	10.0
U.S. No. 5	50.0	51.0	3.0	15.0	5.0	20.0	20.0	10.0	10.0

U.S. Sample grade shall be wheat which does not meet the requirements for any of the grades from U.S. No. 1 to U.S. No. 5, inclusive; or which contains more than two crotalaria seeds (*Crotalaria spp.*) in 1,000 grams of grain, or contains castor beans (*Ricinus communis*), stones, broken glass, animal filth, an unknown foreign substance(s), or a commonly recognized harmful or toxic substance(s); or which is musty, sour, or heating; or which has any commercially objectionable foreign odor except of smut or garlic; or which contains a quantity of smut so great that any one or more of the grade requirements cannot be applied accurately; or which is otherwise of distinctly low quality.

[1] Red Durum Wheat of any grade may contain not more than 10.0 percent of wheat of other classes.

Source: Inglett, G. E. (editor) (1974). In *Wheat: Production and Utilization*. AVI Publishing Co., Westport, Connecticut.

Wheat Grain

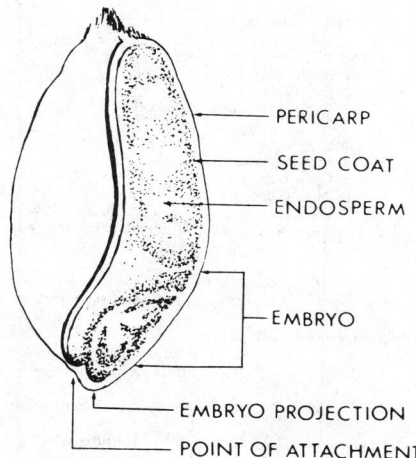

PERICARP

SEED COAT

ENDOSPERM

EMBRYO

EMBRYO PROJECTION

POINT OF ATTACHMENT

FIGURE 2.W.2

Semidiagrammatic of longitudinal section of a wheat seed

Source: Wallace, H. A. H. (1973). Fungi and other organisms associated with stored grain. In *Grain Storage: Part of a System*. R. N. Sinha, and W. E. Muir (editors). AVI Publishing Co., Westport, Connecticut.

Wheat Kernel

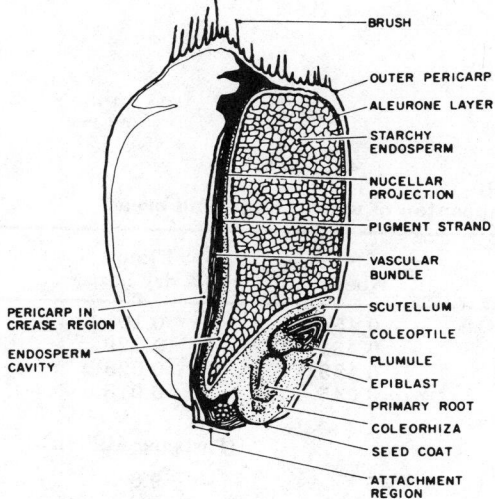

BRUSH

OUTER PERICARP

ALEURONE LAYER

STARCHY ENDOSPERM

NUCELLAR PROJECTION

PIGMENT STRAND

VASCULAR BUNDLE

SCUTELLUM

COLEOPTILE

PLUMULE

EPIBLAST

PRIMARY ROOT

COLEORHIZA

SEED COAT

ATTACHMENT REGION

PERICARP IN CREASE REGION

ENDOSPERM CAVITY

FIGURE 2.W.3

Cross section of a wheat kernel

Source: Brooker, D. B., Bakker-Arkema, F. W., and Hall, C. W. (editors) (1974). Principles of grain drying. In *Drying Cereal Grains*. AVI Publishing Co., Westport, Connecticut.

Wheat Kernel Parts

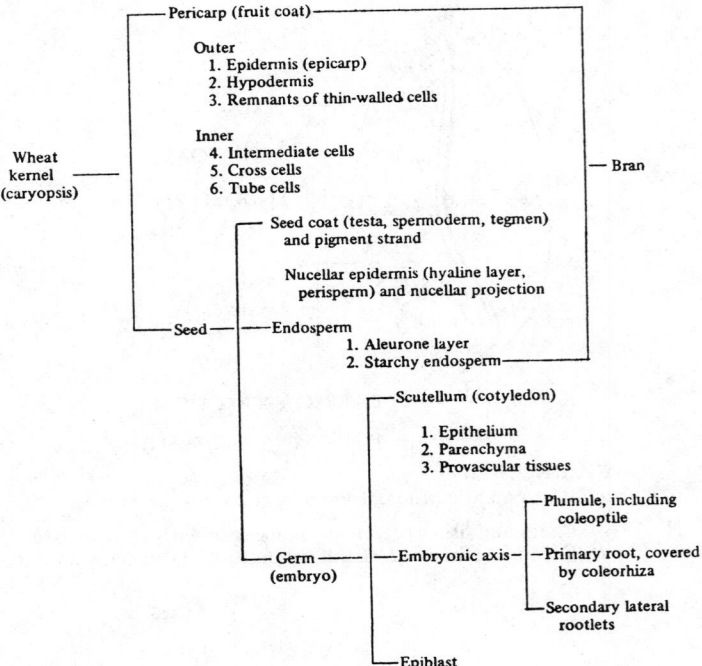

FIGURE 2.W.4
Parts of the wheat kernel and their relation to each other

Source: Pomeranz, Y. (editor) (1971). *Wheat Chemistry and Technology*, 2nd Edition. American Association of Cereal Chemists, St. Paul, Minnesota.

Wheat, Minerals

TABLE 2.W.15
Mineral composition of wheat, flour, and bread

	Wheat	Flour (% dry basis)	Bread
Potassium	0.454	0.105	0.191
Phosphorus	0.433	0.126	0.183
Magnesium	0.183	0.028	0.034
Calcium	0.045	0.018	0.127
		(Parts per Million)	
Sodium	45	9.8	0.858%
Zinc	35	7.8	9.7
Iron	43	10.5	27.3
Manganese	46	6.5	5.9
Copper	5.3	1.7	2.3
Molybdenum	0.48	0.25	0.32
Cobalt	0.026	0.003	0.022

Source: Pomeranz, Y. (editor) (1971). *Wheat Chemistry and Technology*, 2nd Edition. American Association of Cereal Chemists, St. Paul, Minnesota.

Wheat, Parts of Grain

TABLE 2.W.16
Constituents and calorie yields[1] of different parts of the wheat grain[2]

Part of Grain	Starch (g)	Reducing Sugars (g)	Pentosans and Similar Carbohy-drates (g)	Cellulose (g)	Crude Protein (g)	Fatty Material (g)	Ash (g)	Calories (g)
Entire kernel	58.5	2.0	6.6	2.3	12.0	1.8	1.8	310
Pericarp	0.0	0.0	34.5	38.0	7.5	0.0	5.0	175
Testa and hyaline layer	0.0	0.0	50.5	11.0	15.5	0.0	8.0	175
Aleurone layer	0.0	0.0	38.5	3.5	24.0	8.0	11.0	244
Outer endosperm	62.7	1.6	1.4	0.3	16.0	2.2	0.8	345
Inner endosperm	71.7	1.6	1.4	0.3	7.9	1.6	0.5	344
Embryo and scutellum	0.0	26.0	6.5	2.0	26.0	10.0	4.5	350

[1] Per 100 g.
[2] Moisture content: 15%.

Source: Aykroyd, W. R., and Doughty, J. (1970). Wheat in Human Nutrition. Food and Agriculture Organization, United Nations, Rome.

Wheat, Parts of Grain, Vitamins

TABLE 2.W.17
Content of certain vitamins[1] in different parts of the wheat grain

	Kind of Wheat				
	Soft English	Manitoba			
Part of Grain	Thiamin (mg)	Nicotinic Acid (mg)		Pyridoxine Hydro-chloride (mg)	Pantothenic Acid (mg)	Riboflavin (mg)
---	---	---	---	---	---	---
Pericarp, testa and hyaline layer	0.06	2.00	2.57	0.60	0.78	0.10
Aleurone layer	1.65	61.30	74.10	3.60	4.51	1.00
Outer endosperm	0.03	1.50	2.70	0.06	0.39	0.07
Inner endosperm	0.01	0.47	0.55	0.03		
Embryo	0.84	5.20	3.85	2.11	1.71	1.38
Scutellum	15.6	3.80	3.82	2.32	1.41	1.27

[1] Per 100 g; moisture content: 13%.

Source: Aykroyd, W. R., and Doughty, J. (1970). Wheat in Human Nutrition. Food and Agriculture Organization, United Nations, Rome.

Wheat Production in the U.S.

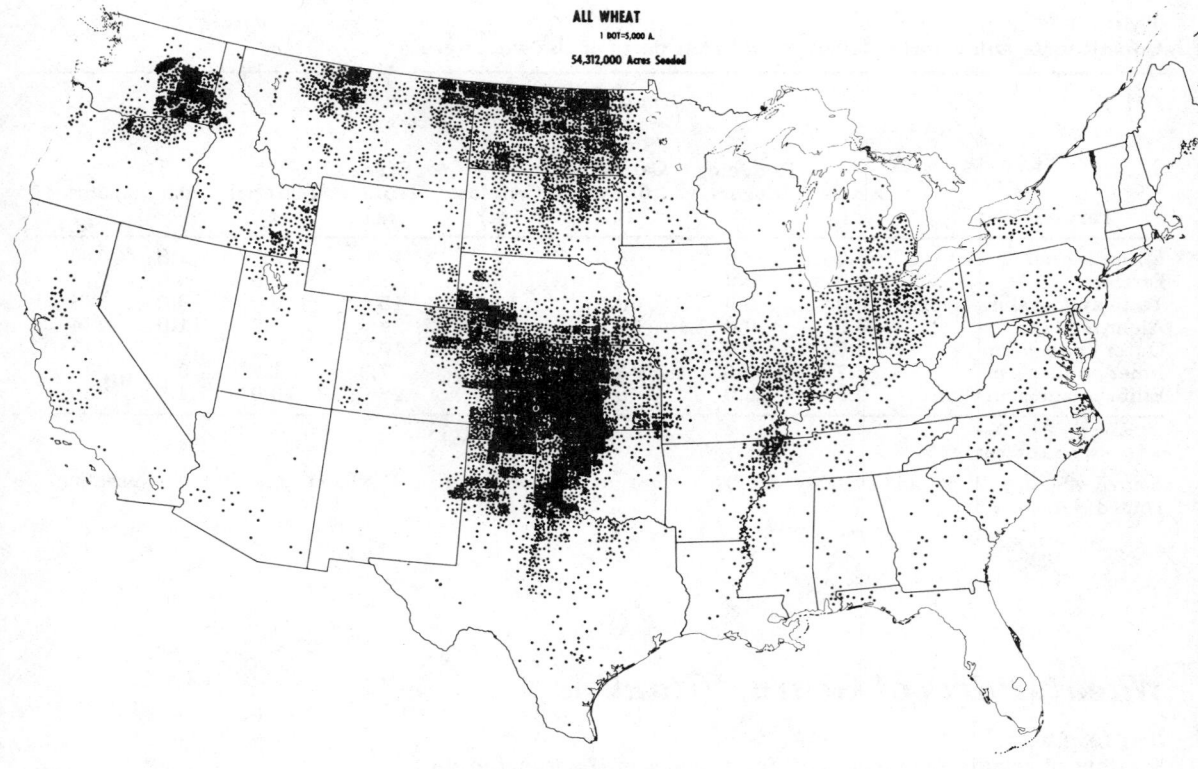

ALL WHEAT
1 DOT=5,000 A.
54,312,000 Acres Seeded

FIGURE 2.W.5

Source: USDA (1976). Wheat in the United States. USDA Agricultural. Information Bull. *386.*

Wheat Products, Amino Acid Compositions

TABLE 2.W.18
Amino acid compositions of wheat, flour, and flour protein fractions (g per 16 g N)

	Wheat	Flour	Albumin	Globulin	Gliadin	Glutenin	Residue Protein
Tryptophan	1.5	1.5	1.1	1.1	0.7	2.2	2.3
Lysine	2.3	1.9	3.2	5.9	0.5	1.5	2.4
Histidine	2.0	1.9	2.0	2.6	1.6	1.7	1.8
Ammonia	3.5	3.9	2.5	1.9	4.7	3.8	3.5
Arginine	4.0	3.1	5.1	8.3	1.9	3.0	3.2
Aspartic acid	4.7	3.7	5.8	7.0	1.9	2.7	4.2
Threonine	2.4	2.4	3.1	3.3	1.5	2.4	2.7
Serine	4.2	4.4	4.5	4.8	3.8	4.7	4.8
Glutamic acid	30.3	34.7	22.6	15.5	41.1	34.2	31.4
Proline	10.1	11.8	8.9	5.0	14.3	10.7	9.3
Glycine	3.8	3.4	3.6	4.9	1.5	4.2	5.0
Alanine	3.1	2.6	4.3	4.9	1.5	2.3	3.0
Cystine (half)	2.8	2.8	6.2	5.4	2.7	2.2	2.1
Valine	3.6	3.4	4.7	4.6	2.7	3.2	3.6
Methionine	1.2	1.3	1.8	1.7	1.0	1.3	1.3
Isoleucine	3.0	3.1	3.0	3.2	3.2	2.7	2.8
Leucine	6.3	6.6	6.8	6.8	6.1	6.2	6.8
Tyrosine	2.7	2.8	3.4	2.9	2.2	3.4	2.8
Phenylalanine	4.6	4.8	4.0	3.5	6.0	4.1	3.8

Source: Bushuk, W., and Wrigley, C. W. (1974). Proteins: composition, structure and function. In *Wheat: Production and Utilization*. G. E. Inglett (editor). AVI Publishing Co., Westport, Connecticut.

Wheat Products, Composition

TABLE 2.W.19
Typical analytical data for U.S. wheat products

| | Range of Analytical Values[1] in Typical U.S. Millfeeds | | | |
	Bran	Shorts	Red Dog	Wheat Germ
Chemical constituent (%)				
Protein ($N \times 6.25$)	13.3–16.9	15.2–18.2	13.9–16.7	23.9–27.0
Starch	4.6–7.2	15.9–21.7	36.2–47.8	14.0–23.9
Ash	4.7–7.1	3.1–4.3	1.5–2.7	3.5–4.3
Crude fat	3.0–4.2	3.7–6.3	2.3–4.7	6.3–10.6
Crude fiber	9.2–11.6	5.6–7.2	1.2–3.2	2.7–4.0
Essential amino acids (%)				
Lysine	0.56–0.61	0.68–0.86	0.45–0.65	1.30–1.77
Methionine	0.20–0.26	0.23–0.30	0.22–0.27	0.39–0.58
Threonine	0.36–0.53	0.54–0.63	0.42–0.56	0.89–1.09
Minerals				
Phosphorus (%)	0.9–1.5	0.54–0.92	0.36–0.62	0.77–0.96
Potassium (%)	1.2–1.6	0.82–1.1	0.34–0.64	0.86–1.3
Magnesium (%)	0.39–0.64	0.20–0.29	0.08–0.20	0.20–0.25
Zinc (ppm)	56–141	62–149	19–100	100–144
Iron (ppm)	74–103	38–79	28–57	41–58
Manganese (ppm)	72–138	91–142	32–71	95–147
Selenium (ppm)	0.10–0.75	0.03–0.75	0.13–0.60	0.01–0.77
Vitamins (μg/g)				
Niacin	249–359	84–120	22–62	64–85
Pantothenic acid	29–41	17–27	9–17	18–27
Folic acid	0.8–1.4	1.2–2.0	0.4–1.2	1.4–3.0
Thiamin	5.1–7.0	16–22	14–30	19–24
Riboflavin	4.3–5.8	4.0–5.2	1.7–3.1	5.5–6.4
Pyridoxine	7.0–10.7	4.7–9.8	2.1–8.6	6.6–19.8
Alpha-tocopherol	20–28	49–82	26–37	31–200
Betaine	3,000–7,000	3,000–6,000	2,350–4,500	3,000–6,000
Choline	1,800–2,700	1,800–2,300	1,400–2,000	2,600–3,300
Lipids (%)				
Total	3.9–6.1	5.3–7.9	3.5–7.0	9.2–13.5
Nonsaponifiable	0.6–0.7	0.5–0.6	0.3–0.4	0.7–1.4
Saponifiable	2.5–4.0	3.6–5.8	2.3–4.7	6.2–9.9
Stearate	0.7–1.4	0.6–1.2	0.6–1.0	0.5–0.8
Oleate	16–22	15–20	14–20	12–17
Linoleate	59–61	55–60	57–61	56–60
Linolenate	3.7–5.4	4.8–6.4	4.2–5.8	7.3–9.7

[1] All values reported on 14% moisture basis.

Source: Milner, M. (editor) (1969). *Protein-Enriched Cereal Foods for World Needs*. American Association of Cereal Chemists, St. Paul, Minnesota.

Wheat Varieties

TABLE 2.W.20
Typical varieties of wheat by region of adaptation and market type listed in approximate order importance

Region and type of wheat	Adapted varieties	Remarks
IA, White Winter	Genesee Yorkstar Ionia Arrow Avon	Grain is soft in texture; flour is suitable for cak cookies, and breakfast foods.
IB, Soft Red Winter	Arthur Arthur 71 Redcoat Monon Abe Logan Seneca Reed Tiwmin [1] Knox 62 Kenosha Pennoll Blueboy [1] Stadler Riley 67 Benhur	Grain is soft in texture; flour is suitable for cake a cookie flour, pastries, and general purposes.
II, Soft Red Winter	Arthur Blueboy [1] Holley McNair 701 [1] Coker 68–15 [1] Ga. 1123 Redcoat Arthur 71 Coker 68–19 [1] Blueboy II [1] Wakeland Abe	Grain is soft to semihard; flour is used for pastr and general purposes.
III: Hard Red Spring	Waldron Era [1] Lark [1] Fortuna Chris World Seeds 1809 [1] Bounty 208 [1] Thatcher Manitou Crim Olaf [1] Polk Bonanza [1] Shortana [1] Fletcher [1] Sheridan	Grain is hard in texture, high in protein; flour is us for bakery bread.

(Continue

Wheat Varieties *(Continued)*

Region and type of wheat	Adapted varieties	Remarks
-Continued		
mber Durum _____	Rolette _____	Grain is hard in texture, high in protein, and used for
	Leeds	macaroni products.
	Wells	
	Ward	
	Hercules	
	Lakota	
:		
ard Red Winter _____	Lancer _____	Grain is generally hard in texture and high in protein;
	Centurk	flour is used for bread.
	Scout	
	Cheyenne	
	Winalta	
	Warrior	
	Trapper	
	Gage	
	Winoka	
	Froid	
	Itana	
	Hume	
	Minter	
	Sundance	
	Teton	
ard Red Spring _____	Fortuna _____	
	Thatcher	
:		
ard Red Winter _____	Scout _____	Grain is generally hard in texture and high in protein;
	Centurk	flour is used for bread.
	Triumph	
	Eagle	
	Sturdy [1]	
	Scout 66	
	Wichita	
	Parker	
	Gage	
	Scoutland	
	Satanta [1]	
	Danne	
	Chanute [1]	
	Caddo	
	Tascosa	
	Concho	
	Warrior	
	Agent	
	Comanche	
	Pronto [1]	
	Ottawa	
	Baca	
	Caprock [1]	
ard Red Spring _____ ____	Milam _____	
	Chaparral	

(Continued)

Wheat Varieties   (*Continued*)

TABLE 2.W.20   (*Continued*)

Region and type of wheat	Adapted varieties	Remarks
VA:		
White Club	Paha [1]	Grain is soft in texture and low in protein; flour suitable for cakes and cookies.
	Moro	
	Omar	
White Winter	Nugaines [1]	Grain ranges from soft to hard and usually has l protein; flour is used for pastry and general purpos
	Gaines [1]	
	Yamhill	
	Hyslop [1]	
	Coulee [1]	
	Luke [1]	
	Druchamp	
	Burt	
	Brevor	
	Golden	
Hard Red Winter	Wanser	Grain is hard in texture; flour is used for bread blending.
	McCall	
	Cheyenne	
	Crest	
	Ark	
White Spring	Marfed	Grain ranges from soft to hard; flour is used for ge eral purposes.
	Twin [1]	
	Springfield [1]	
	Idaed 59	
	Beaver	
	Adams	
	Baart 46	
Hard Red Spring	World Seeds 1651 [1]	Grain is hard in texture; flour is used for blending a general purposes.
	Fortuna	
	World Seeds 1812 [1]	
	Henry	
	Ceres	
	Selkirk	
VB:		
White Winter	Nugaines [1]	Grain ranges from soft to hard and usually has l protein; flour is used for pastry and general purpos
	Hyslop [1]	
	Yamhill	
	Gaines [1]	
	Druchamp	
	Coulee [1]	
	Luke [1]	
Hard Red Winter	Wanser	Grain is hard in texture; flour is used for bread blending.
	McCall	
	Delmar	
	Cache	
	Crest	
	Bridger	
	Franklin	
	Ranger	
	Itana 65	
	Turkey	

(Continue

Wheat Varieties   (Continued)

ABLE 2.W.20   (Continued)

Region and type of wheat	Adapted varieties	Remarks
—Continued		
White Spring	Lemhi 66	Grain ranges from soft to hard; flour is used for general purposes.
	Springfield [1]	
	Twin [1]	
	Idaed 59	
	Marfed	
	Beaver	
	Adams	
Hard Red Spring	Peak 72 [1]	Grain is hard in texture; flour is used for blending and bread.
	Thatcher	
	Moran	
	Fremont [1]	
	Bannock	
	Henry	
	Komar	
White Club	Moro	Grain is soft and low in protein.
	Paha [1]	
Hard Red Spring	Inia 66 [1]	Grain is hard in texture and usually low in protein; used for blending and feed.
	Anza [1]	
	Bluebird 2 [1]	
	Pitic 62 [1]	
	Cajeme 71 [1]	
	Sonora 64 [1]	
White Spring	Siete Cerros 66 [1]	Grain ranges from soft to hard in texture, and used for blending and feed.
	White Federation 54	
	Maricopa [1]	
	Romona 50	
White Winter	Nugaines [1]	Grain is soft to semihard.
	Gaines [1]	
Club	Big Club 60	Grain is soft to semihard.
Amber Durum	Leeds	Grain is hard in texture, and used for macaroni products.

[1] Semidwarf plant height.

urce: USDA (1976). Wheat in the United States. USDA Agricultural Information Bull. *386*.

Wheat, Vitamins

TABLE 2.W.21
Vitamins of wheat, flour, and bread

	Wheat	Flour	Bread
		(Mg/100 g Dry Weight)	
Thiamin	0.40	0.104	0.46
Riboflavin	0.16	0.035	0.29
Niacin	6.95	1.38	4.39
Biotin	0.016	0.0021	0.0029
Choline	216.0	208.0	202.0
Pantothenic acid	1.37	0.59	0.69
Folic acid	0.049	0.011	0.040
Inositol	370.0	47.0	53.0
p-Aminobenzoic acid	0.51	0.050	0.092

Source: Pomeranz, Y. (editor) (1971). *Wheat Chemistry and Technology*, 2nd Edition. American Association of Cereal Chemists, St. Paul, Minnesota.

White Sauce

TABLE 2.W.22
Ingredients for 1 cup of white sauce

	Measure			
Ingredients	Thin sauce		Medium sauce	
	Standard	Low-fat	Standard	Low-fat
Butter or other fat	1 tablespoon	2 teaspoons	2 tablespoons	1 tablespoon.
All-purpose flour	1 tablespoon	1 tablespoon	2 tablespoons	2 tablespoons.
Salt	¼ teaspoon	¼ teaspoon	¼ teaspoon	¼ teaspoon.
Milk	1 cup[1]	1 cup[1,2]	1 cup[1]	1 cup.[1,2]
Calories in 1 cup white sauce	290	180	420	245.

[1] Vegetable liquid may be used in place of part of milk.
[2] Use skim milk or reconstituted nonfat dry milk for milk in low-fat white sauce.

Source: USDA (1980). Vegetables in family meals. USDA Home and Garden Bull. *105.*

Wine, Sugar Addition

TABLE 2.W.23

What the saccharometer shows	For wine of 10% by volume, add	For wine of 12% by volume, add
	Ounces of sugar per gallon	
10	11.8	16.2
11	10.1	14.8
12	8.9	13.3
13	7.4	11.9
14	5.9	10.4
15	4.6	8.9
16	3.0	7.5
17	1.5	6.0
18		4.3
19		2.9
20		1.4

Source: USDA (1977). Canning, freezing, storing garden produce. USDA Agricultural Information Bull. *410.*

Wine, Sweet

TABLE 2.W.24

Fruit	Average sugar level	Sugar needed per gallon to make a sweet wine	Average acid	Gallons of sugar water [1] to add per gallon
		ounces		
Grapes (eastern)	12–20	1¼–2	med. to high	0–1
Grapes (Calif.)	16–20	1–1½	low [2] to med.	0
Apples	13	2–2¼	low [2] to high	0–½
Apricots	12	2–2½	med. to high	0–¼
Blackberries	6	2–3	high to very high	1 or more
Blueberries	8	2¼–3	low to med.	0
Cherries (sour)	14	2–2¼	high to very high	1 or more
Cherries (sweet)	18	1½–2	medium	0
Pear	12	2¼–2½	med. to high	0–¼
Plum (Damson)	14	2–2¼	med. to high	0–¼
Plum (Prune)	17	1½–2	med. to high	0–¼
Peach	10	2–2½	med. to high	0–¼
Raspberries	8	2½–3	high to very high	1 or more
Strawberries	5	2–3¼	med. to high	0–½

[1] To maintain proper sugar level when the acidity is reduced by adding water, it is easier to make up a sugar solution by dissolving 3 pounds of sugar in enough water to fill a 1-gallon jug.
[2] Addition of some acid (citric or tartaric) may help. This can be done "to taste" after the active fermentation is over.

Source: USDA (1977). Canning, freezing, storing garden produce. USDA Agriculture Information Bull. *410.*

Note: There are no entries for the letter X in this section.

Y

Yield Grade, Meat

TABLE 2.Y.1
Retail yield of carcass according to yield of meat grade

Yield Grade 1: means the carcass will yield 79.8% or more in retail cuts.
Yield Grade 2: 75.2–79.7%.
Yield Grade 3: 70.6–75.1%.
Yield Grade 4: 66–70.5%.
Yield Grade 5: 65.9% or less.

Source: USDA (1969). How to buy meat for your freezer. USDA Home and Garden Bull. *166*.

Note: There are no entries for the letter Z in this section.